HANDBOOK OF MODERN MANUFACTURING MANAGEMENT

HANDBOOK OF
MODERN MANUFACTURING
MANAGEMENT

H. B. MAYNARD *Editor-in-Chief*
President, Maynard Research Council, Inc.
Pittsburgh, Pennsylvania

A McGRAW-HILL
CLASSIC
HANDBOOK
REISSUE

McGRAW-HILL BOOK COMPANY

New York St. Louis San Francisco Auckland Bogotá
Hamburg Johannesburg London Madrid Mexico
Montreal New Delhi Panama Paris São Paulo
Singapore Sydney Tokyo Toronto

HANDBOOK OF MODERN MANUFACTURING MANAGEMENT

Library of Congress Catalog
Card Number 77-83271

1983 REISSUE

ISBN-0-07-041087-9

34567890   VBVB   89876543

*To Modern Manufacturing Managers who, by their dedication
to the task of producing quality products in the right amounts
at the right time at ever-lower real costs, have made possible
a material prosperity unequaled in the history of mankind.*

ADVISORY PLANNING COMMITTEE

MAURICE O. BEVERLEY *General Production Manager,*
Moore Business Forms, Inc.,
Niagara Falls, New York,

LESTER R. BITTEL *Publisher,*
Modern Manufacturing,
New York, New York

WALTER P. CARTUN *Executive Vice President,*
Emhart Corporation,
Hartford, Connecticut

M. JOSEPH DOOHER *Editor,*
Industrial and Business Books,
McGraw-Hill Book Company,
New York, New York

GEORGE H. GUSTAT *Director,*
Industrial Engineering Division,
Kodak Park Division,
Eastman Kodak Company,
Rochester, New York

FREDERICK W. HORNBRUCH, JR. *Vice President,*
Macrodyne-Chatillon Corporation,
New York, New York

ROBERT E. LEVINSON *President,*
The Steelcraft Manufacturing Company,
Cincinnati, Ohio

BENJAMIN W. NIEBEL   *Professor and Head,*
Department of Industrial Engineering,
The Pennsylvania State University,
University Park, Pennsylvania

PAUL D. O'DONNELL   *Director,*
Headquarters Manufacturing Controls,
Westinghouse Electric Corporation,
Pittsburgh, Pennsylvania

CONTRIBUTORS

WILLIAM M. AIKEN *Senior Vice President, H. B. Maynard and Company, Inc., Pittsburgh, Pennsylvania*

GUY J. BACCI *General Supervisor—Industrial Engineering, International Harvester Company, Chicago, Illinois*

LESTER R. BITTEL *Publisher,* Modern Manufacturing, *New York, New York*

THOMAS I. S. BOAK, JR. *Works Manager, Aluminum Company of America, Cressona, Pennsylvania*

RAY F. BOEDECKER *Vice President—Manufacturing, Systems Manufacturing Division, International Business Machines Corporation, White Plains, New York*

DR. DAVID M. BOODMAN *Arthur D. Little, Inc., Cambridge, Massachusetts*

ARTHUR C. BOYDEN *Director, Staff Manufacturing, 3M Company, St. Paul, Minnesota*

RICHARD L. BURDICK *Manager, Industrial Engineering, The Maytag Company, Newton, Iowa*

D. C. BURNHAM *Chairman, Westinghouse Electric Corporation, Pittsburgh, Pennsylvania*

JAMES L. CENTNER *Vice President—Finance and Administration, The Hess & Eisenhardt Company, Cincinnati, Ohio*

CHARLES V. CLARKE *Senior Vice President, H. B. Maynard and Company, Inc., Pittsburgh, Pennsylvania*

HARDY M. COOK, JR. *Head, Quality Assurance Department, Western Electric Company, Inc., Baltimore, Maryland*

RICHARD H. DEHAAN *Director of Security, Fred Meyer, Inc., Portland, Oregon*

DR. DONALD D. DEMING *Professor and Chairman, Management Engineering, Rensselaer Polytechnic Institute, Troy, New York*

M. J. DUBUC *Director, Material, Rocketdyne Division, North American Rockwell Corporation, Canoga Park, California*

WILLIAM K. ENGEMAN *Taft, Stettinius & Hollister, Cincinnati, Ohio*

ix

DR. M. U. ENINGER *Normax Publications, Incorporated, Pittsburgh, Pennsylvania*

THOMAS E. FARRELL *President, National Hose Company, Dover, New Jersey*

DR. A. V. FEIGENBAUM *President, General Systems Company, Pittsfield, Massachusetts*

J. F. FISHER *Vice President, Ogden Corporation, New York, New York*

RICHARD W. FOXEN *Vice President—Manufacturing and Purchasing, Westinghouse Air Brake Company, Pittsburgh, Pennsylvania*

DR. DORMAN G. FREARK *Associate Professor, Department of Industrial Engineering, The Pennsylvania State University, University Park, Pennsylvania*

DUANE C. GEITGEY *Director of Program Development, Maynard Research Council, Inc., Pittsburgh, Pennsylvania*

HERBERT C. GLOEDE *Manager of Manufacturing Operations, Asia-Pacific, International Business Machines Corporation, Fujisawa, Japan*

FREDERICK GOLDEN *Director of Manufacturing, Warnaco Inc., Bridgeport, Connecticut*

DOUGLAS P. GOULD *Vice President, Trundle Consultants Inc., Cleveland, Ohio*

M. W. GRANT *Manager of Manufacturing, Executive Staff, Ingersoll-Rand Company, New York, New York*

G. H. GUSTAT *Director, Industrial Engineering Division, Kodak Park Division, Eastman Kodak Company, Rochester, New York*

DR. INYONG HAM *Associate Professor, Department of Industrial Engineering, The Pennsylvania State University, University Park, Pennsylvania*

ROSS W. HAMMOND *Chief, Industrial Development Division, Georgia Institute of Technology, Atlanta, Georgia*

DR. WALTON M. HANCOCK *Professor, Department of Industrial Engineering, The University of Michigan, Ann Arbor, Michigan*

JOHN W. HANNON *Executive Vice President, Maynard Research Council, Inc., Pittsburgh, Pennsylvania*

WILLIAM K. HODSON *President, H. B. Maynard and Company, Inc., Pittsburgh, Pennsylvania*

FREDERICK W. HORNBRUCH, JR. *Vice President, Macrodyne-Chatillon Corporation, New York, New York*

PARK R. HOYT *Vice President—Manufacturing, Smithcraft Corporation, Wilmington, Massachusetts*

JOHN T. JACKSON *Senior Vice President, International Utilities, Philadelphia, Pennsylvania*

W. J. JAMIESON *Superintendent, Maintenance and Utilities Finishing Works, The Steel Company of Canada, Ltd., Hamilton, Ontario, Canada*

CREED H. JENKINS *National Manager, Warehouse Operations, Kaiser Aluminum and Chemical Corporation, Oakland, California*

REGINALD L. JONES *Partner, Arthur Andersen & Company, New York, New York*

MARION S. KELLOGG *Manager, Individual Development Methods, General Electric Company, New York, New York*

JAMES N. KELLY *President, Management Analysis Center Incorporated, Cambridge, Massachusetts*

T. P. KELLY *Principal, A. T. Kearney & Company, Inc., New York, New York*

ROBERT E. LEVINSON *President, The Steelcraft Manufacturing Company, Cincinnati, Ohio*

PHILIP A. LINK *Production Control Manager, Automatic Electric Company, Northlake, Illinois*

HOWARD E. LOVELY *Cresap, McCormick and Paget, Chicago, Illinois*

JAMES R. LYNCH *Controller, Systems Manufacturing Division, International Business Machines Corporation, White Plains, New York*

FRANK H. McCARTY *Corporate Director—Industrial Engineering, Raytheon Company, Lexington, Massachusetts*

W. M. McFEELY *Vice President—Organization, Riegel Paper/Textile Corporation, New York, New York*

LEWIS H. McGLASHAN *Director of Training, Kodak Park Works, Eastman Kodak Company, Rochester, New York*

FRED C. MANASSE *Vice President—Operations, Automatic Data Processing, Inc., Clifton, New Jersey*

JOHN C. MARTIN *Staff Assistant, Headquarters Manufacturing Controls, Westinghouse Electric Corporation, Pittsburgh, Pennsylvania*

W. F. MASLER, JR. *President, Aero-Corry (Division of Aero-Flow Dynamics, Inc.), Corry, Pennsylvania*

DR. HERBERT H. MEYER *Manager, Corporate Personnel Research, General Electric Company, New York, New York*

L. D. MILES *Miles Associates, Washington, D.C.*

BRUNO A. MOSKI *Assistant to General Manager, Yale Materials Handling Division, Eaton, Yale & Towne, Inc., Philadelphia, Pennsylvania*

RICHARD MUTHER *President, Richard Muther & Associates, Inc., Kansas City, Missouri*

A. D. NEWMAN *Director, The Centre for Organization Analysis, Fulmer, England; and Special Professor of Organization Theory, University of Nottingham, Nottingham, England*

BENJAMIN W. NIEBEL *Professor and Head, Department of Industrial Engineering, The Pennsylvania State University, University Park, Pennsylvania*

PAUL D. O'DONNELL *Director, Headquarters Manufacturing Controls, Westinghouse Electric Corporation, Pittsburgh, Pennsylvania*

DR. HAROLD F. PUFF *Professor, Department of Management, Miami University, Oxford, Ohio*

DR. THOMAS J. PURCELL *Rockwell Manufacturing Company, Pittsburgh, Pennsylvania*

H. K. REAMEY *Plant Engineer, Reynolds Metals Company, Sheffield, Alabama*

JOSEPH H. REDDING *Manager, Management Sciences Division, H. B. Maynard and Company, Inc., Pittsburgh, Pennsylvania*

R. E. RENKEN   *Principal, A. T. Kearney & Company, Inc., New York, New York*

J. A. RICHARDSON   *Supervisor, Industrial Engineering Division, Kodak Park Division, Eastman Kodak Company, Rochester, New York*

DR. W. J. RICHARDSON   *Professor, Department of Industrial Engineering, Lehigh University, Bethlehem, Pennsylvania*

DEAN H. ROSENSTEEL   *Dean H. Rosensteel & Co., Inc., New York, New York*

F. G. SAVIERS   *Assistant Controller, Westinghouse Electric Corporation, Pittsburgh, Pennsylvania*

DAVID I. SCHERAGA   *Consultant, Materials Information and Control Systems, Advanced Materials Service, General Electric Company, New York, New York*

L. WEST SHEA   *Managing Director, The Material Handling Institute, Inc., Pittsburgh, Pennsylvania*

EDWIN S. SHECTER   *Manager—Defense Quality Assurance, RCA Corporation, Moorestown, New Jersey*

JOHN P. SIRLES   *Supervisor of Methods, Industrial Engineering Department, Ingersoll-Rand Co., Athens, Pennsylvania*

WILLIAM. M. STOCKER, JR.   *Director, Industry Information, American Machinist, New York, New York*

GORDON A. SUTTON   *Director of Personnel, North American Rockwell Corporation, Pittsburgh, Pennsylvania*

RICHARD L. SWIFT   *Manager of Instrument Manufacturing, Mine Safety Appliances Company, Pittsburgh, Pennsylvania*

D. E. A. TANNENBERG   *Director of Engineering, International Group, The Singer Company, New York, New York*

JAMES W. THOMPSON   *Vice President of Manufacturing, Schlegel Manufacturing Company, Rochester, New York*

ARTHUR W. TICKNOR   *Director—Acquisition Planning, Westinghouse Air Brake Company, Pittsburgh, Pennsylvania*

ARTHUR W. TODD   *Director of Purchase Engineering, The Lincoln Electric Company, Cleveland, Ohio*

RICHARD W. TRUSLER   *Manager, Manufacturing Engineering, International Business Machines Corporation, Rochester, Minnesota*

WILLIAM J. VALLETTE   *Vice President, Vaule & Company, Inc., Wellesley, Massachusetts*

ROBERT L. WELLS   *Vice President and General Manager, Atomic Equipment Divisions, Westinghouse Electric Corporation, Pittsburgh, Pennsylvania*

LEE S. WHITSON   *President, WR Medical Electronics Company, St. Paul, Minnesota*

JOHN J. WILKINSON   *Vice President, H. B. Maynard and Company, Inc., Pittsburgh, Pennsylvania*

FENWICK M. WINSLOW, JR.   *H. B. Maynard and Company, Inc., Pittsburgh, Pennsylvania*

DAVID N. WISE   *Manager, Production Planning, Mine Safety Appliances Company, Pittsburgh, Pennsylvania*

Modern manufacturing management has become a highly complex task, requiring a good working understanding of a number of rather sophisticated techniques and procedures. The constant need to develop better, lower cost ways of producing goods which will meet the ever-expanding requirements of modern society has forced manufacturing managers to turn to concepts and systems that only yesterday would have been shrugged off as being "too theoretical and impractical." Manufacturing managers as a group tend to take pride in being practical, and their interests tend to concentrate on "things that work." The fact that they have turned increasingly to the newer techniques and procedures is therefore highly significant. It indicates that these techniques and procedures do work and that they produce better operating results than would be attainable without them.

When the need for profit improvement arises, the manufacturing manager finds no lack of available courses of action which have been used successfully by others. His problem becomes one of choosing the course or courses which will be most likely to improve his own situation substantially and quickly, rather than to develop anything radically new. To choose wisely, he must know what courses of action are available and must understand their workings in sufficient depth to be able to see how they might apply in his own case. This is where this Handbook can be helpful.

The purpose of the Handbook is to assist the man with manufacturing responsibility to use or direct the use of both the old and tested manufacturing practices and the newer procedures which have been developed since mid-century. It deals primarily with the human, technical, and financial aspects of manufacturing management. It emphasizes what the functions, techniques, and procedures it discusses can do to help the manufacturing manager carry out his responsibilities effectively and economically. No attempt is made to tell in detail how functions, techniques, or procedures should be performed by the specialists who handle them, for this is well covered in other handbooks and texts designed for the specialists themselves. Rather, this Handbook seeks to give the manufacturing manager the kind of practical information he will need to have to be able to evaluate the applicability of a function, technique, or procedure to his own specific situation and to show him what he must do to ensure its successful application if he decides to use it.

The Handbook was designed to accomplish its stated purpose by an Advisory

Planning Committee composed of men of outstanding practical manufacturing experience. Their names appear on page vii.

The Committee met with the Editor-in-Chief to discuss the subjects that should be covered by the Handbook, and subsequently, during the finalizing stages, advised most helpfully on the outline of contents. They then offered specific recommendations on the men best qualified by experience and background to author the eighty-one chapters of the Handbook. Thus the Handbook was designed for practical manufacturing men by practical manufacturing men.

The usefulness of the Handbook is not limited entirely to manufacturing managers, however. It will be found to serve the needs of three groups of people:

1. Men with line responsibility for manufacturing or production.

This group includes chief executives of smaller companies; operating vice presidents; general managers; division managers; plant, works, or factory managers; manufacturing managers; and plant superintendents.

2. Men who serve manufacturing management in a staff capacity, who wish to broaden and deepen their understanding of the total manufacturing function.

This group includes industrial engineers, quality control men, production planners and schedulers, manufacturing engineers, plant maintenance managers, factory cost accountants, systems analysts, and a host of others.

3. Students of manufacturing management.

This group includes manufacturing supervisors on the way to greater responsibilities, management consultants, teachers of manufacturing-related subjects, and university students taking courses dealing with or related to the manufacturing function.

The Handbook was written by eighty-six different authors. Each one contributed of his experience in the area which he discusses. It might be expected that there would be many divergent viewpoints among so many authors. Yet, as one reads through the Handbook, one becomes impressed with the remarkable similarity of viewpoints and philosophies expressed by the different authors. It leads to the conclusion that there appears to be a generally accepted approach to manufacturing management, and that although the application of the principles of manufacturing management may still be something of an art, the underlying principles themselves border on being a science.

In any event, there are three points on which there seems to be almost complete agreement. The first point, which has already been mentioned, is that manufacturing management is a highly complex task. Gone are the days when the "bull of the woods" type of manager could manage by hunches, prejudice, and force of personality. Modern manufacturing management requires a skillful blending of line and staff functions, using a large number of techniques and procedures, some of them highly sophisticated, applied with balance and proper timing to achieve a predetermined set of objectives.

The second point of agreement is that whatever technique is applied, it must have the wholehearted and understanding support of the manufacturing manager. The manager who sees this thought repeated in chapter after chapter may gain a somewhat dismaying picture of himself sitting in meeting after meeting supporting his specialists as they are attacked by other members of the organization—which is scarcely the case in real life—but it should bring home the fact that he cannot approve the installation of any new technique or procedure and expect it to work if he does not take an active and continuing interest in its day-to-day application.

The third point which emerges is the importance placed on the industrial engineering function by most of the authors. In nearly every chapter, reference is made to industrial engineering. Industrial engineering is relied on to supply factual data needed for the successful application of such techniques as forecasting, production planning and control, process engineering, factory cost accounting, plant layout, maintenance cost control, and many others. Industrial engineering is turned to for improved methods, NC machine programming, evaluating proposed courses of action, and the solution of many people problems. Industrial engineering becomes involved in systems design, operations research, and other aspects of the management sciences. The manufacturing manager who does not have a well-established industrial engineering function should ponder the advisability of adding it as he reads in the Handbook of the many valuable uses to which it may be put.

A handbook, no matter how long, cannot hope to cover every detail of every subject which it discusses. Hopefully, it can give guidance to answers to the problems the reader has on his mind when he consults it. If the subject under discussion seems to have value to the reader, he can turn to other, more detailed descriptions for further information. The authors of most of the chapters have included brief bibliographies which show where additional information can be found.

Of course, the reader does not have to have a specific problem in mind as he consults the Handbook to obtain help from it. All managers have many areas in which they would like to have improvement, even though there may be no major problems existing at the moment. The simple act of reading the Handbook, either systematically or at random, will almost always generate ideas for improvement in one or more areas of concern. There are literally hundreds of helpful ideas mentioned in the Handbook, and some of them are likely to be applicable to almost any manufacturing operation.

A handbook of the scope of this one is possible only because a number of qualified manufacturing men have been willing to take time from their busy lives to record on paper their ideas, philosophies, and experiences in the hope that this will be helpful to others who face the task of managing the manufacturing function wisely and well. To these authors, the Editor-in-Chief expresses his warm appreciation for their valuable contributions. Especial thanks go also to the members of the Advisory Planning Committee for their help in the conceptual stages of the Handbook project.

On the editorial side, appreciation is extended to Rita Carlson, who handled the styling and proofreading work so very well and who coped with the myriad of details involved in scheduling, author follow-up, and liaison with the publisher, which must be skillfully managed if a handbook of this magnitude is to be successfully completed.

Thanks also to Barbara Hattemer for her competent preparation of the index.

The entire team—advisors, authors, and editorial assistants—functioned well and harmoniously. It is the hope of all that the users of this Handbook will find that their work has resulted in a useful tool for increasing the effectiveness of manufacturing management.

H. B. MAYNARD
Editor-in-Chief

CONTENTS

Section Seven   PRODUCTS AND MATERIALS

Section Eight   PERSONNEL

Section Nine   MOTIVATING EMPLOYEES

Section Ten   SUPPORTING SERVICES AND ACTIVITIES

THE MANUFACTURING FUNCTION

CHAPTER ONE

The Role of Manufacturing in the Corporate Organization

D. C. BURNHAM *Chairman, Westinghouse Electric Corporation, Pittsburgh, Pennsylvania*

A significant revolution has been developing since World War II in the way products are made. It is a revolution that reaches from the executive offices of the company to the manufacturing aisles, and it must become a way of life for all progressive companies. In response to many different pressures, the entire concept of manufacturing's role in a company's operation has already changed and is continuing to change. Interestingly, most of the changing concepts and procedures apply equally to large and small companies.

A logical question is: Why is such a revolution necessary in a country that has long prided itself on progressive and modern manufacturing techniques? Many factors are involved, but three are particularly significant.

First, there has been a growing realization that progress—whether it is measured in terms of standard of living, an overall improvement in our culture, or as a better life for all—depends on productivity. Manufacturing people are most responsible for improving productivity because in most industrial companies more people are involved in manufacturing. In the end, then, manufacturing people are the principal determinants of productivity gains.

Second, the billions of dollars spent on research and development since World War II have produced an immensely quickened pace in technology. The practical result of this is that new products are being born at a much faster rate. To be useful, however, they must be brought to market, and in a much shorter time than ever before to keep a company competitive. Obviously this places a heavy burden on manufacturing men to develop dramatic new techniques and methods for shortening the manufacturing cycle, reducing costs, and at the same time maintaining or improving the quality of the product.

And third, both products and the manufacturing techniques used to make them are becoming increasingly complex. For example, one compact airborne radar unit has over 90,000 parts, and this is obviously a product that must oper-

1–3

ate precisely and reliably. Moreover, systems such as this must be production tested; this, in turn, sometimes leads to testing equipment as complex as the product itself. Complexity is by no means limited to military equipment; industrial equipment of all kinds and even products for the home are affected. One important result of this increasing complexity is the need for greater skills at all levels of manufacturing.

Thus the need for ever-increasing productivity, the competitive need for shorter manufacturing cycles and lower costs, and the growing complexity of machines and processes have combined to create a manufacturing revolution that has replaced the steady evolution that existed before World War II.

THE EFFECT ON CORPORATE POLICY AND OPERATION

In the evolutionary days, manufacturing was, in a sense, almost an isolated function in many companies. Its job was to take the designer's blueprints and produce a product. Whether it was always admitted or not, there were barriers in communication and cooperativeness between manufacturing and other functions of the company.

One of the most striking changes in the manufacturing revolution has been the steady disappearance of these traditional barriers. Corporate management has recognized that, under the economic and competitive conditions that have developed, close teamwork between all the functional elements of the corporation—and particularly manufacturing, engineering, purchasing, and marketing—is not only desirable but fast becoming a necessity. Ideally, the teamwork starts at the policy making and staff level and extends throughout the line organization. Probably the most obvious areas where this cooperation pays off is in product cost reduction and in the development of new products, where teams from engineering, manufacturing, and purchasing frequently can achieve improvements that none of them could accomplish if they worked separately.

In the midst of this manufacturing revolution, the need for clear guidelines is essential. This means that companies must have much more definitive objectives and policies for the manufacturing organization. They must be stated in such a way that every member of the manufacturing organization clearly understands them and can use them to guide decision making and operational procedures.

More than likely, everyone interested in this book would think it obvious that any organization must have effective objectives and policies. Yet many organizations flounder, or at best operate at low efficiency, for one of these reasons:

1. Objectives and policies are ambiguous, which leaves their interpretation up to the individual, with resultant confusion, misinterpretations, and conflicts.
2. The objectives and policies are not effectively communicated to the people who need them.

You are undoubtedly in an excellent position to determine whether or not your own company has sound manufacturing objectives and policies. First of all, does it have any policies *in writing* that everyone follows? Do you frequently find yourself having to make decisions based solely on your own judgment, without any policy to guide your decision? Or do you nearly always have to go to a superior for a policy decision? No policy can make decisions for you—but it should provide a guide that will let you evaluate the choices open to you and select the best one.

In general, manufacturing policies of companies, large or small, do not differ substantially from one another, even though the words and the emphasis may change from one organization to another. The objective and policies in Figure 1-1, although they are those formulated for the Westinghouse Electric

MANUFACTURING OBJECTIVE

Manufacture a quality product, on schedule, at the lowest possible cost, with maximum asset turnover, to achieve customer satisfaction.

MANUFACTURING POLICIES

1. Select capable and experienced personnel, and continually improve their capability through training, development, and advancement.
2. Carry on full-time continuous manufacturing planning, coordinated with engineering, marketing, and other functional departments.
3. Carry out manufacturing development in each division, preferably in a laboratory, taking full advantage of the latest improvements in equipment, techniques, and methods.
4. Plan facilities for normal operations of at least two 8-hour shifts, 5 days per week, with all interested people participating, making a complete analysis of the manufacturing system and using three-dimensional layouts where appropriate.
5. Provide new facilities with no greater capacity than needed when the facilities go into operation, but have a plan for future expansion.
6. Provide increased productive capacity by balancing operations to minimize bottlenecks and by improving the manner in which the work is done, rather than by increasing the floor area.
7. Plan the physical arrangement of each plant by products, dividing the facilities into self-contained integrated operations wherever possible.
8. Modernize facilities in both productive and expense operations when projected savings meet or exceed corporate guidelines.
9. Review facilities periodically, and retire those that are not required to produce the current volume, or anticipated volume in the next three years, in a two-shift operation.
10. Accelerate product cost improvements based on specific unit cost goals for each product, using appropriate techniques to reduce materials, labor, and overhead.
11. Administer wage payment plans to reward employees fairly for skill, effort, and time.
12. Expect all employees to perform a fair day's work, following the prescribed method, working the full shift, and using normal effort.
13. Establish standards where possible that measure the performance of all employees, keeping the standards up to date with method changes, and using predetermined time standards where applicable.
14. Use a measured daywork form of payment for productive employees in all new plants.
15. Analyze continually all expense and the number of expense people employed, in order to reduce costs.
16. Plan and control manpower, materials, and facilities, consistent with delivery promises, to balance work force fluctuations and inventory levels and to achieve maximum asset turnover.
17. Control product quality, to meet the engineering specifications and to assure reliable product performance for customer satisfaction.
18. Provide good working conditions—a safe, clean workplace, and adequate facilities to help the employee do his job effectively.
19. Require each foreman to supervise his workmen directly, but limit the number of his people so that he can manage them personally.
20. Maintain and safeguard all company assets to maximize the return over the life of the assets.

Fig. 1-1. Statements of Manufacturing Policy.

Corporation, are by no means unique; they resemble those of some other companies and could be used by most companies. Note that there are exactly twenty individual statements of policy to guide the entire manufacturing function. Note also that although the statements are clear and definitive, they are not so restrictive that they discourage or prohibit innovation. There must be enough inherent flexibility in such policies that no manager is saddled with an unworkable situation; in fact, the policies should, by their simplicity, encourage innovation.

The policies outlined can all be grouped into three categories—planning, operating, and control. These are relatively standard areas in any function, but in some companies the manufacturing organization is actually structured into these three categories; obviously, this is where the manufacturing revolution has its base.

THE MANUFACTURING FUNCTIONS

The planning, operating, and control functions of manufacturing in large organizations may be reflected directly in the organization chart, or in smaller operations the functions may be combined. The important point, however, is that they must exist regardless of the exact organization. The diagram in Figure 1-2 gives a general picture of each of these functions and their related activities.

Planning covers all those actions required to assure that the best plant layout, processes, methods, machines, and tools are being used. The operating function covers all activities involved in the actual manufacture of the product; and the control function is designed to make sure that the product is of consistent quality and constructed on time and in the most efficient manner. The identification of these three functions as individual entities should not be misconstrued, however. Seldom, if ever, do they work independently of one another; in fact, most often they are a unified team, each supporting and assisting the other.

Planning. Although none of the manufacturing functions can be neglected, planning is probably the most critical in a highly competitive and expanding economy, whether the planning is done to upgrade an existing plant, or for a new plant. With the high degree of sophistication possible in methods and machines, an error in the planning stage can be extremely costly or perhaps fatal to the competitiveness of the company. On the other hand, tremendous gains are possible through intelligent planning.

Consider, for example, what one machine accomplished in upgrading the manufacture of a custom-designed product in an existing plant. The huge frames of the generators used in electric utility plants may measure as much as 36 feet long and 14 feet in diameter. During manufacture, both the inside and outside diameters of these cylindrical frames must be milled to close tolerances, and holes drilled at appropriate locations. Originally these milling and drilling operations were carried out by moving the frames from one machine to another for different portions of the process. Then one huge numerically controlled machine was installed to take care of all these operations. It was, in fact, the largest machine tool in the world at the time. The results were spectacular; the old method took seventy-three days, the new method about thirteen, or a net reduction of 80 percent.

Planning a new plant offers a different, although not necessarily greater, challenge than the upgrading of an existing plant. In one new plant built to produce a medium-volume standard product, factory overhead was reduced by

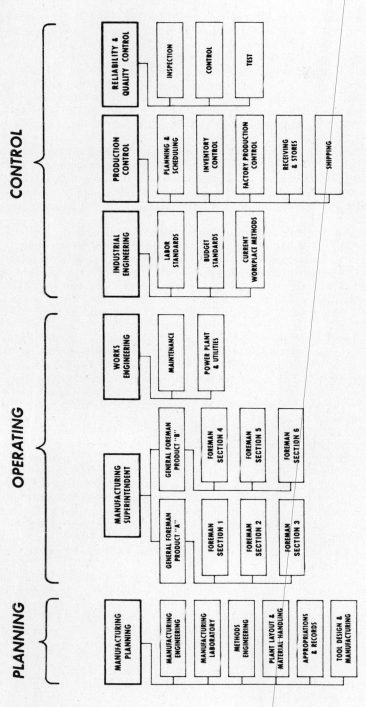

FIG. 1-2. Typical Manufacturing Functions.

1–7

two-thirds, and work-in-process inventory was cut from 2.3 months to 0.7 month, along with a significant decrease in direct labor cost per unit, compared to the older plant. This was made possible by extremely careful planning, and the gains met or exceeded the anticipated results.

One of the most impressive stories of planning, however, involves a company that, in a five-year period, increased its sales by about 300 percent. In this same period, its inventory rose only about 25 percent, its manufacturing floor space decreased by nearly 30 percent, and its return on investment nearly tripled. Most of this improvement can be attributed to very effective manufacturing planning.

Such spectacular improvements as these are not as rare as they might seem at first glance. The technology necessary for the improvements is available. In most instances equipment to do the job is also available, although in others special equipment must be developed by the manufacturer or in cooperation with a machine builder. The necessary ingredient is the simple conviction that anything can be improved.

The tools of the manufacturing planner are many and varied. For example, a manufacturing laboratory serves a valuable function in planning. Here available new tools can be tested and evaluated for various manufacturing operations; new tools can be developed and perfected for specialized operations; and a whole host of other exploratory operations can be conducted. Another significant value of such a laboratory is the ability to test the operation and capabilities of new tools before they are actually installed in a production line.

Other useful tools are models that permit planners to consider the consequences of large numbers of alternatives—both physical and abstract—before major investments are committed. At the physical end of the scale are three-dimensional models. Here for the first time the planners, the operating men, and the control men literally see their new plant before it is built. The model can serve an invaluable function in spotting physical flaws or possible changes in the plant arrangement to improve such things as work flow, traffic patterns, and so on. At the abstract end of the scale are mathematical models used for computer simulations of work flows. Here the manufacturing man can test in a few moments what might happen in weeks or months of experience in complex interactions among product, manpower, and machines on the factory floor.

Manufacturing planning, then, offers the opportunity for large-scale innovations, whether that task is replacing machines, upgrading an old plant, or planning a new one. It requires a careful appraisal of what is economically practical and justifiable. Most of all, however, planning requires an attitude that will inspire men to look beyond the traditional ways of doing things, but with the knowledge and judgment to blend the traditional with the new where this is the best approach.

Operating. Without attempting to evaluate the importance of the various functions of a company, it cannot be denied that the manufacturing operating man has one of the most challenging and difficult jobs. Even though he may have initial assistance from other functions, his is the tough, day-by-day job of manufacturing the product, using the machines and manpower available to him. The operating man usually has the largest work force, consisting of professional people, skilled workers, semiskilled workers, and unskilled workers, all of whom must be trained and motivated to perform their daily tasks well and meet their objectives. Thus, the manufacturing management must truly be man managers, not just work managers.

In general, the operating manager's responsibilities include producing a product in the required quantity, of the specified quality, at a certain cost, while at the same time maintaining high standards of safety, maintenance, and housekeeping. Another definition (which applies equally to all managers) is that a good supervisor gets the people in his department to do what he wants done, when it should be done, and the way he wants it done, because they want to do it.

There is no doubt that training, motivating, and maintaining the proper attitude and morale of the work force are the critical tasks of the manufacturing operating manager. For example, most readers of this Handbook are probably familiar with at least one case in which a foreman of a section or a plant has been replaced by a new man, and in a short time the plant has become more productive and morale and attitude have improved dramatically—all with little or no change in the physical assets of the plant. This kind of result has to be credited to a better understanding of the various human relations factors of managing the work force, and a recognition of the need for better training of supervisors—plus action to improve both the work force and the supervisors.

In the changing world of manufacturing, one fact becomes increasingly important, even though it is by no means a new situation. Highly skilled first-line supervisors are the backbone of the manufacturing operating force. Better educated and better trained professionals in these key positions are essential. Not only must first-line supervisors be better educated technically, to keep up with the technological revolution in our plants, but they must also be more highly skilled in handling any and all situations involving people, and especially those involving the reactions of people to technological change. If the work force is properly motivated and conditioned to change, people can adjust to it; otherwise, people often inherently mistrust and resist change, and the result can be chaos.

Aside from the highly important human relations factors of the operating manager, three distinct and separate factors are figuring in the revolution in the operating function. One is the increasing availability of highly sophisticated tools to help the manufacturing manager achieve his goals. These include not only those tools used in the actual manufacture of the product, but also those used in data processing or in scheduling, such as the computer.

Another is the gradual decentralization, streamlining, and simplification of the manufacturing organization. This is a process that is in its early stages, but that eventually will allow the manager to devote more of his time to managerial duties and leave specialized functions to individual experts in his organization. For example, in Figure 1-2, the general foreman would have planning, scheduling, quality control, and similar specialists reporting directly to him; or, if the operation were large enough, individual foremen might have such specialists in their own sections. This is in contrast to the more common concept of a quality control manager and staff reporting directly to the manufacturing manager. In general, decentralization makes the problems easier to deal with at a lower level in the organization, rather than having, as is frequently the case, too many problems that have to be resolved at the manufacturing manager's level. Having all problems resolved at higher levels is time consuming, and perhaps worst of all, does not allow the operating man sufficient latitude to solve his own problems, which he knows best.

The third factor is the emerging need for more manufacturing engineers as foremen or unit managers in the plant. The technical knowledge and ability that will be needed by foremen, as the machines they deal with and the procedures they use become more sophisticated, will require greater professional skill at the lower levels of supervision.

In summary, however, the operating men in manufacturing, despite efficient new tools and advanced methods, can be successful only to the degree that they are successful in managing the people who work for them. Any manager who ignores or underestimates the fact that basically his job is to manage people cannot succeed for long. A thorough knowledge of human relations and thoughtful preplanning of any actions involving people is an absolute must for any operational manager.

Control. Referring again to Figure 1-2, the control function generally includes industrial engineering, production control, and reliability and quality control. Here again, the technological revolution is inspiring—and sometimes forcing—more and more advanced techniques.

In industrial engineering, perhaps the most noticeable change has been caused by the growing awareness among management of the importance of establishing and maintaining reasonable, accurate standards for the performance of productive workers and motivating the workers to perform to these standards.

Fundamentally, work standards have a direct bearing on many elements of a company's operation. For example, standards establish product manufacturing cost which, in turn, determines the selling price of the product. The cost provides a basis for a change in design to improve the product; and it also establishes a basis for improving the processes and techniques of manufacturing.

Viewed from this perspective, it becomes obvious that standards are essential to much of the planning that goes on in a company—whether it be in production planning, determination of equipment and plant capacity, financial control, or any other affected areas.

Most of the basic techniques for developing work standards have been developed in this century and steadily refined and improved. Techniques for predetermining work standards for a new job are available, as well as many different techniques for actually measuring results as a basis for establishing standards. However, even if predetermined or measured standards cannot be used, good estimates are better than no standards at all.

Closely allied to work standards for productive workers are budget standards that cover other manufacturing costs, including staff people and other workers not working directly on the product. These standards have the same effect on the company's operation as those for productive workers.

The importance of setting good standards cannot be overemphasized. Whether a plant works on an incentive or a daywork basis, good standards are needed for efficient operation. Equally important, however, is a regular program to keep standards up to date. A drastic change in required performance is usually noticeable, but the net effect of many small changes often goes undetected unless the job standard is periodically rechecked. If manufacturing managers truly recognize the tremendous importance of good work standards, they can contribute in a major way to the overall efficiency of their companies by keeping these standards accurate and current.

In production control, data processing and computer equipment are showing the way to new and improved methods. Fast response and minimum manufacturing cycle time are the order of the day. For example, one company uses a system in which, every morning, before its production lines start up, its work scheduling is developed by computer in a matter of minutes. As each employee reports for work, this fact is recorded in a central computer; the computer has been fed information as to how much product must be made and what facilities are available. A computer simulation is run to study the best work assignments and equipment operations to achieve maximum production. A few minutes after check-in time, the computer tells the foreman how to make his daily assignments and what equipment to operate.

Another aid to reducing manufacturing cycle time, sometimes called short-term scheduling, is especially valuable for products with long cycles. Here computer equipment is used in scheduling, and the foreman is given only enough information and material for several days' operation, which shortens the span that he must plan and improves efficiency. The foreman has fewer things to keep track of and therefore can make better use of men and machines.

Reliability and quality control are also assuming entirely new dimensions. In companies such as electric utilities or the various process industries—steel and paper for example—reliability is no longer merely desirable, it is essential. Power outages are less and less tolerable because of increasing dependence on electric power. And downtime in a modern steel processing line is an extremely expensive situation. Add to this the increasing complexity of the equipment such industries use, and the need for stringent quality control in manufacturing the equipment becomes readily apparent.

Actually in many companies there is a distinct difference between the reliability and the quality control functions. In one definition, reliability embraces the entire product cycle—from design, through the manufacturing cycle, to installation and operation of the equipment. A reliability section may in some cases report directly to a general manager because its work cuts across all the functions involved in the plant and some outside the plant. Quality control, on the other hand, is the job of making certain that the product is manufactured according to the standards established for it and that it performs as designed when it is completed. Quality control, therefore, is strictly a manufacturing function.

Ideally, the emphasis on quality control should be in the "preventive" area. It should be directed toward assuring quality during production, rather than relying on reworking completed but faulty products. This is where quality control engineering becomes a major factor. However, the production worker himself can be the most important element in maintaining quality if he is properly motivated. If the worker has a sense of pride in his workmanship and assumes responsibility for inspecting his own work, many of the problems of quality disappear.

Even with the best possible quality control engineering and the finest production workers, however, testing of completed products usually is still a necessity, if only for the reason that human errors will always occur.

The testing of completed products is becoming a highly sophisticated and automatic process. The tendency to test every product that comes off the line, rather than random samples, is more common because of the increasing need and demand for reliable products. For complex products, computers are sometimes used in this process because of the ease with which operating conditions can be simulated. Perhaps the ultimate in this direction is the testing of a process control computer by "plugging it in" to another computer on which all the operating characteristics of the application are programmed, and making the control computer run the process. Regardless of the product, however, automatic testing not only saves time, but also assures a consistently reliable product.

CHANGING CONCEPTS OF MANUFACTURING MANAGEMENT

There was a time when a bright, aggressive young machine operator could work himself up the ladder of manufacturing to become a manufacturing manager. This is now much less likely in most companies, and the possibility seems even more remote in the future. This is no reflection on the bright young man, but merely a condition of our times. The bright young machine operator must constantly upgrade his skills to keep pace with the complexity of manufacturing machinery. Increasingly he must be better trained and educated, because the machine he is now responsible for may be a complex million-dollar tool, and a slight mistake in adjustment, or a few minutes inattention, may cost thousands of dollars of production.

The manufacturing manager who rose from the lowest rung on the ladder, although he knew shop problems intimately, tended to be insulated from other functions of the company because manufacturing was the only thing he knew well. The manufacturing managers of today and tomorrow must, in contrast, know and work hand in hand with all the other functions that relate to manufacturing, including engineering, purchasing, and marketing.

As mentioned, the traditional barriers between functions such as engineering and manufacturing are breaking down, even disappearing. In controlling product costs, for example, design engineers, manufacturing engineers, purchasing men, and others are more and more working as a team. The professional skills of each function are brought to bear simultaneously on the same problem. Frequently, in practice, the manufacturing man may contribute design ideas, as may the purchasing man. As a small example, the purchasing man may well be able to suggest the use of less expensive bolts or a substitute material with which the engineer may not be familiar. The manufacturing man, with his knowledge of his machines and his work force, often can suggest changes in design that will make the product simpler and easier to construct. The important aspect of this is that the tendency is to do this planning in concert and before the product is built. This is in marked contrast to older days, when the manufacturing man took the engineer's design and then altered it to something he could manufacture, sometimes at the expense of performance or usefulness of the product.

The net effect of all the changes discussed here is an increasing professionalism in all areas of manufacturing. The manufacturing manager of the present must be knowledgeable in all the new techniques that are available to him. And, perhaps most important of all, he must have the necessary skills in human relations to inspire people constantly to seek better ways of doing things. In the final analysis, it is the attitude of the men who work for him that determines whether manufacturing performs its function effectively. The attitude must be that *anything* can be improved, no matter how effective or efficient it may seem to be.

CHAPTER TWO

Establishing Manufacturing Objectives

LESTER R. BITTEL *Publisher*, Modern Manufacturing, *New York, New York*

Like any contributing human force of an enterprise, the manufacturing organization is a function of its own objectives. These objectives will determine its size and the characteristics of those who staff it. For this reason, it is dangerous to oversimplify the goals of the manufacturing organization. Clarity is essential, of course. But the entire spectrum of possibilities should be scanned, and its complexity recognized, before isolating either general or specific objectives.

Manufacturing objectives may be classified in these ways:

Ultimate Goals. These are the production-related (or more properly, the product-related) measures associated with the manufacturing operation. At their simplest, these goals can be defined in terms of product cost, product quality, and product availability (as defined by time limitations).

Intermediate Goals. These are the goals which, if reached, usually assure attainment of the ultimate goals. These intermediate goals can be stated as the utilization targets of the manufacturing inputs, including energy, materials, machinery, equipment and facilities, methods, money, and manpower.

Functional Goals. These objectives presume that intermediate and ultimate goals will be reached if the performance targets of the various functional activities are maximized. These functional goals relate to the effectiveness of auxiliary and support departments such as production control, inspection, maintenance, methods engineering, wage incentives, work measurement, tool engineering, and the like.

Restrictive Goals. These represent manufacturing's commitments to other organizations in the corporate complex. More often than not, these committed goals become restrictions on either the establishment or attainment of manufacturing objectives. They must be met concurrently in any event. For example, the manufacturing organization usually must commit itself to goals associated with or imposed by sales and marketing, product design, finance, and distribution operations.

Integrated Goals. These are the goals inherent in the corporate organization itself and increasingly are imposed by it to optimize its efforts. Although the manufacturing function in many companies may conform only to the more obvious procedural or fiscal requirements established by corporate policies and practices, progressive planning of objectives should recognize total cost (system) considerations at work in a manufacturing company.

ULTIMATE GOALS

The primary responsibility of manufacturing is to produce a product or products at (1) a preestablished cost, (2) according to specified characteristics of quality, and (3) within well-defined time limitations.

Manufacturing Costs. Traditionally, cost objectives are divided between (1) those costs directly attributable to labor and materials put into the product, and (2) those indirect costs associated with facilities and services that provide manufacturing support. In setting specific manufacturing objectives, unit cost of the product (which may or may not incorporate both direct and indirect costs) is usually the commanding factor. However, many other manufacturing costs may be well worth setting down as objectives, even though their contribution to total cost may appear insignificant. To attack the cumulative effect of all cost items, many minor ones ultimately deserve attention.

Product Quality Objectives. Product quality requirements often become the restraining factor in accommodating either cost or time objectives or both. And although quality objectives are often established by customer or design specifications, the manufacturing organization must translate these specifications into measurable objectives for its own organization. Here, again, the quality objectives may be of a primary or secondary nature according to whether the objectives relate (1) to a contribution directly associated with the product, or (2) to the services such as quality control which are employed to assure this quality.

Manufacturing Time Goals. In its concern for product cost and quality, a manufacturing organization is most likely to give short shrift to time considerations or to assume that somehow or other the time element will work out. This wishful thinking should be guarded against by the establishment of specific and systematically determined time objectives. It is not enough, however, to establish time objectives for shipments alone. Objectives for subsystems, such as inventory turnover rates and manufacturing cycle times for various parts of the processes, must also be specified.

Typical Measurements for Ultimate Goals.

Costs
   Variable unit cost
   Total unit cost
   Direct costs, gross and detailed
   Indirect costs, gross and detailed
   Cost of delays
   Cost of rework
   Cost of setup and teardown
Quality
   Rejects, number and rate
   Rework, number and rate
   Material yield, percent

Returns, number and rate
Field repairs, cost and rate
Time
Output (dollars and units) per man-hour (direct and indirect)
Man-hours, direct and indirect, per unit produced
Factory schedule performance, deviations and percent compliance
Shipment performance, deviations and percent compliance
Production cycle time
Processing time related to total production cycle time
Machine utilization, rate
Inventory turnover, rate
Hours of backlog; production, maintenance, engineering, and the like
Overtime, total and percent of labor cost
Machine and labor idle time, rate

INTERMEDIATE GOALS

Although the payoff to most operations is ultimately in reduced costs and the like, most organizations are more likely to be guided day by day by how well they are handling their resources. If one conceives of the resources as those inputs peculiar to manufacturing operations and recognizes that the utilization of these inputs determines the ultimate output as measured by cost, quality, and time, he can recognize the need to establish the former with great care.

Production Machinery and Equipment. Objectives in the area of production machinery and equipment can be broken down into (1) acquisition goals and (2) utilization goals. All too often, not enough attention is given to the former. Consequently, production objectives should first be studied with relation to the adequacy of existing equipment. Then the proper additions and replacements to existing facilities should be set forth. Attention must be given to plans that establish alternates depending upon the approval of acquisition objectives and the timing of their eventual availability.

Once the machinery, equipment, and facilities inventory has been established for a particular period, it is time to set utilization goals. And while these goals must harmonize with (*a*) sales commitments, (*b*) production schedules, and (*c*) the inherent characteristics of the equipment, realistic utilization goals will also anticipate (*d*) plans for methods improvement and (*e*) plans for training and improvement of operating personnel.

Manufacturing Materials. Materials can be considered as falling into two classes: (1) those that become part of the product, and (2) those that are merely associated with maintaining the manufacturing operations. The latter materials usually are referred to as operating supplies. Material goals must be set in terms of the amounts required (in units, dollars, and space requirements) and in yield and turnover rates. Yield is the all-important utilization measure, and turnover is a measure of fiscal management of materials. Inventory objectives can be a subject in itself, but should be specific enough in this discussion to include raw materials, in-process materials, and finished goods.

Properly established goals for operating supplies can add materially to the money saved in the manufacturing department. Consequently, target objectives should be set for spare parts inventories, indirect materials such as lubricants, and the like.

Manufacturing Services and Facilities. In a manufacturing plant, proper design and installation of facilities for utilization of energy sources and other utilities contribute decisively to the success or failure of the operation. Long-term goals should be based upon a review of utility and service requirements in much the same way that machinery and equipment acquisition goals are established. Short-term or annual goals can be regarded as conservation objectives. Biggest target areas include economies in use of power or energy sources such as steam, electricity, and compressed air. Other significant savings can be aimed at in the use of utilities such as water, waste disposal (including control or reduction of air and water pollution), and air for heating and cooling.

Housing facilities and space objectives should not be overlooked in terms of both absolute needs and utilization.

Manufacturing Manpower. Manufacturing objectives must be closely allied with objectives for personnel acquisition, selection, placement, training, and utilization. Typically, these objectives are considered (1) under such general personnel management headings as employee turnover rates, safety measurements, labor relations, and absenteeism, (2) under headings more closely allied to manufacturing control, such as direct and indirect labor assignment and use, and finally, (3) under specific manpower requirements and economies for particular operations or departments.

Finance. Manufacturing management is increasingly aware of the contribution and demand that its operations make upon the corporation's financial resources. Inventory management objectives and equipment acquisition objectives are obvious examples, but there are many more. They include timing of hiring and layoff; decisions to employ permanent or temporary manpower; and decisions to subcontract seasonal or one-shot production, construction, or maintenance operations. All these make an impact on company finances. Consequently, when setting manufacturing objectives, these matters—and the timing of them—should get serious consideration.

Typical Measurements for Intermediate Goals.

Machinery and Facilities
  Production equipment utilization rates
  Operating costs, rates
  Maintenance costs, rates
  Machine capacity growth rate
  Obsolete equipment replacement rate
  Capital equipment acquisition rate
  Machine breakdown rate
  Nondurable tools consumption rate
  Manufacturing occupancy, percent of available square feet
Materials
  Production throughput rate
  Materials cost per production unit
  Materials cost per direct man-hour
  Product yield, percent from raw materials
  Materials in process, related to throughput
  Materials discarded because of obsolescence, storage deterioration, and
    the like, rate
  Inventory turnover rate
  Inventory shrinkage
  Stores expense related to throughput
  Expendable supplies consumption rate per unit

Waste recovery rate
Waste disposal costs
Energy
Utilities (electricity, steam, water, air, and so on) consumption rates
Electric power factor
Connected electric horsepower per square foot
Money
Working capital needed for manufacturing activities
Percent return on manufacturing capital investment
Cost reductions attributable to manufacturing activities
Profit attributable to manufacturing activities
Manpower
Productivity per man-hour
Labor cost per production unit
Direct labor and indirect labor
Number of employees—full-time and permanent versus part-time or temporary
Man-hours on daywork
Man-hours on incentives
Man-hours on standards
Man-hours earned
Man-hours off standards
Man-hours of overtime
Man-hours per cost center
Indirect labor distribution
  Tool and fixture making
  Setup
  Maintenance and repair
  Salvage, rework, repossess
  Housekeeping and sanitation
  Clerical, data processing
  Inspection, quality control
  Factory engineering
  Receiving, shipping, warehousing
  Material handling
Employee turnover rate
Employee attendance and punctuality
Accident frequency and severity
Idle time, hours and rate
Work stoppages

FUNCTIONAL GOALS

The further down the operational ladder, the more specific manufacturing goals must be. To the middle-level manager, especially of a staff department, ultimate and intermediate goals are often too remote for him to relate them significantly to his immediate responsibilities. Consequently, a whole series of goals must be set that provide measurable performance targets for the various departments that contribute directly or indirectly to the main manufacturing goals.

Here again, goals tend to fall into either of two categories. The first kind of goal is an indication of how effectively the organization contributes to the effectiveness of the whole manufacturing organization. The second is a measure of how well the organization functions within its own confines. For example, the primary goals for a production control department might be to (1) deliver 92 percent of the orders on time, (2) limit the age of postdue shipments to no more than two weeks, and (3) turn inventory over every three months. However, its secondary objectives, related to the function's internal effectiveness, might be to (1) employ less than 3.5 people on its staff per 100 people in the manufacturing department, (2) contribute no more than 1½ percent to total manufacturing costs, and the like. Sometimes the distinction between the two goal categories is not clear. This should not be an important consideration. It is far better to establish enough meaningful targets than to devote much time to precise identification of the nature of their contribution to plant efficiency.

Typical Measurements for Functional Goals.

Industrial Engineering
Total industrial engineering personnel
Number of industrial engineering personnel per 1,000 factory employees
Number of industrial engineering personnel on standards work per 1,000 factory employees
Percentage of direct employees on incentives
Percentage of indirect employees on incentives
Average earnings as percentage of base rate

Production and Inventory Control
Ratio of production and inventory control employees to total plant employment
Inventory performance
Inventory turnover rate
Dollars in inventory
Surplus inventory
Obsolete inventory
Cost of holding inventories
Estimated material cost versus actual
Percentage of items for which no receipts or distribution was made
Percentage of stock-outs
Scheduled versus actual levels of inventory for raw materials, work in process, and finished goods
Levels of protective stock
Production control performance
Machine utilization
Percentage of orders shipped on time
Overtime attributable to production control
Number of setups
Factory production schedules met
Stockroom tooling and kitting schedules met
Schedule performance in shipping spare parts
Schedule performance in shipping major equipment
Receipt from vendor schedule performance
Processing time related to total production cycle time

Quality Control
Inspection and quality control personnel per 1,000 factory employees
Inspection productivity, percentage of time inspecting
Inspection cost per unit removed
Scrap totals and percentages

Rework totals and percentages

Material Handling

Material handling personnel per 1,000 factory employees

Percentage of time lost by direct labor in material handling

Ratio of total number of moves to total number of operations

Ratio of sum of production operation time to total manufacturing cycle time

Percentage of usable cubic footage usefully occupied

Percentage of available time that material handling equipment is used

Percentage of floor space utilized

Material handling costs as percentage of manufacturing expense

Maintenance

Maintenance employees per 100 production workers

Square feet of manufacturing area per maintenance employee

Horsepower of connected electric load per maintenance worker

Horsepower of connected electric load per 1,000 square feet of manufacturing area

Percentage of total man-hours of maintenance on work planned

Percentage of total man-hours of maintenance on emergency work

Percentage of total man-hours of maintenance on overtime

Crew weeks of current backlog

Crew weeks of total backlog

Percentage of total maintenance man-hours on preventive maintenance

Maintenance costs as percentage of plant investment

Maintenance costs as percentage of costs per unit of product produced

Percentage of operating time lost in downtime owing to maintenance reasons

Number of units of product produced per maintenance dollar

Percentage of time that maintenance force is gainfully employed

Purchasing

Percentage of dollar commitments to gross sales

Percentage of dollar commitments to disbursements

Percentage of rejects in goods received

Percentage of shortages in scheduled production material

Schedule requirements versus on-line delivery

Inventory versus production

Inventory versus sales

Number of requisitions per month and versus forecast

Number of requisitions versus purchasing manpower costs, postage, travel, and freight

Average total costs of issuing a requisition

Labor cost per requisition

Average lead time

Vendors' performance against promised time and quality

Subcontractor performance against time, quality, and cost

Flow time from request to purchase to purchase order issuance

RESTRICTIVE GOALS

Effectiveness of the manufacturing organization is limited, if not prescribed, by commitments imposed upon it by or committed to other departments in the company. Although these commitments are frequently integrated into the three kind of goals already described, it is worthwhile reviewing the commitments to other departments separately to be sure that they are accounted for in planning.

Sales and Marketing. Primary commitments to marketing departments usually involve such things as (1) fulfilling quality promises, product specifications, and reliability, and (2) meeting shipping dates and the like. However, other goals may be included, such as (3) limiting the number of field complaints, or (4) improving communications between production and sales as regards material and design changes, deliveries, and the like.

Accounting and Control Departments. Primary commitments properly include standard costs, inventory turnover, manufacturing cycle times, and so forth, upon which prices and budgets are based. Secondary objectives include speed and accuracy of production reporting, minimizing payroll calculations for incentives, and the like.

Product or Design Engineering. Liaison between production and design departments becomes increasingly important. Many production costs are at the mercy of design decisions and design changes. Mutually beneficial goals established between the two departments are highly desirable. These goals should include restrictions on number, degree, and timing of design changes.

Auxiliaries. Important here are commitments to better communications and improved service to and from purchasing, traffic and distribution, warehousing, personnel, and public and community relations departments. Although many of the commitments in these areas tend to be less specific, they are no less important in attaining the cooperation and support that a manufacturing organization needs in attaining its primary goals.

Corporate Policies and Practices. These tend to be primarily restraining factors and should be realistically reviewed when establishing the manufacturing objectives.

Example of Restrictive Goals Program

1. Reduce number of written customer complaints by 25 percent.
2. Restrict percentage of field repairs costs attributable to manufacturing error to less than 10 percent of sales budget.
3. Accept raw material deliveries for product *F* in bulk quantities of 25,000 gross. Provide handling and storage for these amounts.
4. Ship 25 percent of products *G* and *M* in broken lots, with special packaging and crating.
5. Develop capacity to produce and ship product *A* in ten ton quantities within forty-eight hours after receipt of order.
6. Prepare detailed manufacturing labor reports to support operation-by-operation costing on products *G* and *M*.
7. Paint and clean up processing areas 1 and 2 for stockholders' visits on March 10. Have demonstration equipment operating.

INTEGRATED GOALS

The ultimate in corporate planning takes place when the goals of all its component organizations are integrated into an optimum corporate goal. Parenthetically, the break-even chart which relates fixed and variable costs to sales volumes is one of the simpler although relatively primitive attempts to develop guides for integrated planning of objectives. When the corporation, its suppliers, and its markets can be conceived as a system, then the organization can be treated likewise. Total costs of operating the system then take precedence. System considerations reshape manufacturing's primary goals regarding cost, quality, and time, and of course, its utilization, functional, and restrictive goals. For many corporations, this concept is a long way off. However, it is a concept that should be kept in mind—especially at the higher levels of the manufacturing organization—so that the greatest possible contribution may be made by the manufacturing functions to company profits.

Example of a Manufacturing Objectives Program

1. Reduce total manufacturing unit cost of products A, B, and C by 8 percent. New target units costs as follows: A–$21.35, B–$7.56, C–$12.37.
2. Restrict indirect manufacturing costs for plant to 42 percent of total manufacturing costs.
3. Cut aggregate costs of nonproductive labor time on product B operations to 15 percent of direct costs on that line.
4. Hold aggregate setup and teardown labor costs on both A and C product lines to 25 percent of total labor charges on those lines.
5. Increase material yield on tungsten inserts forming operations on product A from 63 to 72 percent. Attainment target date: April 15.
6. Curtail rejects at final inspection on product line B from present 5.6 to 3.8 percent.
7. Shorten overall production cycle time on product C from 7.25 to 6.85 hours. Attainment target date: October 1.
8. Achieve 90 percent of all shipments on promised dates.
9. Improve screw machine utilization on products A and B by 5 percent. New target rate: 87 percent of rated capacities.
10. Cut hours of preventive maintenance backlog from present 1,258 hours to 1,000 hours by March 31, and 750 by June 30. Hold that level for remainder of year.
11. Raise capacity utilization rate on all class A and class B production equipment to an average of 92 percent on one shift and 75 percent on two shifts. (Annual.)
12. Retire class C production equipment at rate of $125,000 per year, selecting fully depreciated equipment first.
13. Increase manufacturing occupancy of building 3 to 95 percent of available square footage.
14. Hold material cost per unit of product D at present figure while anticipating an increase in raw material costs of 5 percent.
15. Reduce amount of goods in process to 350 percent of weekly finished goods value. Attainment date: September 30.
16. Hold expandable operating supplies cost to 2 percent of total manufacturing costs.
17. Reduce process water consumption by 10 percent. (Annual.)
18. Improve overall plant electric power factor to 85 percent.
19. Reduce working capital needed for manufacturing operations by 5 percent of present figure.
20. Increase product X output per total manufacturing man-hours from 12,575 per thousand hours to 12,955.

ESTABLISHING OBJECTIVES

No one in the entire range of manufacturing management should be excused from entering into the goal planning activity. It should be made clear to everyone, from the president's level to the third-shift foreman of the labor gang, that projecting, forecasting, and goal setting are functions that he must be prepared to perform. Variations in degree and in time spent on these activities, of course, will be marked. But all plans should be built on the principle of integrating the views of every member of the management organization. There is also a very good case for carrying this philosophy and practice all the way down the line to include each employee.

In emulating the military, many companies have gone overboard in designating planning staffs and have lost the greater part of the responsibility for goal setting to the specialists. There are advantages and disadvantages to this practice. In large, complex organizations, the mere logistics of data collection, analysis, and detailing can be overwhelming. Someone other than key executives should perform this work or the bulk of it. On the other hand, the ability to forecast reliably and to choose goals that are both attainable and desirable is one that the important executives must have and exercise. To delegate this activity completely would be to dissipate the organization's greatest strength.

Despite all the difficulties, there are some rules of thumb that can guide a manufacturing manager at any level in handling his planning obligations. For example:

1. Delegate to the next lower level of management all planning responsibilities that can be handled better at that level than at the higher one.
2. Delegate to staff those functions of planning that are most routine, such as making projections and comparing the adequacy of existing plans with newly set goals.
3. Integrate into higher level plans the plans and ideas from all levels subordinate to it.
4. Check with the plans of other major functions to determine the need for coordination of their plans with those of manufacturing.

Time Period of Forecast. Long-range objectives give an organization a fix, an azimuth to guide it. Unfortunately, forecasts upon which long-range objectives should be built are woefully undependable. Happily, in practice, the most frequent kind of planning is of the what-shall-we-do-tomorrow species. Forecasting for such short-range planning is relatively simple and reliable. What is essential in short-range planning is that expedience should not corrupt or obstruct monthly, annual, or five-year goals.

The fact is that both short- and long-range planning involve essentially the same activities. These activities differ only to the degree to which time permits their employment.

Time Interval between Forecasts. There is a distinction between the time period and the time interval. Consideration of the latter is needed because there is a tendency on the part of many manufacturing managers to believe that once a budget has been set, the organization must become like a locomotive charging down a pair of steel rails. Such a concept is dangerous. Business affairs are much too fluid to permit this singlemindedness. The setting and attaining of goals should be "progressive."

Many organizations establish a system of progressive planning which periodically—monthly, quarterly, or annually—reviews attainment of objectives (1) as compared with original objectives and (2) with a view to making a new forecast in light of the additional experience.

Rigidity of Goals. The degree of flexibility maintained in manufacturing goals will depend upon a balance between personal inclinations and the nature of the business. A manufacturing company must achieve some sort of stability to secure operating efficiencies from its investment in plant and equipment; however, it must be supple enough to make adjustments in objectives as economic factors fluctuate.

Systematic Goal Setting. It is useful to look at the plan-ahead process as a systematic series of steps:

First, take measurements of past events, and then in relation to their time occurrence, project or extrapolate them into the future.

Second, make an estimate of what has not happened before or recently, and try to forecast the chances of its happening in the future.

Third, rationalize in what way these new happenings will change the projections made in the first place. These projections, modified by the forecasts, are goals.

Fourth, evaluate existing plans, which were set up sometime in the past to attain previous goals, to determine whether they are now adequate. What is in line, let alone. What is indicated as a weakness or a strength calls for the altering of plans.

The fifth step calls for three things:

1. Alter existing policies and procedures to fit the projected goals.
2. Improve existing organization structure to serve the new goals and the new plans.
3. Check the adequacy of existing staff and its assignments for attaining the new goals and carrying on the new procedures within the new organizational structure. Understaffed or weakly staffed positions will need to be taken care of; overstaffed positions and overqualified incumbents will need reassignment.

Restructuring for New Goals. Organization to support new goals needs a critical assessment. In auditing this area, it should be asked whether the present organization provides:

1. A properly designated management activity to deal with the exceptional problem. In one company, a lag in putting newly developed products into production caused sales to fall behind quotas. What was needed was a liaison group between product design and the manufacturing operation to synchronize start-up tooling and to provide engineering modifications as their need was discovered.
2. A suitable authority to deal with the problem. A multiplant chemical company was irritated by the size of its demurrage charges on railroad tank cars. Forceful instructions from headquarters to the traffic managers at the various plants did not materially improve the situation. Finally the problem was solved by setting up a centralized traffic department with authority to coordinate interplant shipments.
3. Adequate support by communications for measurement and control. A midwestern gray iron foundry was plagued by periodic dips in its working capital. Although the treasurer's plan for control of funds was sound, he was unable to implement it until he appointed a one-man control officer to analyze plant buying activity and sales figures daily—and to report exceptions to projected trends to him each day.
4. A means of avoiding gaps between organizational functions. A home appliance manufacturer found that its inventory of materials in process was becoming a disturbing cost factor. Investigation showed that the purchasing department was ordering an advance in deliveries of subassemblies to conform with production schedules but that no one function was charged with the responsibility of inventory control. The company solved the problem by setting up a materials manage-

ment department designed to control materials inventories from purchase, scheduling, and in-process production and through to shipment.
5. Minimal duplication of effort. Another company detected a persistent rise in indirect charges. Study of the organization showed that each of three manufacturing departments maintained its own clerical accounting group and that almost half of what was reported represented duplication. A solution was brought about by centralizing clerical work for these departments.

BIBLIOGRAPHY

Anderson, Richard C., *Management Practices*, McGraw-Hill Book Company, New York, 1960.
Bittel, Lester R., *Management by Exception*, McGraw-Hill Book Company, New York, 1964.
Carroll, Phil, *How to Control Production Costs*, McGraw-Hill Book Company, New York, 1953.
Enrick, Norbert L., *Management Planning*, McGraw-Hill Book Company, New York, 1967.
Fisch, Gerald G., *Organization for Profit*, McGraw-Hill Book Company, New York, 1964.
Hepner, Harry W., *Perceptive Management and Supervision*, Prentice-Hall, Inc., Englewood Cliffs, N.J., 1961.
Newman, W. H., *Administrative Action*, 2d ed., Prentice-Hall, Inc., Englewood Cliffs, N.J., 1963.

CHAPTER THREE

Organizing for Effective Manufacturing

JOHN T. JACKSON   *Senior Vice President, International Utilities, Philadelphia, Pennsylvania*

Organization consists of arranging work to be done by individuals and by groups of individuals so as to make possible the achievement of the objectives that have been established for the enterprise.   Because managing is getting work done through people, organization clearly requires not only the analysis, measurement, and interrelation of tasks to be done, but also the adjustment of individuals and groups of individuals to their individual and collective tasks.

The philosophy that the arranging of work comes first, that the adjustment of the individual to the task comes next, and that the adjustment of the work to the individual should be considered a last resort is one which has been eloquently articulated by Lyndall Urwick and deserves careful consideration, especially in organizing for effective manufacturing.

The Integrity of Work.   A concept especially useful in organizing for effective manufacturing is that of the "integrity" of work as expounded by Bernard Muller-Thym. This concept reminds us that in the days when a product, such as a piece of furniture, was designed, manufactured piece by piece, assembled, and finished by one man, there could be little doubt that the finished product would at least meet the specifications of the maker if not also of the market. It postulates that there is less and less assurance that this will be true, however, as the manufacturing work is further and further subdivided, as has increasingly become the practice in manufacturing since the turn of the twentieth century.

Integrity of work in this context relates to the possibility or probability that the work or task of any individual worker will be sufficiently understandable to him in its relationship to the end product that he can reasonably be expected to try to meet an expressed or implied requirement of finish, fit, or function on his own volition to satisfy his own pride in his accomplishment.

From this it follows that, as the possibility or probability of the integrity of each individual's direct labor task is diminished, this deficiency must be compensated for by what may become an increasingly complex system of overhead tasks. This accounts to a large extent for the fact that manufacturing overhead costs generally exceed manufacturing direct labor costs, often by a factor of two or more times, and for the bulk of the "boxes" on a manufacturing organization chart.

The Organization Chart. The organization chart may be considered to be the schematic diagram of a communications system. It portrays a system designed to ensure that the objectives of the organization, the plans and programs for achieving them, and the ground rules within the framework of which the organization is to work are known to the responsible participants. The system should provide channels for orderly two-way communication among all the individuals upon whose organized collective efforts the achievement of the objectives depends. Thus, its effectiveness as a system is to a great extent dependent upon the proper positioning and functioning of these interfaces.

Responsibility and Accountability. Probably the most important concepts to be applied in organizing for effective manufacturing are that, wherever possible, responsibility and accountability should go hand in hand and that, with accountability, there must be clearly defined and understood systems of measurement.

In manufacturing management, two primary methods or tools for measurement are cost accounting and some form of quality control. Therefore, in structuring the tasks to be done by individuals or groups of individuals whose primary contribution is the performance of direct labor, some fundamental rules are as follows:

1. Do not establish responsibility for which accountability cannot be established.

2. Do not establish accountability unless adequate tools for performance measurement are available and ready to be applied.

3. If at all possible, give each responsibility-accountability package enough integrity so that the accountable person can have, on an hour-to-hour or at least a day-to-day basis, a pretty shrewd idea of whether he is meeting the objectives, standards, or specifications established for the elements of work for which he is accountable in advance of receiving whatever reports and other performance measurements the accounting function may provide him on a more precise and formal basis.

Obviously, the specific application of these fundamentals to a single product, multiple product, job shop, or process industry varies. In manufacturing operations built around the mass production of a single product or product line, the organization chart, the production flow chart or diagram, and quite possibly, the entire plant layout will be most clearly and almost inextricably interrelated.

In one-of-a-kind or small lot manufacturing of a wide variety of pieces or products, the interrelationship between organizational flow and production flow may be slightly less obvious, but the adherence to these fundamentals in organizing the operation is of even greater importance for this very reason.

In a continuous process operation of the type in which the raw materials flow mechanically from stage to stage of a process, rule 3—the integrity concept—may be difficult to apply or almost totally inapplicable, depending upon the nature of the process and product, but even then it should not be discarded by the organizer without its being given at least a little thought.

Production Planning and Control. Although it may be true that under some circumstances the primary tools of measurement—cost accounting and some form of quality control—could function in the absence of a plan or schedule, it should be evident that, in a manufacturing operation of any complexity, a production planning, scheduling, and control function is an equally essential element.

In the communications system analogy, production control can be compared to the switching system—that is, the manager dials the number to be reached and the switching system proceeds step by step through a series of operations whereby the desired connection is achieved and the call is completed.

A more apt analogy, however, would be to an electronic data processing system in which, in addition to a simple switching system, there is data storage capacity, a calculating capability, and a feedback system which sends a signal back through the system if one or more of the programmed connections cannot be made.

In its fundamental concept, production control is the organizational element which breaks down a total task—an order for a number of units of a product—into a scheduled sequence of subtasks for various organizational elements to perform within the time available for the completion of the total task, taking into account the time available within each organizational element to do the subtasks assigned to it.

Another vital function of production control is the maintenance of control over and the manipulation of at least the work-in-process portion of the inventory; thus, it has an important interface with the cost accounting function, which has already been identified as one of the essential functions in a manufacturing organization, and also with the purchasing function.

Purchasing. The organizational position of the purchasing function varies considerably among manufacturing organizations. In small- or medium-size shoe manufacturing operations, for example, it is not unusual to find the purchasing of leather to be a personal function of the president or general manager, because the cost of the purchased leather varies with market conditions and is by far the greatest single factor in the cost of a finished, popularly priced shoe. For the same reason, the purchasing of copper in a company manufacturing insulated wire is often found to be handled either directly by or under the close personal surveillance of the president or general manager.

On the other hand, in situations where the cost of no one raw material comprises the major portion of the cost of goods sold and the market prices for the material are relatively stable, purchasing may be grouped with both inventory control and production control in what is often called a materials control function.

Another and more sophisticated evolution of purchasing leads into purchasing engineering, which in turn has contributed to the development of the concept and function of value analysis. Both these functions are aimed at the goal of ensuring that the cost and performance of each component, each subassembly, and the total product are optimized with respect to the requirements of the market and as compared with competitive products.

Under any circumstances, the purchasing function must have a good working interface with the total product engineering function and specifically with both the design and production engineering elements of that function.

Engineering Functions. When considering organization for effective manufacturing, one can bypass the relatively pure research and development aspects of what may be broadly termed the engineering function and consider only the four engineering functions which in one form or another exist within the manufacturing organization:

1. Product design and development engineering
2. Production engineering
3. Plant and facilities engineering
4. Industrial engineering

Product design and development engineering is the function which endeavors to develop, from the marketing function's description of customer needs or market requirements, a product which will fill the needs or meet the requirements economically and competitively. Up to a point, this function must respond primarily to stimulus from the marketing function and should not be unduly circumscribed by whatever knowledge it may have of the limitations of the manufacturing facilities and capabilities of the company.

At a fairly early stage in the product development process, however, decisions on which component design approach to follow can save both time and money. Thus, production engineering, which is the interface between product design and the manufacturing floor, must become involved.

Plant and facilities engineering is too often regarded as primarily a maintenance and housekeeping function. However, the lead times and costs involved in the procurement of new facilities or the rearrangement of existing facilities to meet the needs of a new or substantially redesigned product or product line demand close coordination among plant and facilities engineering, production engineering, and the product design and development function.

The industrial engineering function is of paramount importance because it and it alone enables manufacturing management to find, on a scientific and objective basis, the common denominators—the standards on which all cost determinations and evaluations must be based if they are to be valid for use in planning and control of the total operation.

Organization and Personnel Function. The discussion thus far has concentrated on the arrangement of work and the structuring of tasks and has related organization to a large extent to the manufacturing process, whereby raw materials may be subjected to a series of operations which result in their conversion under controlled conditions to a product or products, with some degree of assurance that, if the market assessment has been valid, the products will be competitively marketable.

By applying the fundamentals as outlined, a theoretically workable organizational base can be constructed for any one of many common manufacturing processes. There will be little or no assurance, however, that the organization will be able to achieve its objectives consistently until each responsibility-accountability package is related to the capabilities of the individuals available or potentially available to accept these responsibilities. Thus, the ability of the enterprise to obtain or develop and to maintain a force of workers and supervisors capable of making this ideal organization work must be considered.

This is the unique, highly personal, and critical responsibility of the manufacturing manager. In doing this, he must constantly assess, evaluate, and reevaluate both the structuring and interrelation of the tasks or functions which comprise the work to be done and the present and potential performance of the individuals to whom the tasks or functions are assigned within the structure as it stands, or as he believes it could reasonably be restructured to make better use of the available talent.

To assist manufacturing management in doing this, a staff organization and personnel function should be available—either as a corporate staff service in a large organization, as a part of the manufacturing organization itself, or in some instances, in the form of an outside consulting service.

Depending upon the structure, policies, and practices of the total organization, this function may or may not include labor relations staff assistance. It may be pointed out, however, that experience has shown that comparable degrees of competence in organization planning, compensation and benefits expertise, and labor negotiating ability are seldom found to coexist effectively within a single staff personnel and industrial relations function.

A Philosophy and Approach. This discussion has endeavored to outline a philosophy and approach to the manufacturing manager's job of organizing the work for which he is responsible. How to do this successfully in any specific instance requires, in addition to a knowledge of the philosophy and approach, an objective appraisal of the managerial style of the man who has the total responsibility so that the organization will operate in a manner that capitalizes on his strengths and, insofar as possible, compensates for his weakness. It should also provide enough challenging subordinate positions and sufficient free and clear channels of intercommunications to contribute to the development of strong successors in all its critical elements.

To check this philosophy and approach as they may be reflected in publicly published organization charts, it is interesting to review the study entitled *Corporate Organization Structures* published by the National Industrial Conference Board in 1968.

In those cases in which product line or product group manufacturing organizations are shown in sufficient detail to permit comparison with the philosophy and approach which have been outlined in this discussion, one finds few significant departures in substance, although the same function may be described by a wide variety of terms as, for example, inspection, product assurance, quality control, quality assurance, and reliability assurance. All these terms are directed toward measuring the extent to which the manufactured product meets the performance specifications contemplated in its design and required by its user as a condition of his purchase of the product.

Other Functions. Other functions appearing in the manufacturing organizations depicted in the NICB study which have not been specifically covered in this discussion are traffic, supply and transportation, packaging, warehousing, tool and die design engineering, and pricing or estimating.

Of these, the pricing or estimating function is most deserving of comment, because inherent in its inclusion or exclusion from an organization chart is the question of responsibility and accountability for preparing estimates or price quotes.

What is of fundamental importance here is that responsibility for estimating and accountability for completing the work at or below the cost and within the time estimated must be clearly fixed and measurable. This concept does not preclude the existence of a pricing or estimating function as a manufacturing staff service at any appropriate level in the organization, but it does require that the accountable manager be in a position either to commit himself to or to take specific exception to the validity of the estimates against which his performance will be measured.

Packaging, transportation or traffic, and warehousing as applied to finished goods inventory are all functions with which line manufacturing management must be concerned. Whether they should be the primary responsibility of manufacturing or of the marketing or administrative functions is open to question.

Of the various aspects of packaging, the quantity to be packaged and the styling of the package appear logically to be primarily concerns of the marketing function, whereas the process of packaging is clearly a manufacturing function.

The structure of the package, as it may affect the condition in which the product may be expected to be delivered by whatever forms of transportation and handling are used, is of paramount importance to marketing. It is also logically a problem for a specialized packaging engineering function as a part of, or at least closely and directly coordinated with, the product design and development function so that product and package design can proceed hand in hand.

Transportation or traffic and warehousing can be logically grouped with the marketing and distribution function rather than with manufacturing, because decisions relating to the mode of transportation of the product to the customer and the quantities to be warehoused in various locations are primarily marketing concerns. These decisions, of course, can have a strong influence on packaging design so that wherever the two functions are located organizationally, a good interface is needed between them.

On balance, it appears that packaging, transportation, and warehousing can more logically be grouped with marketing than with manufacturing.

Work Force and Supervision.   Almost obscured by the proliferation of specialized functions on the charts of most large corporations—which in too many cases are diligently duplicated as one descends from the parent corporation to the group, from the group to the division, and from the division to the department, works, or plant at which the manufacturing is done—are the work force and the first-, second-, and even third-line supervisors. Yet, in manufacturing operations in which the performance of direct labor is a substantial factor in the profitable production of a marketable product, it is the arranging of work; the adjustment, training, or development of the individual to meet the requirements of his task; and the motivation of the individual foreman, supervisor, or worker (in which the concept of integrity can play a real part) that are the "guts" of the problem of organizing for effective manufacturing. Without them, no array of sophisticated, specialized overhead functions can ensure that manufacturing management can achieve its objectives.

Conclusion.   An attempt has been made to present an overall picture of the major problems that are involved in organizing for effective manufacturing. Each of the functions mentioned is discussed at greater length in other chapters of this Handbook. In most instances, more detailed information is given about their logical placement within the organization structure. From what has been said, it may be seen that organization is something of an art as well as a science because of the necessity of adjusting the organization structure, no matter how theoretically sound it may be, to the capabilities of the people who are available to staff it.

BIBLIOGRAPHY

Bethel, L. L., and others, *Industrial Organization and Management*, McGraw-Hill Book Company, New York, 1960.

Corporate Organization Structures, National Industrial Conference Board, New York, 1968.

Corporate Structure, American Institute of Management, New York, 1961.

Dale, Ernest, and Lyndall F. Urwick, *Staff in Organization*, McGraw-Hill Book Company, New York, 1960.

Gulick, L. H., L. F. Urwick, and J. D. Mooney, *Papers on the Science of Administration*, edited by L. F. Urwick, Institute of Public Administration, New York ,1937.

Holden, Paul E., Lounsbury S. Fish, and Hubert L. Smith, *Top Management Organization and Control*, Stanford University Press, Stanford, Calif., 1941.

Newman, William H., and James P. Logan, *Management of Expanding Enterprises*, Columbia University Press, New York, 1955.

CHAPTER FOUR

Staffing and Developing the Line Organization

W. M. McFEELY   *Vice President—Organization, Riegel Paper/Textile Corporation, New York, New York*

The line organization is responsible for achieving the economic objectives of an enterprise. This accountability is absolute.

In most organizations, particularly in larger companies, the line organization is provided assistance by various staff groups such as personnel, engineering, industrial engineering, purchasing, and traffic. These staff groups give the line organization advice and counsel in areas requiring sophisticated levels of specialized knowledge, in the preparation of plans, and in the evaluation of alternative courses of action. However, none of these service groups takes from the line organization its accountability for performance.

The day-to-day objectives of a business are attained through people working with plant and equipment. The competitive edge one company may have over another is very largely the result of more effective staffing and developing of the line organization. In a free market economy, the plant and equipment are available to all. The difference in performance, given reasonably similar plant and equipment, is people.

STAFFING THE LINE ORGANIZATION

Inadequate selection cannot be overcome by training. This is true regardless of how good the training may be. This statement is not intended to minimize the effect of good training. Sound training can upgrade the performance of an entire group. However, the gap in performance between those who are well qualified for a job and those who are not will widen as the result of training.

To some line managers, this emphasis on selection may be surprising. The assumption has been that training is the key to effective performance. This is true only if employee selection is equally sound.

The truth of this assertion is perhaps best seen in a plant where an individual employee is matched to a single machine, such as in a sewing plant. Each operator accounts for the total output of a single machine. Thus, the total output of the plant is equal to the number of sewing machine operators.

In a well-managed sewing plant, each operator receives the same quality of training. It is well planned. It is conducted by carefully selected and trained instructors. However, in plants which are considered to have good selection procedures, the most efficient operator may produce 80 to 100 percent more than the least efficient.

In the same kind of operation, random selection of employees could produce a performance gap between the top producers and the poorest producers in the order of 250 percent. Thus, effective employee selection is the focal point for the development of an efficient, productive line organization. This must, of course, be supplemented by good training, good working conditions and policies, and competent supervision.

Employee Selection. All the steps in the employment procedure are designed to accomplish two objectives. First, there is the necessity of matching a prospective employee to a job opening. Second, there is the desire to employ a person capable of advancing beyond the position for which he is being selected. In this sense, people are hired for a company and not merely for a job.

Every step in the selection procedure, including the forms used, should be designed with these two objectives in mind. This is true of employee selection at every level in the organization. It is true of production employees. It is equally true in selecting employees for upgrading into management positions or in promoting persons from one level of management to another.

There is no foolproof way of matching an employee to a job or of selecting a person for upgrading. It is a question of probability. Each step in the selection procedure should add something toward making the odds more favorable. In view of the importance of selection, management should neglect no step that raises the odds, nor should it adopt or continue practices that add nothing toward favoring the probabilities.

Position Specifications. In smaller organizations where the duties, responsibilities, and qualifications for various positions may be well known, position specifications may be unnecessary. This is particularly true where the person who makes the final selection personally performs all the steps in the selection process.

This situation rarely exists in a larger organization. Usually several different persons participate in the process. Often they work in different departments. The personnel department, for example, may have a key role in finding candidates either from within the organization or from the outside, in testing them, and in conducting preliminary or screening interviews. Those considered to be suitable candidates are then referred to appropriate members of the line organization who make the final decisions.

A position specification is a useful tool in the larger organization. It can be quite elaborate or very simple. The form itself is relatively unimportant. The information is important.

The minimum information needed, irrespective of the form used, is: a description of the duties of the positions and of the results expected; a statement concerning the scope of the position (departmental, divisional, company-wide) and reporting relationships; an outline of the knowledge, skill, and experience needed to qualify for the position; and an indication of the compensation or compensation range for the position.

This kind of information is needed by those responsible for finding acceptable candidates. It is of even greater value in screening applicants.

Candidate Data Bank. The application blank, or career resume, is the most commonly used method of providing preliminary factual data concerning a candidate from outside the company. Often this is supplemented by information obtained by reference checks, credit checks, or from other forms of investigation. Additional data are gained from test results and from medical examinations.

There is the same need for providing a data base for present members of the organization who may be candidates for transfer or promotion. Managements tend to shortcut this step because of their familiarity with the persons concerned. In so doing, pertinent factual data may be forgotten or ignored. Or the failure to have adequate information available may mean that a qualified employee is overlooked.

The data bank provides a useful backdrop to decision making. It is another tool for increasing the probabilities of successful selection.

Tests. The use of tests to measure such things as general learning ability, special aptitudes, physical dexterity, levels of skill, knowledge, interests, and temperament is increasing in industry. The use of tests is also being attacked because of their alleged cultural bias and because of lack of evidence in some situations that there is a correlation between test results and success or failure on the job. Some tests, particularly interest inventories and temperament tests, have been criticized also because some people believe the testee can make the test result come out the way he wants it to come out. Thus, the testee can "fudge" the tests, according to their critics. Others attack testing programs on the grounds that they are invasions of privacy.

In the long run, such criticism of testing programs serves a useful purpose. Tests themselves will be improved. Their use will be more carefully considered on the part of management. Tests should not be used unless those who administer them and interpret the results have been adequately trained.

Tests are never the sole means of selection. They add useful information for the candidate's data bank. They supplement other steps in the selection process but do not replace them.

Tests serve as a medium for sorting. They are more useful in indicating those who may not reasonably be expected to succeed in a position than in predicting the degree of success if the candidate passes the minimum requirements of the specific test. A high score does not necessarily mean that the person will be superior in performance. There are too many other factors that influence actual performance. On the other hand, the failure to meet the minimum or cutoff score is a warning that the individual may not be able to measure up to the minimum acceptable standards of performance.

The Interview. In the case of an applicant from outside the company, the interview is the most commonly used method for getting information and for judging the qualifications of the individual. Only in exceptional cases are persons employed without an interview. An exchange of thought concerning the nature of the work and the qualifications of the individual is essential to sound selection.

Good techniques are prerequisites for sound selections based upon interviews. Often, however, interviews are little more than a few obvious questions and their equally obvious answers. This kind of interview may consist of merely a kind of oral checking of the information provided in the application blank. In its extreme form, it may be almost an oral handshake, a most cursory kind of contact. Such interviewing methods are symptomatic of the "hunch" or so-called intuitive method of selection.

Some studies have shown that the interview is not a very reliable method of selection. Other studies have shown that it can be the most reliable process for predicting success on the job. These divergent points of view serve to reinforce the need for sound technique. Good interviewing is not intuitive in nature. It is an acquired discipline.

A good interview is designed to yield facts concerning the candidate's character, temperament, disposition, motivation, interests, inclinations, accomplishments, and aspirations. Such information is usually best ascertained indirectly rather than by direct confrontation.

An interview of this type is a conversation with a purpose. It must be adapted to the individual being interviewed and must be so directed as to bring out information with as little shading and reserve as possible. The conversation is a give and take of thought between the interviewer and the interviewee.

The interviewer is only in part acting as a judge of the merits and qualifications of the applicant. He does act as a judge of the degree that the candidate possesses the qualifications needed for success in the job. He is also an agent of the company responsible for giving the applicant all the information he is entitled to concerning the nature of the work and the results expected. It is an indictment of the interviewer if the successful applicant finds the work significantly different from his expectation.

The interviewer is also a salesman. The company is on trial, with the applicant being the judge.

For many positions, particularly those at key levels in the line organization, multiple interviews are useful. Companies have found that for such key positions it is desirable to have the opinions of several individuals before a final decision is made concerning a candidate. Pooled judgment is often more reliable than that of a single person. Furthermore, this practice gives the candidate a better opportunity to determine whether his own interests and aspirations are consistent with those of the organization he is seeking to join.

Pooled judgment is useful because everyone tends to have a constant error of selection. Thus, each interviewer has a built-in bias. This is unintentional. He may not even recognize that he has a bias. But his own background, experience, and beliefs tend to cause him consistently to give preference to a certain type of person. This tendency is repeated in every interview and results in a constant bias or error in selection. Multiple interviews are one way of trying to offset the biases of the persons participating in the selection procedure.

SOURCES OF CANDIDATES

In staffing the line organization, management should look first within the company. In increasing numbers, companies maintain an inventory system of their employees. This includes the educational background, any additional special training, the skills, and the experience of each employee. The larger the organization, the greater the need for such an inventory. This provides some assurance that, in filling openings in the line organization, qualified candidates for promotion or transfer will not be overlooked.

The reason for looking first within the organization is clear. The principle of upward mobility within the organization is well established in industry.

Most companies employ a person for the company rather than for a specific job. They are looking for people who can be moved up in the organization. When a person joins an organization, he does not expect to remain immobile in his entry position. He does not expect to remain stratified. Opportunities for upward movement are an essential condition of good morale among the employee group.

One further reason for looking first within the organization is that the work record of the employee is known. In the process of selection, a person's track record to date is one of the more reliable indicators of his probable future performance. Thus, a judgment of the probabilities for success of the inside candidate is better than that of an outside applicant.

There is, of course, a danger that proximity and friendship may lead a manager to magnify an insider's strengths and to minimize his weaknesses or to want to give him the opportunity merely because he is on the scene and available. Often, too, managers will give the nod to an insider because they know they will be comfortable working with him.

The reverse may also be true. The insider's faults are so well known that managers sometimes fail to see the whole person. Qualified persons are thus passed by. The desire to give first consideration to inside candidates must be coupled with the same degree of objectivity that characterizes selection from outside the organization.

Well-managed companies do not hesitate to go into the outside market to find the right man for the right job. This is particularly true when there is a need for persons with educational training, skills, or experience not currently found within the organization. Such a situation may exist when a company is moving into a new technology, or is setting up an entirely new method or process, or is planning a new product line. For example, companies entering into an electronic data processing program often find that they must go outside to get the man they need to initiate the activity. Similarly, expansions in research and development activities usually require outside recruitment.

The outside search may be made in a variety of ways. There is no one best way. Each channel is appropriate for a given situation. Each should be examined in terms of the specific situation before a decision is made to move ahead.

Specific channels for finding candidates on the outside are: personal acquaintances, inquiries made of friends and acquaintances, direct advertising in newspapers and professional or trade journals, employment agencies, and executive search firms. These methods are not mutually exclusive. They may be used singly or in appropriate combinations.

Many companies, particularly the larger ones, use college recruiting as a means of filling specific openings or for the purpose of building a reservoir of competent talent capable of being developed for a variety of functional positions.

As one of the means for staffing the line organization, college recruiting should be looked upon as a long-term program. It takes time, careful planning, and sustained effort to build an effective college recruiting program.

In deciding whether to attempt a program of college recruitment, management must consider such things as its ability to plan future manpower needs and the lead time it has or needs to prepare college graduates for foreseeable openings in the organization. Management must also give careful consideration to its ability to train and to challenge such recruits adequately. Failures in either of these areas will result in excessive turnover.

THE WORK OF THE LINE ORGANIZATION

The work of the line organization is distinctive. It is unlike any other kind of work. The work of the manager is not simply an extension of the work of the production or maintenance employee. The different nature of the work, and thus of the knowledge, ability, and skill required to be a good line manager, explains why many good, efficient production or maintenance employees fail to make good supervisors or managers. The job requisites are different.

The operating line organization deals with some very basic economic principles. Its objective is to produce profits which are fully commensurate with the profit opportunities available in the businesses involved. To do this, line management deals in four basic elements: quantity, quality, cost, and time. Obviously, the goals established for each of these elements are met through the management of people.

The functions of line management cover the full range of operations. These include staffing so as to meet the requirement for success in the particular business, planning within the operation, directing the activities of the operating work force, measuring and evaluating the effectiveness of operations, and making the changes and adjustments in any element of the production cycle that are essential to the achievement of approved goals.

Specific Duties of the Line Foreman. A more specific analysis of the duties and responsibilities of a line foreman will serve to illustrate both the uniqueness of managerial work and the skills that must be developed within the line organization.

The essential job elements of a foreman are to direct and supervise the efficient, safe, and profitable operation of his department or shift. To do this, he is responsible for the following functions and any additional responsibilities which may be assigned to him by his superior in the line organization.

1. *Production Scheduling.* Develops or collaborates in the development of production schedules. Checks daily production against schedule. Investigates and determines reasons when schedule is not met and takes corrective action.

2. *Production Control.* Ensures adherence to standard operating procedures and accepted techniques in all operations and activities.

3. *Cost Control.* Directs work force so as to meet cost standards. Eliminates unnecessary indirect costs. Sees that tools and supplies are used properly and efficiently. Keeps waste, scrap, and seconds to a minimum.

4. *Personnel.* Trains new employees and retrains older employees to develop highest skills of each. Makes job assignments for members of his department or shift. Communicates and interprets company policies and practices. Handles employee grievances in accordance with established procedures. Develops employee morale by building employee confidence and pride in his job and in the company.

5. *Facilities.* Exercises proper care and utilization of buildings, equipment, and services. Cooperates with the maintenance personnel in the accomplishment of maintenance activities. Reports and makes requests for routine or emergency maintenance.

6. *Processes.* Makes recommendations to improve processes and yields and to reduce waste, labor, material, maintenance, material handling, and other costs.

7. *Records.* Provides required information concerning the activity of his department or shift, including personnel, raw material usage, process information, finished goods produced, maintenance, and the like.

This description is not intended to be all-inclusive, for the duties and responsibilities of a line foreman or manager will vary somewhat depending upon the industry and the specific company. It is sufficiently comprehensive, however, to be indicative of the scope and magnitude of the task of developing capable members of the line management organization.

THE DEVELOPMENT OF THE LINE ORGANIZATION

Management development is the development of the individual. It is the process of growing leadership. Thus, management development includes all the actions or influence, whether generated by the manager who is being developed, his boss, his associates, or his company, that affects what he knows and can do, how he thinks, how he works, and how he grows as a member of the line organization. Some of the major objectives of a development program are:

1. To assure a supply of foremen or managers in the required numbers and with the required skills to meet the present and the future anticipated needs of the company
2. To encourage members of the management group to grow as individuals in their capacity to handle greater responsibility of any nature
3. To improve performance of the members of management in their present jobs
4. To sustain good performance of members of the management group throughout their entire careers

Before World War II, there was little formalized management development activity in American industry. Many companies had supervisory training programs, but there was little or no organized development activity for middle or upper management personnel.

It was assumed that if men were selected who had both the capacity and the will to succeed, and if these men were given the opportunity, they would develop themselves. This is true. Given time, cream will rise to the top, but the question is always whether there is adequate time for this natural process to take place. Most growing companies have found that there is a need to force-feed or to accelerate the development of individuals. This is one way in which such companies make sure that their growth is not circumscribed by the lack of trained personnel.

Principles Underlying Development Activities. Every development and training technique should be studied objectively in terms of the organization's present and future needs and of how the usual or expected results of such training techniques meet these needs. Each program or activity should also be examined in terms of how the procedures and actions of the techniques being taught may influence the organizational climate and its people.

Every management must make its own decision concerning the principles it uses to evaluate development activities. Today, it would be fair to say that management development activities in American industry are based upon the following ideas.

1. All development is self-development. No one really develops another person. He develops himself. Developmental and training activities merely provide the opportunity for this process of self-development to be appropriately directed and accelerated.

2. Development activity should be tailored to the man. Sophisticated managements do not jump headlong or blindly into one or more programs in the hope that they will do some good. They identify the needs of individuals

and then adopt the methods or techniques which will be responsive to these needs.

3. Improvement requires action; that is, the participant must have experience which contributes toward the development of the skills he is expected to have. A man cannot learn to ride a bicycle by reading a book. A line manager cannot develop the skills and abilities of a manager without experience as a manager.

4. Measurements and controls aid development. A man cannot be developed in the absence of risk. Accountability is a continuing risk of the line manager. He is responsible for results. Measurements and controls are tools of accountability for the line organization. When these tools are used skillfully as a factor in performance appraisal, they encourage, stimulate, and give direction to individual development.

5. The situation or the climate in which the individual works is important to his development. Experience indicates that the environment in which a man works affects his performance, his ability to learn, and his ability to retain what he has learned. Although a person may have an opportunity to learn, research shows that he will not use what he has learned if it does not fit within the context of his job. Development activity is seldom successful if it moves too far from the normally accepted ways of working in a company.

6. The boss himself and the way in which he operates is a major influence on individual development. It is not unheard of for a man to return to his position after completing a developmental program and to be told by his supervisor, either directly or indirectly, to forget what he has just been told and to "get back on the job." It is even more common for the man to find that any ideas he may have picked up in the development activity are ignored. The developed man will soon give up trying to practice the principles he has learned unless they are consistent with the performance standards which he believes are expected of him by his own superiors.

7. Development is primarily a line responsibility, although the line organization may get important assistance from the staff groups. Research into the effectiveness of various training programs has suggested that there is a correlation between the results attained and the degree of participation on the part of the line organization. The absence of line involvement in the developmental processes may lead the participants to think of such programs merely as mental gymnastic exercises or as games which do not necessarily have any real relationship to their jobs. Thus, the things learned are not necessarily carried over into their job performance.

8. Although the development of an individual may be accelerated, it is still a long-term project. Training is the function of helping others to acquire and apply knowledge, skills, and attitudes which they can use in specific work situations. A complete training concept for an individual thus includes activities to give him knowledge appropriate to his situation, the skills which will enable him to carry out his functional responsibilities, and the attitudes which will enable him to apply his knowledge and his skills wisely. Broadly speaking, the knowledge factors of a job are the easiest to impart to a person in a development situation. The requisite skills come next in order of difficulty. Attitudinal training is the most difficult and usually has a much longer time span because it may involve changing an individual's fundamental behavior patterns. This takes time.

Elements of a Complete Concept of Training. The content of a development program should be such as may reasonably be expected to meet the needs of the organization. It is surprising how few companies have checked their specific needs before inaugurating a training program. There are a host of training and development techniques.

Most of the well-established techniques have been developed through research, experimentation, and the findings of behavioral scientists. Their worth has been proved in specific situations. This does not mean that they will be effective in every situation.

Management must be careful not to adopt a program of developmental activities just because the techniques or programs are readily available, have worked in another company in the neighborhood or industry, or are highly touted at some management meeting. As has been previously emphasized, this does not mean that they will work well in any environment or solve every management's manpower needs.

While tailoring the training content and techniques to their own specific needs, managements find that the training of an individual, to be complete, contains all the following elements:

1. Acquisition of knowledge, through on-the-job experience and coaching, courses, publications, lectures, conversations, visual aids, discussions, and experience sharing.

This element of training is designed to keep the supervisor current with the growing technical and professional knowledge pertaining to his job. It is aimed also at giving him the essential facts concerning his company's history, product lines, policies, practices, procedures, goals, aims, philosophy, and organization.

Knowledge training includes, additionally, such things as keeping the organization up to date with respect to current performance, plans, and problems.

2. Acquisition of skills, through on-the-job coaching and instruction, skill training courses and seminars, guided practice sessions, and experience sharing.

A review of the functional responsibilities of the line supervisor will readily indicate the kinds of skills he needs. These include the skills of planning, organizing, instructing communicating, job analysis, methods improvement, cost analysis and control, process and individual performance appraisal, human relations, and leadership.

3. Acquisition of right attitudes, through personal coaching and counseling, identification with appropriate models among his peers and superiors, and participation in courses, including "sensitivity training" and similar analytical approaches.

As a minimum, attitudinal training is designed to develop supervisors who seek to understand situations and people, who feel a responsibility for the whole enterprise rather than only their particular area of operation, who feel free to make and to give others the freedom to make risk-taking decisions, and who see people as ends as well as means.

Managements who successfully implement a well-rounded, soundly conceived program of training and development activities for the line organization use resources from both inside the company and outside. The key to success is in the proper blend of the two.

Outside Resources. The use of outside resources is based upon the obvious fact that it is impossible, in sophisticated areas of knowledge or skill, for a company to pull itself up by its own bootstraps. When an organization is confronted with the need for new knowledge or new skills, it is prudent to look outside for help.

By their very nature, however, courses or other training activities conducted by people outside the company are not usually tailored to the specific needs of a company but deal with general principles and typical situations. With the increased use of the case study method of instruction, real situations are approached in the classroom. The same observation may be made of certain business games or of simulation exercises.

The use of outside resources and facilities is generally considered to be supplementary to a development program within a business enterprise itself and is not designed to take the place of an effective internal program. Individual companies that are too small to have a program of their own may find the use of outside resources the most practical alternative. Similarly, large companies are often able to employ outside resource persons for research and experimentation and to design and conduct training programs that are specifically tailored to the needs of the particular organization.

Many companies have policies of tuition refunds in all or in part for employees who take courses in outside educational institutions. Typically, such courses have to be reasonably related to the employee's occupation or to one for which he may become qualified. More latitude in approving courses is generally given if the employee is taking courses leading to an undergraduate or graduate degree.

Financial aid is also given by many companies to employees who complete approved correspondence courses. Success with correspondence courses varies widely. It is difficult to maintain interest because they lack personal inspiration and many persons need the stimulus of group activity to sustain their own interest. Group instruction using correspondence course material as the basic text has proved successful in many situations where the number being trained justifies the expense.

Internal Resources. Training is going on all the time in a company, whether it is planned or not. People are being trained as they participate in the activities of the company. The question is whether they are receiving good training. The objective of planned training is to make sure that the line organization is acquiring the knowledge, skills, and attitudes which will result in effective job performance.

The understudy system is obviously the most widespread method of internal training. This kind of training is inherent in any situation where a manager or supervisor has one or more assistants.

The understudy system is well adapted to training a limited number of men who have been well selected for their positions. Where the organization is large enough, this system is an integrated part of the organization itself, with each key person having an understudy. The understudy may have no duties of his own but may have a title such as assistant to the superintendent and perform any duties specifically assigned. On the other hand, the understudy may have specific duties such as a general foreman and still be in training as an understudy for the superintendent. The understudy usually acts for the superior in his absence.

The understudy system is effective if the superior is a good coach, can delegate effectively, and is not psychologically threatened in the process of bringing others along. Its effectiveness depends also upon the qualities of the trainee. The two must be able to interact constructively with each other if the full benefits of the system are to be achieved.

The weakness of this system is that it tends to perpetuate the weaknesses of management style and seldom upgrades prevailing management methods unless the trainee is a superior person. It does offer one advantage. It provides an incentive for the understudy. The strength of this incentive depends upon the likelihood of the trainee's being called upon to fill his superior's position in the reasonably near future.

Many companies have formal training programs providing for trainees spending allotted amounts of time in various departments within the company. Such programs may also include classroom work. Companies select a group of college graduates or promising men of experience within the company to form a training group. Typically, this kind of program has as its primary objective the training of minor executives and prospective foremen.

Planned job rotation is another developmental method used by many companies. This kind of program is designed primarily for "comers" within the enterprise, trainees who are judged capable of climbing high up the ladder. The trainee is moved from one job to another in a sequence designed to give him experience and insight into many facets of the business, with the objective of developing him for key management responsibility. Usually, he will remain in a job until he has mastered the requirements of the department and has demonstrated his ability to produce, although this is not necessarily an essential feature of such a program.

There is a strong trend toward attempts at early identification of comers. This is coupled with career planning programs. Such programs outline a sequence of job experiences for the trainee with the expectation that he will reach a certain position level within a predetermined time span. Such career plans also include the use of outside training resources such as schools, colleges, management associations, and similar opportunities.

Lectures, sound-slide pictures, movies, and other straight classroom techniques are also used in many companies, with persons within the company as the trainers or resource people. They are well adapted to training people in company policies and practices and in informing trainees concerning the importance and functions of departments with which they have contacts but in which they will not have job experience.

Discussion groups and seminars are effective developmental techniques of sharing knowledge and experience and for sharpening skills in areas where the participants already have basic competency. Under skilled leadership, such techniques are also useful as a vehicle for attitude training.

There are many variations of these typical development techniques. The range of possible approaches to personal development is almost without limits.

CONCLUSION

In summary, training by absorption is seldom sufficient, because it almost never results in a significant upgrading in the performance of a succeeding generation of management. Training by intention, through well-planned and organized programs geared to the specific needs of an organization, will tend to raise the general level of supervisory and executive performance, and this is a continuing goal of every successful enterprise.

CHAPTER FIVE

The Operating Force

A. D. NEWMAN   *Director, The Centre for Organization Analysis, Fulmer, England; Special Professor of Organization Theory, University of Nottingham, Nottingham, England*

The corporate organization depends on its operating force to implement the manufacturing plan.   No matter how effective the planning is, nothing will be achieved without an effective operating force.   The operating force thus is part of the company team.   Whether or not the operating force itself recognizes this in its behavior and whether or not it is regarded as such by senior management, it is one of the determinants of the organization's performance.

This chapter has as its objective the spelling out of the main features of the operating force, so that the manufacturing manager can see what factors he must take into account both in his planning and in his subsequent management of the implementation of the operating plan.   We live in an era of rapid social and cultural change.   Employment work is itself a major cultural determinant, and conversely, the attitudes and indeed the activities of people in employment are very much affected by these changes.   Examination of the features of the operating force will therefore be an examination of change.   The manager who deals with the operating force must deal with it in this light.

THE ROLE OF THE OPERATING FORCE

To describe the significant features of the operating force, it is necessary to identify its role.   In doing this, one immediate problem is semantics.   Unlike some other important fields of human endeavor, the field of organization and management has no universally agreed upon technical language.   Thus, semantic problems arise not only in textbooks but also in real management.   There are two courses open.   One is to develop new and in a sense artificial terms (often described as "jargon"); the other is to use everyday words, but in a more specific or limited way.   This latter course will be preferred here.

Organizations come into being when groups—shareholders, employees, and customers and suppliers in the case of a commercial company—cooperate in recognition of their common interest although each group has its own individual interest and although the underlying presence of cooperation may not be reflected in overtly cooperative behavior. Each of these groups has power in relation to the organization, depending on its ownership or control of the resources—financial, human, and material—that the organization needs to carry out the activities which produce the return that the cooperative groups share.

The Executive System. At the center of the organization is a system of people—the human resource—in work roles. This is called the executive system, and it includes everyone in roles at all levels. It is the means whereby the activities of the organization are executed or carried out. As a vital part of the whole team that is the executive system, the operating force has a particular characteristic: it is the bottom, or front, level—the level in direct contact with concrete output. It is the last link in the chain between management and product, between organization objectives and results. Therefore, unless the operating force plays its part, the link will be inadequate and the organization will be ineffective.

Where the operating force ends and management begins is an important question. In some companies, it is observable that there is a gray area, a no-man's-land, between the two that is neither one nor the other, that has not the status of management and yet is not regarded as part of the operating force because the latter is considered to be only the shop floor. This gray area can become a serious communications barrier an inadequate link in the chain of command, and a source of dissatisfaction for those in it. This problem can be solved by recognizing (1) that the executive system is a single team, and (2) that the real differentiation between people in the executive system is one of kind and level of work, not one of "them and us" or "management and labor." These points allow a definition of operating force as that body of people in the executive system in direct contact with concrete output, with all others in the executive system at various levels being adjuncts to or planning or controlling the activities of the operating force.

The executive system carries out the activities that are necessary if the organization is to reach its objectives. To carry out these activities, resources must be available. The determination of objectives, the consequent determination of appropriate and relevant activities, and the necessary deployment of resources to make those activities feasible and effective is a main managerial function in the executive system.

The operating force is the ultimate human resource and may also be the final controller of the physical resource—raw materials, machinery, and the like. Thus the operating force must be deployed in a way that makes the activities it is required to perform feasible and effective. A change in activity due, for example, to a change in technology will therefore require a redeployment of the operating force, that is, of the human resource and not only of the machinery or plant involved. These social and organizational effects of changing technology have been widely studied, but the implications have not yet been adequately appreciated by some managers and managements.

Just as the role of the executive system as a whole involves objectives which are part of the total organization's objectives, activities which should be relevant to those objectives, and the use of the resources necessary for those activities, so the role of the operating force and the individual roles of the people in it involve these features of objectives, activities, and resources. It is essential to recognize them if a proper understanding of the operating force and of the

individuals that man it is to be ach...
part of the company t...
vital if it i...

1–46

tive work, and now this is becoming much more apparent to them as a result of education, formal and informal, as well as to their managers.

It is common to suggest that the problem of matching person to work and work to person in the situation where both work and person are changing is a matter of job enlargement. So indeed it is, but enlargement must be in terms of level as well as kind. Enlarging an individual's role by adding more to it in quantity will not solve a problem of mismatch due to a reducing level of available work or the increasing level of capacity of the individual as he develops through time or is replaced by another whose capacity, as a result of the cultural changes going on in society, is higher. Job enlargement, if it is to be effective, must involve an extension of the area of discretion or freedom available in the role.

OBJECTIVES

It was said earlier that the operating force is the last link, and a vital one, in the chain between organization objectives and results. Thus any weakness or misdirection in the operating force will lead to a less effective relationship between objectives and results, and so to a less successful company. It is essential therefore that the objectives of the work of the operating force are clear and are accepted by that force and all its components. Unless top management is itself clear about its objectives, the necessary clarity cannot be achieved at the level of the operating force. What is more damaging still, a specious clarity may be achieved at that level, which speciousness is then exposed when activities at the top of the organization "give the game away."

Clarity alone, however, is not enough. The company objectives, if they are to be understood and accepted, must be translated into such terms that the operating force can reasonably identify with them. Only the managers in direct contact with the operating force can adequately achieve this translation. Acceptance of the company objectives by the operating force will not occur unless the company recognizes that the operating force has objectives of its own. Its members are husbands, fathers, citizens, and members of trade union churches, political parties, and social systems of many kinds, each involv activities and objectives. Unless there is some common ground betwee company objectives and all the other objectives of the individuals and in the operating force, the acceptance of the company's objectives by t ating force will not occur.

Thus management needs to identify and understand these relate of the operating force and to communicate the common ground o necessity that springs from their interrelationship with the comp In this, the immediate management of the operating force cle role to play.

Theory X and Theory Y. In a sense, this identification ent between the organization's objectives and the related obj ing force may be expressed as the well-known problem admin- and aspirations of individuals and the ends and activ wish to that employ them. McGregor's theory X and theory directed approach is very helpful here. objectives.

Theory X corresponds to the traditional rigidly us that in istration, based on underlying assumptions tha avoid responsibility, want security above all, a into putting forth effort toward the achiever These assumptions were perhaps never entir a modern economy with relative individual security and an educated work force they cannot be valid.

Theory Y postulates that the expenditure of physical and mental effort is natural, that in an adequate context individuals do not inherently abhor work, that external control is not the only means of regulation of work in an organization but that self-control and self-direction are also available, that individuals accept and indeed seek responsibility and want to contribute creatively to the solution of work problems, and that the potential abilities of individuals are not being fully used. There are of course some individuals and some groups for whom these assumptions are obviously invalid, and there are probably circumstances in which these assumptions cannot apply at all. On the whole, however, the trend, if not the actuality yet, is in their direction at the operating force level as well as with management, and so increasingly the theory Y approach is valid.

This approach depends on the creation of conditions such that the members of the organization can achieve their own goals or objectives best by directing their efforts toward the success of the enterprise. This does not mean the abdication of managerial authority but the realization that externally applied and arbitrary authority is not the only nor the most effective means of control. People will exercise self-direction and self-control in doing work if they are committed to the work objectives, that is, if they see and accept that these are not in conflict with their own objectives but rather are the means whereby their own objectives may be reached.

Theory Y also has a bearing on the way in which specialists or staff—for example, industrial engineers—may operate. If staff departments are used to control the operating force in their own specific areas of interest, there is bound to be tension and conflict among the various staff departments, managers, and the operating force. Under theory Y, the role of staff is to provide professional help to all levels in the executive system, including the operating force. From this stems the concept that is rapidly gaining ground of the industrial engineer as a staff assistant to the operating technician.

COMMUNICATION WITH THE OPERATING FORCE

For the operating force to do effective work, the communication link must be effective between it and those managers and specialists in the executive system who are concerned with the operating force. It is helpful to examine and learn what these communications essentially are about and what their basic features are.

In the first place, the communications are about work. A first-class communication system will be of no avail in this context if it is not primarily about work—the work that the operating force and the individuals in it are concerned with. This must be a two-way communication. If managers are not communicated to by the operating force about work, they are isolated from the activities that they are accountable for controlling, however well they themselves communicate to the operating force.

But communications about work must also mean communications about resources, because work and resources are essentially connected. In his two-way communications, the manager must achieve this link between work and resources. As the operation becomes more capital intensive, or less labor intensive, the communications between managers and the operating force about the resources used by the operating force become more important. The manager is concerned not only with work or output, but also with the effect of work on his expensive resources.

As the operating force develops in quality as a result of educational and other cultural changes in modern communities, it becomes necessary to communicate objectives to the operating force—objectives of the organization translated into terms such that they are understood by the operating force and are directly relevant to its work. The communication of "why such work is to be done," or of relevance to objectives, as well as "what work is to be done" is increasingly necessary if the operating force is to be adequately motivated. Of course, the objectives must be not only understood but also accepted by the operating force.

Although objectives, work, and resources are the prime subjects of communications with the operating force, they are not the only content. These prime subjects have to do with what were called earlier in this chapter accountability and authority, that is, the organizational aspects of the operation. There remain, however, the vital features earlier called responsibility and power in individuals and groups. Clearly, therefore, another area of content of communications with the operating force must deal with attitudes to or relationships with objectives, work, and resources as concerning individuals and in the form of group consensus. These features themselves affect and are affected by attitudes toward the conditions of employment that concern the operating force—wages, salaries, benefits, working conditions, and so on. For this reason, clarity and separation of communications about the work features (organizational and personal) and the employment features, where they can be achieved, are very helpful.

It is also extremely helpful to those concerned with communications to and from the operating force to be aware of the basic features of communications per se. The comments so far have been about content of communications. Another important feature is style. The language used and the form of presentation must be appropriate for the receiver of the communication, not only for the sender. Whatever the objective of the communication, some action or reaction by the receiver is required.

It is important that the objective of the communication is clear and that the distinction between content and objective is understood. The content should be relevant to the objective, but relevance involves a recognition of the attitudes and susceptibilities of the receiver and is not necessarily a simple relationship. Being clear about the objective means being clear about what result is intended from the communication. This gives a criterion for communication effectiveness—not "Is the content clear?" but "Does it achieve the intended result?"

Sender and receiver are basic features of a communication, and in the context of organization, they involve role as well as person. If the organizational roles are not clear to the individuals concerned, the communications situation cannot be adequate, however appropriate the content and style of the communication. For example, a supervisor cannot communicate adequately about work to the operating force if there is lack of clarity as to the authority that the role of supervisor involves. A member of the operating force cannot adequately communicate the problems he is having with his work, or the inadequacies in the instructions he is receiving, if he is not clear about the roles, and thus the accountabilities, of those above him. This clarity of role is at least as important as adequacy of personal relationship, but it must be recognized that it is more difficult to achieve adequate communications between the operating force and those above it if there is insufficient personal contact.

A final basic feature is this. The receiver must be willing to receive and act upon the communication if it is to be effective. An acceptor is necessary for results to be achieved. Thus the manager and the operating force must be willing to cooperate and to receive communications from each other. This cannot be achieved in a situation where they are in a state of conflict over other issues, for example, conditions of employment. Until these issues are resolved, there will not be an adequate communication possibility about work, no matter how well constructed is the communication itself.

BIBLIOGRAPHY

Argyris, Chris, *Personality and Organization*, Harper & Row, Publishers, Incorporated, New York, 1957.

Jaques, Elliott, *Equitable Payment*, John Wiley & Sons, Inc., New York, 1961.

March, J., and H. A. Simon, *Organizations*, John Wiley & Sons, Inc., New York, 1958.

McGregor, D., *The Human Side of Enterprise*, McGraw-Hill Book Company, New York, 1960.

Newman, A. D., and R. Rowbottom, *Organization Analysis*, Southern Illinois University Press, Carbondale, Ill., 1968.

Roethlisberger, F. J., and W. J. Dickson, *Management and the Worker*, Harvard University Press, Cambridge, Mass., 1939.

Woodward, J., *Management and Technology*, Her Majesty's Stationery Office, London, England, 1958.

ORGANIZATIONAL RELATIONSHIPS

CHAPTER ONE

Relationship of Manufacturing and Research and Development

RICHARD L. SWIFT *Manager of Instrument Manufacturing, Mine Safety Appliances Company, Pittsburgh, Pennsylvania*

The theme of a good relationship between manufacturing and research and development is "Coordination for Change." Few companies can remain in business without innovation, and to a great extent, the degree of success of a company's products in the marketplace depends on the degree of coordination and communication between the manufacturing and research and development areas. Of the many, many functions performed daily by the manufacturing manager, none is of greater importance than this coordination of his long-range planning with the efforts of research and development. The efficiency and skill with which he accomplishes it will be a major contribution to the success of his organization. The manufacturing management practices established to achieve this end will largely determine the ease and efficiency with which research and development output is translated into finished, salable products.

R&D contributes the information for a product, and manufacturing supplies the skills and materials to produce it. Between these two functions are the vital efforts of the design and packaging engineers. Managers in all areas need to recognize these contributions and communicate to their individual organizations the plan for coordinating these separate and distinct abilities. The better the coordination and understanding of a change, the less will be the cost of developing that change.

DEVELOPING THE RELATIONSHIP

A new development will probably require many changes in manufacturing plans and techniques; and just as certainly, new production techniques demand a new design approach which frequently requires aid from R&D. It is essen-

2–3

tial that a designer-builder relationship be established through a successful plan of men working with men toward a single objective. This can only be accomplished through the establishment of mutual confidence of one profession in the other. First, it is necessary to establish the role of each group toward the ultimate objective of company growth.

Manufacturing. To most people, the term "manufacturing" means the actual act of putting things together in a variety of ways to end up with a recognizable product. Accompanying this act are various supporting functions such as production planning, manufacturing engineering, industrial engineering, quality control, and purchasing.

Research and Development. The role of the R&D function will vary widely according to the purpose and size of the company involved. If the term "research" has to do with laboratory investigation solely to find new horizons, the endeavor is usually referred to as pure research. The conversion of an already established principle to one which can be used on a specific product is normally referred to as applied research. This latter type usually is coupled with development and design to arrive at a specific, finished, marketable product.

Although the manufacturing manager should be aware of the various areas of interest being explored by the pure research area, there is normally very limited contact between the two groups. The day-to-day work of the manufacturing manager will see his coordination and communication for change in the areas of applied research, development, and design.

Has the age of automation altered the designer-builder relationships?

On the one hand, no—people still have to solve problems. Even with computers and other automatic data processing equipment, people still must make decisions on what goes into the equipment and interpret and make decisions on what comes out. This requires that men work together, that they have mutual confidence, and that they respect each other's abilities and opinions.

On the other hand, yes—there are many different methods of purchasing and many new technologies which require different and more complex manufacturing techniques. More R&D is needed to stay ahead of competition on materials and methods. More facts on markets are needed more quickly so that day-to-day operations can be efficiently managed in the face of an ever-increasing rate of change. It is essential that company management develop rapid methods of communication. Ideas, to be effective, require a rapid transition into the finished or revised product.

SOURCE OF A CHANGE

Pure Research. The output of a pure research facility may present an idea for a new product which marketing decides to fund through applied research, development, design, and into manufacturing.

Applied Research. New ideas from pure research, either within or without a given company, or investigations on adapting present products to other uses, can generate innovations from this group.

Development. The function of development is to take ideas from either pure or applied research and translate them into practical plans for the salable product. This plan is usually developed to the preliminary test or "breadboard" stage.

Design. From the breadboard stage, the design engineers then complete the final details, in terms that are adaptable to manufacturing processes, of how the product is to be presented to the market.

The degree to which the above functions are organized depends primarily on the size of a company. The larger corporation will have entire divisions for each of the four areas. The smaller company will probably combine all the research, development, and design functions into a single department. Indeed, there are many companies that do not sustain any type of R&D group but are entirely dependent on outside sources for their new-product designs.

PERSONALITY CHARACTERISTICS INVOLVED

Although the manufacturing manager does not need to be a psychologist in his dealings with his counterparts in R&D, he requires an understanding of the types of personnel involved in both areas of endeavor. He needs to recognize that the personality traits which lead a man to the profession of research and development are considerably different from those which guide one to the manufacturing field. It is the skill in recognizing these differences in aspirations and goals that is really the basic foundation of a good working relationship between these different functions of the enterprise. The successful manufacturing manager develops the ability to appreciate the other person's situation and to understand why he is the way he is, says the things he says, and does the things he does. At the same time, he cultivates in the R&D mind a recognition of and trust in the professional ability of the manufacturing effort. It takes a great deal of skill to coordinate the efforts of the academic atmosphere of the research laboratory with the pressure-packed "get it shipped" bustle of the producing department.

WHY THE RELATIONSHIP?

One of the primary reasons for developing a true, working communicating relationship is the recurring necessity for a change of the company's position in the marketplace. This may be a result of competition (domestic or international) forcing a change in products which are already on the market, the opportunity to develop new products which will capture a greater portion of the market, or a management decision to enter new markets. Improving the company's position occupies a portion of every manager's daily effort, regardless of his field within the company. With this increased market orientation comes a greater awareness of the implications of cost versus profit versus quality coupled to make greater profitability the common goal.

From the standpoint of new products for the market, the R&D function is continually being pushed to extend the state of the art at least one step beyond that currently achieved on the latest similar new product introduced by the company. For this reason, R&D needs to become deeply aware of and involved in manufacturing processes. Educational curricula, however, are no longer geared to the so-called overall education of the individual. In the age of specialization, time can no longer be devoted to a general course in shop practice for engineers. By the same token, specialists in manufacturing processes are not exposed to design or laboratory practices. For these reasons, it is imperative that R&D teams include manufacturing personnel early in the development of new products.

LIAISON FOR CHANGE

There are several approaches which can be made to the coordination of manufacturing and R&D to accomplish change. The degree to which these are used depends upon the magnitude of the change as it affects a product's contribution to the overall total company output. Top management establishes the overall operating procedures and policies to achieve the required degree of coordination. When an innovation has been agreed upon, it is then imperative that the manufacturing and R&D managers establish the necessary controls by agreeing on the strategic points of development. For example, when the development of the electric circuitry for a given instrument has been completed, quality control electrical specialists should be called in to make sure that critical inspection criteria are spelled out.

New Products. Where the new product is to have a major effect on the company's business, many companies find it advantageous to set up a program manager who will have under his direct guidance all the necessary skills required to develop, design, package, and manufacture it. Products of lesser import may not require such an elaborate plan, but the manufacturing manager should designate a product coordinator to make sure that the transition from design to manufacturing is a smooth one. For either approach, it is vitally important that the authority of this person be established with the complete understanding of all concerned at the very start of a new project.

Product Revision. The other important area of coordination for change occurs when manufacturing needs help from R&D for existing processes or goods already under manufacture. Such requests are usually to determine whether new manufacturing techniques, materials, or equipment are suitable for use in either general or specific areas. For example, a plastic supplier informs the company that it has developed a new material of sufficiently increased strength to justify using it for the manufacture of head protection devices. The supplier further indicates that it is suitable for molding with the manufacturer's present equipment. Before any such change can be made, manufacturing engineers should thoroughly investigate, evaluate, and test the new material in conjunction with R&D personnel.

ATTITUDES TOWARD CHANGE

The attitudes of all parties concerned with an innovation are vitally important to its success before, during, and after its implementation. A thorough analysis and plan of action is necessary for any revision before steps are taken to institute the change. The force initiating the change needs to establish a clear concept of the desired end result. The common failure in the relationship of manufacturing and R&D is the lack of a complete understanding of what is to be accomplished.

Unfortunately, a large percentage of business communications are full of misunderstood, meaningless words. Inevitably one tends to make basic assumptions on a given subject which he then applies to the people and jobs around him. He is likely to feel that everyone with comparable educational and experience exposures will converse and think in the same way. A large percentage of words and ideas concerning a given topic stand a good chance of being misunderstood and misinterpreted. In fact, the chances of this happening are much greater than are those that they will be received clearly and will convey exactly the ideas intended.

It is vital that a common understanding of all aspects of an innovation be clearly established to the satisfaction of all concerned at the very beginning of a project. Some of the more important of these aspects are:

1. The specific long-term objectives or developments to be achieved.
2. The intermediate short-term objectives and the timing for their completion.

3. Specifically, what change is desired?
4. How and by what means is the change to be accomplished?
5. When is the change to occur?
6. Who is involved in the change?
7. What gains are to be realized from the change?

The specific long-term objectives are normally concerned with major new products or significant revisions to old products, and therefore, these are established by those responsible for marketing the product. The short-term objectives, on the other hand, are usually definable intermediate stages which lead to the ultimate completion of the long-term objectives. Generally speaking, these are established by the product manager or coordinator in conjunction with representatives of all company functions associated with the project.

The answers to "What is to be changed?" are usually determined by the marketing stipulations for the new product from which come the results of the efforts of research, development, and design engineering. Likewise, the revision of a product already on the market will depend on a marketing decision on how it is to be changed.

From the manufacturing manager's standpoint, one of the most critical factors of change is "when." It is vital that a timetable be established for the implementation of a change. From the production planning standpoint, the manufacturing manager would like to know at the earliest possible moment who will be involved, what areas of manufacturing will probably be concerned, and what, if any, equipment changes must be made.

PRODUCT LIFE CYCLE

Both manufacturing and R&D need to be completely aware of progress on a project from the day it is initiated. The degree of participation of manufacturing versus R&D at any point in a new-product life cycle almost exactly follows the quantity of that item produced, from the inception of the idea to the point at which it is decided to obsolete the product. Figure 1-1 shows these contributions superimposed on the standard product life cycle curve.

Serious problems can arise when the R&D phases of a product innovation are in essence finished before manufacturing enters the picture. This inevitably means that there has been little or no coordination in the determination of requirements for personnel, equipment, or space.

Many times, the manufacturing manager is faced with a revision of an already established product. This may come from a marketing desire to revitalize a product which is approaching obsolescence in its present form, a manufacturing desire to reduce costs, or a marketing desire to vary the product for competitive reasons. Such considerations require that the manufacturing function establish communication with R&D for confirmation that suggested changes will not affect the design objective of the product. The contribution of R&D in such instances can occur at any point during the marketing phase of a given product. The chart could show a total effort greater than 100 percent, because the major manufacturing effort would be continued so that there would be no void in product availability in the marketplace. Properly coordinated marketing strategy would institute the need for such a change in sufficient time to achieve this goal.

MANUFACTURING STAFF FUNCTIONS

To achieve the ultimate advantage from true coordination between R&D and manufacturing, it is vital that each be aware of the initiation of new changes in

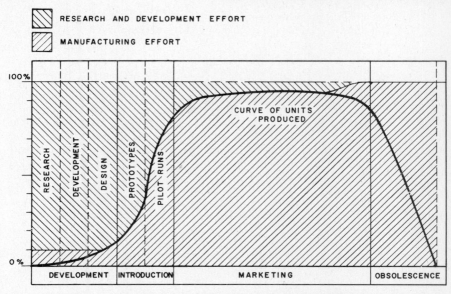

Fɪɢ. 1-1.   Degree of Involvement of Research and Development and Manufacturing at Various Stages of the Product Life Cycle.

either area of responsibility. In the area of new-product development, when a project is initiated by marketing, the manufacturing manager should appoint his product manager or coordinator. The primary assignment of this individual is to follow the progress of the new product, calling upon other manufacturing functions for assistance as required.

There are many ways in which the various manufacturing staff functions can contribute to the transition from idea to product. Depending on the organization of a particular company, these functions may or may not be a direct part of the manufacturing manager's staff. In any case, they are a supporting function to the manufacturing manager and should therefore be included in whatever plans and preparations he makes.

Manufacturing Engineering. The manufacturing engineer is the source of knowledge on techniques and processes available in the organization. This knowledge can be most helpful to R&D personnel in guiding them to a design approach. The manufacturing engineer can provide the information on the capacities and capabilities of available equipment. Should the new product require capabilities not available, the manufacturing engineers are placed on notice of what will be required in time to make a thorough investigation of what can be purchased or needs to be developed. A fuller discussion of the role of manufacturing engineering will be found in Chapter 12 of Section 10.

Industrial Engineering. In a similar fashion, the industrial engineer requires a constant awareness of developments so that he may work with production supervisory personnel on planning for space and personnel requirements for the new products. Before the final release from the research, development, and design stages, the industrial engineer should be consulted for the best ways, from a manufacturing standpoint, to fabricate and assemble the product. What specific types of assembly personnel will be required? Will this be a mass-production item which will be put together by incentive workers, or does the volume or complexity indicate that highly skilled, nonincentive personnel will be required? Are there subassemblies of the end product which will be made in more than one department? Will special manufacturing areas have to be set up, or can this item be produced with other products in a given area? Will new assembly fixtures be required? Will it be necessary to make special test and control devices? Knowledge of requirements in these areas will be of immeasurable assistance to the manufacturing manager in achieving the smooth transition from the drawing board to reality.

Quality Control. Quality control engineers should be made a part of the coordination team at an early stage. This should be no later than the point at which basic design parameters have been developed. They can be most helpful in the period of transition from the laboratory prototype to final design. It is imperative that they be aware of critical inspection and test requirements for component parts, subassemblies, and the final product. This information will provide them with advanced knowledge of test equipment demands and some indication of staffing requirements.

Production Planning. The manufacturing manager, through his production planning staff, requires knowledge of the marketing strategy to relate quantity to methods. Based on this strategy, advanced planning can be started for material requirements long before the ultimate design release. This automatically involves the purchasing function. Availability of vendors, economical purchasing quantities, and lead times are factors to be established. The ability to handle and store the raw materials before use is an important factor. Is it more advantageous to order a large quantity because of price considerations while at the same time accepting the charges for storage facilities, or should a higher per unit cost be accepted with programmed delivery, as required, to offset the cost of storage? The manufacturing manager through his production planning function will need to determine facility requirements. Marketing can aid him in this decision through its knowledge of the anticipated life of the product. The decision on whether to rent or buy facilities can well be dependent on whether a short- or long-term product life is anticipated.

Personnel. The manufacturing manager wants to plan in advance of the implementation of any change what personnel adjustments will be required. Will he need additional supervisory personnel? What types of skill will be required, and does he have them available or must they be hired and trained? How many direct and indirect workers will be involved?

The timing of the dissemination of general information concerning a new product or the revision of an old one is most important from a personnel standpoint. People are always concerned with how they will be affected by a change. Will their jobs be affected? Will they be required to change location? The communication channels established between the manufacturing manager and the R&D manager can help allay fears of people who may be affected, by keeping them informed of progress as it develops.

Budgeting. One of the most important considerations in any plan for innovation is the effect of the change on financial planning. Top management, through the coordination of manufacturing and R&D, needs to be aware of the impact of a new product or major revisions to existing products on capital equipment requirements. Does the new product require a piece of metalworking equipment which will cost $50,000 and will be needed in the next six months? Will it be necessary to allocate $100,000 for the initial inventory of a new product? Answers to these questions and a host of others are required for proper budgetary planning and can only come about through effective communication and coordination for change.

CONCLUSION

Innovation is the very lifeblood of a company. No progressive company can afford to stand still in the marketplace; it requires a continuing development of new products and improvement of the old ones.

It is vital that all areas of a business be coordinated for change. In no area is this more important than in the relationship of manufacturing and research and development. It requires an excellent form of continuing communication to achieve the delicate balance between the research goal of perfection and the manufacturing aim to produce. The good manufacturing manager must be able to determine where the line is to be drawn between these to achieve top management's overall goals for production, growth, and profitability.

BIBLIOGRAPHY

Drucker, Peter F., *The Practice of Management*, Harper & Row, Publishers, Incorporated, New York, 1954.

"Engineering and Manufacturing's Common Goal: Greater Profitability," *Production*, May, 1968.

Judson, Arnold A., *A Manager's Guide to Making Changes*, John Wiley & Sons, Inc., New York, 1966.

Marting, Elizabeth (ed.), *Developing a Product Strategy*, Management Report no. 39, American Management Association, New York, 1959

Maynard, H. B. (ed.), *Top Management Handbook*, sec. 6, McGraw-Hill Book Company, New York, 1960.

Miller, Ernest C., *Objectives and Standards of Performance in Production Management*, Research Study no. 84, American Management Association, New York, 1967.

Newman, William H., *Administrative Action*, Prentice-Hall, Inc., Englewood Cliffs, N.J., 1951.

CHAPTER TWO

Relationship of Manufacturing and Product Design Engineering

ROBERT L. WELLS *Vice President and General Manager, Atomic Equipment Divisions, Westinghouse Electric Corporation, Pittsburgh, Pennsylvania*

Productive and constructive relationships between the manufacturing and product design functions are essential to the success of a manufacturing enterprise. These important relationships can exist only when the personnel in both functions clearly understand and fully accept the objectives of the enterprise of which they are a part.

Broadly speaking, the objectives of a manufacturing company are twofold:
1. To provide goods and services that customers of the organization need and want
2. To make a satisfactory profit while providing these goods and services

It is essential that the needs and desires of the customers are kept in mind in engineering and manufacturing work; otherwise, the organization cannot generate the profits necessary over the long run.

It is important that the operations are managed in such a way that a profit is generated; otherwise, there will be no financial capability to develop and provide the goods and services the customers will need in future years.

On most projects that are undertaken in an industrial organization, the complete accomplishment of the project will require contributions by both engineering and manufacturing, not just one of them. One function is needed to complement efforts of the other function. Saying this another way, it should be noted that seldom, if ever, is there an engineering project; rather, the product design effort is just one part of a more comprehensive project. This same concept is valid for the endeavors of manufacturing or of marketing or of the other functions.

In developing a program to manufacture composite electrical insulators made of both ceramics and epoxy, the initial program plan fell short of recognizing the necessary ingredients for a complete project. The plan showed clearly the product design work, the manufacturing planning, and the equipment procurement. But it did not include getting an order from a customer and the delivery of the first production order. It fell short of scheduling the action to the point where the project justification is completed—satisfying a customer and obtaining a financial return.

Common acceptance by all personnel involved of the total business objectives of the organization is essential to develop and sustain productive relationships between manufacturing and design personnel. This acceptance will enhance the possibilities of producing products at low costs and bringing through needed new products promptly.

PRIMARY FUNCTIONS OF PRODUCT DESIGN ENGINEERING

For a design department or an individual design engineer to contribute to the success of an enterprise, there are several specific functions which must be handled competently. It will be helpful if the manufacturing manager understands what these are.

Development, Maintenance, and Use of Engineering Design Competence. A design engineer must maintain thorough knowledge of the latest developments in the fields of technology pertinent to the businesses in which his design skill is being used. It is recognized that in the extreme an individual can make a full-time job of maintaining his knowledge of his field. As a reasonable rule of thumb, however, a 10 percent expenditure of time should be adequate for keeping in touch with the developments in a given field of technology. With the vast flow of technical knowledge being generated, an individual engineer in any function is hard pressed to keep himself in touch with all the new information even in a narrow field. Rather than attempt this, he will be well advised to select a limited number of good technical sources—perhaps six to ten—and to monitor these regularly and carefully. This approach can generally provide exposure to the bulk of the significant developments in a field. If it is found that too many new ideas are being missed, some of the selected sources can be eliminated and others added. An engineer should strive to keep his continuing research to a practical size.

A competent design engineer should also contribute to the creation of additional knowledge as he tackles new problems for which solutions do not already exist.

This aspect of the engineer's responsibility requires well-planned experiments, carefully recorded pertinent data, and most important, well-documented analyses, results, conclusions, and recommended actions.

It is important that new solutions are recorded carefully so that other engineers do not have to meet and solve the same problems at a later date. One of the inefficiencies that is often encountered in industrial enterprises is the resolution of problems for the second time. This is a particular hazard in project and product line organizations where the informal dialogue between technical people in a single specialty is reduced.

A third important function of the design engineer is to use his knowledge and skill to design products, either new or improved, that perform the functions desired within the cost objectives that must be met to allow commercial success of the products. A competent engineer recognizes the necessity of meeting both the functional and the economic aspects of product design. For example, it is one thing to design a gear train to meet a functional requirement; it is a sharper challenge to meet that requirement at or below a specific product cost.

Organization and Execution of Engineering Design Projects. Engineering design people are most productive when they are results oriented. This is best achieved by tackling specific problems, thinking them through carefully, executing the portions of these tasks that are the proper responsibility of the design engineer, and then passing the results on to the next person who must make his contribution.

In planning product design projects, the following list of steps may be helpful.

1. Definition of functional objectives. This is a statement of what the customer needs functionally in as much or as little detail as is necessary to define these needs clearly.

2. Definition of product cost objectives. Unit cost objectives should be related to the best possible assessment of the market price of the product. Even though only incomplete market data may be available, a judgment determination should be made. Market uncertainty contributes to the financial risk of the project.

3. Definition of development cost objectives. How much money is to be spent to develop the design of this product? Within wide limits, functional and product cost objectives can be achieved with different magnitudes of development effort. But the amount for each project must be estimated beforehand when the total effort is being justified.

4. Detailed schedule showing time objectives of each step. Any effort is enhanced by the establishment in advance of detailed steps and the deadline for each.

The total project schedule should always be extended to include such things as obtaining an order for the first production parts, a shipment date for the first product, and a time at which the first profit shows on the books of the organization. A desirable concept on any program is to schedule the events "all the way to profit."

Evolution of Specifications. The output of any design engineering effort is a product or component or assembly that will be used by someone—generally a customer from the outside, but sometimes a customer within the organization. Because of this ultimate objective, it is important that the specifications to which the design engineer works should have been evolved recognizing the functional needs of the customer. Also, of course, the specifications must recognize the state of the art in both design and manufacturing. The process of evolving these specifications requires give and take between the customer and the design engineer, as well as discussions between the design engineer and the manufacturing people. It generally consumes a substantial amount of time.

Creating Product Designs to Meet Specifications. The central and crucial responsibility of the design engineer is to create the detailed design of a salable product—one that fills the functional specifications of the customer. This detailed design will tax the ingenuity and will draw on the accumulated experience of the design engineer in spelling out clearly and understandably the exact configuration of the product to be made and assembled by the manufacturing organization. During this design phase, the design engineer must draw heavily not only on his own competence but also on that of other people, particularly the manufacturing personnel who know the latest and best manufacturing techniques. The flashes of genius that will define a better product may come from many different sources, and the design engineer must look for and evaluate all ideas that may make a meaningful contribution to the product design.

During this part of the design engineer's task, he needs to recognize the total cycle time of the product's development and manufacture, and also develop a general feeling of the life cycle of the product. He must consider the use of new and advanced technology if the development cycle time is long and if the product life cycle is apt to be long. If the development cycle time is short, the burden is not so heavy on him to use new developments on the frontiers of technology because these can be introduced later on when once they are fully developed. For example, compare the perspective needed by an atomic power plant designer with that required by a man working on a new ceramic insulator.

Product cost considerations cannot be overemphasized. The financial success or failure of the product venture is dependent on product cost levels. The best levels will be achieved when there is close and frequent dialogue between the design engineers and professional people in the manufacturing organization— the manufacturing engineers, the methods engineers, and the industrial engineers.

Product Information.   Information related to the design of a product can be transmitted to people outside the engineering department in many ways. It is important that each of these information transmittals be prepared in a way that is usable by the people to whom it is directed. Product design information prepared by the design engineering personnel may include the following forms:

1. Detailed drawings and assembly drawings to show the configuration of each part and its relationship in the assembled product
2. Process specifications related to such things as a heat-treating sequence or the application of a special finish to a part
3. Standards information related to such things as surface finish, roundness of corners and edges, deviation from true position, and the like
4. Test specifications describing component tests and functional tests of the assembled products
5. Manuals which may be needed to provide information in connection with many parts of the product life cycle such as: installation of the product, operating instructions, maintenance suggestions and procedures, and often, complete product overhaul information

It may be that the design engineering personnel will not themselves prepare all these types of information. If not, however, they must provide a substantial block of assistance to whatever group in the organization is charged with the actual preparation. Once again, close involvement between the design engineers and whoever has the responsibility of preparation is essential to make sure that accurate information is conveyed to the person who ultimately needs it.

MANUFACTURING UTILIZATION OF DESIGN ENGINEERING COMPETENCE

The manufacturing organization in an industrial enterprise carries the heavy responsibility of making the parts and the assemblies that will be delivered to customers to satisfy their needs. In carrying out their responsibilities, manufacturing people should draw on the skills of the product design engineers to help on manufacturing problems.

Manufacturing Yield Problems.   Circumstances are often encountered where a product has been made satisfactorily according to existing process specifications and design information for some time, and then for no readily apparent reason, the yield of the product drops off. Even though the manufacturing function may feel that the problem should be solved by its own staff, the design engineers can often provide assistance.

Recently in a special metals manufacturing plant, several batches of forgings of one of the alloys showed lower creep-to-rupture strength than was acceptable. It was also lower than had been encountered during many months of production of that alloy. Recheck of the process, the heat temperatures, and all the normal controlling factors showed that no deviation had taken place. The design engineers were called in to see whether they could help solve the problem. After much discussion and a number of tests, a tiny amount of an impurity, a trace element, was found to be present in a base metal procured from a new supplier, which did not exist in the base metal procured from other suppliers. The shop reverted to a prior supplier of the metal, and the low-yield problem disappeared. Precautions were taken to avoid recurrences of this problem.

Analysis of High Material and Labor Cost Variances. Eternal vigilance on product, labor, and material costs, as manufacturing personnel fully recognize, is one of the essential keys to business success. When cost variances start to increase, manufacturing personnel must be prompt and aggressive in seeking out the causes and endeavoring to eliminate them. In most instances their efforts are successful, although often the time expended can be quite large.

It is sometimes quite helpful to have design engineers study with the manufacturing people some of the product situations that are substantial contributors to high variances in manufacturing cost. Even though the responsibility for taking action to eliminate these excess variances lies within the manufacturing organization, a faster and less expensive way to eliminate the problem may be achieved through design change.

One fruitful practice that can be used is periodic meetings between the design engineers and the manufacturing engineers to review the top five or so problems that are causing high manufacturing cost variances. Out of these discussions and subsequent analysis, changes can be evolved that may help significantly in the cost problem. For example, a little extra length can be provided in a wire for a control panel door, or a requirement can be added for rounding an edge of a part which has caused damage to an adjacent part during assembly. Changed tolerance on the location of a hole may make assembly easier. Certainly an extra degree of freedom is provided to the manufacturing people by drawing on the expertise of design engineers in instances of this nature.

Quality Improvement. Design engineering personnel may be able to help the shop in tracing and handling quality problems in products and assembly. For example, design engineers can participate in training sessions for production people to show clearly the reasons why certain design requirements are necessary and how parts that deviate from these specifications can cause trouble in the hands of customers. Participation by design engineers in seeking out and eliminating the causes of a low-quality part can be most helpful. For the long-range good of the organization, it is not enough to correct or replace a low-quality part. It is essential to seek out the causes that led to the low-quality part and to apply ingenuity to eliminating or at least minimizing these causes.

Promptness in Development. Often a development effort is needed to be accomplished jointly by design engineering and manufacturing personnel to resolve a problem. In the execution of any development program, the elapsed time is generally longer than the time during which the project is actually being worked on. The lost time occurs between steps or is caused by interruptions of an individual while working on a step.

If the development has a high priority, and this priority is agreed on by the heads of design engineering, manufacturing, and the division, a special effort can be exerted to make sure that work on this development never stops. This does not mean that any individual works any harder or any faster. It means that time can be saved by making sure that as one step of the program is completed, the individual to work on the next step has been alerted, is ready, and starts immediately.

In one critical problem, a new gearbox for driving accessories on a marine turbine was designed, manufactured, tested, and shipped in about one-third of the scheduled time by making sure that the job never stopped. No one really worked any harder, but the job moved steadily, enjoying top priority at each step of the process.

Admittedly this approach can be used on only a limited number of projects, but if a project is important enough, the approach is worthwhile.

Approval of Requested Design Changes. Manufacturing personnel often have ideas for desirable design changes which would help in the manufacturing operation. These are normally passed along to the responsible design engineers through some established procedure in the organization. Some of these ideas may be accepted and incorporated promptly. Others may be rejected for what the manufacturing people feel are unsatisfactory or unconvincing reasons.

In these instances, the manufacturing people should stay with their suggested changes, perhaps restating the reasons, and try again in a dialogue with the design personnel. Often it is necessary to approach the problem from a different standpoint. The approval or rejection of any proposed change should in the last analysis depend on prudent business reasoning, the total economics of the effort related to the change, and the contribution the change makes to the customer who buys the product. Focusing persuasive reasoning on these key objectives helps keep the discussion of any proposed change objective.

There is another factor which should be weighed and agreed on between the engineering and manufacturing personnel. This is the priority assigned to each problem or project. It is always true that both manufacturing personnel and the design engineers have more problems or projects to work on than time permits. Therefore, a judgment must be made on the order in which projects should be worked on. Once again, the basis of judgment should be the economic health of the enterprise and the probable contribution of the project to the satisfaction of the customer.

MEASUREMENT OF ACCOMPLISHMENTS

It is difficult to measure the success of efforts expended on projects, problems, or programs undertaken in design engineering or in manufacturing engineering. The best way to approach measurement is to require the documentation of a detailed plan of action to accomplish the objective desired. This detailed plan can be the basis on which the program is approved and the funds allocated for its execution. The measurement process then becomes one of comparing the accomplishments of the people involved against the plan that they themselves submitted when they undertook the project.

Measurement of people's accomplishments against a subjective, verbalized objective is most difficult. Measurement against a detailed plan of action is vastly more successful.

TECHNIQUES FOR JOINT EFFORT

There are many ways in which the joint efforts of engineering and manufacturing personnel can be marshalled to contribute to the success of the enterprise. Listed below are a few techniques that may be useful in a given manufacturing enterprise.

Design Reviews. A design review is a scheduled systematic study of a product design by specialist personnel, including marketing, manufacturing, purchasing, field service, and appropriate consultants, as well, of course, as design engineering. In the conduct of these reviews, the design engineer presents his proposed design and seeks suggestions, comments, and criticisms from those in attendance. Generally, the engineering manager, or some person senior to the design engineer making the presentation, serves as chairman.

The ideas and suggestions generated at these reviews are carefully recorded for subsequent evaluation and action. The prime purpose of a design review of a new product is to achieve optimum product design from a standpoint of function, cost, reliability, and appearance.

The focusing of multiple minds simultaneously on the design is a powerful technique for making improvements and avoiding costly problems. Bringing a variety of skills and experiences together at one time usually generates more usable ideas than a series of individual discussions.

In a design review of a large power transformer, twenty-three desirable design changes were identified and programmed for incorporation. In reviewing a motor generator set for a gas line pumping operation under high-ambient condition, a suggestion led to a substantial improvement in cooling the stator windings.

Formal design reviews conducted at appropriate points during the design cycle can yield solid cost improvements, increase product reliability, and contribute significantly to the long-range profit of the enterprise.

Value Analysis Seminars. A value analysis seminar, as the term is used here, is a two-week training program which aims at teaching three-man teams the basic skills of the value analysis approach to product design. Generally the value analysis team includes a responsible design engineer, a manufacturing man familiar with the way in which the product is made, and a man from some other function in the company. A team follows the questioning technique of: What does this part do? What does it cost? What else might do the same job? What would that cost? This approach provides the value analysis team with an appreciable amount of protected time during which the engineering, manufacturing, and other functional personnel can boldly and imaginatively explore opportunities to improve product performance or provide the function with less material or less manufacturing cost.

For example, during a value analysis seminar, a team studying an electrical disconnect switch came up with several valuable improvements. The design of the blade of the switch was changed to permit use of a blade-forming die, a method not possible with the original blade design. Several casting designs were altered to allow the use of shell cores in permanent molds, the lowest cost alternative to high-cost collapsible cores or high machining costs of conventional castings. The design of a hinge assembly was modified to enable manufacturing to replace an expensive brazing operation with lower cost arc welding.

Product Cost Laboratory. The product cost laboratory is another powerful device for tackling the eternally present cost problems encountered in design and manufacturing. It is an approach more applicable to large companies which have headquarters staff specialists who can be made available to help line people with the serious cost problems they encounter.

For example, if a division of the Westinghouse Electric Company has a cost problem on one of its products and would like some help from extra talent, the division design engineer and a manufacturing man bring the problem to the product cost laboratory. This laboratory is staffed by experts in headquarters engineering, manufacturing, and research. The headquarters people and the division people study in depth for two full weeks all sorts of ideas relating to the possible improvement of the product. In these studies, the division people have the responsibility for deciding which ideas are useful and usable in the manufacturing operation.

Typical products that have been successfully studied in the product cost laboratory include:

1. Elevator doors and doorways
2. Heat exchangers used in atomic power plants
3. Electric toasters
4. Portable X-ray units

With competent and properly motivated headquarters personnel, the two-week product cost lab session can evolve many valuable and promptly usable ideas. In three years' operation of this approach, cost savings on all products brought in have averaged over 25 percent of the product cost.

COMMUNICATIONS BETWEEN ENGINEERING AND MANUFACTURING

It is essential that frequent communication take place between engineering and manufacturing personnel. Where the people in the two functions are physically separated, special efforts must be made by management to remove the barriers between the two functions. An enterprise having free communications between these two functions will always be faster on its feet, more responsive to customer needs, and more successful from a business standpoint than enterprises in which there is a significant restriction to communications.

To achieve the needed continuous communication, there should be:

1. Regular communication that takes place at predetermined and periodic times
2. Random communication between the two functions that takes place when there is something to be discussed of interest to both functions
3. Mutual involvement on programs or projects that require extended joint effort

A key responsibility of the management personnel in a manufacturing enterprise is to monitor the quality and frequency of the dialogue that takes place between the two functions.

CONCLUSION

In modern industrial organizations, the interdependence of design engineering and manufacturing is essential. A profitable manufacturing organization cannot continue to exist unless this interdependence is recognized and utilized.

All efforts of both design engineering and manufacturing people should be oriented toward the business objectives of the enterprise, namely, providing the customer with the products that he needs and making a satisfactory profit in serving his needs.

And, finally, the attitude that must pervade the thinking of both design engineering and manufacturing personnel is that there is always a better way to handle any existing problem or to make any product. The basic judgment that needs to be exercised is whether or not a particular problem is the one on which to expend the available professional talent.

BIBLIOGRAPHY

"Almanac of Cost Reduction for 1966," *Factory*, November, 1965.

Ansley, Arthur C., *Manufacturing Methods and Processes*, Chilton Company, Philadelphia, Pa., 1957.

Clark, Charles, *Brainstorming*, Doubleday & Company, Garden City, N.Y., 1958.

Dubin, Robert, *Human Relations in Administration*, Prentice-Hall, Inc., Englewood Cliffs, N.J., 1951.

Farrell, Paul V., "VA at Westinghouse," *Purchasing*, May 5, 1966.

Gardner, Fred, *Profit Management and Control*, McGraw-Hill Book Company, New York, 1955.

Miles, Lawrence D., *Techniques of Value Analysis and Engineering*, McGraw-Hill Book Company, New York, 1961.

"Turnaround at Westinghouse," *American Machinist*, Dec. 19, 1966.

VonFange, Eugene K., *Professional Creativity*, Prentice-Hall, Inc., Englewood Cliffs, N.J., 1958.

CHAPTER THREE

Relationship of Manufacturing and Marketing

THOMAS E. FARRELL *President, National Hose Company, Dover, New Jersey*

For the manufacturing executive to become a complete and integrated manager within the corporation, it is necessary that he learn not only the manufacturing processes of his company, but also all facets of how the product ultimately arrives at its end use.

In addition, the organization must be managed in such a way that the working relationship between marketing and manufacturing will be so close that management will have all sorts of information available from these two functions. This can be accomplished by the development of a common working rapport between them through good communication at all levels. The organization will then be able to deal properly with decisions which affect its present and future courses of action.

For the marketing and manufacturing managers to perform their business activities properly within the company policy structure, it is imperative that they thoroughly understand the requirements of one another's functions within the organization. They must also develop the necessary procedures for working together toward their common goal of fulfilling the customers' needs economically so that their company realizes its own ultimate goal of maximizing profits and service.

RELATIONSHIP OF MANUFACTURING TO MARKETING

There is only one compelling reason why a corporation is in business, and that is to earn a return on the invested capital of its stockholders. This profit is attained, however, only by satisfying the requirements of its customers in the various markets in which the company is active. A company satisfies these customer requirements through two major functions: manufacturing and marketing.

2–20

Manufacturing has the responsibility of producing goods of the highest quality at the lowest cost and of making them available when and where the customer desires.

The function of marketing is to find out what customers' needs and requirements are and to have them met to the customers' complete satisfaction.

These two major functions are so interrelated that it is impractical to expect them to operate independently with any degree of success. For this reason, the establishment and maintenance of a close working relationship between marketing and manufacturing is essential for the well-being of the entire company. In doing this, however, it should be realized that, because of the basic differences between the two functions, the personalities of the individuals who head them tend to be quite different.

The manufacturing executive in discharging his responsibilities tends to be introspective, continually considering new ways and means of producing the products. He must be constantly alert to eliminate all obstacles that deter him from his goal of producing a quality product, on schedule, and at the lowest cost. He must abhor waste; therefore he is continually looking for (1) long and economical production runs, (2) wider manufacturing tolerances, and (3) the elimination of all obstacles which would prevent him from lowering the costs of the product and increasing productive capacity.

The marketing executive, on the other hand, is too often thought of as limiting his function to the selling operation. The difference between selling and marketing is more than semantic. Selling, which is often placed organizationally under marketing, is focused entirely on the seller's need to convert his product or service into cash; marketing is concerned with discovering and satisfying the product or service needs of the customers through the following four major functions:

1. The marketing analysis function, which has to do with devising techniques of gathering information and interpreting what customers want and translating this information into the design and packaging of a product. It includes deciding how much shall be produced in a given period of time.
2. The supply function, which has to do with the scheduling, transportation, and storage of the product so that it will be available when and where it is needed.
3. The demand creation function, which includes informing and influencing consumers through advertising, pricing, transferring product ownership, finance, and credit.
4. The function of product performance information, which involves gathering of data on how a product is used, its performance in the field, quality requirements, customer complaints, and changing customer needs.

Marketing, then, takes on the planning strategy for the business: what it wants and expects to sell, what it costs to sell, and what is needed to implement the plans.

The marketing executive is normally an expansive, outgoing type of individual, highly cognizant of his role as the company's number one public relations ambassador. He generates the creative thinking necessary to increase the available markets for his company's products.

The personalities of the manufacturing and marketing functions may be quite different; yet when it is recognized how interrelated and overlapping are the goals of both of these functions, it can be seen that their main objective is really the same: fulfilling the customers' needs and requirements with the highest quality and lowest priced merchandise available at the time the customers need them. If the company accomplishes this, it will satisfy its basic objective: to maximize its profits and services.

The relationship between manufacturing and marketing must be healthy and viable if the company is to exist, grow, and prosper. Neither function should become dominant. A company that is dominated by marketing—to the exclusion of its manufacturing capability—will find itself a follower in its chosen marketing field. Competition will always be ahead with new products, new costs, and new resources. Similarly, the company that is dominated by the manufacturing function and permits that function to establish its market is heading for eventual disaster, primarily because of lack of knowledge of the customers' product needs.

The Penalty of One-function Dominance. A typical example of a manufacturing-oriented company was the Latex Foam Rubber Company. This company had developed during the 1950s an outstanding production setup for manufacturing foam at low cost and high quality. All the planning and expenditures for the company went into the production process, with little thought given to marketing the product after it was produced. The feeling was that with low cost and good quality there would be no problem in selling the latex foam. Production began and inventories grew rapidly. The small sales department set up to move the product was inexperienced, and the company was relatively unknown in the foam marketing area. Soon additional warehouses had to be built to store the foam products.

Losses mounted steadily. After a thorough analysis by top management, a complete marketing program was initiated to complement the manufacturing facilities. After that, Latex Foam Rubber Company became widely known in the industry and began to show healthy profits. However, if the company had balanced its marketing and manufacturing functions based upon proper analysis of needs at the inception of the program, the losses it incurred would not have developed.

A marketing-oriented company can also find itself in chaos. A typical example of this was the Western Latex Company. This company was exceptionally marketing oriented and sold most of the latex foam rubber used on the West Coast in the early fifties. All this company's top management personnel were oriented toward the marketing function exclusively. Their efforts, policies, and planning were concentrated in this field to the exclusion of manufacturing. Western Latex was very profitable during the first half of the 1950s.

In the early part of the mid-1950s, a well-balanced major rubber company made some significant breakthroughs in the manufacturing of rubber latex foam. The result was a decrease in costs and a drop in the selling price to the consumer. Western Latex Company had to meet these prices to maintain its position in the market. Unfortunately, because of its lack of emphasis on manufacturing processes, its costs continued to rise. By the late fifties, Western Latex was in a loss position. Belatedly, realizing its neglect of the manufacturing function, its management began to modernize the company's facilities, but the efforts were too late. Competition kept increasing its lead in production process facilities. This, added to an excellent marketing program, enabled it to stay ahead of Western Latex's efforts. Western Latex closed its doors in the early sixties.

The above are illustrations of how the fortunes of marketing and manufacturing are intertwined. Unless they work together harmoniously and toward the common company goal, the entire organization will suffer.

INFORMATION REQUIREMENTS OF MANUFACTURING AND MARKETING

Coordination and integration of the efforts of marketing and manufacturing will result only if the managers of these functions accept common aims and participate in putting together and accepting common policies. These policies and goals can be generated if the two functions will learn the requirements of each department. From this knowledge can then be developed the reports, statistics, and information needed to enable them to interrelate their activities toward common company objectives.

Information Needs of Marketing. The information needs of the typical marketing function may be outlined as follows:

1. *Information on the Operating Results of the Business Activity.*

GROSS MARGIN CHANGES. These are changes to gross margin that can be attributed to pricing. From this, the marketing executive can review his pricing policies and make changes if necessary.

FACTORY VARIANCES. Factory variances are negative variances in factory overhead brought about by lower sales than were budgeted. With this information, marketing can institute any short- or long-range changes necessary in budgeted sales so that a corresponding change can be made in manufacturing overhead.

BUDGET COMPARISONS. These are comparisons of orders booked to sales forecast, and actual year-to-date shipments to budget. This latter information will show how the manufacturing organization is performing.

CURRENT COSTS. The individuals in marketing who have the prime responsibilities of pricing and profit need accurate information on all costs, including raw material costs, processing costs, shipping costs, and fixed costs.

QUALITY REPORTS. These reports are needed by marketing as a guide to the consistency of product quality and the ability of manufacturing to meet delivery promises because of low spoilage losses.

2. *Delivery Status Information.* Lack of information on deliveries is one of the most serious causes of difficulty between manufacturing and marketing. Marketing must keep its customers informed on deliveries at all times. If not, it will lose them to competition. A few missed delivery dates will be accepted by customers if they are informed far enough in advance to enable them to make the necessary changes in their programs to eliminate or reduce the problems caused by these missed delivery dates.

DELIVERY PROMISES. Most customer orders have acknowledgement copies attached which request delivery information. These acknowledgement copies should be forwarded to manufacturing for the appropriate delivery information, returned to sales, and then sent to the customer. Customer order and delivery information should be logged into the order book which should be kept up to date daily.

CUSTOMER ORDER STATUS. A report should be issued each week to the sales department showing the analysis of the deliveries of all incoming orders. All missed delivery dates and anticipated missed delivery promises should be shown on this report, including reasons why delivery dates were missed and what the new promised delivery dates are. Sales can then notify customers of any changes in the delivery status of its orders.

SPLIT ORDERS. A weekly report should be made to sales on all split-order shipments, showing amounts shipped and the promised date for the remainder of the order. Split orders should be avoided if at all possible, because they become an irritant to sales and to the customer. They cause considerable additional paperwork, higher freight costs, and increased receiving costs on the customer's part. This report is necessary only as a control means to keep split orders to a minimum.

3. *Inventory Condition Information.*

FINISHED GOODS AND GOODS IN-PROCESS. A weekly finished goods and goods in-process inventory report should be provided for the use of the sales order department of the marketing division to enable it to keep customers advised of the availability of products.

WAREHOUSE SHIPPING AND INVENTORY. A weekly or monthly warehouse shipping and inventory report should be made available to marketing so that it may maintain its warehouse minimum-maximum stock status reports.

OBSOLETE INVENTORY. Obsolete inventory should be covered by an updated monthly report on all obsolete and second-grade merchandise. This report is used by marketing to move the material at lower selling prices before it reaches a condition of obsolescence that would require scrapping.

4. *Plant Facilities and Capacity Utilization.* When setting up sales forecasts and deciding upon sales and advertising expenditures which will be needed to keep the plant at capacity, marketing should know of all major projects included in the manufacturing department's facilities plans, together with their status and anticipated completion dates.

MANUFACTURING CAPABILITY. Marketing personnel should be informed of any new equipment installation, process improvements, or added production space that will become available for increased production during the fiscal year. This information should be made available before setting up the yearly sales forecast.

EQUIPMENT UTILIZATION. Marketing should be informed of any anticipated open production time on any machines or process facilities. Marketing can then set up a special sales program for short-range soliciting of business to keep the manufacturing facilities in full production.

ECONOMIC PRODUCTION RUNS. Sales requires information on the minimum economic production runs of all manufacturing equipment and processes so that it may inform customers of the minimum order acceptable without special charges.

Information Needs of Manufacturing. Manufacturing, in turn, needs certain information from marketing. Typically this includes the following:

1. *Sales Forecast Information.* Yearly forecasts of sales requirements must be broken down into units, preferably by monthly requirements for the first six months of the fiscal year and a total for the final six months of the fiscal year. These monthly forecast requirements are then used to prepare a monthly schedule similar to that shown by Figure 3-1.

SALES FORECAST TIMING. The unit needs of the sales department should be in the hands of manufacturing no later than four months prior to the beginning of the fiscal year. Sales should prepare the monthly breakdown of the last fiscal six months' total requirements so that it can be available to manufacturing's scheduling department no later than three months prior to the beginning of the period. This provides the necessary lead time to prepare the proper manufacturing facilities, order long-term delivery raw materials, and in general inform all manufacturing personnel of marketing's needs.

FORECAST DEPENDABILITY. Sales forecasts are usually developed from historical data and include market research and analysis information on new products, economic factors, market trends, competitors' developments, and all other factors that will affect sales. Although they represent the best estimate of what will occur, they cannot be expected to be completely accurate.

MONTHLY UNIT PRODUCTION SCHEDULE

NATIONAL HOSE CO.

MONTH _____

PRODUCT – RUBBER HOSE		UNFILLED ORDERS	MONTHLY SALES FORECAST	MINIMUM INVENTORY QUANTITY	TOTAL MONTHLY REQUIRE- MENTS	OPENING INVENTORY	PRODUCTION UNITS REQUIRED	SPECIAL PRODUCTION REQUIRE- MENTS
SIZE	TYPE							
3/4"	Super Flex	10,000'	30,000'	25,000'	65,000'	20,000'	45,000'	1*
3/4"	All Purpose	4,000'	3,000'	3,000'	10,000'	4,000'	6,000'	
3/4"	H. D. Air	1,000'	2,000'	1,000'	4,000'	2,000'	2,000'	
1"	Super Flex	1,200'	3,000'	5,000'	9,200'	0'	9,200'	2*
1"	All Purpose	15,000'	20,000'	30,000'	65,000'	15,000'	50,000'	3*
1"	H. D. Air	2,500'	1,500'	2,000'	6,000'	3,000'	3,000'	
1-1/2"	Aircraft	1,000'	3,000'	3,000'	7,000'	8,000'	0'	

1* 10,000 MANUFACTURED TO RED COLOR SPEC. # 698
2* 2,000 UNBRANDED – SPECIAL ORDER
3* 10,000 BRANDED "AMES PART # 39872"

FIG. 3-1. Typical Monthly Production Schedule.

FORECAST REVISIONS. Because of the viable conditions of the sales forecast, each fiscal quarter must be reexamined by sales, and revisions made in product requirements where necessary. This safeguard will prevent the company from overstocking slow-moving items and will enable it to switch manufacturing facilities to the faster selling items.

2. *Product Quality Information.* Quality is that property of a product which creates a desire for continued use or ownership.

SPECIFICATIONS. Sales must provide available detailed customer specifications including blueprints, test requirements, end use, size, color, quantity, packaging, shipping instructions, and other pertinent information necessary to enable manufacturing to handle customer product needs.

TOLERANCES. Information is required from sales of the "acceptable quality limits" of manufacturing tolerances. This information is needed to eliminate holding to costly close manufacturing tolerances not required by the customer's end use of the product.

PRODUCT USE. Complete data on how the company's product is used by its customers are vital to continued improvement of the quality of the product. Information from salesmen's reports on product use must be channeled to manufacturing by means of a monthly product use report prepared by the marketing analysis group of the marketing department.

CUSTOMER COMMENTS. Complete copies of salesmen's reports of customer product complaints, customer test data, and other basic information regarding a product's inability to meet customer needs must be forwarded to manufacturing upon receipt. By using these salesman's reports, manufacturing can detect trends of product malfunction and eliminate them before they become major catastrophes.

PRODUCT COST COMMITTEE. This is a group established by manufacturing and includes marketing personnel. It has the basic responsibility of ascertaining whether the product meets customer needs. By working closely together, the acceptable quality limits mentioned above can be constantly reevaluated with the customer so that the best product is continually made available at the lowest cost. This committee will help ensure that the company continually produces profitable products for customer needs.

3. *Competition Status.* Production has no way of knowing what is occurring in the field. The sales department, however, has a tremendous array of competitive and customer intelligence coming at all times. This is gleaned by the marketing people from the salesmen's call reports, customers' letters, marketing research, and the like. This information is as important to the manufacturing department as it is to the sales department. There must be a continuing dialogue between the two departments.

COMPETITION DELIVERY POSITION. Marketing should keep manufacturing advised of how competition's deliveries compare. If competition's deliveries are better and customers require these better deliveries, the company's sales will be eroded unless steps are taken to improve its own delivery situation.

PRODUCT COMPARISONS. Data comparing competition versus company product on life cycle, tests, prices, customer preference, packaging, shipping, and the like enable manufacturing to reevaluate the company product continually and to make any necessary changes to maintain customer loyalty.

NEW PRODUCTS. Samples and data of any new competitive products should be forwarded to manufacturing immediately for evaluation and comparison tests. This information enables the company to remain competitive.

4. *Customers' Changing Needs.*

SHORT-RANGE MARKET ANALYSIS. The marketing department should keep manufacturing informed of customers' changing product needs so that production facilities are not expanded or replaced if customer requirements are to be eliminated or changed in the near future.

LONG-RANGE MARKET ANALYSIS. Long-range (five to ten years) product needs of the company's customers should be projected by marketing research so that future production requirements can be planned and the manufacturing facilities can be made available at the time the customers' future needs arise.

TECHNIQUES FOR IMPROVING WORKING RELATIONSHIPS BETWEEN MARKETING AND MANUFACTURING

Management is one of the so-called behavioral sciences, but it is also an art. It is the art of bringing ends and means together. The combination of the people who do this constitutes management. Good planning by manufacturing requires constant communication with marketing so that plant capacity can be adequately employed to satisfy customer needs, quality- and delivery-wise. Good personnel relations between the two departments require mutual exchange of information.

Interdepartmental Contacts. The following are some commonly used methods of encouraging contacts between marketing and manufacturing personnel.

1. *Sales Seminars.* Manufacturing personnel should request that they be included in sales meetings attended by field salesmen so that they can meet the salesmen and keep them informed of present and future plans of manufacturing.

   a. The time allotted to manufacturing during the sales meeting can be used to discuss all the current mutual problems of product acceptance, customer requirements, deliveries, quality, facilities, processes, new-product needs, packaging, transportation, and other matters that arise during the normal operation of the two departments.

   b. Sales seminars can be used by manufacturing executives to acquaint
   sales with the manufacturing facilities, personnel, procedures, and processes so that they can become familiar with not only the good features
   of the manufacturing process but also their limitations.   These meetings should be open and frank discussions of the abilities and needs of
   each function.

   2. *Production Control Meetings.*   These are meetings held periodically to
keep manufacturing supervision informed on the progress of work through the
plant.   They also provide an ideal opportunity for a marketing executive to
explain the marketing function.

   a. The how and why of marketing can be discussed, including information
   on what a salesman's life is like; how their goals are established; how
   their expenses are monitored; and the reasons for expenditures on advertising, conventions, and meetings.   The more each knows of the
   other's activities, the greater the cooperation between the departments
   is likely to be.

   b. Marketing policy can also be discussed at these meetings by the marketing executive, so that manufacturing can learn and thus understand
   the reasons for such things as unusual customer requests, warehousing
   and shipping requirements, packaging requirements, off-brand markings, and freight allowances.   Basic information such as this will eliminate many frustrations between the two departments.

   3. *Production Scheduling Meetings.*   Manufacturing departments usually
have weekly production scheduling meetings to set daily process and machine
load schedules.   Someone from sales with customer product experience should
attend these meetings.   Mutual information can then be exchanged.

   a. Current market status can be explained to enable manufacturing to
   maintain proper inventory balances.

   b. Sales can use this opportunity to revise yearly forecasts to reflect current trends and future changes in customer needs that have become
   known since the forecast was used for production scheduling.

   c. Manufacturing can be advised of any preferential handling of certain
   orders or customers as shown on the monthly unit production schedule
   (Figure 3-1, under the column headed "Special Production Requirements").

   d. These meetings also give sales the assurance that the various products
   needed will be available in the quantity required to complete customers' orders in the specified time.

   These weekly production scheduling meetings can become a prime means to
both manufacturing and marketing for keeping communication lines open and
building a common close working relationship.

   4. *Reporting Procedures.*   A continuing dialogue can be maintained through
information reports.   For example:

   a. Manufacturing can establish a monthly report to sales, advising them
   of any changes within the manufacturing processes, new raw materials
   available, open facilities, lowered costs, machine or process breakdowns, labor market conditions, supervision changes, and other information that will keep marketing informed.

   b. Sales can set up a report form to complete and return, giving the information that manufacturing needs from marketing.   This report
   should cover such items as field reports on quality and delivery, future
   sales needs not included in original yearly forecast, changes in marketing patterns, possible phasing out of various products, competitive in-

formation, new competitor products, samples of new products available, transportation trends, and any changes in product design being considered that would require equipment or material changes in the manufacturing process.

Customer Contacts. By arranging for joint contacts with customers by manufacturing and marketing personnel, working relationships between these two functions can be further strengthened.

1. *Field Visits by Manufacturing Personnel and Salesmen.* Using production people to call on customers produces benefits for both departments. Sales benefits from the resulting improvement of customer relations, and manufacturing can see the product use in the field and gain much information valuable to product and process improvement.

   a. Customers welcome the visits of manufacturing experts who have intimate product knowledge. From these experts they can learn more of the capabilities of the product they are purchasing.

   b. Salesmen also are glad to have experts from manufacturing make customer calls with them so that they, too, can learn more about manufacturing processes and product application. Field visits by salesmen and knowledgeable manufacturing people stabilize customer loyalty and many times open customer doors that are normally closed to sales personnel, such as engineering or research and development.

2. *Product Complaint Calls.* Manufacturing engineers can be a great help to salesmen on product complaint calls and should be made available to the marketing function. There is no one more informed on the manufacturing facilities of the company than the manufacturing engineer, and no one more informed on the customer requirements than the salesman and the customer himself. By having the manufacturing engineer work with the salesman on a customer's complaint, the company will profit considerably by maintaining a satisfied customer. This also eliminates the possibility of reports by sales personnel being misunderstood, thus lengthening the time required to make the changes necessary to eliminate the customer's complaint.

It is good practice to use a standard form for reporting on customer complaint contacts. The form should be filled out for each contact and kept on file in the manufacturing department, a copy being sent to marketing. Figure 3-2 shows a "Field Reliability Analysis Feedback Form" (customer complaint report) developed by the Electric Service Division of the Westinghouse Electric Company. It is considered to be an outstanding customer information report. It includes all the information necessary for marketing and manufacturing to analyze the customer problem completely and leads to taking the action needed to eliminate the complaint.

3. *Customer Education.* If a company is manufacturing a somewhat complex product, the customers' engineering and design departments will need and want all the detailed information available on the application of the product to their needs. This can be accomplished by:

   a. Making available to sales the manufacturing personnel capable of putting on a product seminar at customers' plants. These seminars should be geared to professional people in the customers' engineering, design, and quality control departments and should cover specific product application information.

   b. Advising sales of manufacturing's desire to help inform customers on product use by scheduling time at the factory for product seminars that can be attended by a number of customers at one time. These seminars can be more effective than those held at customers' places of business because of the availability of all manufacturing engineers. The customers can actually see the product being manufactured, inspected, tested, and prepared for shipment.

4. *Conventions.* Manufacturing should request marketing to keep them advised of the dates of all major conventions that the company customers attend so that someone can be assigned to work with sales at these conventions. Complete written reports should be submitted by this individual on any product discussions with customers.

Customer contacts of all sorts by manufacturing, properly carried out in conjunction with marketing, will help develop the strong communications needed between these two departments.

ADVICE OF TROUBLE
FIELD REPORT
SERVICE ORDER

ELECTRIC SERVICE DIVISION
FIELD RELIABILITY ANALYSIS FEEDBACK
WESTINGHOUSE PROPRIETARY

TO (LOCATION) | (RELIABILITY MGR.) | CONTROL ACCOUNT | JOB NO.

(SERV. OFF.) (MGR.) | RESPONSIBILITY | SERVICE ESTIMATE | R. R. NO.
(SALES OFF.) (SALESMAN)
(WORKS) (ACCTG. MGR.) | CUSTOMER NAME

PRELIMINARY APPROVAL | TROUBLE AT (NAME OF PLANT) | LOCATION

TO BE FILLED IN BY SALES ENGINEER

APPARATUS (PRIME) | REPORT TO | TITLE | TELEPHONE
APPLICATION | APPARATUS SOLD TO | LOCATION
STYLE NO. | DWG. | SUB. NO. | ITEM | SERIAL NO. | G.O. (INCLUDE SUFFIX) | S.O.

1. CUSTOMER COMPLAINT – ACTION DESIRED (USE EXTRA SHEET WHEN NECESSARY)

DATE OF TROUBLE OR FAILURE | TIME IN SERVICE EST. ACT. | DATE WARRANTY STARTED | SHIPPING DAMAGE – TERMS FOB DEST. ☐ FACTORY ☐ | CLAIM ENTERED YES ☐ NO ☐ BY

WILL THERE BE A CHARGE CUSTOMER ORDER FOR THIS WORK? YES ☐ NO ☐ | SEND RECOMMENDED BILLING TO SALESMAN FOR DISPOSITION ☐ | CUSTOMER ORDER NO.

CREDIT APPROVAL (BY & DATE) | BKG. DIST. | SALES OFFICE | WESTINGHOUSE SALESMAN | DATE WRITTEN

ANALYSIS FEEDBACK

ACCURACY OF APPARATUS IDENTIFICATION WILL BE VERIFIED BY ENGINEER | TO BE FILLED IN BY INVESTIGATING ENGINEER RETURN PROMPTLY (WITHIN 2 DAYS AFTER ARRIVAL) → | DATE REPORTED ON JOB

PHYSICAL LOCATION OF TROUBLE | PANEL NO. | CABINET NO. | CAGE NO. | LOCATION NO. | SCHEMATIC

ENVIRONMENTAL CONDITIONS WET DRY DIRTY DUSTY CLEAN | CHEMICAL ATMOSPHERE ☐ TYPE | AMBIENT TEMP. MAX. MIN.

2. PROBLEM AS FOUND (GIVE COMPONENT N. P. DATA WHEN REQUIRED)

PROBLEM DUE TO CHECK APPROPRIATE BLOCK(S)	A. DESIGN	B. MFG.	C. COORDINATION	D. PKG.	E. BRACING	F. TRANSP.	G. IDENT.	H. INSTR. MATL.	I. STORAGE	J. INSTALL. PROD.	K. OPER. PROB.	L. MAINT.	M. APPLI.

3. ACTION NEEDED TO CORRECT TROUBLE – IS JOB COMPLETE? YES ☐ NO ☐ | EST. MAN HOURS TO FINISH

4. MATERIAL REQUIRED: YES ☐ NO ☐ REQ. NO. | DATE OF FINAL GREEN SHEET

CITY OFFICE | INVESTIGATING SERVICE ENGINEER | DATE | REPORT NO. OF | PRELIM. | FINAL

TO BE FILLED IN BY DIVISION RELIABILITY MGR.

CORRECTIVE ACTION (SEND XEROX COPY TO SERVICE OFFICE)

RELIABILITY MANAGER | DATE CLOSED

RECORD OF SPLIT DECISION
CONTROL ACCT. | COST
TOTAL COST CLEARED
FINAL APPROVAL | DATE

FORM 35661 B

FIG. 3-2. Field Reliability Analysis Feedback Form.

Performance Review. A method should be established by the manufacturing executive of reflecting the degree of coordination and cooperation achieved by his department with the marketing department. This might take the form of a quarterly performance review report showing general and specific areas of cooperation between the two departments, with a set of symbols to denote the degree of cooperation achieved. The results of this review can then be used to pinpoint areas needing further attention.

CONCLUSION

The relationship between manufacturing and marketing should always be developing to newer levels of cooperation in all areas of both functions. This relationship enables a company to maintain the operating stability needed so that top management can spend its time furthering the company's growth in its chosen markets.

Customers, too, will become cognizant of the empathy between marketing and manufacturing and will turn more and more to the company with their problems, knowing that they will receive the full benefits of the experienced personnel of both functions. They will come to recognize that they will receive better solutions to their problems much faster than from a company that is dominated by one function.

By building a good rapport between manufacturing and marketing, the entire company benefits enormously. Interdepartmental cooperation will exist, and manufacturing will assist the sales personnel in eliminating customers' reasons for not buying. Marketing will help manufacturing by enabling it to stay current with competitive products. It will assist in many other ways including lowering of inventory requirements, thus making more economic scheduling possible; eliminating overbuilding of products; creating adequate quality and inventory controls; and moving obsolete stock from inventory. Through this constructive cooperation, the company will realize additional sales, lower operating costs, and more profitable operation.

BIBLIOGRAPHY

Allen, L. A., *Management and Organization*, McGraw-Hill Book Company, New York, 1958.
Berger, G. L., and W. V. Haney, *Organizational Relationships and Management Action*, McGraw-Hill Book Company, New York, 1966.
Converse, P. D., H. W. Huegy, and R. V. Mitchell, *Elements of Marketing*, 7th ed., Prentice-Hall, Inc., Englewood Cliffs, N.J., 1965.
Finley, R. E., and H. R. Ziobro, *The Manufacturing Man and His Job*, American Management Association, New York, 1966.
Fisch, G. G., *Organization for Profit*, McGraw-Hill Book Company, New York, 1964.
Mills, E. S., *Price, Output and Inventory Policy*, John Wiley & Sons, Inc., New York, 1962.
Morse, Stephen, *The Practical Approach to Marketing Management*, McGraw-Hill Book Company, New York, 1967.
Phillips, C. F., *Marketing by Manufacturers*, Richard D. Irwin, Inc., Homewood, Ill., 1951.
Stanton, William J., *Fundamentals of Marketing*, 2d ed., McGraw-Hill Book Company, New York, 1967.

CHAPTER FOUR

Relationship of Manufacturing and Finance and Control

JAMES R. LYNCH *Controller, Systems Manufacturing Division, International Business Machines Corporation, White Plains, New York*

The traditional roles of both the manufacturing manager and the corporate controller have been altered and expanded by the faster pace of technological change and continuing growth in the productivity and complexity of industry. The manufacturing manager is still primarily responsible for making and shipping products, but he can no longer do so effectively without a more comprehensive understanding and an intense application of financial controls in both day-to-day operations and short- and long-term business planning. Given a projected production schedule as the fundamental objective in his planning and control, he must be able to observe and measure performance in terms of not only customer shipping dates, cost, and expense, but product profitability as well. In a true sense, happily or not, the manufacturing manager is now, more than ever before, a full-fledged businessman.

The controller and his staff in the same way are still responsible for the many time-honored essential accounting functions—payroll, accounts receivable, accounts payable, and cashiering, to name just a few. In addition, the dynamic business environment today demands that he become deeply involved in the critical area of short- and long-range financial planning, closely oriented to the operations and schedules of the production department, as well as to all other staff and line functions in the company. For the very reasons that cost, expenses, and product profitability are now vital measurements of performance to the manufacturing manager, the controller—no longer concerned only with reporting what happened yesterday—must also take an active part in planning what will (or should) happen tomorrow.

The manufacturing manager continues to make the decisions and take the actions needed to meet production schedules and customer commitments, but the controller must provide him with the tools to do so: timely, complete, useful information on cost and expense for planning and control—in a form geared to management needs and production and financial control requirements. Again, happily or not, the controller must now know more than ever before what is happening on the production floor. Many industries are faced with such rapidly changing technologies that financial decisions made today can be obsoleted at the same pace as production decisions.

The manufacturing manager and the controller then, no longer isolated functions on the organization chart, must work together more closely. How should they work together constructively and positively? How can they help each other in setting cost goals and in measuring actual performance against these goals? The specific procedures for planning and control that these functions develop together may be expected to vary widely from company to company, depending on such factors as types and variety of products, size of the company, and top management's overall administrative philosophy. The degree to which the computer has been applied in handling manufacturing and financial information, as well as conventional accounting tasks, also strongly influences these procedures. As a matter of fact, the joint participation of the manufacturing manager and controller in specifying, contributing to, and benefiting from a corporate data processing system promotes and encourages the day-to-day teamwork that is essential in modern industry. Although the specific procedures may thus vary widely whether or not the computer is involved, the underlying concepts and basic techniques of financial planning and control— and the relationship between the manufacturing manager and the controller— are the same. These are the subjects of this chapter.

THE MANUFACTURING AND FINANCIAL ORGANIZATIONS

Manufacturing Operations and Services. The specific organization of an industrial concern may differ from one company to another, as does terminology for various activities, but the basic operating and service functions reporting to the operations manager and general manager are as given in Figure 4-1. Although quality control may occasionally report directly to the general manager, all other functions almost always are under the supervision of the plant or operations manager.

Most significantly with regard to the subject of this chapter, each function has specific responsibilities in financial planning and control and, to some degree, must work with the company's financial departments. Work standards, job procedures, manpower planning, and space planning, all primarily tasks of industrial engineering, for example, originate information important to the financial department that is not available anywhere else. Conversely, these industrial engineering responsibilities cannot be discharged without the payroll and overhead assignments that are maintained by the controller. Materials management, which includes both inventory control and procurement, certainly must originate much of the information needed in a corporate data processing system.

The manufacturing operations are the primary source of both income and expense, and so the manufacturing manager is deeply involved in many phases of financial planning and control from the point of personal commitment as well as accurate planning. The managers of the various services, such as industrial engineering and manufacturing engineering, are equally deeply concerned with budgets but within a far narrower scope. References to the manufacturing manager alone in the remainder of this chapter, therefore, will often apply also to the managers of manufacturing services.

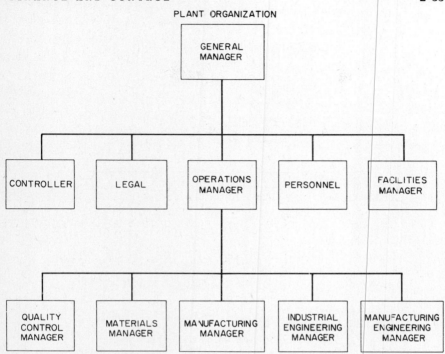

FIG. 4-1. Organization Chart Showing Basic Operating and Service Functions, Typically Reporting to Manufacturing General Manager, Which Work Together to Some Degree in Financial Planning and Control.

The Financial Department. Although he certainly knows the development of financial data and its application to production operations, the manufacturing manager is often unfamiliar with the responsibilities of the financial department, particularly as it is run in the modern industrial organization. As shown in Figure 4-2, the financial department, under the direction of the corporate controller, has three primary functions: (1) accounting services, (2) plans and operations, and (3) data processing. The last function includes all computer equipment operations, computer programming, and systems and procedures involved in maintaining a corporate data processing system. This responsibility is most likely to be found in the financial department, because digital computers were originally devoted entirely to traditional accounting services and so were naturally introduced under the controller's direction.

Traditional accounting services include the ledger, accounting distributions, payroll, labor accounting, and accounts payable. Although these services may occupy the largest proportion of the time of the financial staff and data processing system, the procedures are firmly established and change very little from month to month. The financial controller, then, spends only a small fraction of his time in supervising traditional accounting work.

The controller instead tends to concentrate on the plans and operations activities of the financial department. Here, management action and decision become more important than standardized procedures and paperwork mechanization. In addition, plans and operations constitute the financial activity

CONTROLLER'S ORGANIZATION

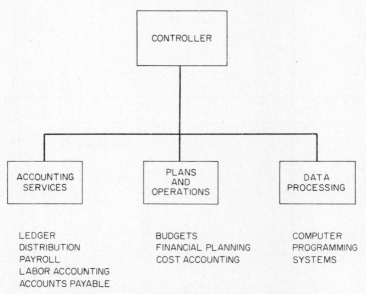

FIG. 4-2. Typical Controller's Organization.

where most of the interaction between manufacturing and finance takes place. There are six major activities in financial plans and operations:

1. Cost accounting and control
2. Inventory accounting and control
3. Overhead budget
4. Financial planning (including cash planning)
5. Capital budgets
6. Assets control and appropriations evaluation

Although these financial activities certainly do not seem to indicate any radical change in the controller's responsibilities, the real difference is that planning and control have changed from periodic studies to establish bench marks and operating limits to dynamic, day-to-day activities that are constantly changing to fulfill present and projected needs.

MAJOR JOINT MANUFACTURING AND FINANCE FUNCTIONS

The key planning mechanism in any manufacturing organization is the Plan of Operation, an overall plant program that is essentially a commitment or contract by the plant manager to the general manager and company president. The controller's job is to help the plant manager and manufacturing manager fulfill this commitment. In doing so, his responsibility is to coordinate the development of the plan by the various manufacturing functions, help set cost and expense ground rules, and trigger reviews in the control activity.

A Plan of Operation logically requires a procedure for performance measurement and operations control. Its content must be specific and identifiable. In measuring performance, there must be timely, accurate information that describes all manufacturing activities with respect to the Plan of Operation and in forms and terms that are meaningful to the manufacturing managers involved. The key management control mechanism might be called a "Plans/Operations Progress Report," a periodic summary of performance measured against the commitment in the Plan of Operation. A monthly Plans/Operations Progress Report is both frequent enough to maintain satisfactory control and yet not so frequent as to be beyond the capacity of a data processing system consistent with reasonable administrative expense. In addition, too frequent progress reports may require too much personnel and computer time in recording and processing data and may also be unnecessarily sensitive to small changes.

The Plan of Operation itself is developed periodically—annually, every two years, or perhaps as long as every five years—the period depending in large degree on the nature of the firm's product line and markets and the pace of its growth. Whatever the period, however, the Plan of Operation must be changed to meet the demands of new production schedules, which rarely stay at the same level as at the time the Plan of Operation is approved by top management. It unfortunately can happen that when a production schedule goes down—shipments to customers are lower than expected—retrenchment becomes necessary. On the other hand, increases in production schedules, although certainly a pleasant problem, can be one of manufacturing management's most difficult tasks. It is then necessary to determine the resources in cash, inventory, manpower, and space that are needed beyond those in the existing Plan of Operation and their impact on product cost. Thus, the controller and manufacturing manager must engage in what might best be called continuous planning, so that the Plan of Operation can be revised to keep pace with the production schedule.

The Plan of Operation. The primary element of a Plan of Operation is the production schedule, which records anticipated product manufacture and shipments each month over the period of the plan. The short-term schedule, of course, will be largely controlled by the customer orders already known. Beyond that, the production schedule is based on many factors, including forecasts by the sales department, corporate expansion objectives, and the general business climate. New products are the most difficult to establish production schedules for: first, they are usually the most difficult to keep on schedule, and second, are most likely to undergo schedule changes (hopefully, in the upward direction).

The next major subject of a Plan of Operation is product cost—what it costs to make the product and its components today, and trends that may be expected during the period of the Plan of Operation. Cost reduction and cost effectiveness programs, which are a continuing activity in any manufacturing concern (or at least should be), may be directed at cost goals that are specified in the Plan of Operation. The tendency is to be optimistic in this area, which may cause a manufacturing manager to be excessively harsh on himself.

All the other elements of a Plan of Operation, including the main planning categories within elements, may be listed as follows:

1. Production schedule
2. Product cost
   a. Product cost today
   b. Cost trends
   c. Analysis of cost for volume changes
3. Manpower
   a. Manpower plan by time

      b. Manpower plan by function
      c. Staffing plan
      d. Nonregular manpower
  4. Facilities
  5. Inventory
      a. Assumptions
      b. Data sheet
      c. Plan-to-plan comparison
  6. **Manufacturing expense**
  7. Procurement
  8. Quality assurance
      a. Quality assurance plan
      b. Manufacturing reliability test
      c. Failure analysis
      d. Early entry
      e. Reduced inspection
      f. Measurement indicators
  9. Industrial engineering
      a. Industrial engineering activity distribution
      b. Cost engineering
      c. Work measurement program
      d. Total improvement program
      e. Indices
      f. Planned product cost reduction
 10. Manufacturing engineering
      a. Major problems, objectives, and programs
      b. Manpower requirements and plans
      c. Financial requirements
 11. Cash
      a. Cash expenditures
      b. Reconciliation of production cost to cash cost
 12. Capital
      a. Capital plan summary
      b. Tooling and test equipment
      c. Plant and equipment requirements

A Plan of Operation is normally developed under the direction of the financial controller but is not a financial plan. It is an overall plant operating plan that integrates and summarizes the plans of all manufacturing operations and services. The development of a Plan of Operation then requires a large degree of interaction among all functions involved. Cohesiveness and commitment are two key ingredients of a successful pan.

One approach in initiating a Plan of Operation is for the plant manager to call a "kickoff" meeting perhaps six weeks before the plan is due. At this meeting, the controller explains the ground rules, key dates, and broad assumptions on which the plan is to be based. Even though the department managers present at these meetings may have contributed to previous Plans of Operation, many of the ground rules are likely to have changed, and managers may have shifted to other responsibilities. Much of this initial meeting may be expected to be occupied with questions and answers dealing with the details of procedure, such as the key schedule of events and the individuals responsible.

The managers of the various manufacturing functions can then follow with their own kickoff meetings. Here, plans are drawn, costs are estimated, and figures may be sharply adjusted and rearranged. The managers may then be expected to have numerous informal meetings with other operating or service managers on budgetary subjects in which both are involved. For example, industrial engineering may propose new processes to achieve product cost reductions. Although the manager of industrial engineering has primary responsibility in this area, he must coordinate with the manager of manufacturing engineering with regard to the resulting effects on manpower requirements, one of manufacturing engineering's main planning jobs. The manpower plan is established for direct and indirect labor on the basis of production schedules, and, in building the plan department by department, industrial engineering must review their requirements with all operating and service managers. The controller must be consulted, too, in order to maintain acceptable cash flow.

The staff of the financial department is naturally involved in any estimating or cost projections and so may be expected to be frequently involved in inter-function planning meetings. Certainly, the cost estimators in industrial engineering must work closely with cost accountants in establishing product cost targets. To do so, the cost accountant must have some understanding of the product itself, and conversely, the manufacturing manager must be familiar with costing and estimating procedures.

Large capital expenditures for process equipment are usually worked out for the capital budget by manufacturing engineering. These expenditures must be justified by the existing and projected needs of the production schedule. The controller advises manufacturing engineering on development of the most realistic and convincing justification of capital expenditure with respect to cost reductions and return on investment. Conversely, the finance department must call on industrial engineering for data on utilization of plant space (what manufacturing groups occupy what space?) to determine a realistic monthly burden rate.

Cost reductions are customarily considered the responsibility of industrial engineering and yet heavily involve manufacturing engineering on process changes, and procurement on contract negotiations and vendor relations. For example, industrial engineering, manufacturing engineering, and the materials manager must together work out a budget for automated material handling equipment in a warehouse. In general, however, the role of the financial controller is primarily advisory in the area of cost reduction programs.

The contributions of the operating, service, and staff functions in developing a Plan of Operation are shown schematically in Figure 4-3. The flow of activity in developing the plan starts with the market forecast and ends with the completed operating plan for approval by top management. The involvement of manufacturing functions in budgetary and accounting considerations is demonstrated in the major planning activities given for the various functions.

Note that the review by the general manager is best held off until agreement has been reached by all other functions. Although the general manager may be called on to settle disputes and certainly is willing to contribute informally, the plant manager and managers of the various manufacturing functions must feel that the Plan of Operation constitutes their commitments or contracts over the planning period with the general manager. Once the general manager has approved the Plan of Operation, which is unlikely to occur without at least some revision, he must then present the Plan to the company president as his own commitment to performance. Approval of the Plan should be confirmed in writing, including any reservations or qualifications.

Plans/Operations Progress Reports. The plant manager and operating and

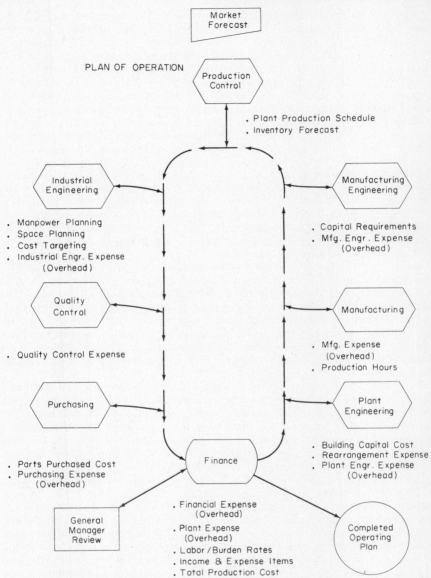

FIG. 4-3. Contributions of Operating, Service, and Staff Functions in Developing a
Plan of Operation.

service managers cannot realistically be expected to fulfill the Plan of Operation
in their areas without periodic progress reports that give them accurate, complete measurements of actual performance in comparison to planned or projected figures.

A Plans/Operations (P/O) Progress Report tabulates in dollars the performance commitment of each manufacturing group and what was actually done

during the month (or over whatever other period the report covers). Although detailed reports in each functional area may be made available to appropriate managers as described below, it is good procedure to distribute the concentrated summary in the P/O Progress Report to all managers. This summary should include the kind of subject organization shown in the following list.

1. Cost of production highlights
2. Direct labor
   a. Direct labor performance
   b. Direct hour utilization
   c. Direct manufacturing improvement trends
3. Factory expense
   a. Summary
   b. Administrative comparison
   c. Manpower analysis (indirect-direct)
   d. Overtime
   e. Absenteeism
   f. Cash analysis
4. Purchasing and interplant
   a. Vendor purchases
   b. Vendor receipts and shipments
   c. Interplant shipments

DIRECT HOURS

UTILIZATION

CURRENT MONTH JUNE 19__

AVERAGE UTILIZATION OF DIRECT HOURS WORKED

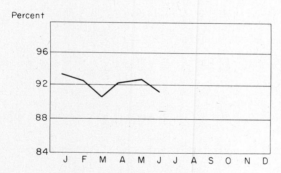

Function	Current Month			Year to Date		
	Total Hours Worked	Prod. Hours	Percent Utilized	Total Hours Worked	Prod. Hours	Percent Utilized
Machining	200	180	90.0	1270	1180	92.9
Process Manufacturing	176	160	90.9	1156	1055	91.3
Assembly	125	118	94.4	710	655	92.3
Total Manufacturing	501	458	91.4	3136	2890	92.2

Fig. 4-4.   Report of Direct Hours Utilization.

Indiret-Direct Manpower Comparison, June 19—

	Indirect			Direct			Total			O.P. Year-end ceiling
	Quarter ceiling	Actual	Variance	Quarter on-board ceiling	Actual	Variance	Quarter ceiling	Actual	Variance	
Plant services:										
General administration	6	5	1				6	5	(1)	6
Plant controller	20	20	—				20	20	—	19
Personnel	40	41	1				40	41	1	36
Plant engineering	64	60	(4)				64	60	(4)	61
Subtotal	130	126	(4)				130	126	(4)	122
Manufacturing services:										
Quality control	45	46	1				45	46	1	45
Materials management	65	64	(1)				65	64	(1)	61
Manufacturing engineering	55	53	(2)				55	53	(2)	55
Industrial engineering	39	41	2				39	41	2	39
Subtotal	204	204	—				204	204	—	200
Manufacturing:										
Administration	2	2	—	—	—	—	2	2	—	2
Machining	5	4	(1)	60	62	2	65	66	1	63
Process manufacturing	5	5	—	50	50	—	55	55	—	52
Assembly	4	4	—	40	33	(7)	44	37	(7)	41
Subtotal	16	15	(1)	150	145	(5)	166	160	(6)	158
Total	350	345	(5)	150	145	(5)	500	490	(10)	480

FIG. 4-5.   Comparison of Actual Indirect and Direct Manpower with Targets.

2–40

5. Product cost
   a. Product cost summary
   b. Product cost detail
   c. Subproduct cost detail
6. Standard quality report
7. Schedules and inventory
   a. Production completed
   b. Production in-process
   c. Schedule analysis
   d. Inventory
   e. Input-output reconciliation
8. Related report data
   a. Income and expense items
   b. Engineering changes
   c. Measurement coverage
   d. Appraisal and counseling

The "cost of production highlights" merely gives an itemized dollar break-down of production of all products matched against manufacturing and procurement expenses, purchases from vendors, and total inventory changes. Typical data formats in the remainder of the report are shown in Figures 4-4, 4-5, and 4-6.

Direct hour utilization is plotted in Figure 4-4 as average utilization of direct hours worked in the current month and for the year-to-date. Below the graph, direct labor utilization for the current month and year-to-date is summarized in total hours and actual productive hours. In Figure 4-5, the indirect-direct manpower analysis summarizes indirect and direct labor in plant services, manufacturing services, and manufacturing. The quarter ceiling gives the maximum hours established for that quarter in the plan of operation in comparison with the actual hours (indirect, direct, and total) worked in that quarter. The Product Cost Comparison Report in Figure 4-6 gives both the

Product Cost Comparison, June 19—

Product	Current month				Year-to-date				
	Product quantity	Unit cost		Total dollar variance	Product quantity		Unit cost		Total dollar variance
	Actual	Forecast	Actual		Forecast	Actual	Forecast	Actual	
xy	100	10	9	100	600	650	14	13	650
ab	75	110	115	(375)	500	450	125	120	2250
cd	80	80	80	—	300	250	90	90	—
gi	75	60	60	—	400	400	70	75	(2000)
fg	75	65	70	(375)	300	350	75	78	1050

Fig. 4-6. Product Cost Comparison Report.

actual unit product cost and the cost forecast in the Plan of Operation for both the current month and year-to-date.

In addition to recording performance in the P/O Progress Report, it is good practice for the plant manager to hold a manager's meeting a few days before the report is published. Here, the controller's review of the figures is followed by informal discussion by the managers of the service and operating departments. Of course, the manufacturing manager may follow the issuance of the progress report with separate meetings with his department managers where actual and target performances can be reviewed, necessary decisions made, and actions planned. The manufacturing manager may request that a cost accountant from the finance department be present to help in evaluating budgetary figures, although decision naturally remains with the department managers involved.

SPECIAL REPORTS ON MANUFACTURING PERFORMANCE

The special performance reports used by the manufacturing manager and his department heads must be produced at the frequency, with the data, and in the format that will be most useful to the managers involved. In a relatively small firm with a limited product line, it is possible to develop these periodic reports manually, with the help of standard office machinery. For most manufacturing concerns, however, the need for timely, accurate information immediately after the period covered by the report—whether a day, week, or month—demands the high data processing speed and information handling capacity of a computer system. Because most firms already have a central computer facility, and often have special computers in various departments, many of the data needed for periodic performance reports are already in machine-readable form. Of course, computer programs must be developed to produce the reports specified by the operating and service managers, examples of which are shown below.

Major Reports by Department within a Function. The Manufacturing Improvement Report (Figure 4-7) compares the unit productivity in the current month with production of the same part in the same operation last year. The measured hours and burden are for the current month, the base figure represents production of the same quantity of parts twelve months before, and the index is the ratio of measured hours to base quantities. In summary for this particular department, for example, the index of 1.278 indicates that the total measured labor and burden for the month is a .278 improvement in productivity over the last year. With a periodic report like this, the department manager is able to evaluate the performance of machines and their operators from month to month, pinpointing both upward and downward trends at individual work stations.

The Labor Utilization Report in Figure 4-8 is generated monthly to detail the distribution of labor hours among regular operations (actually making the product) and in such nonregular operations as rework, training off the job, waiting time, absence, and sickness. This report is generated on two levels. First, the manufacturing manager receives a summary for all operating departments; second, each department manager receives a summary for his area of responsibility alone. The percent effective utilization and equivalent manpower at the bottom of the report give the manager useful indices of performance from month to month; he knows what percent of available time is actually used to make the product. With a computerized data processing system, all key

MANUFACTURING IMPROVEMENT
DEPT. 092

DEPT			MEASURED		HOURS	
092	PART NO.	OPER.	QUAN-TITY	BASE	MEAS-URED	INDEX
1	0365780	0015	86	.1	.1	1.000
5	0365780	0017	86	.4	.4	1.092
8	0411544	0350	6	4.0	6.0	.660
3	0743642	0017	20	.7	.2	3.333
11	2501019	0005	55,780	171.8	163.0	1.055
11	2501019	0010	69,148	385.8	131.2	2.937
12	2501019	0015	55,450	69.9	45.8	1.518
11	2501019	0020	11,506	27.0	30.8	0.877
10	2501019	0025	11,350	123.7	23.0	5.369
11	2501019	0030	11,020	12.0	10.7	1.121
11	2501019	0035	10,814	74.3	69.2	1.073
11	2501019	0040	10,560	8.4	8.4	1.000
10	2501019	0045	9,440	29.5	29.5	1.000
9	2501019	0055	5,388	77.6	38.2	2.031
10	2501019	0060	5,066	88.0	59.2	1.486
2	2510660	0095	774	.9	1.0	.922
3	2510665	0095	21,761	25.0	37.7	.665
3	2510666	0095	6,485	8.2	8.5	.962
1	2570665	0095	1,315	1.7	1.7	1.000
2	5414276	0035	311	22.7	138.7	.163
3	5414276	0045	2,913	69.9	71.2	.982
1	5417929	0590	182	28.0	28.0	1.000
1	5417929	0605	84	6.0	6.0	1.000
1	5417930	0590	231	41.6	41.6	1.000
2	5417930	0600	1,470	103.5	55.7	1.858
1	5417930	0605	84	6.0	6.0	1.000
3	5417931	0590	794	88.8	127.0	.700
3	5417931	0605	1,302	79.0	89.5	.882
00				1,507.1	1,178.4	1.278

Fig. 4-7. Manufacturing Improvement Report (monthly).

monthly reports such as this can be made available to operating managers by the tenth working day of the following month.

The Performance Work Measurement Report in Figure 4-9 is an example of the type of data that may be produced daily, weekly, or monthly, depending on the needs of the department manager. In this report, standard hours for various operations are compared to earned (or paid) hours, and performance figures are given for earned hours as a percentage of standards. The manager of an assembly department, who needs such a report daily to maintain proper control, may expect to receive the report at 9:00 A.M. the following day, the report having been generated overnight in the computer system from labor time reports.

Other Types of Reports. Detailed cost reports may also be produced on the main activities in manufacturing, both in terms of labor, burden, and materials and in product and subassembly breakdowns. Monthly operating budgets at

DIRECT LABOR UTILIZATION

MC	DESCRIPTION	JAN	FEB	MAR
11	REGULAR OPERATION	36029	39448	45689
16	SPECIAL-PARTS SHORTAGE		148	1
19	MODIFIED-ADDED OPERATION	1839	4761	4413
21	REGULAR SETUP OPERATION	1590	1996	2005
29	IRREGULAR SETUP OPERATION	117	359	277
61	REWORK CAUSED BY OWN DEPT	22	27	25
81	REWORK CHGD TO DEPT. XXX	381	436	622
83	EXTRA WORK FOR DEPT. XXX	3269	4064	4850
89	E/C REWORK	825	990	577
**	TOTAL UTILIZED HOURS	44072	52229	58459
33	TRAINING OFF THE JOB	41	3	15
39	MISCELLANEOUS	110	131	553
51	DIRECT-MISC HRS	752	847	541
53	DIRECT MACH TOOL DUTIES	1357	1549	2028
59	DIRECT MISC INDIRECT HRS	152	182	157
74	MULTI-JOB ASSIGNMENT	154	115	148
**	TOTAL NONUTILIZED HRS LESS ABS	2566	2827	3442
93	ABS-SICK&ACCIDENT-DIRECT	1661	2184	2540
94	ABS-OTHER AUTH DIRECT	2805	1565	647
**	TOTAL NONUTILIZED HRS PLUS ABS	7032	6576	6629
**	% UTILIZATION LESS DIRECT ABS	94.4	94.4	94.4
**	% UTILIZATION PLUS DIRECT ABS	86.2	88.8	89.8
91	ABS-VACATION-DIRECT	472	640	1128
92	ABS-HOLIDAY-DIRECT	2360		2432
**	TOTAL DIRECT HRS MISC	2832	640	3560
**	TOTAL DIRECT HRS	53936	59445	68648
41	INDIRECT-DISPATCHING	5137	5757	6683
95	ABS-INDIRECT	828	521	826
**	TOTAL INDIRECT HRS	5965	6278	7509
**	TOTAL HOURS	59901	65723	76157
**	% EFFECTIVE UTILIZATION	76.7	78.5	79.1
**	EQUIVALENT MANPOWER	358.2	371.5	344.9

FIG. 4-8.   Labor Utilization Report (monthly).

the department level give in detail budgetary information that is only summarized in the P/O Progress Report.   Each department manager then receives
budgetary information in the degree of detail he needs.

Inventory reports might include a monthly turnover report which compares
actual inventory changes for the current month with respect to the previous
month.   A separate report on inventory activity might detail weekly inventory
changes by product and subassembly.

In purchasing, a purchasing performance report might summarize monthly
the actual performance in parts procurement with respect to the target stated

DAILY DEPARTMENTAL PERFORMANCE
DEPT. XX

DATE	EMP. NO.	PART NO.	OPER. NO.	JOB NO.	QTY. CLMD.	C L	G R	LBR. CODE	DESCRIPTION	ERND. HRS.	PAID HRS.	PERF. %
0648	507090	0232224	0015	0024	126.00	1	A	11	Regular Operation	7.0	7.0	100.0
	507090	0232224	4015	0024	47.00			19	Modified—Added Operation	—	1.0	—
									Total Paid Hours		8.0	
									Standard Hours (Earned)	7.0	7.0	100.0
	625230	0346902	0093	9020	1.00	3	A	11	Regular Operation	4.0	4.2	105.0
	625230	0231043	0090	0019	9.00	1	A	11	Regular Operation	8.0	8.0	100.0
	625230	0346902	0093	8129	1.00	3	A	11	Regular Operation	4.0	3.8	95.0
									Total Paid Hours		16.0	
									Standard Hours (Earned)	16.0	16.0	100.0
	630080	0231021	9020	0018	1.00			61	Rework caused by own dept.	—	.5	—
	630080	0369549	9020	0018	1.00			81	Rework charged to Dept. xxx	—	1.5	—
	630080	0231021	0010	0018	8.00	1	A	11	Regular Operation	6.0	6.0	100.0
	630080	0231021	9020	0018	1.00			61	Rework caused by own dept.	—	.5	—
	630080	0231021	4010	0018	8.00			19	Modified—Added Operation	—	.5	—
									Total Paid Hours		9.0	
									Standard Hours (Earned)	6.0	6.0	100.0

FIG. 4-9. Performance Work Measurement Report (daily).

in the Plan of Operation, giving in detail information summarized in the P/O Progress Report. Similar to the Manufacturing Improvement Report, a Purchasing Improvement Report might tabulate indices on procurement costs in the current month in comparison to the same time last year for identical parts.

MAINTAINING CLOSE MANUFACTURING AND FINANCE RELATIONSHIP

The operating and service managers' awareness of financial requirements, of course, develops as they contribute to a Plan of Operation and use periodic reports in the administration of their departments. It is important, however, to ensure a firm base of understanding by familiarizing them first with budgetary procedures and the function of the financial department, whether this is done informally by the manufacturing manager or as part of a formal plant course. A new manager should spend some time in the finance department to learn how the controller and his staff are organized to help him and then how he can best use their services. Similarly, cost accountants and other professional personnel in the finance department should be assigned to learn the needs of the manufacturing departments and become accustomed to working with manufacturing personnel on the plant floor. As companies have developed a close working relationship between manufacturing and finance, it is not unusual to find that financial and manufacturing personnel are advanced to higher positions in each other's area.

In solving problems related to the joint commitment to the Plan of Operation, the manufacturing and finance departments may establish joint programs with special staffs. For example, accurate reporting of data for bills-of-material and labor claims is traditionally a difficult task for manufacturing. In a joint program, a manufacturing engineer, a production control representative, and a cost accountant might study the problem, propose a solution, and develop a procedure to make it work.

CONTINUOUS PLANNING AND THE FLEXIBLE BUDGET

A Plan of Operation and control with respect to performance targets in such a plan, as reviewed above, are workable in a dynamic manufacturing environment only when the budgetary levels in the plan can change. An increase (or decrease) in the output volume of standard products—a change in the production schedule—certainly requires a change in the operating budget for manpower, space, materials, and equipment. In addition, as new products are introduced, changes in the production schedule are likely to be even more abrupt. Thus, a Plan of Operation, which itself projects what is expected over a long period, must constantly change—and change demands, in essence, continuous planning by manufacturing operations and service managers.

Continuous planning itself leads to the need for some system for flexible budgeting. Although manufacturing department managers are responsible for operating budgets, it must be made as easy as possible for them to prepare their budgets in the first place and then modify these budgets as changes occur in the production schedule. Increased expenses on any item due to an increase in the production schedule must be differentiated from expense increases that represent a loss of control or unanticipated developments.

Most expense items that fluctuate with a production schedule are functions of such variables as manpower, manpower utilization, labor rates, floor space, and production volume. The concept of flexible budgeting assumes that variable overhead costs and the variable elements of semivariable costs are functions of production volume (or rate of operation) and can be expressed as such. Certainly materials expense for parts is proportional to the number of product units made. In addition to proportional direct labor expense, it is possible to develop from experience expense rates per indirect employee and then the number of indirect employees per unit of production.

The elements of a computerized flexible budgeting system include tables, factors, and formulas. The tables are major sources of expense which are categorized and grouped, such as plant manpower, plant labor rates, machine production, direct hours, department manpower, and department labor rates. Each table of expense categories is broken down into factors. In a manpower table, for example, the factors include direct, indirect, management, exempt indirect, and nonexempt direct. The manager of a department sets up a budget by selecting a formula which best represents the source of each expense item, and budgetary figures are determined from known rates and indices using these formulas. As shown in Figure 4-10, monthly budgets can then be automatically computed for a year in advance on the basis of a given production schedule. And these twelve-month budgets are recomputed and reported each month as the production schedule changes.

Once the formulas have been selected, budget changes are unnecessary unless a change in conditions makes a formula inapplicable to a particular item of expense. Because budgets derived from the monthly updated tables are based on current data, constant resubmissions of budgets are unnecessary as conditions change. Most importantly, operating and service managers need only input projected manpower in order to make necessary changes in their operating budgets, both for the subsequent month and the following year.

MONTHLY BUDGET SPREAD

ACCOUNT NAME	ACCT. NO.	FOR-MULA	JAN.	FEB.	SEPT.	DEC.	TOTAL
MFG. SPT.	102	023	$487	$576	$454	$797	$7192
MFG. SPT.	102	057	147	109	32	65	876
		TOTAL	634	685	486	862	8068
MFG. DIR.	101	039	81	105	91	202	1623
SHIFT PREM.	177	035	225	202	212	312	2946
JOB TRNG.	162	039	70	87	79	176	1410
CONF. MTGS.	165	039	62	83	69	154	1237
S&A BEN.	184	097	270	326	188	319	3510
AUTH. ABS.	185	097	116	140	81	137	1506
ACID, CHEM.	301	085	45	60	63	85	754
TOOLS, GAGE	307	006	65	64	40	69	721
LOC TRAV.	501	016	3	3	3	2	33
EDPM SVC.	605	001	10	10	10	10	120
DEPT. TOTALS			$1581	$1765	$1322	$2328	$21928

Fig. 4-10. Monthly Departmental Budget, as Automatically Computed on the Basis of Projected Manpower Alone, in a Computerized Flexible Budgeting System.

BIBLIOGRAPHY

Finney, H., and H. Miller, *Principles of Accounting*, Prentice-Hall, Inc., Englewood Cliffs, N.J., 1964.

Grant, Eugene, and Lawrence Bell, *Basic Accounting and Cost Accounting*, McGraw-Hill Book Company, New York, 1956.

Gross, Bertram, *Organizations and Their Managing*, The Free Press of Glencoe, Inc., New York, 1968.

Johnson, Arnold, *Elementary Accounting*, Holt, Rinehart & Winston, Inc., New York, 1962.

Lasser, J. K., *Business Management Handbook*, McGraw-Hill Book Company, New York, 1960.

Robichaud, B., *Understanding Modern Business Data Processing*, McGraw-Hill Book Company, New York, 1966.

CHAPTER FIVE

Relationship of Manufacturing and Personnel Relations

GORDON A. SUTTON *Director of Personnel, North American Rockwell Corporation, Pittsburgh, Pennsylvania*

The continually increasing complexities of modern business require manufacturing managers at all levels to have a broad knowledge of an ever-widening array of functions. Many of these functions are individually highly complex and specialized activities. No matter how capable he is, no manufacturing manager can be an expert on all the functional activities relating to his operation. However, he must possess sufficient knowledge to handle the more common day-to-day problems effectively. He must also recognize when he should consult the various staff specialists available. Knowing *when* to seek staff assistance, however, is not sufficient. The manufacturing manager must also know *how* to use these staff services most effectively.

Of all the staff members whose services are usually available to the manufacturing manager, the one that potentially can have the greatest impact on his operations is the personnel specialist. The manager's job has often been described as one of "getting results through other people." Therefore it is obvious that a manager's results can only be as good as the combined results of his subordinates. To get the maximum effective results requires the combined efforts of the line manager and the personnel staff specialist. Too frequently, however, this desired team effort is marred by misunderstanding, differences of opinion, conflicts of objectives, and lack of communication. This chapter presents some basic guidelines that can lead to a fully effective and coordinated effort between the manufacturing manager and the personnel staff in dealing with "people management" matters. Emphasis will be placed on the proper interrelationships of line and staff management. Specific personnel techniques will be discussed only for illustrative purposes.

ORIGIN OF LINE-STAFF CONFLICTS

One of the most common obstacles to establishing rapport between line management and personnel departments is insufficient clarification of accountability and authority with respect to personnel matters. Put another way, it frequently is not clearly established "who's in charge," who has the authority to make final decisions on various personnel matters, and who is accountable for the consequences of such decisions.

It is a basic premise of sound organization that an individual should have appropriate authority and control over matters for which he is accountable. Because each line manager unquestionably is accountable for the results achieved by his subordinates, it logically follows that he, not the personnel department, must make the final decisions on such matters as employment, promotions, discharge, transfer, discipline, and so forth.

Theoretically, the primary accountability for sound employee relations rests with line managers. They are in the command decision position. The personnel staff are expert advisors and consultants who assist line management, but they are accountable only for the quality and reliability of the service, advice, and assistance that they provide. Few, if any, companies actually operate under such a pure line-staff concept. Practical operating requirements, differences in the size and complexity of operations, and varying capabilities of individuals all affect the actual line-staff relationship that realistically exists. Consequently, the authority of most line managers is limited to some degree with respect to personnel matters by established policies, formal procedures, and union agreements.

The degree to which a manufacturing operation adheres to the theoretical concepts of line-staff relationship is of relatively minor significance. The really important considerations are:

1. Are the established working relations between manufacturing managers and the personnel department effective in achieving the operations' overall goals or objectives; that is, are the present relationships working well?
2. Are the delegated responsibilities and corresponding authority of both line and staff personnel clearly understood by all concerned, and do they actually operate accordingly?
3. Within the limits of required formal policies and procedures, does line management have the authority to make the final decision with respect to personnel matters for which it will be held accountable?

Positive answers to these questions are prerequisites to sound relationships between the manufacturing and personnel relations functions. Unfortunately, in many operations the answers to these questions are at best qualified noes.

Responsibilities and Authority. The first step in establishing effective line-staff relationships is to be sure that all individuals involved understand the extent of their responsibilities and authority. Informal verbal communications on these matters seldom work well. Because most day-to-day communications are at best imperfect, what a manager says and how his subordinate understands it are frequently two different things. In defining responsibilities and authority, formal written documents are a necessity. Even the written word has its limitations, but it is nevertheless a highly desirable first step.

Many companies have written job descriptions containing somewhat general statements of responsibility. These descriptions have usually been written for job evaluation, rather than as a communication tool, to assist the incumbent to understand his responsibilities better. To be truly meaningful, the description should contain clear statements of limits of authority and spell out the more significant interdepartment coordination that is expected. This type of description frequently results in a fairly lengthy document and one that is not simple to prepare. However, the very process of preparing it can be an invaluable aid to effective communications.

The most significant step in job description preparation is the joint review that must be carried out between the incumbent and his superior. The discussion of the written description provides an excellent opportunity to answer questions which may arise and to make certain that the individual has a realistic understanding of his responsibilities and authority.

There is no one best format for job descriptions. There are some good books on the subject which can assist in selecting the most appropriate approach consistent with a given company's needs.[1,2] The most important consideration from the standpoint of line-staff relationships is to assure that, in addition to basic responsibility (that is, what is to be done), all significant limitations of authority and working relationships between positions be concisely but clearly spelled out. A comparative review of job descriptions, by organizational levels and across departmental lines, serves to point out possible omissions, conflicts, or overlaps in responsibilities and authority.

Position descriptions are not a panacea for sound line-staff relationships. However, if used properly, they can preclude many misunderstandings and conflicts between functions. A typical example of how the authority and working relationships between line and staff positions can be specified in job descriptions is contained in the following excerpts from the description of the positions of a foreman, a labor relations supervisor, and a manufacturing department superintendent.

Foreman. In matters of employee discipline, the foreman's authority is limited to imposing temporary suspension, pending review of the facts involved by the labor relations supervisor and final decision by the foreman's department superintendent.

Labor Relations Supervisor. He is responsible for reviewing or investigating all proposed disciplinary cases and for recommending for decision by the appropriate line manager, the disciplinary penalty, if any, that may be imposed consistent with the offense and the provisions of the labor agreement.

Department Superintendent. The incumbent shall have final authority to direct the imposing of disciplinary penalties on bargaining unit employees in his department after full consideration of the facts of each case and the recommendations of the labor relations supervisor.

Personnel Policies and Procedures. Other means of maintaining proper relationships between line management and the personnel department are written personnel policies and procedures. In essence, they are the rules of the game and cover the multitude of subjects not practical to detail in individual job descriptions.

The word "policy" means different things to different companies. There are innumerable definitions of policy that are, at best, perplexing. However, there is one common, brief, unperplexing definition: "A policy is a guide for carrying out action."[3] In the context of manufacturing management–personnel depart-

[1] Gordon H. Evans, *Managerial Job Descriptions in Manufacturing,* Research Study no. 65, American Management Association, New York, 1964.

[2] Carl Heyel, *Management for Modern Supervisors,* chaps. 5 and 6, American Management Association, New York, 1962.

[3] M. Valliant Higgins, *Management Policies I,* Research Study no. 76, American Management Association, New York, 1966, p. 21.

ment relationships, policies actually constitute limitations on management authority. The policy statement spells out what is to be done in a given situation and defines how much or how little latitude management is granted in dealing with a particular subject. Procedures, in turn, are supplements to a policy statement. A procedure specifies the "how, when, and by whom" of policy application.

No attempt will be made here to spell out the various personnel subjects that should be reduced to writing. This decision again depends on the requirements of each company. Usually, written policies and procedures are desirable where:

1. Consistent uniform application and action are necessary or desirable on a specific subject.
2. The coordinated action of several departments or units is necessary to achieve a desired result.
3. There have been or it can reasonably be expected that there may be misunderstandings on significant personnel matters.

Development of Policies and Procedures. Maximizing the positive benefits of sound personnel policies and procedures requires a team effort with both line management and the personnel department having appropriate input. Policies should be designed as an aid to line managers in carrying out their job responsibilities. They should not act as a hindrance. Preferably, line management should take the initiative for and be encouraged to identify personnel matters needing the clarification that can be provided by written policies and procedures and to play a major role in determining their content.

The personnel department should be responsible for gathering the facts and preparing written drafts of necessary policy and procedural statements. Drafts of all personnel policies and procedures should be reviewed by the appropriate line managers to assure that they are applicable to practical operating needs. No policy or procedural statement should be issued without top line management approval.

Administration of Policies and Procedures. The primary purpose of most personnel policies and procedures is to provide guidelines that will help assure fair, impartial, and uniform treatment of all employees. It is impossible to write a policy or procedure on a given personnel subject that will cover all possible contingencies. They are guides that will be applicable to the majority of situations. As a result, the need for interpretation of intent or approval of "exceptions" to policies or procedures in certain instances is not unusual. The interpretation and review of exceptions require a central point of administration. To permit each line manager to make his own interpretations or authorized exceptions would be contrary to the whole purpose of having a written policy or procedure.

The personnel department is the logical administrator of personnel policies and procedures. Normally, it should be the primary authority on matters of interpretation and approval of exceptions, and no line manager should be permitted to go around it to higher management or to make his own decisions on policy and procedural matters. However, when line management and the personnel department cannot resolve differences of opinion, the top operating executive must act as the arbitrator. He has the final authority to support or overrule either side or establish a compromise.

By nature and purpose, formal policies and procedures put some degree of limitation on the inherent authority of line management positions. Some line managers resent any limitations on their discretion in dealing with their subordinates. Others may legitimately disagree with the equity of a given personnel policy or procedure. Much of this natural resistance can be overcome if line managers properly participate in determining the policies and procedures that will govern their actions.

DAY-TO-DAY LINE-STAFF RELATIONSHIPS

Position descriptions, personnel policies, procedural statements, and similar formal documents provide the necessary basic guidelines of how the relationships between manufacturing management and the personnel department should be conducted. However, it is the attitude on the part of both the line manager and the personnel specialist in dealing with day-to-day personnel matters that determines the real effectiveness of their relationship. Therefore, in the remainder of this chapter the interrelationships of line managers and the personnel department in dealing with a few specific, major personnel activities will be discussed. The relationships described are not put forth as absolutes. They are intended only to illustrate basic line-staff relationships that can be applied to any aspect of the personnel function.

Employment. The first step in establishing sound line-staff working relationships with respect to employment is to clarify the part that each party will play in achieving the common goal of having qualified employees available when they are needed. In this respect, the following premises should be valid in most situations:

1. Because line managers are ultimately accountable for the results of the people working for them, line managers should make the final employment decision.
2. Establishing employment standards or qualifications requirements is primarily the responsibility of line management.
3. The employment department is responsible for the quality of candidates submitted to line management and should recommend only those who, in its judgment, are fully qualified to meet the standards established by the line manager.
4. The employment department is responsible for assuring that qualified candidates are available when needed by line management.

To enable both line management and the personnel department to fulfill the responsibilities outlined above, a high degree of cooperation and mutual recognition of each other's problems are necessary.

Employment Lead Time. An employment department usually faces the same type of problems with respect to allocating time and resources properly that occur in a production department. In both instances, reasonable lead time is necessary if the result is expected to be a quality product.

In the employment situation, the definition of "reasonable" will vary according to the current situation of the market for the type of employee skills required. An understanding by line management of the problems of employment lead time is necessary to avoid panic employment efforts and the resulting compromises in quality. Advance notice to the employment department of anticipated increases or cutbacks in production personnel is essential to maintaining an effective employment service. Therefore, the timeliness with which line managers anticipate and communicate their requirements to the employment department will substantially influence the service they will receive.

Specifications. No line manager would want to be held accountable for producing an acceptable product from a blueprint that contained only partial drawings, incorrect dimensions, or impossible tolerances. However, it is not uncommon for an employment department to be placed in such a position where employment specifications are concerned.

Line managers must accept the responsibility for providing complete, accurate, and realistic specifications for the employee qualifications they want. The end product will only be as good as the blueprint specifies. A little extra thought and time on the part of line management to make sure initially that the employment department understands what is needed will often save a lot of time and prevent frustrations in the long run.

Written employment specifications prepared in accordance with some type of uniform format are frequently helpful. However, whether the specifications are conveyed in writing, verbally, or in both ways, the key to good employment screening lies in maintaining a high degree of cooperative understanding between line management and the employment department.

Employment Selection. The degree to which the line manager participates in selecting an employee is frequently a bone of contention in line-staff relationships. As stated earlier, it is the line manager who is responsible for overall results, and therefore he must make the final employment decision. However, a busy line manager cannot be expected to spend excessive amounts of time in interviewing multitudes of applicants. The screening job is the responsibility of the employment department. In a well-run employment function, the line manager would normally interview two or perhaps three candidates before he makes his selection depending, of course, on the level of the position involved. If the employment department has clear specifications to work against and has been given reasonable lead time, the line manager should logically expect that all candidates referred to him have been carefully screened against those specifications, that they have met minimum formal testing requirements if such a program is used, and that the appropriate references have been checked and meet the company's employment standards. The line manager then needs only to satisfy himself about the details of the candidate's skills and whether or not the prospective employee will "fit" into his operation from the standpoint of personality and other personal characteristics.

The line manager can be of substantial assistance to the employment department if he will take the time to explain his reasons clearly for rejecting candidates who are referred to him. Each individual has his own personal preferences when it comes to the selection of subordinates, and these factors are not always reflected in the specifications. In addition to these more intangible considerations, a constructive playback from the line manager can also point out certain aspects of basic skills requirements that may have inadvertently been overlooked by the employment department. This type of playback will help assure more effective screening in the future.

There are two extremes in the attitudes of line managers when it comes to employment selection, both of which can cause problems in their relationships with the employment department. First is the manager who, regardless of the degree of competency with which the employment department screens candidates for his review, will not make a decision until he has seen three, four, or more candidates. There may be some merit in this approach if a company is fortunate enough to find itself in an employment market where there are many qualified candidates. If the market is tight, however, a qualified applicant will be quickly hired by another company if the line manager does not make a prompt decision.

The other extreme is the line manager who simply cannot be bothered to take the time to interview the candidates referred to him. This type of manager can be counted on to hire any candidate that personnel refers to him. He is also the manager who complains the loudest about the employment department giving him nothing but warm bodies. The result of this type of attitude is that the line manager in essence abdicates his responsibility for the final employment decision, and the personnel department ends up assuming it for him. In other words, the personnel department assumes the line authority for an employment decision, while the line manager is accountable for the consequences of that decision.

New-employee Orientation. Many line managers consider the initial orientation of new employees as the sole responsibility of the personnel department. They expect the personnel department to brief the new employee on his benefits programs, work rules, safety procedures, and so forth. Actually, new-employee orientation is a shared responsibility between line management and the personnel department. Unquestionably, the discussion of employee benefits, the completion of necessary employment forms, arrangements for physical examinations, and similar activities rest with the personnel department. However, the discussion of work rules, review of safety procedures, the introduction of the employee to others in the department, and similar factors directly involved with the day-to-day work environment should be handled by the line manager.

In instances where the whole procedure of employee indoctrination is left entirely to the personnel department, it is not unusual to find the employee looking to personnel for the answers to day-to-day questions and problems that arise instead of to his supervisor. As a result, the line manager again abdicates part of his supervisory responsibility to the personnel department and becomes merely the person who gives instructions on how the employee should do his job.

Training. The word "training" means substantially different things to different people. Ask any ten managers to define training, and you will get ten substantially different definitions, each of which probably would be accurate as far as it goes. This is because training is such a broad subject that each manager is usually looking at only one aspect of the overall picture. Training, in its broadest context, might be defined as "any activity directed toward preparing an employee to perform his job effectively, to increase his skills and knowledge, or to prepare him to assume greater future responsibilities." For the purpose of our discussion of line-staff relationships as they pertain to training, this very broad definition will be subdivided into formal and informal training activities.

Going back to our original definitions of line-staff responsibilities, it was indicated that line management has the primary accountability for effective employee relations, with the staff being responsible for providing specialized knowledge, assistance, and guidance. Because many personnel departments have individuals who specialize in training activities, this primary accountability of line management is frequently forgotten, and it is this factor that is often at the root of much of the confusion that occurs concerning training activities.

One of the major complaints of personnel department training specialists is that they have difficulty in selling line management on the need for training. If it is recognized that line management has the primary accountability for assuring that their subordinates are properly equipped to do their jobs, it should not be necessary for the personnel department to "sell" management on the need for training.

Formal Training Programs. Formal training programs are usually those devoted to conveying information or techniques in a uniform manner to groups of employees. Normally, these programs take the form of classroom-type sessions as opposed to individual employee instruction.

Training programs are expensive, and many companies waste a substantial amount of money on training efforts because they first fail to identify clearly their most pertinent training requirements. Unfortunately, many programs are designed to train for training's sake rather than to meet specific preconceived and clearly identified needs. Line managers must assume the responsibility for identifying their training needs. They are closest to this problem and have the best insight into where their subordinates may be deficient in specific skills. The training specialist can assist in identifying needs, but the primary input must come from the line managers.

Once the needs are clearly identified, the training specialist can then make his contribution. Line management should look to and be able to rely upon the training specialist to provide the techniques and methods that will achieve the maximum training effectiveness in the shortest practical period of time. The training department should also function as the coordinator of established training activities and provide for the necessary instruction, materials, and personnel. It should also monitor the progress and effectiveness of each program.

Once training programs are established, they often have the habit of perpetuating themselves long after they have achieved their original purpose. Training programs must be kept vital. To achieve this requires regular review of the results being achieved per dollar expended and making any necessary revisions and changes in the program. To facilitate effective communication between line and staff management with respect to the training activities, training plans should provide for periodic personal discussions between the appropriate line managers and the training specialist to review the program effectiveness.

Informal Training. Authorities in the training field generally agree that the most effective training takes place on the job and on a day-to-day basis. Formal training programs can be a valuable supplement to but cannot substitute for this informal on-the-job training. It is obvious that the regular counseling, guidance, and direction that is inherent in on-the-job training places the major burden for training on the employee's immediate supervisor. The type of close personal boss-subordinate relationship required by informal on-the-job training precludes any delegation or relegation of this type of training responsibility to the personnel department. In this respect, each line manager must be his own training specialist. The input from the personnel department normally takes the form of formal training for the manager in the various approaches to providing proper instruction and guidance to his individual subordinates.

Labor Relations. Of the many aspects of employee relations, none requires closer coordination or a higher degree of communication between manufacturing management and the personnel department than does labor relations. Labor relations are constantly becoming more complex as a result of the continuing increase in governmental regulations and the highly involved and complicated nature of labor agreements. As a result, the services of the labor relations specialist are very much a necessity. However, it is the manufacturing manager who must live with the labor agreement and who must learn to operate effectively within its limitations. Because the labor relations specialist and line management are both highly dependent on each other in carrying out their job responsibilities, a truly effective team relationship is imperative.

Contract Negotiations. The makeup of a company's negotiating team and the selection of the individual to function as chief spokesman at the negotiating table will vary from company to company. Because the chief manufacturing executive or a higher level executive in direct chain of command above him is accountable for all final decisions concerning agreements with the union, it is usually preferable that the chief line executive function as the company spokesman. If the labor relations specialist acts as spokesman, it is extremely important that he conduct himself in such a manner as to make it obvious that he is speaking for the chief manufacturing executive.

The company's negotiating strategy must be well planned in advance of the actual negotiation meetings with the union. Each member of the negotiating team should clearly understand his position and the input that is expected from him. Whether or not he functions as spokesman, the labor relations specialist should have the responsibility of being the company's chief strategist. Frequently, he functions much like the director of a motion picture, with the majority of his work taking place behind the scenes during the prenegotiation planning and in the caucus sessions during negotiation. To put it another way, the labor relations specialist should write the script and cue the other members of the negotiating team when their input is required.

Although the majority of the line managers will seldom have direct involvement at the negotiating table, they nevertheless have a highly significant contribution to make to the success of negotiations. Both before and during negotiations, it is the first-line foreman, department superintendent, and comparable levels of manufacturing management who can obtain the real grass roots feel for what the union employees are seeking and how they are reacting to the progress of negotiations. This type of input is imperative in planning initial negotiation strategy and also in readjusting strategy during the course of negotiations. Prenegotiation briefing sessions with all levels of manufacturing managers are frequently advisable so that they understand the importance of the part they are to play and how they should conduct themselves. During the course of negotiations, there should be a continuous, confidential, two-way flow of information between the labor relations specialist and the manufacturing managers.

Grievances and Arbitration. Whether organized or not, production employees should have some sort of practical procedure that will permit them to gain a fair hearing on any grievances they may have. In non-union situations, the steps of the grievance hearing procedure should normally progress up through the hierarchy of line management. In such instances, the personnel department functions in an impartial advisory capacity with no responsibility for rendering decisions with respect to a grievance.

Under many union contracts, the labor relations manager does have decision making authority at some step in the grievance procedure. However, this function is of minor significance in comparison to his primary grievance processing responsibility which is to analyze the facts in a given grievance and advise line management on the appropriate action that should be taken within the limitations imposed by the union agreement. The key word in the preceding statement is *facts*. Nothing is more frustrating to a labor relations specialist than to go to a grievance hearing session with the union or, even worse, to appear in front of an arbitrator and then find that he has not been supplied with all the facts in the case or that he has been provided with inaccurate facts. Many grievances progress far beyond the point they should; and frequently arbitrations are lost for companies, not because of lack of proper counsel or skill on the part of the labor relations specialist, but because line management errs in its responsibility for frankly and objectively providing him with complete and factual information concerning the grievance.

If the labor relations specialist is given all the proper facts and improperly advises line management on the disposition of a grievance or subsequently loses an arbitration, he is accountable for the consequences. Conversely, insufficient or improper facts place the burden of accountability on the line managers involved.

Union Contract Interpretation and Administration. It should be the labor relations specialist's responsibility to be the expert on all matters concerning union contract interpretation and other matters involving its administration. The complexity of present-day union agreements is such that the average line manager cannot be expected to have an intimate knowledge of the implications of its numerous provisions. On the other hand, the line manager cannot run to the labor relations specialist in every instance in which he has to make a decision concerning his subordinates. The line manager should have sufficient knowledge of the contract provisions to handle the majority of his day-to-day supervisory responsibilities.

He must also be provided with clear guidelines that will enable him to recognize situations in which he should seek the advice of the labor relations specialist before taking action that might get him into trouble. To minimize labor relations problems, all proposed actions with respect to such matters as discharge, discipline, transfer, promotion, layoff, recall, and so forth should be reviewed with the labor relations specialist before the action is taken. This is not to imply that the labor specialist should be the decision maker. The appropriate line manager must still make whatever decisions are required, but he should do so with full knowledge of the probable consequences.

CONCLUSION

Frank communications, close cooperation and understanding of each other's problems, and a recognition of their common objectives are essential to a sound working relationship between manufacturing management and personnel relations. Such relationships are most likely to exist in organizations in which the division of responsibilities between functions and individuals has been clearly defined and is thoroughly understood by all concerned. The actual assignment of the various responsibilities relating to personnel matters will be determined by practical operating requirements and the capabilities of the individuals concerned.

However, to the degree possible, manufacturing managers should retain the final decision making authority on personnel matters affecting their operations. The day-to-day relationship between line and staff has much in common with a successful marriage. It requires that both parties conduct themselves in such a manner as to warrant the respect and confidence of the other. Also required are a sincere effort and desire to consider the other party's point of view and problems. And finally, it calls for a give and take on both sides and frequent compromises.

BIBLIOGRAPHY

Black, James M., and Guy B. Ford, *Front-line Management*, chaps. 13 and 36, McGraw-Hill Book Company, New York, 1963.

Evans, Gordon H., *Managerial Job Descriptions in Manufacturing*, Research Study no. 65, American Management Association, New York, 1964.

Higgins, M. Valliant, *Management Policies I*, chaps. 2 and 6, Research Study no. 76, American Management Association, New York, 1966.

Pigors, P. J., C. A. Myers, and F. T. Malm, *Management of Human Resources*, sec. 1A, chaps. 5, 6, and 7, McGraw-Hill Book Company, New York, 1964.

Sostain, Aaron Q., *The Supervisor and His Job*, chaps. 7, 19, and 20, McGraw-Hill Book Company, New York, 1965.

"What's Not on the Organization Chart," *Conference Board Record*, National Industrial Conference Board, November, 1964, pp. 7–10.

CHAPTER SIX

Relationship of Manufacturing and Community and Public Relations Activities

FREDERICK GOLDEN   *Director of Manufacturing, Warnaco Inc., Bridgeport, Connecticut*

The manufacturing manager is a community and public relations executive whether he wishes to be or not. Consider what might happen on a typical day.

First call of the day. The school principal urges him to speak about his company and industry on Career Day. There he is—involved in community and public relations.

A six-color press will be installed in the Box Beauty packaging plant. It will produce extra-fine packages for a cosmetic company known to most women. A hole will be cut in the wall to get the press into the building. It will cost $500,000. The plant will now get more high-quality work, its industry position will be strengthened, and additional people will be hired. Here is a story to enhance the company image.

It is 2:00 A.M. The phone rings impatiently. Fire at the plant. The reporter gets there before the manufacturing manager.

A professional public relations department is a valuable asset to the manufacturing manager in situations like these. He can use an expert news release, some slides and movies with dramatic impact, perhaps a little advice on the speech, and perhaps some special advice on how to talk with that newspaper reporter.

These short examples give clues on why a manufacturing manager cannot escape involvement in community and public relations. They show that there is a reason to call upon a professional for direction, plans, and policies and for a better understanding of how to handle the line manager's prominent role in the execution of community and public relations. This is not a "do it yourself" situation to be played by ear.

Yet even where professional advice is available, the manufacturing manager must also be his own public relations expert, especially on community relations. The fact is that community relations is a major part of public relations and is executed at the local plant level by local management. And everyone in the company is involved—the manager, his supervisors, the operators—all the people in the company.

Line management also influences the company image in the wide area covered by other functions of public relations, such as supplier contacts, product publicity, participation in trade and technical associations, and similar actions beyond the local precincts.

Automatically involved in community and public relations, the manufacturing manager will want to understand:

1. The definitions and functions of community and public relations
2. Why good relations are important to the manufacturing manager and the success of his operation
3. How manufacturing management affects community and public relations
4. What manufacturing managers can do to create favorable community relations
5. How manufacturing managers can work with public and community relations departments or advisors to further company success, and why a professional approach is essential
6. Where to get the detailed information to execute the manager's important role in good community and public relations

DEFINITION OF PUBLIC AND COMMUNITY RELATIONS

Community relations involves the interaction between the company and the local community area—people-to-people relationships among civic, business, religious, professional, and social agencies.

Plant community relations is the management function that appraises plant community attitudes, identifies and relates company policies with community interests, and initiates programs of action to earn community respect and confidence for the company.[1]

Public relations is far-reaching in scope and geography and is concerned with public reaction to the company and its activities, not confined to the local community. It includes stockholder relations, effect of advertising on the market, dealing with financial analysts and suppliers and creditors, major company announcements, product publicity, government relations, contacts with trade associations and technical societies, and similar actions beyond the local precincts.

Public relations is not publicity. Publicity is just one of many tools. Keeping employees and management informed on company activities and achievements is a function of public relations.

THE IMPORTANCE OF COMMUNITY RELATIONS
TO THE MANUFACTURING MANAGER

Manufacturing management profits from a good image and suffers from a negative impression.

[1] John T. McCarty, *Community Relations for Business*, Bureau of National Affairs, Washington, D.C., 1956, p. 1.

Suppose that the zoning calls for the use of 50 percent of the land for light industrial, and the company needs to put up an addition that will take 60 percent. It will be beautifully landscaped. If a favorable climate has been created in the community, there will be a good chance for acceptance of this reasonable variance.

Affirmative community reactions to special requests, such as variances, is just one way in which community relations is important. A good community relations program is vital to the success of the manufacturing operations in other ways that include:

1. Hiring competent personnel
2. Getting help on training people in local schools and through social work programs
3. Obtaining assistance on community facilities—roads, street lights, water, sewers, transportation, regulations, police and fire protection, and the like
4. Getting more sympathetic acceptance of unavoidable minor nuisances such as noise and smoke
5. Gaining community understanding and help on unfavorable news—a fire, an accident, layoffs beyond the manufacturing manager's control
6. Obtaining fair tax assessments
7. Establishing better public understanding of changes such as automation equipment, plant relocations, or changes in management

HOW MANUFACTURING MANAGEMENT AFFECTS COMMUNITY RELATIONS

The ways in which manufacturing management can affect community relations and help mold the company image include:

1. Company policies and their effect on employees
2. What employees say about the company in the community
3. Participation in community activities
   a. Schools
   b. Civic affairs—taxes, bond issues, ordinances
   c. Social agencies—contributions, company actions, personal actions of managers and employees
   d. Service clubs—Rotary, Lions, sports
4. Stability of employment, frequency of layoffs
5. Attitudes on minority groups and how company policies are actually executed at all levels
6. The company as a neighbor
   a. Noise controls, pollution controls, handling of rubbish, dirt and smoke control, landscaping, parking
   b. Uncluttered grounds and building areas
   c. Well-kept building—clean, neat, painted
   d. Attractive rather than offensive signs and displays
7. Relations with other businessmen
   a. Treatment of suppliers
   b. Participation in community projects by local businesses
8. Image from telephone service and conversations
9. Manner of handling complaints and criticism
10. Tone and attitudes revealed by letter correspondence
11. How union matters are handled
12. Handling of emergencies
    a. Fires, accidents, deaths, fights, and altercations
    b. Disasters in local areas, such as floods, explosions, and the like

MANUFACTURING MANAGER'S ACTIONS TO
CREATE FAVORABLE COMMUNITY RELATIONS

Among the great many things that the manufacturing manager can do to create favorable community relations are the following actions:

1. Hold an annual open house.
2. Conduct plant tours.
3. Provide informative news stories on key events—promotions, new equipment, management changes, union activities, emergencies such as accidents.
4. Sponsor community projects—Junior Achievement, training programs, Little League and other sports activities.
5. Establish enlightened policies and active leadership on minority problems—hiring, training, vocational guidance, local housing, elimination of discrimination.
6. Permit use of company facilities, such as auditorium, for community events.
7. Support community improvement programs.
8. Buy locally where possible.
9. Maintain clean, neat physical facilities.
10. Eliminate nuisances such as smoke, noise, or fumes, and explain remaining irritants that cannot be avoided.
11. Avoid polluting water or air.
12. Participate in local community services.
13. Encourage other supervisors and employees to participate in local community, social, and political affairs.
14. Participate in professional societies.
15. Provide special exhibits at local trade shows, airport lobbies, train stations, and other public places.
16. Keep all employees informed on company policies, achievements, goals, and purposes.
17. Handle matters involving individual employees quickly.
18. Have systematic feedback on employee attitudes.
19. Be frank in relations with news media. Do not hold back facts that bear on the matter in question.
20. Know the community. Survey community attitudes periodically.
21. Have a plan for community and public relations and company policies. Teach this plan to the supervisors.
22. Know the community thought leaders and keep them informed—religious leaders, doctors, lawyers, teachers, business managers, school authorities, municipal officials, and others.
23. Develop community mailing lists for distributing company booklets, newspapers, and similar material to civic leaders.
24. Provide jobs for older and handicapped people.
25. Engage in local institutional advertising.
26. Make the factory a landmark (fountain, large clock).
27. Help set up training programs in the schools and colleges, and support with equipment and trainers.
28. Speak at clubs, schools, colleges, and other places where the public image can be influenced.
29. Hold Career Day programs at the local schools.
30. Have anniversary celebrations.
31. Support important legislation.

32. Sponsor pops concerts.
33. Explain major new equipment that may have impact on employees.
34. Show movies of operations and industry.
35. Insist on friendly handling of all applicants, even though they are not accepted for employment.
36. Sponsor ads in local papers and over the radio or television.

Planning Open House and Plant Tours. Open house and plant tours are among the most important organized community relations functions that can be handled by the manufacturing manager. Key steps in planning a successful open house for the general public are:

1. Define the objective.
2. Set the date.
3. Determine finances.
4. Prepare guest list and invitations.
5. Prepare the housekeeping.
6. Arrange transportation.
7. Organize publicity.
8. Determine tour routes and escorts; train the guides.
9. Prepare displays and visual aids.
10. Plan refreshments.
11. Decide on souvenirs.
12. Follow up.

One of the key points of a good plant tour or open house is to make it mean something to the visitor through explanation and interpretation.

Special tours may be arranged for small groups and special visitors such as suppliers, out-of-towners, and community leaders. Many of the same principles of open house tours apply. The *Public Relations Handbook*[2] has a long checklist for staging a successful open house.

EMERGENCIES, FIRE, ACCIDENTS, FIGHTS

The manufacturing manager must expect the press when a plant has an emergency and must be prepared to work with news media. Honesty is the best policy. It is hard to hide unfavorable news.

Access to the scene of the emergency will be requested. If it is safe and the area is not confidential, access should generally be granted. Factual information should be given, but guesses should be avoided. If the manufacturing manager does not know, he should say so and should agree to get the information. He should then be sure to get back with the facts as promised.

When an emergency occurs, news and information should be centralized at one point. An action plan that the supervisors understand should be ready ahead of time, so that conflicting information will not be passed out. The public relations department should give written instructions on how to handle news on emergencies.

Cooperation with news media helps keep incidents in proper perspective. Coy or fearful withholding of information may lead to an unfavorable story and a prolonged series of articles on the incident.

[2] John C. Aspley and L. F. Van Houten, *Public Relations Handbook*, The Dartnell Corporation, Chicago, Ill., 1956, pp. 287–290.

MANUFACTURING MANAGER'S RELATIONSHIP WITH THE PUBLIC RELATIONS DEPARTMENT

Neither community relations nor public relations should be done on an intuitive basis, rationalized by "Oh, I understand human relations," or "I know how to handle local leaders." They should not be done on a basis of playing it by ear when a situation arises.

It pays to consult a professional on public relations, whether he is the company manager of community and public relations or an outside consultant. But the manufacturing manager must know how to distinguish between the action taken and information given without prior reference to public and community relations, and what should be discussed with or even released by those functional areas. The public relations department can spell this out.

In general, public relations must be based upon specific plans meeting definite, articulated objectives. Guidelines for the manufacturing manager's role in sound public relations include:

1. Know the role of community and public relations.
2. Have a plan.
3. Know the program.
4. Understand when to consult with the public relations manager.
5. Systematically spell out plans and policies to all manufacturing people involved.
6. Indoctrinate the public relations function within the organization.
7. Elicit cooperation from all supervisors and manufacturing staff to keep public relations personnel informed, to explain department functions and activities as background for the public relations specialist, and to consult with public relations on matters and statements that could affect the company image on outside relations.
8. Encourage good internal relations through application of public relations principles within the company to keep employees informed. A corporate newspaper is properly the function of a public relations department. Major company actions—an acquisition, a new plant, a plant move—should be told to employees before they read about it in the newspapers.
9. Utilize public relations knowledge and talents internally as a service for the manufacturing management. Help can be obtained on:
   a. Indoctrinating employees on general management policies
   b. Preparing bulletins and announcements
   c. Preparing speeches and articles
   d. Attracting technical and management personnel
   e. Gathering outside information
   f. Getting objective playback on public and employee reactions to policies and activities
   g. Representing the manager at public affairs and trade association activities

   Utilizing the talents and judgment of the public relations department will:

   h. Save the manufacturing manager's time
   i. Provide consistent statements on important company matters
   j. Protect against release of information that would have legal implications, give competitors an advantage, require coordinated timing, and so on
   k. Provide professional quality releases to news media

10. Advance public relations activities by supplying news on:
    a. Management changes
    b. Promotions
    c. New executive appointments
    d. Anniversaries and retirements
    e. Employees attending training courses
    f. Expansion and modernization of facilities
    g. Installation of new or different equipment
    h. New ideas and methods which are not confidential
    i. Celebrities visiting plant
    j. Personnel policies involving bonus, insurance, retirement, profit sharing, and the like
    k. Awards for achievements
    l. Speeches
    m. Attendance at technical or trade group meetings
    n. Unusual hobbies or activities of employees

    Local news releases and contacts with news media, not otherwise distributed by the community and public relations department, should follow guidelines set up by that department. Guidelines on news releases are described in *Working with News Media,* a booklet published by United Gas public relations department, as well as in the *Handbook of Public Relations.*[3]

11. Try to avoid overcontrolling public relations activities, just as research activities should not be overcontrolled.
12. Follow up, measure, and report results.

Company policy manuals and booklets are essential to build a good working relationship between manufacturing managers and public relations.

THE PLACE OF PUBLIC RELATIONS IN THE ORGANIZATION

The public relations manager in a multiplant, multidivision company frequently reports directly to the executive vice president or president, operating on a vice presidential level with other line and staff officers.

In some companies, public relations may be under marketing because of heavy support to product area, but this is considered least desirable in view of broad involvement among all functions of business. As a compromise, a general public relations activity may be organized directly under the executive vice president, and the marketing department of each division may have its own sales promotion or publicity department.

Community relations, though a part of public relations, may be treated as a separate function in the organization structure. Because community relations is so closely aligned to local manufacturing management, it is often logical to place this function under the manufacturing manager, with direction from a central public relations executive.

In a smaller company, someone in the company should be designated for the public relations and community relations functions, even when he has other assignments. If the company is not big enough to have its own public relations manager, there are many competent consultants in this field, happy to advise smaller clients at a reasonable cost.

[3] Howard Stephenson (ed.), *Handbook of Public Relations,* McGraw-Hill Book Company, New York, 1960.

MEASURING RESULTS

Heavily concerned with community relations, manufacturing managers must know where they really stand in their community. Community attitude surveys are one of the best ways to evaluate how well community relations objectives have been advanced.

Answers to the following questions will also give a clue to how effective community relations activities have been.

1. Do the best of the local high school or vocational school graduates eagerly seek jobs with us?
2. Do local graduates of colleges tend to come home to seek employment with us?
3. Do the reporters of the communication media respect us, or do they frequently pillory the company and its officials?
4. Do our employees "talk up" our company as a good place to work and encourage their families' members and friends to seek employment with us?
5. Are city and county government officials helpful when a new access road or land for expansion is needed, or do they consider it good politics to be overtly hostile and to harass us with restrictive ordinances?
6. Are local tax assessment and policies fair to the enterprise?
7. Can we be sure of impartial enforcement of local laws and ordinances if our plant is struck or plagued with picketing?
8. If we are a public corporation, do our neighbors invest some of their savings in our stock?
9. If we produce consumer goods or services, do our local sales markedly exceed regional, state, or national sales?[4]

CONCLUSION

The manufacturing manager, frequently the executor of community relations programs and often facing public relations situations that come up unexpectedly without a plan, must understand the working relations with the public relations department and be prepared to carry through on his own. Prime resources for details on community and public relations of special interest to line managers are listed in the bibliography.

Booklets addressed to line managers and employees by major companies and trade associations are practical guides to community and public relations. Some of these are in the American Management Association New York library. Plant visits—especially at an open house—are another way to discover how other managers succeed in their community and public relations activities.

BIBLIOGRAPHY

Aspley, John C., and L. F. Van Houten, *Public Relations Handbook*, The Dartnell Corporation, Chicago, Ill., 1956.
Canfield, Bertrand R., *Public Relations: Principles, Cases, and Problems*, Richard D. Irwin, Inc., Homewood, Ill., 1960.
Evans, Henry S., and Theon Wright, *Public Relations and the Line Manager*, American Management Association, New York, 1964.
Hodges, Wayne, *Company and Community*, Harper & Row, Publishers, Incorporated, New York, 1958.
Lesly, Philip (ed.), *Public Relations Handbook*, 2d ed., Prentice-Hall, Inc., Englewood Cliffs, N.J., 1962.

[4] Willard V. Merrihue, "Community Relations" in H. B. Maynard (ed.), *Handbook of Business Administration*, sec. 12, chap. 5, McGraw-Hill Book Company, New York, 1967, p. 41.

Maynard, H. B. (ed.), *Handbook of Business Administration*, McGraw-Hill Book Company, New York, 1967.

McCarty, John T., *Community Relations for Business*, Bureau of National Affairs, Washington, D.C., 1956.

Nielander, William A., *A Selected and Annotated Bibliography of Public Relations*, Bureau of Business Research, University of Texas, Austin, Texas, 1961.

Planning an Effective Career Day, American Apparel Manufacturers Association, Washington, D.C., February, 1968.

Stephenson, Howard (ed.), *Handbook of Public Relations*, McGraw-Hill Book Company, New York, 1960.

CHAPTER SEVEN

Relationship of Manufacturing and the Legal Department

THOMAS J. PURCELL *Esquire, Rockwell Manufacturing Company, Pittsburgh, Pennsylvania*

The laws and regulations applicable to each of the separate functions of designing, making, and marketing a product tend to spill over and influence the entire process. So, although designing and marketing are not strictly the concern of the manufacturing manager, the legal problems which they generate often affect him either directly or indirectly. Therefore, in this discussion, the legal problems faced by a manufacturing business as a whole will be considered, for practically all of them have some effect on the manufacturing manager.

There are important areas of the law which will be experienced knowingly or unknowingly as the product moves through the designing, making, and marketing stages to the consumer. The object of the manufacturer is to get the product to the customer with as little delay as possible and at a profit. He is concerned with plant capacity, labor, machinery and equipment, and the other physical considerations which must be brought together at the right time to accomplish this objective. He cannot pause to meditate on the changing legal pattern and its possible effect on his efforts.

Yet, because the object is to make a product that can be sold to a purchaser, the manufacturing company is ultimately going to have a legal relationship with that purchaser. Because it may require a labor force to assemble the product, the company can experience the assertion of employment rights within its own organization. In the design of a product, intellectual property must be protected. Because the company must market the product in an atmosphere of competition and must purchase its raw material in the same competitive economy, it necessarily has involved itself with the then existing laws and regulations which protect that economy.

This chapter will explore the relationship of the lawyer or legal department with the manufacturer, pointing up some specific areas of the law where both must cooperate. It will deal with the responsibility of each to the other and suggest some techniques to help make this relationship work. Although it is geared to the broad definition of manufacturing, the specific areas of the law applicable to the manufacturing function itself are set forth where possible. The object is to assist in establishing an efficient workable relationship so that some assurance can be given to the company that the product will be free of legal as well as engineering defects and will not end up in the caldron of legal potpourri consisting of antitrust regulations and product liability claims.

BACKGROUND OF THE RELATIONSHIP BETWEEN MANUFACTURING AND THE LEGAL DEPARTMENT

The experienced manufacturer does not consider himself to be a legal expert. He is as aware as any informed businessman of the more apparent aspects of the law. He normally will not sign a contract, lease, or other legal document without legal advice. In the event that a claim is made against the company, he knows the role of the lawyer. He knows that it will be to his advantage to cooperate with his legal advisors in the defense of such a claim. In short, he is more than willing to consult with his advisors about matters which he knows are outside his expertise.

But how can he be made aware of the latent or more subtle aspects of the law as they might affect his operation? When a third party triggers the relationship by making a claim against the company, it is obvious that both departments should get together to consider the problem. The manufacturer vaguely suspects, and rightly so, that there must be hundreds of court cases and just as many broad regulations and laws which may have a substantial impact on his operation and of which he cannot be aware. As to these, he knowingly or unknowingly relies wholly on his lawyers or the legal department to tell him when one of these cases, laws, or regulations affects his operation.

The legal department in this situation must call their relationship into action. This is the most significant and difficult area between the two, the one in which most misunderstandings arise, and the one which, at best, rarely satisfies either department.

Traditionally, lawyers are advisors. Before the advent of the corporate legal department, they were consulted by manufacturers and businessmen generally only when there was an immediate legal difficulty. The relationship of attorney and client was begun by the client. Legal ethics dictated this procedure. With the beginning of the corporate legal department, both manufacturer and lawyer found themselves employed by the same company, both working to the same end. Laws and regulations had gotten so complicated and all-inclusive that only a legal department with lawyers on the scene could adequately advise the company. But this is a different relationship from the traditional one brought about by the circumstances of law, regulation, and the economy. It is by no means suggested that the lawyer should in any way alter his high standard of ethics. It is suggested that, because of the traditions of the profession, there is a tendency sometimes not to get as actively involved in many aspects of the business as might be desirable. Of course, the organization of the legal department in the particular company can have a direct influence on this relationship.

Some departments have completely staff functions. They are composed of attorneys who are concerned with the general law and other attorneys who are specialists in some aspect of the law such as labor, antitrust, or tax. This system provides greater communication among the lawyers but sometimes serves to isolate the lawyer from the line operation of manufacturing unless this problem is realized and procedures for communication are established.

Other departments are structured into what might be called semi-line departments. As an example, the company may establish a patent department which will operate within the research and development area and which will be composed of lawyers who exercise direct and constant relationship with the manufacturer. These departments have direct contact with outside lawyers and communicate daily with the manufacturer. Sometimes, in this situation, liaison with the other lawyers in the corporation is not maintained, and the overall legal picture tends to get out of focus.

These are both ends of the legal pole. In between, there are numerous variations and arrangements depending upon the size of the company and the personalities of the people involved. Whatever the organization and whatever the viewpoint, it is important to establish a working relationship within the company which can bring these two functions together. Any workable arrangement must take into account, provide for, and be flexible enough to adapt to the special talents of both the manufacturer and the lawyer.

SOME TECHNIQUES FOR WORKING TOGETHER

The activities of manufacturing and law do not always have a natural day-to-day relationship. The cooperation of each, however, is demanded by the complexity of our economy and society. Because this association does not often happen in the normal routines of either, it is necessary to structure some automatic meeting points to make sure that the two activities get together.

Whether or not these meeting points can be set by the manufacturing executive alone depends upon the organization of the company. If the legal department occupies a strictly staff function, then this probably can be done. If the legal department or some part of it occupies a line or semi-line capacity, then it very well could be the lawyers' job to arrange this schedule of meeting points. No matter who has this responsibility, it is preferable that it should be a joint effort. Certainly the legal department should be consulted on the priority of the schedule. This is so because the subject of these automatic meetings will be the discussion of the prevention of legal difficulty by recognizing the hidden legal dangers rather than the discussion of current litigation in which the company may be engaged and which will, as stated above, call for the more apparent and recognized relationship of the legal department to manufacturing. Some ideas for establishing these meeting points are as follows.

The Legal Audit. Just as the financial progress of a company is determined by an audit of its records, a periodic legal review can determine the legal health of a company in the light of current law. The periods covered by such an audit can be from one year to several years. The audit itself should be conducted every few years. The period will be determined by the size of the company and the complexity of its operation. The audit results in a report to the company and to manufacturing, which comments on the status of the various contracts, leases, patents, and other written documents and also on the company's general position regarding current antitrust laws and governmental regulatory agencies. This kind of report not only informs the company of its current legal status but also can bare whatever weaknesses exist and perhaps can suggest procedures to be adopted to correct them.

Product Records and Checklists. Every product has a beginning, whether it was originally conceived by the company or was suggested by a customer or came from some other source. Companies generally keep a written record of how the product originated and have a checklist which includes an original legal review for patentability and other intellectual property aspects. The product record may also contain estimates of potential sales and other computed information. There can be built into this record an automatic legal review of its marketing, distribution, and liability factors. This review can occur at the times that management reviews the product history and profitability. The legal review can be more definitive than the general legal audit, because it is confined to one product. If such a record is not kept, almost any other engineering or marketing checklist which is available can include a legal inspection. Even if no legal problem is solved by this technique, it serves the very useful purpose of educating the legal department about the manufacturing activity, and this can aid in preventing future legal problems.

Meetings. The more that manufacturing can expose the legal department to its activities, the more the lawyers will be in a position to make intelligent legal appraisals of its operation. In addition to checklists, the manufacturer can invite representatives of the legal department to selected product meetings. These should be product review meetings of general scope which would include comments about engineering, sales and marketing, improvements to the product, and customer history.

In the antitrust area and possibly some other legal area of special interest to the manufacturer, the legal department can send lawyers into the plant to speak to the plant management. During these talks, the law is explained and some background given so that the plant management can respond correctly in the event of contact with these fields of law.

Public Statements. All statements and claims, whether written or spoken, describing what the product can or will do should be automatically reviewed by the legal department to ascertain whether such announcements conform to the company's warranty policy. Such statements can expand the warranty and may be the basis for liability claims. Of course, all statements which respond to legal questions or to questions put by governmental agencies should be given to the legal department for review and, in most cases, for answer.

SOME SPECIFIC AREAS WHERE LEGAL REVIEW IS REQUIRED

During the process of manufacturing, there are some major areas where the law must be specifically invoked to protect the company's interest in the property of the product. There are also areas where the law may be self-operating to the detriment of the company unless precautions are taken. This is why the checklist or any technique which brings manufacturing and legal together is important. There must be procedures which provide a method whereby the legal department can take positive action where it is required and review situations where safeguards must be posted. These areas are mentioned and some limited background is given to emphasize the reasons for cooperation and review.

Designing the Product—Intellectual Property. Whether the organization of the company includes its own patent office or depends upon outside patent lawyers for its intellectual property advice, a formal method of protecting the intangible property of patents, copyrights, trademarks, and special know-how is necessary. For those ideas which are patentable, it must be decided at the very beginning whether to file for a patent and get statutory protection or to rely for protection on the common law. For instance, an idea which will be disclosed by using it in the manufacturing process must be patented for protection. A secret which will not be disclosed by its use will be safe as long as it can be kept secret, and this period may exceed the statutory term of protection. For property which cannot be the subject of statutory protection, such as know-how and special processes, protective measures must be taken to list this property as confidential, supervise its release, and catalog it.

At the time of employment, all employees, except perhaps clerical or stenographic employees, should execute an agreement with the company under which, as part of the employment, all patentable ideas are to be assigned to the company. These agreements can avoid the possibility of cloudy title to this kind of property and misunderstanding where an employee develops a patentable idea while working on company time. Although no special promise is made in the agreement, the company generally rewards an employee for patentable ideas on a discretionary judgment basis. In most companies, the personnel department is responsible for the implementation of this program.

There must also be a strict procedure for accepting ideas from those outside the organization. The company must require full disclosure to evaluate the idea and at the same time avoid the problem of confidential disclosure. Where the idea is patentable, it should be required that the inventor, before disclosure, either apply for a patent or protect himself by affidavits of third parties to the effect that they were aware and understood the idea before disclosure. Nonpatentable ideas should be submitted with no special promises and for evaluation only. All material should be submitted in duplicate, the company retaining a copy in its file. This should be done because if a claim is made, the company will want to know the extent of the disclosure which was made to it.

Those actually engaged in designing or making the product should keep diaries in which to log all new developments and improvements for possible patent protection. The diaries should also include avenues of failure, because this information may also be valuable in evaluating the extent of possible patent protection.

When it is necessary to reveal nonpatentable secret information, manufacturing know-how, engineering drawings, and like property to outsiders, the company should do so under agreement that the disclosure is confidential and that the property will be returned on demand. This is a dangerous area, especially when the manufacturer has a prospective licensee and the disclosure of this kind of know-how without agreement in order to make a contract seems normal. It should not be done otherwise than under agreement.

Where the company has foreign operations, it must be remembered that each country has its own intellectual property laws. If it is contemplated that the product will be manufactured in a foreign country, these laws should be explored to determine whether or not a foreign application should be made. Finally, the company should have a strong policy of defending its property rights. Even a small infringement should be called to the legal department's attention for action.

Making the Product—Product Liability. The manufacturer is one of those potentially liable for damages when a product or part of a product that he has produced causes personal or property damage to a third party. This liability can be founded on negligence, warranty, or misrepresentation in the advertising of his product. With the advent of highly industrialized products which are complicated in both design and use and the large advertising campaigns which are launched to market these products, the threat of product liability has increased. Consumer research organizations have warned the public of the potential dangers in the product, and where accidents have happened, the courts have not been unsympathetic to the claims of the injured persons.

The law of product liability has developed generally from the theory of nonliability in negligence in the absence of a contractual relationship, to negligence liability, then to strict warranty liability, and now to strict liability. The manufacturer must decide how much of his operation he will self-insure and how much he will protect with product liability insurance. Here the legal department can help. Product liability insurance generally is effective to cover accidents happening only after the product has left the premises and control of the manufacturer. Other forms of insurance will be necessary while the product is still in process.

Under the negligence theory, the manufacturer's duty to exercise care includes the making of reasonable tests and inspections to discover latent defects and to warn the prospective purchaser adequately if such latent defects exist. Also, he must use ordinary care in designing or developing his product so that it is safe for its purpose. The initial product checklist should contain an examination of the design for unsafe features. A lack of these precautionary steps may result in negligence. Even if the product is perfectly made, there still may be a duty to warn of latent dangers. This duty to warn may arise subsequent to the sale of the product when new facts are discovered. In addition, the manufacturer must give adequate directions for the use of the product. Violation of the several Federal and state acts or safety standard laws may be evidence of negligence or negligence in itself, because these laws generally set a minimum standard of conduct.

The manufacturer must be careful with his warranty program because, aside or alternatively from liability in negligence, he may incur product liability on the warranty theory. An express warranty arises where a positive representation of the product is made. An implied warranty of fitness for use is imposed by operation of law. Liability in warranty arises when the product does not measure up to the claims of the manufacturer. The measure of dangers for breach of warranty can be as great as in negligence where there is personal injury. The express warranty can be made in the advertising or marketing campaign, and as stated above, this activity should be reviewed by the legal department.

Marketing the Product—Contracts. It has previously been suggested that a contract should act as a reminder to the manufacturer to consult with the legal department about its provisions. However, the contract sometimes seems so clear on its face that there is a temptation to avoid legal advice to save time. Such a contract can be misleading. For instance, the provisions of a seemingly simple contract to produce a product for a customer may contain such hidden legal considerations as antitrust and product liability problems; questions of passage of title; tax, delivery, and shipment problems; credit; and a host of other latent situations. The point to be made here is that, even though the relationship has been triggered, there is a danger that needed consideration will be dismissed before it is explored.

If a contract is negotiable, the manufacturer may or may not want to enlist the legal department in the initial stages as direct negotiators. In most cases, he will prefer to do his own bargaining, and after the general framework of the bargain is set, will ask his lawyers to prepare a formal agreement. This procedure works if the manufacturer is familiar with the general business customs applicable to the contract; but if it is a new field, he should have his lawyers with him initially. As an example, if the contract is the first one with

the Federal Government and is renegotiable, the company may have to institute special accounting procedures and keep special records for that particular
contract, which may be quite different from the usual records of the company.
All this may influence the manufacturer's decision and certainly his profit.

To make the product, new or different equipment may be required. Before
acquisition of this property, it is generally advantageous to consider the possible merits of leasing it rather than purchasing it outright. The legal department tax specialist can provide figures to demonstrate the financial and tax
effects of purchasing or leasing. A different type of agreement will be required in each case.

The company's labor contract, if it has one, may be administered by a separate department such as the industrial relations department. This department
may have its own labor specialist and staff, or it may work through the legal
department. As in the case of the seemingly simple contract, the general
framework of a labor agreement should not be approved without legal assistance. Again, this is because of the hidden problems which may exist.

What has been pointed out here regarding contracts is equally applicable
to all other written legal documents. The manufacturer should not assume
that his interpretation of these documents is correct or that the language of
the document is so clear that it obviously has only one meaning.

Marketing the Product—Antitrust Laws. Before launching a new product or an
extension of a product line, the manufacturer and his marketing staff should
check with the legal department to determine whether or not the company is
currently under any restraining order which would interfere with the sale of the
product. Even if the company has no prior history in this area, a new marketing method or a new product should be considered in relation to the position
of the company in the industry. Whether or not the product will be marketed
in the United States or in a foreign country, one of the Federal antitrust laws
may be violated if the activity in the end affects United States trade.

United States trade is affected by agreements among competition not to
compete, setting prices, allocating customers or markets, boycotting a customer who is a supplier of another competitor, or controlling the kind or volume of goods manufactured and sold. All these activities violate the Sherman
Act, one of the Federal antitrust laws which prohibits contracts, combinations,
and conspiracies in restraint of trade and monopolies.

The Clayton Act, another Federal antitrust law, prohibits the sale or lease
of a product on the condition that the purchaser not deal with a competing
supplier. It has been applied against long-term total requirement contracts
and against blanket contracts. An agreement calling for continuing purchases
and sales running for more than a year and affecting a substantial part of a
total market is subject to challenge under this law. In the situation where the
customer is required to buy two or more products to get the product he wants,
there is also a violation of this act.

The Robinson-Patman Act, another Federal antitrust law, requires a supplier to sell his merchandise at the same price to those of his customers who
compete with each other, unless they are not actually in competition because
they are not in the same geographical location or are on different levels of
distribution. However, a supplier who must reduce his price to meet a price
that his competitor has offered to his customer does not have to extend this
same price to his other customers provided he acts in good faith. Also, where
he is able to realize a cost savings because of quantity sales, he may pass this
savings along to the customer. Except in these situations, he may refuse to

sell, but once he agrees to sell the same product to two competing customers, he must not discriminate in price between them.

The Federal Trade Commission Act, another Federal antitrust law, is a broad statute prohibiting unfair methods of competition and giving the Federal Trade Commission the power to contest any situation which the Commission believes to be unfair.

Any situation in this area should be explored with the legal department before final action. Some of these problems have their roots in manufacturing. Others may affect manufacturing by subsequent action where, for instance, the later distribution of the product is in violation of one of the acts. Perhaps just making the product would violate an existing order. Nothing in this field should be passed without legal review.

SUMMARY

Where the legal problem is apparent, as where the manufacturer receives a summons or claim, the situation is immediately related to the legal department. Traditionally, lawyers handle such matters. Where, however, the legal problem is latent and is hidden from the view of the manufacturer, he has no known signal to warn him of a dangerous course. This is the part of the relationship which must be governed by some automatic review system, regardless of the structure of the company's organization. With increasing regulations by state and Federal government agencies and foreign governments in the international market, no manufacturer can exclude his legal advisors from his operation. In turn, his legal advisors can no longer advise the manufacturer properly unless they actively involve themselves in his manufacturing process.

CHAPTER EIGHT

Relationship of Manufacturing and Top Management

J. F. FISHER   *Vice President, Ogden Corporation, New York, New York*

This chapter describes how manufacturing management can participate effectively in directing the enterprise. Top management expects the manufacturing manager to plan his operations and report exceptions, along with the action taken or recommended to correct exceptions. Manufacturing can competently assist top management only when its own activities are planned and controlled. Two techniques which assist manufacturing management in planning, follow-up, and reporting are:

Bottom-up Budgeting. Preparation of operating and capital improvement plans by each supervisor, which, when summed, provide the manufacturing program which will accomplish top management objectives.

Project Planning and Follow-up. Projects are not limited to large-scale jobs, but include definition, assignment, and follow-up of all significant manufacturing management tasks.

Areas in which clear and timely manufacturing–top management intercourse is especially critical are: organization and development of key personnel, balance between quality and cost, methods research and development, and policy and procedures.

PLANNING

Few, if any, significant manufacturing businesses can operate successfully by responding to unplanned events. Planning is a way of life. Particularly this is so if a business is cyclical. It is important that the manufacturing function integrate its planning with overall company objectives and provide adequate mechanisms which will assure timely response to changes in any of the factors upon which operating plans have been based.

Manufacturing managers often hear sounds such as these arising from the shop:

How do they expect to make money when we have half the lead time we need to finish the order?

How can we produce quality parts when the engineering is incomplete?

We've got to find work for the second shift. Just as soon as we lay them off, there'll be a rush order for our most important customer.

The bills of material are out of date so we ran out of seals.

The business agent is only interested in the dues, not in settling these grievances.

We never get the performance reports back from accounting in time to do anything about the exceptions.

We can't schedule shutdowns with all these rush orders.

As long as we've made the setup, we'd better run a few extra pieces.

The new management will probably want to make a clean sweep.

In one way or another, each of these comments holds the germ of surprise for top management. Top management seeks to operate the manufacturing enterprise so that it will provide a sound and profitable investment for its owners. To assure continuing or improving profits requires that, in addition to meeting its responsibilities to customers, employees, and the community, top management must cope with and in many instances initiate changes—often changes which impinge finally and with the most force upon the manufacturing manager. Manufacturing management abhors a change.

The counsels of top management often produce sounds such as these:

We are getting too many failures because of the design of the rear bearing support.

Our most important customers are accelerating their usage of disposables.

There will be a realignment of power and policy at the national level in our bargaining agent after the election.

Let's face it. The marketing study's conclusions were haywire.

We can't provide sufficient capital or solve the estate problem unless we sell.

The time has come for us to install a computerized management information system.

Such remarks more often than not herald changes which will pose difficult problems in manufacturing.

What Is Manufacturing? For this discussion, it will be assumed that manufacturing comprises the following functions:

1. Production and processing
2. Field service and product repair
3. Maintenance of equipment and facilities
4. Provision of tools, supplies, and utilities
5. Industrial engineering, including performance measurement, value analysis, and methods research and improvement
6. Quality control
7. Manufacturing planning
8. Manufacturing engineering
9. Material management, including
   a. Purchasing
   b. Inventory control and storage
   c. Production control and scheduling
   d. Traffic
10. Security
11. Safety
12. Industrial relations

In large companies, some of these functions, such as inventory control, purchasing, traffic, industrial relations, quality control, or even industrial engineering or maintenance, may report to top management other than through manufacturing management. However, manufacturing management's success closely depends upon the effectiveness of these functions, whatever organizational arrangements exist within a particular company. Consequently, the manufacturing manager must find means of keeping in touch with operations in each of these functions and assure himself that he will not be surprised by results in any area upon which his productive capability depends.

Who Is Top Managment? As with "manufacturing," the connotation of "top management" varies among companies. Size, extent of product or geographical decentralization, management organization and philosophy, type of manufacture, degree of vertical integration, all these factors affect structure. For this discussion, it will be assumed that top management includes the individuals responsible for overall profit at both divisional and corporate levels, including product managers to the extent that they are responsible for profit. In other words, top management comprises all those individuals who are responsible for setting overall objectives and for coordinating all organizational elements to achieve these objectives.

In widely diversified corporations, there may also be functional top management—the headquarters staff executive whose primary interest is to optimize manufacturing effectiveness in each different subsidiary or division.

With the probable exception of the functional headquarters manufacturing executive in a diversified conglomerate, top management may have had little firsthand shop background; in many companies, top managers arrive through sales, engineering, financial, or legal channels. Consequently, manufacturing managers should take special pains to assure that their communications are meaningful to nonmanufacturing top management and, in turn, make sure that top management problems and objectives are clearly understood by all elements of the manufacturing organization.

Communications. How can communication with top management best be maintained? The answer will vary in different organizations, but there are important common requirements:

Sound Internal Systems. The manufacturing manager, among all the other functional executives in most manufacturing enterprises, spends the most money and supervises the largest number of employees. It follows then that the effectiveness of the entire company depends to a large extent upon the soundness of the organization, planning techniques, and control system within manufacturing.

A dangerous aspect of the manufacturing function is momentum. Large or fast-growing businesses require sufficient lead time to alter a course. As with ships, successful companies find it imperative to have sensing devices to discover threats to navigation far enough in advance to avoid disaster. Because he is down in the engine room, so to speak, it is easy for the manufacturing manager to lose sight of the course and problems of the company as a whole and thus find himself unfavorably situated for effective response to the needs of the business. Manufacturing must therefore organize and plan its own operations in accordance with the best state of management art. A good deal of judgment is required if the best fit of technique to problem is to be achieved.

The manufacturing manager whose experience has been entirely within the company or even narrowly within a particular industry should make definite efforts to obtain the benefit of broader outside viewpoints through participation in industrial and management association activities, courses, and a regular reading program.

Likewise, the manufacturing manager whose experience has been from outside the company must do sufficient research and analysis to provide himself adequate insight for evaluating the adequacy of the manufacturing management system with which he operates.

In any event, periodic audits of manufacturing organizational arrangements, planning procedures, and information systems should be made. Audits are most effective when conducted by an agency outside manufacturing. An objective, widely experienced point of view with clear understanding of the company's history and future plans is desirable. In a large corporation, this point of view is usually provided in the corporate central staff. Smaller companies often employ outside consultants for such audits.

Bottom-up Budgeting—Operations. Manufacturing management should review costs for past periods in relation to sales and determine costs for projected sales, taking into account product mix and cyclical effects. Targets should then be set for major cost areas, adjusting for changes anticipated in wages, benefits, and prices. These targets should incorporate desired improvement in utilization of labor, material, supplies, and equipment as well as process and method improvements. Targets should be broken down for each supervisor into dollars of expense and units of output (standard hours, pounds of product, number of orders, service calls, or other units of measure) for each of his subordinates' cost centers.

Each cost center manager now has his own goals. He must analyze his operations in detail and calculate the changes which will be necessary to achieve them. At this point, the manufacturing manager must see that communication is maintained among all levels of his supervisory staff and that individuals are given whatever help they need in working out their plans. In some instances, goals may have to be modified. Finally, each budget will be approved level by level and summarized into the overall manufacturing plan. Each supervisor is responsible for his own budget and for the performance of each of his next-level subordinates.

Capital Budgets. Because capital resources are seldom sufficient to finance all improvement opportunities, management must periodically decide which projects should be authorized. To choose effectively among capital expenditures, it is essential that management consistently rank projected returns on major investments through analysis of expected cash flows. It is equally important, once a capital project has been authorized, that provision be made for monitoring actual results, not only cost of the project, but also performance after it is completed. No important manufacturing capital project should proceed without a regular report to top management which clearly indicates any deviation from the assumptions which governed approval of the expenditure.

The question of whether or not a particular investment is paying off as predicted is not always readily answered by classical cost accounting or performance reporting systems, and even when the system does provide for such analysis, results are often ignored—especially when performance is worse than expected. Top management looks to both manufacturing and accounting for whatever special analyses are required to keep track of results. Accounting can prepare reports based upon cash flow, unit cost, and payroll information and should certainly review any analyses prepared by others to assure proper treatment of accounting data. Nevertheless, manufacturing management must provide explanations of significant exceptions to planned performance as well as recommendations for action.

Reporting. The manufacturing executive should assure himself that significant operating data are collected accurately and compiled in meaningful reports which provide usage and productivity information for processes, machinery, crews, and individual employees in each manufacturing work center. Quality control and yield statistics as well as usage of materials, supplies, and tools should also be compiled in a manner which will enable management to gage the results for which each supervisor is responsible. If information needed for operating control cannot be processed by computer or manual accounting systems, it must be recorded and summarized in manufacturing. It is no excuse to state that a surprising situation arises because another service department did not notify manufacturing of occurrences that were not anticipated in the plan or budget.

Record keeping at best is onerous, even when much of the iterative work is mechanized. But detailed input and output data for manufacturing operations must be recorded and summarized in some form. In the small garage-type shop, more can be left to experience and scratch pad memoirs. But if planning is to be meaningful, that is, if it is to prevent surprises, projections must be founded on facts which can be verified and assumptions which can be quantified. Effective planning requires abstraction of the essential elements of the manufacturing environment in accurate records.

The more extensive the enterprise, the more complicated the record keeping chores become. Obviously not all reports will be provided by service departments outside of manufacturing. But top management relies on manufacturing to assure that the data necessary to predict events are provided as well as explanations of significant variations from predictions.

Goal Setting and Follow-up. Budgets—operating budgets particularly—should be based upon realistic assumptions. Often these assumptions involve performance compromises which prevent top management's full achievement of its objectives or, at the least, delay their achievement. A key operating department may produce at a rate which is 50 percent of its potential for reasons such as shortage of skilled employees, obsolete tooling, poorly designed process, or whatever. Improvement projects which are included as budget items may involve extensive action, the progress of which cannot be included in regular control reports. How best can manufacturing management assure itself that surprises will not occur and that changes are accomplished as scheduled?

Accurate performance measurement for any operation or activity depends upon standards. There is a real analogy between production standards and management plans. A production standard sums up a method; it details inputs and results. Comparing actual to standard performance provides the control through which management can take timely action indicated by significant exceptions.

The above discussion has dealt with the details of interpreting top management performance and investment objectives to the manufacturing organization and describing the steps that manufacturing management must take to assure itself of logical plans and effective operating controls. Sound operating and capital budget procedures are not the only techniques which must be applied to achieve the best use of manufacturing staff, minimize surprises, and manage change with the least friction.

Budgets and operating controls measure the most obvious aspects of performance which have immediate impact on the success of top management in meeting its objectives. The manufacturing manager must also continuously assess the strengths and weaknesses of his staff; organize his human resources in a manner which will capitalize on their know-how and ability as well as prevent to the extent possible, errors, omissions, or excessive costs. Further, the manufacturing manager must devise an effective goal setting and progress follow-up procedure for himself—and ultimately top management—such that improvement projects and other necessary tasks, not specifically covered by the operating and capital budgets, are performed effectively.

Project Management. The same idea applies to the more complex aspects of management. The departmental budgets provide standards in terms of which the economic aspects of each manager's performance and judgment can be assessed; summed, these budgets provide a standard for the manufacturing manager himself. However, there are other vital aspects of each manager's job which cannot be appraised by budgetary items. Action plans covering the near-term future as well as long-range goals should be formalized to the extent that when the manufacturing manager meets with one of his lieutenants, their lists of things which should have been done will be the same.

The manufacturing manager himself will need a project plan for his own nonbudgeted activity, even though top management may not have requested it. This planning on the part of the manufacturing manager will serve the highly desirable purpose of encouraging top management to think through and verbalize is own objectives. At the same time, the plan and regular review procedure will structure a relationship between top management and manufacturing in which progress or lack of it can be evaluated objectively. Some targets will of course be missed, but if review sessions are programmed with reasonable frequency, surprises should be held to a minimum and top management can give timely assistance when needed.

Changes. A further advantage of using project plans as well as budgets for each link in the chain of command is that when the welfare of the enterprise depends on changing policy, practice, products, or performance levels, the rationale for such changes should be clear to all. Communications will be much more efficient and less fraught with people problems caused by oversights or misunderstandings.

Elements of Project Planning. The elements of a project plan are very simple, but although it may be simple to list them, patient consultation and follow-up are necessary if those who are responsible for implementation are to understand fully the objectives, action steps, timetables, and expected results.

Objectives. The reasons for the plan should be clearly stated with whatever background information is necessary to give a picture of the importance of the project as well as of the difficulties which may be anticipated.

Action Steps. The approach to achieving the objective should be agreed upon, and the events which indicate completion of each necessary action should be defined. Specific assignment of responsibility for each task is most important. If more than one person is to be involved in a given task, the part that each is to play should be defined, but primary responsibility for completing the step should rest with one person. If the plan involves other jurisdictions within the enterprise or even outside, communication and authorization procedures should be agreed upon.

Timetables. Complicated projects, such as the construction of a plant or building a special machine which may take several months, may warrant sophisticated techniques for ordering events and keeping track of their scheduling. Critical path and performance evaluation and review procedures are sometimes employed, using computer programs to provide a graphic picture of the network of interdependent events and periodic summaries of progress.

Simpler methods suffice in most manufacturing situations. A target event for each of the key action steps should be established which will allow reasonable time for contingencies and yet permit meeting the project date. If there are but one or two action steps or events, some other criteria of degree of completion must be found, for at each review a new target date must be established if there is any doubt that the original plan can be completed as scheduled.

Expected Results. Some of the bitterest management disappointments occur because it is assumed that if a planned course of action or project has been completed, ipso facto the plan's objective has been accomplished.

A supervisory training program is completed; a new tape-controlled mill is installed; inventory controls are computerized—projects such as these may be planned and executed in accordance with authorized expenditures and timetables. Then what? Some concrete criteria of success must be agreed upon and means of evaluation established to determine if and when such criteria have been met.

ORGANIZATION AND DEVELOPMENT OF KEY PERSONNEL

Organizational maintenance is a prime top management concern. The manufacturing manager can be of great assistance in this task as can the heads of the other key departments. Organizational maintenance has two aspects: (1) providing for orderly succession, and (2) ensuring appropriate, smooth, and flexible relationships among functional units of the enterprise.

Perhaps it is trite to point out that no manager fulfills his job completely unless he selects and trains his successor, but no homely rule is honored more in the breach than this one except in very large businesses where the momentum of profitability enables a company to staff in depth for all its key positions.

Nevertheless, the manufacturing manager almost always commands by far the largest number of employees; his operations usually provide opportunity for the most comprehensive and meaningful inside view of the business. Consequently, he should be in the best position to cooperate with top management in staffing to meet overall and longer term needs not only in manufacturing but in other departments as well.

Much experience has been gathered and distilled into useful guidelines for designing effective manufacturing organization structures, a subject beyond the scope of this chapter. In the most logical patterns of organization, however, situations arise which make it necessary or advisable to depart from strict interpretation of the scope of traditional organizational units. Training, for example, is a prime responsibility at all levels of management; yet aptitude for conducting effective training may be seriously lacking in manufacturing and engineering organizations. Work measurement and performance evaluation are also major management tasks. These skills may be undeveloped in accounting and sales departments, but are usually strong in manufacturing.

The manufacturing manager should regularly review his resources and needs—annually at least—with heads of other major functions and particularly with top management to the end that the best overall interests of the enterprise are served efficiently. Thoughtful consideration of individual strengths and shortcomings, as these are confirmed in the processes of goal setting and monitoring progress, should enable manufacturing and top management to design jobs which will provide the likeliest environment for success and therefore the best motivation and morale.

BALANCING QUALITY AND COST

It is essential for effective contribution to overall corporate performance that the manufacturing manager have complete knowledge of customer requirements. Wherever feasible, the manufacturing manager should familiarize himself firsthand with the customer's use of his products. If he cannot arrange to do this personally, he should assure himself of such knowledge through contact with those in the company who are personally in contact with the customer and his needs.

A key objective for manufacturing management is to achieve and maintain a consistent, optimum level of product quality. Optimum in this context means the best possible balance between cost and end use performance. Determination of the optimum balance is not always simple. Marketing people usually want a level which provides a wide safety margin over competitors and reluctantly sponsor research which may be needed to define product performance characteristics precisely unless assured of price reduction.

Appropriate quality and service standards can be established and maintained only when there is throughout the company a correct and common understanding of customer requirements. Significant recurring problems should be investigated in the field whenever possible by manufacturing management as well as by marketing, sales, and design engineering. In some instances, the customer himself may not be fully aware of his true needs—he may be specifying unrealistic standards. Such customer misconceptions often prove difficult or impossible to change; but the manufacturing manager, the one who finally assembles the product, is often best able to assist in bringing about a true meeting of minds.

The point here is that manufacturing begets insights into problems which frequently find their way to top management through other channels such as product management, design and development, marketing, and sales. Consequently, the alert manufacturing manager should purposefully program his relationship with top management to include communication of his point of view, based upon firsthand knowledge of end use with respect to product quality and service standards. It is assumed, of course, that manufacturing management always presents its best judgment on these matters clearly and completely to marketing and engineering.

Example. A large South American food canning company exports all its production and imports all its tinplate, the most significant expense element next to raw product cost.

Various weights of tinplate were used for different products, but nearly all products were canned in 90-pound plate. Test shipments using lighter weight plate were conducted. These experiments indicated that a lighter weight plate would result in no greater loss due to damaged cans. Because of better tinplate uniformity, the safety margin for quality could be narrowed, permitting significant freight and raw material saving with no loss in end use performance. Thirty years' practice was changed because manufacturing convinced top management that a key policy on quality should be audited.

Top Management and Value Analysis. The foregoing is an example of value analysis or value engineering, a widely used technique which is fully described in Chapter 6 of Section 7. When value engineering involves quality standards, manufacturing must make sure that top management gets a clear view of the balance between cost and performance. Market pressure is heavy on prices, but it is impossible to build a cheap Cadillac. Top management must thoroughly understand the reasons for the quality and performance requirements of its product. Manufacturing is the custodian of these standards just as certainly as it is responsible for making the products profitably. The manufacturing manager can maintain the quality-cost balance effectively only if he fully understands top management's market objectives and makes sure that top management understands the quality-cost relationships inherent in the company's products.

This mutual understanding is especially important and yet difficult to maintain when the manufacturing enterprise becomes a subsidiary or division of a widely diversified corporation. Pressure on division management for quick profits may tempt it to cheapen products whose quality built the company's market reputation over the years before it became a subsidiary. Customers may put up with such deterioration for a time, but eventually they will leave.

METHODS RESEARCH AND DEVELOPMENT

The enterprise must maintain its profitability and continue to meet competitive challenges. Product research and development are aimed at these objectives. The relationship between ignoring product innovation and eventual deterioration of profit is well known to top management. Not so well recognized, unless top management includes considerable shop experience, is the necessity for manufacturing or processing R&D, a necessity which becomes more acute as wages and automation possibilities increase. No one objects to methods improvement, but very few businesses operate continuously in a level state or a state of steady economic progress. There are ups and downs with which top management must deal. The temptation to cut manufacturing overhead is strong when volume dips. Manufacturing management should provide itself with the capability for improving productivity and should see that top management is regularly informed of productivity improvement accomplishments and opportunities. Only when it is convinced that methods and process research are paying off will top management resist the temptation to cut vital industrial engineering strength when times are tough.

Consultants in Manufacturing. Situations occasionally arise in cases of plant relocation, introduction of new products, company reorganization, large-scale redesign of processes, and the like, when the in-house manufacturing R&D capability may be inadequate. Or it may be desirable to have an outside audit of the company's manufacturing organization. There are many competent and ethical consultants who specialize in the manufacturing phase of business and who can be helpful in such circumstances.

Engagement of a consultant to assist manufacturing management should involve thoughtful collaboration with top management on at least the following points:

Nature of the Problem. What is the nature of the problem from the company's point of view? A management definition of the proposed project should be written. The consultant will, of course, submit his idea of the work statement and a proposal for his part in it.

Selecting the Consultant. If the need for consulting assistance has been established, it should be possible to select a consultant in whom both manufacturing and top management can place confidence. Both should work closely with him to define completely and accurately the purpose and scope of the project as well as the approach to be used, a reasonable budget, timetable, and provision for progress checks or reviews and the expected results.

Manufacturing management should meet the individual or individuals who propose to work with the organization and be fully familiar with their professional records before a consultant or consulting firm is chosen.

Division of Labor. What will be the division of labor between company staff and the consultant? Few manufacturing problems, with the possible exception of an organizational audit, can ever be completely resolved through a consulting assignment. Participation by company personnel at the working, supervisory, and executive levels is essential for lasting benefit.

POLICIES AND PROCEDURES

Policies. A policy defines what is to be done or not done and why, in regularly recurring situations. It explains the background of such situations as well as the attitude and philosophy of management in relationship to them. But policy does not detail action; it does not describe how a job is to be done.

The degree to which top management's policies are understood and followed is influenced in large measure by the accessibility of these policies. Supervisors in the shop daily interpret policies, especially in matters of industrial relations, housekeeping, safety, personnel development, and quality. Manufacturing management must see that top management's objectives are understood and that top management is informed when conditions inimical to its objectives arise. Thus it follows that policies should be recorded and explained to every supervisor so that he can represent management consistently.

Procedures. A procedure defines how action is to be taken. Procedures describe methods and work assignments. Procedures often flow from policies, because action is usually required to make policies effective. Procedures should be recorded for all repetitive work routines to define the best methods and eliminate unnecessary decision making.

Maintenance of Policies and Procedures. Changing conditions require review and revision of policies and procedures, particularly those governing the relationships with others such as unions, suppliers, customers, and governmental agencies.

Many companies assign policy and procedure writing to an individual or department outside of manufacturing. Manufacturing, having usually by far the greatest range of activities under its direction, must see that those which should be covered are covered by current, clear, and accessible records.

Top Management Changes. Adequate policy and procedure records are particularly advantageous whenever there is a change in top management. Although there may be no change in local top management when company ownership is transferred, it is especially necessary for new ownership to understand the policies and methods of operation which have governed the enterprise. Communication with new owners will be enhanced if up-to-date manuals of policy and procedure are available. Usually, new ownership is reluctant to alter organization, policy, or procedure in a successful organization if the basis for success is well understood.

The prospect of synergistic benefits often is a motivating factor in acquisitions. The realization of such benefits may require changes in operations. Full communication and understanding of overall objectives and the means for their accomplishment are required to avoid rumors, deterioration of morale, or loss of key personnel when ownership changes or management succession from outside the company occurs.

CONCLUSION

The relationship of manufacturing and top management is the most important of all organizational links. A large part of the firm's human resources and a significant proportion of its controllable costs are bound up in manufacturing. If top management is to be spared avoidable surprises and if manufacturing is to accommodate necessary changes successfully, both groups must use every effort to make sure that the link is soundly forged and frequently inspected for flaws. The chances of maintaining effective manufacturing–top management relationships will be greatly enhanced by clear communication using practical management information systems, painstaking attention to setting objectives, designing jobs to capitalize on strengths, and systematic follow-up of tasks at each organizational level.

BIBLIOGRAPHY

Bierman, Harold, and Seymour Smidt, *The Capital Budgeting Decision*, 2d ed., The Macmillan Company, New York, 1966.

Bower, Marvin, *The Will to Manage*, McGraw-Hill Book Company, New York, 1966.

"Cashing in on Goodwill," *Wall Street Journal*, Aug. 12, 1968, p. 13.

Dale, Ernest, *Management Theory and Practice*, McGraw-Hill Book Company, New York, 1965.

Drucker, Peter F., *The Effective Executive*, Harper & Row, Publishers, Incorporated, New York, 1966.

Drucker, Peter F., *Managing for Results*, Harper & Row, Publishers, Incorporated, New York, 1964.

Drucker, Peter F., *The Practice of Management*, Harper & Row, Publishers, Incorporated, New York, 1954.

Finley, Robert E., and Henry R. Ziobro (eds.), *The Manufacturing Man and His Job*, American Management Association, New York, 1966.

Haskins, Caryl P., "Evolution or Catastrophe," *Science*, Mar. 8, 1968, p. 1055.

Odiorne, George S., *Management by Objectives*, G. P. Putnam's Sons, New York, 1965.

Schleh, Edward C., *Management by Results*, McGraw-Hill Book Company, New York, 1961.

MANUFACTURING PLANNING

CHAPTER ONE

Manufacturing Systems Design

DORMAN G. FREARK *Associate Professor, Department of Industrial Engineering, The Pennsylvania State University, University Park, Pennsylvania*

A broad understanding of presently used manufacturing systems is helpful to the manager interested in improving the excellence of his own operation. Within each industry, production problems have been solved in some general characteristic way different from the solution of similar problems in other industries. For example, uniform thickness control in assembling plywood sheet is accomplished by letting the glue layers compensate for variations in wood layer thicknesses. In metal fabrication, on the other hand, the approach is much more difficult because each part in the assembly is held to tight dimensional tolerances. Advantages are thus gained by learning ways to solve problems that are new to one's competitors or one's own industry, but because they are known in other industries, do not need expensive or risky development.

After the manager has learned of other industries and reviewed the composition of the key manufacturing subsystems, he will be better able to create the optimum manufacturing system to reach his own company's objectives. Each system design is unique, and as it is a living embodiment of the minds of people, it requires continual appraisal and modification. One way to predict its outcome is to apply the analytical skills of the organizational units that will be affected if the plan is initiated. By an imaginative process of itemizing each step in the plan and assessing the interactions with each function, the results may be visualized. These results may then be fed back into a modified plan that is much more effective. If the original plan lends itself to mathematical modeling, then simulation may prove even more advantageous in providing feedback information.

MANUFACTURING SYSTEMS DESIGN PRINCIPLES

Manufacturing systems design is a broad function that includes all the planning, analysis, selection, assembly, and utilization of the company resources used to convert raw materials into salable products at optimum cost. The design usually evolves over a span of time as a key segment of the business system used by the company, and is the cumulative creation of many people under the general guidance of top manufacturing management. It not only embodies past achievement and present goals, but it also channels the future progress of the company.

In the broadest sense, the manufacturing system extends into and overlaps the boundaries of other business systems, especially those of marketing and engineering. In particular, the customers' needs and the product's design influence are influenced by the manufacturing system. Because of the system's uniqueness and complexity, it is not readily analyzed in detail, and because of investment costs, it is not readily adjusted. From a practical viewpoint, however, the situation may be greatly simplified by first reviewing the industry classifications and then the four key subsystems that are the essence of the manufacturing system:

1. Types of production
2. Manufacturing processes
3. Installation of the manufacturing processes
4. Production management

Each subsystem is interdependent on the others, and the selection of each is also influenced by the following major considerations:

1. The designs of the products which include their size, shape, material composition, and intended function
2. The product marketing objectives which include order quantities, order frequencies, delivery responsiveness, and product line configuration
3. The typical systems and subsystems of the industry including those classically used, new ones which are being generally adopted, experimental developments still on trial, and exciting new ideas which hold great promise
4. The present system and subsystem used by the company

There is no ranking implied by the order of any of the above. It is obvious that the instantaneous relative importance of each is determined by dynamically changing conditions.

MANUFACTURING SYSTEMS CLASSIFICATION

Manufacturing systems are broadly classified as either processing or fabrication, because these are the basic material conversion techniques. In processing, the raw materials are chemically and physically changed into new materials with different compositions and forms. These new materials, in turn, serve as raw materials for further processing or for fabrication. The processing classification is further subdivided into heavy processing and light or fine processing. In fabrication, the raw materials are physically reshaped into parts. Usually these parts are combined with others to make a final product assembly. The fabrication subdivisions are heavy fabrication, light fabrication, and bench operations.

Heavy Processing. Both the primary metals industries, such as steel and copper, and the heavy chemicals industries, such as sulfuric acid and heavy alkalies, use heavy processing manufacturing systems. The steel industry is an excellent example and can be used to illustrate the general system design. About 90 percent of the total steelmaking capacity is in the hands of fully integrated companies which mine the raw materials: iron ore, coal, and limestone; smelt the pig iron; refine the steel; and roll or form the steel into semi-finished or finished stock products.

The keynote of the steel industry is bigness. Its size resulted directly from the requirements of an expanding United States in the mid-1800s and of steel's prime customers of that time, the rapidly growing railroad lines. These demands could not be met at a reasonable cost by the existing crucible process which was limited to making slowly a few hundred pounds at a time of relatively high grade steel. The steel converter introduced in the United States by William Kelly and used at Cambria Iron Works in 1861–1862 and the open-hearth furnace brought to the United States in 1868 had immediate and explosive effects. The converter made tons in minutes, not pounds in days; and low-cost steel of suitable quality to meet the demands of the railroads became available. As competition grew, the answer to reducing cost was to increase the batch or "heat" size until the 200-ton open-hearth heat became typical.

The use of the word "heat" to designate a batch of steel is certainly appropriate, because from beginning to end, steel manufacture is characterized by heat. As shown in Figure 1-1, the principal steps include making coke in ovens, pig iron in the blast furnace, and steel in the refining furnace; casting large ingots; and then hot-working these ingots down into products like thin sheet and wire. From a technical standpoint, these are the same processing steps taken over one hundred years ago. The present manufacturing system grew from increases in batch size, as well as process integrations and simplifications. In heavy processing, such as refining the common low-cost metals, the really significant process economies result from heating, shaping, and moving the product in large rather than small masses. Large bodies do not lose their heat as rapidly as do small ones; thus the very important costs of fuel and power have been greatly reduced over the years by increasing batch size. The great masses of pig iron and steel are moved mechanically and are kept hot throughout manufacture to eliminate waste from the repeated reheating needed with nonintegrated processing.

The significant cost factors in the heavy process industries are the basic raw materials and the energy for heat and power. Labor tends to be less costly than it otherwise would be, because of the tremendous batch sizes, the extent of material handling mechanization, and the general overall simplicity of the processes. The equipment for heating, shaping, and moving such heavy products results in correspondingly large fixed capital investments which in an integrated steel company may range over $2,500 million.

Geographically, the heavy process industries are usually located near their customers. In addition, they are frequently located on large rivers or lakes or at ocean harbors where seagoing ships can bring in the necessary raw materials and take away shiploads of finished product. Plant location is a balance between the short delivery cycle demands of the customers and the costs in moving and processing a huge bulk and weight of material. The balancing factors change as the better or closer sources of ore and fuel are depleted and as markets shift owing to changes in population centers or invention and growth of new fabricated products.

Another change that has taken place as heavy process industries have been integrated is the general type of production that is used. Production in these

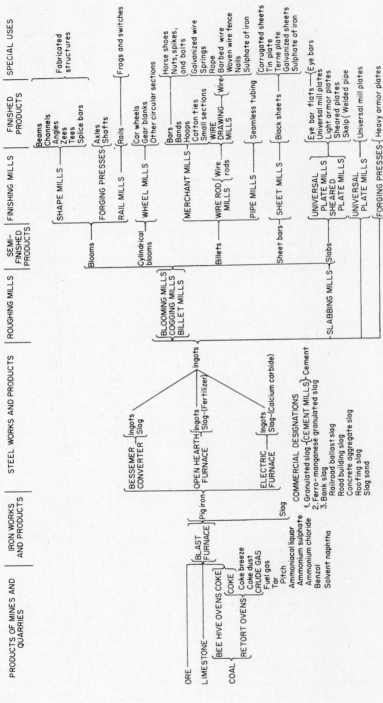

Fig. 1-1. Steelmaking, a Heavy Processing Industry. (*From Economics of American Industry, by E. B. Alderfer and H. E. Michl. Copyright 1957, McGraw-Hill Book Company. Used by permission of McGraw-Hill Book Company.*)

industries is now virtually continuous. Conversion furnaces and chemical processing equipment either run every day and night or are shut down completely for repair, replacement, or lack of demand. Finished and semifinished product is made and stored in inventory in anticipation of future sales, because it takes continuous operation at nearly full capacity to break even.

The heavy process industries have become responsive to increasingly sophisticated and demanding customers. Most of these customers are fabricators who order to stringent specifications. Having strict inventory control systems, they often order their raw materials on a hand-to-mouth basis.

Light Processing. Most light processing is done by the industry that calls itself the fine chemical industry and produces the more intricate chemical compounds, drugs, analytical chemicals, and metals like boron, lithium, and titanium. These materials are carefully made to grade or specification for special uses at high unit price and in relatively small volume. Price and volume are not the sole criteria, however, as shown by plastics, which may be classified as products of the fine chemical industry owing to their relatively high price, even though they are produced in very large volume.

Since 1900, the chemical industry has grown from a relatively small industry into one of the largest in the United States. This growth resulted from the concept of the unit process, an individual step involving a single chemical reaction, and the unit operation, an individual step involving a single physical change. Chemical engineers who have studied these unit procedures construct flow sheets which show the coordinated sequence required to manufacture the desired product and by-products. The chemical engineer also supervises the skilled laborers who later operate the manufacturing equipment.

After the chemical engineer has first tested his process sequence in the laboratory, he constructs a pilot plant which replicates the planned production system but with the smallest equipment available. The small-scale pilot plant is used to test the process design, detect the corrosion and maintenance problems, evaluate plant efficiency, and train foremen and other skilled labor.

When labor was plentiful and inexpensive, chemical operations were carried out in small-scale batches. As the scale of operations increased, continuous rather than small-batch operations were introduced, and it was found that more uniform results could be obtained with automatic control instrumentation. These instruments not only record process variables such as pressure, temperature, and material flow rates, but are able to regulate or adjust them as the process reactions take place. The automatic instruments perform the function of process supervision, and the workmen and supervising engineers assure continued operation by maintaining the plant in the proper running order.

Chemical processing is usually done in enclosed systems. The materials flow in a rigid sequence from step to step and are moved as solids, liquids, or gases within the system by pipe, tube, conveyor, screw feeder, or other similar mechanical means. Material flow is especially important in the process industries. One reason for this is that time is always an essential part of reaction process control, and improper flow can easily cause out-of-specification product. Erratic product quality can result from an improperly designed system where in-process material is trapped for irregular periods in dead-flow regions or pockets. The design of the material transfer system is as important as the selection of the proper unit operations.

As a result of the tendency toward completely self-contained, automatically controlled processing systems, the fine chemical industries have a high ratio of capital investment per employee. The plants have relatively few but highly skilled operating employees, most of whom control, maintain, or repair equipment. The higher price of the fine chemicals results not so much from the scarcity of the raw materials, which are often very abundant, as from the many process or operation steps and the high degree of careful control that must be exercised at each step. This basic nature of fine chemical processing may be understood by reviewing briefly the manufacture of viscose rayon, a typical member of the relatively common cellulosics family. The basic raw materials, wood chips or cotton linters, are plentiful and fairly inexpensive. Figure 1-2 shows the twelve unit operations and five unit processes needed to convert wood chips into wood pulp, the basic ingredient of the cellulosics. The pulp is then processed through eleven more unit operations and eight more unit processes to manufacture the viscose rayon filament, as shown in Figure 1-3. It is evident that these highly technical operations are much more complex and costly than those used in heavy processing.

In heavy processing, raw material and customer location in relation to the plant are critical, and to some extent this problem is solved by multiplant facilities widely separated geographically. The need for the light processing plants to be located close to either the customer or the raw materials is not so great, because the bulk of material movement is much less and fewer plants serve a bigger geographical area. The plant can be located well away from large cities, which has the advantage of easier waste disposal, an increasingly significant factor.

Chemical processing equipment is frequently located outdoors. The system is self-enclosing, and the typical construction materials must resist process chemicals much more corrosive than normal atmospheric exposure. Layout of the equipment is in accordance with the process flow sheet developed by the chemical engineer, plus any modifications indicated by pilot plant operation. Equipment is arranged to give the highest possible product yield at the lowest cost. The equipment layout is geared to suit the process needs rather than those of the operating personnel, because they need not be close to the equipment to supervise or control it.

Heavy Fabrication. The products of the heavy fabrication manufacturing industries are large heavy parts or assemblies, mostly made of iron and steel. The companies tend to specialize either by making roughly formed shapes such as castings, forgings, weldments, and parts from plate stock or by making large machinery or equipment. The facilities and equipment used by each are essentially dissimilar. In many instances, the larger formed steel shapes are made by a division of the primary steel producer, because he already has the furnaces and metalworking and material handling equipment, plus the starting material. On the other hand, the assemblies are most often complex power-driven machines of unique design and custom built either as a single order or as part of a fairly standard product line. Included are such products as railroad locomotives and cars, large farm machinery and construction equipment, electric power generating equipment, and a wide variety of industrial production equipment like large machine tools and the huge Fourdrinier papermaking machine.

The industry is characterized not only by the large, heavy products but also by the correspondingly large plant facilities, production machines, and material handling equipment. The manufacturing system is comparatively simple, because each job order is usually treated as an entity, and little or no manufacturing action is taken until the customer's order is actually received. Heavy machinery and equipment are ordered singly or in small quantities

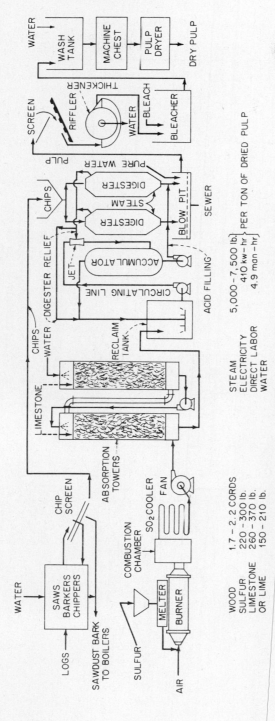

Fig. 1-2. Flow Sheet for Sulfite Pulp. (*From The Chemical Process Industries, 3d ed., by R. N. Shreve. Copyright 1967, McGraw-Hill Book Company. Used by permission of McGraw-Hill Book Company.*)

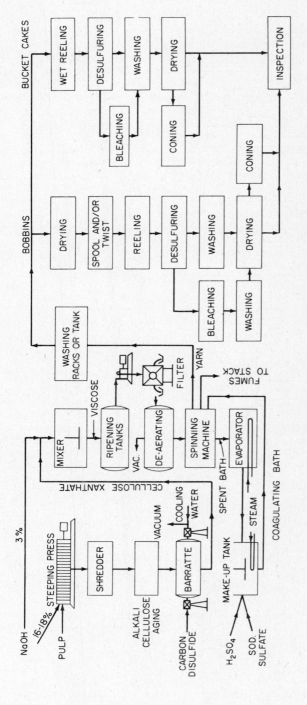

Fig. 1-3. Flow Sheet for Viscose Rayon. (*From The Chemical Process Industries, 3d ed., by R. N. Shreve. Copyright 1967, McGraw-Hill Book Company. Used by permission of McGraw-Hill Book Company.*)

CONSUMPTION PER LB. OF VISCOSE RAYON

WOOD PULP	1.12 LB.	DIRECT LABOR	0.05 MAN-HR.
CAUSTIC SODA, 76 %	0.9 LB.	STEAM	150 LB.
CARBON DISULFIDE	0.35 LB.	REFRIGERATION	0.02 TON
SULFURIC ACID (AS 100 %)	1.3 LB.	ELECTRICITY	2-3 KW.-HR.
CORN SUGAR	0.09 LB.	WATER	170 GAL.

because individual pieces are expensive and because their solid long-lasting construction makes replacement orders infrequent.

Large parts for heavy machinery and equipment are made from castings, forgings, and weldments whose bulk, weight, and rough irregular form make finishing operation setup difficult and time consuming. Much metal is often cut away during machining, which further contributes to the long production cycles. Specifically designed tooling is infrequently used because of the small production quantities and because dimensional tolerances tend to be liberal with a minimum amount of precision machining. Such tooling as is used is generally some type of template, drill jig, or holding fixture. These large parts are usually designed so that the only machining operations needed are those used to provide smooth, accurate surfaces for mating parts. The rest of the surfaces are left in the rough, semifinished cast or hot-worked form. Location, accuracy, and alignment are frequently obtained by shimming and adjusting to fit parts together at assembly rather than using the concept of interchangeability. The main structural part of the fabrication is machined first and taken to an assembly area where the other parts are added in succession until the apparatus is completed. Workmen and tools must be brought to this area. Due to the varied mixture of skills, there may be a supervision problem.

Most material handling is done with the aid of overhead cranes or hoists. Material is transported through the shop on large carts or on cars running on tracks. If the ceiling clearance and plant layout permit, large traveling cranes are used to move work between stations. These cranes are especially important in large fabrication shops not only for loading and unloading production equipment but also for greatly reducing aisle space requirements.

There is a wide range in the extent of quality control employed in the heavy fabrication industry. The casting or forging customer specifies his requirements in considerable detail. He may require any combination of dimensional, material chemistry, material soundness, or mechanical property tests, both nondestructive and destructive. Tests, other than dimensional measurements, commonly include chemical analysis, X-ray, magnetic particle, ultrasonic, tensile, impact, and fatigue.

Manufacturers of large assembled products rely heavily on functional tests to verify product quality. It is common practice to depend on the skilled workers to perform the necessary dimensional inspections as the work proceeds. The fact that mating parts fit together and function properly during assembly is accepted as evidence that manufacture up to that point is proper and may continue. The possibility of design errors also requires that manufacturing personnel be especially alert and careful when a new machine model is first built.

The manufacturing facilities needed to make items like castings are mostly melting furnaces and molding sand-conditioning equipment. Those needed to make items like forgings and plate shapes are mostly heating furnaces, drop hammers, hydraulic presses, and forming tools.

The facilities used for the fabricated machine assemblies are more extensive and varied. Emphasis is on general purpose manufacturing equipment like horizontal and vertical boring mills, planers, shapers, radial drills, and large-size lathes and milling machines. These general purpose types of equipment permit a great deal of flexibility and versatility, although skilled labor requirements are proportionately high. Facility utilization is often poor, because each job must be set up individually with relatively long unproductive tie-ups of machine tools and floor space. Difficulty in setting up and in handling encourages that in-process inspection be done while the parts are on the machines, which further decreases productivity.

The plant buildings are large to permit movement of material and to provide adequate room for fabrication. In addition, they are often high bay buildings with 30- or 40-foot ceilings to permit flexibility in manufacturing the many sizes and shapes of products and to permit the traveling cranes to move overhead.

The heavy equipment manufacturing system must provide for close integration with the design engineering function if delivery schedules are to be met. The engineers must complete their designs in a sequence that permits manufacturing to start work first on the long lead time items. Usually these are the newly designed large castings or forgings ordered for the first time and the drive motors and controls purchased from subcontractors. Liaison with engineering must continue throughout manufacture because mistakes will invariably be made in machining or assembly. Scrapping of partially completed work is often unnecessary if engineering and manufacturing personnel work together cooperatively either to modify the design slightly or to agree on a repair and rework procedure to salvage the part.

The system must also provide for careful concurrent cost control because the total manufacturing cycle time on a single order may extend over many months. Manufacturing cost estimates should be used as a basis for budget objectives against which actual costs are continually compared. This cost control problem is made more difficult by the combination of high facility investment, high skilled labor cost, poor machine utilization, and considerable idle time while workmen wait for parts, tools, inspectors, material handling equipment, and the like.

Light Fabrication. There are significant differences between light and heavy fabrication that are difficult or impractical to express. There is no defined size or weight that permits classifying a product as being specifically either light or heavy. In seeking such boundaries, it rapidly becomes apparent that the variations present in light fabrication make any general discussion full of exceptions. In brief, there are hundreds of different products for nearly every single material made by a process industry, the work force ranges from the one-man shop to industrial giants with over a quarter of a million employees, and the facilities and equipment numbers correspond in proportion to the work force. The equipment itself ranges from small, simple hand tools to very large, complex, fully automated process systems. A review of light fabrication may only be made if one keeps both the variety and host of exceptions in mind.

Products that are in the transition zone between heavy and light fabrication include spacecraft, missiles, aircraft, and automobiles. These all require forgings or castings from the heavy industries; yet the levels of quality and machining precision are as high as are found in the most demanding light work. The facilities and equipment also reflect this combination of largeness to accommodate the product physically, and excellent precision capability to meet product specifications. From a manufacturing systems viewpoint, they are best included with the light fabrication industries because of their complexity and variety.

Light fabrication products may also be grouped into the two broad categories of single formed parts and multipart, finished assemblies. Even though entire books have been written about the manufacturing processes used to form metallic materials alone, appreciable simplification and improvement in understanding can be achieved by considering a few basic ideas. Only four principles are applied in changing shape: deformation, division, chemical reaction, or physical change of state. All processing methods employ one or more of these principles. Die casting, for example, involves deformation and change of state as the metal is melted, squeezed into a die cavity, and solidified. Virtually the same principles apply to injection-molded thermoplastics. Some processing methods are very simple; forging involves only deformation and divisions. Others, such as deposition of metallic films by chemical decomposition of vaporized metallic compounds, are complex and may have rather limited application.

Each light fabrication industry has its own habitual manufacturing methods, and each company or plant uses one or more of these in making its products. The manufacturing manager knows something about the technology of his particular industry and recognizes that improvement of his processing methods may give him a competitive advantage. The light fabrication industries are particularly susceptible to the effect of technological advancements because of the intense competition among products. A new product may widely supplant an old one even though the old one is being efficiently and inexpensively manufactured. The replacement of the fountain pen by the ball-point pen is a familiar example.

Scientific research creates these new products and the processes to make them. Technical knowledge and industrial skills need to be fused into a practical production process, and manufacturing engineering is the means by which management meets this need. The manufacturing engineer has the responsibility of analyzing manufacturing techniques to identify areas where technical improvement is necessary and of taking action to implement these improvements. In some instances, modifications may be minor; in others, new equipment, new methods, or special tool design may be quite extensive and have a profound effect on the company's entire manufacturing system. In a copper-alloy fabricating plant for example, a single new extrusion press may double the plant capacity and require a building addition to house the new press, billet heating furnace, and other peripheral equipment, all at a cost of over $2.5 million. In a case like this, a senior industrial engineer may be given a full-time project management assignment for the complete installation.

In addition to new equipment and methods improvement, the manufacturing engineer has the general responsibility for analyzing product engineering specifications and determining the manufacturing operations required to produce the product. Sometimes the production process details have a significant effect on final product material quality. A detail like abusive surface grinding causing cracking in steel parts is relatively common knowledge, but the advantage of using molten salt in preference to oil for quenching during heat treatment is a detail not so well known. The light fabrication industry's companies have been especially eager to utilize the talents of the industrial engineer for these and other manufacturing systems design functions, particularly those requiring analytical planning or control such as quality assurance, materials procurement, and inventory and production management.

Bench Operations. In bench operations, the product is small and light enough for the manufacturing personnel to stand or sit at a bench or table while working. The essential similarity in all the products is the very high proportion of hand labor, particularly in assembly. In most instances, the bench worker stays at the work station. All needed parts and materials are arranged within easy reach. Work functions include both making parts and placing them in the assembly. The kinds of products that are frequently made in this fashion are tools and dies, instruments, electronic assemblies, typewriters, and watches. It is obvious that there is a wide range of worker skills in the various companies using this manufacturing technique so that in many instances benchwork is done in a single, small internal company department. The tool-and-diemaker will use several machine tools away from his bench, and he is one of the most highly skilled and highly trained industrial workers. In many companies, he designs as well as builds special tools. On the other hand, a worker assembling an electric toaster has a relatively simple repetitive task, uses few tools, and needs little skill or training.

Bench operations apply to either single-unit or mass-produced products. They are used when the relative complexity of the product does not justify redesign at that time for automated assembly of the current production quantity. Electronic products such as radios were once entirely made by bench assembly methods. The worker not only selected the standard parts, resistors, capacitors, tubes, and the like, but also cut and trimmed the connecting wires before soldering them all in place. As production quantities increased, printed circuit boards, mechanical placement of parts, and dip soldering came into general use as standard mass production methods. The electronics industry today combines both automated and benchwork assembly methods, the application of each still depending on the balance between product complexity, quantities, and competitive pressure.

In many cases, it is virtually impossible to inspect benchwork products except by functional tests. These tests are made both as in-process and as final product tests. The tests may include adjustment and may be considered part of the total production process as well as a quality determination. The almost complete dependence upon the individual worker for product quality and the total amount of hand labor make proper supervision especially important in this type of manufacture.

Costs due to the high proportion of labor are countered by the much lower plant or equipment capital investment costs for even large production volumes. The small plant and facility costs make idle capacity relatively unimportant, and if the operations require little skill or training, work force adjustments to meet changing market demands can be readily made. It is feasible to make a profit while operating at a small fraction of full plant capacity, which is impossible to do in, say, the heavy process industry.

TYPES OF PRODUCTION SYSTEMS

A major facet of manufacturing systems design is to establish the type of production to be used. There are three major types or classes of production and eight subclasses.

Job Production. Companies using this class tend to specialize in the production of particular types of products or in the application of particular types of manufacturing equipment or processes. In a sense, they are service organizations and respond to the needs of their customers by providing some sort of unique capability rather than by producing and selling their own proprietary product. Order quantities, delivery dates, detailed product specifications, and other special instructions are provided by the customer. In most cases, the customer places his order only after he has received a quotation from the company. Various activities performed by different job production companies include making such products as a nuclear-powered electric generating system, a special heat of steel, a transfer mechanism for an automated machine, or an electroformed mirror for a solar-powered satellite.

The three subclasses of job production are:

1. Custom designs produced once in small quantities
2. Custom or semistandard designs produced intermittently at irregular intervals, usually in small quantities
3. Custom or semistandard designs produced intermittently at regular intervals, in small or large quantities

The custom producer, say a model shop, is often a small business concern and may have few or no technical personnel. This, combined with small order quantities, tends to preclude detailed methods improvement analyses or special tool designs except where critical customer specifications or process requirements, like patterns needed for castings, demand them. Work on the customer's order does not normally begin until a firm contract has been made.

If the customer anticipates repeat orders, then special tools, jigs, fixtures, gages, or other production aids may be advisable. In these cases, the tool investment risk must be taken by the customer unless the producer is willing to gamble that he can both amortize the tooling and make a greater profit on future orders. It is generally and incorrectly assumed that repeat orders for the same item can be produced for a lower cost because they do not require repeated planning. Variabilities in labor output, in material costs, and in costs for parts or service from subvendors necessitate a review of the previous actual costs incurred and a reestimate including supplier quotations.

The job production company is continually faced with two conflicting objectives which are not easy to achieve because they are mutually contradictory and change in importance with time. Customer satisfaction and profit are both essential to success. Customers attracted by the unique capability offered by the producer are often willing to wait a reasonable time for delivery or service. Too little plant capacity may result in short-range high profit because the shop load is filled, but customers become dissatisfied and are lost. Too much plant capacity results in excellent customer satisfaction for a while, but lack of work causes poor return on investment and lowered profits and can necessitate layoff of key personnel with subsequent customer dissatisfaction and loss. The dangers from plant overcapacity are obviously more serious, and the job producer usually seeks one or more products of his own that can be produced in slack periods. These periods are inevitable if the producer intends to be responsive to customer needs.

Batch Production. Batch production is similar to job production except that the number of parts manufactured is large rather than small. This class is used both by product manufacturers and by vendor- or supplier-type companies who take advantage of a field of speciality and offer a production service. Specialties that are more familiar include forge shops, foundries, heat treaters, automatic lathe shops, and electroplaters.

The three subclasses of batch production are:

1. Semistandard or standard designs manufactured once in a large quantity
2. Standard designs manufactured intermittently at irregular intervals to meet varying production needs
3. Standard designs manufactured intermittently at regular intervals and often in fixed amounts

In the process industries, batch size is regulated by the capacity of the equipment. Equipment capacity is often originally established on the basis of optimum batch size. When the equipment is operated by a vendor-producer, however, the corresponding batch size is not optimum for all potential customers, and so there is obviously very little adjustment flexibility to meet customer needs.

The specialty batch producer also relies on customer satisfaction for repeat orders, but his customer often sets up his own proprietary facility to produce the desired product when the required quantities get large. Batch size is an important consideration, and regardless of whether a vendor or the product manufacturer is the producer, optimum batch size depends on the comparison of setup costs versus carrying costs to hold the batch in stock until used. The product manufacturer makes the batch-size decision. Continued use of a specialty vendor may well depend on his ability to meet tight and frequent delivery schedules. This is particularly true of automobile parts suppliers who function almost as an adjunct of the manufacturer.

As a result of the large production quantities, special tools and other production aids are frequently used in batch production. In many instances, tools used for one batch can be adapted or modified for use on another; therefore, tools are well designed and retained for future use. A skillful designer will incorporate capacity for such future use in the design of his tools if he foresees the production of similar parts or products. Technical manufacturing personnel are more prevalent in companies producing on a batch as compared to a job basis, because appreciable savings are possible from better methods selection, more extensive use of specially designed tools, and other industrial engineering techniques.

Continuous Production. In continuous production, the manufacturing equipment produces a single item or material uninterruptedly during all normal plant operation hours. A high output rate is usually characteristic of continuous production, which can only be supported by an equally high market consumption rate. The need for technical competence in selecting the productive process operations and nonproductive auxiliary functions becomes most important in this type of production. The need for maximum equipment utilization likewise becomes more critical so that high-speed work feeders, material handling equipment, and process control equipment are introduced to achieve better process efficiency. Quality control systems also make their appearance both to reduce process costs and to assure that the product will meet final inspection specifications.

The two subclasses of continuous production are:
1. Repetitive or mass production of a single item
2. Repetitive production of a material or assembly in a fixed sequence of steps

A single item may be produced in very large quantities, possibly by a battery of high-speed automatic machines. These machines are designed with the flexibility of producing a variety of sizes and shapes of a particular class of parts. Production machines such as broaches, four-slide wire benders, and cold headers are typical examples of equipment that can be tooled up to produce one part over and over. The only physical change needed to manufacture a different item is to use a different set of tools. This type of change has no discernable effect on the plant operation.

The most popular method of handling materials in the process industries is to flow them through pipes. Similarly, fast-moving parts appear to flow through highly mechanized repetitive fabrication production or assembly operations. This type of production is sometimes termed flow production because of this smooth and unchanging movement of material or parts. Flow production is extremely efficient, but minor product design changes may be prohibitively expensive.

MANUFACTURING PROCESS SYSTEMS

Men, materials, and machines are most frequently named as the company's resources. Business success comes from man's skillful use of machines to convert materials into salable products. Unless the proper manufacturing equipment is selected, the profit necessary for business survival and growth cannot be achieved, regardless of how good the management. It is understandable then that the phase of manufacturing system design known as process design is frequently approached with much caution and conservatism.

The use of a pilot plant to test the feasibility and practicality of chemical operations prior to building a full-scale plant has been mentioned. The pilot-plant objective is to eliminate all the risks, economic and technical, in the final plant before its construction. Mechanical methods of manufacture are typically used in the fabrication industries, however, and it is not really practical to employ pilot plants to test the manufacturing process design. Here it is normal practice to adhere to the well-known methods customarily used in the industry to make products similar to those under consideration. There are some rather distinct advantages in this approach. First and most obvious, the overall process has been proved successful in that other businesses are using it and making a profit. Second, these other businesses will have already trained supervisors, technicians, and plant personnel, some of whom may be hired as a work force cadre. Third, manufacturing process details and tricks of the trade will have already been worked out and, to the extent that this information is obtainable, need not be duplicated. Although the cost savings in this approach are apparent and may be high, they are difficult to estimate exactly.

On the other hand, the customary methods may be obsolete and should not be followed slavishly and blindly. The risk in trying something new in production methods can be minimized in various ways. For example, innovation is relative. Some companies have discovered that by visiting companies in quite unrelated industries, they learn of methods unknown in their own industry that they may adopt with considerable cost and time savings.

An excellent technique for logically and analytically designing the manufacturing process is to use a series of process charts. These charts are especially valuable because they are a pictorial presentation and permit a rapid visual perception of the entire manufacturing process plan. There are several types of charts which are discussed briefly in Chapter 8 of this Section.

INSTALLATION OF THE MANUFACTURING PROCESS

After the technical manufacturing process operation decisions are made, the next step is to plan the implementation of these decisions. In the fabrication industries, it is common practice to make this the plant layout phase and treat it as a purely technical specialist task. A creative and imaginative management, however, will recognize the need for careful manufacturing strategy planning at this point to assure achieving major company objectives.

Of the management decisions that should be made, two are particularly important to plant layout planning. The first is to define company growth objectives: Is the company size going to increase, decrease, or stay the same? The second is the product market plan: Is it a mass-consumption product at a low price, a premium product at a high price, or a product line at different quality and price levels? Although the need for these decisions is evident, it is often erroneously assumed that the plant layout specialist has all this information and has made the necessary provisions in his layout.

It is customary in the fabrication industries to designate three classical types of layout as line production, process, and fixed position, depending on the elemental consideration of how material moves through the plant during product manufacture.

Line Production Layout. The equipment, facilities, and a material handling system are combined into a production line which is arranged identically with the product manufacturing operation sequence. High-speed, automatic production machines are grouped closely together to minimize travel distances as the material moves steadily from station to station. The concept is essentially the same as that employed in the chemical process industries where continuous production is achieved by flowing materials through the unit operations and processes.

The very high cost to set up and tool for line production carries with it some severe technical and managerial problems. The most significant is the useful life of the line in terms of the quantity produced. An extreme example is the automotive industry which spends many millions to set up lines for a single make of car, but if the public likes the car and buys it, the cost per car is reduced to only a few dollars. Another important problem is maintenance to keep the line moving. It is customary to treat shutdown of a long production line as a major plant emergency with all emphasis on getting the line moving again. Also, the line must be fed continuously. Raw material and parts must be received on schedule from suppliers, flowing steadily into the plant just as the work flows steadily through it. An efficient line requires the highest level of technical thought and planning. Much care must be taken to make each station in the line as simple as possible both to minimize cost and maximize operational reliability. Complex and complicated special tools and work-transfer mechanisms should be avoided.

The high level of automated productive capacity afforded by a line production layout permits mass production at the lowest possible cost.

Process Layout. When a wide variety of products with different manufacturing operations is to be produced, individual product line layouts are impractical. A better solution is the grouping of similar pieces or families of production equipment into a single area in the plant. Each equipment area has a different process capability with the capacity and arrangement that the layout specialist has decided best suits the manufacturing sequence. Work proceeds from area to area in batches or lots in single containers or single collective groups.

As compared to the line production layout, the process layout requires less preliminary technical planning and much less investment, but the production capacity is also less. Single pieces of material handling equipment carry batches of work from one process area to the next and then sometimes back to the first area for a later step. The smooth flowing efficiency is missing. The small or medium lot sizes do not justify the expense of many special tools or other production aids. Setup costs per part must be kept low if unit costs are to be competitive, and numerically controlled equipment is particularly attractive in this regard. Fewer special tools and simpler setups mean that skilled or semiskilled labor rather than unskilled operators must be employed. Also, workers must be provided with detailed written process instructions to assure proper product quality and cost control. Malfunction of a single piece of equipment or failure of a vendor to deliver exactly on time seldom causes a plant crisis as either would do in line production.

As production quantities increase, it is advisable to consider at least a partial transition toward line production. Short lines for repetitive operations are frequently practical and should be used whenever possible to reduce costs.

Fixed-position Layout. The fixed-position layout is used only when some characteristics of the work make its movement from station to station impractical or inefficient. A familiar example is very large and heavy machinery that is unwieldy and inconvenient to move frequently. A less familiar example is the classified product kept in a single, closed work area for security. The fixed-position type of layout is the least common but is usually rather simple physically.

Nearly all the equipment used in this type of layout is either general purpose or portable, and neither kind has high productivity. Special tools are seldom used, and setup time per part is high because of the small lot sizes that normally exist. Detailed operation instruction sheets are seldom used. The highly skilled workers have the ability to plan their own work, and the sequence of operations may be altered depending on the availability of a piece of equipment. Each worker usually operates several different pieces of equipment and can perform several different related work functions. Work measurement with this type of layout is quite difficult. To some extent, management must rely on worker loyalty and self-supervision for both cost and quality control.

The combination of the inherent inefficiency of the layout, poor utilization of equipment, and high labor costs make this type of layout the most costly. If quantities permit, heavy material handling equipment mounted on tracks is used to change all or part of the operation to a variety of line production. A group of operations are performed at each station, and although hand tools are still prevalent, the restricted scope and repetitive nature of the work permit fewer skilled and more semiskilled workers. Work measurement becomes more practical and supervision less difficult. Some tooling also becomes feasible. All these combine to reduce the unit cost. This modified fixed-position—line production layout is used to make products like subway coaches and airplanes.

PRODUCTION MANAGEMENT SYSTEMS

Design of the manufacturing system must include some means of steering it toward the goal of efficient, low-cost production. The production management system provides this means by cross-linking the manufacturing system components into a useful, effective unit. Organizationally, production management is most commonly divided into production planning and production control. Manufacturing management is usually well aware of the utility of production control and normally takes an active part in frequently reviewing production status, production problems, and corrective actions with production personnel.

Manufacture for Inventory. Nearly all companies, including many who produce to individual customer order, manufacture wholly or partially to inventory. Any of the three major types of production—job, batch, or continuous—may be used. When manufacturing for inventory, it is necessary to anticipate customer demands, operate the plant at a rate that will permit meeting market requirements, yet minimize finished goods holding costs. If the demand rate fluctuates widely, it is probably more profitable to be out of stock occasionally and delay some shipments. The continuous type of production which is widely used in producing for inventory normally involves a high investment cost. In this case, equipment utilization is a dominant cost factor, and production management must focus attention on maintaining production without a break. Many companies, especially those in the process industries, operate equipment at virtually full capacity or shut it down completely. It is obviously impossible always to have a good match between plant capacity and customer demands, as for example, when sales are being increased in line with company growth objectives.

Standard items are also manufactured for inventory in job lots or batches, with correspondingly smaller quantities than in continuous production. The production control problems also tend to change with less emphasis on equipment utilization and more on scheduling, particularly vendor shipments. These standard items tend to be larger, more complex, and more expensive products that include forged or cast components, electric drive units and controls, and other items that often have long procurement lead times.

Manufacture for Custom Order. Continuous line production is not as common in fabrication for custom order as it is in fabrication for inventory. If the custom products differ in appearance rather than functional detail, it is possible to make a new line setup for each order at an acceptable cost. This is usually more feasible in the process industries and is commonly done. Fabricated products may be manufactured on a continuous production line with a mixture of some for custom order and the rest for inventory. The assembly of automobiles is a well-known example, where specially ordered cars of a specific color and accessory combination are intermingled with others intended for dealer stock. Production control is simplified by treating each car as an individual order.

A major control problem in custom order manufacture is maintaining the identity of the various customer orders and handling them in the right sequence to meet delivery promises.

Production management in custom manufacture is generally more difficult and complex than in manufacture for inventory so that higher skills are needed. Some custom producers prefer to keep their company size small enough to maintain direct operational control by top management. In some instances, hand-punched data cards may be adequate production control aids; in others, mechanized data processing systems may be required, or if the production volume and complexity warrant, electronic computer systems may be appropriate.

Operation research techniques and computerized data processing systems have been widely adopted by manufacturing organizations. The competent production manager recognizes that the added information permits him to make better decisions only because he is able to put his own good judgment to better use. He takes care to prevent the elegant but impersonal mathematics and computer printouts from replacing the personal rapport necessary for a smooth-running production system.

BIBLIOGRAPHY

Alderfer, E. B., and H. E. Michl, *Economics of American Industry*, McGraw-Hill Book Company, New York, 1957.

Begeman, M. L., and B. H. Amstead, *Manufacturing Processes*, John Wiley & Sons, Inc., New York, 1969.

Bethel, L. L., F. S. Atwater, G. H. E. Smith, and H. A. Stackman, Jr., *Industrial Organization and Management*, McGraw-Hill Book Company, New York, 1962.

Clauser, H. E. (ed.), *The Encyclopedia of Engineering Materials and Processes*, Reinhold Publishing Corp., New York, 1963.

Doyle, L. E., J. L. Morris, J. L. Leach, and G. G. Schrader, *Manufacturing Processes and Materials for Engineers*, Prentice-Hall, Inc., Englewood Cliffs, N.J., 1961.

Eilon, S., *Elements of Production Planning and Control*, The Macmillan Company, New York, 1962.

Greene, J. H., *Production Control: Systems and Decisions*, Richard D. Irwin, Inc., Homewood, Ill., 1965.

Moore, J. M., *Plant Layout and Design*, The Macmillan Company, New York, 1962.

Muther, Richard, *Practical Plant Layout*, McGraw-Hill Book Company, New York, 1955.

Russell, E. L., *Automated Manufacturing Planning*, Manufacturing Division Bulletin no. 107, American Management Association, New York, 1967.

Shreve, R. N., *The Chemical Process Industries*, 3d ed., McGraw-Hill Book Company, New York, 1967.

Thompson, S., *How Companies Plan*, Research Study no. 54, American Management Association, New York, 1962.

CHAPTER TWO

Information Systems Design

DAVID I. SCHERAGA *Consultant, Materials Information and Control Systems, Advanced Materials Service, General Electric Company, New York, New York*

This chapter will provide an overview of the information systems that are typically found in a manufacturing business, the steps in designing and implementing such systems, and the role that management must play in information systems work.

More than any other technology functioning in a business environment, information systems design is the one most enmeshed with the vital processes of business management. However, beyond their own personal information needs and those of their immediate organizational environment, most managers possess little knowledge of business information systems, how they are developed, how they are operated, and how to key them to effective decision making and control. That this situation ought to be otherwise in a modern business environment need hardly be argued. Management has a vital stake in information systems and an active role to play in their development. Consider some of the cogent reasons for this:

1. Information is the common denominator underlying the managerial functions of planning, organizing, implementing, and controlling.

2. To be effective, information systems must be closely coupled to the basic business objectives, policies, and strategies established by management. In other words, management sets the specifications for the information system by first structuring the business system.

3. By being forced to think through their information requirements, managers will gain valuable insight into the parameters most significant to the planning and control of their operations. Often, gaps in goal setting, policy determination, organizational planning, and the like will also become apparent.

4. Information systems have a major impact on the utilization of physical, human, and monetary resources, particularly in factory operations.

5. Information systems technology can and must be managed. As with any technology, an understanding of its capabilities and limitations will enable management better to direct and measure its contribution to business objectives.

6. An appreciation of information systems will make it easier to distinguish between information-oriented problems and those which have other underlying causes. (Are inventories too high because of poor stocking strategies or because of confusion and chaos in the inventory control information system?)

WHAT IS AN INFORMATION SYSTEM?

There are many ways of defining information systems. Heany[1] states that an information system is ". . . a set of well-defined rules, practices, and procedures by which men, equipment, or both, are to operate on given input so as to generate information satisfying specifications derived from the needs of given individuals in a given business situation." Others view information systems essentially as communications systems consisting of all the means, formal and informal, manual and mechanized, by which information flows through an organization. Still others consider the decision and control processes of a business to be its information system.

No matter how it is defined, an information system will always contain the following elements:

Input Data. These are the raw data which, in the process of passing through the system, will be transformed into useful information to satisfy the needs of an individual or group. Data can enter the system in a variety of forms and through a multiplicity of channels—paper forms, punched cards, telephone, telegraph, United States mail, and even face-to-face communication.

A File Structure. This is the means by which data are stored and indexed within the system. In manual systems, data files are usually maintained on file cards or in notebooks. In mechanized systems, the file structure can grow to quite complex proportions, requiring elaborate design and sophisticated computer hardware.

Procedural Logic. A procedure is a definable course of action consisting of one or more predetermined steps for accomplishing a task. In an information system, procedures are the steps which are followed in gathering information, feeding it to the system, storing it, manipulating it, analyzing it, making decisions, reporting results, and acting upon the system's output.

Obviously, there can be a wide range in the complexity of system procedures. In mechanized systems, much of the procedural logic is written into computer programs. However, even in such systems there is always a need for manual procedures to complement those that are computer executed.

Paperwork. Paperwork consists of the various types of documents that are needed to transmit, record, and report information. Documents can be handwritten, computer prepared, or both.

Information Processing Equipment. Just as machines exist for materials processing, so do they for information processing. The most obvious example, of course, is the computer. But equally important in their own fashion are

[1] Donald F. Heany, *Development of Information Systems*, The Ronald Press Company, New York, 1968, p. 7.

desk calculators, tabulating machines, telephones, typewriters, display terminals, and an entire array of other electromechanical equipment. The proper combination of equipment to choose for a particular information system will depend on the economics of the data processing involved.

Output. An information system needs some means of communicating results to its external environment. It does this through a variety of media, the most common of which is printed hard copy. However, systems can also output punched cards, magnetic tape, punched paper tape, cathode-ray tube displays, and even spoken messages.

THE INFORMATION SYSTEM OF A MANUFACTURING BUSINESS

Unfortunately, a universal information system applicable to any type of manufacturing business does not exist and probably never will. The information and control requirements of a job shop producing custom-designed products can hardly be expected to be the same as those of a flow shop producing standard designs to forecast. Furthermore, even when comparing businesses that are physically similar, differing managerial philosophies are apt to be found. Because the information system must ultimately be keyed to business objectives, policies, and operating strategies, it is bound to reflect the individual styles, backgrounds, and personal information needs of the management team. Notwithstanding this, it is possible to identify certain system elements which are common to virtually every manufacturing business. An understanding of these elements and how they interrelate will provide a framework for the design of customized information systems.

One view of a business information system shows how it can be layered in a fashion similar to an organization hierarchy. This view is depicted in Figure 2-1. At the top level are the executive control elements concerned with basic policy formulation, long-range planning, and overall measurement of the health of the enterprise. The next level down consists of the information elements serving that area often referred to as middle management. Here, decisions are made as to the specific products to be manufactured, the processes to be used in manufacturing, the rules by which physical resources will be allocated, market strategy, and the like.

Finally the level of operating systems involving day-to-day work is reached. As might be expected, this is where most information systems work has historically been done and will continue to be done. The bulk of a company's administrative expense and cost of goods sold occurs at this level.

The Major Operating Systems. Experience has shown that certain operating systems, each consisting of a set of logically related work elements, can readily be identified in a typical manufacturing business. These systems do not in all cases bear functional component names, such as engineering or inventory control, because they often cross functional lines.

Presale. Major work elements: market intelligence, proposal preparation, sales statistics analysis, advertising, long-range forecasting, short-range forecasting, and analysis of lost business.

Essentially, the work of this system is geared to market planning and to capturing the orders of potential customers.

Order Processing. Major work elements: order entry, editing and acknowledgement, pricing, credit checking, maintenance of open-order backlog, finished goods allocation, factory requisitioning, billing, and collection.

This system is the primary interface with the customer. Its main function

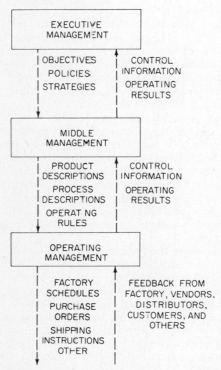

FIG. 2-1. A Business System Can Be Structured into Multiple Levels of Decision Making and Control.

is to accept orders and to interpret them into a form which is compatible with internal product design structures and practices.

Design and Documentation. Major work elements: technical information storage and retrieval, product documentation (preparation of bills of material, where-used lists, and the like), engineering/scientific computations, design automation, and reproduction work.

In build-to-forecast businesses, this system translates product plans into standard designs which state to manufacturing how the product is to be built and tested. In build-to-order businesses, it translates customer specifications into unique designs which will satisfy those specifications.

Production. Major work elements: production planning (master scheduling), raw and in-process inventory control, material requirements planning, operations planning, work measurement, detailed scheduling and loading, dispatching, shop paper preparation, production feedback reporting, and plant engineering and maintenance.

These activities constitute the bulk of day-to-day manufacturing information processing. They govern the ongoing physical processes in the factory. The production system is essentially a logistics system whose primary function is to plan and control material flow in response to customer demands. More than any other, it will determine how effectively the human, physical, and capital resources of the business are utilized.

Purchasing. Major work elements: quotation request and analysis, negotiation, vendor selection, purchase order preparation, purchase order control, incoming material traffic planning, receiving, incoming inspection and test, invoice matching and payment, vendor rating, and material cost analysis.

The purchasing system operates to satisfy the demands of the production system for vendor materials and is sometimes considered a part of that system. However, because of the high material content of most manufactured products, special emphasis is given to this system which can play more than a routine role in holding down the cost of goods sold.

Quality Control. Major work elements: quality operations planning, process capability analysis, reliability prediction and reporting, postsale quality analysis, vendor quality analysis, and factory quality data collection and reduction.

This system, too, might be considered part of the production system, but it is broken out because of the important role that quality plays in achieving and maintaining market position, not to mention its impact on manufacturing cost.

Distribution and Service. Major work elements: traffic planning, finished goods inventory control, warehousing, packing and shipping, installation and testing, and field service.

This system begins where the production system leaves off. It sees that the manufactured product is shipped to the customer in accordance with his instructions and is properly installed and serviced as needed.

Personnel. Major work elements: labor measurement, labor distribution, payroll, employee skills inventory, and candidate selection.

This system is concerned with the hiring, training, and development of employees and with the proper distribution of labor costs for control purposes.

Financial. Major work elements: cost accounting, general and tax accounting, budgets and measurements, evaluation of alternate business plans, and product cost structuring.

Historically, most systems work has occurred in this area, primarily because of the clerical savings to be gained and because much of the work was already well structured. Not surprisingly, the financial functions are usually the first to be mechanized in computer-based information systems.

THE MAIN-LINE INFORMATION SYSTEM

So far, only a static picture of operating level information systems has been presented. To bring it to life, the flow of information through the various elements must be depicted to illuminate the relationships which exist. Perhaps the best way to do this is to follow the course of events that are triggered as current demands (customer orders) and estimates of future demand (forecasts) are received. By so doing, the elements which are in the so-called "main line" of day-to-day information processing will necessarily be emphasized. This should by no means imply that elements not in the main line are unimportant or can be dispensed with. No one would argue against payroll processing, sales statistics analysis, or keeping plant maintenance records, even though these functions are not triggered each time demands enter the business.

The main-line system is the one closest to the physical resources of the business; it deals most intimately with the planning and control of material flow from vendor to customer and concomitantly with the allocation of manpower, factory equipment, storage space, and transportation equipment essential to this flow. Conceptually, this relationship is pictured in Figure 2-2. Here the main-line system is shown superimposed on the factory-warehouse complex.

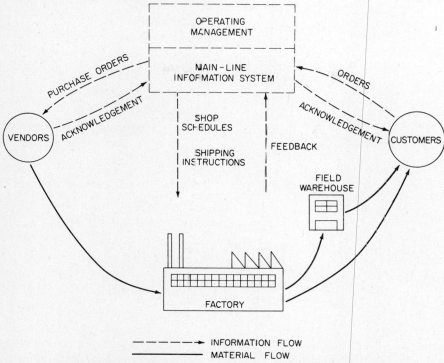

FIG. 2-2. The Main-line Information System Plans and Controls the Flow of Material and the Allocation of Resources to Satisfy Customer Demands.

Note that a series of information loops exist between the information system and the physical system. One half of each loop consists of a demand function (for example, purchase order, shipping instruction, factory schedule), while the other half consists of the feedback or control function. These demand-feedback loops are characteristic of all information systems controlling physical processes.

There also exists a network of information flow paths within the main-line system. This network, a simplified version of which is pictured in Figure 2-3, can grow to quite complex proportions. Successfully systematizing it and, where feasible, mechanizing it constitute two of the outstanding challenges in a manufacturing business.

Main-line information processing typically starts with the receipt of an order from the customer, district sales office, field warehouse, dealer, jobber, manufacturer's representative, or some combination of these.

The order processing function will validate the order to ensure that it contains all the requisite information, that the request date can be met, and that the products requested fall within the scope of the business.

If the incoming order has not already had a price assigned to it by marketing, it will be priced out together with a check of the customer's credit rating and his accounts receivable balance.

Next, a check is made to see whether the order can be satisfied from finished goods inventory. If it can, the system will mortgage the inventory and prepare the necessary documentation for shipping and billing. If not, the order

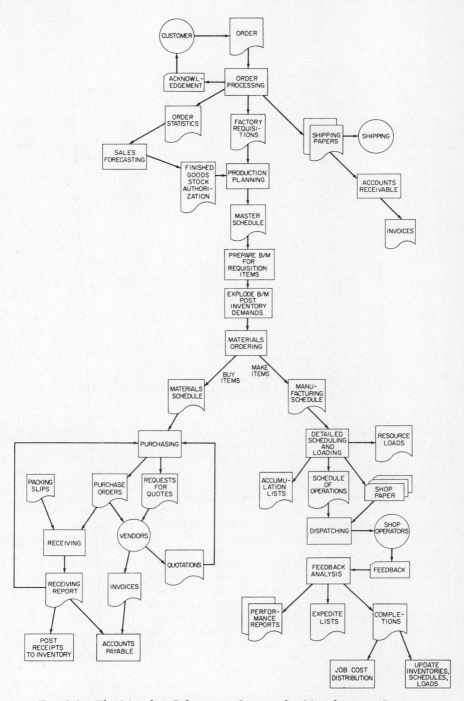

FIG. 2-3. The Main-line Information System of a Manufacturing Business.

will be entered into the backlog, and a requisition or stock replenishment order will be placed upon the factory. The factory will also respond with a delivery commitment, so that a proper acknowledgement can be given to the customer. Order processing will maintain the backlog and see that finished goods are properly allocated to open orders.

Factory requisitions and warehouse replenishment orders are routed to production planning which has top-level control of factory schedules. Basically, this function must decide on how to utilize available factory capacity to make the required number and variety of products at the lowest manufacturing cost. It sets the master production plan, and its importance cannot be overstated. The degree to which lower levels of shop scheduling, dispatching, and control succeed depends very much on the quality of the production planning job.

Production planning is not only concerned with scheduling the factory. In the case of products which require design engineering, it is the responsibility of production planning also to schedule and control the engineering and drafting components so that drawings and specifications are available when needed. Likewise, when new tools, jigs, fixtures, test and inspection equipment, operation planning, quality planning, and the like must be procured, production planning must make sure that the manufacturing engineering and quality control components supply these items to support plant schedules.

In build-to-order businesses or job shops, production planning is a continuous process which occurs each time an order or request for quotation is received. In businesses which produce essentially to forecast, production planning is done on a periodic basis, generally weekly or monthly, and consists primarily of resetting production line rates and product mix to bring finished goods inventories into line with levels authorized by marketing.

Most businesses, of course, work to a combination of sales forecasts and customer orders, as denoted by the dual information flow paths entering the production planning block in Figure 2-3. Though it is only performed periodically, short-range sales forecasting has been included in the main-line system because of the vital role it plays in establishing demand on the factory. In businesses producing a large variety of items for off-the-shelf delivery, a fairly elegant forecasting system using statistical techniques can be justified.

The master schedule generated by production planning is stated in terms of finished products and, occasionally, major subassemblies. Thus, the next step is to "explode" the master schedule to pick up the demands for lower level subassemblies, parts, and raw materials. To do this, a clearly delineated product structure is required, prepared by engineering, which states in unambiguous terms the component genealogy of the end product. This is commonly referred to as a bill of material. A simple product structure is shown in Figure 2-4.

If three of product A were required, the explosion process would yield gross requirements for six B, three $P1$, and twelve $P3$. Explosion continues until level 4, the lowest level in the structure, is reached, at which point the gross requirements for all items going into product A would be tabulated. What then remains is to match the gross requirements with the inventory status of these items. Where inventory can be applied, the gross requirements are reduced or netted out.

The time periods in which materials are needed are also calculated as part of the explosion process. In the simplest case, the dates are determined by working backward from the scheduled shipping date of the end product, using standard lead times for each material item in the product structure. A more sophisticated scheduling approach is to calculate the lead time as a func-

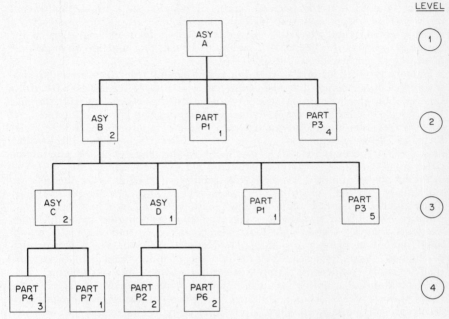

LEVEL

FIG. 2-4.   A Simple Product Structure Diagram.

tion of the quantity of each component required, taking into consideration the existing and projected status of shop loads. This method will naturally improve scheduling accuracy, but it requires considerably more computation. Consequently, it is not too practical for manual systems.

The material ordering phase of the system calculates economic order quantities for both make and buy items. The ordering logic revolves around the basic questions of when to order and how much to order, considering the net requirements pattern, on-hand inventories, open orders, shrinkage allowances, shelf life, maximum allowable inventories, the cost of carrying inventory, and a host of other factors. The decisions made at this point in the system will have a major impact on the magnitude of raw and in-process inventories. The output of the ordering function will be a materials schedule, which will be routed to purchasing, and a manufacturing schedule, which will enter the detail scheduling phase of the system.

In purchasing, requests for buy items will first be recorded. Where an established source of supply already exists, the purchase order can be placed immediately; otherwise, requests for quotations must be issued, followed in some cases by negotiation. The purchasing routine takes into account price breaks, special buys on material, vendor quality and delivery performance, the cost of incoming transportation, and the like. After orders are placed, it is purchasing's responsibility to control them and to expedite them, if necessary, to protect production schedules.

When material arrives at the plant and has cleared through incoming inspection, receiving will report back to purchasing so that open orders can be deleted. The receiving report also goes to accounting which will match it against invoices when they arrive. Approved invoices constitute authorization to issue pay warrants and to make the proper accounting distribution of costs.

Orders for make items (manufacturing schedule) must now be routed and detail scheduled through each shop operation. (In flow-type production, detail scheduling by operation is often unnecessary. Start and completion dates for the orders will generally suffice.) In calculating the operation cycle times, not only should setup and processing times be considered, but so also should move times, queuing, and miscellaneous delays. In fact, any manufacturing flow process chart will show that setup and processing times normally account for a minor portion of the total time it takes to move a job through the shop. It is unrealistic to detail-schedule without recognizing this.

It is likewise unrealistic to detail-schedule without considering the availability of labor and machine capacity. By scheduling to available capacity, more intelligent decisions can be made as to overtime, alternate routing, load leveling, and farm-out. Intelligent loading requires a thorough knowledge of the normal capacities of labor, tools, equipment, floor space, and the like, as well as accurate and timely data on current loads and the resource requirements of each new order being scheduled.

Up to this point, the main-line system has been involved only with the planning of work. Production does not actually begin until work is released from the system by the dispatching function. However, before work is released, the system should check to see if production resources and materials are available to complete the job. If so, dispatching must then decide upon the best job sequence for each work station. Alternative sequencing disciplines are numerous and each has its advantages and limitations. The main-line system should be designed to accommodate the sequencing rule that is best for each individual work station.

Because events on the factory floor seldom occur exactly as planned, the system requires a feedback element for control purposes. Feedback is also required to update the system's files as work is done. Completions must be posted to inventory, resource loads have to be relieved, order progress must be maintained, and new work must be made available for release. The frequency of feedback reporting depends on a number of factors including the rate of material flow through the shop, the performance of the shop in meeting its schedule commitments, the accuracy with which the aforementioned main-line planning functions are performed, and the reliability of shop processes. Because factory feedback involves extremely large quantities of data and is an error-prone process, feedback reporting should be kept to the minimum commensurate with adequate control. Electromechanical feedback equipment, though not inexpensive, can sometimes relieve the feedback burden.

DESIGNING THE INFORMATION SYSTEM

The process of developing and implementing an information system can be divided into twelve discrete steps:

1. Establish the need for systems work.
2. Conduct a feasibility study.
3. Obtain management approval.
4. Train the system's users.
5. Develop the overall design concept.
6. Design the system in detail.
7. Test the system.
8. Construct the data files.
9. Document the system.
10. Implement the system.
11. Evaluate the system.
12. Maintain the system.

Though these steps are listed sequentially, some may proceed in parallel with others, as shown on the task network of Figure 2-5. Furthermore, there can be considerable recycling through the network because of changing business conditions, fresh design insights, and human error.

Establish the Need for Systems Work. Though this should be obvious, it is surprising how often this step is haphazardly performed. It is at this point that management support, participation, and active leadership must be engaged if the system is to address real business needs. A common failing is to allow systems technicians to determine the need for new or revised systems; to do this is to abdicate a management responsibility.

Recognizing the need for systems work can materialize in many ways, both formal and informal. If the business performs systems work as an ongoing process and has taken the trouble to formulate a long-range systems plan, there will always be an array of potential projects from which to select. The problem then reduces to one of establishing project priorities so that resources may be properly allocated.

In other cases, systems work may result from the need to respond to a sudden change in business conditions as, for instance, when a competitor advertises a dramatic cut in delivery cycles. Immediately, management is forced to reevaluate its whole philosophy of doing business. Among the questions that will be asked are: Is our factory equipment outmoded? Should we stock subassemblies? Are our information systems adequate, and if not, how can they be redesigned to achieve shorter cycles?

Often the need for systems work exists just at or below the threshold of awareness, but is not acted upon until conditions become intolerable. A production control manager, for example, may be plagued by scheduling problems in his machine shop. He knows they must be tackled, but he has come to rely on expediting effort to achieve a fair degree of schedule realization. He accepts this as a way of life until expediting expense grows to unacceptable proportions and he decides to "straighten out the mess in the machine shop."

Common symptoms of the need for systems work in a manufacturing business are:

1. A high ratio of indirect to direct manufacturing costs
2. Poor delivery performance relative to promises made
3. Frequent stock-outs at all levels of inventory
4. No statistical techniques used in sales or inventory forecasting
5. Frequent changes to short-range sales forecasts
6. Excessive raw and in-process inventories
7. Long manufacturing cycle relative to the sum of setup and processing times
8. Much obvious paperwork
9. Long response time to inquiries on order and inventory status, or poor quality of status information
10. Frequent schedule changes
11. Low degree of component standardization between products
12. Unsatisfactory labor and machine utilization
13. Excessive confusion and stock obsolescence resulting from engineering changes
14. Poor or nonexistent labor standards
15. Excessive overtime
16. Low inventory turnover

Conduct a Feasibility Study. Once a firm statement of system objectives has been established by management, it remains to determine the technical and economic feasibility of the proposed systems work. This is the purpose

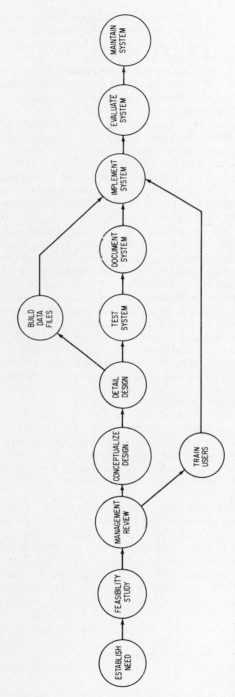

Fig. 2-5. Steps in Systems Development and Implementation.

of the feasibility study. The study team should consist of representatives from the information systems component and from all the functional areas affected. Whether they participate formally or not, the managers of the functional areas should also be party to the study. If the system is to be multifunctional, then the next higher level manager, at the very least, should participate. These are the men from whom the systems team will derive its authority should the project receive approval and on whom they will lean for support if troubles later arise.

On the technical side, the feasibility study will consider such things as the status of existing systems, the types and volumes of data that must be handled and stored, the response requirements of the system, system outputs, and the opportunities to employ data processing equipment. Just as important, the study will be concerned with human factors—the strengths and weaknesses of the people who will ultimately use and maintain the system, the basic health of the organizations involved, the willingness of people to accept a new system, and their desire to make it succeed.

On the economic side, a preliminary estimate of cost reduction and other anticipated benefits to be obtained must be made, together with an estimate of systems design, implementation, operating, and maintenance costs.

In the area of savings, management must resist the urge to justify systems work primarily on the basis of reduced clerical costs. Whereas substantial savings can be achieved in businesses with large pools of clerical labor and much obvious paper handling, such as banking, finance, and insurance, the major systems payoffs in manufacturing stem from better performance of operating work. Examples of such payoffs are reduction in inventory coupled with fewer stock-outs, reduced manufacturing cycles, improved delivery performance, improved utilization of factory resources, and increased share of the market. These are tangible benefits, and every attempt should be made during the feasibility study to translate them into economic terms. In value, they will far surpass direct clerical savings.

The feasibility study will produce two other important outputs. One is a preliminary set of specifications from which the actual system design can begin. The other is a project schedule, spelling out the important milestones and the people required to meet the schedule. It is useful to present the schedule in the form of a network diagram, as in Figure 2-5. This type of presentation highlights relationships between project activities and can be used later for project control purposes.

Obtain Management Approval. Before committing resources to a formal system project, a management review of the feasibility study is mandatory. Even if the findings are favorable, there is an array of higher order considerations which must be factored into the decision on whether or not to proceed. Some of the questions which must be asked are: Will organization changes required by the new system unduly disrupt operations and lower employee morale? Considering the financial demands of other projects, can we afford the kind of expenditure the new system will require? What are the elements of risk affecting the success of the project? Are product designs or process technology likely to change sufficiently before the system investment is recouped, so that a major redesign will be required? Do sufficient systems design and implementation skills exist in-house to conclude the project successfully? Not until satisfactory answers are obtained should approval be given to the systems project.

Management approval should denote an active commitment to the project. It should put everyone on firm notice that the project has solid management backing.

Train the System's Users. It may seem strange that this step should appear even before the detail design of the system has begun. However, in many situations where new or revised systems are being planned, it is necessary to condition the operating people (and their managers) for the changes which are to come. Conditioning can take different forms. Where a computer is involved for the first time, it may be desirable to offer an introductory course in computer technology to arrest irrational fears. There is also a selling and communications job to do regarding any new system. People have to be emotionally prepared for it and must be made aware not only of its expected benefits, but also of anticipated changes in their work loads. Training in advance of system design also provides an opportunity to enlist the aid of the system's users in the design process that is to follow. Users will be responsible for supplying many of the data on which the systems analyst will base his design decisions. If their confidence can be gained, they can also be an excellent source of ideas.

Needless to say, training and communication should continue until the system has been installed and is operating smoothly. Before implementation, all involved employees must be thoroughly indoctrinated as to their responsibilities. This is particularly critical with regard to preparing input data. If poor information enters the system, some of it is bound to be operated upon. Not only is the data processing effort wasted, but worse, incorrect results will be fed into the business mainstream. Painstaking care must be taken to explain the meaning of each item of input, the proper way of filling out input forms, the importance of supplying data on time, and the importance of keeping the data in the system's files current.

Likewise, employees must be instructed on how to read and interpret system outputs, regardless of the form they take. They should know how to recognize irrational or unreasonable output and should be counseled explicitly as to when they may override system results.

Develop the Overall Design Concept. This is the conceptualization phase of systems work, probably the most creative of all. Here the basic approach to meeting the system's objectives will be mapped out. All further detail design (and programming in a computerized system) will be keyed to the procedural framework established in this step. The basic costs of detail design, implementation, and systems operation will also be determined here. For these reasons, it is desirable to assign the most experienced and creative people to this phase of the project and to have functional operating people work as part of the design team.

As with any creative process, systems conceptualization cannot be reduced to a formal procedure. Each designer will employ the approach with which he is most comfortable. However, it is possible to identify some of the tools and techniques that systems designers use, not only in this step, but also in steps 1 and 6 (p. 3-31). They are:

Organization surveys	Process flow charting
Statistical sampling	Collation charting
Interviewing	(redundancy charting)
Work simplification	Logic structuring
Simulation modeling	Electronic data processing

At the conclusion of this phase, the system's design can be expressed in terms of top-level information flow charts, a file structure showing the major record types, their basic contents and relationships, and a broad description of system inputs and outputs.

Design the System in Detail. Detail design is a continuing refinement of the work begun in the last step (p. 3-31). If the system is a large one, the design effort is commonly divided among less experienced analysts, the senior designer retaining overall project control. During this phase, the system will be sufficiently detailed so that its procedural logic is explicit enough for manual execution if the system is to be manual, or capable of being coded into computer programs if the system is to be mechanized. The various forms, punched cards, and other system inputs and outputs will also be detailed.

If the system is to be mechanized, the designer will specify the file storage media, such as magnetic tapes, discs, or drums, and any specialized equipment which may be needed, such as Flexowriters, data communications equipment, and shop feedback terminals.

Test the System. Murphy's law, "Anything that can go wrong, will go wrong" is well known to systems designers. For this reason, they take every precaution to detect flaws before a system becomes operational. Considerable effort is expended in three types of testing—desk checking, program debugging, and systems testing. As the name implies, desk checking involves manually reviewing each step of a system's logic—its file structure, inputs, and outputs. The designer will often run test data through the system to spot logic errors, omissions, or impractical methods of processing.

Program debugging and systems testing are normally associated with mechanized systems. Program debugging must be done to ensure that the programmer has properly encoded the designer's logic. Though individual programs may test out satisfactorily, their performance when run together as a system must still be determined. This is the function of systems testing.

Construct the Data Files. As previously mentioned, one of the elements of an information system is its file structure. This must be in place before the system can operate. Constructing the system files can be a very time-consuming and expensive task, particularly if many of the data are being gathered for the first time. Even when data are available, they will often be obsolete and of little value. It is also common to find considerable redundancy, inconsistency, and gaps in business files.

Because of the effort normally required to construct files, this work should begin as soon as possible in parallel with systems design.

Document the System. Documentation is the key to communicating the system's design and operation to users, to other systems designers, and in the case of mechanized systems, to programmers and computer operators. Two types of documentation are needed. The first is oriented to systems and programming people and includes a narrative description of the system, top-level information flow charts, detailed flow charts, file layouts, input-output formats, program listings, audit and control procedures, and instructions for operating any data processing equipment which may be called for. These are usually compiled into what is called a systems manual. The second type of documentation is oriented to the system's users and should include an overall description of the system, its objectives and expected benefits, the role each individual is to play in the operation of the system, and explicit instructions for preparing data and for handling system outputs. It is good practice to incorporate these into a user's manual.

Implement the System. By this stage, training and documentation should be complete. The only question that remains is one of strategy. Should the new system be run in parallel with the old one until its operation is secure, or should it immediately replace the old system? The first approach is favored by conservatives and may have considerable merit if there are substantial risks associated with the new system. However, this approach has the drawback of providing a crutch for people and thereby possibly delaying cutover to the new system. Furthermore, in cases where the old and new systems are computer oriented, there may be insufficient computer capacity to handle both.

The "go for broke" or immediate replacement approach is favored by this author. Risk can be minimized by devoting sufficient effort to systems testing, training, and documentation.

Regardless of which approach is taken, management must be prepared for a certain amount of confusion and system debugging during the early stages of operation. This is to be expected and should not be discouraging. (Unfortunately, this is also the time when critics who have been waiting for the first mistake are the most vocal.) Just as with machine tools, it takes a certain amount of time to tune a system up to its peak performance.

Evaluate the System. After the system has achieved steady-state operation and periodically thereafter, it is wise to measure its performance. Is it meeting the initial objectives established by management? Are these objectives still valid? Have the expected payoffs occurred? Are operating costs in line with those projected? Is the system being used as its designers intended?

A well-engineered system will also have certain characteristics which should be sought for in the evaluation.

1. Its response capabilities will be adequate to meet the information needs of its environment; that is, the system's users should at no time be delayed waiting for information.
2. There will be harmony between the human and mechanized elements of the system. Everyone will be properly trained for his job and will know how it fits into the overall system.
3. Standard forms will be in use, and operating procedures will be well documented and maintained.
4. Exception reporting principles will be used extensively, eliminating the need for large volumes of hard copy.
5. Information, once having entered the system, will not be recopied in its original form over and over; information files will contain a minimum of redundant data.
6. Reliability of the system will be high; breakdowns will be infrequent and of short duration.
7. The system will adapt to changes in business conditions without requiring major redesign; changes in procedures, data, or logic will be made without confusion and without disrupting production.

Maintain the System. A business does not operate in a static environment. Internal and external factors are always in a state of flux—market tastes shift, product and process technology evolves, and government passes new laws. Change, naturally, also impacts on information systems. For this reason, the maintenance of an ongoing system never really ceases. Unfortunately, the maintenance function, like plant maintentance, is easy to neglect until trouble strikes. The price of neglecting system maintenance will be a slow widening of the gap between system capabilities and user information needs. This will generally be accompanied by a progressive deterioration of the system's data files. Eventually, output quality drops to the point where the user will find ways to work around the system. A good maintenance program coupled with periodic evaluation should prevent this.

ORGANIZING FOR INFORMATION SYSTEMS WORK

Because of the financial character of most early information systems, the information systems component is most often found in the financial function.

There is nothing sacred or inviolable about this. In fact, as the focus of systems development shifts toward operating work and cross-functional systems, a good argument can be made for eliminating the functional affiliation of the systems organization.

The location of the systems group also depends upon the degree of company decentralization. Highly decentralized companies typically place systems groups in each of their operations on the presumption that systems problems are best solved at the local level. On the other hand, this makes the development of common systems very difficult. It is not unusual to find a multiplicity of systems performing essentially the same functions within the same company, an extremely wasteful practice. To counter this, many decentralized companies will also have a corporate systems group to provide overall guidance, counsel, and evaluation of systems planning.

Regardless of how systems work is organized, it is important that it be conducted jointly with functional people. A blending of systems talent with business know-how is the ideal team mix. There are several ways to achieve this:

1. Rotate functional people through the information systems organization. These assignments can be of the "detached duty" variety, or long-term, if advantageous.
2. Assign functional people to work full time as coequal members of a joint systems/functional project team.
3. Hire systems designers to work directly for the functional organization, either to do the entire systems job themselves or to work with people from the systems component.
4. Appoint functional liaison men to work on an "as needed" basis with the systems team.

It is also well to remember that neither systems nor functional responsibilities cease after system implementation. They continue indefinitely if the system is to be properly maintained.

BIBLIOGRAPHY

Chestnut, Harold, *Systems Engineering Tools*, John Wiley & Sons, Inc., New York, 1965.

Heany, Donald F., *Development of Information Systems*, The Ronald Press Company, New York, 1968.

Information—A Scientific American Book, W. H. Freeman and Company, San Francisco, 1966.

Orlicky, Joseph A., "Designing a System for Production and Inventory Control," *Automation*, February, 1967, pp. 74–78.

Prince, Thomas R., *Information Systems for Management Planning and Control*, Richard D. Irwin, Inc., Homewood, Ill., 1966.

Putnam, Arnold O., E. Robert Barlow, and Gabriel N. Stilian, *Unified Operations Management*, McGraw-Hill Book Company, New York, 1963.

Rosove, Perry E., *Developing Computer-based Information Systems*, John Wiley & Sons, Inc., New York, 1967.

Sisson, Roger L., and Richard G. Canning, *A Manager's Guide to Computer Processing*, John Wiley & Sons, Inc., New York, 1967.

Unlocking the Computer's Profit Potential, McKinsey & Company, New York, 1968.

Wilson, Ira G., and Marthann E. Wilson, *Information, Computers, and Systems Design*, John Wiley & Sons, Inc., New York, 1965.

CHAPTER THREE

Process Engineering

BENJAMIN W. NIEBEL *Professor and Head of Department of Industrial Engineering, The Pennsylvania State University, University Park, Pennsylvania.*

Process engineering encompasses selecting the processes to be used in the most advantageous sequence, selecting the specific equipment to be employed, selecting the tooling to be used, and specifying the locating points of the special tools.

This chapter discusses methods of selecting the best operations and their sequence for manufacturing a given component or product; locating-point fundamentals; the place of process engineering in various types of industry; and securing and developing competent process engineers.

IMPORTANCE OF PROCESS ENGINEERING

Unless a product can be produced at a price that will attract the potential customer, it is as much a failure as though the design were incapable of correct function. Thus, process engineering is important to the successful operation of any business or industry. Some type of product or service is the output of all businesses; and in a dynamic society, the nature of existing products is continually changing and new products are being developed as a result of ongoing industrial research and development programs.

Process engineering helps assure that the best methods are used for current products as well as for those that are planned for the future. Process engineering is a systematic procedure for determining the best process or processes for producing a part or performing a service and for specifying the operation sequence and special tooling required, giving careful consideration to the parameters of quality, quantity, cost, and date of delivery.

Timing of Process Engineering. Process engineering should take place before the completion of the final engineering drawings for a new design. It logically should begin after the initial product design sketches and testing of prototype models have been completed. By scheduling process engineering at this stage, the final product design will mate the functional design to the selected manufacturing processes, and the product will be well designed for efficient manufacture. By performing process engineering in conjunction with and before the completion of the final product drawings, much engineering and production time will be saved. Only after process engineering has been carried out can the final design be completed, and equipment, material, and tooling be ordered.

PROCESS ENGINEERING FUNDAMENTALS

Process engineering involves:
1. Selecting the most advantageous process to be used in the best sequence
2. Selecting the most advantageous specific equipment to be used
3. Selecting the special tooling required
4. Specifying the locating points for standard or special tooling

To select the most advantageous manufacturing method, process engineering must consider all available processes. In every enterprise, there usually are several ways to make a part. One way is the best for a given set of conditions. The process engineer must determine the best process. Therefore, he should have information of available processes within his organization as well as those located elsewhere which are capable of competing with company processes.

A manufacturer seldom finds it economical to maintain all possible processes. Usually, outside suppliers provide a source of alternative processes that should be considered. In considering an outside source, however, the manufacturer must know the potential of any outside supplier's process. Effective process engineering will provide such knowledge.

One of the most difficult decisions in process analysis is whether to make a part or to purchase it. Often the supplier's cost is less than the factory cost of the part; in this case, it is generally economical to purchase from the supplier. However, the department may have an overhead charge which has no relation to the manufactured part. If this expense is disregarded, the factory cost may be favorable. Given the same equipment and materials and an overhead charge applicable to the product, the shop should be able to meet competition. Modern process engineering encourages competition among divisions and encourages suppliers to bid in order to improve products and reduce costs. Good accounting practice should avoid unrealistic accounting procedures that distort costs and cause unfair competition.

Limited quantities of standard products such as bearings, machine screws, cotter pins, or lockwire usually can be purchased at less than the cost of manufacturing them. Likewise, it may be more economical to procure specialized processes such as plating and heat treating at a supplier's plant.

CLASSIFYING THE PRODUCTION EQUIPMENT

No one person can retain mentally all the information that it is necessary to have to do a first-class job of process engineering in a plant which manufactures a broad variety of products. Thus, it is necessary to identify the pertinent information needed for process engineering for all the capital production equipment in a company's plant and also for competitive equipment that is available in suppliers' plants.

Equipment may generally be classified into one of six categories:
1. Basic process forming facilities
2. Secondary operation facilities
3. Joining and assembly facilities
4. Decorative and protective coating facilities
5. Inspection and test facilities
6. Packaging facilities

Each of these six classes of equipment should be coded by an alphabetical, numerical, or mnemonic symbol. For example, facilities used in basic forming processes might be coded with the letter "A," facilities for performing secondary operations the letter "B," equipment for joining and assembly the letter "C," decorative and protective coating facilities the letter "D," inspection and test facilities the letter "E," and packaging facilities the letter "F."

Each piece of equipment that is used by the company or that may have application in the manufacture of the company's products should be given an identifying number on a 5″ x 8″ process engineering facility card. Color coding can also be used to identify further the class of equipment described on the process engineering card. For example, light blue cards may be used for basic process forming facilities, white cards for secondary operation facilities, salmon cards for joining and assembly facilities, and so on.

Information that should be included on the process engineering card includes: equipment size and capacity, feed capabilities, power capability, special tooling that is available, condition of the equipment, the overhead rate assigned to the equipment, the base rate of the operator assigned to the equipment, the current location of the equipment, the surface finish that is typically produced by the equipment, and the like. A typical process engineering facility card for a 17-ton punch press is shown in Figure 3-1. Note that this process engineering card is filed by its code number. This code number, B 12 017 03 11, carries the following significance. The Prefix B indicates that this equipment is used in conjunction with secondary operations. This is also indicated by the fact that the card is white. The first two digits, 12,

---

FACILITY __V. & O. #2 Press__ INVENTORY NO. __11-2187__ CODE NO. __B 12 017 03 11__

DESCRIPTION __Inclinable open-back press; width of opening in back 9-1/2 in.; inclination − 28°;__

height from bed to center of shaft − 31 in.; bed area − 12-3/4 x 17-1/2 in.; shut height − 9 in.;

thickness of bolster − 1-1/2 in.; stroke − 2 in.; force near bottom of stroke − 17 tons;

thickness of steel blanks cut − 1/16 in.; diameter of blanks cut − 5 in.

FEEDS __Equipped with roll feed; hitch feed available__

SPEEDS __360 rpm; 6:1 ratio of gearing; 60 strokes per min.__

H.P. __1-1/2, 1200 rpm__

OBTAINED __9/69__ FROM __V. & O. Press Company__ ORIGINAL COST __$6000__

MACHINE OVERHEAD RATE __$4.00/hr.__ OPERATOR RATE __$3.60/hr.__

PRESENT LOCATION OF EQUIPMENT __Dept. 11 − two; Dept. 22 − one__

REMARKS __This equipment has been used to produce shells for SK-1410.__

FIG. 3-1. Process Engineering Facility Record.

indicate that the equipment is in the punch press family. The following three digits are used to provide an approximation of the size or the capacity of the facility. In this case, the 017 indicates a 17-ton press. The next two digits indicate the number of those presses in the plant; the 03 shows that there are three. The final two digits provide information concerning the number of the department where the equipment currently is located, in this case department 11.

CONSTRAINTS AFFECTING PROCESS SELECTION

The principal constraints that must be considered in the selection of a given basic process to bring raw material more closely to the specifications of a functional design are:

1. Type and condition of raw material used
2. Size of raw material that the equipment can handle
3. Geometrical configurations that the equipment is capable of imparting to the raw material
4. Tolerance and surface finish capabilities of the equipment
5. Quantity of finished parts needed and their delivery requirements
6. Economic analysis of the process

Material as a Process Constraint. Not all materials can be processed economically by a given manufacturing method. Thus the material specified by the functional designer limits to some extent the processes available for production parts. For example, ferrous parts generally are not die cast or plaster mold cast. Again it usually is not economical to extrude intricate sections of ferrous materials. Some materials are more easily welded than others. Thermosetting plastics are not injection molded, and it usually does not pay to compression-mold thermoplastic materials in large quantities.

Because the ability to choose the best material is limited by the design engineer's knowledge of materials and because it is difficult to choose the most satisfactory material on account of the great variety available, many times it is possible for the process engineer to suggest a better and more economical material for an existing design.

The process engineer is in an excellent position to suggest using a material that is less expensive or easier to manufacture, yet which will meet product specifications.

Size as an Equipment Constraint. Every process has a size or capacity constraint which can be on either a maximum basis, minimum basis, or both a maximum and minimum basis. Thus every facility has a limitation where it would be impractical or impossible to use the equipment because the work is either too large or too small.

Such limitations can be based on:

1. Dimensional limitations of the facility, such as the swing on a lathe or the size of a furnace for heat treating or stress relieving
2. Dimensional limitations of the perishable tooling associated with the facility, such as the minimum- or maximum-size drill that the chuck can accommodate
3. Power limitations such as the tonnage available in a blanking press or the current-carrying capacity in welding equipment
4. Size and capacity limitations resulting from the process, such as the stroke of a press for deep drawing

This limitation information should be recorded on the process engineering facility record.

Geometry as an Equipment Constraint. All processes have some geometry limitations. For example, in metal forging, the hot plastic metal can be moved only a limited distance before folding or cracking will take place. In considering basic forming processes, the following geometry classifications can be used for metallic items:

Class 1. Solid or partly hollow rounds involving one or more outside diameters along one axis. If partly hollow, the depth of the hollow is less than two-thirds the diameter of the hollow. Class 1 geometry, illustrated by Figure 3-2*a*, can usually be achieved or approximated by such basic processes as casting, forging, powder metals, extrusion, and screw machining within specific size constraints. It would not apply to such basic processes as stamping, press forming, spinning, roll forming, or impact extrusion.

Class 2. Partly hollow or hollow rounds involving one or more outside diameters along one axis. If partly hollow, the depth of the hollow is more than two-thirds the diameter of the hollow. Class 2 geometry, illustrated by Figure 3-2*b*, can usually be produced or approximated by casting, extrusion, impact extrusion, roll forming, powder metals, and screw machining with due regard for size constraints. Class 2 geometry usually is not economically achieved by forging, cold heading, spinning, or press forming.

Class 3. Solid or partly hollow shapes other than rounds, such as square, triangular, or octagonal, including one or more cross-sectional areas along one axis. Class 3 geometry, illustrated by Figure 3-2*c*, can usually be achieved or approximated by the basic processes of casting, forging, cold heading, extrusion, powder metals, electroforming, and rough machining from mill stock. This geometry is usually not economically produced by impact extrusion, roll forming, stamping and press forming, spinning, or screw machining.

Class 4. Partly hollow or hollow solids other than rounds, involving one or more cross-sectional areas along one axis. The depth of the hollow is more than two-thirds the major diameter of the hollow. Class 4 geometry, illustrated by Figure 3-2*d*, or its approximation usually can economically be achieved by casting, extrusion, impact extrusion, roll forming, powder metals, electroforming, and rough machining from mill stock. It usually cannot be economically achieved by forging, stamping and press forming, spinning, and automatic screw machining.

Class 5. Bow-shaped concentric geometry. Class 5 geometry, illustrated by Figure 3-2*e*, or its approximation can usually be readily produced by casting, forging, impact extrusion, press forming, powder metals, spinning, and automatic screw machining. It usually is not economically adapted to cold heading, extrusion, and roll forming.

Class 6. Dish-shaped nonconcentric geometry. The processes that usually can be considered for class 6 geometry, illustrated by Figure 3-2*f*, include casting, forging, impact extrusion, powder metals, press forming, electroforming, and rough machining from mill stock. Those processes that usually do not apply include cold heading, extrusion, upset forging, spinning, and automatic screw machining.

Class 7. Flat shapes with or without configurations. The flat shape may be square, rectangular, triangular, or any other geometrical pattern. Although class 7 geometry, illustrated by Figure 3-2*g*, can be cast or forged, it usually is produced as a stamping. Of course, as in every case, consideration must be given to size constraints.

Class 8. Flanged geometry. As in the case of class 7 geometry, class 8, illustrated in Figure 3-2*h*, is produced in lighter sections most readily in press operations, although in heavy sections it can be economically produced as a casting, forging, or weldment.

Class 9. Complex geometry, characterized by unsymmetrical shapes.

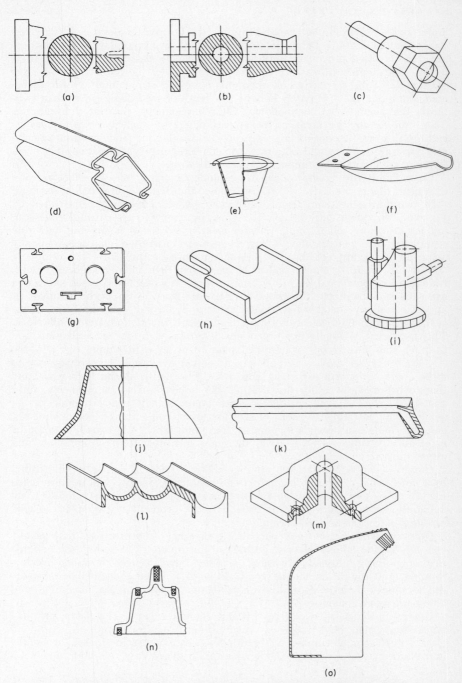

Fig. 3-2. Classes of Primary Operation Geometry. (a) Class 1; (b) Class 2; (c) Class 3; (d) Class 4; (e) Class 5; (f) Class 6; (g) Class 7; (h) Class 8; (i) Class 9; (j) Class 10; (k) Class 11; (l) Class 12; (m) Class 13; (n) Class 14; (o) Class 15.

Class 9 geometry, illustrated by Figure 3-2*i*, is usually obtained from one of the casting methods or else made up as a weldment.

For plastics, geometry will involve different limitations than for metals. From the standpoint of primary geometry classification, the following classes will apply to both thermosetting and thermoplastic plastics.

Class 10.   Cup-shaped geometry, either concentric or nonconcentric.   Class 10 geometry, illustrated by Figure 3-2*j*, can be readily produced by compression molding, transfer molding, injection molding, casting, cold molding, or thermoforming, and is usually not adaptable to blow molding or extrusion.

Class 11.   Continuous geometrical forms such as rods, tubes, filaments, films, and simple shapes.   Class 11 geometry, illustrated by Figure 3-2*k*, is produced only by extrusion.

Class 12.   Simple outlines involving plain cross sections with wall thicknesses under $\frac{1}{2}$ inch.   Class 12 geometry, illustrated by Figure 3-2*l*, is usually economically produced by compression molding, injection molding, casting, or cold molding.   It is not economically produced by transfer molding, extrusion, thermoforming, or blow molding.

Class 13.   Simple outlines involving plain cross sections with wall thicknesses over $\frac{1}{2}$ inch.   Class 13 geometry, illustrated by Figure 3-2*m*, is usually produced by transfer molding, injection molding, casting, or cold molding, and usually is not economically made by compression molding, extrusion, thermoforming, or blow molding.

Class 14.   Complex shapes, intricate sections, thin or heavy walls, with or without fragile inserts.   Class 14 geometry, illustrated by Figure 3-2*n*, is usually economical to produce by either transfer molding, injection molding, or casting.

Class 15.   Thin-walled and bottle-shaped.   Class 15 geometry, illustrated by Figure 3-2*o*, is usually produced by the blow molding process.

As in the case with primary operations, so is it that secondary operations are constrained by geometry.   In the fabrication of metal components, twelve geometrical classifications have been identified, which permit the assignment of any surface into a specific classification.   These twelve classifications (which should not be confused with the classes of primary operation geometry) with typical pictorial illustrations are shown by Figure 3-3.

Tolerance and Surface Finish as an Equipment Constraint.   Just as every process has a geometry constraint, so does every process have a limitation on the tolerance and surface finish that it is capable of achieving under normal operation.   For example, a $\frac{1}{2}''$ drill will not consistently hold a 0.002″ tolerance, whereas a $\frac{1}{2}''$ reamer can consistently hold this tolerance and even a closer tolerance.   Again a 20-microinch finish is not consistently held by turning on a lathe; yet this finish may be consistently held by grinding.

A press brake formed section will have a wider piece-to-piece accuracy than the same section that is roll formed.

The process engineer should be familiar with tolerance and finish capabilities of the facilities within his plant.   He also should have a knowledge of the tolerance capabilities of the basic forming processes and competitive facilities in suppliers' plants.

Tables 3-1 and 3-2 provide typical tolerances and surface finishes that can be expected in producing medium-sized work (work between 5 and 25 pounds).

Several factors influence the tolerance capability of a process.   Equipment that is old and poorly maintained may have substantial wear in its spindle

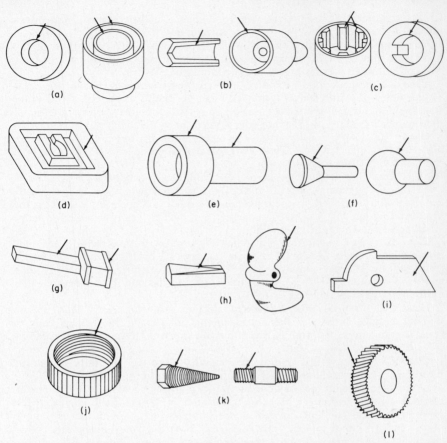

FIG. 3-3. Classes of Secondary Operation Geometry. (*a*) Class 1: Circular Inside Geometry—One Diameter; (*b*) Class 2: Circular Inside Geometry—More than One Diameter; (*c*) Class 3: Noncircular Inside Geometry—One Cross Section; (*d*) Class 4: Noncircular Inside Geometry—More than One Cross Section; (*e*) Class 5: Circular Outside Geometry—One Diameter; (*f*) Class 6: Circular Outside Geometry—More than One Diameter; (*g*) Class 7: Noncircular Outside Geometry—Uniform Cross Section; (*h*) Class 8: Noncircular Outside Geometry—Nonuniform Cross Section; (*i*) Class 9: Flat Surface Finishing; (*j*) Class 10: Inside Threading; (*k*) Class 11: External Threading; (*l*) Class 12: Gear Cutting.

bearings. This will result in loss of accuracy in holding the work or the tool, with resulting widening tolerance capability.

Environmental factors can cause substantial change in tolerance capabilities. For example, equipment producing heavy vibrations when operating close to another facility can cause substantial variation in tolerance in that facility.

Dull and improperly ground cutting tools will have a pronounced effect upon both the tolerance being maintained and the surface finish.

Quantity as a Process Selection Constraint. The quantity of parts required and the delivery schedule associated with the total quantity requirements have a pronounced effect on the process to be selected. Where quantity re-

TABLE 3-1. Typical Tolerances and Surface Finishes Maintained with Primary Process Equipment

Basic processes	Expected tolerance, inches	Expected surface finish, micro-inches	Remarks
Die casting	0.006	75	0.014 inch across parting line
Investment casting	0.010	125	
Permanent molding	0.030	150	
Plaster molding	0.016	125	
Shell molding	0.016	125	0.024 inch across parting line
Sand casting	0.030	250	0.075 inch across parting line
Drop forging	0.030	150	
Press forging	0.020	150	
Cold heading	0.006	100	0.125 inch on length
Extrusion	0.008	125	0.024 inch on flatness
Impact extrusion	0.008	150	
Roll forming	0.006	100	
Stamping and press forming	0.004	150	
Powder metals	0.006	100	
Automatic screw machining	0.004	100	
Electroforming	0.002	75	
Turret lathe	0.004	100	
Rough machining from mill stock	0.004	100	
Upset forging	0.036	175	
Spinning	0.030	125	
Compression molding	0.005	50	
Transfer molding	0.005	50	
Injection molding	0.005	50	
Extrusion	0.005	50	
Casting (plastics)	0.005	50	
Cold molding	0.008	50	
Thermoforming	0.010	50	
Blow molding	0.008	50	
Machining from stock (plastics)	0.006	100	

quirements are low, it will be economically advisable to select processes involving low tool and setup costs. Conversely, where quantity requirements are high, more efficient processes involving more elaborate tooling and longer setup times may be considered. Once material, size, and geometry constraints have been evaluated, those processes that qualify should be studied from the standpoint of quantity requirements. There generally is a minimum quantity that is required before a process can be economically considered.

Closely related to the quantity requirement is the economics of the process itself. The process engineer must be concerned with total cost; thus he considers the total cost of all competing processes. Perhaps the most advantageous method for this type of study is with the break-even or crossover chart. This chart presents those quantities below which a certain process offers economic advantage and above which a different process is more economical.

TABLE 3-2. Typical Tolerances and Surface Finishes Maintained with Secondary Process Equipment

Secondary process	Expected tolerance, inches	Expected surface finish, micro-inches	Remarks
Drilling (size 61–80)	+0.001	80	
Drilling (size 30–60)	+0.002	80	
Drilling (size 1–29)	+0.003	80	
Drilling (size ¼″–½″)	+0.005	100	
Drilling (size ½″–¾″)	+0.007	125	
Drilling (size ¾″–1″)	+0.009	150	
Drilling (size 1″–2″)	+0.011	200	
Boring (small inside diameters)	±0.005	80	
Boring (medium inside diameters)	±0.001	100	
Boring (large inside diameters)	±0.003	150	
Reaming (to ¼″)	±0.0005	80	
Reaming (above ¼″)	±0.0007	80	
Honing (small work)	±0.0001	15	
Honing (medium work)	±0.0002	20	
Honing (large work)	±0.0003	30	
Lapping (small work)	±0.00005	5	
Lapping (medium work)	±0.00007	7	
Lapping (large work)	±0.00010	10	
Broaching (small work)	±0.0005	50	
Broaching (medium work)	±0.0007	75	
Broaching (large work)	±0.0010	100	
Piercing (small work)	±0.003	150	
Piercing (medium work)	±0.004	150	
Piercing (large work)	±0.005	150	
Superfinishing (small work)	±0.00005	5	
Superfinishing (medium work)	±0.00007	7	
Superfinishing (large work)	±0.00008	10	
Internal grinding (small work)	±0.00001	15	
Internal grinding (medium work)	±0.00003	20	
Internal grinding (large work)	±0.00005	25	
Electric discharge (small work)	±0.00003	20	
Electric discharge (medium work)	±0.00004	25	
Electric discharge (large work)	±0.00007	25	
Chem-milling (small work)	±0.005	50	
Chem-milling (medium work)	±0.007	50	
Chem-milling (large work)	±0.010	50	
Ultrasonic (small work)	±0.0001	20	
Ultrasonic (medium work)	±0.0002	25	
Ultrasonic (large work)	±0.0004	25	
Electrolytic (small work)	±0.001	20	
Electrolytic (medium work)	±0.002	25	
Electrolytic (large work)	±0.002	25	
Turning (small work)	±0.001	60	
Turning (medium work)	±0.002	100	
Turning (large work)	±0.005	150	
Milling (small work)	±0.001	75	
Milling (medium work)	±0.002	100	

TABLE 3-2. (*Continued*)

Secondary process	Expected tolerance, inches	Expected surface finish, micro- inches	Remarks
Milling (large work)	±0.005	200	
Forming (small work)	±0.001	100	
Forming (medium work)	±0.002	125	
Forming (large work)	±0.002	150	
Planing and shaping (small work)	±0.005	125	
Planing and shaping (medium work)	±0.006	150	
Planing and shaping (large work)	±0.009	250	
Flame cutting (small work)	±0.040	350	
Flame cutting (medium work)	±0.060	350	
Flame cutting (large work)	±0.060	350	
Contour sawing (small work)	±0.010	250	
Contour sawing (medium work)	±0.015	250	
Contour sawing (large work)	±0.015	250	
Abrasive belt machining (small work)	±0.001	50	
Abrasive belt machining (medium work)	±0.003	60	
External grinding (small work)	±0.0002	20	
External grinding (medium work)	±0.0003	30	
External grinding (large work)	±0.001	40	
Tapping (small work)	±0.002	125	Tolerance on pitch diameter
Tapping (medium work)	±0.003	150	Tolerance on pitch diameter
Tapping (large work)	±0.004	150	Tolerance on pitch diameter
Thread grinding (small work)	±0.0002	15	Tolerance on pitch diameter
Thread grinding (medium work)	±0.0003	20	Tolerance on pitch diameter
Thread grinding (large work)	±0.0004	20	Tolerance on pitch diameter
Gear shaper generating (small work)	±0.0002	80	
Gear shaper generating (medium work)	±0.0004	100	
Gear shaper generating (large work)	±0.001	150	
Gear hobbing (small work)	±0.0002	100	
Gear hobbing (medium work)	±0.0004	125	
Gear hobbing (large work)	±0.001	150	
Thread and form rolling (small work)	±0.001	10	
Thread and form rolling (medium work)	±0.001	20	
Thread and form rolling (large work)	±0.0015	30	
Blanking (small work)	±0.004	250	
Blanking (medium work)	±0.005	250	
Blanking (large work)	±0.007	300	
Brake forming and bending (small work)	±0.015		
Brake forming and bending (medium work)	±0.020		
Brake forming and bending (large work)	±0.025		
Spinning (small work)	±0.005	125	
Spinning (medium work)	±0.007	150	

TABLE 3-2. (Continued)

Secondary process	Expected tolerance, inches	Expected surface finish, micro-inches	Remarks
Spinning (large work)	±0.010	150	
Drawing and forming (small work)	±0.003	100	
Drawing and forming (medium work)	±0.005	100	
Drawing and forming (large work)	±0.007	100	
Beading or curling (small work)	±0.010		
Beading or curling (medium work)	±0.010		
Extruding (small work)	±0.002	100	
Extruding (medium work)	±0.003	125	
Extruding (large work)	±0.003	150	
Swaging (small work)	±0.0005	100	
Swaging (medium work)	±0.0007	100	
Swaging (large work)	±0.001	150	
Embossing (small work)	±0.0005	100	
Embossing (medium work)	±0.0007	100	
Embossing (large work)	±0.0009	100	
Cold heading (small work)	±0.002	250	
Cold heading (medium work)	±0.002	250	
Hobbing (small work)	±0.001	100	
Hobbing (medium work)	±0.002	100	
Stretch forming (medium work)	±0.0125		
Stretch forming (large work)	±0.015		
High energy forming (medium work)	±0.015	100	
High energy forming (large work)	±0.020	100	

For example, Figure 3-4 shows that for the design under study when quantities are less than 1,000 pieces, the most economic process from the standpoint of total cost (tooling plus setup plus production cost) is permanent molding. Between 1,000 and 3,000 pieces, it would be more economical to use die casting, and at a production quantity of over 3,000 pieces, it would be advisable to go to a four-cavity plastic mold. The unit costs of each of the three methods of manufacture for different quantity levels are shown in the upper portion of Figure 3-4.

DETERMINING THE BEST PROCESS OR PROCESSES

The choice of one process over another is dependent upon the constraints already discussed. However, the factors influencing these constraints will vary with time. An economical process may be chosen today, and tomorrow changes in the cost of labor or material, quantity to be manufactured, or equipment available may make it economical to manufacture the part from another material or by a different process. Thus process engineering is a continuing activity even in standard designs.

In many instances, the number of alternative ways to perform an operation is limited. Quick analysis of the functional design and identification of the constraints may indicate that there may be but two or three possible ways to

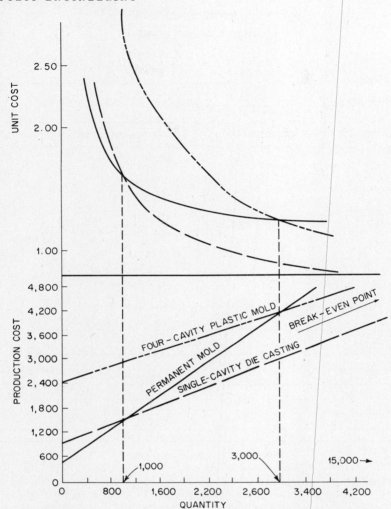

FIG. 3-4.   Break-even or Cross-over Chart for Determining Most Economical Process for Various Quantities.

accomplish the work.   In such cases, the use of a right-wrong form, shown in Figure 3-5, will facilitate arriving at the best solution.   This form provides for a statement of the general problem at the top.   A vertical line then separates the left- and right-hand portions of the form.   To the left of this line are placed the positive factors; to the right the negative factors.   The process engineer should endeavor to utilize quantitative data for each factor.   If a particular process is not capable of maintaining a good surface finish, this fact should be recorded on the right-hand side of the form along with the surface finish that normally is expected.   Thus the form should show not just good or bad, but how good or how bad.

After a right-wrong form has been completed, a conclusion should be reached.   This conclusion should be either to accept the process for further

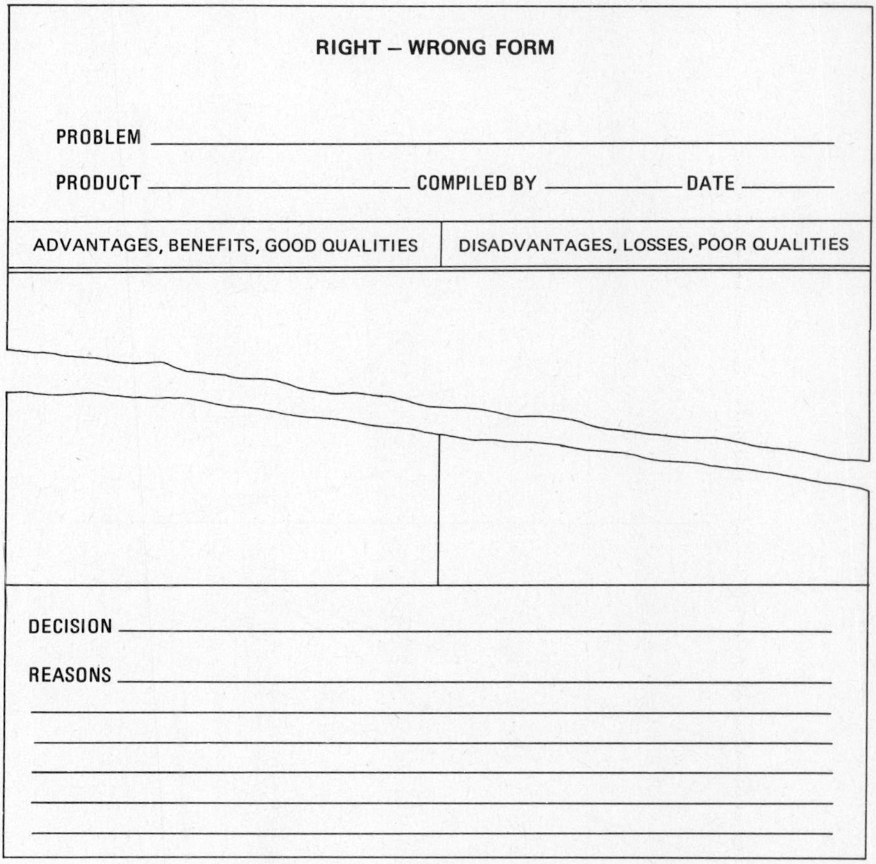

RIGHT – WRONG FORM

PROBLEM _____

PRODUCT _____ COMPILED BY _____ DATE _____

ADVANTAGES, BENEFITS, GOOD QUALITIES	DISADVANTAGES, LOSSES, POOR QUALITIES

DECISION _____

REASONS _____

_____

_____

_____

_____

FIG. 3-5.   Right-Wrong Form.

consideration or to reject it. The reasons for the conclusion should be indicated. One reason such as cost may outbalance all others on the form.

There are times when the number of processes that need to be considered in planning for a design is considerable. The right-wrong type of analysis in such cases may not prove adequate to handle the selection. To tabulate the necessary information related to all applicable processes in workable form, a matrix is recommended. This permits the tabulation of both the controllable and noncontrollable factors related to a design or situation. For example, let us assume that we have n applicable processes which we shall refer to as "strategies" and m different design parameters (size, geometry, tolerance level, material, and cost) which characterize a specific design. We can refer to the design parameters as "states of nature."

Each strategy can be identified, that is, $S_1, S_2, \ldots, S_i, \ldots, S_n$. Likewise each state of nature may be symbolized: $N_1, N_2, \ldots, N_j, \ldots, N_m$. At the intersection of each row (strategy) and column (state of nature), we can establish an outcome measure which we can identify by O_{ij} ($i = 1, 2, \ldots, n$; and $j = 1, 2, \ldots, m$). Figure 3-6 illustrates the format of a decision matrix of this sort.

	P_1	P_2	P_3	. . .	. . .	. . .	P_j	. . .	. . .	. . .	P_m
	N_1	N_2	N_3	. . .	. . .	. . .	N_j	. . .	. . .	. . .	N_m
S_1	O_{11}	O_{12}	O_{13}	. . .	. . .	. . .	O_{1j}	. . .	. . .	. . .	O_{1m}
S_2	O_{21}	O_{22}	O_{23}	. . .	. . .	. . .	O_{2j}	. . .	. . .	. . .	O_{2m}
. . .											
. . .											
. . .											
S_i	O_{i1}	O_{i2}	O_{i3}	. . .	. . .	. . .	O_{ij}	. . .	. . .	. . .	O_{im}
. . .											
. . .											
. . .											
S_n	O_{n1}	O_{n2}	O_{n3}	. . .	. . .	. . .	O_{nj}	. . .	. . .	. . .	O_{nm}

Fig. 3-6. Decision Matrix Involving n Strategies and m States of Nature.

It frequently is convenient to assign probability values to each state of nature tabulated. This can be done from historical data or estimated information. For example, it might be possible to estimate that the probability of a design being produced to a tolerance of 0.0005 to 0.0007 is 0.15. The P spaces provided in Figure 3-6 allow the assignment of probability values associated with each state of nature. Process analysis can be simplified when the probability of the various states of nature is considered. The size of the decision matrix can be reduced by eliminating from further analysis all states of nature where the probability of occurrence is below some value that is regarded as being significant.

It must be recognized that seldom can an optimum decision be made by consideration of only one state of nature. Thus, in process analysis, it is usually necessary to consider several states of nature before specifying the most appropriate process to be used for the design under study. States of nature that will have a bearing on most mechanical designs include the general size of the part under study, the geometry of the part, the material being used, the quantity requirements, and the delivery time. Obviously, it is not necessary for the process engineer to consider all states of nature. Only those having a significant effect on the process selection need be considered.

It should be apparent that the decision matrix concept can be extended to provide outcomes when states of nature are composed of more than one factor. In such situations, the outcome of the first state of nature and strategy will provide the strategy in the second matrix. The various strategies in the second matrix will be plotted against the second state of nature that is applicable to the design under consideration.

The strategies considered will be all those processes capable of producing the part or performing the function under study. Outcomes of significance to the analyst will include the adaptability of the process to the state of nature and the cost involved.

Although it is a relatively rapid and simple matter to use the matrix technique in process planning, considerable planning time can be saved (if much planning needs to be done) by using the digital computer to make the selection. The format of a FORTRAN formula that may be used is

$$D_t = A_{ijk*}N + B_{ij}$$

where D_t = the value printed in the output (total estimated cost of order through primary operation)

A = the coefficient of N, the number of units to be processed

i = the size of the part (this can be expressed as a size class, for example, class 2 = 5 to 25 pounds)

j = the process

k = the material (for example, 3 = aluminum or 4 = magnesium, and so on)

B_{ij} = the fixed element in the process

The values of A and B will be developed for a specific plant.

The information on the several matrices can usually be combined to facilitate the process planning. Table 3-3 illustrates how this can be accomplished. This table reflects information applicable to a given size classification (in this case, metal components less than one ounce). Similar tabular information can be summarized for other size components that are characteristic of the operation of the enterprise.

Once the analyst refers to the correct size-classification data sheet, he then reviews those processes capable of producing the geometry of the part under study. For example, let us assume that the part being analyzed is characteristic of class 4 geometry (Table 3-3). The processes capable of producing this geometry are die casting, investment casting, permanent molding, plaster molding, shell molding, drop forging, extrusion, impact extrusion, roll forming, powder metals, electroforming, and rough machining from mill stock. If this component were to be made from a ferrous material, we could eliminate the processes of die casting, permanent molding, and plaster molding. In Table 3-3, the number 2 signifies nonferrous and 1 ferrous.

Assuming that 300 parts are required, it is possible to eliminate shell molding, drop forging, extrusion, impact extrusion, roll forming, and powder metals from further consideration.

The analyst now considers only those processes remaining to produce the functional design under study. These are investment casting, electroforming, and rough machining from mill stock. He now solves the decision equations for those three processes to obtain a minimum D value. The D_s equation is used when ferrous materials are involved and the D_t equation when nonferrous materials are specified. The process giving the smallest value of D will be the process that should be given final consideration. The variable N in the decision equations refers to the number of units to be made.

Classifying the Secondary Operations. Once the production engineer has determined the basic process that the design will be produced from, he will need to determine the secondary operations required to transform the work to product specifications.

Secondary operations can be classified into four categories. These are: critical operations, placement operations, tie-in operations, and protection operations.

Critical manufacturing operations are those that are applied to areas of the

TABLE 3-3. Processing Information Applicable to Metal Components Weighing Less than One Ounce

Process	Applicable geometry	Applicable materials	Minimum lot size	Decision equation for primary process
Die casting.......	1, 2, 3, 4, 5, 6, 7, 8, 9	2	20,000	$D_t = 0.0268N + 515$
Investment casting	1, 2, 3, 4, 5, 6, 7, 8, 9	1, 2	300	$D_t = 0.3205N + 120$
				$D_s = 0.3043N + 120$
Permanent molding........	1, 2, 3, 4, 5, 6, 7, 8	2	2,000	$D_t = 0.1955N + 215$
Plaster molding....	1, 2, 3, 4, 5, 6, 7, 8, 9	2	400	$D_t = 0.2505N + 120$
Shell molding......	1, 2, 3, 4, 5, 6, 7, 8, 9	1, 2	1,000	$D_t = 0.1475N + 120$
				$D_s = 0.1313N + 120$
Drop forging......	1, 2, 3, 4, 5, 6, 7, 8	1, 2	12,000	$D_t = 0.0542N + 370$
				$D_s = 0.0350N + 370$
Press forging......	1, 3, 5, 6, 7, 8	1, 2	12,000	$D_t = 0.0527N + 370$
				$D_s = 0.0338N + 370$
Cold heading......	1, 3	1, 2	20,000	$D_t = 0.0233N + 265$
				$D_s = 0.0061N + 265$
Extrusion.........	1, 2, 3, 4, 8	1, 2	1,000	$D_t = 0.0301N + 140$
				$D_s = 0.0064N + 140$
Impact extrusion.......	2, 4, 5, 6	1, 2	15,000	$D_t = 0.0323N + 260$
				$D_s = 0.0122N + 260$
Roll forming......	2, 4, 8	1, 2	50,000	$D_t = 0.0307N + 380$
				$D_s = 0.0077N + 380$
Stamping and press forming.........	5, 6, 7, 8	1, 2	5,000	$D_t = 0.0342N + 310$
				$D_s = 0.0163N + 310$
Powder metals.....	1, 2, 3, 4, 5, 6	1, 2	5,000	$D_t = 0.0400N + 210$
				$D_s = 0.0150N + 210$
Screw machining...	1, 2, 5	1, 2	5,000	$D_t = 0.0295N + 95$
				$D_s = 0.0081N + 95$
Electroforming....	3, 4, 6, 9	1, 2	100	$D_t = 0.2124N + 135$
				$D_s = 0.1926N + 135$
Turret lathe.......	1, 2, 5	1, 2	500	$D_t = 0.0967N + 30$
				$D_s = 0.0753N + 30$
Rough machining from mill stock..	1, 2, 3, 4, 5, 6, 7, 8	1, 2	10	$D_t = 0.2017N + 125$
				$D_s = 0.1803N + 125$

part where dimensional or surface specifications are sufficiently exacting to require quality control or are used for locating the workpiece in relation to other areas or mating parts. Critical surfaces almost always mate with other machined surfaces.

A critical manufacturing area can be recognized in one of three ways:

1. The surface or area represents a location to which other surfaces or areas are shown as having a relationship.
2. The surface or area has close dimensional tolerances. Close tolerances are usually thought of as those being within 0.005″. Tolerances can be applied not only to size but also to roundness, straightness, and concentricity.
3. The surface or area has specified conditions such as surface finish, flatness requirements, or squareness requirements.

Placement operations are those whose method and sequence are determined principally by the nature and occurrence of the critical operations. Placement operations may be thought of as being of two types: (1) Those operations that take place to prepare for a critical operation: for example, it may be necessary to machine a surface to provide a suitable stable location for a subsequent critical operation. (2) Those operations that take place to correct the workpiece to return it to its required geometry or characteristic: for example, a press blanking operation may result in portions of the part curling so that it will be necessary to add a flattening placement operation.

Tie-in operations are those productive operations whose sequence and method are determined by the geometry to be accomplished on the work as it comes out of a founding or critical operation in order to satisfy the specifications of the finished part. Tie-in operations may be thought of as those secondary productive operations which are necessary to produce the part, but which are not thought of as being critical. Tie-in operations usually are performed to standard machine tolerances and do not identify a mastering surface, from which other surfaces are located to close tolerances.

Protection operations are those operations, nonproductive in nature, that are performed to protect the product from the environment and handling during its progress through the plant and to the customer, and also those operations that control the product's level of quality. Broadly speaking, all protection operations may be classified as falling into one of three groups. These are: (1) application of protective coatings, (2) inspection and test, and (3) packaging for shipment.

Protective coatings may be applied at several stages in the manufacture of a product. Frequently a rust preventive coating is applied to raw material as soon as it is received to protect it against corrosion in the processor's plant. Similarly, semifinished products may be given a protective coating before being sent to temporary storage. The finished product frequently is treated to protect it from the elements until it arrives safely at the customer's plant.

Protective and decorative coatings specified on the drawings are not operations falling under the classification of protection operations. The applications of these decorative and protective coatings are usually tie-in operations that are performed late in the process.

Determining the Sequence of Secondary Operations. After the process engineer has identified all the critical, tie-in, placement, and protection operations necessary to produce the part under study, he will need to determine the best sequence of these secondary operations. This is determined by considering: (1) the logical process order and (2) the geometrical and dimensional control that can be maintained during processing.

When considering the logical process order, it is obvious that basic operations are performed first, and final inspection is near the end of the process—just before packaging for shipment. Holes that require reaming would of course have to be drilled before being reamed, and threaded inside diameters would have to be drilled before tapping. In general, the final finishing of internal work is done in advance of external work. The principal reason for this is that internal surfaces are less likely to be damaged in material handling and subsequent processes; therefore, their surfaces can be completed earlier in the sequence. When internal work is performed, the logical sequence is: drilling, boring, recessing, reaming, and tapping. The logical sequence of external work is: turning, facing, grooving, forming, and threading.

Another point related to the logical process order is that rough work involving heavy cuts and liberal tolerances should be performed early in the sequence, because heavy cuts will reveal defects in castings or forgings more readily than light cuts. It is better to find out that raw material is defective early in the process rather than late. Because both tolerance and finish of external surfaces can be adversely affected by subsequent material handling and clamping, close-tolerance-type operations should be performed late in the operation sequence.

In considering the geometrical and dimensional control that can be maintained during processing, the analyst should keep in mind those critical operations that establish locating or mastering points. These should be established early in the process. Because it is usually easier to maintain control from a large plane surface than from a curved, irregular, or small surface, the process engineer will establish a surface best qualified for location and will finish that surface early in the sequence.

In planning the operation sequence, it is good practice for the analyst to record on 3″ x 5″ cards all the operations that must be performed. On each card, he should indicate the class of operation, the best surface for location in order to perform the work, the equipment recommended, and any other pertinent information related to the operation. These cards can then be arranged in sequence to arrive at the most favorable order in which the work should be performed. A typical card is shown by Figure 3-7.

The process engineer must also consider the physical location of the equipment that he plans to use in processing the work. If certain equipment is remotely located, it may be more advantageous for small orders to use a less favorable process that involves equipment in a nearby physical location. Similarly, the process engineer will need to consider the number of parts required, the delivery schedule, and the existing loads on the various machines. Larger volume permits using more costly setups and more advanced tooling. Thus larger volumes permit usage of multiple and combined cuts. Multiple cuts refer to the taking of two or more cuts from one tool post or station such as the hexagon turret station on a turret lathe. Combined cuts represent cuts taken at the same time from two or more different stations, for example, the square turret and the hexagon turret.

A sequence of planned operations may appear as in Figure 3-8. The key

---

Part No.____J-1968_____ Operation No.____7_____

Operation ___Drill two 13/32″ lug holes_____

_____

_____

Operation Class____Tie-in_____

Performed On_____Cincinnati-Bickford 21″ Drill Press____

Location of Equipment _____Dept. 11_____

Locate From ___Housing face. Use three points of location on

___this surface, two points on ribbed face, and one point on

___back surface._____

Estimated Setup Time __15 min.___ Each Pc. Time __2 min.___

FIG. 3-7.   Process Planning Card.

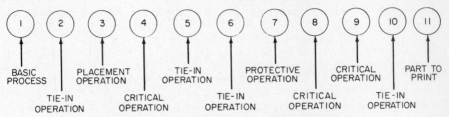

FIG. 3-8.   Example of a Sequence of Planned Operations.

points in this sequence are: Number 11 tells us what is wanted in detail. Numbers 4, 8, and 9 are the critical operations.   It is quite probable that number 4 is critical because a locating surface is being finished, and numbers 8 and 9 are critical because of close dimensional or surface requirements. Number 3 is a placement operation that makes the part from the founding process acceptable for the tooling provided in critical operation 4.

ORDERING THE SPECIAL TOOLING

Process engineering not only involves the planning of the best manufacturing processes in the correct sequence to produce a given functional design, but also the ordering of the special tools in the correct amount and detail.

Once the manufacturing operations have been decided upon, the process engineer will need to determine how the work should be located and held in position while the various operations are being performed.   He will need to determine: (1) those points or areas that are best suited for locating the workpiece while it is being processed; (2) that portion of the workpiece that is suited to supporting or holding it while it is being processed; and (3) that portion or area that is best suited for clamping so that it is securely held during the processing.

Although the process engineering function does not usually involve the design of jigs, fixtures, dies, gages, and the like, it does include the ordering of the special and standard tools necessary to produce the part in the required quantities at the required time.   When ordering the design and making of all durable tools (those that hold the work), as much detail as possible should be provided.

The Use of Locators.   Locators refer to those points on the work which contact the holding device so that the work has a known relationship with the cutting or forming tools.   Three locators are needed to locate a plane, two are needed to determine a line, and one will determine a point.

A workpiece can move in either of two opposed directions along three perpendicular axes (X, Y, and Z).   Also the work may rotate, either clockwise or counterclockwise, around each of these three axes.   If we consider each of these possible movements as a degree of freedom, it can be understood that twelve degrees of freedom can exist.   These twelve degrees of freedom are illustrated in Figure 3-9.

Work can be located positively by six points of contact in the tooling.   These six points include three points on one plane.   For example, in Figure 3-10, the three locations on the bottom of the block prevent the work from moving downward and also prevent it from rotating about the X and Y axes.

By adding two locating points on a plane parallel to the plane containing the X and Z axes, the work is prevented from rotating about the Z axis and also from moving to the left.

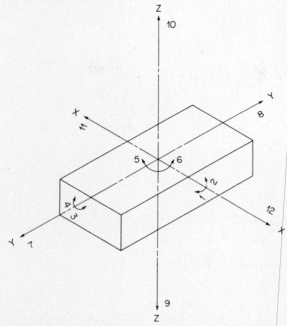

FIG. 3-9.   Twelve Degrees of Freedom.   Arrowheads Indicate Direction of Possible
Movement.

When the sixth and final locating point is added on a plane parallel to the
Y and Z axes, movement upward is prevented.

Thus the first three locators prevent movements 1, 2, 3, 4, and 9, as shown
in Figure 3-9.   The next locators prevent movements 5, 6, 7; and the final
locator prevents movement 11.   This 3-2-1 locating system prevents movement
in nine of the twelve possibilities.   The three degrees of freedom remaining
(8, 10, and 12) must not be restricted as they are needed to provide clearance
to load and unload the tooling.

Generally, the first surface machined is the one which will be subsequently
used as a locating surface.   This surface should be geometrically, dimension-
ally, and mechanically qualified for locating the workpiece.   The area that
lends itself to be machined first should have one or more of the following
characteristics:

1. The area can be easily machined from the rough state in a relatively
    short period of time.

2. The area can be machined while locating the work on the same side
    of the parting line that the cut will be taken.

3. The machined area will provide a flat surface with relatively good
    finish that will facilitate subsequent location.

4. The machining operation will provide a relatively close tolerance in
    relation to other surfaces that will eventually be classified as being
    critical.

The locators should be chosen at positions so that when the work is clamped
in the holding device, it will be stable and will not lift or rock away from the
locators during the processing operation.   Instability of the work in the fixture
may be due to insufficient locators, positioning of the locators too close to-

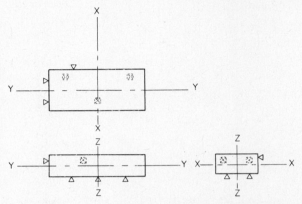

FIG. 3-10.   Work Can be Located Positively by Six Points of Contact.

gether, inadequate support of the workpiece, or inadequate holding or clamping force.

Locators also should be placed on one of the two surfaces that identify a close tolerance. If close dimensions are shown to center lines, it is a good idea to place locators approximately equally distant from either side of the center lines from which dimensioning takes place. When a surface has a close tolerance on squareness, parallelism, or concentricity, then this surface should have either two or three locators placed against it. The engineer should avoid placing locators where they may come in contact with surface irregularities such as parting lines, gates, or burrs.

Supporting the Work. When ordering the special tooling, the process engineer should indicate how the work should be supported, in addition to specifying the position of the locators. To assure that the work is held in a correct position throughout the process, it must be rigidly supported so that it does not deflect because of its own static weight or the holding and tool forces that are applied to it. The process engineer should recognize that adding a support to avoid deflection during processing does not mean adding another locator. The support should not provide a point of location. The workpiece should never contact the support until the tool or tooling forces are applied, because the only purpose of the support is to avoid or limit deflection and distortion.

Clamping the Work. The holding force must be of sufficient magnitude so that all locators contact the workpiece during the processing cycle. It is also important not to have holding forces so large that the work becomes marred. Some general principles that should be followed with regard to the magnitude and location of holding forces include:

1. It is usually advantageous to place holding forces directly opposite locators.
2. A nonrigid workpiece may require holding forces at several locations to hold the work against all locators.
3. Holding forces should be applied on surfaces that do not require a fine finish.
4. The holding force needs to be of sufficient magnitude to hold the work against the locators despite tool forces.

ESTIMATING THE SETUP AND EACH-PIECE TIMES

Immediately after determining the required operations to be performed and their best sequence, the process engineer will need to make time estimates of each operation. This will include an estimate of both setup time and operation time. These time estimates will serve as the basis of the cost estimate of the work.

In estimating the time required to produce a part, the process engineer will need to consider three classes of time that may be part of the cycle. These are:

1. Machine time
2. Effort time
3. Delay time
   a. Unavoidable delays
   b. Avoidable delays
   c. Personal delays

All delays are usually handled by providing an adequate allowance to the effort time and the machine time.

Estimating the Machine Time. To determine quickly and accurately the machine time required for a given operation in advance of production, it is necessary to have valid standard data available covering the equipment on which the work is to be performed. Standard time data are elemental time standards taken from time studies that have been proved to be satisfactory. These elemental standards are classified and filed so that they can readily be found when needed. Standard data is the name given to all the tabulated elemental standards, curves, alignment charts, and tables that are compiled to permit the determination of a time estimate without the necessity of a timing device such as a stopwatch.

By knowing the feeds and the speeds at which the machine should be operated for the material being used and the number of cuts planned, it is an elementary procedure to compute the cutting time. Table 3-4 shows characteristic speed standard data for various materials machined with either high-speed steel or carbide cutters. For example, to determine the time to drill a 1″ diameter hole through a 2″ section of a medium cast iron housing, we would estimate the cutting speed to be 65 feet per minute from Table 3-4. This would be 248 revolutions per minute.

$$\text{RPM} = \frac{65}{(\pi)(1)/12} = 248$$

Perhaps the closest setting on the drill press planned for this work would be 225 revolutions per minute.

Assuming a recommended feed of 0.013″ per revolution, we would have a feed rate of 2.92″ per minute. The total length that the drill must move is 2″ plus the lead of the drill (see Figure 3-11).

The lead of the drill is:

$$\frac{0.5}{\tan 59°} = 0.3 \text{ inch}$$

and the estimated drilling time would be $2.3/2.92 = 0.788$ minute.

The cutting time so calculated does not include any allowance. The allowance will cover time for variations in material thickness and tolerance in the setting of stops, personal and unavoidable delays, and fatigue. The total of this allowance usually lies between 10 and 20 percent of the cutting time on this type of work.

Material		Machina-bility index	Turning with high-speed steel tools	Turning with carbide tools	Milling with high-speed steel tools	Milling with carbide tools	Drilling with high-speed steel tools	Tapping with high-speed steel tools
C-1025	H.R.	54	75	225	80	280	50	20
	C.F.	68	110	300	120	420	70	30
C-1040	H.R.	62	90	280	100	350	65	25
	C.F.	64	90	280	100	350	65	25
C-1045	H.R.	62	90	280	100	350	65	25
	C.F.	60	90	280	100	350	65	25
C-1050	H.R.	62	90	280	100	350	65	25
	C.F.	60	90	280	100	350	65	25
3140	H.R.	58	90	280	100	350	65	25
	C.F.	65	110	300	120	420	70	30
4140	H.R.	60	90	280	100	350	65	25
	C.F.	68	110	300	120	420	70	30
H.T. 300	BHN	43	55	180	60	210	35	10
52100	H.R.	36	55	180	60	210	35	10
	C.F.	34	55	180	60	210	35	10
Forge annealed		44	75	225	80	280	50	20
302 Stainless C.F.		40	55	180	60	210	35	10
303 Stainless C.F.		60	90	280	100	350	65	25
216 Stainless C.F.		40	55	180	60	210	35	30
Nichrome H.R.		55	90	280	100	350	65	25
Cast steel—carbon:								
60,000 psi		55	90	280	100	350	70	30
80,000 psi		70	110	300	120	420		
100,000 psi		64	90	280	100	350	65	25

TABLE 3-4. (Continued)

Material	Machinability index	Turning with high-speed steel tools	Turning with carbide tools	Milling with high-speed steel tools	Milling with carbide tools	Drilling with high-speed steel tools	Tapping with high-speed steel tools
Cast steel—low alloy:							
70,000 psi	64	90	280	100	350	65	25
100,000 psi	65	110	300	120	420	70	30
110,000 psi	55	90	280	100	350	65	25
120,000 psi	50	75	225	80	280	50	20
150,000 psi	44	75	225	80	280	50	20
175,000 psi	36	55	180	60	210	35	10
200,000 psi	30	30	130	35	125	35	10
Cast iron:							
Soft	75	120	325	130	455	80	35
Medium	60	90	280	100	350	65	25
Hard	50	75	225	80	280	50	20
Ingot	50	75	225	80	280	50	20
Chilled (460 BHN)	10		30		35		
Meehanite:							
175 BHN	44	75	225	80	280	50	20
205 BHN	43	55	180	60	210	35	10
220 BHN	30	30	130	35	125	35	10
Aluminum CD	275	375	1000	410	1435	260	90
Cast	150	225	600	165	575	160	55
Forged	200	225	600	220	770	160	55
Brass:							
Al Brass	60	90	280	65	225	65	25
Free cutting	200	225	600	220	770	160	55
Naval	60	90	280	65	225	65	25
Bronze:							
Phosphor bronze cast	55	90	280	65	225	65	25
Ampco 18-22	65	110	300	120	420	70	30
Plastics and fibers	200	225	600	250	875	160	55

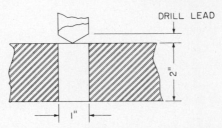

FIG. 3-11. To Drill a Hole 2″ Deep, Drill Must Move 2″ Plus the Lead of the Drill.

Estimating the Effort Time. To estimate the effort time with precision, it is important that reliable standard data are available. The process engineer then needs only to make a record of the work elements involved in the operation, look up the appropriate standard time values, summarize the data, and apply the necessary allowance.

Setup time is usually comprised principally of effort time elements. As in the development of each-piece times, setup times are established with greatest consistency in the least amount of time when reliable standard data exist. If standard data do not exist for determining effort times, the process engineer must use his best judgment in estimating the effort portions of each operation. Once this is done, he should tabulate his estimates as follows:

Setup time estimate .... = _____
Allowance for setup time .... = _____
   Estimated allowed setup time .... = _____
Effort each-piece time estimate .... = _____
Allowance for effort each-piece time ... = _____
Machine time each piece .... = _____
Allowance for machine time each piece = _____
   Estimated allowed each-piece time ... = _____

PLACE OF PROCESS ENGINEERING IN THE ORGANIZATION

Process engineering usually reports to manufacturing engineering which in turn reports to the general manager of the plant or division. Thus, process engineering, along with machine and tool design, material handling and equipment engineering, quality control, standards, and production control, is at a second level of supervision. Manufacturing engineering, product engineering, and research and development are at a first level of supervision reporting to the general manager who is at the plant responsibility level.

A typical organization chart illustrating the place of process engineering is given in Figure 3-12.

Principal Concerns of Process Engineering. Some of the responsibilities of process engineering are as follows:

1. Determine the manufacturing feasibility of product design, and plan for the most favorable processes to be utilized in producing the functional design.
2. Determine the sequence of operations.
3. Analyze tooling requirements.
4. Select the most favorable facilities to be used for each operation.
5. Specify nonproduction material usage, including perishable tools.
6. Specify initial complement of durable tools (jigs, gages, and fixtures).

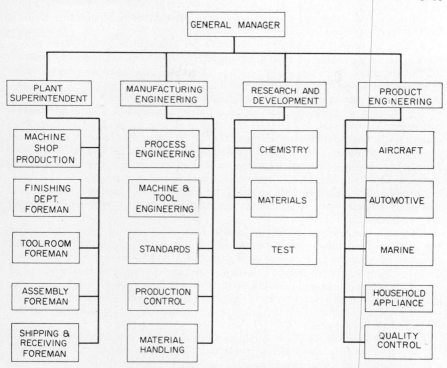

FIG. 3-12.   Typical Organization Location of Process Engineering.

7. Prepare data (feeds, speeds, depths of cut, time estimates) for operational instructions.
8. Prepare and issue in-process drawings for semifinished parts.
9. Review engineering deviations or change requests.
10. Assist in correction of production difficulties, including assistance to purchasing on vendor items.
11. Specify in-process gaging requirements and inspection frequencies.
12. Request required machine tool capability studies and review results.
13. Analyze and develop data for make or buy determination.
14. Maintain available equipment records.
15. Assist quality control in resolution of quality problems.
16. Authorize disposition of special tools no longer required for production or service.

SECURING AND DEVELOPING COMPETENT PROCESS ENGINEERS

To do an effective job of process engineering, it is important that the analyst have a good background in shop mathematics (algebra, trigonometry, and statistics), engineering graphics, elementary physical chemistry, and manufacturing processes. Engineering graduates who have a flare for the practical aspects of technical work usually make excellent process engineers after completion of a training program involving process and machine capabilities.

Graduates from two- and four-year engineering associate degree programs also have the background for this type of work.

Universities and technical institutes do not provide the education or training for the new graduate immediately to do process engineering work. It is necessary for the young technical graduate to be given at least a three- to six-month training program within his company before he can effectively perform all the functions of process engineering. This training program should introduce the trainee to the company products; the materials utilized in their construction; the processes used in the fabrication of the products; the limitations of size, tolerance, geometry, and surface finish; and cost of all the production processes. He should understand the nature of the specialized tooling associated with the production facilities, the typical tool life, and the problems caused by tool wear. He should understand the reasons for the recommended speeds and feeds associated with the various processes and the depths of cut associated with surface finish requirements and power limitations.

Specialized training usually should be provided in product quality and reliability requirements, methods of nondestructive testing, mechanical inspection, and statistical quality control.

Although the background of the trainees will vary considerably, the following schedule provides a guide which usually represents the minimum training requirements for the young engineering graduate.

1. Introduction to company organization and procedures related to product design, process design, manufacturing, and sales—2 weeks.
2. Introduction to product engineering. Review company products, sales volumes, delivery requirements, quality and reliability requirements—2 weeks.
3. Introduction to plant facilities and work of subcontractors. Review all process capabilities; understand recommended feeds, speeds, depths of cut, surface finishes, tolerances, power utilization—4 weeks.
4. Introduction to tool engineering and toolroom. Review types of tools made internally and purchased. Develop appreciation of methods used for holding, locating, and clamping work. Understand the tool steels utilized, heat-treatment procedures—2 weeks.
5. Introduction to development of standards. Short course on time study, methods engineering, standard data, and predetermined motion time data—4 weeks.

BIBLIOGRAPHY

American Society of Tool and Manufacturing Engineers, *Fundamentals of Tool Design*, Prentice-Hall, Inc., Englewood Cliffs, N.J., 1962.

Eary, Donald F., and Gerald E. Johnson, *Process Engineering for Manufacturing*, Prentice-Hall, Inc., Englewood Cliffs, N.J., 1962.

Niebel, Benjamin W., *Mechanized Process Selections for Planning New Designs*, American Society of Tool and Manufacturing Engineers, Paper no. 737, Detroit, 1965.

Niebel, Benjamin W., *Selector Guide for Primary Forming Processes*, AMCP 706, U.S. Army Materiel Command, Management Engineering Training Agency, Rock Island Arsenal, Rock Island, Ill.

Niebel, Benjamin W., and Edward N. Baldwin, *Designing for Production*, Richard D. Irwin, Inc., Homewood, Ill., 1963.

Starr, Martin Kenneth, *Product Design and Decision Theory*, Prentice-Hall, Inc., Englewood Cliffs, N.J., 1963.

CHAPTER FOUR

Tool Engineering

INYONG HAM *Associate Professor, Department of Industrial Engineering, The Pennsylvania State University, University Park, Pennsylvania*

Tool engineering is concerned with the economic production of manufactured goods and deals with the development, design, analysis, planning, construction, operation, application, supervision, and follow-up of production methods, tools, equipment, and facilities for the manufacture of industrial and consumer goods.

The general areas of tool engineering include:
1. Analysis and selection of optimum production process and tooling
2. Planning and control of production processes

The specific areas of tool engineering are analysis, design, selection, construction, and control of:
1. Cutting tools and accessories
2. Workholding devices (jigs and fixtures)
3. Pressworking and forming tools (punches and dies)
4. Measuring instruments and gages
5. Tooling for welding, casing, assembling, and the like
6. Programming and tooling for numerical control (NC) machining and processes
7. Tooling for nonconventional processes such as electrochemical machining, electrical discharge machining, electron beam machining and welding, and laser beam machining and welding
8. Machine tools and components

Tool engineers are responsible for carrying out the functions of tool engineering. A tool engineer helps organize men, materials, methods, and machines so that quality products may be manufactured economically and efficiently. A continuous task of the tool engineer is the development of improved manufacturing processes, methods, and tools which will lead to greater productivity. The complexity of modern manufacturing requires that many functions of tool engineering be carried out by specialists who usually are graduate engineers in either industrial or mechanical engineering and by engineering technicians.

ORGANIZATION

A schematic diagram showing the functions and interrelationships of tool engineering in manufacturing is given in Figure 4-1. Tool engineering is one of the staff and service functions in an industrial organization. The tool engineering department may be an independent unit providing services to various departments in the organization, or it may be subdivided and assigned to several related departments. In most cases, the tool engineering efforts are coordinated and directed by a chief tool engineer, or in some cases, by the heads of other manufacturing, industrial, or production engineering departments, who in turn report to the manager responsible for overall manufacturing. The tool engineering department may be further subdivided into several specific areas, such as process analysis and planning, tool design, and the like, to suit the needs for production.

One of the major functions of tool engineering is process analysis and planning to implement the policies and decisions of management. Process analysis and planning is used to select or design an optimum process for a

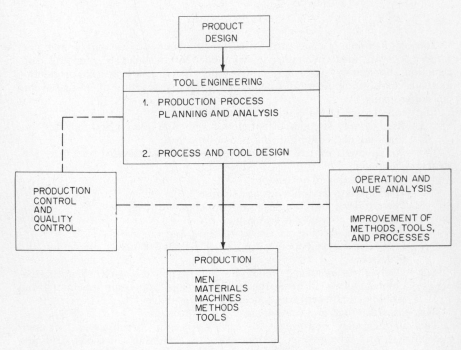

Fig. 4-1. Tool Engineering in Manufacturing.

specific operation in producing a product. Methods of accomplishing this are discussed in detail in Chapter 3 of this section.

Process analysis and planning is a somewhat continuous process. It should always be guided by the simple objective of achieving optimum productive efficiency, that is, of meeting the conditions for minimum cost per piece, for maximum production rate, or for maximum profit while maintaining the required quality standard. Thus, tool engineers should always look for better ways to improve the production process, such as selecting a new alternative process, improving product design, changing specifications, improving tool design, altering operation sequence, choosing better operating conditions, or using new cutting tools.

MACHINE TOOLS AND TOOLS

A machine tool for material processing is a device in which energy is expended in processing a product for removing excess material by shearing or by deforming the material by shaping, sizing, or forming. A machine tool is therefore a machine having a combination of mechanisms whereby a tool is able to operate upon work material, secured in some suitable workholding device, to produce the desired shape, size, and degree of finish under proper operating conditions. Machine tools are the most versatile and the most needed equipment for almost all material processing operations in manufacturing.

A tool used in manufacturing is a device for:

1. Removing or forming a work material into a desired size and shape, such as a cutting tool and a punch and die set
2. Holding workpieces or guiding tools, for example, jigs and fixtures, and machine tool accessories such as chucks and vises
3. Measuring parts or products for inspection, such as gages
4. Sensing necessary information for operational control of machine tools, as, for example, a tool force dynamometer
5. Transmitting instructions to machine tools for desired operations, such as NC tapes and control units

The functions of machine tools are (1) to hold the workpiece and the tool at proper, related positions, and (2) to generate movement between the workpiece and tool for the productive motion of cutting, forming, and the like. To perform the desired functions, the transformation of motion from the power input is accomplished by suitable driving and transmission systems such as mechanical, electric, hydraulic, pneumatic, or fluidic.

A machine tool must be able to satisfy the following general requirements for production operations:

1. Production quality: dimensional accuracy of product and operational accuracy of machine
2. Operational range: operational conditions (speeds and feeds available) and power for high productivity
3. Production capacity: high efficiency and capability for desired production quantity
4. Structural rigidity: freedom from undesirable external and internal vibrations by proper design of sufficient strength and damping
5. Reliability and maintenance: consistent performance accuracy, ease of operation, and maintenance
6. Economic justification

TOOLING FOR MATERIAL REMOVAL PROCESSES

Material removal[1,2] in machining is accomplished by a relative motion between the workpiece and the cutting tool, and involves the interaction of the machine tool, the cutting tool, the workholding and toolholding devices, and the work material. The typical conventional machining processes are classified and shown in Table 4-1, depending upon the nature of the relative motion, the machine tool, the cutting tool, the shape of the generated surface, and the degree of finish and accuracy obtainable.

Cutting Tool Materials.[3] Cutting tools may be subjected to very high pressures (up to or above 100,000 pounds per square inch) and temperatures (1000 to 2000°F or higher). Furthermore, the interface friction between the tool and chip and the tool and workpiece will cause wear at the face and flank surfaces of the cutting tools.

A cutting tool usually fails by one of or a combination of the following: (1) gradual wear, (2) brittle fracture, or (3) plastic deformation. For an ideal cutting tool, the tool material should possess certain essential requirements. It should (1) retain its hardness and strength at high operating temperature; (2) have sufficient wear resistance to all possible wear processes such as mechanical, abrasive, adhesion, diffusion, and oxidation in the operating temperature range; (3) withstand severe impact and not fail by brittle fracture; (4) possess favorable thermal properties so as not to retain too much of the generated heat; and (5) be obtainable at reasonable cost.

Although it is quite difficult to find a cutting tool material to meet all these requirements, there are a number that do possess most of them and are used in machining, namely: (1) carbon steels, (2) high-speed steels, (3) cast alloys, (4) cemented carbides, (5) cemented oxides (ceramics), (6) diamonds (natural and artificial), and (7) other tool materials (high melting point refractory compounds).

Design of Cutting Tools.[4,5] One of the most important factors affecting the performance of any cutting tool is the rigidity of the machine tool—cutting tool—workpiece—workholding device system. For a single point tool, the size of tool shank and the overhang should be designed or selected not only to meet the rigidity requirement for minimum deflection, but also to eliminate undesirable chatter. An improvement of cutting tool rigidity, along with proper workpiece support and machine tool rigidity, ensures vast improvement in tool life and surface finish. In the design of multipoint tools such as drills or milling cutters, the rigidity requirement is sometimes compromised with other essential requirements such as adequate chip space, tooth spacing, and the like.

Tool Life.[6] Tool life is a main factor for evaluating machinability. The

[1] M. Kronenberg, *Machining Science and Applications*, Pergamon Press, New York, 1966.

[2] *Machining Data Handbook*, Metcut Research Associates, Inc., Cincinnati, Ohio, 1966.

[3] H. J. Swinehart, *Cutting Tool Material Selection*, American Society of Tool and Manufacturing Engineers, Detroit, Mich., 1968.

[4] I. Ham and A. Bhattacharyya, *Design of Cutting Tools: Use of Metal Cutting Theory*, American Society of Tool and Manufacturing Engineers, Detroit, Mich., 1969.

[5] L. J. St. Clair, *Design and Use of Cutting Tools*, McGraw-Hill Book Company, New York, 1952.

[6] I. Ham, "Fundamentals of Tool Wear," Technical Paper no. MR 68-617, American Society of Tool and Manufacturing Engineers, Detroit, Mich., 1968.

TABLE 4–1. Conventional Machining Operations: Classification and Features

Operation	Relative motion		Machine tool	Cutting tool	Form generated	Surface roughness, microinches	Accuracy obtainable, inches
	Tool	Work					
Turning	↕	↻	Lathes	Single point tools	Cylindrical and conical surfaces	500 ~ 32	±0.001
Shaping and planing	→|←	↕ ↔	Shaper planer	Single point tools	Straight-cut plane surfaces	500 ~ 32	±0.001 ±0.0025
Drilling	⟳↓	Stationary	Drill press	Drills (double edge tools)	Holes (generate)	250 ~ 125	±0.005
Boring	⟳	↻ ↕	Boring machine	Single point tools	Holes (enlarge)	250 ~ 16	±0.0001
Milling	⟳	↕	Milling machine	Milling cutters (multiedge tools)	Plane and complex surfaces	500 ~ 16	±0.0005
Grinding	⟳↔	↕	Grinding machine	Grinding wheels (multi-edge tools)	Cylindrical and plane surfaces	250 ~ 8	±0.0001

most common criteria of tool life are (1) complete failure, (2) predetermined tool wear limit, (3) surface finish limit, (4) size failure, and (5) cutting forces or power limit. The criteria that should be used in defining tool life depend upon the object of a particular machining operation. However, for most machining operations, surface finish limit and size failure are the most commonly used criteria.

There are various ways of expressing tool life, namely: (1) time of actual cutting, (2) volume of metal removed, (3) total length of cut, and (4) number of pieces machined.

Economics of Machining. Any metal cutting operation must usually meet the most important requirement—making a profit. Continuous effort should be made to find the optimum machining conditions for a given operation to: (1) minimize the production cost per piece; (2) maximize the production rate per unit time; or (3) maximize the profit. The annual expenditure for metal cutting in the United States is more than $35 billion, and the annual expenditure for cutting tools is more than $350 million. Because of these large annual expenditures, it is essential to analyze carefully every metal cutting operation and tooling setup to obtain optimum conditions. Any amount of saving in machining and tooling will greatly affect the total saving. For optimization of machining conditions and tooling, it is essential to apply not only knowledge of production economy but also metal cutting theory. The optimum machining and tooling conditions vary from job to job, machine to machine, and plant to plant. Therefore, it is necessary that every operation should be analyzed individually and continuously as other related conditions change.

A specific analysis of the costs in machining and tooling involves four cost elements: (1) nonproductive cost, (2) machining cost, (3) tool-changing cost, and (4) tool cost. These are a function of cutting speed at a given cutting condition. A graphical presentation of the cost elements is shown in Figure 4-2.

The cutting speed and the corresponding tool life for the minimum cost per piece and for the maximum production rate, namely, V_{mc}, T_{mc}, V_{mp}, and T_{mp}, respectively, can be computed mathematically or found graphically as illustrated in Figure 4-2. Unless V_{mc} and V_{mp} are close together, it is difficult

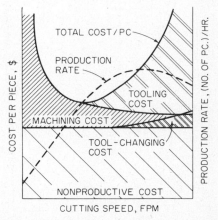

FIG. 4-2. Effect of Cutting Speed on the Cost Elements of Machining Operations.

to satisfy the conditions for both minimum cost and maximum production rate. Therefore it is usually necessary to find a compromise between the two requirements.

Using a computer,[7] it is possible not only to calculate a desired solution for a particular optimum condition, but also to compute all possible combinations of machining variables and tooling cost elements, and show their interrelationships on graphs for making a proper decision.

ECONOMICS OF TOOLING

In designing, selecting, and purchasing various tools required in manufacturing operations, such as cutting tools, workholding devices, assembly fixtures, special instruments, and the like, it is necessary first to analyze their economic effects. Although the technical requirements and functional necessity of the tool are of prime concern, its economic justification should be considered equally for efficient manufacturing.

In dealing with the economic problems of tools, there are many types of problems and many factors to be considered. For a simple case of comparison of two different tooling setups, the saving S occasioned by the new improved method or tool will be $S = N\ (A-B)$. For the saving to be equal to or larger than the cost of the new tool,

$$S \geqq C$$

where S = total annual saving, \$
    N = number of pieces produced per year
    A = annual cost of machining the part with the old method, \$
    B = annual cost of machining the part with the new method, \$
    C = cost of the tool for the new method, \$

However, where quantity production is concerned, many other factors must be taken into account. In dealing with the many factors involved, typical questions most frequently asked to analyze the economic problem are:

1. How many pieces must be run to pay for a tool of given estimated cost which will show a given estimated saving in direct labor cost per piece?
2. How much may a tool cost which will show a given estimated unit saving in direct labor cost on a given number of pieces?
3. How long will it take a proposed tool, under given conditions, to pay for itself, carrying its fixed charges while so doing?
4. What will be the profit earned by a fixture, of a given cost, for an estimated unit saving in direct labor cost and given output?

The answers to these and similar questions are relatively easy to compute.

TOOLING FOR WORKHOLDING DEVICES

The term "workholding devices"[8,9] includes, in general, all devices that hold, chuck, or support a workpiece in a desired manner and location, and

[7] I. Ham, "Economics of Machining: Analyzing Optimum Machining Condition by Computers," Technical Paper no. SP 64-60, American Society of Tool and Manufacturing Engineers, Detroit, Mich., 1964.

[8] American Society of Tool and Manufacturing Engineers, *Fundamentals of Tool Design*, Prentice-Hall, Inc., Englewood Cliffs, N.J., 1962.

[9] American Society of Tool and Manufacturing Engineers, *Handbook of Fixture Design*, McGraw-Hill Book Company, New York, 1962.

that also guide the tool to perform a manufacturing operation. These devices are commonly known as jigs and fixtures and are extensively used in the machining and processing of repetitive, mass-produced parts. A jig is a device for positively locating and guiding both the work and the cutting tool. A fixture is a device for holding and positioning a workpiece, but does not necessarily guide the tool.

A workholding device must meet two basic requirements: (1) positioning and locating a workpiece in definite relation to the cutting tool and the machine tool component, and (2) withstanding holding, clamping, and cutting forces while maintaining the precise position or location required for the desired operations. There are many different types and varieties of workholding devices. Jigs are usually classified by their structural design. Common types of jigs are template, plate, channel, open, box, and leaf. One of the standard components of a drill jig is the drill bushing which guides the drill into proper position. Fixtures are usually classified as vises, milling, boring, tapping, broaching, grinding, welding, assembly, inspection, and the like. Many components of fixtures, such as clamping devices, jaws, or pins, are usually standardized for economic and efficient design and interchangeability.

Design and Selection Procedure. The design or selection of any workholding device should be on sound economic and technical bases, considering many related factors as illustrated in Figure 4-3. A workholding device has four basic elements: (1) locating element, (2) structural element, (3) clamping element, and (4) attaching element. To ensure proper operation of the workholding device as designed or specified, the locating element should position the workpiece accurately, and the structure should withstand the forces. The clamps should apply adequate forces for maintaining the position of the workpiece, and the attachment should hold the device on the machine properly. There are many types of workholding devices which are used for operations other than machining, such as welding, assembly, and inspection. However, the basic design features, requirements, and procedures are similar. Locating, clamping, and their mechanisms are common to all and important in the design and selection of the required fixture.

Locating Methods. For consistent production results in mass production, it is essential to locate the workpiece accurately in order to establish a definite relationship between the tool and some points or surfaces of the workpiece. This desired and specified relationship is established by locators of the workholding device.

To locate a workpiece accurately, it must be confined and restricted against movement in all degrees of freedom except those needed for operation or handling. (See Chapter 3 of this section.)

Clamping and Clamping Devices. Almost all workholding devices have clamps of some kind to hold the workpiece firmly against the locating points or surfaces and securely against all disturbing forces such as cutting forces. All clamping devices must meet some common requirements, and the selection of a proper clamp demands definite considerations. They are: (1) rigid holding of workpiece during the production operation, (2) quick-acting and easy operation, (3) clamping with no damage to the surfaces of the workpiece, (4) magnitude of clamping force and its direction and location, (5) types of clamping device, mechanism, power sources, and the like, and (6) economy of clamping. The types of clamps used in workholding devices are numerous, but the majority exhibit several basic, common mechanical features such as a screw, cam, wedge, hook, toggle, or lever. Clamping by pneumatic, hydraulic,

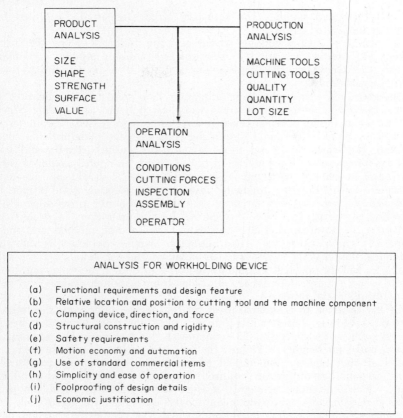

FIG. 4-3. Design and Selection Procedure for Workholding Devices.

or electrical means is also common in supplementing manual operations for quick and easy operation of clamping devices for high production rates.

Because the clamps hold the workpiece against a locator and must also counteract any disturbing forces, it is essential to estimate the required clamping force when designing a clamp. The clamping force must neither disturb the location of the workpiece nor distort or damage it. The direction, location, and magnitude of the clamping force should be analyzed to provide satisfactory functioning of the clamping device. Locating and clamping should not be thought of as the same operation. Locating obtains the most effective position of the workpiece, whereas clamping gives stability to the location chosen.

TOOLING FOR MATERIAL FORMING PROCESSES

Material forming is performed in numerous ways by various processes and operations. Shearing, bending, drawing, squeezing, forging, rolling, and extrusion are among the most common forming processes. The majority of these employ pressworking operations by which a large force is applied by press tools, usually punches and dies, to shear or deform the work material into a desired form and shape. The actuating forces are usually supplied by a machine tool called a press.

In planning a pressworking operation,[10] the following steps are usually taken: (1) product analysis, (2) selection of a suitable process, (3) analysis of the operations required, (4) selection or design of a die set, and (5) selection of a punch press.

Shearing. Blanking, piercing, trimming, and shaving are shearing processes in which the material is stressed in shear between two cutting edges of the punch and die. As the load is applied and increased, the material is subject to both tensile and compressive stresses, plastic deformation occurs through the elastic limit and then the ultimate tensile strength, and finally the fracture occurs. Knowing the pressure (pounds or tons) required for the operation, a die set with the necessary components should be selected or designed considering the following factors: (1) selection of a proper type and size of press, (2) evaluation of the conditions of the press selected, (3) selection of the general type of a die set for the operation, (4) selection of the proper tool steels and heat treatment, (5) feeding method and mechanism, (6) scrap-strip layout, (7) stripping or ejecting method, (8) shaving or trimming that may be necessary, (9) standard die set, and (10) die space. For a typical die set, it is commonly required to design the following components or accessories: scrap strip, die block, punch, punch plate, pilot, gages, stops, stripper, and fasteners.

In the selection of a suitable press for the desired operation, the following factors should be considered: (1) capacity of the press (tonnage, flywheel energy, and motor capacity; (2) type and size of the press (bed opening and space, and shut height); (3) feed of the press (direction and method); (4) speed of operation and amount of stroke (crank velocity and ram stroke); and (5) number of presses required (production quantity and production rate). For production economy, it is most important to select the proper press and to design a scrap-strip layout for the least amount of scrap.

Bending.[11] The bending operation involves the plastic deformation of the metal by exceeding its elastic limit but not its ultimate tensile strength.

There are three basic forms of sheet metal stampings: flat, bent, and formed. Bending processes usually combine all three of these basic shapes and produce various types of bends such as straight-line bends, formed bends, seaming, curling and hemming, flanging tabs and lugs, bridges or louvers, and ribbing.

In designing a bending die, the following items are essential and should be analyzed carefully: (1) bend method, (2) bend radii, (3) bending allowance, (4) bending pressure, (5) spring back, (6) stock size and final dimensions, and (7) bend location tolerances.

Drawing.[12] Various cylindrical, conical, spherical, square, rectangular, and other shapes are produced by a drawing operation in which the metal is subjected to extreme plastic deformation not exceeding its ultimate strength. In drawing operations, the punch forces the metal down into the die to flow along the die face and through the clearance between the punch and die.

[10] *Power Press Handbook*, Bliss Company, Canton, Ohio, 1950.

[11] R. LeGrand, "How to Select Press Brake," *American Machinist*, Special Report no. 604, May 22, 1967.

[12] S. P. Keeler, "Understanding Sheet Metal Formability," *Machinery*, February, March, April, and May, 1968.

The metal is subject to compression on the rim of the blank and tension on the cup wall.

In an analysis of a drawing operation, the following items should be considered, particularly in designing the drawing die set: (1) development of the approximate blank size, (2) reduction factor, for determining the amount of maximum single drawing diameter, (3) reduction ratio, for design of drawing cycle and intermediate blank size, (4) drawing pressure, for selection of the press, (5) blank holding pressure, for design of pressure pad, (6) punch-die dimensions (clearance, draw radii, and the like), (7) lubrication method and lubricant, (8) selection of proper die material, tolerances, and treatment, (9) prevention of undesirable wrinkling and ironing, and (10) follow-up operations such as redrawing, ironing, or trimming.

Forging.[13,14] Forging is a process by which metal is shaped into a desired form and size, refined structurally, and improved in its mechanical properties through controlled plastic deformation in open or closed dies under compressive forces. The compressive forces may be applied by slow-speed squeezing (press forging) or by impact (drop forging). The forging operations can be performed either at atmospheric or at high temperatures, but usually at the temperature range above the recrystallization temperature of the metal. Typical forging operations are: (1) open die forging (upsetting), (2) closed die forging (impression or drop forging), (3) upsetting (closed die), (4) roll forging, (5) cold forging, and (6) hand forging. For press forging, hydraulic presses are commonly used, whereas drop hammers are generally used for drop forging. Special forging machines are often used for producing some other forms of forging operations such as upsetting.

Various metals respond quite differently when they are subject to deformation. Plastic deformation is limited by buckling, necking, fracture, or by a combination of these defects. "Forgeability" is a term commonly used to denote a material's relative resistance to deformation and its plasticity, and is evaluated by various test methods such as: (1) hot-twist test, (2) upset test, (3) notched-bar upset test, (4) hot-impact tensile test, and (5) tensile and compression tests.

It is often necessary to consider forgings in designing a new product or in the redesign of existing components. To select the most efficient forging methods for a given job there are two distinct approaches: (1) to design the part to meet the functional and technical needs for the forging, and (2) to design a forging sequence and die.

TOOLING FOR INSPECTION

Maintaining the desired quality standards is a prime requirement in manufacturing and is essential in mass production systems for interchangeability and continuous assembly of many complex components. Careful control of inspection with adequate policy and system, appropriate standards for tolerances and fits system, and proper measuring instruments and gages are important in enforcing quality control.

Limits and Tolerances. It is never possible to produce a product exactly to a given size or dimension. In engineering practice, therefore, it is neces-

[13] *Forging Handbook*, Forging Industry Association, Cleveland, Ohio, 1966.
[14] F. E. Chepko, "Forging Today," *American Machinist*, Special Report no. 596, Nov. 2, 1966.

sary to allow a certain amount of tolerance which is the permissible variation on a specified dimension of a part. Limits are the limiting dimensions permitted by a given tolerance. Tolerances on a dimension may be specified by either a unilateral or bilateral system. Tolerances may also be classified into the following three basic groups: (1) size tolerances—length, diameter, and angle; (2) geometrical tolerances—straightness, flatness, parallelism, angularity, and perpendicularity; (3) positional tolerances—positions given by tolerancing coordinates.

Fits and Allowances. The fit between two mating parts such as shaft and hole falls into one of two extreme conditions, interference or clearance. Between these two conditions lies a range of fits known as transition fits. Allowance is the minimum clearance or the maximum interference permissible between mating parts.

In developing manufacturing specifications, the tolerances should be assigned with consideration not only to technical and functional requirements but also to economical justification. A small tolerance of a given dimension is more difficult to produce and costs much more to produce than a larger tolerance specification on the same dimension. Minor variations in tolerances sometimes make a great difference in production cost, production method, inspection, and assembly, and may eventually affect the sales price of the product. Therefore, it is important to select the tolerance and fit for a dimension and mating part not only to satisfy the technical requirements but also to justify the cost requirements, whenever possible.

Gages. A gage is used to determine dimensional acceptability of a workpiece as compared with the tolerance specifications for (1) subsequent manufacturing operations, (2) proper assembly operations, and (3) proper functioning as a finished product. There are three classes of gages: (1) workshop gages which are used by an operator at the work station during the production operation, (2) inspection gages which are used by inspectors during routine inspections, and (3) reference or master gages for checking the size or condition of other gages. Although there are many types of gages, they may be grouped into the following five major groups depending upon their shapes and purposes: (1) plug gages—hole diameter and taper, internal thread; (2) snap gages—shaft diameter and taper, length, thickness; (3) ring gages—shaft diameter and taper, external threads; (4) form gages—thread, curvature, template; and (5) pin gages—hole depth, large diameter.

Usually a gage has two sizes of limits provided by the tolerance on a dimension. This type of gage is sometimes referred to as a limit gage which has two measuring elements, go and no-go.

Gage Tolerances and Wear Allowances. Tolerances are required for gages for the same reasons as for workpieces, because it is impossible to produce the gages to exact dimensions. Gage tolerances are usually determined by the amount of work tolerance in the product dimensions.

A gage wears as it is being used. Therefore it is necessary to provide gage wear allowances which are added to the nominal size of the "go" side of a plug gage or subtracted from that size of a snap or ring gage.

Management of Inspection. There is no unified standard for gaging policy; for determining gage tolerances, wear allowances, and their allocations; or for ordering, making, inspecting, and using gages. Each company adapts its own standards to meet its own requirements. Management should be informed periodically of the status of inspection and should review its policies in regard to the effectiveness of its programs, considering overall effects of inspection on the prime objective of manufacturing quality products for profit.

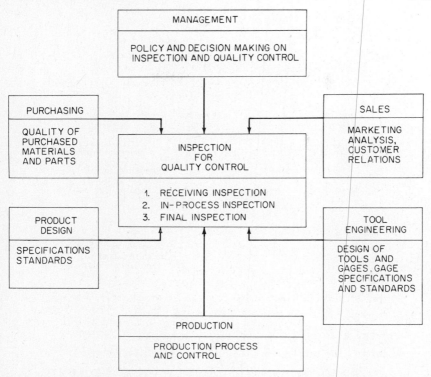

Fig. 4-4. Interrelationships of the Quality Control Inspection Function in a Manufacturing Organization.

The relative position of the inspection function in relation to other areas in a manufacturing organization is shown by Figure 4-4. The fundamental policies on inspection and gaging should be decided by the management concerned with meeting the particular requirements of its plant, considering such factors as: (1) design specifications and quality standards; (2) customer needs, price, and sales requirements; (3) quality and quantity, equipment, and facilities; (4) tools, processes, and gages; (5) inspection organization and personnel; (6) cost; and (7) overall policy.

TOOLING FOR NONCONVENTIONAL MATERIAL REMOVAL PROCESSES

Although the majority of manufacturing operations employ such conventional processes as machining and shearing by pressworking for material removal, there are many other kinds of processes, referred to as nonconventional processes, which are used principally for machining high-strength materials such as precision dies with complex shapes. The nonconventional material removal processes employ various forms of energy—mechanical, chemical, electrical, magnetic, and thermal—for production of useful goods. Some representative nonconventional processes used for material removal classified according to the type of energy are shown in Figure 4-5.

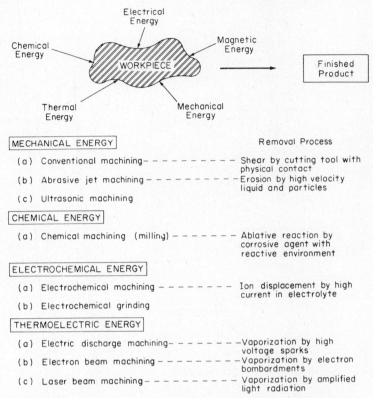

FIG. 4-5. Classification of Nonconventional Material Removal Processes.

TOOLING FOR NUMERICAL CONTROL

A numerically controlled machine tool system[15,16] essentially consists of: (1) machine tool, (2) director, (3) data processing medium (tapes), (4) servo drives, (5) feedback devices, and (6) cutting tools and fixtures. The machine tool is thus equipped to perform automatically, through activation of devices that respond to the control given by signals transmitted by a certain information medium such as coded tapes.

The typical problems involved in NC operations, once NC machines are installed, are: (1) selection of products for NC machining; (2) selection of a suitable NC machine to be used; (3) design of the product with specifications and dimensions for NC programming; (4) programming for NC operations (manual and computer); (5) selection and use of appropriate computer language for NC programming; (6) preparation of coded tapes; (7) NC data processing by director; (8) selection, design, fabrication, and application of optimum tooling setups for workholding and cutting tools; and (9) operational problems such as training, maintenance, and inspection. Management

[15] W. C. Leone, *Production Automation and Numerical Control*, The Ronald Press Company, New York, 1967.
[16] R. Chandler, "Design for NC Machining," *Machine Design*, Feb. 15, 1968.

should, however, be aware that the main problems in NC operations are programming and tooling as shown in Figure 4-6.

Programming for NC Operations. There are two forms of NC operations: (1) point-to-point positioning system and (2) continuous path or contouring system. Point-to-point programming is relatively simple and can usually be done manually. On the other hand, continuous path programming is quite complex and usually requires computers with special languages for programming. The point-to-point system is used for straight-line cuts or for positioning tools in drilling, boring, and the like, while the continuous path system is used for machining any type of curved path and complex shape. Another important consideration to be given in NC programming is the number of axes available for the cutting tool motion. With proper combination of the axial movements of the cutting tool (two, three, and five axial movements) and either a point-to-point or continuous path system, it is possible to machine a desired configuration precisely.

Manual Programming. Manual programming and tape preparation are comparatively easy. All instructions required for NC operations as input data are transcribed on a data processing medium such as punched cards, paper tapes, or magnetic tapes. The most commonly used medium is an eight-hole paper tape, using binary-coded decimal systems for numbers. The

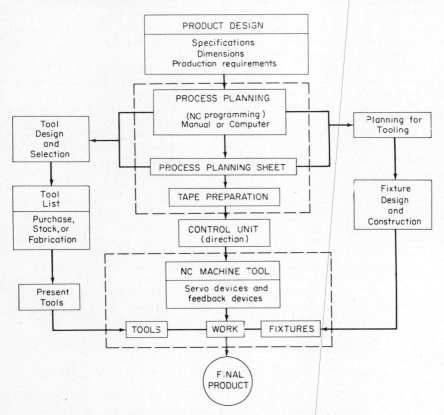

FIG. 4-6.   Flow Diagram of NC Programming and Tooling.

standard tape code characters are specified by the Electronic Industries Association (EIA) Standard.

Computer Programming. Often the complexity of the part requires a computer-assisted programming technique. To facilitate the computer programming for NC operations, many NC programming languages[17] have been developed. Among these languages, the most commonly used for the majority of NC systems in industry is APT (automatically programmed tools),[18] which consists of over three hundred words to describe (1) geometric definitions, (2) tool and motion statements, (3) machine tool functions, and (4) computer system commands.

The typical procedures in NC computer programming are: (1) preparation of manuscript, (2) preparation of punched cards (program deck processor) for the manuscript information, (3) part programming by a computer with the processor for a particular part and operations, (4) programming by the postprocessor for a particular NC machine tool system, (5) preparation of coded tapes for converting the output from the computer, which contains all necessary instructions, and (6) use of the tape for NC operations.

Tooling for NC Operations. Providing tools required for NC machining is an essential part of an NC manufacturing system. The basic factors involved for NC tooling are: (1) workpiece specifications—work material, size, configuration, tolerance, and finish; (2) cutting tool requirements—type, size, shape, geometry, material, grade, holder, tool life, and cost; (3) machining requirements—part configuration and tolerances, machining allowances (depth of cut), production rate (feed and cutting speed); and (4) tooling setups—workhandling devices for optimum handling of workpiece.

Therefore, the main objectives of NC tooling are to reduce tooling costs, to eliminate operator errors, and to provide the tooling setups for maximum productivity and efficiency of the NC machine and operations required. The specific actions to be taken for achieving these objectives are to: (1) program the operation sequence for minimum tooling and machining time, (2) select and design for simple tooling, requiring minimum setup and workhandling times, (3) eliminate unnecessary tools and reduce the number of tools required by combining the operations and by using new improved tools and tooling setups, (4) select standard tools rather than special tools, (5) redesign the program using the same tooling with minor changes in design, rather than using another tool or tooling setup, (6) maintain close coordination among product design, production process design, tool design, and manufacturing, (7) preset tools for automatic, quick selection and change, (8) reduce needs for in-process adjustment of tools, and (9) design the system for continuous operation, without interruption for workhandling and tool changing.

Management Implications for NC Manufacturing.[19] It is management's decision to plan and install an NC manufacturing system and to ensure good utilization of the NC facilities. There are many factors influencing this management decision: (1) capability of NC equipment; (2) production quantity, quality, cost, and future requirements of the work; (3) capital in-

[17] R. A. Thomas, "Language of Tapes," *American Machinist*, Special Report no. 545, 1964.

[18] *Proceedings*, APT Technical Meetings, IIT Research Institute, Chicago, Ill., June, 1964.

[19] R. P. Risch, "Getting Started with NC Installation," *American Machinist*, Nov. 9, 1966.

vestment required; (4) programming and tooling; (5) maintenance and repair; (6) personnel and training; (7) overall operation costs; (8) environmental and customer requirements; (9) company policy; and (10) knowledge of NC.

CONCLUSION

The above somewhat simplified discussion of the tool engineering function will serve to indicate to the manufacturing manager that considerable technical competence is necessary to carry it out properly. A company can either employ a staff of competent tool engineers to do the work in-house, or it can turn to outside toolmaking companies which specialize in the design and making of various kinds of tools. Often it will be desirable to combine these two approaches. The simpler tools or those for certain processes are designed by the company's own tool engineers, and the complex tools or those for processes for which the company's tool engineers have insufficient technical knowledge are purchased outside.

In any case, it is important for the manufacturing manager to have a general understanding of what constitutes satisfactory tooling. This chapter has attempted to provide a start in this direction. More detailed information may be found in the reference works named in the bibliography and the footnotes.

BIBLIOGRAPHY

American Society of Tool and Manufacturing Engineers, *Die Design Handbook*, McGraw-Hill Book Company, New York, 1955.

American Society of Tool and Manufacturing Engineers, *Fundamentals of Tool Design*, Prentice-Hall, Inc., Englewood Cliffs, N.J., 1962.

American Society of Tool and Manufacturing Engineers, *Handbook of Fixture Design*, McGraw-Hill Book Company, New York, 1962.

American Society of Tool and Manufacturing Engineers, *Handbook of Industrial Metrology*, Prentice-Hall, Inc., Englewood Cliffs, N.J., 1967.

American Society of Tool and Manufacturing Engineers, *Machining with Carbides and Oxides*, McGraw-Hill Book Company, New York, 1962.

American Society of Tool and Manufacturing Engineers, *Tool Engineer's Handbook*, McGraw-Hill Book Company, New York, 1959.

Forging Industry Handbook, Forging Industry Association, 1966.

Ham, I., and A. Bhattacharyya, *Design of Cutting Tools: Use of Metal Cutting Theory*, American Society of Tool and Manufacturing Engineers, Detroit, Mich., 1969.

Metals Handbook, vols. I, II, and III, American Society for Metals, Metals Park, Ohio, 1967.

NC Handbook, Bendix Corporation, 1967.

Nontraditional Machining Processes, American Society of Tool and Manufacturing Engineers, Detroit, Mich., 1967.

Numerical Control in Manufacturing, American Society of Tool and Manufacturing Engineers, Detroit, Mich., 1963.

Sen, G. C., and A. Bhattacharyya, *Principles of Metal Cutting*, New Central Book Agency, Calcutta, India, 1969.

CHAPTER FIVE

Production Planning, Scheduling, and Control Techniques*

DAVID M. BOODMAN *Arthur D. Little, Inc., Cambridge, Massachusetts*

Manufacturing is a complex activity involving labor, materials, and equipment in the production of marketable goods. Successful manufacturing requires the management of the resources available for the manufacturing operations to produce the desired goods in the required quantities at the appropriate times and at the lowest possible total cost. As with all management, manufacturing management requires the planning, direction, and control of the resources made available for it. The degree of success achieved in these manufacturing operations depends to a large extent on the skill with which these management functions can be conducted.

Production planning involves management decisions on the resources that the firm will require for its manufacturing operations and the selection of these resources to produce the desired goods at the appropriate time and at the least possible cost. In short, it requires the commitment of resources in preparation for a less-than-certain future. Production control is the adjustment of plans in response to the noted departures of plan from actuality arising out of the uncertainties of the future. Production scheduling is that management activity which directs production operations toward the planned smooth and timely flow of product through the manufacturing steps by means of detailed instructions on the quantities, routings, and time at which each product is to be made.

SCOPE OF PRODUCTION PLANNING

Production planning is the process of deciding on the resources that the firm will require for its future manufacturing operations and of allocating these

---

* Adapted from *Production Planning and Inventory Control*, 2d ed., by John F. Magee and David M. Boodman, published by McGraw-Hill Book Company, New York, 1967.

resources to produce the desired product in the required amounts at the least total cost.

Production planning therefore involves setting the limits or levels of manufacturing operations in the future. Arriving at a production plan requires that management make a number of important decisions. Some of these include deciding the size of the labor force during the period planned, and if hiring campaigns or layoffs are necessary, when these will be; setting plant and equipment capacities where these are flexible; and setting the desired or objective levels for inventory control. Production planning sets the framework within which detailed schedules and inventory control schemes must operate.

Production planning is specifically concerned with the future—with layout of production operations to meet future anticipated sales with facilities which in some cases may not even yet exist. The plan may cover a few months or several years. Typically, in a well-designed control system, production plans may be drawn simultaneously and in possibly different degrees of detail for varying periods in the future. For example:

1. Plans covering the next several months or year may be used to set labor budgets and inventory goals.
2. Plans covering, say, five years may be used to govern capital equipment budgeting for increased capacity.
3. Plans covering, say, five to fifteen years may be used to govern plant construction and product development.

Production plans are designed to fix some or all of the characteristics of manufacturing and distribution operations that are assumed given in more detailed planning or control.

Thus the objective of production planning is to arrive at statements about the general characteristics—the framework—of manufacturing operations during the period planned. This framework should be designed to meet recognized company goals: filling customers' requirements to the extent they can be foreseen, meeting obligations to employees and the community for stable operations, and minimizing total costs. The costs in this case include facility and capital costs, including equipment capacity and inventory costs, costs of labor turnover, and costs of setting up multishift operations.

Production planning methods have two important uses that need to be distinguished. One is direct planning, or drawing up production plans to be followed, subject to costs that have been estimated and policies that have been agreed on with respect to finances, customer service, and labor stability. These plans can be used to decide where extra capacity is needed and to set manufacturing operations.

The other important function of these planning techniques is to give business management guides for use in setting the basic policies themselves. Business management often must make judgments about qualitative factors they find difficult to weigh. One method of helping to make these judgments is to lay out plans under alternative assumptions about policy decisions to make clear the impact on capacity and labor requirements, customer service, and financial needs of alternative decisions in judgment areas.

PLANNING TO MEET SEASONAL DEMAND

Anticipation stocks are carried to meet planned or expected increases in demand rates. Such stocks are built to buffer production rates and capacities from the effects of seasonal demand or surges in demand due to promotional efforts, and to support sales over periods of planned shutdown such as for plant vacation or maintenance shutdown. This buffering is one of the major

functions of inventory. The approach to the control of all forms of anticipation stocks is identical to that which applies to seasonally fluctuating sales.
The following discussion of planning for seasonal demand is intended to treat
all forms of anticipation stocks.

Seasonal demand patterns result in new types of planning problems. It is
useful, perhaps, to think of two types of seasonal problems:

1. The "crash" or short peak-season problems
2. More conventional seasonal problems arising in industries where sales
   show a pronounced seasonal swing, but where these may be of less
   relative importance or where the peak season may extend over several
   weeks or months

In crash-type problems, the effects of uncertainty tend to be concentrated in
the critical high-demand period, often when little can be done to correct for
the discrepanices that materialize between forecast and actual demand. The
kind of seasonal problem where uncertainty is less important arises in industries which are stable but whose demand patterns are subject to external seasonal influences. The basic yearly pattern of demand may be quite predictable, and the overall volume may be reasonably well estimated. There may be
a small error, perhaps only a few percent, in estimating either the total volume
or the size of the peak.

Problems of this latter sort resolve into three considerations.

1. *Maintenance of Safety Stocks.* It is necessary to adjust the forecast of
expected demand to allow for safety stocks to protect against forecast errors.
In most businesses, the risks and costs of back orders so outweigh inventory
cost that substantial protection in the form of safety stocks is justified. These
safety stocks must be large enough so that, after a sudden unexpected sales
spurt, they can be restored by a smooth and moderate adjustment in production rate, but small enough so that the amount of inventory carried after the
season is not excessive.

2. *Setting the Production Rate.* A production plan or pattern must be
laid out to meet the adjusted forecast. Once the adjusted demand forecast or
forecast plus safety stock has been obtained, the next task is to plan the production rate. The difference between forecast and production plan will result in
a planned inventory. The total costs of inventory and production depend on
the form of the production curve, and characteristically the object is to choose
this production plan to minimize the expected total of these costs. The techniques for achieving the solution to the second or planning problem may range
from complex computing techniques for solving sizable problems stated as
linear programs to very simple graphical techniques—a chart of cumulative
sales forecast plus safety stock, and a straightedge.

3. *Short-term Adjustment.* The production plan must be controlled or
adjusted to keep it aligned with the demand forecast, as actual experience
modifies the forecast or results in depleted or excessive inventory compared
with plan. Control methods are discussed later.

Demand Forecasts and the Planning Horizon. A demand forecast may represent an anticipated level of demand or a pattern of demand. The opportunity to take advantage of seasonal inventories in planning production requires a more detailed forecast of demand than a mere knowledge or estimate
of the level or average rate of demand. If seasonal or other cycles can be predicted, production can be planned to take advantage of the predicted pattern
of demand. Thus an important question in determining the approach to planning problems is the degree to which demand cycles, such as seasonal variations in demand, can be predicted.

The forecast must be in sufficient detail and over a sufficient span to permit the plan to be drawn. Seasonal plans may be thought of as employment or operating schedules rather than as detailed specifications of precisely which items would be made at a particular time. Although it may be necessary to forecast by items or groups of items to build up the demand forecast, the objective is to forecast demand on operating units or pools in terms of man-hours, machine hours, or some other appropriate measure of activity. The demand forecast should ultimately be constituted in these terms.

Where demand exhibits cyclical characteristics, it is rarely, if ever, necessary to forecast more than one full cycle in advance. The important point, however, is to recognize and define the planning cycle appropriately. Too frequently, plans are worked out on the basis of calendar year forecasts when the planning cycle should run from, say, September to September. The beginning of the planning cycle should characteristically be the point after the peak demand period when the demand rate first falls below the average for the cycle—the point where inventories characteristically reach minimum.

Specification of Production Requirements. A forecast of the expected pattern of customer demand is not in itself an adequate basis for production planning. The demand forecast must be converted into a specification of production requirements. At least three types of adjustments must be made.

1. To put the forecast of demand on a calendar consistent with production operations
2. To allow for possible errors in the forecast
3. To account for inventories in storage points serving later operating stages (later manufacturing operations, in transit, or in branch distribution points)

Demand forecasts are characteristically quoted as a schedule of anticipated demand for each, say, month covered, or alternatively as a statement of cumulative expected demand by the end of each week, month, or quarter. (It is assumed that this forecast has been converted into a measure of production for the operation being planned.) This must be adjusted to be consistent with available production days, which of course are not uniform in each period. For example, Table 5-1 illustrates a schedule of available production days. Suppose that a forecast of demand on a packaging operation has been made as shown in Table 5-2. Then the demand forecast can be converted to the production time scale by direct comparison of the cumulative entries in Tables 5-1 and 5-2. For example, the tables show that demand equal to 1,075 line hours is expected during the first 83 days of the production year (end of April), or 1,960 hours are expected in the first 137 days of the production year.

The next type of adjustment required is an allowance for necessary operating inventories in the manufacturing and distribution system. These include, for example, stocks in transit. If the transit time averages two weeks from factory warehouse to branch points, then stock equal to two weeks' sales will be in transit. The material must be produced at least two weeks in advance to allow time for transportation. Where inventories are built up between later operations or in field stock points to allow for economical shipment, to protect against short-term demand fluctuations, to permit subsequent production operations to respond smoothly to demand fluctuations, or even to allow more uniform rates of operation at subsequent stages in the face of seasonal demand fluctuations, these must all be allowed for.

For example, suppose in the instance cited above that two weeks (ten production days) must be allowed for packing and transport to field branches, that branches in total carry an average of 300 line hours in safety and cycle

TABLE 5-1. Schedule of Available Production Days

| Month | Production days | | Month | Production days | |
	Per month	Cumu- lative		Per month	Cumu- lative
January	22	22	July	12*	137
February	19	41	August	22	159
March	21	62	September	20	179
April	21	83	October	23	202
May	22	105	November	19	221
June	20	125	December	21	242

* Two-week vacation shutdown in July.

stocks (to protect against short-term sales fluctuations and to allow replenishment shipments of reasonable size), and that it is planned that the factory warehouse should carry 250 line hours to allow economical runs of individual items (products and package sizes) and to permit smooth adjustment to short-run sales fluctuations. Then required cumulative production must stay ahead of expected demand at any time by at least 550 line hours plus 10 production days.

One further adjustment is necessary. No forecast can be assumed to be accurate; in fact, the opposite must be assumed. Expecting a forecast to be in error in some degree is not a reflection on the forecaster but a recognition that a forecast is a measure of *expectation*; no degree of sophistication in forecasting has yet been demonstrated which will eliminate uncertainty, and thus error. A forecast only of expected demand versus time is incomplete without a specification of the range and likelihood of possible departures of actual from expected demand.

It is important to realize that any longer range production plan, for example a plan for meeting seasonally fluctuating demand, requires (1) a forecast of expected demand and (2) a recognition and estimate of possible errors in the

TABLE 5-2. Forecast of Demand—Packing Line Hours

| Month | Demand in line hours | | Month | Demand in line hours | |
	Per month	Cumu- lative		Per month	Cumu- lative
January	275	275	July	310	1,960
February	260	535	August	320	2,280
March	265	800	September	330	2,610
April	275	1,075	October	350	2,960
May	280	1,355	November	340	3,300
June	295	1,650	December	300	3,600

forecast during the period. These two can then be converted by various devices into an estimate of production requirements to give an adequate guarantee of meeting actual conditions as these develop.

There is no satisfactory general way for taking account of expected forecast error to adjust the demand forecast as a basis for production planning. The adjustment to be made is not difficult in principle, but the numbers or values going into the adjustment are hard to estimate with any great accuracy. The adjustment to be made is one of increasing or cutting the quantities shown in the demand forecast until the risks and cost of carrying inventory versus running out of stock are in balance. The difficulty comes in estimating the cost of run-out and the likelihood of an error of any magnitude. It is thus usually necessary to choose the adjustment method that is most expedient in view of information available and the characteristics of the people who must make the necessary policy or operating decisions.

This note of resignation, however, should not be interpreted as implying that arbitrary, unsystematic "judgment" adjustments are to be tolerated. The adjustments will depend ultimately on judgment, but the method should be sufficiently systematic to assign responsibility for judgments, to make clear the influence of governing policies in case these are changed, and to permit review of results to improve the quality of basic data and judgments as experience builds up.

One approach is to attempt an explicit balance of the costs and risks of inventory versus stock run-out. The cost of carrying a unit of inventory per unit time is usually reasonably determinable. The cost of having an extra unit in inventory at any one time depends not only on the cost per unit time but also on the sales rate—the time a unit must be held before it can be sold. In advance of the main selling season, the cost is fairly low; the inventory can be liquidated during heavy sales. However, when the inventory is large enough or when the time is near enough to the end of peak sales, the risk or cost of inventory is considerably increased, especially if there is any likelihood that the inventory will have to be carried over or liquidated in the period of slack sales. Thus the two elements which influence inventory cost are the cost of holding a unit of inventory per unit time and the approximate sales rate which influences how long the item must be held.

The cost of running out of stock is usually much less easy to obtain, but frequently a satisfactory estimate can be reached. This cost, too, may depend on the time in the cycle. In some industries, the cost early in the cycle, when sales are low, is merely the clerical cost of rehandling the order to fill it later. This is true, for example, where off-season sales are largely convenience orders placed by dealers in anticipation of later sales. Sometimes the cost of run-outs can be equated to the gross contribution to overhead and profit on demand diverted elsewhere. Sometimes this is a minimum and must be increased to take some account of possible loss of customers. In some cases, the cost of run-outs can be equated to the cost of emergency action to avoid them, such as emergency overtime, special subcontracting, and the like. Fortunately, in most cases a reasonable adjustment to the forecast can be arrived at if only approximate estimates or ranges for these costs can be established.

How can these costs be used to arrive at an adjustment? The essential procedure is to plan extra inventory up to a point where the cost of carrying the next unit in stock multiplied by the expected time that it will remain in stock just equals or offsets the risk that this unit will be needed to avoid back orders or run-out multiplied by the saving if a back order is avoided.

Another approach is to use the maximum demand concept. Under this concept the sales organization provides a cumulative forecast of the maximum that they reasonably expect to sell rather than an estimate of what they think most likely. This approach does not avoid the issue, but it does restate it. Sometimes it is easier to obtain a forecast of what production operations must be prepared to meet. Such a forecast must be an estimate of maximum *reasonable* demand, not a blue-sky estimate of what might happen in the best of all possible worlds, but an estimate of demand below which orders should be filled routinely and service maintained but above which emergency action, including possible delay in filling orders, may be tolerated.

Returning to the examples of Tables 5-1 and 5-2, let us suppose that the sales department has agreed to a maximum demand forecast 10 percent above the cumulative expected demand. This is shown in Figure 5-1 as a dashed line above the original estimate. To determine production requirements, transit and other inventory requirements must be added to these. These were 10 days' sales in transit plus 550 line hours in inventories at the factory and in the field. When these are added to the maximum demand forecast, the production requirements schedule results, as shown by the upper line in Figure 5-1. The production requirements define what the production plan must be laid out to meet.

Once the adjusted demand forecast, or original forecast plus safety stock, has been obtained, the task is to plan the production rate or draw in the production curve corresponding to cumulative production requirements in Figure 5-1

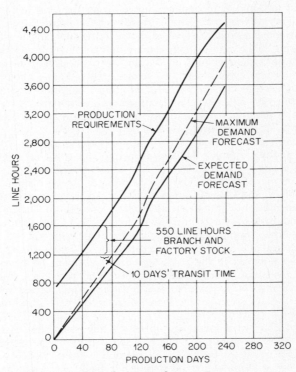

FIG. 5-1. Cumulative Production Requirements.

that will minimize the total of production and inventory costs. A number of techniques have been found useful for doing this job.

Setting the Production Rate by Graphical Techniques. Where the problem of planning production against forecast seasonal demand is not made too complicated by a variety of items, processes, and stages, graphical or arithmetic techniques can be used. They offer the great advantage of being relatively simple to use and easy to understand. For example: Suppose a company has a forecast at the beginning of the year which calls for requirements as outlined in Table 5-3. The first column shows expected demand month by month; the second column shows accumulated expected demand; the third column shows reserves for inventories required for various purposes; the fourth column shows the total amount that must be produced by the end of each month, allowing for an opening stock of 3,500 units; and the last column shows the number of production days available.

The cumulative requirements, after subtracting opening stock, are shown in Figure 5-2. The company might decide to produce at an average annual rate of 100,000 units, the production plan shown as a straight line in Figure 5-2. This plan would produce just enough inventory at the end-of-year peak to meet requirements. The month-end seasonal inventories (equal to the difference between the production plan and the cumulative production requirements) are shown in Table 5-4. They average 9,600 units, plus 3,400 units as safety or other reserve stock, giving a total average inventory of 13,000 units. If the annual inventory carrying cost were $45 per unit, the seasonal anticipation stocks would be costing about $430,000 per year.

Various alternatives might be tried to reduce this cost. For example, operations might be run at the rate of 250 units per day during the low months of the year, building up to a peak rate of over 950 units per day in September. This plan, shown by the dashed line segments in Figure 5-2, would result in substantially lower anticipation stocks. The average inventory would be 4,450 units, with 3,400 units safety stock, or 1,140 units seasonal anticipation

TABLE 5-3. Forecast of Sales and Safety Stocks Needed

(In units)

Month	Expected demand	Cumulative demand forecast	Required inventories	Cumulative production requirements*	Cumulative production days
January	6,000	6,000	3,000	5,500	22
February	4,000	10,000	2,500	9,000	41
March	3,000	13,000	2,100	11,600	62
April	4,000	17,000	2,500	16,000	83
May	6,000	23,000	3,000	22,500	105
June	9,000	32,000	3,500	32,000	125
July	11,000	43,000	4,000	43,500	137
August	12,000	55,000	4,200	55,700	159
September	13,000	68,000	4,400	68,900	179
October	12,000	80,000	4,200	80,700	202
November	11,000	91,000	4,000	91,500	221
December	9,000	100,000	3,500	100,000	242

* After allowances for opening stock of 3,500.

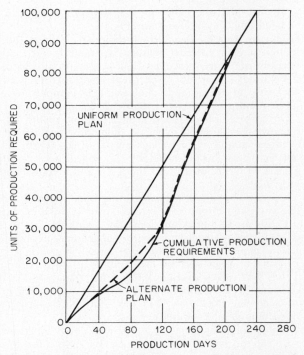

FIG. 5-2. Cumulative Production Requirements and Alternate Production Plans.

stock. At $45 per unit, the cost of seasonal stock under this plan would be only $51,500 per year, a saving in inventory cost of over $375,000 per year.

This, of course, is not all net saving, because it is gained at the cost of adding and laying off the equivalent of some 700 units of daily production capacity. If the company involved were a chemical plant operating well under capacity, and the variation from 250 to 950 units of production a day could be managed by adding and then laying off some 100 semiskilled men, the saving

TABLE 5-4. Monthly Ending Seasonal Inventory

Month	Units	Month	Units
January	3,590	July	13,110
February	7,940	August	10,000
March	14,020	September	5,070
April	18,300	October	2,770
May	20,890	November	240
June	19,650	December	0

Average seasonal anticipation inventory.......	9,600
Average reserve............................	3,400
Average total inventory.....................	13,000

in inventory cost, equivalent to $4,000 per man hired and released, might well justify the change. On the other hand, if the change in operating levels meant adding and laying off some 1,000 to 1,500 employees of various skills, the inventory saving might fall short of offsetting the hiring, training, and layoff costs, not to speak of its effect on community relations. Under these circumstances, the change might not be worthwhile.

This alternative production plan, of course, calls for substantially increased plant capacity—nearly 60 percent more—for the same average throughput. If the capacity were not available and had to be added, or if it would be gained at the cost of overtime or second-shift premiums or additional equipment installations, the simple cost calculation just outlined would have to be extended to include these extra costs and investments (not a difficult task if the procedures are well laid out).

By making similar trial calculations under other operating patterns, one can reasonably quickly get a picture of the influence of the operating pattern on cost and can arrive at a pattern which comes close to giving the minimum overall cost. This plan then represents the basis for procurement, employment, and inventory control during the coming months until new forecasts call for an adjustment.

The operating plan summarized in Table 5-5 is essentially a minimum cost plan, under the conditions that (1) annual inventory holding costs are $45 per unit, (2) the cost of hiring and training an employee is $300 (typical of many industries), and (3) a change of 40 units in the daily rate of output requires employment or release of 100 men. The cost of seasonal inventory equals 2,275 units (average seasonal anticipation stocks) at $45 per unit, or about $102,000. The plan calls for varying the production rate from a low of 250 units per day to a maximum of 550 units—a change of 300 units; this requires hiring and training 750 new employees at a cost of $225,000. (If the

TABLE 5-5. Minimum Total Cost Plan

Month	Monthly production plan, units	End-of-month seasonal inventory, units
January	5,500	0
February	4,750	1,250
March	5,250	3,900
April	5,250	4,750
May	7,450	5,700
June	11,000	7,200
July	6,600	2,300
August	12,100	2,200
September	11,000	0
October	11,800	0
November	10,800	0
December	8,500	0

Average seasonal anticipation stock..	2,275
Average safety reserve..............	3,400
Average monthly inventory.........	5,675

hiring and subsequent layoff of 750 employees is considered an undesirable employment variation, the solution must be sought within whatever are set as the feasible or tolerable levels.)

Thus, under the plan in Table 5-5, the total of seasonal anticipation inventory stocks and hiring and training costs is $327,000. This represents a net saving of over $100,000 per year compared with the uniform production plan in Figure 5-2. If the same cost factors are used to evaluate the two extremes described above—one calling for a production rate varying from a low of 250 units to a high of 950 units, the other being the uniform plan in Figure 5-2— the total cost of these plans is roughly the same, $430,000 to $450,000 annually.

A number of devices can be used to help work out the seasonal plan graphically. Frequently, for example, the production level can take on only discrete values; that is, production must operate on a 0-, 1-, 2-, or 3-shift basis. This tends to be true particularly of assembly or product line operations, especially where overtime on a planned basis is not allowed by policy. Some production planners have found it useful to lay these alternatives out on a plastic sheet. The scale on the plastic sheet is the same as that on the planning graph. Lines are cut through the sheet representing cumulative production or output versus time for each of several levels of operation. The slopes of the lines cut in the sheet are the effective rates of output. Then the plastic sheet and cumulative production requirements graph can be used together to lay out alternative production plans for test. A number of other devices and methods have been used successfully to meet the same objectives.

Graphical methods usually do not allow one to arrive directly at a minimum cost plan that takes into acount the various inventory, hiring and layoff, and overtime penalties which may exist. It is necessary to work out and cost two or three alternative plans to find one that is close to optimum.

Linear Programming Methods. Various mathematical programming methods have been used for production planning in the face of seasonal production requirements. Linear programming has been found useful both as a routine planning procedure and as an investigative tool to determine how important seasonal inventories were and how critical different cost elements were in determining optimum plans.

The use of linear programming in production planning is based on certain assumptions which may appear on first inspection to be rather rigid:

1. Production requirements are assumed known and exact. This, of course, is rarely true, but the requirements schedule does represent the best estimate, including an allowance for demand forecast error.
2. Cost functions or relationships are assumed to be linear; that is, cost relations are assumed to consist of fixed elements plus elements which vary directly in proportion to the variables specified in the plan— amount of overtime, amount of inventory, and so on.

Devices for avoiding the dangers implicit in the first assumption have been noted in connection with converting the demand forecast into a schedule of production requirements. The seriousness of the second assumption depends entirely on the particular problem. However, in production planning problems, costs are usually known only approximately, and to the extent that they are known they can usually be approximated by linear relation or combinations of linear relations.

Linear programming has been found useful in circumstances where the problem is complicated by one or more of the following conditions:

1. Several product lines using the same facilities or staff

2. Possibilities of planned use of overtime to meet peak needs
3. Need for considering extra-shift premiums
4. Several stages in manufacturing, with seasonal storage possibilities between
5. A number of alternate plants, with different cost and employment situations, to meet demand
6. Joint planning of plant operations and of the assignment of branch warehouses to the plant

When the seasonal planning problem is attacked as a linear programming problem, the objective is to minimize the total of costs incurred in carrying inventories forward in slack periods to meet future sales peaks, changing the production level to meet sales requirements, or resorting to overtime. The objective has to be reached within the limitations imposed by: (a) capacity restrictions on the amount which can be produced at normal or overtime rates in any month; (b) the requirement that inventories in each line or product be planned large enough to meet sales requirements; and possibly (c) the amount of variation that can be tolerated in the planned production rate. Illustrations of production planning problems formulated in linear programming terms can be found in technical literature on the subject.[1]

OBJECTIVES OF PRODUCTION CONTROL

Control, in the sense in which the term is used here, means the adjustment of operations to conform to plans. As noted earlier, a principal source of difficulty in the management of production is the uncertainty of future requirements. The fundamental function of production control is the timely issuance of orders to the production facility for replenishment stocks in response to short-term fluctuations in demand. Safety stocks give short-term protection against sales or demand uncertainty. For example, they protect individual products over the period required for delivery of an order or between inventory reviews. The effectiveness of control, however, depends on the ability of the control system to restore these safety stocks in case of depletion.

If total demand varies and stocks are being restored from production operations, the ability to restore stocks depends on the ability of the production facilities to react to chance fluctuations in demand. To get low inventories, the process must have fast reactions properly controlled or, equivalently in some cases, large *capacity*. If reactions are slow or limited then inventories must be large. Inventory, in effect, serves another type of protective function, namely, protection of production rate or capacity from the stresses of demand fluctuation.

Problems resulting from demand fluctuation arise in a variety of types of manufacturing organizations. For example, changes in the throughput rate of chemical processing equipment may be slow and difficult or expensive. The output level of an assembly line operation may depend on the number of stations that are manned or on the number of shifts working. Some time may be required to effect changes in the production rate by, say, changing the number of stations manned at each point along the line. The production output of

[1] See A. Charnes, W. W. Cooper, and Donald Farr and staff, "Linear Programming and Profit Preference Scheduling for a Manufacturing Firm," *Journal of the Operations Research Society of America*, vol. 1, no. 3, May, 1953, pp. 114–129; and J. F. Magee, in *Notes on Summer Course in Operations Research*, Massachusetts Institute of Technology, Cambridge, Mass., June 16–July 3, 1953.

job shop operation may likewise be influenced by the rate at which new workers can be hired and trained, or by the cost of making changes in the manning level by bringing in new untrained workers or laying off people.

Simultaneous control of production rates and inventories requires a clear-cut control system with well-specified rules of operation. Sometimes a company will devote great effort to "inventory control," setting "economical" reorder levels, fixing safety stocks or reorder points, and the like, without clearly taking the effect of production fluctuations into account. The management calmly assumes that the replenishment orders which the system generates will give production operations a reasonable load. A system which might be reasonably efficient for controlling inventories of purchased items may be inefficient where production and inventories are under single management.

ELEMENTS OF A SOUND CONTROL PLAN

A sound production control system depends on:
1. A forecast of demand expressed in units of production capacity
2. A production plan or preliminary budget which establishes the inventory and production budget
3. A control procedure for deciding how fast to restore inventories to budget levels when errors in the demand forecast cause inventories to exceed or fall below budget

A first requirement is to get a measure of production or demand that is useful and can be applied to production, inventories, and demand equally well. Production, inventories, and demand—especially the latter two—are frequently quoted in physical units such as ounces, dozens, or carloads, and sometimes in dollars sold. On the other hand, a company's business can be thought of as selling time of its employees and time of use of its physical assets. The finished product demanded by a customer, or the finished or processed item in stock, is a block of processing time plus raw materials in more or less permanent form. Production control decisions are answers to questions about how much time to make available and how to use it in view of customer demand for time and the time "stored" in inventory.

How does this bear on the question of a measure of demand? It means, first, that production control is concerned with the availability and use of common—interchangeable—pools of machine and employee time. Second, product forecasts, actual demand, and inventories must be convertible into amounts of time of each of the common production pools.

For example, many consumer packaged and bottled goods are produced on mechanized blending and packaging lines. This equipment is readily shifted from one product or package to another, and the same employees are required, whatever the item. Sometimes two or more lines may be set up in parallel, but employees can be shifted from one line to another without retraining. In cases like this, there is no point in forecasting demand for each item in detail for purposes of controlling the line operation. A forecast and control of the hours of line operation in total is needed to plan the proper number of shifts and arrange for appropriate employees. If the right amount of employee and line time is planned, decisions on what product to make can be reached day to day to keep stocks balanced as actual demand materializes.

Many companies, particularly those supplying industrial customers with items like meters, tools, small-volume chemicals, motors, or equipment, have a different problem. They supply a wide range—often many thousands—of items. Manufacture of different groups of items will call for distinctly different routings through the plant, and each routing may require a number of processing and assembly steps. However, different routings may call for use of common equipment or people, for example, a particular machining center.

Despite apparent differences between the two cases, the control principles are the same. In the second case, products should be grouped for forecasting purposes so that within each group all products go through the same pools of interchangeable employees and machines as far as possible. The forecast demand for product groups can then be exploded into forecast demand for individual production pools. The available time in the several production pools can then be controlled by methods such as those described below.

Cost Factors. Control of production operations in a particular center amounts to deciding how fast production time should be changed to account for differences between times needed to meet forecast and actual demand. Determining how fast production operations should respond to sales fluctuations and to what extent these fluctuations should be absorbed by means of inventory depends on a balance of costs—the costs of warehousing and cash investment in inventory as opposed to the costs of changing production rates or building in excess capacity in the production system. In some cases, the production rate may be changed by changing the level at which the plant is manned, thus incurring hiring, training, and layoff costs. In other cases, flexibility in production rates may be obtainable only by the device of building and manning facilities with excess capacity. In these cases, the cost of production capacity includes the capital cost of excess facilities and the cost of unused labor. A third element of cost, sometimes important, is the actual cost of making out schedules, which depends on the frequency with which these are made and the degree of precision required. The degree of production flexibility to be built into the control system also depends on the speed of reaction of production which is physically possible, for example, the time needed to train new employees.

OPERATING WITH PRODUCTION CONTROL RULES

Under a periodic reorder rule, the warehouse would place an order in each period equal to anticipated requirements over the lead time plus the reorder period, less the amount on order, plus the amount by which desired inventory on hand and on order exceeds actual. This rule is set up on the assumption that there is no cost of changing the size of order from period to period.

How would this work as a production control procedure? First, a preliminary production budget is drawn up based on the demand forecast. The preliminary production budget or plan takes the place of anticipated requirements, and the "reorder amount" specifies the production or employment level for the coming period. Fluctuations in demand from period to period are passed on to production to their full extent; production will fluctuate around the preliminary budget by the same amount that demand fluctuates around the forecast. Inventories will fluctuate about desired levels to the extent of differences between actual and forecast demand over the period of the lead time plus one review interval. Thus the desired or planned inventories must be set high enough to account for differences between the production budget and demand forecast *plus* inventory fluctuations.

This production rule has one clear and serious difficulty as a basis for controlling production: it passes back to production the full period-to-period fluctuation in demand about the forecast. If this rule were used directly to control production, the fluctuations from one period to the next in the production rate might be uneconomical. In many circumstances, it is desirable to make greater use of inventories to even out changes in production rates.

One frequently useful method is to adjust the production rate by some fixed fraction of the discrepancy between planned and actual stock on hand or scheduled. Suppose we change the rule to adjust the production rate by only some fraction of the discrepancy between planned and actual stock on hand or scheduled. If k represents the fraction used (k being some number between 0.0 and 1.0), the control rule would call for current production equal to the planned level adjusted by a fraction k of the discrepancy.

When the control number or fraction k is set equal to 1.0, we have the same rule as before. If the control number were set equal to 0, the correction term would be eliminated, and production would follow the preliminary plan regardless of demand. In such a case, of course, planned inventories would necessarily have to be huge to maintain service. In general, the larger the value of k—the closer to 1.0—used, the more responsive is the control system to forecast errors: production-level fluctuations are larger, and inventory requirements are reduced. This type of control method keeps production levels close to preliminary plan but allows them to fluctuate above or below to take up deviations in planned versus actual stocks.

In some circumstances, another type of rule may be useful. One scheme allows for modifying the production rate based on departures of inventory from plan. The modification is based on the existing rate rather than on the preliminary plan. The production level for the period being planned is given by

1. The level to be in effect during the preceding period (already planned)
2. Plus a fraction of the difference between desired and expected inventory at the end of the period being planned if the preceding rate is continued

Each of these alternatives is useful in certain types of plants, depending, for example, on whether the cost of production fluctuations comes primarily from fluctuations about some long-run desired normal of such things as overtime and undertime costs or work guarantees, or from changing the rate from one time to another of such things as hiring, training, and layoff costs. Each in appropriate circumstances will lead to smoother production at the expense of extra inventory to maintain the desired level of service.

Information Flow. The information flow under control rules of the type described can be shown schematically as in Figure 5-3. The inventory of material on hand at the beginning of any period plus material on order during the period less demand during the period determines the inventory discrepancy versus the "normal" level for the period being planned. (The "normal" may be a fixed amount—the same for all periods—or it may vary from period to period according to a preliminary plan in the case of seasonal items.) The inventory discrepancy plus the normal production level for the period being planned determines the production order or final plan. The normal production level may be the level set in a preliminary plan or the level planned for the preceding period. The control rule specifies how the normal level and inventory discrepancy are to be combined to obtain the production order or final plan for the period under consideration.

FORMS OF PRODUCTION ORGANIZATION

Production scheduling and related control systems strongly reflect the organization and functions of the production system. Two forms are generally

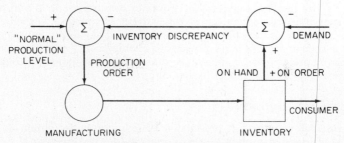

FIG. 5-3.   Information Flow for Production Control.

recognized: the functional organization and the product line organization. The functional form is better known as the "job shop" organization. The product line organization is probably best known in the automotive industry. Because it is most often found in the automotive and similar industries where assembly operations are important, it is generally referred to as "assembly line" manufacture.

In the functional organization, departments or work centers are organized about types of equipment or operations such as drilling, forging, spinning, or assembly. Products flow through departments in batches corresponding to individual orders. These may be finished-stock orders on the plant or, in the extreme, individual customer orders. Theoretically, any sequence of operations from one department to the next is possible.

The functional type of organization is found in industries characterized by substantial basic product diversity. It has the advantages of flexibility and adaptability to change in demand. Moreover, equipment is not specialized or tied to other units; as a result, better equipment utilization and lower equipment capacity requirements are in theory possible. On the other hand, the functional form of organization typically results in slow movement of product through manufacturing stages, resulting in sizable process inventory requirements.

Under the product line form of organization, all operations on a product or set of related products are combined. Equipment is devoted to a single product or product group. It is generally physically contiguous, and capacities of the several manufacturing stages are related to permit uniform product flow. Under this form of organization, individual product orders are merged, and only superficial product differences, from the point of view of manufacturing procedures, exist within a given line.

This form of organization is typical in industries with stable demand and limited basic product diversity. It has the advantages of rapid flow of product through manufacturing stages, resulting in lower process inventory requirements and the need for less paperwork in scheduling material, routing, and control. Opportunities for using specialized tools and less versatile people permit lowered operating cost. On the other hand, rigidity, extra equipment costs, sensitivity to disruption due to breakdown of component units of the line or due to fluctuations in output of individual units or stations, and feasible limitations on product diversity have limited the extended adoption of this form of organization.

Intermediate Forms.   Most manufacturing organizations contain elements of both organization forms, functional and product line; and almost all products and product lines—whether several hundred or several tens of thousands of items—are capable of being manufactured under a wide range of organizational forms intermediate between the extremes of pure job shop and assembly line operation. Taking advantage of this latitude has been a source of considerable operating economy in some businesses and could be in many more. Analysis of specific product and processing characteristics has revealed opportunities for improvements in inventory and production control ranging from better forecasting to more efficient scheduling.

THE SCHEDULING FUNCTION

The principal function of production scheduling is to obtain a smooth, timely flow of product through manufacturing steps. It starts with the specification of what to make, from customer orders or from the operation of the inventory control system. It includes the loading of items to be made into manufacturing centers and covers the dispatching of manufacturing instructions to operating centers.

The objectives of the scheduling function are to prevent unbalanced use of time among departments and work centers, to keep labor on hand employed, and to meet established lead times. The scheduling methods used are closely allied to the production planning and inventory control methods used. These methods determine the resources available for scheduling. On the other hand, the lead times which the scheduling system permits in turn have a strong influence on inventory stocks and policies.

Scheduling practices depend in detail on the nature of the product and facilities, although considerable effort has gone into the development of techniques such as board displays, filing systems, and card systems to facilitate scheduling and control of progress on orders scheduled. Conventional scheduling techniques or procedures are typically designed to cope with the complexities of job shop scheduling, where each order is unique and no predetermined sequence of operations exists. Most such procedures are basically schemes for recording and keeping track of center loadings, expected delivery times, and work progress. In examining approaches to scheduling, it is helpful to break these down into

1. Techniques for deciding which item to make and how to make it
2. Methods for loading production orders or fitting orders to available facilities
3. Methods for dispatching orders and watching progress

SCHEDULING TECHNIQUES

The systems described earlier are useful in planning and controlling overall inventory levels and production operating levels. They do not, however, necessarily indicate how much of which particular item to manufacture. This is a day-to-day decision to be made in the face of actual demand and inventories on hand. If any type of "damped" response to inventory fluctuations is employed, some decision must be made on how to allocate available production time among the items in question.

One approach to this rests on the concept of run-out time, the time when inventory on hand plus production of the item already scheduled will be used up. The object is to assign available production capacity in such a way that run-out times for all items are the same.

The inventory of each item expected on hand at the end of the period being scheduled is: Inventory on hand or scheduled in production on the scheduling date plus scheduled production of the item less expected usage of the item during the period equals inventory expected on hand at end of period scheduled. This expected inventory divided by the current usage rate gives the expected time over which demand for the item is covered.

This formula can be applied equally well to the total inventory of all items produced by the facility being scheduled as long as inventories, production, and usage are expressed in commensurable units such as machine hours or man-hours. Because the total production to be scheduled is known from the employment plan or overall control, knowledge of total inventory on hand and an estimate of expected usage are all that are needed to determine how long the total expected inventory will last—the total run-out time.

The production of each item should then be scheduled so that the run-out time for the item is the same as for the inventory as a whole. This can be done as follows:

1. Multiply the usage rate for the item by the run-out time for the total inventory planned for the end of the period scheduled.
2. Add expected usage during the period scheduled.
3. Subtract the total of inventory on hand or currently scheduled in production. This gives the production of the item to be scheduled.

A run-out list can be used for scheduling production in an operation which makes a number of stock items that are to be made in economical fixed or minimum batches or lots and where the operating level has been set. Some examples include: a machining center making parts for stock; an assembly line used to make a series of items; a paint, petroleum, or powder blending operation; a textile dyeing operation. In such cases, either setup costs or physical limitations such as equipment capacity will dictate batch or run sizes, and items must be scheduled in batches or runs to meet these conditions.

Where items are in continuous production on multipurpose equipment, the principle of run-out time can be employed to adjust machine assignments. In the spinning operations of the textile industry, for example, several types of yarn may be produced on a battery of spinning frames. The assignment of spindles to yarn grades must be kept in adjustment with yarn requirements. In spinning and similar continuous operations, the allocation of equipment among products can be determined in each scheduling period by fixing the proportion of equipment producing each item so that the expected run-out time is constant among all items.

Loading. The production order being scheduled may pass through one or several departments or common pools of employees and may require time on a variety of types of equipment. The types of equipment such as drill presses and grinders may perform basically different functions. They may be of different sizes, such as presses with different capacities, mixing vats of varying sizes, or packaging lines equipped to handle cartoned and bulk-packaged material. In this case, each item must carry a designation of the type of equipment preferred or required to process it on the operation master list. The job of loading is to fit the production order onto the required machine or process centers in the uncommitted time available and within a total time no greater than the promised delivery time on special items or lead time on stock items.

The first essential piece of information needed is a list of available equipment and processing time. For convenience, similar machines should be grouped into single centers. In the simplest circumstances, where each machine or processing unit is operated independently of others, the number of machines in each group multiplied by the number of hours to be worked each day gives the total time available for processing orders. In other circumstances, individual employees in a department may work on a number of types of machines. Loading may have to be consistent with the capacities of individual machine groups as well as with the total time available of employees working in the area.

Loading may be accomplished by a number of graphical means. A load chart may be used to show the cumulative work load for each center represented by the unprocessed order backlog. The work load report may be drawn up in a variety of ways using mechanical and display techniques. In its simplest form, the report may show the total backlog in hours or days for each department or center, with no attempt to display the effect of a large backlog in one center on completion opportunities in another. As an operation on a job is completed, the work done, represented by the *estimated* time for that operation, is subtracted from the approximate backlog. This type of load control is easy to maintain; it gives an approximate idea of job completion lead times which can be quoted, and it shows up work center imbalances for labor and equipment procurement.

A variety of display boards are used to make detailed production scheduling and control data available for easy inspection, many of which date back to the Gantt chart.[2] The Gantt chart is designed to display load and work progress as a function of time, for example, planned load and progress by machine center, or planned versus actual progress on individual orders. Gantt charts make use of a horizontal scale marked in time units. A series of horizontal lines, each representing a controlled machine or order, is used to display control data.

A number of other types of techniques can be used for assigning and keeping track of machine or center loads. One common technique is to set up a register for each machine center for each time period considered. Anyone familiar with an old-fashioned hotel register can recognize this approach. As each order is loaded, a notation is made on the register for each machine showing the estimated time the order is due to go on the machine and the estimated time off.

Some companies find it convenient to use open boxes with a section for each machine, each period. As an order is loaded, a copy of the job ticket can be inserted in the box section for reference. A running total of time assigned each section may be maintained. Other companies have found tag systems convenient, with tags representing orders hung on hooks representing machine capacity. Such a system is less flexible and less easy to interpret than a chart loading system in conventional machining operations. However, it is often quite satisfactory where time estimates are not precise or where the best measure of load is the number of orders assigned. Some mixing operations, such as paint or chemical blending and sometimes dyeing operations, show this characteristic.

Dispatching. Once the production order has been drawn up, routing and time requirements have been determined, and the order has been loaded on operating centers, the production control center has the general responsibility for informing operating centers and departments of work to be done and completion dates, and for reviewing progress against orders released. This is the general function of dispatching.

A primary dispatching job is to make up the production order set including necessary job tickets, material requisitions, and the like. A number of reproducing or copying systems have been devised for selective reproduction of job tickets, material requisitions, and move tickets from an operation master list specially prepared or kept on file. The production order papers, including

    [2] H. B. Maynard (ed.), "The Gantt Chart," *Industrial Engineering Handbook,* 2d ed., sec. 7, chap. 3, McGraw-Hill Book Company, New York, 1963.

drawings, will normally be sent to the first department in the sequence to move with the order in process to subsequent departments. Frequently, job tickets will be forwarded directly to each department as an indication of work ahead.

Another dispatching function of the production scheduling unit is often to check on availability of parts or materials before release of an order. Normally, if intermediate inventories are properly controlled, stocks will be on hand. This is a particular characteristic of inventories controlled against exploded customer demand under a base stock system. From time to time, unanticipated usage, delays in processing parts replenishment production orders, or delays in receipt of materials from suppliers will cause depletion of inventory on hand.

Other dispatching functions of the production scheduling unit include maintenance of a log or record of releases, an order status file for answering inquiries, an expediting list, and often a file of drawings and other data descriptive of the order.

PRODUCT LINE CONTROL

Where the product line organization is used, the loading and control problem is easier. Loading by means of run-out lists and the like is possible. The control problem is not so much one of following individual orders from center to center as it is a job of seeing that the flow through each center is on schedule and that bottlenecks are not allowed to develop.

SUMMARY

The principles discussed here are those generally applicable to the management of production operations. Refinements in the details of the techniques of the planning, scheduling, and control of manufacturing operations are developing at a rapid rate and are finding wide application as they prove their value. The advent of high-speed data processing and computation has facilitated these applications and made possible the wide use of these more technical methods of manufacturing management.

BIBLIOGRAPHY

Bierman, H. R., L. E. Fouraker, and R. K. Jaedicke, *Quantitative Analysis for Business Decisions*, Richard D. Irwin, Inc., Homewood, Ill., 1961.

Charnes, A., and W. W. Cooper, *Management Models and Industrial Applications of Linear Programming*, vols. I and II, John Wiley & Sons, Inc., New York, 1961.

Eilon, S., *Elements of Production Planning and Control*, The Macmillan Company, New York, 1962.

Holt, C. C., F. Modigliani, J. F. Muth, and H. A. Simon, *Planning Production, Inventories and Work Force*, Prentice-Hall, Inc., Englewood Cliffs, N.J., 1960.

Klein, Morton, "On Production Smoothing, October, 1960," *Management Science*, April, 1961, pp. 286–293.

Magee, John F., and David M. Boodman, *Production Planning and Inventory Control*, 2d ed., McGraw-Hill Book Company, New York, 1967.

McGarrah, Robert E., *Production and Logistics Management: Text and Cases*, John Wiley & Sons, Inc., New York, 1963.

Moore, F. G., *Production Control*, 2d ed., McGraw-Hill Book Company, New York, 1959.

Silver, Edward A., "A Tutorial on Production Smoothing and Work Force Balancing," *Operations Research*, vol. 15, no. 6, November–December, 1967, pp. 985–1010.

CHAPTER SIX

Network Planning Techniques

JOSEPH H. REDDING *Manager, Management Sciences Division, H. B. Maynard and Company, Incorporated, Pittsburgh, Pennsylvania*

The two principal network planning techniques are PERT (Program Evaluation and Review Technique) and CPM (Critical Path Method). Both these techniques were developed in the late 1950s. PERT had its origin in the development program for the Polaris missile; CPM was first used to facilitate a faster plant turnaround at DuPont. PERT has been used to schedule and control massive government development programs, while CPM has been used to schedule and control smaller but equally complicated industrial projects. The passage of time has caused a merging of these two techniques so that it is very difficult to tell one from the other in actual application.

The new network planning techniques are a refinement of the older technique of Gantt charting. All are means of planning, scheduling, and controlling projects.

The benefits to be gained through the use of PERT or CPM are the benefits to be gained through the application of detailed planning to any project. A chemical manufacturer cut the cycle time for the overhaul of its stone docking crane by 18 percent; a defense contractor spotted a delay in the procurement of a special wiring harness and by redesign and expediting was able to avoid a contract penalty; a contractor planned a new shopping center with CPM and was able to finish two weeks ahead of schedule, saving two weeks of overhead charges; another contracting company found that the overtime that was being applied to a job was not really expediting its completion and therefore cut back on overtime and saved 12 percent on the contract cost; a consumer goods manufacturer developed a PERT network for the introduction of one of his new products and was able to speed it to the marketplace four months ahead of normal schedule; and there are many more examples of the application of network planning techniques.

This chapter will explain the technical aspects of network planning, how a manufacturing manager can initiate the use of network planning, and how a computer—the company's or a service bureau's—can be used to facilitate the implementation of network planning techniques.

NETWORK PLANNING TECHNIQUES

At the center of the network planning techniques is the network diagram. The network diagram is a shorthand approach to showing in one picture both the activities of a project and their performance sequences; such a network diagram is shown in Figure 6-1 for a simple project involving installation of an electric motor.

In a network diagram, each project activity is represented by an arrow. The arrows are not drawn to a time scale at this point. The sequence of arrows indicates the progression of project activities or the flow of work. Where project activities can be done in parallel, the arrows are shown in parallel. The junctions between activities are called events or milestones. By indicating project activities on the network diagram, project elapsed time can be calculated by adding up the time along various paths through the network diagram; the longest path represents the critical path or project duration. By specifying project activities and manpower requirements for these activities, total resource requirements can be planned.

Figure 6-2 shows how to apply network planning to the motor installation project. The first requirement is for an activity summary which indicates the tasks involved in the project. The arrows for all the activities are arranged in a network diagram reflecting their sequence and the opportunity for paralleling them. The next step is to calculate the critical path, using a simple computational procedure, thereby identifying the bottleneck activities. Finally, it is desirable to frame the network diagram in an activity schedule drawn on a time scale. At this point, the appearance of the network diagram more closely approximates the Gantt chart, with which most people are familiar.

Network planning is most often compared with Gantt charting. Both are effective planning techniques. However, network planning techniques are more explicit about activity interrelationships. Further, because the network diagram is not drawn to a time scale, it does not have to be redrawn to reflect changes in activity durations; the Gantt chart typically must be redrawn.

An additional advantage of the network planning techniques is that there is a substantial amount of computer software available to permit calculation and

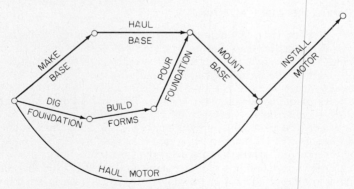

FIG. 6-1. Network Diagram for Motor Installation.

PLANNING

states the problem
using

ACTIVITY SUMMARY SHEET		
Activity	Duration	Resources
Make base	1 day	2 iron workers 1 welder
Dig foundation	1 day	2 laborers

AN ACTIVITY SUMMARY

and
AN ARROW DIAGRAM

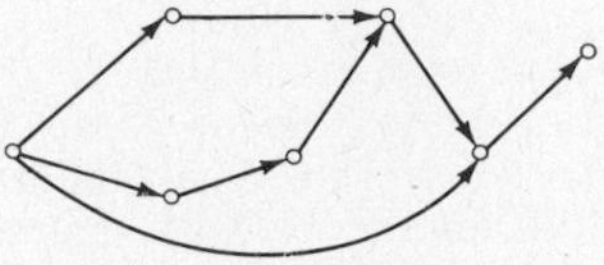

SCHEDULING

provides the problem solution
with

THE CRITICAL PATH

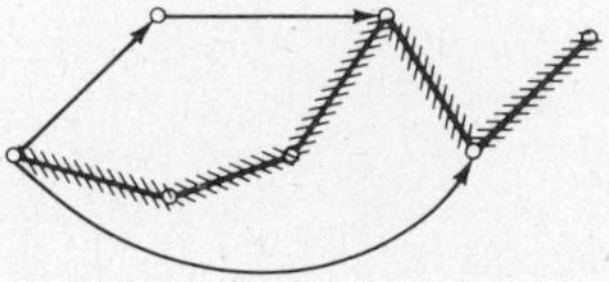

AN ACTIVITY SCHEDULE
The arrow diagram drawn
on a time scale

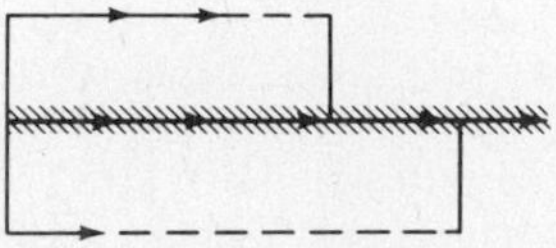

FIG. 6-2.   Application of Network Planning.

recalculation of schedules.   Such computer techniques are not readily available for the Gantt charting procedures.

IMPLEMENTING NETWORK PLANNING

Network planning is easy to implement.   For very large projects, a staff group such as industrial engineering typically will prepare network diagrams and schedules.   The computer department implements the computer procedures and modifies the format of output reports to suit individual user needs.

On smaller projects, it is not essential that highly skilled staff personnel apply network planning techniques.   A major chemical company trained all its maintenance foremen in network planning and now requires them to draw a very simple network plan for any maintenance work order they submit.   An interesting benefit from this approach is that it has reduced labor requirements by calling for men only when they are needed on the job.

Although network planning techniques are simple and readily learned, some instruction is required.   There are textbooks readily available on the subject from a number of sources.   The use of the textbooks is recommended primarily when application will be made by a competent staff organization. When it is desired to broaden the use of network planning techniques, it is best to conduct a seminar in-plant or to send the key people to outside seminars on network planning techniques. These are conducted by the American Management Association and a number of private organizations. Anyone interested in sending someone to a network planning seminar should contact any one of the training firms which regularly send out announcements regarding educational seminars. These seminars typically run from three days to a week. In-plant seminars may involve one week of classroom instruction followed by a period of pilot applications.

USE OF THE COMPANY COMPUTER FACILITY

There is a considerable amount of computer software available to produce network plans. Every major computer vendor will make such programs available to its customers without charge.

Because network techniques have been available for some time and have been quite popular, the programs for running network schedules are highly sophisticated and will require very little modification by a company's own programming staff.

The computer companies will also supply manuals which describe the application of network planning techniques and the specific computer program. Input to these computer programs typically involves a listing of project activities, the time that they require, and the nature of the interrelationships among the activities.

CONCLUSION

Network planning techniques provide an excellent approach to planning important projects. The benefits of this form of project planning include the assurance that sufficient time will be allowed for the project, that the project will be planned to be accomplished in the time available, that the necessary resources in terms of manpower and equipment will be available to accomplish the project, and that materials for the project will be available when required. Further, the technique permits rapid replanning in the event of the now well-known "Murphy's Law" which says that "if anything can go wrong, it will!"

Network planning techniques are readily learned by most people in any organization and can be facilitated by the use of an electronic computer. The technology for network planning is well developed and will require little research on the part of the user.

BIBLIOGRAPHY

"Choosing a Critical Path Scheduling Program," *Engineering News Record*, June, 1964.

"Give Foremen Fact in Familiar Form," *Factory*, January, 1968.

"How PERT/COST Helps the General Managers," *Harvard Business Review*, November, 1963.

"How to Shrink Lead Time in New Product Production," *Business Management*, May, 1966.

Stilian, Gabriel N., *PERT, A New Management Planning and Control Technique*, American Management Association, New York, 1962.

Stires, David M., and Maurice M. Murphy, *Modern Management Methods—PERT and CPM*, Materials Management Institute, Boston, Mass., 1962.

"Third Generation PERT LOB," *Harvard Business Review*, September, 1967.

Project Management

FRED C. MANASSE *Vice President—Operations, Automatic Data Processing, Inc., Clifton, New Jersey*

Project management is probably one of the most important and least understood activities of manufacturing management. It is not uncommon that the manufacturing process proper is well managed and that the utilization of operators, materials, and equipment is close to 100 percent, while at the same time the effectiveness of the professional specialists who are conducting staff projects, such as engineers, computer programmers, and operation analysts, is less than 25 percent of optimum.

It is the objective of this chapter to contribute to the understanding of the basic principles and conditions which determine the effectiveness of project management and to outline practical steps leading to the successful direction, execution, and control of manufacturing projects. It is specifically designed for the character and magnitude of the projects which are commonly encountered within the area of the practicing manufacturing manager—projects which are assigned to individuals or small teams of five or fewer members and which are of one to thirty-five weeks' duration.

THE PHASES OF PROJECT MANAGEMENT

The process by which projects are managed consists of five basic phases:
1. Specification
2. Direction
3. Authorization
4. Implementation
5. Evaluation

These phases and their principal documents are shown by Figure 7-1.

Specification. Any project which takes more than five man-days for its execution should be clearly defined in writing by means of a project specifica-

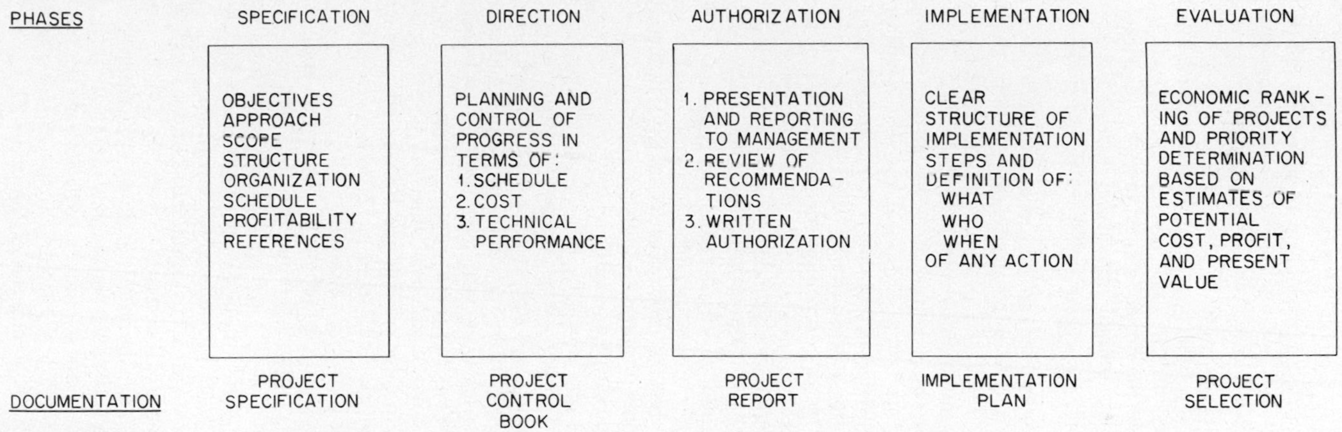

PHASES

SPECIFICATION	DIRECTION	AUTHORIZATION	IMPLEMENTATION	EVALUATION
OBJECTIVES APPROACH SCOPE STRUCTURE ORGANIZATION SCHEDULE PROFITABILITY REFERENCES	PLANNING AND CONTROL OF PROGRESS IN TERMS OF: 1. SCHEDULE 2. COST 3. TECHNICAL PERFORMANCE	1. PRESENTATION AND REPORTING TO MANAGEMENT 2. REVIEW OF RECOMMENDA-TIONS 3. WRITTEN AUTHORIZATION	CLEAR STRUCTURE OF IMPLEMENTATION STEPS AND DEFINITION OF: WHAT WHO WHEN OF ANY ACTION	ECONOMIC RANK-ING OF PROJECTS AND PRIORITY DETERMINATION BASED ON ESTIMATES OF POTENTIAL COST, PROFIT, AND PRESENT VALUE
PROJECT SPECIFICATION	PROJECT CONTROL BOOK	PROJECT REPORT	IMPLEMENTATION PLAN	PROJECT SELECTION

DOCUMENTATION

FIG. 7-1. Phases and Documentation for Project Management.

tion. This document should cover the points listed in the left-hand box on Figure 7-1.

Objectives. Every project must have an objective. The two basic requirements of a statement of objectives in the manufacturing industry are that it must be meaningful and that it must be related to the overall objective of the company.

To be meaningful, the objective must be quantified and defined in operational terms. In other words, it must be measurable, and the conditions which determine the success of the project should be fully described.

Nonspecific and nonquantified objectives such as "improved morale of the labor force," "better quality," or "reduced cost" are meaningless because they are unverifiable.

Objectives such as improvement of the annual labor turnover rate from 24 to 17 percent, reduction of the reject rate of camshafts due to brittleness from 2.1 to 1.3 percent, or increased productivity in the milling department from 108 to 122 percent are much more meaningful.

Objectives should be expressed not in terms of professional excellence but as business goals. It is unsound to state that the end result of a systems project should be a sound purchasing system; the objectives of a good purchasing system might better be quantitatively expressed as a specific reduction in clerical cost, improved pricing, less incidence of fraud, and the like.

Approach. The adequate guidance by the manager of a project in the areas of the correct approach and methodology may mean the difference between delegation and abdication. This guidance is especially necessary in the case of inexperienced and junior members of the organization.

One major item which should be specified is the level of sophistication. It is sometimes overlooked that the most efficient solution to a problem is not always the most advanced, most modern, or most powerful—but the most economic method that leads to the desired result.

This is illustrated by the execution and the results of two similar projects in different companies. In each case, the raw material inventory consisting of about two thousand items was excessive, and a project was undertaken to reduce the inventory level within the limits of a specified stock-out probability.

In Company A, the project was given to a well-qualified management analyst who was somewhat computer happy and mathematically oriented. He spent eighteen man-weeks of analysis plus fourteen programming weeks and eight weeks of testing and debugging, and developed a computerized inventory management system which resulted in a 22 percent reduction of the inventory level. It cost $28,000 annually to administer.

In Company B, a seasoned practical management analyst decided to use a different approach; he confined detailed control to 10 percent of the inventory items which accounted for 76 percent of the inventory volume. This permitted close manual control by means of simple rules for the establishment of order points and lead times for delivery. This project was completed in seven man-weeks. The annual cost of its administration was $12,000, and the inventory reduction amounted to 19 percent.

Specifying the approach, the depth of study, the amount of necessary detail, and the level of sophistication prevents cases in which the distance to the moon is measured in inches or a nut is cracked with a steam hammer.

Scope. The scope section of the project specification outlines the organizational, geographic, or other boundaries of the project.

This is essential to avoid unnecessary effort and organizational conflict. In many cases, it serves as one of the bases for savings calculations.

Structure. One of the prerequisites of effective control is the breakdown of complex processes into smaller homogeneous manageable activities. Poorly structured or unstructured processes or projects are poorly controlled or uncontrolled.

Projects are most commonly structured into phases or milestones, and these are further broken down into steps or activities.

Phases are parts of a project which lead to definite review or decision points and which require different crafts or professional experience for their execution.

Steps or activities are parts of phases which lead to clearly identifiable events. The rule of thumb is often used that a step or activity should be not less than one and not more than five man-days.

All phases and activities of a program should be clearly coded and numbered. For example, the phases of a work study project might be:

A. Cultivation of attitudes
B. Methods improvement
C. Work measurement
D. Report to management and authorization
E. Implementation
F. Follow-up

Phase A, cultivation of attitudes, could be further broken down into steps:

1. Introduction and orientation by department head
2. Information sessions with foreman
3. Meetings with union representatives
4. Informal discussions with key employees
5. Article for company newsletter

Organization. The organization section of the project specification should clearly state who is responsible for the success of the project. In the case of a team, it should define the organizational relationship of its members.

It should further outline the machinery for review and decision making regarding the findings and recommendations of the project team. In case the project is directed by a committee, the jurisdiction and frequency of meetings should be spelled out. Responsibilities for implementation, subcontracting, and follow-up should be defined.

Schedule. The method and detail of program scheduling depend on its size, complexity, and nature. For major complex projects, the various techniques of network planning have been found appropriate. Chapter 6 of this section of the Handbook gives a detailed description of network planning.

For many projects in the intermediate size range of one to thirty-five man-weeks, it is sufficient to use Gantt charts or to compile a table as illustrated by Figure 7-2.

Profitability. The cost and benefits of each project should be estimated as part of the project specification. The out-of-pocket savings should be separated from non-out-of-pocket savings such as increases in capacity. It is furthermore important to be specific as to where—in which account—and when —at which point in time—savings should accrue. Figure 7-3 is an example of such a profitability estimate.

References. This last section of the project specification is a listing of information and a bibliography necessary for the conduct of the project.

One of the most wasteful practices in the execution of projects is duplication of effort. In numerous cases, persons tackle a problem which has been solved several times before, in some cases even in the same company or the same department.

This is mostly due to a poor information retrieval system. It is therefore essential that all material which is relevant to the project, such as progress reports of similar projects, minutes of preparatory discussions and meetings,

Phase		Number of man-weeks	Due week number
Code	Description		
A	Cultivation of attitude......................	3	5
B	Method improvement........................	6	8
C	Work measurement.........................	4	10
D	Progress report............................	1	11
E	Implementation............................	3	14
F	Follow-up.................................	2	16
	Total man-weeks........................	19	

FIG. 7-2.   Project Master Schedule.

texts, and statistics, be listed for ease of reference and incorporation in the project specification.

Direction.   A project which is well specified, scheduled, and planned in all its aspects is likely to be well directed.

The main task that remains to be done is follow-up, which means to control progress in terms of:

1. Schedule
2. Cost and savings
3. Technical performance

Single-project Control.   The duration of each phase and its activities can readily be controlled by means of a comparison between actual and scheduled

AUTOMATIC DATA PROCESSING, INC.

PROJECT 44-08-69 IMPROVEMENTS IN PRODUCTION SCHEDULING SYSTEM

PROFITABILITY ESTIMATE

Data Are Thousands of Dollars

No.	ACCOUNT Item	FISCAL YEAR 1970/71				Total	FISCAL YEAR 1971/72				Total	GRAND TOTAL 1970/71 AND 1971/72
		Quarters					Quarters					
		1	2	3	4		1	2	3	4		
14	A. Cost Engineers' salaries		.9	.9	.5	2.3	.5	.5			1.0	3.3
28	Technicians' salaries		.4	.4		.8	.4				.4	1.2
59	Equipment						1.2	1.2	1.2	1.2	4.8	4.8
	Total cost		1.3	1.3	.5	3.1	2.1	1.7	1.2	1.2	6.2	9.3
11	B. Savings, out of pocket Direct labor				1.8	1.8	4.2	4.5	4.8	5.3	18.8	20.6
63	Overtime						1.4	1.5	1.5	1.8	6.2	6.2
37	Reduced expediting						.5	.5	.5	.5	2.0	2.0
	Total savings				1.8	1.8	6.1	6.5	6.8	7.6	27.0	28.8
(59)	C. Memo savings Machine utilization						.7	.7	.7	.7	2.8	2.8
	Total cash flow (B-A)		(1.3)	(1.3)	1.3	(1.3)	4.0	4.8	5.6	6.4	20.8	19.5

FIG. 7-3.   Profitability Estimate.

man-days or man-hours. This can be represented graphically by means of bar charts or Gantt charts.

In the case of projects which are scheduled by network planning, the appropriate techniques described in the preceding chapter should be considered.

It is important to bear in mind, however, that completion ahead of schedule does not necessarily reflect good performance, for it may be due to poor scheduling. Planners and foremen alike sometimes develop the habit of estimating ample times to ensure early completion; they feel that this enhances their reputation. This is likely to become an extremely costly practice. If loose estimating is suspected, it is advisable to spot-check productivity by means of work sampling studies of critical operations.

An example will illustrate this point. A heavy rolling mill had to be installed in a steel mill; one of the critical operations was digging the foundations. The foreman estimated he would need ninety-six man-days to complete this portion of the project, using a crew of eight men. He actually completed the job in eighty-eight man-days, and one day ahead of schedule. This certainly looked good. A work sampling study, however, revealed that the average productivity of his men amounted to only 50 percent. Therefore, he could have completed the work in forty-four man-days. The practice of "padding" the schedule is more prevalent in project work than is commonly realized, and the project manager must recognize it.

Most of these comments apply equally to the control of cost and technical performance.

Multiproject Control. Robert A. Howell developed a simple practical technique for the control of a number of simultaneous projects of varying duration, cost, and technical complexity.

The heart of the system is a color-coded project status board, Figure 7-4, here modified for black-and-white presentation. Projects are reviewed at predetermined intervals for technical status, "T"; schedule status, "S"; and cost status, "C." In each of these areas, the question is asked, "Are things going well?" If the answer is "Yes," the appropriate field is coded by a circle, ○; if the answer is qualified, if progress has to be watched, or if serious potential trouble is ahead, the code is a triangle, ▽. An asterisk, *, means in trouble or out of control.

In this simple manner, up to one hundred projects can be controlled simultaneously without the aid of a computer.

Authorization. Most projects contain definite decision points. Part of a project, for instance, may be a study which results in findings and recommendations. In such cases, these recommendations must be compiled as a report to management which is to serve as a basis for a rational selection of a course of action.

Project reports do not have to be long or elaborate, but it is advisable that they cover the following subjects:
1. The title page
2. Objectives of the report
3. Summary of findings (This should be no more than two pages and should permit a busy executive to evaluate quickly the progress and potential results of the project.)
4. Description of the study
   a. The true nature of the problem
   b. Methodology of study
   c. Presentation of relevant data
5. Recommendations
6. Appendix (if necessary), references, and bibliography

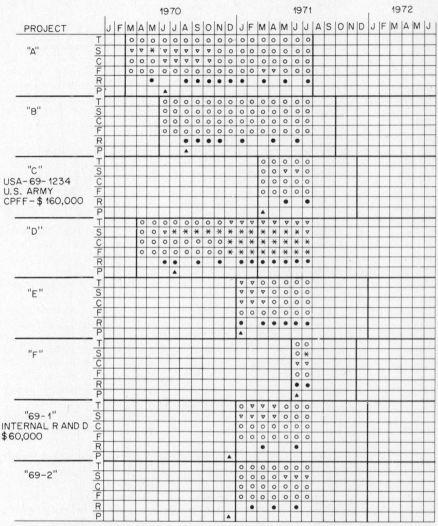

FIG. 7-4.   Project Status Board. (*Source:* Harvard Business Review, *March–April, 1968.*)

The recommendations should be clearly listed and numbered for ease of reference and well-structured authorization. The actual authorization is frequently preceded by a formal presentation to a committee or an appropriate group of executives. It is highly desirable that the authorization be given in writing.

Implementation. It sounds like a platitude that even the best project is of little use unless it is translated into action; yet it is surprising how many well-conducted projects remain shelved in the reporting stage.

One of the best ways to overcome this is to develop a clear-cut implementation plan. This plan should basically cover three aspects:

1. What should be implemented
2. Who should do it
3. When it should be done

Figure 7-5 shows an example of an implementation plan.

Implementation in most cases means change; change in turn may mean reluctance or even resistance.

It is important to anticipate the dislocations and ill feelings which the implementation of a project may cause. Especially in the case of cost reduction projects which result in staff reduction, problems should be faced with candor.

In an incorrectly handled case of an automation project where a piece of equipment was designed to replace sixty-two operators, it was presented to the work force as a quality improvement project which would have no significant impact on employment. When the members of the department suddenly found out that layoffs were imminent, the morale of the whole plant was affected adversely.

Another case illustrates correct handling. In the early stages of a mechanization project, the company newsletter announced that it was intended to acquire ten modern stamping presses which would greatly improve the competitive position of the company. At the same time, it was indicated that this would result in reduced manpower requirements, but that employment was safeguarded for all employees. A massive program of retraining was initiated. A good deal of the reduction in the labor force was accomplished by attrition. The employee morale remained on a high level.

EVALUATION

One highly critical aspect of project management remains to be described. This is the problem of project selection. There are commonly more projects than can be economically handled. Are the right ones being selected? Are correct priorities being assigned? Unless these questions find satisfactory answers, the manufacturing manager can fall into the well-known trap of merely causing people to do unnecessary work faster.

Figure 7-6 shows a practical format for project evaluation and selection. The example in this illustration is a developmental project carried out over a number of years. The evaluation covers a ten-year period. The ten individual years are listed in the left-hand column. The next column to the right contains estimates of the profit impact of the project over the same period. These profit benefits are not always direct; they may be obtained through cost reduction, improvements in quality, or increases in capacity. The cost incurred in the conduct of the projects as well as its implementation is listed in the cost column. The difference between the profit and the cost is the cash flow, which is listed next. In evaluating the project, it is essential to reflect the timing of the potential profit and cost. A profit next year is of greater value than the same amount of profit estimated far in the future. This is considered by means of the present value factor. As can be seen, the cash flow of the current year is multiplied by a present value factor of 1.00, whereas the profit of $780,000 in 1980 is adjusted by a present value factor of 0.25. This present value factor represents an application of an interest rate, in this case

AUTOMATIC DATA PROCESSING, INC.

PROJECT 36-07-69

INSTALLATION OF CONVEYOR SYSTEM
FOR DEPARTMENT 200

IMPLEMENTATION PLAN

What	Who	When
1. List components and color code locations	F.M.	Wk. 25
2. Inspect conveyors at subcontractor's plant	A.B.	Wk. 27
3. Determine delivery schedule	A.B.	Wk. 29
4. Change layout to make room for conveyor	C.F.	Wk. 30
5. Prepare foundations	B.D.	Wk. 31
6. Install motor	A.D.	Wk. 33
7. Erect conveyor bed	A.D.	Wk. 34
8. Adjust belt	B.G.	Wk. 31
9. Trial run	F.M.	Wk. 32
10. Final furniture move	A.D.	Wk. 34
11. Final personnel orientation	B.F.	Wk. 35
12. Full operation	A.D.	Wk. 36
13. Final adjustments	A.D.	Wk. 38

FIG. 7-5. Implementation Plan.

PROJECT EVALUATION

DEPT. 211	PROJECT LEADER A. SMITH		DATE 11/8/69	PROJECT NUMBER BSF 244

TITLE
WELDING ELECTRODE 72 x 14

PRESENT VALUE AND PRIORITY DETERMINATION

YEAR	PROFIT	COST	CASH FLOW	PRESENT VALUE FACTOR	PRESENT VALUE
1970		27,000	− 27,000	1.00	− 27,000
1971		147,000	− 147,000	0.87	− 128,000
1972		225,000	− 225,000	0.76	− 171,000
1973	8,000	145,000	− 137,000	0.66	− 90,000
1974	40,000	95,000	− 55,000	0.57	− 31,000
1975	158,000	145,000	13,000	0.50	6,000
1976	314,000		314,000	0.43	135,000
1977	450,000		450,000	0.38	171,000
1978	700,000		700,000	0.33	231,000
1979	780,000		780,000	0.28	218,000
1980	780,000		780,000	0.25	195,000
TOTAL PRESENT VALUE					509,000

RISK	RESEARCH 0.7 SALES 0.7	RISK FACTOR 0.50	ADJUSTED VALUE	254,500

CAPACITY	(ENGINEER WEEKS)	AVAILABLE 4	REQUIRED 9	SHORTAGE 5	BASIC 1 PRIORITY

PRIORITY ADJUSTMENT OF OTHER PROJECT
REDUCE BSF 96 CRACKING OF CHROMSTEEL FROM 1 TO 2

RESEARCH DIRECTOR'S DECISION   APPROVED ☐
REJECTED ☐

FINAL PRIORITY | 1 |

FIG. 7-6. Method of Project Evaluation and Selection.

15 percent. Figuratively, it represents the amount of money that an investor must deposit in a bank paying 15 percent interest to reach the value of one dollar after one year, two years, and so on, up to ten years.

The product of the cash flow and the present value factor for each year is the present value of the project for the same year. The sum of the present values for the evaluation period of the project is a sound measure of its economic value. This method is widely used for ranking or selection.

The fact that in some cases estimates have to be made under conditions of uncertainty should not deter the project manager from using this technique. Such uncertainties may be compensated for by the use of one or more risk factors. If, for instance, the probability that the project will be successful is estimated to be 70 percent, a risk factor of 0.7 can be used. Furthermore, if profit is anticipated from future sales gains and the probability that the sales will materialize is likewise 70 percent, an additional risk factor of 0.7 for sales risk may be built into the evaluation.

CONCLUSION

The practicing manufacturing manager is faced with the problem of managing a variety of projects. The normal tools of cost control and scheduling employed in the control of the manufacturing process are of little use owing to the nonrepetitive and creative nature of most project activities. The problem is further complicated by the characteristics of project engineers who are often highly qualified professionals, somewhat allergic to most forms of administration and control.

This chapter outlines a number of practical and noncomplex steps which will help the manufacturing executive to control projects successfully without the aid of computers.

BIBLIOGRAPHY

Baumgartner, John Stanley, *Project Management*, Richard D. Irwin, Inc., Homewood, Ill., 1963.

Gibson, Robert E., "How to Increase Executive Productiveness," *Business Management*, February, 1968.

Hirsch, Irving, William Milwitt, and William J. Oakes, "Increasing the Productivity of Scientists," *Harvard Business Review*, March–April, 1958.

Howell, Robert A., "Multiproject Control," *Harvard Business Review*, March–April, 1968.

Manasse, Fred C., "Increase Engineering Productivity," *American Engineer*, December, 1967.

Martino, R. L., *Project Management and Control*, American Management Association, New York, 1964.

CHAPTER EIGHT

Developing Improved Methods

PAUL D. O'DONNELL *Director, Headquarters Manufacturing Controls, Westinghouse Electric Corporation, Pittsburgh, Pennsylvania*

JOHN C. MARTIN *Staff Assistant, Headquarters Manufacturing Controls, Westinghouse Electric Corporation, Pittsburgh, Pennsylvania*

Direct manufacturing costs can be reduced in two general ways: (1) getting operators to work with increased effort, or (2) making improvements in the ways of applying operator effort to achieve desired results. Although the second approach has many variations, it may generally be described by the term "methods improvements."

There is always a practical limit to the first of the two approaches, no matter how well operators are motivated. On the other hand, the potential cost reductions through better methods are almost unlimited. If a steady rate of improvement can be maintained, the total savings within a few years can far surpass any results through extra effort by the operators. Or to put it another way, a company that neglects to place emphasis on regular methods improvement can find itself no longer competitive.

Changes in method may be as simple as moving a hopper of parts closer to an operator to shorten the motions involved. Or changes may be expensive and complex, such as the installation of numerically controlled lathes to reduce setup and machining time. The first type requires little more than common sense to put into effect. The new machine installation may require a series of studies to estimate possible savings and to show that the investment is justified. Methods improvements are usually the result of applying both common sense and detailed analyses.

Not very often, however, will either of these key steps to better methods "just happen." Carefully planned action by management is usually required to obtain the desired results. In recognition of this, many methods improvement programs and techniques have been developed over the years. But the best methods programs will fail if there does not exist within the plant a policy of encouraging those who have ideas to apply them to improve methods.

ESTABLISHING A CLIMATE FOR METHODS IMPROVEMENT

For more than just occasional ideas to take root and grow to fruition, an organization must be receptive to the introduction of changes. There are approaches which management can take to establish such a receptive climate. The manner in which operators react to change is often influenced negatively by existing conditions. Once these conditions have been identified, steps can be taken to reduce their influence. Industrial history shows that continued improvements have been accompanied by better working conditions and increased employment. Getting such points across to operators should be one of management's objectives.

Effect of Wage Plans on Resistance to Change. Wage incentive systems sometimes act as roadblocks to constructive methods changes. This is because the operators tend to resist changes that may lower their bonus earnings. For example, a greater percentage of machine-controlled time within a cycle will reduce the opportunity to apply extra effort during manual portions of the job. Or an operator who may have built up unusual proficiency on a job—perhaps accompanied by hidden methods changes that help add to the bonus—will probably not want that job changed and a new time value established. When operators strongly oppose a change, they tend to find ways to keep it from being introduced successfully. A firm management policy regarding methods revisions is called for when wage incentives are in effect.

Incentive plans have the advantage of inducing operators to look for methods improvements that the job analyst may have missed when setting a time value. This advantage tends to diminish when close follow-up by the job analyst results in the time values being revised to bring them in line with the changed methods. Yet if this follow-up is not made, the incentive application will deteriorate and lose its effectiveness. Management should insist that standards be revised as methods are changed.

A daywork wage plan does not involve as strong a "reverse incentive" to resist changes. When the daywork method of wage payment is accompanied by carefully applied work measurement plus effective supervision and staff assistance, it is possible to obtain a fair day's work from operators while at the same time keeping the door open to methods improvement. Referred to as "measured daywork," this framework for manufacturing control makes it possible for industrial engineers within a plant to concentrate on sound standards plus ever-improving methods. They are not as burdened with the time-consuming discussions about rates that wage incentive programs tend to require.

Positive-attitude Builders. *Suggestion Award Programs.* The value of suggestion systems is only partially in the methods improvements generated by the suggestions themselves. The attitudes that suggestion systems help create can be of even greater importance. A strong emphasis on employee suggestions is a way of saying, "We want everyone in the plant to help work toward better methods."

Stress "The Easier Way." Most cost reducing methods changes result in making jobs easier for the operators. For example, a transfer device to move heavy sheet metal parts from one punch press die to another may reduce labor requirements on the two presses by one third, while at the same time performing mechanically what was previously a difficult manual job. The introduction of a power screwdriver to replace a hand tool may have the same effect; or a minor change in a motion pattern may eliminate the transfer of a part between the hands. In each of these cases, introduction of the new method should be accompanied by emphasis on the reduced effort involved. Making every job easier to perform is a valid objective for both operators and management.

Avoid Downgrading Due to Methods Changes. A sure way to cause employee resentment that can counteract efforts to build cooperation is through making force reductions or downgrading job classifications after major methods changes. There may be occasions where this is unavoidable. However, such action will inevitably affect the climate for generating future improvements. The introduction of improvements involving reduced labor content should be done during expanding business periods where possible. Net force reductions can then be avoided, and the employees concerned can be shifted to other work of similar classification.

Reflect Cooperation in Merit Rating. Where employee merit rating plans are in effect, one of the factors taken into account should be the cooperation given in developing improved methods during both the planning and the implementing stages.

Include Indirect, Clerical, and Technical Personnel. Methods improvement should be a plant-wide endeavor, without stopping at the shop boundaries. The accounting, maintenance, or receiving departments, for example, should be as concerned about the procedures, tools, and manual methods affecting their work as any of the direct manufacturing sections.

Enlisting the Support of Foremen and Other Supervisors. Foremen are close to many of the problems that occur in the work situation, such as heavy lifting, unnecessary hand motions, or extra handling between operations. They may tend to accept existing conditions as just part of the job unless their attention is directed to solving the problems that undesirable conditions create.

Regular Training Programs. An hour per month on methods training is a reasonable program to establish on a continuing basis. Subjects that can profitably be covered are discussed later in this chapter. One of the best training aids is to film before-and-after views where manual methods have been improved and then to use the films to illustrate the general principles involved.

Promote Cooperative Action. When there are procedures for rating the effectiveness of supervisors, such ratings can properly consider whether they exhibit a willingness to have the methods which they supervise improved. Good cooperation between line supervisors and staff specialists is essential. To increase this, the recognition accorded by management for improvements should, where appropriate, be shared between the staff specialists who develop the ideas and the supervisors who help with their implementation.

Provide Staff Assistance. The control of the manual methods used by the operators is basically the responsibility of the direct supervisor. For example, if a foreman does not insist that operators develop motion patterns which utilize both hands effectively, the manual methods in his department will probably not be acceptable. Thus, it is important that supervisors should not be tied up too long on production planning, time reporting, stock chasing, equipment problems, and the like. It should be possible for supervisors to check the methods on newly assigned jobs and make changes as justified. Management should consider the need for clerical personnel or staff specialists to relieve the direct supervisors of routine duties so that they can do a sound job of controlling methods.

Act on Ideas That Are Practical. Those who make suggestions expect a prompt answer. If an idea has merit and is economically sound, it should be carried out. Slow action in doing this will tend to stifle good ideas.

Staff Personnel. Industry practices differ both in the number of staff specialists provided and in the terms used to describe their functions. For staff work concerned with the development of manufacturing methods, such titles as industrial engineer, manufacturing engineer, production engineer, process engineer, tool engineer, or methods engineer are used. The design engineering function is an important contributor to manufacturing methods, as are the purchasing, plant maintenance, and production control functions. The personnel department affects methods indirectly through its selection of new employees.

Get Qualified Men. Qualified men are desirable on any job. Because management may for some time not know whether an effective methods improvement job is being accomplished, it is essential to select capable men for this work.

Provide Time for Analysis. An industrial engineer whose major duty is to establish incentive time standards may be so busy doing the nonpostponable parts of this job that he has little time to think about better methods. Having potential methods analysts within the plant does not assure that the required job of improvement will be accomplished. There must be time for the analysts to utilize methods improvement techniques. There must be time to think, in addition to "putting out fires."

Give Adequate Methods Training. Some of the training required for staff methods specialists is included within the framework of certain college courses. Part of the needed training can come from technical reference sources, provided there is a background of analysis capability. Other phases of methods training can best be provided through on-the-job associations along with competent guidance.

DETAILED METHODS ANALYSIS TECHNIQUES

There are several commonly applied techniques for analyzing industrial industrial operations to develop methods improvements. A brief description is given of each so that the general approach will be clear. Additional details about specific techniques may be obtained from industrial engineering handbooks or texts such as those listed in the bibliography. Although there is an area of overlap between several of these techniques, they are considered sufficiently different to merit individual discussion.

Perhaps the first "technique" that should be mentioned is common sense combined with a background of shop experience. This in itself will accomplish much in the way of methods improvement, provided time for careful thought is available and an orderly approach is taken. To go further requires ways of directing the analyst's attention to points that would otherwise be overlooked. That is what the more advanced techniques for analysis attempt to do.

Motion Study. Motion study involves a study of the hand and body motions required to perform an operation. For clarity, a chart of the right- and left-hand motions is usually prepared. The breakdown may be as fine as the sequence of finger and arm motions involved, or a grouping of motion aggregates may be employed to designate the functions of get, place, process, and dispose.

The purpose of motion study is to find ways of eliminating, shortening, or combining certain motions so that the work cycle can be performed more effectively. Because this approach is time consuming, motion study in fine detail is applicable chiefly to short-cycle, high-volume operations.

The diagramming of a motion pattern involves some estimation of time content. This may be determined from direct observation with a stopwatch or—more precisely—through the frame-by-frame analysis of motion picture films.

Predetermined Motion Times. There are several predetermined motion-time systems in general use which extend the scope of motion study in two ways: (1) they define practical rules for the combination of elemental finger, arm, and body motions to build up an effective motion pattern; and (2) they provide motion times which can be added together to determine cycle times.

The work pace level that is built into the predetermined time system is not consistent for all systems, and a conversion factor must in some cases be used in applying the resulting time values to a given plant's wage payment plan.

The most widely used system of predetermined times is Methods-Time Measurement or MTM. Continued refinement of this technique is carried out through the MTM Association for Standards and Research, Fairlawn, New Jersey. The fourth book in the bibliography describes MTM in detail. The time required for MTM application training is approximately three weeks, assuming adequate background of the individual and a competent instructor.

Other predetermined time systems in general use are Work Factor, Motion Time Analysis, and Basic Motion Timestudy.

Advantages for Motion Study. Through the use of a predetermined time system, it is practical to make valid comparisons between the cycle times for alternative methods without actually setting up the job for any of the methods. In this way, the method and standard time for an operation can be predesigned so that it approaches the optimum for given conditions of layout and equipment. In addition, the justification for making needed changes in the equipment can be determined ahead of time. Thus the job can be set up with improved methods that are known to be economically sound.

Trained analysts can be expected to utilize the principles of motion economy to develop sound methods and time standards through the use of predetermined time systems without the need for repeated trial-and-error analyses. It should be recognized, however, that the application time involved may be appreciable. As a rough guide, the use of detailed predetermined time systems for methods and time standard development will be justified if the expected repetition for short-cycle jobs is in the range of 15,000 or more.

Use of Condensed Predetermined Time Systems or Standard Data. Application of predetermined times for improving methods or establishing standards is not limited to high-volume work, however. There are condensed forms of data within MTM and other systems which specify the time required to perform groups of motions. Typical breakdowns include the "get" and "place" categories that have long been a part of motion study techniques.

In addition, it is common practice to apply either the detailed or the condensed systems of predetermined times through the use of standard data tables for a family of related jobs. Such data permit the quick selection of standard times for a given method. For example, standard data for single-fed punch press operations have been developed in this way. A valid standard time for any of twenty to thirty possible methods can be determined in about one minute. In case of doubt about which method should be specified, comparisons can easily be made. Standard data can also be developed through time study observation.

Time Study. A fundamental step in using time study for establishing job rates or time standards is a preliminary methods review. During this review, the analyst determines whether the methods being followed are acceptable. If not, one of two approaches should be followed: (1) revise the method before making the study, working through the supervisor involved; or (2) establish the time standard on the best method that can be set up currently, and then initiate action to obtain any further improvements that may be justified.

It is easy for the methods phase of time study work to be neglected. Given a belligerent operator, a busy or uncooperative foreman, or an analyst without sound methods training, the tendency is to make the study to cover the way the job is being performed. Management should guard against this tendency.

Process Charts. The techniques described so far have dealt with the details of specific operations. The area for methods improvement within manufacturing is much more than this, of course. Often, it is not clear where analysis should be undertaken. Consider the job of making a refrigerator door, for example. There may be dozens of parts, a series of operations to fabricate each of them, and an assembly sequence to complete the door assembly.

A methods analyst could begin at random to look for possible improvements, and he might possibly do a creditable job. Those who make such studies repeatedly, however, find that it saves time and helps accomplish more if a "picture" is first prepared of the overall process. This picture can take different formats but usually is in process chart form. Essentially it is an orderly listing of pertinent work details. Process charts are tailored to fit specific needs, but they can to some extent be standardized in format. Figure 8-1 shows the symbols adopted by the American Society of Mechanical Engineers for process charting.

Operation Process Charts. A typical operation process chart shows on one page the operations and inspections required to make each component of a product, arranged to indicate how parts came together for subassembly and assembly. Time standards are usually shown for each operation. Figure 8-2 illustrates the arrangement of a simple operation process chart with time standards and other details omitted.

Flow Process Charts. Somewhat like the operation process chart in that it lists operations and inspections, a flow process chart also indicates the han-

OPERATION

TRANSPORTATION

INSPECTION

DELAY

STORAGE

Fɪɢ. 8-1. Process Chart Symbols.

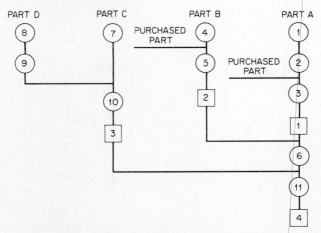

FIG. 8-2. Typical Operation Process Chart Format.

dling activities, delays, and storages. A short portion of a typical flow process chart is shown by Figure 8-3.

Man and Machine Charts. "Man and machine" charts are used to show the relation between the working cycles of the operator and of his machine. The purpose is to identify the idle time of both man and machine, so that both can be better utilized.

Operator Process Charts. Shown by Figure 8-4 is a typical right- and left-hand motion analysis based on MTM. The idle time increments for each hand are clearly shown. The usual worksheet used for developing a predetermined time standard involves one-line entries for each motion, but a graphic picture drawn to scale like the one shown facilitates discussion and understanding of the method.

Purpose of Process Charts. The four charts described are simple, basic types. Many variations are possible to show special situations. In all cases, the purpose is to bring out clearly, for analysis, information about manufacturing conditions that would otherwise be hidden and vague. It becomes possible in this way for various members of the organization to participate in the analysis. Management can more easily review the backup data to check the conclusions reached.

Work Sampling. Work sampling is a procedure often used to obtain information about the activities of a group. Observations are made at random intervals of what each individual in the group is doing. The activities are classified according to selected categories such as working or idle. The time spent on each category is expressed as a percentage. Either mathematical relationships or simple charting can be applied to determine the number of observations required to obtain answers that fall within a specified reliability range.

A work sampling study made of a maintenance function where problems are known to exist might provide the following information:

1. Actual maintenance work (38%)
2. Walking (12%)

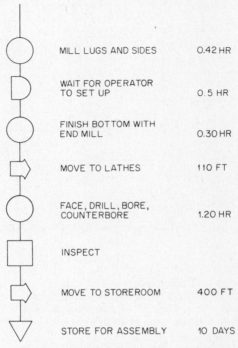

	MILL LUGS AND SIDES	0.42 HR
	WAIT FOR OPERATOR TO SET UP	0.5 HR
	FINISH BOTTOM WITH END MILL	0.30 HR
	MOVE TO LATHES	110 FT
	FACE, DRILL, BORE, COUNTERBORE	1.20 HR
	INSPECT	
	MOVE TO STOREROOM	400 FT
	STORE FOR ASSEMBLY	10 DAYS

Fig. 8-3.   Portion of a Flow Process Chart.

3. Waiting
   a. At storeroom (3%)
   b. For other maintenance men (11%)
   c. Other reasons (8%)
4. Obtain information (8%)
5. Personal delays (20%)

The low percentage of item 1 indicates that considerable improvement is possible. Analysis of the remaining data shows the need for improved methods of work planning and scheduling that will specify a full day's work for each man. Other possibilities for improvement are also suggested by the data. The work sampling study provides a factual basis which shows the need for better methods. When the improvements have been put into effect, a second study will show whether the expected results have been achieved.

Performance Reports.   Performance reports show the efficiencies of the operators. This has a direct relation to bonus earnings in the case of incentive payment. Performance reports generally show a combination of performance against standards plus extra allowances due to conditions that are beyond the control of the operators. The reports should show the amount of extra allowances for various specific categories. The need for better methods of work planning, machine maintenance, material inspection, or drawing control constitutes some of the possible improvements which will be brought to management's attention by well-designed performance reports.

Line Balancing.   A well-balanced assembly line will tend to minimize labor costs. Thus a line balancing study made for the purpose of distributing the

ELEMENT 3: Assemble bracket to fixture and place washer on rotor shaft.

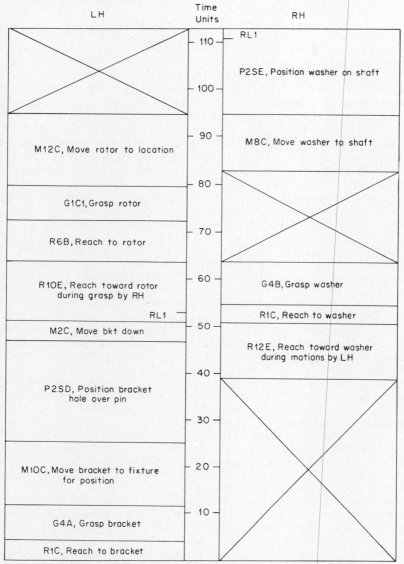

FIG. 8-4. Right- and Left-hand Operator Process Chart.

assembly work equally among the line operators will often result in increased production and reduced costs.

The first step is to list all job elements involved in the assembly process, together with the standard time for each. The elements should be as small as practical. They are then recombined to arrive at balanced work assignments for each operator. If computer methods of line balancing are used, it is necessary to specify the conditions that control the sequence in which each job element may be performed.

Complete Manufacturing Information. Methods improvement often results when clear, detailed information is sent to the shop floor to define authorized work.

Where the work to be done is nonrepetitive in nature, the listing of detailed operation descriptions can help avoid wasted effort through faulty methods. For example, consider the phrase "machine per print" in comparison with the following operation description: "Turn 1.39" dimension with carbide cutter; two roughing cuts with 1/32" feed and 300 rpm; one finish cut of 0.01" with 0.004" feed and 1,000 rpm." It is apparent that the probability that the correct method will be used is much greater in the second case.

For repetitive operations, providing even more detailed methods instruction can be advantageous. Right- and left-hand charts somewhat like Figure 8-4 are often used. With good supervision to see that these detailed instructions are actually followed, management can feel confident that the operators will not drift into the use of poor methods.

In work of a processing nature, process specifications should be carefully prepared, kept up to date, and enforced by supervision. Good process specifications that are rigidly applied can often make the difference between acceptable and unacceptable products.

Mathematical Analysis Techniques. When manufacturing conditions are difficult to analyze because of multiple variables that affect one another, it may be necessary to apply mathematical analysis techniques. As a simple example, consider the problem of slitting wide steel sheets to fill shop requirements for strip stock in many variations of width, thickness, and quantity. Inevitably, some waste will occur in the slitting process. The problem is to determine the mix of widths for each slitting operation which will minimize inventory and scrap costs. Questions of this kind can be answered by using the mathematical analysis technique known as linear programming. There are other analysis techniques that fit other kinds of problems. Approximate answers to such problems may often be obtained through nonmathematical approaches. There will be cases, however, when reliable answers require considering the variables in a precise manner using mathematical techniques.

Equipment Usage Data. It has already been pointed out that reports showing labor downtime can help indicate potential areas for methods improvement. Similarly, equipment downtime records can be used to answer questions such as the following. Should little-used equipment be removed and replaced with more useful types? Should production planning methods be improved to use equipment more effectively?

Ideas from Outside the Plant. Management should not be content to rely on ideas generated from within the plant organization. A wealth of ideas may often be obtained from other sources. Multiplant companies can exchange ideas among plants. Visits to other plants often serve as a stimulus to new lines of thought. Review of technical literature or discussions at meetings of technical organizations help generate ideas. Sales representatives from equipment or machine tool companies can be helpful if they are given a chance. These sources of methods improvement ideas are discussed more fully in the next chapter.

METHODS IMPROVEMENT PROGRAMS

There are a number of methods improvement programs in general use that are broad in scope. They may be distinguished from the specific techniques described above by the fact that the broader programs often include the application of a number of the techniques.

Most of the programs overlap to some extent. Their content and scope are less definite than those of the techniques on which they are based. For example, work sampling (a technique) is a clearly definable procedure used to determine activity percentages. But work simplification (a broad program) is a concept that can involve a number of techniques, depending upon the needs and conditions within a given organization.

Methods Engineering. Methods engineering is almost synonymous with "methods improvement." It implies not so much a program as a field of endeavor. Applied to denote the collective concepts for methods improvement in the 1930s, the term is still descriptive and applicable. Methods engineering may be thought of as a major subdivision of industrial engineering. Management will find that the term "methods engineer" is a descriptive job title for those within the general field of industrial engineering whose function is to develop improvements and follow up on their application.

Work Simplification. Almost self-defining, this name is often applied to plant programs aimed largely at the improvement of manual operations. Work simplification training courses are typically developed within the industrial engineering departments of large plants and given to such groups as manufacturing supervisors, other staff personnel, and even to key operators. The name carries with it the implication that jobs will be made easier to perform, which is a sound industrial relations approach. It is likely to be much more successful to discuss with an operator the ways of making his job easier than to emphasize the cost reduction aspects. Yet both results occur through work simplification.

A typical work simplification training program will start with how to prepare flow process charts. Process charts may be developed for the plant area with which each course participant is most familiar. By applying the questioning attitude to the charts, commonsense principles for improvement are stressed, such as:

> Eliminate unnecessary operations.
> Combine operations to reduce handling.
> Reduce handling between necessary operations.
> Shorten the hand motions involved.
> Rearrange or revise hand motions to simplify the operation cycle.

Work simplification training generally includes some form of right- and left-hand analysis, as in Figure 8-4. Management should recognize that there are possibilities for large cost reductions in this approach.

The work simplification training program should be augmented by motion picture films showing steps taken previously within the plant to simplify manual jobs. With some planning ahead, before-and-after shots can be taken that will illustrate the different methods improvement principles.

Operation Analysis. Operation analysis is about as broad in scope as methods engineering. However, it is perhaps more descriptive of specific programs that are commonly applied through plant training to reach a wide segment of the manufacturing staff and line management.

Operation analysis includes all of work simplification plus concepts of part design, tool design, equipment selection, plant layout, and similar manufacturing functions. The subjects discussed in the operation analysis training program given by the Westinghouse Electric Corporation include the following:

A. Make a preliminary survey.
B. Ask questions to get needed information.
C. Determine extent of analysis justified.
D. Organize information by means of process charts.
E. Review the data through ten primary approaches for asking questions to develop methods improvements. (These are discussed below under "Systematic Approach to Methods Analysis.")
F. Compare proposed methods with existing methods.
G. Present the proposed methods to obtain approval.
H. Install new methods after approval.
I. Establish new time standards.
J. Follow up the new method.

Value Analysis. The operation analysis program just described may be considered an overall review of areas where improvements can be made in manufacturing methods. Work simplification programs are largely an expansion of operation analysis principles as applied to manual work. Similarly, value analysis may be thought of as an expansion of the portion of operation analysis related to part function, design, and material utilization. Chapter 6 of Section 7 covers value analysis in detail.

Systems Analysis. A system may be thought of as an interrelated series of functions required to accomplish a given object. The term is often applied to procedures for the processing of manufacturing information, such as a production control system or a maintenance planning and scheduling system. The key in systems analysis is to account for all the necessary components, including any feedback of information that is required. Analysis techniques should then proceed with the usual questioning approach, considering each element to determine whether it can be eliminated, combined, or simplified to improve the methods that are involved.

Because of the complex interactions that occur within extensive systems, it may be advantageous to look for improvements through simulation of the interactions. This can be done through computer applications. A model of the system may be programmed so that the computer simulates the system. By injecting specific changes into the model, their effects can be determined and improvements worked out.

Operations Research. Based on the scientific method of approach, operations research has the objective of providing a quantitative basis for management decisions. Mathematical analysis techniques are frequently employed, requiring analysts who have obtained special training. A mathematical model of the functions in question may be derived to aid in the analysis.

Suggestion Award Plans. The suggestion plan approach to methods improvement is closely associated with the area of employee relations.

Cost Improvement Programs. The subject of methods improvement is of sufficient importance for many plants to establish an organized procedure to aid in searching for ideas, identifying them, and following them to conclusion. The typical features of a cost improvement program are:

1. Committee action
2. Cost improvement goals
3. Identifying ideas and reporting results

Committee Action. Because many ideas for improvement involve participation or approval by various departments, the committee should have representatives from manufacturing, design engineering, purchasing, and the other plant functions chiefly concerned. The duties assigned to the committee usually include: (1) searching for ideas through group discussions, (2) identifying ideas that deserve committe action, and (3) providing required follow-up by individual committee members.

Cost Improvement Goals. Management may designate specific amounts of net yearly cost reductions which should be effected by the manufacturing staff and line departments. This has the obvious advantage of spurring action, but it can also have the disadvantage of causing conflicts in claiming "credit" for ideas that are carried out. An alternative approach is to let it be clearly understood that a primary key to advancement is a demonstrated proficiency and interest in getting better methods into effect.

Identifying Ideas and Reporting Results. When improvement ideas are considered significant and worthy of follow-up, they should be recorded and reported on at intervals until acceptable action has been taken. An individual may be designated to do this, on either a part-time or a full-time basis. Wherever time standards are applied, the savings from labor cost reductions should be based on the reduction in time standards. To aid in classifying the results from a cost improvement program, it may be helpful to separate "cost avoidance" from "cost reduction." Cost avoidance may be defined as savings through ideas that lower the cost of planned action before the action is taken— for example, before manufacture begins. Cost reduction, on the other hand, may be defined as savings resulting from changes in existing conditions.

SYSTEMATIC APPROACH TO METHODS ANALYSIS

Whatever the methods improvement program is called or whatever techniques are applied, a systematic approach to analysis will accomplish more than a random searching for ideas. After the existing methods have been surveyed and recorded in process chart form or otherwise, this systematic approach will include asking questions from a number of standpoints. The following ten-point summary of questions that lead to improvement indicates the kind of questions that should be asked and—equally important—thoughtfully answered. There are, of course, many additional similar questions that can and should be asked.

1. *Purpose of Operation.* Is the operation required because of the improper performance of a previous operation? Would the operation be necessary if subsequent operations were performed differently? If the operation was originally required to give the product greater sales appeal, is this reason still valid? Would the operation be unnecessary if tools and equipment were adequate?

2. *Design of Part.* Can a better or less expensive material be used? Can parts be joined better? Can machining be made easier? Can the design be simplified?

3. *Tolerances and Specifications.* Are existing specifications reasonable and clearly defined? Are causes of rejects corrected when they first occur? Are the methods by which inspection operations are performed effective?

4. *Material.* Is the material relatively inexpensive, yet economical to process? Is the material economical in both size and condition? Is the material utilized most effectively? Are tools and supplies utilized so as to avoid waste?

5. *Process of Manufacture.* If an operation has been or can be changed, will this change affect any of the other operations involved? If the operation is manual, can it be done mechanically? If done mechanically, should more effective equipment be utilized? If the operation is performed with the proper equipment, can the equipment be operated more effectively?

6. *Setup and Tools.* Can setup time be reduced by better planning? Can

the setup be changed to utilize more fully the capacity of the machine? Are better methods needed for holding the work?

7. *Working Conditions.* Is it possible to reduce working hazards? Are lighting, temperature, and ventilation adequate? Is housekeeping within the area satisfactory? Can operator fatigue be reduced?

8. *Material Handling.* Has the need for handling been minimized? Can the time spent in picking up material be reduced? Can manual handling be reduced by using mechanical equipment? Can better use be made of existing handling facilities? Should parts be handled with greater care?

9. *Plant Layout.* For straight-line, high-volume production, is material laid aside in position for the next operation? For diversified production, does the layout permit short moves and delivery of material convenient to the next operator? For multiple machine operation, is walking time minimized? Are storage areas arranged to minimize searching and rehandling? Are service centers located close to production areas?

10. *Principles of Motion Study.* Are operators making maximum use of both hands? Have unnecessary motions been eliminated? Is the workplace arranged to avoid long reaches or moves? Can use of the hand as a holding device be avoided? Have positioning or grasp motions been simplified?

PRESENTING AND INSTALLING NEW METHODS

Just as there are gradations in the costs of putting ideas into effect, so are there differences in the steps that must be followed to do so. A manufacturing supervisor can go directly to the operator if the change he wants made is a minor one such as a change in the hand motion pattern. He should, of course, always let the industrial engineer know that a change has been made, so that he can revise the standard if necessary. But if the industrial engineer wants to make a change, he must do a certain amount of "selling" to convince the supervisor of its desirability. Usually a brief discussion will suffice.

For more involved or more expensive changes, the necessary steps to get action may be much more extensive. Management should use care in establishing the chain of events which must take place if a fixture is to be made, a tool purchased, an operation revised, or a part design altered. There should be workable safeguards against both unnecessary expense and product quality deterioration. But making changes unnecessarily difficult to accomplish can act as a roadblock to progress and should be avoided.

In any case, there will always be a need to get approval at various levels for certain types of methods improvements. Such approval should involve the clear understanding that the methods change will be followed up to its successful conclusion.

A written proposal describing the new method is usually desirable. Often it should include backup material such as the process charts used in the preliminary stages of the development of the new method. Costs and savings should be summarized and due credit should be given to all who participated. The necessary detailed information should be kept available to answer questions. It is good practice for the backers of a proposal to be armed with an alternative plan in case of unforeseen objections. A clear decision should be obtained from the individual whose approval is needed.

Before the new method is installed, all concerned should be informed of what is to be done and the reasons for doing it. Instructions should be provided to operators and others concerned. Management should be certain that the commitment to spend money on making the change is not given unless there is full assurance that the new installation will be followed closely to handle problems that arise. As a final check, procedures may be established to ensure that actual savings are subsequently measured and compared with the estimate.

THE TEAM APPROACH TO COST REDUCTION

Cooperation and teamwork by all concerned can establish continuing methods improvement as a dynamic force within the manufacturing organization. When this is done, costs will be reduced continuingly and in significant amounts. Each member of the team should accept and carry out certain responsibilities described as follows.

Manufacturing Manager. See that staff and line personnel have both the time and the ability to make methods analyses, and assign duties. Consider establishing a full-time or part-time cost improvement coordinator, and assign duties. Consider also establishing a cost improvement committee with representatives from design engineering as well as from manufacturing. Indicate areas for special analysis, and set goals for accomplishment. Establish procedures for follow-up after installation of changes.

Staff Analytical Departments. Initiate surveys both on a broad scale and in specific areas where the need for improvement is known to exist. Work closely with the manufacturing supervisors in making the analyses. Participate in cost improvement committee meetings as assigned. Develop proposals for submission to management. Advise the cost improvement coordinator of action taken or in process so that adequate attention is assured. Follow up new method installations to see that expected results are obtained.

Manufacturing Supervisors. Accept methods improvement as a full-scale activity to be given close attention. Encourage cooperative attitudes by operators so that changes can be made without undue resistance. Call for assistance from staff specialists as required to check out ideas. Cooperate closely with staff specialists in providing information. Assist in the follow-up of new installations. In smaller organizations with few staff functions, take the lead in initiating improvements.

BIBLIOGRAPHY

Barnes, Ralph M., *Work Sampling,* 2d ed., John Wiley & Sons, Inc., New York, 1964.

Buffa, Elwood S., *Modern Production Management,* 2d ed., John Wiley & Sons, Inc., New York, 1965.

Carson, Gordon B. (ed.), *Production Handbook,* 2d ed., The Ronald Press Company, New York, 1958.

Karger, Delmar W., and Franklin H. Bayha, *Engineered Work Measurement,* 2d ed., Industrial Press, New York, 1966.

Maynard, H. B. (ed.), *Industrial Engineering Handbook,* 2d ed., McGraw-Hill Book Company, New York, 1963.

Niebel, Benjamin W., *Motion and Time Study,* Richard D. Irwin, Inc., Homewood, Ill., 1967.

CHAPTER NINE

Keeping Abreast of New Process, Tool, Equipment, and Methods Developments

W. J. RICHARDSON *Professor, Department of Industrial Engineering, Lehigh University, Bethlehem, Pennsylvania*

Every manufacturing manager knows that change is inevitable and that people institute change. The manager bears the responsibility both for creating a climate in which new ideas will flourish and for making certain that these ideas are put to use.

The following concepts will be discussed in this chapter.
1. The need for a systematic cost improvement program as a stimulus to new thinking. Such programs are fundamental to change.
2. The information system which exists external to the company and which contains the new knowledge which may be useful.
3. The information system which exists internally and is under the direct control of the manager. This system not only must collect and appraise new ideas from outside the company, but must also provide the means for exchanging ideas within the company.

The manager works through people, and the same administrative philosophies apply to the acquisition and processing of ideas that apply to the acquisition and processing of material. Nothing just happens in manufacturing. The manager, directly or indirectly, must make things happen.

THE PROBLEM OF KEEPING ABREAST

Methods, processes, and equipment change at a rapid pace. The environment in which manufacturing managers operate is also constantly changing. It is reasonable to suppose that these changes should be reflected in manufacturing, and of course they are. The basic question, however, is whether or not the manufacturing operation is taking full advantage of the new ideas available. The manager is constantly beset by the nagging doubt that per-

3–134

haps there exists—somewhere—a better way than he is now using to obtain a seal, bake on a finish, fasten a joint, or package a part. The manager also knows that he himself should not do the technical work—he pays people for that. So he must try to make sure that some systematic attempt is being made in his own organization to keep abreast of the new developments which exist outside his organization.

COST IMPROVEMENT PROGRAMS

New ideas can be forced upon the manufacturing organization by means of an organized cost reduction or cost improvement program. Such programs have proved to be the one sure way to obtain the necessary motivation for change.

Cost improvement programs are fundamental to manufacturing management in that they provide the frame of reference for other programs such as value analysis and work simplification. Without an organized cost improvement program, the manager has no way in which he can systematically drive for better cost performance. Cost improvement goals really represent plans for change. United Air Lines, for example, uses the term "profit plan" in describing this. The hallmark of the good manager is that he plans, executes, and controls. If he has no plan for cost improvement and no scheme for motivating his subordinates in this area, he cannot expect real progress. The demands made on his subordinates to produce good product on time are controlled by specifications and schedules. The need for cost improvement is very likely to be lost in the shuffle unless there is an equally strong demand, expressed in a formal program.

Characteristics of Cost Improvement Programs. Although cost improvement programs vary from company to company, they have certain features in common. These are:

1. *Active Support by Management.* This support is characterized by the selection of a strong director of cost improvement and by the use of performance under the cost improvement plan as a basis for granting or withholding salary increases and promotions.

2. *Company-wide Participation.* Even though the program may be introduced in stages, the ultimate goal should be the inclusion of all departments. Many changes are the result of a joint effort. The cost improvement program allows the sharing of credit and breaks down the reluctance to change which may exist when the savings show up in one department, but another department is accepting some of the responsibility.

3. *Line Responsibility for Meeting Goals.* The departmental supervisor has the basic authority and responsibility for running his department. He should participate in the setting of his goals for cost improvement and be held responsible for meeting them. This should be just as much part of his job as meeting schedules, reducing lost-time accidents, or maintaining quality. Also, if he must meet the goals, he is in a better position to require that those who are working for him should cooperate.

4. *Staff Specialists at the Working Level.* A formal cost improvement program usually establishes a team approach in which the staff specialist works as part of a group whose mission it is to introduce change. This encourages a real drive toward new ideas and makes it easy to have them accepted.

5. *Formal Goals for Each Supervisor.* After the appropriate analyses of budget, process capability, and work patterns have been made, specific goals of cost improvement should be set. A committee usually coordinates this, but

the supervisor participates in setting his own goals. Once set, these goals provide the driving force to the introduction of new ideas, because it is obvious to all that continuing to operate in the same old way will not be acceptable.

6. *Systematic Audit.* Once a change has been made and savings claimed, there should be a systematic procedure to audit results to see whether or not the expected savings actually are being realized.

From the manager's point of view, a systematic approach to cost improvement is invaluable. It provides the thrust which forces his organization to improve. This in turn provides a climate in which new ideas are actively sought; it also puts everyone on notice that the manager is not satisfied with the status quo, but expects a planned drive toward changes which will improve cost. It provides the motivation to seek new ideas and keep up to date, and the people who introduce the new ideas do not have to explain why they are deliberately seeking change. The manager, through the cost improvement program, sets this policy.

Management's problem is to provide both the motivation for change and the procedures with which change can be introduced systematically. Figure 9-1 shows a typical form used to ensure the systematic introduction of improvements.

Every change carries with it an implied criticism of the status quo. The people who are very much at home with present methods must accept new methods. This acceptance is absolutely vital to the success of the new method; yet it does not exist and therefore must be created. This is management's job.

THE EXTERNAL INFORMATION SYSTEM

Knowledge of new developments may be thought of as existing within an information system. The concept of the information system is not just an artificial notion. Information is the basic commodity in management, and the manager himself depends upon the information available to him when he makes decisions. In a similar way, technically oriented people must depend upon information systems for knowledge which they themselves do not generate. This includes by far the major part of the knowledge which they use.

The basic characteristics of any system can be shown very simply in the form of a block diagram (Figure 9-2). Reference to this basic concept is necessary, because the type of information needed to remain current in any field varies widely and thus is found in many different systems. For example, the advanced design group for a complex electromechanical assembly manufacturer will not consult the same external sources of information as will the material handling group of that same manufacturer.

External information systems can most easily be characterized by their outputs. These are known and hopefully can be matched against needs.

Information Systems for Highly Technical Knowledge. There are three places in which people systematically developing new ideas at a high technical level are likely to be found. These are the universities, government research agencies, and private business research and commercial consulting operations. Both the objectives and the ultimate availability of information differ for each.

Universities. The general pattern prevailing in universities for the development of new ideas is that individual professors with a particular area of interest obtain support for their work from a government agency or from private industry. The Federal government is by far the major contributor to research. At the date of writing, about 93 percent of university research was government supported. The principal investigator supervises the research, hiring graduate

AMP 1743 (10/63) PROFIT IMPROVEMENT PROJECT RECORD	PREPARED BY RICHARDSON, Wallace J.	LOG NO.

INSTRUCTIONS: PREPARE IN FIVE COPIES, AND SUBMIT THRU INDUSTRIAL ENGINEERING AND/OR SYSTEMS AND PROCEDURES

PROJECT TITLE		TYPE PROJECT ☐ DATA ☐ MFG. OR OTHER
DATE INSTALLED	DIVISION	ORIGINATOR
DEPARTMENT NAME NO.	PROJECT RESULT OF ☐ WORK SIMPLIFICATION ☐ WORK SAMPLING ☐ VALUE ANALYSIS	OTHER

DESCRIPTION OF FORMER/PRESENT METHOD

DESCRIPTION OF PRESENT/PROPOSED METHOD

ADVANTAGES OF PRESENT/PROPOSED METHOD

ESTIMATE OF ANNUAL SAVINGS	FORMER/PRESENT METHOD	PRESENT/PROP. METHOD	SAVINGS
LABOR COSTS	$	$	$
MATERIAL AND SUPPLY COSTS			
OUTSIDE SERVICE COST			
OTHER COSTS (SPECIFY)			
SUB TOTAL	$	$	$
LESS COST OF NEW EQUIPMENT (COST OF ITEM / EXPECTED LIFE)			$
TOTAL ANNUAL SAVINGS			$

SAVINGS ☐ IMMEDIATE ☐ POTENTIAL	SUPERVISOR	DATE	PLANT OR FUNCTION MGR.	DATE
MGR. OF OTHER DEPT. AFFECTED DATE	MGR. OF OTHER DEPT. AFFECTED	DATE	AUDITED BY	DATE

DISTRIBUTION: WHITE - PERSONNEL DEPT.   CANARY - ADMIN. ASS'T. OF DIV. MGR.   PINK - PLANT OR FUNCTION MGR.
GOLDENROD - INDUSTRIAL ENGINEERING OR SYSTEMS AND PROCEDURES   GREEN - FILE

FIG. 9-1.   Profit Improvement Project Report.

students who work for advanced degrees as they help in the experimental work. The results are usually published as technical papers or doctoral dissertations and are thus available. The private report for the sponsoring agency usually is restricted in its distribution.

The manager who wants to give his people the opportunity to keep abreast of this type of research and development should:

1. Maintain a technical library resource. This need not be in-house, but can be some arrangement with a larger library, public or private.

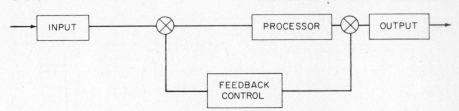

Fig. 9-2.   Basic Concept of a System.

2. Encourage, within well-defined limits, attendance and participation in the multitude of special seminars which are conducted by universities at a rigorous level. These are usually of one or two weeks' duration. Technical people will recognize the right ones for them to attend by the subject matter, academic or professional background, and seminar leaders. At the conclusion, the manager should require a written report as well as a follow-up report after a month or so, giving the use, if any, to which the information gained at the seminar is being put.

3. Encourage postgraduate education by individual employees, leading to advanced degrees. Such programs, taking advantage of local university facilities, have proved to be of value. Some companies, such as Western Electric and International Business Machines, have entered into formal arrangements with universities, but the usual pattern is to do this on an individual basis. The only caution here is that upon completion of the work toward an advanced degree, the employee's record and potential should be reviewed carefully. If he merits promotion, this should be arranged—or else he may seek recognition elsewhere.

4. Enter into an agreement with a university to do some research work of interest to the company. This has the advantage of establishing personal relationships between company and academic personnel. It also should result in worthwhile contributions to the bank of knowledge in the field of the research. Working with universities can sometimes be a frustrating experience, because their basic objectives will differ from those of business, but there usually is much common interest. In any case, it will be helpful to industrial personnel to be exposed to such joint undertakings, for the basic objective is to broaden individual viewpoints.

5. Participate as one of a group of companies supporting research in a particular technical area. Many universities have research centers which deal with general problems in a field and get their support from a group of companies which have this as a common interest. Lehigh University's Materials Research Center is an example of this. Seminars are arranged for the benefit of the members, and projects are undertaken to increase the general knowledge of all.

6. Engage university personnel in a consulting capacity to work with company people at company facilities. This is a common arrangement and can be quite satisfactory to both parties. Aside from the added income, the professor maintains contact with the real world. The company, in addition to the problem solving part of the consultant's job, should plan some sort of semiformal educational activity which involves the consultant and a few selected management personnel. Such sessions usually are a sure way to broaden the viewpoint of the managers. Sometimes it is the most efficient way to give them an appreciation of the technical problems.

Government Research and Development. At first glance, it might seem that research done for the government is not a promising source of new ideas for industry. Yet it is common knowledge that the electronics industry has taken advantage of work done primarily for the government to expand its sales tremendously; that nuclear expertise was developed under contract; and that medicine, the behavioral sciences, and the construction industries all have benefited enormously from technical advances which occurred as the result of government research.

Even though a governmental agency quite properly may place initial restrictions on the free dissemination of some of its research—which the taxpayer should applaud—it is nevertheless true that much of the work done finds its way eventually into the public domain.

The manager's concern is how he can have his people take advantage of new ideas of a highly technical nature which are generated by government agencies and by government-sponsored research. There is some duplication in the approach here and with universities. This is primarily true because universities do much government-sponsored research, because results tend to be published in a similar manner, and because in many cases men of quite similar interests do the work.

To allow his people to keep current in government research, the manager should:

1. Maintain in his technical library resource some competence in the area of government-sponsored research reporting. These reports take various forms and are issued by literally hundreds of agencies, but they are cataloged as they become available and can be obtained. Many government reports have become industry standards.
2. Encourage his people to develop contacts with appropriate government agency personnel. By "appropriate" is meant the various people whose direct interest is in areas important to the company. The normal ethics apply, of course, but there is no reason to feel that any contact with civil servants brings with it the stigma of an improper relationship.
3. Take advantage of opportunities to do work for the government—as either a contractor or a subcontractor. Despite some of the difficulties, the government is the world's largest customer, and an alert person can learn a great deal in the course of doing business with government agencies who deal in highly technical procurement.

Private Business Research and Commercial Consulting Operations. "Private business research" means work done at facilities such as the Bell Telephone Laboratories. This is of course proprietary in nature and protected by patents. Some of it is published in papers, but only after careful editing and internal clearance. Even with these restrictions, new ideas do emerge; eventually they may be incorporated in products which are sold. The best lead at the highly technical level again is a matter of keeping current through the literature and by attendance at selected seminars and meetings. Usually, the information is useful in sharpening up processes; it is unrealistic to expect someone else to solve a company's problems directly. But in many cases careful attention to private research will be very useful. At the very least, the company's people will keep in touch with first-class effort in the research area.

"Commercial consulting operations" means work done by firms such as the Battelle Institute, Arthur D. Little, and the Stanford Research Institute. These firms, for a fee, will do work at a high technical level. The advantage of employing such firms is that it relieves the client of the responsibility of maintaining a large staff of experts. The manager might use their services with the understanding that his own people participate in the research. Or the firm might be retained to conduct an investigation, and its report made the basis for further internal study. This last procedure is at times used as a means of broadening the thinking of company men and providing a bench mark for appraising their progress. The services of commercial research firms are contracted for in the same manner as those of any consulting service. The manager should realize, however, that what he is buying is expert knowledge of individuals, and he should try to satisfy himself that those working on his problem are in fact the experts and not merely competent men who may not be as good as his own employees.

One other source of new ideas at the technical level is the industry-sponsored research activity. Although such research is available to all participating members, every company which contributes to the support of the activity obviously should be sure to get its money's worth. The bituminous coal industry, the printing ink industry, and the portland cement industry furnish examples of such groups.

Information Systems for Applied Technical Knowledge. "Applied technical knowledge" means ideas which have been incorporated in existing products, materials, or designs, or methods of operating which now exist. The basic distinction between this kind of knowledge and "highly technical knowledge" is that applied knowledge has already taken a marketable form, and someone somewhere is making a profit from it. This applied knowledge may be in the form of a new type of plastic squeeze bottle, a new fastener, or a new way of scheduling job shop production.

There are in general three main sources of new product or process ideas: vendors, competitors, and professional societies and trade organizations.

Vendors. The vendors with whom design people do business can be a most important source of new ideas. Their salesmen are anxious to sell, and the appeal of a new material or a new component is useful in opening the door to new business. Further, the good salesman attempts to build up an association with his customers, and within the limits of business ethics, can keep the company's people in touch with what the trade is doing.

A good example of a management's stimulation of vendor interest occurred in a plant making electrical controls. A table was placed in the lobby where all salesmen called. On this table were placed several parts which were purchased. On each was a sign giving the price. Over the table was a sign saying: "This is what we pay for these parts. Can you do better?" The implications here are obvious. Not only are new vendors shown opportunities, but also present vendors are put on notice that this particular account is not an automatic reorder.

Many vendors also will undertake fairly extensive development, working with customers to expand uses of their products. In the area of process applications, machine tool manufacturers often will take customer jobs to show how their particular equipment will do the job. Such extraordinary cooperation by the vendor is most common, of course, when a process or product is new and a market is being developed.

The ordinary day-to-day contact with vendors also brings some insight into general industry practices. It is management's job to keep before its employees the need for real exploitation of such contacts. Some sort of log might be kept of the product or process changes which result from vendor contacts. This is a simple way of reminding designers and process engineers that the vendor is useful. It also gives some indication of how many changes, from whatever source, are being introduced.

Vendors also exhibit their products at trade shows and make sure that they are included in the standard catalogs used by designers. The catalogs are universal and not generally a source of new ideas. The trade show is not a surefire source of new ideas which will be useful, but if a vendor does have something different, he will show it. A trade show represents a meeting of people with considerable know-how in a field, and as such can be valuable. Here again, some sort of trip report is useful.

Competitors. The company's sales force is probably as good a source as any for finding out the new ideas in products which competitors offer. Although vendors will give some information, a careful analysis of competitors' products is essential. All manufacturing managers have had the experience of underestimating the competition. Sometimes this is just the challenge that the design and process engineers need. Implicit here is the necessity to improve and "be different," because there usually is a competitive advantage to be overcome. At the very least, consideration of the competitors' products makes one think.

Professional Societies and Trade Organizations. Many companies have their technical interest in a field represented by a professional society. For example, boiler and piping manufacturers keep informed of progress through individual employees' membership in the American Society of Mechanical Engineers. Not only is there an interest here in the codes governing performance, but also in the papers presented at various meetings, which describe new concepts and new techniques. Similarly, in the field of manufacturing processing, the American Society of Tool and Manufacturing Engineers serves as a forum for many ideas in the field of metal cutting, tooling, and materials.

The manager again should encourage active participation in society affairs, but also should be sure that this participation results in some tangible benefit to his company. Trip reports, analysis of the source of improvement, and a personal follow-up by a short chat with those participating all are useful.

Most industries have some sort of trade association, usually with information exchange (within the law) for commerce problems. Although no one will be completely frank on matters properly confidential to his own company, the general pattern of the information discussed is informative. In addition, publishing houses such as McGraw-Hill and Cahners Publications issue trade journals. Even though these are available to all, they at least are an avenue for vendors and hopefully a means of introducing new ideas of all kinds. If the manager provides the incentive for change, all these may provide knowledge of new materials and processes.

All the sources of information discussed above are known to the manager's own people. What the manager must do is to stimulate interest and provide the pressure which keeps these sources under constant review. In many cases, all that is needed is a discussion with his own people to appraise periodically the potential of each. Even a brief review sometimes is valuable, because it reminds the design and process engineers that other people are solving problems of a similar nature and suggests the possibility of profiting from their experience.

Information Systems for New Techniques of Operations. In addition to the generation of knowledge about new products or processes, there is a constant flow of new ideas about what may be called techniques of operation. System simulation, dynamic programming, and the expanding use of electronic computers are examples. The manager hears and reads about such things, and he is of course anxious that his people are at least aware of their possibilities and that there is a systematic appraisal of their specific applications within the company.

Techniques of operation are not tangible. It is not as easy to determine if they apply to a company problem as when testing a sample of new material. But such techniques may be of equal importance in terms of making a profit. Application of them may lead to a better inventory position, smoother scheduling, or better labor control. Because it is universally recognized that eventually any application must be run by people in the company, it is important that they be involved from the beginning. Willingness to change operating methods is hard to come by, however, because there is an implied criticism of present operation. It is sometimes difficult, for example, to stimulate the manager of production control to investigate the use of linear programming when he himself originated the system that is now in use and in fact may feel uneasy in the face of new concepts of mathematics.

For new techniques to be effective, they should be supported and eventually applied by the people in the company. This means that they must have both the motivation and opportunity to keep up to date. Again, an organized cost improvement program is the manager's best way to give motivation. Through such a program he forces change, and gives the impression that he is not bound to present practice. He also must be careful not to discourage change in the area of operating techniques, because this is his own domain, and his example is important. He has to expect that some of the things he does will come under examination in the course of evaluating new operating techniques.

There are three major sources of information outside the company which deal with techniques of operation. These are: (1) universities, (2) professional societies, and (3) private consultants. New techniques come to a company from these sources either directly, in the form of person-to-person exchanges, or indirectly, in the form of publications.

Universities. The universities are probably the prime source of new concepts in operating techniques. Even in those cases in which the universities do not originate technique, they are the principal channel for refining and publishing, in the broad sense of the word "publishing." Universities have a basic interest in research and in teaching. A body of knowledge must be developed in an organized form before a course can be taught. The university is not under the strenuous pressure of time and can afford to look into interesting ideas and follow them to a conclusion without deadlines.

There is one point, however, which should be made clear. This is that it is difficult to teach application of operating techniques in a university. Also, the man who is quite competent in mathematical modeling may not have the somewhat different skills needed to apply the model to a real-world situation. He may not even have an interest in this. So the manager looks to the university as a source of knowledge but must realize that applications in his own company should be under his control.

The most direct connection between the university and industry is through the hiring of university graduates by industry. Even though the manager realizes that the recent graduate has much to learn about the company, he may expect that each new man will bring new ideas with him. In particular, because new techniques are taught, he may hope that the new hire will be a resource. This is a long-range view, because the new man does not have the experience or position to make much of an impact at first. But the manager should pay attention to the recruiting program. He should be sure that his division sees its share of promising new men.

The actual introduction of new ideas by recent graduates, once hired, is something which does not just happen. The manager must set up some scheme to ensure this. One method which works well is to use a team approach to the solution of operating problems. One member of the team is a recent graduate, and another is a more experienced man. The new man is strong in technique and the older man in knowledge of the area of application and company personalities and procedures. Working together and jointly responsible for results, the new man learns how to get data and the experienced man learns new ideas. This meets two obvious objectives.

In addition to hiring the graduate, direct contact with the university to learn new concepts can be had through short courses offered by the university and by university extension divisions. Such courses are taught by members of the staff, as a rule, and are directed at a very specific topic or group. The courses run for a week or two or for one night a week for longer periods. They are not offered for credit and do not require prerequisites of a formal nature. Such courses can be valuable in teaching techniques; they have the advantages that they are held in an educational environment and that those attending become acquainted with university personnel and facilities.

Finally, many companies use the services of university professors as private consultants. The usual pattern is to have the professor build an in-plant course around a specific management technique, using examples from within the company.

Professional Societies. Professional societies are an important source of new ideas in operating techniques. From the presentation of papers by F. W. Taylor and H. R. Towne to the American Society of Mechanical Engineers in 1890 to the latest papers of the American Institute of Industrial Engineers, the professional society has provided a platform for new ideas. The tradition is for open discussion on a professional level. Papers are usually screened for quality and are widely discussed. Perhaps in no place else is there such freedom to advance new ideas or to learn as an individual, not representing the company formally. In addition, many of the journals which go to members are worthwhile.

The manager should encourage individual employees to participate actively in one society. Many companies pay dues and expenses where the employee is directly involved. Active participation is worth a great deal, whereas merely joining is not worth much to the employee's personal development. Working with others from other plants or industries gives exposure to different viewpoints and can be useful in solving common problems.

Private Consultants. The term "private consultants" is taken here to include not only consulting firms which offer training and project work to their clients, but also the many organizations which, for a registration charge, conduct seminars and conferences on new techniques which are open meetings. The consulting firms usually are strong in the application of new techniques. In the process of solving a problem for a client, the good consulting firm will train company personnel in the methods involved. Consulting firms make it a point to keep up to date and have competent people. As with the use of professors as consultants, members of the company staff should be designated to work with the consultants and be responsible for mastering the new methods.

A number of organizations, both profit making and nonprofit, offer seminars and conferences designed to present new techniques in a condensed, informational style. The usual format is a classroom-type presentation of one to five days' duration. These feature speakers who are knowledgeable and who have a well-constructed exposition of limited scope. Speakers are drawn from colleges and industry. Those attending have an opportunity to learn about operational techniques in an efficient manner. The strength of this approach is that it exposes the registrant to new ideas and does not commit the company in any way. The weakness is that the subject usually is not presented in depth and that follow-up depends upon the perseverance of the individual who attends. Such seminars have much to recommend them as a means of finding out about new techniques. The manager should insist upon some sort of trip report, with a tickler file item for future audit.

It is of course possible to overdo trips to seminars and conferences. But whether they are conducted by a university, a professional society, or a consulting firm, they do have in common the feature that the sponsor is trying to present something new which will attract registrants. The manager should at least consider these as a source of new ideas for his employees and make it possible for them to attend when appropriate.

THE INTERNAL INFORMATION SYSTEM

There is another aspect of the process of keeping up to date which is vital. This is the internal arrangements by which ideas from any source are made available to the right people inside the company. This internal information system acquires knowledge, organizes it, and matches the needs of the user at all levels.

At one time a company which had a reasonably good library and an efficient office mail system could feel that it was competitive in providing facilities for information handling. The words "information systems," while almost self-explanatory, did not have any particular meaning in terms of facilities or expertise. Three things have changed this.

First, there is more to know. Research and publication have been proceeding rapidly, and this knowledge explosion has increased the mass of information available which might be useful.

Second, the pace at which new products and ideas are put on the market has accelerated. The time from development to production has been shortened.

Third, new information processing equipment and the development of a body of knowledge in what is termed information science have become available.

The result of these developments is that manufacturing managers must expand their thinking and become conversant with yet another new discipline. Of course, no one expects the manager to become expert in linguistics or information retrieval. What he should do, however, is to set objectives for and plan and control this activity just as he does any other. He must realize that information science has become a profession, and that unless some serious thought is given to the problem, a sensible system will not be devised.

Because the objective is the handling of new ideas expressed in writing, the logical starting point is to place on the users of information a requirement that they define their needs. Then those presently responsible for the system should appraise these needs and evaluate them in terms of cost. It is quite difficult to distinguish between what one wants and what one needs. Just because some areas of organic chemistry knowledge have been reduced to a form which can be stored in a computer memory does not mean that this should be done for every product which the design engineers might use. Perhaps a first-rate file of periodicals will serve as the best source of new ideas.

Despite the complexity of the problem, the manager can demand that the subject be investigated and presented to him for formulation of policy. In essence, this policy will balance the cost of information versus its value. Basic characteristics of internal information systems include:

1. The ability to obtain quickly books, papers, and articles requested by a user. This probably includes some arrangement with a university library.
2. The ability to search the literature and to prepare a bibliography for a general rather than a specific request. For example, one might ask for "definitive works on static electricity."
3. An awareness and continuing appraisal of new advances in the fields of cataloging, storing, and retrieving data and the proprietary services available.
4. Orientation sessions, conducted regularly, so that the users will be made aware of what is available and what others in the company are doing.
5. Systematic evaluation of actual use of various services offered, so that evaluation of return for expenditures can be made.

CONCLUSION

This chapter has discussed some of the actions which can be taken to keep abreast of new ideas in materials, processes, and methods of manufacture. There has also been presented background material on the sources from which new ideas are likely to come. The basic problems to be faced are motivation and opportunity. The quality of the people with whom the manager works is of course important, but this is something which is fixed over the short term.

The primary motivation for the introduction of new ideas comes from three general sources:

1. The professional pride of engineers, designers, or managers
2. The need to meet competition or expand sources of revenue
3. The demands for improvement inherent in a cost improvement program

The opportunity to be exposed to new ideas exists outside the company in what may be termed an external information system. These ideas are generated and presented by universities, professional societies, vendors, competitors, consultants, and governmental agencies. None of these sources should be neglected.

A problem of equal importance is the internal information system which exists in every company. The manager should become aware of the operation of his system as it affects the problem of keeping up to date.

Finally, the manufacturing manager should use his regular accounting system, cost improvement audits, personnel evaluations, salary administration incentives, and promotions, which are his standard administrative tools, to translate his efforts in updating into profit. He must remember that manufacturing does not involve pure research, that his basic interest is application for profit, and that it is his responsibility to exert administrative skill to meet this objective.

MANUFACTURING CONTROL

CHAPTER ONE

Manufacturing and the Computer

RAY F. BOEDECKER   *Vice President—Manufacturing, Systems Manufacturing Division, International Business Machines Corporation, White Plains, New York*

Data processing is a vital tool in most industries.   In manufacturing, however, it offers unique opportunities.   Traditionally, the manufacturing plant has been composed of a series of separate though interrelated entities—departments contributing to a final product but collecting, storing, and using data in individual fashion.   But this has changed.   Through computers, many factories tie their operational needs into one neat data package.   In this way, managers and executives are able to get a timely, accurate, detailed, and graphic picture of what is going on in their particular function and in the plant as a whole.

THE PROBLEMS OF MANUFACTURING

Despite differences in size, method of operation, product, and so forth, most manufacturers share similar operational problems.

The Cost of Manufacturing.   Most manufacturing organizations face periodically rising manpower, material, and operational costs.   Material cost, for example, is compounded by the burgeoning price of handling and storing goods, plus the drain caused by obsolescence and taxes.   These costs reach the point where they can represent up to one-quarter the inventory value of goods.   And it is essential that the manufacturer keep a close watch on these items lest they price him right out of the field.

Competition.   Competition is always a major manufacturing problem.   To stay competitive, companies must be able to retool, reorder, and reorganize rapidly.   The only way this can be done is to get answers to questions such as order status, scheduled shipment dates, material availability, and other factors which have an influence on ability to put new designs into production.

4–3

Meeting Delivery Commitments. Another problem, allied to competition, is the ability to meet delivery commitments on a timely and accurate basis. Many wholesalers and retailers manage their inventories on a scientific basis. When they place an order, it is with the expectation that the manufacturer will deliver it on time and as requested. For this reason, it is incumbent on the manufacturer to maintain materials, manpower, and facilities in a way that permits rapid production and prompt delivery.

Meeting Cost Targets and Estimates. As the manufacturer tackles these problems, however, he is faced with the critical job of keeping a watchful eye on production costs. Indirect labor and overhead costs often rise to a point where they have a dramatic impact on the price tag of a given item. Thus the manufacturer must develop a means for measuring these costs while the item is still in manufacture—not after it has gone off to the customer.

Quantifying and Meeting Quality Criteria. Holding the cost line, however, cannot be done at the expense of quality. As part of his system, the manufacturer must establish quality parameters and then have some means for measuring them as production progresses.

Timely, Detailed, and Summarized Operating Information. Although most departments in a plant have varying need for the same bits of basic data (part number, order number, and the like), they usually gather and record information in individual fashion. This may be fine for the department involved, but it turns out to be extremely costly when management requests an overall view. This is where data processing comes into the picture.

Response to Changing Environment. Changing customer demand means a changing product mix, a changing schedule, changing work loads, changing technology, and so on. All this has a direct effect on the manufacturer's most valuable resource: people. Therefore, a major problem faced by the manufacturer is utilizing his workers so that they can make an optimum contribution to the company, the customers, and to themselves—all in a dynamic, changing environment.

THE ROLE OF DATA PROCESSING

A data processing system, by its very nature, requires that records be maintained in a centralized file. In a typical electronic digital computer system, information is stored on magnetic tape, on direct access magnetic discs, or in punched card form. In any case, management has a readily available source of centralized, timely, and detailed information which can be tapped when it is needed. Moreover, if the system includes remote terminals (input-output devices linked directly to the computer via telephone or private wire lines), the data can be brought directly to the point of use.

History of Data Processing. Dr. Herman Hollerith, a statistician from Buffalo, New York, devised the punched card system of accounting for the U.S. Bureau of the Census in the late 1880s. Census information was recorded as a series of holes in cards; then the cards were positioned one by one over mercury-filled cups. At the touch of a lever, telescoping pins descended onto the surface of the card. Where there was a hole, a pin dropped through into the mercury and made an electric circuit. The circuit, in turn, caused a pointer to move one position on a dial, adding another unit to the census count.

The technique caught on, and by the early 1900s many industrial firms were using Dr. Hollerith's unit record system for a variety of accounting functions.

New machines were added to the line for sorting, merging, verifying, collating, printing, and calculating information.

But punched card machines have limitations. The physical manipulation of cards takes time and carries with it a certain amount of error potential (lost cards, for example). The next step was to coordinate the various operations achieved with separate machines into a single, multipurpose data processing device. This device turned out to be the digital computer.

Electronic Digital Computer. The first electronic digital computer—that is, a machine using vacuum tubes instead of electric relays to produce impulses—was the Electronic Numerical Integrator and Computer (ENIAC), developed by Drs. J. Presper Eckert, Jr., and John W. Mauchly at the Moore School of Engineering at the University of Pennsylvania.

ENIAC, however, did not have a true stored program memory. Instructions for operating the machine (the program steps that guide a computer through its chores) were recorded through removable plug wires, just as instructions for punched card machines are programmed on interchangeable control panels. As a result, the computer was unable to depart from a fixed sequence of steps.

In 1948, the Selective Sequence Electronic Calculator was introduced—smaller than ENIAC in size, speed, and capacity. The important difference, however, was that the SSEC employed an internal storage system for recording program steps. Thus it became possible, for the first time, for a machine to modify its operating steps in line with the developing stages of work.

A program, as one observer put it, is the stuff that turns an electronic computer from an inert complex of metal into a versatile tool capable of performing an endless variety of jobs. This includes not only "application" programs which present a specific business or manufacturing problem to the computer in a form that it can understand, but also a great variety of instructions that enable the machine to control much of its own work.

The important thing to remember about programs is that they do not just happen automatically. They are written by people—men and women who design, devise, and dream up every instruction needed to turn the machine into a useful tool. So it has always been; so it will always be.

First Generation Computers. The first generation of stored program computers utilized vacuum tubes to create the impulses that enabled the machine to operate. Many of the early computers were restricted to fairly mundane accounting chores: keeping track of inventory, maintaining personnel records, processing accounts receivable, and so forth.

Second Generation Computers. The second generation computers replaced the vacuum tubes with transistors, resistors, and similar solid state componentry. Aside from being faster and more compact than earlier models, they could be relied on to perform many essential jobs. As a result, second generation machines were, and still are, used for manufacturing operations such as preparation of numerical control instructions, dynamic scientific maintenance of inventory records, and on-line control of production machines. More significantly, a few were used to provide a unified approach to manufacturing by taking inputs from many areas—sales order processing, materials management, manufacturing control, numerical control, quality control, and so forth—and using the information to provide management with a single, coherent, timely, and detailed picture of what was taking place in the plant at any given time.

Third Generation Computers. The third generation of computers features microminiaturized circuit modules, new forms of internal memory, and a variety of other innovations designed to make them faster, more compact, and more flexible. The latter improvement—flexibility—is probably the most significant from the manufacturing point of view. It means, in effect, that every facet of a manufacturing operation can eventually be "plugged in" to the computer, interrelated through programming, and finally wind up as outputs that have specific meaning to specific areas of plant operations. In this way, a manufacturing company can reach a so-called total system whereby the computer becomes a "personal" tool for every manager and every facet of manufacturing. Top management, for instance, can receive meaningful overviews of the company on a routine or special basis; middle management can get periodic listings which highlight potential trouble spots; specialists, such as design engineers, can use the computer whenever they need it for computations and trial approaches to various problems; and even line workers can benefit from on-line feedback, computer-produced instructions, education systems, and so forth.

Preparing for a Total System. To reach the goal of such an all-encompassing system, however, takes time, effort, and most of all, advance preparation. A manufacturing man contemplating computer usage either initially or in expanded form should first understand his plant or small business as a total system. That is, he should define: (1) all the inputs and outputs of this system (the data that literally enable him to perform day-to-day operations), (2) the facets or subsystems that are most important to him and his company, (3) the interrelationships among these subsystems (how each uses a particular piece of information such as part number or purchase order number), (4) how raw input data from the customer's sales order or from engineering design affect the functions of materials control, fabrication, assembly, quality control, purchasing, and so forth, (5) the areas which are in need of tighter managerial control, and (6) the importance or priority of subsystems in terms of their contribution to the whole. Then, based on the premise that it may take three to five years to attain a goal of a total system, these subsystems should be automated (put on the computer) in an order that reflects their importance in terms of immediate contributions to the company and the role they will play in creating a framework for a total system.

An example of the type of thinking needed for preparation is the flow diagram of the COMPASS (Computer-oriented Management Planning and Scheduling System), Figure 1-1, presently used by a plant of a major electronics manufacturer.

Note in the diagram the order of priority assigned by management to the various functions within the plant. Highest priority for implementation is given to product entry, followed by scheduling and parts planning, cost control, and procurement. This would indicate a certain amount of manufacturing to order which causes fluctuations in the needs of the various subsystems. For this reason, they are considered more critical than quality control and management planning and control.

As for interrelationships between functional areas, the arrows on the diagram graphically illustrate how much information is exchanged, and how essential one subsystem is to the functioning of another.

Developing a Framework. It cannot be overemphasized that the success of any data processing system in a manufacturing environment is dependent on the strength of the framework (as exemplified by the flow diagram of COMPASS). This framework is, in effect, a series of individual data processing applications, all using the same centralized computer and, most important, all contributing to the same data base. It also includes people—

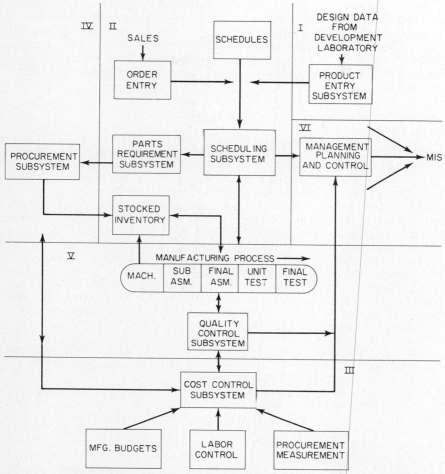

FIG. 1-1. COMPASS (Computer-oriented Management Planning and Scheduling System) Flow Diagram.

managers and skilled workers who generate and use these data. Ideally, this information which consists of all the operational data needed to handle the company's business should be stored on disc files where it is easily, rapidly, and randomly available to the computer. In this manner, both summary and detailed information needed by the various subsystems can be accessed, updated, and retrieved in a minimum amount of processing time; fewer programs have to be written to get at the data; the information is stored under a common format; output can be printed any way desired by its users; and multiple entry points can be used to update and retrieve essential data.

Building Bridges. Once a well-founded data base is established, the company can then go ahead to build links or bridges between the various subsystems. This is, in effect, the final approach to a total system. The bridges, in reality program steps, ensure that a change in one area will automatically update the records of all other affected areas. As an example, if engineering design should suddenly make changes to a product by altering a subassembly, an input of this information to the computer will automatically cause changes to be reflected in the records of all operations involved with this subassembly, from materials control who must buy parts to quality control who must be aware of new parameters in testing of final products. Thus, building bridges means that the entire data base is updated, rather than just one or two related records.

SALES ORDER PROCESSING

Although a total system is the ultimate objective, the manufacturing man contemplating computer usage will have to start somewhere. The decision as to which application area should be implemented first will be influenced by the size of the company, its products and problems, and so forth. In most cases, though, sales order processing will be among the first jobs to go on the data processing system. The reasons for this are evident: the sales order is a basic source of data, improved efficiency here means almost immediately improved service to the customer (by virtue of the fact that the sales order goes into work much faster), and the data appearing on a sales order are used by virtually every department in the manufacturing organization. Therefore, a first objective (as it is on the COMPASS diagram) will be to capture sales order information quickly, convert it into a machine language form (punched codes in cards or direct input to a computer), and then utilize the data processing system to prepare related paperwork (invoice, shipping notice, and the like) and update related records (accounts receivable and inventory).

Ordering from Stock. For the manufacturer who is in a position to fill orders from stock, sales order processing is a straightforward, uncomplicated process. Perhaps the best illustration of this is the system used by a small upstate New York specialty steel manufacturer:

Orders for specialty steel items come into the company by mail, telephone, or through data transmission terminals. The data transmission system features terminals at customer offices (usually those with a large enough volume to justify this type of equipment), linked via regular dial-up telephone lines to the data processing department of the steel company. When the customer wants to place an order, he dials the steel company supplier and, once contact has been made, feeds a prepunched card into the data transmission terminal. The card completely identifies the item in question, and a keyboard on the terminal is used to enter variable quantity information. At the receiving end of the line, a card punch machine senses the transmitted information and creates a duplicate set of punched cards.

As for manually received orders, these are converted to punched card form by keypunch operators. Either way, the cards, which now contain all the order information, are fed into a computer for preparation and printing of the packing list, inventory control form, and customer invoice. At the same time, the computer updates its direct access records to reflect inventory deductions caused by the order and to update the accounts receivable record of the customer.

Customized Orders. Satisfying an order from stock is one thing; satisfying an order for a complex, multicomponent custom-made product is another. In a large manufacturing organization, the processing of a custom order may have widespread reverberations. Even in a small manufacturing firm, many different departments in as many different locations may be affected by the information on an order.

Although initial customer order processing may be the same (the objective still is to get information into the system as quickly and accurately as possible), processing within the computer will be far more sophisticated. In this case, the program will be required to "explode" the order so that it shows all the components, subassemblies, and assemblies involved, and so that it generates all the paperwork needed to alert and inform each manufacturing location. In a large company, this may be done through the facilities of remote terminals. In any event, though, sales order processing will involve quite a bit of advance preparation and programming work.

MATERIALS MANAGEMENT

Sales order processing, whether for custom or stock items, has immediate and profound impact on inventory. This impact influences the company's ability to maintain a competitive level of service to customers, stabilize or reduce work loads, purchase goods on favorable terms, and generally maintain tight control over its investment in stock. Therefore, it is most critical that materials management, including forecasting, inventory control, purchasing, and receiving, be carried out as efficiently and effectively as possible.

Manual System. Under a manual system, it is virtually impossible to attain any degree of accuracy or efficiency in materials management—at least in a typical manufacturing company where thousands of items are involved. No matter how conscientious personnel may be, practical considerations force the use of shortcuts and generalizations. For example:

Simple ordering rules such as "when inventory drops below a one-month supply, order a three-month supply"

Use of the same ordering rules for all items, regardless of vendor, lead time, forecast error, and service objective

Inability to revise rules in line with changing customer, market, and vendor conditions

Lack of time to forecast demand, review items, anticipate seasonal conditions, or estimate in advance the results of changing key objectives

Inability to maintain inventory policies to the point where they are followed diligently and consistently

Scientific Inventory Management. In contrast to manual control, a scientific inventory management system utilizes mathematical techniques to determine "when to order" and "how much to order" of inventory items. Far from being an inflexible set of rules, scientific management allows the company to look at each item on an individual basis and determine an order based on: (1) the customer service level desired, (2) an equitable balance between inventory level and the number of sales orders processed, and (3) estimates in advance of results expected from management decisions.

Computer as a Tool. More effective inventory control brings both short- and long-term benefits in terms of cost, service, and control. Nevertheless, attaining these results is no simple matter. It requires frequent and individual analysis of the items in inventory; it must take into account a multitude of facts and constraints such as lead time, service desired, expected demand, stock on hand, pack size, minimums and maximums, discounts, freight rates, and the like; and it must do all these things regularly and accurately.

The powerful logical ability and speed of modern data processing systems make them an ideal tool for this type of job. Once programmed with the formulas that make up the scientific inventory management system, the computer can apply them to all or part of the inventory, on an item-by-item basis, and as frequently as required. Moreover, the difference between doing this for 1,000 items and 10,000 items is only a matter of minutes. Thus, with a computer available, both large and small manufacturing firms can utilize highly sophisticated techniques for managing materials.

Forecasting. In the forefront of these sophisticated techniques is forecasting. A forecast of future inventory demand can be the foundation of the entire scientific inventory management program. Typically, forecasts are made on the basis of projecting past demand patterns into the future. As an example, if past data show a demand uptrend, coupled with seasonal patterns, the computer will take these characteristics into account in forecasting future demand. In this way, all the factors encountered in real-life management are written into the program that guides the computer.

To forecast, a simple yet effective technique called "exponential smoothing" is built into the program. It is a form of moving average that gives more weight to recent demand history than to older demand data. It can be used for both horizontal items (those whose average demand level is fairly stable) and trend items whose average level is constantly on the move.

Seasonal items are handled by adding a base index, or series of multipliers, for each seasonal period of the year. For example, if August has twice the demand of an average month, the base index value for the month would be two. Seasonal forecasting is then accomplished by using exponential smoothing to reach an average yearly demand level and multiplying by the base index to find the demand for the month in question.

It should be emphasized that no forecast technique, regardless of how carefully programmed and run, is perfect. At best, forecasting is a calculated guess as to what will happen in any given time period. Nevertheless, experience has proved that forecasts are a necessary and valuable part of materials management, particularly in view of the trend toward long-range contract buying. For this reason, it is strongly advised that all companies, regardless of size or manufactured product, consider forecasting as an essential part of their inventory management program. If this means starting with just one major item, then this should by all means be done. Eventually, however, forecasting is bound to become an ingredient in the control of all items.

Inventory Control. In essence, forecasting serves to monitor any significant discrepancies between actual and predicted demand. The real "payoff" in materials management, however, comes in the frequent analysis of inventory records and the use of this information in issuing orders to purchasing and production.

There are many forms and variations of inventory control systems. As already seen, some companies update inventory records as customer orders are processed through their data processing system; others wait for notification of actual shipment. Where complex, multiassembly products are involved, variations of input and processing may be even greater.

Nevertheless, the basic objective of an inventory control system is to take daily transactions, such as stock issues, receipts, transfers, adjustments, engineering changes, and so forth; translate them at the earliest possible opportunity into machine language form; and use the information to update inventory records stored on tape or disc. These inventory records are then analyzed periodically by an inventory control program which prepares reports for the individuals who determine when and how much to order.

The computer, it must be stressed, is only a tool to aid management in the analysis and evaluation of current inventory positions. The man-written program which guides the computer through its operations offers mathematical and statistical techniques designed to meet the company's service objectives. These may include forecasting, materials planning, cost control, inventory management, customer order processing, inventory analysis, stock status summaries, and accounting. In the final analysis, though, the output generated by these various materials management modules serves only to inform, guide, and alert management to existing or potential inventory conditions.

Purchasing and Receiving. The purchasing and receiving functions can also be included in a materials management system, with the same number of options for carrying them out. In some cases, purchasing decisions and the paperwork associated with them are handled entirely on the computer, with purchasing management having the power of veto. In others, the data processing system is used only to prepare pertinent reports and listings, with management then making all purchasing decisions from this printed information. Either way, there is a feedback mechanism built into the system whereby whatever purchasing or production decisions made will be fed back into the computer, stored in the appropriate record file, and analyzed periodically to find out if the vendor or production department is meeting its commitments.

The other end of this system is receiving—notification to the computer that the items in question have been received and are available for use. This, too, can be handled in many ways depending on company size, function, physical layout, and so forth. One example is a "dock to stock" system used by a large manufacturer, featuring terminals located in the receiving department, receiving inspection, and stockroom. With the terminals on-line to the computer, control of incoming orders is established immediately upon their arrival at the dock. Moreover, once the information is received by the computer, a program is called into play to analyze the record and determine if there are any special considerations involved in it. This may include a special notice for quality control because previous history indicates that all items should be inspected, or it may be a notice to management that the item has been received either over or under the order amount.

IMPACT. The manufacturer contemplating a materials management system may very well be staggered by the various approaches and interrelationships that can exist in such an operation. For this reason an inventory management package has been put together—in actuality, a series of program modules which can be used either "as is" or adapted piecemeal to the needs of the factory. The system, called IBM IMPACT (Inventory Management Program and Control Techniques), provides management with a unique type of control over the routine decision making that affects inventory. Figure 1-2 is a schematic drawing of an IMPACT system showing what goes in and what comes out.

As can be seen from the schematic diagram, it becomes possible with IMPACT to base policy decisions on knowledge, in advance, of the results expected from using alternative sets of operating objectives. And, once having selected these objectives, it allows management to be confident that they will be carried out in a consistent and sound manner.

PRODUCTION INFORMATION AND CONTROL

Production is the heart of a manufacturing organization. The subsystems described up to now—sales order processing, forecasting, inventory control, purchasing, and receiving—all exist to help maintain the efficient, productive, and economical employment of men and machines. To make the picture

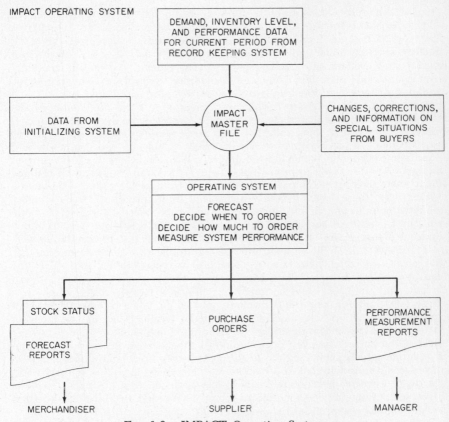

IMPACT OPERATING SYSTEM

FIG. 1-2. IMPACT Operating System.

complete, however, requires still more subsystems whose function, in effect, is to take information from the data base and use it in the planning, scheduling, and control of production.

Capacity Planning.   One such subsystem is capacity planning.   This forms the base from which a plant's operational schedules are developed.   Capacity planning determines from the data base the load of jobs to be run and places this information against available men and machines within the required time period.   The output of this program is starting dates which reflect a leveled load pattern.

PRISM.   Production Requirements for Industrial Scheduling of Manpower is a program written for a computer system manufacturing plant which shows just how effective capacity planning can be.   Using as its inputs labor hours, learning curves, performance, improvement, and configuration ratios, PRISM develops the manpower and space needed for a job.   The program actually explodes computer systems into units, and units into subproducts; applies lead times; and extends quantities by hours to develop the work load.   Information is then sorted by department, skills, product, project, function, and division, and distributed appropriately so that management can assess the impact of schedule changes and plan future plant work loads.

Operation Scheduling. Another production subsystem is operation scheduling. This program involves the assignment of dates on which a job is expected to start and finish. In a typical manufacturing operation, this procedure can become extremely complex, because start and finish dates must be established for large numbers of orders moving through the plant at the same time, each contending for limited production facilities, each dependent on prior and subsequent processing, and each having an assigned priority but subject to change. Nevertheless, with all data available within the data base, operation scheduling can be accomplished accurately and effectively.

Shop Floor Control. Finally there is the timely flow of information regarding the status of production orders. It is important to know the orders that are on time, the orders that are behind schedule, the location of jobs, and the work centers in which they have to be processed. In addition, all exceptional conditions (excessive cost, unusual delays, and the like) should be brought to management's attention at the earliest possible time. The shop floor control subsystem accomplishes this through a series of prepunched routing tickets, job tickets, and the like, which, when entered into the system either through plant terminals or directly in the data processing department, serve to update the data base with current production information.

MANUFACTURING AND THE COMPUTER

In production information and control, as well as in materials control, the objective of data processing is to build up the files stored on the computer's direct access discs and then interrelate this information to satisfy a variety of subsystems.

But a computer in a manufacturing environment need not be restricted to jobs of supervision and control. As a matter of fact, the classic role of computers in manufacturing has been that of a computational tool—a superfast slide rule, if you will, which engineers use for a variety of routine jobs such as the following.

Numerical Control. One of these jobs is the preparation of instructions for numerically controlled machine tools. There are several simplified programming languages available which allow a production engineer to describe in English-like statements the various machining steps required of a numerically controlled machine tool. The computer then translates these statements into the specific codes needed by the machine tool. In this way, numerically controlled machines can be reinstructed and put back into productive work far faster, and with more accuracy, than is possible under any manual or semiautomated system.

Process Control. Another important job for computers in a manufacturing environment is on-line process control. In this case, manufacturing machines, and in some instances entire manufacturing or production lines, are linked directly to one or more process control computers. Through various electronic or mechanical sensing devices, the activities that take place on the machine or line are measured or evaluated and fed back to the computer where they are compared with previously stored parameters. Should anything appear out of line—the acidity of a chemical bath too high or too low, the temperature of a part beyond normal range, the rate of turn above a safety limit—the computer will then generate signals to alert management, correct the condition, or shut down the production machine.

Design Engineering. Still another area is design engineering—utilizing a computer system to reduce the time and effort involved in preparing new designs. Many industrial firms do this through the facilities of a graphic display terminal. The computer controls a cathode-ray screen on which an engineer draws designs with a "light pen." To initiate these designs, he may call forth specific drawings from the computer's memory. Then, when they appear on the screen, he may rearrange, delete, or add lines to the drawing through use of the light pen. To get an idea of how his design might look from another perspective, he can request that it be shown from the left or right side, in three dimensions, and so forth. These perspective changes, by the way, are made possible through prior programming. In this manner, the company gains the flexibility to try many approaches to a given design problem and, once a final design is reached, use the same computer to produce manufacturing instructions.

Simulation. The characteristics of a computer are ideally suited for use in simulation. Utilizing one of the many general purpose languages that come with a system, the manufacturer can model a given problem—or even describe the workings of his entire plant. Then, by feeding variables against the model, he can get a realistic idea of what will happen under actual conditions.

An excellent example of simulation may be found at most aerospace firms. One manufacturer, deeply committed to space work, uses a computer to simulate thousands of missile configurations before building a prototype. The missiles are modeled in the computer in mathematical terms—formulas to show the height, thrust, strength, and so on. Then, using this mathematical model, engineers subject it to varying wind, velocity, pressure, and other conditions. In this way, they are able to get a good idea of how a real missile will behave under actual conditions. And if it does not stand up under computer processing, they have the flexibility to try another, and another, and another "model" until they reach a satisfactory point.

MANAGEMENT INFORMATION SYSTEM

Finally, we come to the management information system—a system which has been defined as meeting the information needs of executives and managers at all levels of an enterprise. Once again, this system is dependent on the data base built up on the computer's direct access files. As shown in the diagram (Figure 1-3), all departments of a plant contribute to and use these data.

To utilize data on the direct access files for management decision making, a package of programs is provided which has the capability of going in and locating information needed for a given report. Thus data which may have originated on a customer's sales order are utilized by the computer to meet all the informational needs of a manufacturing firm.

SUMMARY

In essence, a major purpose of an information system is to broaden the vision of a manager, allowing him to make more timely decisions and giving him better controls. The computer serves merely as a means for storing and presenting far more information than he could gather under a manual system. In the era of first generation computers, this information usually related only to a single application such as payroll processing. With the second generation computers, there were multiple applications which pretty well covered the total information of a particular plant. In the third generation, two additional factors have been added: a higher degree of stress on transaction-oriented

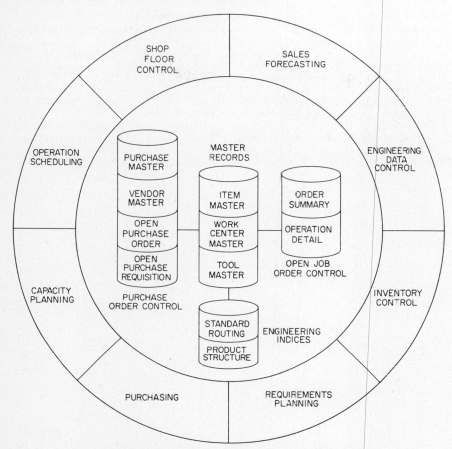

FIG. 1-3.   Diagram of Integrated Manufacturing Information System.

processing which makes the interrelated data synchronous in relation to time, and the ability to pull together data from multiple facilities so that management has a current picture of company-wide operations.

A computer, in the final analysis, is only a tool. It does what management wants it to do—on the basis of programs put into it by man. Experience has shown, however, that the range of these uses is limited only by imagination.

BIBLIOGRAPHY

Bellman, Richard, "Control Theory," *Scientific American*, September, 1964.

Computer and Management, The Leatherbee Lectures, Harvard University, Graduate School of Business Administration, Boston, 1967.

Englebardt, Stanley L., *Computers,* Pyramid Publications, Inc., New York, 1965.

International Business Machines Corporation, *Basic Principles of Wholesale Impact,* Data Processing Division, White Plains, N.Y., 1967.

International Business Machines Corporation, *The Dock to Stock Receiving System at the IBM Rochester and Raleigh Plants,* Data Processing Division, White Plains, N.Y., 1966.

International Business Machines Corporation, *Management Operating System Forecasting, Materials Planning, and Inventory Management—General,* Data Processing Division, White Plains, N.Y., 1967.

International Business Machines Corporation, *The Production Information and Control System,* Data Processing Division, White Plains, N.Y., 1967.

Magee, J. F., *Production Planning and Inventory Control,* McGraw-Hill Book Company, New York, 1958.

Plossl, G. W., and O. W. Wight, *Production and Inventory Control: Principles and Techniques,* Prentice-Hall, Inc., Englewood Cliffs, N.J., 1967.

Scheele, Evan D., William L. Westerman, and Robert J. Wimmert, *Principles and Design of Production Control Systems,* Prentice-Hall, Inc., Englewood Cliffs, N.J., 1960.

Wall, Herbert M., "Using a Computer for Circuit Analysis," *Electronics,* Nov. 2, 1964.

CHAPTER TWO

Noncomputerized Data Reporting and Processing

FENWICK M. WINSLOW, JR. *H. B. Maynard and Company, Incorporated, Pittsburgh, Pennsylvania*

The successful operation of a manufacturing enterprise depends on two factors: (1) being able to make a product which the market desires, and (2) being able to make that product at a competitive price, in the quantity and at the time the customer wants it. The second condition is related to manufacturing economically and dictates the need for an effective flow of information from the production floor to manufacturing management. Manufacturing paperwork systems provide the flow.

The proper manipulation of data emanating from the production floor provides manufacturing management with information relative to product costs, production quantities, and projected deliveries.

Basic information is required in every manufacturing situation. It must be provided by a data reporting and processing system. The tools used to collect and report this information will be discussed in this chapter, but first it is important to identify the data which are to be reported.

BASIC MANUFACTURING DATA

There are two types of information which are a part of any manufacturing information system. The first is the information required to initiate the manufacturing process, or input. The second is the information which should emanate from the manufacturing process, or output. The tools used to handle the two forms of data will be discussed later.

Input Data. The minimum input information necessary to initiate manufacturing activity in most companies is as follows.

1. Production order
2. Route sheet
3. Material or parts requisition
4. Tool requisition

4–17

The separate pieces of data may sometimes be combined in one form, but they will be discussed separately for clarity of understanding.

The production order is an authorization for work to be performed. It generally contains the following information.

1. Part or assembly number
2. Description
3. Production order number
4. Date to be shipped
5. Identification of part or assembly to be produced

The production order is accompanied by a route sheet which basically describes the processes to be used in making the part or assembly and tells how long each process will take. An example of a route sheet is shown in Figure 2-1. The route sheet identifies the following information for shop personnel.

1. Operation sequence
2. Time for each operation
3. Machines on which operations are to be performed
4. Material or part from which the basic part is to be made

The material requisition is used to identify to the storekeeper the type and amount of parts or material needed and to authorize him to disburse it to the shop floor for processing. The material requisition contains the following information.

1. Part number
2. Material to be drawn from stores
3. Quantity
4. Production order number
5. Date material will be required

OPERATION – ROUTE SHEET

DATE 2-15___			PART NAME GEARCASE				PART NO. M0463			
MAKE FROM 1174			MATERIAL CAST IRON		NEXT ASSY. R-42 SHELDON			MFG. ENG. NL		
REVISION								SHEET 1	OF 2	
LINE NO.	OPER. NO.	DEPT.	OPERATION DESCRIPTION	MACHINE	JIG	FIXT.	GAGE	STD. HOURS	REV.	
1	10		RECEIVING INSPECTION							
2										
3	20		GRIND & PAINT							
4										
5	30	M	FINISH REGISTER & ROUGH BORE BRGS.	POTTER	T-365F	T-369F	T-360G	1.62	M-20	
6			INPUT 3.135/3.137 DIA.	#199	T-366F		T-351G			
7			OUTPUT 2.822/2.820 DIA.		T-367F					
8										
9	40	M	FINISH BEARINGS CONCENTRIC	LE BLOND	T-613F1	T-611F		.95	TS	
10			WITH REGISTER 3.1495 +.0008 – .0000 DIA.	LATHE #573	PLATE	BAR				
11			2.8345 +.0008 –.0000							
12										
13	50	M	QUALIFY OUTPUT END 9.011 +.005 –.000	ACME LATHE	T-376F		T-213G	.67	M-11	
14			AND 11-57/64	#208			T-215G			
15										
16	60	M	MILL FEET & BASE PLATE SURFACE	MILL #198	T-371F		T-309F1	1.04	M-15	
17			1-11/16 +0 –1/32 FROM REGISTER		T-360F					
18			O.D. 3-5/16 FROM CENTER LINE 2PL. 1/2 DEEP							
19										
20	70	M	DRILL RAIL & C' SHAFT HOLES	YOSHIDA DRILL	T-285J	T-537J1	T-216G	.75	M-18	
21			41/64 DRILL THRU .640 LINE REAM	#304	T-359F		T-222G			
22			2 PL. – 47/64 DRILL .750 LINE REAM		T-537J					
23			FOR .7505 ×.0005 AND .7495 ±.0005							
24										
25	80	M	MILL BOSSES 6.577 +.005 –.000	MILL #115	T-603F	T-609F8	T-214G	.50	M-15	
26					T-603F2	T-604F9	T-212G			
27					T-604F					
28										
29	90	M	DRILL & TAP OUTSIDE OF CASE 27/64	AVEY #196	T-292J1			.84	M-19	
30			DRILL 1/2–13 TAP 23/32 DRILL 1/2 PIPE		T-292J					
31			TAP 3 PL. – 5/8 DP. THRU 2 PL. –7/8C' BORE		T-293					
START DATE_____			W.O. #_____				QUANTITY_____			
			FINISH DATE_____				SHOP ORDER NO._____			

FIG. 2-1. Route Sheet.

The tool requisition lists:
1. Jig, fixture, and gage numbers
2. Date required

It may be a special form, or it may be a copy of the route sheet.

When furnished to production supervision, the four types of information authorize them to begin production and identify in some detail what has to be produced, how it will be produced, during what period of time, and in what quantity.

Output Data.   The output data from a shop reporting system will vary from company to company.   Generally it is only the format in which it is arranged that varies, for the basic information is pretty much the same. The types of information required from a shop reporting system are as follows.

1. Time and activity reporting
2. Material movement
3. Material or purchased parts receipts
4. Material or parts disbursements
5. Shipments
6. Scrap and rejections

The following pages discuss in detail the type of information required, where it originates, and how often it is required.

Time and Activity Reporting.   Time and activity reporting is the basic information dealing with the attendance and the activity of each production employee.   The attendance record is a basic record of time worked.   Generally it is in the form of a card which has a provision for seven days' recordings on it.   Each day, as an employee reports for work, he inserts his card in a time clock which punches the arrival time on the card. He clocks out in the same manner when he leaves at the end of a shift.

The daily activity reporting of an employee has to do with the way in which his time was used while he was at work, including the amount of work produced. What jobs did he work on? How long did he spend on each job? Did he complete the job? What machine was used? The summary of the time spent on all jobs should equal the amount of time that his attendance record indicates he was at work.

Material Movement.   To maintain information at a central control point about the location of parts, subassemblies, or materials, it is necessary to have information reported which indicates the last significant movement of each item.   In a job shop, it is important to know exactly where an order is located in the shop.   This information can be used to make delivery promises, to schedule production, and to expedite overdue orders.   In a production line operation, the detailed location of an order is not particularly important, but it is necessary to know when that order is produced and goes into test if testing is time consuming or into stock or to the shipping room.   The important point is not the detail required, which is determined by the characteristics of each situation, but that provision must be made for some type of order location information.

Material or Purchased Parts Receipts.   Timely information should be provided on the receipt of materials in a plant.   Material or purchased parts receipts will be used to replenish low inventories or to release production orders waiting for the material.   Material receipt information should clearly indicate the specific lot received if the order has been scheduled for receipt in several lots over a period of time.

Material Disbursements. Material disbursements are authorized movements of material or parts from stock to an in-process state. Disbursement information must identify the part number to which the material or part is to be converted and the production order number authorizing the transaction. Material disbursements are used to relieve stores inventory records as well as to initiate in-process inventory records. Any variations of actual quantities disbursed from those authorized must be noted, and reasons for the variance must be shown.

Shipments. Shipments represent the transfer of finished product from the manufacturing plant to the customer. Information concerning the physical movement out of the plant should be transmitted in a timely manner to reflect accurately the status of the remaining open orders in the plant.

Shipment information should include freight class, quantity, carrier waybill, and weight which can be used to inform customers of shipment and to trace lost shipments where necessary.

Scrap and Rejections. Inspection and quality control reports are essential for the overall guidance of manufacturing toward more economical production. Information on parts which must be reworked or scrapped must be transmitted to manufacturing management expeditiously so that they can do whatever is required to assure that customer orders can still be produced in the right quantity at the right time.

NONCOMPUTERIZED DATA REPORTING AND PROCESSING SYSTEMS

Within the general definition of noncomputerized data reporting and processing there are several methods of handling data. The obvious one is manual, with little or no mechanical aid except calculators, comptometers, and duplicating equipment. Punched card systems using unit record equipment are another means of reporting and processing data. In addition, there are specially designed types of electromechanical equipment used. All these will be discussed.

Attendance Reporting. Time reporting is accomplished by having a special time clock located near the entrance of the department in which an employee works. As the employee enters the department at the beginning of the day or leaves at the end of the day, he punches the time on his card. The card is generally of stiff cardboard and provides for recording seven days of attendance. Each day, attendance cards are collected and the total time worked is calculated and recorded for each employee.

In situations where data collection stations are used for gathering other information, they can also be used for attendance reporting. The data collection stations are connected by cable to a keypunch at a central timekeeping station. As an employee reports for work, he inserts a permanent badge—assigned to him when he was hired—into the data collection equipment. This creates a card at the keypunch with employee's name, number, and the time when he reported for work. When the same procedure is repeated at the end of a shift, another card is created which indicates when the employee went home. These cards can be used daily to develop an attendance record by sorting and listing on an accounting machine. Monthly and annually, they can be used to compile overall absentee and tardiness reports for management information.

Labor Activity and Production Reporting. Labor activity and production reporting are usually combined because they are so interrelated. All the information relative to work accomplished is included in the labor activity report; it merely needs to be drawn off and summarized in a different form for production reporting. For labor activity reports, management is generally concerned with hours worked; for production reports, management is concerned with units produced and operations completed. Labor activity reporting systems should be designed bearing in mind that both hours and units are desirable and necessary pieces of information.

Alternative Reporting Methods. There are several noncomputerized methods which can be used to obtain meaningful and accurate labor activity and production reporting. The selection of the best method depends upon the needs which are to be satisfied. Figure 2-2 illustrates six different methods for reporting and the characteristics of each as they pertain to:

1. Paperwork complexity
2. Production status definition
3. Work center load definition
4. Job costing capability
5. Labor performance measurement
6. Attendance card verification
7. Indirect labor performance measurement

The most detailed approach to production status monitoring is one where each production worker submits a card—punched or handwritten—for each operation that he completes. At the end of the day, if he has not completed all work on the part that he is producing, he indicates partial completion and thereby accounts for his entire day's work. In the most complete systems, indirect charges such as unavoidable delays and machine downtime

CHARACTERISTICS

STATUS MONITORING APPROACH

PAPERWORK COMPLEXITY	PRODUCTION STATUS DEFINITION	WORK CENTER LOAD DEFINITION	JOB COSTING CAPABILITY	LABOR PERFORMANCE MEASUREMENT	ATTENDANCE CARD VERIFICATION	INDIRECT LABOR PERFORMANCE MEASUREMENT		
HIGH	GOOD	GOOD	GOOD	GOOD	GOOD	GOOD		SUBMIT CARD FOR EACH OPERATION; REPORT PARTIALS AT END OF DAY. INCLUDE INDIRECT CHARGES.
MED	GOOD	GOOD	GOOD	GOOD	FAIR	GOOD		SUBMIT CARD FOR EACH OPERATION; REPORT PARTIALS AT END OF WEEK. INCLUDE INDIRECT CHARGES.
MED	GOOD	GOOD	GOOD	GOOD	GOOD	FA R		SUBMIT DAILY TIME SLIP SHOWING ALL OPERATIONS AND PARTIALS AT END OF DAY. INCLUDE INDIRECT CHARGES.
MED	GOOD	FAIR	GOOD	FAIR	FAIR	FAIR		SUBMIT WEEKLY TIME SLIP SHOWING ALL OPERATIONS AND PARTIALS AT END OF WEEK. INCLUDE INDIRECT CHARGES. / SUBMIT OPERATION COMPLETION CARDS INCLUDED IN SHOP PACKET.
MED	GOOD	FAIR						SUBMIT OPERATION COMPLETION CARDS INCLUDED IN SHOP PACKET.
LOW	VAGUE	VAGUE						SUBMIT NOTICE OF INTERDEPARTMENT OR INTERBUILDING MOVEMENT.

Fig. 2-2. Alternative Methods of Labor Activity and Production Reporting.

are recorded on other individual cards. It is simpler, however, and generally equally effective to include the indirect charges on the card reporting the direct operation during which the indirect charges occurred.

This system can produce an unnecessary amount of paperwork for the information it provides. In cases where machining operations require several days, the preparation of a daily time card produces several time reports for one operation on one part, and these cards have to be summarized before production status, job costs, or labor performance can be determined. The same procedure also must be repeated for each work shift.

The second approach shown on Figure 2-2 is a simpler variation of the first. Partial operations are accounted for only at the end of the week. Thus, if an operation takes three days, only one activity card is submitted for that operation; the production worker reports the fact that he spent three 8-hour days to produce the job.

A still simpler approach is to ask production workers to submit a daily time slip showing all operations at the end of the day on one sheet. Again, because there may be operations which require several days, showing partial operations will inevitably produce confusion and extra work in the monitoring of production status as well as job costs and performance reporting. The weekly time slip which shows all operations and partial operations completed by the end of the week may therefore be preferable. Coupled with this simpler time reporting system must necessarily be a system for more rapidly notifying the production control section of the completion of individual operations. This can be accomplished by including in the job packet sent to the shop preprinted or prepunched cards indicating the part number and all operation numbers. These are turned in to the production control office as operations are completed. The progress of machining and fabricating the various parts and subassemblies can thus be monitored.

Simpler still is the system which utilizes only operation completion cards and ignores time reporting. Such a system will provide good definition of production status but will reduce the accuracy of the definition of work center load.

Finally, perhaps the simplest approach of all is to monitor the movement of parts between departments or buildings in a plant rather than to monitor the movement of parts between operations. This approach is extremely simple, but it will provide only vague information on the status of jobs and work center loads.

Material Movement. In the case of a small manufacturing operation with only two or three major departments, it usually is not necessary to set up a system to report the movement of materials within the plant. The labor activity and production reporting system will provide the information needed to locate orders in process. In large or multiplant operations, it will usually be desirable to have a reporting system which reflects the movement of material from one department to another, from one plant to another, or from a plant to an outside company for processing.

A material movement reporting system similar to the labor activity and production reporting system just discussed will in most situations satisfy the need. A material handler turns in a card for each order that he transfers from one department to another. The card can be a punched card or manually prepared and should show "moved from" and "moved to" information. In addition, provision should be made for a responsible person in the department to receive the material or parts and acknowledge their receipt.

Material movement cards, in addition to providing the source for an order locator file, can be effectively used to measure the performance of the material handling organization.

Material and Purchased Parts Receipts.   Material and purchased parts receipt procedures must recognize and accommodate two conditions which are generally prevalent in a receiving department. The first is that receipt information must be furnished on material and parts in two stages: (1) received but not inspected, and (2) received and inspected. The second is that the procedures must be built around multiple receipts against a single order.   In most receiving situations, split receipts are a fact of life, and provision must be made for recording them meaningfully, accurately, and economically.

The most effective noncomputerized paperwork system for handling receiving transactions is one which begins with a set of preprinted purchase order forms.   The set includes a duplicating master.   When the set is typed and copies are created, one of the copies is the typed duplicating master. This is the receiving department's copy.   The masters are filed in the receiving department and represent an open purchase order file.   Each time a shipment from a vendor is received, the receiving clerk removes the duplicating master, posts in a prescribed place on the form the item and quantity received, and shows the balance yet to be received.   Then by running off copies of the updated master, the receipt information can be sent to all interested parties, with full information relative to the purchase order contained on a copy of that order.   Each time a shipment is received, the procedure is repeated.   The duplicate master is the one and only master record, and the purchasing department need only retain the copy created by the most recent receipt to have a complete record available for reference.

A copy of the received order accompanies the material until it is placed in storage or received in a using department.   A second copy for inspection can accompany the material to inspection and then be given to the production or inventory control department when the material has been inspected.

Prepunched cards created at the time that a purchase order is issued can be used in receiving, but they are less flexible in meeting the required conditions than are other manual systems.   The significant liability of prepunched cards is that they require the reproduction of a new card when split shipments are received. This generally must be done on an office machine physically removed from the receiving location.   Therefore, while the original card is out of the open order file in receiving and before the reproduced card is available, the open order card file is not complete.

Manual material and purchased parts receipt information systems can be independent of most other manufacturing-related information systems.   They should therefore be designed to satisfy the unique requirements of the receiving function without worrying about the interface with other systems.

Material Disbursements.   Materials or parts are disbursed from a stockroom only when authorized by a material requisition.   The important information on any material requisition is as follows.
1. Part number of item wanted
2. Description of item wanted
3. Quantity requisitioned
4. Unit of measure (each, feet, pounds)
5. Date to be delivered to production department
6. Order number of assembly on which part is to be used
7. Location in the stockroom
8. Authorized signature

Material requisitions fall into two general categories—planned and unplanned.

Planned Requisitions. A planned requisition accompanies a production order as it is released from production control. It is a list of the parts required to produce a given order. Prior to an order being scheduled, a bill of material is prepared identifying the parts required to make the order. The bill of material identifies all parts required, regardless of whether or not they are subassembled and stored in a stockroom. Production control reviews the bill of material and takes off a parts list for the parts that are carried in a stockroom. This parts list is used as the material requisition for planned disbursements. It can be set up on a duplicating master and used over and over again. When the parts list is pulled for an order, the quantities of each part are extended for that order and the requirements are reviewed against an inventory record for availability. If parts are available, the parts list is released with the production order to authorize disbursement of parts to the production floor. It is used in the stockroom to pull the parts and is signed and returned to the issuing department to report the actual disbursement.

Prepunched cards can be used instead of parts lists, but they are more susceptible to misplacement and loss in handling.

Unplanned Requisitions. Unplanned requisitions are authorizations for parts disbursements which cannot be anticipated. They generally are of an emergency nature resulting from rush orders, defective quality, spoilage in production, or loss or misplacement of previously issued parts. Unplanned disbursements should be authorized on a card or paper form identifying, in addition to the basic information, the reason for the requisition. The requisition forms should be turned in to the inventory control department for posting to inventory records.

Unplanned requisitions should be summarized periodically by cause to analyze in some detail the reasons for them. This analysis can point out serious defects in the inventory control function.

EQUIPMENT FOR MANUFACTURING PAPERWORK SYSTEMS

The development of manual systems in a manufacturing situation can vary, depending upon the best estimate of the future pattern of growth. For example, the type of industry and market may indicate only a modest opportunity for expansion. In this case, the systems in operation at the present time should be evaluated to determine how well they serve the needs of the company now. In a situation where planned substantial growth is a factor, however, the current systems must be evaluated not only for present effectiveness, but also to determine how well they are laying the groundwork for the information reporting and processing which will be required in the future when the volume of paperwork will be much greater.

Where current systems are only a prelude to better, more sophisticated procedures in the future, more thought must be directed toward how the individual systems can eventually be integrated to provide a total manufacturing information system. The core of the longer range systems plan is in most instances a computer. Therefore, companies who can look down the road to a transition from noncomputerized systems to computerized systems should give serious thought to how the information which is being gathered, reported, and processed today can eventually be used in a computerized system.

The use of punched cards offers the most obvious method for reporting and processing data which can tie in at some time in the future with a computerized system. Therefore, punched card systems using electrical or electromechanical equipment are often economical solutions to data processing problems. They also lay the groundwork for tomorrow's more advanced computerized systems.

Punched Card Systems. A data collection system using punched cards has many applications in a manufacturing plant. It can cover many of the separate reporting functions as a system. For example, time reporting, labor activity, production reporting, material movement, order dispatching, order status reporting, and in-process inventory reporting can be tied into one system using only data collection equipment and a keypunch or keypunches. The value of this type of system lies primarily in the fact that the information transmitted is current and consequently most useful for solving today's problems. In addition, it provides for the accumulation of operating data in the form of punched cards which can be used for analysis of such things as machine utilization, labor efficiency, delay times, lead times, and material move times.

In its simplest form, a shop floor control system employing data collection equipment can be used by providing an input of two punched cards and a production order on a paper form. The production order should contain the following basic information.

1. Order number
2. Part number
3. Quantity
4. Date due
5. Routing (if known)

After the production order is created, two cards are punched containing the order number, part number, and due date. One of these cards is kept in a central control office and the other card is sent out with the production order when it is released. For every activity that takes place in the shop relative to that order, the information is transmitted back to the keypunch in the central control office through the data collection equipment. For example, when the material is issued from stock and delivered to the initiating production department, the material handler records this activity by inserting the punched card accompanying the order in the data collection station in the department to which he made the delivery. This creates a card back in the central control room where it is reviewed by a dispatcher. In this way, every movement, every setup, and every completed production operation can be reported in a timely and useful manner.

With this basic information, all forms of scheduling, control, and reporting functions can be set up. Production control can set up a central dispatching function and monitor progress versus schedules. Timekeeping information can be obtained as a by-product. Order status information is maintained on an up-to-the-minute basis.

In addition, after serving their initial purpose, the cards can be accumulated and used for analysis at a later date. This system also provides a practical forerunner for a computerized system later on because it depends on punched cards but requires manual evaluation of data inputs. This monitoring will, over a period of time, improve the accuracy of input data to a point where they can be used in a computerized system with a known degree of validation. This is extremely important for the introduction of an on-line computer operation in the manufacturing planning and control functions.

Voice Communication Systems. Voice communication systems or intercoms can be used as data collection systems, particularly in the labor activity and production reporting systems. However, their disadvantages as compared with electric data collection using punched cards are twofold. First, they require the manual recording of information by the person receiving it. This offers possibilities for recording inaccurately, transposing figures, poor penmanship, and the like. Second, voice communication systems cause a queuing up of senders at an input station at busy times. Thus operators can be forced to wait in turn for their chance to report when the receiving station is available. This can be a serious deterrent to voice communication if a large volume of reporting information is required.

Other Reporting Equipment. There are other types of electrical, mechanical, and manual equipment which can be used to gather, report, evaluate, or assist in manipulating operating data. In the proper environment, each of these systems has a value far in excess of its cost.

Telecontrol Equipment. Telecontrol equipment produced by the Telecontrol Division of Hancock Telecontrol Corporation is electronic in nature. A typical Telecontrol monitoring system consists of six components:

1. Piece sensor
2. Work station terminal
3. Display cabinet
4. Count memory unit
5. Data output unit
6. Master console

The piece sensor is attached to each production machine being monitored and counts the number of pieces produced. A work station terminal is installed at every sensing station to control signaling and voice communications between each work station and a central control room where the display cabinet is installed. The information detected by the piece sensor is transmitted to the control center. The display cabinet provides visual information on the status of work for each work station, such as whether or not the job is running, pieces produced, balance to be produced, and so on. The count memory unit contains the electronic arithmetic unit, data storage drum, and the systems electronic control circuitry. The storage drum is divided into two sections and stores current working data as well as data for completed jobs. The data output unit is any standard output device which may include printers, paper tape punches, magnetic tape units, card punches, and central processing units. The master console controls the input, interrogation or display, and output of all data from the system.

In concept, then, Telecontrol equipment provides for fast, accurate reporting of production data, quick recognition of problems and a communications network for corrective action, an up-to-the-minute display in a central area of current production activity, and a storage and output device for the purpose of reporting significant information.

Telecontrol equipment has its greatest application in manufacturing operations using large numbers of similar types of production equipment such as screw machines and presses. It has been used effectively to reduce downtime, setups, and in-process inventories and to increase machine utilization.

TelAutograph Transcriber. The TelAutograph Transcriber is an electrically operated instrument which transmits handwritten messages instantaneously from one central point to a remote point or points. The use of this instrument ensures that messages will be received in exactly the form transmitted. It therefore provides insurance against misunderstandings which can arise from verbal orders.

Applications for TelAutograph Transcriber equipment are warranted where it is desirable to initiate an action immediately with precise information. For example, instructions to a shipping department or a stockroom can be quickly and accurately transmitted. The instrument is particularly useful in areas where noisy conditions make verbal communications difficult.

Teletype. Teletype equipment manufactured by the Teletype Corporation consists of sending and receiving stations connected by wires.

The sending and receiving stations may be separated physically, as for example in several plants in one general location or in several sales offices and a main plant in widely dispersed locations. The Teletype sending device resembles a typewriter. When the various keys are hit, telegraph code signals are transmitted to the designated receiving station or stations. The receiving stations record the message exactly as sent.

Teletype equipment has the obvious advantage of being able to transmit, in a timely manner, information to remote operations to direct that operation's activity toward satisfying the most current needs. Production schedules can be reviewed and sent to outlying plants as soon as they are available. Sales orders can be relayed from sales offices to the nearest shipping points for fast, accurate delivery service. In-plant, Teletype equipment can be used to transmit shipping orders from the sales office to the shipping department to hold paperwork handling time to a minimum.

Two-way Radio. Two-way radio communications are used effectively in manufacturing operations to schedule and control the operations of material handling and transportation equipment. Lift trucks can be guided without delay to departments requiring services. Urgent orders can be expedited by directing material handling equipment to move them as soon as each operation is finished. Trucks and trailers on the road can be dispatched from a central point to make additional pickups without returning to the central point for further orders. The utilization of material handling equipment and trucks and trailers can be improved with two-way radio equipment.

Keysort System. The Keysort system developed by the Royal McBee Company is a manual system used for scheduling and controlling manufacturing operations. The core of this system is a series of edge-punched cards which can be used to sort, classify, and summarize all forms of production and labor activity. The edge-punched cards are the basic information file used to produce all information relative to plant activity. Because of their manipulative characteristics, they can be used to control machines, materials, and tools.

The Keysort system is employed in small- to medium-sized plants to obtain effective results with reasonable clerical costs.

CONCLUSION

Noncomputerized data processing and reporting systems must be viewed from two directions. How do they satisfy today's information requirements? How will they satisfy tomorrow's information requirements? The answers to these questions will go a long way in determining how a noncomputerized system should be developed. If a company is expected to grow vertically with more of the same type of production equipment, perhaps today's reporting and monitoring system will still provide fast and accurate operating data. However, if the company is expected to grow horizontally with more complex operations, with more diverse product lines, and with many more pieces of paper to be handled, today's noncomputerized systems probably should be developed to meet today's needs, but also so that they can be adapted to computers in the future.

BIBLIOGRAPHY

Carson, Gordon B. (ed.), *Production Handbook*, 2d ed., The Ronald Press Company, New York, 1958.
Spriegel, W. R., *Industrial Management*, 5th ed., John Wiley & Sons, Inc., New York, 1955.
Westing, J. H., and I. V. Pine, *Industrial Purchasing*, John Wiley & Sons, Inc., New York, 1961.

CHAPTER THREE

Establishing Output Standards

RICHARD L. BURDICK *Manager—Industrial Engineering, The Maytag Company, Newton, Iowa*

The manufacturing manager must continually search for ways to obtain maximum operating effectiveness from the facilities under his direction. To attain that effectiveness, managerial action must be directed toward deficiencies and areas for improvement that can have the greatest impact on total operating results. This requires that the manager and his organization must not only have appropriate, timely information on what the results are, but most importantly, they must also know how those results compare with the potential capabilities of the operation. It is within this context that properly selected and established output standards become an essential part of any useful systems of control.

The purpose of this chapter is to discuss the importance of standards in obtaining maximum effectiveness of the manufacturing function and some of the significant considerations in their selection, development, and application.

IMPORTANCE OF STANDARDS

Standards have long been recognized as necessary parts of a wide range of control systems. Historically, their early applications were largely centered on labor output—predominantly direct labor operations—where they proved to be effective in obtaining labor efficiency. As newer systems of control were designed, including production control, standard costs, budgets, and numerous others, the importance of standards expanded.

More scientific and less time-consuming techniques for establishing standards have emerged, largely replacing intuitive judgments and historical data. But most important, these developments, along with the design of even more sophisticated systems for manufacturing control, have provided management with the tools necessary to determine accurately and economically not only what is happening in a plant, but also how those results compare with what should be happening. Although information systems that merely identify results can undoubtedly be of value to a manager, his effectiveness in initiating actions that produce desirable changes can be far greater if deficiencies or opportunities for improvement are specifically identified. This requires that appropriate standards be incorporated in the control systems.

Perhaps an even more important reason for having a well-designed standards program is associated with the ever-accelerating rate of change. Rapid advancements in manufacturing technology, shifting ratios of indirect to direct labor, and competitive forces causing frequent changes in products which also exert pressures for improved quality and costs are but a few of the many influences that are characteristic of most manufacturing operations. No longer can a manager rely largely on experience to evaluate performance. It may be impractical for him to gain enough experience to know the performance capabilities of all that is new before he is confronted with an even newer set of conditions. Within that kind of environment, it is difficult at best for the manager to have assurance that the organization's resources are being properly directed toward those things that will produce optimum operating results. Without reliable standards to judge performance, his task may be impossible.

DETERMINING ESSENTIAL AREAS FOR STANDARDS APPLICATION

Determining essential areas for standards application is of primary importance in any system of control. Although there may be some benefits in having measured output standards for all the activities of an organization, there is a point of diminishing returns from a practical standpoint where the costs of developing, applying, and administering standards in certain areas outweigh their potential value.

It becomes the manager's responsibility to be sure that proper evaluations are made in selecting the areas for standards application. Fortunately, techniques are available for accurately measuring output of practically all activities within the manufacturing function, with perhaps the exception of some highly creative jobs. Consequently, the use of standards is normally not restricted by technical limitations. The major evaluating consideration becomes one of economics—the potential value of standards in contributing to improved operating results against the costs of their application and administration.

The evaluating process for determining appropriate applications is as important to ongoing standards activities as it is in deciding what programs should be started. Over a period of time, the characteristics of most manufacturing operations change significantly, causing shifts in costs and control needs that affect the relative importance of standards application. Using but one illustration, mechanization normally reduces direct labor content extensively and places greater relative value on the costs of indirect labor, machine downtime, maintenance, and other factors that previously were of lesser significance. As mechanization expands, to continue to emphasize standards designed for direct labor efficiency to the exclusion of standards for machine utilization, maintenance, and other indirect labor is to ignore economic reality.

Areas for Effective Standards Applications. Because each plant has unique operating characteristics that create different control needs, it is impractical to attempt to outline a standards application program that would be of universal value. Further, most managers are well aware of the use of standards for control of certain labor classifications, especially direct labor, through either measured daywork or incentive sytems. To elaborate here on these particular facets of standards applications would appear unnecessary.

There are, however, other types of industrial work where standards have not been so extensively used, but which offer very real potential for increasing productivity. One of the more lucrative areas is in the skilled trades—the maintenance crafts and toolroom work.

Standards Application to Maintenance and Toolroom Work. With the greater complexity of industrial machines and equipment coupled with expanding mechanization, an increasing proportion of total manufacturing expenditures is required for skilled trades work. Yet, with some exceptions, this seems to be a part of many organizations where fundamental management principles and techniques long used in other areas are often last applied. Undoubtedly this is influenced by widely held concepts that craftwork is uniquely different, an idea often promoted by craft supervisors, and that it does not lend itself to systematic management. This is far from being true. Systems for planning, scheduling, and measuring maintenance and toolroom work have been successful in increasing productivity and, where properly designed and installed, have been well accepted by the craftsmen.

Those systems are, in principle, little different from other control systems such as production control, usually being based on some form of measured work data from which jobs are planned and scheduled. Improvements in results are predominantly obtained through eliminating waste time caused by inadequate work standards and related low output expectations of craft supervisors, poorly planned and scheduled craftsmen assignments including crew manning, delays caused by equipment and materials not being available at the right time and place, and similar inefficiencies.

Where a good understanding has been established of the character, potentials, and requirements of such a system and where the responsible manager has a high degree of conviction of its value, improvements in operating costs can far outweigh the cost of installing and maintaining the system, even in relatively small organizations. Because of the wide variety of work performed in most maintenance and toolroom functions, it is often uneconomical for a company to develop its own standard time data. However, a number of consulting firms have developed data that are broadly applicable and economical to use.

To be more specific about the value of standards and the associated system for planning and scheduling maintenance work, in one company having what was considered a good maintenance organization of about 280 employees, labor effectiveness increased by more than 50 percent under a measured daywork application—from around 60 percent average performance of all crafts to nearly 95 percent. In one craft the productivity doubled, while others had dramatic improvement. These changes were accomplished within approximately three years after the program's introduction, with most of the improvement occurring during the first two years.

Other benefits, particularly reduction of downtime and better maintenance service, were also obtained, while added costs of operating the new system were relatively inconsequential in comparison with the savings. Of particular interest is that the program was introduced with practically no labor complaints in two plants represented by a major industrial union. As a matter of fact, most craftsmen welcomed the changes that eliminated delays and allowed them to do the kind of job that provided a personal sense of accomplishment.

In the same company, where a system of planning, scheduling, and measuring similar to that used in the maintenance organization was applied to toolroom work, the improvements were also substantial. The improved performance again exceeded the costs of applying and maintaining the program.

To managers seeking significant improvements in operating results, well-designed programs directed toward maintenance and toolroom work, based on properly established output standards and incorporating planning and scheduling procedures, provide potentially lucrative areas for consideration.

Standards for Other Indirect Labor. In evaluating opportunities for improved operating results, consideration should be given to the use of output standards for all classifications of indirect labor having a substantial number of people. As indicated previously, new techniques for measuring a wide variety of work, along with refinements in standard data development and systems for computer processing of labor standards, have made it economical to use standards extensively for control of indirect labor.

Where measured standards are not broadly applied to indirect labor, the assumption is often made that labor budgets provide adequate controls. But budgets, as important as they are, are usually designed for profit planning purposes and must therefore represent the best estimates of what future results *will* be, not necessarily what they *should* be. To the manager whose responsibilities include initiating effective actions to correct deficiencies and exploit opportunities for improvement, the usual budget data are not adequate. Neither is it usually sufficient to rely on a supervisor's evaluation of indirect labor performance unless the supervisor uses appropriate, objective data in making his determinations or is provided with measurement results from some other competent source.

Standards have been usefully applied in industry for practically all classifications of indirect labor including material handling, general labor, janitorial, and clerical work. The developments in general purpose data and other forms of standard time data, along with work sampling techniques, have resulted in vastly reducing the time and cost of applying standards to indirect work.

In those organizations that may be too small to afford a separate work measurement unit, work sampling provides a particularly effective measurement technique that can be used by any shop supervisor after a short period of instruction. Through random observations and simple recording of data, reliable measurements of efficiency of even a large number of indirect workers can be obtained with relatively little time required by the observer. Although work sampling has far broader application as a measurement tool than indicated here and is extensively used by industrial engineers, it has been particularly useful for quickly determining manpower needs for all indirect labor in a production department, leading to planned adjustments by shop supervisors to obtain efficient utilization of personnel.

Multifactor Standards. There are some industrial plants where labor costs, particularly direct labor, are small in comparison to operating costs of machines and equipment. In most industrial operations, there are departments or perhaps particular machines where controls on machine utilization, quality, tool costs, materials, or supplies are economically far more important than high labor efficiency. Mechanization has had a major influence on this changing characteristic of manufacturing. Multifactor standards, used for either management control or incentive payment, may be the most effective way of obtaining optimum overall results under these conditions.

Where relatively low-cost standard machine tools are used and labor content is high, the normal labor standards can generally be used with reasonable assurance that acceptable costs will be obtained. But when a number of standard machines and their operators are replaced by a single transfer machine or similar equipment costing perhaps a million dollars, the control needs to be drastically changed if the best operating results are to be expected.

Using the transfer machine as a representative illustration, too frequently the approach has been to establish separate controls for machine utilization, tool costs, quality (scrap and rework), maintenance, and other significant economic factors, with the expectation that this approach will produce optimum total results.

The fallacy of this expectation is quite evident when one examines the interrelating effect of tool changes (representing one aspect of tool costs) on machine utilization, particularly on a machine that may have over a hundred tools. An objective of minimum tool costs dictates, among other things, changing tools at the point of maximum tool life. But if that objective is strictly adhered to, tool changes would undoubtedly occur in a frequency pattern that would cause excessive downtime, reducing machine utilization and very likely increasing overall costs.

Similar conflicts may exist among other economic factors, making it imperative to use optimizing techniques if one expects to obtain the best total cost results. When the capabilities and costs for each of the several factors have been determined, the optimizing computations are often reasonably simple and can be made by most industrial engineers having mathematical training.

Criteria for Determining Areas for Standards Applications. The preceding pages have attempted to identify some of the less common areas of standards application that may provide unusual potential for improved operating results. In summary, there are a relatively few, but important, criteria for selecting areas for standards applications:

1. The standards applications must have the potential for making important contributions to operating results.
2. The costs of development, application, and administration must be economically sound.
3. The organization must be competent to develop, apply, and maintain the standards.

It is evident from these criteria that the more important and perhaps most difficult determinations are in evaluating both the potentials from the standards applications and the competency of the organization to obtain those potentials.

For several reasons, the operating manager must actively participate in these determinations. Even though an economic evaluation of possible standards applications may show opportunities for substantial cost reductions, operating supervision may not be knowledgeable enough of the new requirements that will be imposed on them or may not be adequately motivated to provide assurance that the potential savings will materialize. The operating manager may be the only competent person to make that judgment or to determine what training is required if the organization is to obtain the potential benefits. Further, he must objectively consider the technical competency of the standards setting group, an important consideration if new techniques are to be used or unfamiliar types of standards applications are planned.

SETTING STANDARDS

An often overlooked truism is that substantially lower manufacturing costs can be obtained if standards are set by properly trained, competent people. There are companies where the time standard is viewed as the only important product of a standards program and little consideration is given to other benefits that could be obtained. Often associated with this situation are poorly trained analysts whose performances are largely evaluated by the number of standards established each day. As a result, they usually produce standards of questionable reliability, do not significantly contribute to improved work methods and costs, and inevitably create labor problems.

On the other hand, competent work measurement engineers or analysts who make really significant contributions must have knowledge and capabilities in a number of areas, including:

1. Work design
2. Measurement techniques best adapted to the characteristics of the work studied
3. The process of establishing standards and administering the measurement program
4. Characteristics and capabilities of machines, equipment, and processes studied
5. Communications and motivation skills
6. Labor relations activities, including a thorough understanding of relevant contractual requirements
7. The management process for accomplishing results

Some observations on several of these areas may be appropriate.

Work Design. In some situations, basic work design can have the greatest single effect on combined investment and operating costs; yet engineers often will follow traditional patterns existing in an industry without giving more than superficial consideration to the alternatives available. For example, in assembly of large-volume, medium- or large-sized products, the powered assembly line with its short-cycle, highly specialized jobs became the standard for efficiency and was broadly copied for smaller products and subassemblies. More recently, mechanization has challenged the manned line in popularity for the latter classes of work, while job enlargement provides yet another practical alternative.

Job Enlargement. Enlargement of jobs is certainly not new in concept, but although it often can produce superior results in quality and costs, it may not be seriously considered by the engineer even for assembly work to which it may be ideally adapted. Job enlargement as used here is defined as being the expansion of job content to include a wider variety of tasks and to increase the worker's freedom of pace, responsibility for quality, and discretion of method.

There are, of course, definite limitations in the practicability of enlarging some assembly jobs. These limitations are generally associated with job complexity, processing characteristics, space requirements for equipment and materials, component part size, material handling needs, and the cost of equipment where production volume requires duplicate work stations. However, many initially perceived restrictions can be practically and economically overcome by thorough analysis and proper application of work design and motion economy principles.

When selectively applied to even high-volume production requiring multiple work stations, equipment investment for enlarged jobs is often less than for powered assembly lines and is usually a fraction of the cost of mechanized installations. Properly selected job enlargement applications will provide lower operating costs than the line and will compare favorably with mechanized assembly for many products.

In one company, conversion to job enlargement of about twenty-five powered assembly line installations involving well over a hundred operators resulted in a number of distinct benefits:

1. IMPROVED QUALITY. Continuous movement of a powered assembly line usually prevents an operator from correcting defects caused by minor material variations or his own mistakes. This problem is not encountered in fixed-station, enlarged jobs, thus reducing defects while improving product reliability. But more influential to quality is the operator's greater interest and awareness of the importance of his work resulting from a job design requiring complete assembly of a major component and responsibility for functional testing.

Where the operator is provided broader control of job conditions and maximum personal identification with the product of his work, improvements in quality and reliability are inevitable.

2. INCREASED PRODUCTIVITY. Inherent in the powered assembly line are line balance delays caused by variations in work content among jobs which, for short-cycle operations, can be a significant percentage of the productive work. Enlarged jobs do not have this characteristic. Other productivity improvements can often be obtained through better tooling, more compact locations of materials and tools, and other similar refinements.

For certain products, mechanized assembly provides the only feasible solution to productivity requirements, but for other products where job enlargement is a possible design alternative, productivity may compare favorably even with the mechanized line.

3. REDUCED DIRECT AND INDIRECT LABOR COSTS. There are several influences that tend to lower labor costs of enlarged jobs in comparison to those of the powered assembly line. As previously noted, direct labor reductions are obtained from elimination of line balance delays; materials and tools can normally be located closer to the point of use, reducing the work content; and fixture designs can often be more highly refined, allowing more frequent use of simultaneous motions and other motion economies. Reduction in direct labor costs of 10 to 15 percent is not uncommon for exactly the same assemblies converted from a powered line to enlarged jobs.

Reductions of indirect labor costs are obtained primarily from substantially improved quality that reduces rework. Other benefits result from greater flexibility in using conveyor equipment for delivering larger parts to assembly locations and in eliminating much of the inherent inefficiencies of stockmen servicing a powered line.

Because enlarged jobs have more work content than the comparable line jobs, longer training time is usually required for new operators. However, these costs are offset to varying degrees by cost advantages noted in the following paragraph.

4. GREATER FLEXIBILITY IN CHANGING PRODUCTION RATES. Unlike assembly line operations, the work content of an enlarged job is not changed with increases or decreases in production schedules. With a sufficient number of enlarged work stations to accommodate variations in production schedules, increases in schedules require only the assignment of additional operator time, either through extending the work time of currently assigned employees or by adding operators. Lower schedules are obtained by merely reducing

operators. A stable level of productivity is maintained by all operators except those newly assigned, while the powered line requires rebalancing and at least some retraining of all operators. The line's production is limited to the capabilities of the slowest man, or additional costs are generated by assignment of additional labor.

New operators on the enlarged job know by observation what the experienced operators' capabilities are in attaining standard output and therefore are influenced to achieve maximum production more quickly. Grievances against new line standards resulting from rebalancing because of schedule changes are eliminated when job enlargement is used, a particularly important consideration with incentive payment plans. Another saving comes from eliminating engineering and other management time required in rebalancing the line.

5. IMPROVED EMPLOYEE SATISFACTION AND MOTIVATION. In the company referred to, greater operator satisfaction with enlarged jobs is quite apparent, but most important are the tangible evidences of high levels of quality and production.

An independent study conducted in that company by a major university, involving a sizable number of operators who had worked on both line and enlarged jobs assembling the same components, provided several conclusions relating to operator satisfaction: (1) an almost universal preference for the enlarged jobs and for most of the specific attributes of that work; (2) strong evidence that inherent characteristics of assembly lines, which prevent the worker from exercising his maximum capabilities to contribute to the quality of the product and obtaining recognition for that contribution, are the most important source of his dissatisfaction with the line; but (3) even with the strong preference for enlarged jobs, somewhat over half of the employees had favorable attitudes toward line specialization and were not as totally alienated from line jobs as some commentaries have depicted them to be.

6. BETTER WORKPLACE LAYOUTS. Designing workplace layouts for enlarged jobs, particularly if a large number of sizable parts is involved, usually requires the engineer to exercise a high degree of ingenuity in fixture design, tool and material location, and use of handling equipment, along with other considerations that provide a compact, economical work arrangement. Often, enlarged jobs are more adaptable to being set up as integral parts of a larger processing system, such as the machining of major components, than is a powered assembly line. These characteristics very often provide opportunities for additional cost reductions from both methods efficiencies and material handling that would be impractical to obtain from the powered line.

Job enlargement is not a panacea, but rather is a work design alternative that under certain conditions can produce better total results than either specialization or mechanization. Neither is it restricted solely to assembly work—the underlying principles can be effectively applied to many other industrial jobs where there is a high degree of specialization. Undoubtedly, the concentration of job enlargement attention to assembly work has been influenced by the thoughtful questioning by some engineers and managers of the assembly line's effectiveness in attaining optimum results and by the research of industrial psychologists and behavioral scientists suggesting that a high degree of specialization may not be the best approach to achieving maximum productivity.

Work Design Summary. If the potential of standards as effective tools for improving operating results is to be fully realized, the process of setting standards must begin with the work design. Alternative possibilities should be identified and evaluated rather than merely accepting traditional approaches. For the more complicated manufacturing processes, use of newer mathematical techniques and computer simulation may be necessary in determining the best work design and can in many cases help produce large savings in investment and operating costs. At the other extreme of job complexity, application of motion economy principles may be sufficient.

Whatever the complexity of operating characteristics is, measurement engineers or analysts appropriately trained in the principles and tools of work design can make important contributions. When these capabilities are coupled with a management policy establishing optimum work design as the only acceptable criterion, and that policy is well understood by all management personnel, the engineer can then be most effective.

Measurement Techniques. Limiting consideration of measurement techniques to nonmanagement jobs, the work performed in most industrial plants has broad ranges of characteristics, from routine clerical and production operations to highly skilled jobs and from repetitive, short-cycle work to that of a nonrepetitive or long-cycle nature. The use of standards may also be quite different even within a single plant, ranging from spot-checking performances in relatively isolated areas to continuing, plant-wide measured daywork or incentive programs. Both the work characteristics and the use of standards are significant considerations in determining the measurement techniques to be used.

Available to the engineer is a wide variety of measurement techniques which, if properly selected and applied, can measure practically any industrial work to the degree of accuracy required by the ultimate use of the data. It is therefore important that manufacturing management have an understanding of the techniques that can be efficiently and effectively used to provide information for improved operating control, and equally important for the engineer to be able to select and apply the most appropriate technique for the particular characteristics of work to be measured.

The more common measurement techniques include:
1. Stopwatch time study
2. Motion pictures
3. Predetermined time systems
4. Standard data
5. Work sampling
6. Electronic measuring devices and computers

Stopwatch Time Study. Stopwatch time study for industrial work originated in the latter part of the nineteenth century, when Frederick W. Taylor proposed that to establish work standards the operation should be subdivided into elements, a description of each element written, the elements timed with a stopwatch, and allowances added for fatigue and unavoidable delays. From Taylor's first use, stopwatch time study has had broad application in establishing standards and when used by well-trained engineers or analysts is an important technique for measuring work.

Inappropriate use by unskilled people has resulted in the stopwatch being broadly condemned as a tool for exploiting labor, and unfortunately in some cases, that accusation undoubtedly has historical justification. Because of that reputation, operators are often suspicious of stopwatch studies even when made by well-trained, skilled engineers. Complete understanding by all employees in a plant of the process of establishing standards is essential if operator confidence is to be expected and labor problems are to be prevented.

Too often management assumes the unrealistic attitude that practically anyone can make a stopwatch study, only to discover later that the standards are inaccurate, inconsistent, and ineffective and that labor difficulties are the only significant product. These results, however, are unnecessary. With the recognition that applicators must be provided extensive and continuing training in performance rating, that they must know the statistical techniques for determining the number of cycles to be studied, and that they have the skills to communicate effectively with employees to establish understanding and confidence, along with other necessary capabilities, standards established by stopwatch can be reliable and acceptable to the vast majority of workers.

Motion Pictures. A few years after Taylor had begun his work in time study, Frank B. Gilbreth began using motion pictures to study the motions of certain kinds of work. From those studies, Gilbreth established basic work motions which he called "therbligs" and used these motions to build operation standards. Over the ensuing years, motion pictures have found many uses in work analysis and standards setting. Two predominant techniques have emerged—micromotion and memomotion.

Micromotion is the process of taking motion pictures with a high-speed clocking device in the picture, or with the camera operating at a constant speed, most often at 1,000 frames a minute. Because of the high-speed capability of the motion picture camera, it is particularly adaptable where motion analysis in small increments of time is needed. The uses of micromotion are quite diverse and include simultaneous study of more than one person in a work group, determining activities of man-machine relationships, developing the most efficient method of doing work, training people in understanding and applying motion economy principles, timing operations to establish standards, and as a tool for obtaining motion-time data for developing predetermined time systems.

Memomotion is essentially a process of time-lapse photography where the camera is driven at a fixed speed, usually in the range of 50 to 100 frames a minute. The slower speed allows camera use under conditions where costs would be prohibitive if operated at normal speeds or where lengthy operating time is desired between film changes. Memomotion can be particularly effective, if a wide angle lens is used, for simultaneous study of a number of people. Other applications include studies extending over long periods of time, long or irregular cycle jobs, and multiple activities including machine and crew balancing.

Two outstanding advantages of motion pictures are in accurately recording time-motion relationships and in providing a permanent visual record of conditions studied.

Predetermined Time Systems. Following the work of Taylor and Gilbreth, industrial engineers have continued their search for more effective procedures of work measurement. Perhaps the most significant advancements have been in the development of predetermined time systems, where time is directly related to basic motions required in performing work. Some of the better known systems using that approach are Methods-Time Measurement (MTM), Work-Factor System (WF), Motion-Time-Analysis (MTA) and Basic Motion Timestudy (BMT).

Methods-Time Measurement (MTM), the most widely used of the predetermined time systems, is by definition a system of predetermined time values which analyzes any manual motion into the basic motions required to perform the operation and assigns a time value to each motion, which is determined by the nature of the motion and the conditions under which it is performed. The basic motions for MTM are Reach, Move, Turn, Apply

Pressure, Grasp, Position, Release, Disengage, Eye Travel, Eye Focus, and Body, Leg, and Foot motions. Using the basic motion for Reach for illustration, the time value assigned is determined by the distance reached, the destination of the Reach, and whether or not the hand is in motion at either the beginning or end of the motion.

Although predetermined time systems are not particularly complicated and are being used by thousands of practitioners, training should be conducted by instructors well qualified in both the theory and application of the particular system. Independent study of textbooks is not adequate to develop the knowledge for competent use in setting standards.

In the extensive application of the various predetermined time systems to a broad range of industrial work, a number of important uses have developed:[1]

1. Developing effective methods in advance of beginning production
2. Improving existing methods
3. Establishing time standards
4. Developing time formulas or standard data
5. Estimating
6. Guiding product design
7. Developing effective tool designs
8. Selecting effective equipment
9. Training supervisors to become highly methods conscious
10. Settling grievances
11. Research—particularly in connection with methods, learning time, and performance rating

Predetermined time systems are being used extensively for establishing standards for a wide variety of work ranging from clerical and service jobs through all types of factory operations. One of the major advantages of predetermined time systems is their broad adaptability—either from direct application of the basic motion times or from standard data developed from the basic motions—for application to specific classes of work. In addition to the detailed basic motion times, many of the systems provide broader, general purpose data that allow economical application to nonrepetitive or long-cycle jobs where the use of the detailed data would be too time consuming. General purpose data are also useful for repetitive or short-cycle operations if the greater accuracy obtained from the basic motion times is not of significant importance.

In industrial organizations where predetermined time systems have been used extensively, distinct benefits have resulted. Some of the more prominent ones are:

1. BETTER WORK DESIGN. Before starting production, alternative methods for doing the job can easily be compared and the most efficient one selected. If tool engineers have been trained to use the technique in evaluating the motion economy effect of their designs, additional efficiencies can be obtained. Other advantages of this approach to engineering the method in advance of production include accurate cost estimates, better operator training, and perhaps eliminating costly changes after production has started.

2. CONSISTENCY OF PRODUCTION STANDARDS. Where standards are used for measured daywork control or incentive payment, inconsistent standards are a major problem. When standards are developed from the motions re-

[1] H. B. Maynard, G. J. Stegemerten, and J. L. Schwab, *Methods-Time Measurement*, McGraw-Hill Book Company, New York, 1948, p. 13.

quired to perform the work and performance rating of observed elemental times is eliminated, greater consistency is inevitable.

3. REDUCED LABOR RELATION PROBLEMS. In comparison with standards established by stopwatch time study, predetermined systems have several characteristics that reduce labor conflict. First, the method, not the operator, is studied, eliminating the employee's concern about being directly observed and particularly his fear of performance rating. Second, a much more detailed and accurate record of the method is obtained, allowing easier resolution of questions that may arise when changes in job conditions occur. And third, if the correctness of the standard is disputed, resolution is more objectively obtained when the method, not the operator's performance, is the basis for examination.

Although affording many advantages over other techniques of work measurement, predetermined time systems have several limitations in their application. They are not designed to measure machine times, nor are they generally applicable to pure mental time requirements, certain physically restricted motions, and a few other similar conditions.

Standard Data. Although standard data may not be properly considered a measurement technique, their importance in establishing standards warrants consideration here.

Unlike predetermined times, which are associated with basic motions, standard data times are normally identified with elements of work. In industrial work, common elements are employed in many different jobs. For certain classes of work, all jobs may consist of essentially the same elements, having only minor variations in conditions that influence the time for doing the job. To study every operation independently can be a time-consuming, costly, and often unnecessary procedure. The purpose of standard data is to provide elemental time values that incorporate significant variables and that are formulated so that they can be broadly applied to operations without requiring individual time study.

Before the development of predetermined time systems, stopwatch time study was primarily used for preparing standard data. To make enough studies to measure all conditions and variables accurately was a lengthy and costly process, especially for nonrepetitive work like maintenance and toolmaking. Reconstruction of questioned standard data was often difficult or impossible because of inadequate information about the methods and conditions under which the original studies were taken.

Predetermined time systems have largely overcome these problems in standard data development. They allow construction of the data with increased accuracy in much less time than is required by other techniques. Variables can be isolated better and described more precisely, and records of the work methods are more exact, making it possible to answer better any questions which may arise during application of the data.

Work Sampling. Work sampling is based on the laws of probability, where a random sample tends to have the same pattern of distribution as the larger group from which it was taken. It has been increasingly used in industry since its introduction in the United States as "ratio delay" in 1940.

Work sampling is an effective and economical tool for obtaining accurate information on the percentage of time that people are working or machines are operating. If performance ratings are applied to manual work observations, measures of work time can also be obtained and time standards can be established. This technique is most useful where studies of a number of people are needed and for long-cycle or nonrepetitive work.   Other techniques of work measurement are more adaptable to repetitive, short-cycle operations.

One of the major attributes of work sampling is its simplicity of application, allowing foremen or other nontechnically trained people to evaluate operating efficiencies more objectively.   Where applicable, it can also save considerable time.   In many situations, the cost can be less than half that required to obtain comparable data by continuous study.

The simplest application of work sampling is the making of random observations of one or more operators or machines and recording whether they are working or idle.   From that record, the percentages of work time and idle time can easily be calculated.   Quite obviously, most applications will be more elaborate, and statistical techniques will be required to assure accuracy of the data.

The work sampling procedure, however, can be quickly learned.   Its potential value is extensive, and with its relative simplicity of application, it can be an important control tool in any manufacturing organization.

Electronic Measuring Devices and Computers.   With the rapid advances in electronics and computers, increasing use has been made of such equipment for work measurement.   Many of the techniques are in the development stage, but broad use of mechanization for work measurement and standards setting is becoming an increasing reality.

Electronic time recorders tied to standard computers are being used on a limited basis for measuring industrial jobs.   The recorder, key-operated by an observer, provides elemental data for computer tapes, which are then converted to punched cards and processed by the computer to produce a time standard.

Electronic devices, either separate units or connected to a computer, are being used on mechanized machines where machine utilization is of major importance and continuing records of downtime are needed to determine corrective actions to be taken.   When used on a transfer machine, for example, a daily (or more frequent if desired) printout showing all downtime, its causes, the station on the machine having problems, and other data can be provided. Analytical programs can be incorporated to furnish the manager with essentially any control data important to achieving maximum production and optimum costs.

Several systems have been applied for using computers for processing work measurement data and establishing time standards.   One general approach has been to enter elemental standard data in computer storage, and from the analyst's determination of the elements of a job, process the data through the computer to obtain a printout of the time standard, operation description, and relevant equipment characteristics.   A second, more advanced approach has been to code predetermined motion-time data and then store the necessary data, including word descriptions of the motions, in the computer.   In developing a standard, the engineer provides a sequential list of coded work elements and their frequencies, along with the machine identification and other necessary data.   The computer printout shows all machine, tool, and inspection data; a word description of the elements; and the standard time for the operation.

Another even more sophisticated system has been used by one computer company in some of its own manufacturing facilities.   Through the use of a desk-top optical terminal and projected filmstrips along with certain computer programming techniques, it is possible for an engineer to use a light-sensitive probe to provide input data for complete determination of the manufacturing processing of a part. The engineer identifies such things as the type of material, material specifications, the operations required, and dimensional specifications, along with similar processing information. The computer provides output data for the part that include plant routing, descriptions and data for the operations performed, standard times, material and labor cost estimates, and other pertinent information. In essence, the system is designed to generate all the needed manufacturing processing and cost data from an engineer's analysis of a part drawing, with the data being simply and directly entered in the computer through the optical terminal. Although extensive programming is required for broad application of such a system, it also offers a large potential for reducing manufacturing engineering time, particularly in plants processing a large volume of new parts or numerous specification changes.

Use of computers for assembly line balancing is one of the more extensive, specialized applications to work measurement. Manual line balancing has always been a time-consuming process for the many companies having long, high-volume assembly lines. Frequent changes in product design and production schedules greatly compound the problem, making it difficult to maintain efficient assignment of work elements so that the operator's available time is fully utilized at each work station. With the newer generation of computers having the capacity to handle the many restrictions characteristic of a large assembly line, this technique has even greater potential application. The principal advantages are in savings of engineering time and reduced labor requirements resulting from better balancing of work elements. Cost reduction from both these sources can, in some situations, be substantial.

Computers and other electronic devices will be increasingly used for establishing time standards and for providing other information for the effective control of industrial output. Developments in this area are important, and the manufacturing manager should keep informed of new applications so that he can evaluate their adaptability to his needs.

Establishing Standards and Administering the Measurement Program. Even with the newer tools and techniques that have expanded measurements to broader areas of industrial work, the vast majority of standards will continue to be set on repetitive, relatively short-cycle production operations. Most of these standards will undoubtedly be established from direct observation of the operations and applying stopwatch measurement or predetermined time data.

No measurement program, either daywork or incentive, can produce worthwhile results or be effectively maintained unless the process of establishing standards is well understood and competently applied by both the measurement people and operating supervisors. Neither can the program succeed unless it is properly administered.

The process of establishing standards essentially involves the following steps:
1. Prepare the job.
2. Study the operation.
3. Prepare the time standard.
4. Apply the standard.
5. Follow up the standard.

Prepare the Job. The importance of engineered work design and application of motion economy principles in obtaining optimum costs has been discussed previously. If that work has been properly accomplished, the job preparation will have been largely done and, hopefully, the operator's ideas already incorporated. Unfortunately, this is often not the situation confronting the measurement observer and the supervisor when the job is supposedly ready for study. They must therefore collaborate in taking care of any remaining problems before the study is started. If economics is not a sufficient motivation for refining the job before it is studied, potential labor problems certainly should be.

Many of the operators' complaints about time standards result from the standards established on jobs having frequent changes in conditions—where the method has not been stabilized, where equipment and tooling are not functioning properly, or where changes in the quality of materials cause fluctuations in the time required to perform the operation. By resolving these kinds of problems, establishing adequate safety and quality controls, and involving the operator in any plans affecting his job, future problems with employees can be greatly reduced.

Study the Operation. Assuming that the method has been well designed and all job conditions affecting the performance of the work are satisfactory, the next important consideration is the relationship existing among the people involved—the operator, the supervisor, and the observer. Their understanding of the purpose of time standards and their individual attitudes toward that purpose are most crucial at this point. Each has certain natural concerns that can only be overcome by confidence in the intent and capabilities of the others.

From the operator's viewpoint, too often the mystery of time study has not been removed by either formal training or competent and thorough explanation by his supervisor. His knowledge may have been largely obtained from comments of fellow employees, often those who complain about tight standards, tough supervisors, and to put it mildly, stupid time study observers. Further, if his supervisor has not exhibited enough interest in him to explain the what and why of standards, he probably has little confidence that he will be treated fairly. Because most employees are willing to produce a good day's output if they have been adequately trained in the skills of the job and have confidence that the standards will be fairly established and administered, the results from the job study are largely dependent on how realistically management has treated with the obvious concerns of the operators. To expect the supervisor and the observer, at the time of a study, to overcome any deep-seated, adverse employee attitudes is unreasonable.

The supervisor recognizes that to carry out his responsibilities to both the company and his employees, he too must have a thorough knowledge of the purposes and process of work measurement. Along with that, he realizes he must be sensitive to the operators' concerns and that his personal capability for communicating effectively with his employees about standards is essential in preventing problems. He, like the employee, must be confident that the time study observer is well qualified to establish a standard which properly reflects all the job requirements. But the supervisor also has an additional problem—the concern that if the standard is not properly set, he may have more difficulties than benefits from the standard. He must not only have confidence in his own capabilities, but he must also have assurance that the time study man can do his job well.

The time study observer also has certain attitudes and reservations when studying an operation. Even though he may know that he has been well trained and is technically competent to measure the work, he also knows that the accuracy of his standard and its acceptance by the operator are greatly influenced by a number of things. Among these are the consistency of the job methods and conditions, the knowledge and attitude of the operator concerning work measurement, the skill and pace of the operator, and the capabilities and involvement of the supervisor in providing necessary help to obtain an accurate standard. Like the supervisor, the observer knows that the results of his efforts are largely influenced by the importance management has placed on the standards program and by the training provided to assure effective results.

Obviously, there are also many technical requirements in studying an operation. But if management personnel have been competently developed to handle the human relations needs, they will, of necessity, have also been trained in the technical requirements.

Prepare the Time Standard. There are normally two essential parts of a time standard—the standard time value and some form of a job instruction write-up.

Calculation of the standard time depends, of course, on the technique used for measuring the job. Usually the process consists of computing the time required for each element of the operation, calculating the total operational time, applying necessary allowances (personal time, fatigue, and unavoidable delays), and then determining the standard time. The last mentioned is most often expressed in hours per piece or per hundred pieces produced (standard hours) and in output required per hour at the standard rate. If the time standard is used for incentive payment, output per hour may also be shown at the normal incentive performance level, such as 120 or 125 percent of standard.

The importance of a well-written job instruction sheet is often underestimated. Quite commonly, this consists of only the identification of the operation and a very brief description of the operation or possibly of the elements performed. Such a description is totally inadequate for practically all standards, particularly repetitive production jobs.

A properly detailed job instruction sheet serves a number of essential purposes. Most important of these is its use in instructing operators and in providing a record, readily available to both the supervisor and operator, of the method and job conditions under which the standard was established. Although the description may not include all the information to identify every change in job conditions, such as data on tool details, part dimensions, or other detailed engineering specifications, it should be complete enough to identify changes easily that might affect the standard time significantly.

An adequate job instruction sheet will provide several categories of information. These include operation identification information and dates; the standard time value and production output requirements; machine and equipment information such as speeds, feeds, or cycle times; any special instructions relating to such areas as safety and quality; a sketch of the workplace layout, showing dimensional relationships of locations of materials, tools, equipment, or any similar dimensional characteristics; and a detailed description of the method.

The last mentioned should provide a right- and left-hand word description showing distances of reaches and moves for all repetitive elements and should include any needed special instructions. Nonrepetitive elements need not be so precisely described if they are a relatively small part of the total standard time. The job instruction sheet should be hung at the workplace or should be available in some other location readily accessible to the operator and supervisor. Although this thoroughness may appear unnecessarily time consuming, it is well worth the effort, for it provides greater assurance that the operators will be adequately instructed in the standard method of running the job and that changes in job conditions which affect the standard will be identified.

Apply the Standard. The first step in applying the standard is a thorough review by the operating supervisor. He should be satisfied that all required work elements are included, that the job instructions provide the best safe method of performing the work, that necessary special instructions are covered, and that a qualified operator can attain the required output. If there are any doubts about the output requirements, he and the time study observer should immediately resolve the differences before the standard is issued to the operator. The review should be thorough enough for the supervisor to be able to explain the standard to the operator and to answer any questions the operator may have.

There are several other checks that the supervisor and observer should make before discussing the standard with the operator. The first is to determine if the equipment and tooling are operating properly and if the material quality is satisfactory; second, that there is a procedure established for obtaining accurate production counts and time; and third, that an adequately skilled operator, or one who has the ability to attain the required skills in a reasonable period of time, is assigned to the job.

At this point, the standard should be discussed with the operator so that he has a complete understanding of the method and other requirements, including expected output. Questions must be adequately answered, and periodic observation of the operator's performance maintained until consistent, satisfactory output is achieved.

Follow up the Standard. The greatest single cause of failure of measured daywork or incentive programs, outside of allowing untrained or incompetent people to establish standards, is inadequate administration of the program. Application of standards is not the final step, but rather is the beginning of the essential responsibility for administration. This is not a simple task, for there are many influences exerted that make it easier to live with undesirable conditions than to deal with them effectively. For example, a foreman who is meeting production schedules—perhaps largely because of a standards program—may find it difficult to report a change in method, knowing that the standard will be revised and that the operator may, as a result, enter a grievance or even withhold production so that schedules will be missed.

The manager who is responsible for an existing standards program, or is considering installing one, must recognize that along with the benefits are certain administrative requirements which, if either ignored or extensively compromised, will inevitably cause ineffective results. The more important administrative needs are:

1. Every employee assigned to a job must be thoroughly instructed in the method and other requirements of the operation, and his performance must be followed until consistent, adequate production is obtained.

2. Known permanent changes in methods or job conditions must be promptly reported by the supervisor and measured by an engineer or analyst, and the standard must be revised to reflect the changes.

3. There should be a continuing, effective procedure for periodic review of all standards to provide assurance that changes in job conditions are resulting in appropriate modifications in standards.

4. Temporary changes in job conditions, resulting from such things as

equipment, tool, and material variances, should be promptly covered by time allowances or disallowances measured by an engineer or analyst when possible.

5. Operators' complaints must be thoroughly investigated and prompt resolution obtained.

6. A procedure for obtaining accurate production counts and time records must be maintained.

7. Conformity with all provisions of any labor agreement in effect must be adhered to. It might be noted here that often problems in application and administration result from management's willingness to negotiate contractual requirements that compromise sound standards principles.

PREVENTING LABOR RELATIONS PROBLEMS

There are companies whose work standards programs have totally failed within a few months after installation, while others have had programs, including incentive plans, that have produced effective results for decades. Either result can usually be traced to management's knowledge of the needs of a good standards program and the degree of its commitment to those needs. Often the blame for failure is placed on labor unions, but in reality, the difficulties are more often of management's own making—inadequately trained people applying and administering the program, allowing unnecessary compromises of sound standards principles to be negotiated into the labor agreement, and similar things, often solely within management's control. If a standards program is properly designed and if management has knowledgeably and realistically committed itself to the requirements for its successful application and administration, labor conflicts need not become a major problem.

Preventing labor relations problems starts, therefore, with management's perceived importance of work standards and the responsibility it assumes in obtaining effective results. There are several important, tangible evidences of that responsibility being exercised:

1. Labor agreement clauses which provide employees assurance that they will be fairly treated, but which do not compromise fundamentally sound standards principles or restrict the application of appropriate work measurement techniques and procedures

2. Selection of competent work measurement personnel who are provided adequate training to become skilled in both the technical and human relations needs

3. Training of operating supervisors to become fully knowledgeable of the standards program's characteristics and requirements, development of their capabilities to communicate with the employees effectively, and assurance that they carry out their responsibilities in applying and administering the program

4. Providing employees and union representatives with thorough knowledge of the purposes and techniques of the standards program, including necessary training, and openly discussing all relevant information or data about specific standards that may be questioned

5. Maintaining open channels of communications among employees, supervisors, union representatives, and labor relations and work standards personnel, which properly consider lines of authority, but which are also effective in preventing problems or in promptly resolving those that occur

6. Directly involving the appropriate standards personnel in grievances, contract negotiations, or other labor relations activities affecting the standards program

If it were possible to identify the complex labor relations characteristics of a standards program by only two simple objectives, these would be competency of all management personnel involved in the standards activities, and mutual confidence among operators, management people, and union representatives. The needs described above are all associated directly with the achievement of these objectives.

It would be misleading to leave the implication that with a standards program, particularly where wage incentives are used, labor relations are not a problem or that they can be simply handled. The significant point is that standards need not cause any greater problems than any other areas of labor relations if management knows what is needed and intelligently treats with those needs.

ROLE OF THE MANUFACTURING MANAGER IN THE STANDARDS PROGRAM

There is essentially but one reason for the manager's interest in a standards program—the contribution it can make to better operating results. Because of its potential in serving that purpose, the manager inevitably becomes involved, first in evaluating the importance of using standards in various areas of potential application, and second in providing the managerial attention necessary to assure effective results from the applications which are made. Perhaps somewhat oversimplified, his role becomes one of evaluating and facilitating.

To carry out the evaluating responsibility, the manager must determine how important standards are to the various control systems either in use or to be developed. If, for example, there are no standards being applied to a large group of general laborers or maintenance craftsmen, but from information available the manager suspects that there are opportunities for substantially greater efficiency, he might conclude that work sampling studies should be made to determine the potential value of applying standards in those areas. This requires that he also have an awareness of various measurement techniques available and their uses, or as an alternative, that he have someone in his organization to turn to who is competent to make these determinations.

Another important evaluating responsibility is in assessing the capabilities of the organization to handle any standards activities undertaken. As has been mentioned earlier in this chapter, to obtain effectiveness from a standards program requires not only well-trained, capable work standards personnel, but also operating supervisors who are knowledgeable of the purposes and needs of the program and can competently carry out their responsibilities.

From the manager's evaluation of potential standards applications evolves the character and scope of the activities. Requirements to carry out these activities, including personnel, training, or any other needs, can then be determined and provided. But probably a more demanding facilitating responsibility of the manager will occur when the standards activities are underway. The manager must be sensitive to major problems that may develop, such as widespread failure of supervisors to report changes in job conditions, or indications of broad conflict between operators and standards people, or evidences of consistently tight or loose standards, and he must initiate or support the actions necessary for correction.

CONCLUSION

To the manufacturing manager looking for ways of improving operating results, output standards may provide an important tool. When standards are included as a part of control systems, the manager not only has timely information on what the operating results are, but he also knows how those results compare with the potential capabilities of the plant. Deficiencies or areas of possible improvement can be pinpointed, and managerial action can be directed toward the needs that can have the greatest influence on total results.

With the advancements which have been made in measurement tools and techniques, standards can be accurately and economically established for practically all industrial work. This provides the manager opportunities to extend effective controls to classes of work that in the past may not have been considered possible for time standards. The expanding use of computers adapted to work measurement systems and performance data collection opens broader areas for standards applications and provides flexibilities to adjust the standards activities to keep pace with rapid changes in manufacturing conditions.

Although the tools and techniques are available for effective use of standards, their benefits in improving operating results are largely dependent on proper selection of areas of application and particularly on management's knowledge of the needs of a good standards program and the importance it places on those needs. With competent management people, well trained in both the technical and human relations requirements, a properly designed standards program can produce effective results.

BIBLIOGRAPHY

Annual Conference Proceedings and other publications, MTM Association for Standards and Research, 9-10 Saddle River Road, Fairlawn, N.J.

Barnes, R. M., *Motion and Time Study*, 6th ed., John Wiley & Sons, Inc., New York, 1968.

Drucker, P. F., *The Effective Executive*, Harper & Row, Publishers, Incorporated, New York, 1967.

Gellerman, S. W., *Motivation and Productivity*, American Management Association, New York, 1963.

Heiland, R. E., and W. J. Richardson, *Work Sampling*, McGraw-Hill Book Company, New York, 1957.

Karger, D. W., and F. H. Bayha, *Engineered Work Measurement*, 2d ed., The Industrial Press, New York, 1965.

Lewis, W. E. (ed.), *The Journal of Industrial Engineering*, American Institute of Industrial Engineers, Inc., New York (monthly).

Maynard, H. B. (ed.), *Industrial Engineering Handbook*, 2d ed., McGraw-Hill Book Company, New York, 1963.

Nadler, G., *Work Design*, Richard D. Irwin, Inc., Homewood, Ill., 1963.

Stewart, P. A., "Job Enlargement," *Monograph Series no. 3*, Center for Labor and Management, College of Business Administration, University of Iowa, Iowa City, Iowa, 1967.

CHAPTER FOUR

Budgeting

REGINALD L. JONES *Partner, Arthur Andersen & Co., New York, New York*

Modern business budgeting is a systematic process of planning the best use of resources to achieve business objectives. The end result of this process is a set of projected statements of profit and loss and cash flow over a period of time—usually a year, with a breakdown by month—and a balance sheet at the end of each period. The value of budgeting, however, is far greater than the preparation of financial projections. Benefits of a good budgeting process include:

1. A disciplined approach to coordinating the planning of all functional executives in the company
2. The opportunity to predetermine what profits and costs should be under various alternative operating conditions
3. A basis for assigning responsibility for business results among managers
4. Provision for management control on an exception basis by providing a "bench mark" for comparison with actual results

Budgeting is a tool for the use of management. The preparation of a budget in itself does not ensure good planning, nor does a budget control business results. Planning and control are management functions, and only managers can plan ahead and exercise control over people and operating events.

In this chapter, the techniques of good budgeting will be covered, with particular emphasis on what manufacturing managers must do to make budgeting an effective tool. It should be kept in mind that the budget department and budget accountants can provide the best techniques of financial and economic analysis, but only operating management can make budgeting work.

4–49

THE REQUIREMENTS AND OBJECTIVES OF BUDGETING

The environmental requirements for good business budgeting are essentially the same as for sound business management. Every successful business firm, regardless of size, must:

1. Develop a statement of profit objectives and policies to guide management in reaching its business goals
2. Develop a sound plan of organization with clearly defined responsibilities and authorities for each management and supervisory position
3. Establish a clear understanding of cost behavior and product cost structure
4. Develop a plan of operations over a given period of time to achieve objectives with a minimum of waste and inefficiency
5. Provide for measurement of performance through timely, comparative control reports
6. Take necessary action in execution of plans to correct unsatisfactory performance

The concept of budgeting formalizes the process implied in these requirements by incorporating the above steps into a comprehensive financial plan or budget.

It should be obvious that the financial plan or budget is not just a forecast of business results a year ahead. It is instead a plan of operations. The plan must be based on good operating practices and soundly conceived management strategy. It should have "stretch" in it. This means that operating men should incorporate in the budget performance goals that are attainable by hard work and dedicated effort.

An easy test of whether or not a company budget has been built on good planning and control concepts is to check these points:

1. Sales and production requirements should be defined in terms of quantities by product.
2. The variable and total costs of producing each product should be identified on a predetermined basis in the budget.
3. Budgeted costs and expenses should be stated for each responsibility center.
4. The degree of capacity utilization of major equipment and facilities should be clearly defined in the budget plan.
5. All departmental budgets should be based on the same volumes of product and service requirements and should meet an acceptable profit goal.

If a company's budgeting cannot meet these tests, manufacturing management should discuss the defects with the budget personnel to seek improvements in the budgeting process.

RESPONSIBILITIES OF OPERATING MANAGERS AND BUDGET PERSONNEL IN BUDGETARY PLANNING AND CONTROL

In any coordinated activity, teamwork is important. Budget personnel, under the direction of the budget officer or controller, play an important but by no means exclusive role in budgeting. The best way to view their role is as a staff or service function to line or operating management. Operating management must develop objectives, plans, and policies and must exercise control. The budget department puts the budget together based on these objectives, plans, and policies and "dollarizes" the results. The budget department also prepares budget and cost reports and helps operating men explain the nature and causes of variances from plan.

A convenient way to look at the role of the two functional areas is by the steps required in the budgeting process as illustrated in Table 4-1.

FLEXIBLE BUDGETING—THE KEY TO CONTROL OF OPERATIONS

Experienced manufacturing managers recognize intuitively the value of good budgeting. Several reasons exist. One is that manufacturing consumes or spends a large share of the revenue received for product sales and also controls a large part of the company's assets. Therefore, control of manufacturing cost is crucial to profitability. Second, structuring and laying out production operations requires good organization and assignment of responsibilities—another key to good budgeting. Third, manufacturing executives must know the flow of material and accumulation of conversion cost in a product.

Nevertheless, in many companies, manufacturing personnel are frustrated with budgeting. The reasons cluster around the way in which budgets are established and their value for control under (1) changing levels of operations and (2) changes in the mix of products manufactured.

All too frequently, business budgeting fails to meet the real needs of operating personnel. Where this happens, it is because of failure to understand

TABLE 4–1. Role of Operating Management and Budget Management
in the Budgeting Process

Budgeting requirement	Primary area of responsibility	
	Operating management	Budget management
1. Monitor budget process		X
2. Perform economic analysis		X
3. Determine sales potential and plan	X	
4. Establish inventory levels	X	
5. Prescribe operating methods	X	
6. Determine production processes	X	
7. Develop cost center structure	X	
8. Establish equipment capacity and operating rates	X	
9. Develop quantitative standards	X	
10. Identify material measurement points	X	
11. Analyze cost behavior		X
12. Establish budget determinants		X
13. Determine manning requirements	X	
14. Apply dollar rates to physical estimates or standards		X
15. Develop product/service transfer costs		X
16. Develop product costs		X
17. Prepare budget and cost reports		X
18. Consolidate profit plan		X
19. Prepare statistical variance analysis		X
20. Explain cause of variance	X	
21. Prescribe and initiate corrective action	X	

the system and techniques of modern business budgeting. Typical of the failure is the concept of budgeting, frequently found in government agencies, which provides fixed appropriations or allowances to each department based on one revenue projection.

Business management does use this form of appropriation or fixed budget in certain areas of expense management where it is appropriate, but good managers know that for many types of costs such a fixed allowance is totally useless because no one sales revenue projection is ever completely realistic. Therefore the budget system must provide for flexibility in establishing budget allowances under varying operating conditions. This is particularly important in manufacturing.

In a very generalized way, costs can be described as being a function of either (1) the passage of time (such as the president's salary) or (2) the volume of activity (such as the direct material in units produced). Fixed budgets assume that the dollars allowed in the budget are triggered by the passage of time irrespective of production levels or the volume of activity. Flexible budgets assume that costs will vary with the volume of activity.

Flexible budgeting can be incorporated in one of two ways—the step budget, wherein budgets are developed for different levels of operation, or the variable budget, where budgets are prepared on a variable cost basis providing progressively greater budget allowances as the volume of activity increases.

Advantages of Flexible Budgeting. The value of the techniques of flexible budgeting can be easily understood by production executives because of the realistic way in which such budgets accommodate actual operating conditions in the plant. Furthermore, the ability to incorporate variable budgeting in the budgetary control process deemphasizes the need for precision in forecasting sales and production volumes, and this benefit is enormous when one considers that such forecasting is crude at best.

Figure 4-1 contrasts the application of the fixed, step, and variable types of budgeting for the manufacturing expense of a machine shop. The fixed budget is based on a projection of operating hours related to the original sales plan. Its realism is destroyed if sales vary markedly from the projected level. The flexible forms of budgets are constructed to show what costs and expenses should be over a range of operations. The step budget approach offers some advantages, but it does not offer as good a control mechanism at the point where operating hours move from one step level to another because in practice the budget requirements do not change that sharply with small changes in operating hours. Also, to develop step budgets for every expense account at several levels of activity can be inordinately time consuming and costly.

The variable budget is constructed under the principle that some costs are fixed over a range of activities and others vary in proportion with the activity. This requires the budgetary accountant to separate cost accounts on the basis of cost behavior.

Cost Variability. When we think of the total costs of a factory, we immediately recognize that they will increase or decrease depending upon the level of activity or the production plan in the factory. If a second shift is authorized, additional costs of raw materials, labor, supervision, and utilities, to mention just a few, will be incurred. Therefore it is clear that costs can vary with the level of activity in the operating plant. It is also true, however, that some costs vary with the volume of operations whereas others do not. Where certain costs are variable, others are fixed. Still others are mixed in that they are semivariable.

Budgeted Operating Level—11,000 Machine Hours

Annual Fixed Budget

Supervision and indirect labor	$ 28,000
Payroll	60,000
Repairs and maintenance	22,000
Utilities	11,000
Supplies	6,500
Services	16,000
Depreciation	50,000
	$193,500

Annual Step Budget

Level of operating hours	6,000 to 7,999	8,000 to 9,999	10,000 to 11,999	12,000 to 13,999
Budgeted operating hours			11,000	
Supervision and indirect labor	$ 23,200	$ 25,600	$ 28,000	$ 30,400
Payroll costs	40,000	50,000	60,000	70,000
Repairs and maintenance	17,600	19,800	22,000	24,200
Utilities	7,000	9,000	11,000	13,000
Supplies	5,500	6,000	6,500	7,500
Services	13,000	14,500	16,000	17,500
Depreciation	50,000	50,000	50,000	50,000
	$156,300	$174,900	$193,500	$212,600

Annual Variable Budget

	Total	Fixed	Variable (11,000 hours)	Variable rate per operating hour
Supervision and indirect labor	$ 28,000	$ 14,800	$ 13,200	$1.20
Payroll costs	60,000	5,000	55,000	5.00
Repairs and maintenance	22,000	9,900	12,100	1.10
Utilities	11,000	—	11,000	1.00
Supplies	6,500	1,000	5,500	0.50
Services	16,000	7,750	8,250	0.75
Depreciation	50,000	50,000		
	$193,500	$ 88,450	$105,050	$9.55

FIG. 4-1. Three Approaches to a Manufacturing Department Budget.

Budget Determinants. In budgeting each of these costs, manufacturing management must identify the measure of activity that will cause the cost to vary, such as units of product manufactured, tons or gallons of output, machine hours operated, or maintenance hours demanded. These quantitative measures of activity are called budget determinants. They determine the amount of budgeted cost required to meet the level of activity.

The proper identification of budget determinants is an important part of budgetary control. The determinants must make sense to manufacturing managers who are in the best position to understand the nature of the production processes. The best determinant is that measure which is most likely to reflect the factors which cause costs to change.

Fixed costs are those where the budget determinant is the passage of time. For example, depreciation and real property taxes accrue over the passage of time during the calendar year irrespective of operating levels in the plant. Similarly, in the area of direct material, the best budget determinant is usually the amount of finished or semifinished material or product completed at the cost center. For example, in a paper mill, the best determinant of paper pulp required on the paper machine is the amount of finished paper produced on the reel at the end of the paper machine. And of course, direct material is a fully variable cost.

The difficult costs to classify are those of a semifixed nature where the relationship of resource consumption to output is not as clear as in the case of depreciation or materials. These semivariable costs must be analyzed in each cost center to determine what portion of the cost is fixed and what portion is variable with some measure of activity. There are a variety of ways in which this analysis can be carried out. Many of them are based on the historical relationship of the amount of cost to activity. A frequently used technique is the scatter chart illustrated by Figure 4-2, where the amount of cost is plotted against the activity and a linear relationship is assumed by drawing a line of best fit. This line can be drawn by eye or can be developed by a mathematical technique called the method of least squares. The illustration shows the amount of indirect labor cost, including setup men and material handlers, related to machine hours ~ ' '~ ~chi...ing department.

A more costly me~' ~st h~havior is to conduct engineering studies to predete   ie manuf   ' ~ expenses should be under given le\   iethod is s~   '~ved wh the amount of cost i~   _~~~r believes that the potential for cost reduction is significant.

Whether historical correlation or engineering studies are used, the result is the development of budget worksheets which show by cost category the amount of fixed expense and the variable budget rate for the variable portion of expense. From these schedules, a budgeted amount for the cost category can be determined at any given volume of activity.

To determine the effectiveness of cost performance, manufacturing executives can then compare, for the actual volume of activity, the allowable budget on the flexible budget scale with the actual costs incurred. This is a powerful control tool. It eliminates arguments about assumptions in forecasting production volumes and focuses on management spending and productivity. It enables managers to concentrate attention on controllable problem areas and take corrective action to keep costs in line.

Flexible budgets are vital to operational control, but they have a double advantage because they make it possible to develop good profit planning.

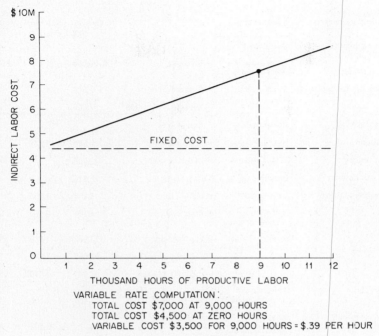

VARIABLE RATE COMPUTATION :
TOTAL COST $7,000 AT 9,000 HOURS
TOTAL COST $4,500 AT ZERO HOURS
VARIABLE COST $3,500 FOR 9,000 HOURS = $.39 PER HOUR

FIG. 4-2. Scatter Chart of Indirect Labor Cost.

PROFIT PLANNING

A free enterprise economy evaluates business performance typically by means of financial performance criteria. Therefore, a universal and predominant objective of all business firms is adequate profitability. As a result, comprehensive budgeting must include profit planning. A profit plan represents the combination of all the functional and departmental budgets into an integrated plan of operations for the entire business. Top management can compare the indicated results with profit objectives and management policies. If the results are unsatisfactory, top management can call for changes in the sales or operating plans to correct the unsatisfactory conditions.

Relationship of the Manufacturing Budget to the Profit Plan. The profit target set by top management will indicate a competitive return on investment for shareholders and reflect what the board of directors feels is an adequate level of profitability in the company's industry and in the economy generally. The process of profit planning will also enable management to anticipate and coordinate functional plans and operating needs so as to minimize the amount of decision making in crisis and permit managers to focus on problem areas in each function as operations progress. Profit planning and its component budgets facilitate "management by exception."

A schematic illustration of the components of the profit plan is given by Figure 4-3.

The components of the profit plan include a marketing or sales plan, an inventory plan, an operations plan, and selling and administrative department staffing levels. These are converted into a sales budget; bills of material; labor

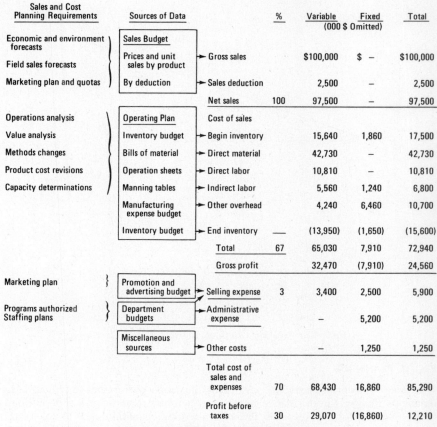

Sales and Cost Planning Requirements	Sources of Data		%	Variable	Fixed	Total
				(000 $ Omitted)		
Economic and environment forecasts	Sales Budget					
	Prices and unit sales by product	Gross sales		$100,000	$ –	$100,000
Field sales forecasts						
Marketing plan and quotas	By deduction	Sales deduction		2,500	–	2,500
		Net sales	100	97,500	–	97,500
Operations analysis	Operating Plan	Cost of sales				
Value analysis	Inventory budget	Begin inventory		15,640	1,860	17,500
Methods changes	Bills of material	Direct material		42,730	–	42,730
Product cost revisions	Operation sheets	Direct labor		10,810	–	10,810
Capacity determinations	Manning tables	Indirect labor		5,560	1,240	6,800
	Manufacturing expense budget	Other overhead		4,240	6,460	10,700
	Inventory budget	End inventory	___	(13,950)	(1,650)	(15,600)
		Total	67	65,030	7,910	72,940
		Gross profit		32,470	(7,910)	24,560
Marketing plan	Promotion and advertising budget	Selling expense	3	3,400	2,500	5,900
Programs authorized Staffing plans	Department budgets	Administrative expense		–	5,200	5,200
	Miscellaneous sources	Other costs		–	1,250	1,250
		Total cost of sales and expenses	70	68,430	16,860	85,290
		Profit before taxes	30	29,070	(16,860)	12,210

FIG. 4-3.   Profit Plan Components.

requirements; manning tables; manufacturing expense budgets; promotion and advertising budgets; selling, general, and administrative department budgets; and miscellaneous input.   Note that the combination of these components produces a profit and loss statement for an assumed volume of business—$100 million of gross sales.   By incorporating flexible budgeting, the variable costs and expenses can be separated from fixed costs and expenses.

Break-even Analysis.   The breakdown permits the budget department to prepare a break-even chart (Figure 4-4), which depicts graphically the revenue, the variable cost rate, and the level of fixed costs.

The break-even point reflects the point at which the sales revenue equals the sum of fixed and variable costs.   Additional sales revenue yields pretax profit at the marginal income rate or the difference between 100 percent and the variable cost rate.   In Figure 4-3, the variable cost rate is 70 percent of sales, and the marginal income rate is 30 percent.   Therefore, within the area of applicability of the chart—the volume range where fixed costs will not change— a change in the volume of sales of $100 will produce a change in profit of $30.

The break-even point in revenue dollars can be calculated for any company by dividing the fixed costs by the marginal income rate.   In the example

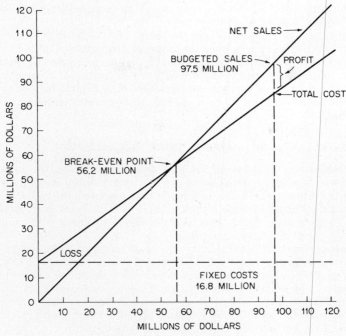

FIG. 4-4. Break-even Chart.

given, the break-even point is $16,860,000 of fixed costs divided by 30 percent or $56,200,000 of net sales.

Admittedly, the break-even chart is only a representation of reality, but it is useful for profit planning. It can be expanded to incorporate marginal income rates for each product line. A profit plan is put together to test the acceptability of all functional budgets in meeting the profit target. If in fact the indicated result is not adequate, the break-even chart helps show the economics of the potential for change. A change can be brought about only by a change in one or more of the following:

1. Increase in selling prices
2. Increase in unit sales volume
3. Change in product mix
4. Decrease in variable costs
5. Decrease in fixed costs

Each of these prospective changes can be plotted on a new break-even chart to show the impact on profits. Consider, for example, a manufacturing proposal to install a new piece of equipment (increasing the fixed cost of depreciation) which will reduce direct labor cost (decrease in variable cost rate). On the chart, the result will be to raise the fixed cost level but reduce the slope of the variable cost line and increase the marginal income rate.

From the manufacturing planning point of view, budgeting as a part of profit planning should provide management with answers to three areas of questioning:

1. Product-based costs—What should products cost, in terms of variable costs and fixed costs, under an assumed production plan?

2. Organization-based costs—What should responsibility centers spend and "output" under an assumed production plan?

3. Production balance—Where is there excess capacity or restrictions on available capacity under an assumed production plan?

In addition, the budgeting system should permit management to evaluate alternative courses of action because this is at the very heart of planning itself. These alternatives could include consideration of a capital budget project to relieve a restraint on capacity or a specific cost reduction program to reduce product costs.

COST CONTROL AND THE MANUFACTURING ORGANIZATION

The problems of budgetary planning and control from the organization point of view necessitate consideration of the responsibility structure of manufacturing operations. Decisions are made and executed by various organizational units in a plant, factory, or mill. Each of these units is a responsibility center. It is through these units that management plans and controls the operation of the organization as a whole.

The lowest level of responsibility center is the cost center. In a well-organized manufacturing operation, each cost center performs a single function or a group of closely related functions. The budgeting of costs and the accumulation and reporting of costs should be by cost center, so that deviations from budget plans can be analyzed and corrective action taken at the responsibility center level. This is commonly called responsibility accounting and is one of the key ingredients of good budgetary control.

Cost Center Structure. The cost center structure in a manufacturing complex is the responsibility of manufacturing management. Certain criteria form useful guidelines in establishing the plan of organization that results in the best responsibility center structure for budgeting and operating control. These criteria include:

1. Can one individual be assigned responsibility for the entire performance of the responsibility center?

2. Is each cost center clearly defined in terms of physical boundaries and responsibility for equipment, material, and personnel within that cost center?

3. Can product or service transfer points in and out of the responsibility center be clearly stated?

4. Is there no ambiguity about where authority for activities lies among cost centers?

5. Does the structure provide the best basis for planning operations and controlling performance in the plant, or would a finer or less fine breakdown of responsibility accomplish the job better?

It is valuable to document the organization structure on an organization chart. In addition, the use of cost center specifications can add importantly to the definition of responsibility centers. The specifications deal directly with documenting the application of the above criteria and assure the adequate understanding of foremen and superintendents of their responsibility for planning and control. Figure 4-5 is a sample of a simple cost center specification questionnaire.

Discussion of the development of budgets for individual cost centers immediately raises the questions of what costs come under the responsibility of the cost center and what benefits or outputs result from the cost center perform-

Cost Center _____

Supervisor _____ Date _____

Please answer the following questions as completely as possible:

1. What functions are performed in your cost center?

2. When does responsibility for goods or services begin in your cost center?

3. When does responsibility for goods or services end in your cost center?

4. Are there any functions or services performed within your cost center for which you are not responsible?

5. What is the best measure of the activity performed in your cost center?

6. What type of costs are incurred in your cost center?

7. Attach a list of all equipment, including office equipment, showing property number and description, in your cost center.

8. Exceptions to responsibilities and incurred costs:

Signature _____

FIG. 4-5. Cost Center Specification Questionnaire.

ance. This gets at the heart of performance budgeting. Schematically it can be viewed as shown in the following diagram.

$$\text{Cost input} \rightarrow \begin{array}{c} \text{Cost center} \\ \text{activities} \end{array} \rightarrow \begin{array}{c} \text{Product, service, or} \\ \text{benefit output} \end{array}$$

It is a fundamental requirement of management to determine that the output results are achieving the maximum effectiveness for the cost input or resources consumed. To do this, output must be measured. In many centers, this is possible; in some it is not, because the nature of the work of the responsibility center cannot be quantified in a discrete way.

Consider, for example, a cost center fabricating parts in a plant. The function of the cost center is clear and the responsibility for performance easily ascertained. Assume that in the budgetary process the cost of the part has been determined under good operating practices. From the standpoint of output, then, for any given period of time, the number of parts produced can be multiplied by the predetermined budgeted cost to establish the quantified measure of output from the cost center. It is useful to think of this measure as "earnings." In effect, it represents an earned budget for the production of the cost center. In many production operations, the parts would be accumulated in inventory, and from an accounting point of view, a bookkeeping entry would be made to transfer these parts into an inventory account. This is perhaps one of the clearest examples of "earning" a budget. It is similar in concept to the earnings or revenue associated with the sale of products to customers, but with one important distinction. When a sale is made to a customer, the revenue includes an element of profit over and above the costs of the firm. In manufacturing operations, the concept of earnings associated with output measurement should be on the basis of earned budget allowances, because in fact no profit can be made until the final sale of products to customers.

If the earnings associated with the production of the part are based on predetermined cost by cost element, that is, material, direct labor, and allowed overhead in the cost center, then the earnings for good production can be stated by cost element to create the variable budget as a basis for comparison with the actual accumulation of material, labor, and overhead cost within the cost center.

The example demonstrates the application of a concept of budgetary management to a production cost center. Generally it is useful to classify responsibility or cost centers into categories describing the nature of cost center activity. These categories include production cost centers, service cost centers, and administrative cost centers. The ability to apply cost effectiveness measurement varies somewhat among the three cost centers. In many service or auxiliary cost centers, the notion of output measurement can be applied similarly to production cost centers on the premise that the service cost center is "selling" services to production cost centers. Generally in the administrative cost center area, however, although there are benefits from activities performed, it is not practical to measure them in a quantified way.

Predetermined Product Costs. Sound budgetary management for manufacturing operations requires consideration of the nature, classification, and behavior of costs that are incurred in manufacturing operations by responsibility center. It is useful to remember that costs can be looked upon as being associated both with organizational entities (organization-based costs) and with products (product-based costs). If one thinks of a manufacturing budget as the financial blueprint of an operating plan for a given business year, one will recognize that it can be viewed in terms of costs and expenses allowed by department and cost center, and as a blueprint of costs predetermined for each product if operations are conducted according to plan. The purposes of preparing this budget include:

1. A clear definition of responsibility for cost performance
2. Development of what product cost should be
3. An effective basis for subsequent measurement of individual performance within a coordinated operating plan.

Some people tend to distinguish budgeting from standard cost accounting, but to do so fails to take maximum advantage of the power of both tools. It is true that budgets can be developed in a business that does not operate a standard cost system. In this situation, accountants say that the budgetary system is not integrated with the accounting system. This means that predetermined product costs based on budgeting are developed on a memorandum basis and are not charged through the inventory and cost of sales accounts of the manufacturer. Nevertheless, whether budgeting is integrated in this way or not, the essential value of predetermined product costs, which should always flow from good budgetary practice, is one of the important purposes of both budgeting and standard cost accounting. Therefore in this chapter no semantical difference is made.

Manufacturing management must assure that the responsibility center structure is defined as above. In a large production facility, there may be more than one hundred cost centers; in a very small plant perhaps only ten or a dozen. The point is that such definition relates cost control and budget development to physical area and function.

The budget department can help define: (1) the cost accounts that apply to costs controlled in a cost center, (2) the output or earnings that measure the value of the function, and (3) the budget determinants that should apply for developing the flexible budgets by expense category. The output or earnings of a cost center are, of course, the primary budget determinant for that cost center.

With the proper definition and communication of the responsibility center structure, manufacturing is ready to prepare the manufacturing budget and the operating plan.

THE BUDGET AND THE OPERATING PLAN

Much of what has been discussed so far has been to set the stage for actual budget preparation. The manufacturing manager's budget is his operating plan. To prepare it, two things are required:

1. Manufacturing management must be satisfied that responsibilities have been properly defined and costs analyzed so as to get the most efficient control of cost performance.
2. Manufacturing management must receive a sales plan which shows the expected sales of each product and must agree with sales management on finished goods inventory plans.

The latter requirement is important because of policy considerations. Policy considerations related to production planning will include:

1. The cost of carrying inventory
2. The delivery policy of the company with respect to servicing customer orders
3. The desired level of performance against delivery policy, that is, the out-of-stock or back-order level that is considered acceptable by management
4. The degree of fluctuation in employment levels that is going to be acceptable

These areas of policy determination involve more than just manufacturing operations and thus require approval by the top management of the company. Once these policies have been stated, manufacturing and sales management can agree on finished goods inventory levels, and manufacturing management can determine from these levels and the sales plan what the requirements will be on the factory.

The starting point then is to determine the volume of production required for each product. This can be viewed as a gross explosion of manufacturing requirements on production responsibility centers. Manufacturing management must then convert these product requirements into budget determinant quantities for all the responsibility centers in manufacturing. One can see why care is required in developing the proper budget determinants and the relationship of cost incurrence. It should also be apparent that the amount of cost required in each cost center depends upon operating methods, sequences of scheduling, and operating conditions which must be specified by management to develop proper budgets for planning and control.

The production plan must be converted to budgets for direct materials, direct labor, and manufacturing expenses or overhead. Each of these costs will be budgeted by cost center as appropriate and will represent a subplan part of the manufacturing budget.

Direct Materials. The direct materials budget is developed from raw materials and purchased parts requirements. These requirements flow from the explosion of product requirements in the manufacturing or production plan. The budget determinant for material consumption has already been described as the products or semifinished products produced and transferred to subsequent cost centers. Working backward from finished product output, raw material and purchased parts requirements can be calculated, taking into account yield or scrap loss factors and possible changes in work-in-process and parts inventories.

The manager must develop, in detail, not only what materials will be purchased, but also when these materials must be available, in both raw and in-process stages, and what the purchase costs will be. Timing and price factors require evaluation of lead times, reorder point policy, economic order quantities, and production run size and setup costs.

The materials budget is important because it guides purchasing activity and becomes a purchasing plan or budget. In addition, this budget has a significant effect on the cash and working capital budgets of the company.

Direct Labor. The direct labor budget is a projection of manpower requirements, based on the gross explosion of production needed, in terms of labor hours and dollars. Manufacturing management should establish the basic time standards and labor classifications required. The budget department will develop wage rate projections by labor grade based on wage payment plans and union contract provisions.

Although most companies have good information on direct labor time requirements for products, management should be especially alert for the impact of methods changes and standards revisions. Budget personnel may not be aware of the effect on direct labor requirements of a capital project, for example, and manufacturing executives must be sure that changes in operating practices are reflected in the budget.

Manufacturing Expenses. Manufacturing expenses can initially be classified in terms of their reaction to changes in activity levels or the passage of time. This classification between fixed and variable is the first step in preparing for the budget of overhead and has been discussed.

Fixed costs can be identified from historical information, salary schedules, or planned program costs. In this category are included only the classic fixed costs such as depreciation, rental, base cost for utilities and power, supervisory salaries, clerical salaries, and contract-type maintenance.

The remaining overhead costs can be categorized into the four groupings which relate them to a level of activity. The use of determinants for flexible budgets has been discussed earlier. These determinants are the four general categories of variable costs. They are:

1. Material unit of cost
2. Labor cost
3. Labor time
4. Facility time

All the variable costs in a manufacturing operation can generally be related to these specific determinants.

Overhead costs related to material can be identified as those related to ordering, receiving, handling, storage, and protection. These generally include the costs of the following departments:

1. Purchasing
2. Production control
3. Stores
4. Material handling
5. Receiving
6. Inventory record keeping, plus insurance and warehousing costs

The overhead costs related to labor costs are generally limited to fringe and other labor benefits applicable to the labor dollar, such as employment taxes and employer-paid insurance costs.

The overhead costs related to the labor hour generally cover the types of services necessary to support an hour of man time. They include various types of janitorial and maintenance services, timekeeping, payroll records, and consumable supplies such as safety supplies and equipment.

Manufacturing expense related to the facility hour includes the cost of maintenance, utilities, and tooling.

In each of these four categories of variable costs, the basic approach to budgeting involves the identification of units of activity anticipated. Under ideal conditions, standards are available—engineered, historical, or estimated—to calculate from planned volume what the allowances should be.

The historical analysis is always useful in relating the trend of overheads and their correlation to the basic determinants. However, in practice, the overhead budget is generally approached on the basis of last year's spending adjusted to rising price changes. To effect better budgetary control, the gross step can be taken of requesting a percentage reduction after adjustments have been made for appropriate price and wage level changes.

No discussion of manufacturing overhead budgets would be complete without commenting on the ability of front-line supervision to control expenditures of these costs. In the case of labor-related costs, the control is limited to the control that can be exercised over the utilization and control of direct labor personnel. Expenditures for tools and supplies can also be controlled by the front-line supervisor.

Costs charged to a department by service departments, however, are very difficult to control from the front-line level. For this reason, it is better to agree on predetermined budget rates for services to be charged to cost centers. Costs expended in excess of this should be absorbed by the service cost center and should result in a budget variance in the service center.

The following grouping of costs has been found convenient for use in identifying and reporting overhead costs:
1. Indirect labor
2. Labor-related payroll costs
3. Repairs and maintenance
4. Fuels and utilities
5. Services
6. Supplies
7. Transportation and material handling
8. Departmental administrative costs
9. Fixed costs

BUDGET CONTROL REPORTS

The final building block of a good budget control system is the ability to produce timely control reports which will highlight problem areas and permit management by exception. Once the budget has been approved, the system should provide regular budget control reports by cost center and for the plant as a whole on a responsibility reporting basis. This means that each manager will receive reports showing actual versus budgeted costs for areas and cost classifications under his control or responsibility. Ideally, each of these reports is summarized along responsibility lines so that top manufacturing management can see where actual costs exceeded budget and by how much for the period, usually monthly. Under this system, top management can follow overspending or substandard performance to the specific responsibility center where the condition exists and review corrective action proposed or taken. At the cost center level, the budget control report should include a statistical analysis of the cause for deviations from budget earnings or fixed budget amounts. As an illustration, Figure 4-6 shows a responsibility report for the machine shop cost center in a hypothetical company.

BUDGET CONTROL REPORT

Area: MACHINE SHOP – 150
Responsibility of: MR. GENERAL FOREMAN
Month: JUNE

| Description | Acct Class | Month Results | | |
		Budget	Actual	Better or Worse (–) Than Budget
DIRECT LABOR	010	$ 49,946	$ 56,663	$ 6,717–
CONTROLLABLE OVERHEAD				
SUPERVISION	110	3,925	5,008	1,083–
CLERICAL	120	421	396	25
MATERIAL HDLG	130	3,502	4,080	578–
LOST TIME	140	277	797	520–
SUNDRY	150	4,105	4,408	303–
TOTAL INDR. LABOR	100	12,230	14,689	2,459–
VACATION PAY	210	3,097	4,102	1,005–
HOLIDAY PAY	220	2,724	2,204	520
SOC. SECURITY	230	1,912	2,548	636–
UNEMPL. TAX	240	1,027	2,444	1,417–
WORK. COMP.	250	451	520	69–
INSURANCE	260	1,273	1,827	554–
PENSIONS	270	1,827	2,598	771–
OVERTIME PREM.	280		41	41–
SHIFT PREM.	290	1,022	1,148	126–
TOTAL PAYROLL COSTS	200	13,333	17,432	4,099–
TOOLING	300	1,737	886	851
TOTAL SERVICE CHARGES	700	43,900	39,445	4,455
TOTAL NONCONTROLLABLE EXPENSE	900	9,987	7,767	2,220
TOTAL AREA COSTS		$140,427	$149,273	$ 8,846–
EARNINGS VARIANCE		$ 23,012	XXXXX	$23,012–
TOTAL EARNINGS		$117,415	$149,273	$31,858–

COST CENTER STATISTICS	
EARNED HOURS – D.L.	21,253
ACTUAL HOURS – D.L.	23,909
BUDGETED D.L. HOURS	29,700
DIR. LABOR RATE – STD.	$ 2.35
DIR. LABOR RATE – ACTUAL	$ 2.37
VARIABLE O.H. RATE	$ 2.16
FIXED O.H. RATE	$ 1.43

VARIANCE ANALYSIS	
LABOR EFFICIENCY	$ 6,240–
LABOR RATE	477–
LABOR	6,717–
O.H. – EFFICIENCY	5,735–
O.H. – SPENDING	1,386
O.H. – NONCONTROLLABLE	2,220
OVERHEAD	2,129–
EARNINGS – PROD. MIX	14,730–
EARNINGS – VOLUME	8,282–
TOTAL	23,012–

Fig. 4-6.   Budget Control Report.

Let us look at this report in terms of the discussion in this chapter. First of all, in the last line in the comparison of budget and actual costs for the month, there is an unfavorable variance of $31,858, the difference between the total actual expenses of the general foreman of $149,273 and the value of his output which is $117,415. The total value of the output is the aggregate of the budgeted labor and overhead for the machine shop responsibility center for all the parts and products processed in or produced by the machine shop during the month of June. The calculation of this value or "earnings" is a function of production reporting and the predetermined budgets of allowable labor and overhead for each part developed from the annual budget plan. If in fact this company developed standard product costs from its budgetary management system, this value of output would represent the standard cost added to inventory accounts. This variance measures the total performance during June of the general foreman in charge of this cost center. Further analysis is necessary to determine the contributing factors producing this result, but the simple fact is that the management of this cost center spent $31,858 of planned profits during June by incurring excessive costs. As will be seen, not all this amount was controllable by the general foreman. Budgetary control must distinguish this fact.

The first step in the variance analysis is to subdivide the total variance shown for the machine shop into earnings variance and total cost variance. These figures are shown on the budget control report just above the total earnings summary line. They reveal that the cost center had an earnings variance of $23,012 and a total area cost variance of $8,846. This distinction is important to the general foreman because it separates the area of his control from the control of others. The machine shop foreman is accountable for the $8,846 that represents his total area cost variance. The accountability for the earnings variance in this hypothetical company rests elsewhere. It is shown in this cost center report in this specific example so that higher levels of management can have an easy facility for determining the impact of scheduling and production volume decisions by cost center.

As can be seen from the table at the bottom of the exhibit, the dollar variances are described by basic cause. The total earnings variances attributed to product mix and volume are shown. To make the actual calculations requires reference to certain cost center statistics which are also summarized at the bottom of the report. For example, the volume portion of the earnings variance is the difference between the budgeted direct labor hours of 29,700 hours for the month of June and the actual direct labor hours of 23,909 worked during the month of June multiplied by the fixed overhead rate of $1.43 per hour. Obviously, fixed costs were budgeted to be recovered out of the budgeted direct labor hours of 29,700 to develop the fixed overhead rate of $1.43 per hour. The fact that direct labor was not utilized at that budgeted level is due to lack of volume of work produced in the machine shop.

The remainder of the earnings variance is a function of product mix and can be calculated by subtracting the volume variance from the total earnings variance. To derive the figure independently requires a somewhat more detailed calculation which will not be illustrated here. The product mix variance, however, represents the fact that, after assuming a certain mix of products and operations in the machine shop, a variable overhead rate of $2.16 per direct labor hour was developed. In this company, the specific variable overhead rate assigned to any part or product is a function of its routing and the specific machine centers involved in production. The actual mix of products provides a different overhead recovery from the planned mix, and this difference represents the variance.

To reduce the total earnings variance, manufacturing management should review production scheduling and discuss with sales management what steps might be taken to improve the volume or product mix picture. From the standpoint of the general foreman, his performance control covers the results shown on the total area costs line or the variance of $8,846 representing excess costs during June. The body of the control report shows the composition of this variance by natural expense account, that is, direct labor, indirect labor, payroll costs, and so on. The manufacturing manager will recognize that this is not fully informative because the difference between budget and actual expense as shown for any natural expense account is due to efficiency as well as spending. For example, the unfavorable variance for social security of $636 does not mean that Federal social security rates were increased. Therefore, the foreman needs to refer again to his cost center statistics and variance analysis at the bottom of the report.

In terms of direct labor he can see substandard performance of $6,717. The analysis shows how much is due to efficiency and how much to the wage rate paid. The efficiency portion relates to the difference between the actual direct labor hours worked and the flexible budget determinant of earned direct labor hours for productive work. This difference, when multiplied by the standard or the budgeted direct labor rate of $2.35 per hour, tells the foreman the cost of paying for excess direct labor time on production jobs. The rate variance is the difference between the actual direct labor rate and the budgeted rate times the actual direct labor hours worked. This difference may reflect higher wage rates than were incorporated in the budget, or it may reflect the use of men in higher job categories on lower rated operations or jobs. To determine this more precisely will require more detailed investigation by the foreman and his cost or budget analyst. Here he can use management by exception based on the size of the amount of the variance.

In the area of overhead, similar breakdowns are made to reflect the extent to which substandard direct labor performance has caused excessive overhead spending in terms of payroll costs, indirect labor, and so on (the efficiency portion). He also knows the amount that is attributable to noncontrollable overhead—for example, an increase in the real estate tax. The remainder of the overhead variance is spending and tells the foreman where he authorized more expense than his flexible budget allowed him for the level of operations.

The purpose of this analysis is to show the significance of cost variances for the month and to get to the operating reasons behind the reflected level of cost performance.

The budgeting principles applied to this cost center include the application of flexible budgeting, the association of costs to determinants, and the distinguishing of controllability and noncontrollability. Two main budget determinants apply in the structure reviewed in this exhibit:

1. Total earnings are determined on the basis of good parts and products manufactured.
2. Labor and overhead dollars are earned in the budget on the basis of hours of direct labor time. For direct labor and variable overhead, the budget is triggered by the earned hours. For fixed overhead, the budget is created on the basis of actual hours.

Variance Letter. It is good budget practice for foremen and higher levels of management to prepare in writing a variance letter which discusses the operating causes behind any unfavorable figures and proposes action to eliminate substandard performance and improve dollar results. This letter should be concise but fully informative on the management by exception principle.

It represents a demanding but potent documentation of the way in which total manufacturing management is controlling its business.

CONCLUSION

The kind of budget control discussed above provides management with the basis for looking at profit improvement and cost reduction. High-cost areas frequently pinpoint problems where management can take aggressive action to reduce costs. Alternatives will be considered in terms of changes in methods and materials. Consideration will be given to more efficient utilization of labor. Where new equipment with greater productivity is a possibility, manufacturing management may suggest important capital budget projects.

Under a good system of budgetary control, management should be motivated to look for such opportunities for cost reduction and profit improvement. Where they are found and implemented, the results should be reflected in changes in budget rates or time standards with a resulting change in budgeted product cost. This completes the cycle of the cost reduction program, because it creates new budget amounts and a new bench mark for performance control.

BIBLIOGRAPHY

Bunge, Walter R., *Managerial Budgeting for Profit Improvement*, McGraw-Hill Book Company, New York, 1968.

Dearden, John, *Cost and Budget Analysis*, Prentice-Hall, Inc., Englewood Cliffs, N.J., 1962.

Heiser, Herman C., *Budgeting Principles and Practice*, The Ronald Press Company, New York, 1959.

Horngren, Charles R., *Accounting for Management Control*, Prentice-Hall, Inc., Englewood Cliffs, N.J., 1965.

Jones, Reginald L., and H. George Trentin, *Budgeting: Key to Planning and Control*, American Management Association, New York, 1966.

Wellington, C. Oliver, *A Primer on Budgeting*, D. Van Nostrand Company, Inc., Princeton, N.J., 1960.

Welsch, Glenn A., *Budgeting: Profit Planning and Control*, 2d ed., Prentice-Hall, Inc., Englewood Cliffs, N.J., 1963.

CHAPTER FIVE

Factory Cost Systems

F. G. SAVIERS *Assistant Controller, Westinghouse Electric Corporation, Pittsburgh, Pennsylvania*

The development and implementation of a cost accounting system tailored to an individual manufacturing location will provide the necessary framework to control manufacturing expenses. The system and the methods of analysis and control are a product of the method of manufacture, the floor time of the product, and the ability to analyze and use the information provided. Each system, if properly designed and implemented, will provide:
1. Costs of products produced
2. Costs for pricing
3. Value of work-in-process and finished goods inventories
4. Information required by regulatory agencies
5. Information for formulation of long- and short-range profit plans
6. Information necessary to analyze and control deviations from the plan
This chapter, although not intended to make cost accountants of manufacturing managers, is designed to explain and clarify various cost systems, their usage in modern manufacturing, and their advantages and disadvantages.

TYPES OF COST SYSTEMS

Manufacturing systems can be broken down into two basic categories:
1. Continuous manufacture or process systems
2. Job order systems
Cost accounting systems have been developed to accommodate these two basic forms. These systems should not be confused with methods of applying cost to the system or methods of analyzing the results obtained. Standard or actual methods of cost determination can be used with either of the two systems. Two alternative methods of recording and analyzing the results are also available—the "absorption" method and the "direct cost" method. Both are acceptable methods of recording and analyzing manufacturing costs.

4–68

Continuous Cost System. The continuous cost system may be defined as a cost procedure used in continuous manufacturing environments where costs are added as the manufacturing process progresses from beginning to end. The prerequisites for this type of system are:

1. Departmentalization of factory processes
2. Ability to identify material, labor, and overhead to these classified processes
3. Mass production of similar products
4. Short manufacturing cycle time

Job Order. The job order system may be defined as a system of recording all costs which are caused by the manufacture of that job or order. The basic characteristics of a job order system are:

1. Departmentalization of factory processes
2. Ability to identify material, labor, and overhead to these classified processes
3. Each job is assigned an identification, and a separate accounting control is established and maintained throughout the manufacturing cycle
4. All direct material and direct labor required in processing are identified to individual jobs and applied to their specific control
5. The in-process inventory is equal to the sum of the values of the unfinished job orders

Factory expense allocations to a specific job may present some difficulty. At this point, it will be necessary to determine what portion of such expenses may be identified to a specific job and what portion must be prorated. As an example, depreciation expense may be charged to a job based on machine hours within a given department. However, the same job must bear a portion of total plant depreciation, exclusive of machine tools and fixtures directly identified. Many methods have been devised to accomplish this allocation; some of the most commonly used are:

1. Machine time
2. Allocation to department on floor space and then to job on productive hours
3. As a percent of direct labor

A careful examination of each prorated expense is necessary to determine which method of allocation is best suited for each type of expense in a given manufacturing situation.

Manufacturing environments are not normally restricted to the use of a single system. A continuous manufacturing operation can also be recorded on a job order basis if necessary.

A standard product can be changed or modified to an individual customer requirement by using a specific identification to which all standard product and deviation material and labor are charged. This deviation will necessitate charging the order with the process cost of the product and the labor, material, and overhead necessary to make the modifications.

MANUFACTURING COSTS

Once the basic system is determined, it will be necessary to establish tight control over the costs incurred in the manufacturing process. These costs can be classified into three general categories:

1. *Direct labor*, which may be defined as labor specifically identifiable to a unit of production and is measurable on an hours-expended basis.

2. *Direct material*, which is material directly identifiable to a unit of production, where quantities used can be measured and costed.

3. *Manufacturing overhead*, which may be defined as all other expense necessary to produce a product as well as maintain the manufacturing facilities. A chart of typical manufacturing overhead accounts is shown in Figure 5-1.

Depending upon the degree of control desired, overhead accounts can be expanded or contracted. A greater degree of control will exist with an expanded account structure. Monthly budgets for each account should be established for purposes of analysis and control. With a report showing actual charges and budget allowances, management can easily determine any variance from budgets within a given department. A typical factory control budget is illustrated by Figure 5-2.

METHODS OF CHARGING MANUFACTURING COST SYSTEMS

There are two commonly used methods of charging cost to the manufacturing process which are:

1. Actual cost
2. Standard cost

Actual Cost Method. All charges to work-in-process inventory are made at the actual value incurred. Because of the difficulty of measuring performance, consideration of the use of actual cost methods should be restricted to as few applications as possible. "Cost plus fixed fee" contracts by nature are prime examples of an application where actual methods of costing will produce the desired results. In most other instances, analysis is hampered by the fact that all costs are not known until the product is shipped.

XYZ Manufacturing Company

Account number	Title	Description of overhead
501	Factory supervision	Salaries of factory supervision
502	Industrial engineering	Industrial engineering department expense
503	Production department	Production department expense
504	Inspection	Expense of all quality control inspectors
505	Material handlers	In-plant transportation and salaries of material handlers
506	Utilities	Fuel, electricity, water, and so on, used in manufacturing process
507	Miscellaneous shop supplies	Cost of rags, gloves, safety glasses, and so on
508	Storeroom expense	Cost of storekeeping and storeroom control
509	Receiving	Expense of receiving department
510	Purchasing	The portion of purchasing expenses identifiable to the manufacturing process
511	Defective work	Defective work at point of disposition
512	Depreciation—building	Depreciation—building
513	Depreciation—machinery fixtures	Depreciation—machinery
520	Employee benefits	Cost of employee benefit program

Fɪɢ. 5-1.   Chart of Typical Manufacturing Overhead Accounts.

EXPENSE CONTROL STATEMENT

Department: A – Unit – Mfg.	Month: February		Responsibility: J. C. Jones			Budget No. 5128		
Current Month			Acct. No.	No. of Empl. Bud. 22	Description	No. of Empl. 23 Act.	Year to Date	
Budget	Actual	Variance					Variance	Actual	Budget
1 200	1 260	* 60	501		Supervision		* 250	2 650	2 400
600	580	20	505		Material handling		–	1 200	1 200
150	153	* 3	507		Miscellaneous shop supplies		* 60	360	300
90	80	10	511		Defective work		220	140	360
120	126	* 6	520		Employee benefits		* 12	252	240
2 160	2 199	* 39			TOTAL		* 102	4 602	4 500

FIG. 5-2.   Factory Control Budget.

Standard Cost Method.   The standard cost method requires the establishment of certain predetermined rates for all factory charges.   These predetermined or expected rates should cover direct labor, direct material, and manufacturing overheads, and should be established based on the expected level of production for a yearly period.   The standard cost method is often considered to be preferable to an actual method, in that the results may be compared against the predetermined standards and control exerted on the causes of variances for the benefit of future operations.

Standard Labor Rate per Hour.   A method of establishing a standard labor rate per hour is shown in Figure 5-3.   The standard labor rate should include

XYZ Corporation

Department 201

(1) Labor grade	(2) No. of people Total	(3) Night turn	(4) Hourly rate	(5) Night-turn bonus	(6) Total hourly rate	(7) Total night turn
1						
2						
3	6	1	2.100	0.210	12.600	0.210
4						
5	2	2	2.540	0.254	5.080	0.508
Total	8	3			17.680	0.718

Col. 6 + col. 7 = $18.40
Col. 6 + col. 7 ÷ col. 2 = hourly rate chargeable to work-in-process = $2.30

FIG. 5-3.   Method of Establishing a Standard Hourly Labor Rate for a Department.

a portion of machine setup time (if performed by productive personnel) and any extra allowances that management is aware of and does not desire to analyze as a variance. For example, it is possible to have two machines in a manufacturing section capable of producing at different levels. If allowed hours are calculated on the faster machine, then a differential in the form of an extra allowance for the difference between the capacities may be included in the standard labor rate. The combination of several departments performing similar operations and the provision for extra allowances and setups are illustrated in Figure 5-4.

Figures 5-3 and 5-4 illustrate that for each hour of actual production time generated in cost center 200, work-in-process inventory will be valued at $2.49.

Standard Material Values. Standard material values should be established by the cost accountant in cooperation with the design engineer and purchasing agent. These standards should take into consideration economic ordering quantities, volume discounts, inbound transportation, and expected short-range pricing trends. In calculating the raw material required to be included in the standard, consideration must be given to manufacturing scrap, such as short ends or punchings, where no use can be made of them. This type of scrap is generally termed work-in-process scrap, in that it is cleared in the standard cost of the product from work-in-process and is not charged to manufacturing overhead as in the case of defective workmanship.

Standard Overhead Rates. Overhead rates are generally calculated and applied as a rate per productive hour or as a percent of direct labor. Using a sampling from the chart of factory expense accounts shown by Figure 5-1, the calculation of an overhead rate per productive hour at forecasted standard volume would be determined as shown in Figure 5-5. Standard overhead rates should be developed on a departmental basis and applied to the actual allowed manufacturing hours for that department.

Combined Cost Methods. A standard cost method may be applied to a job order or a continuous process system to determine a product's cost to manufacture. If this method is used with a job order system, each job order should bear a portion of the total variance created because of using the standard cost method. The assignments of these variances to each job will be arbitrary, and in most cases will have to be analyzed to determine the best method of allocation (hours, dollars of material, or the like).

XYZ Corporation

Cost Center 200

Department	No. of employees	Setup ratio	Extra allowance	Standard labor	Direct labor	Setup	Extra allowance	Total
201	8	–0–	–0–	18.40	2.30			
202	6	0.04	–0–	14.18	2.36	0.09		
203	4	–0–	0.03	9.32	2.43		0.07	
Total	18	0.04	0.03	41.90	2.33	0.09	0.07	$2.49

FIG. 5-4. Method of Establishing a Standard Hourly Labor Rate for a Cost Center with Provision for Extra Allowances and Setups.

XYZ Corporation

Department 201

Prorated Expense from Staff Functions
501—Superintendent and staff.................................... $ 1,200
502—Industrial engineering..................................... 600
510—Purchasing... 450

Direct Departmental Expense
501—Departmental foreman..................................... $ 8,100
507—Miscellaneous shop supplies............................... 1,300
511—Defective workmanship.................................... 100

Total expense... $11,750

Allowed manufacturing hours at forecasted standard volume............... 6,000
Rate per allowed manufacturing hours to be charged to work-in-process.... $1.96

FIG. 5-5. Standard Manufacturing Overhead Rate Calculation.

Costs of Products Produced. The costs of products produced may be determined by applying the standards previously developed in Figures 5-3, 5-4, and 5-5 to manufacturing drawings and the estimated time requirements obtained from the industrial engineering department. The combination of the labor, material, and overhead into a product cost is illustrated by Figure 5-6.

When using either an actual or standard cost system for product costing, it is necessary to be assured that current data are being used. Therefore, it is imperative that all drawing changes or time value changes be included in product cost as soon as possible after they occur. The lag time between changes and inclusion in product cost will cause a variance between the actual work-in-process and the predetermined standard cost. If product is moved from work-in-process to a shipping stock account, it is a normal practice to clear from work-in-process to the shipping stock account at the predetermined standard cost. If this is done, the variance must be calculated and the work-in-process adjusted accordingly. It is necessary to know the actual production units produced at previous costs or rates, and the units produced at the new costs or rates to calculate this variance accurately.

VARIANCE ANALYSIS—THE KEY TO CONTROL

Variance may be defined as the difference between actual cost and standard cost. The control of variances is one of the primary responsibilities of the manufacturing manager, for herein lies the key to profitable operation. Variance reporting can be a very sophisticated system or a relatively simple one, depending again upon the degree of control required and the personnel available to perform the analysis. Some of the most important manufacturing variances and the controls available are listed by type.

Material Variances. Included in material variance reports are variances of four different types:
1. Material price variance
2. Material usage variance
3. Defective workmanship
4. Inactive inventory

Material Price Variance. Material price variance is the difference between the expected or standard price and the actual price charged by the supplier of the material.

Product A

XYZ Corporation Material Requirements

Style	Description	Quantity	Material code	Department routing	Allowed manufacturing hours each
C-52400........	Painted disc	1	Self-manufacture	100 400	0.02 0.05
C-41200........	Painted sides	3	Self-manufacture	200 500	0.03 0.06
C-21300........	Screws	4	Bought outside		
C-32500........	Cover	1	Bought outside		
C-16200........	Wire leads	2	Self-manufacture	300	0.05

Cost Determination

Style	Description	Quantity	Department	Material	Labor	Overhead	Total	
C-52400........	Painted disc	1	100 400	0.13	0.052 0.200	0.044 0.155	0.130 0.096 0.355	
Subtotal........								0.581
C-41200........	Painted sides	3	200 500	0.30	0.021 0.090	0.012 0.022	0.300 0.033 0.112	
Subtotal........								0.445
C-16160........	Wire	2	300	0.04			0.040	
C-16170........	Terminals	4	300	0.016			0.016	
C-16200........	Wire leads	2	300		0.012	0.008	0.020	
							0.076	
Assembly cost........			700	—	0.150	0.090	0.240	
Total cost........				0.486	0.525	0.331	1.342	

Fig. 5-6. Development of a Product Cost.

This variance can be subdivided into three subcategories: true price, premium transportation, and premium price. By analysis, it can be determined where the variance occurred. In the case of premium transportation, it may be determined that the economic ordering quantity of a given part is in error or that production schedules do not provide sufficient lead time. This may also account for a premium price if the supplier is forced into an overtime situation. True price variance is generally the responsibility of the purchasing agent and the design engineering department. It is the result of either poor estimating or economic factors not taken into consideration, such as price increases or decreases not known at the time of making the estimates and setting the standards.

Material Usage Variance. Material usage variance is the difference between the planned usage of material at standard and the actual usage. As an example, assume that ninety 3′ × 5′ sheets of steel are calculated to be obtainable from a coil weighing 8,000 pounds, and that 12 parts can be made from one sheet. If the actual number of scrap parts reported is 5, the calculation of material usage variance is:

Beginning inventory.. 0
Requisition: 8,000 pounds
Conversion to sheets: 90
Conversion to pieces: 12 × 90   Expected deliveries............... 1,080
                                Actual deliveries................. 1,060
                                Difference....................... 20 pieces
Analysis of variance: Scrap....................................... 5 pieces
                    Material usage............................ 15 pieces

After calculating this variance, it is necessary to determine the cause. In this example, the cause may be:

1. Loss of material due to scrap not reported by operator
2. Usage of substitute material of a different gage
3. Incorrect weight on the original material requisition

Additional possibilities will come to light as the investigation progresses to an explanation. Thereafter, control can be exercised on the particular reason.

One important area in which a usage calculation can be of great value is where a liquid or gas is used. If the quantity used per unit of product can be determined and the input can be measured at a central point, a usage calculation can be made.

Beginning meter reading..................................... 10,345 gallons
Add receipts.. +5,000 gallons
Less ending meter reading................................... −6,800 gallons
Actual usage of material.................................... 8,545 gallons
Production deliveries....................................... 136,450 units
Standard usage... 0.0625 gallon
Calculated usage... 8,528 gallons
Material usage variance.................................... 17 gallons

This type of usage variance will provide information which can lead to the detection of leaks in the system or excess use of materials in the product.

Usage variances are an extremely important analysis technique designed to aid manufacturing management in controlling costs.

Defective Workmanship. Defective workmanship should be measured against a preplanned budget based on historical information, and the difference if significant should be analyzed. In many instances, it will be of value to publish scrap reports by production style number. Such reports will enable management to detect areas, personnel, or machines that are causing problems.

Inactive Inventory. Inactive inventory has a habit of building up in a manufacturing inventory, and unless strict control is exercised and programs established to utilize this inventory, serious future profit problems can arise. Inactive stock can be generated in several ways. Two of the most common are changes in the manufacturing drawings and overpurchases. Both these reasons are controllable. When drawing changes are made, an inventory of the superseded part should be taken, and based on management decision, parts should be scrapped or used. If the superseded part is not a critical functional part, in most cases the superseded part should be used, and the use of the new part should be postponed until after the surplus of the old part is exhausted. If management makes the decision to scrap the superseded inventory, it should be scrapped currently, instead of allowing a buildup of inactive inventory. Another method that can sometimes be used to minimize the write-off of this stock is to rework it into another style. The cost of rework is normally charged to the material usage account, and the cost difference between the two styles is charged or credited to work-in-process inventory.

Labor Variances. Labor variances are determined by comparing predetermined labor standards with the actual cost of productive labor. These variances fall into the three general categories of:

1. Rates of pay
2. Labor efficiency
3. Extra allowances and setup

Rates of Pay Variances. Rates of pay variances occur when operators at a higher or lower pay scale are substituted for operators on whom the standard was based.

Labor Efficiency Variance. Labor efficiency variance is the difference between the standard labor hours and the actual labor hours required to manufacture the product.

Extra Allowances and Setup. Where these two operations are included in the labor rate, variance measurement against actual expenditures is desirable.

Analysis of these labor variances will provide management with information which will pinpoint inefficient departments, as well as those areas where the standard labor force is not being maintained in accordance with predetermined plans.

Overhead Variances. Overhead variances are generally controlled by comparing the actual against the budget. To make a valid comparison between budget and actual, it has become a generally accepted practice to adjust the budget base when a significant change occurs in mix or volume. This technique is usually referred to as variable budgeting. (See Figure 5-2.)

MANUFACTURING ANALYSIS USING
ABSORPTION OR DIRECT COST METHODS

The basic difference between the absorption costing and direct costing methods is in the recording of inventory values.

Absorption costing is a cost method that charges to inventory, in addition to direct labor and direct material, all manufacturing overhead. These overhead costs are considered to be inventoriable until the unit is sold.

Direct costing is a cost method which charges to inventory, in addition to direct labor and direct material, those manufacturing overhead costs which vary directly as a result of manufacturing the product.

All expenses which are not a direct result of manufacturing the product are termed period costs and are charged to operations in the month in which they are incurred. These period expenses may include such items as foremen's salaries, sales and marketing, maintenance, administration, warehousing, and production department activities.

Direct and absorption costing methods both will provide management with the same income figures when sales and production are equal. The major differences between the two methods occur when production and sales volumes are significantly out of phase. In the short run, the advantage of a direct cost system can be related to the ease with which analysis of period cost variances can be made and therefore controlled. This can be demonstrated by using the following example: For a two-month period—January and February—assume that the following condition occurs.

1. Sales = $100,000 each month or 10,000 units.
2. Production is 10 percent above normal in January and 10 percent below normal in February.
3. Total factory expense is $20,000 per month.
4. Selling and administrative expenses are $5,000.
5. Unit manufacturing costs are as follows:

Direct labor....................................	$1.50
Unit material....................................	3.00
Manufacturing overhead direct...................	1.00
Period cost.................................	1.00
Total....................................	$6.50

We are now in a position to analyze the effect of direct versus absorption costing on the profit level. (See Figure 5-7.)

This illustration highlights the difficulty of analysis using the absorption system. Varying levels of production will result in either favorable or unfavorable changes in operating results. Thus, erroneous decisions may be made if proper consideration of inventory levels is not assured.

In general practice, under the absorption method, analyses produced for manufacturing levels of management usually reflect the favorable or unfavorable variance without considering the long-range profitability of the business. If improper consideration is given to the fact that production volume is not in phase with either the sales volume or the predetermined normal shop activity, it will produce a short-term favorable effect on profits which will cause an adverse effect on profits at a later time. This condition is eliminated under the direct cost system as illustrated in the analysis. This brings us to a more basic question—What level of manufacturing management is the analysis being prepared for? In most environments, there are several levels of management involved in the manufacturing process.

1. Line foreman
2. General foreman
3. Superintendents
4. Manufacturing manager
5. Plant manager

In a small- to medium-size manufacturing organization, either of the last

	Absorption costing		Direct costing	
	January	February	January	February
Sales 10,000 units...................	$100,000	$100,000	$100,000	$100,000
Cost of Sales				
Labor.........................	15,000	15,000	15,000	15,000
Material......................	30,000	30,000	30,000	30,000
Factory expense: Direct..........	10,000	10,000	—	—
Period.........	10,000	10,000	10,000	10,000
Total.............................	$ 65,000	$ 65,000	$ 55,000	$ 55,000
Manufacturing margin...............	35,000	35,000	45,000	45,000
Volume variance*..................	+1,000	−1,000		
Period Cost				
Factory.......................	—	—	10,000	10,000
Selling........................	3,000	3,000	3,000	3,000
Administrative and general.......	2,000	2,000	2,000	2,000
Income before taxes.................	$ 31,000	$ 29,000	$ 30,000	$ 30,000

* Since period cost does not fluctuate with volume, the January favorable variance as reflected on the profit statement is created as follows:

$$\frac{\text{Normal period costs}}{\text{Normal activity}} = \frac{\$10,000}{10,000 \text{ units}} = \$1 \text{ per unit} \times 11,000 \text{ units}$$

$$= \$11,000 \text{ charge to inventory}$$

$11,000 charge to inventory − $10,000 actual cost = $1,000 favorable variance

Conversely the $1,000 unfavorable variance in February is caused by production at a lower volume than normal.

$9,000 charge to inventory − $10,000 actual cost = $1,000 unfavorable variance

FIG. 5-7.   Direct versus Absorption Costing.

two categories may be the president of the company, and if the analysis is being addressed to him, it must involve such items as:

1. Marginal income by product
2. Total product cost
3. Selling price calculated to realize a specific return on investment
4. Maximum machine and manpower utilization
5. Total income presented in such a manner that analysis will point out deviation from the income plan
6. Break-even points

The detail required for analysis and control will vary with the level of management to which it is directed. Conversely, the decision making process will emanate from a broad base to a focal point. This is illustrated by Figure 5-8.

In most instances, when using a direct costing method, management will be able to estimate the monthly profits shortly after determining its sales volume. This occurs because it is not necessary to know the production level and calculate the volume variance to apply to the month's operations. As an example, assume that the company in Figure 5-7 sells 25,000 units in March. A quick calculation will establish the manufacturing margin at $112,500. The expected profit at this level will be $97,500.

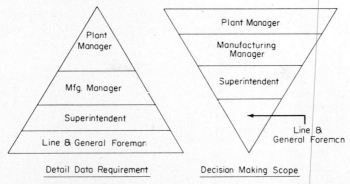

Fig. 5-8. Detailed Data Requirement versus Decision Making Scope.

Sales.....................................	$250,000
Cost: 5.50 per unit......................	137,500
Margin.................................	$112,500
Period cost.............................	15,000
Expected income......................	$ 97,500

Note that this calculation did not require knowledge of actual production data to arrive at the expected income. To determine the expected income under the absorption cost method, it is necessary to know if the actual production level was less than, equal to, or greater than the standard level of production, and if this production was in phase with sales. The ability to make advance determinations of income can be of significant benefit in shortening the response time to changing conditions.

Quick Calculations Using Direct Costing. Direct costing can be of considerable help to management in the areas of:

1. Break-even analysis
2. Make or buy decisions
3. Price determination
4. Machine usage decisions

Break-even Analysis. A break-even analysis indicates the level of activity required to produce a break-even condition, assuming fixed expense to remain constant throughout the year. The calculation, based on Figure 5-7 data, is:

Total yearly period cost: $15,000 per month............................		$180,000
Sales to date: two months.....:........................	$200,000	
Less variable cost.......................................	110,000	
Marginal profits: two months................................		90,000
Period cost to be covered...		$ 90,000
Additional months required to break even at current sales level...........		2
Total months required to break even..................................		4

This quick-type calculation is not readily available under absorption costing because of the necessity of determining past and succeeding months' production levels to determine the over or under clearance of period expenses.

Make versus Buy. Make versus buy analysis can differ, depending upon the method used. In the following example, it is assumed that facilities are available:

Part A

	Absorption	Direct
Direct materials	0.060	0.060
Direct labor	0.015	0.015
Factory expense: Direct	0.010	0.010
Period	0.035	
Total unit cost	0.120	0.085
Supplier's price	0.100	0.100

Under absorption costing, if only total unit cost is used, the obvious decision is to purchase the part. Under the direct costing system, the decision is exactly opposite. As stated earlier, the decision to make under the direct cost system is predicated on the fact that no new facility or period expense will be necessary. If, in fact, additional costs will be incurred because of the addition of facilities, then these expected increases must be taken into consideration and the calculation adjusted.

Price Determination. Assume from our prior example that the direct cost is $5.50, fixed yearly expense is $180,000, capital employed is $100,000, return on investment is required to be 15 percent, and units of sale are predicted to be 120,000 units.

$$\text{Direct cost} + \frac{\text{period cost} + \text{return on investment}}{\text{units}} = \text{selling price}$$

$$\$5.50 + \frac{\$180,000 + \$15,000}{120,000} = \text{selling price}$$

$$\$5.50 + \$1.625 \text{ or } \$7.13 = \text{selling price}$$

Alternative selling prices can be determined by adjusting the unit volume.

Machine Usage Decisions. The decision to use a newer piece of equipment as opposed to using an older, fully depreciated piece of equipment in the production of a given job will differ, depending upon the method used in calculation.

	Old machine	New machine
Absorption Costing		
Material	$3.00	$3.00
Labor	2.80	1.60
Overhead	1.30	2.95
Total	$7.10	$7.55
Direct Costing		
Material	$3.00	$3.00
Labor	2.80	1.50
Overhead	0.84	0.45
Total	$6.64	$4.95

It appears that a lower cost will result by producing on the old machine, using the absorption method. Conversely, the direct cost method would suggest the use of the newer machine. This difference occurs because of the elimination of the depreciation expense that is a portion of overhead under the absorption method from consideration under the direct cost method.

The answer obtained from this analysis should be to produce on the newer equipment, for regardless of whether the machine is used or not, the additional depreciation will continue by virtue of management's original decision to purchase the machine.

Price Consideration and Direct Costing. The direct costing approach can, in many instances, provide a means of faster and more meaningful short-range analysis. A problem arises when a high degree of automation is reached, and the direct labor and variable overhead content of the production drops. Can it be said with all sincerity that the product cost has been reduced when in fact the classification of expenses has only been shifted? If the answer to this question is yes, then it becomes necessary to be assured that all fixed expenses are covered in the selling price.

It cannot be pointed out too strongly that, although direct costing methods can be used to record, report, and analyze monthly operations within a manufacturing organization, they should be used with caution in pricing. Full absorption pricing will provide total costs for pricing whereas direct costing will provide only marginal income unless additional factors are considered. Before making price cuts or accepting marginal income business, management should check the profit plan and determine the impact on planned profits regardless of the contention that, by producing and selling marginal income items, some of the fixed costs will be absorbed.

COST REDUCTIONS

Cost reduction efforts by manufacturing management should be a continuing program. To be effective, cost reduction efforts must be accumulated, recorded, and reported. The reporting of cost reductions should be on an annualized basis, so that the full impact of the project will be available; however, for control and analysis purposes, the savings should be identified to fiscal periods. Once the base cost of a product has been established, it will be necessary to measure all increases and decreases from the base cost.

Increases. Increases in the base cost of a product should be given priority of attention in cost reduction efforts. The manufacturing manager must require detailed reasons for each increase over the base cost. These increases can occur because of changes in material specifications and labor time values. When increases are annualized and the impact on profit is understood, it is often possible to reverse the cause of the increase.

In many instances, changes of nonfunctional parts are made without regard to the effect on income. To evaluate these changes, it is necessary to have up-to-date detailed cost records available. There are several control methods for establishing the relative value of production parts and their cost. A technique which can be used with certain products is the reduction of all material used in the product to a cost per pound basis. Then by comparing products of a similar family, the individual products where the standard or price may be out of line can be identified and cost reduction efforts applied. Another analysis used by cost accountants is comparison. Using this method, the part is reduced to its basic shape and compared to costs of similar basic shapes. Any significant differences in costs are investigated.

Decreases. Decreases in the basic product cost should also be documented. Each planned decrease should be docketed and the actual results compared to the docketed expectation. Cost reduction dockets can originate from any function. The four most likely to establish the greatest cost savings are purchasing, through negotiation with suppliers; production, by better scheduling; engineering, through design; and manufacturing, through improved manufacturing efficiencies.

Many of today's manufacturing organizations rely on a suggestion system to involve all plant personnel in the cost reduction effort. The financial effect of the suggestion is normally annualized, and the suggester given a portion of the annual savings, normally 10 to 15 percent. The suggestion system can be a highly profitable segment of the cost reduction program and should not be overlooked.

SUMMARY

Systems in themselves will not produce profits. It is the information which they provide and the analysis therefrom that will assist in the profitable management of the business. Although in this chapter comparison has been made between the absorption method and the direct cost method, and certain advantages are illustrated in the uses of the direct method, it should not be construed that in all circumstances the direct method is preferable. The system and the methods selected should be those that provide the most accurate and timely information which best satisfies the needs of the enterprise.

BIBLIOGRAPHY

Current Application of Direct Costing, Research Report no. 37, National Association of Accountants New York, 1961.

Haseman, Wilbur C., *Managerial Uses of Accounting,* Allyn & Bacon, Inc., Boston, Mass., 1963.

Henrici, Stanley B., *Standard Costs for Manufacturing,* McGraw-Hill Book Company, New York, 1960.

Staley, John D., *The Cost-minded Manager,* American Management Association, New York, 1961.

Taggart, Herbert F. (ed.), *Paton on Accounting,* University of Michigan Press, Ann Arbor, Mich., 1964.

Van Voorhis, Robert H., Clarence L. Dunn, and Fritz A. McCameron, *Using Accounting in Business,* Wadsworth Publishing Company, Belmont, Calif., 1962.

Whiteside, Conon D., *Accounting Systems for the Small and Medium-sized Business,* Prentice-Hall, Inc., Englewood Cliffs, N.J., 1961.

CHAPTER SIX

Labor Performance Control

WILLIAM M. AIKEN   *Senior Vice President, H. B. Maynard and
Company, Incorporated, Pittsburgh, Pennsylvania*

An important element of manufacturing management is the establishment
of controls over labor performance. Controls naturally have a strong bearing on the cost of labor which goes either directly into the product or indirectly into the functions which support direct labor. They also have a strong
bearing on how well a company utilizes its capacity to maximize return on
investment or to have an adequate means of planning plant operations.
Without reliable labor performance controls, it is extremely difficult, if not
impossible, to manage a manufacturing enterprise effectively.

For many years, it has been common practice for management to have performance controls for direct labor costs. This has been accomplished through
the use of work measurement techniques or, in many cases, piece rates. The
effect has been that management generally knows rather well what its direct
labor costs are and what they should be. This knowledge has led to continued efforts to refine and further reduce direct labor costs.

Significant steps have also been taken to establish similar controls over the
performance of indirect labor and salaried costs. The development of new
industrial engineering techniques and approaches has made it practical and
economical to control indirect labor costs. Managers in many progressive companies control the performance of workers in such diverse activities as plant
and equipment, maintenance, toolrooms, warehouses, design and drafting departments, shipping departments, and offices.

MEASUREMENT—THE KEY TO CONTROL

The key to the establishment of reliable labor performance controls is the
ability of management to measure the work with reasonable accuracy. Some
years ago H. B. Maynard stated, "Scientific management is based on measure-

ment plus control." This points out clearly and simply that for a man to manage a function in an enlightened way, he must first measure the work and then establish controls based on the measurement. For labor performance controls, this requires the use of work measurement techniques such as time study, work sampling, standard data, and predetermined motion time systems like Methods-Time Measurement (MTM) or other similar systems. The measurement of the work determines the time, expressed in minutes or hours, required to complete an operation on one unit (or one hundred or one thousand units) of product. For indirect labor activities, the measurement expresses the time required to complete a task such as typing one letter, repairing one valve, or handling one carton.

The measurement must be of sufficient accuracy that the ensuing controls will realistically represent the true performance of the individual or group of workers being controlled. Thus, it is very important that management select the work measurement technique or combination of techniques that will provide a solid base for the control reports and do it economically. If an operation is performed thousands of times daily, the operation should be studied carefully with a very precise technique such as MTM. If the operation is performed infrequently, such as a maintenance task, a combination of standard data, work sampling, and statistical analysis should be used to arrive at the proper standard economically.

CONTROL INFORMATION

There are two basic types of information needed to control labor costs. First is the performance report. This report shows the degree to which the time standards have been attained for the operations that are measured. It is the quotient, expressed in percent, of the standard hours of work earned divided by the actual total hours worked on measured operations. Performance by itself, however, is not meaningful unless a substantial portion of the operations have measured standards. Thus, the second type of information needed is a report on standards coverage. This report shows the proportion of hours worked on operations covered by measured standards to the total hours clocked in as time worked. It is the quotient, expressed in percent, of the hours worked on measured operations divided by the total hours worked.

For example, assume that in a 40-hour week an operator works 32 hours on operations covered by standards. In that time, he accumulates earned standard hours amounting to 28 hours. Thus, his performance is

$$\frac{28 \text{ earned hours}}{32 \text{ actual hours}} \times 100 = 87.5\%$$

The standards coverage for his work is

$$\frac{32 \text{ actual hours}}{40 \text{ clock hours}} \times 100 = 80\%$$

From these two basic types of information, many kinds of control reports can be developed to handle particular situations. One very useful labor performance control is the cost per standard hour. It is unusual to find an operator who works as diligently on an unmeasured job as he would work on a measured job where he has a specific target at which to shoot. This, of course, is one of the principal reasons why work measurement is desirable and why standards coverage should be high. The cost per standard hour is a control that measures the combined effect of performance and coverage.

The Performance Report. The performance report shows how effective an individual worker or a group of workers is when working on measured operations. When operators work on an unmeasured daywork basis, their performances customarily are somewhere between 50 and 60 percent. When the work is measured and normal allowances and controls are applied on a measured daywork basis, the performances generally range between 80 and 90 percent. In most companies, performances of over 90 percent on measured daywork are unusual because there is little motivation for this effort level. Thus, measured daywork performances below 80 and over 90 percent should be investigated to determine the reasons. They may be due to inaccurate standards applications, methods changes, inadequate training or supervision, or material changes.

When wage incentives are applied to the measured work, performances are considerably higher. Whereas standards on a measured daywork basis will yield performances of approximately 85 percent, the same standards will yield incentive performances of 115 to 130 percent. This is a healthy range of incentive performances. Higher than normal performances can indicate an undesirable condition which should be investigated and corrected. This could lead to the discovery of such things as deficiencies in standards application, timekeeping, or quality. If incentive performances fall below 100 percent, an equally serious situation may be indicated. Investigation might show such things as material shortages or changes, improper supervision or training, or work added which was not included in the standards. Thus, the performance report can be used effectively as a barometer of the conditions under which the people work. If the performances go above or below the limits established by management, the report should trigger investigation into the possibility of abnormal and potentially serious situations.

Performance reports are developed in varying degrees of detail for the different levels of management who can use them effectively. Figure 6-1 is a chart showing weekly performance plus the trend of performance using a six-week moving average. This highlights current performance and gives management an effective warning of any unhealthy trends. At the right of the chart is shown the degrees of some of the control information needed by various management levels to direct the work for which they are responsible.

The foreman should have detailed reports on the performances of individual workers or small groups of workers where their efforts are pooled. A superintendent or general foreman would most likely be interested in summary reports showing the performance of entire sections with some detail on the exceptionally high or low performances. A division manager would generally require a report covering the performance of departments or plants as a whole. With modern data processing equipment available, the reports can be tailored to fit the organization and the management requirements of any company. The key to the preparation of the reports is that sufficient detail must be provided to each level of management to trigger good control action.

Standards Coverage Report. It means little for a worker to attain good performance unless that performance is attained on a large portion of the total work performed. Otherwise, no real control is possible. Thus, to give performance figures significant meaning, a measure of the extent of standards coverage must be considered at the same time. It means very little if a worker performs at 125 percent if it is done on only two hours of his eight-hour day. His performance for the other six unmeasured hours may only be

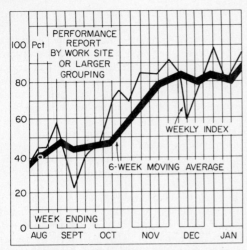

PERFORMANCE REPORT – Comparison of standard hours to actual hours.

GENERAL MANAGER

Total Plant

        Cost per standard hour
        Backlog
        Missed deliveries

PLANT MANAGER

Total Plant by Departments

        Performance
        Coverage
        Backlog
        Schedule exceptions

SUPERINTENDENT

Department by Areas

        Performance
        Coverage
        Backlog
        Equipment utilization
        Schedule compliance

GENERAL FOREMAN

Areas

        Performance
        Coverage
        Schedule compliance
        Equipment utilization

FOREMAN

Area by Work Group

        Performance
        Coverage
        Schedule compliance
        Actions to improve
         performance

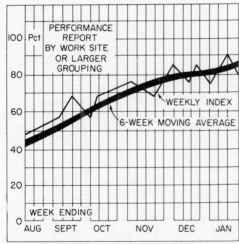

COVERAGE REPORT – Actual hours worked on standard work.

FIG. 6-1. Control Reports by Responsibility Level. A Typical System for Informing Various Levels of Supervision of Accomplishment, So That Action Will Be Taken When Necessary.

50 percent. This low coverage can encourage abuses such as "time juggling" in that the time reported as being worked on measured work can be minimized to make the performance report look good. Although such abuses can be a serious problem to management, the principal reason for controlling coverage is the lost productivity represented by the difference in controlled

measured performance (85 to 125 percent) and uncontrolled unmeasured work (50 to 60 percent). Each hour spent on unmeasured work can cost a company the equivalent of two hours' pay.

The ideal goal for standards coverage is 100 percent. A realistic minimum figure for repetitive operations is 95 percent. For job shop and indirect operations, standards coverage should equal at least 80 to 85 percent of the total hours worked in the department. If coverage drops below these levels, management must make extraordinary efforts to bring coverage up to the correct level by extending measurement to more work.

Because the reports of standards coverage are used in conjunction with the performance reports, their scope and time periods must coincide. This then provides the manager with complete information on the effectiveness of his work force in terms of hours spent on the job, hours worked on measured work, and performance while working on measured work. If control is needed on principal causes of downtime, the coverage report may also be detailed to show the classifications of off-standard work, such as machine breakdown, material shortage, or rework.

Figure 6-1 illustrates a new standards installation where performance and coverage start off at relatively low percentages. As the installation progresses, both performance and coverage improve until they reach satisfactory levels. Charts of this type are particularly useful to indicate progress or lack of progress in new installations. When performance and coverage reach and stay at a satisfactory level for an extended period of time, it may no longer be necessary to chart the information. Thereafter, management will watch that the percentages stay within acceptable ranges.

Labor Cost per Standard Hour. A single control which combines the effect of both performance and coverage into a single figure is the labor cost per standard hour. It represents the total labor cost of producing one standard hour of work or one hour of measured work. It is computed by dividing the total labor cost for a group—both measured and unmeasured—by the standard hours of work produced.

The ideal cost per standard hour is achieved when it is equal to the average hourly labor base rate of the group being measured. If this ideal were achieved, it would signify that all standards were met or bettered and that all work was measured. In other words, performance and coverage would both be at or above 100 percent. Cost per standard hour will never be less than the average hourly labor base rate. The further it rises above the base rate, the more it means that performance or coverage must be improved to keep the labor costs in line. For example, if performance and coverage of a group are both at the 80 percent level, the cost per standard hour will be approximately 50 percent above the ideal.

In some incentive installations, the ideal cost per standard hour can be and often is achieved. It is more common, however, that there is some loss due to incomplete standards coverage. In measured daywork installations, the ideal is generally achieved only when the workers are paced by an assembly line or preset machine process speeds. In these cases, management can establish the ideal cost per standard hour as the target for line management to achieve. In the more typical measured daywork situation where a performance level of 80 to 90 percent and coverage of 85 percent should be expected, a target of 130 percent of the average hourly base rate is reasonable.

An example of a report showing performance, coverage, and cost per standard hour for an incentive installation is shown by Figure 6-2. The method of computation is summarized at the bottom of the report.

DEPARTMENT 4 PERFORMANCE REPORT   May 10

Operator	Hours Worked	Hours Meas. Work	Hours Nonmeas. Work	Std. Hours Produced	Rate	Earnings	Performance	Standards Coverage	Cost per Std. Hour
	(1)	(2)	(3)	(4)	(5)	(6)	(7)	(8)	(9)
Sam Abel	8.0	7.0	1.0	7.7	$ 2.25	$ 19.58	110%		
Robert Benton	8.0	8.0	0.0	9.0	2.40	21.60	113%		
Harry Case	8.0	6.0	2.0	7.2	2.32	21.34	120%		
Earl Davis	8.0	7.5	0.5	8.5	2.32	20.88	113%		
John Mavis	6.0	5.5	0.5	5.0	2.32	13.92	91%		
Department Summary	154.0	136.0	18.0	152.0	$ 2.32	$394.40	112%	88%	$ 2.59

Summary of Columns (1), (2), (3), (4), and (6) is the sum of the respective columns.
(5) is the Department Average Hourly Base Rate
(6) = [(4) + (3)] x (5)
(7) = (4) ÷ (2)
(8) = (2) ÷ (1)
(9) = (6) ÷ (4)

FIG. 6-2.   Labor Performance Control Report.

To show how the performance controls reflect changes in conditions, Figure 6-3 illustrates the hours worked and earned by Department 4 over a four-week period.   Notice that in weeks 2, 3, and 4 the performance was much better than in week 1.   The cost per standard hour, however, was higher in each of these weeks because the standards coverage was considerably lower.

Other Control Reports.   Although work measurement coverage and performance reports provide the basis for labor performance control, there are many situations which require control reports of a different nature.   The purpose of these reports is to emphasize clearly and concisely the main objectives for which management is striving.   For example, Figure 6-4 illustrates reports prepared for a company starting a new product line.   Here it was essential that the necessary man-hours be spent on the job and that the

WEEK	HOURS WORKED	HOURS MEAS. WORK	HOURS NONMEAS. WORK	STD. HOURS PRODUCED	RATE	EARNINGS	PERFORM-ANCE	STANDARDS COVERAGE	COST PER STD. HOUR
	(1)	(2)	(3)	(4)	(5)	(6)	(7)	(8)	(9)
1	154.0	150.0	4.0	156.2	2.32	371.66	104%	97%	$ 2.38
2	154.0	124.0	30.0	146.2	2.32	408.78	118%	81%	2.80
3	154.0	136.0	18.0	161.0	2.32	415.28	118%	88%	2.58
4	154.0	136.0	18.0	152.0	2.32	394.40	112%	88%	2.59

FIG. 6-3.   Summary of Department 4 Labor Performance Control Reports.

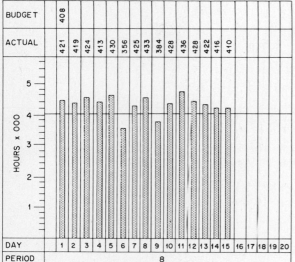

ACTUAL LABOR HOURS VS. BUDGET
(408 HOURS PER SCHEDULED DAY)

Press____Department
Labor Hours and Production
        Daily
Period No. _8____
Date__April 22 – May 19,19__

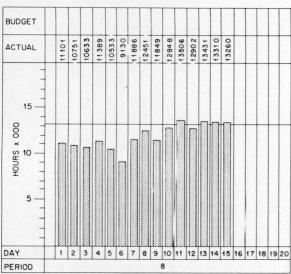

ACTUAL PRODUCTION VS. BUDGET
(13,200 PIECES PER SCHEDULED DAY)

Fig. 6-4.   Actual Labor Hours and Production versus Budget.

targeted number of pieces be produced. Both items were put into chart
form and displayed prominently so that everyone concerned would be well
aware of the status of the progress being made. As the effectiveness of the
workers improved, the desired amount of production was accomplished with
fewer hours until both targets were reached.

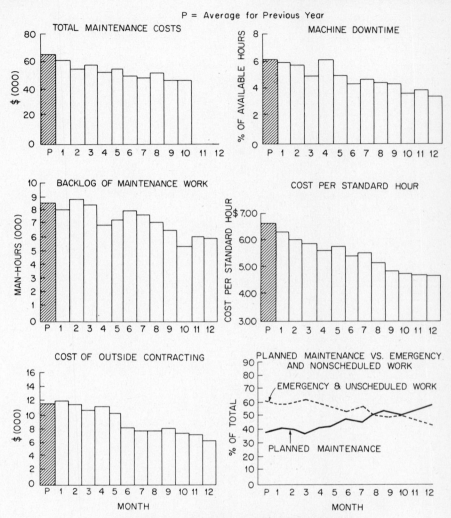

FIG. 6-5.　Maintenance Control Reports.

Figure 6-5 shows a set of typical control reports used by one company to establish control over maintenance costs. Most of these reports have work standards as a basis, with accurate reports of performance and coverage. Each report, however, highlights a different aspect of the maintenance management problem by showing important trends in cost or utilization of equipment and man-hours.

CONCLUSION

Although a great variety of reports are used by many companies to control labor performances, they are generally variations of two basic indices—performance and coverage. For the controls to be truly effective, they must be built on reliable standards established by work measurement. With measured standards as a base, management has the means to maintain good control over labor performance.

BIBLIOGRAPHY

Crossan, R. M., and H. W. Nance, *Master Standard Data*, McGraw-Hill Book Company, New York, 1962.

Drucker, Peter F., *The Practice of Management*, Harper & Row, Publishers, Incorporated, New York, 1954.

Gellerman, Saul W., *Motivation and Productivity*, American Management Association, New York, 1963.

Karger, Delmar W., and Franklin H. Bayha, *Engineered Work Measurement*, 2d ed., Industrial Press, New York, 1965.

Maynard, H. B. (ed.), *Handbook of Business Administration*, McGraw-Hill Book Company, New York, 1967.

Maynard, H. B. (ed.), *Industrial Engineering Handbook*, 2d ed., McGraw-Hill Book Company, New York, 1963.

Pappas, F. G., and R. A. Dimberg, *Practical Work Standards*, McGraw-Hill Book Company, New York, 1962.

MANUFACTURING FACILITIES

CHAPTER ONE

Plant Location

FREDERICK W. HORNBRUCH, JR. *Vice President, Macrodyne-Chatillon Corporation, New York, New York*

A variety of situations may precipitate a desire on the part of management to seek a new plant location. Some conditions, like urban redevelopment or new highway construction, leave no choice and require relocating. Others are associated with a need for additional capacity or an improved competitive position. Usually, however, management is interested in a new location for one of two fundamental reasons. Either the business is not successful in its present location and management seeks a plant in a new area that promises improved profit margins and growth potentials; or the enterprise is successful, in which case management strives to keep pace with the demand for its products and services through strategic expansion of facilities.

Either reason—problems or success—may justify a new plant in a new location, but first management should be confident that optimum costs and maximum utilization of facilities are being or will be achieved at the present location. The easiest course of action is to invest in additional plant sites, buildings, and equipment. By doing this, however, it is entirely possible that the old problems, in reality, will be exchanged for a new set that is just as complex and just as difficult to solve. Such a turn of events, together with the added investment, can lead to disappointing consequences. The alert management, then, makes certain that the existing operations are well tuned, soundly organized, and functioning effectively before deciding to relocate or to expand at a new plant site.

RETURN ON INVESTMENT

Modern management has the responsibility of maintaining an adequate return on the capital invested in the business. In manufacturing, this return is the result of two dynamic factors:

(1) $$\% \text{ profit on sales} = \frac{\text{net profit after taxes}}{\text{net sales}} \times 100$$

(2) $$\text{Turnover} = \frac{\text{net sales annualized}}{\text{gross assets employed}}$$

The return on investment is the product of these two factors. Hence, to maintain or increase the ROI, management must make certain that any expenditure for relocation or expansion will maintain or improve both the profit in relation to sales and the sales in relation to the total investment. This calculation should be projected for a variety of alternative situations. The resulting analysis can provide management with several choices in mathematical terms that can be compared readily and later can serve as the objectives to be achieved for the decided course of action.

PRESENT LOCATION

The operation of the present plant and its location should be analyzed thoroughly to avoid its apparent shortcomings and to understand and amplify its competitive advantages. An important feature of such a study should be to ascertain whether or not the location is being successfully exploited to the fullest. For example, the output of a daywork plant, where the employees are paid for the time they put in rather than for the product they turn out, can be increased as much as 40 percent by the installation of sound time standards and wage incentives. The resulting increase in salable output, accompanied by substantial reductions in unit costs, can have a beneficial compounding impact on sales and on the ROI. Other ways to utilize the present plant more fully include value analysis, methods improvements, automation, line production, latest generation machinery, elimination of bottlenecks, minimizing manufacturing cycles, and second and third shift operation.

ACQUISITIONS

Another step before irretrievably pursuing the new location route is to consider making a carefully selected acquisition of a company with a related product line. An acquisition initially may involve substantally greater amounts of capital than the purchase of a new plant. However, acquisitions can be made with an exchange of stock or a combination of stock and money so that the cash requirement need be no more, and could be less, than that needed to build and equip a new plant. A well-timed acquisition, although presenting a different set of conditions, makes it possible to gain time; additional sales and markets; skilled manpower, management, and engineering talent; immediate profits; new products; and advanced processes, equipment, and tools. The opportunity for synergism with an acquisition is substantial compared to adding more of the same in a new location.

PREPARE SPECIFICATIONS

The major problem in searching for a new plant location is to sort out the important conditions from those that should have relatively little bearing on the ultimate choice. Management can save both time and effort by preparing specifications for the desired location. A systematic approach can reduce the amount of data needed for a decision, can simplify the analysis and facilitate comparisons, can help solidify management thinking behind the project, and can make it possible to obtain factual information from a variety of outside sources concurrently. Consultants, area development commissions, railroads, utilities, state and local Chambers and Associations of Commerce, banks, and other organizations can be of considerable assistance. These sources have up-to-date information on file, are pleased to arrange trips and meetings, and have available to their staffs a wealth of statistics relating to their specific geographical areas. A set of specifications and questions placed with several of these sources can bring quick response for a preliminary analysis.

The many factors to be considered in designing the set of specifications and questions may be classified as general information, market influences, employee considerations, cost elements, and future conditions. The following outlines typical questions that should be raised and the kind of information generally needed to provide a composite factual picture of each area under consideration.

General Information

1. The community of _____, _____ is in the _____ of the state approximately _____ miles from _____, _____, _____.

2. The climate is revealed by the following official statistics taken from the records of the last ten years:

Item	Low	Annual average	High	Days per year
Temperature, °F	_____	_____	_____	
Rainfall, inches	_____	_____	_____	
Snowfall, inches	_____	_____	_____	
Relative humidity, %	_____	_____	_____	
Tornadoes				_____
Hurricanes				_____
Floods				_____

3. The major manufacturing companies in the community are:

		Employment		
Company	Products	Male	Female	Unions
_____	_____	_____	_____	_____
_____	_____	_____	_____	_____
_____	_____	_____	_____	_____
_____	_____	_____	_____	_____
_____	_____	_____	_____	_____
_____	_____	_____	_____	_____
_____	_____	_____	_____	_____

4. The population growth is as follows:

Group	19__	19__	Current	19__ estimate
Male	_____	_____	_____	_____
Female	_____	_____	_____	_____
Total	_____	_____	_____	_____

5. The education levels attained by the citizens are:

Level	% population completed
Elementary school	_____
High school	_____
Junior college (2 years)	_____
College (4 years or more)	_____

6. The financial institutions in the community are:

Name	Number of branches	Total assets as of last Dec. 31
_____	_____	_____
_____	_____	_____
_____	_____	_____
_____	_____	_____

7. The hotels and motels in the area are:

Name	Year opened	Rooms	Single room rate From	To	Dining room	Air cond.
_____	_____	_____	_____	_____	_____	_____
_____	_____	_____	_____	_____	_____	_____

8. Residential construction has followed this trend:

	Houses built			Apartments built	
Year	Number	Avg. selling price		Number	Avg. annual rental
19__	_____	_____		_____	_____
19__	_____	_____		_____	_____
19__	_____	_____		_____	_____
19__ est.	_____	_____		_____	_____

9. Residential land sells at prices about as follows:

Lot size, square feet	Minimum	Price range Nominal	Maximum
Minimum _____	_____	_____	_____
5,000	_____	_____	_____
10,000	_____	_____	_____
20,000	_____	_____	_____
40,000	_____	_____	_____

10. Area newspapers and magazines with advertising space include:

Name	Circulation
_____	_____
_____	_____

11. Television and local radio stations received in the area are:

Name	TV	Radio	Network affiliation
_____	_____	_____	_____
_____	_____	_____	_____
_____	_____	_____	_____

12. The municipal government is the _____ type.
The officials and department heads are:

Name	Position and department
_____	_____
_____	_____
_____	_____

13. The police department is composed of _____ full-time police officers, _____ special officers, _____ radio-equipped patrol cars, and _____ motorcycles.

14. The fire department consists of:

Fire station	Firemen Paid	Volunteer	Engine equipment Pumper	Ladder	Foam	Rescue
_____	_____	_____	_____	_____	_____	_____
_____	_____	_____	_____	_____	_____	_____
_____	_____	_____	_____	_____	_____	_____

Market Influences

1. The community is located as follows:

City	Miles distant	Air	Hours by rail	Truck
New York	_____	_____	_____	_____
Chicago	_____	_____	_____	_____
Los Angeles	_____	_____	_____	_____
New Orleans	_____	_____	_____	_____
_____	_____	_____	_____	_____
_____	_____	_____	_____	_____

2. The community is served directly by the following airlines, railroads, steamships, and trucking companies:

Carrier	Type	Special services

3. International, national, and municipal airports in the area include:

Airport	Type	Miles distant	Airlines

4. The Post Office is _____ class with _____ postal stations. Deliveries are made _____ times daily in the business districts and _____ times daily in the residential areas.

5. The community is in close proximity to U.S. Highways _____, _____, _____, _____ and State Primary Highways _____, _____, _____, _____.

6. Telephone service is provided by _____ with the home office at _____ and dial offices located at _____, _____, _____.

Employee Considerations

1. Bus lines serving the community are:

Line	North	South	Number of buses daily East	West	Airport

2. Taxi companies operating in the area:

Name	Number of taxis	Airport service

3. The public schools are:

School	Number of schools	Enrollment	Teachers	Graduates
Elementary				
High				
Total				

4. The capital investment per pupil is _____ and the public school debt per capita is _____.

5. Teachers' annual salaries range as follows:

School	Minimum	Average	Maximum
Elementary			
High			

6. The private, church, and nursery schools in the area include:

School	Address	Type	Grades	Enrollment Male	Female	Teachers

7. Colleges and universities in the area are:

| | | Offers degrees in | |
Name	Bachelor	Master	Doctor

8. Adult education facilities include:

Name	Address	Specialty

9. Libraries in the community are:

Name	Address	Volumes	Bookmobiles

10. The hospitals serving the area are:

Hospital	Beds	Doctors	Surgeons	Registered nurses	Ambulances

11. Practicing within the area and in addition to the hospital staffs are _____ doctors, _____ surgeons, _____ obstetricians, _____ pediatricians, _____ dentists, and _____ optometrists.

12. The cultural, fraternal, and civic organizations functioning in the community are:

13. The professional societies with chapters in the area are:

14. Churches in the community include:

Church	Denomination

15. Facilities for recreational activities are available at the following lakes, parks, stadiums, theaters, camps, and schools in the area:

Name	Location	Activities

16. Private clubs include:

Name	Address	Type of club

17. Sports within 150 miles of the community include: _____, _____, _____, _____.

18. Municipal taxes on residents are:

Class of tax	Tax rate per $1,000	Tax rate, %	Assessed % of actual value
Real estate	_____		_____
Personal property	_____		_____
City wage		_____	
State income		_____	
City sales		_____	
State sales		_____	

19. The state does _____ have "right to work" legislation.

Cost Elements

1. Employment and wages within the area approximate the following:

	Male		Female	
Industry	Employees	Average annual wage	Employees	Average annual wage
Manufacturing	_____	_____	_____	_____
Construction	_____	_____	_____	_____
Commercial	_____	_____	_____	_____
Financial	_____	_____	_____	_____
Federal government	_____	_____	_____	_____
State government	_____	_____	_____	_____
Municipal government	_____	_____	_____	_____
Utilities	_____	_____	_____	_____

2. Electricity is supplied to the area by _____ with offices at _____. The electric power rate schedule in effect is: _____

3. Natural gas is available at a rating of _____ Btu per cubic foot and the rate schedule in effect is: _____

Fuel oil costs _____ per gallon in bulk quantities.

4. Municipal water is processed in treatment plants at the maximum rate of _____ gallons per day. The process is _____

Current average daily usage is _____ gallons per day. Treated water is stored in _____ with a total capacity of _____ gallons. Municipal water can be made available _____ miles beyond the corporate limits. The treated water has a hardness of _____ parts per million.

5. Municipal sewage is treated and discharged to _____. The maximum total capacity of the treatment plants is _____ gallons per day and the current average daily flow is _____ gallons per day. The sewage treatment is _____. Municipal sewage services can be made available _____ miles beyond the corporate limits.

6. Trash collections are made _____ per week in residential areas and _____ per week in commercial districts. Municipal dumps are located at _____ _____.

7. Municipal, county, and state tax rates are as follows:

Class of property	Tax rate per $1,000	Tax rate, %	Assessed % of actual value
Real estate	_____		_____
Personal property	_____		_____
Machinery and tools	_____		_____
Inventories	_____		_____
_____	_____		_____
Municipal sales		_____	
State sales		_____	

8. The outstanding municipal debt is as follows:

Project	Type of bond	Amount	Expires
Water system	_____	_____	_____
Sewage system	_____	_____	_____
Roads and bridges	_____	_____	_____
Schools	_____	_____	_____
_____	_____	_____	_____
_____	_____	_____	_____
Total debt		_____	

9. The municipal budget for the following fiscal years was:

Major items	19__	19__	Amount 19__	19__	19__
_____	____	____	____	____	____
_____	____	____	____	____	____
_____	____	____	____	____	____
_____	____	____	____	____	____
Total budget	____	____	____	____	____

10. Welfare payments totaling _____ were made to _____ persons last year.
11. The fire insurance rating is class _____ for the community.
12. Typical fringe benefits given in the area are:

Benefit	_____Co.	_____Co.	_____Co.
Vacation schedule, exempt	_____	_____	_____
Vacation schedule, nonexempt	_____	_____	_____
Vacation schedule, hourly	_____	_____	_____
Total insurance premium per employee	_____	_____	_____
Paid by employee	_____	_____	_____
Paid by company	_____	_____	_____
Insurance coverage			
Group life	_____	_____	_____
Hospitalization	_____	_____	_____
Major medical	_____	_____	_____

13. Payroll taxes are:

Benefit	Tax rate
State unemployment insurance	_____
Federal unemployment insurance	_____
Federal insurance Contribution account (FICA)	_____
Workmen's compensation	_____

14. Job training programs in effect and sponsored by the community are:

Program	Sponsoring agencies	Type of training
_____	_____	_____
_____	_____	_____
_____	_____	_____
_____	_____	_____

Future Conditions

1. Area plans currently under consideration include:

Redevelopment _____
Zoning _____
Bond issues _____
Transportation _____
Schools _____
Recreation _____
Industrial parks _____
Shopping centers _____
Highway construction _____

EVALUATE AREAS

The volume and variety of information collected may make the evaluation appear so formidable as to defy arriving at a proper comparison of the areas under consideration. One way to solve this type of complex problem at least partially is to use a system for weighting the criteria. In one typical system, management selects the factors considered most important and necessary, assigns numerical rating values to these factors, and establishes the relative importance of each factor on a numerical scale. For example:

Factors

Rating value		*Relative importance*	
Poor	1	Low	1
Fair	2	Medium	2
Average	3	High	3
Good	4		
Excellent	5		

This method of rating and weighting then may be summarized as illustrated in the Area Evaluation Rating Chart (Figure 1-1). It is important to recognize that this method is a management tool and not a substitute for management judgment. Its correctness is proportional to the soundness of the management thinking contributed to its formulation and compilation. Perhaps its greatest value is that the method forces the management decision makers to get into the specifics of the analysis.

GENERAL GUIDELINES

The manufacturing manager must assume an overall viewpoint in the search for a new plant location. The customers want service, the employees want job satisfaction and good living, and the stockholders want growth and profits. These are universal wants, and several general rules can serve in most instances to guide management in satisfying these wants in the most effective combination.

Locate Near the Customers. It may be economical to locate adjacent to the source of raw materials or major elements used in processing, such as fuel, water, pulp, or minerals. In general, however, the rule is to locate as near as practical to the customers. Customers want service. They have demonstrated dramatically that they will give their business to those companies that recognize and cater to their needs and desires. The customers want service not only in the traditional sense of price, delivery, and quality, but in a much broader context. The customers have problems. They need and want real help from their suppliers in solving these problems. Timeliness and effectiveness are significant in determining the degree of assistance a company can give. Being strategically situated in close proximity to the customers makes it possible for a company to be much more aware of their needs. The very nearness can improve responsiveness substantially. Nearness today is measured both in miles and in time. Thus, a company serving a national market can achieve nearness by locating its manufacturing plants geographically close to major customers and aeronautically near concentrations of medium and small accounts.

Settle Close to a Major Airport. The desirability of close proximity to the

Factors	Rating value		Relative importance	Weighted rating	
	Area 1	Area 2		Area 1	Area 2
General information					
Population growth..............	4	2	2	8	4
Education.....................	3	3	3	9	9
Residential construction..........	2	3	1	2	3
Municipal government...........	4	3	2	8	6
Climate.......................	2	3	1	2	3
Subtotal...................	15	14		29	25
Market influences					
Location of community...........	5	3	3	15	9
Transportation.................	3	3	2	6	6
Airport.......................	3	4	2	6	8
Subtotal...................	11	10		27	23
Employee considerations					
Schools........................	3	3	3	9	9
Colleges.......................	4	2	3	12	6
Hospitals......................	3	1	2	6	2
Professional societies............	3	1	1	3	1
Recreational facilities............	3	5	2	6	10
Taxes on residents...............	2	3	2	4	6
Subtotal...................	18	15		40	34
Cost elements					
Wages.........................	3	4	3	9	12
Tax rates......................	2	3	3	6	9
Utilities.......................	3	2	2	6	4
Municipal debt.................	2	4	1	2	4
Subtotal...................	10	13		23	29
Total........................	54	52		119	111

FIG. 1-1.   Area Evaluation Rating Chart.

customers suggests seeking a plant location in an area with ready access to national air transportation. The airlines have a reputation for service, and in addition, they have been working diligently to make air freight more economical. The advent of faster and larger aircraft promises substantial opportunities in this direction. Servicing customers involves personal attention by executives, salesmen, engineers, installation and maintenance personnel, and others. A handy airport can conserve the time of these employees, can improve responsiveness to customer needs, and can contribute to lower operating costs and increased sales.

Think of the Employees. Modern employees are affluent, and with affluence comes independence and a desire for more knowledge and recreation. A plant location that possesses inherently desirable features can be expected to attract and keep capable people. A comfortable climate is conducive to outdoor living that people of all ages enjoy. One requisite given top priority is the local school system. Transferred and prospective employees will want to know if graduates are readily accepted at colleges and universities. Some will be interested in the vocational opportunities. Others will want special courses for advanced study, particularly in scientific, engineering, and technical subjects. The continual upgrading of the employees and their families is a very necessary motivating force for the company that wants to grow. Community attitudes and attributes of the right kind can amplify management's efforts to build and operate a successful plant.

Look for Reasonable Taxes. Taxes are a significant part of costs both to the company and to the employees. The search for a new plant location should include a study of the taxes in effect, the tax rates, and a projection of the tax structure into the future. This is necessary to avoid unpleasant surprises later and to evaluate the tax cost in relation to what the community provides to its citizens. Real estate, personal property, income, and sales taxes levied on residents in many areas tend to elevate local salary and wage scales. Some states continue to function without state sales and income taxes.

Seek High Productivity and Creativity. The pace of progress is accelerating. Above all, seek an area where the people not only possess the necessary skills but also have a talent for producing. The people in some areas have more pride in their ability to create and to produce. This attitude can be developed. Obviously, however, a new plant is off to an earlier and more successful start if the new employees believe in doing good work, in turning out a "fair day's work for a fair day's pay," and in originating and trying new ideas and new ways of operating the business. This is probably the most important and at the same time the most difficult condition to appraise. Certainly it requires and justifies several visits to each area, meetings and discussions with local management people, and observations of local manufacturing plants in operation. An experienced industrial engineer with his manufacturing manager should be able to evaluate realistically the productivity and ingenuity of the employees in each area. This information should then be used in establishing cost projections. In this way, the estimated costs can be related to forecasted outputs for a more accurate comparison.

Separate Distribution and Production Costs. The logistics problems involved in physical distribution activities such as inventory, warehousing, and transportation, when solved in combination, can have a favorable impact on costs and on the service offered to the customers. By separating distribution costs from production costs, it is possible to seek both distribution efficiency and production efficiency. Production efficiency in a plant tends to improve as volume increases. Distribution efficiency, however, may very well be lowered as the volume increases if the added volume is distributed over a greater geographical area. An analysis along the lines shown in the Production-Distribution Efficiency Chart (Figure 1-2) can serve to focus management attention on the point where further improvement in total costs may be accomplished by a second plant in a proper new location.

Look Out for the Expensive Incidentals. The small, easily overlooked incidentals can accumulate to substantial cost totals. Will the new plant need a cafeteria? Most in-plant cafeterias increase the investment and provide no direct return. A cafeteria may be a desirable service, if not a necessity, but make certain it is anticipated in the cost calculations. Have the expenses of making the move and the subsequent start-up costs been included? Will the statistics on available manpower prove misleading if the new plant is located

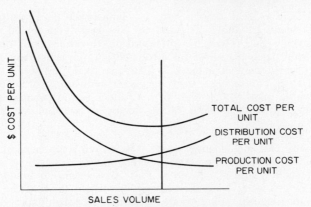

FIG. 1-2. Production-Distribution Efficiency Chart.

in the suburbs or the countryside? Jobs in the suburbs with employable people in the cities is not an uncommon situation. If this is so, are there adequate public transportation and highways connecting the two sections? Have adequate parking facilities been provided with paving and fencing costs included? Does the plant site allow for future expansion? Will the insurance carrier approve the community fire department or must company fire-fighting apparatus be provided to obtain a low insurance premium rate?

ANALYSIS, COMPARISON, DECISION

The mass of information collected, sorted, and projected for the locations under consideration needs to be distilled in an orderly, systematic manner and arranged so as to facilitate reliable comparison of alternatives leading to the best overall decision. Essentially three simple steps can serve this purpose.

Break-even Charts. The preparation of break-even charts similar to that shown by Figure 1-3 relates sales volumes and total costs for the present location and for each of the locations being compared. The break-even charts then reveal the fixed costs inherent in each situation, including amortization

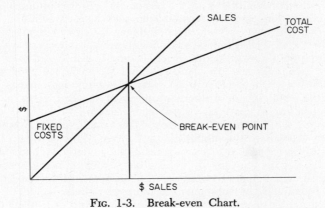

FIG. 1-3. Break-even Chart.

of the initial investments. The break-even charts indicate the sales volume at which a plant at each location can be expected to begin earning a profit and also establish the basis for operating budgets and profit planning.

Return on Investment. The projected profits obtained from the break-even charts for a selected annual sales volume produce percent of profits on sales. The annual sales volume divided by the gross assets employed in each location establishes the expected turnovers. These two indices when multiplied combine into an ROI for each location under study. (See page 5-4 for formulas.)

Comparison Chart. A chart may be prepared to show for the present and each contemplated new location the above indices plus the many other facets that should be considered in the final decision making session. This chart will facilitate the comparison of the extensive detailed data which have been collected for each location.

SUMMARY

The final analysis will bring to management's attention one or perhaps several locations that would be suitable. One thing certain, however, is that it is virtually impossible not to find a location that will meet the desired specifications. These United States contain almost all the potential a company could desire in terms of climate, topography, communities, markets, facilities, taxes, transportation, communications, services, talents, skills, wage scales, and recreational, educational, and spiritual benefits. Then, of course, there is the rest of the world offering an even greater range of conditions. Management, however, must be willing to devote time and effort to making a thorough analytical search. The location of a plant is a long-range matter. A new plant site is an opportunity to gain on competition for years to come. Plant location is an important element of strategic planning. It is a complex top management assignment in which the manufacturing manager should participate in a key role.

BIBLIOGRAPHY

Kinnard, William N., *Industrial Real Estate*, Society of Industrial Realtors of the National Association of Real Estate Boards, Washington, D.C., 1967.
Kotler, Phillip, *Marketing Management*, Prentice-Hall, Inc., Englewood Cliffs, N.J., 1967.
The Management Publishing Group, "Relocation," *Business Management*, April, 1968.
Perrow, J. Randolph, *Our Community Inventory*, Area Development Department, Virginia Electric and Power Co., Richmond, Va., 1968.
Will, Robert A., "Can Your Schools Attract New Industry?" *Plant Location Surveys*, The Austin Company, Cleveland, Ohio, 1965.
Will, Robert A., "Finding the Best Plant Location," *Chemical Engineering*, Mar. 1, 1965.
Will, Robert A., "Move or Stay—It Pays to Know," *Plant Location Surveys*, The Austin Company, Cleveland, Ohio, 1965.
Yaseen, Leonard C., "Plant Location," sec. 7, chap. 2 in H. B. Maynard (ed.), *Handbook of Business Administration*, McGraw-Hill Book Company, New York 1967.

CHAPTER TWO

Plant Layout and Design*

RICHARD MUTHER *President, Richard Muther & Associates, Inc., Kansas City, Missouri*

Plant layout and design deals with the physical arrangement of factories, plants, warehouses, office and laboratory areas, and commercial establishments. This arrangement involves processing equipment, the people and their workplaces, the supporting services—utilities, auxiliaries, and communication and control equipment—and the building itself.

Providing these facilities is a responsibility of management. Actual planning of the arrangement and installation of the facilities is generally assigned to some specialist or staff group either within or outside the company. Regardless of where the responsibility lies, modern business and industry are so competitive and specialized that it becomes almost mandatory to have an effective arrangement of machinery, equipment, and buildings to remain profitable. Most well-managed companies recognize both this need and the time required to plan properly to achieve it.

OBJECTIVES OF PLANT LAYOUT

Making a layout plan is not the end result, even of those responsible for the planning. Rather, improved operations, increased output, reduced costs, better service to customers, and convenience and satisfaction for company personnel are likely to be the chief objectives. It is important to target on these real aims; otherwise it becomes easy to drift into the viewpoint that

---

* Much of the material in this chapter is drawn from the same sources as that for the *Handbook of Business Administration*, edited by H. B. Maynard, published by McGraw-Hill Book Company, New York, 1967. The treatment there is directed to business or commercial managers; the treatment here is for the manufacturing manager.

the plan—rather than what the plan can accomplish when properly installed—is the only accomplishment required.

Each planning or rearrangement project will have its own individual objectives, and these will vary with different management viewpoints, operating policies, and the specific considerations surrounding the project. For efficiency in planning layouts and plant designs, it is important that the real objectives be clearly stated early in the planning.

PLANT LAYOUT FUNDAMENTALS

It is probably impossible to achieve all the benefits of a good facility in any one plant. By its very nature, a plant facility involves a multitude of factors and considerations: products, materials, sales volume, people, buildings, services, utilities, and the like. All these must be blended into a facility that will give the greatest benefits and have the fewest limitations. This is complicated by the short- versus long-time measurement of the benefits and limitations and by the relative importance of each. Essentially, then, a plant facility is a combination of factors or considerations, and its planning rests on a compromise of various isolated benefits and limitations which in turn are modified by time, degree of relative importance, and management attitude or policy.

A manager should aim at certain fundamentals in his facility. These include:

1. Integration—of all pertinent factors affecting the layout
2. Utilization—an effective use of machinery, people, and plant space
3. Expansion—easy to expand
4. Flexibility—easy to rearrange
5. Versatility—readily adaptable to changes in product design, sales requirements, and process improvements
6. Regularity—a regular or straight division of areas and relatively even sizes and heights of areas, especially when separated by building walls, floors, main aisles, and the like
7. Closeness—a practical minimum distance for moving materials, supporting services, and people
8. Orderliness—a sequence of logical work flow and clean work areas with suitable equipment for scrap, trash, and wastes
9. Convenience—for all employees, both in day-to-day and periodic operations
10. Satisfaction and safety for all employees

Layout Planning. Basically every layout or arrangement of functional areas or activities involves three fundamentals:

1. Relationships—closeness desired between various activities or functional areas
2. Space—in amount, kind, and shape for each activity or functional area
3. Adjustment—of the activity areas into a layout plan

See Figure 2-1.

TYPES OF LAYOUTS

There are three so-called classical types of layout: fixed position, process or function, and product or production line.

Fixed position layout holds the chief material in one place and brings men and machines to it. This layout is generally most economical when the

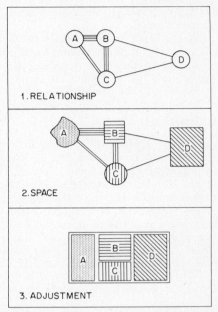

Fig. 2-1.   Every Layout Plan Rests on Relationships, Space, and Adjustment.

product or material is physically large and heavy, the quantity of each item is small, and the process is simple.

Process layout or layout by function is generally most economical when the process or nature of the operations is relatively complex or costly, the products or materials are diversified or variable, and the quantities of each item are relatively small.

Product layout or line production is generally most economical when the quantity is large, the process is fairly simple, and the product or material is relatively standardized, constant, and not too large.

From the above, it may be seen that the decision as to type of layout rests chiefly on three elements:

P—Product (or material)
Q—Quantity (or sales volume)
R—Routing (or process or operations)

These three elements determine the flow of materials—a certain P, in a certain Q, moving through a certain R.

Actually, most plants are a combination of these classical types of layout, part of their products being segregated on the basis of their physical characteristics (say size, shape, or metallurgy), and part segregated because of the peculiar processing required (say heat treating or plating), and possibly part divided in terms of fast-moving, standard items versus slow-moving specials.

In other cases, the division may be by special grouping: a particular group of products with a particular grouping of machines which are laid out like none of the three classical types of layout but, instead, halfway between. This type of layout lends itself to conditions where neither P nor Q nor R dominates.

Modern managements look very seriously at the way in which they split or combine their *P*'s, *Q*'s, and *R*'s when a new layout offers them the opportunity. Basically, each of these elements is traditionally under the control of a different department or division of the firm. This means that integration of product design, sales and marketing, and production or process engineering is truly important if major savings are to be gained from the plant layout.

METHODS OF APPROACHING PLANT LAYOUT PROJECTS

There are several approaches to layout planning which companies tend to follow.

1. *Instinct and Intuition.* Planning layouts by instinct and intuition is often fast, direct, and timesaving; but it is limited generally to situations where there is strong, deep experience and a record of sound decisions in the past.

2. *Find One Ready Made.* Magazine articles, visits to other plants, discussions with other company managers at lunch or social events, trade shows, or professional society meetings may lead to "finding" a layout—one that is spoken of enthusiastically and could be "just the thing." New ideas and methods are essential in this day of rapid change and certainly should be sought out; but what is good for one situation is not necessarily suitable for another, and without at least some modifications, it is likely not to be.

3. *Full Participation or "Keep Everyone Happy" Approach.* This approach involves the democratic process: get all ideas from everyone, discuss them, and translate them into a visual presentation; then call the group together for comment, make changes, and again solicit agreement of the group. This gives everyone involved a chance to participate and therefore to support the ultimate plan. But this approach draws only on the experience of those solicited, it is usually time consuming, and it does not take advantage of the analytical techniques so important to moving the company forward at the very time when it has the opportunity to do something progressive and constructive. Additionally, it tends to put emphasis on discussion and visualization rather than on problem analysis.

4. *Flow of Materials.* Many years ago, engineers discovered that to move material directly from each operation to the next afforded a logical sequence for control and reduced the cost of handling materials. By analyzing the sequence of necessary moves and arranging the layout accordingly, these benefits are gained. This is the approach most frequently taught in colleges and universities. It is ideal for process-type industries such as oil refineries or flour mills. But this approach is limited to those situations where there are dominant patterns of material flow, for it does not fully recognize that relationships other than flow of materials may be equally or more important.

5. *Organized Systematic Methodology.* This approach employs a universally applicable methodology known as Systematic Layout Planning.[1] It recognizes the differences of overall versus detail planning; follows a pattern of logical steps; employs a set of meaningful rating codes, symbols, and colors; and forces a systematic documentation of the planning. It is recognized as the most realistically analytical of any approach yet developed. As a result, it develops plans more soundly and gets approvals faster. Learn-

[1] Richard Muther, *Systematic Layout Planning*, Industrial Education Institute, Boston, 1961.

ing the approach initially takes time and some training, and once learned, there is a tendency to become intrigued with the methodology itself and to substitute mechanics of problem solving for the intelligent analysis and creative synthesis that should accompany the procedures.

Systematic Layout Planning (SLP) identifies four phases through which every layout planning project passes:

    I.   Location
    II.   Overall (block) layout
    III. Detail layouts
    IV. Installation

These phases come in sequence chronologically, and for best results from the layout planner's standpoint, they should overlap. See Figure 2-2. The phases recognize the distinction between large projects and small: overall layout involves blocking out departments, buildings, or entire sites; and detail layouts involve the arrangement of specific pieces of machinery and equipment.

SLP follows the philosophy of planning the whole and then the details. There is a desirable overlap between each phase and the one following it; the choice of a location, for example, will depend in part on what can be done with the layout of the facility that will fit into or onto that location.

ORGANIZING FOR PLANT LAYOUT AND DESIGN

In setting up to plan a new layout or plant, the project may be organized in several ways. The most prevalent way is to assign the responsibility to a trained staff specialist or staff group. If the individual has extensive prior experience, he should need little help other than a clear statement of what is wanted and the plan-for input data on products, quantities, routing (including process equipment), supporting services, and time or timing. If the individual does not have experience, he should be supported with outside technical knowledge and experience. In most industrial operations, the layout planning group or individual reports to a technically oriented department.

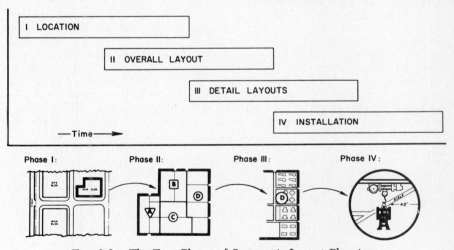

FIG. 2-2. The Four Phases of Systematic Layout Planning.

When the labor content of the operations is high and the process simple (garment work or hand assembly, for example), this department is generally industrial engineering or a similar group. When the equipment dominates and layouts are built into the building (steel rolling mills or wood pulp mills), this is generally plant engineering or a similar group. When the processing is usually complex or special (oil refinery or ethical drugs), this is generally process engineering.

Companies not infrequently use a task force or committee. Although this spreads the participation and presumably focuses on the project the attention of all interested departments, it falls short of expectations more often than not. The looseness and inaction associated with committee projects may be offset when a knowledgeable and directive chairman is in charge and when the committee is small and dedicated and its members are individually compatible with one another.

It is possible to let the manager of the area involved plan his own layout. After all, he knows most about his operations. The difficulty is that he is often too close to the problem and too unfamiliar with analytical planning methods. This works most effectively where the manager knows he will be responsible for the long-range operation of the plant and for achieving the budgeted profits or return on investment, and when he is relieved of day-to-day direction and control problems so that he can devote full time to the layout planning. Usually, the manager doing his own layout planning is familiar with only his operations, and he misses the big opportunity because of lack of breadth. Moreover, he is likely to be a doer rather than a planner and therefore short on integrative capacity.

Still another way to organize the project is by the use of outside specialists. This category includes a variety of management consultants, professional engineers, and architectural or construction firms. Properly selected, the specialist can be a real aid in factory, office, or laboratory planning. He can handle the entire planning, or he can be engaged to guide, assist, and consult with those who are internally responsible. Additionally, an outside specialist can be employed as "added insurance" to audit a layout, or layout alternatives, planned by the firm. It is usually preferable to retain someone who has broad layout planning experience rather than knowledge of a particular industry.

Shortcomings in Planning. Lack of long-range planning, failure to communicate corporate plans to the layout planners, and hesitancy to start planning sufficiently early are frequent top management faults.[2]

At the same time, the manufacturing manager should recognize typical shortcomings on the part of his planners. Most frequently these include not having the knowledge, the ability, and an organized approach to get the planning done quickly and convincingly and not being as cost conscious and as realistic or practical as top management and the operating people would like them to be.

One of the most prevalent complaints is about time. Planners frequently feel they do not have time to do the planning, and managements frequently feel planners take too long. In reality, this is an outward result; the underlying causes chiefly are those mentioned just above.

---

[2] This and the next two paragraphs are based on a survey conducted by the Technical Services Division, AMHS (now IMMS), and reported in "Who Lays Out the Plant?" *Modern Materials Handling* Magazine, June, 1963.

SPACE REQUIREMENTS

There are at least five ways to establish space requirements.

1. *Calculation.* Determine the amount of space required for each kind of machine or equipment, including areas for workers, maintenance service, material setdown, and access to aisle; extend this by the number required of each kind of machine; and add in space allowances for aisles and general or support areas.

2. *Conversion.* Determine the amount of space now used for each machine, machine group, or activity area; adjust this to what should be used now to do the job more efficiently; then convert this by some factor or multiplier to what will be needed for the new requirements.

3. *Rough Layout.* Prepare a rough detail layout plan to scale of a proposed or at least possible arrangement. It will in all likelihood not be the final, approved layout, but it will indicate approximate spacing between the activity areas or equipment involved and will allow measuring the rough plan for total area requirements.

4. *Space Standards.* In cases where certain types of areas are subject to repetitive layout planning, it is highly practical to develop standard amounts of space. This is particularly applicable for office areas or standard assembly bench layouts. There is danger in using any standard if it is not understood. For example "300 square feet per car" for parking lots and "75 square feet per draftsman" for engineering offices are good only if it is specified whether they are gross, net, or somewhere in between.

5. *Ratio Trend and Projection.* There are a number of ratios that can be of value. The first type is "space-to-space ratio." This includes the land-to-building ratios. For example, the ratio of open land to land under roof may be considered as 3 to 1; if one acre is to be under roof with this ratio of land, four acres will have to be obtained. Many new plants are established on sites too small for adequate growth, flexibility, parking, green frontage, and outbuilding services. Ratios of 10 to 1 are considered minimum for new sites by several multiplant manufacturing firms. A minimum ratio of 5 to 1 is frequently suggested for medium-sized manufacturing plants moving from downtown to the suburbs.

A second type of ratio is the "space-to-function ratio": so many square feet per dollar of inventory, per unit produced, or per employee. A company can build a record of certain meaningful ratios of this kind for several previous periods. From a plot of each ratio against time, a trend of that ratio is noted. This in turn can be projected into the future. Thus, when the projected ratio is known, the square feet required (numerator) can then be calculated for any projected denominator. For example, if 105 gross square feet per office employee is projected, 105 times a five-year-plan figure of 100 office employees means that 10,500 square feet of office will be required to meet the five-year plan.

In practice, space requirements are not established quite this simply. In fact, several of the five methods may be employed on the same project. Moreover, space requirements must be balanced against space available. Here it may be most helpful to rate each of the activity areas on the relative importance of maintaining its established space requirement. The areas rated lowest are squeezed the most when reducing area requirements to a smaller area available. In industrial plants, these areas usually end up being storage, office, and flexible service areas, as compared with production areas or fixed equipment services.

In any case, it is important to summarize the total plan for space figures. Space comes in three basic forms: amount, kind or nature, and shape or configuration. Most experienced planners want to know early in their projects all three of these aspects of the space with which they are working. As a result, the activity area and features sheet is recommended. Figure 2-3 shows how these data can be recorded.

Long-range Plans. The bigger the project, the more important is the need to give sound, long-range plans to the planners. This is especially true when relocating and moving onto a new site. One of the biggest wastes in industry is the failure—when the opportunity presents itself—to make a master site plan with fully thought-out assignment of its activity areas for future use, its total handling or movement plan, its utilities and auxiliary services plan, its dedicated areas for buildings and site features, and its communications and coordinative procedures.

For a facility that is supposed to serve a company for, say, the next twenty-five years, current managements are all too prone to wash away their long-range responsibility under the guise of "nobody can know what is going to happen in the future." There is a serious neglect in this area on the part of too many companies. It is easy to understand why. Most managers have the opportunity to plan a new site only once in a lifetime. Therefore, it is not surprising that they fail to recognize the long-range implications, and so they put the first-needed building in the corner of the new site that is most convenient at the moment.

Most companies consider long-range plans to be four to five years. This is really not long enough for plant facilities. Also, most industrial companies plan their sites for current needs with a look ahead about three to ten years to the most likely next general move or logical next expansion. This really is not good enough for long-term investments. As a result, the method of allocating now all space on the total site to certain probable types of functional use, as it is likely to be when the site will become fully occupied, is receiving much acceptance. Although less precise, the totality of this full-density viewpoint often makes it more realistic.

PLANT DESIGN

There are typical patterns of building arrangement and growth. Those that have proved the most successful over the long pull all have a regularity of some kind. This regularity can come from equality or consistency in the bay sizes or column spacing, in the overall building dimensions, in the spacing between buildings, or in the blocked-out allocation of space for various types of different activities. Straight, dedicated access ways (roads and main aisles), clearly segregated areas for the increasingly important utility and auxiliary service activities, and simple rectangular departmental areas are all indications of good planning that lead to regularity.

There are several questions regarding buildings that planners usually must face and answer:

> One location or branch locations?
> One building or several on one site?
> One-story building or multiple floors?
> Basement, part basement, or no basement?
> Ceiling heights and floor loading?
> Module size and column spacings?
> Degree of permanency wanted?
> General type of construction?

ACTIVITIES AREA & FEATURES SHEET

No.	Name	Area in Sq. Ft.	O'head Clearance Ft.	Max. Overhead Supported Load PSF	Min. Column Spacing	Water & Drains	Steam	Compressed Air	Foundations or Pits	Fire or Explosion Hazard	Special Ventilation	Special Electrification	Requirements for Shape or Configuration of Area (Space)
	Total:	3925											
1.	Fittings Storage	550	12	250		–	–	–	–	–	–	–	
2.	Valve Storage	600	12	250	20' x 20' ASSUMED	–	–	–	–	–	–	–	
3.	Hi-Value Items Storage	500	10	150		–	–	–	–	–	–	(a)	
4.	Tubing Storage	250	12	150		–	–	–	–	–	–	–	
5.	Misc. Supplies	800	12	150	NORMAL BUILDING ROOF LOAD ONLY (ALREADY ASSUMED)	–	–	–	–	–	–	–	
6.	Floor Dry	300	12	200		E	–	E	–	–	–	–	
7.	Fabrication Shop	400	14	200		–	–	E	O	O	I	–	
8.	Wrap, Pack and Trash Accumulation	200	12	150		O	–	–	O	–	–	–	
9.	Office	150	9	–	50' x 20'	–	–	–	–	–	–	(b)	
10.	Shipping, Receiving & Dock Area	100	12	250		–	–	–	–	–	–	–	ONE TRUCK DOOR ONLY WITH OUTDOOR DOCK
11.	Toilets	75	9	150		A	–	–	–	O	–	–	(b)
12.													
13.													
14.													
15.													

Physical Features Required — Relative Importance of Features
A – Absolutely Necessary
E – Especially Important
I – Important
O – Ordinary Importance
– – Not Required

Notation
a — WIRE-MESH, FENCED-OFF AREA
b — AIR-CONDITIONED AREA
c
References d

No. _____ Activity _____ Sheet _____ of _____

Sub-Activities or Areas

RICHARD MUTHER & ASSOCIATES — 150

Fig. 2-3. Activities Area and Features Sheet.

Flow Patterns. As for overall flow patterns, there is generally a choice of:
1. Straight through (in one side and out the other)
2. U shape (in and out the same side or end)
3. L shape (in one end and out one side)

Much has been written about the straight-through pattern. It provides relatively direct flow and simple control and allows expansion on both sides with addition(s) of approximately equal amounts of space for each activity.

The U shape offers the advantage of having incoming and outgoing areas near each other. This usually saves dock space, road paving, and number of doors in the building. It also frequently allows combining receiving and shipping (areas and personnel); puts raw and finished goods storage next to each other for occasional convenient exchange of space; and allows moves in to production to be combined on the same vehicle as moves out from production, with a resultant reduction in material handling effort.

The L-shaped pattern frequently is selected in congested areas or where rail lines or ship docks dominate one side of a plant. Moreover, the L usually permits a more segregated arrangement of departments and product groups, especially likely when there is a mixture of different products and processes in the same plant.

The older a plant becomes in terms of product life or process life, the more likely it is to depart from one of these three flow patterns and to become a combination. Figure 2-4 shows the chief advantages of different types of basic flow patterns.

Note that these patterns hold for total site areas as well as for areas within one building.

Five Components of Plant Facilities. There are five components or physical aspects of an industrial plant:
1. The layout
2. The material handling methods
3. The communications or controls
4. The utilities and auxiliaries
5. The building itself

These five components are involved in almost every modern industrial plant. In different plants, different emphasis is placed on each of the five. The important point is that all five must be integrated to have a dynamic, operating plant.

All too often, managers tend to fragment the problem. They may look at layout alone or isolate the building as a separate architectural problem. But experience has shown that best results are achieved when each of the five is integrated into a logical whole. In this sense, the layout plan is only one element or subsystem of the total plant facility.

Plant Utilities. Plant utilities, when properly planned, installed, and operated, permit the production organization to devote maximum attention to production problems.

Plant utilities or auxiliaries typically include:
1. Electric power (for lighting and processing)
2. Water (for drinking, processing, cooling, and fire protection)
3. Heating, cooling, and ventilating
4. Sewage (storm runoff and sanitary)
5. Gas (or gases)
6. Oil (fuel and lubricants)
7. Process waste disposal
8. Smoke, fume, dust, and dirt control

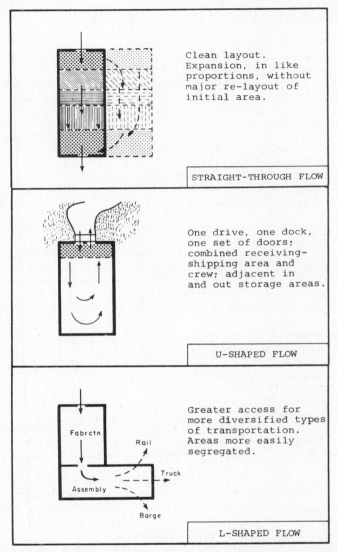

Clean layout.
Expansion, in like
proportions, without
major re-layout of
initial area.

STRAIGHT-THROUGH FLOW

One drive, one dock,
one set of doors;
combined receiving-
shipping area and
crew; adjacent in
and out storage areas.

U-SHAPED FLOW

Greater access for
more diversified types
of transportation.
Areas more easily
segregated.

Fabrctn

Rail

Truck

Assembly

Barge

L-SHAPED FLOW

FIG. 2-4. Examples of the Chief Advantages of Different Types of Basic Flow
Patterns.

    9. Compressed air or vacuum
   10. Telephone and communication wiring

In planning these utilities, one should check for reliability of service, reserve capacity for expansion, safety of personnel and plant facilities, flexibility
of distribution to allow changes in layout and plant equipment, and ease of
maintenance and rearrangement of the utility distribution system itself.

Companies with only conventional requirements for utilities find that although they must have these services available, it is possible to install them
to suit almost any layout or design of plant. On the other hand, in process-
dominated plants or so-called heavy industry, the utilities frequently dictate

the design of the plant.   An example is shown in Figure 2-5.   Note also, that when gathering data for planning space requirements, it is desirable to include the type and amount of utility service for each activity area right on the same worksheet.   See Figure 2-3.

Lighting.   The design of a plant's lighting system is usually the responsibility of a plant or architectural engineer.   However, management must assure that adequate light is provided.   Lighting factors of particular importance are:

1. Adequate illumination requirements
2. Avoidance of glare and eye fatigue
3. Proper type of lighting fixture
4. Location and height of fixture
5. Proper wiring layout or grid[3]

[3] Ruddell Reed, Jr., *Plant Layout—Factors, Principles, and Techniques*, Richard D. Irwin, Inc., Homewood, Ill., 1961.

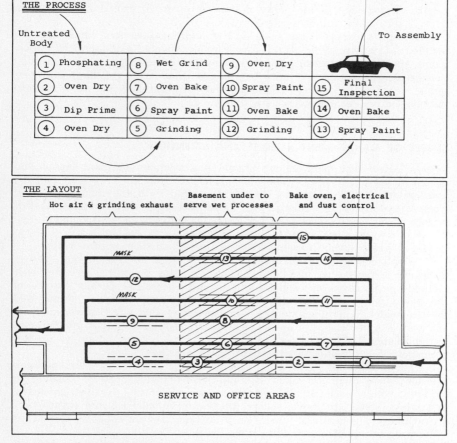

FIG. 2-5.   Plant Arrangement for Rust-proofing and Painting Automobile Bodies. The body threads its way back and forth to keep the major spray paint booths and critical baking ovens in line; thus keeping water, drains, pumps, air ducts, exhaust, electric lines, blowers, and the like together (with resultant savings in installations and maintenance).

The general rules for type of plant lighting are:

1. Use fluorescent lights for general interior lighting.
2. Use incandescent for close, localized lighting.
3. Use mercury vapor or cold cathode for exterior or high-ceiling interior installations.

Heating, Cooling, and Ventilating. The comfort one must provide for workers is important. Because this provision can be a large portion of the initial plant investment, a significant element of operating expense, and a major factor in employee morale, managers must give it realistic attention in their plant design. This usually involves looking at several alternative systems, both at the overall (block layout and preliminary building design) phase, and later at the departmental or detail plant design phase. It usually involves looking at the systems both separately and together.

Certain specific requirements here will influence the plant design:

1. The temperature and humidity range limits required
2. The quantity or exchanges of fresh air needed
3. The degree of air purity desired in terms of freedom from fumes, dirt, odors, and contaminants

Auxiliary Services. There are a host of additional services which must be planned into any modern plant. These usually involve plant services (stock-rooms, maintenance, salvage depot, cooling pond, filter bed, trash accumulation areas, incinerator, tool cribs, compressor room, and the like) and personnel services (lavatories, cafeterias, car parking, first aid and medical stations, lockers, recreation area, and so on).

DEGREE OF MANAGEMENT INTEREST AND ATTENTION

It is logical that managements should pay attention to plant layout and design in varying degrees. The manager of a cotton gin or a feed mill devotes relatively little attention to this compared with the manufacturer of electric appliances or automobiles. The extent of this interest depends largely on how continuous a project layout planning is for any company, and this in turn rests on the nature of the conditions involved.

This degree of layout planning continuity can be classified in three ways:

1. Plants requiring major attention before initial installation but little or no layout analysis after installation. This condition prevails where the basic methods or processes are expected to remain unchanged during the life of the plant; where installed machinery and equipment—including those used for production, handling, storage, and service—are lasting, very expensive, and very fixed or costly to move; where products and materials are not subject to change for long periods of time; and where plant buildings are less permanent than the process, equipment, and life of the products.

2. Plants requiring periodic or irregular layout attention. This condition prevails where there are occasional improvements in process or changes in methods; where machinery and equipment are moderately durable, expensive, and fairly difficult to move; where products and materials are occasionally or irregularly changed; and where the plant buildings are about as permanent as the process, equipment, and life of the products.

3. Plants requiring more or less continuous attention to layout problems. This condition prevails where there are frequent changes in process and methods, both minor and major; where machinery and equipment are short-lived, inexpensive, and easily moved; where products and materials change fre-

quently; and where the plant buildings are more permanent than the process, equipment, and life of the products.

Supervision of Facilities Planning. Regardless of the degree of attention and interest as described above, each management must be responsible for supervising its layout and plant design function. Generally, this involves the following:

1. Specify who is responsible for doing the layout planning.
2. Specify the basic objective and purpose of the layout planning project, with specific targeted goals.
3. Break down the project into logical phases and steps within phases.
4. Put these phases and steps in sequence, assign a specific person responsible for each, and set a time when each step will be completed.
5. Check the progress at periodic steps, especially during Phases I and II of the project. Certainly management should approve the final decisions made at the end of Phases I, II, and III. See Figure 2-2.
6. Make sure planners are not held up for lack of clear data or information from management.
7. Balance forcing accomplishment with getting good results.
8. Do not overlook the opportunity to build morale, improve methods, and sweep away bad practices as a part of the new layout or new plant.

In approving the layout, executives who are asked to approve plans normally look at six things:

1. How sound and reliable are the analysis and planning that support the proposed layout or plant design?
2. What does this installation cost? Can we afford it relative to our available funds?
3. What do we stand to gain from this layout? How much will it reduce our basic costs, and will it make our work easier, more convenient, and safer?
4. What are the risks in this layout? What could happen to us if certain of the features of the layout went wrong or failed or did not function as planned?
5. How does this layout affect me personally and the group for which I am responsible?
6. How well will this layout or plant function in the long run as well as in the immediate future?

When to Move. It is usually impossible to satisfy everyone when picking a time to make an installation. An attempt can be made to maintain production schedules during the move; or the move can be made on weekends, holidays, or during vacations or seasonal lulls when production is normally down. It is frequently advisable to suspend operations and make the move all at once rather than tangle with everyone during the move. Once the schedule of moves is set, it is usually better to go ahead than to hold up because something is not quite ready.

When the move takes place, the layout planner should be on the floor or at least readily available for consultation with the movers. No matter how well the planning has been done, there will be some adjustments or questions at installation time. Therefore, the layout planner must be available to answer questions, interpret plans, inspect for completeness, and secure as early a resumption of production as possible.

Before the move, it is well to condition employees for the change. Operation and supporting service supervisors should be briefed. In some cases, elaborate training of operating people may pay off handsomely, depending in large measure on the relative newness of the product, process, and personnel.

CONCLUSION

The important points for management to consider in managing a new layout or new plant project include the following:
1. Look far enough ahead, soon enough.
2. Provide planners with management-approved inputs.
3. See that the project is properly assigned and organized.
4. Be sure that the planners involve the operating people.
5. Check project results at Phases I, II, and III.
6. Recognize that all five components (layout, handling, communications, utilities, and the building) must integrate at each phase of the planning.

BIBLIOGRAPHY

Apple, James M., *Plant Layout and Materials Handling*, 2d ed., The Ronald Press Company, New York, 1963.
Bolz, Harold (ed.), *Materials Handling Handbook*, The Ronald Press Company, New York, 1958.
Briggs, Andrew J., *Warehouse Operations Planning and Management*, John Wiley & Sons, Inc., New York, 1960.
Haynes, D. Oliphant, *Materials Handling Application*, Chilton Company, Philadelphia, Pa., 1958.
Mallik, R. W., and A. T. Gaudreau, *Plant Layout—Planning and Practice*, John Wiley & Sons, Inc., New York, 1951.
Moore, James M., *Plant Layout and Design*, The Macmillan Company, New York, 1962.
Muther, Richard, *Practical Plant Layout*, McGraw-Hill Book Company, New York, 1955.
Muther, Richard, *Systematic Layout Planning*, Industrial Education Institute, Boston, Mass., 1961.
Muther, R., and J. D. Wheeler, *Simplified Systematic Layout Planning*, Management & Industrial Research Publications, Kansas City, Mo., 1962.
Reed, Ruddell, Jr., *Plant Layout—Factors, Principles, and Techniques*, Richard D. Irwin, Inc., Homewood, Ill., 1961.
Ripen, Kenneth H., *Office Building and Office Layout Planning*, McGraw-Hill Book Company, New York, 1960.
Robichaud, Beryl, *Selecting, Planning, and Managing Office Space*, McGraw-Hill Book Company, New York, 1958.

CHAPTER THREE

Capital Budgeting

DONALD D. DEMING *Professor and Chairman, Management Engineering, Rensselaer Polytechnic Institute, Troy, New York*

Capital budgeting refers to the practice of allocating, on a regular, periodic basis, money to be used for acquiring capital goods. Two basic purposes are served by this practice: the first is to increase existing productive capacity and to broaden operating capabilities; the second is to replace equipment as it becomes uneconomic as the result of wear and obsolescence. The first purpose (expansion) is to a large degree a marketing problem—estimating the manufacturing capacity required to meet the anticipated demand for a new product or increased demand for an existing product. The other purpose (replacement) is nearly the sole responsibility of operating management. This chapter will deal primarily with the replacement problem. Many if not most of the procedures described apply to budgeting for expansion as well as for replacement.

BUDGETING FOR EQUIPMENT REPLACEMENT

Many things contribute to the success and growth of a company. The manufacturing arm makes numerous vital contributions. Very high on the list of contributions will be an item which can be called utilization of assets. By effectively utilizing the manpower, materials, and facilities available, costs may be kept low, quality kept high, and output maximized.

It may be that in accomplishing this feat manufacturing management still becomes the cause of company failure. The reason for this is that cost, quality, and productivity are entirely relative. To prove this fact for himself, let the reader look back twenty or thirty years in his own industry and compare what was then thought to be good performance with that of today. In nearly all instances, one will realize that conditions have changed and that today's success, or lack of it, is very often due to the improvements made in the industry and by manufacturing in keeping abreast or ahead of these improvements.

Equipment replacement is a key factor in maintaining and improving manufacturing effectiveness. To deal with this problem effectively, certain basic assumptions are necessary:

1. Existing facilities must be continuously upgraded by replacement of worn and obsolescent equipment. To do this, funds must regularly be budgeted for this purpose.
2. Opportunities for most effective equipment investments do not present themselves automatically; they must be sought out.
3. Demands for reinvestment funds will (or at least should) exceed the funds available.
4. Organization, including methods, procedures, and assigned responsibilities, is necessary to secure expeditious implementation of funded proposals.

Little need be said about the importance of regularly budgeting funds for equipment replacement. Suffice to say that if a portion of earnings is not set aside for this purpose, the company is gradually liquidating its original equipment investment and in due course will cease producing. Because most companies would not knowingly do this, they should consider a systematic plan for replacement. The annual budgeting of replacement funds is the first step of a systematic method for accomplishing the objective of continuing production effectiveness.

Identifying Replacement Needs and Opportunities. It is important to establish effective and broadly understood methods for bringing to light replacement needs and opportunities. Two universally employed methods are the "squeaking wheel" method and the "why don't cha" method. These are both useful methods and when properly organized can accomplish very satisfactory results. There are other more complex and sophisticated methods that should receive careful consideration and should as a rule be incorporated in any systematic approach to replacement. One fairly common analytical technique is employed when computers are used to keep track of the cost trends of all equipment. Continuous records of all repairs, downtime, scrap, accidents, and quality for each piece of equipment can reveal when a certain piece of equipment "goes out of control" relative to any one of these cost factors, the rule of exception mechanized. There is no reason, of course, why this type of analysis cannot be made manually—except, perhaps, time and cost.

Another analytical approach is to identify and rank high-cost operations where relatively small improvements will yield high returns. Very high cost operations suggest investment in R&D for these areas because of high rate of return for each increment of improvement.

Squeaking Wheel Approach. Because of the widespread use of the squeaking wheel approach, its good and bad points should be considered. Its main good point is that such a grass roots request usually reflects a strongly felt need of people who have a genuine problem.

Its weaknesses are:

1. It is untimely—the problem usually could and should have been identified before the squeaking became apparent.
2. It is subject to many abuses and is often used as an excuse for poor human performance.
3. The allocation of money tends to be based on the loudness of the squeak rather than on relative importance.
4. Remedial action is often hasty and poorly conceived.

Despite these shortcomings, the squeaking wheel approach is likely to be a part of any replacement procedure.

"Why Don't Cha" Approach. The "why don't cha" approach is essentially preventive in nature, and as such is highly commendable, whereas "squeaking wheel" is an after-the-fact approach. The problem with "why don't cha" is that organizations are seldom adjusted to exploit the potential of random ideas coming from unpredictable sources. The well-known but little understood suggestion box can, when properly exploited, be a gold mine of otherwise missed opportunities.

Assigning Capital Expenditure Priorities. If we organize to utilize all the sources mentioned for finding replacement opportunities, it seems a foregone conclusion that the in-basket of proposed expenditures will exceed our financial and organizational capability at any given time. Such being the case, we need to apply priorities so as to get the most important things done first.

Given a rational system for assigning priorities, we can make up an ordered list starting with the most desirable proposal and ending with the least. If proposals have to do with improving profit, we could make a running summary of required funds and stop with the proposal that consumes the last of budgeted funds, or we might stop at the item with a rate of return which equals a predetermined minimum rate of return.

A problem comes up when we recognize that many highly desirable proposals are desirable for nonmonetary benefits—safety, quality, flexibility, and the like.

To deal with this rather mixed situation, let us assume that we utilize one of the sound approaches for determining the relative or absolute profitability of all equipment proposals that are up for consideration. Having made these computations, we will list them in descending order of profitability. Next we will look at the list of items yielding intangible benefits, and rank them in order of importance to the organization. If there are unbreakable ties due to difference of viewpoints, let ties occupy the same "line" or preference rating. One list might be safety proposals. Make a similar ranked list for these items. Do the same for proposals leading to improved customer service, quality, and so on. The final listings reflect the number of separate categories considered to be significant by individual organizations.

We now have a number of ranked lists, and what we want is a single list which ranks all proposals in all categories relative to desirability to the organization. With such a list in hand, we can go down the list until reinvestment funds are exhausted or until the return rate falls below some desired limit.

The first step is to examine and compare all items at the top of each list. Enter the most desirable single item at the top of the final, merged list. Removal of the number one choice puts another item at the top of that particular list. Now look at all first items again including the new one brought into consideration by removal of the first choice. Again choose the most desirable alternative to place second on the final list. Continue in this manner until you have a finally merged list. Ties on the finally merged list produce no problem unless budgeted investment funds run out on a line occupied by more than one investment item. In this case, a choice may have to be made, but it is likely that funds can be found if contenders are equally and highly desirable.

Follow-up of Approved Expenditures. At this point, it may seem that the work is done; but really it is only now ready to begin. What must be done finally is to make sure that approved expenditures result in purchase contracts which specify clearly what is expected from the supplier and that a responsible organization is set up that will ensure that the equipment is brought up to the anticipated level of performance at an early, probably planned date and that benefits begin flowing in without delay. Sometimes this results in project management assignments; often something less formal and expensive will suffice, but it is necessary in any event clearly to assign individual responsibility and to require systematic planning and follow-up. In the end, an appraisal of conformance of initial plan to actual results must be made to ensure planned achievement.

Documentation of Expenditure Requests. A common characteristic of all but the smallest organizations is the practice of securing approval of proposals at a reasonably high level in an organization, well above the level at which the proposal originates. This is particularly true for replacement proposals, perhaps less true for expansion proposals. In either event, documentation is important for effective communication without which poor results are inevitable.

Standard forms, if well designed, can assist materially to assure complete information systematically presented in an understandable manner, thus ensuring for each proposal an objective appraisal. Standard procedures make comparisons easier and more valid.

The form shown by Figure 3-1 is a good example of an effective one. As the "Summary" block of information suggests, there is more than one way to compute the economic benefits of cost saving proposals. This particular form mentions four possible ways of evaluating potential cost benefits: "first year's operating savings," "MAPI comparison factor," "discounted cash flow rate of return on investment (after tax)," and "payback period." The example shows results of computing first-year operating savings and the payback period. Why were the other two computations not made? The answer is that they are somewhat complicated to make, and in this case they were unnecessary. The substantial cost benefits of $19,332 for the first year for a $14,100 investment giving an equivalent inflow of cash in 8.8 months suggests that this proposal be funded without further ado. If savings were a half or a quarter of the indicated amount, it might still be a worthwhile investment, but we would then wish to get a more accurate estimate of return on investment.

Simple Method of Estimating Return on Investment. Figure 3-2 shows a chart which makes the reasonably accurate determination of rate of return both quick and easy. To use the chart, the anticipated yearly saving from the equipment, S, is divided by the cost of the investment, C, to get the S/C ratio. The curve on the chart is selected that most nearly matches the useful life and depreciation period of the investment.

The percent return on investment may then be read directly from the chart. The answer is directly comparable to a bank interest rate. The method is exact under four conditions:

1. The cost of the investment must all be paid at the same time; for example, the $1,000 paid out for a machine foundation should not be a year in advance of the $10,000 paid out for the machine itself.
2. Year-to-year savings must be constant.
3. Depreciation must be figured by the sum-of-digits method.
4. Income tax must be 52 percent.

For other more precise methods of determining rate of return on investment, the reader is referred to the sources given in the bibliography.

CONCLUSION

At this point, only one basic question remains to be dealt with: How much should a company budget annually for equipment? Of course there is no

CAPITAL EXPENDITURE APPROPRIATION
TPEC-671 111 -2 PRINTED IN U.S.A.

DIVISION – WORKS	DEPARTMENT	PROJECT NO.
Smith Mining – Denver	Electronics	68-65012-S
PROJECT TITLE	PRODUCT LINE	
Automatic Assembly Machine	Mining Batteries	Supp. offset Aband. $14,000
QUARTERLY ESTIMATE OF EXPENDITURE	ESTIMATED LEAD TIME REQUIRED FOR DELIVERY	TOTAL COMMITMENTS YEAR TO DATE
2nd	13 wks.	-0-

ITEM	QTY.	DESCRIPTION	EST. LIFE YEARS	PURCHASED AMOUNT	FREIGHT	SHOP ORDER	TOTAL
1	2	Automatic assembly machines for mining batteries (part fabricated in-house	6	$ 10,240	$ 360	$ 3,500	$ 14,100
		TOTAL		$ 10,240	$ 360	$ 3,500	$ 14,100

PROJECT OBJECTIVE

To reduce labor costs in producing mining battery subassemblies and provide a backup in the event of our current machine failure. 85% of our battery production is dependent on the existing two machines.

PRIMARY OBJECTIVE

- ☐ NEW PRODUCT
- ☐ INCREASED CAPACITY
- ☐ REPLACEMENT
- ☒ COST REDUCTION
- ☐ R & D. TECHNICAL CAPABILITY
- ☐ OTHER

ECONOMIC JUSTIFICATION

Based on our present production schedule requiring 146,000 subassemblies/week, the following labor figures were obtained:

Present method (2 mach.)   Proposed (4 mach.)
Monthly $3671 $ 2060

Est. monthly savings $1611

SUMMARY

	$
1ST YEAR'S OPERATING SAVINGS	19,332
MAPI COMPARISON FACTOR	
DISCOUNTED CASH FLOW RATE OF RETURN ON INVESTMENT (AFTER TAX)	
PAYBACK PERIOD	8.8 mos.
NUMBER OF YEARS USED IN RATE OF RETURN CALCULATIONS	YRS.

ALTERNATIVES CONSIDERED

Continue operation with only two machines and incur the higher labor costs as well as the continued risk of machine breakdown.

APPROVALS

	DATE		DATE
PREPARED BY			
INDUSTRIAL ENGINEERING		GROUP VICE PRESIDENT	
WORKS MANAGER		STAFF MANUFACTURING SERVICES	
ACCOUNTING		CORPORATE CONTROLLER	
DIVISION MANAGER		POLICY COMMITTEE	

DISTRIBUTION OF COPIES   WHITE – DIVISION ACCOUNTING   BLUE – STAFF MANUFACTURING SERVICES   BUFF – DIVISION INDUSTRIAL ENGINEERING
GOLDENROD – CAPITAL PLANNING   GREEN – PLANT AND PROPERTY ACCTG.   PINK – ORIGINATOR

FIG. 3-1. Capital Expenditure Appropriation Request Form.

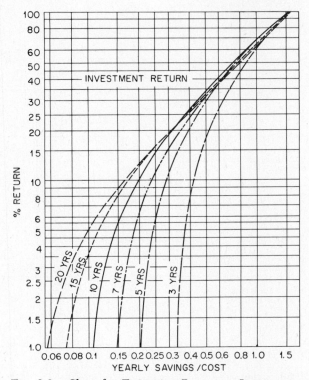

FIG. 3-2.   Chart for Estimating Return on Investment.

single answer to this question.   A seemingly rational approach would be to budget an amount equal to annual depreciation.   Such an approach implies an intention to stand still; less would suggest slow liquidation; more might suggest aggressiveness in upgrading as well as in replacing equipment.   Each management must decide, within its limits of capability, how aggressive and expansive it chooses to be.

BIBLIOGRAPHY

Bierman, Harold, Jr., and Seymour Smidt, *The Capital Budgeting Decision*, The Macmillan Company, New York, 1960.
Dean, Joel, *Capital Budgeting*, Columbia University Press, New York, 1951.
Deming, D. D., and R. G. Murdick, "Equipment Replacement Analysis" in H. B. Maynard (ed.), *Handbook of Business Administration*, sec. 7, chap. 6, McGraw-Hill Book Company, New York, 1967.
Morris, William T., *The Capacity Decision System*, Richard D. Irwin, Inc., Homewood, Ill., 1967.
Murdick, R. G., and D. D. Deming, *The Management of Capital Expenditures*, McGraw-Hill Book Company, New York, 1968.
Terborgh, George, *Business Investment Management*, Machinery and Allied Products Institute, Washington, D.C., 1967.

CHAPTER FOUR

Equipment Selection and Procurement*

M. J. DUBUC   *Director, Material, Rocketdyne Division, North American Rockwell Corporation, Canoga Park, California*

The importance of selecting and procuring capital equipment is clearly seen from the truism: A sound market, a competent organization, and adequate capital and capital facilities are the three basic elements required to initiate and maintain a profitable operation.

Capital facilities and equipment additionally provide the immediate means to augment and multiply human effort, thereby increasing productivity. Because such acquisitions must be paid for initially or ultimately from earned profits, they are subject to stern mathematical constraints, which in turn interact with the soundness of the market and the competitiveness of the organization to control rates of profit or loss, growth or decline.

EQUIPMENT DEFINED

The term "equipment" means many things to the manufacturing and industrial sales people. The following descriptive commodity list has been evolved from many years of experience in the purchase of capital equipment and services, and should serve as a fairly accurate guide to identifying in clear terms the general field of equipment and services.

    Air conditioning and refrigeration equipment
    Communication equipment
    Containers and closures

* Grateful acknowledgement is made to J. R. Norris, Manager, National Water Lift Division, Pneumodynamics Corporation, El Segundo, California, and D. J. Novelli, Senior Management Systems Analyst, Rocketdyne Division, North American Rockwell Corporation, Canoga Park, California.

Conveying, elevation, and material handling equipment
Cooling towers
Cryogenic equipment (design and construct)
Electrical and electronic measuring and testing apparatus
Electric generators, motors, and other rotating electric equipment
Electronic welding equipment and systems (design and construct)
Furniture and fixtures
Gas welding, heat cutting, and metalizing equipment
Heat exchanger equipment (evaporators and condensers)
Industrial furnaces, kilns, lehrs, and ovens
Inspection, testing, and measuring machines
Laboratory instruments and apparatus
Measuring and controlling apparatus (industrial and laboratory precision
    quality)
Mechanical power transmission equipment
Metalworking machinery
Miscellaneous industrial machinery and equipment
Miscellaneous machine tools
Miscellaneous transport equipment
Motor vehicles
Office machines and equipment
Photographic and optical equipment
Plumbing and nonelectric heating equipment
Portable communications equipment
Power pumps
Power supply and switchgear equipment
Prefabricated buildings, partitions, and panels
Radio and television equipment (systems/design and construct)
Reciprocating and rotary compressors
Safety and sanitation equipment
Signal-alarm devices
Special testing equipment (electrical, pneumatic, and hydraulic)
Ultrasonic cleaning, testing, and inspection equipment
Vacuum pumps
Valves, regulators, and actuators
Vessels—pressure, vacuum, storage, and processing

EQUIPMENT SELECTION AND PROCUREMENT, A KEY FUNCTION

From the viewpoint of the manager responsible for the establishment of new or modified manufacturing facilities, the process of selecting and procuring the right type of manufacturing, processing, and handling equipment is of great importance. It is at this point in time that delineation of the function to be performed, capital outlay authorized, expected life term, versatility, and other characteristics of the desired equipment should be clearly spelled out.

Responsibility for handling the preliminary phases of equipment procurement rests with various management representatives in various business organizations. However, certain key points should be considered before and during the approval and procurement phases of capital equipment and facilities:

1. Can the equipment be used for more than one program over a long period of time, and does it fit into a sound business objective which is supported by a strong continuing market? The answer to this question must be in the affirmative or the request should be dropped.

2. Recognizing that the equipment will directly or indirectly affect the output of direct labor hours upon which the entire overhead cost system is based, the cost penalty for inefficiency, breakdown, or noncompetitive output will rapidly exceed the purchase price of a wrong choice. Therefore, selection of correct equipment is imperative.

3. There is no substitute for a well-prepared proposal for each proposed procurement taking care to include these salient parts:

   a. What the equipment must accomplish.
   b. How and if this function fits into the long-term business picture.
   c. Why it will accomplish the job with the highest productivity at the least near-term and long-term costs.
   d. Is the proposed supplier reliable—dependable for equipment, service, and warranty recourse with no loss of production time.

In summary, the responsible manager will realize, after viewing capital equipment and facility requirements in the critical way described above, that the odds for success are increasingly favorable. As the approval cycle concludes, the manager will be assured that the procurement function is fully aware of the proposed procurement and understands it sufficiently to make good, clear decisions in effecting its procurement, installation, and performance in keeping with planned objectives.

SPECIFICATION PREPARATION

Treating specification preparation as one of the most important steps will avoid needless expenditures of time and funds later brought about by rectifying actions due to specification oversights. Key requirement questions were suggested in the previous paragraph, answers to which will provide the key points for inclusion in the specification writing process.

Simply stated, the main purpose of a specification is to relay in clear, concise terms what is wanted, the task it is expected to perform under given conditions, and the area displacement allowable. Additional considerations such as complexity, life cycle, budgetary allowance, proof of compliance, and the like may be included.

Writing an effective specification need not entail the compilation of a highly abstract work statement. Most manufacturers, distributors, or dealers provide preprinted specifications or descriptive brochures which readily provide most specification details desired. In those cases where certain information might be lacking, a telephone call to the local representative, preferably through the purchasing department to avoid later contractual problems, will provide the needed details without delay.

Whether the specification is written as a part of the purchase order copy or as a separate enclosure is a matter of choice, but one precaution is suggested for either approach. Carefully describe all the features and characteristics desired. References may be made to the seller's or distributor's specifications or brochures including specification identifying numbers, model numbers, page numbers, figure numbers, dates, and other pertinent information. The specification should be written so that it may be reproduced in multiple copies for the bidding and ordering steps that follow.

Although a certain manufacturer's model designation may be specified, the addition of the words "or equivalent" should make it possible for the purchasing department to obtain proposals from several qualified sources. Proposal information is generally submitted by interested suppliers on a no-charge basis as part of their service to the trade. This information should prove useful in making up evaluation and recommendation studies before proceeding with the next step, procurement. One word of warning. Do not add the "or equivalent" proviso to specification data calling for the supplying of a proprietary product or process by a sole source of supply. Rely upon the purchasing representative to negotiate the best possible price and delivery. There is no practical alternative, unless one has the time and perseverance to write a comprehensive basic specification and to proceed with a market availability and proposal action.

Sources of Information. Industrial organizations have their names entered on mailing lists for trade papers, certain free service directories, and unsolicited spot mailing campaigns, all of which provide good preliminary information. Additionally, there are usually available within the industrial engineering or purchasing functions paid-for information files in catalog or microfilm arrangements that can provide extensive information simply for the asking. Some of the better known sources of information are listed in the bibliography at the end of this chapter. Finally, do not overlook the fact that the purchasing department has continuous contact with sources of supply, and can obtain urgently needed information by telephone, telegram, letter, or sales representative visitation to the home office or plant.

AUTHORIZATION TO PURCHASE

Good business practice dictates that the expenditure of short-term or long-term capital equipment funds should be accomplished according to well-defined procedures that provide for:

1. The determination of needs in keeping with top management's plans and policies
2. Justification of the proposed equipment procurement in terms of operational savings to be realized, marketing advantages to be gained, modification or replacement of obsolescent methods and equipment, and other likely objectives too numerous to mention
3. Setting aside funds for the procurement action recommended on a programmed basis—neither too soon nor too late
4. A reporting method or system that provides complete information in a readily accessible manner from the planning stage through the final installation report
5. Strict adherence to budgetary dollar allocations and timetables by all parties concerned, including the supplier of the procured equipment or service

A typical flow diagram and controlling document that will ensure conformance with the foregoing objectives are illustrated by Figures 4-1 and 4-2.

PURCHASING ACTION COMPLETES PROCUREMENT PHASE

All the achievements described in previous paragraphs have now led to the final step. Upon release of the requirement, the purchasing department has all the necessary data readily available and consequently is in a position to take timely and superior procurement action.

In summary, the following key points are reviewed to assist in completing an effort whose successful conclusion will optimize the company's fixed capital position in relation to that of its competitors.

Bidding Data. Copies of the specifications written to support the capital expenditure request action may be included as part of the purchasing depart-

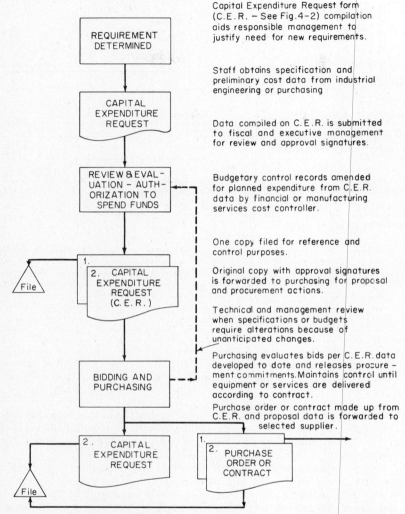

FIG. 4-1. Flow Diagram Illustrating the Basic Steps in Their Logical Order Required to Accomplish the Procurement Cycle.

ment's invitation-to-bid package. Oversights or updating information disclosed by the bidders can be fed back with minimum effort to the requisitioner as purchasing accumulates its proposal data, thereby assuring current and accurate procurement data being available in all control files.

Further, if significant changes or deviations are recommended during the bidding process, they can be recycled through management's control system before capital funds are erroneously committed. Another look at Figure 4-1 will clearly illustrate this point.

Selection of Qualified Suppliers. The selection of qualified suppliers was virtually assured when the buyer obtained preliminary proposals to evaluate the need for the requirement in the first step of the procurement loop. If

JOB IMPROVEMENT REQUEST

REGULAR ☐   MINOR-SERVICE ☐

TO: DATE _____

INDUSTRIAL ENGINEERING DEPARTMENT_____

CODE _____ SERIAL NO. _____
JO REL.   JO COMP.
DUE _____   DUE _____

ASSIGNED TO _____
THIS BLOCK FOR INDUSTRIAL ENGINEERING USE ONLY.

REQUESTED BY _____   DEPT. _____ EXT. _____

APPROVED BY _____   REQUIRED DEL. DATE _____

APPROVED BY _____   DELIVER TO _____

THE FOLLOWING CONDITION EXISTS _____
_____
_____
_____

IN THIS LOCATION (REQUIRED ONLY IF "DELIVER TO" LOCATION NOT SPECIFIED) _____
_____

WHICH CAN BE IMPROVED BY _____
_____
_____
_____
_____

TO GIVE THE FOLLOWING RESULT _____
_____
_____
_____

Approved budget allocation. _____
_____
_____

Fig. 4-2.   Capital Expenditure Request Form.

unqualified selections of equipment or supplier had been made at the outset, the evaluation routine recommended earlier should have automatically sifted them out. Nevertheless, one precaution should be noted at this point. There is no substitute for competent purchasing services.

Advantages of Competition.   The tendency to follow traditional paths in the selection of capital equipment and associated sources of supply will prevail unless the total procurement procedure is closely examined by management. As mentioned, the use of well-considered and well-written specifications or work statements will make it relatively easy for the purchasing department to interest suppliers, both established and potential, and to provide a cross section of the market, thus obtaining price, relative quality comparisons, and firm delivery information with a reasonable amount of effort applied.

Budgetary Control within Purchasing.   The purchasing function will always know exactly how much of the company's capital funds are on hand for the procurement of equipment. Such information is available on the authorization-to-purchase document, the Capital Expenditure Request.

CONCLUSION

Planned equipment selection and procurement is attainable with reasonable effort and is essential to the success of a business in a competitive environment. It is wise to follow up all authorized procurement actions through the user and the purchasing department to see that expected performance and service are being obtained.

BIBLIOGRAPHY

Equipment Reporter, "Product News for Western Industry," published monthly, De Roche Publishing Company, Glendale, Calif.

Product News International, published bimonthly, PNI Publishing Company, New York.

Purchasing Week, published weekly, McGraw-Hill Book Company, New York.

Surplus Record—Index of Available Machinery and Equipment, Surplus Record, Inc., Chicago, Ill.

Used Equipment Directory, published monthly, Chapman and Rheinhold, Jersey City, N.J.

Western Machinery and Steel World Buyer's Directory, San Francisco, Calif.

CHAPTER FIVE

Equipment Replacement

M. W. GRANT *Manager of Manufacturing, Executive Staff, Ingersoll-Rand Company, New York, New York*

Equipment replacement programs are important to overall corporate planning because rapid technological change is a permanent factor in industrial corporate life. Corporations must look for competitive advantages through the use of a total, systematic approach to the replacement of equipment.

To have a successful equipment replacement program, it is important that it be organized properly. Ideas must flow up from operating levels and down from the corporate level. At operating levels, there are essentially two approaches used—operating and staff.

The operating approach holds the operating supervisor responsible for acceptance of specific recommendations for equipment replacement and therefore accountable for installation, utilization, and return on investment of the equipment involved.

Usually, the detailed study of a specific project, leading to exact equipment recommendations, will be made by an industrial engineering, methods, or tooling section. To a large degree, the amount of direct involvement of the operating supervision depends on the size of the organization.

A second method of organization places the responsibility with a staff department, usually industrial engineering, to develop a specific program and be accountable for the installation, utilization, and return on investment for an initial period of time. When the project has sufficiently proved itself, it is then turned over to operating personnel.

Whether the operating approach or the staff approach is used, the important organizational consideration is to fix responsibility and accountability.

Because manufacturing is represented at the corporate executive level, it is the corporate manufacturing responsibility to monitor the capital equipment replacement program, to contribute to the establishment of priorities for various projects, and to make operating divisions aware of new and advanced technological thinking that can contribute to recommendations for equipment.

5–44

SYSTEMATIC APPROACH TO EQUIPMENT REPLACEMENT

In an equipment replacement program, there are great dangers of a "hit or miss" analysis. This can be avoided only by a systematic approach to equipment replacement.

A systematic approach must be compatible with the overall goals of manufacturing operations and must be coordinated with plans and forecasts of the sales organization and the engineering organization. This concept is represented graphically by Figure 5-1. It facilitates establishing priorities on various equipment replacement studies and avoids unnecessary and unprofitable studies. It eliminates the acquisition of equipment that is not compatible with long-range plans.

Total Equipment Replacement Program. A total program for equipment replacement is necessary because, in corporations that have more than one type of product or more than one manufacturing location, results of the systematic studies at each location must be put together in the form of an overall or total program.

This total program can then become the corporate plan, and priorities can be established and funding requirements allocated to meet it.

It is also important to recognize that the equipment replacement program is one of the essential pieces of a long-range plan. In planning ahead at least five years, the equipment replacement program charts a long-range course for equipment replacement. This program is in depth for the initial years and represents a general approach for the latter years.

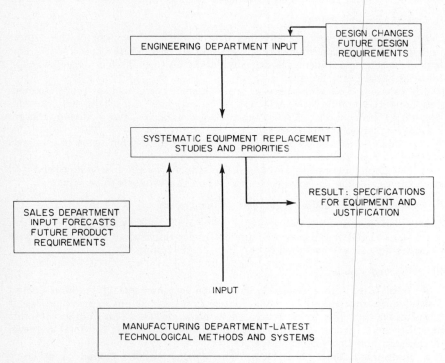

FIG. 5-1. Inputs Required for Systematic Equipment Replacement Studies.

STAFFING FOR EQUIPMENT REPLACEMENT

To make sound equipment replacement studies, specialized personnel are required. These persons usually form the industrial engineering team. They draw on specialized knowledge from operating supervision and outside sources. Many specialized data and services are available from suppliers of equipment.

It is important that the manufacturing manager make sure that these people keep up to date in areas of their specialized knowledge. This can be accomplished in part by having them visit suppliers and attend seminars and expositions.

The specialized personnel required for any equipment replacement study will be determined by the nature of the equipment under consideration. Specialized knowledge may be required in the areas of tooling, numerical control, material handling, facilities, systems, foundries, warehousing and distribution, and the like. Process specialists may be required for such processes as welding, painting, packaging, heat treating, plating, assembly, or fabrication.

JUSTIFICATION OF EQUIPMENT REPLACEMENT

The justification for the expenditure of a large sum of money for a piece of new equipment must be based on an in-depth study of all the costs and savings involved. The study must be carefully made so that no factor is overlooked. Figure 5-2 shows a Project Justification Summary Sheet which has been found useful for summarizing the information collected during an equipment replacement study. The meaning of each item on the form is as follows.

I. Cost of Proposed Project

A. Capital. The amount included here is the total amount of the project that will be capitalized, consistent with present accounting procedures. This includes cost of equipment, freight, foundation, and installation, as well as capitalized standard attachments.

B. Expense. This is the portion of the project costs, such as rearrangement and abnormal tooling cost, which will be expensed consistent with present accounting procedures. These expenses are expected nonrecurring charges due to installation of this project.

C. Value of Assets to Be Salvaged. This is the disposition value of all assets sold due to this project.

D. Net Cash Investment. Net cash investment is equal to the capitalized and expense portion of the project, minus the value of assets to be salvaged.

II. Expenditures Avoided by Investment in This Project

Included in this category are nonrecurring costs such as major repairs which must be incurred if the proposed project is not undertaken. Note that these expenses may also be included in costs for the old system.

III. Estimated Volume

A. Total Direct Labor Hours for Production Requirements in Machine Center. This includes the direct labor hours required on the machine or machine center based upon the units to be produced in each period. The number of units must be equal for the old and the new systems. Note that the total required direct labor hours may exceed capacity.

B. Anticipated Direct Labor Hours Expended in Machine Center. This entry shows the expected direct labor hours that will be expended in the machine

CER. NO. _____   Date _____

Present equipment: Describe name, model No.,
year built, year installed.

      6 Cincinnati Model Y Mills
      Built and installed 1949

Proposed equipment: Preferred-alternate

      Model XX milling machine

Estimated life of project   18   years

I.   Cost of Proposed Project

Capital _250,000_ Expense _12,000_ Total _262,000_
Less value of assets to be salvaged   12,000
Net cash investment $250,000

II.   Expenditures Avoided by Investment in this Project

Recondition or replace existing equipment $10,000   In year 1969
Other — list

III. Estimated Volume

	First Year 19			Second Year 19		
	Old System	New System	Net Change	Old System	New System	Net Change
Machine center (direct labor hours in thousands)						
A. Total D.L. hours for production requirements	42,000	35,700	6,300	42,000	35,700	6,300
B. Anticipated D.L. hours expended in machine center	31,824	31,824	–	31,824	31,824	–
C. Capacity in D.L. hours (basis 120 hrs./week)	37,440	37,440	–	37,440	37,440	–
D. Machine tool utilization (B/C)	85%	85%	–	85%	85%	–
E. Total number of machines in center	6	6	–	6	6	–

IV. Operating Cost Analysis

	Old System	New System	Net Change	Old System	New System	Net Change
A. Continuing cash flow benefits						
1. Direct labor – basis present production	15,912	7,956	7,956	15,912	7,956	7,956
2. Direct labor – in lieu of subcontracting	xxx	7,956	(7,956)	xxx	7,956	(7,956)
3. Subcontracting	132,275	63,336	68,939	132,275	63,336	68,939
4. Direct material	–	–	–	–	–	–
5. Overhead						
a. Industrial engineering	–	8,000	(8,000)	–	8,000	(8,000)
b. Tooling	3,000	1,500	1,500	3,000	1,500	1,500
c. Repairs and maintenance	10,000	–	10,000	–	–	–
d. Spoilage	–	–	–	–	–	–
e. Fringe benefits						
f. Overtime						
g. Other overhead						
Total continuing cash flow	161,187	88,748	72,439	151,187	88,748	62,439
Return on investment	xxx	xxx	29.0%	xxx	xxx	25.0%
B. Operating income effect						
1. Total continuing cash flow	–	–	72,439	–	–	62,439
2. Less depreciation	–	29,400	(29,400)	–	27,600	(27,600)
3. Less expense portion of project	–	12,000	(12,000)	–	–	–
Total operating income effect	–	–	31,039	–	–	34,839
Rate of return	xxx	xxx	12.4%	xxx	xxx	14.0%

FIG. 5-2. Project Justification Summary Sheet.

center under the old and the new systems. Note this may be less than A if subcontracting is anticipated.

C. Capacity in Direct Labor Hours. This is established as 120 hours per week.

D. Machine Tool Utilization. Machine utilization is defined as the direct labor hours to be expended in the machine center, as defined in B, divided by the capacity in direct labor hours which is considered to be 120 hours per week.

E. Number of Machines in Center. The number of machines in the applicable center are listed for the old and new systems.

IV. Operating Cost Analysis

The operating cost analysis section shows benefits expected to accrue from the project. Benefits are separated so that return on investment on a cash flow basis is available as well as the income statement return on the capitalized portion of the project. Note that all expenses are stated on an alternative basis; thus the old system corresponds to the estimated results if this project is not approved. Units produced and subcontracted for the old system and the new system must be comparable; therefore all expenses are stated assuming that output does not exceed 100 percent of present capacity plus a feasible amount of subcontracting.

A. Continuing Cash Flow Benefits

1. *Direct Labor—Basis Present Production.* Expected direct labor costs, excluding fringe benefits, are recorded for a comparable number of units for the old system and the new system if approved. This corresponds to the direct labor on the number of units in "Anticipated direct labor hours expended" for the old system. For the new system, direct labor on additional units produced in the factory instead of subcontracting are included on the next line.

2. *Direct Labor—in Lieu of Subcontracting.* The expected direct labor costs are recorded for those units that will be produced internally under the new system, which would otherwise be subcontracted.

3. *Subcontracting.* Subcontracting cost is shown for the old system as total cost for work performed by the subcontractor. For the new system, the cost for any work to be performed by the subcontractor is included. Note that the number of units produced for the old and the new systems may not be comparable.

4. *Direct Material.* Expected costs are shown if a material saving is anticipated. Units for both systems must be comparable except where material and labor are subcontracted.

5. *Overhead.* Changes in overhead are stated exclusive of the expected expense portion of the project. The expense portion of the project shows abnormal nonrecurring expenses due to installation of the project. Changes in overhead in this category thus reflect expected continuing cost reductions or increases attributable to this project. (See IVB3 for expense portion of the project.)

Where significant changes are anticipated, the following should be treated separately:

a. INDUSTRIAL ENGINEERING.[1] The net change corresponds to the increased number of industrial engineers, method engineers, time study men, programmers, and the like necessitated by the project.

b. TOOLING.[1] Expenses under the old and the new systems are shown as

---

[1] Industrial engineering and tooling expenses, required solely to convert to the new production method, apply to the expense portion of the project.

totals and should include tool design, toolroom, and purchased tools costs, which are of a continuing nature.

c. REPAIRS AND MAINTENANCE. Repairs and maintenance under the old system should correspond to the expected expense if the old machinery were to be used. Note that major repairs included in "II, Expenditures Avoided by Investment in This Project," may apply to the old system.

d, e, f, AND g. Changes in expected spoilage, fringe benefits, overtime, and other overhead should be thoroughly documented.

Total Continuing Cash Flow Benefits. The sum of items 1 through 5g equals the expected continuing cash flow effect of this project.

RETURN ON INVESTMENT. Return on investment is defined as continuing cash flow benefits divided by the net cash investment (defined in I above) times 100.

B. Operating Income Effect. This item shows the effect that the project will have on the profit and loss statement. Thus, noncash charges will be included. This section is completed as follows.

1. Total Continuing Cash Flow Benefits. This figure corresponds to the total cash flow benefits shown under IVA.

2. Depreciation. Depreciation is stated as total for the old and the new systems using the sum-of-the-years digits method or the method normally used by the company. The net increase will be due to installation of the project. Using the sum-of-the-years digits for sixteen-year life yields depreciation of 0.118 and 0.110 of the capitalized portion of the project for the first and second years, respectively.

3. Expense Portion of the Project. This is the figure shown in I above and corresponds to abnormal expenses associated with the project, such as rearrangement, original tooling costs, training, and traveling.

Total Operating Income Effect. This is the sum of items 1, 2, and 3.

RATE OF RETURN. The rate of return is defined as the "Total operating income effect" divided by the "Capitalized portion of the project" times 100.

Project Justification Example

The Project Justification Summary Sheet (Figure 5-2) is filled in with figures gathered during an equipment replacement study. It was proposed that one model XX milling machine should be bought. At the time, there were six milling machines in operation in the machine center, one of which was to be replaced, with the five others remaining in operation. The following describes the completion of sections I through IV of the Project Justification Summary Sheet for this example.

I. Cost of Proposed Project

Capital
Rockford model XX mill (delivered and installed) $220,000
Auxiliary equipment (permanent fixtures, gages, and the like). .   30,000

                                                                  $250,000
Expense
Rearrangement, start-up, training. . . . . $ 12,000
    Total. $262,000

Salvage Value
Selling price of replaced mill.   12,000

Net Cash Investment. $250,000

II. Expenditures Avoided by Investment in This Project

The mill that was to be replaced was in need of extensive rebuilding. It was anticipated that this would cost $10,000 in 1969. Because this expense would be incurred if the new machine were not purchased, it was also considered as an expense of the old system.

III. Estimated Volume

It was expected that in 1969 and 1970, after this machine was installed, 21,000 units would be required. Five old machines plus the proposed machine would be available. Each unit produced requires two hours on present equipment or one hour on the proposed machine.

A. Total Direct Labor Hours for Production Requirements

OLD SYSTEM

$$21,000 \text{ units @ 2 hours per unit} = 42,000 \text{ hours required}$$

NEW SYSTEM. On average, production would take 1.7 hours per unit; that is, in two hours, five old machines produce five units and one new machine produces two units, for a total of seven.

$$\frac{12 \text{ hours}}{7 \text{ units}} = 1.7 \text{ hours per unit}$$

$$21,000 \text{ units} \times 1.7 \text{ hours per unit} = 35,700 \text{ hours required}$$

B. Anticipated Direct Labor Expended in Machine Center.
Under each system, six machines are available. Assuming three-shift operation and 85 percent utilization, it is estimated that direct labor hours expended = 6 machines × 120 hours per week × 52 weeks per machine × 0.85 = 31,824. No weekend work was anticipated.

C. Capacity in Direct Labor Hours

$$120 \text{ hours per week} \times 6 \text{ machines} \times 52 \text{ weeks} = 37,440 \text{ hours}$$

D. Machine Tool Utilization

$$\frac{31,824}{37,440} \times 100 = 85\%$$

IV. Operating Cost Analysis

A. Continuing Cash Flow Benefits.
Because of the interrelationship of the various direct labor and subcontracting alternatives, it was necessary to deal with these in total. For this example, the following approach was used.

1. *Direct Labor.* It was assumed that the direct labor rate would be $3 in 1969 and 1970. Note that for both the old and the new systems the same number of units are produced on the five present machines. For the machine to be replaced, production would be as follows.

OLD SYSTEM

$$\text{Direct labor hours} = 120 \text{ hours per week} \times 52 \text{ weeks} \times 0.85$$
$$= 5,304 \text{ hours or 2,652 units}$$
$$\text{Direct labor hours} = 5,304 \text{ hours @ \$3 per hour} = \$15,912$$

NEW SYSTEM. For the new system to produce an equal number of units, 2,652, would take 2,652 hours.

$$\text{Direct labor dollars} = 2,652 \text{ hours} \times \$3 = \$7,956$$

Note that the anticipated direct labor rate should be used for the applicable period.

2. *Direct Labor in Lieu of Subcontracting.* An additional 2,652 hours would still be available on the new machine. This corresponds to 5,304 hours that were subcontracted under the old system. Direct labor in lieu of subcontracting = 2,652 hours × $3 = $7,956.

3. *Subcontracting.* Under the old system, it would be necessary to subcontract 42,000 − 31,824 = 10,176 hours, or 5,088 units. Assuming a subcontracting cost of $26 per unit, subcontract cost (old system) = 5,088 × $26 = $132,288.

Under the new system, 2,652 more units would be produced in-house; therefore 5,088 − 2,652 = 2,436 units would be subcontracted. Cost = 2,436 × $26 = $63,336.

4. *Direct Material.* The use of this machine would not allow for part redesign that would result in direct material savings.

5. *Overhead*

a. INDUSTRIAL ENGINEERING. Excluding the initial industrial engineering expense included in the expense portion of this project, it was assumed that additional expenses would be incurred each year because the new machine would be numerically controlled. Programming tapes for this machine would require one programmer full time. Therefore, the new system additional expenses were estimated at $8,000 for programming each year.

b. TOOLING. Because of the properties of the new machine, it was estimated that simplified jigs and fixtures could be used. Assuming $3,000 of expenses per year for these items under the old system and only $1,500 per year under the new, a saving of $1,500 per year would result.

c. REPAIRS AND MAINTENANCE. It was assumed that maintenance of the new machine would be essentially the same as on the one to be replaced. However, if the old machine were kept, the $10,000 for rebuilding expense would be incurred in 1969. This, then, became a net saving. Note that for this case it was assumed that this repair would all be expensed.

No other overhead savings or extra expenses were anticipated.

Total Continuing Cash Flow. This is the sum of items 1 through 5g above.

RETURN ON INVESTMENT

1969: $\dfrac{72,439}{250,000} \times 100 = 29.0\%$

1970: $\dfrac{62,439}{250,000} \times 100 = 25.0\%$

B. Operating Income Effect

1. *Total Continuing Cash Flow.* This is as shown above.

2. *Depreciation.* The present six machines would be twenty years old in 1969 and would thus be fully depreciated. Old system depreciation is zero. Using sum-of-the-years digits method for the new machine and start-up at the beginning of the year would yield depreciation as follows.

1969: $\dfrac{16}{136} \times 250,000 = 29,400$

1970: $\dfrac{15}{136} \times 250,000 = 27,600$

3. *Expense Portion of Project.* It was anticipated that all the expense portion of the project shown in section I would be incurred in 1969.

RATE OF RETURN

1969: $\dfrac{31,039}{250,000} \times 100 = 12.4\%$

1970: $\dfrac{34,839}{250,000} \times 100 = 14\%$

TYPES OF EQUIPMENT REPLACEMENT PROJECTS

Generally, the major reasons for equipment replacement can be reduced to the following types:

1. Replacement to reduce or eliminate excessive downtime on worn-out machines (obsolescence)
2. Replacement to reduce product costs that have increased due to inaccurate or permanently damaged machine tools (bent ways or excessive wear in bearings, gears, and the like)
3. Replacement due to new metal removal technology or fabricating methods
4. Replacement to eliminate the need for highly skilled setup men and machine tool operators
5. Replacement to reduce cost of jigs, tools, and fixtures
6. Replacement to reduce lead time and inventories
7. Replacement to accomplish product design requirements (tolerances, finishes, and the like)

Each of these will require record keeping and documentation to measure relative performance. "Excessive downtime" can be interpreted many ways, but sufficient documentation from well-maintained records will greatly add to the presentation and in the justification.

FOLLOW-UP AND MEASUREMENT

Equipment replacement projects as part of a total capital equipment program must be measured and controlled. Naturally, the magnitude of the project will have an important bearing on the degree of measurement and control established.

The important areas to be measured are project start-up time, equipment utilization, and equipment savings. All three areas will affect the return on investment.

The Investment Report. Figure 5-3 shows a typical four-part capital investment report.

Columns 1, 2, 3, and 4 of part A identify the project, its priority, the individual who is the project head, and the total cost of the investment.

Columns 5 through 15 of part B identify important progress checkpoints to ensure prompt start-up of the project. This covers the progress from date of approval of funds until the date the division actually starts reporting savings.

Important areas for consideration are checked along the way. An illustration is column 8, "Operator and Maintenance Training." The report ensures that the division will consider the training of the personnel who will man the equipment and those who will maintain it. It encourages the division to accomplish the training so that the project start-up time will not be adversely influenced by failure to do so.

Columns 18 through 28 of parts C and D show monthly savings and then convert these to an annualized rate. They show the number of months that the project has been reporting savings. The number of months that a project should be followed will vary according to company policy, but as an example, the following ground rules might be used.

$500,000 and over	24 months
$100,000 to $499,999	12 months
Under $100,000	6 months

CER or Project No.	Priority Hi=1,Low=5	Description of Project	Project Head Responsible	Cost	
				Capital	Expense
(1)	(1a)	(2)	(3)	(4)	(4)

(A)

Progress Checkpoints (By Date)													Mach. No.
Approved	Order Placed	NC Preparation	Oper. & Maint. Training	Found. Installed	Equip. Installed	Equip. Rec'd.	Equip. Installed	Est or Act. (Approve Pay.)	Operational (Incl. Time All.)	Report Act. Saving	Est. Date Rep. Saving		
(5)	(6)	(7)	(8)	(9)	(10)	(11)	(12)	(13)	(14)	(15)	(16)		(17)

(B)

Current Monthly Savings					No. Mos. Reporting
Direct Labor		Other		Cum. Total Actual	
CER Est.	Act.	CER Est.	Act.		
(18)	(19)	(20)	(21)	(22)	(23)

(C)

External Distribution: 1. Group Vice Pres.
2. Mgr. Mfg, Exec. Staff
3. Division Gen. Mgr.
4. Manufacturing Engineering Services, F.S.D.

Sheet _____
of ____ Sheets

Projected Annual Savings Rate (Average last 3 mos. Actual ×12)					% Utilization of :				% Rate of Return	
Direct Labor		Other		Total Variance + (−)	Hrs. Available (120/wk.)		Hrs. Scheduled			
CER Est.	Act.	CER Est.	Act.		CER Est.	Act.	CER Est.	Act.	CER Est.	Act.
(24)	(25)	(26)	(27)	(28)	(29)	(30)	(31)	(32)	(33)	(34)

(D)

FIG. 5-3. The Investment Report.

Colums 29 through 32 of part *D* report the utilization of equipment against a three-shift, forty-hour-per-week operation, showing estimates versus actuals and what the division is scheduling for equipment versus the 120 hours that are available.

Columns 33 and 34 reflect the rate of return, showing the actual versus the estimate. For this analysis, the straight payback method is used.

Report Distribution. The external distribution of the capital investment report shows how operating management (division general manager and group vice president), corporate staff management (manager of manufacturing—executive staff), and manufacturing engineering services are involved in the follow-up procedure.

In conclusion, it is well to summarize that equipment replacement programs depend upon the following:

1. A total systematic approach
2. Proper manpower organization
3. Suitable financial justification
4. Necessary follow-up procedures

BIBLIOGRAPHY

Burder, C. H., "Machine Tool Purchase and Replacement Costs," *Machinery and Production Engineering,* June 29, 1966.
Haynes, W. W., *Managerial Economics,* Dorsey Press, Homewood, Ill., 1963.

CHAPTER SIX

Equipment Leasing and Rental

JAMES N. KELLY *President, Manager Analysis Center Incorporated, Cambridge, Massachusetts*

Leasing has become a commonly accepted method of obtaining practically any type of equipment used by a manufacturer, retailer, or consumer. Pictures, glasses, beds, construction equipment, airplanes, trucks—almost anything can be obtained through a lease transaction. The very omnipresence of leasing makes it essential that the manufacturing manager be familiar with the nature of leasing transactions and with commonly used techniques for determining the desirability of entering into a lease arrangement.

Unfortunately there is no easy rule of thumb which can be applied to determine when a leasing arrangement might make economic sense. Each leasing transaction must be evaluated in light of the company's financial condition and the terms of the lease.

ADVANTAGES AND DISADVANTAGES OF LEASING

The advantages attributed to leasing rather than buying equipment are numerous, often redundant, and usually unclear. To many manufacturing managers, the following claims about leasing will be quite familiar:

A company is absolutely insane if it owns its own forklift trucks. The headaches of maintenance and taxes alone make it worthwhile to sign an operating lease with a firm which specializes in forklift rentals and therefore has a huge fleet of trucks at its disposal.

This machine is available on a long-term lease basis. If you prefer to conserve your working capital and not tie it up in capital assets, you can still obtain the use of the machine by paying a very low monthly lease payment.

By leasing this mixing machine you can receive 100 percent financing, which will never appear on the company's balance sheet and will leave your normal lines of bank credit undisturbed.

The advantages attributed to leasing are practically as numerous as the number of lease plans available to the equipment purchaser. Professor Richard F. Vancil compiled the following list of advantages and disadvantages of leasing in his comprehensive book, *Leasing of Industrial Equipment:*[1]

Advantages of Leasing. From the point of view of the lessee, some writers claim that equipment leasing offers the following advantages:

1. Frees working capital for more productive use (since money is not tied up in low-yielding fixed assets)
2. May cost less than other methods of acquiring equipment
3. May permit more rapid amortization of the equipment than would be possible using Schedule F depreciation
4. May increase the firm's ability to acquire funds
5. Avoids the restrictions frequently found in loan agreements
6. Establishes only a restricted (not a general) obligation against the company which may be satisfied by payment of one year's rent in bankruptcy or three years' rent in reorganization
7. Does not appear as a liability on the lessee's balance sheet
8. Leaves normal lines of bank credit undisturbed
9. Permits 100 percent financing (as against 75 or 80 percent through other methods)
10. Creates an allowable cost (including interest cost) under government contracts
11. Permits hedging of business risks (primarily the risk of obsolescence)
12. Minimizes danger of being oversold
13. Assures more adequate servicing
14. Offers the convenience of making only one periodic lease payment (rather than separate payments for debt service, maintenance costs, insurance, property taxes, etc.)
15. May be tailored to the lessee's needs more easily than ordinary financing
16. Avoids the necessity of selling equipment no longer wanted
17. Permits middle management executives to acquire new equipment without going through formal appropriation request procedures
18. Provides cost cutting equipment to be installed immediately
19. Acts as a hedge against inflation
20. Provides long-term financing without diluting ownership or control
21. Pays for equipment out of before-tax savings rather than after-tax profits

Disadvantages of Leasing. From the point of view of the lessee, some writers claim that equipment leasing has the following disadvantages:

1. Charges a higher interest rate (than the lessee's regular interest rate)
2. May provide less attractive tax deductions (than interest plus accelerated depreciation)
3. Gives any residual value of the equipment to the lessor
4. Establishes a fixed obligation against the company
5. Reduces the flexibility to dispose of obsolete equipment (before the end of the lease term)
6. Does not provide the prestige that goes with ownership
7. Raises the fear of dispossession if payments are not made during hard times

Many of these advantages and disadvantages are purely subjective and cannot by themselves be scrutinized by quantitative analysis. It is impossible to quantify the advantage of the convenience often attributed to leasing, or the disadvantage that leasing rather than owning equipment might reduce the lessee's feeling of prestige. In most cases, lessors who make these subjective claims about leasing expect that their arguments will be accepted without

[1] Richard F. Vancil, *Leasing of Industrial Equipment,* McGraw-Hill Book Company, New York, 1963, pp. 6–7.

further analysis. They act as though the mere compilation of a large number of stated advantages for leasing is enough to allow the decision maker to decide to enter a lease transaction. Rarely does a lessor mention the true effective rate of interest that is included in the lease payment. Lessors want you to accept their plan with no greater analysis than deciding that you need equipment and that the lessor is offering a very convenient method of obtaining it.

The fact is that leasing can and should be subjected to quantitative analysis and need not be accepted on merely subjective grounds. This does not mean that these subjective arguments are meaningless, but rather that a potential lessee should accurately quantify what it costs to obtain the convenience of lease financing or what is saved by sacrificing the prestige of equipment ownership. Quantifying the cost of leasing is not easy and should probably be done by the financial department of the company. However, the manufacturing manager should know enough about the analysis of leasing to be able to determine (1) when lease financing might be worth pursuing, (2) what policies should be established within his department concerning leasing, and (3) when the financial department should be consulted.

CLASSIFICATION OF LEASING PLANS

For analytical purposes, leases are commonly divided into two categories: financial leases and operating leases or rentals. As the leasing industry expands and becomes more complex, the difference between these two transactions becomes shaded, but still it is possible and necessary to draw a distinction between them to talk intelligently and meaningfully about leasing. Financial leases, in the general use of the word, are leases that commit the lessee to a series of payments which in total will exceed the original cost of the equipment. The crucial word in this definition is "commit." A financial lease, like an installment loan, is a legal commitment to pay for the entire cost of the equipment plus interest over a specified period of time. In normal circumstances, a financial lease will not include provisions for maintenance or taxes, which are therefore paid separately by the lessee. In a financial lease, the lessor is fulfilling a primarily financial function.

At the other extreme, an operating lease or rental agreement is defined as a contract in which the lessee is not committed to paying more than the original cost of the equipment during the contractual period. An operating lease usually includes maintenance and taxes so that the lessee has no other significant expenses in obtaining and using the equipment than what is paid to the lessor. In this type of transaction, the lessor is assuming the risk of obsolescence or underutilization of the equipment. The lease might be for a day, a week, a month, or a year, but it is the lessor's responsibility to see that when the lease period ends, another lessee will be ready to utilize the equipment. By the same token, in this type of contract the financial function fulfilled by the lessor is insignificant—the most important service performed is assuming the risk of obsolescence.

These two types of leases are radically different and therefore require radically different policies and procedures on the part of a manufacturing manager. As in any capital investment, both an operating lease and a financial lease should be economically justified before they are approved. Thus, it is important that policies concerning lease transactions be included in the company's capital budgeting procedures and that a manager be aware of the pitfalls connected with evaluating either an operating or a financial lease.

LEASING POLICIES FOR THE MANUFACTURING MANAGER

Financial Leasing Policies. The basic principle of capital budgeting is that the decision concerning how capital is to be used should be separated from the decision concerning how capital is to be obtained. This division of responsibility between the use of funds and the source of funds is evident in most companies' capital budgeting procedures. The manufacturing manager determines a need for capital equipment and submits an estimate of the savings associated with the equipment to the financial manager. If the equipment satisfies the company's minimum requirement for return on investment, it is approved, and the financial manager is charged with the responsibility of obtaining the funds to finance the equipment.

The difficulty of financial leases is that these two different decisions in the capital budgeting process, the use of funds and the source of funds, are closely intertwined. The intertwining of traditionally separate capital budgeting decisions is often exploited by the leasing company to the detriment of the lessee. By leasing, the manufacturing manager can often avoid the normal capital budgeting procedures and make decisions concerning both the use and source of funds by himself, without the approval of the financial department.

In many instances, a financial leasing company's success has resulted, not from the economy of its service to lessees, but from its ability to short-circuit the normal capital budgeting channels, thereby giving the manufacturing manager the power to obtain capital equipment quickly without authorization from the financial department. Consider the following real case histories.

1. One plant manager in a large manufacturing operation obtained a $10,000 lathe by signing a five-year financial lease. The lease included interest at 13 percent, twice the company's bank borrowing rate, but the manager signed the lease because he (1) did not know the rate of interest included in the lease and (2) did not want to submit the normal capital requests to the financial department.

2. The division manager of a diversified company avoided the normal capital budgeting procedures for a new warehouse facility by signing a twenty-five-year financial lease. The manager claimed that "the warehouse would not have met the company's minimum return on investment (15 percent) but was essential for the division. Anyway, the interest rate in the lease was only 11 percent."

3. A warehouse manager signed a three-year financial lease for five forklift trucks. The manager knew that there was enough surplus in his annual budget to cover the lease payments and was afraid that it would be difficult to obtain approval of the trucks through the capital budgeting system.

The danger of this kind of independent action by nonfinancial managers is not only that the savings from the equipment leased might not be as high as the company's minimum standards, but also that the interest cost included in the lease payments might be higher than the company needs to pay to borrow capital. In general, leasing is more expensive than financing equipment through a banking institution. This higher cost is sometimes justified by special considerations such as the company's tax situation, the company's feeling about showing debt on its balance sheet, or the mere convenience of lease financing. Thus, preventing financial leasing from being used improperly is not as simple as establishing a policy that the company will under no circumstances enter into financial leases. Rather, the policy should be designed to permit the consideration of leasing, but at the same time preserve the traditional split between the manufacturing manager and the financial manager in the capital budgeting process.

The best policy for the manufacturing manager to follow, regardless of the size of the company and, within reason, the size of the lease, is that all financial leases should be presented to and approved by the financial department. The manufacturing manager should restrict his attention to (1) determining that the equipment is worth obtaining regardless of how it is financed, and (2) making certain that the financial department is aware of leasing plans through which the equipment can be obtained.

Policies for Operating Leases (Rentals). In operating leases, the company is not committed to paying more than the cost of the equipment, and therefore financial considerations are not as important as in financial leases. The important considerations in operating leases are (1) the utilization of equipment and (2) the risk of equipment obsolescence. Both these considerations are the domain of the manufacturing manager, not the financial manager. Thus, although policies for financial leases exclude the manufacturing manager, policies for operating leases must directly involve the manufacturing manager.

Operating leases are understandably expensive. Renting a forklift truck on a monthly basis for a solid year would cost almost as much as the original cost of the equipment. This is understandable because the lessor plans to have some months when the equipment will not be leased at all—the lessor is absorbing the risk of underutilization of the equipment.

Recognizing the legitimately high cost of operating leases, there are at least two dangers which the manufacturing manager must prevent. First, a short-term, one-week or one-month rental can become a permanent part of the company's equipment by neglect or default. Examples of this danger are numerous. They are caused by a lack of control over rental equipment which the manager must act to prevent.

The second danger results not from a lack of control, but from failure to analyze the economics of an operating lease transaction. The following example is not unusual:

A large electronic appliance manufacturer operates a fleet of twenty-five forklift trucks in one of its manufacturing facilities. The trucks are all rented under a rental agreement requiring only thirty days' notice for cancellation. The rental arrangement is justified because: "We are in the appliance business, not the forklift business. We just can't worry about maintaining a few forklift trucks and at the same time accomplish our primary mission—producing appliances."

This argument is not without merit. However, it is impossible to judge the strength of the argument without measuring the extra cost which the company is incurring in exchange for the convenience of renting its trucks. How to analyze this type of lease will be discussed in a moment. From a policy standpoint, the most important consideration is ensuring that a large rental expenditure will be quantitatively evaluated as a normal procedure.

Probably the best way to ensure that rentals do not get out of control is to maintain a tickler file of rental equipment according to when the equipment was originally scheduled to go off rental. Continuation of the rental beyond the original completion date will then have to be reevaluated and approved. If the volume of rental equipment is not large, a simple notation and review by a lower manager or secretary might be all that is required.

At a broader level, the best way to ensure that rental expenditures are controlled and periodically evaluated is to include an analysis of large rentals in the normal annual capital budgeting review. The manufacturing manager should make it a policy to review annually the company's rental status and determine what the company might save by owning rather than renting equipment.

EVALUATING LEASE OPPORTUNITIES

It would be convenient to know unequivocally that leasing is desirable under certain general conditions and not desirable under other conditions. However, this is not possible. The only general condition which might make leasing unusually attractive occurs when a company is in a tax situation which prohibits the use of investment tax credits, accelerated depreciation, or other tax benefits. In normal circumstances, and even in unusual tax circumstances, each individual leasing opportunity has to be analyzed quantitatively before a decision can be made to lease, rent, or buy the equipment.

Analyzing Financial Leases. A financial lease commits a company to pay the full cost of the equipment plus interest over a specified period of time. Thus, even though the liability is not always reflected on a balance sheet, a financial lease places a company in debt just as though a loan had been taken from a bank. Analyzing financial leases, therefore, involves two steps: (1) justifying the equipment independently of how it is to be financed, and (2) if the equipment can be justified, determining the desirability of financing the equipment with a financial lease.

The first step is no different from any other capital budgeting analysis. The hardest part of the analysis is measuring the cash flows associated with the investment. These cash flows include such items as the future savings or income which will be received by buying the equipment, the tax shield from depreciating the equipment, and the original cost of the equipment. The equipment can be economically justified if the cash flows discounted at the company's minimum return on investment results in a positive "net present value" to the company.

The entire capital budgeting technique cannot be explained in one short paragraph or without giving examples. It is not the intention of this chapter to explain capital budgeting, but rather to point out that before any analysis of lease financing is conducted, the equipment should first meet the test of the company's traditional capital budgeting procedures.

If the equipment under consideration meets the requirements of the capital budgeting system, the second step is to analyze the desirability of financing the equipment through a financial lease. The issue to be determined at this stage of the analysis is: "Should the company lease or borrow to finance the equipment?" Analyzing this issue is not easy and, as indicated earlier, should be done by the financial department. The best technique developed to complete this analysis is called the "Borrowing Opportunity Rate" method. This method is described in depth in Richard F. Vancil's Book, *Leasing of Industrial Equipment.*[2]

Analyzing a financial lease is complicated and should be done by a financial specialist. From the manufacturing manager's point of view, the important thing to realize is that a financial lease involves a financial commitment to the company similar to a bank loan. Thus, although it is the manufacturing manager's responsibility to inform the treasurer of leasing programs, he should

[2] *Ibid.*, p. 101.

not take it upon himself to analyze financial leases or to commit the company to a long-term financial leasing contract.

Analyzing Operating Leases. The analysis of operating leases is more directly the responsibility of the manufacturing manager. An operating lease does not require a financial commitment from the company and is therefore not of direct concern to the treasurer or financial officer.

As in a financial lease, analyzing an operating lease involves two steps. First, the equipment must be economically justified. This is accomplished by comparing the savings or income which the company will realize with the cost of obtaining the equipment under an operating lease. If the savings are less than the lease cost, the operating lease is ruled out, but an additional analysis must be made to determine if it might be economical for the company to purchase the equipment. This is a normal capital budgeting analysis and does not require additional explanation.

If the income or savings exceed the operating lease cost, the second stage of analysis is required. This stage involves comparing the annual cost of the operating lease with the cost of owning the equipment directly. The savings or income resulting from the equipment are not relevant at this point. The savings have already been used to justify the rental of the equipment. The purpose of this second stage is to determine the economic benefit of committing the company financially by investing in the equipment rather than renting.

The most difficult aspect of this analysis is determining all the costs, including maintenance, taxes, insurance, and so on, which are included in the lease payment but must be paid separately if the company owns the equipment. This difficulty causes many managers to avoid comparing owning and leasing in any formal way. They are willing to decide subjectively that it is or is not economical to pay their own maintenance, insurance, and taxes. However, the difficulty of estimating costs need not stop the manager from calculating what these expenses would have to total to make leasing more attractive than owning. The following simple example demonstrates how this is possible.

Lease or Buy—Sample Calculation. The Meyer Manufacturing Company leased five of the twenty-five forklift trucks utilized in its plant. These five trucks were required to fill the company's peak demand which occurred from August to December. The lease contract was for a minimum of four months, with thirty days' notice of cancellation after the minimum period. Historically, the company used these five trucks an average of five months per year. Maintenance, taxes, insurance, and equipment cost were included in the monthly lease payment of $225 per truck. A new truck had an estimated useful life of five years and a cost of $3,600.

Mr. Parker, the manufacturing manager, was considering buying some or all of the five rented forklift trucks and asked a member of the treasurer's office to calculate the cost of owning the equipment before consideration of maintenance and other variable expenses. The analyst prepared Tables 1 and 2 for Mr. Parker's review. These tables were constructed as follows:

Table 6-1. Equivalent Annual Cost of Forklift Equipment. This table contains a calculation of, first, the net present value cost of one forklift truck. This cost includes the original cost ($3,600) less the present value of the depreciation tax shield which the equipment will generate. Thus, after considering taxes and the time value of money, the net present value cost is $2,147. Using a 10 percent discount factor, $2,147 is equivalent to $566 of

TABLE 6-1.   Equivalent Annual Cost of Forklift Equipment

	Sum of years' depreciation	Depreciation tax shield, 50%	Present value factor, 10%	Present value
Original cost......................				$ 3,600
Less: Depreciation tax shield				
Year 1..........................	$1,200	$ 600	0.91	$ (546)
2..........................	970	485	0.83	(403)
3..........................	720	360	0.75	(270)
4..........................	470	235	0.68	(160)
5..........................	240	120	0.62	(74)
Total..........................	$3,600	$1,800	3.79	$(1,453)
Net present value cost..............				$ 2,147

Equivalent annual cost: $2,147 ÷ 3.79 = $566

cost per year.   Thus, the equivalent annual cost of just the capital expense of owning one forklift truck is $566.

Table 6-2.   Comparison of Owning and Renting Forklift Equipment. Table 6-2 compares the after-tax cost of renting for 4, 5, 6, and 7 months per year with the equivalent annual cost of owning the equipment. The difference between these two costs is available to pay for maintenance, insurance, taxes, and the like each year.   As shown in the table, leasing for five months per year is less expensive than owning, even before variable expenses are considered.   However, if the machines were to be rented for six months per year, $218 would be available annually to cover the cost of owning and maintaining the equipment. On the basis of this analysis, Mr. Parker decided to continue renting the equipment for at least another year.

TABLE 6-2.   Comparison of Owning and Renting Forklift Equipment

Months of utilization per year	Rental cost	Rental cost after taxes, 50%	Equivalent annual cost of equipment (Table 6-1)	Funds available for maintenance, insurance, and taxes per year	
				After tax	Before tax
4	$ 900	$450	$566	$(116)	
5	1,125	562	566	(4)	
6	1,350	675	566	109	$218
7	1,575	787	566	221	442

CONCLUSION

Convenience alone is not enough justification for entering into either a financial or an operating lease. Each individual lease can and should be analyzed to determine whether the company should lease or borrow, in the case of financial leases; or whether it should lease or buy, in the case of operating leases. Once such an analysis has been made, it is then possible to relate the cost or savings of leasing with the subjective benefits or weaknesses of leasing, to arrive at a final decision.

BIBLIOGRAPHY

Abate, R. P., "Understanding Leasing and Lease Financing," *Robert Morris Associates Bulletin*, May, 1967.

Bower, R. S., "Lease Evaluation," *Accounting Review*, April, 1966.

Engelbourg, S., "Some Consequences of the Leasing of Industrial Machinery," *Journal of Business*, January, 1966.

Hata, K., "Decision Curve for Lease or Buy," *Management Services*, January, 1967.

Shaw, R. B., "Beating High Cost Capital Spending by Leasing and Renting," *Magazine of Wall Street*, June 25, 1966.

Steinberg, S., "Why Lease Capital Equipment?" *Systems*, July, 1966.

"Unscrambling the Claims about Leasing," *Administrative Management*, May, 1966.

Vancil, Richard F., *Leasing of Industrial Equipment*, McGraw-Hill Book Company, New York, 1963.

White, H. R., "Lease or Buy Equipment?" *Graphic Arts Monthly*, January, 1967.

Material Handling Devices

L. WEST SHEA *Managing Director, The Material Handling Institute, Inc., Pittsburgh, Pennsylvania*

Material flow is one of the major factors in determining the size, shape, and general arrangement of any manufacturing facility. It also dictates the placement of machines. Material flow depends upon—and is almost synonymous with—material handling.

A product, part, or material is of little value unless it is in the right place at the right time. Movements of material must mesh with other operations in as nearly perfect a sequence as possible. Storage of raw materials, parts, and semifinished or finished products involves material handling, as does the positioning of parts and materials convenient to operators and machines in work areas.

Material handling also is concerned with the transportation of raw materials and finished products and the warehousing (stocking, order picking, assembly of orders, packing, shipping) and distribution of raw materials and finished products.

Therefore, in any manufacturing facility, material handling plays a major role. It embraces all the basic operations involved in the movement of any kind of material by any means—from the receiving of raw materials to the shipping and distribution of finished products.

NATURE AND ORGANIZATION OF MATERIAL HANDLING

In following a raw material through production to finished product, there are seven fairly definable material handling functions:
1. Transportation of raw materials
2. Receiving
3. Storage
4. In-process handling

5. Handling at the workplace
6. Warehousing
7. Distribution

The handling of materials usually does not shape, form, process, or change a material or product in any way. In some cases, however, material handling operations are performed within a processing operation. For example, a conveyor may move products through an oven, paint booth, testing room, or freezer, and the product is processed during movement.

Perhaps the best way to grasp the true meaning of material handling is to consider the basic processes and procedures in any manufacturing facility that are affected by material handling.

Motion. Parts, materials, and finished products must be moved from one place to another. Material handling is the process of moving them in the most efficient manner.

Time. Each step or process in a particular industry requires that supplies be available at the moment that they are needed. Material handling techniques must assure that no plant or customer need will be hampered by having materials arrive on location too late or even too early. Materials must arrive at a workplace, service location, or customer at the right time.

Quantity. Rate of demand varies among operations in any particular production process. It is the responsibility of the material handling function to provide each operation with the exact quantity of the right materials.

Space. Storage space, used and unused, is a major element in any facility —it costs money. Space requirements and control of inventory are greatly influenced by the material flow pattern.

Add the above four elements together, and the basic purpose of material handling is defined. These four elements cannot be considered independently —each affects the other. To design an optimum system, all elements must be properly integrated so that their combined performance results in smooth, efficient, safe handling of materials, parts, and products.

To summarize, the overall success of any manufacturing operation, large or small, depends to a great extent on the efficiency of material handling.

SELECTING MATERIAL HANDLING EQUIPMENT

There are so many types and kinds of material handling equipment—from wheelbarrows to computer-controlled robots—that merely choosing the right equipment, in terms of size, degree of sophistication, function, and cost, is sometimes difficult. However, a nonexpert in the field can make a reasonably intelligent selection for his particular industry or specific job if he approaches the problem in a logical manner.

Reduced to its simplest form, equipment selection involves the following nonmathematical relationship (see Figure 7-1):

What + where + when → how   (equipment specifications)

What. What covers the material to be handled (solid, liquid, gas); its characteristics (fragile, rugged); and its size, shape, and weight.

Where. Where includes everything involved with the path to be followed by material from the point of origin through various production processes, until it is in the customer's hands. Factors involved are: type of movement (horizontal, elevating, lowering, incline), length of movement, limitations to movement, and in-transit operations (processing, inspecting, storing, weighing).

When. When involves scheduling of parts, products, or materials so that

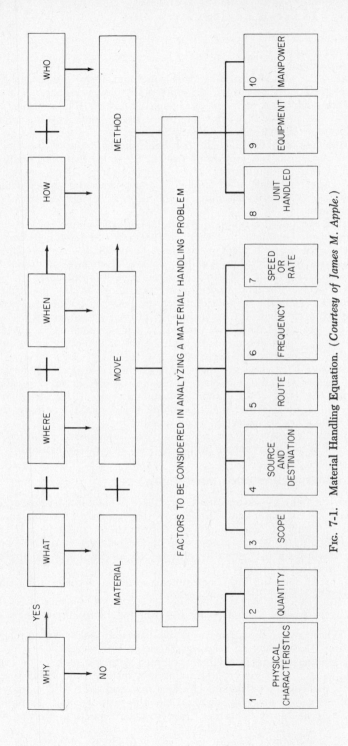

Fig. 7-1. Material Handling Equation. (*Courtesy of James M. Apple.*)

they arrive in the right place, at the right time, in the right quantity. Each cycle of need throughout the total production and distribution system must be considered.

Nature of the materials to be moved affects not only the choice of basic handling equipment, but also pallets, tote boxes, and pickup, loading, or holding devices, if they are not integral with the handling equipment. Affinities between the form of the material and a particular holding attachment often make a choice obvious, and the variety of slings, clamps, push-pull, rotating, and vacuum handling devices available gives the user a number of choices.

Another factor that influences the choice of material handling equipment is the difference in form of materials before and after processing. The spectrum of forms encountered during processing also influences equipment choice, because manufacturing is principally dedicated to changing the shape of things. Materials, parts, or finished products will vary in configuration from the worst possible—which may be something awkward in shape, unbalanced in weight, bristling with protuberances, and practically impossible to grab hold of—to simple shapes like rigid and nonrigid sheets and bars, tote boxes, and other symmetrical forms.

The ideal manufacturing operation is one in which the raw materials arrive at the starting point at exactly the right time and in the quantities required and are transformed in size and shape as they move in a straight line for the shortest possible distance. The customer picks up the finished product as soon as it comes off the final assembly line. This, of course, is an ideal and highly unlikely sequence.

However, the manufacturing process itself—all that goes on between the receiving and the shipping docks—can and must be rigorously controlled if costs are to be kept in line.

Common carriers—trucks, freight cars, aircraft, ships—condition both ends of the manufacturing process. Vehicles that deliver incoming or dispatch outgoing materials influence the type of handling devices needed on loading docks.

Similarly, many other factors determine specific equipment requirements. For example, could more efficient handling equipment be used by changing the form, shape, or container in which material is handled? Should certain raw materials be purchased in different form or be packaged differently for quicker unloading and storage?

These and many other questions often can be discussed and evaluated by suppliers and customers, resulting in advantages to both. They also illustrate how material handling is related intimately to other industrial operations.

TYPES OF MATERIAL HANDLING EQUIPMENT

For convenience, material handling equipment can be grouped under the following classifications:

1. Conveyors
2. Industrial vehicles
3. Overhead equipment
4. Containers and supports
5. Positioning, weighing, and control equipment

Each of these major types of equipment can be further divided into sub-groups, as shown in Table 7-1.

There is a sharp division among equipment for handling liquids; bulk

TABLE 7–1.   Selected Types of Material Handling Equipment

Conveyors	Industrial Vehicles
Belt	*Floor Trucks*
Closed	Dollies
Flat	Hand lift
Troughed	Platform
Bucket	Portable elevator
Cable	Sheet feed table
Chain	Two-wheel hand
Apron	*Industrial Tractor*
Arm	*Powered Industrial Truck*
Car or pallet	Crane
Cross bar	Forklift
Drag chain	Load carrier
Flight	Narrow aisle
Power and free	Platform
Pusher bar	Side loading
Rolling chain	Straddle
Slat	Travel loader
Sliding chain	
Suspended tray	
Tow	
Trolley	**Overhead Equipment**
Chute	
Pneumatic	*Cranes*
Roller	Bridge
Gravity	Gantry
Live	Jib
Rack	Pillar
Spiral	*Hoists*
Screw	*Monorails*
Tube	
Trough	
Wheel	
Ball table	**Containers and Supports**
Gravity	
Live	Pallets
Rack	Pallet boxes
Spiral	Racks
Wheel table	Skids
Special	Skid boxes
Pallet loader	Shipping containers

(loose) solids; parts and equipment; and packaged products. Yet pipelines, traditionally reserved for liquids, are suitable for many finely divided solids. A belt conveyor that will handle parts and equipment will also handle packages or bulk materials.

Thus, equipment for handling inherently different types of materials is often more versatile than realized and may defy rigid classification. As stated above, however, there are five major classes of equipment on which there is fairly general agreement.

Conveyors.   By definition, a conveyor is a device used to carry material over a fixed route.   The breadth of this definition, however, makes the classification, "conveyor," a veritable catch-all.

Equipment classed as conveyors includes the familiar moving belt, screw conveyors which use a propellerlike screw to move materials, and pneumatic and hydraulic conveyors which are actually pipelines through which materials are sucked or pumped.

Each of these types has myriad subdivisions. There are flat-belt conveyors, bucket conveyors, slat conveyors, monorail conveyors, gravity-roller conveyors, and many other types. There are conveyors to handle bulk or packaged material, small items or big ones; to move parts up, down, or horizontally; or merely to hold them suspended.

Not every type of conveyor can do every job or move in all directions. A screw conveyor, for example, will handle only bulk materials—and only those which will not be damaged by crushing—and it will move them in only one direction. A belt conveyor, on the other hand, can be designed to handle almost anything except liquids (unless they are containerized).

Although conveyors carry materials along a fixed path, this does not imply lack of flexibility. For example, conveyors may remain fixed, but materials can be directed to any one of several end points by arranging the conveyor system so that material can be fed from one conveyor to another by a gate or switching system. Furthermore, conveyors need not be stationary except while in operation. It is possible to obtain portable, lightweight units that can be moved easily from one location to another and set up as needed.

Monorail systems, sometimes classed as conveyors and sometimes considered as hoists or cranes, also are versatile. A monorail usually consists of an overhead track from which can be hung any one of a number of types of wheeled hooks, racks, baskets, and operator cabs for transporting a variety of parts and materials.

Overhead trolley conveyors are particularly useful as "live storage" conveyors. Racks or baskets suspended from a closed-circuit track will ride parts around overhead—in space often wasted—until the parts are needed, bringing them past the point of use at regular intervals.

Industrial Vehicles. This category contains a vast panorama of trucks and tractors developed for in-plant, warehouse, or other areas in and immediately around manufacturing, warehousing, or receiving and shipping facilities. These vehicles range from the wheelbarrow to powered equipment like forklift and platform trucks.

Powered industrial vehicles are versatile pieces of handling equipment. They have great mobility and can handle almost any type of material with proper palletization or containerization. In addition to the standard forklift and platform types which are used to pick up and carry unit loads, pallets, and skids, industrial trucks can be fitted with a variety of special attachments—rams for handling rolls of paper or metal, special clamps for packaged unit loads, rotating heads to facilitate dumping of bins, and numerous other special purpose manipulating mechanisms.

Available in both guided and driven models, industrial trucks can be powered by diesel, gasoline, propane, or electric propulsion. They are available in almost any desired lifting capacity, based on the size or weight of materials that they are expected to handle.

In addition, there are industrial tractor-trailer systems which combine a puller unit (lift truck or tractor) with a train of wheeled carts on which loads, including pallets, can be handled. Less maneuverable than the individual trucks, the train systems are particularly useful for moving large amounts of material over a considerable distance, and they have the ability to deliver material to several different points merely by unhooking one or more carts. These tractor units can be operator driven or remotely controlled and programmed.

For handling material in unit loads, there are many types of pallets, skids, skid boxes, and special racks. It is also possible to make up unit loads without skids or pallets.

Any manufacturing enterprise that transports materials by highway truck, rail, air freight, or ship should be aware that standard size pallets and shipping containers have been adopted by these industries. Therefore, it may save money and time if pallets, containers, or unit loads are sized to be compatible with the standardized units being used in the general freight industry.

Overhead Equipment. Except for small cranes, hoists, and lifts mounted on casters or on small motorized vehicles, overhead equipment generally operates over a limited area, because it moves on a fixed track. But it does permit area coverage. Specific types of equipment may be hand or power operated and may range from a simple fixed chain hoist to highly complex and expensive overhead traveling cranes, complete with air conditioning for the operator or remotely controlled by an operator on the floor without wires or other fixed connections.

In general, cranes and hoists are used where space is at a premium or where parts or materials to be moved are especially heavy or bulky. Areas which can be covered by a crane or hoist are limited only by the rails or overhead trolleys on which the equipment travels and by structural barriers within the plant. Overhead equipment is usually expensive, and the volume or nature of material being handled must be such that the cost is justified.

Containers and Supports. The varieties of pallets, skids, baskets, and containers available are too numerous to list. It is almost certain that off-the-shelf containers and supports are readily available from a number of sources to accommodate any material handling job. If standard items cannot be found, most large manufacturers of container and support equipment are prepared to supply special purpose units.

Positioning, Weighing, and Control Equipment. Here again, the person selecting material handling equipment can be inundated by the vast variety of equipment available. Much is designed for highly automated systems. Many specific kinds of manufacturing, processing, and material handling equipment will have built-in positioning, weighing, or control mechanisms.

ORGANIZATION PRINCIPLES

Rules for organizing material handling operations are similar to those used in organizing other departmental efforts. The more important factors are: (1) Material handling, like any other department or organization, should be set up to achieve a specific goal (profit, ultimately). (2) Authority and responsibility should never be separated. The authority for determining methods and equipment must be accompanied by the responsibility for their successful operation. Authority for arranging handling layouts must be accompanied by the responsibility for the resulting flow of materials. Authority for establishing training programs must be accompanied by the responsibility for their effectiveness. Results achieved from any reorganization will be directly proportional to the degree of both authority and responsibility being placed with a single person. (3) Overall material handling activities must be divided into functional segments, with methods and equipment chosen accordingly. (4) Adoption of one new method or system does not necessarily lead to a permanent solution to cost reduction and increased productivity. An organization must be flexible—capable of changing promptly and continuously to maintain maximum effectiveness.

Thus, there is little fundamental difference between organizing an effective material handling operation and organizing any other manufacturing operation. The difference is in detail only.

Four Major Functions. Functions of the material handling activity can be divided into four broad categories:

1. Planning and equipping (or engineering)
2. Training
3. Operation (movement and storage of materials)
4. Maintenance

Each of these deserves detailed analysis.

Planning and Equipping. Engineering of a material handling job or system starts with an analysis of the design of the product and follows through to customers' packaging specifications. Product engineers can be encouraged to design parts which are easier to handle and store. Manufacturing engineers can design production tooling which minimizes or eliminates handling at work stations and reduces handling between processes. They can also design production tooling layouts which eliminate the movement of bulky, expensive parts between remote points. Production engineers can contribute scheduling plans which minimize handling and storage. Purchasing agents can help by negotiating better lot-buying plans, shipping schedules, and packaging specifications.

Ideally, the material handling supervisor acts as a liaison between design, production, and sales departments. He stands between these departments and the various handling activities they require.

Training. To maintain an effective material handling organization, training is necessary on a continuing basis. There are three important requirements for an effective training program: (1) aim of the program must be clearly understood, (2) training material must be prepared with both physical and psychological factors in mind, and (3) presentation must be vigorous, comprehensive, and interesting.

Training required for supervisors obviously is different than that for operators, and there are few training programs that explain the full spectrum of the job. Also, the proliferation of routing functions in the material handling, packaging, and transportation activities has resulted in a corresponding increase in the variety of labor classifications required to perform these functions.

Operation. Personnel assigned to the various material handling jobs carry out a plan developed by the material handling supervisor or systems engineer. Performance is directly proportional to the operators' understanding of the job to be done and their knowing how to do it in the most efficient manner.

No company can devise a completely satisfactory system unless a method of leveling work loads is devised. And the leveling problem will never be satisfactorily solved merely by directing traffic. Solution requires knowledge of the basic work flow generated by three activities: receiving, production, and shipping.

Maintenance. The best material handling system will cease to perform effectively if equipment is not properly serviced on a regular schedule.

SOLVING COMMON PROBLEMS

Planned buying to assure proper inventory quantity can help level the receiving and storage work loads. Similarly, careful planning of production schedules can level the service operation work load. Sales planning, inventory control of finished parts, and distribution controls also can level the shipping work load.

Every company is different—no one formula will determine the leveling media for everyone. Each requires individual study to determine where the leveling media are and how they can be controlled to enhance material handling effectiveness and costs.

A handling activity must accommodate physical movement of material, and there should be a definite and organized plan for that movement. Generally, there are three material handling zones:

1. Receiving and into storage
2. Out of storage, into, and through production and assembly
3. From production and assembly through shipping

Receiving and into storage is governed and controlled by the volume of material received. Out of storage and through production is governed by production schedules. From production and assembly through shipping is governed by the sales schedules.

These three zones provide an opportunity to organize accordingly. In a small operation, all three can be covered by a single supervisor. In a medium-sized operation, perhaps each of the three should be covered by a foreman. In a large operation, the three may supply enough work for a department superintendent. In any case, they represent separate categories of handling which must be recognized in any attempt to organize the overall job.

This categorical approach to the improvement of material handling is less costly than new methods and new equipment and should be carefully studied before new methods or equipment are ordered.

Plant Layout. Perhaps the single most important factor affecting handling efficiency and cost in any manufacturing facility is physical layout or ground plan. Every time parts or materials move, it costs money. In the ideal plant, raw materials enter at one end, go through the various processing steps in exact order, and emerge at the other end ready for shipment.

Obviously, this is not possible in most plants. For most companies, existing plant layout represents a compromise between this ideal and the existing constraints (space available, location of departments which cannot be moved, manufacturing processes, and production equipment).

Practically every company, however, can find opportunities to reduce handling costs by studying layout and processing sequences and by rearranging ground plans to achieve minimum total travel for each part and material. In addition, it is possible to speed the flow of materials, reduce accident hazards, and eliminate handling bottlenecks.

In planning a new plant, it is possible to avoid built-in handling costs by considering layout long before construction starts. The likelihood of future problems can be minimized by making the new plant as flexible as possible from the handling point of view. In other words, plan the plant not only for the processing system now being used, but also for possible future changes.

If a plant is already built, there is little that can be done about location of girders and other structural obstacles or of certain special equipment. But it will pay to keep next year's needs in mind when planning tomorrow's changes. For example, it might be better to spend more money for portable rather than fixed conveyors, so that when methods change, conveyors can be easily rearranged.

Naturally, there are occasions when permanent installations should be made. But they should be studied carefully, with a view to alternate arrangements. It is often worth paying a premium—in money or in a slightly less than perfect setup—to keep the layout flexible and ready for future changes.

Planning Spatial Relationships. What steps can be taken in finding the best possible compromise between the space available and the ideal layout? The first step is the same whether planning a new plant or rearranging an old one. That is, without reference to present physical layout, a process chart and a flow diagram should be made, listing the operations involved in making each product and the paths to be followed by major components.

Starting with the receipt of raw material, the process chart should trace material movement through to final shipping. In addition to noting each operation, it should indicate the approximate amount of material that must be moved per hour, day, or week and the frequency of movement.

Spatial location is only one of the factors to be considered. Another important consideration is the type of handling equipment that is to be used. Type of equipment affects layout, and layout affects the type of equipment that is chosen.

For example, if forklift trucks are to be used, it may be important to have aisles wide enough to permit easy passage of two fully loaded trucks without danger of bumping. Cross aisles should be avoided; blind intersections are extremely hazardous; doors must be wide enough to accommodate fully loaded trucks; separate pedestrian exits are often necessary as a safety precaution; lighting above aisles is important to safety; and floors should be smooth and able to stand constant travel by fully loaded trucks.

If cranes or monorail systems are to be used for handling, floor smoothness is less important, but it is still necessary to leave plenty of aisle space for maneuvering loads, to make sure there are no tall machines projecting into the freeway, and of course, to make sure that the building structure will bear the largest possible load that might be handled.

Material handling affects plant layout in still another way—as a limiting factor. For example, good utilization of space calls for high stacking in storage areas. But that means the area chosen for storage must have a floor capable of sustaining a stacked load.

Thus, a plant layout that does not properly analyze material handling problems is likely to be unsatisfactory. When handling and layout are planned together, positive results are realized in terms of cost, safety, and general efficiency. The end result: increased profits.

Process Charts and Flow Diagrams. Almost any material handling problem can be solved if it is clearly stated. Usually, it is merely a matter of setting down available facts. Furthermore, there are means of picturing or diagraming material handling activities so clearly that logical solutions become quite apparent.

Production is materials in motion. This being true, why not apply motion study and process analysis to material handling operations? A general analysis should be applied to the problem as a whole first, because it would be foolish to study an operation singly which might be eliminated or combined with another.

Step-by-step analysis is thus essential, and for this, a flow process chart accompanied by a simple flow diagram is recommended. These give more information than a mere list of operations and equipment needed. They show the direct relationship between operations and the movement or handling required.

A flow process chart (Figure 7-2) is a simple means of collecting and tabulating, in direct sequence, data about present material handling operations. It can include information on storage, temporary delays, transport distance, time involved, and type of equipment used for moving materials, plus other required facts.

A flow diagram (Figure 7-3) might be compared to a road map, with a

PART NAME___ Gizmo

PROCESS DESCRIPTION Machine base and assemble, and finish

DEPARTMENT Machine shop, Assembly and Finishing

PLANT XYZ Products Co.

RECORDED BY___ I. M. Looking ____ DATE ___ Jan. 15 _____

SUMMARY	
	NO.
O OPERATIONS	
▷ TRANSPORTATIONS	
□ INSPECTIONS	
D DELAYS	
▽ STORAGES	
TOTAL STEPS	
DISTANCE TRAVELED	

STEP	Operations / Transport / Inspect / Delay / Storage	DESCRIPTION OF PRESENT METHOD	Meth. of Handl.	Dist-ance	No. Men	Cost per Move
1	O ▷ □ D ▽1	in storage at receiving				
2	O ▷1 □ D ▽	to skid	walkie	6'		
3	O ▷ □ D ▽2	on skid				
4	O ▷2 □ D ▽	into machine 2	hand	4'		
5	1O ▷ □ D ▽	turn				
6	O ▷3 □ D ▽	to table	hand	4'		
7	O ▷ □ D ▽3	on table				
8	O ▷4 □ D ▽	to machine 3	hand	4'		
9	2O ▷ □ D ▽	drill				
10	O ▷5 □ D ▽	to table	hand	4'		
11	O ▷ □ D ▽4	on table				
12	O ▷6 □ D ▽	into machine 4	hand	3'		
13	3O ▷ □ D ▽	drill				
14	O ▷7 □ D ▽	to skid	hand	4'		
15	O ▷ □ D ▽5	on skid				
16	O ▷8 □ D ▽	to assembly dept.	walkie	10'		
17	O ▷ □ D ▽6	at end of assembly bench				
18	O ▷9 □ D ▽	on to bench to assembly position	hand	5'		
19	4O ▷ □ D ▽	assemble				
20	O ▷10 □ D ▽	to inspection position	hand	3'		
21	O ▷ □1 D ▽	inspect				
22	O ▷11 □ D ▽	to skid at end of assembly bench	hand	8'		

FIG. 7-2. Flow Process Chart. (*Prepared by James M. Apple.*)

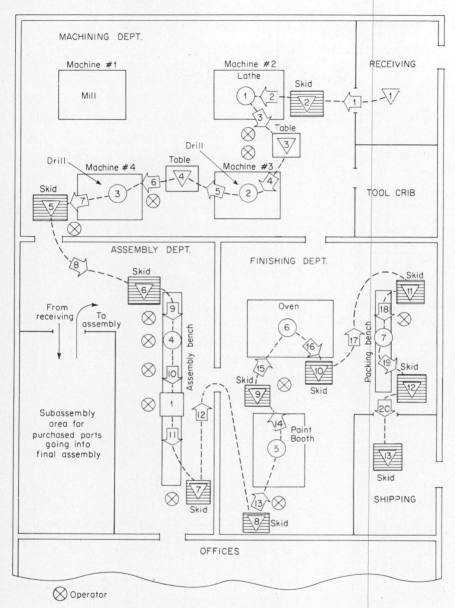

FIG. 7-3. Flow Diagram. (*Prepared by James M. Apple.*)

line drawn through the area through which the material passes. It not only depicts handling and transportation problems, but also pictures the obstacles encountered by materials in transit. Flow process charts and flow diagrams are relatively easy to construct. There are even standard symbols used in drawing them, as shown in Figure 7-4.

There are several common mistakes that should be avoided in making flow

OPERATION A large circle indicates an operation such as	Drive nail	Mixer	Type letter
TRANSPORTATION An arrow indicates a transportation such as	Move material by truck	Move material by conveyor	Move material by hand (messenger)
STORAGE A triangle indicates a storage such as	Material in truck or on floor at bench waiting to be processed	Finished stock stacked on pallets	Papers waiting to be filed
DELAY A large capital D indicates a delay such as	Wait for elevator	Broken belt on lathe	Erase pencil writing
INSPECTION A square indicates an inspection such as	Examine material for quality or quantity	Read steam gage on boiler	Examine printed form for information

FIG. 7-4.   Process Chart Symbols.

process charts. One is the tendency to confuse an operator with the material being handled. A chart must indicate movements of either the material or the operator. Also, it is almost impossible for anyone to sit at a desk and develop an accurate chart, no matter how familiar he is with the overall operation of his company or with the specific phase of the manufacturing process being charted. Materials must be followed step-by-step through each process.

Every flow process chart should contain a summary of the number of operations, the number of delays and storages, the number of moves, the number of feet traveled in each step, and the total elapsed time. If the chart depicts a new or improved material handling method, it should clearly illustrate the difference between the present and the proposed methods, indicating the advantages of the latter.

After a chart of the present handling method is completed, it can be evaluated by answering four vital questions:

1. Can any step be eliminated?
2. Can it be combined with another?
3. Can it be simplified?
4. Can the sequence be changed to advantage?

Going through a chart step by step and questioning every symbol may prove tedious, but experience has shown that it is well worthwhile.

Material Handling Costs. From an average of 30 to 40 percent all the way up to 80 percent of the cost of any manufactured product can be traced to material handling.

When accountants analyze a manufacturing process, they often lump costs into two general categories: (1) direct manufacturing costs—buying raw materials, processing them, and packing the final product; and (2) indirect manufacturing costs which include everything else.

Invariably, a large proportion of the indirect costs can be traced to material handling. These costs can be segregated into four categories: (1) transporting raw material to the plant and shipping finished products (costs are a function of plant location in regard to raw material supply and location of the market); (2) in-plant receiving and storage, movement of materials between processing operations, and warehousing; (3) handling of material by machine operators, assemblers, and inspectors; and (4) distribution of finished products, which includes assembly of unit loads on trucks or other common carriers, and delivery to area warehouses, where products must be unloaded and restacked in the area warehouse, or to customers.

Cost Comparisons. What information is needed to predict accurately the cost of a new material handling method? The first question quite obviously concerns initial cost and installation cost of the equipment required by the new method. The second question is: What will the installation accomplish . . . how much will it save?

The first step in the analysis is to review the present method being used. A good guide for determining basic cost data is the flow process chart. It shows the various operational steps—inspection, transportation, storage, and distance traveled by the material being processed—and it describes them systematically.

Next, flow layout and route of travel can be illustrated on a flow diagram. A process chart of present methods can then be compared to a similar chart showing proposed changes. With these as a guide, each move can be costed.

From these charts, the standard hours per unit of handling or standard hours per foot of travel can be computed. Standard hours can then be converted into cost per unit of handling or foot of travel.

This type of basic data can be used effectively for budgetary control of operations by helping measure current handling costs and by providing a quick means of appraising new material handling methods.

Cost Reduction Techniques. To control costs effectively in a material handling operation, it is necessary to know where to look for waste and inefficiency. Certain handling activities may contain inefficiencies, or they may affect other production operations in such a way that costs are increased. Therefore, to analyze any cost saving step thoroughly, it is usually necessary to investigate the whole production operation.

The following list of danger signs has been compiled as an aid in searching for cost reductions:

Idle Machine Time. Machine downtime means lost productivity, which costs money. When a machine is slowed down or stopped because of inadequate material flow, the cost should be charged to inefficient material handling.

Production Bottlenecks. An interruption of production through lack of material can shut down a whole line of machines—disrupt the entire manufacturing operation.

Rehandling of Material. Every time an item is handled, it costs money. Material handling techniques should be devised and refined to reduce the number of times that an item is handled.

Large Inventories. Inventories tie up capital and require storage facilities. Usually, the more efficient a material handling system, the smaller the inventory required.

Poor Space Utilization. Space represents money. Effective material handling can optimize the use of space.

Excessive Maintenance. Maintenance costs for material handling equipment represent a double loss—the time and material spent for corrective action, plus the loss of the equipment's useful time. Improper or careless use of material handling equipment is the major contributing factor to such losses.

Inefficient Use of Labor. Production employees are paid to produce. Every minute they spend handling material is a minute lost to the productive effort.

Damaged Material. Breakage is frequently a high cost factor. Proper material handling methods and equipment can minimize this cost.

Demurrage. When transportation facilities are kept idle beyond specified limitations, extra charges are incurred. Efficient material handling can minimize these charges.

Inefficient Use of Equipment. Material handling equipment costs money. When a piece of equipment that costs $10 per hour is used on a job that could be handled by a device costing $5 per hour, the penalty is obvious. Material handling equipment should be selected for function and efficiency.

Cost of New Equipment. When a manufacturing manager decides that his company needs a new piece of equipment or a new system, he knows that management is going to require much more from him in the way of information than initial cost of the equipment. He is not faced with the simple matter of calling a lift truck dealer, for example, to ask what a specific model costs. Basic price is important, of course. But far more important is a determination of how much the new equipment will reduce production costs. In other words, will the equipment pay for itself and add to company profits in the relatively near future?

A key factor in evaluating equipment cost is labor—how much direct labor is required to do a certain job with the old machine or system compared with the new. As employee fringe benefits increase, managers in industry are willing to spend more and more on capital equipment that saves labor.

In addition to labor, another important factor, especially to management, is the time value of money. New machinery requires capital, and it is important to show that this capital is being used in a productive manner.

Accumulation of cost data is generally done on an annual basis and is most familiar to management on an annual cost and return basis. Methods shown by Tables 7-2 and 7-3 are based on annual cost, and they also are useful in

TABLE 7–2. Equipment Operating Cost Determination*

Item	Alternative 1	Alternative 2
Equipment data		
Make	Acme	Whirlwind
Type	Direct	Direct
Model	46	B–3
Capacity	5,000 per hr	5,200 per hr
Accessories		
Attachments		
Operating characteristics		

Item	Alternative 1	Alternative 2
Investment		
Invoice price	$39,000	$33,000
Installation charges	4,000	5,000
Maintenance facilities	1,000	1,500
Fueling and/or power facilities	2,800	2,800
Alterations to present facilities	6,000	6,000
Freight and/or transportation	800	1,000
Design work	1,800	1,400
Supplies	1,600	1,800
Other charges (travel and training)	3,000	2,500
Credits		
Total investment cost	$60,000	$55,000

Item	8 hours	16 hours	8 hours	16 hours
Fixed charges				
Depreciation (5-year, straight line, 20%)	$12,000		$11,000	
Interest on investment (10%)	6,000		5,500	
Taxes (25%) at 30% assessment	530		420	
Insurance (5%) at 75% coverage	230		180	
Supervision (50% × $5,000 wage)	2,500		2,500	
Clerical (25% × $4,000 wage)	1,000		1,000	
Maintenance personnel (10% × $8,000 wage)	800		800	
Other	170		100	
Total fixed cost	$23,200		$21,500	
Variable charges				
Operating personnel (percent × dollars wage)	$ 9,750	(3 men)	$ 6,500	(2 men)
Power and/or fuel costs	250		200	
Lubricants	100		100	
Maintenance parts and materials	500		600	
Maintenance labor	6,200		5,100	
Other				
Total variable cost	$16,800		$12,500	
Other overhead (percent × dollars)				
Total annual cost	$40,000		$34,000	
Operating hours per year	2,000		2,000	
Cost per hour of operation	$ 20.00		$ 17.00	

*Prepared by James M. Apple.

TABLE 7–3. Equipment Investment Analysis*

Direct costs	Indirect costs	Indeterminate costs	Intangible factors
Fixed Depreciation Interest on investment Taxes Insurance Supervisory personnel Clerical help Maintenance personnel Other *Variable* Operating personnel Fuel, power Lubrication Maintenance, parts, and supplies Maintenance labor	*Equipment/Method* Space occupied Effect on taxes Effect on inventory value Value of repair parts Demurrage costs Downtime charges Changes in production rate *Management* Travel expenses incurred in investigation Cost of follow-up Re-layout costs Training of personnel Overtime required to make up for lost production Volume of work in process Charges to operation after full depreciation Handling returned goods	*Equipment/Method* Space lost or gained Changes in overhead Inventory control savings Inventory taking savings Production control savings Changes in product or material quality Life of job using equipment Reduction in physical effort *Management* Lost production due to delay in installation Percent of time equipment will be utilized Additional labor required for increased capacity Turnover of work in process Changes in line balance Trends in business volume Trends in equipment costs Improved work flow Ease of supervision Reduction in paperwork	*Equipment* Quality Durability Compatibility Standardization of equipment and components Flexibility Adaptability Complexity Safety Rate of obsolescence Manufacturer's reputation Availability Postsale advice/service Availability of service Availability of repair parts Quality of service *Management* Financial policy Economic survival goals Effect of future changes Plans for expansion Labor relations aspect Effect on morale Increased salability of product Improved customer service Pride in installation

*Developed by James M. Apple.

quickly determining cost factors when a decision (or necessity) dictates the immediate purchase of a piece of equipment.

More sophisticated, detailed methods of costing material handling equipment are available. Some sources of information on them are given below in the bibliography.

BIBLIOGRAPHY

Apple, James M., *Lesson Guide Outline on Material Handling Education*, The Material Handling Institute, Inc., Pittsburgh, Pa., 1969.

Bolz, H. A., and G. E. Hagemann, *Materials Handling Handbook*, The Ronald Press Company, New York, 1958.

Conveyor Terms and Definitions, Conveyor Equipment Manufacturers Association, Washington, D.C., 1952.

Department of Army, *Storage and Material Handling*, TM743-200, U.S. Government Printing Office, Washington, D.C., 1955.

Haynes, D. O., *Material Handling Applications*, Chilton Company, Philadelphia, Pa., 1958.

Haynes, D. O., *Material Handling Equipment*, Chilton Company, Philadelphia, Pa., 1957.

An Introduction to Material Handling, The Material Handling Institute, Inc., Pittsburgh, Pa., 1967.

Material Handling Engineering Directory and Handbook, Industrial Publishing Company, Cleveland, Ohio, biennial.

Small Business Administration, U.S. Department of Commerce, *Improving Material Handling in Small Business*, U.S. Government Printing Office, Washington, D.C., 1969.

Periodicals

Automation, Penton Publishing Company, Cleveland, Ohio.

Handling & Shipping, Industrial Publishing Company, Cleveland, Ohio.

Material Handling Engineering, Industrial Publishing Company, Cleveland, Ohio.

Mechanical Handling, Dorset House, London, England.

Modern Manufacturing, McGraw-Hill Publications, New York.

Modern Materials Handling, Cahners Publishing Company, Boston, Mass.

Transportation and Distribution Management, Traffic Service Corporation, Washington, D.C.

CHAPTER EIGHT

Mechanization and Automation

BRUNO A. MOSKI *Assistant to General Manager, Yale Materials Handling Division, Eaton, Yale & Towne, Inc., Philadelphia, Pennsylvania*

Progress in manufacturing demands a constantly increasing rate of financial return upon capital investment. Two successive years of similar volumes of physical product at comparable total costs signal retrogression in the marketplace. The third year may well demonstrate that a competitor has seized the opportunity to increase his share of market at the expense of the "static cost" supplier.

The most expensive source of power in industry is human energy. While the cost of electric, electronic, and nuclear power tends to decrease year by year, the cost per hour of employee wages, including fringe benefits, tends to increase steadily. Fresh decisions must be made continuously, consistent with the relative costs of power sources.

To take advantage of the great disparity in cost between human and electric energy, investments in capital equipment are necessary. Comparatively minor investments, which mechanize operations and decrease fatigue without displacing the employees, are welcomed by the work force. Major investments which result in automation, displacing one or more employees, are strongly resisted.

Manufacturing management has a responsibility to maintain a vigilant eye upon all internal operations and weigh them in the light of technological advances in the field of mechanization and automation. After evaluation of the economic factors in specific cases, decisions must be made to increase return on investment, and action must be taken, giving due regard to the solution of the human problems which are involved.

EXAMPLES OF MECHANIZATION AND AUTOMATION

Industry abounds with examples of mechanization and automation. A few examples are given here in progressively higher degrees of mechanization to illustrate some basic principles.

Layout versus Drill Jig. A simple manufacturing operation is to take a piece of steel and lay out the points where several holes are to be drilled, as called for by the engineering drawing. Using a single spindle drill press, the piece of steel is moved under the drill spindle from one point to another, with each hole drilled individually. This method may be used to build the first prototype unit of a new product.

After the product is marketed in reasonably substantial volume, the layout operation is eliminated by designing a drill jig which holds several pieces of steel. A multiple spindle drill press is used which drills all holes at the same time.

Additional capital equipment is required, but a lower level of employee skill is used and the cost per piece is substantially reduced.

Engine Lathe versus Automatic Bar Machine. The versatile engine lathe can take a piece of bar stock and turn it to form a shaft, with several different steps or dimensions. With low-quantity production, this method is eminently acceptable.

With increased volume, an automatic bar machine can be tooled to produce the same shaft at substantially higher speeds and lower cost. The automatic character of the machine permits the assignment of two or more machines to a single operator, amply justifying the greater capital investment in the automatic bar machine.

Progressive Line versus Special Purpose Machine. A large, intricate steel casting, housing a set of gears in a transmission unit, requires a number of facing, drilling, boring, and milling operations. With a large volume of production, a progressive machining line may be installed, consisting of a series of turning, drill press, boring, and milling machines.

In this example, the material handling cost of moving the heavy castings from one machine to the next, together with the cost of placing the castings in fixtures and removing them from fixtures, is quite large in comparison with the machining time alone.

Economics justifies a heavy investment in a special purpose machine which performs the several operations with a major reduction in the cost of handling the castings.

Fork Truck versus Stacker Crane. The use of forklift trucks, together with pallets, skid bins, and various attachments, is prevalent in manufacturing operations of an intermittent nature. Fork trucks transport work in process between manufacturing operations, place materials in storage locations, and remove materials from storage.

In storage locations, particularly of a large-scale warehouse nature, stacker cranes can demonstrate considerable superiority over forklift trucks. More refined planning and programming are necessary, but the cost per ton-mile is significantly reduced.

Integrated Handling System. The majority of American manufacturing plants use a wide variety of material handling equipment. Conveyors, forklift trucks, hoists, and overhead cranes are but a few of the devices which handle material. Each piece of equipment is selected for a specific purpose.

The systems approach to material handling, resulting in completely integrated or automated movement of materials, can be applied to many industries. In an all-inclusive material handling system, all the carrier elements are coordinated to provide continuous flow throughout the plant, with electronically coded bypassing of storage banks and heavy traffic areas. Full utilization of air space is attained, with overhead monorails supplementing floor conveyors and sophisticated stacker cranes.

Well-designed systems result in substantial reductions of operating costs and greatly improve turnover of manufacturing inventories. With the excellent potential profit improvement from an automated material handling system, management must plan, well in advance of the installation, the steps it will take to solve the problem of the considerable number of employees who will be available when the system becomes operative.

MECHANIZATION IN MANUFACTURING

In the approach to mechanization and automation in a specific company, it is well for manufacturing management to take a broad view of the total scope of the field. This view may be attained by a mental survey of the various degrees of mechanization which exist throughout industry. A review of the status of mechanization in all fields of manufacturing stimulates the manager to compare his operations with general practice and to suggest individual areas for improvement.

Figure 8-1, "Mechanization in Manufacturing," is presented with the permission of James R. Bright of the Harvard Business School, author of *Automation and Management*. It is intended to provide the manufacturing manager with a tangible and concise picture of progress which has been made and the factors which influence increases in mechanization.

As the type of activity progresses from physical to mental, it might be expected that the amount of mechanization would decrease. The illustration indicates such a trend, with some notable exceptions. In the fields of production control and inventory control, where the activity is entirely mental, advances in automated data processing have resulted in considerable mechanization.

Within the fields of activity which are largely physical, the amount of mechanization is proportional to the volume of similar components and products.

The law of diminishing returns plays a large part in the practical economics associated with the transition from manual efforts to any form of mechanization.

The manufacturing manager should evaluate the possibility of mechanizing his own operations, using Figure 8-1 as a guide. Areas may exist which will lend themselves to improvement and justify more detailed feasibility studies.

SEVENTEEN LEVELS OF MECHANIZATION AND AUTOMATION

Figure 8-2, "Seventeen Levels of Mechanization and Automation," is a more refined guide for the manufacturing manager. It identifies specific steps in the evolution of mechanization. It covers the complete field from the basic hand effort of man to complete automation in which a machine, operating under nonmanual power, responds with action to a variable in the working environment by modifying its own action over a wide range of variation, with the capability of anticipating the action required, and by making adjustments to provide for that action.

This illustration indicates the steps which are taken to transfer the control of action from man to the machine, the increase in the sophistication of the machine response, and the change from human to mechanical power.

Type of action	Basic function	Typical activities	Level of mechanization	Amount of mechanization
Largely physical	Processing, creation of utility	Forming	Medium to extremely high	Almost entirely mechanized
		Assembly	Very low, with a few exceptions	Very little, with exceptions
		Packaging	Very low to extremely high	Much in mass production and bulk materials; little elsewhere
	Movement, creation of time and place utility	Material handling	Low to extremely high	Moderate but increasing rapidly
		Transportation	Medium	Almost entirely mechanized
	Storage, creation of time and place utility	Raw materials and finished goods storage	Medium to very high	Roughly proportional to the size of the volume; much in bulk materials
		In-process storage	Low to medium	Very low, with a few exceptions
		Warehousing	Low to moderate, with a few high exceptions	Roughly proportional to volume and size of the material stored
Both physical and mental	Maintenance, retention of utility	Maintenance	Very low, except for some mechanized lubrication	Hand and hand tools universally used, except for mechanized lubrication
Largely mental	Design, conception, analysis interpretation, planning	Product design	Low to moderate, with a few high exceptions	Very little, except in highly engineered products
		Process design	Low	Very little
	Measurements, verification of time, place, and form utility	Inspection	Low to moderate, with a few high exceptions	Very little, except in mass production
		Testing	Moderate to very high	Much
		Production control	Very low, with slight exceptions	Fairly common
		Inventory control	Low to moderate, with a few high exceptions	Much low-level mechanization

FIG. 8-1. Mechanization in Manufacturing. (*Courtesy of James R. Bright*, Automation and Management, *Division of Research, Harvard Business School, Boston, Mass.*, 1958.)

Initiating control source	Type of machine response		Power source	Level number	Level of mechanization
From a variable in the environment	Responds with action	Modifies own action over a wide range of variation	Mechanical (nonmanual)	17	Anticipates action required and adjusts to provide it
				16	Corrects performance while operating
				15	Corrects performance after operating
		Selects from a limited range of possible prefixed actions		14	Identifies and selects appropriate set of actions
				13	Segregates or rejects according to measurement
				12	Changes speed, position, direction, according to measurement signal
	Responds with signal			11	Records performance
				10	Signals preselected values of measurement (includes error detection)
				9	Measures characteristic of work
From a control mechanism that directs a predetermined pattern of action	Fixed within the machine			8	Activated by introduction of workpiece or material
				7	Power tool system, remote controlled
				6	Power tool, program control (sequence of fixed functions)
				5	Power tool, fixed cycle (single function)
From man	Variable			4	Power tool, hand control
				3	Powered hand tool
			Manual	2	Hand tool
				1	Hand

Fig. 8-2. Seventeen Levels of Mechanization and Automation. (*Courtesy of James R. Bright,* Automation and Management, *Division of Research, Harvard Business School, Boston, Mass.,* 1958.)

Figure 8-2 provides a practical approach to the conduct of a detailed survey of current manufacturing practices from the viewpoint of mechanization and automation. For each manufacturing department, for each product, or for the entire plant, a series of vertical columns can be added to the right-hand side of the figure, with each column representing a specific step in the manufacturing processes from the receipt of raw materials to the shipment of finished products. Each step or operation in the manufacturing process is then evaluated with respect to the seventeen levels indicated, and the appropriate level is checked in the proper column. A solid line connecting the check marks in the series of columns provides a mechanization and automation profile for the department, product, or plant.

A mechanization and automation profile for each manufacturing department, for each product, or for the entire plant pinpoints the specific steps or operations where detailed feasibility studies are required to increase the level of mechanization and automation.

SURVEY OF WORK SKILLS

Within a given manufacturing situation, another sound step which may be taken in the development of the potential economics of mechanization and automation is to prepare a survey of existing work skills in the plant. Such a survey should include all nonsupervisory employees who are paid on an hourly basis.

Figure 8-3, "Survey of Work Skills," is a typical example of such an analysis. Within the general categories of machining, structural fabrication, product assembly, material handling, inspect and test, tool services, maintenance services, and clerical, it identifies the work skills which are employed and the number of employees within each work skill.

A review of Figure 8-3 indicates that 233 employees, or 16 percent of the total of 1,457, are engaged in material handling. This does not add value to the product itself, but it does provide time and place utility within the plant. Of the 233 employees, a total of 143 employees are stock keepers and stock selectors, whose essential functions are to place materials in bins and racks and to remove materials from those same bins and racks. The magnitude of this cost appears to justify a complete reappraisal of the flow of materials in this plant, including the application of the principle of point-of-use storage, and mechanization refinements at specific points of use to provide a steady flow of components to the productive employees involved.

A total of 240 employees, or 23.3 percent of all employees, is assigned to assembly and repair. It is quite possible that a substantial amount of this work is truly at Level 1 of mechanization, using the hand only, and will remain so. A more detailed analysis, particularly at the subassembly operations, should result in upgrading the work from Level 1 to at least Level 2 by introducing hand tools. The very consideration of hand tools can increase the work to Level 3, involving powered hand tools, or Level 4, with power tools under hand control. Once these levels have been fully reached, occasional instances may be found to introduce Level 5, utilizing a single function power tool with a fixed cycle, or even Level 6, where a sequence of fixed functions with program control is applied to a power tool. The economics in this area should be extremely favorable.

Within the structural work skills, a total of 107 employees, or 7.4 percent of all employees, is engaged in welding. The substantial technological progress being made in this field may warrant inviting a number of representa-

Work skill	Number of employees	Percent to total
1. Machining		
a. Saws and cutoff..................................	14	1.0
b. Layout...	7	0.5
c. Engine lathe....................................	17	1.2
d. Turret lathe....................................	78	5.4
e. Vertical turret lathe............................	39	2.7
f. Drill...	91	6.3
g. Bore...	16	1.1
h. Mill...	48	3.3
i. Grind..	28	1.9
j. Gear cutting....................................	8	0.5
k. Deburr..	16	1.1
l. Heat treat......................................	15	1.0
m. Total machining................................	377	26.0
2. Structural Fabrication		
a. Shear..	8	0.5
b. Burn..	12	0.8
c. Brake...	11	0.8
d. Punch and draw press...........................	8	0.5
e. Weld..	107	7.4
f. Hand grind.....................................	21	1.4
g. Straighten.....................................	28	2.0
h. Surface treat...................................	12	0.8
i. Miscellaneous equipment........................	23	1.6
j. Total structural fabrication......................	230	15.8
3. Product Assembly		
a. Assemble and repair............................	340	23.3
b. Paint..	19	1.3
c. Total product assembly..........................	359	24.6
4. Material Handling		
a. Receive and ship...............................	9	0.6
b Material handling equipment......................	81	5.6
c. Stock keepers and selectors......................	143	9.8
d. Total material handling..........................	233	16.0
5. Inspect and Test		
a. Inspectors.....................................	83	5.7
6. Tool Services		
a. Toolmakers and apprentices......................	33	2.3
b. Tool grinding...................................	20	1.3
c. Total tool services..............................	53	3.6
7. Maintenance Services		
a. Maintenance trades.............................	64	4.4
b. Maintenance helpers............................	37	2.5
c. Total maintenance services.......................	101	6.9
8. Clerical		
a. Clerks...	21	1.4
9. Total hourly paid employees......................	1,457	100.0

FIG. 8-3. Survey of Work Skills.

tives of welding equipment manufacturers to survey the major operations involved and present specific recommendations.

In the more traditional machining work skills, 91 employees, or 6.3 percent of the total, are required for drilling operations. It is quite possible that the most sophisticated types of numerical control equipment may be feasible, increasing the level of mechanization as high as Level 17, where the machine anticipates action required and adjusts to provide such action. Similar considerations should be given to turret lathe and milling operations, which include 78 and 48 employees, respectively, or 5.4 and 3.3 percent of the total.

ORGANIZATION FOR AUTOMATION

Consideration of Figures 8-1, 8-2, and 8-3, as related to the manufacturing characteristics of a specific plant, leads to the question of practical organization for automation. A preliminary analysis by manufacturing management can establish an approximate evaluation of the potential extent of automation which is feasible, but considerable detailed work is necessary to make tangible progress.

As an absolute minimum, should any significant potential be apparent, a full-time manufacturing engineer should be assigned to the development of automation. Demonstrated competence in existing manufacturing engineering techniques is essential, but the outstanding characteristics to be sought are intense curiosity, a keen desire to reshape the status quo, and the ability to glean technological know-how from outside vendor representatives.

As a maximum, where the advantages of automation are obvious, particularly when it is known that competitors have made great strides in this area, it may be necessary to establish a complete automation engineering department capable of developing and designing specialized machines and equipment. In general, steps in this direction should be of an evolutionary nature, progressing from the one-man manufacturing engineering concept in direct proportion to the tangible improvements which are made.

EVOLUTION OF AUTOMATION ORGANIZATION

In the possible evolution of an internal organization for automation, several major stages may be considered. Each stage involves specific advantages and disadvantages to be recognized and accepted before a decision is made to enter that stage of evolution.

User and Traditional Vendors. The first stage involves discussions among the existing manufacturing engineering staff and the representatives of traditional vendors of machine tools and other equipment for the development of specialized automation equipment.

In this stage, the clear-cut advantages are those of past relationships and mutual understanding. The possible problems are clearly discussed and vendor limitations are defined.

In general, the disadvantages may well outweigh the advantages. The vendor is very apt to hesitate to approach problems which are beyond his current capabilities. He must gain experience in a new field. Considerable engineering assistance from the user may be required. To obtain the desired results, the user may need to integrate several different units of equipment. The limitations of traditional vendors may force the acceptance of technical compromises.

User and Vendor of Special Systems. In this stage, the manufacturing engineers search out vendors of special systems which may be applied to existing problems. Conversely, the vendors may approach specific plants where a need may exist for their systems.

The advantages include a fresh approach to traditional manufacturing concepts. It is possible that less engineering effort on the part of the user may be required. The vendor assumes total responsibility for the system and has a special incentive to please the user because of the impact of the installation upon his own future sales.

The disadvantages include the necessity of developing new business relationships between the user and the vendor and may involve some inherent risks. It may prove that the special system was developed for a particular set of conditions and cannot be adapted to the needs of the user plant.

User, Consulting Firm, and Vendors. In this stage, the user deals with a consulting engineering firm. That firm, in turn, represents the user in gaining the specialized services of various vendors.

The advantages include the assumption that the user is obtaining the last word in advanced practice. The user is not committed to his historical manufacturing practice or skills. There is minimum company responsibility, and no demand upon company engineering time.

The disadvantages include a possibly higher cost for the complete installation. There may be a lack of understanding of the full manufacturing problem. Unless properly clarified, the consulting firm may not accept adequate responsibility for the end results.

User, Own Engineering Design, and Vendors. In this stage, the user prepares the detailed engineering design for all pieces of equipment and deals with various vendors for the construction and installation of the system.

Major advantages include the development of an engineering design which is compatible with the remaining segments of the production system. Desirable standards of performance can be obtained and maintained.

The disadvantages include the basic problem of integrating design requirements and construction details with a number of different vendors. Another problem is coordinating and controlling delivery and installation schedules. It becomes apparent that a highly competent engineering staff is required.

User, Own Engineering Specifications, and Vendor Projects. In this stage, the user limits his engineering work to the development of broad engineering specifications for the entire system. Negotiations are conducted with individual vendors to accept responsibility for various segments of the system as complete projects. Each project includes responsibility for detailed design, construction of all tooling and accessories, and "run-in" of the segment, to the satisfaction of the user.

The advantages include less division of responsibility and increased certainty of performance. A minimum drain upon the talents and time of the user engineering staff is involved. The automation line is received in complete working order. An overall shorter procurement time should result.

The most important disadvantage is the strong possibility of higher costs because of vendor reluctance to assume entire responsibility for the projects. Quotations will be increased substantially to compensate for unplanned contingencies which may develop.

User and Own Complete Automation Department. At this final stage of evolution, the user organizes a complete automation department with full responsibility for initial concepts, development and detailed design of equipment, construction, and installation of the entire system.

The advantages include total control of all projects as well as excellent integration of the projects with plant and process capabilities. With the proper administration, lower overall costs should be incurred.

Major disadvantages include the cost and difficulty of maintaining the variety of machine design and development skills which are required. A possibility exists of becoming stereotyped and not seeing fresh approaches. Extreme difficulty may be encountered in keeping the design engineers busy unless the corporation is of a multiplant and diversified nature.

ADVANTAGES OF AUTOMATION

At all stages in the evolution of automation from the initial concept in the mind of manufacturing management to the completion of the most sophisticated installation, it is necessary to be prepared for resistance from many directions. Production employees, manufacturing supervision, maintenance personnel, and even manufacturing engineers and top level management are either concerned with job security, question their own ability to adjust to the new environment, or have grave doubts regarding the overall economics of specific installations. An analytical evaluation is essential to dispel objections as they are encountered.

Lower Direct Labor Cost. The most obvious advantage, which creates maximum resistance on the part of production employees, is the reduction of direct labor cost. Employees must be convinced that technological progress is essential for the survival of the enterprise itself. Management must be prepared with a concrete program which makes equitable provisions for the employees who will be affected by automation.

Lower Indirect Labor Cost. Automation installations generally combine the operations of several productive units of equipment, thereby decreasing the number of cost centers in the plant. With fewer productive units to service, the amount of indirect labor, principally of a material handling, tool services, and quality control nature, is decreased. The impact of this reduction is less apparent in the minds of hourly paid employees than is the decrease of direct labor employees.

Lower Setup Time. With several productive operations combined in one automation unit and with more control features built into the design, the probability is strong that total setup time will be reduced. In addition to decreasing total cost, this factor has the effect of increasing the total utilization time of the equipment.

Increased Quality. At the higher levels of mechanization leading to automation, as the skill of the employee is transferred to the machine, increased product quality is assured. The effect of random human errors is decreased and consistent quality is produced, subject to care being taken that the critical wear points of the equipment are checked before the operations go out of control.

Decreased Floor Space. The combination of productive operations and the need for fewer temporary storage locations result in decreased floor space requirements for an equivalent volume of production. In effect, the lower investment for floor space increases the potential capacity of existing facilities, which is highly important in a growth situation.

Shorter Lead Time. Manufacturing lead time—the calendar time which elapses between the instant that the demand for a component part is known and the instant that the component part becomes available after all productive operations are performed—is extremely vital in meeting competitive delivery schedules. With several operations in a single piece of automated equipment decreasing the total time for material handling, setup, and direct labor, manufacturing lead time is significantly reduced.

Decreased Work-in-process Inventory. As a corollary to manufacturing lead time, work-in-process inventory is substantially lower as the result of automation. Not only is the time for setup and the productive operations reduced, but also the need for several temporary storage locations between individual operations is eliminated. Once the material has entered the automation cycle, it is continually in motion for all practical purposes, and the rate of inventory turnover is remarkable.

Increased Capacity. Taking into account the decreased floor space and the higher productivity of the equipment itself, the productive capacity within the scope of the automation installation is increased considerably. If comparable improvements can be made in other areas of the plant, the impact upon total capacity will be highly profitable.

Increased Production with Minimum Increased Labor. A truly effective installation of automation may result in sufficient productive capacity with a single working shift to balance former volume which required two working shifts. With a significantly lower direct labor requirement, an increase in production may be obtained by a moderate overtime schedule, with the percentage increase in volume considerably more than the former percentage of direct labor that would have been needed. On the basis of two or more full shifts, the "production to former direct labor ratio" becomes very impressive.

Easier Production Control. With the fewer and higher capacity production centers which are developed by automation, the planning and administration of production control become relatively simpler. There is less paperwork to generate and a smaller number of control points to check in meeting a given schedule. In principle, the total cost of production control should decrease.

Easier Plant Administration. For similar reasons, the total task of routine plant administration is reduced through automation. For a given volume of production, there are fewer employees to supervise, fewer productive units to service, and less floor space to maintain. Administrative cost per unit of product should be markedly lower.

Easier Housekeeping. As one phase of plant administration, the problem of housekeeping is considerably reduced. A larger percentage of product material is in motion, with fewer temporary storage locations. An important phase of plant housekeeping is the orderly control of work in process, and automation assists in the improvement of this control.

Improved Safety. Automation equipment requires more meticulous engineering design than does conventional productive equipment. More of the physical work of the installation is built into the machines, requiring less intimate and less frequent contact by the machine operator. With inherently better design and the reduced possibilities for personal injury, overall safety is considerably improved.

More Attractive Working Conditions. Automation assumes a substantial share of the routine work associated with productive operations. It also requires a more orderly flow of materials to and from the equipment. These factors, together with the logical organization of associated tooling, create excellent working conditions.

Less Skill and Training Required of Some Employees. Conventional productive equipment requires considerable detailed training of employees in the setting and adjustment of tooling and in the care that is essential to maintain consistent quality. With automation, such a large percentage of employee skill is transferred to the machine that the residual skill requirements of the employee are less technical in character and more of a surveillance nature. Discriminating judgment is not eliminated, but the need for continuous mechanical know-how is reduced.

Improved Employee Morale. Considering the more attractive working conditions, the decreased need for continuous mechanical work, and the resultant improved safety, automation improves employee morale substantially. In the earlier days of the Industrial Revolution, the pride of individual workmanship was an outstanding attribute. In the automation stage of the Industrial Revolution, the employee has an opportunity to develop pride in his responsibility for an ingenious robot with a productive capacity which has multiplied his own potential output.

Increased Return on Capital Investment. The acid test of any business venture is the annual rate of return on capital investment. The basic economics of any automation project must demonstrate an increased rate of return on investment if management approval to install the project is to be obtained. With decreased direct labor, indirect labor, floor space, setup, lead time, and inventory, together with increased quality, capacity, safety, and employee morale, the combined benefits of automation should demonstrate a dramatic improvement in return on capital investment.

DISADVANTAGES OF AUTOMATION

There are two sides to every coin. Distinct disadvantages in the installation of automation, as well as basic changes in operating conditions, must be recognized. A realistic evaluation of such disadvantages is required to ensure that tangible advantages outweigh the disadvantages and to prepare for effective administration of automation.

Greater Capital Investment. Each of the seventeen levels of mechanization as portrayed in Figure 8-2 involves a progressively higher investment in tooling and equipment. A simple hand tool requires a relatively small expenditure to permit the employee to increase his productivity. Every additional transfer of skill from man to the machine must be purchased through correspondingly greater expenditures of capital. Automation demands substantial capital investments beyond the levels which are normally presented to top management for approval.

Difficulty in Securing Adequate Engineering Personnel. The complex demands of automation design require a high grade of engineering talent to lay out and detail all the features. Several engineering disciplines are involved, and comparatively few engineers are sufficiently broad in scope to master all aspects of automation. Highly qualified specialists in some phases will be found wanting in other areas. The constant pressure for profitability does not permit a large staff of specialists and places a greater burden on engineering supervisory personnel.

Longer Design and Build Time. Whether the automation installations are developed within the organization or are planned in conjunction with outside firms, a lengthy period of time for designing and building the various pieces of equipment is necessary. More conventional productive facilities are relatively standardized, whereas automation involves a tailor-made approach to each project. Between the instant of conception and the final installation, overall economic conditions may change, possibly increasing management problems associated with automation.

Troublesome Debugging–Start-up Period. The more advanced an automation project, the greater will be the difficulty in proving in the installation at the initial stage. With a host of detailed links in the system, the statistical probability of imperfections is of large magnitude. Considerable time must be devoted to the diagnosis and correction of each problem before going on to the next one.

Need for Greater Maintenance Skills. Automation does not permit the continuance or simple enlargement of a conventional force of maintenance employees. Depending upon the specific features of the installation, some greater maintenance skills will be needed. The ability to analyze specific difficulties promptly and to make repairs as quickly as possible is of the utmost importance.

Higher Maintenance Cost. The need for greater maintenance skills, the availability of expensive replacement components, and the urgency of keeping equipment in operation all contribute to higher maintenance costs. To repair breakdowns, a crew of mechanics and electricians may be required to work continuously until the problem is corrected, and substantial overtime premium costs may be incurred. A sound preventive maintenance program is much more important in the case of automation equipment than in the case of conventional productive facilities.

Serious Compounding of Downtime. The most costly operating problem associated with automation is downtime. The entire production control system is planned around the capabilities of the automation equipment, and log jams occur throughout the plant when breakdowns occur. When using conventional equipment, there are usually alternate methods available to compensate for machine breakdowns. In the case of automation, practical economics does not justify the luxury of standby equipment. All corrective resources must be pressed into action to prevent a significant halt in production as the result of a defect in the automation system.

Need for Higher Caliber Foremen. The substantial investment in automation and the imperative need for continuous operation call for higher caliber foremen than were previously acceptable. Constant vigilance is required on the part of foremen to detect difficulties before they become serious and to exert all the pressure that is necessary to eliminate downtime immediately after it occurs. Similar alertness is demanded in maintaining the flow of incoming material and the availability of trained employees to obtain maximum utilization of the equipment.

Need for Faster Administrative Reaction Time. Even with superior foremen, their personal efforts are to no avail if they do not receive the support of the entire manufacturing organization. Specialists associated with the production control, tool services, material handling, maintenance, and industrial relations functions must be oriented to the principles of effective automation administration and must respond promptly when the need arises. Management and supervisory personnel have an obligation to recognize the top priority requirements of the automation system and to act immediately and decisively at a moment's notice.

Reduced Flexibility in Products Manufactured. Unless considerable long-range planning is incorporated in the design of automation equipment, thus increasing the capital investment substantially, automation tends to reduce flexibility in the variety of products manufactured. One of the principal advantages of automation is to permit the standardization of manufacture of large quantities of components. Introducing design changes or considering completely different products involves major costs in the changes of automation equipment to provide the required manufacturing capability.

Reduced Flexibility in Raw Material Supply Sources. To a lesser degree, automation reduces flexibility in raw material supply sources. In attaining minimum operating costs, specifications and tolerances of raw materials must be controlled within narrow limits. When problems occur with certain suppliers, other suppliers may not be prepared to meet the same specifications and tolerances at short notice.

Reduced Flexibility in Scheduling. Automation involves a highly standardized program throughout the entire production cycle. It is difficult to provide for temporary variations from the planned program to compensate for problems of raw materials, employee availability, or equipment delays. For that reason, production scheduling, which is capable of various alternatives when dealing with conventional equipment, is much less flexible in an automation installation.

Need for Some Greater Employee Skills. The electronic controls associated with automation, together with the punched tapes and cards, raise the level of manufacturing operations above the purely mechanical processes of typical productive equipment. Skills of a manual and mechanical nature are not adequate for the effective operation of the installation. Considerably increased analytical skill, judgment, and understanding of the entire system, approaching the level required of supervisory personnel, are essential.

Reluctance or Inability of Some Employees to Adjust. The vast majority of employees become accustomed to established work patterns and accept both the advantages and disadvantages of known habits. Even minor method changes tend to unsettle some employees. With the advent of automation introducing a complete revision of the work environment, psychological blocks enter the picture strongly, creating a genuine problem for management.

Widespread Employee Resistance. The instinct for survival, expressed in a deep concern for job security, comes to the fore with intensity when automation is being introduced. Genuine or irrational fears are expressed by employees, and management must be prepared to cope with them. Sound planning for automation extends beyond the physical concept of the installation and must include a constructive program for the equitable solution of problems relating to the employees affected by automation.

Higher Break-even Point. The substantial capital investment required by automation, coupled with the decreased variable increments of direct and indirect labor costs, significantly raises the break-even point of profitability in the manufacturing plant. It is important, therefore, to evaluate the future demand for products sufficiently far in advance to avoid the possibility of lengthy periods of low production and associated financial losses. Automation installations are most successful when a growth pattern of the enterprise is clearly indicated.

EVOLUTION OF MACHINE TOOLS

Figure 8-4, "Evolution of Machine Tools," provides a graphical record of technological progress in machine tools as prepared by Ben C. Brosheer, senior editor of *American Machinist,* and James C. DeSollar, vice-president of Cincinnati Milling and Grinding Machines, Inc. It illustrates the decrease in manufacturing cost per piece proportional to the increase in production requirement quantities.

Three major curves are drawn for nonnumerical control machines, conventional numerical control machines, and a combination of the two types, identified as a variable mission system.

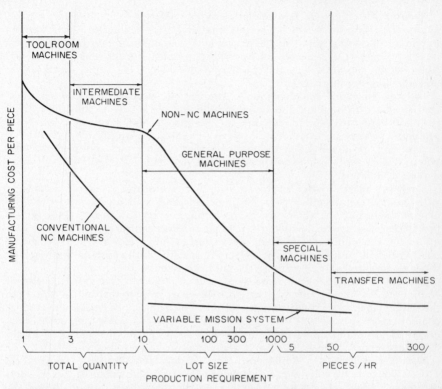

Fig. 8-4.   Evolution of Machine Tools. (*Courtesy of Ben C. Brosheer and James C. DeSollar, "Variable Mission Machining,"* American Machinist, *September, 1968.*)

Nonnumerical Control Machines.   When the total production quantity is only 1 to 3 pieces, the use of toolroom machines, such as jig borers, planers, shapers, engine lathes, and drill presses, with no associated tooling, is justified.

With quantities of 3 to 10 pieces, intermediate machines—including engine lathes, drill presses, milling machines, and grinding machines—with a minimum of tooling are appropriate.

When the lot increases to 10 to 1,000 pieces, general purpose machines with considerable tooling are the rule. Such machines include turret lathes, multiple-head drill presses, large milling machines, and a variety of grinding machines.

When production requirements increase to 5 to 300 pieces per hour over extended periods, special purpose machines and transfer machines with built-in tooling are economically justified.

Conventional Numerical Control Machines.   The ability of numerical control machines to minimize the need for special tooling increases substantially the range of potential application. Figure 8-4 indicates that such machines substantially reduce manufacturing costs in the areas where toolroom machines, intermediate machines, and general purpose machines have been generally accepted.

Variable Mission System.   A variable mission system is designed to process parts of medium complexity in lots of 20 to 1,000 pieces at rates of 5 to 50 pieces per hour. It consists of a combination of numerical control machines and conventional machines specially tooled, linked together with conveyors and an electronic workpiece address system. The features of this plan justify a more detailed explanation.

VARIABLE MISSION SYSTEM

Figure 8-5, is the schematic layout of a typical variable mission system as developed by Cincinnati Milling and Grinding Machines, Inc.

Each variable mission system is designed to attain low manufacturing costs, consistent quality, and the smooth flow of production in the middle-ground area between low-quantity and mass production. It is particularly intended to meet the model proliferation problem which exists in the automotive, farm tractor, earthmoving machinery, and forklift industries, among others. Competition and the desires of individual customers are constantly developing additional optional features, while a demand always exists for replacements of out-of-date parts on a variable need basis.

A variable mission system, developed for families of similar parts, processes a variable mix of components with minimum delays for setup changes and the replacement of worn tools. It provides for automatic, random order machining of a variety of parts, utilizing a series of programmable work stations interconnected with a power conveyor and a workpiece address system which controls both work movement and station operation.

A major key to the success of a variable mission system is the pallet address system. Each work load must go to the proper work station in the correct sequence. To complete the system, provisions are made for queuing workpieces ahead of each work station and for locating and locking the work-carrying pallets at each station.

Each work station is assigned an identification code symbol different from that assigned to any other station, except that identical stations tooled for identical operations are assigned duplicate symbols to permit sharing the work load.

In the staging area at the left-hand end of Figure 8-5, each pallet is identified with a symbol indicating the workpiece that it is carrying and the address of each work station to which it is scheduled. Addressing can be performed manually when different workpieces are loaded on the same conveyor spur, or automatically when separate spurs are provided for each different workpiece.

The address system is so designed that the work can travel from station to station in either a fixed or a random sequence, depending on process requirements and station availability. This is accomplished by determining which operations can be performed in any sequence and therefore can be assigned independent addresses, and which operations must be performed in a specified sequence and therefore must be assigned dependent addresses. The ability to distinguish between independent and dependent addresses is important for automatic load balancing.

When a loaded pallet passes the address setter in the staging area, it is coded to show all the independent operations it will be seeking, but only the first of the dependent operations is scheduled.

After leaving the staging area, each coded pallet orbits around the conveyor loop until a queue line ahead of a work station to which it is addressed is free to accept incoming work. As each pallet approaches the loading end of a queue line, along the upper side of the conveyor loop in Figure 8-5, a station

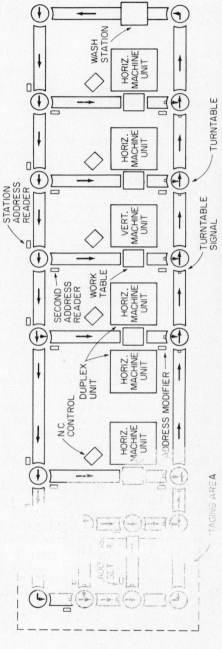

FIG. 8-5. Variable Mission Machining. (*Courtesy of Ben C. Brosheer and James C. DeSollar, "Variable Mission Machining," American Machinist, September, 1968.*)

address reader determines whether any address on the pallet coincides with the adjacent work station. If so and there is room in that station's queue line, a turntable is actuated to shunt the fixture onto the queue line conveyor. There, a second address reader checks the pallet to make sure that it was correctly shunted onto the line.

If there is no coincidence of address or if the queue line is filled, the turntable remains stationary to allow the pallet to bypass that station. It continues along the main conveyor loop seeking an addressed station that can accept it. This helps keep the work load at the several stations in balance and eliminates pileups at some stations while other stations are looking for work.

When work assigned to a station is completed on a workpiece and the pallet is released to the discharge conveyor, an address modifier automatically erases the coded address of that station. If it is a dependent operation, the modifier replaces the address with the address of the next dependent operation on the schedule. If it is the last dependent operation, no new address will be applied.

A turntable at the end of the discharge conveyor returns pallets to the main conveyor loop when they have been released by the address modifier. When all addresses are erased from a pallet, it is returned to its proper spur in the staging area for unloading.

Because the sensors in the address readers can easily be moved from position to position, the address identity of each work station can be changed quickly. Thus, if a machine is deactivated temporarily for a change in setup or for the replacement of worn tools, removal of the sensor from the address reader ahead of that station will cause pallets on the conveyor line to bypass the station.

With this feature, standby machines may be included in a variable mission system for quick substitution of identical units should an abnormal shutdown be required. It is necessary only to install the proper tools, operating numerical control tape, and a station address sensor to substitute a standby machine in the line. When changeovers must be made frequently, the use of standby machines may be a profitable investment.

At each work station, an indexable locating table lies in the path of the queue line conveyor to receive, locate, and lock in place the loaded pallet when it reaches the station. This table is capable of only rotationally indexing the workpiece. All traverses of the machine spindle are accomplished by moving the machine column or the spindle.

The work locating table is an important element of the fixture-to-machine connector system devised to ensure accurate and rigid support of the workpiece. The top face of each table carries a precision multitooth ring which mates with a similar ring on the under face of the pallet. Clamping force is equalized all around the mating rings to eliminate distortion.

To facilitate loading of workpieces onto palletized fixtures in the staging area, the workpieces must be qualified before delivery to the variable mission system. In some instances where qualifying operations are not difficult and do not involve much time, the qualifying machine may be located in or near the staging area. In such cases, the employee responsible for loading and unloading the system may have ample time to mill locating pads or drill manufacturing location holes in the workpieces and still perform his primary task effectively.

EMPLOYEE PROTECTION PROGRAM

With substantial progress in mechanization and automation, the most serious problem which must be faced by management is the protection of the employees who are affected by technological improvements. This problem requires major policy decisions on the part of top management, but manufacturing management must be prepared to implement such decisions in a manner which minimizes friction and gains the active support of the employees.

Essentially, it is desirable that annual wage increases which are negotiated be emphasized as justified only on the basis of increased productivity. Productivity must be stressed as the composite result of employee effort and the tools and equipment which are provided by management. At the lower levels of mechanization and automation, physical manual effort of the employees may have a greater influence upon productivity than the tools used by the employees. At the higher levels, tools and equipment may have a greater influence upon productivity, but only if employees exercise the proper alertness, judgment, and initiative which are necessary for maximum productivity.

Management concepts of job evaluation and work measurement must take into consideration the total productivity of the man-machine combination if basic wage rates and productivity standards are to be equitable. Unless there is tangible evidence that employees are obtaining a share of the benefits of improved technology, strong employee resistance may dissipate the economic advantages of technical progress.

In the larger manufacturing plants where high levels of mechanization and automation may be justified, the total employment is generally substantial. The normal rate of attrition due to voluntary terminations, retirements, and deaths may be greater than the number of employees who are being displaced by modernized manufacturing equipment. Under such circumstances, management should have no difficulty in adapting a firm policy that no employee will be terminated as the direct result of mechanization.

In the majority of manufacturing plants, seniority clauses in labor contracts provide for specific steps which are taken when displaced employees are to be assigned to other occupations. In the absence of contractual provisions in this area, management has an obligation to provide whatever retraining is necessary to enable displaced employees to qualify for other occupations which may be available.

The crux of the problem comes to the fore when the number of employees displaced by automation exceeds the number of jobs which are available in the immediate future as the result of normal attrition. In such cases, generous financial termination settlements are recommended and should be included in the calculation of economic justification of the automation installation. An alternative solution which may be suggested is that management take the initiative to locate fairly comparable jobs in other manufacturing plants in the area for the employees involved before they are terminated.

SUMMARY

Competition demands continuous progress in the improvement of manufacturing facilities. A host of alternatives is available to manufacturing management in its quest for the optimum level of mechanization and automation. Management must have a deep appreciation of all the advantages and disadvantages of technological progress to provide sound and persuasive guidance in attaining its objectives. It is necessary to anticipate strong employee resistance and to be prepared with a constructive program which protects job security and wins the active support of the entire organization.

BIBLIOGRAPHY

Bright, James R., *Automation and Management,* Division of Research, Harvard Business School, Boston, 1958.

Brosheer, Ben C., and James C. DeSollar, "Variable Mission Machining," *American Machinist,* September, 1968.

DeGroot, George, "Numerical Control on the Production Line," *American Machinist,* September, 1968.

Turnkey Systems for Moving Materials, Automated Handling Systems, Inc., Eaton, Yale & Towne, Inc., Washington, D.C., 1968.

Weir, Stanley M., *Order Selection: A Focal Point for Developing Warehouse Machine Systems,* American Management Association, New York, 1968.

CHAPTER NINE

Numerical Control Machines

WILLIAM M. STOCKER, JR. *Director, Industry Information,* American Machinist, *New York, New York*

In only a single decade, numerical control became firmly entrenched as a fundamental concept for manufacturing equipment control. More than a technical concept, numerical control evolved a philosophy of manufacturing organization, of system practice, which is as pertinent to management as it is to engineering and operations. Numerical control is widely recognized as the most significant manufacturing development of the twentieth century. From 1960 to 1967, installations increased tenfold.

Numerical control is significant because it provides a practical means of closing the communications gap between management and the specific functions of manufacturing equipment. In effect, it places control of the manufacturing processes directly in the hands of management, minimizing the need for interpretation of design ideas and thus the dangers of misunderstanding.

From an engineering standpoint, numerical control is significant because it offers the first feasible means of bypassing the limitations of mechanical technology. By eliminating or at least minimizing the need for drill jigs, workholding fixtures, cams, templates, and similar hardware, the factors of tooling, setup, and lead time are reduced to a small fraction of their role in conventional practice. Inherent in this reduction is a high degree of manufacturing flexibility. Thus the immediate advantage of numerical control is found in short-run manufacturing requirements.

DEFINITION OF NUMERICAL CONTROL

Any system (of control plus controlled equipment) is said to provide numerical control if it accepts commands—data and instructions—in symbolic form as an input and converts this information into a physical output—into physical values such as dimensions or quantities. Numerical control is sometimes called symbolic control.

Any input signal source or energy form may be used. Inputs may be electric, electronic, hydraulic, mechanical, pneumatic, optical, or the like. Although electric or electronic inputs are most common, the concept is not limited to any one form. The only criterion is that the signal be applied as a symbolic value and be converted to a physical value by the system.

Output motions, too, usually provided by drives, can be energized electrically, hydraulically, pneumatically, and otherwise. The form of output is determined only by its suitability to the function.

Information can be put into the system symbolically with a simple push button. More commonly, the input is via dial, perforated paper or Mylar tape, punched cards, or magnetic tape. Although the term "tape control" is widely used as a synonym for numerical control, a system does not have to include tape or cards to be numerically controlled. The input device can be as simple as a push button or as sophisticated as a general purpose computer.

Tape and cards serve only as information storage media—as external memories to feed data to the control. Their role is not unlike that of the jig and fixture, which remember position and location data, or the operation sheet given to a machine operator in conventional practice.

Record playback systems, in which an operator's procedure in making a first piece is recorded on magnetic tape and then is played back to the machine to control manufacture of additional pieces, are not numerical control. The operator has put in physical movements rather than symbolic values. He has merely used a tape recorder to memorize his motions.

Similarly, machines which are preprogrammed by physically setting length measures and limit stops, or are controlled by tape templates, are not numerically controlled. In such systems, too, the input is physical measurement. (Tape templates, such as are used to position large riveters, have holes physically spaced in the tape in relation to the desired hole location in the work. Numerical control tapes carry only symbolic data; they have no physical relationship to the workpiece.)

In selecting and evaluating control systems, it is important to recognize these distinctions. Costs, capability, accuracy, process flexibility—all are affected by them. Program control is a broad field in which numerical control is only one area, albeit basic and extensive.

Numbers in Control. As a philosophy, numerical control has carried manufacturing engineers into a whole new area of process control—the finite commands involving numbers. Complicated as they may appear, numbers provide information symbols for only three functions—counting, measuring, and predicting. Numbers are only symbols for values. They are not values in themselves. And Arabic numerals are only one of many ways to symbolize these values visually.

For conventional manufacturing equipment and the simpler NC machines, numbers are relegated to just two functions—counting and measuring. Prediction has been a function limited to the human mind until recently it became a particular capability of the computer.

The mind of man can manipulate and interpret highly complex numbers. His ten fingers led him into widespread use of the decimal system of numeration, using Arabic numerals. However, the less intelligent machine requires a simpler numeration system. Thus, numerically controlled equipment is instructed in a binary number system.

Binary numbers are numbers based on 2, rather than the base 10 used in the decimal system. The binary system requires only two numerals, 0 and 1. Where the decimal system calls for both position and value to establish total value, binary numbers use only position. Thus, for a simple electric switch, 1 is on and 0 is off, and the counting or measuring begins. A hole in a tape is 1; no hole is 0. Combining four switches in parallel permits counting from 0 to 15 in decimal—2^{n-1}, where n is the number of switches.

Most numerical control systems are designed to accept data in a numeration technique called "binary-coded decimal" or BCD. This notational form uses a block of binary positions on the tape to represent a decimal value, as shown by Figure 9-1. It is easier to read visually, and it simplifies programming. For complex parts, BCD can mean a longer tape than straight binary, but the extra length seldom causes much concern.

Whenever perforated tape or data processing cards are used, switches in the reader are actuated by the presence of the holes. With magnetic tape, magnetic impulses in the tape trigger the switches. In combination with logic devices, the switches interpret both numerical and instructive information.

Holes are arranged in channels on tape and in columns on cards. The standard Electronic Industries Association tape is one inch wide and has eight channels plus a row of sprocket holes to locate and drive it.

Although there are many information handling and directing techniques used in applying numerical controls, there are two basic types of systems which should be recognized by anyone studying the subject. These systems are defined in terms of the signals used to transmit information. They are called digital and analog. Signals are the information carriers which make up both the quantity, or dimensions, in which operations must be performed and the means by which operations can be performed. In each system, signals are amplified, transmitted, and switched.

The digital signal is, as the name connotes, a single, sharp, discrete signal of definite duration—usually a pulse. Frequently, in electrical terms, the signal pulse is a square wave. The analog signal is continuous; it gives a continuous representation of (is analogous to) some quantity or process. The signal from a light switch is digital; from an automobile speedometer, analog. Input to most NC systems for machine tools is essentially digital.

Each pulse has a definite value, such as 0.001 or 0.0001 inch, or the like. Thus a stream of one thousand 0.001-inch pulses would move a slide one inch. In addition, pulse patterns are used to actuate logic circuits which select the drive to receive the pulses, turn on coolant, change tools, and perform many other programmed commands. Full numerical control calls for:

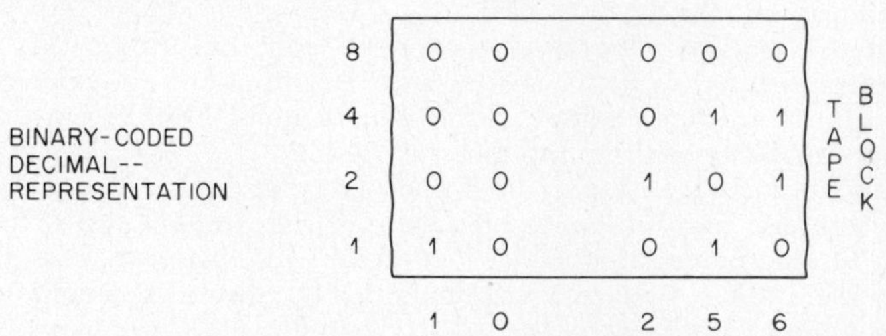

DECIMAL QUANTITY-- 10.256

	1	0		2	5	6	
8	0	0		0	0	0	
4	0	0		0	1	1	T A P E
2	0	0		1	0	1	
1	1	0		0	1	0	
	1	0		2	5	6	

BINARY-CODED DECIMAL-- REPRESENTATION   BLOCK

Fig. 9-1. Binary-coded Decimal Representation on Tape of the Decimal 10.256.

1. Instructions to the machine, such as direction of motion, start, stop, reverse, rapid traverse, and so on
2. Numerical values including dimensions, length of travel, speeds, feeds, number of pieces, and tool length from spindle
3. Auxiliary functions involving tool changing, coolant flow, chuck open or closed, lubrication, end-of-cycle signal, and so forth

Feedback. One other characteristic of NC systems is significant to their performance. This part of the system is called feedback. Generally, it is desirable but, depending upon the inherent accuracy of the system and its drives, it is not always essential.

Feedback devices in control systems monitor execution of the command. They return signals to the director to indicate that the given instruction and numerical value have been achieved—or, if incorrect, how much error exists. Feedback is applied in three principal forms: (1) to indicate how accurately the command has been carried out, (2) to feed correction signals into the director which provide automatic error compensation, and (3) to establish a control principle in continually reporting the position of a motion and, when this position signal is in balance or null with the input command signal, the motion stops.

Systems using feedback for self-compensation are called closed loop. Without feedback, or with feedback that serves only to indicate response, they are termed open loop. Some systems have a limited form of feedback applied to individual internal functions, such as between the input and output of each drive. Although these systems are considered open loop, they can be highly reliable.

To assume that feedback guarantees accuracy is highly dangerous. The characteristics of the system must be understood. Feedback from the end of a lead screw may not compensate for windup in the screw. Similarly, it will not compensate for misaligned or improperly sharpened cutting tools, nor for any error introduced between the spindle and the table. Stable friction characteristics in the slides and ample torque in the drives are as vital as feedback.

Other Characteristics. Numerically controlled machines must have certain characteristics which may or may not be present in conventional machines. Frequency response is a measure of the machine and control system's ability to change speed or direction quickly. It is probably the most critical factor in this technology. For continuous path (contouring and profiling) systems, it is even more critical than in positioning systems. In any case, frequency response should be as high as possible. Essentially, it is a function of the power elements and the stiffness of the mechanism. Other significant factors include friction, system sensitivity, windup, and play.

Adaptive control (see Figure 9-2) is a function designed to provide the inanimate machine control system with something akin to but far more sensitive than operator feel. Adaptive control continuously monitors all significant parameters of a metalworking operation and then feeds the information back to the control system so that it can modify machine action. Tool tip temperature, vibration, cutting force or torque, and spindle end thrust are some of the conditions which might be measured. The control can, for example, vary feed and speed to compensate for changes in material hardness or structure.

There is nothing complicated about the idea of controlling machine tools and a great variety of other equipment by feeding them numbers. The complexity is inside the system—and the manufacturing manager need concern himself only with its use.

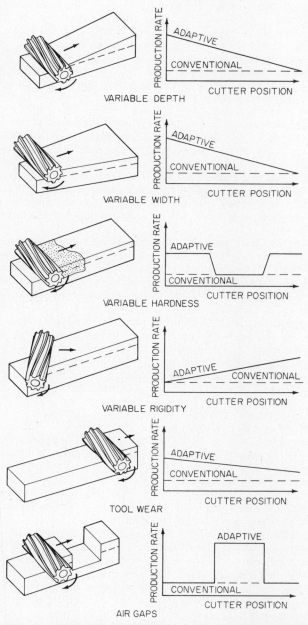

FIG. 9-2. Adaptive Control Illustrated. For a given combination of tool and work-piece, there are five major process variables: depth of cut, width of cut, workpiece hardness, stiffness between tool and work, and tool wear. By compensating for these variables, plus other minor ones, adaptive control increases productivity by minimizing noncutting time and maintains optimum rates. It also simplifies programming.

GETTING STARTED WITH NC

Several problems are virtually certain to arise when the suggestion to use numerical control is introduced.

1. NC is foreign to all the traditions and experiences of conventional manufacturing practice. It shifts authority and control from the shop floor to middle management. Rather than the customary functions in sequential steps, NC demands performance of several functions simultaneously. Traditional organization structures are disturbed. Some resistance, perhaps a great deal, is inevitable. Management must understand this resistance and allow for it.

2. Numerical control cannot succeed unless and until it has the enthusiastic support of top management. The impact of this technology, the changes it requires, and the financial investment demand top management involvement.

3. On first exposure, the dollar investment required for numerical control is staggering. This reaction stems from the tendency to look at cost rather than return, and to judge value on historical criteria. Many firms have had difficulty in justifying this investment because their cost accounting systems are outdated and do not reflect the unique cost considerations and differences in modern manufacturing processes. Frequently, the first NC machine is bought on faith. It establishes justification for further investment.

Planning. The era of pioneering in NC is past. Nevertheless, each new marriage has a critical trial period. It demands mature, detailed planning of all phases for the first acquisition to achieve profitable manufacturing practice. Nothing can destroy motivation and enthusiasm faster than an installation without a plan. And the content of the plan is quite different from that for acquiring conventional facilities.

Evolution of an NC acquisition can be planned in six stages, the first three of which are diagrammed in some detail in Figure 9-3.

1. With initial interest in the concept, investigate the characteristics of NC as a manufacturing procedure and as a solution to manufacturing problems. Evaluate the manufacturing needs plus the kinds of equipment available to meet those needs. Choose several alternatives. Based on return on investment, or even payback, justify the amount of investment which is appropriate to the need. Explore the intangible values of NC. Select the most suitable equipment. Visit plants where the equipment is in use. Observe the procedures related to its use.

2. The time has come to procure the equipment. Place the order. Avoid overdoing the extras. As in buying an automobile, once enthusiasm sets in, there is a tendency to order all the options. This practice runs up the bill. Stick to the plan. Include options only as the need is obvious. As soon as the order is placed, prepare to use the equipment. Preplan the work to be done, including redistribution of machine loading and analysis of NC effects on other processes. Predetermine the tooling to be used, then set a completion date for it. Design or order the tools—both cutting and workholding. Pretrain for programming, operation, and maintenance. Select apt personnel and set up a formal training program. Allow for an open-end continuing program.

From the first planning step, maintain a detailed log of the plan and each element of its completion. Also, even though the plan includes only one machine at first, structure it to consider broader use of NC in the plant.

3. When the machine is installed, everything should be ready for it to go into operation—people, programs, parts, and procedures. At first, experiment.

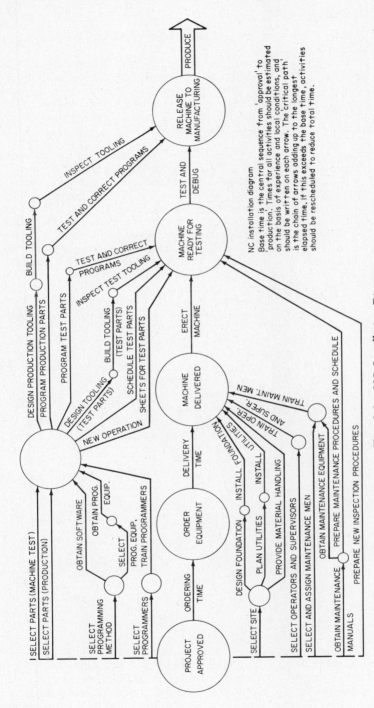

Fig. 9-3. NC Installation Diagram.

Test the programs and tooling. Get familiar with the machine, with its capabilities and its idiosyncrasies. Then go into full production, optimizing its use as capability develops.

4. For efficient use of the NC concept, plan to expand its application; take time to restudy peripheral effects. If the first three phases have been reasonably successful and the manufacturing requirement is sufficiently large, it is logical to add more NC facilities and organize an NC department. Now it is more feasible to schedule subsequent installations based upon their relative importance from a plant-wide viewpoint. Take a fresh look at procedures, programming, maintenance, inspection, product design, tooling (fixtures and cutting tools), personnel, supervision, assembly, and make-or-buy policies.

5. Departmentalization of NC is the keynote of the transition to the "new" NC organizational structure. Now the initial plan should be restudied and rewritten for total involvement. The basics of all manufacturing functions in the plant, including design and purchasing, must be analyzed. How can the NC concept be used to integrate these functions? Then the plan must provide for converting, without disruption, from the traditional structure to the NC configuration. Finally, the plan must provide for optimizing output. As the operational plan is developed, a financial plan should parallel it. From a department, NC can be expanded to the entire plant.

6. The final phase of NC planning introduces computer assistance. If even the first machine must do contouring, some computer assistance is necessary for programming. Even positioning (point-to-point) programs can be prepared more efficiently with computer assistance, but the latter is not essential. Initially, it might be prudent to hire the services of a consultant or a programming service to provide computer know-how in the manner illustrated by Figure 9-4. Large plants will, very likely, have a general purpose computer. Smaller plants may have one too. If not, they have several choices: installing a small general purpose computer; contracting for remote access, time-sharing computer service which offers large computer capability at nominal cost; or contracting for outside computer programming service.

To move to NC at a departmental level, and certainly for plant-wide use, some in-house computer competence is highly desirable. At this stage, emphasis should be placed on correlating the NC functions with computer functions, design functions, production control functions, and the like, plus the functions of manufacturing and business management. Here, too, professional counsel is advisable.

Every manufacturing organization, large or small, should go through the steps listed in phase 1. There are enough successful and profitable NC installations to warrant investigation. The extent of the detail that may be involved is a matter of the individual firm's internal policy and procedures. However, stinting on the study in time or talent can prove costly. Time, effort, and profit can be lost in an installation that takes place without a plan and grows without control.

Anyone experienced in manufacturing and engaged in NC operations or familiar with its primary values can evaluate the NC potential with a quick survey. Recognizing where NC definitely belongs is not hard. However, to decide fringe area applications is sometimes difficult.

Reasons Vary. Justification of NC installations varies in many ways. One company bought NC to give it the capability for handling work that the management would like to do rather than the work they were doing. Another firm bought NC to reduce the cost of inventory. In a third instance, reduction of inspection time by 85 percent with the first NC machine warranted

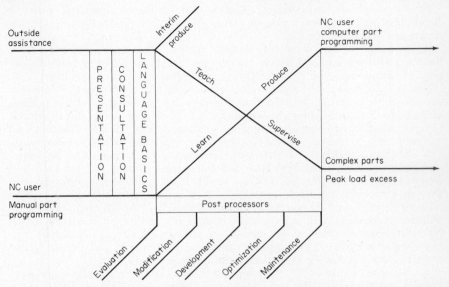

Fig. 9-4. Method of Using Outside Consultants to Provide Computer Know-how.

purchase and installation of a second machine. Many firms buy NC machines to reduce tooling and setup costs. For some of these installations, the reduction in lead time is more significant than the cost saving.

One example of selection initially involved a machining center and a turret drill combination. It ideally suited the work involved. Eighteen months later, an expansion was needed. Initial judgment had proved sound by post-audit figures. The simplest and least risky action was to duplicate the initial setup.

Instead, the company restudied its current requirement. New ideas and new machines had been developed. A completely different machining center was procured, producing at nearly twice the rate of the first equipment.

Work Selection. Originally, numerical control was developed to meet the need to generate the intricate mathematically defined shapes used in aerodynamic structures. After several years of development in this direction, based on complex, contouring profilers and skin mills—"elephant machines" —manufacturing engineers realized that NC offered a machine tool having an inherent measuring system and memory. It could remember and locate any point, line, or path in space.

Suddenly, manufacturing had found a breakthrough in what had become a major obstacle to any significant increase in productivity—the limitation of mechanical control of manufacturing variables. NC offered, in electronic control, a fresh opportunity.

There is no part configuration or lot size which should not be considered for manufacture by numerical control. This claim does not mean that every possibility is practical. It does mean that all parts and quantities should be studied in the context of the NC opportunity.

Parts machined on NC equipment range from simple motor shafts to such things as the shells (housings) for large steam turbines, from bushing plates to complex aerodynamic structures and forging dies. In addition, NC is used to punch electronic chassis, form tubing, assemble various products, control flame cutting, apply paint, and for many other purposes. Generally, the more distinct the operations, the more individual the measurements, and the more surfaces which require work, the better the opportunity to apply NC. This concept is the only way to machine mathematically defined irregular curves.

Quantity is another important consideration. NC is best known for the benefits that it offers in short-run manufacturing. Most of the workpieces processed by NC are in lots of 1 to 50 pieces, with the majority 5 to 25. However, lots of 500 or more are proving practical. The real criterion is found in piece complexity—the more complicated and precise the part, the more tooling and setup time required, the smaller is the number of pieces that can be processed advantageously. In many instances, companies program a tape for one piece. Figure 9-5 shows the cost/quantity relationships when machining complex castings by various methods.

With the availability of NC, it pays to restudy all lot sizes. Frequently, parts are produced in large lots and then put in inventory for use over a long period, merely to reduce the tooling and setup cost per piece. Processing these parts by NC in smaller lots at more frequent intervals can result in substantial inventory savings. Part family grouping increases productivity.

NC also is applied to transfer machines for some part requirements. Reductions in setup time of 90 percent and more make production of 500 pieces or more profitable. This application is especially practical when frequent design changes are called for within a family of parts.

NC AND DESIGN

Every management problem, it is said, stems from a change. Yet without change there is no management. One of the major managerial worries is

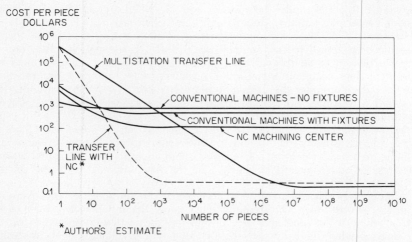

Fig. 9-5. Cost of Machining Complex Castings. (*Data courtesy of General Electric Company.*)

interpretation of instructions; hence every point of information transfer is critical. As an innovation in communications, NC offers significant improvement in the accuracy of information management.

Product or finished part design traditionally includes two basic functions: development of the concept and specifications by the designer, plus drafting of the product characteristics into a formal engineering communication for use by manufacturing. NC simplifies both the design function and manual drafting. Also, closely correlated with NC and readily integrated into a total NC system, computer-aided design brings new freedoms to the designer as well as improved manufacturing data.

Freedoms. One of the major advantages of NC is the greater freedom that it offers designers in using mathematical constructions, especially regular and irregular curves. Where traditional manufacturing practices frequently force a compromise, NC permits optimum shapes. If a mathematical definition is possible, the NC machine can generate the shape. Where three-dimensional models are used or the desired curve is "art" and not capable of mathematical expression, the data can be digitized in an NC measuring machine (digitizer), points blended to smooth the curves, and machine tool control tapes prepared to produce the shape.

For use in NC part programming, drawings can be simpler than for conventional operations. They require less time to produce and less effort to read. Dimensions and pertinent lettering can be applied with a typewriter.

Tolerancing of the drawing is less critical with NC because the NC machine used to produce the part will hold its inherent tolerance regardless of the drawing call-out. The designer must know machine capability. The variability introduced by manual control is absent.

In theory, no drawing is required for NC manufacturing. The designer, using at most a rough sketch, can define the part directly as an NC manuscript from which the tape is prepared. However, many people, including many parts programmers, need a visual aid to help them understand the part configuration. Hence drawings and prints still are common. Some saving can be made by using a single drawing for a family of parts and by using matrix programming. The latter shows, for example, one bolt circle on the drawing; all other similar bolt circles are identified by the location of the circle's center plus a note to describe its characteristics.

Restraints. NC provides greater control of manufacturing variables than is possible or practical in conventional equipment. However, NC also requires closer attention to all the variables that affect satisfactory completion of the part than does an operator-controlled machine. One reason is that relatively few NC machines offer the degree of adaptive control over these variables that is found in the hands of a skilled operator. The time and place to plan for control of these variables is in design.

Materials introduce one of the most influential sets of variables. The designer should specify materials with sufficient care to assure cohesive and reliable structural integrity. Blowholes, sand inclusions, hard spots, warped castings, excessive overall hardness, and the like will not be "seen" by the cutting tool until it is too late.

Although the lack of need to put tolerances on drawings is an advantage, it also is a restraint. The designer must know the inherent accuracy of the NC machine to be used and then design mating parts within this restriction. No matter what he calls out, the machine will give only what its design, construction, and maintenance permit.

NC machines should be selected to work with a specific category of part shapes. Part of the selection process is a determination of the number and variety of cuts (surfaces, holes, threads, angles, curves, and so on) needed to complete the parts. The machine, as a result, should include the necessary cutting tool capacity, work capacity, degrees of freedom (axes and motions), and the like to complete the parts in one setup. Thus, if a machining center is used, for example, it might include ten tools, thirty tools, sixty tools, a rotary table, table tilt, and other features.

The designer should know the extent of this capability and should strive to hold the variety of operations within it. The number of cuts should be as small as is practical, of course, but productivity is more seriously affected by the variety of different cuts, especially if the part must be put through the machine twice.

Similarly, the designer should know the capacity of the NC machine and then keep all parts within that "envelope." At the time of selection, it pays to buy the largest capacity machine that the budget will permit. Most first-machine users find themselves wishing for larger capacity. As they get accustomed to using NC, they tend to schedule larger parts.

Standardization. The designer should reevaluate all the characteristics of the part and then simplify it. For example, studies show that one-third of the commercial drill sizes smaller than one inch meet all normal design needs for drilled holes.

Changes, even with NC, cost money. Another restraint, which more often is considered a freedom, is limiting design changes to those which truly make sense. In other words, change just for the sake of change should be avoided. Companies using NC equipment find that design changes are so easily absorbed into the manufacturing schedule, compared with conventional practice, that design becomes an unchained tiger. With NC, a value analysis program is more important than ever.

Computer-aided Design. By using the computer as a design tool, with or without numerical control, management has a unique man-machine capability. Computer-aided design permits the designer to contribute what he does best—his thinking, his creativity, his concepts—while the computer performs its role of calculating and predicting. The part design is developed as a result of the direct, on-line dialog between the designer and the computer. One output of the computer can be a design master tape from which NC machine control tapes can be generated to manufacture the part.

CAD, computer-aided design, is available in several degrees of sophistication. The simplest form uses the computer as a catalog to store part descriptions. The designer tells the computer the performance requirements of a product, and the computer then selects the appropriate parts for assembly.

The more advanced CAD system combines a large general purpose computer with several input-output consoles which include light-sensitive cathode-ray tubes. The designer sketches his ideas on the screen of the cathode-ray tube (CRT) with a light-pen and then inserts values or symbols through an adjacent keyboard. The input shapes and data are analyzed by the computer and returned to the designer for evaluation, correction, or elaboration. This exchange continues until the design is complete. One computer can serve six or more consoles.

CAD requires a substantial capital investment. However, the direct benefits justify this expenditure, and the indirect benefits amplify the return. For example:

1. Design productivity is increased from five to sixty times.
2. Drawing changes are much easier to make and control.

3. Design data, as output, are suitable for direct evaluation or for application in other phases of the total design procedure.
4. NC tapes can be prepared from the design data output.
5. Lead time for the design function on major new-product programs (aerospace, automotive, shipbuilding, and the like) can be reduced by as much as 90 percent.
6. Cost estimating is made faster and more accurate.
7. Savings are significant in avoiding overdesign and interferences.

Management Challenge. Numerical control in manufacturing has created an astonishing integration of all manufacturing functions. It is inherent in the need for simultaneous rather than sequential functions as control is shifted out of the shop and closer to the design phase. NC forces closer liaison between design engineers and manufacturing engineers. Decisions must be shared. Designers must be educated to define and specify the part configurations to accommodate the NC requirements. Manufacturing managers and engineers must understand the significance of design conditions and criteria.

The transition to NC demands that management introduce modern drafting practices where they are not already in use. Drafting for NC has three fundamentals:

1. Dimensioning should be done in the decimal system.
2. True-position dimensioning should be used for both location and tolerance of part characteristics.
3. Datum surfaces are critical to good part programming; hence draftsmen must be taught how to select them.

Decimal system dimensioning does not mean that the dimensions should inherently suggest more precise work. Where fractions are shown to the nearest $\frac{1}{64}$ inch, it is normally satisfactory to replace them with increments of 0.02 inch. Where, in the conversion of old drawings, parts are interchangeable or tooling is involved, it is essential to analyze all related dimensions before conversion. It can add considerably to the cost of a part, tool expense, acceptable quality level, and the like, if draftsmen casually use 0.0156 or even 0.016 inch to replace $\frac{1}{64}$ inch.

Datum points or surfaces are critical to NC performance. As the "zero-zero" reference for measurement to the various motion end points, one datum point is determined for all dimensions or motions in X, one for Y, and one for Z (see Figure 9-6). Datum points and planes must be determined so that the part programmer can use the print dimensions without further calculation. Also, consideration must be given to workholding devices and other conditions which can cause interference with table and tool motions. Carefully selected datum references also expedite quality control inspection.

Zero offset is supplied for each axis of most NC machines to permit final adjustment of the machine's measuring system relative to the datum plane.

Generally, drawings for numerical control should be made to a base-line coordinate system in which all dimensions are perpendicular or parallel to the predetermined datum planes. Coordinates of significant points should be specified or readily determinable. For general curves, either an algebraic equation or a list of points from which a smooth curve can be approximated should be given, with points close enough to permit quadratic interpolation between them, unless a computer program is available to generate these data. Ultimately, this coordinate, true-position system will improve the productivity and the accuracy of the designer, the draftsman, the checker, the programmer, the machine operator, and the inspector. It also implements tool design and development.

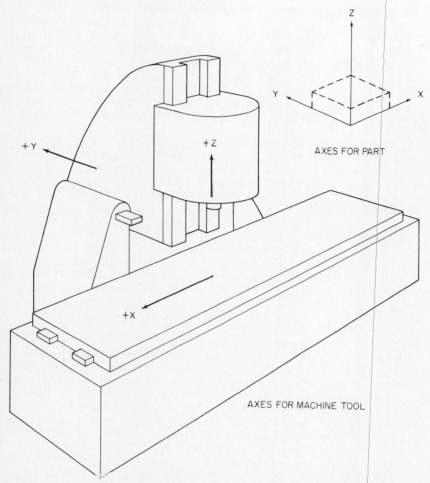

FIG. 9-6. Axes for Machine Tool and Part. Axes for a specific machine tool are selected to give the standard cartesian coordinates X, Y, and Z on the part. Around each of the primary axes is an axis of rotation. A machine cannot have more than six axes. Beyond that scope are multiple motions within the same axis.

NC AND QUALITY

"Quality control" is another way of saying "limiting variability (of part features) within the tolerances specified for proper performance of the product." Inspection is used to determine whether these limits have been held—after the fact. As a procedure intended to increase control of manufacturing variables markedly, numerical control is inherently quality control.

Quality control procedures, including the inspection function, in plants using NC will be sharply influenced by NC. In fact, this influence will pervade even the conventional operations. With NC, quality control is no less important, but it may have a different role.

What traditionally was man-machine capability now becomes machine and control capability—and more significant than frequent sampling. Parts manufactured on NC equipment are generally more accurate than conventionally produced parts. Furthermore, consistency from part to part and from one lot to the next is outstanding. In lots of two or more, the proximity to identical form resulting from this consistency will upgrade the quality level and productivity of operations which follow NC.

One company president who agreed to purchase an NC machine but had serious misgivings about the concept was pleasantly astounded. He saw, for the first time in his firm's history, the men in the shop assembling the parts without files and taper reamers.

Normally with NC, the tape is checked against the first piece produced from it. If the piece and hence the tape are satisfactory, the same level of quality can be anticipated for the remainder of pieces in the lot. For large lots or highly complex pieces, sampling inspection of key dimensions can be done from time to time. However, because even the metal removal rate is predetermined in the program, it is possible to predict such factors as tool wear and then compensate to hold dimensions within limits.

First-piece inspection is important. As the job and the machine must wait until it is complete, this inspection also can be a costly bottleneck. Several hours may be needed to inspect a part which was machined in minutes.

Coordinate measuring machines offer one very practical solution to this delay. For point-to-point work, these machines can cut inspection time as much as 90 percent. One part requiring eight hours to inspect on a surface plate with a height gage, angle blocks, and other conventional inspection tools was finished in twenty minutes.

Simpler CMM's use a manually moved probe and some form of decimal digital readout of X and Y or X, Y, and Z dimensions. More sophisticated machines provide a printout of the dimensions, with out-of-tolerance dimensions shown in red. The latter is made possible by feeding the probe reading to a small general purpose computer adjacent to the measuring machine.

If the computer is fed design data, or the machine control tape data, along with the readings of the actual part dimensions, it can output errors as well as wall thicknesses, clearances, hole straightness, roundness, and the like. Of course, the CMM is useful for non-NC parts too.

Traditional inspection methods, as well as much of the equipment used to implement these methods, are more susceptible to error than is the NC equipment used to make the parts to be inspected. Thus, effective inspection is one of the critical challenges in NC use.

The requirement has brought about greater use of the laser for interferometry, as well as other optical and electronic gaging innovations. It opens a whole new field of manufacturing metrology.

NC Inspection Machines. Both to measure highly complex parts produced by NC and to inspect critical components whether or not NC was involved, another application of NC has had substantial growth. The NC inspection machine has some of the characteristics of the coordinate measuring machine, but in addition, the probe (or probes) is tape- or computer-directed according to a predetermined program. Thus it can take thousands of readings of discrete points, curves, thicknesses, and the like in a very short time.

An "inversion" of the measuring capability is used to provide a digitizer. The probe travels over the surface of the three-dimensional model, as of an automobile body, to obtain the data for programming machine control tapes.

Management and Quality Control. Quality control is a by-product of NC. At the operating level, NC provides substantial freedom from conventional inspection problems. Restraints, or at least quality awareness, must take place at earlier stages such as design, manufacturing engineering, part programming, and production control. Facilities selection and maintenance also are critical to quality.

Normally, quality control personnel will devote more time to the accuracy of tape preparation, tooling, and the NC equipment itself than they will to the parts which result from the equipment. As one result, some reevaluation of direct versus indirect labor may be advisable.

NC AND LABOR

It has been said that as automation affects human effort, so numerical control affects human skill. Never before NC, in the entire history of civilization, has it been possible to translate an idea into physical reality except through the skill in human hands. Now that restriction has ended. A whole new frontier of technological challenge has opened. A threshold has been crossed.

The impact of this technological change is so overwhelming in its portents that some managers even reject NC because they consider it too demoralizing to their skilled employees. In actual practice, negative reaction by labor has not been significant. Conversely, there is considerable demand by shop people to be assigned to NC equipment. It is a prestige assignment.

All the impact of NC on labor, and it can be far-reaching, stems from just a single change in the job requirement—digital skill. Of course, no element of manufacturing practice is more fundamental. In selecting operators for NC equipment, attitude is the predominant trait to consider.

Other than digital skill, NC in no way minimizes the competency, training, and experience of manufacturing personnel. In fact, optimum use of NC requires that personnel be well versed in machine function, manufacturing (operational) sequence, tooling, setup, cutting tool geometry, methods, shop mathematics, and the like. However, the point of application of this knowledge is shifted from the machine site to planning and part programming. The machine operator, essentially an observer, need not have this level of competency.

Understandably, NC equipment, which has the productivity of two to ten conventional machines, will ultimately displace workers. Only a greatly expanded and highly diversified market can postpone this situation. However, to date there have not been enough people trained in these metalworking skills to meet the demand by industry. NC has merely helped offset the skill shortage, a condition which is likely to exist for some years to come.

Operator skills, wage plans, and incentive systems must be reviewed and adjusted to suit the NC environment. Many workers must be relocated within the plant and trained for new jobs to replace those assumed by the NC equipment. Some of these people will do well as programmers and as NC maintenance specialists. Others can be used in the toolroom and in quality control. These tasks offer equivalent compensation or, especially for programming, better compensation. It will, nevertheless, require highly knowledgeable and enlightened management to make this transition without damaging employee morale or straining union relationships.

It is the practice of some firms to assign highly skilled personnel as operators of NC equipment. The principle is that the hourly rate paid these people is not significant as related to the investment in the equipment and the productivity obtained from it. Using a knowledgeable operator is good insurance, a practical form of training, and a constant source of counsel to improve both programming and equipment performance.

In some companies, operators have requested supplemental work to avoid boredom. At least one company has an incentive system based not on the productivity of the NC machine, but on the additional work done by the NC operator while assigned to the NC equipment. He can be assigned any of a series of rated tasks.

Under NC, the climate of industrial relations still is influenced by management's ability to develop sound personnel policies as well as procedures for consulting, communicating, and negotiating. However, the way in which the work to be done is organized and controlled is becoming a far more critical factor. The influence of the manufacturing engineer himself can be more meaningful than that of the personnel manager or the shop steward.

Rather than demoralizing, NC in the plant seems to spark a new enthusiasm and spirit among manufacturing employees. NC fosters better organization and control.

BIBLIOGRAPHY

"AM on NC," a 200-page compendium of NC articles, *American Machinist*, McGraw-Hill Book Company, New York, 1967.

American Machinist 10th Inventory of Metalworking Equipment, McGraw-Hill Book Company, New York, 1968.

Childs, James J., *Principles of Numerical Control*, The Industrial Press, New York, 1965.

Dyke, R. M., *Numerical Control*, Prentice-Hall, Inc., Englewood Cliffs, N.J., 1967.

Leone, William C., *Production Automation and Numerical Control*, The Ronald Press Company, New York, 1967.

Proceedings—Numerical Control Society, Numerical Control Society, Princeton, N.J., published annually.

Stocker, W. M., Jr., "How to Prove the Profit in Numerical Control," special report no. 513, *American Machinist*, Oct. 30, 1961.

CHAPTER TEN

Facility Records

T. P. KELLY   *Principal, A. T. Kearney & Company, Inc., New York, New York*

R. E. RENKEN   *Principal, A. T. Kearney & Company, Inc., New York, New York*

This chapter deals with various types of facility records and the necessary systems and procedures required to support them. As with most records systems, some form of paperwork is a necessity for proper control, although caution must be exercised to ensure that only the optimum amount is generated. Too little paperwork may result in the loss of control, whereas too much can create an unmanageable maze of forms and red tape. Where appropriate, the advantages and disadvantages of any recommended systems are discussed to assist the manufacturing manager in evaluating them against his own requirements.

DESIGN OF FACILITY IDENTIFICATION SYSTEM

An important consideration in implementing a facility records system is the identification of the property itself. In situations where the equipment is a self-contained unit, that is, where there are no supplementary components such as motors, pumps, or drives, identification of the facility as a whole seems fairly obvious. However, where the facility is comprised of many major components which are interchangeable with other pieces of equipment, it may be necessary to identify the components also. An example of the latter would be a reactor in the chemical industry, which is comprised of a motor, drive, cover, agitator, and the main shell.

In designing a facility identification system, it must be decided if the identification numerals and letters should be coded so that they identify the type of equipment, its location, and whether it is the original installation or a replacement.

Aftercooler	AFC		Heat exchanger	HEX
Agitator	AGT		Heater	HTR
Air conditioner	AC		Intercooler	INC
Air handling unit	AHU		Kettle	KTL
Autoclave	AUT		Kettle coil	KCL
Centrifuge	CRF		Meter	M
Coil	CL		Motor	MO
Column	COL		Motor generator	MG
Compressor	COM		Precipitator	PRC
Concentrator	CNL		Pump	PMP
Condenser	CND		Reactor	REA
Conveyor	CNY		Recorder	RCD
Cylinder	CYL		Regulator	REG
Drill press	DP		Safety valve	SV
Dryer	DRY		Screen	SCR
Elevator	ELV		Scrubber	SCB
Evaporator	EVP		Speed reducer	SPR
Exhauster	FAN		Tank	TNK
Fan	FAN		Trap	TP
Filter	FIL		Turbine	TUR
Gage	GA		Valve	V
Generator	GEN			

FIG. 10-1. Typical Equipment Abbreviations.

As an example, the type of equipment can readily be identified by a prefix of two or three letters which is an abbreviation of its name. In this manner, all drill presses may be prefixed with DP, motors with MO, air handling units with AHU, and so on. Figure 10-1 shows a list of typical equipment abbreviations. Specific identification is accomplished by assigning an individual number to each piece of equipment within a grouping.

In multibuilding plants, the location of the equipment also can be coded by building number. In the case of drill press 1073 located in building 61, the identification number would be 61-DP1073.

Finally, in plants where it is advantageous to determine whether the equipment is the original installation or a replacement, an additional letter may be employed. Using the previous illustration, the original drill press would be identified by 61-DP1073. In the event it was scrapped, its replacement would be 61-DP1073A; if it were replaced again, it would be 61-DP1073B, and so on.

Other Considerations. There are also some instances where the costs of maintaining a building are significant and a breakdown by type of repair is needed. In this case, building services are grouped into categories such as miscellaneous piping, electrical repairs, masonry work, and structural steel repairs, and an identification number different from that used for equipment is assigned. If structural steel repairs were assigned an identification code of 101, then 61-101 would represent structural steel repairs in building 61 and 62-101 would represent the same type of repair in building 62.

Another Approach. Another numbering system consists of six digits divided into three groups—system, item, and unit numbers. Any piece of equipment is identified by referring to its number in the following sequence:

System Number		Item Number		Unit Number
00	-	00	-	00

The first two digits identify the general category of the equipment. This number applies to a broad classification of equipment performing a similar function. For example, a compressed air system could have the system number 15 which would be written as follows:

15-00-00

The system number alone is too broad to pinpoint the costs associated with some equipment. For this reason, the second two digits are used to identify particular items in a given system and are referred to as the item number. The compressed air system could then be subdivided into an air compressor which would be given the item number 10 and a distribution system which would be given the item number 11. Additional item numbers could be added if a further breakdown were required. The equipment numbers for the compressed air system would then be:

15-10-00
15-11-00

These would identify the air compressor and its distribution system individually.

The third group of digits in the equipment number is the unit number. Unit numbers are assigned consecutively, beginning with 10, to identify different pieces of equipment under the same system and item classification. Thus, in a system intended to collect detailed information on two compressed air stations, the equipment would be numbered as follows:

15-10-10   (first air compressor)
15-10-11   (second air compressor)
15-11-10   (first distribution system)
15-11-11   (second distribution system)

The actual numbering will depend upon the needs of a particular facility. Depending on the system, item or unit numbers may not be required. In the case of furniture and office equipment, only system data may be desired. The equipment number for all this equipment might then be 51-00-00. The equipment records would show the total costs charged for the maintenance of all furniture and office equipment without a distinction as to how the charges were distributed. In some cases, the item number but no unit number may be desirable. The equipment number 51-10-00 would apply to all furniture repair. The equipment number 51-11-00 would apply to all mechanical office equipment repair. In other instances, the item number may be unnecessary but the unit number may be important, such as: 51-00-10, referring to all furniture and office equipment in a certain building. 51-00-11 would apply to similar items in another building.

It should be recognized that the size of the plant and the number of units to be identified will be the major factors in determining the degree of sophistication required. It is obvious that a small plant encompassing one building with only 100 units can utilize a simple three-digit number. In developing a system, however, provisions should be made for expansion so that redesign will not be required as new facilities are added.

INSTALLATION OF FACILITY IDENTIFICATION SYSTEM

The method of installing the facility identification system will vary slightly depending on whether a new or an existing facility is involved. In a new facility, the installation phase can begin with the delivery of the first piece of equipment. In an existing facility, there may be thousands of units to be identified and a physical inventory may initially be required. Although both cases utilize the same principles, the existing facility presents the more difficult task and therefore will be discussed in more detail.

Selecting the Personnel. The individual selected to make the facility inventory need not be technically trained. A well-qualified maintenance clerk who will later be working with the system is often an excellent choice, because this initial exposure will acquaint him with the system and the equipment involved. Regardless of the person selected, it is important that he be thoroughly familiar with the proper method of assigning equipment identification codes or numbers and collecting the information required to develop the records. The design of an equipment record form is discussed later in this chapter.

Identification Tags. Another facet to be considered in designing the system is the type of identification tag to be used and how it will be installed. In the chemical and oil industries, where equipment may be exposed to an extremely severe environment, it is important that the tag be made of corrosion resistant material and firmly attached to the equipment with fasteners which will not readily be affected by the elements. In a relatively clean environment, such as in an office, a paste-on tag may be suitable. Other types of tags frequently used are brass discs and lead plates. In both cases, the identifying numbers and letters are stamped on the tag.

If possible, the tag should be installed by the person taking the inventory. However, local policies and union agreements may require that it be installed by a craftsman. In this situation, it would be advisable for the person taking the inventory to write the identifying number on the equipment with a marking pencil and have the craftsman install the permanent tag later.

Equipment Inventory Procedure. The method by which the equipment inventory is taken is another important consideration. Two approaches are:

1. Select a specific type of equipment such as motor generators and concentrate on it until all units are inventoried. Then proceed to the next type. This method is often employed in situations where the information obtained during the inventory will also be used to develop preventive maintenance inspection procedures on critical equipment.

2. Concentrate on a physical area such as a building or a department and inventory all existing equipment. Under this approach, there is less likelihood that the one-of-a-kind type of equipment will be missed.

EQUIPMENT INVENTORY RECORDS

Equipment inventory records are important in manufacturing operations, regardless of the size of the operation. A small model shop operation with fifty pieces of equipment, or a large manufacturing facility with thousands, should maintain a record for each individual unit. While many companies maintain such records for accounting purposes, such as depreciation, they should also be used in plant maintenance for accumulating repair information and recording lubrication specifications, spare parts information, inspection schedules, and equipment modifications.

Many companies keep two sets of records for the same equipment. The accounting records are concerned primarily with original costs and depreciation schedules, while the maintenance records cover detailed information pertaining to the servicing and repair of the equipment. It is usually possible, however, to design one system which will accommodate both.

Field Inventory Sheets. The field inventory form should be completed, where possible, by the individual taking the physical inventory and assigning the identification number. Its design is contingent on the type of equipment

FIELD INVENTORY SHEET

DATE_____

PLANT_____

BLDG/EQUIP. NO. _____

ITEM_____

MANUFACTURER_____

P. O. NO._____DATE PURCH. _____

PURCH. FROM_____

MODEL NO._____SERIAL NO. _____

TYPE_____SIZE_____CAPACITY_____

HORSEPOWER _____VOLTS_____AMPS_____

RPM_____PHASE_____CYCLES_____

OTHER DESCRIPTIVE DATA_____

_____

_____

BEARING DATA_____

_____

LUBRICATION DATA_____

_____

DRIVE SPECIFICATIONS_____

_____

PACKING OR MECHANICAL SEAL SPECS_____

_____

OTHER SPECIFICATIONS OR COMMENTS_____

_____

FIG. 10-2. Field Inventory Sheet Used in Taking the Physical Inventory.

to be inventoried, that is, mechanical, electronic, and the like, and more than one form may be needed in a given system. An example is shown in Figure 10-2.

When completed, the field inventory sheets should be reviewed by an engineer or a knowledgeable person who can add any additional data that may be required.

EQUIPMENT RECORD

ITEM			BLDG/EQUIP. NO.	
MANUFACTURER				
P.O. NO.		DATE PURCH.	PURCH. PRICE	
PURCH. FROM				
MODEL NO.		SERIAL NO.		
STYLE		CAT. NO.	DWG. NO.	
TYPE		SIZE	CAPACITY	
HORSEPOWER		VOLTS	AMPS.	
RPM		PHASE	CYCLES	
OTHER DESCRIPTIVE DATA				

BEARING DATA

LUBRICATION DATA

DRIVE SPECIFICATIONS

PACKING OR MECH. SEAL SPECS

AUXILIARY EQUIPMENT

OTHER SPECIFICATIONS OR COMMENTS

RECOMMENDED P.M.

INTERNAL TRANSFER

DATE	FROM	TO	REMARKS

SPARE PARTS

PART NO.	DESCRIPTION	RECOMMENDED STOCK	
		MAX.	MIN.

FIG. 10-3.   Equipment Record Form.

Equipment Records.   Equipment records are usually permanently filed in the plant engineering or the maintenance department so that they will be readily available.   They include information such as size, type, motor specifications, packing or mechanical seal specifications, manufacturer's name and address, availability of replacement parts, power transmission information, and similar important details.

Information from the field inventory sheets should be transferred to the equipment record form.   A typewriter should be used rather than pen or pencil because this will be a permanent record.   Field inventory sheets can be destroyed once the permanent record has been established.

A filing system based on the identification code or number is most commonly used. If the identification code is designed to include the location and type of equipment, it will permit quick retrieval of the record, thereby minimizing time spent in searching for the information. An example of an equipment record form is shown by Figure 10-3.

Other Information. It is important that all information pertaining to a specific piece of equipment be available in one location and not scattered throughout several files. For this reason, many plants utilize the equipment record for recording periodic preventive maintenance inspections, a list of spare parts to be inventoried, minimum and maximum inventory levels, and maintenance costs.

Where possible, the space required to record the above information should be included in the original design of the equipment record form. However, if this is not possible, an auxiliary form which can be attached to the original record may be utilized.

MAINTENANCE COST RECORDS

Equipment identification is a necessity if maintenance and repair costs for individual units are to be identified. Proper cost records cannot be developed, however, unless work order, timekeeping, and material cost systems are functioning effectively.

Work Order System. A work order system serves many purposes. However, in the case of facility records, it can be used to isolate the cost of individual repairs. Even though total maintenance and repair costs can still be identified if labor and material are charged to the equipment identification code, the work order system permits the isolation of the various types of repairs and the cost of each.

A quarterly repair cost of one thousand dollars representing twenty separate repairs on twenty different units may not be significant. However, the same quarterly expenditure representing twenty repair occurrences on the same unit may indicate improper design, poor maintenance, or lack of preventive maintenance, and may highlight areas for further investigation.

Figure 10-4 is an illustration of a work order form. Although it is important that the information required be complete, caution must be taken to design the system so that it does not require excessive effort by the persons using the document. Space should be provided on the form to insert the equipment identification code and identify the type of repair.

To avoid excessive paperwork for minor repairs or adjustments, it is usually convenient to establish a few blanket or yearly work orders. These are collection accounts in which labor and material charges can be accumulated without generating a work order for individual jobs. Each blanket order should include an identification number so that minor labor and material costs can be accumulated by piece of equipment. Because there is often a tendency by craftsmen and foremen to charge major repairs to the blanket work order merely because of the convenience, it is imperative that a minor repair be closely defined and that blanket order charges be periodically monitored.

Timekeeping System. The development of good maintenance cost records is dependent upon an accurate timekeeping system.

Figure 10-5 shows a sample labor distribution card used by maintenance personnel to identify the jobs on which they worked and the hours spent on each. Space is provided for the man's name and the clock number, work order number, and hours worked. The card must account for all hours worked

				WORK ORDER		WORK ORDER	№ 30		
UNIT NO.	DATE ISSUED	DATE REQ'D		J.O. NO.					

WORK ORDER

							MAN HOURS		
EQUIP. DESCRIPTION				DEPT. TO BE CHG'D					
WORK REQUESTED _____					CRAFT		EST.	ACT.	%
					ELECT.				
					PIPEFITTER				
					TINNER				
					MACH. RIGGER				
REQUESTED BY _____ APPROVED BY _____					MACH. SHOP				
PLEASE ATTACH SKETCH OR ADDITIONAL INFORMATION AS NEEDED					MACH. CRANE				
MAT'L'S – TOOLS – EQUIP. REQ'D _____					MASON				
					PAINTER				
					BLACKSMITH				
WORK ACTUALLY PERFORMED _____					TOTAL MAN HOURS				
					LABOR	$			
					MAT'L	$			
					TOTAL	$			
WORK ORDER № 30		FOREMAN'S SIGNATURE			PLAN BY		EST. BY		
		DATE COMPLETED		BRIEF JOB DESCRIPTION					

FIG. 10-4. Work Order Form.

and should be verified against time clock information. Although some companies use a weekly labor distribution card, most prepare them on a daily basis to minimize the problem of error correction at the beginning of the following week.

Material Cost System. Material for a job can be issued through an in-plant stores operation or purchased directly from an outside vendor. In either case, a system should be established so that material can be charged through the use of a work order number to the equipment on which it was used.

In the case of in-plant storerooms, a materials issue form (Figure 10-6)

DAILY TIME TICKET

CRAFT	MAN NO.		MAN'S NAME			DATE	SHIFT
Occ. No.	Total Hours	Cost Center	Work Order No.	Item No.	Brief Description		
TOTAL HOURS							

Foreman's Signature

FIG. 10-5. Labor Distribution Card.

STORES WITHDRAWAL

Maintenance Use Only

☐ INSTR.   ☐ PIPE

☐ ELEC.   ☐ MECHANICAL

☐ MACHINE   ☐ SHEET METAL

CENTER #	ACCOUNT #	DATE	WORK ORDER # I.E. PROJ. #	CODE
18	22 24	28 30	35 43 48	79 80 8 5

STOCK NO. 1 6	QUANTITY 12 16	DESCRIPTION

DELIVERED BY:	RECEIVED BY:	APPROVED BY:

Fig. 10-6.   Materials Issue Form.

is normally required to withdraw materials.   Under this system, the individual using the material presents the completed form to the storeroom personnel as an authorization for withdrawal.   In addition to material identification information, the form should include space for the work order number so that accounting can accumulate job material costs and relate them to the equipment involved.   Purchases from outside vendors for direct consumption on a specific job are handled in a similar manner by cross-referencing the work order to the purchase order.

Recording Maintenance Costs.   Where an equipment inventory file is already in existence, many companies use it as a vehicle for recording facility maintenance costs.   In plants where a copy of the completed work order is available, labor and material costs can be recorded on the work order and the copy filed with the equipment record.   This results in easy access to the original repair record for review but may create a bulky and unwieldy filing system in a large plant.

The reverse side of the equipment record card can also be used for posting maintenance and repair costs.   This minimizes the size of the filing system but requires additional clerical work for posting.   If the original work order is of value, a separate file for completed work orders can also be maintained.

Data Processing Assistance.   A more sophisticated record system is possible if data processing assistance is available.   Although the initial programming effort may be significant, it is a one-time charge which eliminates a continuous clerical posting effort.   Also, exception reporting techniques can be used to highlight the relatively few areas requiring further investigation, thus reducing the time required to search manually through the records developed in the initial system.

This technique involves the use of a computer program in which maintenance costs are totaled by month and year to date and compared with previously determined parameters. If current costs exceed the defined parameters, the cost record is printed out as an exception; if not, the information is stored in the computer for future reference. In this manner, management personnel concentrate their efforts on equipment with excessive maintenance costs. It is advisable, however, to request periodically a complete printout of all equipment costs to review and adjust the parameters.

BIBLIOGRAPHY

Collins, James F., Jr., "The Manufacturing Manager's Job," *A Control System for Maintenance of Plant and Equipment*, American Management Association, New York, 1966.

"Equipment Records," in Gordon B. Carson (ed.), *Production Handbook*, The Ronald Press Company, New York, 1953.

"Filing and Records Control," in Harry L. Wylie (ed.), *Office Management Handbook*, The Ronald Press Company, New York, 1958.

"Identifying Codes and Numbers," in F. W. Wilson (ed.), *Tool Engineers Handbook*, McGraw-Hill Book Company, New York, 1959.

Knight, Charles E., "Recording, Summarizing and Distributing Cost Data," in L. C. Morrow (ed.), *Maintenance Engineering Handbook*, 2d ed., McGraw-Hill Book Company, New York, 1960.

Lewis, Bernard T., *Controlling Maintenance Costs*, National Foremen's Institute, Waterford, Conn., 1966.

Lewis, Bernard T., and William W. Pearson, *Maintenance Management*, John F. Rider Publishers, Inc., New York, 1963.

Newbrough, E. Truett, "Action Idea—Reduce Your Maintenance Costs," *Business Management*, March, 1968.

CHAPTER ELEVEN

Manufacturing Research

D. E. A. TANNENBERG *Director of Engineering, International Group, The Singer Company, New York, New York*

The explosion of new products and new technology has placed emphasis upon effective and economical methods of manufacture in all industries. There is constant pressure placed on the manufacturing manager to provide the means to build new products efficiently and at the lowest possible cost consistent with high quality. Profitable corporate growth is tied closely to the effective use of existing processes and manufacturing equipment and to the development or adaptation of new methods, machinery, and factory systems.

Manufacturing research formalizes the procedures for developing, investigating, and implementing new processes, methods, and production equipment that have existed since man began making things. From the first crude ax to industry's most complex machine, there has always existed a need to find the better way, a faster and more economical way to fabricate a product.

Manufacturing research as a separate and distinct function in an industrial organization is a relatively new concept, for research and development work in the past has been primarily focused on the invention or creation of new products. Throughout the history of product creation, there have been new ideas that could not be put into practice until process and manufacturing technology could catch up and make economical and practical production a reality. Manufacturing research can provide for improvement in current shop practices and more importantly in future practices by sharing with the product designer the task of bringing a new idea to the marketplace in the shortest possible time.

GOALS AND DEFINITION OF MANUFACTURING RESEARCH

As its main goal, manufacturing research must find and apply new manufacturing technology which will reduce manufacturing costs and contribute heavily toward improved product quality. It must further provide for the future growth and improved utilization of the company's facilities and resources. As applied research, it must open up new fields and push back the technological frontier of manufacturing knowledge.

Manufacturing research and development as practiced by most manufacturers can be separated into three basic areas:

1. Process improvement and process development performed on a day-to-day basis in cost improvement programs by manufacturing engineers, production supervisors, and operators
2. Manufacturing process research and development as a by-product or a necessary part of new product invention and development
3. Manufacturing research separated from day-to-day product and production problems comprised of:
    a. Original research into processes, equipment, and methods
    b. Adaptation of known process, equipment, and methods technology

This chapter concerns itself with manufacturing research as a separate function in industrial organizational structures, identified and supported by management, with well-developed objectives and performance measurements.

OBJECTIVES IN DIFFERENT INDUSTRY SEGMENTS

There are essentially three segments in industry, and each one has its own needs and objectives in manufacturing research. Depending upon the end product manufactured, the emphasis on the method employed to seek out improvements and new technology varies.

Industry segment	Manufacturing research	
	Original	Adaptation
Material manufacturer................	×	
Equipment manufacturer.............	×	×
Fabricator.........................		×

The majority of manufacturers concentrate their efforts and technical resources on the development of new products and rely heavily on equipment manufacturers to provide economical processes and equipment. In addition, assistance is usually available from the material suppliers in developing the most effective methods of using their products. True manufacturing research was performed in the steel industry in the development and application of the basic oxygen furnace, a process that has revolutionized steel production. The development of electrical discharge machining, chemical blanking, and electron beam welding are examples of technological breakthroughs achieved in the equipment industry. Automated assembly of light bulbs developed by the General Electric Company is a fine example of adaptation of equipment and methods technology by a fabricator.

Objectives Examined. The basic material manufacturer will have as his objective the creation and development of new proprietary processes to provide for high quality and low cost in the production of his commodity. These methods and processes can be the key competitive advantage that he holds in his particular field.

The equipment manufacturer, in seeking new ideas, will emphasize the areas which will give him the widest possible application for his machinery and processes. With a broad base over which to amortize his research and development costs, the equipment maker will have the ability to support a combination of original research and development of improved machinery and processes through application of known technology.

The emphasis by the fabricator is generally on adaptation of known technology with modifications of these methods to suit specific needs. Cost reduction and short payback periods are generally one of the most important objectives in this segment of industry.

THE CENTRAL RESEARCH LABORATORY

Many large industrial companies have well-established and separate central research laboratories engaged in product and manufacturing research. Some of the well-known companies with such facilities include Ford, General Motors, Western Electric, DuPont, SCM, and Singer. Separate facilities like these provide an environment free from specific production problems, schedules, and commitments. Therefore, engineers and scientists have the opportunity to concentrate on areas of basic research and applied science in the product and process fields. This environment will attract the researcher or scientist who might otherwise shun the factory climate. Central laboratories play an important role in disseminating technical information to operating divisions and in providing a clearinghouse for ideas and proposals generated by operating and factory support personnel. New technology investigations that could not be economically justified in a single operating unit can be performed for the benefit of the entire company.

STARTING A MANUFACTURING RESEARCH PROGRAM

The manufacturing manager may well ask himself why he should establish a separate function for manufacturing research. Most companies already have engineers and scientists who develop manufacturing sequences, select processes, select or develop equipment, and develop material flow and plant layouts best suited to their current needs. The separate manufacturing research organization, however, will be able to concentrate on investigating and finding the way to implement new technology for the maximum benefit of the company. It will eliminate duplication and concentrate on work areas with the greatest potential.

Assessment of Existing Capabilities. One of the first steps in a formalized program of manufacturing research is the definition of current processes and equipment capabilities. An analysis of manufacturing work areas will help identify those which will provide the maximum potential return on invested effort. One method that can be employed is the charting of processes used, showing manufacturing and support costs:

Major process	Subprocess	Costs	% of total
Machining	Milling	____	_____
	Drilling	____	_____
	Turning, etc.	____	_____
Metals joining	Welding	____	_____
	Brazing	____	_____
	Bonding, etc.	____	_____
Chemical	Pickling	____	_____
	Plating, etc.	____	_____
Assembling	Automatic	____	_____
	Manual	____	_____
	Semiautomatic	____	_____

This method illustrates one means for determining the small number of processes that consume the largest proportion of the manufacturing dollar. In addition to cataloging current capabilities, new-product planning will have a strong influence on the work areas that should be explored. In this cooperative phase of manufacturing research, the early implementation of new-product ideas can be assured through concurrent development of efficient and economical production methods and equipment. In the same fashion, product ideas that are not economically feasible can be identified early, and efforts in both product and process development can be channeled in more promising directions.

Search of Known Technology. Technical journals, trade magazines, and the wealth of other technical publications provide one of the most fertile grounds for seeking out new manufacturing technology. Most probably, the greatest immediate gain for any manufacturing research activity can be made by a well-organized, systematic review of methods employed by other manufacturers, not necessarily those in the same field. As an example, the electronics industry looked to photography for development of printed circuits and their economical manufacture. Processes such as explosive forming, first developed in the aerospace industry, may well have application in the appliance field.

EVOLUTION OF THE MANUFACTURING RESEARCH ORGANIZATION

Manufacturing research organizations grow from modest and informal efforts in a natural manner, either as an offshoot of a product research and development function or as an outgrowth of manufacturing engineering or a similar operating staff function. Many times, they begin with the assignment of a project to an individual within one of these departments, who conducts the investigation of available technology, determines applicable processes or equipment that can be adapted to fit the needs of the project, develops the necessary cost justifications and payback information, and submits his recommendation to his superiors for a decision to proceed or terminate the program. Upon approval, he oversees installation of the process and verifies his financial projections. Temporary assignments to manufacturing research projects can become permanent as projects and project results warrant; and with this step, the beginnings of a formalized manufacturing research function take shape.

The Project Team Concept. Recognizing the benefits of a continuing effort in process improvement and new-process development, the manufacturing manager may elect to install the project team concept in his manufacturing engineering department. In this concept, specific individuals are assigned and organized into an overlay function with the manufacturing engineering manager serving as the head of both the production support staff and the research project team.

Figure 11-1 shows a typical manufacturing engineering department in a small- to medium-sized company. Here the manufacturing research effort is carried out by the various development engineers with the full project team operating as a screening committee and a review board in determining work areas, setting cost improvement objectives, developing measurements of performance, and establishing project priorities. One of the prime advantages of the approach is the ability of the manufacturing engineering function not only to find a new process or a new machine, but also to test it and install the improvement, thus truly completing the project. The prime disadvantage of the project team concept is the interference of day-to-day problems and production emergencies which must come first in an operating staff department.

Manufacturing Research as a Separate Department. The best opportunity for manufacturing research is in a separate function with its own operating budget, performance goals, and facilities for research and experimentation. Here, too, the function will grow, depending on the extent of project assignments and success in their implementation. Figure 11-2 illustrates a separate manufacturing research function as a parallel department to manufacturing engineering, both reporting to the manufacturing manager. With this type of organization, a healthy combination of long-range and short-range projects is possible through simple lines of communication. Although the assignments of the manufacturing engineering group are directly related to the support requirements of the production departments, manufacturing research can concentrate on new projects. It can take a longer range look at existing processes and machinery and, in combination with a thorough understanding of the company's product plans, seek out the tasks that will have the greatest overall effect on manufacturing costs. The basic functions of the separate manufacturing research organization can be summarized as:

1. Operating research and laboratory facilities for the conception, development, test, adaptation, and application of new processes, new machinery and equipment, new methods, and new factory systems
2. Communicating to operating and staff departments the knowledge and information developed in original and applied research and in the adaptation of known manufacturing technology
3. Training of operating and staff personnel at the interface between development work and practical installation
4. Advising and counseling product research and development on technological breakthroughs that may provide the basis for new products

MANUFACTURING RESEARCH FACILITIES

Engineering and scientific personnel need facilities for proving out concepts, for debugging processes and equipment, and for educated tinkering. The question arises whether a laboratory facility can be integrated with existing plant space or whether a completely separate laboratory should be established. The industrial giants have in many cases chosen the latter approach. The majority of companies considering the establishment of a manu-

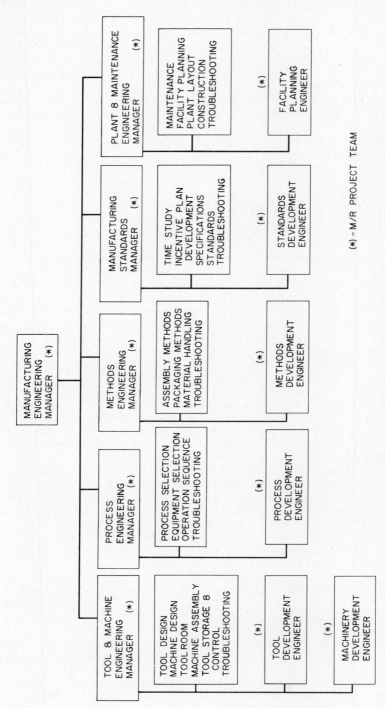

FIG. 11-1. Manufacturing Research Project Team Concept—Small- to Medium-sized Company.

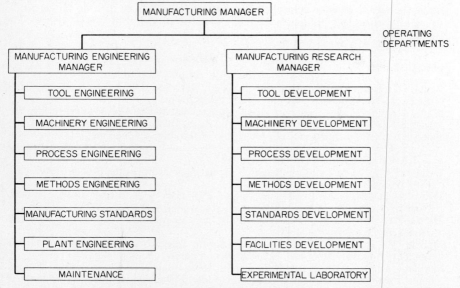

FIG. 11-2. Manufacturing Research Department—Medium- to Large-sized Company.

facturing research function may not initially be able to justify such plans. A laboratory is a must, however, because the promise of some running time in the shop or of a temporary tryout area in production will not provide the atmosphere for a detached analysis of test observations. Often, the initial space for a manufacturing laboratory can be made available in a product research area where limited process development is performed by the product developers.

Flexibility a Prerequisite. In setting up a manufacturing laboratory, effort must be made not to overequip, because this tends to limit projects to those that utilize available facilities. In terms of occupied space, there should probably be about 30 to 40 percent vacant area available for temporary pilot process installations. The equipment selected for permanent installation will vary with the kind of company. It will generally include some basic toolroom equipment, metallurgical and chemical facilities, and limited force, motion, and environmental measurement equipment.

BENEFITS OF MANUFACTURING RESEARCH

The activities of manufacturing research are all directed toward improving the efficiency, cost, and quality of the manufacturing function through new discoveries and improvements in process, machinery and equipment, and methods technology. Original research and development is vital for long-range planning and growth. However, the greatest immediate gains are available in the application of known technology through search and analysis of processes, techniques, equipment, and factory systems developed by other companies in both related and unrelated industrial fields. Through effective communication within the total organization, new-product ideas can become a reality sooner than ever before, and an integrated program of long-range product and process planning can provide a more predictable future course for the company and for its profitable growth.

BIBLIOGRAPHY

Bixler, H. H., *The Manufacturing Research Function*, Research Study no. 60, American Management Association, New York, 1963.

Black, T. W., "Engineering with Ideas: A Look at Space Age Manufacturing Research," *Tool and Manufacturing Engineer*, April, 1962.

Bond, E. E., "Management and Interfaces of Product Development from Design Concept to Final Test," *International Convention Record*, Institute of Electrical and Electronics Engineers, New York, 1965.

Cathey, P. J., "Manufacturing Research Opens New Pathway to Profits," *Iron Age*, Oct. 11, 1962.

DelGatto, J., "DuPont's Textile Laboratory—Prototype of Industry," *Rubber World*, November, 1965.

Hafstad, L. R., "Making Research Pay—One Corporation's Approach," *Research Management*, September, 1965.

Morsilli, W. F., and M. Nelles, "Manufacturing Research and Development Is Essential to Survival," *Tool and Manufacturing Engineer*, September, 1965.

Simmons, G. R., "Manufacturing Research: Developing New Processes and Equipment," in R. E. Finley and H. R. Ziobro (eds.), *The Manufacturing Man and His Job*, American Management Association, New York, 1966.

CHAPTER TWELVE

Relocation of Manufacturing Facilities

PARK R. HOYT *Vice President—Manufacturing, Smithcraft Corporation, Wilmington, Massachusetts*

Moving to new manufacturing facilities, though a not uncommon undertaking, involves an area in which there exists a dearth of reference information. For most company executives, it represents a once-in-a-lifetime experience. Few who have been through a plant move have chosen to commit their findings and ideas to writing.

This chapter highlights the critical areas and discusses briefly the techniques and procedures that will prove helpful in developing and administering a move program. Actual experience gained during a plant relocation from a large metropolitan area to a suburban industrial park fourteen miles away provided the basis for much of this material. Whether the distance moved is a few miles or many miles, however, the comments which follow will be applicable to a great extent.

IMPORTANCE AND SIGNIFICANCE OF RELOCATION

The decision to relocate is the result of a combination of company needs and motives. High on the list might be potential cost reduction and provision for future growth and expansion. During the planning and implementation of the move, these objectives must be kept in sharp focus and the ultimate realization carefully provided for.

A relocation of manufacturing facilities, be it near or far away, is one of the most important undertakings that a company will make in its lifetime. Until the move is imminent, one does not appreciate the permanence and finality of the undertaking. After a given point, the many decisions become irrevocable, and there is no stopping—no turnback, no luxury of second thoughts, no benefit of hindsight. Murphy's laws apply perfectly to plant relocation programs:

1. Nothing is as easy as it looks.
2. Everything takes longer than you think it will.
3. If anything can go wrong, it will.

Use of Established Management Techniques. The relocation program should be approached in the same careful manner as any other important management undertaking. All management resources, techniques, and knowledge should be brought to bear on the program. Techniques which are especially useful include:

1. Management by objectives and measurement
2. Management by exception
3. PERT or critical path scheduling
4. Gantt charts
5. Effective communications
6. Budgets

PREPARING THE ORGANIZATION FOR THE MOVE

During the period of making the decision to move and the ensuing search for a suitable location, it is advisable to treat this as confidential information restricted to the absolute minimum number of people. The reasons for doing this are to prevent wild rumors and to ensure complete freedom of choice of location in the most objective manner possible. Once the new location has been selected, an early announcement from the chief executive to all employees is in order. The announcement should cover such items as when, where, who will move, why the decision to move, and the like. This announcement, which is frequently in the form of a letter mailed to the employee's home, should be issued promptly before the factory "grapevine" begins to function.

To maintain good community relations, thoughtfully worded announcements should be placed in the local papers of the present plant community and the community of the new plant. The projection of a favorable company image in the new community can be helpful in future dealings with civic officials and in creating a desirable labor market.

The advertising department can make good copy of the impending move by stressing improved quality, better deliveries, new processes, and the like.

Organizational Setup. Many plans will have to be developed, implemented, and executed. To accomplish this effectively, an organizational structure should be developed, job assignments made, and accountabilities established.

Each company will probably tailor the organization to its own particular needs and circumstances. Most small- and medium-sized companies will give additional assignments to people already wearing "one or more hats."

A typical organization structure would be:

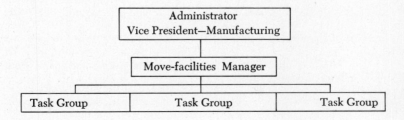

Task Groups. Task teams with specific assignments are an effective means of bringing expertise to bear on various facets of the move program.

Typical task groups, their assignments, and their personnel composition are:

Task Group A—move sequence
   Plant manager
   Materials manager
   Production and inventory control manager
Task Group B—move schedule
   Move-facilities manager
   Materials manager
   Departmental foremen
Task Group C—trucking and rigging
   Move-facilities manager
   Traffic manager
   Maintenance supervisor
Task Group D—equipment and inventory records documentation
   Materials manager
   Company auditor
   Receiving foreman
Task Group E—old facilities cleanup
   Plant manager
   Maintenance supervisor
Task Group F—methods and standards
   Plant manager
   Chief industrial engineer

MAJOR PROBLEMS

Timing of the Move. If there is any freedom of choice of the calendar time of the move, full advantage should be taken of it. Every effort should be made to optimize the following criteria:

1. Move during a slack period.
2. Move during good weather.
3. Move during a period when inventories are in good shape.
4. Move during a period of good labor relations.

Continuity of Operations. Unless it is possible to build up an inventory of finished and in-process goods in advance of the move, it will be necessary to continue production during the move. This necessitates some extremely difficult production scheduling at both the old and new plants. In critical areas, production must be continued to the last minute at the old plant, and as the move progresses, people must be shifted as soon as new facilities become available.

Phasing Production out of Old into New Facility. Inventories permitting, every effort should be made to move complete departments quickly. If they are not moved promptly and in their entirety, needless confusion and extra transportation between plants will be involved. Care and judgment must be exercised to ensure that facilities, services, and in-process work are available immediately upon movement to the new plant.

If a department must be moved piecemeal over an extended period, duplicate provisions must be made for supervision, controls, and materials at the old and the new locations.

Debugging and Start-up. Start-up may or may not involve mechanical debugging, depending upon whether the transferred operation involves methods changes. Almost for a certainty, people debugging will become a way of life for a while.

The process of "cranking up" operations to an acceptable level of productivity is more frustrating than debugging a new-process system or new equipment. With the latter, the problem can usually be readily pinpointed and corrective action initiated. People problems are difficult to identify and frequently do not lend themselves to ready solutions.

The fewer the methods changes, the quicker the operation at the new plant will reach satisfactory productivity. However, this is a situation where a short-term gain is traded off for a long-term loss. The ideal situation is to initiate a cost reduction program before the move and implement it and the accompanying methods changes upon start-up at the new facility.

People Problems. The nature of the people problems is keyed closely to whether the move involves transferring existing personnel or whether recruiting new employees at the new location is contemplated. Most likely, it will be a combination of the two.

Transferred personnel will present many problems, some of which are difficult to identify and cope with. The bulk of the anxieties will fall into the following categories:

1. Instinctive resistance to change
2. Fear of loss of job or decreased earnings
   a. Job change or transfer
   b. Job elimination
3. Transportation
4. New plant working hours
5. Available lunch facilities

Management must maintain good communications concerning the move with all employees, starting several months in advance of the actual move date. These communications can take the form of letters from the president sent to the employee's home, foreman and employee conferences, bulletin board announcements, progress reports, employee surveys, posted pictures of new facilities, and the like.

Policies must be established and factual answers provided for items 2 to 5 above. It may be desirable to work closely with the union in formulating policies, so that they can assist in the communications problem. An alert foreman should know his employees well enough to elicit worries from them and to answer their questions.

Union Problems. The union is normally concerned with the protection of its members relative to wages, hours, and working conditions. The move to new facilities injects additional areas of concern, such as:

1. Employee displacement
2. Transportation
3. Hardship cases
4. Separation pay
5. Longer workday in situation where new plant location is a greater distance from employee's home

It may be desirable at an early stage to negotiate a supplemental labor contract agreement with the union, generalizing on the new location in order to allow complete freedom in selecting the final plant location. The following is a specific example of such a supplemental agreement.

SUPPLEMENTAL AGREEMENT made and entered into by and between SMITHCRAFT CORPORATION at 217 Everett Avenue, Chelsea, Massachusetts, hereinafter sometimes called the "COMPANY," and LOCAL UNION NO. 1499, of the INTERNATIONAL BROTHERHOOD OF ELECTRICAL WORKERS, affiliated with the AFL–CIO, sometimes hereinafter called the "UNION."

WITNESSETH:

The COMPANY is now planning to relocate its premises from 217 Everett Avenue, Chelsea, Massachusetts, to a location in the Greater Boston area.

The COMPANY and the UNION have discussed the effect of such relocation upon the persons employed by the COMPANY, and have entered into this Agreement, supplemental to the Collective Bargaining Agreement of even date, in order to provide an orderly procedure to be followed if and when such relocation takes place.

NOW THEREFORE, in consideration of the mutual promises and agreements herein contained, the parties agree as follows:

Article I

Notice will be given to all employees of the date on which production will be commenced at the new premises.

Since it is not now known whether all departments will be moved at the same time or whether the move will take place by moving departments or operations at different intervals, each Employee or group of Employees will be notified at least sixty (60) days before the date on which their work assignments will be transferred to the new premises.

Such notice(s) will state the location of the new premises and the approximate moving schedule.

In such notice, provision will be made for each employee to state whether or not he or she will continue employment at the new premises. Each employee will be required to notify the COMPANY in writing (on a form to be provided by the COMPANY) whether or not he or she will continue employment at the new premises.

Article II

Any employee who notifies the COMPANY that he or she intends to be employed at the new premises will be continued at the new premises on his or her regular job assignment unless that assignment shall be discontinued or the number of persons so employed shall be reduced. Any employee so affected shall, on a seniority basis, be offered employment in the same Labor Grade if work is available in that Labor Grade or, if work is not available in the same Labor Grade, work shall be offered in the next lower Labor Grade.

If the COMPANY shall not be able to find employment for any such employee in the same Labor Grade or in the next lower Labor Grade, then such employee shall be separated and receive severance pay as hereinafter provided.

Any employee whose regular work assignment carried incentive pay shall not be required to accept employment on a nonincentive basis if his or her total average earnings would be less than 90% of his or her average earnings in the preceding six (6) months, and may request separation with severance pay as hereinafter provided.

Article III

Any employee who shall be given a new job assignment (as provided above) shall be retrained by the COMPANY to the extent required for proper job performance.

Article IV

Severance pay shall be at the rate of twenty (20) hours' straight time pay for each full year of employment with the COMPANY up to a maximum of ten (10) years' seniority or 200 hours' pay. The hourly rate for severance pay shall be the hourly Labor Grade rate of the employee at the time of severance. Severance pay will be paid only to persons with at least two (2) years of seniority.

Article V

Unless the parties shall otherwise agree, commencing with the start of production at the new premises and for a period of twelve (12) weeks thereafter, the COMPANY will provide free daily bus transportation from a central point in Chelsea to the new premises and return to Chelsea.

Article VI

Commencing at least thirty (30) days prior to the first commencement of production at the new premises and approximately monthly thereafter for a period of three (3) months, the COMPANY and the UNION shall have Labor-Management meetings to review and discuss matters affecting production and the effect of relocation upon work assignments. The purpose of such Labor-Management meetings shall be to bring about an orderly transition in production and work assignments resulting from relocation.

To the extent that any matters relating to production and/or work assignments shall present problems, the solution to which cannot be reached by agreement, such matter(s) may be considered by either party as a grievance within the meaning of the Collective Bargaining Agreement and shall be processed as such.

This SUPPLEMENTAL AGREEMENT shall be and remain in full force and effect for a period ending six (6) months after the date of first commencement of production at the relocated premises.

Labor Force. A well-trained, effective labor force is essential for low-cost operation. It is costly to recruit, train, and impart product knowledge to new hires. It is therefore desirable to move as many employees as possible to the new location, providing that moving costs do not exceed rehiring and training costs. With all the attendant problems of start-up, it is reassuring to have knowledgeable and experienced employees on the job.

To get an early evaluation of how many present employees are likely to move, all foremen and department heads may be requested to prepare, several months prior to the scheduled move, a guesstimate of their respective departments, as follows:

Name	Will move	Will not move	Doubtful

If a substantial number plan to remain with the company, a new plant visitation should be arranged about two months before the move for all employees to orient them to travel conditions and the new plant facilities and to "sell" those who are doubtful about moving. The visitation can be followed immediately by a formal written survey to obtain a fairly accurate appraisal of how much new hiring will have to be done. Figure 12-1 shows an example of a survey form.

Methods Improvement and Revision of Wage Incentives. One of the justifications for a plant move is usually the achievement of lower labor costs through more efficient plant layout and work flow. This is fine as a starter, but advantage should be taken of the situation to institute method changes, eliminate loose incentive practices, and review all existing time standards.

MASTER PLAN AND MOVE SCHEDULE FOR NEW PLANT

Many small plans and schedules must be developed, working backward from move day, in order to develop the master plan. Plans and schedules must be worked out in minute detail, showing dates, action, allowed time for accomplishment, and persons responsible. Techniques such as Gantt charts and critical path scheduling are useful tools for this procedure.

Smithcraft

CORPORATION

CHELSEA, MASSACHUSETTS 02150, TEL. 884-4560

PARK R. HOYT
VICE PRESIDENT MANUFACTURING

TO:

FROM: PARK R. HOYT   SENIORITY DATE_____

SUBJECT: NEW WILMINGTON PLANT

Each of you has now had an opportunity to visit your new plant at Wilmington. We
hope that you were pleased with what you saw and that you plan to continue working
with Smithcraft in Wilmington after your vacation.

In order to assist both you and ourselves, we need the following information:

1. Do you plan to take advantage of the 12 weeks' free bus service to Wilmington
   starting after vacation?_____

2. Do you plan to continue working at Wilmington when the free bussing period
   ends?_____ .

3. Will you need transportation when the bussing period ends? _____

4. Do you have a car that you can use to drive to Wilmington? _____

5. Would you be interested in carrying passengers after the bussing ends?_____
   How many?_____

6. If you do not plan to move to the new plant, when do you think that you will
   be leaving us?_____

Please return this questionnaire to your foreman.

Park R. Hoyt
Vice President - Manufacturing

Look to Smithcraft for Lighting Leadership

FIG. 12-1.   Survey Form for Determining Approaching Requirements for New
Employees.

Plans, schedules, or programs should be developed for the following areas:
1. New facilities availability, including utilities and necessary supporting
   services
2. Equipment move schedule by departments
3. Raw materials and in-process inventory move schedule
4. Finished inventory move schedule

5. Steps to avoid union crafts' jurisdictional disputes and walkouts
6. Employee visitation to new facility
7. Hiring and training schedule
8. Transportation:
    a. Company-furnished (if any)
    b. Car pools
    c. Public

For each department to be moved, the following must be considered.

1. The move
    a. When
    b. How
    c. By whom
    d. Who is responsible
2. Closing out facilities
    a. Reconditioning of area
    b. Removal of all salvageable equipment
    c. Discontinuance of services
    d. Ultimate disposition of old facility

Checklist.   With all the details involved in a plant move, it is all too easy to overlook items of considerable importance.   The following checklist, which is by no means exhaustive, may help avoid such oversights.

1. Old facilities
    a. Watchman service during vacancy
    b. Renovation and cleanup
    c. Discontinuance of services
    d. List of equipment and appurtenances that are to be:
        (1) Removed
        (2) Left
        (3) May or may not be removed
2. New facilities
    a. Lights, power, heat, and air conditioning
    b. Fire protection
    c. Security protection
    d. First aid facilities
    e. Eating facilities
    f. Parking facilities
    g. Scrap and waste disposal
    h. Communications system
    i. Transportation
    j. Time clocks
3. Area practices
    a. Starting time
    b. Length of lunch period
    c. Check-cashing policy
4. Transportation
    a. Temporary company-furnished transportation
    b. Available public transportation
    c. Car pools
5. New area surveys
    a. Wage and salary
    b. Fringe benefits
    c. Available labor market

CONCLUSION

The relocation of manufacturing facilities is a challenging and complex undertaking. Operating under severe pressures of time, a large variety of problems must be solved; decisions rendered; plans made, implemented, and executed; and a myriad of details coordinated and followed.

Frequently some facets of the overall plan will go astray, and provisions must be made for immediate identification and the application of corrective action to these areas. No two plant moves will ever be executed under identical situations, nor for that matter, will any single plant move be carried out exactly as planned. One can, however, optimize the controllable conditions and minimize the adverse effects of the uncontrollable areas.

BIBLIOGRAPHY

Carson, Gordon (ed.), *Production Handbook*, 2d ed., The Ronald Press Company, New York, 1958.

Dooley, Arch, *Administering Industrial Relocation*, thesis, Harvard University Graduate School of Business Administration, Cambridge, Massachusetts.

Fourre, James, *Critical Path Scheduling*, American Management Association, New York.

Maynard, H. B. (ed.), *Industrial Engineering Handbook*, 2d ed., McGraw-Hill Book Company, New York, 1963.

PLANT ENGINEERING AND MAINTENANCE

CHAPTER ONE

Organization of Plant Engineering and Maintenance

W. J. JAMIESON   *Superintendent, Maintenance and Utilities Finishing Works, The Steel Company of Canada, Ltd., Hamilton, Ontario, Canada*

Every plant, regardless of size, must have a technical service group which will look after the physical plant, its utilities, and its equipment. This group is referred to normally as the plant engineering department or sometimes as the maintenance department. The organization of the department will vary from industry to industry and from plant to plant; however, the major functions are the same everywhere. This chapter will outline briefly the engineering functions required of this group but will deal primarily with the human, technical, and financial aspects of the maintenance function. The techniques involved and the controls necessary for effective maintenance performance will be described.

GENERAL ORGANIZATION

The plant engineering and maintenance department must be an integral part of the plant production effort. The department consists of engineers, tradesmen, and other technical personnel qualified and trained to maintain the buildings, the manufacturing equipment, and the necessary utilities for the manufacturing plant to function efficiently. The head of the department may be called plant engineer, superintendent of maintenance, master mechanic, supervisor of engineering and maintenance, or some similar title. To be most effective, he should report directly to the man responsible for the operations in the plant which are serviced by the maintenance group. This will normally be the plant superintendent, plant manager, or manager of manufacturing, depending on the organization structure. There are manufacturing plants which contract out their complete maintenance needs. In such cases, the responsibility for decision and control must still be delegated to the plant engineer. A typical organization chart is shown by Figure 1-1.

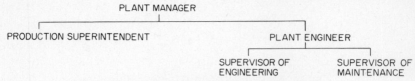

FIG. 1-1.   Typical Plant Organization Chart.

The duties of the plant engineering department can be divided into those concerned with engineering functions and those concerned with maintenance functions.   The principal duties assigned to each function are as follows:

Engineering

1. The production and maintenance of all drawings pertaining to property, plant, and equipment
2. The design specifications of all buildings and plant equipment
3. Major construction and equipment installation
4. Studies pertaining to equipment modifications and product process
5. Help and guidance on technical matters to plant maintenance staff upon request
6. Consultant to the plant manager on all engineering matters

Maintenance

1. The efficient maintenance of all plant buildings, roads, and production equipment
2. The supply of uninterrupted utility requirements of air, steam, water, power, and gas and the disposal of all waste products
3. A proper procedure for the maintenance function to provide control of such things as work orders, schedules, budgets, and the efficiency of the work force
4. Limited trial and development work with production processes
5. Proper procedure and control of inventory levels on spares and maintenance materials
6. Labor for "labor gang" work and control of janitorial service in the plant
7. Consultant to the plant manager on all maintenance matters

Traditionally, the plant engineering function includes the engineering and maintenance duties listed above.   It is becoming more and more evident, however, that these functions should be divided and that the heads of both these departments should report to the plant manager.   This is illustrated by Figure 1-2.   This is necessary because the major functions involved are so specialized that no one plant engineer can do justice to both requirements.   On the one hand, a good professional engineer is needed to spend most of his efforts to ensure that his department produces sound engineering designs and specifications, and who has enough time to tackle the engineering problems of the

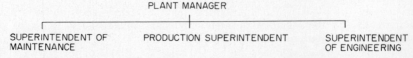

FIG. 1-2.   Organization Chart Showing Separation of Engineering and Maintenance Functions.

plant. On the other hand, an engineer who spends most of his effort in dealing with craft foremen who direct the work of a maintenance force is also needed. He has to be much more oriented to the production effort of the plant and involved in all the day-to-day production decisions. The amount of knowledge, experience, and time required to manage an efficient maintenance organization makes it mandatory that this function be headed by a man reporting directly to the works manager. It goes without saying that the maintenance and engineering departments should work closely together to complement each other's efforts and to act as a check and balance system for each other.

FUNCTIONAL CHART

A typical functional organization chart for a maintenance group is shown by Figure 1-3. As in any organizational setup, the chart should be considered as a guide only. It must be flexible enough to accommodate any special personal attributes and characteristics of the people available. Figure 1-3 represents an actual organization of approximately one hundred maintenance employees involved in maintaining a steel finishing operation, but it illustrates most of the human and technical considerations involved in any kind of maintenance work.

Master Mechanic. The master mechanic should be a graduate engineer

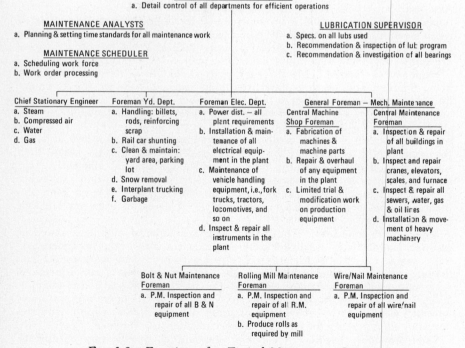

Fig. 1-3. Functions of a Typical Maintenance Group.

(usually mechanical) who has had practical shop experience in some trade work (summer employment) and has served under a competent plant engineer for three to four years. His main function is to weld together a strong, competent team which is well motivated and which will cooperate to the fullest extent with the production departments. His main strength should lie in his administrative abilities, but he must possess a sound, practical technical background to appreciate the effects of his decisions on a craft organization.

Assistant Master Mechanic. The size of the organization, imminent retirement of the master mechanic, and similar factors will determine whether an assistant master mechanic is needed. If he is, he should be considered the heir apparent. His main function is to coordinate the different activities of the maintenance group to ensure that they function efficiently. He must use all the control tools available and should be examining constantly better and more economical controls. To fulfill his responsibilities well, the incumbent must show an aptitude for working with and getting along with people.

Lubrication Supervisor. The staff position of lubrication supervisor is one that a maintenance department should almost always fill. The science of lubrication for modern equipment has grown so rapidly that it is practically impossible to expect a maintenance foreman to keep up with the technology. Here again, the size of the organization and the complexity of the lubrication program will determine whether this position is needed. Background requirements should include sound mechanical experience and a broad knowledge of industrial equipment. The lubrication supervisor must be a "self-starter," aggressive, and able to influence people. Thorough technical training in lubricants from an oil firm is recommended, and he should continue to upgrade this training through seminars, technical magazines, and the like. The American Society of Lubrication Engineers is an excellent source for continued development. The main function of the lubrication supervisor is to recommend proper lubricants at proper intervals with proper controls. He may be channeled into other special projects, such as a bearing program or a preventive maintenance program, depending upon his work load.

Maintenance Analyst. Ideally, each craft should have its own analyst to plan, organize, and set time standards for its work. To be practical, it may be necessary for one analyst to cover a number of trades. First of all, an analyst should be a recognized expert in his own trade. He should be constantly looking for better methods, and most importantly, should think of himself as a member of management. His main function is to plan and organize the work which comes into his area of responsibility and to assign time standards so that the work can be scheduled and measured efficiently. He must be trained in the fundamentals of industrial engineering and preferably in MTM and the use of basic standard data. A good analyst must know the plant and the work required to maintain it. This is an excellent training ground for future foremen.

Maintenance Scheduler. The maintenance scheduler should be a practical maintenance man with a flair for clerical work. He is truly the bookkeeper of the organization. He is primarily concerned with processing work orders and drawing up weekly work schedules with the foreman. He is also concerned with maintaining an accurate record of the backlog of work and a running account of expenditures on major projects. He keeps the operating personnel informed as to the state of work in progress. He must work closely with the operating departments, the analysts, and the maintenance foremen.

Chief Stationary Engineer. A proper standard of qualification to operate specific horsepower or therm-hour rating of an installation is generally required by law; therefore, the department must be staffed with qualified people so that proper controls can be provided to ensure efficient and safe operations.   An active preventive maintenance program is necessary to maintain uninterrupted service.   Studies for improvements and long-term requirements should be made constantly.   The chief stationary engineer must maintain his equipment in top condition and be constantly on the alert for waste use of his utilities.

Foreman—Yard Department.   Many organizations may not find the need for a department commonly referred to as the "bull gang," but someone is needed to look after the functions listed under this department in Figure 1-3.   Good leadership qualities are required, for this foreman, under normal circumstances, ends up with the least-skilled people from all other departments in the plant.   This whole function literally bulges with opportunities for innovation.   Manpower can be saved by the introduction of fast cranes and loaders for material handling, mechanical sweepers and vacuum cleaners, dumper-type scrap and garbage units, and the like.   The man in charge of this department should be given an opportunity to learn the fundamentals of industrial engineering.   An exposure of several months is recommended.

Foreman—Electrical Department.   The electrical foreman should be a first-class tradesman holding the necessary certificates required by law as a "master electrician" or equivalent.   As in any foreman position, good leadership qualities are desirable.   His main function is to ensure the uninterrupted, efficient, and safe distribution of electric power for all plant requirements.   He must staff his department with competent people to carry out the maintenance functions required in the electrical, instrument, and motor mechanics field.   It should be noted that size and complexity may demand separate instrument and motor mechanic departments.   This foreman must keep himself and his staff familiar with technological advances.

General Foreman—Mechanical Maintenance.   The general foreman of mechanical maintenance should be the best mechanical foreman who has the most experience in the plant and who can get the best effort out of his organization.   His main function is to ensure that efficient service is given to production departments by departments under his control.   Both central and area shops are under his control.   He must take maximum advantage of both systems.   Generally speaking, he should require the area shops to perform preventive maintenance and emergency work while the central shops perform major overhaul and plant-wide functions, giving support to the area shops when required.   The area shop foremen are fully responsible to him for the maintenance of production equipment in their areas.   They may request help from the central shops, but cannot abandon their responsibilities merely by writing a work order.   The main strength of the general foreman lies in his intimate and detailed knowledge of the plant and his ability to foresee problems so that his departments can respond quickly and efficiently to the demands placed upon them.

Central Machine Shop Foreman.   The central machine shop foreman should be a good leader and a first-class machinist.   His main function is to make sure that the machine tools under his control are adequately manned and efficiently operated.   He must work closely with the scheduler and the analyst to ensure that the necessary machining work is performed by "best method" techniques.   He must keep abreast of recent innovations such as numerical control, electric discharge machining, and electrochemical machining, and where possible take advantage of them in his own shop applications.   His main strength should lie in his technical knowledge, experience, and ability to direct his force effectively.

Central Maintenance Foreman. It is best to have a craft foreman come from the craft he is directing. There are times, however, when this is not possible because of the small size of each trade group required in the plant. Such a situation is shown in Figure 1-3 where the central maintenance foreman directs painters, carpenters, tinsmiths, bricklayers, pipe fitters, millwrights, and repairmen. The foreman should be a first-class tradesmen from one of these groups who understands the rudiments of the other trades and by good leadership methods gets the best out of his group. He must work closely with his analyst and get full cooperation from his many specialist trades. Innovations are being introduced constantly in all the trades that he controls, and so his job requires him to be fully aware of them. This man must have a good technical background, have a desire to learn more about his business, and be a good leader.

The Bolt and Nut Foreman, the Rolling Mill Maintenance Foreman, and the Wire Nail Foreman. Three "area shop foremen" are shown in Figure 1-3. They are tradesmen who have worked in a particular plant maintenance group and displayed leadership qualities. Much has been written on the theory of area shops versus central shops. Each has certain advantages and certain disadvantages. The decision on which to use must be made on the basis of efficiency. The main functions of the area foreman are to ensure that his preventive maintenance program is efficiently carried out and to deal with any emergency situations. In the situation where the central shops are emphasized, the area foreman's scope of work is limited by the equipment that he is allowed to have to avoid duplication and low utilization of machine tools. Roll turning lathes are given to the rolling mill foreman to produce rolls on specialty machines which are fully utilized for this function. The reason for having an area shop is to capitalize on location and specialization. However, unless there are definite economic gains to be made, the advantages of area specialization are dubious.

Maintenance Stores. Another function of the Figure 1-3 organization is the control and operation of maintenance stores. Normally maintenance stores are centrally located to avoid duplication of stock and attendants. This may not always be possible because of the geographic location of different maintenance departments. The central shops may have tool crib attendants to order and control the spares and materials they are required to carry, while the foremen of the other departments perform this clerical function themselves.

Maintenance stores is a vital part of any maintenance organization and can either add to or detract from the efficiency of the whole group. A proper inventory control system is essential to a good stores operation. A realistic, practical, and economic approach has to be taken when deciding on what stores are to be kept. Investigation in most shops will reveal that maintenance stores are overstocked with wrong amounts of stock and often with the wrong stocks, and thousands of dollars can be saved by a managed inventory approach. A typical example is where maintenance stores carries thousands of dollars of inventory in bearings, although four blocks away there is a bearing supplier advertising twenty-four hour service; on the other hand, a vital hydraulic valve with an eight-week delivery time is not stocked at all.

In organizing maintenance stores, clear policies should be established on authority to sign requisitions and on free issue and company-owned tools. Many items must be considered, but generally it is considered good practice to:

1. Allow foremen and analysts to sign stores requisitions
2. Place nuts, bolts, washers, springs, and so on in convenient "lazy Susan" bins near the stores department or near a foreman's office

3. Insist that each tradesman have his own tool kit and maintain it

The company should provide special and large tools such as torque wrenches, 36-inch pipe wrenches, and gear and bearing pullers.

ORGANIZING MAINTENANCE PAPERWORK AND RECORDS

Generally speaking, it should be the policy to process the minimum amount of paper necessary to provide adequate control. Certain forms and procedures, however, are a must if *any* control is to be exercised; to these, more sophisticated paperwork systems can be added if and when they can be justified in terms of useful information for initiating action.

The Work Order. One of the most important pieces of paper in the function of a maintenance department is the work order. It provides

1. The necessary information to:
   - *a.* Perform the work required
   - *b.* Perform the work on the proper piece of equipment
   - *c.* Perform the work when it is required
   - *d.* Plan the work and set the time allowed for it
   - *e.* Charge the proper account
   - *f.* Allow the scheduling of men and equipment economically
2. The necessary signing authority to expend labor and materials
3. The necessary control of labor and material against a specific job
4. A historical record of maintenance work performed or modifications made to a piece of machinery

There are many forms which can be used, one of which is shown by Figures 1-4*a* and *b*. The variations are not important; what is important is that there should be a work order procedure specifying the critical items mentioned above. The following are four classic problems encountered in a work order procedure.

1. Should a work order request be issued first, and after the work is analyzed should a specific work order be issued to the tradesmen to do that work? The use of one initial work order is generally preferable. At first, the line supervisor issuing the directions involving the necessary work may not be explicit. For example, he may describe the work he wants done merely as "fix machine." This problem can be overcome with patient and diligent training. When the originator of the work order is trained properly, he then be-

(a)

FIG. 1-4*a*. Maintenance Work Order Form (front).

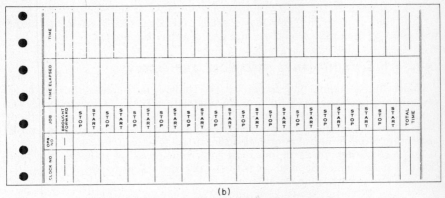

(b)

FIG. 1-4b. Maintenance Work Order Form (back).

comes in effect a vitally interested and unpaid member of the maintenance department.

2. "No tickee—no washee" concept—is this practical? The answer is yes. Without a work order, a maintenance department has no chance to organize and plan to perform its work efficiently. Of course, there will be emergencies, but these too can be handled in such a way that when the maintenance foreman is lining up men and material to face the emergency, the production foreman can write out the vital facts and authorize the necessary work.

3. Should standing work orders be used? Yes, but only on previously agreed to, well-defined, and time-analyzed tasks such as preventive maintenance work. There is a tendency to extend this concept to short emergency "call-in" work. If this is done, be sure that each task is properly logged and the exact time to perform it is also noted. Generally speaking, standing orders are like blank checks and should be avoided.

4. What priority system should be used? No priority system will work unless the people involved with it work diligently toward making it work. An effective system is based on "date required." When making out a work order, the production foreman states clearly the date by which he requires the service to be performed. This date is taken seriously by the maintenance organization. They will try to meet it if at all possible. The minute they discover that they cannot meet the required date, they notify the production foreman and suggest a date which can be met. If this does not satisfy the production foreman, a discussion is held which may require some schedule juggling to meet a compromise solution. Words like "Rush," "Emergency," or "ASAP" have no meaning and therefore no place in a priority system.

The Monthly Cost Report. To determine the actual time to perform each job, a method of recording time must be used. The simplest and most accurate method of accumulating time against a work order is by means of a time clock. With the accumulation of time against each work order, and therefore against each charge account or subaccount, a monthly cost report can be developed to indicate the totals. To have better control of the total maintenance expenditures, it is usual to break them down further. For example:

1. Maintenance labor charges by service departments
2. Major maintenance projects (over $1,000)

3. Maintenance labor by production department
4. Purchased maintenance spares and services

These monthly charges can be compared with the budgeted amounts in each category for control purposes.

The Downtime Report. A downtime report is usually presented as percentage of scheduled time or paid clock hours and represents the actual time that equipment was not able to produce because of maintenance problems. In its own way, this report is a useful indicator of the relative efficiency of the maintenance force.

The Labor Efficiency Report. A measure of the efficiency of the maintenance work force is given by a labor efficiency report. The hours allowed to do a job (based on historical, estimated, or accurate engineered standards) are accumulated and compared to the actual hours required. The figure is usually expressed as a percentage and is a good control tool, providing that accurate standards are used and at least 80 percent of the maintenance work force is covered.

The Service Labor Report. The service labor report indicates how service labor is used. It is usually expressed as a percentage of total hours. The types generally listed are:

1. Preventive maintenance
2. Regular scheduled
3. Regular nonscheduled
4. Emergency
5. Indirect maintenance work such as moving machinery or setting up production equipment

It is fairly obvious that this report may be used for goal setting. The prime objective should be to have a maximum of regular scheduled work and a minimum of emergency work.

The Ratio Report. There are a number of ratio reports which may be useful if they are used to measure trends and not for absolute judgment of the efficiency of the maintenance department. These include:

1. Total maintenance costs compared to total plant worth
2. Total maintenance costs compared to total sales
3. Maintenance labor compared to total plant labor force

Maintenance costs per unit of product is a very meaningful figure and may be used to justify equipment purchase, modifications, and the like.

The Backlog Report. Another useful report is the backlog report. It is usually expressed in crew weeks of backlog in a particular maintenance department. This is an accurate gage to use when the question of increasing or decreasing the work force has to be considered.

The Random Sampling or Ratio Delay Report. Work sampling studies will indicate relative activity, idle time, and the like. They provide an inexpensive method of measuring the relative efficiency of a maintenance group. Relative efficiency should not be confused with effective effort. Effective effort takes into account use of proper methods and standard times. Sampling is usually a preliminary review before a more effective control program in a maintenance group is established.

Other necessary paperwork required in a maintenance organization generally includes several additional items.

Man-hour Scheduling and Machine Loading (Machine Tool) Forms. Appropriate forms are required to schedule and control work during the successive steps of the maintenance operation. Scheduling should be done weekly and cover 70 to 80 percent of the work force.

Preventive Maintenance Inspection Forms and Control Forms. There is a great variety involved in preventive maintenance forms, but individual preference should be encouraged as long as certain basic principles are not violated. These are:

1. The control form should:
   a. Clearly schedule each and every inspection task and state who should do it
   b. Indicate whether or not the scheduled work was done
   c. Indicate that follow-up action was taken when it was required
2. The inspection or task form should:
   a. Be different for every type of equipment
   b. Clearly indicate all items to be inspected or work to be performed
   c. Use specific instructions like "adjust to 10 psi" or "shim to 0.010"
   d. Have a remarks column for the inspector to indicate faults and any recommended action that he deems advisable

Without these specific forms and controls, a preventive maintenance program can be a waste of time and money. Many a plant manager can be deluded into a false sense of security by being informed that his plant is being patrolled by competent people and that there are always competent people available to meet any emergency. This "baby-sitting" concept is costly and is diametrically opposed to the concept of preventive maintenance which requires these "competent, available people" to perform specific tasks and submit written reports of their inspections.

Estimate Sheets. Estimate sheets are a necessary form of control, especially on major jobs. These should indicate the estimated cost in man-hours and material for the complete job. The estimating done is a form of discipline which requires the person involved to plan and organize his work in the most effective way.

Major Maintenance Projects Planning Control. If a system of highlighting major repairs or purchases for maintenance work is adopted, a scheduling control feature of spreading these throughout the year should also be adopted. In this way, labor requirements are evened out.

Logbooks or Equipment Record Forms. Historical records are needed for some kinds of equipment. They can pinpoint troublesome areas readily and often suggest the resolution of problems either by modification or by change of equipment. Maintaining such records is a costly process, and a selective approach should be used. From time to time, the plant engineer may wish to introduce a new flow of paperwork to place some aspect of his function under closer scrutiny. This should be encouraged, but it should also be discontinued when it has served the original purpose.

MANAGEMENT PROBLEM AREAS

Typical recurring management problems in the field of plant maintenance are listed below.

Budgets. Like any other well-managed function which requires the establishment of targets, maintenance requires the establishment of budgets. Maintenance budgets should be set cooperatively by operating and maintenance personnel. This requires the maintenance people to recommend a suitable budget for a department and the operating people to study and approve when they agree. The procedure should go something like this:

1. The plant manager asks the plant engineer to recommend a maintenance budget for the next year's operations at certain levels of activity.

2. The plant engineer, after consultation with his department heads, spells out specifically:

   a. The type and amount of craft and maintenance labor (in hours) which will be required for each production department (accounting unit).

   b. The amount of money required to purchase spares, materials, and services for each production department.

   c. The type of labor man-hours and cost of materials required to perform the major overhauls and repairs during the year for each building and production department.

   d. The amount of maintenance hours required by the production department which tends to use its own labor for maintenance purposes.

3. The above recommendation is sent to the production superintendent. He in turn reviews it with his people. If there are any differences of opinion, they are straightened out and agreed to. Rarely should the plant manager get involved in referreeing differences here.

4. Once the production and maintenance people agree to a maintenance budget, it becomes in fact a production maintenance budget. The production people are obliged to authorize maintenance work and to explain any variances. The maintenance people are obliged to work efficiently and to stay within the budget which has been based upon their recommendations.

This procedure places the authority for spending money where it belongs, with the production people. They alone are responsible for getting quality "widgets" out of the door economically. To do this they must control the machinery, the raw material, the manpower, and the maintenance costs. The maintenance superintendent must be in tune with the objective of the production shops and do everything necessary to help the production people meet their objectives.

Contract Maintenance. Virtually every plant uses outside contractors for some of its maintenance work. Some plants have gone the whole way and depend on contractors to do all the necessary work in their plants, although this usually is not altogether desirable.

Maintenance work often handled by outside maintenance contractors includes:

1. All major roof and building repairs
2. All larger painting tasks
3. Office janitorial service
4. Plant window washing tasks
5. Plant lighting fixture washing
6. Work for craftsmen not in work force, such as bricklayers or carpenters
7. Pest control and sanitation
8. Railroad repairs
9. Large floor repairs
10. Gardening
11. Snow removal tasks
12. Garbage removal tasks
13. Manufacture of components which cannot be produced in plant because of manpower limitations (skill or available man-hours)

Generally speaking, work should be contracted out if it can be done more economically by specialists or if the internal group cannot do the necessary work because of skill, equipment, or manpower limitations. Occasionally, it will be necessary to use contract work because of peak demands on the available work force. There should always be a hard core of company-employed tradesmen, however, who are experienced on the plant's own equipment and who should be able to compete successfully against contract workers. It is a good idea to obtain competitive quotes for certain trades to see if the shop force measures up to the competitive market.

Training. Training of supervisors in the plant engineering organization takes on great importance, for the supervisors should be trained in the best man-management techniques as well as in the latest innovations in their field. Usually these supervisors are included in all training plans for production supervisors; so the first training requirement is satisfied. The technical aspect of training is much more flexible and sometimes will take on the role of training programs for plant engineering supervisors only. At other times, department heads may be sent to specialized schools, seminars, and conferences. Membership in technical societies should be encouraged, for these groups tend to be great disseminators of knowledge in specific fields.

Training of tradesmen and maintenance people is important, particularly in view of the more sophisticated equipment that is coming into most plants. Updating training of the work force can be done by various methods. A popular one is to send tradesmen to a supplier's school where they get the basic and advanced training required to maintain a specific piece of equipment. Another method is to encourage tradesmen to take specialized courses in local technical schools by offering to pay their tuition. The most common method is to assign a tradesman to the installation phase of new equipment where he works with the commissioning engineer and learns by doing and observing. A supplier or a local technical teacher might also come to the plant to cover a specific subject. Whatever avenue is chosen, the investment will generally be returned many times.

CONCLUSION

With the advent of automation in manufacturing plants, more and more emphasis must of necessity be placed on good maintenance of plants and equipment. That is why it is suggested that serious consideration be given to dividing the engineering and maintenance groups so that they may both report to the plant manager. Good plant engineering and maintenance can contribute greatly to the profitability of a company. These functions should therefore be staffed with well-qualified and dynamic individuals. To function efficiently, they should be encouraged to adopt currently available management tools and modify them as necessary for their own use. A certain amount of paperwork is necessary for proper controls; the relative amount and sophistication involved depends on the size, complexity, and requirements of a particular plant. As good management depends on controls and controls depend on accurate measurement, it should be the ultimate goal of every maintenance group to plan and measure the work of its force.

BIBLIOGRAPHY

Kapner, Sylvan L., "Maintenance Management," sec. 7, chap. 5, in H. B. Maynard (ed.), *Handbook of Business Administration,* McGraw-Hill Book Company, New York, 1967.

Morrow, L. C., *Maintenance Engineering Handbook,* McGraw-Hill Book Company, New York, 1960.

Newbrough, E. T., *Effective Maintenance Management,* McGraw-Hill Book Company, New York, 1967.

CHAPTER TWO

Preventive Maintenance

CHARLES V. CLARKE *Senior Vice President, H. B. Maynard and Company, Incorporated, Pittsburgh, Pennsylvania*

The purpose of this chapter is to help the manufacturing manager understand and evaluate preventive maintenance. In too many plants, the concept prevails that the breakdown method of maintenance is the best. Some maintenance foremen and superintendents grew up with it; hence they prefer it and tend to influence the manufacturing manager. Some production foremen and superintendents accept breakdown maintenance or at least do little to push the installation of preventive maintenance.

The acceptance of organized and integrated preventive maintenance, as distinguished from simple lubrication preventive maintenance, comes slowly. The maintenance supervisor often prefers having a force of top maintenance men available to send out when he receives word that there is a machine breakdown. His unwitting ally is the production supervisor who is interested in obtaining maximum machine utilization right now. This utilization is fine, but its attainment requires expensive standby maintenance men to appear just at breakdown time and get the equipment under way again. The fact that the breakdown need not have happened is not considered, nor is it recognized that the repair is often temporary, with the result that another breakdown impends.

In the face of these attitudes, the manufacturing manager must make a decision:

1. Shall breakdown maintenance be practiced in an attempt to obtain apparent maximum machine utilization?
2. Shall preventive maintenance be introduced to reduce emergency breakdowns, regardless of periods of lost production during preventive maintenance inspections?

Experience has shown that the second course is best, but persistent effort is necessary to make it operative.

The plant engineer can help if he is given responsibility for the reduction of emergency and breakdown work and for maximum utilization and performance of maintenance personnel on a definite planned and scheduled basis. Also, of course, he should share the responsibility for convincing production and maintenance supervisors that preventive maintenance is beneficial and profitable.

Preventive maintenance must have the support and approval of the manufacturing manager in both word and deed. Production supervision must be led to recognize that preventive maintenance is here to stay. Maintenance management must be indoctrinated to provide prompt but low-cost service to production. Although preventive maintenance is only a part of the total maintenance system, it is a most important part that must be integrated into the total effort.

BENEFITS OF INTEGRATED PREVENTIVE MAINTENANCE

The benefits that will result from a properly conceived and installed preventive maintenance program are many. The benefits realized from halfway preventive maintenance measures are few and constitute a poor investment. A preventive maintenance program costs money initially, but in the long run one of its purposes is to help minimize costs, both maintenance costs and production costs. A good program can help correct the imbalance between a force of maintenance personnel available for any eventuality and the excess manufacturing costs resulting from productive equipment downtime due to breakdown maintenance.

The facts are that preventive maintenance:

1. Is based upon economic aspects that are measurable and controllable.
2. Will help reduce maintenance costs by eliminating more costly maintenance work and by detecting and correcting potential troubles and reducing emergency shutdowns.
3. Lends itself readily to work measurement and the resulting labor cost control.
4. Can be planned and scheduled well in advance.
5. Generates additional maintenance work orders that can be planned and scheduled.
6. Permits the preparation of a more factual maintenance budget, because the work is largely predictable.
7. Can reduce the emergency hours to approximately 10 percent of the direct maintenance hours. Without preventive maintenance, up to 75 percent of these hours may be devoted to breakdowns and emergency work.
8. Can reduce the need for standby equipment.
9. Results in less production downtime and production delays.
10. Reduces safety hazards.
11. Will increase the life of fixed assets.
12. Can be profitable.

THE PREVENTIVE MAINTENANCE PROGRAM

The steps necessary to introduce a preventive maintenance program properly can be understood by analyzing unsuccessful installations. Programs have failed for a few reasons. Chief among these are lack of support, understanding, and interest evidenced by the manufacturing manager; failure to sell the benefits to the production and maintenance departments, with the result that the preventive maintenance philosophy was really never accepted; failure to train the preventive maintenance staff in its duties and responsibilities and to train all supervision to an appropriate degree in the operation of the program; and finally, failure to establish and reduce to writing those policies that should govern the program. A significant and positive step that the manufacturing manager can take is to set up a steering committee to help keep the program progressing. Included on this committee should be personnel from maintenance, maintenance planning, production, industrial engineering, and plant engineering.

In the limited sense, preventive maintenance is considered as the scheduled and systematic inspection, cleaning, lubrication, and servicing required to maintain equipment and buildings in optimum condition. A complete program, however, also includes the planned and scheduled replacement of troublesome, costly items of production equipment in the coming year or the next. In addition, it includes shutdown inspection with resulting overhaul and reconditioning of productive and auxiliary equipment.

A preventive maintenance program has two distinct parts that have equal importance in the development, installation, and operation of the system: (1) the paperwork procedures and (2) the manual portion. The paperwork consists of preventive maintenance checklists, route sheets, planning and scheduling forms, work orders, equipment records, and control reports. These are used in the day-to-day operation to organize and prescribe the work and to provide for feedback to update and control the preventive maintenance effort. They all are essential.

Allied and integrated with the paperwork procedures is the manual work comprising cleaning, adjustment, minor repair, lubrication, and inspection—both visual and shutdown.

Installing the Program. As with production, the preventive maintenance worker will do a better job when he knows what must be done, where the job is, when it must be done, and how long it should take him to do it.

Preventive maintenance is best introduced by analyzing and installing the program in the total operating entity—a plant, a mill, a refinery—a section at a time. The plant engineer and an industrial engineer with knowledge of preventive maintenance procedures, together with the maintenance supervisor, should first conduct an overall survey. With carefully selected and trained maintenance inspectors, industrial engineering then makes the first installation. Extension of the plan from a pilot installation should be accomplished gradually. For example, in a pulp and paper mill, the actual program development work for preparation of initial checklists may be confined to the pulp mill, bleach plant, or wood yard, or it may be confined to an item, such as instruments, plantwide. After checklists have been completed and tested for one area, the next area may be started, and so on, until the entire complex is covered.

A manager should be certain that policies are written and followed. Preventive maintenance failures have occurred because of lack of written policies resulting in maintenance personnel being loosely assigned. Management in those cases relied on the experience and initiative of the maintenance staff to provide the equipment with the service required. If everything happened to be just right, some successes were realized, principally in the area of lubrication. All too often, however, with a loose approach, accessible equipment is overmaintained while the more inaccessible equipment does not receive enough maintenance. Also, even though a good job is currently being done there is no guarantee that this will continue as time goes by. Organization and control must be established by specifying the servicing to be performed at production units, by providing the means to do it, and by follow-up to see that the work has been done as specified.

Checklists. Checklists are prepared for certain equipment or groups of equipment. There are generally considered to be two types of checklists that should cover about 85 percent of the productive equipment: periodic checklists and routine checklists.

Figure 2-1 shows an example of the former, and Figure 2-2 illustrates a routine preventive maintenance checklist.

Information relative to checklists and route sheets for various tours, crafts, and equipment may often be preprinted on different-colored forms. Color coding of preventive maintenance documents for classification is desirable. Companies with computer facilities have incorporated many of their preventive maintenance routines into the computer, with a daily run indicating exactly what work is to be carried out that day for inspection work and for lubrication routines.

PERIODIC PREVENTIVE MAINTENANCE ELECTRICAL INSPECTION		Checklist No. E7 Sheet 1 of 1				
EQUIPMENT	Henley, G.E.C., Warbrick & McKellan Spark-testers					
Part or Component	Instructions		Weeks			
		Freq.	4	12	24	A
General	Remove mains plug.		x	x	x	x
Electrode chamber	Open electrode chamber		x	x	x	x
	Look and feel for broken or displaced electrode chains.		x	x	x	x
	Examine H.T. lead for loose connections, tighten if necessary.				x	x
	Look at interlock micro-switches for cracked insulation. Test operation for sticking plungers. Replace if necessary.		x	x	x	x
	Close electrode chamber. Test latches for faulty locking and adjust if possible.		x	x	x	x
Earth connection	Look and feel for loose connection to capacitor, transformer, and rheostat. Tighten if necessary.				x	x
	. . . . . and so on.					

Fig. 2-1. Periodic Preventive Maintenance Checklist.

ROUTINE PREVENTIVE MAINTENANCE CHECKLIST

Production Unit___Brown Stock Washer___   List No.___Mechanical___
Dept._____Kraft Pulp Mill_____   Rev. No._____
Plant No._____742A_____   Sheet___1___of___1___
                                                 Issued___5/13/xx_____

Part or Component	Instructions	Frequency			
		S	D	W	2W
A. Repulper	4/M/4 Look at stuffing box for leaks front and back. If leaking, adjust.			x	x
B. Vat	4/M/4 Look at stuffing box for leaks front and back. If leaking, adjust.		x	x	x
C. Main worm drive	1/L/3 Look for lubricant leaks around shaft seals, case, or shaft.		x	x	x
F. General instructions	19/M/1 Inspect general condition of piping and valves on this route — report leaks.	x	x	x	x
	20/M/1 Look at condition of tanks and chests along this route — report leaks.	x	x	x	x
	6/E/5 ..... and so on.				

Fig. 2-2.   Routine Preventive Maintenance Checklist.

Checklists and route sheets generally fall into five classes:
1. Mechanical (millwright)
2. Lubrication
3. Instrument
4. Electrical
5. Pipe

Other classes may be added if needed. These checklists should comprise the basis for a policy and procedure manual.

Figures 2-3 and 2-4 represent daily and summary type working route sheets. They are used in conjunction with checklists. They are designed to save the inspector from backtracking as he completes the inspection and servicing on one production unit and moves on to the next one on the route sheet. When the inspector is following a route, he refers to the checklist for the specific operation that he is to perform for each production unit on his route. By using these basic forms, the manual portion of the preventive maintenance work is carried out.

ABC PAPER COMPANY
Z MILL

Route Sheet No. _121_ Rev. _____   Sheet ____1____ of ____1____
Frequency____Daily____   Cost Center_____

Service Area ____02____   Date Scheduled ___6/15/xx___
Craft No. ____92 – Oilers____   Certified Complete_____
Assigned to_____   Standard Hours ___2.1_____

Production unit	Check-list	Codes missed	Adjustments or additional work – report defects	Std. hours
Conveyors	003			
Brown stock washer fans	001			
Brown stock washer	005			

Evaporator pumps				
Stock chest agitator & pumps				
Time & date completed			Total Std. Hours	
Time & date started			Certified complete_____	
Total time used			Posted records & filed by _____	Date
Are checklists adequate	Yes	No		

Fɪɢ. 2-3. Daily Route Sheet.

The size of the preventive maintenance group varies with the area of the plant and the level of maintenance decided upon by the manufacturing manager together with his production and maintenance staff. As a bench mark, however, the size of the group should be about 10 percent of the total maintenance force. The organization can vary. Each craft may inspect and service equipment related to its craft; that is, electricians for electrical equipment, pipe fitters for valves and pipelines, and so on; or a separate section may be set up to handle all preventive maintenance work. The organization will be influenced by the physical plant and by jurisdictional agreements with unions. There are advantages and disadvantages to both operating procedures, but both of them work. A separate preventive maintenance section under a qualified supervisor is generally the more desirable.

A successful inspection program is basic to a successful preventive maintenance program. By reporting and recording conditions, it helps correct defects before they become major. The key to all instructions on checklists is to direct the action of the inspector to finding faults. Note in Figures 2-1 and

SUMMARY ROUTE SHEET

PM INSPECTION – ELECTRICAL

Eff. Date – 7/10/xx

Dept.	Name and Plant	Weekly		Monthly		Quarterly	
		Sheet No.	Work Group	Sheet No.	Work Group	Sheet No.	Work Group
2	General plant	114	A	–	–	–	–
4	Extrusion	115	A	–	–	–	–
5	Large rod	–	–	116	C	–	–
6	Forge	–	–	118	H	–	–
7	Trim	117	C	–	–	–	–
8	Automatic	–	–	111	G	–	–
33	Die cast	112	B	–	–	–	–
5 & 7	Hoists and furnaces	–	–	–	–	127	E
	Plant 1	–	E	–	K	–	E
	Plant 6	113	A	–	–	–	–
	Total plants 1 and 6	–	E	–	K	–	E

Fig. 2-4.   Summary Route Sheet.

2-2 that the inspector looks or feels for something broken. He does not just examine connections; he examines for loose connections. He does not just test a latch; he tests a latch for faulty locking.

If an operator fails to look for loose anchor bolts on a reducer and no corrective action is taken until the reducer foot breaks, the workman has not performed the preventive maintenance required for that reducer. Also, if a workman, in taking up a packing gland on a critical fluid valve, knows that there is not enough take-up left to stop another leak and does not report it, he is not helping to reduce emergencies. The next time that the valve leaks, it will have to be repacked or replaced on an emergency basis.

On one typical installation, the first time that a preventive maintenance inspection for an electrical route of two and one-half hours' duration was performed, over 240 man-hours of legitimate electrical maintenance work were uncovered for which work orders were prepared. The first run on another installation produced nineteen valid pipe fitter work orders.

Preventive maintenance routines should be planned to require not more than two to three hours to complete. At the end of this time, the inspector may start another two-hour route, and so on through the day. The reason for this relatively short time is to have management control over the time of the preventive maintenance staff. Experience has shown that blanket eight-hour routes usually cause the schedule to become out of balance after a short period of time. If not out of balance, then the equipment at the end of a long tour is neglected or given just a cursory examination. Shorter routes permit a second go-around if necessary, and missed work is picked up more readily in subsequent tours.

The route sheet in Figure 2-3 shows a time of 2.1 standard hours. This represents an engineered time standard and not an estimated time. Through the use of such time standards and scheduling boards, some inspection and lubrication work may be planned and scheduled by days for up to a year in advance. At the completion of each route, the time actually taken is shown so that performance can be calculated in the same way that performance is computed for productive work covered by engineered time standards. Thus the manufacturing manager has a major tool for the control of preventive maintenance labor, and the supervisor and plant engineer have a device for balancing manpower requirements.

Lubrication. Lubrication operations occur regularly, are prescheduled, and should carry a standard time. They are seldom combined with inspection operations. Lubrication consists of oiling and greasing mechanical checkpoints of equipment. One of the five generally accepted classes of checklists and route sheets is devoted to lubrication.

An interesting procedure that is simple, effective, but often overlooked is the use of color coding. Grease fittings, grease cups, oil cups, and other lubrication points in color can show type and quality of lubricant to be used as well as frequency or even the specific day for lubrication. Lubricant dispensers can be similarly coded. New employees with less than average education are able to perform successfully the oiling and greasing routines with an absolute minimum of training when provided with proper checklists, route sheets, and color codes to follow.

A final point with respect to lubrication is the advisability of a careful study of oils and greases on the market. Usually only a few of the total available need be used. Through standardization of oils and greases, savings of up to 15 percent of lubrication material costs may be realized.

Work Orders. Preventive maintenance work is predetermined and scheduled, and the operations should be reduced to writing. The written checklist is a form of work order. There are other work orders that are essential for successful operation. They, too, must be written so as to bring all work out into the open where it can be analyzed, evaluated, measured, and controlled.

Unfortunately, the written work order for other than production work is sometimes considered an evil and consequently something to be avoided. The manufacturing manager, however, should have a firm policy that there will be written work orders applying to all maintenance work requiring over fifteen minutes to perform. To eliminate work orders in order to eliminate paperwork is false economy. Meaningful written work orders provide a means of control. Even a waitress in a diner uses a written work order form to process something as simple as an order for a hamburger.

Written preventive maintenance work orders should describe clearly the exact work content of the job. They originate in several ways. Besides the checklist, one of the principal sources is the inspector while making his tour. Minor repairs and adjustments requiring no more than fifteen minutes are made immediately by the inspector. The need for other maintenance work that is uncovered during the round is noted on the route sheet. Upon completion of the route or at the end of the day, the results are reviewed with the supervisor, and appropriate work orders are written for standards application and inclusion into the maintenance backlog and schedule.

Follow-up and completion of this repair work are essential to prevent a breakdown in the preventive maintenance program. Nothing is more disheartening to a craftsman than to report the same fault again and again and realize that no action is being taken to correct it.

One plant solved this problem by providing inspectors with colored tags having various markings. As the inspector makes his rounds and uncovers a fault, he tags the equipment or valve or motor with the appropriate colored tag showing the date of inspection. Figure 2-5 shows a two-part tag where the paper tear-off sheet is submitted for the preparation of the work order while the card remains fixed to the equipment. This tag remains in place until the repair is made. This, by the way, eliminates the necessity of an inspector having to make out a second work order for the same repair on a subsequent tour.

This procedure provides the manager with an excellent visual means of determining the effectiveness of his preventive maintenance follow-up. After the first few weeks of the installation, this plant took on the appearance of a gaily decorated Christmas tree. During his plant tours, the manager had no difficulty in observing the growing number of tags; neither did the maintenance foremen who took appropriate action to process the work orders and eliminate the majority of tags. Because the tags are dated and color coded, the manager can make spot checks to sample craft delay time between inspection and repair.

Maintenance requests also originate with the production supervisors. These may be work orders related to the preventive maintenance activity or directly for maintenance work. Production personnel should be included in the operation of the preventive maintenance program. They have intimate knowledge of and familiarity with the equipment and can contribute considerably with respect to equipment checkpoints, frequencies, lubrication, and perhaps minor adjustments. Their preventive maintenance duties, however, must be clearly specified in writing.

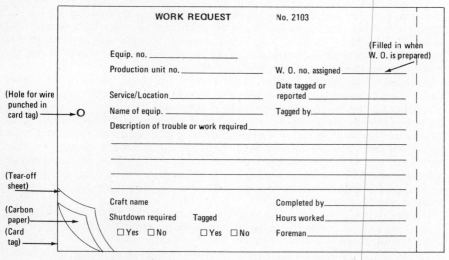

Fig. 2-5. Tag to Be Placed on Equipment Requiring Maintenance.

A final major source for work orders, for adjustments in preventive maintenance routines, and for maintenance work directly is the equipment records. Periodic analysis of these records will show where there is a high incidence of breakdown or emergency work. It will also indicate the desirability of issuing new or adjusted preventive maintenance checklists.

Equipment Records. The preventive maintenance program includes a systematic inspection of critical equipment to detect and prevent emergencies. To help adjust and maintain the inspection routines to keep them functioning properly, there must be feedback into the system. This feedback is obtained through another phase of paperwork—the equipment history record data. It is an essential ingredient of a preventive maintenance program. Without an inspection and equipment record system, valuable information is lost or at least must be constantly rediscovered.

These equipment records with auxiliary files and work order jackets should include the important but not total plant equipment. With minor, fairly trouble-free equipment, there will be excess clerical costs in proportion to value received. Optimum preventive maintenance develops through the judicious use of feedback data and the analysis of records for each production unit and component at least once every six months. Care should be taken that the repair histories of components or assemblies can be identified, and that faults with such items as oil seals, bearings, shafts, and the like are not concealed.

The manager should see that equipment records are analyzed systematically. The frequencies and contents of preventive maintenance checklists and route sheets must be revised constantly until the optimum balance between cost of emergencies and cost of preventive maintenance is approached.

Some companies set up their equipment record data in card files, while others make use of their computers. With computers, it is possible to make data available in numerous forms. Repair histories, costs, frequencies, probabilities, and the like may be obtained rapidly at the manager's request. However, the cost for this method for analysis and retrieval must be compared with other procedures.

Care should be taken not to keep records, even with computers, just for the sake of record keeping. Managers are interested in record keeping for the purpose of receiving timely and accurate information upon which to base decisions. The plant engineer uses these records to make adjustments in his preventive maintenance program, to make recommendations for equipment replacement, or to institute repair, modification, or overhaul work.

Shutdown Inspection. Another major phase of planned and scheduled preventive maintenance work is classed as shutdown inspection. In this, the inspector or the mechanics determine the general condition of a piece of equipment when it is not running and perhaps requires dismantling. This procedure can involve either a small pump or equipment as significant as a paper machine. In the inspection of shutdown equipment, it is also desirable to follow written prescribed inspection procedures. The planned maintenance overhaul should be in conjunction with these inspections, perhaps following a critical path schedule, comprising work uncovered during previous preventive maintenance shutdown inspections.

At the outset of a preventive maintenance program and while establishing inspection procedures and assumed frequencies, all critical equipment, including support items, should be listed. A decision should then be made on whether they will be inspected visually while operating or when shut down. Preventive maintenance work performed on a shutdown basis must be coordinated with production schedules. This is perhaps the most difficult phase of the preventive maintenance program because of varying production schedules and the manufacturing manager's understandable desire to get out production. Shutdown for preventive maintenance is often postponed and all too often cut short in order to get the equipment back in operation. To optimize preventive maintenance costs, other maintenance costs, and production costs, the manufacturing manager should establish shutdown policies based on equipment records as well as on production schedules. Policies can and should be changed when the equipment history records show that new circumstances have arisen. Inspection schedules for shutdown equipment should be developed from frequency analysis and production performance.

Frequency is an essential part of any preventive maintenance inspection plan. Too long a delay from a scheduled inspection will not pick up the potential breakdown on time; too short an interval results in excess production costs and excess inspection costs.

Planned Replacement. Planned replacement, although constantly under consideration, is formalized each year with the preparation of the preventive maintenance budget. This is when the manager directs his attention to the replacement of items of production equipment in the coming year. Usually, replacement comes about as a result of either excess maintenance costs or excess production costs. In either case, replacement may be the necessary step to reduce the amount of breakdowns or emergencies.

MEASUREMENT AND CONTROL

Work measurement can be applied in advance of the work being performed to at least 80 to 90 percent of the total preventive maintenance labor hours. The standard times for preventive maintenance work orders should be known by the inspectors before they start their rounds or do any work. How long it should take to do a job can be determined accurately and in advance by using engineered work measurement through the Universal Maintenance Standards approach discussed in the next chapter. It is no longer necessary to rely on the use of estimated or historical times for this type of work.

Work measurement for preventive maintenance will provide the manufacturing manager with a practical means for cost control for this group. Resulting reports will point out where improvements in the program and in cost reductions can be made. It will provide the means for establishing manpower requirements balanced to the prescribed level of maintenance and assist in providing equalized work loads requiring good worker performance and utilization.

Figure 2-6 is a sample analysis sheet for a preventive maintenance inspection route. Such basic data and reference data are available for practically all work in all crafts and have been applied successfully in most industries. Of importance also is the fact that numerous companies have wage incentive plans based on engineered work measurement for their preventive maintenance labor and are obtaining additional outstanding results.

Control over the functioning of the preventive maintenance system is as vital as the existence of the system itself. It is necessary to accumulate data, histories, frequencies, and costs over a period of time. Using these data, checklists, route sheets, time standards, and frequencies can be adjusted to reflect current conditions and realize optimum performance for total plant equipment and building maintenance.

Figure 2-7 illustrates a communications loop for the control of the preventive

BENCH MARK ANALYSIS SHEET
STANDARD TIME

CODE___0690.69_____

Description: Inspection route – finishing mill	Date: 4/21/xx BM 8		
	Craft: Pipe fitter		
	Dwgs:		
No. of Men 1	Analyst: M.P.		Pg. 1 of 1

Line	Men	Operation Description	Ref. Symbol	Unit Time	Freq.	Total Time
1	1	Walking time for inspection	03.0104	.0015	150 x 1½	.3375
2	1	Check gas on all salamanders	13.0002	.0025	8	.0200
3	1	Drain water from air line receivers	13.0003	.0050	8	.0400
4	1	Check all air lubricators	13.0002	.0025	16	.0400
5	1	Check tube round bed kickers and piping	13.0001	.0012	24	.0288
6	1	Check Siemag lube and hydraulic systems	13.0002	.0025	12	.0300
7	1	Check beam turnups and piping	13.0001	.0012	12	.0144
8	1	Check and drain rail pull-off	13.0001	.0012	6	.0072
9	1	Check rail pull-off lubricators	13.0003	.0050	6	.0300
10	1	Check rail drill press water	13.0002	.0025	8	.0200
11	1	Check Heller saw skilly pump	13.0003	.0050	4	.0200
12	1	Check tie-plate skilly pump	13.0003	.0050	4	.0200
13	1	Check air line, hoses for leaks	13.0001	.0012	48	.0576
14	1	Check rail hardeners air and anti-freeze	13.0002	.0025	12	.0300
15	1	Check gag press hydraulic hoses and pumps	13.0002	.0025	12	.0300
16	1	Check gag press sump pumps	13.0003	.0050	2	.0100
17	1	Check Kling saws, pumps, hoses, and sprays	13.0001	.0012	12	.0144
18	1	Check Ball Mill water, air, and gas	13.0002	.0025	32	.0800
19	1	Check Ball Mill quenchers' water	13.0002	.0025	4	.0100
20						

30						
Notes:			Bench mark time			.8399
			Standard work group			D

FIG. 2-6.   Analysis Sheet for a Preventive Maintenance Inspection Route.

maintenance function.   Preventive maintenance work is scheduled and performed in accordance with a plan.   This may be the checklist, route sheet, or work order.   As a result of the work, certain information or data are generated that must be fed back into the system or loop.   Pertinent feedback data are entered into the equipment history records directly from the work order form after the work has been completed.

These data are then subject, at least twice a year, to a periodic analysis and evaluation.   Also, certain of the data from the completed work order, such as performance to time standards, may be analyzed and evaluated promptly by the maintenance planning section for comparison of standard hours to actual hours taken to obtain individual or departmental performance.

Based on these analyses and evaluations, certain decisions are made relative to the program.   These may be to change preventive maintenance routines,

PREVENTIVE MAINTENANCE WORK

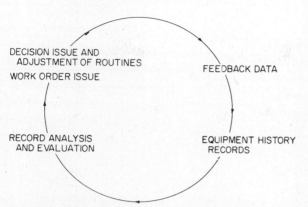

Fɪɢ. 2-7. Communications Loop for Controlling Preventive Maintenance Work.

adjust frequencies, shut down equipment, adjust manpower, plan for new equipment, modify lubrication practices, or the like. These decisions are fed back into the system by new work orders or checklists, and communication and control continue to flow smoothly around the loop. Regular or special reports desired by the manufacturing manager should be generated from within this loop, preferably by the maintenance planning section.

The manager should receive, as appropriate, certain control reports showing, for example, the number of work orders generated from the equipment record analysis and the relation of hours worked to the total maintenance standard hours of work accomplished in the same period. These numbers and percentages will vary considerably according to industry, equipment type, plant investment, and the like. A pattern will form, however, providing the manager with pertinent bench marks.

During the initial stages of the preventive maintenance installation, it is usual to find that emergency hours account for a high percentage of total maintenance hours. Unfortunately, emergency work cannot be eliminated completely. The manager should receive an emergency control report weekly showing:

$$\% \text{ emergencies} = \frac{\text{emergency hours}}{\text{direct maintenance hours}} \times 100$$

The manager should also receive weekly a composite preventive maintenance performance report showing:

$$\% \text{ performance} = \frac{\text{preventive maintenance hours}}{\text{actual preventive maintenance hours work on standard}} \times 100$$

If performance is low, it may point out either poor worker utilization or poor methods being followed. A coverage report is desirable that indicates how well the industrial engineering department has done in establishing standard time data for preventive maintenance work and how well the maintenance planning section has done in applying it.

$$\% \text{ coverage} = \frac{\text{preventive maintenance hours on standard}}{\text{total preventive maintenance hours available}} \times 100$$

	Dept. "A"		Dept. "B"	
	This week	Last week	This week	Last week
No. of inspections scheduled				
No. of inspections completed				
No. of faults found				
No. of repairs initiated				
No. of repairs completed				
No. of breakdowns				
No. of recurring breakdowns (within 6 months)				
Preventive maintenance hours				
Production downtime				

Fig. 2-8.　Preventive Maintenance Inspection Effectiveness Report.

Figure 2-8 shows a Preventive Maintenance Inspection Effectiveness Report. This provides the manager with a comprehensive summary of preventive maintenance activities, especially when coupled with the above performance and coverage reports. This report will also give an indication of whether the work was stopped or interrupted for other maintenance work. Interruptions to preventive maintenance constitute poor practice and as policy should be avoided. As part of this control report, the manager should receive a copy of all breakdown work orders. Periodically, he should review the preventive maintenance reports in conjunction with the breakdown records of given equipment to see what maintenance work may have been reported or recommended.

CONCLUSION

An integrated preventive maintenance program, properly installed and operating and supported by the manufacturing manager, will result in cost reduction. The cost of a given level of maintenance will be reduced. The cost of production will be reduced because of a decrease in the effect of breakdowns on output.

Preventive maintenance inspection is carried out for the detection of potential trouble spots or breakdown points. This should be an aggressive part of the program. Consideration should be given to setting up a research and development project to further the preventive maintenance effort in the plant. As automobile diagnostic centers ferret out potential problems, the manager of a plant, mill, or refinery can take similar action and make use of diagnostic tools as part of the preventive maintenance and overall cost reduction effort. Use should be made of electronic devices, vibration studies, monitoring, automatic control mechanisms, ultrasonic detectors and probe microphones, and the like to determine the interior conditions of equipment.

BIBLIOGRAPHY

Baumeister, Theodore, and Lionel S. Marks (eds.), *Standard Handbook for Mechanical Engineers*, 7th ed., McGraw-Hill Book Company, New York, 1967.

Carson, Gordon B., *Production Handbook*, 2d ed., The Ronald Press Company, New York, 1959.

Corder, G. G., *Organizing Maintenance*, British Institute of Management, London, England, 1963.

Grothus, H., *Arbeitsstudium und Instandhaltung—Band 2*, Beuth-Vertrieb GmbH, Berlin, Germany, 1964.

Jorgenson, D. W., and J. J. McCall, *Optimal Replacement Policy*, Rand McNally & Company, Chicago, Ill., 1967.

Lewis, Bernard T., and William W. Pearson, *Management Guide for Preventive Maintenance*, John F. Rider Publishers, Inc., New York, 1960.

Maynard, H. B. (ed.), *Handbook of Business Administration*, McGraw-Hill Book Company, New York, 1967.

Maynard, H. B. (ed.), *Industrial Engineering Handbook* 2d ed., McGraw-Hill Book Company, New York, 1963.

Morrow, L. C. (ed.), *Maintenance Engineering Handbook*, 2d ed., McGraw-Hill Book Company, New York, 1960.

Staniar, William (ed.), *Plant Engineering Handbook*, 2d ed., McGraw-Hill Book Company, New York, 1959.

CHAPTER THREE

Maintenance Cost Control

JOHN J. WILKINSON *Vice President, H. B. Maynard and Company, Incorporated, Pittsburgh, Pennsylvania*

Maintenance costs have always been a major part of total costs in process industries, and they have increased appreciably over the years. In general manufacturing, maintenance costs have increased to a point where manufacturing managers are forced to take action because they are such a large part of their total costs.

Maintenance costs can be reduced if better management can increase the productivity and overall effectiveness of maintenance labor. This involves improved procedures for planning, scheduling, and controlling all maintenance activities in the plant. Some form of measurement is required, because without measurement, good control is impossible.

In this chapter, some of the basic requirements for good maintenance cost control will be discussed, including organization, work orders and related procedures, planning and scheduling, maintenance work measurement, and performance measurement and control.

ORGANIZATION

A manager must make sure that the organization structure, the duties and responsibilities of his people, and the lines of authority are spelled out and understood by everyone involved. Unfortunately, owing to the relative smallness of the typical maintenance department, the maintenance organization is frequently only vaguely defined and is quite hazy in many people's minds.

There is no single organization concept that can be specified as right for every plant. Basically, good maintenance departments can be any of the following:

1. Functionally organized—where the division of responsibilities is based on

function, type of service rendered, and craftwork involved, as shown in Figure 3-1.

2. Geographically organized—where there is a real and logical need for division of responsibilities based primarily on geographic, process, or specialized manufacturing areas. Frequently, as shown in Figure 3-2, an area supervisor is responsible for all craftwork in his area. The more specialized crafts which are not closely allied to any one area are then centrally located, to be called in as needed. Some inefficiencies that are inherent in decentralized groups can be offset by quicker availability and "loyalty" to a given area. In both types of organization, a separate control section is set up, reporting to the highest level of management in the engineering and maintenance department. Many of the improvements and controls discussed later are originated or processed by this control section.

3. A combination of these two organizational concepts—where circumstances dictate a combination of functional and geographic organization, as when a certain building or area justifies its own multicraft group shop (Figure 3-3) or when certain key craftsmen have to be assigned the responsibility for a key area or a specific piece of equipment which is vital for continuous plant operation. Inefficient utilization of manpower is kept to a minimum by assigning minimum crews; and hopefully these inefficiencies are offset by reduced equipment downtime.

The late Professor Berenschot of Holland always stressed that, "If you delegate, you must educate." All too often when considering maintenance organization, duties, and responsibilities, this principle is forgotten. The result is a built-in weakness due to people. Supervisors and workers must be trained to do their jobs properly and to understand their contribution to the whole orga-

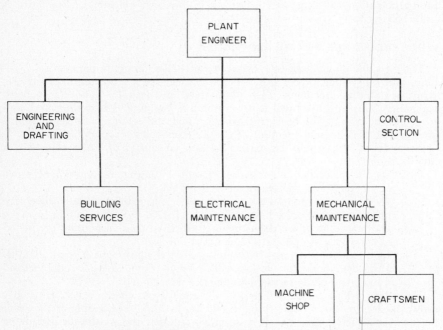

Fig. 3-1. Functionally Organized Maintenance Department.

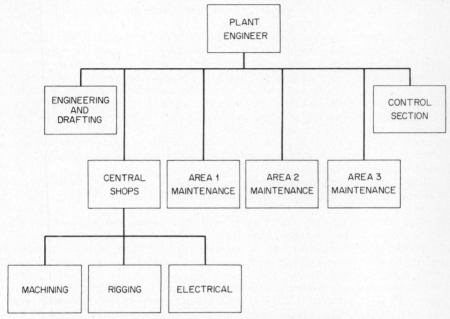

FIG. 3-2. Geographically Organized Maintenance Department.

nization. Management must follow up on these efforts. There is a vital need for participation, training, and follow-up if low-cost, efficient maintenance is to be achieved.

WORK ORDERS AND RELATED PROCEDURES

The effective maintenance department must have adequate paperwork, planning, and scheduling procedures. There is need for a work order procedure, with an initiating document and information feedback to maintenance management. This approach will ensure optimum planning, scheduling, and control. It will provide the basis for cost allocation and equipment records which are essential for effective operation of the maintenance department.

A work order is usually originated by one of several different sources. A few examples are:

1. By the plant engineering department—initiating an equipment move or an equipment modification
2. By a specific procedure or routine—for lubrication, oiling, preventive maintenance, and the like
3. By the maintenance department itself—from troubleshooting or special observations throughout the plant
4. By production people—by sending work requests which serve as initiating documents for more specific or more detailed work orders subsequently prepared in the maintenance department

The work order may be written on a standard punched card such as that shown by Figure 3-4. These cards should be as simple as possible or they will not be used. They must have minimum complexity and maximum usefulness for the maintenance department. The front side usually contains realistic

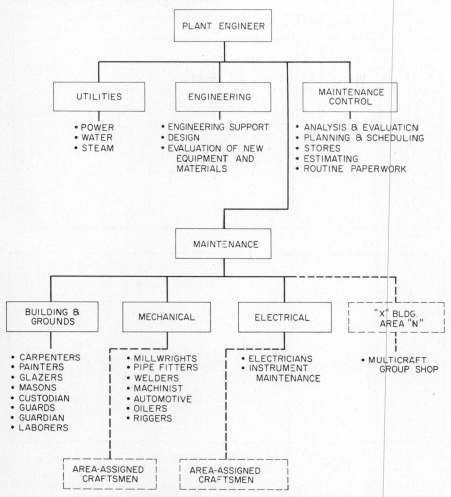

FIG. 3-3. Combined Functional and Geographic Organization.

maintenance and cost allocation information, and it is usually tailored to specific plant needs. Figure 3-4 shows the information which is normally required. The work order is more of a useful maintenance management tool than a cost accounting tool. It enables the cost department to assign costs in the manner they require, but it is designed primarily for maintenance department needs.

On the reverse side of the card, the hours charged against the job are posted, either from a time clock or as entered by the craftsmen or foremen responsible.

This type of work order and information permits an effective job of planning and scheduling of maintenance work. It gives the supervisors certain important information necessary to police and control the maintenance work and costs for which they are responsible.

Use of punched cards does not automatically involve data processing, as

MAINTENANCE JOB ORDER
M-483-A (REV. 1-67)

DATE ISSUED	DATE REQUIRED	MACH NO	WORK REQUEST NUMBER
			91455

MAINTENANCE JOB ORDER
M-483-A (REV. 1-67)

DATE ISSUED	DATE REQUIRED	MACH. NO	WORK REQUEST NUMBER
			91455

WORK DONE BY — WORKS & GRP: 517 717 727 737 OTHER N O OC S H MC
CRAFT COST CENTRE: 272 301 308 311 312 316 342 355
DATE COMP D: MO. DAY YR
CLOCK NO — TOTAL HRS

CHARGE TO — WORKS GRP CENTRE EXP CLASS SUB
MAINTENANCE TYPE: 1 PM 2 RS 3 RN 4 EM 5 OH 6 CS 7 OR
GROUP — STANDARD

DESCRIPTION OF WORK

SPECIAL TOOLS & MATL S.

DEPARTMENT FOREMAN　ANALYST　MAINTENANCE FOREMAN

DWG NO

TIME

TIME ELAPSED

JOB — BROUGHT FORWARD — STOP START STOP START STOP START STOP START STOP START STOP START STOP START STOP START STOP START STOP START STOP START STOP START STOP START STOP START — TOTAL TIME

OPR NO

CLOCK NO

FIG. 3-4.　Maintenance Work Order.

might be inferred from Figure 3-4. These cards have several advantages even if they are never used for data processing. The card is an ideal size for pocket or hard hat; it is rigid enough to write on without a firm backing; it looks rather important because it is a card and has a corner chamfered, and thus is treated with respect; and it is inexpensive to buy because of the competitive situation in its high-usage market. All sorts of card racks and storage boxes can be bought off the shelf for these standard cards. They can be printed singly or they can be interleaved with carbons, with either thick or flimsy copies, in whatever form is required by the particular plant situation. Many plants start out with multiple copies of these work orders, because each department originator and recipient feels that it has to defend itself by distributing copies and keeping detailed records. However, when confidence has been built up between the production and maintenance people for the service provided, the feeling of need for multiple copies and notifications is drastically reduced—often to a point where a single card copy may suffice. Some plants use only a single-copy work order and have a small backup copy machine in the department so that there is an absolute minimum of manual rewriting of information once the original work order is prepared. The accent is on sim-

CRAFT & NAME	TO START	IN PROGRESS	INTERRUPTED	COMPLETED
ELECTRICIANS:				
JOHN DOE				
BILL SMITH				
MIKE BROWN				
HENRY JONES				
PIPE FITTERS:				
JIM ROE				
JACK PYE				
JAKE QUINN				
BOB MILLS				
CHAS. TATE				
MECHANICS:				

FIG. 3-5. Job Dispatch and Work Order Board for Maintenance Department.

plicity. The whole procedure must be simple to ensure maximum use and benefit from this paperwork.

PLANNING AND SCHEDULING

In conjunction with a simple, easy-to-use work order, any plant with more than twenty maintenance craftsmen will find it advisable to set up a dispatching, scheduling, and manpower control board as shown in Figure 3-5. This simple four-column scheduling board, along with reasonable communication among craft foremen, facilitates the day-to-day planning and scheduling of maintenance work in the shop and indicates the current position of every job and the assignment of every craftsman.

For this simple scheduling and dispatching board, a standard punched card rack is used, with the lines assigned either to each group of craftsmen or to each individual craftsman. In Figure 3-5, all the electricians and pipe fitters are listed by name, one to a line. The next vertical column is headed "To Start." In this column are the work orders assigned by the craft foreman to each man for each day. The procedure works in this way. The foreman has a work load or backlog box of cards for his people plus work orders which come in during the day with various degrees of priority. He decides the sequence in which the jobs are to be worked on. He then places the work orders in the "To Start" pockets according to his assignment of men. There may be one rather long job for Mike and perhaps two or three smaller job cards for Bill. These are assigned as the next jobs for these men. Thus, in a very simple manner, the priority and sequencing of jobs are accomplished, and an automatic means of ensuring that there is always work ahead for each craftsman is provided. Along with good communication among craft foremen, this may be all that is needed for preplanning and dispatching work orders.

A few useful and practical embellishments can be added if desired. For instance, if there is need for sequencing a pipe fitter onto an electrical job at a specific time, say three o'clock in the afternoon, a small, colored clip-on tag can be put on the pipe fitter's job card to signal the foremen that there is need for this man at a specific time. Thus the pipe fitting foreman and dispatcher will have a memory jogger to supplement direct contact with the electrical foreman who is the main contractor on that job.

The next column on the dispatch board is headed "In Progress." When a craftsman starts his job, the card is moved from the "To Start" column to the "In Progress" column. This procedure provides a record of where each man is working, which job he is working on, and which jobs are in progress.

The column headed "Interrupted" is a very important column from a management control point of view. Whenever a job is interrupted for a man to go onto a more urgent job or because of a wait or delay caused by lack of parts or materials or unavailability of equipment, the job card goes into the "Interrupted" column. This column should be policed carefully by maintenance supervision and by general management, because in effect every job in this column is costing the company unnecessary expense. Every job interrupted costs the company an extra "prepare and put aside" time, extra "travel to and from the job" time, and the spinning of wheels that inevitably occurs when a job has to stop and restart.

When a job is at length completed, the work order card is moved to the column of the dispatch board headed "Completed." The work orders for completed jobs can be observed and recorded throughout the day, or they can be collected at the end of the day. In either case, the originator can be notified that the job is finished, hours and costs can be collected, machine and equipment records can be updated, and the cards can then be used for reconciliation with the man's time card and for actual cost allocation.

In smaller companies, the work order procedure may be carried out manually and the cards never used for data processing. Alternatively, the small- or medium-size company may choose to use a data processing service bureau if it does not have in-house facilities. The larger and more sophisticated company with its own data processing department will be able to use these cards in an optimum manner. It may have preplanning and preloading of the maintenance department processed by the tabulating department; it may have preventive maintenance and lubrication schedules printed out and work orders generated ahead of time by the data processing department; and of course it will have all information gathering, in many forms, done by the same function.

With this simple work order approach and the scheduling and dispatching board illustrated, the means for effectively implementing good paperwork, planning, and scheduling procedures for the maintenance department are inexpensively provided.

MAINTENANCE WORK MEASUREMENT

To achieve good management control and optimum benefits from the work orders and the scheduling and dispatching board, some form of maintenance work measurement is needed. In fact, the work cannot be properly scheduled unless the time that each job or each work order should take is known. Job standards applied to the work orders when they are issued to the shop are therefore greatly to be desired. In addition, benefits are realized when the man doing the job knows the time that should be taken and when he knows that his supervisor knows the time as well.

It is essential that management and supervisors at all levels have a thorough understanding of the procedures used to measure maintenance work of all types, and that they recognize the validity of the standards used for their performance reports and controls.

Universal Maintenance Standards. The Universal Maintenance Standards (UMS) technique for developing standards for maintenance work has three major features:

1. Range of time concept
2. Bench mark jobs
3. Work content comparison

Range of Time Concept. It is a practical and economic impossibility to set a standard of pinpoint accuracy for each maintenance job. Variations exist as jobs recur. For instance, if a water line valve is changed, sometimes the bolts in the flanges can be easily removed. Other times, the bolts will be badly rusted and cannot be removed by merely using a wrench. They may have to be burned or broken off, or at least penetrating oil will have to be applied before removal. Thus, even though the job is the same, time variations exist. To deal with this problem, the "range of time concept" of UMS is used. This concept states that for the completion of a given job a certain standard time will be allowed, but that the standard is the median of a range of time in which the job should be completed. This range allows for variations in the amount of work required to do the job and makes it possible to set standards economically. When a number of jobs are done over a period of time such as a pay period, the highs and the lows tend to average out, and a reasonably true measure of performance is obtained.

Bench Mark Jobs. Using the range of time concept, standard job times are easily developed for representative or bench mark jobs. These are then cataloged in a series of standard work groupings by type of craft involved and according to the range of time or work group into which they fall. Figure 3-6 shows a number of slots, each representing a standard work group. Work Group E, for example, is shown to have a median time of 1.2 hours. The range of time in which jobs in this work group may normally be expected to be done is 0.90 to 1.5 hours. The time slots gradually broaden as they progress to larger time values.

Work Content Comparison. When the catalog of reasonably accurate bench mark jobs has been developed, setting job times from the catalog becomes easy. To deal with work tasks not described in the catalog, the "work content comparison" aspect of UMS is applied.

Work content comparison involves comparing the work content of a given job with the work content of a job already in the catalog. When there is appreciable similarity in this work content, the same work group time can be safely used. For instance, an expansion joint or tee fitting change will have the same work content as a valve change in a similar size line.

This approach will be made clearer by referring to the top third of Figure 3-7, which shows a typical catalog spread sheet. The illustration depicts a series of bench mark jobs slotted into their proper work groups. This provides a good sampling of jobs covering most of the work in this craft. If, for example, a work order is received for the job of changing twenty single-pole switches in a multiple switch box, the planner-analyst calculating the standard time for the job (a former electrical craftsman) can easily compare the work content for this project with the work content of bench mark 0790-2, shown in Group E. The twenty-switch change job will now be given the Group E time of 1.2 hours, and this standard will be close to the actual time required to complete the job.

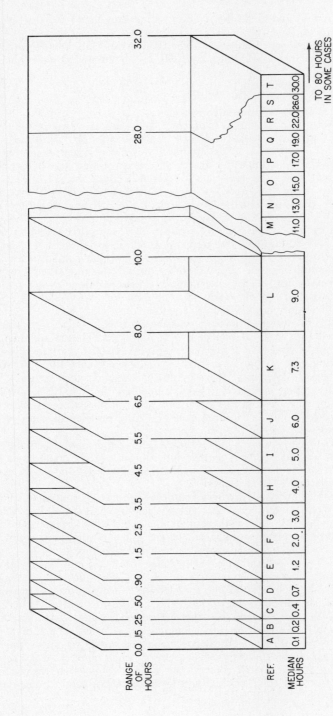

Fig. 3-6. Standard Work Groupings.

Task Area: General Installation

Code: 0795
Craft: Electrical

(0.5)	Group D 0.7	(0.9)	Group E 1.2	(1.5)	Group F 2.0	(2.5)	Group G 3.0	(3.5)
	0790-6 -- Medium-size junction box, 4 tapped holes, 26 wires #12, screw clamp connection, mount and connect		0790-16 -- Conduit, 15'-1¼'' 2-30° bends, 2 condulets, 2 nipples between junction boxes, prepare conduit and install; 2 men		0790-15 -- Conduit, 35'-2'', 2-30° bends, 2 condulets, 2 nipples between junction boxes, prepare conduit and install; 2 men		0790-3 -- Medium-size junction box, 4 holes, 85 wires #12, crimped connections, mount and connect	
	0790-7 -- Medium-size junction box, 4 tapped holes, 17 wires #12, screw clamp connections, mount and connect		0790-2 -- Medium-size junction box, 4 holes, 37 wires #12, crimped connections, mount and connect		0790-17 -- Conduit, 15'-1½'', 2-30° bends, 2 condulets, 2 nipples between junction boxes, prepare conduit and install; 2 men		0790-11 -- Wires, 54-#12, measure, cut, identify, install in 80' then 50' conduit	
	0790-10 -- Wires, 14-#12, 15', measure, cut off, identify, and install in 15' of conduit		0790-5 -- Medium-size junction box, 4 holes, 28 wires #12, crimped connections, mount and connect		0790-8 -- Wires, 37-#12, measure, cut, identify, install in 35' conduit		0790-19 -- Medium-size junction box, splice, #12, wire, make 54	
			0790-9 -- Wires 22-#12, measure, cut, identify, install in 15' conduit					

BLOCK 1

BENCH MARK ANALYSIS SHEET   CODE 0790

Description: Medium-size junction box, 4 holes, 85 wires #12, crimped connections, mount and connect.   Date: 4/26/61   B.M. 0790-3

Craft-Elect.: Gen. Install.   Dwgs.: None   Analyst: No. of men 1   W.M.   Sh. 1 of 1

Line	Men	Operation Description	Reference Symbol	Unit Time	Freq.	Total Time
1		Mount medium-size junction box	750.0207			.3243
2		Select proper wire	13.0002	.0035	85	.2975
3		Move marker on wire	720.0660	.0094	85	.7990
4		Cut off 85-#12 wires	720.0101	.0021	85	.1785
5		Skin 85-#12 wires	720.0211	.0023	85	.1955
6		Connect 85-#12 wires	720.0323	.0110	85	.9350
7						
30			Bench Mark Time			2.7298
		Notes:	Standard Work Group			G

BLOCK 2

UNIVERSAL STANDARD DATA   CODE 0720.02

SKINNING

Skin Electrical Conductor #18 thru MCM

Symbol					Hours
720.0211	Single	Small	#10, 12 gage and smaller		.0023
720.0212	Conductor	Medium	#4, 6 0 gage		.0034
720.0213	Cable	Large	#2 thru MCM gage		.0076
720.0214	Multiple	2	#10, 12 gage and smaller (Romex)		.0031
720.0215	Conductor Cable		#10, 12 gage and smaller (BX)		.0077
720.0216	Does not			Unarmored	.0096
720.0217	include	3	#4, 6, 8 gage	Armored	.0167
720.0218	inside Conductor		#2 thru MCM gage (4-6') Armored		.0558

Table values are for skinning only. They include tool and material handling, but no cutoff.

BLOCK 3

OPERATION SYNTHESIS   CODE 0720.02

Symbol	Ref.	Operation or element description	TMU	Freq.	Total
720.0211		Skin wire; #10, 12, and smaller (Leveled Hrs. .0023)			
	05.0004	Handle knife	100.5		
	04.0001	Handle wire	34.2		
	A	Skin end of wire	96.5		
			231.2		

BLOCK 4

ELEMENT ANALYSIS CHART   CODE 0720.02

Description – Left Hand	No.	LH	TMU	RH	No.	Description – Right Hand
A Skin end of wire with knife – #10 or smaller						A
Move to area	M10B	18.7		M16C		Move knife to work
		16.2		P2SE		Align
		2.9		M1B		
		16.2		AP1		Skin wire
		5.4		T90S		
		16.2		AP1		
		7.5		D2E		
		13.4		M12B		Move knife away
		96.5				

FIG. 3-7. Spread Sheet and Method of Developing the Standard for a Bench Mark Job.

Task Area: General Installation

The time required to do the bench mark jobs can be measured with a stop-watch if an acceptable assessment is made of the methods used and the effort and skill applied. Though feasible, this is a time-consuming approach. The use of MTM (Methods-Time Measurement) standard data and the building block concept is far more effective.

Figure 3-7 illustrates how bench mark job time is derived. Block 1 shows the six operations required to perform the bench mark job coded 0790-3 in Group G. Each operation has a unit time developed from Universal Standard Data tables, as shown in Block 2. These unit times in turn are built up by operation synthesis (Block 3) from basic MTM motions as shown in Block 4. This is the "one shot" development of a typical bench mark job time as entered in the UMS catalog. The procedure is *not* used for setting a job standard on any maintenance work order. Job standards for each work order are developed using work content comparison with existing measured bench mark jobs.

PERFORMANCE MEASUREMENT AND CONTROL

A good manager does not need to know all the details of his maintenance operation, but he does need to know what is going on. He cannot control his activity effectively if he does not have some form of measurement. He needs to know, for instance, when he is getting 85 percent instead of 60 percent efficiency from his department. In addition, he should know the trend of the value received for a dollar spent on maintenance. This trend may be based on unit of production, per mile operated, or a similar criterion.

Basic Control Reports. Assuming that capable technical maintenance engineers and supervisors are employed in the department, certain basic reports prepared for each reporting period will prove most helpful.

1. A report of dollars expended for maintenance labor and materials is obviously required. The trends of these costs should be included. Figure 3-8

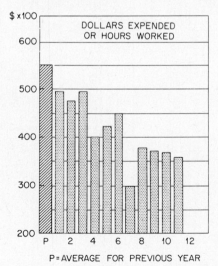

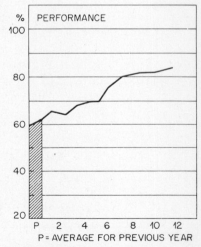

Fig. 3-8. Chart of Average Monthly Maintenance Costs for Previous Year and This Year's Monthly Maintenance Costs to Date.

Fig. 3-9. Chart of Performance Efficiency.

shows a chart indicating the average monthly costs for the previous year and the costs per month to date for the current year. This comparison, together with a comparison with budgeted costs, is useful for controlling the maintenance function.

2. Charting the performance or effectiveness of maintenance labor is a relatively simple matter when job standards and time reporting are set up. In most cases, this is best shown as a percentage against a 100 percent norm. The data in Figure 3-9 are typical in many respects. Before any major improvement program, it is likely that maintenance effectiveness will be in the 50 to 60 percent range, as shown. Poor methods, wrong tools, unnecessary travel, and idle time, plus interruptions or delays caused by management, contribute to this level of performance. When these negative features are eliminated, efficiency rises; as shown in the exhibit, it will increase to about 85 percent of the measured daywork standard.

If true measured performance is 80 percent, departmental effectiveness is reasonably good. At 90 percent or over, planning and control are outstanding. Higher than 100 percent effectiveness is rarely achieved in either production or maintenance work unless incentive payments are made for performance above 100 percent. With incentives, total departmental effectiveness will usually go to the 115 or 120 percent level when measured against the same 100 percent standard.

3. A report can be prepared to show the maintenance manager how much lost time on key pieces of productive equipment was due directly to equipment breakdown or repair. This may be charted as shown in Figure 3-10. A decreasing trend of maintenance downtime shows improved effectiveness of maintenance and vice versa.

4. Some form of work load record is vital, even if it is only a count of the number of work orders on the foreman's desk waiting to be started. The simplest procedure is to record orders received and delete orders completed each day, thus deriving a daily backlog.

However, a much more useful current backlog report is shown by Figure

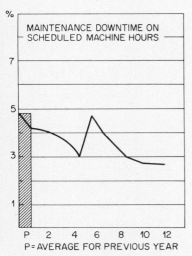

FIG. 3-10. Percent Downtime Caused by Equipment Breakdown or Repair.

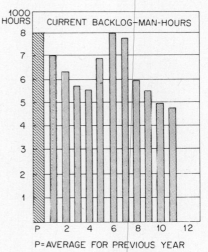

FIG. 3-11. Backlog Report.

3-11. This report is a chart of the number of standard hours covered by work orders to be completed by the maintenance department. It is designed so as to indicate the trend. Backlog trends indicate the need for management action. If the backlog continues to reduce from period to period, action must be taken. If it drops too low, men will be idled by lack of work. To prevent this from happening, it may be desirable to bring in work that is currently subcontracted, to start a major overhaul which has been deferred, to start on otherwise deferred maintenance projects, or to reduce eventually the number of maintenance men on the payroll.

If the maintenance backlog continues to increase, action must also be taken. Some work may have to subcontracted and some deferred; less critical jobs may have to be forgotten to "see if they will go away." Perhaps the hiring of more maintenance men can be factually justified.

Backlog records make an effective tool for manpower planning, both on a long-term and on a day-to-day basis. Control becomes most effective if the reports are broken down by key crafts and labor groups. This facilitates the transfer of people from group to group (where union craft boundaries permit). It also sets guidelines for preplanned overtime work in key areas.

5. There is often a need for reports of current actual costs compared to budgeted costs and expenditures during the previous year. Plotting these figures on a chart, thus making them available currently to the people responsible for the costs, is an effective management control procedure.

When these cost and performance figures are available, an excellent measure of department progress and the savings achieved is the cost per standard hour figure calculated each period and plotted to show a trend, as shown by Figure 3-12.

6. Another report that will sometimes provide useful information to management is a monthly breakdown of maintenance labor costs. One such breakdown is shown by Figure 3-13. The amount of detail which is desirable and the best manner of separating the component costs will vary from company to

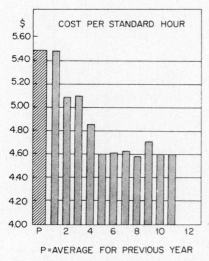

FIG. 3-12. Chart of Cost per Standard Hour.

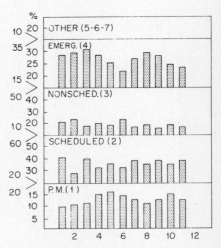

FIG. 3-13. Chart of Maintenance Labor Costs by Classification.

company depending on departmental needs, tax reporting requirements, overhead considerations, and other factors.

7. Properly kept equipment and machine records show what has been done and provide a dynamic tool for improving plant equipment. It is of small value to keep a file of past work orders charged against a given equipment number or area in the hope of some day being able to thumb through it. A careful machine maintenance record should be kept of all time spent on maintenance work on each major piece of equipment and each key machine in the plant. The type of information retained is important. It is not necessary to record that a forklift truck was driven into the gear unit and broke off the foot. On the other hand, it is important to know that belts repeatedly had to be changed on a certain motor drive or that a motor was rewound unusually often, thus indicating that corrective action is necessary.

There are other means of measuring the performance of the maintenance group. For example, comparing the number of labor hours with a fixed base is one means of showing graphically the results from an improvement program. This approach is illustrated by Figure 3-14, which was prepared for one department of an integrated steel mill operation. The chart shows a reduction of 40 percent in the maintenance man-hours expended over a two-and-one-half year period—despite the fact that the current production index for the plant increased about 15 percent over the same period.

Work sampling can be used for assessing maintenance efforts. Combined with improvement steps in other areas, work sampling is useful for indicating trends. It can also be useful for highlighting areas where improvement is required and then for indicating the amount of improvement that is achieved. It offers no real measure of the actual performance or the effectiveness of people, but only indicates the way things are going. It does not measure the skill and effort applied to the job or the adequacy of the methods used.

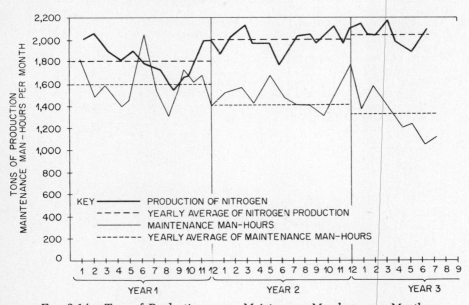

FIG. 3-14.   Tons of Production versus Maintenance Man-hours per Month.

CONCLUSION

Companies with energetic and realistic management teams, willing to overcome misconceptions about the impossibility of improving maintenance work, have proved that dramatic results can be achieved when team effort is applied to the improvement of maintenance. The team approach is essential because of the need for a large number of skills which rarely exist in one individual. Maintenance improvement programs require industrial engineering experience combined with practical maintenance experience. Maintenance departments often have some of the best and most able people in the plant. These men are willing—but they expect management to do its part to reduce delays, irritations, and useless work or travel time.

Maintenance improvement and cost reduction may be difficult, but certainly they are not impossible to achieve. Good management requires measurement and control. Long-cycle, nonrepetitive maintenance operations definitely are measurable and controllable. Good planning and scheduling, used together with consistent job standards and modern methods, can and do achieve major benefits for many companies, including savings of 20 to 40 percent in maintenance labor costs as well as superior operating performance.

BIBLIOGRAPHY

"How Maintenance Managers Feel about Using Work Standards," *Factory*, December, 1967.

Lewis, Bernard T., *Developing Maintenance Time Standards*, Industrial Education Institute, Boston, 1967.

Maynard, H. B. (ed.), *Handbook of Business Administration*, McGraw-Hill Book Company, New York, 1967.

Maynard, H. B. (ed.), *Industrial Engineering Handbook*, 2d ed., McGraw-Hill Book Company, New York, 1963.

Newbrough, E. T., *Effective Maintenance Management*, McGraw-Hill Book Company, New York, 1967.

"Time Slotting Helps Cut Costs," *The Oil and Gas Journal*, May 1, 1967.

"Universal Maintenance Standards," *Factory Management and Maintenance*, November, 1955.

Wilkinson, John J., "How to Manage Maintenance," *Harvard Business Review*, March–April, 1968.

Wilkinson, John J., "Maintenance Management," *Plant Engineering*, four parts: Jan. 9, Apr. 17, May 15, and June 12, 1969.

Wilkinson, John J., "Measuring and Controlling Maintenance Operations," *Journal of Methods-Time Measurement*, March–April, 1966.

CHAPTER FOUR

Plant Engineering and Maintenance Facilities

H. K. REAMEY   *Plant Engineer, Reynolds Metals Company, Sheffield, Alabama*

Plant engineering and maintenance include the plant engineering department, whose prime responsibility is the design and installation of tools and facilities; the maintenance department, whose responsibility is the maintenance of all tools and facilities; and the utilities department, whose main function is to supply utilities, such as water, gas, steam, and sewage disposal, as required by the work being performed.

In discussing the facilities for these activities, physical arrangements, environment, and tools which increase the effectiveness of plant engineering and maintenance work will be covered. It will be assumed that the plant engineer has department head status comparable to that of the production superintendent and that he reports to the manager of the facility. It is further assumed that the production superintendent has full responsibility for plant operation and that he calls for assistance as needed from the various service departments, among which are plant engineering and maintenance. It is the responsibility of the plant engineering and maintenance departments to provide this assistance in a professional manner, giving high-quality service at a low cost.

PLANT ENGINEERING FACILITIES

Plant engineering normally requires engineers of professional competence to deal with the complex problems confronting the manufacturing manager. In keeping with this professional stature, and to attract the proper type of person to the job, it is necessary that the plant engineer's working conditions be at least equal to those in other companies who compete for the same professional people.

Any good architect can supply the basic requirements of good surroundings. Certainly privacy ranks high for promoting efficiency. Privacy may be supplied by individual cubicle-type offices or by the use of movable partitions. The movable partition is generally preferable because of the flexibility it provides as engineering services change. A minimum space of 100 square feet should be provided for each engineer. This minimum will be acceptable only if good layout provides for the storage of clothes, safety equipment, and other personal items that must be kept in the office.

Engineering office furniture should include a conventional desk and a table large enough to handle a large print and preferably convertible into a drawing board. The lighting, acoustical insulation, and air-conditioning equipment should compare with good practice elsewhere.

The office should be located near the reproduction department and so that the casual visitor can be prevented from having free access to the engineering department. Each engineer should have his own telephone. Background music is acceptable if control is provided within each office.

The plant engineer should preferably be located close to the production superintendent because of their need for frequent contacts. The project engineers in widely spread facilities should be as near as possible to the plant so that an undue effort is not required for facility visitation.

Tools. The following general tools are essential to good engineering work. A technical library, the extent of which is determined by the availability of the libraries of public and educational institutions, is a necessity. Vendor catalogs should be centrally filed, but each office should have a bookcase where each engineer can keep the most used reference materials. The catalog files should be indexed, cross-indexed, and kept up to date, so that time is not lost in seeking reference materials. In many instances, a catalog file is maintained by the purchasing department. If the engineers are located too far from the purchasing department to permit easy access to the file, then separate files should be maintained. Calculating equipment, adding machines, and dictating machines should be readily available either on an individual basis or in a pool. The project engineer should be able to use available computing and data processing equipment for the solution of difficult problems. The slide rule is no longer adequate for any except the most general problems. The computer is a necessary adjunct for a group responsible for the design and installation of tools and facilities.

Cameras, levels (including micrometer levels), transits, and the like should be available in a central, locked storage area, preferably in the drafting room.

Vehicles should sometimes be provided to reduce the time spent by high-salaried engineers in travel to and from the plant. Golf carts for in-plant travel and jeeps for larger areas should be given consideration.

The drafting room should be large enough to accommodate the needed draftsmen. The furniture should provide the most comfort available for these persons who spend so much time on stools bending over their drawing boards. In addition to a board and a desk, adequate lighting, drafting machines, erasing equipment, and templates should be supplied to each drafting station. The desk top should be large enough to hold reference drawings. The desk itself is required for storage of tools and instruments. The drafting room should be located close to the reproduction room where tracings and other drawings are usually stored in flat files. Drawings of specialty products, if numerous, should be microfilmed and made available for examination on a microfilm reader adjacent to the drafting room.

Print-making machinery should generally be of more than one type, because making copies of tracings requires one kind of unit and making reproductions of photographs and existing drawings and sketches on opaque paper requires another. If much time is spent by engineers in using this equipment, it may be less costly to provide a lower-paid clerk to operate it.

Special furniture for the storage of tracings is commercially available. If the heights are selected wisely, the tops of the cabinets may be used for examining the tracings and prints being selected.

An adequate number of supporting technicians and secretarial people should be provided for the engineering department. Numerous studies have shown repeatedly that much of the work done by the professional person is work that could be done, not only less expensively, but often more efficiently, by a person with clerical or secretarial training. Each engineer should have available to him a secretary and a clerk, supplied usually from a pool. The use of dictating equipment allows the dictator to dictate when he chooses and the transcriber to transcribe and perform the directed function at his own convenience.

MAINTENANCE FACILITIES

The ratio of maintenance employees to production employees has increased steadily owing to mechanization, automation, specialization, and sometimes negotiation. Because the trend shows very little sign of changing, all maintenance facilities should be designed with flexibility in mind.

With maintenance, as with plant engineering, the service aspect of the function needs to be emphasized. The maintenance department does not make anything for sale. Without the production which it supports, there would be no need for maintenance. A level of maintenance costs which results in optimum production costs is generally a sound goal for the maintenance manager. For optimum production costs, the maintenance costs may be relatively high or they may be low. In any event, maintenance crafts are among the highest paid in industry. The facilities in which they operate and the techniques and tools which they use should be the very finest.

In any facility discussion, often the first question asked is: "Do you have area or central maintenance?" In most companies, there is a combination. In any case, regardless of whether a company has area maintenance, central maintenance, or a blend of the two, central maintenance control is necessary for good maintenance cost management.

Maintenance Control Center. The flow of information from and to a maintenance control center is illustrated in Figure 4-1. The hub of the system is the maintenance control center. The shop satellites surround and feed information to the center. This concept makes the maintenance control center the nerve center of the maintenance department.

The maintenance control center is also the communications center. Various forms of communications may be used. The most common is the telephone. Paging by telephone or radio is also widely used. Radio communications are in many instances the prime contact with mechanics and foremen in the field. Remote writers are used for dispatching if the backlog of work orders is maintained in the central office of the control center where primary sources of information are located. It is not uncommon to have all truck deliveries dispatched from the maintenance control center by radio. Also it is not uncommon for a roving shift mechanic to be contacted from the control center by radio. His radio may be the cigarette-type walkie-talkie, or it may be a buzzer type that requests him to use the phone to call a certain number specified by code.

For communication and cost control purposes, clock stations are often located throughout the plant where job start and stop information is communicated to a data processing center by inserting a card into the clock. The data

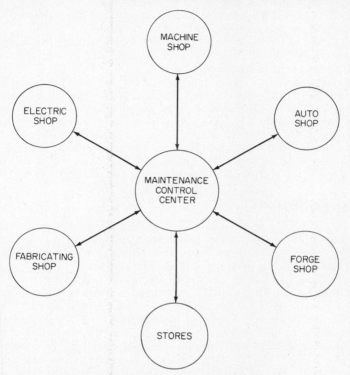

Fig. 4-1.   Maintenance Control Flow.

processing center for large maintenance activities is frequently located next to the control center. Maintenance shares its services with the production department.

The delivery schedule of maintenance jobs has the same level of importance as the delivery schedule of production items. One is essential to the other. Electronic data processing is most useful in project status reporting, project cost control, and maintenance analyses.

Office Facilities.   Normally the maintenance control center will have facilities for the maintenance superintendent, for the maintenance control supervisor, and for one maintenance control analyst or clerk for approximately every thirty maintenance employees. Many times, the maintenance engineers and general foremen are located in this same facility. Their offices should be similar to those of the project engineers. Privacy for the general foremen and for the maintenance superintendent is a must because much of their time is spent in discussions of a highly personal nature with their employees.

Because the maintenance control center is often located adjacent to heavy traffic and operating machinery, provision for noise insulation of the floors and foundation is essential at the time of design. A conference room subjected to noise transmission through a common floor is a classic design error.

Maintenance Shops.   Every manufacturing facility should have a central stores area. The stores may be broken down into manufacturing and maintenance supplies. Many times the categories overlap. For estimating and sizing purposes, it can be assumed that the central maintenance stores will have a value of 1 percent of the total plant capital investment.

In addition to the central stores area, each maintenance shop should have a smaller stores area of its own, where a day's or a week's needs should be available. It is necessary that these small stores areas have good inventory control.

The permissible environment in the maintenance shop stores area will depend upon the nature of the items being stored. Climatic conditions in certain portions of the country allow all hot-rolled steel, for instance, to be stored outside. At the other extreme, all bearings should be stored in a dust-free and humidity-controlled room. An analysis of the components will reveal the nature of the storage required.

The shop storage bins should have labels, part numbers, and catalog numbers that match those of the central storage system. Often the tool crib attendant can serve as the storeroom dispatcher also. Naturally, the storeroom for the maintenance shops should be reasonably accessible. One point worth mentioning, however, is that crane-covered areas in most shops are the most expensive in cost per square foot of any of the facilities. It would be unwise, therefore, to place office and storage areas, traffic ways, and the like under the crane-covered areas.

In laying out the shop, the flow of material through the shop should be considered. As a general rule, a storage area and a cleaning area must be provided ahead of the shop which makes parts and equipment repairs. The cleaning area may include steam cleaning and degreasing facilities. A surge area after the steam cleaning or degreasing is necessary. A storage area for the completed parts or overhauled components should also be provided. Good scheduling by maintenance control will reduce the storage areas in the shop, keeping the work areas reasonably clear and providing for good cost control.

Because the cost of traveling on foot is expensive, vehicles are often provided. They may be bicycles, golfsters, jeeps, or trucks. In any event, a parking area should be provided. Climatic conditions may make parking in a covered area necessary, but it should not be in expensive crane-covered areas.

Many maintenance shops find it economical to crane-cover the complete maintenance area where work stations are located, with the exception of hand-bench work stations where the items are small enough to be moved from tote trays to the bench by hand. In providing the crane, consideration should be given to whether it should have a cab and a crane operator or whether it can be operated more economically from a pendant attached to it or by radio control. The size and speed of the crane generally dictate the most practical type of control. It is not uncommon to have two types of controls on a crane.

Some special tools may be needed, such as equipment for handling loaded buckets with a minimum of manpower, telescoping scaffolds for high work in close areas, fork trucks, and bucket lifts. Specialty equipment normally requires a special storage facility. It may be preferable to use contract maintenance for certain specialty jobs so that the needed special equipment will be provided and maintained by the contractor.

Each shop foreman should have available to him a private office. Ideally, a view of the work area while doing administrative work should be provided. The handling of labor and disciplinary problems is a major concern of the foreman, and complete privacy is required for this.

The working conditions in maintenance shops should be compatible with the type of work being done. The maintenance craftsman is a skilled, highly paid technician. His working conditions should be such that he can work effectively. In addition, he needs a lunch area, a rest area, and perhaps a vending machine area. Generally these areas are combined into one. They should be reasonably accessible to his work area. These areas, with lighting, music, and bulletin boards, provide an atmosphere conducive to good employee morale.

The maintenance shop should have adequate door accessibility. In many instances, this will mean a door to every shop bay. If the machine shop is broken into various craft shops, each shop should have door accessibility to provide proper flow into and out of the shop with minimum surge storage at the work station.

General Arrangement of Maintenance Shops. In considering the general arrangement of the maintenance shops, the question arises of whether or not to join the shops. The answer depends on the nature of the work. It would be foolish, for instance, to join a smoky foundry operation with a highly sophisticated machine shop.

The satellite concept of shop location is often desirable. The maintenance control center is the hub, and located around it are the various maintenance shops.

Machine Shop. The maintenance machine shop should have a stores area and a tool crib. This tool crib is often the finest in the plant. It may be the only tool crib in the plant. In all probability, it will have a tool crib attendant. Located in the crib will be certain specialty tool items such as diamond grinders for sharpening tool bits, automatic saw sharpening equipment, and optical apparatus used for inspecting precision tools and dies. The tool crib attendant may be required to maintain manufacturing tools and may also be responsible for tool storage.

As a general rule, the machine shop tool crib is enclosed in a humidity-controlled, air-conditioned environment approaching that of the cleaning room.

The basic machine shop will have a shaper, a shear, a press brake, a combination punch and specialty shape shear, a planer, and several lathes, drill presses, and milling machines. It will in all probability have an automatic cutoff saw.

It is generally necessary to provide coolant reclamation facilities and metal chip disposal bins. Flexibility should be provided for in locating the equipment. The ideal arrangement is to have complete crane coverage over all facilities except office and storage areas. Trenches or complete utility subfloors permit relocating machines or adding new equipment comparatively inexpensively.

If the shops are combined, it is not uncommon to find a bench repair shop adjacent to the machine shop, a pipe shop adjacent to the machine shop, and in many cases, a welding shop in the machine shop. The welding shop should not be tied into the machine shop unless adequate ventilating equipment is used in the welding shop area. The gases and fumes many times generate a corrosive atmosphere that is detrimental to the nearby machine tool equipment.

Fabricating Shop. The fabricating shop is often an independent shop of the maintenance facility. Here the ironwork and sheet metal work are done for the plant. Flexibility is the basic requirement. The shop is generally piped for the air, oxygen, acetylene, natural gas, and other gases required in welding or burning processes. Electric outlets must be provided. The shop should have a large crane, a good layout area, accessibility to large steel plate and bar stock, a large brake, a roll bender, straightening apparatus, and a level bedplate area for the setup of large fabricated items. Racks for tools and jigs are necessary in the tool storage area.

Special provisions should be made for large templates, layout tools, and multihead tracing mechanisms for burning equipment. Blacksmith forging hammers may be located in this area along with heat treating equipment, forges, and benders. With this type of equipment and large floor areas for assembly, it is evident that a fabricating shop is particularly difficult to heat properly in cold weather and to cool properly in warm weather.

Auto Repair Shop. The modern industrial plant invariably uses many pieces of industrial rolling stock for handling and transportation, and therefore an automotive repair shop is often an important maintenance facility. In no other maintenance installation is the shop arrangement and flow as important.

Figure 4-2 shows the usual flow of auto repair work. Storage for incoming vehicles must be provided. Steam cleaning or degreasing is the second step, and storage ahead of repair the next one. Failure to provide adequate storage areas causes congestion, with resulting expensive multiple handling. Many repair shops have two doors for each work station with storage on either side.

Separate facilities should be provided for electric-powered vehicles and for internal combustion-powered vehicles. Crane service is essential over every work station. The commonly used filling station-type lift for greasing is excellent for over-the-road conventional automotive vehicles, but it is generally unsatisfactory for industrial vehicles. The industrial vehicle is much more compact, and the bottom of the lift in many instances will block the accessibility required for proper maintenance diagnosis and repair.

Ventilation is a must for the internal combustion vehicles. Tool storage and work station cabinet space should be provided at each work station. Oil disposition, both hydraulic and engine, may present a problem. Oils dumped into conventional storm drains must be removed at some later point to prevent water contamination. If the volume is high enough, oil reclamation stations should be considered. If the volume is not high enough, separate receptacles for incineration or further use in the plant should be provided.

The work stations should provide the necessary utilities for the operation of the many power tools, such as air-driven or electric nut runners, impact wrenches, and screwdrivers, used for equipment overhaul.

Important preventive maintenance work normally consists of lubrication and the checking of various electrical and hydraulic components. This station may be separate from the auto repair shop proper. It should be accessible to the steam cleaner, because cleaning is often required for satisfactory mechanical diagnosis and overhaul. Degreasing racks should be provided inside the maintenance shop.

A clean storage room should be available for parts storage and for the storage of the instruments and analyzers used for automotive maintenance work. The size of the storage facility will be determined by the plant location. In highly industrialized areas, it is possible to have daily deliveries of

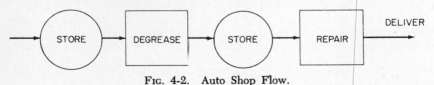

Fig. 4-2. Auto Shop Flow.

the parts needed for vehicle overhaul. In remote sections, the probability of quick delivery is decreased, and provisions must be made in central departmental stores for a stock of spare parts.

Hydraulic and electrical testing and analyzing equipment should be provided for the proper diagnosis of needed repairs. Proper tools and training are necessary, however, for these techniques to be effective.

Fuel and Charging Stations. Water hoses, gasoline pumps, and a battery charging station should be available in the auto repair shop and at the grease racks. Other gasoline and water pumps and battery charging stations should be set up throughout the plant to prevent the congestion often found in large centers. When a plant operates continuously, it is necessary that the vehicles in twenty-four-hour service have their gasoline, water, and oil checked for each shift. Battery charging stations should be provided for electric vehicles. Checking and battery replacement can be done by the vehicle operator.

Multiple pump installations should follow the techniques generally used in service stations to allow for convenient servicing of the vehicles with minimum delay. Automatic cutoff nozzles, quick-opening pressure valves, and similar devices are a necessity. At the battery charging stations, one-man lifts should be provided to replace the large industrial-type batteries. This should be the operator's responsibility, with routine checking of the units on charge being the responsibility of the maintenance department.

Office and Records. The analysis of automotive records provides valuable insights into how to reduce maintenance costs. It is therefore necessary that the record keeping systems be compatible with the data processing system, card sorting equipment, and other types of analytical devices normally associated with good maintenance procedures. Each mechanic normally does much of the record keeping to minimize the administrative burden on the supervisor.

Instrument Repair Shops. An instrument repair shop normally services all electric, hydraulic, and pneumatic instruments and analyzing equipment. Standards for comparing measured quantities provide the essence of control. It is necessary, therefore, that standard pressure gages, voltage meters, linear measures, and the like be readily available. In addition to the standard gages in the laboratory, it is often an advantage to have portable standards that can be taken into the field for routine checking.

The shop work stations should consist of adequate tables with good lighting. High intensity lighting should be available to use with magnifying lenses on movable arms that can be brought over small objects. Equipment should include such devices as complex analyzers for diagnosing difficulties in electrical apparatus, combustion analyzers for use in setting air-fuel ratios, and atmosphere analyzers for determining protective atmosphere makeup. Setting controls correctly is normally the responsibility of the instrument repair department. It is not uncommon for the instrument repairman to be the real troubleshooter for the control equipment used by several crafts.

Closed-cabinet storage, humidity-controlled storage, and air-conditioned work areas are basic requisites for the up-to-date instrument repair shop.

The storage areas for the small components may be well-labeled drawers, properly protected from dust and moisture. The supervisor's office again should have good records. Instruction books, parts lists, and drawings should be kept on file. The complexities of modern equipment demand that schematics, detailed drawings, and parts lists be readily available to the mechanic to aid him in his diagnosis and maintenance activities.

UTILITIES

The utilities group of the plant engineering and maintenance department normally is responsible for supplying and maintaining the various utilities required for the operation and maintenance of the facility. These utilities include electricity, gas, air, water, steam, sewage disposal, industrial waste reclamation, and any special fluids such as chlorine, acids, and the like normally used in the plant.

In the design of the original installation, it is desirable to anticipate the ultimate in size of transmission components, recognizing that the cost of the carrying device is normally a relatively small portion of the total. For example, the difference in cost between two- and four-inch-diameter pipes is not appreciable when compared with the total equipment and installation costs.

Loop design is often desirable in that, in the closed loop system, it allows various components to be isolated for maintenance and repair without interrupting the entire operation. This, of course, is of particular importance in processes that operate continuously.

The reduction of labor costs in utility operations is of prime importance. Recognizing this, manufacturers have made available to industry package units that require very little attention. Fully packaged steam plants and fully automatic air compressor stations are no longer the exception. Unattended water filtration plants and sewage disposal plants are available. If the units are complex, with possible high cost resulting from failure, alarms and perhaps remote closed-circuit television monitoring should be provided.

CONCLUSION

The applicability of the suggestions made in this chapter will depend upon the size and nature of the plant engineering and maintenance activities and the limitations of the physical facilities available. When analyzing existing facilities or contemplating the provision of new ones, the fact that plant engineering and maintenance are almost always high-cost activities should be kept always in mind. In the long run, the best facilities will usually prove to be the lowest cost facilities.

BIBLIOGRAPHY

Baumeister, Theodore, and Lionel S. Marks (eds.), *Standard Handbook for Mechanical Engineers*, 7th ed., McGraw-Hill Book Company, New York, 1967.

Beeman, Donald, *Industrial Power Systems Handbook*, McGraw-Hill Book Company, New York, 1955.

Maynard, H. B. (ed.), *Industrial Engineering Handbook*, 2d ed., McGraw-Hill Book Company, New York, 1963.

Morrow, L. C., *Maintenance Engineering Handbook*, 2d ed., McGraw-Hill Book Company, New York, 1960.

Staniar, William, *Plant Engineering Handbook*, 2d ed., McGraw-Hill Book Company, New York, 1959.

PRODUCTS AND MATERIALS

CHAPTER ONE

Initiating the Manufacture of a New Product

LEE S. WHITSON *President, WR Medical Electronics Co., St. Paul, Minnesota*

This chapter tells how the manufacturing function fits into the overall corporate program for the development and introduction of new products. It defines manufacturing's responsibilities for new-product introductions and outlines the planning and preparation for manufacture. It discusses how the manufacturing staff functions are used in initiating the manufacture of new products. The functions and procedures themselves are covered more fully in other chapters.

THE CORPORATE NEW-PRODUCT PROGRAM

To succeed in developing and exploiting new products, a company must have systematic procedures for finding and developing product ideas, analyzing their potential, initiating production, and getting the products onto the market. There also needs to be a close working relationship among the product design, manufacturing, marketing, and accounting functions in carrying out the new-product program. Specific objectives should be set for each new product, the accomplishment of which will reasonably assure its success.

Product Development and Appraisal. A new product must yield an adequate return on the expense of developing it and on the additional working capital and investment in manufacturing facilities required. Before management decides to go ahead with the development of a prospective new item, preliminary studies should be made to determine the required features or properties and to indicate potential demand, possible selling price, and the probable cost, profit, and required capital. At this stage, only rough estimates are possible, but they do give an indication of the product's commercial feasibility and aid in guiding its further development.

Management must also decide whether the new product is suited to the company's capabilities in development and design, manufacturing, and marketing and how it will fit in with existing products and operations. It must also determine that the company can absorb the development and introduction expense and provide the manufacturing facilities and additional working capital without overtaxing its resources.

As the product development progresses, the data for evaluating the product should be brought up to date and refined, and the project should be reviewed at appropriate intervals. A project review may bring out that the profit margin is too low, indicating the need for either a higher selling price or restudy of the design and manufacturing procedures to reduce the cost. If it is necessary to give up certain product features to get the cost down, the effect on the possible selling price and sales volume will have to be considered. If a satisfactory balance of cost, selling price, and sales volume cannot be attained, the project may have to be abandoned. It is better to reach such a conclusion at an early stage rather than after the product is on the market.

If the new product is to replace one already on the market, it may be feasible to go ahead with full-scale production at the outset. More commonly, however, production is started on a limited basis with only minimum expenditures. This initial introduction provides more reliable data on the product's acceptance and its possible selling price and sales volume and may bring out needed design changes. Experience with the initial production also helps in planning the final manufacturing procedures.

When the product design is final and the planning for manufacture has been completed, an up-to-date cost study, a profit projection, and an estimate of capital requirements are prepared. If management decides to go ahead with the product introduction, funds are appropriated for tooling and manufacturing facilities.

How the Program Is Carried Out. The new-product program involves not only the development laboratory or design group, but also the marketing, manufacturing, and accounting functions. Marketing makes the surveys to determine the needed product features and possible selling prices and sales volumes. Manufacturing furnishes the data for estimating product costs and capital expenditures and advises the product designers on the production and cost aspects of the designs. Accounting prepares the cost studies, summaries of capital requirements, and profit projections.

The heads of product design, marketing, manufacturing, and accounting, along with the general manager of the company or product division, may act as a product review committee which selects potential products, guides their development, and decides when they should be released for production. Sometimes the committee function is only advisory, with the decisions being made by the general manager.

A typical product development program from the initial product concept to the start of production is shown by Figure 1-1. This chart shows the time allotted to each phase of the program, the activities included in each phase, and the person or function responsible for it. Dates of the periodic project reviews and the start of production are indicated by the heavy arrows at the top. This chart is a prototype for the specific schedules to be made for actual projects.

There are many variations in the way in which new-product programs are handled. A project manager may direct the new-product development and coordinate the related activities of the product design, manufacturing, marketing, and accounting functions. Large companies often have separate new-products departments for commercial development of new items up to the point that they are either turned over to an existing product division or become the basis for a new division.

Defining Objectives of the Product Introduction. The decision to proceed with the manufacture of a new product is based on specified product features, performance, and quality and on projections of product cost, selling price, profit margin, sales volume, and capital requirements. All these factors should be set forth as specific results for which the design, manufacturing, and marketing functions are accountable. Accomplishment of these results should give reasonable assurance that the product introduction will succeed. Any unfavorable deviations can easily turn the expected profit into a loss.

Release of the Product for Manufacture. The product design department is responsible for issuing complete and accurate drawings, parts lists, and material specifications. Any errors or omissions are likely to result in material shortages, added operations, scrap, rework, and delays in starting production.

Any special quality, performance, or appearance requirements beyond the usual tolerances, finishes, and the like which are shown on the drawings must also be specified to ensure their being provided for in the manufacturing operations and inspection procedures. Requirements that come to light after production is started may necessitate costly retooling or changes in procedure.

Any design changes or corrections in drawings or bills of material after they are released should be handled by a formal reissue superseding the original one. Informal changes and corrections made by manufacturing may solve an immediate problem but will lead to later confusion.

THE MANUFACTURING PROGRAM

Planning and preparing for the manufacture of a new product are highly complex tasks. They can be carried out successfully only if there is an adequate and competent manufacturing staff to analyze requirements, plan and develop procedures, and design the facilities. Close working relationships must be maintained between the manufacturing staff and the line supervisors and between manufacturing and the other corporate divisions concerned with the new product.

The entire program must be thoroughly planned so that no details are overlooked, and it must be closely scheduled to meet the production deadline. Specific objectives must be established for the overall program, and the work assignments and results expected of each individual must be clearly defined. Reporting procedures must be set up to keep track of progress and to monitor quality, costs, and expenditures as the work progresses.

Staff Requirements. The planning and preparation for manufacture of the new product are carried out by the following manufacturing staff departments: process planning, methods engineering, tool design, time standards, plant layout, and plant engineering. Also involved are quality control, inspection, packaging engineering, production planning, materials control, and plant personnel. The organization of these functions varies, and in smaller companies several of them may be combined. It is essential that these staff functions have competent people with the necessary technical, analytical, and creative abilities. They must be able to recognize and evaluate alternative approaches and make sound decisions or recommendations.

Tying Line Supervisors into the Program. With the emphasis that is necessarily placed on manufacturing staff functions, there is sometimes a tendency to neglect the line supervisors until it is time for production to begin. If they are brought actively into the planning phase, however, they will better under-

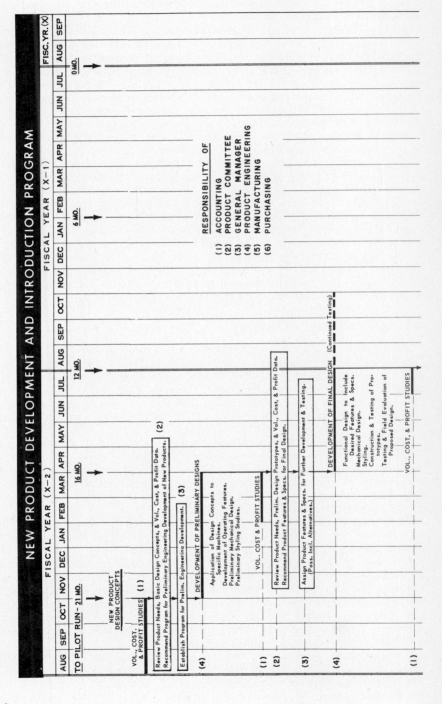

NEW PRODUCT DEVELOPMENT AND INTRODUCTION PROGRAM

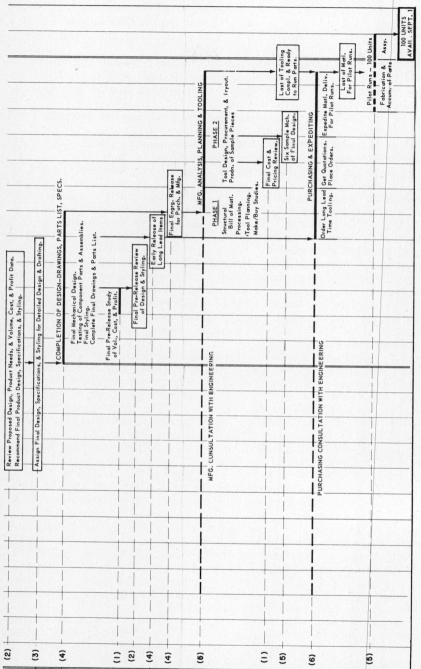

Fig. 1-1. Chart of a Typical Product Development Program Showing Principal Phases, Periodic Reviews, and the Person or Function Responsible for Each.

stand the product requirements and new manufacturing procedures. As a result, production will get off to a smoother start, and the objectives of the program are more likely to be met. In addition, the line people supply a practical viewpoint that should not be overlooked in planning the new operations.

Objectives of the Manufacturing Program. If the manufacturing function is to fulfill its responsibilities for success of the new product, it must:

1. Satisfy the specified requirements of product quality, performance, and appearance
2. Hold the product cost within the limit established as necessary for a satisfactory profit margin
3. Hold capital expenditures within the amount appropriated
4. Provide adequate capacity for projected sales volumes
5. Have the new product available in time for its scheduled market introduction

Each of the manufacturing staff people and production supervisors should know what these objectives are and what specific results are expected of him. Quality requirements, cost targets, and expenditure limits for each phase of the program, together with a detailed work schedule, will help in defining individual responsibilities.

Providing for Product Quality. Three things are essential to assure acceptable quality in the new product: (1) the quality requirements must be provided for in the processes, methods, tooling, and equipment; (2) quality requirements for each operation must be clearly specified and be understood by the foremen and operators; and (3) quality control and inspection procedures must be set up for the new product, covering raw materials, work in process, and finished product.

Quality requirements frequently dictate which processes and machines can be used for an operation, what kind of tooling is needed, and how the job shall be run. For example, tolerance and finish requirements may limit the operation to certain machines or may require an extra rigid fixture, additional finish cuts, or a separate grinding operation. The process engineer must know the capabilities and limitations of the processes, machines, and tooling in order to meet the requirements of each job at the lowest cost.

In manually controlled operations, quality is more dependent on the judgment, skill, and motivation of the worker. Standardization of methods reduces quality deviations such as parts being put together incorrectly or being left out of an assembly. Jigs to hold the work and guides and stops to aid in positioning the parts produce greater uniformity in such operations as drilling, spot welding, and assembly.

Failure to satisfy quality requirements is often due to the operator not understanding what is expected of him. The foreman must know the quality requirements of each operation and make sure the operator understands them. Quality requirements should be stated clearly and completely, and insofar as possible, in measurable terms. In some operations, quality is a matter of workmanship, which cannot be measured precisely. Examples of types and degrees of defects aid in judging what is acceptable.

The purpose of quality control is not just to assure a satisfactory finished product, but to monitor the quality level of work in process and prevent defects from occurring. Statistical techniques are used to determine the percent of the output of each operation to be inspected to assure a given level of quality and to predict when the deviations will exceed acceptable limits.

The quality control and inspection procedures must be tailored to the quality requirements of the new product and to the characteristic variations in the processes. Studies are made to determine at what points the work should be inspected, the percent to be checked, the specific attributes to be measured, and how the data should be plotted or analyzed to monitor quality most effectively. Inspection procedures must be prescribed, measuring instruments and checking fixtures provided, and standards set for acceptance or rejection of the material.

Estimating and Controlling Product Costs. Preliminary cost estimates made while the product is being developed are necessarily rough, because the design has not been set and manufacturing procedures cannot be anticipated precisely. Such estimates are based on judgment, past experience, and comparison with similar products. The final cost study on which management bases the decision to proceed with the new product is based on actual material quotations and a more detailed study of the operations on each part and assembly. Operation times are estimated by comparison with similar jobs or by use of predetermined motion-time data.

In planning methods and designing tooling for each operation, the manufacturing engineers and foremen should have the objective of equaling or bettering the estimated time per piece used in the cost study. If this can be done consistently, the overall cost objective will be met. The time per piece used in the cost study should be checked against the method actually developed for each operation to determine whether the time still appears to be reasonable. Any operation which seems to take a significantly longer time should be reviewed.

Actual production times can be checked during the pilot run, but they will usually be high because of unfamiliarity with the new operations. The latter part of the first regular production run gives a truer indication of actual costs. Learning curve data can be used to project probable results after further experience.

Estimating and Controlling Capital Expenditures. Any capital expenditures above the minimum necessary to satisfy quality requirements and provide the necessary production capacity should be justified by corresponding reductions in unit costs. Such optional expenditures should also be justified in comparison with any alternatives that would require a smaller outlay. In one plant, a $20,000 capital expenditure for a special forming machine appeared justified by an annual saving of $11,000. However, an alternate type of equipment was found which cost only half as much and produced 80 percent of the savings. The additional $10,000 expenditure was not justified by the added savings.

When the manufacturing planning is completed, an itemized schedule of capital expenditures is prepared. Each major item of tooling, equipment, plant facilities, plant rearrangement, and construction is shown, but minor items are usually grouped. Dollar amounts are based on quotations if possible, but otherwise on detailed estimates. If a major program will extend over several months, a breakdown of expenditures by month may be needed for planning cash requirements.

When the product introduction is approved, funds are appropriated for the capital expenditures as represented in the schedule. Those who control the actual expenditures must make sure that they are held within the budgeted amounts. Each expenditure should be compared with the original estimate, and any significant differences should be reviewed. Any excess expenditures, even though they may be justified by savings, should have management approval.

Sales Forecast for Manufacturing Planning. Despite the uncertainties in forecasting the demand for a new product, it is necessary to set some level of sales and production as the basis for designing the product and planning its manufacture. The design of the product and selection of manufacturing processes, tooling, and equipment are greatly influenced by the quantity to be produced. At higher volumes, the savings in direct labor and handling may justify more extensive tooling, higher capacity equipment, line production, or automation, which would not be economical at lower volumes. Furthermore, the only way to be sure that the product will be available in sufficient quantities is to forecast the sales so that adequate capacity can be provided in advance.

Any seasonal pattern in sales should be anticipated, because it means either providing enough capacity to meet the peak demand or building inventories during the slack season. The probable life of the product and frequency of model changes also influence the selection of manufacturing processes and design of tooling.

Sound decisions on the initial tooling, equipment, and plant facilities must take into account future as well as immediate requirements. Planning for manufacture cannot be done effectively on a year-at-a-time basis. Consequently, sales should be forecast for at least three years and preferably longer, recognizing the uncertainties in such predictions. After the product is on the market, the sales forecast can be revised periodically and manufacturing plans adjusted accordingly, but at least there will be some basis for advance planning.

Scheduling the Manufacturing Program. A definite date must be set for availability of the new product because sales promotion and advertising commitments must be made months in advance. Delay in production of a seasonal item can mean the loss of virtually the entire first year's sales. This emphasizes the importance of a realistic schedule for the start of production to assure that the product will be available on time and in adequate quantities.

The activities in planning and preparing for the manufacture of each part usually follow a definite sequence such as process planning, tool design, tool construction, and tool tryout. The total number of days or weeks needed for each sequence is determined by estimating and totaling the times for the individual activities. The longest sequences must be identified and given priority, because they determine the elasped time for the entire program. Other jobs are scheduled around these critical ones to utilize the available personnel and facilities most effectively. The estimated hours for each type of activity should be summarized to check whether the work can be accomplished in the allotted time with the available personnel.

In one plant, the overall tool design program appeared to be on schedule, with 80 percent of the work completed at a given date. Unfortunately, the remaining 20 percent included a die that took sixteen weeks to build, and this delayed the start of production by ten weeks. With more careful scheduling and earlier concentration on this one item, the delay would not have occurred.

Certain sequences of activities are interrelated, and this can extend the overall time. As an example, it might appear that a die-casting die and a fixture for machining the casting could be designed and built at the same time. However, a sample casting may be needed in order to complete the fixture design, and the fixture may have to be built and checked before the die is hardened in case changes are required. The sequence becomes: (1) design the die, (2) build the die and run samples pieces, (3) complete the fixture design, (4) build the fixture and run sample pieces, (5) modify the die if necessary, and (6) harden and polish the die.

Network planning and critical path scheduling techniques are well suited to this kind of programming. Activities are shown in sequence on a diagram which brings out clearly any activities that must be completed before the next step can begin. The estimated time for each activity is shown on the diagram, and the sequence with the greatest elapsed time (called the "critical path") is readily identified. Activities in the critical path are given priority because this sequence determines the overall time for the program.

The network diagram is the basis for establishing priorities and scheduling the work of the manufacturing engineers and for setting due dates for completion of tooling, delivery of materials, and installation of equipment. These detailed schedules may be in tabular form or may be represented on a bar chart having a time scale. Close follow-up by the supervisor of each function is needed to keep all activities on schedule.

PLANNING AND PREPARATION FOR MANUFACTURE

The planning and preparation for manufacture depend on the nature of the new product, its similarity to existing products, the anticipated production volume, and whether the initial production is to be on a limited or full-scale basis.

A simple product similar to existing ones may require only limited process and methods planning and routine scheduling of the operations, and the entire program may take only a few weeks. In contrast, large-volume production of a complex product usually requires extensive tooling, new equipment, and plant rearrangement or expansion. Such a program may involve thousands of hours of manufacturing staff time and a large capital outlay and may take several months to accomplish.

In a limited product introduction, the emphasis is on producing the required quantity of the product at a mimimum total expenditure. This may dictate using temporary tooling and improvised equipment, even though unit costs will be higher as a result. The limited introduction affords an opportunity to try out manufacturing procedures and gather data for planning full-scale production.

If the product involves bulk or continuous flow processing, the process is usually developed in a laboratory, and the transition to full production is through a pilot-plant operation to determine the type of facilities and establish such parameters as temperature, pressure, and rate of flow. The pilot plant also produces material for initial marketing of the product. Facilities for full-scale production are designed from the data provided by the pilot-plant operation. Transition from pilot-plant to full-scale production and the planning and layout of facilities usually involve extensive engineering and construction which may take several months.

Much of the planning for manufacture of the new product is carried out in a preliminary fashion while the product is being developed. Periodic management appraisals of the new-product program require estimates of costs and capital outlays. These are based on preliminary studies of the manufacturing procedures, estimates of operation times, and projections of tooling and facilities requirements. The final planning of processes, methods, tooling, facilities, and personnel is, in effect, a refinement of the plans made during product development.

The task of getting ready for manufacture of a new product is not finished when production begins. Most new products start with relatively small volumes which build up as the product gains acceptance. Preparing for manufacture is not merely a matter of meeting immediate needs but should include a step-by-step program for increasing capacity as the need develops.

Manufacturability of the Product. Product designs and material specifications determine or at least influence the selection of fabricating techniques. The decision whether a particular part shall be a casting or a weldment determines how it will be made and what it will cost. The designer can make a sound decision only if he knows the part cost and tooling expenditure for each alternative and considers the quantity to be produced. Too often, such decisions are made without the necessary knowledge, and excess costs are inadvertently designed into the product. Unnecessary tolerances and finish requirements and parts that are difficult to fabricate or assemble represent costs that can be avoided if the designer knows the manufacturing processes and their limitations.

Advance consultations between the designer and the process and tool engineers will provide information for sound design decisions. If necessary, detailed cost studies can be made from rough sketches of alternate designs. Such consultations also broaden the designer's understanding of manufacturing processes and of the cost implications in his designs. Advance consultation is more effective than reviewing completed designs, and avoids the expense of revisions.

Value analysis has the specific aim of reducing the cost of a product without detracting from its true value. It is a group approach to analyzing the function of each part or feature and putting a value on it. If the cost of the function exceeds its value, this suggests alternative approaches to reduce the cost. If a particular function is of marginal value, it may be eliminated entirely. Value analysis thus calls attention to possible material substitutions, designs which are easier to fabricate, and parts and operations which can be eliminated. If the designer open-mindedly accepts this approach, it can be effective in reducing costs and improving the manufacturability of the product.

Standardization of parts and materials is a significant source of savings. Fewer varieties, with larger quantities of each, bring lower purchase prices and manufacturing costs and reduce inventory carrying charges and obsolescence. A company standards manual cataloging shafts, spindles, bushings, and other common components that are already in use will aid in specifying one of these rather than designing a new one. The varieties of commercial parts such as fasteners and connectors should be limited except for unusual circumstances.

A prototype of the product should be built, conforming so far as possible to the final design. This serves as a check on the drawings and bills of material and uncovers discrepancies which might cause difficulties in the plant. It may also suggest design modifications to improve the product or simplify its manufacture. The final prototype is helpful in planning the fabricating and assembly operations and in acquainting production supervisors with the new product.

When the product is released for production, a final design review may bring out possible cost reductions or potential production problems that were overlooked in the earlier consultations. Further possibilities may be recognized during the process and methods planning and tool design. If the savings are large enough, the changes should be made, even though they require drawing revisions.

Packaging Requirements. Packaging is an integral part of the manufacturing process and must be planned for, the same as other operations. Packaging operations and materials represent the major part of the cost of some consumer products. Package design usually cannot start until a prototype of the final product is available, and time must be allotted for developing and testing alternative designs and planning the packaging operations and facilities.

An internal packaging engineering department is usually responsible for determining requirements, overseeing the design and testing of the package, and providing instructions to the factory. Package designs are frequently developed by the supplier, but the company must be able to evaluate them and, if necessary, propose alternatives to reduce the cost, facilitate the packaging operations, or meet shipping requirements. Assembly instructions may be needed if a container has several parts which must go together in a certain way. Packaging engineering is usually a manufacturing staff function, but if merchandising is the primary consideration, it is sometimes attached to marketing.

Make-or-Buy Decisions. A company may have been purchasing certain classes of work such as plating or die casting because the volume has been too low to justify in-plant facilities. If the new product adds sufficient volume, it may become economical to take on such operations. Some jobs that the plant is already equipped to do can be purchased at a lower cost from specialized job shops. As an example, a part might be run on a hand screw machine in the plant in contrast to an automatic in an outside shop.

The process engineer can frequently recognize from past experience which jobs clearly belong in the plant and which should go outside. If the choice is not clear-cut, a cost study should be made for comparison with outside quotations. If capacity is available, the internal cost should include only materials, direct labor, and those variable expenses which would be increased by the added work load. If the added work required overtime or additional equipment which would not be fully used, the increment of expense associated with the added work would be quite high. This would favor putting it in an outside shop until the volume builds up enough to justify the added facilities. As the circumstances affecting make-or-buy decisions change, the decisions should be reviewed.

Process Planning. Three principal factors to be considered in process planning are: (1) the operations to be performed on each component part or material, (2) the buildup of the product from its component parts, and (3) integrating related operations.

Operations on Each Component. For each component part or material, it is necessary to plan what operations are to be performed, the equipment to be used, the tooling required, and the optimum machine settings or processing conditions such as speeds and feeds, pressure, temperature, and the like.

There are usually several alternative processes which might be used for a given operation; for example, a flat surface on a part might be produced by milling, facing in a lathe, or broaching. For each of these processes, the job might be run on any of several machines. The selection of the process and equipment to satisfy the quality requirements at the lowest cost is governed by the production rate, hourly cost, tooling expenditure, production quantity, and expected life of the job.

An experienced process engineer familiar with equipment capabilities can often select the most suitable process on the basis of experience and judgment, but if there is any question, a cost study should be made. The choice is limited to the equipment available in the plant unless the production volume requires additional equipment or unless new equipment can be justified by reductions in unit costs. The process engineer should be experienced in methods and tool design in order to specify the operations without excessive revisions after the methods planning and tool design have been completed.

The processing information for each part and assembly is recorded on an operation sheet. The operations are listed in sequence and are numbered in a series such as 10, 20, 30, . . . , to permit adding operations without changing the numbers. The information to be shown and the form of the sheet depend on the nature of the operations. For machining, columns are typically provided for operation number; description of operation; department; machine; speed, feed, and depth of cut; setup hours and hours per piece; special tooling; and standard tools (drills, taps, and the like).

The operation sheet provides all the information needed each time the job is to be run and is referred to by the foremen, operators, and inspectors. It is used by production control in routing, machine loading, and scheduling and is the basis for determining equipment and personnel requirements for the new product. The operation sheet should be revised and reissued if there are any changes.

Buildup of the Product from Components. If a product involves a large number of individual parts or materials, the process of putting it together is simplified by breaking it down into a number of subassemblies or semifinished materials. An assembly operation with fewer parts involved is simpler and easier to learn, and the workplace can be more compact. Subassemblies or semifinished materials common to several models of the product may be processed in larger quantities to meet the total requirements. If, however, there are too many subassemblies including only a few parts each, the process becomes unduly complicated and handling is excessive.

Arriving at the most suitable pattern for the overall process is largely a matter of judgment and knowing how the alternatives will affect costs. Assembly of small parts should usually be separated from the assembly of larger components because of differences in work procedures, skills, and workplace arrangement. As an example, preassembling the clutch mechanism of a large wrapping machine reduced the time for the clutch assembly as well as for the rest of the main assembly. Similarly, making up a wiring harness for an electric appliance is less costly than running the wires individually during final assembly.

The structural bill of material as shown in Figure 1-2 is a convenient tool for planning and recording the buildup of the product. It shows which groups of parts go together in subassemblies and how the subassemblies and other components go together in building up the final product. The structural bill of material is the basis for planning the assembly operations and flow of work. It also helps production control to coordinate the processing of components with the assembly operations.

If the product has a large number of parts, tabulating equipment is helpful in making up the structural bill of material. Punched cards for the parts can be manually grouped by subassemblies and an extra card inserted ahead of each group to identify the subassembly and indicate in which column it should appear. The cards are run through a printer to produce the structural bill. If the pattern of assembly is changed, the cards are rearranged and a new structural bill is printed.

The operation process chart shows graphically the pattern in which a product is built up from component parts and subassemblies and the operations on each. It is particularly useful in planning the flow of work and laying out production facilities.

Structural Bill of Material

Electric Motor: ½ hp, 115/230 volt, cap/ind, continuous duty, sleeve bearing
Assembly drawing 5463d 3/6/___

Description	Part no.	No. required
Stator Assembly..	4736d	1
Frame assembly...	4749d	1
Frame..	4750d	1
Stator lamination assembly............................	4753c	1
Laminations..	4754b	130
Rivets...	4755a	4
Main coils...	4809c	4
Main coil leads..	4810a	2
Lead wire..	4811a	2
Connector...	4813	2
Starting coil..	4825c	4
Starting coil leads......................................	4827a	2
Lead wire..	4828a	2
Connector...	4829	2
Condenser assembly compl...............................	4900	1
Condenser mounting screws.............................	4901	2
Slot insulation..	4912b	36
Coil insulation..	4914b	36
Wedges..	4917b	36
Grommet..	4920	1
Rotor Assembly..	4976d	1
Shaft assembly...	4978d	1
Shaft...	4980d	1
Rotor lamination assembly............................	4982c	1
Laminations..	4983b	130
End rings..	4985b	2
Copper bars..	4986b	26
Fan assembly..	4995c	1
Fan plate..	4996b	1
Fan blades...	4997b	8
Starting switch assembly................................	5001c	1
Bearing ring..	5003b	1
Fiber ring..	5004b	1

FIG. 1-2. Structural Bill of Material Shows How a Product Is Built Up from Component Parts and Subassemblies.

Integrating Related Operations. There are several alternatives that should be considered when deciding how the equipment for the new product should be grouped and how closely the succeeding operations should be integrated. A related question is how closely the fabricating operations on component parts should be tied to the assembly operations. The most suitable pattern depends on the production volume and the nature of the operations.

With equipment grouped by function or type of process, materials are transported from department to department for the succeeding operations.

Detailed scheduling is necessary to coordinate the operations and keep production moving.

If the production volume is great enough to utilize the equipment capacities, all the operations on a particular component or assembly may be brought together in one area. This affords a more direct flow of materials, reduces handling, and makes one supervisor responsible for all the related operations. The product grouping ties up the equipment for the one product, however, so that it is not available for other work. Consequently, more equipment may be required and will have to be justified by the savings.

If the cycle times of the succeeding operations can be balanced, the process may be tied together still more closely in a continuous production line. The part or assembly is transferred directly between work stations by chute or conveyor with only a nominal accumulation between operations. Manual handling is virtually eliminated, and the work may be broken down into simpler individual operations than would otherwise be economical. The elapsed time for a given unit to go through the process is reduced from several days to a matter of minutes. Quality control can react more quickly because of the small quantity of material in process. Production control is simplified because the entire line is scheduled as a unit.

At still higher volumes, the operations may be more closely integrated in an automated production system. Parts are automatically fed into the beginning of the process and are moved between operations by mechanical transfer devices. The workpiece is automatically positioned at each station, the equipment cycles automatically, and automatic gaging devices check the work and readjust the settings as required. Such a system offers the maximum economy of manufacture, but it requires a higher capital investment and affords very little flexibility in accommodating product variations or different levels of output.

In summary, as related operations are more closely integrated, direct costs are reduced, the elapsed processing time is shortened, less space is needed, quality control is more direct, scheduling is simplified, and a single supervisor can be made responsible for an entire series of operations. However, the equipment investment tends to be higher, and the system becomes progressively less adaptable to changes and variations. Trouble with any of the individual operations or with the materials is likely to shut down the entire system.

Methods Development. Well-planned production methods reduce costs, improve equipment utilization, and result in better quality. These results can be accomplished only if methods for the new operations are developed in advance. Trying to improvise procedures in the plant when production is ready to start only leads to confusion and delays.

Work procedures are synthesized in terms of work elements or fundamental motions. Motion economy principles related to the different types of elements or motions suggest effective ways of performing each of them. Visualizing the individual elements or motions suggests how the workplace should be arranged for economy of motion and the possible use of jigs and mechanical devices to aid in positioning or holding the work. Other possibilities include processing two or more pieces at a time or using an indexing fixture to overlap the operator and machine portions of the work cycle. Standard times may be applied to the work elements or fundamental motions to evaluate alternate procedures. For large-volume operations, experimental workplace setups should be developed in a methods laboratory.

The methods engineer should work closely with the foreman, who will be responsible for seeing that the job is set up correctly and for training workers in the correct procedure. The method for each operation should be recorded on a job instruction sheet which outlines the step-by-step procedure and explains any points that require special attention. It also includes a sketch of the workplace layout and lists the tools, jigs, and equipment to be used.

Tooling and Special Equipment. The first requisite in tool design is to satisfy the quality requirements of the part. As an example, the tolerance and finish specified for a milling operation may necessitate a special fixture to minimize distortion and vibration of the work. If a deep-drawn part must be free of minor wrinkles and draw marks, it may have to be drawn in three or four stages rather than one or two. The tool designer must know what can be done with different grades of tooling and how to provide for the specific requirements of each job.

Tooling should be designed for maximum efficiency of the machine and operator. Such features as easy loading, quick-acting clamps, and automatic ejection increase production significantly but add little to the cost of the tooling. Gang milling setups, compound dies which combine blanking and drawing operations, and progressive dies which combine an entire series of operations can cut production costs to a fraction of what they would otherwise be. Indexing fixtures which can be loaded during the machine cycle reduce idle time of both operator and machine.

For high production quantities where versatility is not required, special machines should be considered. Standard components such as air-actuated drilling and boring heads, clamping fixtures, and the like can be combined in special configurations to fit specific jobs. This often permits combining two or more operations that would have to be done separately on standard machines. The cost of such a special machine is frequently no more than the total cost of the standard machines for the separate operations.

Equipment and Personnel Requirements. Lead times for delivery of new equipment may range from a few weeks for smaller standard machines to a year or more for large units that are built to order. Consequently, equipment deliveries may be the limiting factor in getting the new product into production. For this reason, requirements must be determined and the equipment ordered as early as possible.

The required number of machine hours per week for each operation is calculated by multiplying the scheduled number of pieces per week by the hours per piece. Summarizing the weekly machine hours required for all the operations by types and sizes of equipment gives the aggregate weekly hours for each type and size. The total weekly hours divided by the available hours per week in the work schedule gives the number of machines required. The available hours depend on the shift schedule and whether the equipment will run continuously or be shut down during lunch and rest periods. Idle machine time due to rest periods, setups, and delays is either deducted from the scheduled working time in arriving at the available hours or is added as a percentage allowance to the time per piece. If the analysis pertains to equipment already in use in the plant rather than to new equipment, the hours per week assigned to other work must of course be deducted in calculating the available hours for the new product.

The preferred method of determining operation times is to make a detailed methods analysis of each operation and synthesize the time per piece by use of predetermined motion-time data. If the company does not use standard data or if the equipment lead time is critical and there are too many operations to analyze in the available time, estimates will have to be used. Scanning the part drawings or reviewing a prototype of the new product will give some indication of the types of equipment that will be needed and the approximate hours per unit. If it is recognized that there will be a large work load for certain critical equipment, the parts involving such operations can be singled out for process planning and analysis ahead of the others.

In selecting additional equipment for the new product, consideration should be given to present operations that use similar equipment. The aggregate volume of the old and new operations may justify replacing existing machines with higher capacity units rather than adding capacity only for the new product. Projected future needs should also be considered. Detailed cost comparisons are made to determine the return on the investment for each of the alternatives.

The number of people in each labor grade needed for the new operations must be determined far enough in advance so that the positions can be filled in accordance with the policies governing job posting, transfers, and hiring. Ample time must be allowed for recruiting qualified workers and for the necessary training. The number of people for machine operations can be determined from the analysis of machine requirements. The number needed for such operations as assembly and packaging may be calculated on the basis of operation times and production quantities. The number needed for indirect work such as material handling, inspection, and setup can be estimated from ratios of indirect to direct employees in similar production departments.

Plant Layout and Facilities Planning. If the new product is similar to existing ones and represents only a modest work load, it can often be fitted into existing production departments with only minor layout adjustments. With a higher volume of production, however, an extensive rearrangement of facilities may be required to accommodate both the old and new operations efficiently.

If the operations and facilities for the new product are better adapted to being set up as a separate department, the layout study is concerned mainly with the new product. Existing operations are involved only to the extent that they may have to be shifted to make space available. Common facilities such as shipping, receiving, and storage must of course be expanded to accommodate the added volume. The added requirements for plant utility services such as power, compressed air, water, and steam and for employee facilities such as washrooms and locker rooms must be provided for.

The usual layout planning techniques are employed in analyzing production flow, determining space requirements, planning workplace arrangements, providing for material handling, and developing the complete detailed plan. Several alternative arrangements are usually considered in arriving at the final plan. Projected future requirements should be considered in the planning so that they can be provided for with a minimum of rearrangement.

MATERIALS PLANNING AND PROCUREMENT

The purchasing and materials control functions must be closely coordinated with the new-product manufacturing program to ensure correct material specifications, acceptable quality, proper quantities, and delivery at the right time. There must be procedures for routinely developing and transmitting the necessary information.

The bill of material issued by product engineering includes all the commercial and manufactured parts. However, material specifications for the manufactured parts cannot be determined until process planning has been completed. In addition, the quantities of any materials used for more than one part must be summarized, and manufacturing lead times must be established for scheduling deliveries. The necessary information for ordering materials is summarized in a special purchasing bill of material.

Purchasing Specifications. Both the product design and the processing requirements determine material specifications for ordering purposes. The type and gage of steel, for example, are specified in the design of a stamping, but whether the material is to be bought in the form of sheets, strips, or coils depends on how the part is to be run, and the slit width will depend on the die design. Bar stock should be purchased in multiples of the lengths to be used. The dimensions of sheet materials should be selected to minimize cutting waste. In-plant handling and storage facilities should be considered in specifying how the materials will be packed and shipped.

Purchasing specifications for materials to be processed in the plant are usually written up by the process engineer, reflecting both design and processing requirements. Specifications for commercial parts can be taken directly from the engineering bill of material. Any requirements beyond the usual commercial standards must be clearly specified.

Quantity Requirements. The same commercial parts may be used repeatedly in the product, and certain materials may be common to several manufactured parts. These requirements must be summarized to get the total quantities per unit of product. For a product with many parts and materials, this is most easily handled by a computer or tabulating equipment.

Material requirements for the new product should be correlated with requirements for existing products to take advantage of combined purchase quantities. Price breaks for quantity purchases should be considered, but if an item is to be used only for the new product, it is probably better to forego any price advantage and buy only what is needed for the first production run. Materials obsoleted by design changes after the first run can represent a substantial loss.

Ordering Materials and Scheduling Deliveries. The primary considerations in selecting suppliers are price, ability to meet specifications and quality requirements, capacity to supply the required quantities, reliability in meeting delivery schedules, and willingness to make good on any substandard shipments. Trial orders, plant visits, and checking with other customers help in evaluating the capabilities of new vendors. Those that the company has dealt with before can be rated on the basis of past experience.

Materials for the pilot run should be ordered and delivered early to allow maximum time for production and for getting replacements in case these first shipments are not satisfactory. Delivery of materials for regular production should be scheduled in accordance with the manufacturing lead times for the individual parts. This will get the materials into the plant when needed but avoid excessive inventories which take up plant space and tie up working capital. The vendor's lead time and the time in transit must be anticipated in placing orders. Delivery schedules must be closely watched and the orders expedited to ensure delivery on time.

START-UP OF PRODUCTION

Training Production Personnel. Participation in the planning for manufacture of the new product is the best way to familiarize the foremen with the quality requirements and manufacturing procedures. Further experience with the pilot production run should enable them to handle the start of production effectively.

Production workers are trained in the new job procedures during the pilot run. Training is easier and more effective if methods have already been developed and if the work procedures are outlined on job instruction sheets for reference by both foremen and operators. Any new and unfamiliar equipment should be set up in the plant early enough so that it can be run experimentally in advance of actual production.

Tool Tryout and Pilot Models. As the tooling for each part is completed, enough parts should be run to verify that they meet all quality requirements. Several sets of parts should be built up into subassemblies and into the final product to check on how they go together. The pilot models uncover design errors and production discrepancies and are useful in the study of assembly methods, for product testing, and for package design and testing.

Pilot Production Run. The pilot production run uses regular production equipment, tooling, and methods, but is limited to around 10 to 15 percent of the quantity in a normal production run. Its purpose is to test and refine the methods for all operations, recheck the tooling and equipment under regular operating conditions, and train the workers in the new operations. It also affords a final check on the product design, fit of parts, and product performance. Some of the units should be sold as soon as possible for early field evaluation of the product.

The product designers, manufacturing engineers, and quality control people should be in the plant during the pilot run to work with the foremen in resolving any difficulties and to study the operations for possible improvements and cost reductions. The pilot run should be far enough in advance of regular production to allow for any necessary corrections in the product design, materials, and manufacturing procedures.

Starting Regular Production. At the start of regular production, special attention should be given to the flow of materials, work procedures, and functioning of tooling and equipment. Any production lines or continuous flow processes should be checked for bottlenecks or idle time which indicate the need for rebalancing the operations. The foremen should make sure that each worker is doing his job correctly and give any additional instruction that is needed. Inspection reports on raw materials, work in process, and the finished product should be reviewed for deviations needing special attention.

Bills of material, purchasing specifications, and operation sheets should be checked to be sure that they are accurate and up to date. It is essential to get everything running smoothly so that operations can henceforth be on a routine basis.

FOLLOW-UP AND APPRAISAL OF RESULTS

At the beginning of the manufacturing program, specific objectives were set with respect to quality, product cost, capital expenditures, production capacity, and meeting the deadline for the product introduction. The final results after production is established should be compared with these objectives to measure the effectiveness of the manufacturing program. This will point out anything that still needs attention and will serve as a guide to more effective handling of future new products. The overall results should be broken down by areas of responsibility for appraisal of the individuals concerned with different phases of the program.

Even though the objectives have been met, a continuing effort should be made to refine and improve the manufacturing procedures to reduce costs and improve the product. As sales volumes increase, the procedures and facilities will have to be restudied and updated to handle the increases efficiently.

BIBLIOGRAPHY

Karger, Delmar W., *The New Product*, The Industrial Press, New York, 1960.

Marting, Elizabeth (ed.), *Developing a Product Strategy*, American Management Association, New York, 1959.

Marting, Elizabeth (ed.), *New Products—New Profits*, American Management Association, New York, 1964.

Tietjen, Karl H., *Organizing the Product Planning Function*, American Management Association, New York, 1963.

CHAPTER TWO

Total Quality Control *

A. V. FEIGENBAUM *President, General Systems Company, Pittsfield, Massachusetts*

Product quality is one of the most significant factors in customer decisions. This is true whether the purchaser is a housewife, a large industrial corporation, or a government agency. Recognition of this fact—and dealing with it adequately in business planning and action—is one of the great management challenges.

Thoughtful managers will wish to evaluate carefully the place of product quality in their company plans and programs. They should key their programs to a twin objective: first, to achieve better ways of obtaining much-improved product quality-in-use-by-the-customer, and second, to do this with much-reduced quality costs.

THE TOTAL CONTROL OF QUALITY

Total quality control is based upon the principle that, to provide genuine quality effectiveness, control must start with the planning and design of a product and end only when a trouble-free product has been placed in the hands of a customer who remains satisfied.

The basis for this concept becomes clear upon examination of the total effort required to contribute to trouble-free product quality. Such effort is far more than a matter of inspection alone, or reliability engineering alone, or quality assurance work alone—important as each of these techniques is. This is because the quality of a product is affected at many more stages of the production cycle than those susceptible to inspection, or reliability, or quality assurance effort.

* Adapted in part from *Total Quality Control—Engineering and Management*, by A. V. Feigenbaum, published by McGraw-Hill Book Company, New York, 1961.

The total weight of quality is actually created in nine sequential stages:

1. Quality is influenced by the marketing function which evaluates the level of quality that customers want and for which they are willing to pay.
2. Quality is influenced to a major degree by engineering which must reduce marketing's evaluation to exact drawing specifications.
3. Quality is influenced by purchasing which must choose, contract with, and retain vendors for parts and materials.
4. Quality is influenced by manufacturing engineering in its selection of the jigs, tools, and processes which will vitally affect it throughout production.
5. Manufacturing supervision and shop operators have had a major quality influence during parts making, subassembly, and final assembly.
6. It goes almost without saying that the job of mechanical inspection and functional test is necessary to check the product's conformance to specifications.
7. Shipping has its influence on quality—an influence seen in the caliber of packaging and the excellence of transportation.
8. Field engineering has a major influence on quality and customer satisfaction through the adequacy of its installation work and the instructions it gives the user.
9. Field testing has a great responsibility to study the reliability inherent in the product under actual operating conditions.

THE TECHNICAL AREAS OF QUALITY CONTROL

From an organizational point of view, therefore, customer satisfaction is actually created and influenced throughout the industrial cycle—whether the product is an electric toothbrush or a turbine, or whether it is a motor or a missile. True customer satisfaction in all its major characteristics, such as performance, reliability, maintainability, serviceability, appearance, and features, can be accomplished only through a deep, well-planned, organization-wide program. Such a total quality control program smoothly dovetails all quality effort into an integrated effort that is truly directed toward customer satisfaction at costs that are reasonable.

Fundamental to building the organization which puts quality control to work is the identification of the four technical work areas involved. These are:

1. New design control—which involves new or modified products prior to the start of production
2. Incoming material control—that is, control of incoming purchased parts and materials
3. Product control—or the shop floor control of materials, parts, and batches from machines, processes, and assembly line
4. Special process studies—which involve conducting special analyses of factory and processing problems

These major jobs of a total quality control program cut across the entire production cycle, and they come to grips with the first principle of quality control organization: *product quality is everybody's job in the business.* To implement this principle, part of the management approach to total quality control is in reemphasizing the significance of product quality and its cost in the specific responsibilities of all major individuals and functions in the company.

Corollary to this first principle is a second one: *if product quality is everybody's job, it may very well become nobody's job.* The second step required in total quality control programs is management recognition that the many individual responsibilities for quality will be exercised most effectively when they are buttressed and serviced by a well-organized, genuinely modern management and engineering function. For this function, the only area of specialization is product quality; the only area of operation is in the quality control jobs; the major responsibilities are to be sure that products shipped are right— and at the right quality costs.

THE QUALITY SYSTEM

The quality control component makes this organization work administratively and technically through the development and maintenance for the company of what may be properly termed a quality system. This system integrates the many individual responsibilities and decisions for product quality throughout the enterprise into a single operative system which is truly targeted on proper quality-in-use performance at appropriate quality costs. The quality system provides the network of technology and procedures which marketing, engineering, and manufacturing people follow while working closely together to get the four jobs of total quality control done. The importance of the proper design of this quality system is substantial.

It is not possible to review the complete requirements for a quality system in this Handbook. However, some of the most important subsystems will be noted, and two will be explained briefly.

First, there is preproduction quality evaluation that deals with the product design and the product manufacturing plan to make certain that the end product, as designed and manufactured, will fulfill customer requirements. During this phase, important technical tasks are accomplished such as identification of major quality characteristics along with their classification of importance; review of specifications for clarity, compatibility, and economy; identifying and eliminating possible sources of manufacturing problems before production starts; and the identification of design requirements to process capabilities to make certain that the design dovetails with these capabilities rather than "fights" them.

Second, there is product and process quality planning, the work that determines what quality characteristics should be measured, how they should be measured, to what extent, where in the process flow, who should take and record the measurement, and the limits beyond which corrective action should be taken, along with other important process requirements.

The other major quality subsystems are: purchased material quality planning and control; product and process quality evaluation and control; quality information feedback; quality information equipment; quality training, orientation, and manpower development; postproduction customer servicing; management of the quality control function; and special quality studies. Figure 2-1 shows each subsystem in relation to the four basic jobs of quality control.

This kind of quality system provides distinct, recognizable channels through which the stream of quality-related activities and contributions flows for the enterprise. Quality requirements and product quality parameters change, of course, but the quality system remains fundamentally the same, always providing the proper technical channels through which essential product quality-related activities, such as reliability, maintainability, and serviceability, must proceed.

This, in essence, is total quality control, which deals with the design of a product on through the industrial cycle and places quality products into the

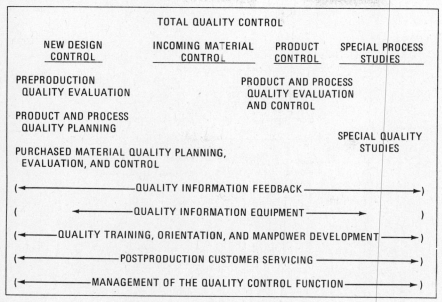

FIG. 2-1.   Total Quality Control System.

hands of customers: military, industrial, or private consumer.   Anything less than this kind of total business quality effort falls short of serving the real purpose of quality control work.

THE TECHNOLOGICAL TRIANGLE

The quality control function makes this quality system real and effective through the application of three distinct technologies.   Figure 2-2 shows the technological triangle, which provides a useful structure for relating the technologies of quality control to one another.

The apex of the triangle provides the caption for the field, in this case, total quality control.   The first tier divides the field into the technical work areas or jobs of quality control: new design control, incoming material control, product control, and special process studies.

The jobs of quality control are accomplished by three technologies:

1.   Quality control engineering
2.   Process control engineering
3.   Quality information equipment engineering

These are shown on the second tier of the technological triangle and are overlaid by training in many associated technologies and disciplines.

The third tier shows the techniques employed by the technologies.   It is important to point out that any single technique or combination of techniques may be selected by any one of the three technologies for use in any of the technical work areas.   This area of techniques can be looked upon as a storehouse of tools from which all the technologies are free to draw in accomplishing work in the technical work areas.

The fourth, and bottom, tier shows the applications for the various techniques in accomplishing certain parts of the work.   For example, the technique

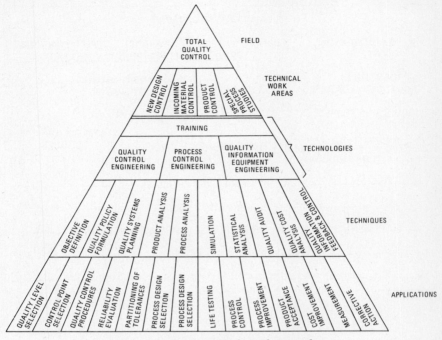

FIG. 2-2.   The Technological Triangle.

of quality cost optimization may be applied to cost reduction, product design selection, and many other listed applications.

Quality Control Engineering Technology

Quality control engineering technology may be defined as: The body of technical knowledge for formulating policy and for analyzing and planning product quality to establish that quality system which will yield full customer satisfaction at minimum cost.

The entire range of techniques used in quality control engineering technology may be grouped under three major headings as shown by Figure 2-3:

1. *Formulation of Quality Policy.* Included here are techniques for identifying quality objectives. Also included are techniques for developing guidelines that are related to the realization of these objectives and that serve as a foundation for quality analysis and planning.

2. *Product Quality Analysis.* Techniques for analyzing include those for isolating and identifying all the factors that relate to the quality of the product in its served market. These factors are then studied for their effects toward producing the desired quality result.

3. *Quality Planning.* Techniques for planning emphasize the development in advance of a proposed course of action and of methods for accomplishing the desired quality result. These are the techniques used for planning the procedures which, when taken together, comprise the documented elements of the quality system discussed earlier.

Techniques for Formulation of Quality Policy.   *Quality Objectives and Quality Policy.* A prerequisite to any quality analysis work is the clear delineation of

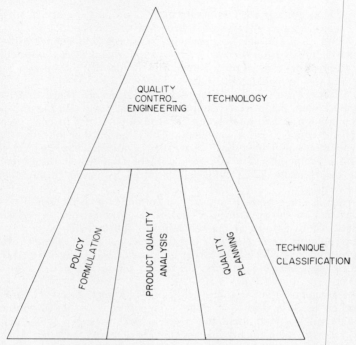

FIG. 2-3. Quality Control Engineering Techniques.

the quality objectives and the quality policy of a company. Until the company knows where it is going with respect to product quality standards and product quality levels, no foundation is provided on which to build functional quality plans. Policy must be established to provide the limits within which quality-related decisions by the functions of the business will assure a proper course of action in meeting quality objectives.

Helping to formulate quality policy is one of the major contributions that the quality control engineer makes to the business. To do this effectively, he must see the broad quality picture, particularly as it relates to the customer and his desires. In particular, he must identify (1) the quality decisions that must be made and (2) the quality problems that must be solved. He can then (3) help in the specific documentation of the quality policy for the company.

Decision Identification. First, the integrated product plan for the business is charted step by step from inception of a product idea on through all the actions required to deliver the product to the customer and to service that product. All the quality-related decisions are identified at each step.

Then the limitations are identified that have to be placed on each decision to assure meeting the quality objectives of the business. These limitations provide the guidelines within which managers are free to make alternative decisions and take courses of action toward reaching quality objectives.

For example, when a product design concept has been completed for a company by one of its design engineers, a decision must be made by the company whether to accept the concept as developed or to subject it to review. Individual cases, taken of and by themselves, may cause internal frictions incident to such a decision. If it has been established by policy that design reviews always are necessary to assure desired product quality, then the issue, instead, becomes merely how the design review will be conducted.

Guidelines, in the form of supporting procedures, will delineate the components or individuals from the various functional organizations who will participate in the review. These procedures also will identify the criteria to be used in accepting the design concept.

Problem Identification. All the quality problems are listed that have been encountered with the product under any circumstance, during development, in customer service, and elsewhere. The question is put in each case of how the problem came to be a problem. Then the further question is posed: "What decision could have been made that would have prevented this from becoming a problem?" The required element of policy is then identified by putting the question: "What policy is required to assure getting these 'right kinds' of decisions?"

For example, in a western company, a consumer product model was rushed to market to gain the advantage of an innovation in design. Insufficient time was scheduled to determine the reliability of the model. As a result, many quality complaints were received from the field. A policy element was subsequently established which required a 98 percent reliability at an 80 percent confidence level before future models in the product line could be released for market.

Policy Documentation. There are many different forms of presentation that can be used to document policy, depending upon individual company requirements. Many of these forms are equally effective in communicating written policy to the company managers. The majority include a basic format that covers the following points:

1. Policy title.
2. Need for policy.
3. Policy statement—this defines the basic quality interests that must be preserved for the company.
4. Courses of action—these are the procedures that are followed for implementing the policy.
5. Responsibility and authority—this area defines the position assignments in the organization that have responsibility for enforcing the policy and for interpreting it.
6. Definition of terms, if needed.

To assure adherence to the quality policy and to provide for its proper implementation, the required step is a formal communication to the managers responsible for administering the functional work within the company. This is best accomplished by equipping each manager with a loose-leaf binder containing all elements of the quality policy. As issues become superseded, they can be replaced in the binder with new issues.

Figure 2-4 shows a representative section of a quality policy formulated by an eastern electronics manufacturer.

Techniques for Product Quality Analysis. *Approaches to Analysis.* Before planning of the quality system is undertaken, not only should the objective and quality policy of the business be developed, but also the quality aspects of the product itself and those of the served market should be analyzed.

Analysis of all the quality factors bearing on the product defines the areas in which courses of action must be established to meet business objectives. After those needed have been identified, planning can then be undertaken to establish methods for carrying out the courses of action.

The act of analyzing involves breaking down a situation into all its elements

---

XYZ ELECTRONICS COMPANY
PRODUCT QUALITY POLICY

Need for Policy

To enhance the Company reputation, competitive position, and profitability, it is necessary to produce products of good quality. Meeting this objective requires a properly directed approach by all functions to the elements which concern product quality.

Statement of Policy

It is the policy of the XYZ Electronics Company to market only products of a quality that will merit and earn customer satisfaction by performing expected functions reliably and effectively in accordance with customer expectations, and which are discernibly better than competitive offerings. In support of this objective, the XYZ Electronics Company continuously strives to lead its product field in research and development, design, manufacture, and marketing of work related to its area of business responsibility.

Courses of Action

1. **Selection of Business Opportunities**

   This Company will not accept business which will compromise its product quality reputation. In this regard the customer's specifications will be reviewed to determine that they serve the common interests of the customer and the Company and to ensure that minimum quality standards can be met. When these conditions are not met, the Company will not submit a proposal. A comprehensive contract review will be carried out by all functional areas before a contract is signed in accordance with Company instructions.

2. **Product Development and Design**

   1) Only approved components and processes shall be used. In cases where new components and processes are needed to meet product requirements, adequate qualification tests or process capability measurements will be carried out prior to their use. Department instructions shall specify procedures for obtaining component and process approval.

FIG. 2-4. Typical Product Quality Policy.

and then synthesizing these elements back into the whole. In quality control work, there are many separate elements to any product quality situation. Some examples are:

1. Function to be performed by the product
2. Environments encountered by the product
3. Life or durability requirements
4. Product design
5. Manufacturing process
6. Shipping conditions
7. Installation
8. Maintenance
9. Characteristics of served market
10. Competitive offerings

Each of these items can be further analyzed. For example, item 4, product design, can be described in terms of each individual quality characteristic of the product, and even further analysis can be made by considering various aspects of these quality characteristics. They can be analyzed on the basis of their importance in supporting the principal functions of the product. They also can be analyzed by considering each quality characteristic with respect to its ability to be manufactured easily and economically.

Here, the reliability requirements and the product quality levels are established and translated into quality planning that will dovetail with manufacturing capabilities rather than fight these capabilities. The importance of this contribution lies in the fact that, before costly trial and redesign are necessary, each major or critical part and subassembly is carefully reviewed and classified in relation to its importance to product performance and acceptance.

This may involve, for example, establishing the standards for mean time to failure along with whatever other reliability targets may be indicated to meet the inherent reliability required for the product. The quality control engineer must carefully balance the cost of attaining an incremental increase in quality or reliability against the total costs in dollars and in loss of business with not attaining it. This work provides the information from which quality control planning will be developed.

To accomplish such preproduction planning, the quality control engineer performs a vital role in the product planning area by reviewing the design from a quality-ability aspect. It is not sufficient for quality engineers to accept specifications only. In addition, they must know the design so thoroughly that they can—with authority of knowledge—assist in recommending all quality requirements including the reliability elements required.

To do this, the quality control engineer must employ many techniques which have become a part of the technology of this field of engineering. A few of these are: delineation of quality requirements; designed experiments; economic partitioning of tolerances; analysis of prototype tests; analysis of environmental and end use effects; review of designs using earlier experience on quality aspects; evaluation of effects of new methods, new processes, and new materials; adjustment of product and process for compatibility; vendor facilities evaluation; quality cost optimization; and simulation.

Techniques Used in Planning. *Approaches to Planning.* The act of planning is thinking out in advance the sequence of actions to accomplish a proposed course of action in doing work to accomplish certain objectives. So that the planner may communicate his plan to the person or persons expected to execute it, the plan is written out with necessary diagrams, formulas, and tables.

Planning in the field of quality control must, of course, fundamentally be geared for delivering satisfactory product quality to the customer at minimum quality cost. These objectives are realized only by carefully planning many individual procedures which relate properly to one another and make up the documented elements of the quality system.

Many different pieces of work must be performed by many people and in a certain time-phased sequence. Different techniques are used in accomplishing the work. Therefore, the development of a quality control plan is based on using the results of the techniques of analysis progressively to answer the following questions:

1. What specific elements of quality work need to be done?
2. When, during the product development cycle, does each element of work need to be done?
3. How is it to be done: by what method, procedure, or device?
4. Who does it: what position in what organizational component?

5. Where is it to be done: at what location in the plant, on the assembly line, in the laboratory, by the vendor, or in the field?
6. What tools or equipment are to be used?
7. What are the inputs to the work? What is needed in the way of information and material inputs to get the work accomplished?
8. What are the outputs? Do any decisions have to be made? What are they, and what criteria should be used for making them? Does any material have to be identified and routed?
9. Is any record of the action to be made? If so, what is the form of the data? What kind of analysis is required? To whom is it sent? What form of feedback is to be used?
10. Are there alternative courses of action to be taken, depending on certain differences in the product quality encountered?
11. What are the criteria for these courses of action?
12. Is any time limit imposed on the work? If so, what is it?

Many more questions are developed as the planning assumes a finer degree of detail.

The final output of the planning process is the set of detailed procedures necessary to accomplish the prescribed courses of action in meeting the quality objectives of the business and in carrying out the established quality policy. Fundamental elements of a portion of such a quality system plan, which require documentation applying to the incoming material control job of quality control, are shown by Figure 2-5. Figure 2-6 shows a page of an instruction covering one of these elements within this system plan, giving the detailed procedure for sampling and testing one type of purchased material, fuel oil.

This planning clearly spells out to process control engineers, to manufacturing supervision, to inspectors and testers, and to the operators themselves, the step-by-step requirements for accurately measuring and controlling inputs and outputs of the many processes required to produce the final product.

This product quality plan includes the exact measurement equipment to be used and the exact auditing station to perform the necessary audits. It spells out the system for receiving and accepting purchased material, and for the quality and reliability control of parts, subassemblies, and assemblies as they progress through the manufacturing line. It establishes the final audit weighting of important quality characteristics as close as possible to actual customer reaction.

Here, again, the quality control engineer brings his specialized techniques into play. He employs such techniques as classification of characteristics; acceptance sampling; determination of quality measurements to be made; determination of quality measuring equipment requirements; quality personnel requirements; documentation of quality planning; review of technical instructions, procedures, and manuals; making quality requirements understood by vendors; servicing of vendors; material certification plans; quality information feedback; data processing and use of computers; communicating with other functions; feedback of information from the field; quality control in the field; renewal parts quality control; and promotion of quality to the customer.

Process Control Engineering Technology

Process control engineering technology may be defined as: The body of technical knowledge for analysis and control of process quality, including direct control of the quality of materials, parts, components, and assemblies as they are processed throughout the entire industrial cycle.

Materials

1. Incoming material control procedures
   a. Sampling plans
   b. Instructions
   c. Data recording
   d. Reporting
2. Vendor relationships
   a. Delineation of quality requirements to vendors, including classification of quality characteristics and acceptable quality levels
   b. Correlation of measurement methods
   c. Vendor quality capability, facilities, and quality systems surveys and evaluations
   d. Incoming material rating
   e. Feedback of quality information to vendors
   f. Corrective action and follow-up
   g. Servicing to assure scheduled quality output
   h. Certification of incoming material
   i. Interpretations
3. Incoming material control measuring devices
   a. Specification (method, accuracy, precision, capacity, service connections, floor space, and so on)
   b. Maintenance
   c. Calibration
   d. Periodic correlation with vendor's devices
4. Laboratory acceptance testing
   a. Test specifications
   b. Samples for laboratory
   c. Request for tests
   d. Laboratory results reporting
5. Material disposition
   a. Identification
   b. Requests for deviation
   c. Routing (scrap, rework, salvage, return to vendor, detail inspection, and so on)
6. Incoming material audit
7. Incoming material quality control personnel requirements
   a. Number
   b. Qualifications
   c. Special training

FIG. 2-5. Quality Control Elements for Incoming Material Which Require Documentation.

The techniques employed by this technology may be grouped under four major headings:

1. *Process Quality Analysis.* Techniques for analyzing the measurements that have been planned by quality control engineering technique. These measurements describe the behavior of the process while it is operating, so that there will be sensitive and rapid means for predicting process trends.

2. *In-process Control.* Techniques for applying results of the process analysis actually to adjust process parameters and environments in order to keep the process in a state of control.

3. *Implementation of the Quality Plan.* Techniques for adjusting and revising elements of the quality system plan to take into account the dynamic changes of the day-by-day production situation.

4. *Quality Effectiveness Audit.* Techniques for performing the constant

---

QUALITY INSTRUCTION

COMPANY R

Subject: Fuels, and Oils, including Process Chemicals

IV. SAMPLING JET FUELS AND LUBRICANTS
   A. Fuels and lubricants are subject to 120-day sampling by ABC Laboratory.
   B. Receiving Inspection will maintain a complete file of records and will be responsible for the schedule of sampling and the preparation and delivery of the samples to the Plant Laboratory.
   C. Samples will be processed in accordance with requirements of military fuel specifications.
      1. All samples will be analyzed by the Plant Laboratory and the composite report of both ABC and Plant Laboratory findings will be reported to the Receiving section submitting the samples.

V. SAMPLING ON 90-DAY BASIS
   A. It is the option of the Quality Supervisor of each section in the Company to require 90-day sampling for the purpose of maintaining a control check on incoming quality of materials.
   B. It is the responsibility of the Receiving section to set up the necessary record control for such sampling program.
   C. The Plant Laboratory will perform the analysis and furnish a report to the Receiving section submitting materials under a 90-day quality control program.

VI. PROCESS CHEMICALS
   A. Process chemicals shall be ordered and received in the same manner as fuels described in paragraph II.
   B. It shall be the responsibility of each Operating Section to issue and to conform to detailed instructions providing the necessary control of these materials.
   C. Sampling shall be performed at the option of the Quality Supervisor of each Operating Department, analysis to be performed by the Plant Laboratory on request.

APPROVED: *John Smith*
Manager – Quality Control
Company R

DATE: *March 10, 19—*
March 12, 19—

Date Issued	Superseded Issue	Dated	Page	No.

Fig. 2-6.   Quality Instruction for Testing Fuel Oil.

monitoring that has been planned by quality control engineering technique. The monitoring covers product and process as well as the attendant costs to assure that the planned quality results are achieved.

Techniques Used in Process Analysis. *Machine and Process Capability Analysis.* Use of this technique permits the prediction of the limits of variation within which a machine or process will operate.   Hence it provides a means for measuring the machine and process capability and comparing this against the tolerance required by the specification.

Every machine and every process has inherent variability.   For example, if a lathe is set up to turn shafts to an outer diameter of 1.000 inch, it is known that not all the shafts produced will be exactly 1.000 inch. The majority will be near this value, but there may be a few percent that are as low as 0.998 or as high as 1.002 inches. Each machine has a natural pattern of variability; machine and process capability analyses establish this pattern on the basis of actual measurements taken under controlled conditions.

On the basis of this behavior pattern, it is possible to predict what the machine or the process is capable of producing. If the spread of the pattern is less than that of the tolerance, the machine is capable of producing parts to tolerance. If it is broader than that of the tolerance, the machine will have to be replaced with one of greater precision or the process will have to be changed.

For example, a process capability study was conducted by a Philadelphia manufacturer to determine the capabilities of a Burgmaster six-spindle automatic turret-drill press with General Electric numerical tape control. Accuracy of hole location was determined under each of the operating conditions ordinarily encountered in practice. Two different methods were employed: one using the master plate to indicate positioning without actually cutting metal, and the other putting a random series of holes in a number of sample pieces.

The sample pieces were measured and analyzed. The study was comprehensive and provided the following information:

1. Accuracy of each of the six spindles when (a) drilling, (b) reaming, and (c) boring
2. Accuracy of hole locations without center drilling
3. Repeatability of the machine in coming back to zero position after performing a series of operations
4. Accuracy of the machine in different areas of the worktable
5. Comparison of accuracy with dial versus tape-controlled operation

This information was used for programming the machine so that it would meet drawing tolerances. This permitted acceptance of the work from the machine with a minimum amount of inspection and a maximum assurance that the pieces were accurate.

Some other process analysis techniques are: quality measuring equipment capability and repeatability analysis; analysis of pilot-run results; incoming material testing, inspection, and laboratory analysis; quality assurance inspection; production testing; process variation analysis; test data analysis; and field complaint analysis.

Techniques Used for In-process Control. *Vendor Rating.* Vendor rating is the technique used in evaluating the performance of each of the suppliers of a business on a comparative basis.

Various vendors may be rated on their quality performance on a given material or part. This may be on the basis of percentage of acceptable lots to total lots received or on some other suitable basis. This quality rating is combined with ratings on price and service, resulting in an overall performance rating. The final index provides a rational basis for the selection of vendors or for dividing the total business among two or more vendors.

When a vendor is compared against his competitors, he may insist that the only fair basis is comparison on a given part or component and not on an overall average performance. This is because some vendors may have more difficult requirements to meet for a particular kind of part not being made by their competitors.

This information can be used to strengthen vendor performance, because when apprised of a poor quality situation, most reputable suppliers will make every effort to improve their standing or reputation.

Structure Table Control. A structure table (Figure 2-7) provides a tech-

MACHINE #273
(LATHE–O.D.)

TABLE 0331

A. Q. L. – %	←				.1 →
CAPABILITY – (% OF TOLERANCE)	≤10	≤25	≤50	≤75	≤75
CHECK–(# PIECES)	1	1	6	10	REJECT
ACCEPTANCE BAND– (% AROUND NOMINAL)	85	64	40	13	REJECT
NEXT TABLE	0332 ————→				NONE

←		1.0			→	←		2.5			→
≤10	≤25	≤50	≤75	≤90	<90	≤10	≤25	≤50	≤75	≤90	≤90
1	1	4	10	10	REJECT	1	1	1	6	10	REJECT
88	70	51	32	18	REJECT	90	73	46	38	29	REJECT
←——— 0332 ———→					NONE	←——— 0332 ———→					NONE

←		5.0			→	←		10			→
≤10	≤25	≤50	≤75	≤90	<90	≤10	≤25	≤50	≤75	≤90	<90
1	1	1	4	6	REJECT	1	1	1	2	4	REJECT
90	76	51	43	35	REJECT	92	79	57	45	42	REJECT
←——— 0332 ———→					NONE	←——— 0332 ———→					NONE

FIG. 2-7.   Structure Table.

nique for the tabulation of knowledge in a logical sequence.   In quality control work, such a table is established for a part or a process.   The knowledge required for control of the quality attributes is contained in the structure table. Planning for similar parts or operations can be quickly extracted from such tables with a minimum of effort.

Quality information in the body of the table includes process capability values and percentage yields.   Analysis of this information provides a basis for machine routing and expected yield.

For example, if production of a given part involves several different turning operations, the process capability data will show which lathes should be used to generate a given dimension to a required tolerance.   By progressing a step further, the tables will show the expected quality levels which will be produced by following the recommended routing.

Some other techniques for in-process control are control charts and work sampling.

Techniques Used for Implementing the Quality Plan.   *Use of Manuals and Standing Instructions.*   Preparation of process quality manuals and standing instructions, within the framework of the quality system plan, represents an important process control technique.   These manuals codify and communicate various procedural details, such as operative procedures and standards of workmanship, which ordinarily are not spelled out on a drawing or in a specification. Too often, these instructions are not written anywhere. They are transmitted verbally, and like all verbal communications, the information will change each time that it is communicated.

Typical manuals are:

1. Process quality procedures manuals, which include such instructions as material disposition procedures, instructions for completion of forms, maintenance of files, gage inspection procedures, and procedures for making process capability studies.

2. Standard shop practice manuals, which include such information as the definition of flatness, finish, squareness, undercut for threading, spot-weld depressions, and the like. Instructions of this type are difficult to write, and so pictures, sketches, and visual or physical samples may be required to convey fully the meaning of the instructions. Manuals of this type become the reference material for judging quality of workmanship and are useful in training new personnel and for reviews by experienced personnel.

Interpretation of Drawings, Specifications, and Quality Planning. Interpretation of drawings, specifications, and quality planning is often a necessary technique for their proper implementation in the shop. Even though these instructions are written as clearly as possible, there is always the chance that they may be misunderstood by shop personnel. These men do not always have the same background information that is available to the product engineer who develops the design or the quality control engineer who develops the plan. The interpretation activity helps to give an image of a good part and emphasizes its important characteristics. Information given in this manner is more acceptable than criticism of mistakes and errors by an operator or assembler that result from lack of understanding.

Drawings, specifications, and quality planning can be interpreted to the operator, using different methods of communication. This can be accomplished in orientation sessions with either groups or individuals. Another method is to communicate the information to supervisors or lead men so that they can instruct their operators. Samples, pictures, and drawings may be used as visual aids. Proper instruction of operators is essential to the "make it right the first time" principle.

Some other implementation techniques are: temporary quality planning, first-piece inspection, and disposition of discrepant material.

Techniques Used for Auditing Quality Effectiveness. *Quality Rating of Organizational Components and Productive Personnel.* A product quality rating for production units or production personnel provides a technique for observing product quality trends. A product quality rating is an index number or ratio which is obtained by taking into account such factors as scrap and rework, level of outgoing quality, the number of rejected lots, and the excess cost in other units due to workmanship errors. Generally, changes in the quality of work produced are small. Any noticeable change is the cumulative effect of a gradual degradation of product quality over time. An index number, plotted on a chart chronologically with time, will indicate a trend, either up or down, when one exists. Action can be taken or an investigation can be made when an unfavorable trend is taking place and before serious problems develop.

Procedures Audits. A procedures audit is a technique for a formal examination and verification that the detailed procedures in the quality plan are being followed. An index can be computed that will indicate the degree that procedures are being adhered to.

The audit is a detailed examination made on a representative sample of procedures. A record is made of each deviation. Demerits are then assessed for each deviation in relation to the importance of the procedure and the degree of departure from the specified procedure.

The result of the procedures audit can then be stated as an index number. A chart on which these index numbers are plotted will indicate trends as periodic audits are taken. The makeup of the sample should be varied at random from audit to audit.

The procedures audit is a measure of managerial control, because the effectiveness of the quality plan depends on its prescribed procedures being followed. The procedures audit indicates areas requiring better instruction and closer supervision.

Product Audits. A product audit is a technique for customer-centered evaluations of a relatively small sample of product. It may use environmental, life, and other reliability tests as a means for evaluating product quality. The purpose is not to control quality but to determine the effectiveness of the quality control system. The audit may be made at the end of the line, it may be made on the completed product, or it may include in-process audits of parts and components. The choice depends on where the different quality characteristics can best be evaluated.

In making an audit, every feature of the product is evaluated with demerits assessed for each discrepancy noted. These demerits are then weighted according to the importance of the quality characteristic. An index is computed by totaling the demerits and relating them to a comparison base such as so many units of product. The index is plotted graphically with time to determine trends of product quality. The audit report is further analyzed to identify specific areas which call for additional investigation of design, processing, control methods, or procedures. Corrective action is applied where the results of the analysis dictate.

Working in the manufacturing environment, the process control engineer becomes the technical advisor to manufacturing supervision and other key specialists in all aspects of producing and controlling product quality and reliability. He applies techniques that involve vendor-vendee relationships; he may arrange for and guide economical quality runs; and he integrates the quality efforts of all the contributing process lines to assure the quality of the final product.

To accomplish this work, he must use his experience and knowledge in physics, electronics, chemistry, or mechanics to assure the continuous flow of acceptable products—not only from a design, reliability, appearance, or feature standpoint, but also from the customer's actual end use viewpoint.

In the final analysis, these process control engineering techniques are directed toward providing immediate quality information to the operator so that he can make parts right the first time and know that he has done so. To do this, however, requires that the necessary quality information be provided for the operator. As this is done and as this method of operation becomes effective in the shop, the inspectors can then back away from routine sorting in favor of more positive activity. Instead of operating as policemen of manufacturing processes, inspection and test personnel can become true parts of the process control subfunction of quality control. These types of process control men can provide positive assistance in the production of the right quality by:

1. Becoming auditors of the good quality practices that have been preplanned
2. Providing as much as possible on-the-spot, shop floor analysis of defects

3. Feeding back facts about these defects for corrective action
4. Beginning truly to understand process behavior as the basis for process analysis and control

Quality Information Equipment Engineering Technology

Quality information equipment engineering technology may be defined as: The body of technical knowledge relating to equipment which measures quality characteristics and which processes the resulting information for use in analysis and control.

There are many techniques used in this technology, any one of which may have several applications. One example is the design of dimensional measuring equipment to send back a signal of the measured characteristics for adjusting the quality of the process. The X-ray gage used to measure the thickness of steel sheets during rolling operations typifies such equipment.

The full complement of techniques of quality information equipment technology may be grouped under four major headings:

1. *Advanced Equipment Development.* Techniques for creating measurement practices and instrumentation procedures for application to those quality information requirements that are established by quality control engineering and process control engineering techniques

2. *Equipment Specification Planning.* Techniques for establishing the actual specification of the quality information equipment which is required within the framework of the quality system plan

3. *Design, Procurement, and Construction.* Techniques for the design and procurement of the individual components for the specified equipment; also techniques for constructing the equipment and for procuring the equipment in total, when this is necessary

4. *Installation, Check-out, and Follow-up.* Techniques for the installation and application of the quality information equipment following its construction

These techniques are important because modern process control demands equipment which can make quality measurements of precision. The thousandths-of-an-inch pocket micrometer, which once epitomized exactness, is rapidly being replaced by optical flats which measure ten-millionths of an inch.

Dimensional characteristics are, as a matter of fact, but one of a long list of quality characteristics needed for the evaluations of modern products. A whole array of electronic parameters must be measured: voltage, current, power, resistance, capacitance, and frequency, in a wide range of values. Chemical measurements are common even in the mechanical goods and electrical industries. Physical strength, thrust, flow, pressures, temperatures, and times (in microseconds) are widely used measurements. An array of radiation measurement devices has been placed on the list.

Often these measurements must be rapidly and accurately made during the manufacturing cycle, must be compatible with it, and often must be made automatically. Furthermore, they may be used to adjust the process itself automatically. This may involve feeding the measurements into a computer, comparing the results with standards, and then feeding back the needed information for correction of the process, all automatically.

Equipment in the field of quality control has thus assumed a new and much more significant role than was played by the traditional inspection and testing devices.

Historically, inspection equipment was essentially a small incident in the work of the factory methods planner, and the primitive equipment and low productivity of such equipment certainly demonstrate this. Even test equipment, although somewhat more extensively covered, was still largely a matter of selecting manually operated flip-switch circuits that could be mounted in a suitable metal box.

These older equipments had the principal job of accepting or rejecting parts. Their being made automatic usually meant only that they would mechanically sort the bad product from the good, which made no other contribution to the plant's quality objective than that bad parts might be identified more quickly than had ever before been possible. These devices were often set up with almost no preplanned relationship to other segments of the plant quality control work.

The Job of Modern Equipment. In contrast, it has been becoming increasingly recognized that the basic job of modern quality control equipment is not merely to inspect or test; it is also to provide usable information about product and process quality. This information may still be used, in part, as the basis for acceptance or rejection. But its other major use is for rapid manual, mechanized, or fully automatic feedback for process control and for true control of product quality—often for the first time in some operations.

In fact, these modern quality information equipment devices are the representation, in physical equipment, of elements of the quality system of the plant. As such, they are an essential segment of this system and must be fully compatible with its other segments.

Testing and inspection equipments that are designed in terms of the quality information concept are often much lower in total cost and less complex in design and operation than are the older testing and inspection devices. This is because bad quality control habits all too frequently have been mechanized in the form of a piece of testing and inspection equipment which turns out to be much more complex and more costly than the planned quality requirements demand.

An example is the midwestern motor plant that purchased a motor tester for final, 100 percent, go–no-go checking of seventeen quality characteristics. This $90,000 piece of checking equipment did nothing to improve the basic quality level of the motors; its principal asset was that it provided much more rapid separation of the bad motors from the good.

Study, employing the techniques of quality control engineering, established a quality system plan for the plant which specified two pieces of in-process equipment to measure and process quality information. These two equipments, whose total cost was $12,000, helped control the motor process. They soon made the costly, elaborate final motor tester unnecessary.

The principle is this: what is significant is not better quality control devices as such, but instead, those information equipments which integrate with low-cost, high-efficiency quality control systems.

PRODUCT RELIABILITY

A reliable product is one that can be counted on to perform the function that it is designed to perform when called upon. To put it another way: "when you press the button, it works."

Emphasis on the reliability segment of product quality has been increasing significantly. This has been due to such trends as:

1. Greater use of automatic or automated products, production processes, and systems
2. The increased complexity of these products, production processes, and systems

When products and systems were manually operated, some person was present to override them and to compensate for maladjustments. For example, the manually operated carburetor choke on an automobile could be overridden by the automobile driver and opened or closed to produce the fuel mixture that would ignite under the conditions encountered.

When such a choke became automatic, however, there no longer was a simple, manual way to override it. If it went out of adjustment, it could not be made to perform by the driver. Hence, the reliability element of automatic choke product quality suddenly became a matter of much greater importance than it had been in manual choke product quality.

When the automatic choke is multiplied by a multitude of modern, more complex products—household automatic washers, automatic machine tools, electronic control equipments, automatic closed-circuit television, automatic electric ranges—the increased significance of product reliability becomes apparent.

In the automatic choke, the importance of reliability was further increased by the fact that, to make a product function automatically, it is sometimes necessary to make it more complex. This increased complexity may tend, in itself, to make the product potentially less reliable because the more parts and functions that there are in a device, the greater the probability that one or more will fail.

Before the development of the total quality control activity, companies too frequently concentrated on testing their products at the start of product life (time t_0) instead of also evaluating product performance at stages during product life (times $t_1, t_2, \ldots, t_n$). In many cases, the related life testing and environmental testing were cursory. This may well explain why, before introducing total quality control programs, companies in all product areas have experienced extremely difficult reliability problems with their increasingly multifunction products when they were put to use by the customer.

Reliability and Costs. In the final analysis, the reliability requirements of a product are determined by its customer's requirements. There is a certain product reliability standard that provides him with the most economical system to meet his needs. If this standard is set too low, actual total cost to the customer may be high because of excessive repair, maintenance, and out-of-use costs. If an unduly high reliability standard is specified, total costs may still be excessive because of the greater requirements for components and assemblies.

At some point, there is an optimum reliability value—determined as a balance with other product quality parameters—that provides lowest overall costs, both to the purchaser and to the manufacturer. This point is probably never fully fixed because of the dynamic efforts of a business toward giving the customer progressively higher reliability without increasing product costs, or even while reducing product costs.

Purchasers have increasingly emphasized that they expect this standard of product reliability without undue premiums in prices that they pay to manufacturers. As one knowledgeable purchaser has noted:

There is a strong tendency in some industries . . . to consider all reliability requirements as something "extra." This is like a haberdasher who offers to sell a new fedora for $10 and a few minutes later qualifies his price by saying that a fedora that really fits will cost $12. One simply does not buy a hat that does not fit.

We all recognize that increased effort in any area necessitates extra expenditures. Just as any other customer . . . [we] must be willing to pay for those specific costs incurred to improve reliability; however, we must separate the traditional and basic elements of good management and engineering from those unusual and justifiable expenditures for higher reliability achievement. We must insist that the term "reliability" not be used as camouflage for additional charges for those functions which are an intrinsic part of an effective industrial operation.

The Definition of Product Reliability. Product reliability is one of the qualities of a product. Quite simply, it is the quality that measures the probability that the product or device will work.

As a definition: Product reliability is the probability of a product performing its intended function over its intended life and under the operating conditions encountered.

Four of the significant elements in the concept of reliability are:

1. Probability
2. Performance
3. Time
4. Enviromental conditions

The first element in reliability is the consideration of variation, which makes a reliability a probability. Each individual unit of product will vary somewhat from other units; some may have a relatively short life and others a relatively long life. Further, a group of units may have a certain average life. Thus it is possible to identify frequency distributions of product failure which permit prediction of the life of units of product.

The second consideration contained in the definition is that reliability is a performance characteristic. For a product to be reliable, it must perform a certain function or do a certain job when called upon. For example, a heating pad must give the intended degree of heat when it is switched onto the low setting and must do the same for the medium and high settings.

Implied in the phrase "performing its intended function" is that the device is intended for a certain application. In the case of the heating pad, the intended application is to apply warmth to various areas of the human body. If, instead, it is used out-of-doors to keep a large container of coffee at a certain temperature, the heating pad might be inadequate because of changes in rate of heat transfer and the greater volume to be heated, as well as a change in environment.

The third element in the definition of reliability is time. Reliability, stated as a probability of the product's performing a function, must be identified for a stated period of time.

An analogy is life insurance actuary tables. The probability of an individual's living through the next year is a different number from the probability of his living through the next decade. By the same token, a statement about the reliability of a product must be coupled to its intended life, whether ten minutes or ten years or whatever the life span is.

The fourth consideration in the definition is environmental conditions. These include the application and operating circumstances under which the product is put to use. These factors establish the stresses that will be imposed on the product. They need to be viewed broadly enough to include storage and transportation conditions, because these also can have significant effects on product reliability.

The environment which a product "sees" will greatly affect its life span and its performance. In the case of the heating pad, for example, the out-of-doors environment of the container of coffee is quite different from the relatively dry environment of a room and would significantly alter the reliability of the pad.

The term "inherent reliability" has become popular for describing the potential reliability that the designer is able to create with his design. This is presumed to be the highest reliability that the particular design will afford. When the design is actually produced in the form of hardware, it has some reliability value always less than the inherent reliability. This is usually considered as the achieved reliability.

The achieved reliability of a device is the reliability demonstrated by the physical product. Hence, it includes the manufacturing effects on product reliability, which in reality are always present for a physical product.

As a practical matter, the physical product is measured and analyzed to determine what effects are causing the achieved reliability to fall short of the inherent reliability. This calls for a study of the failure mechanism for the product under consideration.

Failure mechanism may be defined as the chronological series of events which logically lead to product failure. An understanding of these events and the causes for them permits elimination of those factors responsible for low achieved reliability.

The Measurement of Reliability. A basic measurement of the probability of the reliability of a product—that is, its probability of survival—is that of mean time between failures. This measurement leads, in turn, to the equally basic product parameter of failure rate for the same system, product, or component.

Much of reliability analysis has been founded on statistical studies to identify, product by product and component by component, distinct patterns of failure versus time during the life cycle of products and components. An increasing amount of such reliability data is becoming available, as a result of studies by manufacturers, research institutes, and other agencies, for use by companies that are considering use of the product. Figure 2-8 illustrates such data.

One pattern, for example, that seems basic for most electronic product systems is shown by Figure 2-9. The life cycle consists of three distinct periods.

The first period is termed the infant mortality period and is caused by early failure of weak components due principally to assignable causes of a non-

**General Electric: Tube Temperature Study on Signal Corps Contract
DA-36-039-SC-72-42524**

Bare-bulb temperature, °C		% survival, 1,000 hours	% survival, 2,000 hours	% survival, 3,000 hours
Type 6005/6AQ5W	220	97	97	97
	237	78	64	
	261	34	19	10
	316	8	3	2
	347	0		
Type 5654/6AK5W	125	92	89	57
	192	72	52	43
	263	33	17	50
	312	9	1	

FIG. 2-8.   Typical Reliability Data.

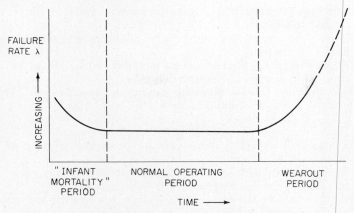

FIG. 2-9.   Common Life Characteristic Curve.

random nature.   This period is typified by a fairly high failure rate which drops off rapidly, perhaps in a period of 100 hours or less.

The second period is typified by a fairly constant rate of failure.   Failures occur in the random manner associated with a constant cause system.

The third period, termed the wear-out period, is one in which the failure rate starts to rise rapidly as the number of survivors approaches zero until all units have failed and no more are left to die.

The reason for establishing these patterns is that when they become known, they permit the application to them of established mathematical probability distributions for measuring and predicting the failure rates of given products and components from sample data.

TOTAL QUALITY CONTROL AND ITS RELIABILITY PROCESS

Because product reliability is one of the more important qualities of the product, it cannot be operationally or systematically separated from other product quality considerations.

As was noted, responsibilities for product quality thread throughout the entire company organization.   This is true for reliability, just as it is for all components of quality, with specific assignments being made to appropriate positions.

Three of the ten subsystems of the quality system will be used as illustrations of how the assurance of reliability results from operation of the system. The are:

1. Preproduction quality evaluation
2. Purchased material quality planning, evaluation, and control
3. Postproduction quality service

Preproduction Quality Evaluation.   This subsystem involves such product reliability activities as:

1. Determining the standard of reliability required by the customer for the product
2. Clearly identifying the environment that the product will encounter
3. Determining the economic balance between reliability and total costs to obtain it
4. Optimizing the design to obtain the required product reliability

    5. Selecting processes and process parameters that contribute to high product reliability

    6. Proving by means of prototype and pilot-run tests that required reliability is attainable

    7. Eliminating from product design and process design, so far as possible, any threats to product reliability

Purchased Material Quality Planning, Evaluation, and Control. This subsystem involves product reliability activities of which the following are examples:

    1. Clear delineation of reliability requirements to vendors

    2. Evaluation of vendors' capabilities for producing products of the required reliability

    3. Evaluation of vendors' product reliability on a continuing basis

    4. Servicing of vendors for product reliability improvement

Postproduction Quality Service. This subsystem involves the following product reliability activities:

    1. Review of guarantees and warranties with respect to product reliability and their equitable adjustment

    2. Reliability evaluations of competitive products

    3. Information flow from factory to field with reference to anticipated reliability problems and corrective action

    4. Information flow from field to factory with reference to reliability problems encountered and corrective action

    5. Certification of product reliability to the customer

    6. Audit of product reliability after shipment, during and after warehousing, after installation, and in use

    7. Reliability maintenance through adequate instructions concerning installation, maintenance, and use; serviceability of product; tools and techniques for repairs; quality cost and timeliness of field service

    8. Measuring of product reliability performance in the field by costs and failure rates

These reliability activities may be grouped under four headings:

    1. Establishing the product reliability requirements

    2. Developing the reliability program to meet the requirements, including product design, manufacturing processes, and transportation

    3. Continuing control of reliability

    4. Continuing reliability analysis

Establishing the Product Reliability Requirements. The initial new design control activity involves establishing the standards for mean time to failure and whatever other reliability targets may be indicated to meet the inherent reliability required for the product. As was discussed, the cost of attaining an incremental increase in reliability must be balanced against the costs associated with not attaining it.

Because this overall balance is of primary interest to the customer, the selected reliability target should be a matter of agreement between the customer (or his representative) and the manufacturer in such areas as industrial products and military equipment. In the case of consumer products, where the customer will not be present at the reliability review, every effort should be made by the manufacturer to represent him as realistically as possible.

The selection of a reliability standard should be a practical matter rather than a speculative exercise. The standard must be chosen with due attention to the state of the technical art and with understanding of what it will take to extend this art beyond current limits. It must be obtainable within economic bounds.

Too often these elements have not been realistically considered when reliability standards have been created, and unrealistic reliability specifications and costs have been the result.

To be meaningful, the reliability targets must be within reach at a planned date.

This means separation of the reliability analysis into two areas:

1. Reliability considerations that can be currently established in relation to current capabilities
2. Considerations that require further analysis, testing, and development before satisfactory data can be considered as established

The reliability specified may thus require further technical advances before it can be attained. To accomplish these advances requires that the greatest effort be placed where it is needed. A careful analysis of the proposed system will reveal the components with the highest failure rates. These should be "split out" of the package for further research and development work.

Required reliability values may ultimately be realized only after the product has been placed in production. Some of the increase in reliability is due to increased skill as a result of the learning process. The major portion, however, is afforded by basic refinements to both product design and process design. This is made possible by sufficient numbers of units and accompanying data on which fundamental decisions can be based for reliability improvement.

Throughout it must be remembered that the objective is to achieve the optimum value for the reliability parameter of product quality rather than to establish any particular special means for this purpose. This means emphasis on simplicity to the extent possible. As an observer has noted, "The present trend toward complexity of missile systems must be reversed before it becomes a limitation. Is it reasonable to expect reliability of an inverted pyramid of four gadgets to cure the bugs in two gadgets which are necessary because the original device was inadequate? How much better to use a simple well-thought-out design in the first place. We fear that many are so confused that they think a clever fix is the equal of good design. Reliability unsupported by crutches, no matter how artistically they are carved, should always be the end in view."

Developing the Reliability Program to Meet the Requirements, including Product Design, Manufacturing Processes, and Transportation. The plan by which the product reliability requirements are to be attained involves the product engineering specification which establishes the system, components, and configuration; the manufacturing process specification by which the product is to be made; the packaging and transportation specifications in which the product will be protected; and the selection of the transportation by which it will be moved to the customer.

Attention is first directed toward determination of product reliability requirements and the design engineering considerations necessary in specifying a product to meet these requirements. It becomes the problem of the design engineer to specify the design, manufactured by a certain process, that will meet certain reliability requirements within the economic limitations involved.

Where does the design engineer start? Usually, the desired product function on which a reliability requirement is placed determines the reliability of the product that is to provide that function. The product, however, is composed of many individual components. Each of these components contributes its share to the reliability of the product.

The design engineer starts by considering the arrangement of components that he must have to provide the supporting functions essential to the overall product function. He then evaluates the reliability of the product on the basis of the individual component reliabilities. If certain individual component reliabilities are unknown, it may be necessary to evaluate them by simulation tests. Where analysis shows certain types of components have a critical effect on the reliability of the product, it may be necessary to alter the design so that less use is made of these critical components. Or it may be necessary to obtain components with a higher reliability or to use components with higher ratings or to provide redundancy in the design.

When the optimum theoretical product design has been created on paper, it is prudent to build a prototype and test it, measuring its performance and thereby determining its reliability. Such tests show up the weak components where additional reliability improvement is required. It is then possible to concentrate on these component types, thereby improving product reliability to the required standard of inherent reliability.

The larger the number of components in a product, the more serious the reliability problem becomes. If a product composed of ten components must have a reliability of 0.90, then the reliability of each component must be approximately 0.99; however, if the product employed 1,000 components, the reliability of each component would have to be 0.9999. When the reliability requirements get this high, an almost unbelievable amount of testing is required. The only practical solution appears to be the designing of products with adequate design margins and the manufacturing of products with satisfactory precision and control.

The important considerations involved in the designing process and related to the product are:

1. Design margin
2. Derating
3. Redundancy

Details of these techniques are now widely available to the quality and reliability engineer.

Continuing Control of Reliability. At the conclusion of preproduction work, the next activity in the reliability program is that of continuing control. The product control job of total quality control includes work in all areas that will affect product reliability: incoming components, process control, transportation, and so forth.

For example, when a manufacturing process is improved and a new standard of reliability is established, it needs to be "pegged" so that there will be no slipping back to old standards.

How can this be accomplished? How can it be determined when the process is slipping? It was shown earlier that variation is inherent in any manufacturing process. How, then, can the difference between a slippage from the newly pegged standard and a normal variation from that standard be determined? This is one of the areas in which the technique of process control engineering contributes to product reliability.

It is possible statistically to determine the limiting values of the pattern that typifies the control state. This is the basis for the control chart. A controlled process is a predictable process, and an uncontrolled process is not predictable; hence, a controlled process is essential to achieving a product with a specific reliability. As has been noted: "A state of statistical control must be the goal of our entire effort—design, production, and testing. This is the only known path to reliability. It is inescapable; it is incontrovertible."

The process control engineer, in endeavoring to bring about a state of control for a process critical to product reliability, should carefully consider the control function served by modern quality information equipment. Especially those processes that are subject to drift due to tool wear, exhaustion of chemicals, temperature effects, and other environmental influences can be automatically adjusted to compensate for such effects and kept in a state of statistical control. Becoming increasingly available are specialized $\overline{X}$, σ computers that can take measurement information, statistically analyze it, and automatically feed back information to adjust the process the amount required to maintain the subject quality characteristic within specified limits.

Measurements of quality characteristics and their analyses by means of control charts or computers detect a change in processing that could have a decided influence on the reliability of the product; however, a process control engineer's responsibility does not end here. What would be the result if some important quality characteristic were completely overlooked and no measurements taken? The only safeguard against such a possibility is actually to measure the end result, specifically the reliability of the product after manufacture. This has to be done on a continuing basis with actual production units to protect against the intrusion of some unknown factor.

Continuing Reliability Analysis. Product reliability is seldom, if ever, a "one-shot" effort. Even in those cases where only a few prototypes are produced as part of a research and development program, intensive study and extensive reliability testing are continuously performed to gain knowledge that can be used for succeeding generations of similar products.

This sustained new design control effort is made to increase reliability in the majority of cases because:

1. State of the art may not yet have advanced to a point where the required reliability has been realized for the product in question.
2. The cost may be excessive because of low reliability and too many premature product failures.
3. Maintenance and repair costs during the expected life of the product may be excessively high.
4. Consequences of product failure may be serious in terms of lost life, property damage, lost income, or inconvenience.
5. Competitive products may be pushing to higher reliability values.
6. Customers may be dissatisfied and may be demanding higher reliability values.

THE COSTS OF QUALITY

A very important feature of a good total quality control program is that better quality and lower costs go hand in hand. Why this is possible is clearly seen as soon as the true character of the three categories of quality costs is considered. These categories are:

1. Failure costs, which are caused by defective materials and products that do not meet company quality specifications. They include such loss elements as rework, scrap, field complaints, and spoilage.
2. Appraisal costs, which include the expenses for maintaining company quality levels by means of formal evaluations of product quality. This involves such cost elements as inspection, test, outside endorsements, and quality audits.
3. Prevention costs, which are for the purpose of keeping defects from occurring in the first place. Included here are such elements as quality control engineering, employee quality training, and the quality maintenance of patterns and tools.

To understand the potency of total quality control, it is important to understand this distinction among failure, appraisal, and prevention costs.

In the absence of formal studies of quality costs in various businesses, it is impossible to generalize about the relative magnitude of these three elements throughout industry. However, it would probably not be far wrong to assume that failure costs may represent about 65 cents out of every quality cost dollar, while appraisal costs probably range in the neighborhood of 25 cents. In many businesses, however, prevention costs probably do not exceed 10 cents out of the total quality cost dollar.

And out of this 10 cents, usually 7 to 9 cents are directed into such traditional channels as pattern and tool maintenance and the specification changing or interpreting work of product engineering. This leaves only 1 or 2 cents of each quality dollar for pure prevention work, or to put it another way, for bona fide quality control engineering technology.

In a nutshell, this cost analysis suggests that we have been spending our quality dollars the wrong way: a fortune down the drain because of product failures; another large sum to support a sort-the-bad-from-the-good appraisal screen to try to keep too many bad products from going to customers; and comparatively nothing for the true defect prevention technology that can do something about reversing the vicious upward cycle of higher quality costs and less reliable product quality.

The fact is that, historically, under the sorting inspection type of quality control function, failure and appraisal expenses have trended upward together, and it has been extremely difficult to pull them down once they have started to rise. The reason is clear.

An unprofitable cycle is at work that operates something like this: the more defects produced, the higher the failure costs. The traditional answer to higher failure costs has been more inspection. This, of course, means a higher appraisal cost.

Now, this tighter inspection screen does not really have much effect in eliminating the defects. Some of the defective products are going to leave the plant and wind up in the hands of complaining customers. Appraisal costs thus stay up as long as failure costs remain high. And the higher these failure and appraisal costs go, the higher they are likely to go without successful preventive activity. So, total quality control's approach is to establish the right amount of prevention to turn this cost cycle downward.

This plainly means an increased expenditure for prevention to bring about reduced failure costs and reduced appraisal costs, with the remainder of quality cost dollars available for profit. The 10 cents out of every dollar that is now being spent for prevention may well need to be doubled, with much of the increase going toward test equipment automation, improved inspection, and quality control engineering. These increases in prevention are financed by a portion of the savings in failure and appraisal cost; they do not represent net long-term additions to total company quality cost.

What actually does happen cost-wise in total quality control should be examined.

First, when prevention costs are increased to pay for the right kind of quality control engineering, a reduction in the number of product defects occurs. This defect reduction means a substantial reduction in failure costs.

Second, the same chain of events takes place with appraisal costs. An increase in prevention costs results in defect reductions which, in turn, have a positive effect on appraisal costs, because defect reduction means a reduced need for routine inspection and test activities.

Finally, when there is an upgrading of quality control equipment, personnel, and practices, an additional reduction in appraisal costs results. Better inspection and test equipment, a general modernization of quality control practices, and the replacement of many routine inspections by less numerous but more effective quality control inspectors and testers have a positive downward pull on the cost of the appraisal function.

The end result is a substantial reduction in the cost of quality and an increase in the level of quality.

No large, long-term personnel increase in the overall quality control function is required. Instead, the amount of quality control expense, as a proportion of total business expense, can be reduced considerably. The personnel mix of the quality control function will, however, change to include a very much higher proportion of quality control engineering professionals and specialists.

ROLE OF THE MANAGER

Many managers have pointed out that the technologies of total quality control provide a strong technical capability that is sufficiently broad and yet specifically oriented to come to grips successfully with major quality problems that the businessman must face and solve. Certainly, truly trouble-free quality, in all its aspects, requires this truly professional quality engineering work throughout the industrial cycle. It requires quality control engineering that becomes an integral part of planning work; process control engineering that brings to bear all the quality and reliability tools to assure trouble-free processes; and quality information equipment engineering that provides the required upgraded equipment for really controlling product quality.

But in a sophisticated marketing and technological environment, the manager cannot fully delegate his quality responsibilities. He must work intimately with these quality control professionals. The manager must devote significant amounts of his personal time and energies to this product quality subject just as he has come to devote time to such other major activities of the business system as marketing and finance.

It is, for example, only the manager who can make the appropriate final decision on what the company quality policy must be both on an overall basis and with respect to specific product offerings. Because quality is an area in which all major functions must be involved, it is only the manager who can give the creative and final direction to major quality programs in the business. It is only the manager who by his leadership and example can inspire and direct the organization with the positive attitudes which alone assure the type of quality impact that his customers wish.

This more intensive and more direct attention to total quality control may be a new role for some managers, but it is one into which more and more managers have been entering with interest and enthusiasm and from whose exercise they and their companies are deriving much benefit. For, although price may sell certain customers the first time and various other kinds of features will impress him, it is quality that keeps the company's customer coming back the second, tenth, and twentieth time. And with the cost of quality amounting to 7 cents or more of the sales dollar, any significant cost improvements that are brought about can have substantial implications for the net income of the business.

Properly understood, properly staffed with the right engineering talent, properly organized, and above all, with sound management leadership, total quality control provides modern business management with tremendous leverage for products that truly yield full customer satisfaction. It helps management orient the enterprise to the highly quality-competitive marketplaces which are one of the important characteristics of modern business operation.

BIBLIOGRAPHY

Control Chart Method of Controlling Quality during Production, American War Standard Z1.3-1942, American Standards Association, New York.

Dodge, Harold, and Harry F. Romig, *Sampling Inspection Tables,* 2d ed., John Wiley & Sons, Inc., New York, 1959, pp. 1–224.

Feigenbaum, A. V., *Total Quality Control—Engineering and Management,* McGraw-Hill Book Company, New York, 1961, pp. 1–627.

Freeman, H. A., Milton Freedman, Frederick Mosteller, and W. Allen Wallis, *Sampling Inspection,* McGraw-Hill Book Company, New York, 1948.

Grant, E. L., *Statistical Quality Control,* 3d ed., McGraw-Hill Book Company, New York, 1964, pp. 1–557.

Guide for Quality Control and Control Chart Method of Analyzing Data, American War Standards Z1.1-1941 and Z1.2-1941, American Standards Association, New York.

Ireson, W. G. (ed.), *Reliability Handbook,* McGraw-Hill Book Company, New York, 1966.

Juran, J. M. (ed.), *Quality Control Handbook,* 2d ed., McGraw-Hill Book Company, New York, 1962, pp. 1–1000.

Lloyd, D. K., and M. Lipow, *Reliability: Management, Methods and Mathematics,* Prentice-Hall, Inc., Englewood Cliffs, N.J., 1962, pp. 1–528.

Quality Program Requirements, MIL-Q-9858A, U.S. Government Printing Office, Washington, D.C., Dec. 16, 1963, pp. 1–9.

Requirements for Reliability Program for Systems and Equipment, MIL-STD-785, U.S. Government Printing Office, Washington, D.C., June 30, 1965.

Sampling Procedures and Tables for Inspection by Attributes, MIL-STD-105D, U.S. Government Printing Office, Washington, D.C., 1963.

Shewhart, W. A., *Economic Control of Quality of Manufactured Product,* D. Van Nostrand Company, Inc., Princeton, N.J., 1931.

CHAPTER THREE

Developing a Quality-minded Work Force

EDWIN S. SHECTER *Manager—Defense Quality Assurance, RCA Corporation, Moorestown, New Jersey*

Consideration must be given in manufacturing to performing work in the most effective manner possible. Industrial engineering approaches and value engineering methodology are designed to determine whether a function needs to be performed and the most effective manner of performing it. The quality cost approach is somewhat different and is designed to subdivide the cost of producing product of satisfactory quality into categories of:
1. Prevention
2. Appraisal
3. Internal failure
4. External failure[1]

The subject of motivation to produce high-quality work falls into the category of prevention.

MOTIVATIONAL APPROACHES

There are two basic kinds of management, termed reductive and facilitative. In the reductive approach, motivation is achieved through the removal of something that the employee has become accustomed to receiving, such as a merit increase, bonuses, or nonfinancial incentives, or in the extreme case, the employee's job itself. A management environment such as this motivates through fear. If the employee does a good job, his incentive is that he gets to keep his job. Studies which have been made of management methods have indicated that this approach does not have a permanent effect. As soon as the motivation is removed, regression begins.

[1] A. V. Feigenbaum, *Total Quality Control,* McGraw-Hill Book Company, New York, 1961.

In the facilitative management approach, something is given to the employee in addition to what he already receives, providing his performance or his group's performance has proved to be outstanding. This method of management is more permanent in nature and is achieved through the development of personal involvement. Its effects are long-lasting and will not regress when the stimulus is removed.

Training and Certification. Indirectly related to motivation, an element which is needed if quality performance is to be achieved, is employee training and certification. The simple fact is that no one can be motivated to do a job properly without the basic skills necessary to do the job. It behooves management, therefore, to produce an adequate training and certification program for the employee. Any training program should include more than the basic skills in its curriculum. It should include reasons for performing a function in a particular way and perhaps some of the technical background. Some time should also be devoted to motivation of the trainee with a view toward establishing a greater degree of involvement on his part. When such a course is offered, the employee invariably improves his quality output and frequently his productivity. Upon completion of any training session, an evaluation of the employee's competence should be reported to him as well as to his supervisor. This evaluation is essentially the difference between training and certification. When an employee passes an examination testing his skill and knowledge, he then becomes certified rather than just trained.

Having achieved the basic skills, the employee must be provided with instruction on how best to do the job on which he is working. In manufacturing, it is necessary for the manufacturing engineer to prepare an instruction on how each task is to be accomplished. With the increase in the labor spent for paperwork and software rather than hardware, instructions must be given for this as well.

The proper tools for performing the job are also mandatory. It is obvious that instruction cannot be given in the training room utilizing one set of tools and equipment without expecting some degradation of performance when the operator is not provided with the same tools when working in the shop. This may seem self-evident, but there have been cases where operators were taught an operation, such as soldering, using a 40-watt soldering iron, and were then asked to perform production operations with a 100-watt soldering iron.

In addition, the attitude of first-line supervision must be correct. If the production supervisor indicates a lack of respect for quality and a high respect for quantity and, further, demands that the operator meet production commitments at all costs, then it will be impossible to achieve high quality.

MOTIVATIONAL PROGRAMS

One of the most popular motivational programs is termed "Zero Defects." This has as its goal the total elimination of operator-caused defects through proper motivation. Thousands of companies throughout the United States and the rest of the world have adopted either a program which they call Zero Defects or one which uses another name but contains the essential elements of the Zero Defects approach. Some of these other terms are: PRIDE, the acronym for Personal Responsibility in Daily Effort or Perfection Requires Identical Defect Elimination; PEP, Personal Excellence Performance: EFP, Error-Free Performance; The Right Way; DRIVE, Do It Right Initially for Value and Effectiveness; and BB, Build Better. Regardless of the name, the object is to do it right the first time.

Professor Abraham Maslow of Brandeis University, in his pyramid of human needs, indicates that there are five basic needs which must be satisfied, shown in the pyramid structure of Figure 3-1. The first of these is the physiological need, the satisfaction of human needs for food and water. This comes before the second need for safety, such as a cave or a shelter, in which the individual can be safe from outside natural environments and other aggressive forces. Once these needs are satisfied, the human seeks satisfaction of social needs through fraternization with other humans.

It is only after these three basic needs are satisfied that the requirement for satisfying the ego needs and self-actualization come into play. The ego is satisfied through public recognition of achievement such as recognition by one's peers, superiors, or subordinates. The self-actualization need is fulfilled only when the individual feels that he himself is making a contribution and has a feeling of self-satisfaction through knowledge that he is doing a good job.

Although there is some aspect of social acceptance involved in motivation, it is primarily in the areas of ego satisfaction and self-actualization that Zero Defects type programs appeal to the individual. The real problem in establishing a motivational program is the identification of specific acts which will prove motivating factors that satisfy the psychological needs of the individual.

The Need for Motivation. One of the major problems confronting management in implementing a Zero Defects program is that making errors is a human trait. Errors are caused by three principal elements.

1. Lack of knowledge
2. Lack of skill
3. Lack of attention

Training, instruction, and experience should take care of the first two elements, but lack of attention must be overcome to a large extent by motivation. It must be recognized first of all that not all defects are caused through human error. Many problems result from manufacturing processes which have excessive material variability or are improperly machine controlled through the inadequacy of machine capability, breakdown, or wear problems. More complex equipment, more sophisticated customer demands, and increased competition place increasing pressures on industry to produce higher quality and more defect-free equipment.

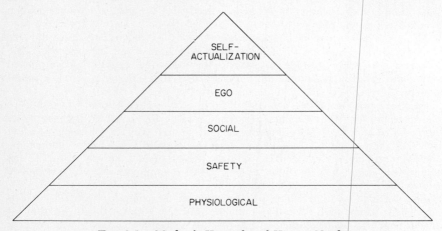

Fig. 3-1. Maslow's Hierarchy of Human Needs.

Quality Control versus Zero Defects. Zero Defects is not a replacement for a quality control program. It is but one element of a quality control program, albeit a very important one. Quality control not only is interested in motivational aspects, but also is involved with the application of statistical methods in such areas as process control, statistical sampling, design of experiments, correlation and regression analyses, and many others. One of the comparisons that can be made is that in a quality control approach, attempts are made to isolate the significant causes. These causes are then worked on by engineering, quality, or manufacturing personnel, or a combination of these, and corrective measures are taken to bring the major problem causes up to standard.

In Zero Defects, similar attempts are made to identify the problem causes. However, emphasis is placed on the areas where problems do not exist, and attempts are made to provide recognition for outstanding performers in such a manner that the remainder of the population strives to achieve the same recognition. It can be seen, then, that to reduce poor performance and raise the overall level of good performance, both methods should be applied simultaneously.

IMPLEMENTATION OF THE ZERO DEFECTS APPROACH

The elements of a Zero Defects program are:
1. Establishing a committee
2. Employee indoctrination
3. Supervisory orientation
4. Pre-kickoff promotions
5. The kickoff
6. Publicity and promotion
7. Employee involvement
   a. Manufacturing
   b. Test
   c. Secretarial and clerical
   d. Engineering
   e. Vendors
8. The measurement system
9. Award system
10. Error cause elimination or error cause identification

The elements of this program in PERT format are shown in Figure 3-2. This identifies events that must be achieved and the time phasing between events and phasing of events.

The approach to establishing a program will vary, depending upon the size of the company and the basic objectives that have been established. The following discussion attempts to establish the tasks that must be accomplished and some recommendations for accomplishing them under varying circumstances.

Establishing a Committee. In establishing a committee to implement a Zero Defects program, the manager must make clear to his staff the company's desire to have a Zero Defects program and should provide for representation from all departments. Individuals who are chosen as members should be creative, articulate, and used to getting things done. Membership on the committee should not be given to just another employee, but rather to one who is a self-starter and is highly motivated.

The department from which the chairman of the committee should come is far less significant than the individual. If, however, a motivational program for all employees is to be implemented, then it is desirable to select someone, if possible, from the department which has a bearing on all functions. For this

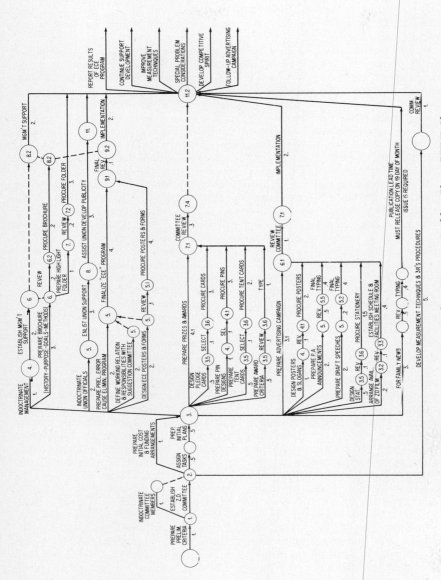

Fig. 3-2. RCA Moorestown Zero Defects Program Buildup Phase PERT Chart.

reason, someone from the quality assurance or personnel department has generally been chosen as chairman of the Zero Defects committee.

The committee must establish a timetable under which it will operate. In addition to the schedule, the elements of the program must be identified, goals must be set, and an approach must be established. Subcommittees should be set up to determine measurement systems, awards and recognition methods, and publicity and promotion.

An effective approach utilized by one major electronics firm is that of the salient interest group concept. This approach recognizes that although the basic factors motivating individuals are the same, the specific items for achieving the basic motivation are different. A female operator working on a production line, for example, responds differently from a scientist in a laboratory. This approach forms the basis for much of the material that follows.

Supervisory Orientation. Obtaining the supervisor's support is a major task that confronts the committee. Many supervisors are themselves not motivated. The most effective way of obtaining supervisory involvement is for top management to address groups of supervisors, explaining the objectives of the program and requesting support. This should be followed with meetings between supervisors and committee members in small groups. No more than six to ten supervisors should meet with either the committee chairman or several of the committee members in an open discussion during which questions can be resolved and support can be solicited. This aspect is probably the single most important element in developing a good program. Supervisors must be made to understand the needs of the company and its obligation in fulfilling these needs. They must also be given some motivating inducement. Supervisory recognition, therefore, must be a part of the total approach. Some companies have found the preparation of a supervisory handbook to be very helpful. In a small firm, letters signed by the president are adequate to satisfy the recognition need.

Gaining Attention. All members of the company must be made to feel that the program is something special and not just another gimmick to speed up production or achieve some other short-range management objective. The benefits that can be obtained can be long-lasting, providing the initial impact is made and the program is sustained properly. One method of launching a program is through a kickoff period. The kickoff is designed to gain employee attention. The general methodology is to start with a series of teaser posters which do not present the entire story but pique the interest of the employees. After a short period, a mass employee meeting is held with appropriate ceremonies, keynote speakers, and other fanfare. This must be properly done, or there will be adverse repercussions from employees. Some people like to see a low-flying airplane towing a banner. More sophisticated, technical people consider this to be an insult to their intelligence. The approach, therefore, must be tailored. It is desirable to do something different. A letter to every employee's home, signed by the general manager, might be one method. A coffee break with free coffee and cake might be another. The approach will depend on the individuals and their backgrounds, the location of the plant, and the amount of money that the company is prepared to spend to initiate the program. It is not necessary to spend a great deal to get started on the right foot.

Union Involvement. Companies which have unions should not start a Zero Defects program without contacting union leadership and securing active support of the program. If the union is overlooked, or if it cannot be convinced that the objectives are in consonance with its own objectives so that it will support the program, the consequences can be disastrous. Enlightened union leadership recognizes that an improved company position will result in increased salaries and wages. If possible, a union representative should be a member of the Zero Defects committee.

Post-kickoff Follow-up. With the program launched, each employee may be given an employee handbook which describes the goals of Zero Defects in somewhat general terms. What remains to be done is to indicate to the employee how he may participate and what is going to happen that is different from what has happened in the past. This involves developing measurement standards which will make it possible to evaluate superior performance and the selection of awards that are appropriate.

Whatever measurement system is established to evaluate individual performance, it must not be so cumbersome that it involves too much additional record keeping. Otherwise, results will merely be a reflection of the time available of the supervisor or the person doing the rating and therefore will not necessarily be a measure of the true performance of the individual. Normal quality control records, when they are maintained on an individual basis, should be adequate for all production functions. The actual records maintained may be determined in advance by a subcommittee or may be submitted for approval by department managers.

Developing an Approach. Zero Defects or motivation should apply to all elements of an organization. Frequently, it is found that production operators are considered to be the ones who are doing the most repetitious job, and assumptions are made that these individuals need additional motivation. In a broad motivational program, however, an attempt must be made to provide this motivation to all elements of the work force. An approach which the author has used successfully is that of the salient interest groups. In this approach, various elements of the work force are subdivided, and each subdivision participates under a separate program. Separate awards, separate measurement criteria, and separate goals are established for each group.

Salient Interest Groups. *Manufacturing.* The best measure of manufacturing department performance is the defect rate that is being experienced. This can be measured in terms of percent defective, defects per 100 units, defects per unit, defects per 100 man-hours, or any other term that relates the number of defects to the actual production rate. The primary problem is to provide a measurement unit in which equal opportunities exist for a defect to occur. When this figure can also be developed in terms of dollars, it is preferable to do so.

If the desire is to recognize individual performance, then records must be maintained on individual operators so that those performing outstandingly good work can be identified. In the event departmental performance is desired, records must be maintained by the department. The programs with which the author has been acquainted have generally utilized both approaches simultaneously.

It is not necessary to establish specific goals, either for individuals or for departments, to accomplish results. In an electrical manufacturing assembly operation where a great deal of hand soldering was done, defect levels were reduced by 80 percent in a period of approximately three years during the time a motivational program was in effect. The initial performance level was very good, and so the improvement was truly significant.

When goals are set, it is preferable to have the group set its own—and this includes the operators. Charting progress on large displays adds interest to the effort. Of course, some appropriate recognition is needed when the goal is achieved.

The awards that can be used in the manufacturing department include an honor roll as a primary item. This can be merely a printed page listing the employee's name and identifying his performance. Inclusion on the honor roll might be for performing defect-free work for a specified time period such as one month or three months. It might be for achieving a low percentage of defective work. The nature of the work being performed determines which type of record can be effectively used.

Supplementing the honor roll, a photograph can be taken of the individual, showing him either at his work station or being congratulated by his supervisor. If this is sent home, with a letter from the vice president or general manager indicating the importance of the employee's contribution to his own future and to the success of the company, his prestige with his family is enhanced (ego need). Family involvement is important, and sending the photograph to the family as a token of appreciation for outstanding performance can be highly rewarding. In addition to the photograph, a token award of the employee's choice can be provided. A typical letter explaining the awards available is shown in Figure 3-3.

Testing. In the testing activity, defects may not be easily measured. A series of evaluations must therefore be applied based on achieving desirable performance. Some of those that may be used are:

1. Attendance record
2. Lateness
3. Error-free test performance
4. Contribution to the suggestion award/error cause identification program
5. Proper completion of test records
6. Keeping work areas clean

Awards in this activity can be similar to those in manufacturing or engineering.

Secretarial and Clerical Program. The large amount of paper utilized by all activities makes the secretarial area one which can be significant in an overall motivational program. One of the difficulties confronting the establishment of a program for secretarial and clerical personnel is that of obtaining a realistic measurement of performance. Most companies do not attempt to set up criteria for letter writing, unless the letter is the output of the company, such as an insurance firm. Other errors, such as in filing, telephoning, and other clerical tasks, are not recorded. Consequently, it is difficult to determine the accuracy of secretarial performance.

An effective way of running a secretarial program involves the establishment of a separate committee composed entirely of secretarial and clerical people. Selecting the committee is crucial to the success of the secretarial program. Those selected must be compatible, able to work together, and willing to try to create a new approach to their jobs. The secretarial committee should decide what approach to take. One of the goals for the program might be the development of a handbook for all secretaries. This handbook might contain helpful hints for the secretary which could assist her in her normal secretarial duties such as filing, typing, making reservations, completing forms, processing forms, and any other daily chores which she may be required to perform. The committee might develop the outline for the book, and secretaries throughout the division might be encouraged to contribute ideas. Token awards might be given for accepted suggestions.

In addition, secretaries may feel that there is a need to identify more with the work being performed in the division. As a result, plant tours might be arranged and small groups of secretarial and clerical operators taken on the tour to see the kind of work being done. They may learn, for example, that

RCA | Defense Electronic Products | Missile and Surface Radar Division
Moorestown, NJ 08057 | Telephone (609) 963-8000

RCA

To:

From: E. S. Shecter

Subject: Zero Defects Award   Date:

Congratulations! You have been selected by supervision in your activity for outstanding performance in the Zero Defects program for the month of

Those in charge of campaign administration wish to add our thanks for your fine efforts. As announced, the monthly winners are to receive one award from the following list:

1. Gold Cross ball-point pen and pencil set
2. Two seat belts (installed)
3. 4000 green stamps
4. A $10.00 Family Store Gift Certificate
5. A textbook (specify title, author, publisher, edition)
6. Subscription to a technical publication
7. Membership in a technical or professional society

Circle the number of your selection, and bring this letter to George Tantum in the Purchasing Department.

_____
E. S. Shecter
Zero Defects Administrator

Items 5, 6, and 7 are limited to $10.00 in value; any cost in excess of $10.00 must be borne by you. For items 5, 6, and 7, provide all necessary information and obtain the signature of your immediate supervisor or leader.

_____   _____
Award winner's signature   Supervisor's approval (if applicable)

FIG. 3-3. Typical Letter Commending Outstanding Performance and Explaining Available Awards.

a harness is a bundle of wires tied together and not something that is used on horses.

The committee may wish to have a periodic award for an outstanding secretary. Because it is costly to establish a measurement system which enables an objective evaluation of all secretaries, it may be decided that the secretary should be identified through recommendations submitted by her supervisor.

A typical evaluation sheet might include the following ratings:

1. Quality of work
2. Quantity of work
3. Attitude toward job

4. Cooperation
5. Reliability
6. Attendance and punctuality
7. Outstanding accomplishments
8. Initiative

The Engineering Department. One of the most difficult areas in which to establish a motivational program has traditionally been the technical or engineering department. One of the difficulties is the inability to establish an objective measurement system. Even more important is the skepticism with which the typical engineer will view a motivational program of this type.

One of the methods that has been used to measure engineering department performance is to record the number of engineering change notices required to correct engineering errors. Although some companies report a high degree of success with this method, others have indicated total dissatisfaction with the approach. Engineers can manage to reduce the number of engineering change notices through methods which bypass the system. Substituting a waiver instead of an engineering change notice, for example, may achieve the same purpose.

Another approach has been to measure engineering performance through design reviews, which in many instances are a normal function within the engineering activity. The design review group can classify engineering performance based upon the review conducted. Recognition can then be given to the engineer or engineers whose designs are outstanding for a given rating period.

A broader and more comprehensive program can be achieved through a separate engineering excellence or technical excellence approach which seeks to measure an individual's performance through achievement in his job function. This, of course, is the supervisor's job anyway, and is really the basis upon which an engineer is evaluated for merit increases. In addition to job performance, other desirable activities may be taken into consideration. For example, participation in professional societies, either in a management capacity or through the presentation of papers, is something that is to be encouraged. Rapid technological advances result in technical obsolescence unless the engineer is encouraged to continue his education in nearby universities. Company courses, and participation in them, are further stimuli to technological advancement.

Publication of technical papers should be encouraged. Patent disclosures are desirable. These activities can be made a portion of an overall measurement system which can be used to select an "Engineer of the Month."

The total selection criteria are as follows:

1. Creativity
2. Technical accomplishment
3. Acceptance and discharge of responsibilities
4. Presentation and subject of technical papers
5. Professional society activities
6. Patent disclosures
7. Identification of new areas of business

An appropriate award is important to provide the engineer additional motivation to strive for achievement of recognition. This may be a key, a plaque, or the presentation by the chief engineer of a desk pen set appropriately engraved. Some awards involve a luncheon with the engineer and his wife and the selection of a technical publication or a subscription to a technical magazine of his choice.

A Vendor Program. An overall Zero Defects program must involve the company's suppliers. The measurement here should be tied into the vendor rating program which may be in effect. In the absence of such a program, vendors must be classified with respect to quality, deliveries, service, and price. Each of these factors provides some measure of vendor excellence. Because the interest is generally in the area of quality and delivery as an adjunct to price, these two factors must particularly be evaluated.

A vendor whose performance has been outstanding for a prolonged period of time can be recognized through the presentation of a certificate of achievement. This provides the supplier with certain benefits which he normally seeks. These are:

1. He can advertise that he is a preferred supplier of the company.
2. He can use this preferential status to expand his business with the company, providing, of course, that his product is competitively priced.

It is often desirable to recognize outstanding performers and publicize this recognition so that other suppliers will attempt to achieve the same recognition. One approach that has been used successfully is to have a poster or a plaque in the lobby recognizing the supplier or suppliers who have been outstanding. This will stimulate interest on the part of other salesmen to see that their companies get added to the list.

The Award System. Awards are an important part of the program. Zero Defects or motivational programs cannot generally afford to issue significantly large awards on a prolonged basis. The objectives of the awards program should be to provide recognition to the individual or group who has earned the award and thereby establish a sense of pride in performance. In addition, the award can be used as a source of internal and external publicity. Such things as public address announcements, publications in the company paper, publications in local paper or national magazines, and involvement of the family through letters home should be utilized to the maximum extent. The point is that the value of the award is not as important as the recognition afforded to the people receiving the award.

The Error Cause Elimination or Error Cause Identification System. Many companies already have employee suggestion programs which result in monetary awards keyed to the value of the suggestion. When attempts have been made to establish a separate ECI (error cause identification) committee to evaluate error cause submissions, the amount of effort involved becomes quite large, and a total duplication of the suggestion evaluation group often results. It is desirable, therefore, to utilize what already exists and perhaps provide some supplementary support to handle the additional work load of ECI's.

The basic difference between an ECI and a suggestion is that the ECI does not contain a recommendation for correction, but merely identifies a possible source for errors.

It is essential that a prompt response in the form of a thank you note (perhaps accompanied by a small token award) be given upon receipt of an ECI. Subsequent evaluation of the ECI's as a group should be used to select the best ones for a specific period of time. Once again, an award for the oustanding ECI should be given.

RESULTS OF A MOTIVATIONAL PROGRAM.

The principal result that should be established as an objective for the motivational program is the development of a work force which feels that it is a participative group in the overall operation of the company. This will result in a major contribution, not only to productivity, but also to the productivity of defect-free products, which will enhance profits for the company. Defect levels experienced in most operations, regardless of whether they are software or hardware oriented, can invariably be reduced.

Quality control, through the isolation of major defect causes, helps direct attention to areas needing corrective measures. Many times, correction is considered to be a resolution of the immediate problem, allowing the basic cause to go undetected. The result is that the problem recurs. True solutions to problems lie in the identification of the causative system and the application of corrective measures to this underlying system. A properly motivated work force will assist management in identifying these problems and will be responsive to needed systems changes. The result is higher yield, greater ability to meet schedules, and less time spent repeating functions that have already been performed.

Many companies have indicated that the return on investment in a motivation program has been in the order of 10 to 1. An additional return is realized from reduction in employee turnover and the attraction of highly competent individuals.

Getting management involved in the motivational program, through its participation in award ceremonies and recognition of individuals, helps break down some of the barriers unknowingly created by management's seemingly greater attention to other problems.

Still another result that can be achieved is the reduction of customer complaints and the enhancement of the sales image of the product lines of the company. Products which contain defects when entering final stages of inspection and test will invariably contain some degree of defectiveness upon leaving the final inspection. Studies have shown that inspection efficiency, which is defined as the ability to detect a defect when one exists, can vary between 20 and 90 percent, depending upon the product line, the inspector's ability, the classification of defects, the inspection area, and many other factors. Products which may contain 10 percent defective material when entering inspection may therefore contain anywhere between 1 and 8 percent defective material after inspection. A Zero Defects program can help to eliminate this or reduce it to a minimum.

Another benefit comes from the reduction of potential product liability claims. In Cook County, Illinois, product liability judgments increased since 1960 from \$4,211 to \$906,640 in 1966,[2] including one award of \$725,000. When considering this fact, the need for "perfect" quality becomes even more important. Judgments are increasingly against the original manufacturer rather than the distributor or retailer or even the manufacturer who integrated a product from one of his suppliers into a product of his own.

The Employee Reaction. The employee frequently thinks of big business as having a bottomless pit containing money which can subsidize all his mistakes. He frequently looks upon management as "them," and feels that "they" do not have his interests at heart. This is quite the contrary to actual practice because management realizes that good employees are the key to corporate success.

A properly conceived Zero Defects program can help overcome the feeling that management does not care. The program does not necessarily have to conform exactly to the approach discussed in this chapter as long as it involves the employees in the solution of company problems. An innovation in Japan,

[2] *Quality Assurance Magazine,* article by Robert J. Scott, June, 1968, pp. 40–42.

called the QC Circle,[3] has sought to overcome the problem of a lack of contribution by the employee. The principle involved is the establishment of small teams of workers consisting of two to four individuals, who, in addition to their regular jobs, perform a problem solving function. Three operators may get together to find out why wrong parts are being inserted in an assembly, and in this way, they can apply more of their human capabilities and in a sense achieve a greater satisfaction through performance.

Another discussion[4] centered around the motivation of maintenance mechanics involved on a high-speed operation with lengthy setup time. To reduce this setup time, operators and setup men were asked to make recommendations regarding ways in which the operation could be improved. In a weekend meeting at a resort hotel, approximately half the recommendations were agreed upon by the maintenance personnel attending. Adoption of the recommendations reduced the setup time by more than 50 percent and resulted in a direct saving to the company of over $250,000 per year.

CONCLUSION

A properly conceived motivation program will benefit management in terms of increased sales, higher profits, and fewer headaches. It will benefit the employee, because he receives the recognition he needs to satisfy his human needs. He will also be employed in a company where job security and job opportunity are maximized. The consumer will benefit through the availability of better quality products.

BIBLIOGRAPHY

Argyris, Chris, "We Must Make Work Worthwhile," *Life,* May 5, 1967.
Buchanan, P. C., *The Leader Looks at Motivation,* Leadership Resources, Inc., Washington, D.C., 1961.
Drucker, Peter F., *Managing for Results,* Harper & Row, Publishers, Incorporated, New York, 1964.
Gellerman, Saul W., *Motivation and Productivity,* American Management Association, New York, 1963.
A Guide to Zero Defects, Department of Defense Quality and Reliability Assurance Handbook no. 4115.12H, Washington, D.C., November, 1965.
Haas, A. R., "The Superior Craftsmanship Program," *Industrial Quality Control,* June, 1966, pp. 665–669.
Halpin, James F., "Zero Defects in Retrospect," *Industrial Quality Control,* June, 1966, pp. 669–682.
Likert, Rensis, *New Patterns of Management,* John Wiley & Sons, Inc., New York, 1961.
Maslow, Abraham H., *Motivation and Personality,* Harper & Row, Publishers, Incorporated, New York, 1954.
Myers, M. Scott, "Who Are Your Motivated Workers?" *Harvard Business Review,* January–February, 1966.
Quality Motivation Workbook, American Society for Quality Control, Milwaukee, Wis., May, 1967.
Rook, L. W., "ZD—Momentary or Momentous," *Quality Assurance,* October, 1965.

[3] J. M. Juran, "The QC Circle Phenomenon," *Industrial Quality Control,* vol. XXIII, January, 1967, pp. 329–336.

[4] 1967 Rutgers Conference—American Society for Quality Control Keynote Speech.

CHAPTER FOUR

Materials Management

PHILIP A. LINK   *Production Control Manager, Automatic Electric Company, Northlake, Illinois*

Materials management has been practiced in various forms since the inception of manufacturing. With the growth of specialized functions in corporate organization, increases in departmental efficiencies have been partially offset by increasing difficulties in communication and dispersion of effort.

Functional self-centeredness tends to create stumbling blocks in the path of cost reduction when crossing departmental lines. As an example, in the determination of an economic lot size for a purchased item, the purchasing agent rightly wants to purchase a quantity of sufficient size to take advantage of a vendor's price break. But the inventory controller objects because of the resulting lower turnover. The stores department may object because the larger lot exceeds space limitations. Production planning may not want to take on added responsibility for long-term commitments to vendors. Likewise, each of the other interested departments may develop separate objections to protect its particular position.

It is possible to have the advantage of the higher efficiencies of specialized functions and gain further improvements through integration of those functions under centralized direction.

This chapter describes the concept and purpose of materials management to help the manufacturing manager determine to what degree this concept can and should be applied in his own company.

DEFINITION

"Materials management is a term to describe the grouping of management functions related to the complete cycle of material flow, from the purchase and internal control of production materials to the planning and control of work in process, to the warehousing, shipping, and distribution of the finished product. It differs from materials control in that the latter term, traditionally, is limited to the internal control of production materials."[1]

CONCEPT

From the definition, it is apparent that materials management is an organizational concept that the control of material costs is an interdepartmental responsibility. "The concept arose from the idea that there are only four key areas to control in manufacturing: men, machines, money, and materials. Logically, then, all the material-related functions—purchasing, production and inventory control, material handling, packaging, traffic, and distribution—should report to a single manager. In this way, the natural conflicts between these departments, each trying to maximize its own performance, could be resolved at one point. The optimum solutions thus arrived at would take account of the company-wide impact of each decision."[2]

Materials management is a vital concept which can result in cost reduction and improved performance in a manufacturing organization when it is understood and properly carried out. It is a concept that must be built into the philosophy of the company and its organization.

PURPOSE OF MATERIALS MANAGEMENT

Why do companies introduce materials management? There is one basic goal: to maximize profits and minimize costs. Centralization of authority and responsibility brings all people with responsibility for materials together under common direction. The most immediate and obvious result is in improved communications. The effect is to reduce finger pointing or buck-passing to transfer blame for parts shortages, missing materials, and late deliveries. Obstacles to change from entrenched functional positions are reduced and can be overcome when departments report to the same boss. Interdepartmental frictions diminish, and cooperation becomes a more normal relationship.

Sometimes the reason is to concentrate control of materials in a single executive as a basic profit center when going through a conversion from centralized to decentralized management. At other times, a materials manager is put in to carry the load for inexperienced subordinates. Some companies have corporate or divisional materials managers for the obvious benefit of obtaining information on the critical areas of dispersed or branch plants. Headquarters can quickly find out about problem areas and assess the managers of the various functions. Other reasons are generally related to problems concerning systems, inventory, cost control, computerization, and cooperation.

IMPORTANCE OF MATERIALS MANAGEMENT

Materials are commonly the largest cost going into finished goods. *Purchasing Week*[3] reports that materials account for 52 percent of the product cost in the average company, and in some cases may be as high as 85 percent. The investment in inventories of materials is typically some one-third of a company's assets.

[1] *APICS Dictionary*, 2d ed., American Production and Inventory Control Society, Washington, D.C., 1966.

[2] *Factory*, McGraw-Hill Publications, New York, December, 1967; name changed to *Modern Manufacturing* with June, 1968, issue.

[3] *Purchasing Week*, McGraw-Hill Publications, New York.

Potentials for savings are enormous. One company reports annual savings in the cost of purchased materials amounting to 5 percent of its total expenditures (saving more than a million dollars annually) since adopting integrated materials management. Some other areas for potential savings are in reduction in number of stock-outs, fewer missed deliveries, reduction in number of orders issued, and reduction in transportation costs.

ORGANIZATION

Divided versus Centralized Management. In most companies, organizational arrangements are the result of evolutionary development, accepted industry practices, or the impact of strong individuals. Even in so-called traditional organizational structures, minor variations are commonplace. The emergence of the materials management concept as an integrated professional management approach is a development resulting from recognition of the problems created by divided or dispersed functions and responsibilities in the control of materials.

Figure 4-1 illustrates one of many possible vertical organizational arrangements showng decentralized management of materials. Although there are numerous variations to the basic structure portrayed, it typifies the chain of command with divided responsibilities for the flow of materials. Planning and ordering, under the production control manager, initiate requirements to be purchased and transported under fiscal control and delivered to the receiving–stores–material handling group under the plant superintendent. Control of material in process is under the production control manager and passes on to shipping under the superintendent. In transit, the traffic manager has responsibility as a part of the fiscal organization, and it is then transferred to marketing for warehousing and distribution. Under this arrangement, the majority of functions are under the vice president of manufacturing but divided between two organizations.

The organizational arrangement of the materials management concept is illustrated in Figure 4-2. Functional responsibility has been separated from various management spheres of influence and joined under one head. This horizontal approach ties together all the operations involved in the planning, procurement, handling, and movement of materials under one manager, reporting to the manufacturing head of the division or company. Some variations in departmental structuring will occur, mainly related to company size. Thus production and inventory control may be considered as one department. Likewise, the four functions of receiving, stores, material handling, and shipping may be combined in various ways, as for instance, in one department under the title, "Plant Materials Department."

Place of Materials Management in the Company. There are usually more compelling reasons for centering materials management under the head of manufacturing, regardless of his title, than in any other area of top management. It should, however, be thought of as a flexible concept and modified to fit the needs and conditions of the company. In process industries where little labor is added to the raw material to produce the product, the cost of materials may be as much as 85 percent of product cost. Here financial consideration may be greater than manufacturing responsibilities, and the materials manager may report to the company president. In the concept that materials is one of the four key areas to control in manufacturing, the materials manager is placed at staff level, reporting directly to the company president as shown in Figure 4-3.

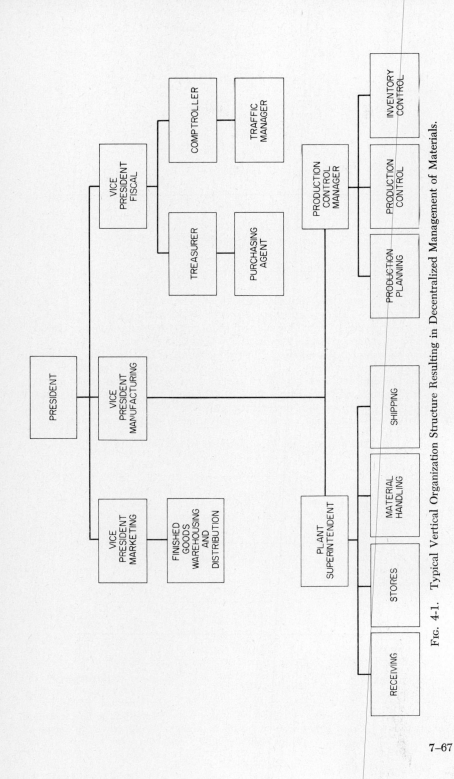

FIG. 4-1. Typical Vertical Organization Structure Resulting in Decentralized Management of Materials.

7–67

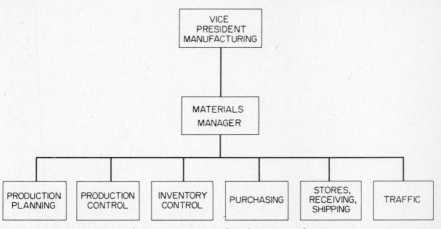

FIG. 4-2. Organizational Arrangement under the Materials Management Concept.

In branch plants, the materials manager will most likely report to the branch manager. Such corporate decentralization may be tied together by having a corporate materials manager, reporting to the company president, with functional authority over the branch materials managers.

Interrelationship of Departments. *Manufacturing.* The flow of materials into and out of manufacturing is vital to the operations of the company. This close relationship requires maximum cooperation between materials management and manufacturing. Every stock-out[4] creates a potential manufacturing problem, but each is the direct responsibility of materials management. Work in process takes place under the direction of shop supervision but ac-

[4] Defined as, "The lack of materials or products which are normally expected to be on hand in stores or stock." *APICS Dictionary, op. cit.*

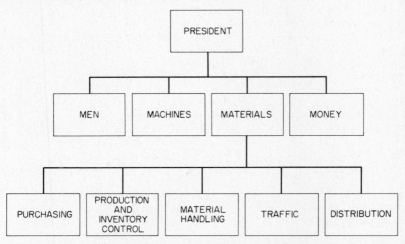

FIG. 4-3. Typical Reporting Arrangement When Material Cost Is a Large Part of Product Cost. [*By special permission of* Modern Manufacturing (*formerly* Factory), *December, 1967. Copyright by McGraw-Hill, Inc.*]

cording to the production plan, schedules, shop orders, and material requisitions prepared by production planning and control.

Marketing. Marketing looks to production planning for effective conversion of the sales forecast into a production plan, then to production control for delivery promises and follow-up. Warehousing and shipping of finished products to support sales with a satisfactory level of service can be an effective competitive tool for marketing.

Engineering. Engineering precedes the beginning of the manufacturing process. Timeliness of engineering releases, engineering changes, preordering information, technical assistance, aid in vendor qualification, and similar initiating and supporting activities tie materials management functions in all their phases closely to engineering.

Finance. The capital to be invested in inventory must be provided by the financial function. It therefore always shows a continuing interest in expenditures for materials, the movement of materials as expressed in turnover, and shipments which bring a return in receivables, earnings, and profits. The accounting and auditing departments of the finance organization are integrally involved with most materials management activities. They audit and approve vendors selected by purchasing, audit and pay invoices, and furnish a variety of reports on purchases. Budgeting looks to production planning for forecasts of labor and production levels. Accounting directs and supervises the periodic taking of physical inventory and provides regular inventory reports. Payroll and production records stem from common or interrelated source documents to the extent that changes in procedures and practice must be jointly agreed upon before implementation. This interrelationship is sometimes so inseparable that joint responsibility is assumed.

Top Management. Having entrusted responsibility for expenditures of proportionately large amounts of money to materials management, top management is always concerned that adequate controls exist and are exercised to protect its investment. It also looks to production control, as the nerve center of manufacturing, for timely and meaningful reports on the status of production. Production planning, working with marketing, engineering, manufacturing, personnel, and finance, provides top management with short- and long-term production plans for evaluation and adoption.

Other Departments. Such departments as personnel, research and development, legal, advertising, public relations, labor relations, and quality control have varying relationships with materials management depending upon the type of business, the industrial climate, management characteristics, and numerous other factors, but generally are not as closely related to materials management as those discussed in the paragraphs above.

Organizing for Materials Management. In setting up any new management arrangement, the action to be taken depends upon the conditions which exist and the ultimate goal. The first step is to take a look at the present manner in which the functions are being carried out and where they are placed in the organization, and then to make a study of the system from initial planning to final shipment.

The next step is to determine the objectives, plan the moves to be made, and establish an approximate timetable of events. If there is a clean-cut separation of functions, the task is simplified. It may only be necessary to select and appoint the materials manager and announce the new organizational arrangement. Conversely, if functions are mixed, untangling those functions will become the first problem to be solved. Usually, purchasing exists as a well-defined and separate function. Receiving, stores, and shipping will also probably be well established as separate departments and may already be under one head. But there are problems if receiving is under the purchasing agent, stores under the plant superintendent, and shipping under the sales manager.

If there is no well-defined department in each case and if the activities are spread throughout a vertical organization, some preliminary steps must be taken. If, for instance, each department does its own purchasing, the first step in organizing for materials management would obviously be to gather all purchasing activities into a single purchasing department. Likewise, if each production department has its individual stockroom under the jurisdiction of the production foreman, control of all the stockrooms must be brought together under one head.

Once the various activities of materials management are organized into identifiable and specialized functions, even though some are combined in the smaller companies, work should begin on an integrated system. Paperwork flow, standardized forms, common use of the same source data, definition of duties and responsibilities to prevent overlapping and duplication of work, procedures, and similar groundwork should be accomplished upon which to build the total system.

Staffing the organization starts with clearly defined and understood requirements for each job, either with or without job descriptions but with some form of job evaluation. Selection may then be made by reshuffling existing personnel, with or without the infusion of new talent.

The final step is to bring about coordination of the major functions. This will depend almost entirely upon the materials manager and the backing he receives from top management. Here his talent as an organizer, leader, and administrator will be called upon, and the final outcome will be largely a measure of his success in bringing together all elements of his organization to work as a team toward common goals.

Characteristics of the Materials Manager. Development or adoption of the materials management concept has been hindered in many companies by the controversy over who is best qualified to be the materials manager. A general specification should call for a man with experience in production planning and control, preferably involving electronic data processing. He should also have experience in purchasing raw materials, parts, and related equipment. If he does not have direct experience in supervising material handling, receiving, stores, shipping, and traffic, he should at least demonstrate sound familiarity with these functions.

The manager should have successful managerial experience with wide responsibilities, coupled with actual experience in handling or supervising activities in these areas. Personal characteristics should include skill in planning for both economical production and customer delivery requirements and the ability to direct a range of functions from complicated paper planning to practical stock handling. He should be capable of exercising initiative in administrating activities involving great detail without losing his perspective or overall control. A degree in business administration or business management would be most appropriate, but depending upon work experience, a degree in engineering, mathematics, economics, or liberal arts could be acceptable.

According to a survey by *Factory* magazine, in practice, about half the materials managers rose via the purchasing route.[5] Production and inven-

[5] Gregory V. Schultz, *Factory*, McGraw-Hill Publications, New York, December, 1967; name changed to *Modern Manufacturing* with June, 1968, issue.

tory control managers ran second but showed increasing success as the business grew in complexity and computerization. Others came from the ranks of traffic, quality control, systems, production, and merchandising. Few rose from beginnings in industrial engineering, material handling, or warehousing.

FUNCTIONS

When identifying or describing the functions of materials control, the impression is created that these are distinct and separate tasks. It is usually true in large companies, but in the smaller companies they may be found combined with one another or with other seemingly unrelated activities. For purposes of clarity, the principal functions are described here with a brief explanation of how each works.

Planning. The philosophy of planning is to perpetuate the goals of the company. Production planning is the first step in materials control. It is defined as: "The function of setting the limits or levels of manufacturing operations in the future, consideration being given to sales forecasts and the requirements and availability of men, machines, materials, and money."[6] Because the planning activity in a company deals with the future, planning starts with the sales forecast, and through various techniques, adjusts the forecast to actual conditions. Once levels of production are established and approved by top management, materials requirements can be worked out in terms of amount and time.

The essential elements of planning are (1) a forecast giving timed requirements, and (2) a knowledge of capacity in terms of labor, machines and equipment, space, and time required to change capacity. Ideally, a planning committee representing sales, engineering, and planning should prepare data for top management decision on levels of production which will balance service against cost. More effort should go into the planning than the execution of the production schedule. Good planning can minimize fluctuations in employment levels and permit maximum utilization of the plant within company policy. (See Section 3, Chapter 5.)

Some of the planning department functions are:

1. Prepares data for top management decision on level of plant activity
2. Forecasts load from three to twelve months in advance
3. Loads shop to planned capacity
4. Makes long-range projections to anticipate increases or decreases in load
5. Adjusts for peaks and valleys in load by varying the production level, inventory level, and delivery interval to the customer
6. Forecasts materials requirements
7. Provides statistical information for all production needs
8. Issues manning tables
9. Analyzes inventory continuously in relation to plan

Production Control. The purpose of production control is to translate the production plan, broadly outlined by the planning department, into action by preparing and issuing orders and schedules. "The function of production control is to direct or regulate the orderly movement of goods through the entire manufacturing cycle from the requisitioning of raw material to the

---

[6] *APICS Dictionary, op. cit.*

delivery of the finished product to meet the objectives of customer service, minimum inventory investment, and maximum manufacturing efficiency."[7]

Manufacturing orders prepared by production control constitute a work authorization which tells the foreman what to make, how much to make, and when to make it. After preparation, manufacturing orders are sent to the scheduler for scheduling and shop loading in accordance with the overall production plan. When issued, the order is a release against capacity to start the production cycle and becomes the basic document for control.

Work is dispatched to workers in the shop according to manufacturing orders and schedules. This production control activity implements the planning, ordering, and scheduling that have gone on beforehand. The dispatcher is the principal source of feedback or flow of information back into the control system, so that actual performance can be compared with planned performance. Progress reporting, generally initiated by the dispatcher, keeps interested supervision informed on a regular periodic basis of production activity.

Finally, expediting as an important element of production control deals with the many variables which upset plans or require quick action. Expediting of orders behind schedule, follow-up on parts shortages, special handling of rush orders, implementation of engineering changes, and similar corrective actions pick up the loose ends to complete the production control function. (See Section 3, Chapter 5.)

Inventory Control. There should be a systematic procedure for ensuring the availability of items necessary to meet production requirements at optimum cost. The technique is called inventory control. The overall limits for control are established by management as, for instance, in deciding levels of production. Then work-in-process inventory is governed by scheduling to those levels. Within that framework, the amount of in-process inventory is determined by the manufacturing interval, size of work banks, and performance to schedule.

Stocking levels to support a rate of production should also be established by management policy. Such policies are expressed by specifying the desired turnover rate, the cost of carrying inventory, the use of an economic lot size formula, the desired service level, the extent to which inventory should be used to balance fluctuations in sales, what constitutes surplus and its disposition, and similar basic directions. Then rules, procedures, and practices will determine the amount and distribution of inventory in the stockroom.

Stock items occupy most of the inventory controller's attention because of the many variables and risks which are involved in making ordering and scheduling decisions. Many techniques have been developed to assist him as discussed in Chapter 7 of this section. The basic concepts involve two decisions which must be made when reviewing the stock position of an item: (1) when to order, and (2) how much to order. In most systems, the point at which to order is established as the time when the quantity on hand will last until the replacement material is received. The real problem in this simple solution is to predetermine how much material will be used during the manufacturing or procurement interval. This makes accurate forecasts an important element in inventory control.

Purchasing. Procurement of materials and components of desired quality in time to meet production requirements and at the lowest ultimate cost is the objective of purchasing. Requirements which originate in inventory control

---

[7] *APICS Dictionary, op. cit.*

are sent to purchasing in the form of requisitions where the first task becomes the selection of vendors. Evaluation of vendors may be the exclusive prerogative of purchasing or may be a joint responsibility with engineering, accounting, quality control, and others.

Purchase orders are placed on the basis of competitive bids or negotiated arrangements according to the item and circumstances. This activity is the center of interest because success or failure in accomplishing purchasing objectives is decided at this point. It is possible to achieve substantial savings in the cost of purchases by adjusting quantities to take advantage of price breaks, gaining approval on material substitutions, and making long-term commitments. (See Chapter 5 of this section.)

An example is the purchasing agent who started a cost reduction program by asking inventory control for a list of all purchased items in their A category under the ABC inventory distribution.[8] The comparatively small number of items which represented a large majority of annual purchases proved a gold mine. Careful analysis of usage, ordering patterns, forecasts, and individual characteristics laid the foundation for new negotiations. In some cases, a change in lot size was sufficient to provide an advantage. In others, long-term commitments enabled suppliers to effect cost reductions which were passed on in their quotations. The result: a 5 percent reduction in the cost of purchased goods.

Receiving, Stores, Material Handling, Shipping. It is common practice to group the receiving, stores, material handling, and shipping functions under one heading because all involve the physical handling of materials. Receiving accepts delivery of purchased materials, identifies with the appropriate purchase order, verifies that the item is correct and suitable, counts, reports receipt to purchasing and accounting, and routes to stores or using department according to directions on the order. (See Section 10, Chapter 8.)

Stores, or stockroom, receives materials and parts from manufacturing and receiving for storage until needed. Items are identified, counted, put away in a storage location, indexed, and reported to inventory control and accounting. Upon receipt of requisitions from production control or shop, items are located, counted, identified, routed to the using department, and reported to inventory control and accounting. (See Section 10, Chapter 7.)

Shipping receives products or parts from manufacturing or stores, identifies with the proper shipping order, packages or packs, labels, and loads onto vehicles for transportation to customers. It prepares shipping documents such as packing lists, bills of lading, and waybills, which are forwarded with the shipment. Copies are held as records for internal use. Shipping also reports each shipment to accounting for billing and inventory purposes, to sales for order closing or customer notification, and to production and inventory control for record purposes. (See Section 10, Chapter 10.)

Material handling, when separated as a function, is responsible for in-plant trucking; care, storage, and control of shop containers; and where branch plants exist, for interplant transportation. One effective arrangement is to have all counting of production output under material handling as a neutral party in incentive payment plans.

The reporting function of this combined group has special interest for materials management, because all systems and controls are dependent upon

---

8 H. F. Dickie, *"ABC Inventory Analysis Shoots for Dollars," Factory,* McGraw-Hill Publications, New York, July, 1951; name changed to *Modern Manufacturing* with June, 1968, issue.

their record accuracy. Timeliness in reporting is often critical and will directly affect expediting effort. Loss or damage of items difficult to replace can seriously affect production performance.

Traffic. Traffic is included in materials management as a control over the transportation costs of inbound shipments of purchased materials and outbound shipments of finished products. These costs are controlled through the administration of freight rates, classification ratings, routings, packaging, containerization, consolidation of shipments, and auditing of shipping practices.

Decision areas which properly belong to traffic concern the selection of carriers, whether contract, private, or common, and the use of purchased versus rented vehicles or equipment. On export shipments, traffic arranges for shipping space either directly with the transportation line or through brokers. Export papers and customs clearance will also fall in the province of traffic.

ADVANTAGES OF MATERIALS MANAGEMENT

Improvement in Communications. The most immediate and obvious advantage obtained through materials management is an improvement in communications. This improvement is mostly between the integrated functions, but other departments also find it easier to deal with a single head on materials problems than to work through various elements of a vertical organization.

Centralization of Authority and Responsibility. Under a single manager, all the people in the unit are brought together under common direction for control of materials. Resistance to change and the natural desire to protect functional positions can be overcome through forced coordination. Cooperation between departments improves, and a more smoothly functioning organization results.

Reduction of Material Costs. The basic goal to maximize profits and minimize costs is achieved in greater degree through reduction in material costs than in any other area. This is accomplished through the elimination of duplication of effort, reduction in inventory investment, and reduction in operating costs as in the handling, packaging, and transportation of materials. Reduction in the cost of materials through opportunities for better purchasing is frequently the most impressive. By taking advantage of price breaks, entering into long-term commitments, obtaining shorter lead times, and obtaining material substitutions, purchasing can make a major contribution to cost reduction. In manufacturing, improved runs because of better lot sizes, greater assurance of availability of materials when needed, less fluctuation in work loads, and shorter production cycles result in lower production costs.

DIFFICULTIES AND DISADVANTAGES

Not a Panacea. There is no substitute for qualified managers. If the materials management concept is adopted to solve problems caused by poor management in the hope that it will bring order out of chaos, it can only succeed if the management problems are first resolved. No system can compensate adequately for improperly led and trained people. If the concept is accepted blindly, it can create personnel problems, particularly with the strong, ambitious contenders who find themselves second best in the new organizational arrangement.

May Result in New Frictions. Although cooperation and communications are improved within the integrated materials management organization, the other elements in the company that were required to give up functions may carry deep and lasting resentment which will be expressed in continual friction.

Possibility of Overemphasis. Most of the spectacular results claimed for materials management have been in purchasing and inventories. These results are usually due to an improvement in doing things the way they have always been done, rather than in doing them differently. Achievement of cost reduction through the creation of a total systems environment in a company-wide approach has been elusive. A number of companies have found their biggest savings in the first few years, after which a leveling off takes place.

MEASURING PERFORMANCE

Evaluation of any function depends upon the point of view. There are, however, some generally accepted approaches in appraising effectiveness. As an example, inventory turnover is a commonly used index of inventory management. Although there is and may always be controversy over the use of this ratio of inventory investment to value of annual usage, it is extremely useful if understood and properly used.

Perhaps one of the most useful devices in attempting to evaluate an activity is a checklist. A checklist will suggest an approach, stimulate thinking, and open up avenues for further questioning or investigation. It is easiest to use when answers can be given objectively in numerical form as quantities, ratios, or percentages. Subjective answers, while requiring interpretation or some means of comparison, possess the same values of stimulation and investigation.

Although a checklist can be made extremely detailed if a searching inquiry is intended, for an overall audit of materials management, the following simplified version may be satisfactory.

Planning

1. Is there a regular sales forecast?
2. How frequently are production levels reviewed:
    a. At calendar intervals?
    b. At each change in forecast?
    c. At time of each production release?
3. Is plant capacity established in terms of:
    a. Labor?
    b. Machines and equipment?
    c. Space?
    d. Time required to increase or decrease?
4. Does planning adjust for peaks and valleys in sales to level factory loads?
5. Does planning make long-range projections?
    a. Two years?
    b. Five years?

Producion Control

1. Are schedules made:
    a. According to the production plan?
    b. To obtain all possible labor efficiency?
    c. To minimize setup costs?
    d. Based upon known manufacturing intervals?
    e. To make allowances for rush orders?

2. Is work dispatched to employees according to schedules?
3. Is expediting organized:
    a. Less than 5 percent of orders expedited?
4. Is feedback of information from the shop:
    a. Factual?
    b. Current?
    c. Comparative: performance versus plan?
5. Are regular reports issued on departmental production performance:
    a. Showing amount of work ahead or behind schedule?
    b. Age of past-due work?

Inventory Control

1. Are inventory levels established by:
    a. Executive opinion?
    b. Historical precedence?
    c. Mathematical methods?
    d. The stock record analyst?
    e. Financial limitations?
2. Are there clearly established and understood policies on:
    a. Authorized maximums and minimums?
    b. Service level (percent)?
    c. Safety stocks?
    d. Surplus and obsolete classifications?
    e. Inventory stages or banks?
    f. Use of inventory to level factory loads?
3. How much money is invested in inventory?
    a. More or less than a year ago?
    b. At the desired turnover?
4. Are inventory control records adequate and accurate?
    a. Stock-outs and in-stock figures?
    b. Adjustments after physical inventory satisfactory?

Purchasing

1. Is there a policy on competitive bidding by:
    a. Type of item or commodity?
    b. Number of bids for each inquiry?
    c. Value of purchase?
2. Is a vendor determined to be an acceptable source by:
    a. Reputation?
    b. Buyer's judgment?
    c. Credit investigation or financial rating?
    d. Vendor qualification team?
    e. Inquiring of his customers?
3. Is a record kept and are reports made on savings:
    a. At regular intervals?
    b. Only when obtained?
    c. By buyer, purchasing agent, or group?
    d. By manner in which it was obtained?
        (Price break, negotiation, value analysis, and the like.)
4. Is corrective action taken when a vendor:
    a. Ships early?
    b. Ships late?
    c. Overships?

5. Does purchasing work with inventory control to:
   a. Take advantage of price breaks?
   b. Program deliveries on large orders?
   c. Make long-term commitments?
   d. Consolidate ordering?

Receiving, Stores, Material Handling, Shipping

1. Does receiving:
   a. Promptly report damaged goods and initiate a claim through traffic?
   b. Verify count and report discrepancies?
   c. Verify shipping weights?
   d. Verify collect or prepaid shipping charges against f.o.b. point on order?
2. Does stockroom:
   a. Count and report each item as received?
   b. Report stock-outs?
   c. Fill shortages before putting away new stock?
   d. Report service for each production period in terms of percentage of requisitions filled?
   e. Identify and store separately various classes of stock, returned goods, obsolete items, and the like?
   f. Have work standards?
3. Is in-plant transportation organized and controlled, with:
   a. Full-time truckers?
   b. Dispatching?
   c. Work measurement?
   d. Control over vehicles and equipment?
4. Does shipping:
   a. Report performance in terms of percentage of on-time shipments?
   b. Report amount of unshipped merchandise at closing dates?
   c. Control labor efficiency by some form of work measurement?

Traffic

1. Are freight bills audited:
   a. For correct rate?
   b. For correct classification?
   c. Against f.o.b. point on purchase or sales order?
2. Are routings specified:
   a. To vendors for inbound shipments?
   b. To the shipping room for outbound shipments?
   c. With preferred or alternate carriers?
3. Is there a program to schedule and combine shipments to obtain optimum transportation costs?
4. Are shipping containers, provided by common carriers, used to reduce packaging costs?
5. Are vehicles and equipment owned or leased? Why?

Total Performance

1. Has a factory performance goal been set? (___percent)
   a. Is it being met?
2. Are lines of communication good?
3. Does the company enjoy the reputation for good customer service?

4. Is overtime required:
   a. Regularly?
   b. To handle periodic overloads?
   c. To make up for lack of capacity?
5. Are there frequent work interruptions or downtime because of parts or material shortages?
6. What is the size of the materials management organization as a percentage of:
   a. Total employment?
   b. Sales cost?

SUMMARY

Materials management is a vital concept which can result in cost reduction and improved performance in a manufacturing organization when it is understood and carried out. It is essentially a management tool to provide better leadership and direction to the multiple functions of acquiring and controlling materials. It should break down departmental barriers to smooth the way for the joint accomplishment of the ultimate goal of the group—minimum cost of material. To do this, a great deal depends upon the materials manager and his ability to train and motivate his people.

BIBLIOGRAPHY

Ammer, Dean S., *Materials Management*, Richard D. Irwin, Inc., Homewood, Ill., 1968.

Boch, Robert H., and William K. Holstein, *Production Planning and Control*, Charles E. Merrill Books, Inc., Columbus, Ohio, 1963.

Briggs, Andrew J., *Warehouse Operations Planning and Management*, John Wiley & Sons, Inc., New York, 1960.

Brown, Robert G., *Statistical Forecasting for Inventory Control*, McGraw-Hill Book Company, New York, 1959.

Cushman, Frank M., *Transportation for Management*, Prentice-Hall, Inc., Englewood Cliffs, N.J., 1953.

England, Wilbur B., *Procurement: Principles and Cases*, 4th ed., Richard D. Irwin, Inc., Homewood, Ill., 1962.

Goubeau, Vincent de P., "Materials Management," in H. B. Maynard (ed.), *Industrial Engineering Handbook*, 2d ed., McGraw-Hill Book Company, New York, 1963.

Heinritz, Stuart F., and P. V. Farrell, *Purchasing Principles and Applications*, 4th ed., Prentice-Hall, Inc., Englewood Cliffs, N.J., 1965.

LaMarr, Lee, Jr., and Donald W. Dobler, *Purchasing and Materials Management*, McGraw-Hill Book Company, New York, 1965.

Plossl, George W., and Oliver W. Wright, *Production and Inventory Control*, Prentice-Hall, Inc., Englewood Cliffs, N.J., 1967.

Pooler, Victor H., Jr., *The Purchasing Man and His Job*, American Management Association, New York, 1964.

Pritchard, James W., and Robert H. Eagle, *Modern Inventory Management*, John Wiley & Sons, Inc., New York, 1965.

Scheele, E. D., W. L. Westerman, and R. J. Wimmert, *Principles and Design of Production Control Systems*, Prentice-Hall, Inc., Englewood Cliffs, N.J., 1960.

Westing, J. H., and I. V. Fine, *Industrial Purchasing*, 2d ed., John Wiley & Sons, Inc., New York, 1961.

CHAPTER FIVE

Purchasing

ARTHUR W. TODD *Director of Purchase Engineering, The Lincoln Electric Company, Cleveland, Ohio*

In the typical manufacturing operation, purchasing people spend 40 to 60 percent of the entire income of the company. It is sometimes assumed that the handling of this large sum of money can efficiently and properly be done by clerks whose sole function is to translate requisitions into purchase orders on the basis of "today's lowest price," or alternatively, to send the purchase orders to suppliers selected by others in the organization, not always on the basis of long-term, economical results for the company.

The purchasing officer, however, faces a variety of economic circumstances and improvement and change in raw materials and in end products, together with wide fluctuations in consumption and irregularities of supply due to labor and transportation conditions. He must so organize his operation that, to the maximum extent possible, there will be a smooth flow of information and materials extending all the way from the basic source of the raw material through the engineering, methods, and manufacturing operations of the company on to the ultimate consumer.

The need is obvious for personnel of integrity, sound judgment, and exacting attention to detail, together with a comprehensive knowledge of the origin, processing, and use of materials pertinent to the manufacturing operation. For every 2 percent saved in the purchasing operation, the net profit of the company is increased by 1 percent, which is the equivalent in most cases to the profit resulting from a 10 percent increase in sales.

RESPONSIBILITY TO THE MANUFACTURING OPERATION

It is the job of the purchasing function to ensure that the company receives the right amount of the right material at the right price and at the right time.

The manufacturing division provides information by requisition or otherwise of its needs for fabrication or assembly at stated times. If this raw information is transmitted to outside suppliers without refinement, it yields:

1. Relatively uneconomical lot sizes from a price standpoint or because of the level of freight charges on shipments of various sizes
2. Substantial variation between the desired and actual time of delivery of certain components (unless expediting is done at substantially higher than standard expense)
3. Deviations from quality standards
4. Prices higher (or occasionally lower) than are warranted on the basis of long-term economic goals

Therefore, purchasing has the responsibility of processing the raw information in a way which will reduce or eliminate these difficulties.

Given a choice between having no goods or having defective goods, the manufacturing manager will probably prefer the former. At least he then knows that he cannot work, whereas with defective goods, he will expect to produce at standard costs but will find the results disappointing. The manufacturing function has no business doing, and cannot afford to do, the inspection for a vendor. High-quality performance by a vendor is not a desirable attribute measurable in degrees—it is an absolute must. A manufacturing manager performs incoming inspection in the same sense that an auditor examines a financial record—not to perform the task, but to assure himself that it has been done properly.

A highly effective communication interchange between manufacturing and purchasing is necessary. In most cases, voice for this purpose is hopelessly slow. Meetings may describe the grand outline to meet particular circumstances, but the details can be accomplished only by an exchange of written information. The traveling requisition shown by Figure 5-1 illustrates a form used for this purpose. It bears on its face the information needed by both

PART NO.	DESCRIPTION										SPEC:	
FLOOR LOCATION											DOCK	
ACCT. NO.	J	F	M	A	M	J	J	A	S	O	N	D
BLANKET ORDER NO.												
BUYER–	VIA–	ORIGIN		Terms:		PPD	Coll.	Lead Time				
DATE		VENDORS						Av. Use per Month				
								Best Buy Quan.				
								Finish: Cad☐ Silver☐ Cu ☐				
								Heat Treat☐ Zinc ☐Chrome☐				
								☐				
Orig|Apd|Ver|PO No| Quan	Unit Cost	Date Reqd	Date & Qty Rcd	Acct No	Orig|Apd|Ver| PO No	Quan	Unit Cost	Date Reqd	Date & Qty Rcd	Acct No

PU-50

FIG. 5-1.   Traveling Requisition.

manufacturing and purchasing and is constantly updated and exchanged between the two.

The goals of manufacturing and purchasing must be harmonious. Among other aspects, there can be no division of responsibility. It is a top management function to define these goals and responsibilities clearly.

Life is seldom ideal. Vendor promises which should be kept are not kept. Prices change. Strikes develop. Fires and floods destroy facilities. Seldom can any purchasing man anticipate these occurrences. All he can do is to learn of these events at the earliest possible moment and transmit the resulting delivery information to manufacturing. Tracing or expediting, in the large sense, must be a purchasing and not a manufacturing function, carrying with it the implication that purchasing must mitigate delaying circumstances by some alternative arrangement if at all possible.

So also it is with defective merchandise. The nature of the defect and its cause must be uncovered and steps taken to remedy the problem. Potentially defective end products must be isolated or recalled. The goods themselves must be physically eliminated from stock, and proper value must be recovered from vendor or salvage.

A manufacturing manager not receiving such service from a purchasing operation has four choices: to request improvement, to sell the need for cooperation, to secure an order through proper channels, or to forget the problem. The first would accomplish little, because it would not be understood; the third would arouse resentment and noncooperation; the fourth would court disaster at the hands of lower cost competitors. Only the second alternative—to show the purchasing people the comparative results of good and bad performance in terms of the ultimate consumer—can ever secure a long-lasting improvement.

Relationship of Purchasing to Other Departments. Purchasing serves as the eyes and ears to the outside world, permitting the other functions to devote their time efficiently to the circumstances, materials, and information directly pertinent to their activities.

For design engineering, purchasing must make a thorough check of all possible sources of desired items, sift out those which are acceptable, and transmit the information properly and accurately.

Working with industrial engineers, purchasing must understand the characteristics of materials needed for economical processing and fabrication and seek those which will result in optimum internal production.

The quality control function should identify inadequate merchandise wherever it can be found—at the original point of receiving, in the manufacturing operation, or by referral, in the hands of customers. The function of purchasing here is not merely to assure restitution to the company of claims for defective merchandise, but to go further and determine the reasons for inadequate purchased products and the steps which should be taken by the supplier to correct them.

In relation to sales and service, purchasing must be attuned to defects, shortcomings, and limited life where they occur. It must ensure that vendor service calls are promptly made where appropriate and be sensitive to any areas where raw materials affect the sales of the company.

In some companies, production control or inventory control is a function of purchasing, and in others the reverse is true. Regardless of organization, there are optimum quantities for production purposes, for inventory, and for purchasing, and they are often widely differing figures. In some way agreeable to the total organization, proper consideration must be given to ordering quantities in the light of all three functions.

In small companies, scrap is often sold by the purchasing department. In larger operations, this should be the function of a specialist. Regardless of whose responsibility it is, purchasing must assist in those areas where return, rework, or adaptation will yield higher returns than scrap value.

Purchasing also has responsibilities for procuring information, samples, and deliveries for other functions such as maintenance, plant engineering, plant protection, research, and advertising.

No purpose is served by having a separate function buy materials for any of the described departments. The central buying function should be able to develop experts who are knowledgeable about any class of material, regardless of the purpose for which it is eventually intended.

SOURCES OF INFORMATION

The traditional concept of a purchasing operation is that buyers should await visits by salesmen to secure information and to place orders. In an efficient manufacturing operation, this is about the most wasteful method that could be devised. Orders, when developed, must be placed immediately; and information, when needed, must be obtained without delay. Salesmen are often poorly prepared to discuss the origins, methods of manufacturing, and methods of application of materials which they represent, and their discipline in the handling of paperwork is not such as to lead to dependable results.

It is far more desirable for the purchasing function to know to what place the order must be sent to assure reliable action, and the persons, regardless of their location, who have sufficient knowledge to answer the many questions which will arise. Calls by salesmen should not be scheduled by the day or the hour. Rather, calls should be requested based on whether or to what extent the salesmen can provide reliable information about specific questions of concern to the company at the time of the interview. Purchasing people who are doing their jobs have no time for routine calls, for conversation when a written communication would suffice, or for various forms of personal intervention when the only function being performed is the exchange between companies of material on the one hand and money on the other.

Evaluation of Suppliers. In too many companies, people spend a great deal of time keeping track of the number of times that various suppliers are late, deliver defective merchandise, or ship substantially more or less than is ordered. This is usually a waste of time.

The proper evaluation of suppliers should determine which one is best able, on the basis of facilities, intentions, and general strength, to assure a continuous supply of the proper material. Purchasing should work closely with a limited number of such suppliers, not recording defective performance, but making any necessary investigations in depth, on a mutual basis, to determine the reasons for shortcomings and how to correct them.

Zero Defects in Purchasing. Zero Defects programs are usually initiated by management for the benefit of the manufacturing operation. They relate to purchasing (1) insofar as vendors follow the program and (2) in connection with the components purchased. One view of this type of program is that management is trying to accomplish by enthusiasm an objective which might better be accomplished by improved supervision or an incentive system. In any case, erroneous components, or the right component at the wrong time or at the wrong price, represent a large and unnecessary waste. It is estimated that every erroneous part or piece of information takes ten times as long to process as a correct one; hence 5 percent rejects equate with 50 percent of value or time.

Maximum efficiency can be achieved only when it is understood and agreed by all that no defects of any kind can be tolerated, regardless of the name under which the program is publicized.

Evaluation of Price. A concern which wishes to operate on the basis of the lowest invoice price at the moment must obviously be prepared to cope with whatever arrives, whenever it arrives, and to have some alternative if it does not arrive at all. This method may be suitable to a trading corporation, but a manufacturing operation, obliged in many cases to accept long lead times from suppliers and generally having an involved manufacturing cycle and long-term continuous demand from customers, cannot operate this way.

Obviously, the repetitive securing of competitive quotations is an extremely time-consuming job, completely preventing the purchasing function from doing any more intelligent type of work. In addition, some aspects of quotations are often overlooked, such as who pays the freight, what kind of cash discount is available, the significance of various forms of packaging and transportation arrangements, variations in lead time, quality variations, and other explanatory information which cannot adequately be supplied on a price quotation form. In addition to searching for, receiving, and evaluating all this information, it may be necessary for the purchaser to evaluate the source by personal inspection to judge whether or not the various aspects of the offering will actually be accomplished.

As a generality, so long as a supplier offers a particular product to one customer under specific circumstances, he cannot refuse, on request, to sell a second customer, similarly situated, merchandise on the same general basis for the same price. As a generality also, a price must be such as to assure a profit and thus a continued interest on the part of the supplier, and it also must be at such a level that, after further processing at the manufacturer's plant, the eventual customer will pay for the final product on a repetitive basis.

Too many purchasing operations claim credit for price reductions due to market price reductions or to increased quantities of single orders, and dismiss price increases due to small quantities or market price rises as circumstances beyond their control.

Quite obviously, the securing of the proper price depends on wholly different circumstances, and only those achievements which result from the proper application of sound purchasing principles are worthy of reporting to management as a purchasing accomplishment.

Value Analysis. The purpose of a value analysis program is to evaluate the long-term, all-inclusive cost implications of a purchased commodity. Value analysis techniques are discussed in detail in the following chapter.

Whether or to what extent a value analysis program, as distinct from a purchasing program, is necessary depends a great deal on the size of the company, the instructions given to the purchasing department, the training and competency of its staff, and the diversity of locations where purchasing decisions are made.

Specifications and Standards. A company which operates with a proper set of specifications and standards for purchasing (equally useful in manufacturing and engineering) may have difficulty in visualizing a situation where they do not exist. Yet in many companies, there are no agreed specifications or standards; but instead brand names, "or equal" clauses, or generic terms such as sodium chloride are used, which might result in delivery of anything from highly refined table salt to crude brine.

Components and parts should, where necessary, be described by a line drawing. They should be numbered and accompanied by a written statement of the nature of the material and all the characteristics which on the one hand will result in proper engineering and manufacturing operations, and on the other will permit purchase at a reasonable cost. The normal procedure is to send a copy of the drawing with the order or to file such drawings with suppliers in a foolproof manner which will ensure that active suppliers always have the most up-to-date drawing. There are numerous materials for which there are trade standards of various kinds such as ASTM, AISI, SAE, and the like. To avoid needless repetition of words, reference may be made to specific categories or paragraphs as published in these sources.

All materials, whether raw materials in the usual sense or fabricated parts, have some leeway or tolerance. It is important that the scope of these be understood and agreed to by vendor and customer alike. If there are particular ways in which the measurement is to be made, these should be carefully spelled out.

Assuming a proper specifications and standards system, deviations from these should be questioned as soon as they are detected. No material should then proceed to manufacture without full agreement on all the special circumstances involved, including chargebacks to vendors where appropriate.

Enforcement of standards should apply to quantity as well as quality. Shipments either short or over proper quantities, or in full for the basic commodity but lacking accessories such as screws, brackets, and so on, must be questioned in the same way as if quality were out of specification. Some vendors build up business by purposeful overshipment. Certain companies have controlled this situation by publishing in advance their intention of retaining such extra shipments gratis and then enforcing that stipulation.

If the name of the vendor or some trade name which is equally revealing is included on the drawing or purchase specification which is sent out for bid, it hinders getting the best price from alternate suppliers. If there is some sound engineering reason for having approved vendors, this information should be kept separately so that such drawings as are distributed do not carry this telltale signal as to what the price should be.

ECONOMIC ORDER QUANTITY

The formula for economic order quantity was developed many years ago on the same premise which underlies the manufacturing lot, which is to say that setup and space and holding costs must be equated when determining how long a manufacturing run to schedule.

The cost of a setup is a fairly precise figure in manufacturing. This is not the case in purchasing. Obviously, some receiving, accounting, and purchasing initiation costs can be established to represent the cost of placing an order. Whether more than a small percentage of the full cost of a purchasing department can be assessed against the order placing function is highly questionable unless the purchasing function is wholly clerical. Even within a company, the per order cost can vary between $2.50 and $15, depending on who looks at it. Likewise the holding cost is speculative. The principal portion usually is money interest which may vary from 3 to 15 percent or more, depending on both money supply and possible alternative use of funds within the company. Real estate and property tax costs are usually low—in the 1 percent area each. Risk of obsolescence has been listed at 4 to 20 percent per year, though a careful inventory management situation should presume virtually no loss from this situation. Thus the holding cost might run from 5 to 35 percent or more.

The influence on the order point of high or low ordering and holding costs is shown by Figure 5-2. The flat curve (or situation in which the actual quantity ordered has almost no significance) is probably characteristic of most ordering conditions in processing operations or when manufacturing for stock.

Timing and Inventory Control. In many cases, lead times can be reduced by a proper understanding with the supplier of what creates the lead time and of the various kinds of information or estimates which, on proper authority, may be given by the customer to the supplier. Nonetheless, lengthy lead times are inevitable in some cases. The only basic handicap in the long lead time is that requirements must be figured earlier than would otherwise be necessary. Beyond this, and provided the vendor-customer relationships are dependable, it is entirely feasible and economical to have with the supplier a series of monthly orders for delivery requirements over a twelve-month period on a twelve-month lead time basis, with a maximum of one month's supply on hand at any time, running down, of course, to the zero point immediately before replenishment.

INFORMATION SYSTEM

Whether by the spoken or written word, telephone or teletype, manual or computer, desk file or library, the purchasing function must act as a channel for accurate, reliable, and up-to-date information for all the issues described

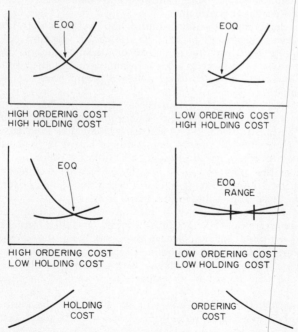

Fig. 5-2. Influence on Order Point of High or Low Ordering and Holding Costs.

in this chapter. For the sake of efficiency, the purchasing function must trim away, discard, or abandon any information scheme which does not pertain to these objectives.

It is vital that the purchasing operation discharge fully all functions charged to it, including such matters as procurement of information, follow-up of orders, and quality details. To the extent that any other function of the company takes over the procurement of this information, first, it is an admission that the purchasing people are not doing their jobs, and second, it results in proliferation of information in different places, which can only lead to confusion and inefficient operation in the long run.

The channeling of information through purchasing should be desirable, not because the purchasing function has the right to do certain things, but because it is best qualified to do them.

A true information system goes far beyond the transmission of selected facts. The relationship between manufacturing and purchasing requires a highly effective exchange of pertinent information, often leading to the selection of the best of a series of alternatives.

Material lists are an important aspect of a total information system. In far too many companies, material lists which were correct at one time have been changed in practice, not on paper, by a series of *de facto* engineering, methods, and customer-inspired changes. When this occurs, materials ordered to the manufacturing list will not be those actually needed for the production operation.

A proper system must provide that each related function, including manufacturing and purchasing, be advised on paper of any changes to be made. There should be a definite time schedule and coding or numbering system so that the time of change will be known throughout the company. This is most important in connection with outstanding orders and later with repairs, replacements, and customer complaints.

An essential segment of the total information system is a forecast, or more possibly a series of forecasts, not only of the present demand but also of the availability of supplies. Any mathematical or machine method used to derive these forecasts must be subject to review by human methods. Without proper forecasting, the control of inventories at the optimum minimum level is completely impossible.

Control Systems. Whoever is responsible for the purchasing function must in one way or another assure himself that proper judgments are made on all purchases. The most obvious way of accomplishing this is to ensure that one responsible person signs all orders, or all orders above a given size, with all other functions of purchasing being assigned to subordinates.

Assuming that the company has a proper cost record, it is necessary that all price changes, or all price changes of a certain total dollar significance, be made known to those responsible for manufacturing costs.

In addition, the person responsible for purchasing activities must see that the use of time is restricted to getting the most needed information, that this information is supplied accurately and promptly, that the proper long-term arrangements are initiated and maintained with suppliers, and that the entire operation is morally and ethically sound. A purchaser who expects his vendors to be dependable and honest in all respects must himself be dependable and honest.

A significant aspect of control concerns the flow of money required to sustain a previously agreed upon volume of purchases. In many companies, expense of operation of the various functions and divisions is closely controlled by a budget, which is a forecast of money required to sustain a management-approved operation at an agreed rate. That most significant outflow of money for purchased goods, however, often remains a need defined by conditions; or in other words, wait until it is seen what bills have to be paid and then do something about it.

If it were economic to buy goods continually at a rate corresponding to sales, there would be no particular problem. Unfortunately, so smooth a flow is not characteristic of the supply situation, in part because of strikes and threats of strikes, price changes, production facility shortages, and quantity purchases. The extension of unit prices on the various purchase orders and tabulation of these money requirements by date when goods are due does not completely define the problem, because in many cases goods are priced "at time of shipment" (notably primary metals and chemicals); and shipment, in whole or in part, may not occur even close to the time when delivery was originally specified. If the customer does not himself alter delivery dates, the supplier likely will. Suffice it to say that a budget for materials purchase is just as necessary as any other budget, but the practical difficulties of accurately developing this budget require the thoughtful preparation of an information system which probably cannot be adequately managed except by a computer.

Accounting and Audit Systems. The purchasing department has the responsibility of creating clear and accurate records without unnecessary duplication of figures. A function separate from purchasing should independently check the authorization to purchase against the ultimate receiving record, the transportation record, the vendor invoice, and the "proper price" before authorizing payment. Audit procedures verify that this procedure is maintained.

An audit system can only probe the integrity of a transaction which has been accomplished. It has no way of determining whether a proper source was used or proper diligence was exercised in securing information and results.

INTERNAL STRUCTURES

No matter how it may be organized otherwise, the purchasing function must assign the total responsibility for each segment of procurement to a single individual. Whenever this responsibility is diluted among assistant buyers, expediters, and so forth, the whole impact of responsibility is lost. Although the pyramidal structure is typical of most larger purchasing operations, experience indicates that a team structure is far preferable and accomplishes maximum results with minimum friction.

Too many people fail to make a distinction between using information and generating it. One does not have to own the local newspaper to read and accept the information it contains. The purchasing operation does not have to own the record generating function of the manufacturing division in order to use it. Indeed, it is preferable that there be a separation, because if one function is separate from the other, then one can ask questions which otherwise would never be asked and challenge facts rather than accept them.

APPRAISAL OF PURCHASING PERFORMANCE

An objective and universal gage of the activities of purchasing people is difficult to design. Certainly any yardsticks, such as number of pieces of paper processed or number of dollars spent, are appraisals of a clerical function and not of one requiring initiative and judgment. In 1965, the National Association of Purchasing Agents initiated an elaborate survey and made tentative conclusions available to the contributors; as of January, 1968, no final conclusions had been reached, and the possibility of the setting of definitive standards did not look bright.

In spite of the high percentage of company income involved and although their qualifications are undoubtedly as pertinent here as anywhere else in business, management consultants are seldom asked to review purchasing operations. The obstacle appears to be a gross lack of understanding of the objectives by management itself, rather than any shortcoming on the part of consultants.

A proper yardstick for measuring purchasing performance might be to expect material savings generated by a purchasing function, other than cost reductions due to market conditions, to be equivalent to, say, twice the annual savings generated by an industrial engineering or methods department.

Inasmuch as there would be no inventory if the purchasing function did not buy it, a reasonable rate of inventory turnover may also indicate proper purchasing performance. Too rapid a rate probably would indicate a great deal of last minute changes and expediting; whereas too slow a rate would imply additional costs in extra handling, space, and monetary investment. If finished goods are built to stock rather than to order, raw materials and in-process inventories should not be greater than finished stock inventories in normal business times.

Any purchasing function which considers itself to be up to date and abreast of the times will probably be in poor shape because this attitude discourages the search for further improvement. The proper objective of purchasing management, like any management, is to design its function today in terms of the needs as of five years from today. The only way to stay ahead is to be ahead.

Guidelines for Optimum Purchasing Performance.

1. Objectives must be defined clearly and accepted: the right amount of the right quality material at the right time and at the right price.
2. The primary function is that of communication and this in turn is chiefly a "people problem."
3. Accuracy is critical, even to small details.
4. A buyer can serve only one master—he has no obligation to any vendor person and must never get into this position.
5. The buyer who buys on price alone is a traitor to his company because he certifies an evaluation job to be completed when, in the full sense, it has only begun.
6. The responsibility for each fraction of the total buying program must be centered exclusively in one person.
7. Every buying transaction is subject to audit, and everyone must accept the need for this audit.
8. Both parties to every transaction must earn a reasonable profit.
9. Beware of mechanical gadgets—they may purport to eliminate work which is not needed in the first place, or eliminate judgment in the only area where judgment is needed.

CONCLUSION

Subject to the forces of inflation, the manufacturing manager should expect from an optimum purchasing operation a combination of lower prices, fewer shutdowns and rescheduling due to missing or defective merchandise, less scrap, and lower manufacturing variances due to better material of somewhere between 2 and 5 percent of total factory costs cumulatively, year in and year out. Like interest on savings, the total can become a highly significant competitive factor in a few years' time.

BIBLIOGRAPHY

Aljian, George W. (ed.), *Purchasing Handbook*, 2d ed., McGraw-Hill Book Company, New York, 1966.

Anyon, F. G. Jay, *Managing an Integrated Purchasing Process*, Holt, Rinehart & Winston, Inc., New York, 1963.

Berry, Harold A., *Purchasing Management*, Prentice-Hall, Inc., Englewood Cliffs, N.J., 1964.

Colton, Raymond R., *Industrial Purchasing*, Charles E. Merrill Books, Inc., Columbus, Ohio, 1962.

England, Wilbur B., *The Purchasing System*, Richard D. Irwin, Inc., Homewood, Ill., 1967.

Hass, George H., Benjamin March, and E. M. Krech, *Purchasing Department Organization and Authority*, Research Study no. 45, American Management Association, New York, 1960.

Heinritz, Stuart F., *Purchasing Principles and Applications*, 4th ed., Prentice-Hall, Inc., Englewood Cliffs, N.J., 1965.

Internal Audit and Control of the Purchasing Department, Institute of Internal Auditors, New York, 1968.

Pooler, Victor H., Jr., *The Purchasing Man and His Job*, American Management Association, New York, 1964.

Smith, Alton E., *New Techniques for Creative Purchasing*, The Dartnell Corporation, Chicago, Ill., 1967.

CHAPTER SIX

Value Analysis

L. D. MILES   *Miles Associates, Washington, D.C.*

If each person in the manufacturing, process, or service area of work achieved fully the purposes for which he works, there would be no need for the techniques and methods of value analysis. If marketing men knew precisely which product or service functions the user wants; if engineers chose the optimum design approach and followed it through with the optimum detailed shapes, tolerances, materials, and processes; if manufacturing work always employed the optimum manufacturing methods, considering volume and all other known factors; and if procurement people always achieved their objective of providing the best functional materials at the lowest cost; then value analysis would not be profitable. In the work of men and organizations, however, this degree of effectiveness is a goal, not a reality.

The purpose of value analysis is to assist each to approach nearer enough to this goal to provide substantial competitive and profit advantages. It provides planned and disciplined thought and action which helps identify unnecessary cost throughout the product or process cycle. Functions are deeply studied and are evaluated in terms of dollars.

Unnecessary cost is defined as cost which contributes neither to the quality of performance which the customer wants nor to the appearance or other aesthetic features which he wants.

VALUE ANALYSIS

Value analysis is a precise, disciplined, one-purpose thinking process. Its one purpose is to retain all the performance and aesthetic factors which now exist in the product, process, or service, which the customer wants and is willing to pay for; and through disciplined thinking procedures, to put together practical alternatives which will accomplish them at still lower cost.

A complete definition of value analysis is: an arrangement of techniques

7–90

which makes clear precisely the functions that the customer wants; establishes the appropriate cost for each function by comparison; and causes required knowledge, creativity, and initiative to be used to accomplish each function for that cost.

Some of the techniques are for the purpose of clarifying functions; some are for establishing appropriate costs by comparison; and some cause the required knowledge, creativity, and initiative to be used.

For example, an evaluation of the function of the electric contacts used in an electric control reduced cost by $26,000 a year. When a new model of an electric control was first designed, it was approved by the Underwriters' Laboratories and manufactured for two years. Value analysis methods were used to evaluate several functions by comparison. The electric contacts were evaluated at about $26,000 a year less than their present cost. Further investigation revealed that, during the design phase, appropriate contacts had been developed by test, and they had been selected. However, it was also found that, during the assembly process when preparing samples to be sent to the Underwriters', something had gone wrong, and the supply of the appropriate contacts had been exhausted. To avoid delay, the engineer had furnished another, more expensive contact to the assemblers. This solved the assembly problem, and the samples were made and sent to Underwriters' Laboratories where they received approval. Two years later, with this information in hand, the appropriate contacts were submitted to the Underwriters and were approved, with the result that the unnecessary, noncontributing cost was eliminated.

SCOPE OF VALUE ANALYSIS

Value in a product or service is the reward for appropriate performance and appropriate cost. Value analysis must therefore employ techniques which will sensitize any "lacking" area so that the need can be identified and satisfied.

The action of the value analysis system is to identify which of the several areas of the manufacturing system holds the solution to each specific component of unnecessary cost. The necessary knowledge, creativity, and initiative can then be used where needed and to the extent needed to solve the cost problem.

Some of these areas are:

1. *Management Organization.* If the organization is not best suited to the task to be performed, it can only produce poorer product performance or extra cost. If poorer performance results, tests will normally follow, and it will be promptly corrected. If, however, higher costs result, they often will continue.

2. *Marketing Concept—Customer Functional Understanding.* The customer purchases a product to accomplish functions for him. These are "use" functions and "esteem" functions. To the extent that the customer has not been led to understand and communicate just what functions he wants to buy and pay for, and to the extent that this information is not basic to the engineering and manufacturing processes, extra cost remains in the system, product, or service.

3. *Engineering Concept and Approach.* After the functions which are to be provided to the customers are determined, the effectiveness used in establishing the engineering concept which will be detailed and implemented introduces either positive or negative factors in the cost area. These remain,

regardless of actions of any others. Often much unnecessary cost is allowed to remain because the work in the engineering concept stage was not optimum.

4. *Engineering Detail.* After the basic approach for accomplishing the functions is established, it must be implemented by choice of materials, shapes, assemblies, methods, functions, tolerances, and so on. Appropriate cost can also be lost in this work area.

5. *Manufacturing Concept or Approach.* How much or how little automation? How much to make? How much to buy? What machines and factory layout? If the manufacturing conceptual and planning work is not competently done, cost can be lost.

For example, forty thousand ¼- by 3-inch screws were required for a certain product. It was necessary that they be threaded all the way to the head. Standard screws had only 1 inch of thread. They were therefore purchased and put in a screw machine for extension of the threads to the head. The cost was 12 cents. The arrangement satisfied all concerned because (1) purchasing could buy available standard screws with no problems, (2) manufacturing had the equipment and welcomed the work which could be put on its machines, and (3) the engineers obtained the screw they needed. As is so often the case, all considerations except those of value were properly cared for. The use of value analysis techniques showed that the function was not worth 12 cents. This resulted in a change to buying screws, for 2½ cents each, that were ready to use.

6. *Manufacturing Operation.* That appropriate cost will be lost in a carelessly, loosely, inefficiently operated factory is so obvious that it needs no elaboration.

7. *Purchasing or Materials Procurement Work.* A significant amount of cost is normally incurred by purchasing. To the extent that purchasing recognizes its potential to contribute to profits, staffs itself with competent buyers and negotiators, buys function as nearly as practicable, and assumes a major role in getting a wide variety of solutions from available suppliers, it eliminates the possibility that significant unnecessary costs may be lost in this area.

WHY VALUE ANALYSIS IS NEEDED

Top emphasis, knowledge, research, and skills have traditionally dealt with the prime task of securing the performance and aesthetic factors that the customer wants. Expertness in developing superior cost alternatives has not been developed to the same extent. As competition increases, similar expertness in dealing with all factors which add unnecessary cost becomes imperative.

In general, the production of a product involves three stages, as illustrated by Figure 6-1. The first is the research and development stage in which knowledge is extended toward innovation to create new functions, to provide additional functions, and to accomplish existing functions more reliably or efficiently. Cost is not usually the vital factor. Value analysis methods are therefore not needed.

Then comes the second stage, the growth stage. The product, having proved that it fills a need, gains in customer demand, and competition enters the field. It becomes evident that to sell the product competitively and profitably, it must be produced at a lower cost.

The third stage, the maturity stage, is reached when the product has matured fully. Research and development are no longer making large contributions to the efficiency with which functions are accomplished, to the life of the product, or to the addition of new functions. Thus the prime task of the manufacturer becomes one of maintaining performance and securing cost leadership. This means that it is good business to commit more resources to the now vital task of effectively identifying unnecessary cost and arranging for its removal.

Whether a business continues to increase in profitable sales volume or starts to decrease and then drops out of the field is normally governed by the degree to which it recognizes this shift from performance to value emphasis at the right time and by the effectiveness with which it shifts its use of resources and competence, as compared with its competitors. The proper timing of this shift is shown by Figure 6-2.

ALL THINKING IS BASED UPON FUNCTIONS, NEVER UPON PARTS

Direct relationships between cost and specifically described functions should be established. The basic purpose of each expenditure, whether it be for hardware, for the work of a group of men, for a procedure, or for whatever, is to accomplish a function. It is necessary to establish the language of function and stay with it to think and communicate clearly.

Evaluation of Functions. Because the purpose of value analysis is to achieve the total function for the lowest overall cost, effective measurements of the value of functions are necessary. Techniques are provided for evaluating functions by comparison. These evaluations must not be made by comparing to the past. Values are established by other valid comparisons and are then used as guides to achieving the functions for that value or cost.

Types of Functions. In the search for basic objective thinking, the functions are divided into types. There are two types. Either or both may cause the

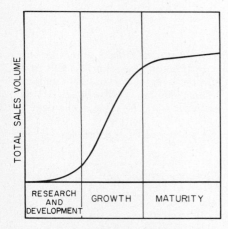

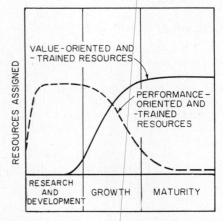

FIG. 6.1. Product Maturity Cycle. (*From* Techniques of Value Analysis and Engineering *by L. D. Miles. Copyright 1961, McGraw-Hill Book Company. Used by permission of McGraw-Hill Book Company.*)

FIG. 6-2. Optimum Change in Use of Performance Engineering and Value Engineering Skills as Product Matures. (*From* Techniques of Value Analysis and Engineering *by L. D. Miles. Copyright 1961, McGraw-Hill Book Company. Used by permission of McGraw-Hill Book Company.*)

user to buy this product. One type is the "use" function. The other is the "aesthetic" function. Each is important. Any cost other than to provide the amount of each of these two functions which the user wants is unnecessary cost.

The cost which is expended to cause the product to perform a use which the buyer wants and is willing to pay for is incurred for the use function.

The elements of cost which are for the purpose of pleasing the buyer through color or shape of feature, causing him to buy, are incurred to achieve the aesthetic function.

Basic Function. The basic function is that function for which the user or buyer buys the product.

Second-degree Functions. Second-degree functions are those functions chosen by the designer to permit effective accomplishment of the basic function. The customer is extremely interested in the basic function; he does not care about the second-degree function. Large amounts of cost are contained in second-degree functions and become the immediate target for high-grade value analysis work.

To illustrate, manufacturing reduced cost from 96 cents to 37 cents on an appliance part by evaluating the function of the mounting holes. Galvanized steel sheet, $\frac{1}{32}$ inch thick and 1½ feet wide by 6 feet long, was used. To perform its function, it was necessary to punch 10,000 holes in each sheet so that it became perforated. This punching cost 68 cents.

To facilitate mounting the sheet, six more holes were punched near the ends at a cost of 28 cents, bringing the punching cost to 96 cents. The 10,000 holes served an essential function in the appliance, while the six additional holes served merely for mounting the part.

When these required functions were brought into clear focus and alternatives were developed, it was found that the material could be continously perforated in the long, uncut strip and that some of the holes could then be used for mounting.

THE VALUE ANALYSIS JOB PLAN

In the value analysis job plan, the problems are approached with the functions to be accomplished clearly in mind. Information surrounding the problem area is intensively and extensively secured. It is thoroughly analyzed for meaning and for sense of direction. The essential creative work is then done. Afterwards, and separately, the judicial work is done, followed by suitable developmental thinking and work.

Before the start of the job plan, a concise statement of the problem should be developed.

1. What, *exactly*, are we really trying to accomplish?
2. Save how much? Increase production how much?
3. Improve exactly what—how much?
4. Precisely what is required to meet the need?

The job plan is a five-step procedure. These steps are carried out as follows.

Information Step. Make three lists:
1. Facts
2. Beliefs
3. Information needed but not known

Allow no interpretation, no analysis, no idea generating. What is known? What is believed? What is done? Where? By whom? When? At what cost? What are the service factors? What are the maintenance factors? What are other customer factors? Why was it done this way? When? What changes? Why changed? Why not other changes? What are marketing engineering, manufacturing, purchasing, inventory, and all other factors?

Write them all down. Surround the situation with more facts than one person has yet viewed in one picture.

At this stage, a review is normally scheduled with the manager or supervisor, who can often make meaningful additions.

Analysis Step. What are the meanings? What are the total problems? The individual problems? The reasonable goals and plans? What are the key problems to be solved first? What solutions seem reasonable? What end result is reasonable? What steps of the five-step job plan are indicated? What additional information is required? What unlisted assumptions are being made? Are the assumptions now valid? What solutions does it make sense to search for? About what savings or benefits might each of the best approaches bring? Exactly what parts of the problem or overall problems shall we seek out better solutions for first? What specific needs, when well met by better solutions, would unlock beneficial solutions to the project?

Select a few approaches which will next receive intense study, search, and creative thought. Normally, there will be one or more specific problems in each of the following classes.

Class I problems—seemingly very difficult, with large benefits if solved.
Class II problems—require penetrating thought and creativity and have substantial benefits when solved.
Class III problems—small need for new search or creativity, and small but probably worthwhile benefits to profitability.

For example, originally a few hundred fiber washers, ⅛ inch thick and 1½ inches in diameter, were needed. They were made by purchasing fiber rod 1½ inches in diameter, drilling the center hole, and cutting the washers off like wafers. This required no special tooling and was easy to accomplish in any machine shop. The cost was 16 cents each. As the product involved became successful and the quantities increased to many thousand per year, the washers continued to be made by the same process. The function was evaluated at much less than 16 cents. As a result, the washers were made from sheet at a cost of 3½ cents each.[1]

Creativity Step. Three to ten people should participate. They should defer all judging, which will be much more difficult than expected.

Use should be made of the various methods to accelerate creative activities of the mind. These methods were originated by the late Alex Osborn and are extended and taught by the Creative Problem Solving Institute of the University of Buffalo, and others.

Because creativity is joining bits of knowledge in new combinations, it may be desirable to include people in this session who have some knowledge related to the subject, but they *must* accept the discipline of deferred judgment or *they must not be there.*

Consider each of the problems in classes I, II, and III thoroughly, listing all suggested approaches.
Encourage free association of ideas.
Use preliminary judgment.

[1] Adapted from *Techniques of Value Analysis and Engineering* by L. D. Miles, published by McGraw-Hill Book Company, New York, 1961.

Select the approaches which show so much promise that it is believed they should be thoroughly studied.

Again, a review is normally scheduled with the manager or supervisor for his contributions.

Judgment Step. One person, consulting others on specific factors as required.

What approaches show promise, and what are the cost advantages of each? What are the advantages and disadvantages? Which is ready now for development? Which should be referred back to another information or analysis or creativity cycle? What disadvantage becomes the new problem?

Development Step. The "better answer" is usually 50 to 90 percent ready to use. Because good development procedures are often in place, no additional comments are made here.

QUALIFICATIONS AND TRAINING FOR VALUE ANALYSIS WORK

Qualifications. To do value analysis work successfully, a combination of knowledge, imagination, initiative, self-organization, mature personality, and experience is required. These traits may be described more fully as follows.

Knowledge. A practical understanding of the properties of materials and their uses and of manufacturing processes, their potentials, and their limitations.

Imagination. A good, practical, creative imagination, with enough mental abilities and skills to discipline thinking processes, that is, to devote the total mind to information gathering, then to analysis, to creativity, and so on, doing each thoroughly. Ability to defer judgment during the creative steps is essential.

High Degree of Initiative. In value analysis, there are often no definite beginning and ending points, and specific instructions are nonexistent. "Self-drive" is essential.

Self-organization. Initiative and drive are not enough. The roadway to better value is not charted. Men must be able to organize their efforts effectively and pursue the worthwhile trails efficiently.

Personality. A mature, stable personality, which is not easily discouraged. All work is in the area of change. The amount of opposition, delay, and even ridicule, which occurs if the work is achieving high success, exceeds the tolerance of the normal individual. Exceptional maturity is required.

Experience. Several years of engineering-related work such as industrial engineering or design engineering. Successful experience in achieving job objectives through harmonious working with others.

Training. Some of the knowledge which must be acquired and some of the new skills which must be developed for value analysis work are:

What the specific techniques and approaches are
How to use each technique
When to apply each technique
How to use each phase of the job plan effectively
How to expect and overcome the stoppers or roadblocks that are sure to come
How to search out successfully new information and new good answers for what is needed
How to acquire enough special knowledge so that it can be used efficiently and can be expanded to continue to be valuable

To accomplish this training, a combination of lecture and "do it" seminar is effective.

Appreciation Training. It is a normal human reaction to discredit that which we do not understand. Thus, if a new activity appears in the industrial or other business setup, it will be subject to suspicion, doubt, discredit, and disfavor by all who do not understand it. It is evident, therefore, that when introducing value analysis, the first task is to explain the work to every individual affected by it. Each person must know what the value analysis work is, how it will be done, and how it will affect him.

Successful orientation may be accomplished under usual conditions by two 2-hour lecture periods, separated by one to two weeks.

ORGANIZATION FOR VALUE ANALYSIS WORK

A broad administrative management base is required for value analysis work because of the fact that the prime reason for unnecessary costs in any situation may rest not only in the area of manufacturing responsibility, but also quite often in the areas of engineering, purchasing, marketing, or even management. Administrative access to and support from these broad areas are essential.

In businesses up to $2 million, one competent and dependable man from the top management group is usually given training in value analysis techniques. This man will himself evaluate functions, services, and benefits secured in important expenditure areas. He will promote suitable group work and action in appropriate areas. He will constantly teach the functional approach and lead activities which bring benefits from it.

Businesses with $2 million or more of annual sales will usually start with one carefully selected and trained value consultant. This man must be respected by his peers and management alike. His background must be exceedingly broad. Extra attention must be given by management to this new work until it becomes understood by, integrated into, and accepted by every phase of the business.

Two men can provide a much more satisfactory degree of the necessary knowledge and experience. Combined in the two should be skill in engineering ideas, in manufacturing methods and processes, and in the very extensive field of using vendor and specialty-vendor competence. Although the two men work together, they do not work as an interlaced team. Rather, they work as consultants to each other on any particular job. In every instance, each project or activity is the responsibility of one of the two. That individual, in turn, to the right extent and at the right time, consults with the other man on the job. One of the two may be the senior man and carry certain responsibility for assigning work to the other. Care must be taken, however, that neither of the two works as an assistant to the other but rather that each accepts responsibility for a specific activity in the plant and consults with the other as needed.

Three men constitute the smallest efficient operating unit for wide-range value analysis work. It is then usually possible to have the necessary depth in the three required areas of skill named above. The three men again act as individual value analysis consultants, each taking responsibility for specific projects and calling on the others as consultants to improve the degree of accomplishment. Again, one man may be a senior member who organizes and assigns work to the others, or else the three may report to the same manager who, in that case, must have a real grasp of value analysis work, its problems, and its opportunities, and must be capable of performing the managing function skillfully. Three men often aid one another during the creative phases of their work studies, and having much in common, they do not readily become frustrated and discouraged.

As the business begins to see the benefit of the activity, additional value analysis consultants may be added. This will provide more penetration in the three identified areas, and besides, additional abilities will be secured. For example, with groups of four persons or more, an individual who has special abilities in teaching and communicating will be very valuable in that education is an important part of the work of value analysis consultants and specialists.

With four or more individuals assigned to the value analysis work, it will be of definite advantage to have the managerial functions delegated to one of them. He then will be the one to:

Set objectives

Establish plans and programs

Provide for proper staffing of the group, augmented by provisions for continued development and growth in the individuals' competence

Motivate appropriate actions

Support each specialist in his work with other segments of the business

Administer work assignments, schedules, compensation, facilities, and the like[2]

BIBLIOGRAPHY

Aljian, George W. (ed.), *Purchasing Handbook*, 2d ed., sec. 11, McGraw-Hill Book Company, New York, 1966.

Brewster, Charles E., et al., *Value Engineering Methods Manual*, Aerospace Division, The Boeing Company, Seattle, Wash.

Crouse, R. L., *Preparing and Conducting a VE Training Seminar*, Honeywell, Inc., Minneapolis, Minn.

Crouse, R. L., *Value Engineering and Analysis Bibliography*, Society of American Value Engineers, Smyrna, Ga.

Directorate of Value Engineering, *Reduce Costs and Improve Equipment through Value Engineering*, U.S. Government Printing Office, Washington, D.C., 1967.

Gage, W. L., *Value Analysis*, McGraw-Hill Book Company, New York, 1967.

Miles, L. D., *Techniques of Value Analysis and Engineering*, McGraw-Hill Book Company, New York, 1961.

[2] *Ibid.*

CHAPTER SEVEN

Inventory Control

RICHARD W. FOXEN *Vice President—Manufacturing and Purchasing, Westinghouse Air Brake Company, Pittsburgh, Pennsylvania*

ARTHUR W. TICKNOR *Director—Acquisition Planning, Westinghouse Air Brake Company, Pittsburgh, Pennsylvania*

American industry has a big investment in inventory—in 1968 it was $86 billion in manufacturing industries and another $60 billion in wholesale and retail trade. The effectiveness with which that capital investment is used may be as significant as that of our fixed investment in plant and equipment, although it is generally given much less attention in industrial planning.

THE NATURE OF INVENTORY

The relative use of inventory, as measured by turnover, varies by industry, but within any given industry did not change much from 1956 to 1966. In Figure 7-1, turnover is computed as total operating cost divided by inventory at year-end.

Why has this tremendous investment in inventory been made? At the finished goods level, the answer essentially is to provide adequate service to an increasingly complex, demanding, and geographically dispersed group of buyers and potential buyers. At the production level, the answer essentially is to operate in the most efficient, lowest cost way. There are other reasons for having inventory investment on the books, as, for example, a hedge against anticipated price increases or as the result of past errors in judgment leading to obsolete stocks. The really significant reasons, however, are customer service on the one hand and production efficiency on the other. Any other reasons would normally be temporary and nonessential.

In the case of finished goods inventories, the average amount on hand for any item can be conveniently viewed as consisting of (1) an amount equal

Industry	1956	1961	1962	1963	1964	1965	1966
Durable goods........................	4.6	4.6	4.8	4.8	4.7	4.7	4.5
Motor vehicles and equipment.........	5.5	5.6	6.0	5.8	5.4	5.6	5.4
Instruments, etc......................	3.6	4.0	4.3	4.1	4.0	4.1	4.3
Stone, clay, and glass................	6.2	5.9	6.4	6.4	6.6	6.7	6.4
Electrical machinery..................	4.5	4.8	4.7	4.6	4.5	4.3	4.1
Machinery...........................	3.8	3.8	3.8	4.0	4.0	3.9	3.9
Furniture and fixtures................	6.2	6.3	6.6	6.7	6.5	6.5	6.3
Fabricated metals....................	4.8	5.4	5.5	5.4	5.3	5.0	5.0
Lumber and wood....................	5.6	5.4	6.0	6.3	5.8	6.1	6.1
Iron and steel.......................	5.5	4.0	4.6	4.8	4.9	5.1	4.9
Nonferrous metals....................	5.2	3.9	4.0	4.2	4.6	4.7	4.5
Aircraft and parts....................	.....	3.9	4.0	3.7	3.8	3.4	2.9
Nondurable goods.....................	5.7	6.1	6.1	6.1	6.2	6.1	6.1
All industries........................	5.1	5.3	5.4	5.4	5.4	5.3	5.1

FIG. 7-1. Inventory Turnover by Industry between 1956 and 1966.

to half the normal (most economic) order quantity, as stock orders are replenished and then worked off; (2) a safety stock, or cushion, which is a function of the pattern of receipts and shipments and the desired level of service; and (3) an amount which is unnecessary and should be eliminated. From this, it can be seen that there is some theoretical relationship between inventory levels and customer service. But the relationship is not direct and should not be accepted without a rigorous test. The specific techniques involved in these analyses will be discussed later.

It is worth pointing out that finished goods inventories may be a very large part of the firm's total inventories—sometimes half or more—and that they are frequently assigned to individuals with little education or experience with the techniques of inventory control. Where that situation has occurred, substantial reduction of investment may be possible with no loss in customer service levels, if suitable inventory control techniques are applied.

Production inventories, which are primarily related to the efficiency of the production process, can be considered to consist of four classes: (1) raw materials, on which work must be performed before assembly; (2) work in process; (3) finished parts, both manufactured and purchased, ahead of assembly; and (4) work in assembly. Although these distinctions may be blurred in any particular case, they are useful for analysis and planning purposes.

Optimum inventory levels for class 1 and class 3 should behave essentially the same as finished goods inventory—that is, they are a function of order size and protective stock allowances. Optimum levels for classes 2 and 4, however, are a function only of the time that the order spends in process or in assembly. This in turn is, up to a point, a function of how much time is allowed in the planning (usually the more time allowed, the longer the actual manufacturing cycle—a form of Parkinson's law), and also the logic of the production process itself, including physical layout, equipment, systems, and organizational assignments.

For all types of inventory, the approach to inventory management is similar to that for value analysis, which seeks to identify "the minimum cost to perform the essential function" and to cut out all the rest.

ORGANIZATION

Modern manufacturing management generally assigns inventory control to the "production and inventory control" function, which in turn is part of the "materials" activity. A typical organization chart is shown by Figure 7-2.

The reason for this arrangement is, of course, that production control and inventory control are usually highly interrelated. Insofar as the effectiveness of plant operations is concerned, the determination of ordering policies and inventory levels at all points in the process is inseparable from the more general goal of production control, which is to see that the scheduling, ordering, dispatching, material handling, and all other functions of the business combine to produce on-time deliveries at the lowest practical total cost.

Of course, there are many variations on this organizational theme. For example, in a smaller operation, inventory control may report directly to the Manager—Materials who may be called the Production Control Manager. He may in turn report to the Manager—Manufacturing who may be called the Plant Manager. In some cases, the materials or production control function may be split off entirely from manufacturing and report at the same level as the Manager—Manufacturing or the Plant Manager, as shown by Figure 7-3. It should be recognized, however, that this solution usually entails significant risk of conflict rather than cooperation at the shop operations level, and for that reason is generally not recommended.

A form of "decentralized" inventory control may be used where there is in fact a physical decentralization of shop operations, such as by production process or product line. In that case, a materials manager may exist as before but with a policy and coordinating role in inventory control, at least from work-in-process through assembly.

In the case of finished goods inventories, a service parts manager or warehouse manager may report to the materials function or to marketing, depending on the nature of the problem and the results desired.

There are many other possibilities for organizing the inventory control function. To help decide which is best in any particular situation, the following questions may be asked: (1) Where is the inventory now, by type and physical distribution? (2) Who is responsible for it, and does he know to what

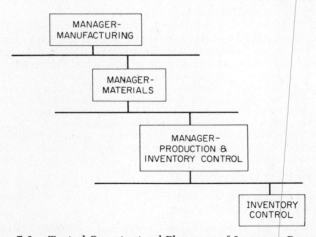

Fig. 7-2. Typical Organizational Placement of Inventory Control.

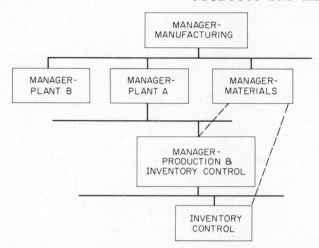

FIG. 7-3.   Alternative Organizational Placement of Inventory Control.

extent he is responsible; also, does he know its value and in detail how it is controlled?   (3) How is the responsibility for production control assigned (inventory control should be assigned at the same point)?   (4) Are certain types of inventory such as raw material and finished goods separable?   (5) Or would better control result from assignment of inventory to a product or process unit, as for example, paint to the paint shop or bar stock to the automatic screw machine section?   The best answer or combination of answers is that which will give clearly defined and measurable responsibility to the individual most able to do something about the results.

Job Description of Supervisor–Inventory Control.   However the function is organized, the work is likely to be similar.   The following is an example of a job description of a Supervisor–Inventory Control, taken from *Managerial Job Descriptions in Manufacturing* by Gordon H. Evans.[1]   This may be used as a general guide, although details will, of course, have to be modified to suit the particular situation.

Supervisor–Inventory Control
A Machinery Maker

FUNCTION: To supervise, directly and through section heads, the activities of the department engaged in insuring that stocks of goods are adequate but not excessive for operating requirements, in accordance with established practice and policy procedures; to provide a basis for recording inventories and movement of goods in the most economical manner consistent with Corporation's procurement and accounting requirements; to determine the most economical quantities and varieties to be carried; to promote more rapid turnover and minimize the investment in inventories to reduce taxes, insurance, storage and handling expense, and minimum losses from obsolescence and physical deterioration, assuring an available supply of materials when needed to facilitate production operations, minimize cost of idle time, and render better service to customers.

ORGANIZATIONAL RELATIONSHIPS

1. Reports to: Manager of Manufacturing: Supervises: Warehousing, internal transportation, and stock ledgers.

[1] Gordon H. Evans, *Managerial Job Descriptions in Manufacturing*, Research Study no. 65, American Management Association, New York, 1964, pp. 304, 305.

2. The Inventory Control Supervisor reports directly to the Manager of Manufacturing. His duties require close collaboration with all Manufacturing, Engineering, and Sales Departments to achieve production schedules.

SPECIFIC RESPONSIBILITIES: The Inventory Control Supervisor shall be accountable for the following broad responsibilities that he shall fulfill through delegation of responsibility and authority and by initiation and execution of action in keeping with the authority vested in his office and the applicable Corporation policies and procedures.

1. To control the delivery of material requirements as to time and quantity, and the purchasing, receiving, storage, and handling of material; to store finished parts, ship finished products, and provide all records necessary to keep track of these materials; to establish inventories of the raw materials and parts items to be carried in stock; to set up order points for the various items based on purchasing and manufacturing lead times in accordance with specified practice; to requisition items when available balance falls below order point.
2. To prepare reports on inventory activities on request.
3. To schedule and conduct meetings to review current status of production schedules and work jointly with the Departments involved to overcome any problems.
4. To provide internal transportation between Warehousing and Production Departments as needed to maintain production schedules.
5. To be constantly on the alert for opportunities to improve methods, materials, and procedures so as to effect economy in the operation of the Department and Division. To prepare and submit recommendations, outlining the features and anticipated savings, to management for approval.
6. To train, instruct, and assign work to employees. To administer the Corporation personnel policies within the Department, enforce safety and health regulations, and take prompt action on employee complaints to encourage good morale. To maintain current status with respect to employee morale and keep management informed about it. To review job performance of subordinates and advise them of their good points and shortcomings; to counsel them on growth potential.
7. To plan and schedule work and make effective use of employees' time. To keep Department operating expense within budget allowance.

AUTHORITY: The Inventory Control Supervisor is vested with the following authority to be exercised in keeping with all established Corporation and Division policies and procedures in carrying out the responsibilities of the office:

1. To hire authorized personnel and recommend salary-rate or employee-status changes in the Department.
2. To penalize or discharge any employee in the Department who is guilty of an infraction of Corporation rules which calls for such penalty.
3. To settle complaints or grievances in the Department within the limits of Corporation personnel policy and labor contract terms.

Relationships of Inventory Control and Other Functions. In any organization, the inventory control function primarily interrelates with scheduling, which supplies it with the inputs that determine ordering action; purchasing and shop operations, which are on the receiving end of those orders; product engineering, which controls the bills of material; manufacturing engineering, which controls the process planning; and higher management, which may have much to say about both customer service and inventory levels resulting from the ordering action.

With the growing use of computers in manufacturing, most of the historical work of the inventory control function, such as translating a given schedule through a set of bills of material and stock status records to a detailed material requirement plan, can, and in most cases probably will, be handled by a computer rather than in the inventory control unit. When that happens, inventory control becomes less of a clerical function, which it has largely been in the past, and more of a logical, analytical activity. It must then be fully cognizant of the manufacturing and distribution activities of the firm, so that its policies can be designed to help achieve one of its primary goals: maximum customer service with minimum inventory investment.

As this transition occurs, the interrelationship mentioned above must become more precise and measurable. The bills of material must be unambiguous, stock status must be accurate, and inventory and customer service goals must be stated and measured rationally. As this happens, the importance of scientific inventory control will more and more be recognized as a key function of the business.

GOAL SETTING

Inventory levels are frequently considered to be merely the result of many other activities, each of which has a logic of its own—in the language of mathematics, it is a dependent variable. The first step in really controlling inventory is the recognition that inventories are controllable, too, and that there are systematic ways of going about the job.

Because inventory control, in spite of its great importance to the success of the company, may have been assigned a relatively low level in the organization structure and may be considered primarily a clerical function, the real drive for better results can typically come from an enlightened top management. Borrowed money is hard to get and expensive, and inventories may be the single best source of cash for the organization. The involvement of top management in this problem is normally very healthy, and when it happens, those directly responsible for inventory control should have reasonable and achievable goals spelled out and understood.

The yardstick used to define those goals is generally "inventory turnover," which is merely some measure of output divided by the inventory balance at the point in time being measured. The output may be expressed as "sales" or "inventory cost of sales" to put it on the same valuation as the inventory itself. The latter is usually preferable for the individual firm and follows the general rule that the numerator and denominator of the turnover fraction should if possible be stated in exactly the same terms (pounds of steel, barrels of oil, dollars of inventory cost, and the like).

Stating the output for goal setting raises another question: Over what period of time? Ideally, it should be the output over the immediate future during which the stocks on hand will be used up. For example, if there are 100 units of a commodity on hand and the usage of that commodity over the next three months will be 25, 35, 40, then there is now exactly three months' usage on hand, and the turnover is 12 divided by 3, or at the rate of 4 times per year. Using future requirements is the best way to make the turnover calculation, if those requirements are fairly definite. The more indefinite the forecasts, the less value that making the calculation on future output has.

An alternative is to make the calculation on current output levels (for example, the current month, annualized), and this is done for gross economic studies. That number may be difficult to define for any one company, and so the output levels of the immediate past—for example, year-to-date annualized output—may be used, recognizing that if volume fluctuates during the year, a distortion is introduced. In any case, it should be realized that turnover is a measuring stick and that if it is used in a consistent manner, it probably will be satisfactory.

Once the means of measurement has been decided on, the next step in goal setting is to define exactly what is to be measured. For this purpose, five basic kinds of inventory have already been mentioned: (1) raw material, (2) work in process, (3) manufactured and purchased parts and components, (4) work in assembly, and (5) finished products. These must be broken down into more meaningful elements. For example, under "raw materials" may come "steel," which can be segregated into "sheet," "plate," "tubing," and the like. "Sheet" will be further classified into size, metallurgical specifications, conditions, and so on. Naturally, this entails a long job, but it is justified for the same reason as the industrial engineer's attention to detailed work elements.

The point in time fixed for making an analysis of this kind may coincide with the taking of physical inventory, when much of the information may be properly coded. Or the job may be done section by section over a longer period of time.

After the inventories are described in detail, the usage pattern (frequency and size of demands) must be determined. Where this is not available through production records, foremen's estimates or other approximations may be good enough. Putting the two sets of figures together will give the number of weeks' usage on hand (a reciprocal function of the turnover) for any item or group of items. For example, if there are 500 tons of plate steel on hand and average usage is 50 tons per week, then there are 10 weeks' usage on hand, and the turnover is $52/10=5.2$.

Now the question of theoretical optimum turnover can be addressed. This concept is similar to the industrial engineering concept of standard data: under normal conditions and good performance, what should we expect? We have ten weeks' usage of plate on hand, for example, but how much should we really have under normal conditions? If all of it can be obtained from local steel warehouses with no cost penalty, perhaps we should expect just enough to protect against the dislocation of that service. If some or all of it requires special mill runs to get an acceptable price, six months' or a year's usage on hand may be "normal." Whatever is chosen as normal, however, should not be considered as unchangeable. One plant had a steel inventory problem because it required over 1,000 different types and sizes of steel on hand. A serious effort at standardization reduced these to about 250 and reduced the value of the steel inventory from about $1 million to $300,000.

Even after all the work of collecting information on balances and usages is completed, if a plant has, say, 30,000 items on hand in all stages of production, it is unlikely that each of these can be considered separately to determine the theoretical optimum inventory turnover. Assigning the analysis of different kinds of inventory to different people will help. But in most cases the items will have to be grouped into classes for goal setting purposes, such as nuts and bolts, transistors, plating solution, and engines. There is no general answer to the question of how they should be put together, but however it is done, each significant group should be laid out as shown by Figure 7-4.

This table, when constructed, will permit (1) the calculation of current weeks on hand or turnover for any significant element or group of elements of inventory, (2) the calculation of the theoretical optimum turnover for each, and (3) the identification of the significant blocks of inventory and surpluses on hand.

Identification raw material	(1) Inventory on hand	(2) Average weekly usage	(3) Weeks on hand	(4) Theo-retical optimum weeks on hand	(5) Theo-retical optimum inventory (1) × (4)/ (2)	(6) Supplies on hand (1) − (5)
Sheet.........						
Plate.........						
etc..........						

Fig. 7-4.   Format of Table for Developing Theoretical Optimum Inventory.

The theoretical optimum turnover levels should be the goals for the organization. It is not true that the higher the turnover the better the inventory performance, because higher-than-optimum turnover will generally result in higher levels of cost. It is important that a finite goal be set so that unlimited pressure for turnover improvement can be avoided.

Figure 7-4 will also identify the principal surpluses on hand. Normally, the "80–20 rule" will hold: 80 percent of the theoretically surplus inventory will be accounted for by 20 percent of the elements studied. Obviously, that is where the attention of the organization should be directed if the goal is the reduction of inventory investment. Some of the specific actions which can then be taken are described later.

What we have tried to present here is a general approach to the setting of rational goals for inventory control. In the absence of such objective goals, the subject tends to become merely a bundle of techniques or, worse, a routine resultant of decisions made elsewhere in the organization. It is true that the above analysis can be a long, tedious job. But it does not usually have to be done very often, and it may result in very significant operating improvements.

BUDGETS AND MEASUREMENTS

After a company has thought enough about inventories to establish (1) clear-cut responsibilities, (2) a means of measuring performance, (3) a good idea of where the main opportunities are, and (4) rational goals and objectives, it can get down to the problem of the controls needed to achieve the desired results. These can generally be broken down into three types: (1) budgets, (2) business forecasts, and (3) operational controls.

Budgets. Most business organizations operate with an annual budget, designed to describe in detail the expected operating results for the year. The two key statements in the budget are the profit and loss statement (sales through net earnings) and the balance sheet (assets, liabilities, net worth) at the beginning and end of the period. Inventories, as has been seen, are usually an important balance sheet item, and the expected changes in inventory during the year must therefore be budgeted with care if the business is to plan its cash needs accurately. There has probably been more financial embarrassment and failure in business on this point than any other, and so it deserves most careful attention.

Having developed the detailed inventory status analysis and the theoretical optimum inventory (Figure 7-4), the business is in a position to set proper, budgeted inventory levels for the year. If the operation is not already performing at the optimum turnover levels, some estimate of time will be required to achieve those results. For example, suppose that inventory turnover is measured by annual output divided by year-end inventory balance, not an accurate measure but suitable for this purpose. Assume that output at cost of sales in Year A was $77 million, and inventory balance at the end of this year was $28.4 million, giving a Year A inventory of 2.7 ($77 divided by $28.4). The theoretical inventory turnover has been determined to be 3.8, but because of slow-moving inventories, it is estimated that a turnover of only 3.4 can be reached by the end of Year A + 1. If cost of sales output in Year A + 1 is budgeted to be $85 million, then ending inventory should be budgeted to be $85 divided by 3.4 = $25 million, a reduction of $3.4 million during the year. Monthly inventory turnovers and balances can then be budgeted by taking into consideration seasonal factors or any other factors that may apply. Once inventory budgets have been set, results should be reported regularly, along with all other financial statements.

The exact format of these reports depends on the use to which they will be put. Inventory balances and turnovers should be shown as of the end of last year, end of last month, end of this month (actual and budgeted), and perhaps forecasted or budgeted as of the end of this year to show what remains to be done. How much detail is shown in the inventory breakdown depends on the use to which it will be put. At the corporate level of a multidivisional company, gross inventories by plant may be sufficient. At the plant level, much finer breakdowns into raw material, work in process, and so on, are necessary, and beyond that into pig iron, fuel oil, engines, Job 1234, or whatever may be significant for control purposes. Because actual output may not match the budget plan, the budgeted inventory turnover should be the controlling factor, and deviations from that should be explored as closely as any other budgeted figure.

Business Forecasts. Another principal control tool for inventories is the periodic forecast. Many businesses make a monthly short-range forecast as a supplement to the annual budget. Changes in inventory during the forecasted period can be very critical. For example, an inventory change of 10 percent over a three-month period may by itself require a change in the level of production (up or down) of 10 to 20 percent. If such changes are not actually recognized in the operating plan, the forecasts may not mean much.

The simplest way to relate the inventory forecasts to the operation plans may be through the standard device of material, labor, and overhead. For a plant or a division, this analysis may be organized as shown by Figure 7-5.

The quantity A is, of course, the actual inventory change over the last three months, and the quantity B is that forecasted over the next three months. The advantage to this display of information is that the implications of those changes are immediately evident. For example, if labor is forecasted to change in a certain way, are the actions in the plant designed to support that change? If incoming material is forecasted at a certain rate, does the material commitment report verify that? Once again, inventory control can be considered as something which interacts with and partly determines other elements of the business, not merely as a resultant.

How these periodic forecasts will be developed depends to some extent on the company's financial control system. But, in any case, the individuals re-

	Last 3 months			Next 3 months		
	Input	Output	Difference	Input	Output	Difference
Material..............						
Labor................						
Overhead @ —%......						
Total.............			A			B

FIG. 7-5.   Format for Relating Inventory Forecasts to Operation Plans.

sponsible for inventory control in the organization should make these analyses regularly and follow up on their conclusions.

Operational Controls. A third group of commonly used inventory control tools can be conveniently termed "operational controls." These may be detailed operating instructions developed on the basis of analysis or experience and assumed to work in general. A power plant may plan always to have thirty days' usage of coal on hand; fabricated steel may be made exactly one week ahead of assembly requirements; twenty finished machines of a certain type may always be kept in the yard. Once these kinds of rules are established, control reports for management can be built to monitor them. If a substantial amount of inventory is involved, it should be verified that the rules are not just customary but have good reasons behind them. But if they make sense, the controls based on them have the great advantage of being easily understood and acted on. They also get lower levels of management quickly involved in the mysterious subject of inventory control.

Carrying that concept further, some plants attempt to keep continuous track of inventories by production unit within the plant and to budget for results accordingly. This approach has obvious appeal and may be very effective. There are two drawbacks, however. First, if there are a large number of material transfers involved from unit to unit, a great deal of paperwork is introduced and the added expense may be more than the control is worth. Second, if each production unit cannot really *affect* the amount of inventory that it has on hand, there may be little reason to budget it for control purposes. If the intent is to get information for action at a higher level in the organization, periodic analyses may be sufficient.

In general, budgeting, measurements, and control of inventories should be approached from the same point of view as budgeting, measurements, and control of costs. Cost control seems to be much better developed, perhaps because it is easier to understand and is familiar to more people. As a result, it is probable that most companies could make substantial gains on their inventory problems by applying to them the kinds of analysis and control techniques with which they are already familiar in controlling costs.

PHYSICAL ASPECTS OF INVENTORY CONTROL

It is generally accepted that the physical arrangement of production facilities can have an important influence on certain kinds of cost—material handling, for example. Perhaps less generally understood is how good manufacturing arrangements can affect levels of inventory and the ease of inventory control.

The general rule seems to be that a plant should be laid out and organized so that a minimum of formal inventory control is necessary. Formal inventory control is expensive and too often operates after the fact. The best plan is to incorporate it into the logic of the production facility itself. It is interesting to note that the inventory investment in operating a plant may be as much as or more than all the investment in the buildings and equipment put together. But how much attention is usually paid to that investment in planning the facility?

Product Shops. Perhaps the best place to start is to make a general distinction between product shops and process shops. A product shop can be organized in accordance with the logic of the product. A good example of this appears in Figure 7-6, which shows the layout for all machining, assembling, testing, and packaging of the WABCOPAC freight car brake system. Although thirty-eight basic models go through this line, all are similar in machining sequence, size of parts, and test code. Total elapsed time from the input of raw materials (castings, forgings, springs, gaskets, and the like) to the packaging of a complete assembly averages about three hours. Inventory control is hardly necessary except at the raw material and finished product levels.

A product may, in fact, be a subproduct—for example, frames for trucks. Here again, a shop may be designed to handle a large variety of frame models but within a strictly defined production logic.

In those cases where a product shop, which may be only a small part of a larger plant facility, is feasible, good inventory control can be made part of the facilities planning itself. Because the amount of in-process inventory is a function of the duration of time spent in production, the shop should be laid out to minimize time between operations. The simplest way to do this is to combine the operations themselves so that there is essentially no time lost between them. Where that is impossible, care should be taken that finished materials move promptly and that large accumulations of work ahead of production equipment are impossible. This approach may require flexibility on the part of operators and a certain amount of carefully placed excess capacity to handle surges, but it may result in substantially lower inventories.

In assembly operations, paced conveyors minimize time between operations; and for fixed-position assembly, performance of operations in parallel rather than in series will minimize the total accumulation of work in process in assembly. Where there are limits on how many men may work on a single assembly at once, the job may be broken down into subassemblies. Or working two shifts instead of one may move the job through assembly in half as much time. However it is done, to keep inventory low, the physical facility should be built to telescope the total assembly time to the shortest possible.

Process Shops. Many of these same comments apply to process shops, except that it is the logic of the process rather than the logic of the product which must be understood. Principal accumulations of inventory in the process should be identified, and every effort made in the facilities planning to reduce them. For example, if the process is an automatic screw machine section, a large amount of inventory may be tied up in bar stock ahead of the machines. Or a long cleaning cycle in a foundry may offer opportunities. The act of identifying the principal inventories in the process will suggest ways to reduce them to a minimum.

It is often overlooked by those responsible for inventory control that it may *not* be necessary to accept the physical plant arrangement and organization as fixed and then work within those limitations. Often a change in layout or organization, even a minor one, may make possible an inventory reduction and

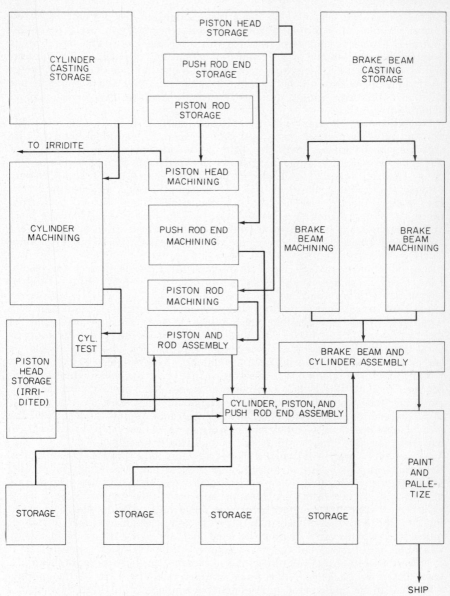

Fig. 7-6.   WABCOPAC Brake Beam Assembly Flow Chart.

a lower cost of inventory control. Consolidating stockrooms, moving one operation next to another and putting it under the same supervisor, or identifying
a unit for product shop organization, all are examples of inventory reduction
projects which may be identified, planned, and implemented in the same way
that cost reduction projects are.

How can the investment and expense involved in such an inventory reduction project be justified? Theoretically, the amount that can be spent to
break even on the project is the present value of the savings due to the in-

ventory reduction during the time that the new arrangement will be in effect. To be conservative, say the savings are evaluated at 10 percent of the inventory reduction (mostly interest on the money), and the reduction is expected to be in effect for three years. With these assumptions, up to 30 percent of the inventory reduction could be spent on the rearrangement and systems work necessary to accomplish it. If any capital investment is involved, it should be subtracted from the inventory reduction before the cutoff calculation is made. Although this is a fairly crude approach, it should help to justify expenditures for inventory reductions which may indeed be economic. And it may also help to throw some new light on the subject of engineering economics, which has spent so much time on the question of capital investment to reduce expense and so little on that of expense to reduce capital investment.

CONTROL TECHNIQUES

There are many different inventory control techniques that may be applied, depending on the level of service required, the type of product, and so on. In every case, however, there are two factors to be considered: (1) when to order, and (2) how much to order.

When to Order

There are basically two different systems used to determine when to order: (1) order point systems, and (2) periodic review systems.

Order Point Systems. Order point systems are systems in which order action takes place when the stock on hand falls below a predetermined level, usually called the order point. Replenishment orders may be placed for either fixed quantities (predetermined, using economic order quantities, for example) or for variable quantities. This type of system is illustrated graphically by Figure 7-7. In this type of system, the following terms are used:

1. Usage during lead time + safety stock.
2. Buffer quantity to prevent stock-outs from exceeding desired frequency because of fluctuations in demand or replenishment lead time. Typically, safety stock is estimated on a statistical basis to provide the desired level of performance.

Three examples of this type of system are as follows.

Bin Reserve or Two-bin Systems. A bin reserve or two-bin system is one in which the available material is divided into two parts. One part is active stock; the other is a reserve which is equivalent to the reorder point. When the open stock is depleted and the reserve is broken into, a replenishment

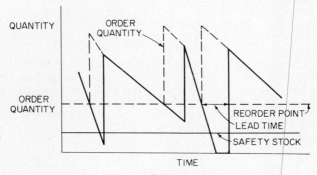

Fig. 7-7. Order Point System.

order for a predetermined quantity is initiated. This is controlled by the store-room, so that it is not necessary to keep elaborate inventory records. This system is generally used for low-cost, high-volume items that have consistent usage. It should be avoided for parts that have low or erratic usage, because for parts of this nature it is difficult to prevent stock-outs without providing excessively high safety stocks.

Min-Max Systems. A min-max system is one in which the stock is always brought back to a predetermined maximum figure when the minimum is reached. Because the minimum figure is set in advance, this is a type of order point system. The order quantity is not fixed as in the bin reserve system, however, but is variable, because the quantity ordered must be sufficient to bring the stock back to the maximum. Like the bin reserve system, this generally is applicable to low-cost, high-volume parts with consistent usage.

Perpetual Inventory Systems. In perpetual inventory systems, inventory status records are maintained so that closer control may be exercised over the ordering of material. In this type of system, all transactions are posted to the inventory record so that judgment may be used in determining when order action is to take place and what quantity is to be ordered. Typical inventory records used in a perpetual inventory system are illustrated by Figure 7-8.

Perpetual inventory systems allow review of all disbursements and requirements to screen out unusual requirements and provide information for close control of inventory. However, for such a system to be effective, it is necessary to process a large number of requirements quickly and accurately. Because all transactions must be posted, this type of system is more expensive to operate than a bin reserve or two-bin system.

Periodic Review Systems. Periodic review systems are those in which the inventory is reviewed at a fixed time interval, such as weekly or monthly, rather than when the material reaches a specific level as in the order point system. A periodic review system is illustrated graphically by Figure 7-9. In this type of system, the following terms are used:

1. Reorder point—Usage during lead time and safety stock. Lead time in this case is the manufacturing lead time plus the review period, because enough stock must be available to allow shipment between reviews.
2. Safety stock—Buffer quantity to prevent stock-outs.

Three examples of this type of system are as follows.

Min-Max Systems. In this type of system, the level of material in all bins is reviewed periodically, and orders are placed to bring the stock level back to the maximum, predetermined level. This type of system is again applicable to low-cost, high-volume items that have consistent usage.

Fixed Order Quantity Systems. In this type of system, all items are re-viewed periodically, and in contrast to the min-max system, a fixed order quantity is ordered each time. Often, the quantity to be ordered is calculated using an economic order quantity formula.

Materials Planning and Control Systems. The basic difference between this type of system and the perpetual inventory type of system described before is that where in the prior system all requirements were grouped or summarized as received, in the materials planning type of systems, requirements and orders are handled on a time-phased basis. What is meant by "time-phased handling" of requirements is shown by Figure 7-10. In this system, requirements are shown as needed in the time period in which they are due to be shipped or withdrawn from stock; orders are shown in the time period in which they are to be delivered to stock. The net is calculated for each time period. The requirements for each time period may be either actual

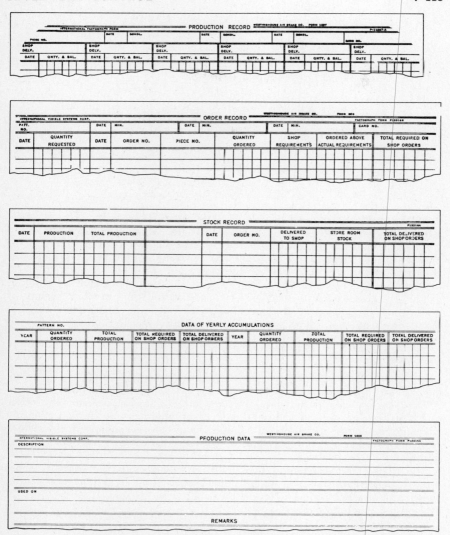

FIG. 7-8. Typical Inventory Records Used in a Perpetual Inventory System.

requirements or forecast requirements or a combination of both. This system is of particular advantage where changes in product mix can be predicted in advance. It is also advantageous where short delivery requirements are coupled with a very restricted inventory. With accurate forecasting, it is possible to schedule into stock the quantity that will be needed in each time period rather than drawing from a larger order quantity over a period of time. This system differs from the perpetual inventory system described earlier, because in the perpetual inventory system, requirements and orders are shown in a summarized fashion, as indicated in the total column of Figure 7-10. They are not netted in each time period.

In the materials planning system, requirements may be processed to show the exact quantities due in each time period, or requirements and orders

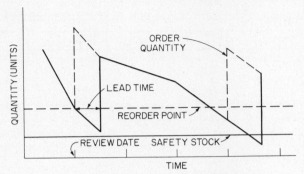

FIG. 7-9. Periodic Review System.

may be accumulated for some period of time such as one year. This accumulation system is illustrated by Figure 7-11. The accumulative system is advantageous in situations where there are a large number of transactions to be processed and where delay in processing is likely. Because all production and shipments are on an accumulative basis, the need for a sharp cutoff in handling data is reduced. In other words, instead of being concerned about clearing the records for a specific lot of material and the attendant danger of duplicating production if the records are not cleared, production may be based on completion of an accumulative quantity by the end of each time period.

How Much to Order

In determining the order quantity, there are principally two types of ordering systems: fixed order quantity systems and variable quantity systems.

Fixed Order Quantity Systems. In fixed order quantity systems, the order quantity may be determined on the basis of judgment or desired monthly coverage, or one of a number of formulas may be used. These formulas are typically called economic order quantity (EOQ) or economic lot size (ELS) formulas.

The EOQ formula is one method used for calculating order quantity. This formula determines the order quantity that results in the least total cost. This is shown graphically by Figure 7-12.

The most simple form of the EOQ formula is

$$\text{EOQ} = \sqrt{\frac{2AS}{I}}$$

where A = annual usage in dollars (annual usage units × unit cost = dollars)
S = setup and ordering costs in dollars
I = inventory carrying cost, percent per year

Time period	1	2	3	4	5	6	Total
Requirements.....	50	25	25	0	100	75	275
On order.........	100 (stock)	....	....	100	100	100	400
Net available.....	+50	−25	−25	+100	0	+25	+125

FIG. 7-10. Time-phased Handling of Requirements.

Time period	1	2	3	4	5	6
Requirements........	50	75	100	100	200	275
On order...........	100	100	100	200	300	400
Net available........	+50	+25	0	+100	+100	+125

Fig. 7-11.   Accumulation System for Requirements and Orders.

Fixed order quantities are most commonly used in conjunction with the bin reserve and perpetual inventory types of systems.

Variable Order Quantity Systems.   There are basically two types of variable order quantity systems.   The first is part of the min-max type of system. In this type of system, the order quantity, although variable, is determined by the predetermined maximum to which the stock level is to be raised.

The second type of variable order quantity is found generally as part of the material planning type of system.   Here, items may be ordered as they are received, that is, on a one-for-one basis or grouped over a period of time. If items are ordered on a one-for-one basis, each customer's order is scheduled and ordered independently of all others.   Except in the case of a pure job shop—one where there are few, if any, repeat orders—this will result in unnecessary repetition of orders.

If items are grouped over a period of time for ordering, requirements are summarized at some control level and combined for scheduling and ordering purposes.   If orders are combined in this way, it is possible to control the loading of the shop more carefully and to vary the size of the order (including such things as scrap allowance) depending on the value of the item, expected or forecast orders, and the like.

SELECTION OF CONTROL TECHNIQUES

To determine the most appropriate control technique—the methods and calculations by which materials are to be ordered and scheduled—the purpose that the inventory is to serve must be defined.   As discussed earlier, the need for good customer service must be balanced against the cost of carrying

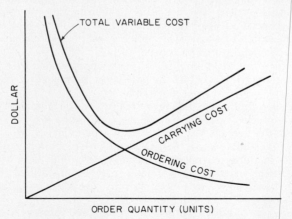

Fig. 7-12.   Graphical Representation of Economic Order Quantity.

the necessary inventory. In determining the type of control to be used, however, specific attention must be given to the lead time (the time from receipt of a customer's order to shipment) and the value of the item to be controlled.

Lead Times. In most manufacturing operations, three types of lead times must be defined: (1) the desired time for delivery of goods to the customer, which must generally be defined by marketing or sales in the light of competition; (2) the total manufacturing lead time, which is the sum of all the individual cycle times, plus waiting times for all operations or parts that must be produced after an order is received; and (3) the individual piece part lead time which is the estimated time to produce a given part. In a job shop, this is generally a function of the number of operations required rather than the actual machining times because of the length of time spent waiting for the next operation to be started. After the desired delivery lead time has been established, the product and part lead times must be reviewed to determine the level and type of inventory to be controlled.

Lead Time Analysis. Figure 7-13 shows a typical lead time analysis of a three-level product (assembly, subassemblies, and parts). Product A is represented by chain $A + E + F = 150$ days. The following table indicates the different levels of inventory that are required to satisfy different customer delivery times:

Desired customer lead time	Stocking level	Typical inventory examples
"Off the shelf":		
Less than 30 days........	A	Finished goods stocked
60 days.................	E, B	Major subassemblies that are stocked to allow assembly of several different top items
90 days.................	F, G, B	Detail parts
120 days...............	F, G, D, C	Raw materials, purchased parts stocked
More than 150 days......	No inventory required	All items ordered as required

In developing the estimated manufacturing lead time, the elapsed time at each point in the process must be considered. If the lead time is defined as the time from receipt of a customer order to delivery, the time to perform the following operations must be considered:

1. Order entry—Interpretation; pricing of order; placing of specific production and purchase orders.
2. Manufacturing lead time—Lead time for specific purchase materials; waiting time for each job to be run on a specific machine; machine run time; inspection and move time.
3. Shipping—Time required to purchase and accumulate material for shipment. If shipments consist of many orders in a carload, this must include the average length of time to accumulate a carload.

The lead time estimate used for EOQ and order point calculation is often based on an estimate based on sampling a given group of parts. From this sample, a statistical analysis can be made to determine the variation in lead times that can be expected and therefore must be taken into consideration to prevent more stock-outs than anticipated.

ABC Analysis. In addition to the lead time, the value of the parts to be

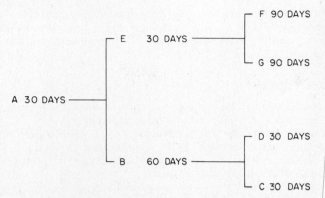

Fig. 7-13. Lead Time Analysis of a Three-level Product.

controlled should be taken into consideration. It is not reasonable to spend as much time on a $0.10 item as on a $1,000 item. Inventory items may usually be grouped so that the control effort and attention may be applied to the high volume or key items. Typically, the distribution of items is as shown by Figure 7-14.

This distribution of items and value, often called the *ABC* analysis, allows concentration of the control effort on those items that are the most significant. The analysis can be made by calculating the annual dollar volume for each individual item, and then ranking the items in descending order. In every case, a relatively small number of items will make up a large percentage of the value to be controlled.

Figure 7-15 shows the selection of some of the inventory control techniques based on the lead time requirements and the value of the item to be controlled.

As illustrated in the table, for high-value items some form of accurate record keeping for inventory control is required. For high-value items which need not be delivered from stock—that is, where some lead time is allowed—the material planning technique is usually used, because it allows greater flexibility and control in ordering and scheduling material than does

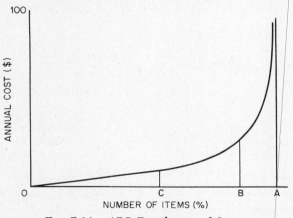

Fig. 7-14. *ABC* Distribution of Items.

the perpetual inventory system. For low-value items, regardless of the delivery requirements, it is usually more economical to order and control material without counting each receipt and disbursement—to use bin reserve or min-max systems.

APPLICATION PROBLEMS

In the application of the various inventory control techniques previously discussed, there are several key areas to be considered.

Generation of Usage for EOQ Formulas. One of the key elements to successful use of the EOQ and ROP (reorder point) formulas is accurate predicting of the usage that will occur in the future. This prediction may be generated in two basically different ways.

1. Extrapolation of actual past usage by moving average or exponential smoothing techniques
2. Forecasting future demands based on known customer demands, specific jobs, and judgment

In practice, both techniques are usually combined in the determination of the usage that is the basis for EOQ and ROP calculations, if material must be delivered off the shelf.

In situations where the materials planning concept is used for high-value items, the specific time-phased requirements scheduled in the future may be the basis for forecasting usage for C (low-value) items. In this way, the forecast of future usage has a base of actual requirements and should tend to be more accurate.

Development of Inventory Control Point. In situations where the delivery lead time conditions require delivery "off the shelf," the inventory control point for an item must be the completed item, so that it may be shipped immediately as orders are received. However, in situations where some lead time can be allowed—generally those situations where the materials planning type of system is used—inventory can often be controlled at some lower level. Thus, depending on the lead time requirements, material may be held as subassemblies ready for final assembly, held as parts ready to go into subassemblies, or held in the form of bar stock and purchased materials. Generally speaking, the further down in the bill of material that the control point is established, the greater the flexibility in the use of inventory and the less inventory required overall. In fact, in operations where it is possible to

Value of item	Delivery	
	Off the shelf	Lead time allowed
High (A and B)	Perpetual inventory	Materials planning
Low (C)	Bin reserve or min-max	

FIG. 7-15. Appropriate Inventory Control Techniques Based on Lead Time and Item Value.

provide many variations in the finished product, the establishment of the control point is one of the basic manufacturing decisions to be made in putting an item into production.

After the control point has been established, customer orders are exploded down to the control point. Parts requirements are then summarized at the control point for periodic order action. In materials planning systems, orders will be compared with forecasts at this point and schedules adjusted accordingly.

Scheduling and Ordering. After the specific order quantities have been established, purchase or production orders must be prepared and released for manufacture. Generally speaking, in an order point system the order should be released immediately, showing the required completion date. In materials planning systems, orders should be held, if possible, until the required start date which is the completion date less lead time.

If orders are released for manufacturing early, two problems may occur.

1. Apparent lead times may be lengthened as the load increases, resulting in increasing the order points and corresponding overloading in the shop.
2. As jobs are fed into the shop early, more urgent jobs may be deferred, resulting in deterioration of performance to schedule dates.

Use of Inventory for Load Leveling. Inventory may be used as a buffer to level the factory load where mix changes and seasonal loading problems exist. In this case, orders may be released to the factory for completion earlier than expected. They should not be released to *start* earlier than needed because of the problems that this may cause.

Inventory Identification System. Fundamental to the problem of inventory control is the identification and classification system that is used. In many cases, items are identified in numerical sequence with little if any logic in the assignment of the numbers. This tends to aggravate many inventory problems.

The ideal system is one that allows the following:

1. Identification of similar manufactured items such as brackets, braces, and so on
2. Identification of similar basic materials such as alloy steels
3. Identification of finished items that use the same basic assemblies

One example of this type of system is:

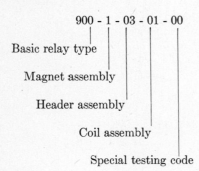

$$900 - 1 - 03 - 01 - 00$$

Basic relay type

Magnet assembly

Header assembly

Coil assembly

Special testing code

In this numbering system, the piece number indicates what the product is and what the basic components used in assembly are. This allows flexibility in the use of material and inventory control.

USE OF COMPUTERS

Much of the work in the inventory control area is ideally suited for modern high-speed computers.   Some of the applications are as follows:

1. Maintaining perpetual inventory records
2. Calculation of order quantities and order points
3. Calculation of average usage—including use of exponential smoothing techniques for forecasting requirements
4. Simulation of the effect on inventory of specific actions; calculation of inventory investment based on forecast production

Basically, the computer may be used to store and manipulate the information needed to create a viable inventory information system.   Some of the information that should be considered for use in a computer-oriented inventory system is as follows:

DATA ELEMENT
PART NUMBER
DRAWING
INVENTORY STATUS
PLANNER CODE
PRODUCT CODE
LEAD TIME
   MANUFACTURING—ALL LEVELS
                    —SINGLE LEVEL
   MARKETING—CUSTOMER DELIVERY TIME
STOREROOM
UNIT OF MEASURE
UNIT COST
   LABOR
   OVERHEAD
   MATERIAL
   TOTAL
STOCK BALANCE
AVAILABLE BALANCE
ACCUMULATED REQUIREMENTS THIS YEAR
USAGE LAST YEAR
USAGE PRIOR YEAR
ORDER POINT
REQUIREMENTS
   TOTAL
   OVERDUE
   BY TIME PERIOD
ON ORDER
   TOTAL
   OVERDUE
   BY TIME PERIOD
NET BALANCE (ORD-REQ)
   TOTAL
   OVERDUE
   BY TIME PERIOD
WRITTEN & UNWRITTEN ORDERS
   DATE ISSUED
   QUANTITY
   COMPLETED
   START DATE
   DUE DATE
   ORDER STATUS
   OPERATION STATUS
   FROM SECTION
   TO SECTION

In the operation of a computer-oriented system, several benefits may be obtained. One of the most important is the use of exception reports to pinpoint areas where action is needed. Typical of these reports are the following:

1. Order point reached reports
2. Date delivery/material overdue from vendor reports
3. Date of last usage report (to flag slow-moving inventory items)

In the installation of computer-oriented systems, great attention must be paid to the accuracy of the data used and to the accuracy of the transactions that take place to update the records. If the accuracy of the records is allowed to deteriorate, the improvements in efficiency gained through the high speed of the computer may be lost.

BIBLIOGRAPHY

Holt, Charles C., Franco Modigliani, John F. Muth, and Herbert A. Simon, *Planning, Production, Inventories and Work Force,* Prentice-Hall, Inc., Englewood Cliffs, N.J., 1960.

Magee, John F., and David M. Boodman, *Production Planning and Inventory Control,* 2d ed., McGraw-Hill Book Company, New York, 1967.

Plossl, G. W., and O. E. Wight, *Production and Inventory Control,* Prentice-Hall, Inc., Englewood Cliffs, N.J., 1967.

Reinfeld, Nyles V., *Production Control,* Prentice-Hall, Inc., Englewood Cliffs, N.J., 1959.

CHAPTER EIGHT

Make or Buy

FRANK H. McCARTY *Corporate Director—Industrial Engineering, Raytheon Company, Lexington, Massachusetts*

In an atmosphere of increasing competition, one of the most perplexing problems that a manufacturing manager faces is arriving at a good make-or-buy decision. Because of the pressures of normal business and the detail required to formulate a make-or-buy decision, he will often delegate this task. Frequently, the eventual decision is made at such a low level that it is ineffective, but the responsibility in terms of profit or loss still rests with the manager. Although this is not one of the more rewarding managerial duties, it is an extremely important one. Consequently, it must be handled in a well-organized fashion. Proper preparation can alleviate much of the routine drudgery associated with a decision of this nature.

A manufacturing manager can expect to face this problem in such circumstances as:

1. The introduction of a new product
2. The reevaluation of an existing product that is failing to contribute to anticipated profits
3. The preparation of competitive bid proposals for new products
4. The development of a second or alternative source
5. The need to stabilize the work force by building in-house rather than purchasing a part or assembly
6. The need to balance shop loading to meet present and future commitments
7. The need to maintain direct control of quality and reliability over a particular product or process

The purpose of this chapter is to develop a logical and systematic approach to the make-or-buy decision.

APPROACH TO MAKE-OR-BUY DECISIONS

Concisely stated, the logical and systematic approach to a make-or-buy decision consists of the five major steps illustrated by Figure 8-1. These are:

1. Utilization of present organization
2. Evaluation and analysis process
3. Decision process
4. Implementation and follow-through
5. Measure, record, and publish final results

Some of the most important factors in any make-or-buy decision involve schedule, costs, facilities, and manpower. This chapter will provide guidelines to assist the manufacturing manager in arriving at good decisions. It will show how to manage a make-or-buy decision process rather than emphasizing the actual mechanics of economic and mathematical analysis.

Uppermost in the mind of the manufacturing manager in the make-or-buy decision process should be a continual awareness of the impact on cost, quality, and delivery. One of the most valuable tools during the decision process is to develop and maintain a questioning attitude.

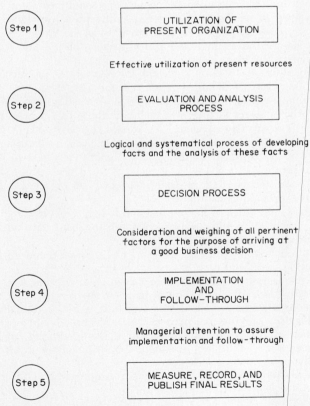

Fig. 8-1. Steps to a Logical and Systematic Make-or-Buy Decision.

THE ORGANIZATION—ITS ROLE

The make-or-buy decision should be reached by a team effort, formally called a "Make-or-Buy Committee." Because of the importance of the decision and the great number of details involved, the scope of such a decision goes beyond the capabilities of any one individual.

The responsibility for the final decision to either make or buy a part, product, or service usually rests with the manufacturing manager. The way in which he organizes and plans the preparatory work is therefore important. The guidelines that follow will only be as good as the caliber of the organization set up to perform the functions involved in make-or-buy decisions.

An organized approach does not imply the adding of another department or increasing the people already in existing departments, but rather involves the effective use of talent already available.

As products, processes, and services become more complicated, there is a greater need for more and more participation by various specialists. These specialists cross not only all lines in manufacturing but those in general management as well. For example, the personnel department will in some cases participate in a make-or-buy decision that affects people in terms of the union contract, special skill requirements, and extraordinary training requirements.

The make-or-buy committee should have representatives from the various functions involved in reaching a decision, as illustrated by Figure 8-2. The information supplied by these representatives must be evaluated, analyzed, and brought before the committee for the purpose of making recommendations to the manager of manufacturing.

There probably never will be sufficient information to permit making the perfect decision. A considerable amount of the risk, however, can be removed by organizing properly to make available all existing information. This, coupled with the manager's experience, will contribute to a successful decision.

Use of the Present Organization. It should be decided at the outset whether the information should be gathered by a formal committee or by an individual especially assigned to this task. Committee action generally produces the best results.

When a committee is used, a chairman must be selected. He should preferably have certain qualifications:

1. A broad knowledge of the product and industry involved
2. The ability to coordinate and evaluate significant data and eliminate superfluous facts
3. A thorough knowledge of the company's present and future manufacturing capabilities
4. Ability to select the necessary talent from other departments

It is generally desirable to set up a make-or-buy committee charter and issue position descriptions for committee members, even though these people perform in this area only on a temporary basis. There should be representatives from each of the major functions within manufacturing, including industrial engineering, purchasing, production and inventory control, quality control, and the production department.

Figure 8-3 illustrates the departments and functions frequently involved in a make-or-buy decision.

Customer Service. Factors which may affect customer service include the effects on products already in the field, the documentation impact on service

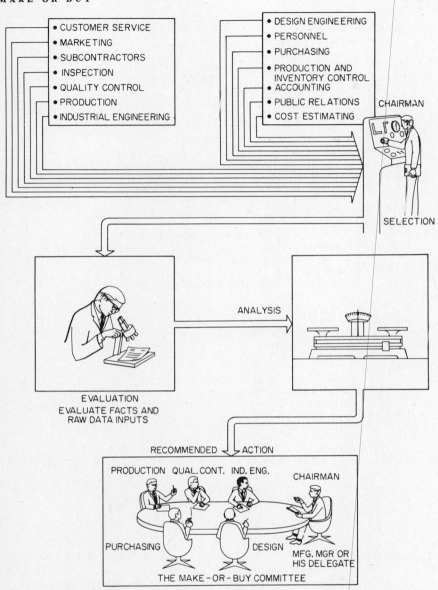

- CUSTOMER SERVICE
- MARKETING
- SUBCONTRACTORS
- INSPECTION
- QUALITY CONTROL
- PRODUCTION
- INDUSTRIAL ENGINEERING

- DESIGN ENGINEERING
- PERSONNEL
- PURCHASING
- PRODUCTION AND INVENTORY CONTROL
- ACCOUNTING
- PUBLIC RELATIONS
- COST ESTIMATING

CHAIRMAN

SELECTION

ANALYSIS

EVALUATION
EVALUATE FACTS AND
RAW DATA INPUTS

RECOMMENDED ACTION

PRODUCTION   QUAL. CONT.   IND. ENG.   CHAIRMAN

PURCHASING   DESIGN   MFG. MGR OR
HIS DELEGATE

THE MAKE-OR-BUY COMMITTEE

FIG. 8-2. Functional Participation in the Evaluation and Analysis Process.

data and technical manuals throughout the country, and the training of field service technicians and engineers.

Marketing. The marketing department can determine such things as the degree of market penetration, the follow-on sales potential, the availability of distribution systems, and the degree of competition faced. A good decision must be based not only on the marketability of the product but also on the effect it will have on the overall manufacturing organization.

1. *Customer Service*
   - ☐ Effect on products already in the field
   - ☐ Documentation impact on service data and technical manuals
   - ☐ Training of field technicians
2. *Marketing*
   - ☐ Determine market potential
   - ☐ Adequate distribution system
   - ☐ Identification of competition
3. *Subcontractors (Major)*
   - ☐ Degree of capability
   - ☐ Solvency
   - ☐ Ability to deliver either raw material or finished product
4. *Inspection and Quality Control*
   - ☐ Inspection and test equipment requirements
   - ☐ Requirement of skilled technicians
   - ☐ Special reliability and maintainability consideration
5. *Production*
   - ☐ Intimate knowledge of both capacity and capability
   - ☐ Experience with similar products
   - ☐ In concert with I.E., determine the best method
6. *Industrial Engineering*
   - ☐ Routing, processing, labor standards, and tooling
   - ☐ Plant and facilities
   - ☐ Prepare labor estimates
7. *Design Engineering*
   - ☐ Degree of manufacturability
   - ☐ Stability of design
   - ☐ Probability of engineering changes
8. *Personnel*
   - ☐ Special manpower acquisition
   - ☐ Possible labor relations implications
   - ☐ Determine special training requirements
9. *Purchasing*
   - ☐ Secure firm quotations during analysis stage
   - ☐ Procurement after ultimate decision is made
   - ☐ Prepare material cost estimate
10. *Production and Inventory Control*
    - ☐ Impact on schedule
    - ☐ Material handling peculiarities
    - ☐ Routing and dispatching in production
11. *Accounting*
    - ☐ Source of necessary funds for such things as capital equipment
    - ☐ Impact on total profit plan
    - ☐ Effect on overhead and future competitiveness
12. *Public Relations*
    - ☐ Will it complement or detract from labor force?
    - ☐ Will plant and process have a detrimental effect on the community?
13. *Cost Estimating*
    - ☐ Coordination of both labor and material estimate
    - ☐ Cost analysis of various alternatives
    - ☐ Effect on other local businesses

Fig. 8-3. Checklist of Departments and Functions Involved in a Make-or-Buy Decision.

Subcontractors. Subcontractors must be investigated before the make-or-buy decision is reached. Factors to consider are financial solvency, ability to meet specification and quality requirements, and ability to deliver raw material or the finished product to an agreed-upon schedule.

Inspection and Quality Control. The inspection and test equipment requirements, in many instances, may be limiting and very demanding. Often make-or-buy decisions are made more difficult by a lack of data in this area or the lack of engineering talent to design and develop the needed equipment. Furthermore, there may be some special reliability and maintainability considerations that are not quite evident at the time a decision is required.

Production. The production people generally have an intrinsic knowledge of both capacity and capability. They are particularly skilled in the quality and quantity inputs that will go into the total decision process. They work in concert with the industrial engineering department in determining the best methods of processing throughout the manufacturing process.

Industrial Engineering. Industrial engineers contribute in the areas of routing, processing, standards, and tooling, as well as in the setting up and maintenance of plant and facilities, the preparation of labor estimates, and the control of labor costs.

Design Engineering. The concern of the design engineer in the make-or-buy decision may not be one of dramatic engineering consequence in terms of the conceptual process of a new product, but it is important in terms of design review for manufacturability later in the production process. Too often, products are engineered that are impossible to produce. There is also the problem of unstable designs which generate numerous engineering changes during the manufacturing cycle.

Personnel. The personnel department must provide information concerning the availability of skilled labor, possible labor relations implications, and any special training requirements.

Purchasing. Purchasing plays an important role in make-or-buy decisions by securing firm quotations, especially during the analysis stage. This department is responsible for the procurement of parts, raw materials, or finished products and also for the preparation of the necessary supporting cost data relative to the material.

Production and Inventory Control. The impact of a given product on scheduling, material handling, routing, and dispatching on the production floor must be taken into consideration if the make-or-buy decision is to be a success.

Accounting. Sources of the necessary funds for such things as capital equipment and payment for material are found in the financial arm of the business. A decision made without consultation with this department could lead to chaos should there not be sufficient capital funds for additional manufacturing process equipment and facilities.

Public Relations. Public relations may become involved if the make-or-buy decision will result in adding to or subtracting from the present work force, or if it may lead to the possibility of installing a process or erecting a building that would be offensive to the community. Also, it may be necessary to consider the added expense of hiring someone to coordinate company-community affairs.

Cost Estimating. Generally, the cost estimating department will coordinate both labor and material costs, perform cost analyses, and determine the effect of the decision on other products.

The number of departments involved in any one decision will depend on the nature of the product. Certainly, not all departments will have to participate in every make-or-buy decision.

When the manufacturing manager has analyzed a particular situation, selected the proper departments to participate in the decision, and made the committee appointments, he is ready to proceed toward a logical make-or-buy decision. The following steps describe a logical approach.

EVALUATION AND ANALYSIS PROCESS

Preliminary evaluation and analysis will pay off considerably by providing sufficient information to enable a good decision to be made. A series of logical steps should be followed which will assure, if not necessarily the right decision, at least a sound decision.

Gather All the Facts. Fact gathering starts with the determination of the real reason for conducting the make-or-buy study, as well as of what specifically is involved. It may be a new product, a new part of an existing product, or the introduction of a new process. Whatever the reason, it should be clearly defined and stated. This eliminates the common problem resulting from a make-or-buy situation that was not clearly understood from the start.

Such things as quantities of items involved and quality levels required should be considered. Special customer requirements must be made clear. Shop loading and capacity must be taken into account. Sometimes a product could be made in-house from a technological point of view, but because of the shop load and previous commitments, it cannot be handled even on a multishift basis. These economic and technical factors must be taken into consideration for a successful make-or-buy decision.

Secure All Physical Aids. Physical aids are such things as engineering drawings, the physical part or assembly, a detailed parts list if it exists, and samples from competitors if they are available. This information will assist in evaluating labor content, material content, and drain on facilities.

Determine That the Right Departments are Represented on the Make-or-Buy Committee. This is especially necessary in organizations that establish a permanent make-or-buy committee of representatives from various departments. For instance, it may be desirable to have design engineering rather than marketing represented on a certain committee. Although the selection of people on the make-or-buy committee should be left up to the chairman, it will be advisable for the manager of manufacturing to approve the functions represented on the committee.

Prepare a Competitive Cost Analysis. The major elements of cost for most industries and products are:

1. Prime material costs
2. Direct labor costs
3. Indirect labor costs
4. Tooling costs
5. Test and inspection costs

In addition to these major elements, possible capital investments in the form of special machinery and plant facilities must be considered. There are many ways in which a detailed cost comparison can be made; the way chosen must be tailored to each particular set of circumstances. Figure 8-4 is but one example of a cost comparison where in-house costs, in terms of a make decision, are compared to an outside vendor's cost in terms of buying the same part.

Unit Product Cost versus Unit Product Cost. If possible, be sure to evaluate like cost elements such as unit product cost versus unit product cost or material cost versus material cost.

Generally, however, when comparing the cost to produce a product against the cost to buy, the comparison will be between a detailed cost to make against a selling price. Rarely will it be possible to get the detailed cost breakdown shown by Figure 8-4 from the prospective vendor.

Another very important point to consider is the effect on overhead should

MAKE-OR-BUY COST ANALYSIS

Date _____

Part number _____   Description _____

Quantity _____

	In-house Make		Buy Outside
Material costs			
Raw	$200.00		$150.00
Finished	500.00		300.00
Min/max	50.00		10.00
Other			
Total	$750.00		$460.00
Overhead application 10%	75.00	10%	46.00
Unit material costs	$825.00		$506.00
Labor costs			
Direct			
Fabrication	$100.00		$ 50.00
Assembly	75.00		35.00
Inspection	10.00		10.00
Test	15.00		20.00
Other	—		
Total	$200.00		$115.00
Support			
Industrial engineering	$ 25.00		$ 15.00
Production control	50.00		5.00
Quality control	10.00		5.00
Other	—		
Total	$285.00		$140.00
Overhead application 100%	285.00	150%	210.00
Unit labor costs	$570.00		$350.00
	$1,395.00		$856.00
Amortized tool costs (total ÷ by qty.)	200.00		175.00
Packaging costs	10.00		10.00
Unit product costs	$1,605.00		$1,041.00
Number of pieces	x 100		x 100
Contract product cost	$160,500.00		$104,100.00

FIG. 8-4.   Typical Cost Comparison.

the vendor's price be less than the cost to make, and it is decided to buy the product. It may be economical to purchase the part outside, but the long-term result may be a higher overhead rate.

Consider the Alternatives. In the decision process, any available alternatives should be considered. A decision to make the product will commit facilities, manpower, and overall company resources. In this instance, it may be wise to consider not only the alternatives of either making the entire product or buying it, but also of making or buying a portion of the product.

Advantages and Disadvantages. It is often desirable to list each significant item on a sheet of paper for examination and comparison. Considering each item in the light of its advantages and disadvantages will help in making a successful make-or-buy decision.

DECISION PROCESS

With the steps of the evaluation and analysis process completed, and with a clear understanding of all the cost elements, relative facts, and alternatives involved, the moment of the final decision approaches.

To ensure success, however, it would be well to give consideration to the predecision checklist shown by Figure 8-5. This checklist, by closing the in-

ENGINEERING QUESTIONS

YES   NO

Is the product, part, or assembly adequately engineered?
Is adequate engineering documentation available?
    1. Engineering drawings
    2. Bills of material
    3. Individual part specifications
    4. Working prototypes, samples, and the like
Is the design pushing the state of the art?

MATERIAL QUESTIONS

HIGH LOW

Level of confidence in material prices
    1. Vendor telephone quotations __% of dollars __% of items
    2. Vendor written quotations __% of dollars __% of items
    3. Buyers' estimates __% of dollars __% of items
    4. Catalog prices __% of dollars __% of items

YES   NO

Are firm delivery dates available?
Have material handling and storage been considered?
Has a purchasing plan been developed?
Has scrap allowance been considered?

LABOR QUESTIONS

YES   NO

Have preliminary processes been written?
Have work standards been applied?
Have tooling requirements been developed?
Is manpower presently available?
Is special manpower training required?
Is adequate manufacturing engineering available?

SPACE AND FACILITIES QUESTIONS

YES   NO

Has capital equipment been considered?
Is sufficient factory space available?
Are there any special plant rearrangement considerations?
Are the necessary utilities available?

FIG. 8-5. Manufacturing Manager's Predecision Checklist.

formation loop, provides an organized means by which a manufacturing manager can make, with some degree of confidence, a make-or-buy decision. It not only assists him in formulating the decision, but also serves as a basis for investigation and analysis at a later date, should the outcome of the decision be less than what was expected. The checklist shown is by no means all-inclusive, but it should help to convey the idea that each manufacturing manager should develop a checklist applicable to his own circumstances.

Generally speaking, for most industrial situations requiring a make-or-buy decision, there are four major categories of questions to consider, namely:

1. Engineering questions
2. Material questions
3. Labor questions
4. Space and facilities questions

By considering these additional factors, further data on which to base the decision will be obtained.

Engineering Questions. *Is the Product, Part, or Assembly Adequately Engineered?* On a complicated piece of equipment, this question can become the sole guiding factor. Without proper design engineering, it will be very difficult to make the part inside, but even more difficult to effect a successful out-of-house purchase. For the most part, the only point at which placing an item of this nature outside should be considered would be in the preplanning stage, especially if it is felt that the product will be completely engineered by the time of release. It is wise to avoid subcontracting work that should be kept in-house because of the state of the engineering design.

Is Adequate Engineering Documentation Available? The availability of adequate engineering documentation will have a bearing on the decision. This documentation includes engineering drawings, bills of material, individual part specifications, working prototypes and samples, and the like. As much of this documentation as possible should be available.

Is the Design Pushing the State of the Art? Extreme caution should be exercised in subcontracting work which is "pushing the state of the art." This also holds true for attempts to bring in-house a product with which the organization has little or no experience, especially if the technology is new.

Material Questions. *Level of Confidence in Material Prices.* An important concern is the level of confidence which may be had in quoted material prices, especially if the product is an assembly. Classifying material costs in terms of percent of dollars and percent of items by vendor telephone quotations received, vendor written quotations on file, buyers' estimates, and catalog prices can give valuable information.

Are Firm Delivery Dates Available? Should the answer to this question be no, then it is important to proceed immediately to establish tentative dates to be used as targets. Many times a part is bought outside because of cost considerations with no thought given to whether or not it can be delivered on time by the vendor.

Have Material Handling and Storage Been Considered? If material handling and storage have not been taken into account, thought must be given to how material will be handled, how adequate storage can be provided, and how storage conditions can be made such that there will be no deterioration in storage.

Has a Purchasing Plan Been Developed? A purchasing plan should include the development of the requisition, the quotation cycle, the placing of the requisitions, and the final purchase order.

Has Scrap Allowance Been Considered? Scrap allowance and any allowances for spoilage and other contingencies must be considered. If left out, especially on large-volume items, unfavorable costs can easily result.

Labor Questions. *Have Preliminary Processes Been Written?* Preliminary processes must be written, especially in areas which are pushing the state of the art or which introduce into the manufacturing system a process that has not been handled before. The ability to develop these processes, and the fact that they are available, will lend a degree of confidence to the final make-or-buy decision. If, however, the industrial engineering people have been unable to provide this information, it may be because it is difficult to develop. Before making a decision, it may be desirable to take another look at how the work can be performed with the manpower and equipment available.

Have Work Standards Been Applied? These can be either engineered work standards developed by MTM or Work Factor, or estimated standards. As a minimum, careful estimates of the time for the various processes should be made to maintain at least some sort of control over labor costs.

Have Tooling Requirements Been Developed? This, of course, refers back to methods and process planning. If tooling has not been considered, it may be another area to look into because of possible special tooling requirements. Tooling costs will affect the piece price of the item, and if they are unduly high, the best decision may be to place the order outside rather than in-house.

Is Manpower Presently Available? Manpower is a critical consideration in areas where manpower and needed skills are scarce. Before bringing a product in-house, the company must be sure that it can either secure the properly skilled manpower or train people in the required skills.

Is Special Manpower Training Required? If special training is required, the company should be equipped to handle it. The cost of the training must be considered in the decision process.

Is Adequate Manufacturing Engineering Available? Too frequently, companies will embark on a "make in-house" program without adequate manufacturing engineering coverage in terms of methods, standards, tooling, and production engineering. Without this technical arm in manufacturing, a decision to make in-house could be disastrous. If the decision is to buy, it is highly desirable to investigate the technical personnel of the vendor's plant to determine whether they are capable of delivering a quality product on time and within cost limitations.

Space and Facilities Questions. *Has Capital Equipment Been Considered?* In many industrial situations, capital funds are not readily available. Therefore, the make-or-buy decision must be weighed in terms of the capital equipment required.

Is Sufficient Factory Space Available? If the decision is to make, sufficient space must be available to house the required new capital equipment and the people that may be required to run it. Space is most important because it is a requirement that cannot be provided rapidly in most situations, especially where the erection of a new facility is necessary.

Are There Any Special Plant Rearrangement Considerations? Generally, costs of rearranging the plant are handled as overhead and are not treated as a direct charge. The reason for bringing up this question at this point is that any extraordinary plant rearrangement will be not only costly but also time consuming.

Are the Necessary Utilities Available? Necessary utilities include such things as electric power, compressed air, water, and gas. "Available" means capacities sufficient for the machinery required to produce the product.

With the predecision evaluation and analysis completed, the moment of truth is at hand. In any industrial situation, there probably will never be at hand all the facts needed to make the perfect decision; but by compiling all the information that the organization can gather, the probability of making a good decision is increased.

IMPLEMENTATION AND FOLLOW-THROUGH

Once the final decision is made, the proper mechanism must be set up to make certain that the decision is carried out. All departments, subsections, and individuals must be informed of the decision, especially those that can influence its outcome. For instance, if the purchasing department and the industrial engineering department are not informed of the final decision, the purchasing department may buy a part that was supposed to be made in-house from raw material, and the industrial engineering department may be unaware of the fact that they have to write the processes, set up the work-place, and provide the necessary machinery and facilities.

Many problems are caused by not disseminating the final information to the people who are required to act. Generally, it is a good idea to develop a detailed bill of material and to code each item on it either manually or by data processing. A simple code can be set up such as P.V.—purchased from vendor, A.H.—assembly in-house, D.S.—drop ship, and so on. Coding each item on the bill of material forms the basis for a master plan. Purchasing now has a firm plan to start the purchasing cycle, and industrial engineering has instructions to set up the production department to provide the necessary manpower and machinery. It is wise always to assume that the decision will not be carried out correctly unless the manufacturing manager gives it his personal attention.

MEASURE, RECORD, AND PUBLISH FINAL RESULTS

Once the decision is made and implemented, there remains one final step, namely, to measure, record, and publish the final results.

Measurement is accomplished by the simple expedient of comparing the original cost analysis (for example, Figure 8-4) with a cost analysis showing actual performance. Simultaneously with this cost analysis, performance should be evaluated in terms of schedule and quality.

Regardless of whether this comparison proves the decision to be good or bad, the important thing is that documentation will be available for review if the company is faced with a similar decision in the future.

It is most important for the chief manufacturing executive to set up a system of regular reporting of the progress and status of the make-or-buy decisions. This, of course, will be tempered by the number of make-or-buy decisions to be made. Along with this reporting, the proper mechanism for periodic published reports should be set up so that the people who participate in the decision—the committee and perhaps people who supplied information to the committee—will get a formal feedback on the accuracy of their predictions and recommendations.

Considerable time may have to elapse before it is possible to evaluate the wisdom of the decision that was made. Each time a company is faced with a make-or-buy decision, it is likely to be approached as though it were the first time the problem came up if nothing is documented from past experience.

CONCLUSION

The make-or-buy decision has little in common with other problems facing the manufacturing manager in that there is no one set of tried and proved guidelines which cover all industrial situations.

Each manufacturing organization has its own unique set of circumstances which are different and which do not lend themselves to any single solution for the make-or-buy decision process.

In spite of this, the same set of ground rules can be used to develop a good make-or-buy decision. They are: organize, evaluate, analyze, decide, implement, and measure.

BIBLIOGRAPHY

Aljian, George W., (ed.), *Purchasing Handbook*, 2d ed., McGraw-Hill Book Company, New York, 1966.

Anthony, Robert N., "The Trouble with Profit Maximization," *Harvard Business Review*, November–December, 1960.

Barish, Norman N., *Economic Analysis for Engineering and Management Decision Making*, McGraw-Hill Book Company, New York, 1962.

Brinkerhoff, J. F., "Make or Buy," *Mill and Factory*, October, 1958.

Carroll, Phil, *How to Control Production Costs*, McGraw-Hill Book Company, New York, 1953.

England, Wilbur B., *Procurement Principles and Cases*, Richard D. Irwin, Inc., Homewood, Ill., 1962.

Schiba, Kenneth F., "Make-or-Buy Decisions, Cost and Non-cost Considerations," *National Association of Accountants Bulletin*, March, 1960.

Tucker, Spencer A., *Cost Estimating and Pricing with Machine Hour Rates*, Prentice-Hall, Inc., Englewood Cliffs, N.J., 1962.

SECTION EIGHT

PERSONNEL

CHAPTER ONE

Manpower Requirements

HAROLD F. PUFF *Professor, Department of Management, Miami University, Oxford, Ohio*

Organization planning forms the basis for manpower requirements and activities. The manufacturing manager utilizes all of management's basic elements of planning, organizing, controlling, staffing, and motivating. He should therefore be familiar with good organization principles and concepts so that he can do an efficient job of organization planning. His task is to organize human effort toward the accomplishment of company objectives. This can best be done with a master plan or organization, spelling out the functions, duties, responsibilities, and authority of the required people.

Once the basic structure and functions are determined, a quantitative assessment of the needed manpower can be made and a planning table of organization established. The objective of manpower planning is to assure that the proper quantity and quality of managers and workers will be available when needed to staff the organization structure that has been formulated to carry out the company's mission.

An annual sales forecast can form the basis for determining the work load, which can be broken down by departments into individual tasks. In plant production, machine data and work standards can be used for establishing the number of people required to meet the daily, weekly, and monthly schedules.

ESTABLISHING COMPANY POLICY

The quality of required manpower, as determined by job analysis and recorded in job specifications and descriptions, forms the basis for recruitment and selection. The staffing tasks of management encompass recruitment, selection, training, promotion, development, and utilization of personnel. In manning large organizations, these activities are handled by a personnel department or a specialized staff department.

For the overall direction of manpower, clearly written policy statements should define objectives and give relevant responsibility and authority. Procedures with stated policies should be available concerning such recurring events as layoffs, terminations, grievances, discipline, holidays, sick leave, hiring and induction of new personnel, and working conditions. Policies are thus guides to action so that the manpower function will be accomplished in a harmonious way with the least amount of conflict.

Even in a relatively stable company, an estimate must be made of the company's future requirements instead of waiting for needs and vacancies to occur. Manpower planning may assess the planned changes in numbers and nature of personnel in the light of such possible changes as expansion of present business, mergers and acquisitions, diversification of products and new markets, changes in objectives, and reorganization plans.

Long-range plans that spell out the future of the company two to five years hence should also include overall manpower planning. In many companies, a moving forecast is made by annually deleting the current year's record and projecting one year further in the future.

Line and Staff Relationships. Manpower planning is basically a line function which should not be delegated to the personnel department and forgotten. Staff personnel departments can assist and advise, but the real responsibility for sound planning of both organization and manpower should rest with the line managers—from the president to the operations manager, from the plant superintendent to the foremen.

Because line and staff conflicts may arise, there should be a definite understanding of who has the authority to do what. For example, while acting in a service and advisory capacity during hiring, the personnel department may recruit, screen, and test a number of job applicants. The final selection, however, is made by the line officer.

FACTORS IN MANPOWER PLANNING

Any corporate planning involves forecasts, objectives, policies, schedules, procedures, and budgets, all of which are also necessary in manpower planning. Manpower planning data do not stem solely from the personnel unit or line operating departments, but from a variety of sources within the organization—from marketing and sales functions, from design and engineering personnel, and from other staff functions.

Starting with a five-year forecast, a rolling five-year plan can be kept up to date by adding each year a new fifth year. The current plans may be rather detailed; future plans may be less concrete. The initial sales forecast must be based on growth trends of the recent past, market research studies, estimates of changes in business conditions, specific industry changes, and geographical area changes. A stable industry may have less risk in forecasting than industries subject to more variables have, but in any case, forecasts can be helpful in determining the volume of goods and services to be produced.

Next, the size and nature of the work force can be estimated, including the number of employees, the functions to be performed, and the needed mix of skills and background. From this analysis, objectives and policies can be set for the next five years, such as whether to fill higher level positions from within, how to recruit at lower levels with this policy in mind, whether supervisory positions ought to be filled with college graduates, and so on. If the available work force in the local population is declining, it may even be necessary to transfer production to another location. Clearly, the objective of manpower planning is to anticipate and meet needs two or three years in advance.

The manufacturing manager implements the manpower plan, objectives, and policies in his recruitment activities by training and development activities designed to upgrade present employees to fill vacancies. The scheduling for procuring the needed personnel depends on the lead time as determined by the situation within the company, by the type of industry in which it operates, and by technological changes.

For a company with multiple divisions and plants, the planning base may be the individual plant; for another, the divisions may form the planning unit, depending upon the accuracy possible in statistical projections.[1]

Determining the Quantities of Needed Manpower. The number of persons required should be established in terms of operator, technical, and managerial requirements. In general the more skilled or technical the position to be filled, the more lead time will be needed for procuring the necessary personnel. Needs for skilled and unskilled operators can be met by short-run estimation, but in a competitive labor market a company should not wait for vacancies to occur before finding replacements. Failure to plan ahead for manpower needs may prove costly in terms of work interruptions or hastily selected personnel who prove to be inadequate.

The manufacturing executive should look still further ahead to future needs for executives and technicians, including top management, middle management, and supervisory positions. The availability of engineers, technical and service maintenance men, and indirect workers is also vital to him. Determining the number needed is difficult, for their number does not necessarily vary with production as does the number of production workers.

In many of the larger companies, sales forecasting is done by economists or the market research department. In some, an annual forecast of sales is prepared by both departments and then compared and correlated to become the basis for all company planning. However, forecasting techniques, although increasingly sophisticated in recent years, are not exact, so that errors still occur.

Nevertheless, the sales forecast is the best available foundation upon which to build the labor estimate. By starting with current sales estimates, comparing them with past sales records, and adjusting for purchasing power and possible economic and political changes, it is possible to arrive at a fairly accurate figure. The past sales records will reflect cyclical and seasonal fluctuations that can be projected into the future, and the combined forecasts of local sales units, which are close to the customers in their areas, will reflect reasonably accurately the sales potential for the new period.

Once the forecast of total sales is reached, production planning begins by making an analysis of the projected work load. The total production program is broken down into department schedules. The objective is to determine the number of workers needed to do the scheduled work.

The production plan should be broken down into work units such as parts produced, products assembled, tons produced, or boxes packed. Work standards for producing these units, if available, may be used to compute manhour work loads.

From these studies, departmental manning tables can be set up showing the various kinds and amounts of labor needed.

[1] "Factors in Manpower Planning," *The Management Record,* National Industrial Conference Board, New York, September, 1960.

Absenteeism and Turnover. At this point, absenteeism and turnover should be taken into account when figuring the manpower requirements.

Absenteeism can be measured by the following formula:

$$\text{Absenteeism} = \frac{\text{man-days lost}}{\text{man-days worked} + \text{man-days lost}}$$

Those absent are not available for production, and so the figure constitutes a needed guide in manpower planning. From 3 to 6 percent absence is normal, but a greater amount will result in unmet schedules, overtime, and perhaps loss of customers unless allowance is made for it.

Estimating turnover may be difficult, because persons leave a company for many unpredictable and unannounced reasons. However, study of past turnover records will usually give usable data on which to base estimates of how many vacancies are likely to occur in the future.

Techniques Which Provide Flexibility. For short-run planning and control of manpower, flexibility is obtained by the use of overtime and expanded shift work.

The use of manpower leasing has mushroomed as a device not only for meeting manpower needs, but also for curbing manufacturing overhead. Leased manpower enters the plant ready for work virtually anywhere from assembly line to warehouse. All paperwork and administrative costs are handled by the leasing agent. This tool is very effective in the short run for emergency operations or for peak seasonal requirements.[2]

Personnel Requisition. The net available manpower of a department can be determined from the number of people on the payroll plus individuals on loan from other departments less the estimated number of quits, transfers and promotions, discharges, people on vacation, and average absenteeism. This figure subtracted from the total labor needs of the department will indicate how much labor must be added to or subtracted from the departmental work force.

The personnel department may then be informed of departmental needs by use of a personnel requisition form similar to the one shown by Figure 1-1. This form specifies what kind of employee is needed and what for.

Mathematical Techniques. Mathematical techniques are sometimes useful for manpower planning. The problem of determining the makeup of the direct-labor force in view of changing and irregular manpower requirements was approached in one company with the linear programming technique.[3]

. . . Essentially, our problem was to determine the least-cost mixture of overtime and newly hired employees for any time interval we wished to analyze. For analytical purposes, we combined the forecast of sales and the probability distribution of forecast errors into the probability distribution of future sales. This was in turn translated into a master manufacturing schedule, denoting the levels of activity in three specific categories of work:

1. Machining of major parts
2. Machining of minor parts
3. Assembly labor

Each category was expressed in attendance hours required to produce the given manufacturing schedule. Next, we measured the probability distribution function

---

[2] "Manpower Leasing," *Factory*, October, 1962.

[3] Josef Klecka, Kearney and Trecker Corporation, "An Application of Linear Programming for the Determination of the Minimum Cost Labor Mixture under Conditions of Varying Production Levels," *Proceedings American Institute of Industrial Engineers Conference*, 1962, pp. 151–157.

PERSONNEL REQUISITION

Forward original and duplicate
to Personnel Department

DEPARTMENT _____ LOCATION _____ DATE _____ SUPERVISOR _____ REQUISITION NO. _____

Date Wanted	Number of Employees Required	JOB TITLE	Grade & No.. or Spec. No.	Wage Rate or Salary Range	CHARGE CODE (Salary Employees only)

Addition ☐   Permanent ☐   Part Time ☐

Replacement ☐   Temporary ☐   Full Time ☐

If temporary, for how long? _____   If part time, what hours or days? _____

Person Replaced _____
(If replacement)

Male ☐   Female ☐

Age Limits   Min. _____   Max. _____

EDUCATION

Grammar ☐   Commercial ☐
High ☐   Engineering ☐
College ☐   Chemical ☐
Other ☐

IF ADDITION TO FORCE, STATE REASONS _____
(Use reverse side if necessary)

STATE DUTIES; ALSO ANY SPECIAL REQUIREMENTS _____
(Use reverse side if necessary)

SIGNED _____
Department Head

APPROVALS _____

(FOR PERSONNEL DEPARTMENT USE)

Position filled by	Starting Date	Starting Rate	Pay Office Notified by	REMARKS

Fig. 1-1. Personnel Requisition Form. (*Source:* How to Establish and Maintain a Personnel Department, *Research Report no. 4, 3d ed., American Management Association, New York, 1944.*)

of the occurrence of vacations throughout the year. By using this approach, we arrived at the available straight time capacity of our labor force.

Cost variables investigated and used as a part of the program were training, straight time, overtime, hiring, layoff, and fringe benefits. Also assumed was that the present work force would produce a standard hour for every hour attended and that normal loss of present employees by death, retirement, and so on would be 5 percent. After formulation of the problem, a computer was used to find the solution.

Another operations research technique useful for manpower planning is multiple regression analysis. "Stepwise multiple regression" is the statistician's name for a method of (1) selecting the significant work load factors, (2) obtaining the conversion coefficients for the work load factors to convert them into a manpower norm, and (3) describing the reliability of the norm.[4]

MANPOWER CONTROLS

The labor budget is a valuable tool for controlling manpower. It can be used for planning manpower requirements and for maintaining financial control.

The budget authorizes a ceiling for labor expenditures for each department. It is based on monthly production schedules, the number of each kind of employee required for each month, and their estimated rates of pay.

In its most common form, the labor budget is included in the conventional annual or semiannual expense budget for each department. It is developed by the department heads and reviewed and adjusted by management. Management must rely upon the judgment, analytical ability, and effectiveness of the departmental supervisors for an accurate plan.

Planning charts which show the assignment of all employees by job classification can be an effective aid in planning a change such as a major expansion of or reduction in the work force. Manning tables, listing all jobs, with the number of employees in each job, may also be of help in manpower control. An analysis from time to time may reveal labor hoarding or underutilization, or overstaffing and waste of manpower in comparison with other firms in the industry.

Some companies make use of a skills inventory which lists skills, areas of knowledge, and special abilities possessed by all company employees. This can be helpful in locating people within the company for special missions or projects, or for planning a manpower development program.

Replacement charts, position guides, and organization charts are helpful tools for management in the control of manpower.

When the work force is relatively stable, control of manpower is maintained by rigid budget allowances. Periodic reports should be made by departments to assure management that the budget plan is being followed. Figure 1-2 shows a report of this kind.

MANPOWER QUALIFICATIONS

After determining the quantities of manpower required by the various departments, the qualifications of persons who can fill these jobs adequately

[4] An explanation of the technique can be found in Richard H. Shaw and William R. Swett, *Manpower Utilization in Production Control,* American Management Association, New York, 1964. See also Raphael R. Thelwell, "An Evaluation of Linear Programming and Multiple Regression for Estimating Manpower Requirements," *Proceedings American Institute of Industrial Engineers Conference,* 1966, pp. 83–93.

J. D. ADAMS MANUFACTURING COMPANY
WEEKLY REPORT ON PERSONNEL
All Employees in U.S.A.

Week Ending September 3, 19—

	Factory production			Factory nonproduction										Total
	#9	#10	#15	#8	#11	#26	#27	#28	#30	#40	#44	#45	#46	
Actual strength 8/27/—	78	140	226	15	60	55	41	12	15	17	35	20	24	738
Actual strength 9/3/—	80	140	230	15	60	57	42	12	15	18	36	20	24	749
Extended leave	2	4	5		1					2			1	15
Standard strength	83	142	234	16	62	59	42	13	17	20	38	20	26	772
Temporary approved overage	1	4	2								1			8
Separations	1		1								1			3
Regular absentee rate (hourly paid only)	2.8	4.2	3.4	0.0	2.1	4.0	2.3	0.0	1.0	2.5		0.0	1.6	

	Other manufacturing											Total
	#2	#4	#5	#6	#12	#13	#14	#18	#22	#31	#42	
Actual strength 8/27/—	11	15	22	4	14	10	21	4	43	7	30	181
Actual strength 9/3/—	11	16	21	4	14	11	21	4	43	8	30	183
Standard strength	12	16	23	4	14	12	22	4	44	9	30	190
Temporary approved overage				1								1
Separations			1		1							1

	Commercial					Total
	#1	#3	#16	#17	#99	
Actual strength 8/27/—	30	12	7	15	7	71
Actual strength 9/3/—	30	12	7	15	7	71
Standard strength	32	12	7	16	7	74

Turnover

Hires	Separations
17	3

TOTAL 19—

160	90

Turnover percent:
J. D. Adams March 19— 0.27
Previous year— Weekly 1.02
BLS 1st 5 mo. 19— Weekly 1.05
BLS previous year— Weekly 1.03

Absentee rate
All prod. and nonprod. departments

Regular	Excluding ext. leave
3.7	2.1

Total employees factory prod. and nonproduction	749
Other mfg.	183
Commercial	71
Ext. leave	15
Grand total	1,018

FIG. 1-2. Manpower Control Report. [*Source:* Personnel Handbook, *John F. Mee (ed.), The Ronald Press Company, New York*, 1951, p. 121.]

need to be specified. The characteristics of the workers needed to perform the tasks must be known before meaningful hiring can be done.

Job Specifications. When hiring experienced workers, the ability to perform the duties and tasks required by the job may be the only criterion needed. However, for inexperienced but potentially suitable workers, formal statements of man characteristics, such as physical capacity, mental ability, emotional stability, and other attributes, may also be helpful.

Physical specifications may note the degree of standing, walking, vision, or hearing required and the extent to which the hands must be used, in part to determine whether the work can be done by handicapped workers.

Mental specifications refer to those mental processes needed on certain jobs, such as ability to solve problems, to think, or to concentrate. Levels of schooling can be specified, or experience levels can be used indirectly to measure the mental processes needed. The intelligence quotient is also an accepted measurement of the mental factor.

Emotional stability is sometimes assessed when screening those who may be emotionally unstable enough to cause labor difficulties. This factor is difficult to measure and define but can be judged by superiors when evaluating candidates for promotion. At higher levels of supervisory positions, such characteristics as judgment, creativity, sensitivity to others, and teaching ability may be important.

Job Analysis. Job analysis is an intensive, direct method of obtaining basic information about jobs. It can be accomplished through observation or by discussions with supervisors and workers. The analysis of each job should cover the following points: (1) what the worker does, (2) how he does it, (3) why he does it, and (4) the skill involved in doing it. From this information, a job description such as the one shown by Figure 1-3 can be prepared.

Job Descriptions. Occupation descriptions are available for many trade jobs. A nationwide compilation of job titles and brief job descriptions can be found in the *Dictionary of Occupational Titles* published by and available from the U.S. Government Printing Office.

One must be careful to differentiate between the analysis of the job and the analysis of the man. In man analysis, the workers who are performing the job successfully are studied to discover the characteristics they must possess. This may be through such personnel techniques as interviewing, testing, and appraisal. In job analysis, the characteristics of the job are the primary interest.

SOURCES OF LABOR SUPPLY

In general, sources for labor are internal or external. Internal sources include another department or division, a subsidiary of a company, and former employees on leave or on layoff. Internal sources are usually preferred by companies whose policy favors promotion from within or where there is considerable union pressure to rehire union members.

External sources include:
1. Applicants who come unsolicited
2. Trade and industrial associations
3. Clergymen
4. Schools and teachers
5. Customers and suppliers
6. State employment agencies (USES)
7. Commercial employment agencies
8. Advertisements in local newspapers and trade magazines

JOB NO._____ JOB COVERS OPERATION_____

JOB TITLE___Machinist — B_____

DEPARTMENT___Machine Shop_____

PLANT LOCATION_____

PRINCIPAL FUNCTION

Operates all machines and equipment in machine shop to make parts and install them in plant equipment or machines.

DUTIES

Works from sketches, blueprints, or drawings to make up simple or complex parts. Occasionally may work from a worn or broken part instead of a drawing. May do some operations on a part or all operations except welding or heat treating. Works to tolerances of $\pm0.005''$ on average jobs. May work on some precision parts that require a tolerance of $\pm0.002''$. Makes up and maintains simple dies and punches for plant equipment. May sharpen production drills and punches. Work may involve the hand fitting of parts to machines and equipment. Works with cast iron, steel, brass, stainless steel, and other materials. May occasionally do some machine rebuilding. Consults with supervisor before proceeding on new, unusual, or difficult jobs. May occasionally travel to other company plants to make emergency repairs or to rebuild machines or equipment.

EQUIPMENT & TOOLS—All machines and equipment in machine shop, i.e., milling machines, lathes, shapers, drill presses, surface grinders, band saws, and hand tools.

MATERIALS

Cast iron, steel, brass, stainless steel, cutting oil, plastics.

FIG. 1-3. Job Description.

Untapped Sources. In addition to the sources of manpower familiar to most managers and personnel departments, a creative management will realize the potential of some relatively untapped reservoirs.

Older workers are a good source of manpower, and their numbers are on the increase. Among them can be found men and women with first-rate experience, good backgrounds, and a mature outlook—qualifications often overlooked by recruiters.

Handicapped workers also represent an important source of manpower, for one out of ten working adults is handicapped in some way. Their skills, abilities, and interests are often obscured by the existence of the handicap. When hired, however, they often prove to be highly imaginative, loyal employees. With the exercise of a little creativity in placement, they can perform satisfactorily. The state rehabilitation agencies and state employment services will assist employers in analyzing vacancies, skills, and physical requirements to match the capabilities of handicapped persons to the job demands.

APPLICATION FOR EMPLOYMENT

Date _____

Print
Name _____

Address _____

City-State _____ Phone No. _____

In case of in-   Name _____
jury notify:

Address _____

Marital   No. of Dependent   Other De-
Status _____ Children _____   pendents _____

Physical Defects (explain) _____

_____

Position
Desired _____

Earnings
Expected _____

Date
Available _____

Soc. Sec. No. [| |]

Height _____ Weight _____

Sex _____   Birth
                   Date _____

Citizen of U. S.: Yes _____ No _____

Have You Ever Been Dis-
charged from a Position? _____

EDUCATION

School	Name and Location	Dates From	To	Years Completed	Dipl./Degree Yes	No	Major Course (Subject/Degree)
Grade							
High School							
College							
Graduate School							
Business or Trade							
Other							

Extracurricular School
Activities _____

_____

Current Hobbies _____

ARMED SERVICES RECORD: Have you served in the U. S. Armed Forces? Yes _____ No _____

Dates: From _____ To _____ Branch _____ Final Rank _____

Type of Discharge _____ Current Draft Status _____

PERSONAL REFERENCES

Name	Address	Occupation

EXPERIENCE (in chronological order)

Present Employer		Address		Kind of Business	
Starting Date	Starting	Salaries	Present	Reason for Leaving	
Job Title		Supervisor's Name			May we Contact?

Description of Work _____

_____

_____

FIG. 1-4. Typical Application Form. (*Source:* Management

EXPERIENCE (continued in chronological order)

Next to Last Employer		Address			Kind of Business	
Starting Date	Leaving Date			Salaries	Reason for Leaving	
			Starting	Leaving		
Job Title		Supervisor's Name				May We Contact?

Description of Work _____

Employer		Address			Kind of Business	
Starting Date	Leaving Date			Salaries	Reason for Leaving	
			Starting	Leaving		
Job Title		Supervisor's Name				May We Contact?

Description of Work _____

Employer		Address			Kind of Business	
Starting Date	Leaving Date			Salaries	Reason for Leaving	
			Starting	Leaving		
Job Title		Supervisor's Name				May We Contact?

Description of Work _____

Employer		Address			Kind of Business	
Starting Date	Leaving Date			Salaries	Reason for Leaving	
			Starting	Leaving		
Job Title		Supervisor's Name				May We Contact?

Description of Work _____

ADDITIONAL EXPERIENCE AND INFORMATION (licenses, special machines, etc.)

_____

_____

_____

_____

_____

INTERVIEWER'S COMMENTS _____

_____

_____

Date of Interview _____ Interviewed By _____

Guides, *Small Business Administration, Washington, D.C.*, 1962.)

RECRUITMENT AND SELECTION

The selection of employees is an important part of manpower management. Some executives feel that they can select people on a snap judgment basis, but there are techniques available which will provide a sounder basis for selection.

The Selection Process. To create a good impression on prospective employees, a pleasant environment for conducting interviews and a pleasant, tactful receptionist should be provided.

A preliminary interview is often helpful to screen out the unqualified and to acquaint the applicant with the company and its job opportunities.

A well-designed application form should be used. It should be complete but not voluminous. Figure 1-4 shows a typical application form. When filled in, it provides a written record of the prospective employee's background, both personal and business, so that his qualifications can be analyzed and evaluated for the job to be filled.

Laws require that persons be hired and promoted without regard to race, color, religion, national origin, age, or sex. Information of this type, including photographs, should not be requested.

Employment Tests. Employment tests are often used for screening applicants. Many kinds of tests are available to measure aptitudes, dexterity, intelligence, and personal characteristics. A comprehensive picture of the applicant's skills and abilities can be gained through a battery or series of tests. Test scores should be recognized as only one aspect of the selection process, however, and should not be unduly emphasized.

Tests commonly used for hourly workers include trade tests, oral or written, containing questions that only a qualified person could answer. An aptitude test may be used to measure capacity to learn various jobs. Dexterity tests measure ability to manipulate objects or equipment.

Tests should be valid (successful in previous uses) and reliable (consistent). If personnel departments are not set up to administer them, professional testing services are available.

The Interview. Interviews may be conducted by one or more persons. The patterned interview is well planned and organized, seeking directly the answers wanted; the nondirective interview gives the applicant a chance to talk at length on any points he cares to discuss.

The interview is where the job and the applicant meet. The applicant finds out the requirements, and the employer finds out the prospective employee's qualifications for the job. Steps in the interview procedure to be remembered are:

1. Review application as a preliminary step, looking for pertinent information, test scores, references, and the like.
2. Put the applicant at ease and establish rapport.
3. Give information; seek information not on application.
4. Make observations; watch for "halo effect" (prejudices and biases).
5. Record results.
6. Evaluate and summarize.
7. Be tactful and diplomatic. Public relations and goodwill are a by-product, regardless of outcome.

Background and Reference Checks. If an applicant meets preliminary requirements, the next step is to check work and personal references. Methods of checking include personal interviews, telephone inquiries, and letters. It is highly desirable to contact former employers, and if possible, immediate supervisors. School references, personal data, and credit bureau financial data should be checked. Watch for inflated wage and salary figures, incorrect dates of employment, and falsification of experience, levels of responsibility, and education.

If the applicant has successfully passed the interviews, testing, and checks, the decision to hire must be made. If the decision is made by the operating executive, his judgment of the predictive value of the available information comes into play at this point.

Physical Examination. Most companies require a physical examination to protect the applicant from work that he is physically incapable of performing, and to protect the employer from the potential hazard of an employee who may injure himself and endanger the health and welfare of other employees.

Induction and Orientation. The last step is to see that the new worker makes a good adjustment to the job, the company, and his fellow workers. This is discussed in some detail in the next chapter.

BIBLIOGRAPHY

"Employment Projections by Industry and Occupation, 1960–75," Special Labor Force Report no. 28, U.S. Department of Labor, U.S. Government Printing Office, Washington, D.C.

Holt, Charles C., Franco Modigliani, John F. Muth, and Herbert A. Simon, *Planning Production, Inventories, and Work Force*, Prentice-Hall, Inc., Englewood Cliffs, N.J., 1960.

Jucius, Michael J., *Personnel Management,* 6th ed., Richard D. Irwin, Inc., Homewood, Ill., 1967.

Management Guides, Small Business Administration, U.S. Government Printing Office, Washington, D.C., 1962.

Manpower Planning: A Research Bibliography, Bulletin no. 45, Industrial Relations Center, University of Minnesota, Minneapolis, October, 1966.

Mee, John F. (ed.), *Personnel Handbook,* The Ronald Press Company, New York, 1951.

Schoblock, Peter, *Manning Tables Used to Project Indirect Manpower,* Technical Bulletin, vol. 1, no. 1, Management Division, American Institute of Industrial Engineers, New York, November, 1963.

Shaw, Richard H., and William R. Swett, *Manpower Utilization in Production Control,* American Management Association, New York, 1964.

Yoder, Dale, *Personnel Management and Industrial Relations,* 5th ed., Prentice-Hall, Inc., Englewood Cliffs, N.J., 1962.

CHAPTER TWO

The New Employee

JOHN W. HANNON *Executive Vice President, Maynard Research Council, Incorporated, Pittsburgh, Pennsylvania*

The new employee's orientation commences the instant he arrives on the premises of his new employer. The impressions that are made upon him, the attitudes that are exhibited toward him, and the manner in which he is received will all contribute to his later behavior within the organization. The new employee represents a sizable investment which has already been made in his recruitment and selection for employment. The investment which will be made in the future is much greater. These investments must be protected and utilized to their fullest extent.

The steps in the successful induction of the new employee into the company, his inclusion into the work force, and his subsequent training and development will be explored in this chapter. The new employee will be considered a male semiskilled worker with prior work experience.

COST COMMITMENT WITH THE NEW EMPLOYEE

The cost commitment of the company because of the new employee is made *before* the employee reports for work. He has been recruited through advertising or other means; he has been interviewed; and he has been screened, tested, examined, and finally notified to report for work. From this point on, management must not only protect the investment already made, but also consider that each hour that the employee works represents not only wages paid to him but also the expense of others involved with his induction. Many of these future costs are obvious, but others are hidden. If the new employee "sticks," becomes a well-adjusted employee, and produces profitably, the investment has been worthwhile. If he becomes an "early quit" or must be terminated early in his employment, the entire investment not only has been lost, but also must be repeated for his replacement. What are some of these obvious and hidden costs?

8–16

Cost of Hiring. These are the costs involved in recruiting, selecting, screening, and examining the employee.

Cost of Administration. Personnel administration, hospitalization and life insurance, payroll processing of records, and supplies used in administration are only a few of the administrative costs involved with the induction of a new employee.

Cost of Supervision. The supervisor is the key figure in a proper induction procedure. To perform his function well requires considerable time and attention on his part. He not only instructs the employee, but he must introduce him to his co-workers, acquaint him with the physical surroundings, evaluate him periodically, and counsel him. While the supervisor is doing these things, his other work continues and must be covered by assistants. Multiplicity of new hires puts the supervisor further "in the hole" and increases costs of supervision, perhaps beyond tolerable limits.

Cost of Lowered Productivity. A new employee lowers the productivity of the production unit until he becomes fully trained and proficient at his new job. Some companies with group incentive plans supplement the wages of the older employees until the newcomer's productivity reaches the accepted standards. This is additional cost. Lower productivity on equipment increases operating costs of that equipment, to say nothing of the costs involved due to scheduling if this is a critical piece of equipment. Thus, the faster the new man can be trained and his productivity raised to standard, the lower the cost of lost production will be. Again, multiplicity of new hires only increases these costs.

Cost of Lowered Quality. Coupled quite closely with lowered productivity is lowered quality. Poor quality can be caused by poor training, poor attitude, or a drive for higher earnings without the necessary skills. The costs involved are those incurred in lowered productivity because the work must be done over, plus increased inspection time, rework of defective but salvageable parts, excess time in assembly if applicable, customer dissatisfaction, and probably increased costs of tooling and equipment.

Cost of Termination. Hopefully a new employee will not be terminated early in his tenure of service. If, however, this step is necessary, it also involves excess costs. In some cases, in a union shop, a grievance will result even if the employee is still probationary. In this instance, time is consumed by not only personnel in management, but by union officials as well, which will result in lowered production with its many implications. Aside from the grievance procedures, the terminated employee or the employee that quits must be administratively processed "out" as he was "in."

These are only a few of the major costs involved when investing in, or reinvesting in, a new employee. Although some of them are not immediately recognizable, they are very real costs and must be considered as preventable by a sound induction program.

OBJECTIVES OF THE INDUCTION PROCEDURE

The overall objective of the employee induction procedure should be to provide the employee with the information, environment, and opportunity to adjust properly to his new work and his new company. His loyalty and enthusiasm are to be encouraged and developed so that he may be sufficiently motivated to accept the challenges and requirements which he will encounter. The goal, then, is to produce a well-adjusted and productive employee.

There are three main functions which must be performed before the final objective can be reached.

Administrate and Communicate. Define the terms of employment in clear, concrete terms. Communicate directly so that there is no question of terms or conditions. Administer all necessary tests, examinations, forms, and agreements.

Introduce and Train. Introduce the new employee to his work group, his job, and the requirements and standards expected. Training starts here by showing him how to do the job so that his work will meet the requirements and standards of performance expected.

Build Confidence. Build the employee's confidence in himself and in his new company. Presenting the proper image from the very beginning of the induction process will build confidence in the company. Proper training and instruction will be instrumental in developing confidence in himself to do the job.

To protect the company's investment in the new employee, management must have an effective, well-planned induction procedure and use it properly. The overall goal is to help the employee make a quick and successful adjustment so that he is producing profitably in the shortest time possible. The key term here is "profitably"—in good quantity and quality, with consistency, and with the proper attitude for sustaining these conditions

IMPORTANCE OF ORIENTATION PROGRAM TO EMPLOYEE

The new employee is a person, a person with certain rights and sensitivities which must be recognized and considered in every phase of the induction process. The new employee walking through the door of the employment office or through the plant gate is entering a strange and bewildering world. Hopefully, he will spend many productive years within this world he is entering—years in which he will contribute his labor and talents to the ultimate objectives of the organization.

To the new man, the first place he enters, the first people he encounters, and the first reception he receives are his first impressions of his new employer. If the physical surroundings, the people and the reception are good, his impression will be good. The reverse is true to an even greater extent. Too many times a new man is quickly ushered through the plant gate or employment office and told to seek out his foreman. This can be a harrowing experience for the new employee, amid unfamiliar surroundings and strange people, to look for someone whom he knows by name only. In such an environment, the foreman in all probability "attaches" the new man to one of the older employees and goes on about his business.

You have an orientation program within your company of one sort or another. The question is: What kind of program do you have? Is it a "let the chips fall where they may" type or one which shows preparation, planning, and a true regard for this new asset your company has acquired?

Why so much emphasis on an orientation program? The reasons can be traced ultimately to costs of operations in most cases.

Settling Effect. A good program puts the new employee in a frame of mind which is conducive to learning and development.

Reduced Turnover. The first few days are the critical period in determining whether or not a new employee stays on the job. Insecurity in a new job is normal to some extent. If a man is merely "turned loose" on his own initiative, the percent of early "quits" will be much higher than if he is properly introduced to his new surroundings, new co-workers, and new job.

Clearing Process for Details. Included in a well-planned and well-executed program are provisions to clear up administrative "loose ends." Are all insurance forms completed? Are all withholding certificates filled out? Have all deductions been explained? Have company vacation policies, holiday pay plans, and other fringe benefits been explained? These are items which can so often be explained insufficiently or possibly forgotten. Such errors can cause ill feelings, confusion, or extra costs to both employee and employer.

Reduction of Employee Grievances. The application of good human relations principles helps form lasting impressions. The attitude of the new employee can deteriorate into one of hostility and antagonism or can develop into one of enthusiasm and cooperation.

The "Unlearning" Process. The new worker with prior experience has formed certain work habits. Many of these may be bad habits which need to be replaced. Proper instruction and familiarization with his new duties can contribute significantly to this retraining process.

Esprit de Corps. By being properly introduced to the company, its history, its people, its products, and its ambitions, the new employee absorbs some of the spirit which has made the company successful and feels that he is a part of this organization. His attitude will be reflected in his new work group and in the results of his work.

Creativity, initiative, and drive can be stimulated by impressing on the new employee how these factors have been key points in the development of the company. Conversely, the absence of this impression can lead the new worker into being satisfied to be a "just get by" employee.

Communications. The orientation and indoctrination period is the time to establish lines of communication. Let the employee know whom he can see regarding his personal problems or work problems, and on whom he can try out any new ideas. Impress on the man that you want him to communicate— to discuss his problems and suggestions.

These factors are all cost oriented. Their presence will ultimately reduce costs; their absence will certainly cause costs to be generated directly or indirectly.

NEEDS OF THE NEW EMPLOYEE

Before the planner can proceed toward building an employee induction program, he must understand certain basic facts about the person—the new employee—for whom he is building the plan. By understanding these facts, he can realize the needs of the new employee and set about satisfying them. The program designer should consider the following points as "bench marks" in setting up a plan.

Attitude toward the Company. The new employee for one reason or another has been impressed by the company. This is particularly true of the more skilled worker for whose services there is a greater demand. By accepting the new job, he is accepting the new challenges and new training requirements that he must meet to perform satisfactorily on the job. He wants to make good; the induction procedure must help him toward that goal.

Knowledge of Company. Again, the new employee probably knows something about the company and what it produces. What he knows is probably no more than enough to stimulate his interest. The induction procedure should answer his questions concerning the company's history, size, products, and people and how he will fit into the organization. This is often more than can be digested in the hour or so usually allotted. He should be given a booklet to study later or, as in some companies, be given the opportunity to see and listen to an audiovisual presentation about the company.

Conditions of Employment. Conditions of employment are of very personal interest to the new man. How long is he on probation? When will he be eligible for vacation? What are the work schedules and lunch periods? What is the pay schedule? When is payday? How soon does insurance coverage start? These are all questions that the newcomer will want answered sooner or later—better sooner than later.

Self-assurance and Confidence. Self-assurance and confidence are important bench marks. The new man is among strange people, in strange surroundings, and in a strange job. He will want to know how he is doing. He must be assured that the company will help him in his adjustment.

The person planning the induction procedure *must* consider the above points to satisfy adequately the needs of the employee. They must be kept in mind throughout the entire planning process.

PLANNING THE INDUCTION PROCEDURE

First impressions are lasting impressions. The objective is to impress the new employee favorably and to get him inducted into his new company in an impressive manner. To accomplish this goal successfully, the induction program must be carefully planned and organized. All plans must be complete and all arrangements made so that the new man will know exactly what is going to happen next. This complete state of readiness indicates to the new employee that his new company considers him a valuable asset. The well-planned program exhibits leadership, orderliness, and efficiency. This influence will at least "rub off" onto the new man.

How does one go about planning an induction program? The planner must put himself in the shoes of the new employee and carefully consider his needs as well as those of the company. The following points are some which must be considered in the induction process.

Time. Sufficient time must be allocated at each step for the employee to grasp the details and complete the various tasks required.

Reporting to Work. Are the instructions of where and when to report and what will then happen clear and concise? Tell the new employee exactly where and when to report and name the person to whom he reports. If any personal equipment, clothing, or records should be brought along the first day, they should be specified. If parking or transportation is a problem, give him advice on this too.

Meet Him. Be sure that someone is prepared to meet him at the specified arrival time. Demonstrate to the new worker that he is expected and that you are looking forward to his arrival.

Welcome Him. The first greeting will come from the person meeting the new employee. Further welcoming can be done, either individually or in a group, by some chief executive. This can be accomplished personally, if practical, or through a short movie or an audiovisual presentation. Incorporated in an audiovisual or a movie can be an introduction to the company products and facilities. Pictures and brief remarks from several company officials can be included also.

Administration. The administrative details of the induction procedure are time consuming but quite important and should be dealt with accordingly. Administration is, in most cases, the responsibility of the personnel department and is carried out immediately upon arrival of the new employee. This activity can have as much impact on the new man as nearly any other single function. Here the first work is encountered—the work of filling out forms. Consider the questions that the new man may ask and provide a counselor to help interpret and answer the questions, thus promoting a friendly atmosphere, not a curt "here, fill out these and come back when finished" atmosphere. Individually counsel the new man, or provide one counselor for a small group if individual counseling is not practical. Payroll information may be completed in the personnel department, or the new employee may be sent to the payroll department.

Personnel Orientation. Each new employee should be individually oriented by a representative of the personnel department, either at the time when the various forms are being completed or immediately after. At this time, the use of a checklist is necessary to ensure that no forms are missed or no necessary information omitted. An example of a typical checklist is shown in Figure 2-1. The new employee should be presented with his identification badge, employee's manual, ticket for a free lunch in the cafeteria, safety glasses, or other materials which he may need to begin work.

This is an appropriate time to include a briefing on union policies and labor agreement and to present the new employee with his copy of the labor agreement. Explain the seniority system, the probationary period, and his rights during the probationary period.

At this point, explain the fringe benefits to the employee, using the employee manual, described later, as a guide. Answer any questions about benefits, and use examples to show the benefits that can be derived from the various insurance plans. While using the employee's manual as a guide, the company rules and regulations can also be covered. Make sure that the new employee understands what he has been told. The use of a checklist will guard against omitting any important points. Note that in Figure 2-1 space has been provided for the employee to acknowledge that he has received and understands each item of information.

A general plant tour can be given at this point showing the location of company facilities such as cafeteria, washrooms, safety equipment, entrances and exits, locker rooms, and tool cribs. The tour should logically end in the department to which the new man will be assigned. Here the new employee is introduced to his supervisor.

Departmental Orientation. The new employee now becomes the responsibility of the supervisor. The importance of the role of the supervisor cannot be overstressed. The new employee will not be oriented to the company, to the department, or to the job until the supervisor becomes involved. Regardless of how well planned all the previous steps have been, the supervisor can make or break the total induction or orientation program.

For purposes of this discussion, assume that the new man has been turned over to the supervisor permanently. All further orientation and training will be done by the supervisor. Other methods of training will be discussed in a later section.

Time is the key point in the supervisor's orientation. The supervisor is a busy man, but he must allocate sufficient time to orient his new employee properly. The saying, "If we don't have time to do it right the first time, we have to take time to do it over" applies here. The effort that the supervisor exerts here will produce dividends in overall time saved and reduce the necessity of having to do the job over again later.

Another key point is leadership. The supervisor must exhibit leadership from the very start. He can begin by gaining the confidence of the new employee—making him feel welcome and needed.

What sequence of events does the supervisor follow in his orientation program?

NEW-EMPLOYEE CHECKLIST

NAME: _____ POSITION: _____

ASSIGNED TO _____ DEPARTMENT DATE: _____

	Dept. Initial	Employee Initial
PERSONNEL DEPARTMENT PREPARATION		
Arrange to meet and welcome employee	☐	—
Advise supervisor of arrival, name, and for what job (duplicate of application to supervisor)	☐	—
Evaluation forms to supervisor	☐	—
Arrange for official welcome by company executive (or audiovisual program)	☐	—
Arrange for training (if applicable)	☐	—
Prepare and assemble orientation materials:		
Employee manual	☐	—
Identification badge	☐	—
Free lunch ticket	☐	—
Labor agreement	☐	—
Withholding authorizations:		
Federal income tax	☐	—
Local income tax	☐	—
Union dues checkoff	☐	—
FICA	☐	—
Insurance premiums	☐	—
Credit union	☐	—
Safety equipment	☐	—
Medical history form	☐	—
Arrange for plant tour guide	☐	—
Arrange for physical exam (if applicable)	☐	—
PERSONNEL ORIENTATION		
Welcome talk or audiovisual program	☐	☐
Physical exam	☐	☐
Administration:		
Complete employment records:		
Personal data card	☐	☐
Social security card (if applicable)	☐	☐
Federal income tax forms	☐	☐
Local income tax forms	☐	☐
FICA forms	☐	☐
Insurance application forms	☐	☐
Union dues checkoff	☐	☐
Credit union deduction	☐	☐
Personnel briefing:		
Position description:		
Read job description	☐	☐
Pay rate	☐	☐
Probationary period and terms	☐	☐
Pay policy	☐	☐
Holiday pay	☐	☐
Vacation policy	☐	☐
Reporting-off procedure	☐	☐
Plant security:		
Identification badges issued	☐	☐
Personal property pass procedure	☐	☐

FIG. 2-1. Orientation Checklist.

Deductions policy.................................... □ □
Union briefing:
   Terms of agreement—contract period.................. □ □
   Seniority system..................................... □ □
   Transfer plan.. □ □
   Progression.. □ □
   Copy of agreement to employee....................... □ □
Work rules (use manual as guide):
   Point out rules in manual............................ □ □
   Personal conduct on job.............................. □ □
   Smoking plan, etc.................................... □ □
   Disciplinary procedure—conditions.................... □ □
Explain accident procedure.............................. □ □
Describe first aid services.............................. □ □
Describe safety regulations............................. □ □
Employee benefits:
   Retirement and pension plans......................... □ □
   Sickness and accident insurance...................... □ □
   Hospitalization insurance............................ □ □
   Bonus plan (if applicable)........................... □ □
   Stock purchase plan (if applicable).................. □ □
   Suggestion system.................................... □ □
   Life insurance....................................... □ □
   Cafeteria.. □ □
   Employee recreation.................................. □ □
   Employee organizations—social........................ □ □
   Employee store....................................... □ □
   Credit union... □ □
   Public transportation................................ □ □
   Parking areas.. □ □
Plant tour... □ □

SUPERVISOR'S CHECKLIST

Departmental policies:
   Work week—hours..................................... □ □
   Attendance... □ □
   Reporting off.. □ □
Function of department................................. □ □
Job description.. □ □
Pay rates.. □ □
Tour of department:
   Introduction of co-workers........................... □ □
   Introduction to union steward........................ □ □
   Safety equipment..................................... □ □
   Departmental facilities.............................. □ □
   Departmental machinery and equipment................. □ □
The job:
   Explain duties....................................... □ □
   Job instruction...................................... □ □
   Explain production standards......................... □ □
   Explain quality standards............................ □ □
   Explain incentive system............................. □ □
   Show how earnings are computed....................... □ □
Follow-up:
   Explain periodic evaluation system................... □ □
   Make periodic evaluations............................ □ □
   Monitor performance.................................. □ □
   Post-induction follow-up by personnel................ □ □

FIG. 2-1 (*Continued*). Orientation Checklist.

Get-acquainted Talk. This is an informal private conversation in which the new employee and the supervisor get to know each other. The supervisor emphasizes that the new man is needed and that the company has an interest in his development and progress on the job. The supervisor is selling a product—the company and the job—with the employee being the customer. The supervisor must "sell" the company policies and rules and the advantages of "playing the game" by the rules.

The newcomer should be given the information that he needs to understand what will be required of him by the job and by the company. Give him a general idea now of what he will do, where he will be doing it, and how he will go about it. These should be generalizations in this conversation, but they are things that the employee needs to know.

Remember, this conversation is not a speech, only a friendly, get-acquainted conversation. Promote questions by the newcomer throughout the talk, not just at the end.

Introduction to the Department. This introduction has dual advantages: the new man meets his future co-workers, and good human relations among the older employees are fostered. When an introduction is made, the supervisor tells the newcomer what job the older employee has and stresses its importance. This promotes the good feeling of the older man. There should be some orderly sequence in the introductions, such as following the flow of work through the department or by machine type.

A special point should be made of introducing the new man to the union steward of the department, if applicable. This little detail can aid in promoting present and future good labor relations.

During the introductory tour, the newcomer can become acquainted with the physical part of the department. He can be shown where the time clock is, the lockers, washroom, boundaries of the department, safety hazards and equipment, unusual machinery, the place where he will be working, and any other points of interest or concern.

Explanation of the Function of the Department. After the tour, the supervisor can explain the function of the department and how it fits into the overall company organization. Effective aids for this explanation are organization charts, product flow charts, the actual parts produced, and the assemblies they go into.

Job Instruction. The training process starts here. The training may be formal and conducted in a separate training center or area, or it may take the form of on-the-job training at the actual workplace. For the immediate purpose of discussion, assume on-the-job training.

The supervisor explains the job in detail to the new man. Included is familiarization with necessary materials, tools, and equipment. Also, if locations such as the tool crib and stockroom have not been previously shown to the newcomer, these should be pointed out now.

The supervisor performs the operation, explaining each step as he goes. Any available operation sheets are used as guides.

The new man performs the operation and explains what he is doing to the supervisor. The supervisor corrects the employee where necessary.

The employee performs several cycles of the job until the supervisor is satisfied that he can perform satisfactorily.

The expected performance is explained to the new operator. Caution should be exercised to be sure the operator knows that he is not expected to reach "standard" until his skills and proficiency develop sufficiently. The supervisor should explain how the standard is determined and what system is used—daywork, measured daywork, or an incentive bonus system. The supervisor should also instruct the employee on how to compute his earnings if an incentive system is used.

The supervisor should check on the new operator at intervals—often at first to review his progress, make suggestions and corrections, and answer any questions that the operator might have; and less frequently as the operator's performance improves.

Just as the supervisor should correct the employee for his mistakes, he should also praise him for his accomplishments. A little praise can show the new employee that he is making progress and that his accomplishments are being noted by the supervisor. A new employee wants to do a good job, and recognition for doing a good job is an indication of appreciation and a positive step in building confidence.

The supervisor must exercise caution in his praise, however. Praise should be given only when deserved or its meaning will be lost. If correction or criticism is deserved, correct or criticize; if praise is deserved, give praise.

Only one of the several training methods available has been discussed here. The other commonly accepted methods will be discussed in the section on "Training and Development" later in the chapter.

Post-induction Follow-up. The induction and orientation procedure does not end when the new employee begins his job. His progress must be noted periodically, his questions answered, and his training and development continued.

A system should be set up for formal evaluations to be made at specified intervals—perhaps after one week, one month, three months, and six months, or at the end of the probationary period—by the supervisor. These evaluations can be recorded on a form such as that shown by Figure 2-2 and retained as part of the permanent record of the employee. It is often advantageous to review these evaluations with the employee.

A follow-up conference or interview should be arranged with the personnel department after about one month's service. The purpose of this interview is to answer any administrative questions, change any forms, or take care of any official business which may have arisen during the early stages of employment. This interview also illustrates to the employee that the company cares about him.

Planning, preparation, presentation, and follow-up are the four key points to a successful orientation program. These points must be kept constantly in mind at all stages of the orientation process. Compare the process to the proverbial chain with a weak link—if one link is weak, the entire chain will be weak. Likewise, if the entire program except the departmental orientation is well planned and well executed, the total program will be weak because of this weak link. Plan and prepare and outline the presentation at *all* levels—leave nothing to chance.

EMPLOYEE MANUALS

On the reporting day and the first few days immediately following, the new employee's head is jammed full of so much new information about his new company and job that he can hardly be expected to remember it all. Details of fringe benefits, work rules, and facts of the business are items that require retention of specific details. The employee manual can serve as a reference to all these details that the new employee needs to retain.

Besides serving as a reference source, the employee manual can deliver a

GRAPHIC PROFILE MERIT RATING PLAN

Date Rated _____   Code _____   Name _____   Clock No. _____

Dept. _____   Job Grade _____

Occupation _____

YEARS — LENGTH OF SERVICE — (Check)

| 10 | 9 | 8½ | 8 | 7½ | 7 | 6½ | 6 | 5½ | 5 | 4½ | 4 | 3¾ | 3½ | 3¼ | 3 |

MONTHS

| 12 | 10 | 8 | 6 | 5 | 4 | 3 | 2 | 1 |

JUDGMENT APPLIED TO JOB

- High degree of judgment used on job.
- Applies somewhat more than usual degree of judgment to job.
- Adequate judgment applied for good performance.
- Could give better performance if more judgment were applied.
- Performs the job but uses little judgment.

QUALITY OF WORK

- Can be depended upon to produce high quality or thorough work above requirements.
- Quality or thoroughness generally somewhat above requirements.
- Adequate quality or thoroughness.
- Quality or thoroughness of work generally border line but usually acceptable.
- Generally below standard and quality or thoroughness, often not acceptable.

RESPECT OF OTHERS

- Held in high regard by most associates.
- Some indications of above average regard of others.
- Neither looked up to nor looked down upon.
- Some indication that others lack respect for this employee.
- Not respected by associates.

ATTITUDE TOWARD OTHERS

- Definitely friendly, cooperative, and tactful.
- Inclined to be friendly, cooperative, and tactful.
- Somewhat friendly and cooperative but with reserve.
- Inclined to be cold, somewhat unfriendly or moody.
- Noticeably surly, uncooperative, or quarrelsome.

RESPONSIBILITY AND SAFETY

- Particularly careful of equipment, materials, and safety of others and self.
- Good care of equipment, materials, and safe practices.
- Adequate regard for equipment, materials, and safe practices.
- Tendency to be careless and to disregard safe practices.
- Careless and indifferent. Invites accidents.

VOLUME OF WORK

- 120 to 130% Performance Hourly — Well above average of others. Incentive — Regularly better than standard.
- 110 to 120% Performance Hourly — Usually above average. Incentive — Usually better than standard.
- 100 to 110% Performance Hourly — Average output. Incentive — Standard, the average.
- 90 to 100% Performance Hourly — Somewhat below average. Incentive — Quite often under standard.
- 80 to 90% Performance Hourly — Unsatisfactory low volume. Incentive — Seldom performs at standard.

JUDGE EMPLOYEE ON PRESENT JOB

Be sure to have qualities clearly in mind. In each quality judge this employee and place a mark in the column to the right of the appropriate definition of this employee's standing in that quality. Connect marked points in columns with lines to form employee's merit rating profile.

Volume of Work: If rating Hourly Work mark "H" in column. If rating Incentive Work mark "I" in column. If both classes are rated draw profile to both marked points.

PROMOTIONAL POSSIBILITIES — (Check)

| Unlikely | Doubtful | Fair | Quite Likely | Most Probable |

Rated By _____

Copyright 1968
MAYNARD RESEARCH COUNCIL—Form No. 265

Fig. 2-2. Example of a Personnel Evaluation Form.

message to the employee. The manual tells the story of the company—the story that the company wants told, the way it wants it told. The manual also serves as a public relations vehicle because the new employee will show it to his family and friends.

The manual is another way in which the company can show the new employee it does care about him. The fact that the company took the time and money to produce something for the convenience of the employee is an indication of the concern of the employer about the employee.

The manual becomes the "official" answer to many questions. The employee obtains the answers to his questions by asking someone who may give him erroneous information, by making a mistake and being disciplined for it, or by seeking the answer through an official source—the employee manual being one of the official sources.

Organization of the Employee Manual. The manual should tell the new employee exactly the same story that he has been told during his personnel orientation and should be planned like a written transcript of the induction process.

Title, Size, and Construction. The title selected for the manual should be a "catchy" one that draws attention and should also indicate the personal nature of the booklet. A title using the word "your" imparts a sense of possession to the new employee.

The manual can range in size from a small pocket-sized booklet to a larger loose-leaf book. Both kinds have their advantages. The smaller variety can be carried in the pocket, it is economical, and the cover can usually be printed more colorfully than in the other styles. Although the loose-leaf manuals are more expensive, they impart a look of quality and are more durable. They can be updated periodically by issuing replacement sheets as, for example, when fringe benefits are changed. Often sheets are included upon which employees may record details of their pay, deductions, and so on. These pages can also be reissued annually; thus the employee will have a permanent record of pay, deductions, and payments if he desires.

Welcome and Story of the Company. Here, as in the induction process, there should be a short introductory remark by the chief executive of the company, along with his picture. This message should be short and chatty, not legal and formal sounding. The message should be followed by a short history of the company, its products, and what it is today, including pertinent statistics such as number of employees and number of plants.

Working Conditions. Items of information about the job in general belong in the section on working conditions. Among these items are:

1. Pay policy—when and how
2. Holiday pay
3. Vacation policy
4. Reporting-off procedure
5. Identification badges or cards
6. Deduction policy
7. Security plan—passes for personal property
8. Advancement—methods and procedures

Company Rules. The section on company rules contains statements concerning rules and regulations of the company. Included are:

1. Smoking policy or plan
2. Personal conduct on job
3. Disciplinary procedure—conditions

Employee Health and Safety. Included in the section on employee health and safety are:

1. The right and wrong way to work, illustrating conditions which cause the greatest number of accidents
2. Procedure to follow in case of accident
3. Description of hospital (or dispensary) services
4. Personal hygiene
5. Proper clothing and equipment
6. Safety devices
7. Rules for health and safety

Employee Benefits. The "Employee Benefits" section probably requires frequent updating as benefits change. This section includes the most detailed information found in the booklet. It is also the section most often referred to by the employee; the contents should be stated in clear, concise, plain language, making full use of tables and examples. As previously mentioned, use can be made of replaceable sheets upon which the employee can keep a record of all deductions and changes. Some of the items which might be covered in this section are:

1. Pension and retirement plans
2. Sickness and accident benefits (insurance)
3. Hospitalization insurance
4. Bonus plans (if applicable)
5. Stock purchase plans (if applicable)
6. Suggestion system or other awards
7. Life insurance

Miscellaneous Information. Miscellaneous information covers descriptions and information about:

1. Cafeteria
2. Employee recreation
3. Employee organizations (recreation and social)
4. Employee store
5. Credit union
6. Public transportation
7. Parking areas

Photographs and Illustrations. The text of the manual will be more interesting and will hold the attention of the employee better if judicious use is made of photographs and illustrations. Many times, important points can be stressed by using an appropriate photograph or illustration. Possible illustrative material might be:

1. Pictures of company facilities
2. Pictures of products
3. Scenes within the plant and offices
4. Pictures of employee activities—sports, clubs, social gatherings, and the like
5. Pictures of company officials
6. Pictures of health facilities
7. Pictures of machinery
8. Charts of company statistics
9. Maps with company locations indicated
10. Examples of company advertising
11. Reproductions of insurance policies
12. Pictures of recreation facilities

Distribution of Manual. The manual should be presented to the employee during the personnel orientation. Each section can be shown to the employee during the time that subject is being discussed during the orientation.

Another way to indicate preparation and to add a personal touch to the orientation is to enter the new employee's name in or on the manual. This act is further proof to the employee that he was expected and that the company *cares*.

FAMILIARIZATION PROGRAMS

Another means of presenting the image and message of the company accurately and consistently is the audiovisual familiarization program. Through this medium, the necessary facts can be presented in an entertaining and colorful manner.

Through audiovisual programs, the new employee can "meet" the company officials as they talk to him about the company and his function within the company. Retention of the subject matter is great because the employee sees as well as listens to what is being said.

Akin to the audiovisual program is the video-tape program. The flexibility of this equipment permits on-the-spot taping of live action which is immediately ready for playback. Tapes can be retained for future showings as the need arises. The advantages of video tape are that revisions to the program can be made quickly, and the cost of producing a tape with available equipment is low. If desired, the video tapes can be converted to standard movie film.

TRAINING AND DEVELOPMENT

Training is a function of leadership. An organization exhibiting well-trained, well-disciplined people will also exhibit a strong leader at the top of the organization. For the supervisor to lead his new employee effectively through the early stages of his employment, he must understand and use sound training practices. The supervisor must train the new employee in the attitudes and skills which will assure good performance.

The training process prepares the employee to make his expected return to the employer. In general, training has the following objectives:

1. *Improved Confidence.* A well-trained operator is a confident operator. He *knows* that he can do the job and does not hesitate to do it. He receives a great deal of satisfaction from learning to do the job right; thus, his morale and general attitude are improved.

2. *Versatility.* Training an operator in a number of jobs or operations provides a versatility and flexibility to the organization.

3. *Quality Assurance.* In his drive for higher earnings, a poorly trained operator lowers the quality level of the product. He has not developed the skills necessary to produce a high-quality product at a high production rate. Proper training teaches him the skills and the method of performing the work so that his productivity rises without a loss in quality.

4. *Tool and Equipment Economy.* A poorly trained operator, one without the necessary skills and attitudes, causes excessive tool wear and machine maintenance. The majority of equipment breakdown and tool breakage can be traced to operator error—excluding, of course, normal wear and tear. Proper training teaches an operator the correct way to use his tools and equipment.

5. *Reduced Turnover.* A confident operator who receives a great deal of personal satisfaction from the job is an operator who will *be* on the job. As

mentioned earlier, a well-trained operator knows that he can do the job and does not hesitate to do it. In times of expansion or reduction of work force, where operators are often transferred to other jobs, the well-trained operator is less inclined to resist the change. Not only is turnover controlled, but absenteeism is also held in check.

6. *Higher Productivity.* Good training teaches the skills and attitudes needed to reach the expected productivity standards quickly and economically. The learning process can be shortened by employing good, sound training practices.

Modern training techniques have been designed to provide the skills and attitudes necessary for the operator to do the job well. These techniques employ the methods—programmed material, audiovisual presentations, learn by doing, motion pictures, video tape, and so on—which will do the job best. Material can be presented in such a way that it becomes self-teaching and, within limits, self-pacing. This is not to say that training has lost the human touch—trainees must be counseled and monitored and have their questions answered by a qualified training specialist or counselor.

The training process consists of three phases or stages: orientation, attitude, and skills training. Attitude training is an extension of the orientation training. The two are so closely related that it is difficult to separate them. The whole idea of the orientation procedure is to develop the proper attitude required for proper acceptance of the skills training.

Again, the line of separation between attitude training and skills training is not clearly defined. There is a definite overlap between the two. Skills training establishes the work habits of the employee. If the skills training and attitude training are sloppy, the work will be sloppy. The greatest retention of learning is gained through actually "doing" something. For this reason, the greatest emphasis in skills training should be placed on actual job performance in a controlled training situation.

The first step in the skills training program is planning. The controlled training situation should be organized in exactly the same manner as the employee's workplace—the same layout, tools, materials, and standards of quality. Substitutes of any kind must be avoided wherever possible. Here again, planning indicates leadership.

Planning applies to the instruction techniques as well as to the physical layout. The instruction must be organized with the job in mind. The job, or operation, should be broken down into easy-to-recognize elements which can then be presented as steps in the total learning process of the job. These steps can be later used by the employee in further developing his proficiency on the job.

Before actually starting the instruction, the abilities of the employee must be determined. This may be done through interviewing or proficiency testing, the latter being preferred.

The instructional or presentation stage of the training follows exactly the same steps used in on-the-job training previously explained. Follow-up of the training process must be reemphasized, however. Checks on the performance of the employee should be continuous and systematic.

CONCLUSION

To be successful, the orientation program must be an integrated effort of many company functions. The overall program can only be as strong as the weakest function.

The program consists of several stages: planning, preparation, presentation, and follow-up. The process starts before the employee arrives and in effect never ends, because follow-up is a continuing process.

The objective of the program is to cultivate a receptive attitude in the new employee which will enable him to accept the training that will transform him from a stranger to a skilled productive worker. He represents an investment—an investment which must be protected.

Although the preceding material has been directed toward the orientation of the factory employee, the same procedures apply with little variation to the white-collar worker as well.

BIBLIOGRAPHY

Aspley, John Cameron, and Eugene Whitmore, *Handbook of Industrial Relations,* 3d rev. ed., Dartnell Corporation, Chicago, 1950.

Bittel, Lester R., *What Every Supervisor Should Know,* 2d ed., McGraw-Hill Book Company, New York, 1968.

Black, James M., and Guy B. Ford, *Front-line Management,* McGraw-Hill Book Company, New York, 1963.

Forms & Records in Personnel Administration, Studies in Personnel Policy, no. 175, National Industrial Conference Board, New York, 1960.

Haire, Mason, *Psychology in Management,* 2d ed., McGraw-Hill Book Company, New York, 1964.

Marting, Elizabeth (ed.), *AMA Book of Employment Forms,* American Management Association, New York, 1967.

Maynard, H. B. (ed.), *Handbook of Business Administration,* McGraw-Hill Book Company, New York, 1967.

Maynard, H. B. (ed.), *Industrial Engineering Handbook,* 2d ed., McGraw-Hill Book Company, New York, 1963.

Nadler, Gerald, *Work Design,* Richard D. Irwin, Inc., Homewood, Ill., 1963.

CHAPTER THREE

Demotion and Severance

MARION S. KELLOGG *Manager, Individual Development Methods, General Electric Company, New York, New York*

One of a manager's least attractive responsibilities is facing up to inadequate employee performance and doing something about it. Whether the man is a laborer or an executive, the basic process is the same.[1] The first steps are:
1. Recognition of serious performance failure
2. Identification of reasons for failure
3. Man-manager problem solving

If this effort fails, the process continues:
4. Warning—probation
5. Managerial decision
6. Notification of decision
7. Help in relocating

Fortunately, managerial actions which tend to increase productivity and prevent failure are also those which make possible rational, fair, and humane decisions on demotion and severance. They also increase the odds that the employee can understand and accept the decision. Both factors are important. If a manager's decisions are unsound, they are certain to affect the attitude and performance of the remaining work force. And if a man feels that he has been treated unjustly, his performance in a lower job may suffer, his attitude may affect his associates, and the likelihood of his remaining a customer of the firm is lowered.

Therefore, as each employee enters a new job or begins work on a new

[1] It should be recognized that contracts covering union-organized employees usually delineate severance and demotion regulations. Many companies also have administrative policies on the subject for unorganized workers. Where they exist, they must, of course, be observed.

phase of his position or undertakes a new set of work goals, the manager should do two things: set the work up properly and review its status frequently.

SET THE WORK UP PROPERLY

Reaching a clear understanding of what an individual is expected to do and how it contributes to the goals of the organization of which he is a member is not easy.

Job Description. Basic to understanding is a job description, preferably in writing, which outlines the reason for the position and the major responsibilities of the incumbent.

The job description provides the long-term framework within which the individual functions. It is necessary but too general to be sufficient to prevent misunderstanding.

Work Standards. For any given period of time, man and manager must agree on how the employee's success in fulfilling his responsibilities will be measured and what the standards for this period of time will be.

A foreman's results, for example, are usually measured in terms of shipments to schedule, waste and spoilage, rework, absenteeism, and similar familiar items. Standards for these may vary from year to year. He is probably expected to meet shipping schedules within a few days if there are no more than the usual production complications this year. Another year when several new models are introduced, the tolerance may be increased. The dollar allowance for waste, spoilage, and rework may be X when both materials and designs are roughly the same as in preceding years. But the figure may be higher if there are many design changes or new materials are introduced.

The point, of course, is that responsibilities must be understood and accepted by both parties, and there must be mutual agreement on what the standards for measurement will be for the current time period.

Work Goals.[2] In addition, in order to work for improvement and promote innovation—especially in professional jobs of both individual and managerial[3] nature—specific, measurable goals should be established in writing for each person. These goals represent the key results of their work and are best suited to projects or programs which the business needs. In this sense, they are tied very directly to the business plans of the firm. As these plans are translated down into the organization, subgoals are created, representing the specific expected contribution of each individual involved.

Goals, too, should be agreed upon between man and manager. If the goal is well specified and supported by detailed courses of action for which there are adequate resources and appropriate due dates, it is more likely that what is being undertaken and the conditions under which it will be considered successful are clear from the beginning to both man and manager.

Typical goals might include such targets as a new factory layout to accommodate expected expansion without additional new plant investment, a specified dollar savings resulting from application of statistical inspection tech-

[2] Goal setting in current managing thinking is usually identified with the work of professional individuals. It can apply to clerical workers, technicians, and blue-collar workers, although there is less freedom of choice for such employees and less experience in applying the concepts to such work.

[3] The term "managerial" is used as a generic term to include all position incumbents who get their work done through other people. It therefore includes such jobs as foreman, supervisor, manager, and executive.

niques, or a streamlined, computerized production control system to speed up the manufacturing cycle by so much time.

In addition to a direct relationship to current business plans, work goals may also be a selected area of needed performance improvement. This is very likely at lower levels in the organization. For example, a foreman in whose department absenteeism is running significantly above standard for the year might be asked to undertake a project to discover why and devise remedial actions and install them. His goal in this case is to bring absenteeism into line with the established standard. Defining this goal, and focusing his attention on it by asking for plans (with dates) to meet it, emphasizes what is expected of him and clarifies the importance placed on it by his manager.

If goals are to serve their purpose, they should be few in number so as to focus effort, and fairly short term so as to generate a sense of urgency. Both the number of goals and the length of time into the future that they project depend on the nature and complexity of the work. Two or three goals at any one time is a reasonable average. Three to six months ahead is also a reasonable average time period, providing that there are long-range plans for the organization which give general direction. If the work will take longer than this, milestones along the way should be identified.

Involving the man in the formulation of his goals, how he will meet them, and how he will know how successful he has been adds to his clear understanding and personal commitment.

REVIEW STATUS FREQUENTLY

Planning brings to most people a sense of excitement and anticipation. When agreement is finally reached on what will be done and on how to do it, commitment is high. As work proceeds, however, earlier thoughts become hazy, specifications shift, and new enthusiasms are generated. Worse still, as barriers occur and progress is blocked in some directions, discouragement may rise, and there may be a loss of interest.

For these reasons, managers must establish follow-up procedures which permit frequent enough informal contact without the old bugaboo of oversupervision. This gives them the opportunity for adequate, rapid feedback to the employee: recognition of results and actions that the manager feels are sound; and suggestions for change if improvement is needed in approach, methods, behavior, and so on. In addition, it is critical that a manager should review progress at specified intervals on a slightly more formal basis. The following are some ground rules for making this procedure effective.

Keep Intervals Short. Intervals for review will vary, depending on the nature of the work and the experience and past performance record of the employee. Monthly reviews appear to be sound for most foremen, production expediters, and buyers, for example; whereas quarterly reviews seem to be more appropriate for quality control specialists, manufacturing engineers, managers, and others whose main work is of a longer term nature.

Focus on Work. The purpose of a status review is to identify work which needs more attention, strengthen future plans where the schedule is slipping, work out solutions to problems that have occurred, and anticipate potential problems which lie ahead. The purpose is not to analyze the employee's performance strengths and weaknesses, although the information obtained may permit it. The man-manager interaction, therefore, should be concerned with work, and the manager should avoid making evaluative statements about the employee's performance.

Ask Employee to Do the Briefing. By placing the employee in charge of analyzing the progress of his work, a manager is able to see how the employee views accomplishment to date. It may permit the manager to add to his understanding of where things stand. Moreover, it keeps responsibility for measuring work status against standards and project plans in the employee's hands, thus reducing his defensiveness and rationalization. Through careful questioning, the manager can be sure that all relevant information is brought out for discusssion.

Engage in Joint Problem Solving. As the employee describes obstacles or barriers to progress, the manager should explore reasons for their existence; obtain employee proposals for eliminating or minimizing them; contribute ideas, information, and suggestions based on his own experience; and finally, reach agreement on the course of action that the employee will pursue in the future to avoid or solve the problem.

Update Plans. Whatever new information may be available since standards and plans were originally developed should be factored into an updated plan. Are there schedule changes based on new orders? Are there revised inspection standards because of customer complaints? Have packaging changes been made to reduce injury in transit? Have whole new projects been introduced so that priorities must be adjusted or resources added? Is engineering running late so that the manufacturing cycle must be compressed?

Get Greater Commitment. By requesting the employee to analyze work status, by engaging him in problem solving, and by asking him to incorporate needed changes into his plans, the involvement level of the employee is high. And because of this involvement, his determination and interest are renewed. Moreover, he should see the new targets as more realistic and therefore more achievable. This, too, upgrades his personal commitment.

Document the Changes. Both man and manager should change planning documents and, if necessary, the work standards records to conform to the newly made decisions.

Why These Prerequisites. Man-manager agreement on work to be done, including standards for routine or continuing kinds of work activities and specified, measurable work goals for more innovative projects, is the foundation on which all personnel decisions should be made. Review of progress against such plans at frequent intervals gives the manager an effective early warning system of discrepancies in performance and roadblocks which stand in the way of needed results.

RECOGNITION OF PERFORMANCE FAILURE

Any serious discrepancy between work output and preestablished standards or between accomplishment and agreed-upon plans is a performance failure. But when is such a discrepancy serious? All individuals, even the most capable, at one time or another find that their work misses its target. When to penalize and when to encourage a man to try again is a difficult judgment, especially for the inexperienced manager. Factors which often mitigate performance failure are shown in Figure 3-1.

How Tough Are the Targets under Current Conditions? If a standard represents substantial improvement over previous performance levels or if a goal is significantly more ambitious than earlier ones, it may be that the target is too tough, not that the employee is inadequate. In addition, a manager should consider the number of such tough goals. One or two may represent stretch and challenge, but five or six may seem unrealistic to the man.

1. The results expected are tough under current conditions.
2. The work requires considerable innovation.
3. Missed targets occur only occasionally.
4. The employee correctly identifies reasons for failure.
5. The employee identifies sound remedial actions that he can take.

FIG. 3-1. Factors Mitigating Performance Failure.

Sometimes the target is sound, but the resources allocated to it or the priority set on it or the schedule to reach it are faulty.

If a manager reviews accomplishment and finds it inadequate, his first question should be: "Did I ask for too much?"

Has It Been Done Before? Closely allied to the issue of toughness of target is that of the innovation required. If work is not new, if the process for accomplishing it is well understood, if adequate information for needed decisions is available or can be obtained, or if similar things have been done before under similar conditions, performance discrepancies are clearly serious.

There are cases, however, where these conditions do not hold. Invention is required to reach the objective. Sometimes work is at the outer limits of existing knowledge. Under these conditions, even though the job description may call for invention and generating of new information, and even though pay is based in part on these things, nonetheless more latitude is allowed.

Does the Man Miss Consistently? An occasional miss is acceptable, but if at each succeeding review the individual continues to miss his targets in spite of the revision, problem solving, and replanning which took place at the previous session, the manager has solid grounds for judging the discrepancy to be serious.

Can the Employee Identify Reasons for Failure? If work is below standard or significantly off schedule, the normal response of an intelligent, involved employee is to attempt to identify the reasons so that he can take corrective action. As a manager reviews progress, his probing should be directed toward this issue. Does the employee blame others, give wary, superficial excuses, or display ignorance or disinterest? If so, the manager has grounds for judging the situation to be serious. If in addition the manager's questions, which should help the man to see new approaches, are unsuccessful in helping him toward a more intelligent evaluation, there is even more evidence of a serious problem.

Can the Employee Suggest Remedial Action? Finally, if an employee whose work is in serious difficulty is able to present a thoughtful, realistic plan for getting himself or his organization out of trouble, a manager has a good reason for deciding to give him the chance to try it. In the absence of such a constructive proposal, it is doubtful that the man can be allowed to continue in the job.

Clearly a mathematical formula cannot be devised for ensuring a proper weighting of the above factors so that a manager is able to judge the seriousness of the situation infallibly. But consideration of the five factors listed should permit a rational evaluation.

Failures outside the Performance Area. Occasionally an employee fails not because he misses his performance targets but because he violates a disciplinary rule or important company policy or uses unethical methods. Such failures in serious matters may be cause for immediate dismissal. If the employee is aware of the firm's position on the matter, the manager simply talks to the man, confronts him with evidence of failure to comply, and outlines the conditions for severance.

In less serious disciplinary matters, it is customary to warn the employee, preferably in writing, and take termination action only if he fails to make the desired change.[4]

EARLY FAILURE RECOGNITION AND REMEDIAL ACTIONS

Because performance failures usually involve more managerial contacts with the employee, the information which follows details what the manager should do, once he has recognized performance discrepancies.

Not only must the manager see the failure, he must also see it early enough to protect the organization from its effects. This means getting quick evidence, recognizing the situation rapidly, and taking immediate remedial action.

Remedial Action No. 1—Employee Appraisal Discussion. During the planning conferences described earlier, the manager focused his attention on the work and on strengthening plans for reaching needed results.

As soon as a serious, persisting discrepancy in employee performance against plans is recognized, the manager must bring his conclusion to the employee's attention. It goes without saying that if the groundwork described above has been properly laid, the man is as aware of failure as the manager. The purpose of the discussion, then, is not to rehash the work, but rather to relate the lack of result to the man himself in an effort to determine reasons for failure. Some suggestions for this discussion are:

State the Situation. This is not the moment to ask the employee how he feels about the situation—there is no choice involved. The manager has reached a conclusion based on a considerable amount of factual information. He should therefore state his position factually, using as matter-of-fact a tone of voice as possible.

He briefly reviews the performance picture in support of his position. He might, for example, say (in his own words):

Bob, I asked that we have a discussion this morning because I am seriously concerned about your work. As you know, we agreed on certain standards to be met and certain necessary results to be accomplished. Each time we have reviewed where work stands, it has been apparent that results are not what we expected. I'm sure you are also concerned about this. It seems essential to me that we should put our heads together this morning to see if we can figure out why you are having so much difficulty and what, if anything, can be done about it.

Notice that in this statement the manager does not try to manipulate the employee into saying that he is in trouble. This would probably only cause defensiveness. Neither does he attempt to pussyfoot around the evaluation. He comes right out with his feeling so that it is in the open for the employee to deal with. He is supportive on the one hand in making it clear that he has not given up; he will work with the employee to find a solution. On the other hand, he also signals that he is not sure that the situation is correctable, when he says that they should try to determine ". . . what, *if anything*, can be done . . ."

Ask for the Employee's Analysis of Causes. It is essential for the manager to know whether the employee can—and is willing to—change his performance in significant ways. He probably has made an estimate of this already, but the employee's insight on these matters can be extremely helpful. There is

---

[4] Union contracts often detail procedure for discipline.

only one way to find out what he thinks and that is to ask. The way the manager asks is important if he wants an honest, thoughtful reply. One way might be something like this: "I'm sure you've been giving a great deal of thought to this situation, Bob. Have you reached any conclusions about yourself in this job? Do you feel you can do it? Or is it a wrong job for you at this point in your career?" If, in reply, Bob admits that there is a mismatch, or that he just has not had enough experience, or that there is too much pressure, or that he dislikes this work immensely, or if he gives any other reasons which suggest that he wants to make a change, the manager can move on to discussing what kind of a change, when, their mutual obligations, and so on.

If, as is more likely, the employee feels that he can do the work if given another chance and says he wants the opportunity, the manager must take a next step.

Describe Short-term Conditions. Clearly some changes must be made, both by the manager and by the employee. The manager improves the odds that the employee can make them by doing three things, subject to the employee's agreement: focusing needed accomplishment even more than before, setting very short-term milestones, and specifying the measures to be used to determine the extent of success at each milestone.

In focusing attention on fewer items to be accomplished, the manager cannot, of course, do this at the expense of other needed results. He merely expands the amount of time and attention that the employee gives to higher priority matters, thus permitting accomplishment of a few key things in a shorter period of time. If the method is successful, the lower priority items are delayed but will take their proper turn. The net result ultimately should be the same.

In setting short-term milestones, the time will vary, depending on how criticial the work is. The milestones might be weekly or biweekly, but more often are monthly. This more frequent look at progress permits the manager to judge how the employee is responding. It provides an opportunity for the manager to give the employee more of his own suggestions and ideas. It does, of course, add to his managing burden substantially and therefore must be considered a short-range, temporary, emergency program.

The measures at each milestone provide for appraisal of progress on as objective a basis as possible. They let both man and manager know whether improvement is taking place.

Get Employee's Agreement. Essential at this point is the employee's agreement that he will work under these conditions. Ideally, he helps evolve them, thus ensuring his acceptance. Practically speaking, however, if the situation has deteriorated seriously, it is most unlikely that he will contribute. If the manager cannot obtain the employee's agreement, the odds of success are so slim that they would do better to move immediately to a consideration of other positions or of termination.

Make Consequences of Failure Clear. At the risk of introducing a destructive note into the discussion, the manager owes it to the employee to make clear to him precisely what the consequences of continued failure will be. Essential in doing this is a calm, matter-of-fact, nonthreatening tone of voice. This is harder than most men realize. There is almost inevitably a small feeling of guilt or embarrassment which may show itself in a curt, blustery way of speaking. It is sometimes the tone rather than the content of the remarks which destroys an employee's confidence in himself or makes him angry or vindictive.

A manager might use words such as these: "This is not easy for me to say,

Bob. But I wouldn't be fair to you if I failed to paint the complete picture. We must meet standards X and Y fully by such and such a date and we must make milestones A and B on the nose. If we don't, Bob, I cannot let you continue in this job. The way we've set it up now, it seems to me you have a reasonable chance of making the grade, but we both know it's going to take a lot of effort. I want you to succeed very much. I hope you feel the same way."

Remedial Action No. 2—Open-minded, Constructive Day-to-day Relationship. When work and conditions have been agreed to and the appraisal discussion is over, the manager's next problem is to maintain a supportive, pleasant, on-the-job, day-to-day relationship with the man. He must display interest, keep communication channels open, stop by to see and chat with him, and the like. This is not the time for the employee to believe that his manager has no confidence in him, has given up on him, or worse still, dislikes or resents him.

Information Giving. It is especially important during this period for the manager to bring to the employee's attention any decisions, actions in other parts of the organization, changes in thinking, new appointments, and similar matters which may relate to the employee's current work program. Failure to do this leaves doubt on both sides as to who is responsible for poor performance.

Rapid Feedback. Equally important is reinforcement by the manager of actions that he sees the employee take which are in the right direction. A quick compliment or word of appreciation is all that is required. He should similarly point out to the employee that certain observed methods or behavior or actions are not likely to help him meet his targets, and if he can explain why and offer suggestions for improvement, so much the better. This procedure increases the odds of employee success.

Respect the Employee's Privacy. It may be a great temptation to discuss with his associates the difficulties that the employee is experiencing. The motive may be good, namely, to enlist their special help and thus give the man a better chance of succeeding. *Do not do it.* If the man wishes to explain the situation, this is his privilege.

Keep Replacement Plans Secret. The manager should observe the employee as closely as he can without taking from him the freedom to work or without giving him the feeling that he is under constant surveillance. As the manager observes, he may decide that the employee does not appear to be improving. Depending on the criticality of the work and the expected difficulty in replacing the employee, it may be necessary to alert the personnel office of the probable opening and to ask for a slate of candidates drawn from within the organization. The manager may wish to examine records of other employees currently employed.

To whatever extent this can be done without the employee's knowledge, it is both wise and necessary to proceed. But avoid internal reference checking, interviews, advertisements, and the like. These are almost certain to come to the employee's attention, and he will feel that his manager has already made his decision without giving the employee the promised chance. What is to the manager merely a parallel program in case it is needed, may seem to the employee to be a clear lack of integrity.

Remedial Action No. 3—Prompt Milestone Checks. Whenever a regular report of work against agreed-upon standards is issued or a milestone is reached, the manager should meet with the employee promptly to review the extent to which he has succeeded. This session should be handled very much like the status reviews discussed earlier. At the end of each such session, however, the manager should make an evaluation of the employee's performance and communicate it to him.

If the manager is pleased, the simple statement: "I'm pleased. You're doing fine," is all that is necessary. If he is not pleased, he might say: "I'm still concerned. We are not up to Standard X; Y looks as though it's improving; but we are not meeting our project schedule. Let's review this again next week to see how it looks then."

THE DECISION

Performance evidence builds during this period until it is clear whether the employee is able to handle the position or is incapable of doing so for the immediate future. It is time for a decision. Before making it, the manager should make sure that he himself has done everything he could to correct the situation. He should ask the questions in the checklist shown by Figure 3-2. If he can answer them all in the affirmative, the decision cannot be postponed further. A change must be made.

How Soon? How many such reviews a manager holds before he feels that the man has had his chance and that it is useless to try further is, naturally, a judgmental matter. The reason for poor performance influences this a great deal. If it is a lack of talent or knowledge or experience, managers will probably give up sooner than if they feel that it is one of motivation.

The importance of the work to the total results of the organization must also be considered. A manager may not be able to risk much loss of time in fairness to the firm and to other employees in the organization.

The probable difficulty in replacing the man is a third major influence. If it is going to be very difficult to recruit his successor, a manager will probably extend the trial period as a practical matter.

The man himself is an important influence, of course. If he is a long-time employee who has succeeded well in other jobs and is trying hard in this one, the trial period should undoubtedly be longer than might otherwise be the case.

If, in the appraisal discussion, the manager gave him a time interval within which he had to meet his targets, this sets the limit for the final decision.

On What Basis? This is critical. If the manager has done a good job of involving the employee in setting clear, well-defined standards and measurable goals or milestones toward goals, there is usually little question about the basis for decision. The evidence is factual and reasonably objective.

As manager, have I:
1. Defined his job in clear, specific terms?
2. Informed him of important policies which he must abide by?
3. Agreed with him on current standards for his work?
4. Agreed on the specific results (goals) he is to achieve and by when?
5. Informed him of changes which affect his work?
6. Provided adequate feedback on his accomplishment and methods of accomplishment?
7. Shared my appraisal of his work with him?
8. Provided constructive suggestions for improvement?
9. Warned him of necessity for improvement and explained consequences of failure?
10. Set a time limit on needed improvement?

Fig. 3-2. Manager's Checklist to Be Reviewed before Deciding to Act.

More important, it is usually as obvious to the man and to his associates as it is to the manager.

Demotion or Severance?   Does the man deserve an opportunity to be considered for other jobs in the firm?   If performance failure involved a serious disciplinary matter or a violation of important policy or unethical behavior, the answer is very likely no.   But what of the man who is mismatched to the job and is in over his head?   From the firm's point of view, if the man is qualified for other jobs, possesses needed skills, and has a good past work record, he should certainly be considered and probably offered work within his abilities.   This is especially true if his service with the company is long.

If, on the other hand, his service is short and his failures are mainly due to poor relationships, ability or attitude, low interest, or lack of drive—factors which are hard to change—termination is usually the better course of action.

Demotion within the same organization presents some problems for both man and manager.   If there is a changed reporting relationship, it may be awkward for the man, his replacement, his associates, and the manager. There may be a loss of self-confidence, and the man's new manager may face a confidence-rebuilding process.   The man's attitude may affect his work unfavorably.

In most cases, however, facing the new problems frankly, discussing them openly with the employee, and letting time do some healing are sufficient. But the manager should be willing to live with the early consequences of his decision and should be prepared to devote a little extra time and attention through the transition period.   The man should think through the new situation in which he will find himself so that he expects and is ready for the change.

HOW TO COMMUNICATE THE DECISION

With the careful build-up outlined, the final communication of the decision represents in many ways the least of the problem.   The man himself, seeing the discrepancy between results and expectations, may ask for permission to look for another job inside the firm or seek employment outside the company.

If, however, he clings to the job, assuring himself and his manager that things are about to take a sudden turn for the better, so that the manager is forced to reach a decision and discuss it, the following are some guidelines for this unpleasant task.

Manager's Preparation.   The manager should begin by reviewing the evidence to be sure that he has the facts well in hand.   He should organize his data so that he is prepared to explain his reasons based on a few key points, rather than belaboring the detail.

Next, with the help of the personnel office, he must work out the conditions under which the man will be removed from his job.   The following lists items to review and decide upon.   Because it is essential to cover these thoroughly and exactly, it is wise to make written notes:

1. Final day of work
2. Length of time that pay will continue
3. Time off to search for new position
4. Specific work to be completed before leaving job
5. Procedure for investigating other jobs in firm, if applicable
6. Help available from manager
7. Help available from personnel office
8. Procedure for investigating status of benefits available to him, if applicable

Finally, opening and closing statements should be prepared so that the stage is set properly for the discussion and so that the session is closed in a way that leaves the man feeling as good about himself, his manager, and the company as is possible under the circumstances. This word-for-word memorization is essential for most managers. The discussion will at best be painful. He should not add to it by groping and fumbling for words to express himself. Some sample dialogue is given below as an aid.

Set the Meeting Time. When the manager sets the time of the meeting, he should signal ahead that the news is not good. He should give the man a little time to get himself ready, say an hour, but not too much longer, for this may be a very strained period for the man. For example, one afternoon two or three days after a milestone check which showed inadequate progress, he might go to Bob's desk and, assuming there is enough privacy, say rather slowly: "Bob, things aren't going too well. We're both aware of it and we'd better discuss it. How about three o'clock in my office?"

Opening Statement. No small talk should be indulged in at this session. The decision should be presented quickly, using a gentle tone of voice and a fairly slow pace. "Bob, we're not on target, as you know. And I see no sign that things will change. Neither of us can be satisfied with this state of affairs. It's not fair to your future nor to this organization for you to go on like this. I'm going to replace you, Bob." It is hard to say words as simple and direct as these. This is why the manager needs to prepare in advance both what he will say and how he will say it.

Body of the Discussion. The content after the opener depends, of course, on the employee's reaction and what the manager has decided about another job within the organization versus outright severance. In general, the manager will cover in some detail the checklist items given earlier.

Manager's Attitude. As the manager talks, it is entirely possible that the man will miss some of the content of his remarks, but he will not miss the attitude which sparks these remarks. It is important for whatever future relationship may exist between the two that the manager let his sincere feeling of sympathy and regret for the man's situation show. He should have as one of his key objectives to display his serious intention to give whatever help he can in the search for another job. He should make it clear that he respects the man and sees his strengths. At all costs, in his efforts to defend his decision, he should avoid overstating the failure or implying a general lack of ability in the man. The failures were specific. They stemmed from specific inadequacies. The manager should make that clear. He should stress the strengths which could be applied in other jobs or other situations. This is not the time to destroy whatever self-confidence and self-respect the man may have.

Closing Remarks. In closing, the manager might say: "This discussion has been painful for both of us. Before we close, may I make one or two suggestions? In a situation like this, we look at what hasn't been done. But you possess some important experience and know-how. Try to concentrate on these and think about the kinds of work which would capitalize on them. The important thing now is to think about yourself and how you can turn this situation into an occasion for embarking on the kind of work you will enjoy doing and will be successful at. This may not be the moment to do it, but I'd like very much to talk to you about the kinds of jobs I believe you would do well . . ." The manager thus lets the man choose whether he wishes to continue the discussion now or return at a later date.

Written Confirmation. The specifics of the terminal agreement probably need to be put in writing within two or three days of the discussion so that there is no misunderstanding of time and monetary arrangements. This can be a brief note:

Dear Bob:

This will confirm the specifics of our discussion of Wednesday, June 23. Your last day of work will be Friday, August 6, and your salary will continue for two weeks after that (through August 20).

The benefits administrator will be happy to review the situation with respect to the status of insurance, pension, and other benefits which have accrued to you during your association with us.

I'm sure you know how much I regret the situation which has forced this action. My very best wishes in your search for a new position. Let me know how I can be of help.

Manager X

WHAT HELP CAN A MANAGER GIVE AFTER NOTICE OF TERMINATION?

There is a natural tendency for man and manager to avoid each other once the decision has been made and the termination arrangements finalized. But there are some constructive things that a manager can do to be of positive help. These are shown in Figure 3-3.

Agree on Recommendation. The need for references should be discussed. Agreement should be reached on what the manager will say that will be truthful but will not kill all chances of another position. The man can then prepare what he will say to a prospective employer about the reasons for leaving his last job.

State Man's Strong Points. A manager should counsel the employee on what he believes are his major talents and most useful experience. This will help the man to prepare his resume properly for a new position.

Suggest Suitable Positions. If the man's strengths can be related to jobs that he can do well or kinds of businesses in which he is most likely to function effectively, this will help him select openings for which to apply.

Recommend Professional Counselors. If there are nearby universities, veteran's counseling services, or similar professional vocational counselors, their objective review of the man's qualifications will be useful and probably more acceptable to him than the manager's views which must inevitably appear biased.

Suggest Consulting Firms or Employment Agencies. If a manager or a personnel specialist is able to recommend consultants, agencies, or other employment services, it will save the employee's time. Better still, an appointment can be made for him with someone who is known to the firm—but only if the employee wishes it, of course.

---

1. Agree on content of future recommendations to prospective employers.
2. Discuss strengths on which the employee should build.
3. Describe positions that the employee could perform well.
4. Suggest counsel that the employee might obtain on: preparing a resume, sources of employment, writing or answering ads, being interviewed, and vocational or career advice.

Fig. 3-3. Help a Manager Can Give after Notice of Termination.

Allow Time off for Job Hunting. This is probably obvious, but some agreement on how it will be handled is necessary. As a minimum, the man should let the manager know when he will be out for this purpose so that someone can cover his responsibilities.

Provide Assistance with Resume. Through the personnel office, the manager should offer advice on how to prepare a resume, how to answer a help wanted ad, and how to write a position wanted ad and where to place it. Recommended reading on how to be interviewed would be helpful too.

Offer Man Another Job. If the situation is that of demotion rather than severance, the manager should offer the man a position in his own organization if at all possible. This forces the manager to stand back of what he says and prevents passing an unqualified individual on to another unsuspecting manager. The man may not accept because he feels that he will lose face, but he should have the choice.

Provide Interview Contacts. If the manager has contacts within or outside the firm and believes there are certain positions the individual could fill satisfactorily, he should be willing to make contacts and pave the way for interviews. It is up to the man to sell himself, but he gets a head start.

Extend the Final Date? Extending the final date is not a good idea—not good for the organization and usually not good for the man. Is the next date final? Really, really final? He may be misled into thinking that there is no end date and may fail to take needed action.

Write "To Whom It May Concern" Letters? Such letters are not much help. If the employee wants one, all right; but contacts are much more effective when handled on an individualized, more personal basis.

CONCLUSION

The basic principles involved in demotion and severance are clear. The work situations should be set up so that the individual has no doubt of what is expected and so that he is involved, in fact, in setting up the expectations. Progress should be reviewed frequently so that standards become clearer and work plans are current. It is this frequent review which provides the needed early warning system for the manager. Effective actions that he can take have been outlined above. The problem is for him to heed the warning and take the needed action quickly when serious performance discrepancies appear.

Often managers delay, feeling that they are being kind or enlightened in doing so. They are, in fact, not only imperiling the results of the total organization but also limiting the development, growth, and future career of the employee.

It is no kindness to leave a man in a job that he cannot or will not do well. It may mislead him into thinking that his level of performance is adequate so that he fails to make the stretch he should. It permits him to continue poor work habits which thus become deeply rooted and difficult to change. In many cases, it merely delays the day of reckoning to a time when he is older, when economic conditions may not be as good, or when his poor reputation is so firmly entrenched that it is difficult to locate a new position.

Early managerial action gives both the man and the organization a better chance. A distinguished industrialist once said of a former manager: "He was a great developer of men. He constantly threw us in over our heads. But he watched us closely, and if he saw we weren't going to make it, he pulled us out before our reputations were gone."

BIBLIOGRAPHY

Baker, Charles, "Expanded Use of the Exit Interview," *Personnel Journal*, December, 1965, pp. 620–623.

Batten, Joseph D., *Beyond Management by Objectives*, American Management Association, New York, 1966.

Drucker, Peter F., *Managing for Results*, Harper & Row, Publishers, Incorporated, New York, 1964.

Kellogg, Marion S., *What to Do about Performance Appraisal*, chap. 10, American Management Association, New York, 1965.

Magoon, Paul M., and John B. Richards, *Discipline or Disaster: Management's Only Choice*, Exposition Press, Inc., New York, 1966.

Mitchell, William Norman, *The Business Executive in a Changing World*, American Management Association, New York, 1965.

"The Operation of Severance Pay Plans and Their Implications for Labor Mobility," U.S. Department of Labor, sponsored by Office of Manpower, Automation and Training, prepared by Bureau of Labor Statistics, Bulletin no. 1462, January, 1966.

Phelps, Orme W., *Discipline and Discharge in the Unionized Firm*, University of California Press, Berkeley and Los Angeles, 1959.

"Severance Pay Plans," *California Industrial Relations Report*, June, 1965.

Stessin, Lawrence, *Employee Discipline*, Bureau of National Affairs, Washington, D.C., 1960.

"Termination Forms, Interviews, and Letters," *The Problem Clinic*, Office Administration Service feature, Dartnell Corporation, Chicago, Ill., 1966.

CHAPTER FOUR

Labor Relations

WILLIAM K. ENGEMAN   *Taft, Stettinius & Hollister, Cincinnati, Ohio*

Labor relations is one aspect of the overall personnel responsibility. In practice, it is primarily concerned with the construction of a working relationship between the manufacturing corporation, as represented by its management, and the production worker, so that corporate aims can be fulfilled.[1]

No manufacturing manager should understimate the importance and complexity of the labor relations function. Like any important job, good performance will generally be reflected in the balance sheet. Poor performance can result in disastrous strikes or the gradual erosion of the plant financial situation. There are few opportunities offered to undo unsound labor relations policies. When bad labor relations policies spoil a work force, the results may be felt for decades.

At any plant, someone with adequate time and ability must be responsible for labor relations planning and must see that plans are carried out. In a plant with relatively few production employees, the job may be adequately performed by a production superintendent with access to advice from a management consultant or attorney specializing in the field. Many larger companies employ a full-time industrial relations manager or equivalent who may combine some or all of the ordinary personnel functions with the labor relations responsibility. The largest corporations have staffs specializing entirely in labor relations problems. The solution in any individual situation will depend upon the time and talents of the available management personnel and the availability of competent specialized professional assistance.

This chapter is intended to assist in structuring the thinking of practical managers in some of the most sensitive areas of labor relations. It is not possible to provide answers to all or even most of the problems that will arise

[1] The problem of the organized clerical or white-collar worker is not treated here except insofar as parallels may be drawn.

requiring responsible management decision. As with many highly specialized areas, however, some knowledge is necessary if responsible management is to be able to recognize that problems exist.

LABOR RELATIONS GOAL

The plant goal is profit. Labor costs are expense items. It takes no economist to recognize that paying an employee $3.50 an hour to perform work for which a competitor pays its employee $3 an hour will result in a fatal disparity in labor costs, unless the first employer enjoys a great advantage in employee productivity. Similarly, paying an employee $3 an hour for work which a competitor completes in half a man-hour will be disastrous although the competitor's wages are $3.50 an hour. Labor relations must continually strive to minimize unit labor costs—this is its ultimate goal.

BUILDING A SOUND LABOR RELATIONS FOUNDATION

To carry out this ultimate goal, management must retain control of the manufacturing operation. A union bargaining committee backed by a picket line and strike fund is a potential threat to effective management present in every negotiating confrontation. The practical manager recognizes what unions offer and provides the alternative.

Fundamentally, the union offers not the better wages, pensions, and other improved conditions so often heard (this is only the sales pitch), but substitute leadership. A union lawyer described the union's real appeal as follows:

Why do you think employees join unions? The business agent doesn't organize them. The employer is the union's best organizer—by his mistakes and his failure to properly display an interest in the men who help make the business go.

. . . union guys are not strong unless management makes them so by either ignorance or default. Their "strength" and I put that word in quotes is in proportion to management's weakness.[2]

The practical manager, therefore, makes sure that he and his staff provide effective leadership, whether or not there is a union in the plant. With leadership down into the grass roots of the organization, frictions are minimized and production employees can be firmly attached to the company goals.

Residual loyalty is there. Each employee, no matter how menial his task or how rabid his union sympathies, is psychologically predisposed to view his company favorably. When he complains about his employer, he is admitting something about himself. Implicit in every gripe, psychologically, is the admission that if his company is so bad only a dummy would work for it, he must be a dummy. The practical manager builds on this residual loyalty.

Build Loyalty through Leadership. Concrete results cannot be expected without hard thought and follow-through. No one of the suggestions below can achieve results if others are seriously neglected. Equally fatal is sporadic attention. When the organizer is at the door or the strike vote is set for next week, it is too late. These areas require vigilance.

Communication. As with customers, face-to-face employee communication is essential. The manager must know something of the production employees' expectations to evaluate them fairly.

[2] *The Wall Street Journal*, Dec. 19, 1966, remarks of Harry J. Lambeth, a union lawyer.

There are many legitimate ways of obtaining employee information, particularly in a nonunion situation. In the absence of a union or employee grievance committee (and such committees must never be selected by or with the assistance of the employer and should never be dealt with unless they have been freely selected by the employees in an NLRB election), the following avenues are frequently used: (1) alert line supervision—men who seek out discontent; (2) an open-door policy by which employees are encouraged to come to representatives of management with problems through the so-called "open door"; (3) periodic interviews between individual employees and a representative of management; (4) group meetings; and (5) some combination of these.

Other methods have been used successfully by some companies in some situations, such as attitude surveys taken by outside consultants. However, these have limited long-range value in most situations. Day in and day out, the cornerstone of an effective labor relations policy is knowledge—knowing the employees' expectations and the employees' knowing that management wants to know.

The ideal situation, of course, in any plant would be to have line supervision so sensitive to labor relations policy that they can be the eyes, ears, brain, and heart of the company in full view of the men they are leading. Where this leadership core can be created, only occasional broad-scale management guidance will be required. A respected foreman will not necessarily know everything that is bothering his men, but he will probably know enough and by his presence inspire confidence. If line supervision, after a careful study, is found to be effective and loyal, it is best left more or less alone. Too much interference from above may be more destructive than none. Through contacts with the supervisors, management can get the information it needs to formulate policy.

Few plants are this fortunate, however. In far too many industrial situations, the insensitivity of line supervision is at the root of worker discontent or at least masks the discontent so that it festers. It was for such situations that the open-door policy, individual interview techniques, group meetings, and the like were developed. All these techniques are valuable to bridge the obstruction created by inefficient line supervision. The practical manager, however, will recognize these as substitutes and will be planning in the long run to remove the obstructions so that the bridge can fall into disuse. Everything said below about the necessity of replacing the inefficient, slovenly, or disruptive employee is trebly applicable to the bad line supervisor.

The most useful bridging system will depend upon individual plant considerations. Where an open-door policy can be utilized, it is informal and serves as an *ad hoc* check on supervisors' actions. The open door is simply a technique for funneling employee suggestions or complaints to a single responsible management representative. This man behind the open door must be prepared to serve as complaint desk, counselor, and representative of higher management. He serves the employees as a safety valve and check on supervision, and if effective, he provides management with a realistic basis for appraising labor relations policy.

A manager contemplating the use of this technique should make every effort to assure that his employees know of the open door and use it. Whether the door is to an executive's office removed from the work area or to a foreman's office on the shop floor, employees should know where it is, know that they are expected to come with problems that they are unable to solve with their supervisors, and know precisely where and when such matters will be heard.

The principal drawback to the open-door system is that it may well fail long before its breakdown is recognized. The natural tendency is to assume that complaints are "smoke" and that where there is no smoke there is no fire. In fact, the opposite is often the case, and the smoke is being blown in another direction—toward the union organizer. As discussed below, this technique should be periodically checked by management interviews.

Another problem is that, as with any other bridging system, there is the danger that it will completely undercut line supervisory authority and be detrimental to line supervisory morale. To ameliorate this, every effort should be made to apprise line supervision of nonconfidential aspects of employee interviews and to assure that the line supervisor takes a part in their solution.

The manager who finds himself repeatedly siding with the employee against the line supervisor is making a serious error. If the supervisor is to function, he must be supported. If he is not worthy of support, he should be replaced.

The individual interview is a variant of the open door. It may also be used either regularly or sporadically to check the workings of the open door. It too must be tailored to the individual plant situation, with quarterly to annual interviews most commonly found effective. Such interviews are often coupled with merit reviews and are opportunities for supervision to sit down with the individual employee away from the work floor and discuss his progress and performance. In some plants, the line supervisor takes this opportunity to discuss problems that he is otherwise too busy to discuss. However, this will usually be a sign that line supervision is less than effective in its labor relations actions on a day-to-day basis. More often, such interviews are conducted by a higher management representative who can use the situation to check the attitudes of both the employee and his line supervisor. Again in such instances, every effort should be made to make the line supervisor a part of effective resolution of grievances and not to undercut his authority.

The third bridging technique, the group meeting, is seldom an acceptable substitute for the open door or individual interviews. It may be useful as a forum for the company's viewpoint, but it can seldom be effective in obtaining employee information. Few employees want to be identified before their fellow employees as complainers. Many are afraid to speak up at all before a group.

Action. With effective communication, problems can be identified and corrected if necessary. The nature of problems requiring management direction will depend upon the individual situation. However, alert management will keep abreast of certain problems which are constant, such as wage and fringe benefit scales. The man responsible for labor relations should know of area and competitor standards in wages, fringes, and other working conditions and continually update his information.

Often membership in employer or trade associations will give access to such information. If not, alternative contacts should be established so that information can be exchanged on a regular basis. Most employers are willing to exchange wage and fringe information where there is no attempt to get actual production costs.

The nonunion manager will want to keep a careful eye on this information and reported union contract settlements in the area. He should not allow plant wages and fringes to lag far behind those of competitors or comparable area companies. This does not mean that an attempt should be made to match such benefits on a one-for-one basis. The manager should attempt to react to the individual plant situation and employees' reasonable expectations. Thus, if wages are behind those of a neighboring plant but vacation benefits are better as the result of management response to employee expectations, the management may be on sound ground.

The union employer will be constantly aware of this competitive pressure. Lacking the nonunion employer's flexibility to make immediate correction, however, he will often be in a position where the lack of a benefit results not only in an expectation for future negotiations but also a friction resulting from employee jealousy. This unfortunate outcome can also be ameliorated to some extent through exchange of information with other similar companies so that management can react with information in the between-negotiation period to counter union propaganda, even though the contract term makes adjustment inappropriate.

Apart from financial considerations, the problem of the ineffective or undisciplined employee stands out as the most frequently found potential trouble spot in any plant. This problem is frequently overlooked or not acted upon. Many employers have had the bitter experience of finding that the root of their labor relations problem is an employee that they may have befriended or tolerated whose performance was not adequate. The ineffective employee or the employee who will not accept discipline is more disruptive to the well-being of the work force than inadequate compensation. His presence demoralizes good employees who will recognize the disparity in performance. These employees cannot but ask why the employer puts up with ineffective or undisciplined co-workers, rewarding them apparently despite their inadequacy.

Moreover, these inadequate workers have an ambivalent attitude toward the employer. Often they are contemptuous of the company for retaining them. Coupled with this attitude is the employees' basic insecurity. They typically know that they are less effective and feel strong need for organized support. They frequently are leaders in organizing efforts or in particularly militant wings of organized groups. The company which does not strive for a uniformly qualified work force is assuring itself of continuous labor relations problems.

Reporting. All too often, good fact-finding and reaction policies are wasted because they are unnoticed. Communication is a two-way street. Each employee must know enough about the company, its objectives, and actions so that he can feel that it deserves his support. Too often the company leaves the employee in the dark on the real issue—with disastrous results.

The union attorney, quoted above, noted:

Examine the average company magazine or newspaper and compare it with the publications distributed by the AFL–CIO. Gentlemen, you won't find the bowling scores or the date of the company picnic in the union mouthpieces. You'll find blatant political and antiemployer propaganda.

If your workers are being fed this stuff week after week, month after month, and year after year—while you offer nothing to counter it—it won't be long before the kid in the shop won't have to see the white hats in order to pick out who he thinks are the "good guys."[3]

If this is the situation in a plant, it should be remedied. Part of the labor relations function is to create loyalty. Get together information showing the employee the company's virtues, and regularly get it to the employees. Area surveys, news clippings, and reports on plant developments, such as new products, promotions, advertising campaigns, sales outlooks, customer problems, planned benefits, and facilities, are all effective. Make sure that em-

[3] *Ibid.*

ployees understand their contribution; the function of executives; problems such as financing, taxation, government regulation, sales and distribution difficulties; and the company's reaction to these problems.

Plant magazines, newsletters, speakers, letters to families, posters, notices, picnics, parties, commercial newspapers, radio, or TV may be effective media for conveying the message. Each manager generally finds a somewhat different solution, depending upon circumstances, and may well change media and approach often. The important thing is to get the message across—dynamically and in human terms.

THE ORGANIZING CAMPAIGN

To the nonunion manager, the organizing campaign is the crucial test of his leadership. For some reason, which he will probably never pinpoint, one of the thousands of labor organizations in this country tries to obtain the right to be the exclusive bargaining agent for his employees.

Generally, the campaign begins in secret. Employees are contacted in their homes or away from work. The union attempts to enlist the aid of respected workers and with their aid to obtain support from a majority of the employees. If the union meets with some success, employees are asked to sign union cards which authorize the union to be their "exclusive bargaining representative." The methods used to obtain such signatures are often highly questionable, and substantial misrepresentations are not uncommon.

The union's goal, of course, is recognition (and the right to force the employer to sign a union shop agreement and collect union dues from the employees). Recognition is usually obtained after an NLRB election but may, in some circumstances, result from the acquisition of union cards alone.

The company with a sound labor relations policy and effective leadership is in the best possible posture to combat a union organizing effort. However, even the soundest leadership cannot guarantee success. Organizing campaigns, like political campaigns, often turn on quite irrational considerations which are often beyond the power of the parties to control. However, by careful preparation and strengthening of labor relations policies before organizing starts, management will be prepared to deal effectively with union propaganda from a position of residual strength.

Anyone faced with a union organizing campaign should immediately seek professional advice. The NLRB rules governing these situations are so complex that any written statement of "do's and don'ts" is sure to be inadequate and likely to be outdated. At the same time, it is worthwhile to understand the outlines and philosophy of the Labor Management Relations Act. All too frequently, an inadvertent violation, before the manager is aware that organizing is in progress, is the basis of an NLRB order. The manufacturing manager should also make sure that all supervisors having contact with production employees have a good working knowledge of the basic rules so that these individuals will not inadvertently violate the Act. The company is responsible for them, and it is generally assumed that they speak for the company.

The manager faced with a union organizing campaign need not hesitate to express his views to employees within the boundaries discussed below. He should give his side. The Labor Management Relations Act expressly guarantees the employer this right,[4] and the NLRB has stated that the policy of the

---

[4] Section 8(c) of the Labor Management Relations Act, 1947, 29 USC §158(c).

Act requires that employees have "an effective opportunity to hear the arguments concerning representation."[5] The reasons for opposition to unionization will not be heard from the union organizer. If employees are to hear this side, they must hear it from the employer.

However, every representative of management must abide by the NLRB's rules in word and deed. The practical effects of mistakes are substantial. Some of the often repeated mistakes can be avoided by operating within the following guidelines: (1) No employer representative may make promises of benefits, either expressly or impliedly, to employees during a union organizing campaign, which are in any way tied to the outcome of the unionizing drive or an employee's participation in it. (2) Employer representatives must not make threats of any kind to employees which could be construed as threats of retaliation for any individual employee's activities in supporting the union or opposing the union. Nor should threats be tied to the outcome of the union organizing drive. (3) Veiled threats are as bad as direct threats, and the same goes for promises. The manager must be ever alert to the possibility that a threat or promise may be found where none was intended by the speaker. Often a comment considered in the context of an earlier comment or a later comment can be given an improper interpretation by the NLRB. (4) Also to be avoided, except on specific advice of a professional, is any change in the conditions of employment, such as wage increases, during a union organizing campaign. Changes, later determined to be adverse, are often regarded as retribution. Improvements are similarly violative if the NLRB considers that the employer's object was to defeat the union organizing effort. (5) Employees should not be questioned by any employer representative about their union activities or views. Nor should any attempt be made to spy on employees' or union meetings. (6) No meeting or discussions regarding the union may be held by management in supervisors' or management offices or in the employees' homes.

Describing a union organizing campaign in detail is beyond the limited scope of this chapter. As pointed out above, it is usually begun without publicity and away from the plant. The manager may first learn of the organizers' efforts when he receives a demand for recognition from the union.

Often this demand is accompanied by copies of the union authorization cards referred to above. The manager desiring to ensure his employees a democratic opportunity to decide for themselves on the union representation question should not meet with a union organizer claiming to represent the employees based upon cards, nor should he inspect cards or facsimiles of cards which are forwarded to him for his attention. These cards are not always what they seem and often do not represent employees' real wishes.[6] If, based upon such cards, a claim of majority representation is made, the manager, after consultation with a professional, should in most instances refuse recognition and ask, or suggest that the union ask, the NLRB to conduct a secret ballot election among the employees. During this election proceeding, both sides will have an opportunity to express their real views on the question, within the NLRB's rules.

---

[5] Excelsior Underwear, Inc., 156 NLRB 1236, 1240 (1966).

[6] For example, the NLRB's chairman compiled data showing that when a union presented authorization cards representing 50 to 70 percent of the employees in the unit, it lost the subsequently held secret election more than 50 percent of the time. 1962 Proceedings, Section of Labor Relations Law, American Bar Association, pp. 14–17.

In the vast majority of organizing campaigns, employees will be permitted to vote in a secret ballot election supervised by the NLRB, and the results of this balloting will control. Such elections are initiated by the union or the employer or the employees filing a petition with the NLRB. A hearing or conference will be arranged by the NLRB to determine when the election will be held and which employees will vote. The election itself is generally held by an NLRB agent at the plant several weeks after the petition is filed.

Up until twenty-four hours before the polls open, the employer is free to express his views in letter form or in speeches, meetings, handbills, posters, and the like, all subject to very careful review by the NLRB for unlawful (objectionable) content or misrepresentations. Within the twenty-four-hour period preceding the election, no speeches or meetings may be held on company time with the employees, although all other forms of contact are still available.

Throughout this period, the union will be propagandizing with meetings, home visits, leaflets, and so on. It is not unusual for a larger campaign to involve sound trucks and commercial radio and television announcements. The management must also be alert to other union tactics such as the provoked discharge or the quickie strike. These are harassments designed to win support or demonstrate management's weakness. They must be dealt with in such a way that management appears firm but fair.

If the employees reject union representation and the election was regular and without objectionable conduct, the union has no status in the plant and the employer may continue to deal with the employees on the preelection basis. If the union obtains a majority of the votes cast and there was no irregularity, it will be certified by the NLRB as the exclusive representative of the employees. This means that the employer may not make any change in the terms and conditions of employment of employees in the unit represented by the union without negotiating with the union and that he must bargain with the union upon request regarding the terms and conditions of such employees' employment and reduce agreements reached to writing. If the employer does not voluntarily bargain with the union, the NLRB will order bargaining. If the employer refuses to comply with the NLRB's bargaining order, the NLRB may obtain enforcement of that order from the Federal courts.

There is an exception to this general rule that the election results control, however. In certain situations, although a majority of the employees have voted against the union (or without an election ever being held), the NLRB will order the employer to bargain with the union.[7] Generally, although not always, these situations will involve some breach of the NLRB's rules by the employer representatives.[8]

The possibility that the employees can be forced into this situation, virtually despite their wishes, and the employer forced to bargain with the union, puts a premium on supervisors understanding the rules. All supervisors should know that unions are alert to this possibility and frequently seize upon seemingly harmless offhand comments or attempt to bait supervisors into hasty remarks. Of course, it is not unheard of to have such remarks embroidered or made up from whole cloth. An alert supervisor will often be able

---

[7] Bernel Foam Products Co., 146 NLRB 1277 (1964).

[8] An example of a case where the NLRB held that an employer was obligated to bargain, although he did nothing illegal but merely looked at the authorization cards, is Snow & Sons, 134 NLRB 709 (1961).

to prevent such situations by knowing the rules, refusing to get cornered, and keeping a clear head.

The goal should be to have a democratic test of the employees' wishes. If they do not support the union and do endorse the management's leadership, management is free to continue its program. If the union is certified or the employer ordered to bargain, the focus of labor relations attention shifts to the bargaining table.

BARGAINING NEGOTIATIONS

A manager with an established collective bargaining relationship or one whose employees are represented by a union for the first time is faced with the bargaining table. Over this table, at intervals, major confrontations will occur. The minor confrontations of contract administration are discussed later.

The practical manager will see that negotiation is not a trial, a game, or an opportunity for good fellowship. It is a confrontation in which the ability of the manager to control the manufacturing facility is challenged. The strength of the challenge will depend to a great extent upon the quality of the manufacturing manager's leadership. If, by and large, there is acceptance of this leadership, the confrontation, although outwardly unpleasant, can be de-escalated to the point where it is susceptible of resolution because the basic control of management is recognized and accepted.

The actual process of negotiation consists of two equally important stages—preparation and presentation. Both require firsthand detailed knowledge, experience in such situations, and a breadth of vision. A practical manager will see that all three are applied. If any is lacking in his organization, he will obtain outside assistance.

Preparation. The details of preparation will depend upon the issues to be negotiated. A first contract will undoubtedly involve a full spectrum, whereas a later contract may involve nothing but wage and fringe issues. In many situations, the union will present its list of demands long before the initial negotiation session. The company may then prepare responses as well as proposals of it own.

In any situation, management must have its priorities firmly fixed long before actual negotiations. In arranging priorities initially, little consideration should be given to tactics. Management must attempt to view each of the potential areas of discussion as an economic matter over the longest foreseeable course of events. In virtually every instance, the key issues to be negotiated, those which have "must" priority from management's viewpoint, do not relate to the size of the wage and fringe package; yet each has a definite economic impact.

Management's Obligation to Maintain Efficiency. Management's interest is in maintaining control of the manufacturing operation. Of course, an uneconomic wage and fringe package is detrimental and occasionally even fatal to the competitive position of the company. However, restrictions on the company's ability to enter new product lines or abandon old ones, to promote in accordance with ability, to lay off when economic conditions warrant, and the like can be far more expensive without any redeeming virtues.

Where these high-priority issues are to be negotiated, management should prepare by reviewing its operational situation from top to bottom. It is sometimes helpful to rethink the entire manufacturing operation—mentally going step by step through the manufacturing procedure. For example, raw materials, semicompleted parts, or totally completed parts are purchased to be worked on. Does management want to continue these practices? These materials move through various departments and work stations. As to each, management might ask: How are these departments and stations manned on a permanent basis? Does the company want to assure that employees promoted or hired into these jobs will have the skills required? If skills are not available or if a new process is developed, might subcontracting be considered? It is frequently necessary to transfer temporarily to fill vacancies caused by vacations or absences or for other reasons. How is this done? Will work stations or entire departments be laid off as units? Will employees be laid off individually? Will production standards have to be changed from time to time? Will new and improved methods of manufacturing, equipment, or materials be developed? These suggest but a few of the problems present in most plants which must be identified for solution.

The preparation should look beyond the present operation. Introducing new products or discontinuing others will require operational changes. How should these be handled? Similarly, the prospect of drastic changes through sale of the business or closure of the particular plant or operation should not be overlooked.

Once management has a firm fix on the labor relations aspects of its manufacturing operation, it can begin to draft concrete proposals designed to guarantee its continued ability to perform these functions in the most efficient way. It is not sufficient to negotiate a general term in the contract giving the management "the right to manage the company's business." The NLRB has held that no matter how basic to "the company's business" a decision is, if it changes the terms and conditions of employment, management may not act unless it has bargained with the union about the change.[9] The very general language discussed above is not considered to constitute a waiver or consent by the union to the company's managing the business without consulting with it on each move.

The net result, of course, is that before employees in a department can be laid off, for example, even for an extremely brief period, the union must be consulted and given an opportunity to bargain about the matter. Of course, in a short-term layoff situation, this bargaining may be taking place while the employees remain present in the plant with nothing to do. Management needs the right to act swiftly. Therefore, it must get express contractual agreement to the exercise of these rights to act.

The Management Rights Clause. At the core of every collective agreement is the management "rights" or "responsibilities" clause. It and various subordinate clauses should be drafted with a view to giving the company the right to act immediately in the areas of management concern—the areas which review of the plant situation shows that management must subject to continuing control.

No two clauses of this kind should be identical. Each should reflect a very careful appraisal by management of the essential elements which must be controlled for operating efficiency. An example of such a clause is the following:

Section 1. The Union recognizes those rights and responsibilities which belong solely and exclusively to the Company, including, without limitation on the generality of the foregoing, the right to manage the Company's business and to direct the working force; the right to hire, promote, or demote employees; the right to maintain order and efficiency; the right to extend, maintain, curtail, or terminate

---

[9] Puerto Rico Telephone Co., 149 NLRB 950 (1964).

the operations of the Company or any part or department thereof, to determine the size and location of the Company's plant or operations and to transfer work between its various plants, operations, and subdivisions thereof; the right to subcontract and to farm out work, and to determine the type and amount of equipment to be used and the assignment of work; the right to determine and revise production schedules, methods, standard processes, means of manufacture, and material to be used, including the right to introduce new and improved methods or facilities and to change existing methods and facilities; the right to transfer employees from job to job, from classification to classification (either temporarily or permanently), and from shift to shift; and the right to discipline, suspend, and discharge employees for just cause and lay off for lack of work or other legitimate reasons; the right to determine the number of hours and starting and quitting times of shifts, the number of hours and days in the work week, and the number of persons to be actively employed by the Company at any time; the right to require employees to observe reasonable rules and regulations established as needed by the Company; the right to determine the products to be manufactured and to set work standards and require job performance to meet the required standards and to maintain performance records for all jobs; the right to establish new classifications and the rates therefor and to eliminate jobs or not fill classifications.

The above is not an exclusive designation of the Company's prerogatives. Any and all of the rights, powers, privileges, prerogatives, and authority which the Employer had possessed prior to its having recognized the Union, are retained and reserved by the Employer, excepting only those specifically and expressly abridged or modified by the express terms of this Agreement.

Section 2.   The exercise by the Company of any of the rights, powers, or authorities defined in Section 1 above, except those specifically modified by this Agreement, shall not be subject to the grievance and arbitration procedure set forth in Article VII.

This clause was designed for a relatively small manufacturer. Each clause must be individually tailored. It can be seen that it is not designed to protect many rights which will generally be significant but which are usually protected in other clauses of the contract. The wording of these clauses should also be given serious consideration in the preparatory stages.

The Seniority Clauses. Most contracts have "seniority" clauses (clauses defining and relating to various plant opportunities the concept of length of service). From an operational standpoint, they are misnomers. Management is interested in protecting its right to select employees for promotion, transfer, layoff, recall, and so on, on the basis of ability—to get the right people in the right jobs. On the other hand, many unions begin negotiation from a position that absolute seniority must govern these matters.

Generally this position is firmly held because it accords with employees' abstract ideas of justice and because often the employees fear that management will play favorites. This is a basic tension present to some extent in virtually every negotiating situation. Where the employees trust management leadership, of course, their will be less pressure to override it.

The working out of these tensions is beyond the scope of a handbook; however, the result is generally an accommodation, that is, a recognition of seniority to some extent where the employee has demonstrated either ability or equal ability with the other employee to perform the job in question. Often resolution takes the form of a more absolute recognition of seniority among a smaller group. Thus, departmental seniority enables management to group similarly skilled employees, minimizing the danger that unqualified employees will be promoted or that the overall mix of skills necessary to operate will be disturbed by layoffs. Seniority proposals must be given very serious study.

Miscellaneous Operating Proposals. The tendency of unions to attempt to limit the company's actions in such matters as hours of work, overtime, vacation scheduling, probationary periods, and discipline also deserves attention. Management proposals in each of these areas should be designed to maintain flexibility. Within reason, management should have the right to schedule hours of work, compel overtime, assign vacations, require adequate probationary periods, and exercise discipline.

Similarly, proposals in areas such as safety or health must be prepared carefully. Of course, management does not intend to operate an unsafe facility. However, it should maintain its ability to operate despite contentions of unsafety. Proposals in this area should be carefully reviewed and should contain nothing permitting an employee or group who contends that an operation is unsafe to discontinue working.

The Resolution of Disputes during the Contract Term. The grievance and no-strike areas should be thoroughly reviewed with professionals familiar with the latest decisions of arbitrators, the NLRB, and the courts before formulating any proposal.

Grievance Resolution. The grievance and arbitration provisions should be structured to preserve management's interest in at least five areas: (1) restricting problems subject to arbitration to those alleging a violation of the express terms of the agreement, (2) defining and limiting the parties to present grievances, (3) barring out-of-date grievances, (4) assuring that proper management representatives review the grievance, and (5) controlling the selection of an arbitrator. Management must be alert to its interest in each of these areas.

Restricting Problems Subject to Arbitration. Management should recognize (the union will surely point it out) that many different discontents may be present in a plant. Most of these gripes are really not susceptible to arbitral resolution. An arbitrator is no more qualified to decide on wall color or sanitary facilities than anyone else. The union would recognize that the amount of its dues or assessments should not be subject to arbitration although there are plenty of gripes on this. Management would not wish to submit the size of its wage and fringe package to an arbitrator's judgment.

The arbitrator should properly function only to interpret and apply the express terms of the parties' collective agreement. The agreement should spell out this limitation. Either the types of grievances submissible to arbitration or the definition of a grievance which may be processed through the grievance procedure should be limited to those "concerning the interpretation, application, or violation of the express terms of this agreement" or something similar. The practical difference between this language and language throwing open the procedure to "any dispute an employee or the union may have with the company" is obvious.

Defining and Limiting the Parties to Present Grievances. There are three potential sources of grievances—the individual employee, the union, and the employer. It is generally recognized that barring union grievances by restricting the procedure to grievances filed and signed by employees will result in fewer manufactured situations clogging the grievance machinery.

Some consider it good policy to bar employer grievances from the procedure, thus leaving management free to process its complaints of breach of contract in the courts. The Supreme Court has held that where an employer has a right to file a grievance and has promised to resolve disputes concerning the contract through this procedure, he may not file suit until his promise has been fulfilled.[10] The thought behind leaving management free to go to court was the expectation that in the most devasting breach of contract situation, that is, the breach of contract or "wildcat" strike, only the court would be available to offer injunctive relief. Because of Supreme Court decisions, no court can any longer be counted upon to provide this assistance.[11]

Some employers negotiate provisions allowing them to file and process grievances with immediate arbitration before an available arbitrator of their selection to stop breach of contract strikes. The manufacturing manager should be alert to this problem and should consult his professional counselor expressly on it with a view to obtaining the maximum no-strike protection.

Barring Out-of-date Grievances. Far too many agreements lack any statute of limitations, and old grievances may be dredged up at any time. All agreements should provide that grievances must be presented promptly—often within five to ten days of the event, with older grievances specifically barred.

Assuring That Proper Management Representatives Review the Grievance. Management personnel with knowledge, authority, and an ability and interest in resolving grievances should be permitted to review them. However, simply repeating fruitless discussions should be avoided. Meetings should be used only in steps where the manager will have sufficient authority to command the union committee's respect and resolve the matter. Other steps should be handled by written communication.

Controlling the Selection of an Arbitrator. The necessity for retaining some control should be obvious. Even where the contract is carefully drafted, extremely important management decisions will be subject to arbitral review. The quality of arbitrators varies widely. However, under most contracts, the arbitrator's award is final and binding, and no court will subject it to more than a cursory review. For this reason, provisions for compulsory selection from a single list or appointment by a third agency such as the American Arbitration Association should be avoided. All too often the list sent will contain no competent people, and of course, there is no control over an outside agency. The very real prospect of placing a multimillion dollar modernization project before some college instructor in labor relations should suggest the reason for control.

An example of language maintaining the requisite control is the following:

After receipt of a notice requesting arbitration, a representative of the company and a representative of the union shall select a mutually agreeable arbitrator to hear and determine the grievance. If the representatives of the parties are unable to agree upon the selection of an arbitrator, either party may request the Federal Mediation and Conciliation Service to submit a list or lists of arbitrators from which one will be selected by the parties.

The No-strike Clause. The no-strike clause has always been central. The prime consideration received by management for the collective agreement, of course, is the assurance of peace for its term. The difficulties of enforcement make ingenuity in drafting these clauses important. The clause should bind the union and covered employees to promises not to authorize, instigate, condone, or engage in work stoppages, strikes, slowdowns, picketing, or other actions which will interrupt or interfere with the operations of the

---

[10] Drake Bakeries, Inc., v. Local 50, American Bakery Workers, 370 U.S. 254 (1962).

[11] Avco Corporation v. Aero Lodge 735, IAM, 390 U.S. 557 (1968); Sinclair Refining Co. v. Atkinson, 370 U.S. 195 (1962).

company. It is often helpful to bind the union to an agreement that, upon notification by the company, it will take immediate affirmative steps with the employees involved, such as letters, bulletins, telegrams, and employee meetings, to bring about an immediate resumption of normal work.

Similarly, the clause should spell out that the company may discharge or otherwise discipline any employee who has violated it. As it is often impossible to discipline all participants or to pinpoint conclusively the leaders, such a clause should permit selective discipline. An example provides:

In the event of violation of this article, the company may discharge or otherwise discipline any employee (whether individually or in a group) who has engaged in the violation. Any employee so discharged or otherwise disciplined who has not participated in or instigated a violation of this article may file a grievance under the grievance provisions of this agreement. Employees who instigated or participated in the violation may not process grievances concerning any discipline under the grievance provisions of this agreement. It is understood that the fact that some employees but not all employees participating in the violation were discharged or otherwise disciplined shall not be held to be a ground for reinstatement or reduction of the penalties imposed and that the only issue before any arbitrator appointed to consider a grievance involving discipline for an alleged violation of this article shall be whether in fact the employee disciplined instigated or participated in the violation.

Other possible provisions which should be considered with a professional restrict the removal of suits for violation of these clauses from state to Federal court, bar discussion or negotiation while a violation is taking place, and provide for liquidated damages in case of violation.

The Wage and Fringe Package. Careful consideration should be given to data from other competitive and area plants. The overall plant situation should be reviewed and potential inequities noted and, if possible, justified. The management should always construct its package with a view to its own needs; that is, it should select those areas for improvement which will most help to keep present employees and hire new ones. All potential fringe items should be reduced to actual cost in terms of cents per hour, so that they can be compared on a one-for-one basis with wage costs.

The package should be constructed in such a way that the increase goes to the employees in areas of greatest competition. These are generally the most productive and highest paid employees. For example, it is generally more difficult to hire a skilled tool and die maker than an assembler, and the established wage relationship should already reflect this difference. Often percentage increases should be considered as a way of maintaining this difference. A wage increase of 5 cents across the board if repeated often enough will tend to flatten the wage curve and result in a smaller percentage difference between the two jobs in each negotiation. However, a 2 percent increase would result in a 4-cent-an-hour increase for the $2-an-hour assembler and a 7-cent increase for a $3.50-an-hour tool and die maker. The wage curve and percentage differential will thus maintain the same relationship. Generally, most employees are in the lower rate ranges. Therefore, a percentage increase can result in very substantial improvement in the high ranges without artificially inflating the cost.

Presentation. There are very few universally accepted principles in the area of negotiation. Of course, if the preparation has not been thorough, negotiations cannot be successful. Like the union, management must have goals and must set out affirmatively to achieve these goals.

The medium for attaining these goals is the negotiating committee. It must have a single spokesman, with other participants selected for their special knowledge of the problems to be discussed, and a single individual competent to take virtually verbatim notes.

The management spokesman or negotiator is attempting to communicate with the union committee. He is building a relationship between the company and this committee, a relationship that must last for many years—in many cases, long after he is gone. The foundation of this relationship must be respect. Tricks are no substitute for ethical standards. If management sticks to high standards, it may demand and receive the same from the other side.

As in any sales proposition, knowledge of the other party, his interests, and his personality is mandatory as are common courtesy and concern.

The actual negotiating procedure depends upon the personality of the company's chief negotiator. There are usually a series of meetings in which this negotiator will attempt to bring the parties to an agreement in line with the company's goal. This requires continuous positive action by the management committee, no matter how awesome the prospect of strike may seem. There is no company that cannot afford a strike, certainly in preference to some concessions. Once this is recognized, the absolute necessity of management's maintaining a positive outlook during the negotiations is obvious.

One harassing tactic to which any management negotiator should be alert is the request for information. The NLRB has held that a union is entitled to certain relevant information.[12] This rule is, of course, subject to abuse, and the management negotiator may find himself peppered with a continuing stream of questions and requests. The union's object is not necessarily to obtain the information requested. The union really wishes to trap the company into refusing to divulge information, thereby committing an unfair labor practice which will allow the union to engage in a strike without fear that the employees will be replaced. Before the management negotiator refuses any request for information, he should get the request in written form and review the question with an experienced professional.

When negotiations have been completed, all details of the settlement should be set down in writing and spelled out clearly. The negotiator should obtain written assurances from the union committee that the settlement will be recommended and that they will use all efforts to obtain ratification.

THE STRIKE

The one virtual absolute in modern labor relations is that no organized company can operate over any extended period without being in a position where it either should or must take a strike. To the union, the strike is first an economic weapon, but also, perhaps more importantly, it is the reason for its existence and a potential rallying point for revivifying a flagging organization. Over the course of a decade of volatile contract negotiations and grievances, it is the unusual situation where no union leader has taken a deliberately outrageous position in hopes of provoking employees to strike. A management which reacts to this outrage by demonstrating its servility only encourages further outrages. At some point, every management must take a strike in such a situation.

There are three basic categories into which strikes fall, with different legal rules applicable to each. The problem of classifying any particular strike,

[12] Truitt Mfg. Co., 110 NLRB 856 (1954), enfd., 351 U.S. 149 (1956).

however, is not easy.   As management must frequently act during the course of the strike, subject to later review by the NLRB, it is always advisable to seek professional advice when faced with a strike situation.

The first major distinction is between the breach of contract strike—a strike during the term of a collective agreement containing a no-strike clause covering the situation—and an ordinary economic strike over the terms of a new collective agreement. The employee's right to engage in an ordinary economic strike, not in breach of a collective agreement, is protected by the Labor Management Relations Act.   Any action taken against an employee because of his participation in such a strike is an unfair labor practice.   Thus, employees may not be disciplined because they have struck, nor may employees be deprived of vacation pay to which they would have been entitled but for the fact that they were on strike on the qualifying date.[13]   On the other hand, the breach of contract striker does not have this protecion and may be disciplined or discharged for engaging in strike action.

The third category of strikes which overlaps the other two is the unfair labor practice strike.   This strike is one which is found by the NLRB to be in protest against an unfair labor practice committed by the employer.   An unfair labor practice strike may be called either during or between contract terms, and employees who participate in such a strike may not be disciplined nor discharged for striking nor replaced.

Combating Strikes.   Essentially the way to combat any of the three types of strikes is to minimize its economic impact.   A strike is called to cost the company money and thereby coerce the company to accede to the union's demands.   Obviously, any action that the company can take to minimize the economic impact of the strike will greatly increase its chances of winning it.

Before any negotiations for a new contract, every effort should be made to prepare for a strike by building up inventory, storing it in remote locations, exploring the possibility of operating the plant during the stoppage, and making arrangements with customers so that their needs can be anticipated and, if possible, supplied.

The decision whether to operate the plant during the strike will depend on local conditions, and professional assistance generally will be helpful.   Competent labor relations counsel should have firsthand knowledge of the potential law enforcement problems in any particular area.

If, after careful consideration, it appears feasible to operate on some basis, it is generally advisable to do so, not only for economic reasons but because of psychological considerations.   An employee faced with the visible evidence that in some manner the company is successfully completing his job begins to question the efficacy of the strike action.   No matter how management attempts to counter union propaganda, it is difficult for employees not to favor, at least in principle, the union's goals in any given strike.   Management makes most of its progress by convincing the employees that the union's goals are not going to be attained.   Once the employee senses this and once the employee is himself faced with the economic pinch that a strike entails, he will put pressure on the union to bring it to an end.   This effect is magnified where the employer, as he generally has a right to do, hires permanent replacements for part of the work force.   Even if very few replacements are actually hired, the impact is great.

The strike in breach of contract presents a somewhat different problem. Everything said above regarding the ordinary economic strike is equally

[13] NLRB v. Great Dane Trailers, Inc., 388 U.S. 26 (1967).

applicable. However, in addition, as this strike is not protected by the Labor Management Relations Act, the employer may discipline employees who engage in it and may sue the union if it has participated. Before either tactic is considered, however, professional advice should be sought so that either the discipline or suit can be brought to a successful conclusion.

The cardinal rule for dealing with breach-of-contract strike situations is that under no circumstances should the company negotiate regarding the supposed cause of the strike while the strike is in progress. If the strike should be successful in the sense that the company concedes something to the strikers' demands, repetitions are virtually assured.

The unfair labor practice strike is an attempt at economic coercion and may be countered as such. However, employees may not be disciplined, nor may they be permanently replaced.

THE OPERATION OF THE GRIEVANCE PROCEDURE

In the intervening periods between contract negotiations, the parties engage in a series of problem-oriented confrontations involving grievances. Grievances are filed and processed for a variety of reasons. Some represent reaction to a legitimate abuse and breach of a contract right. Others are attempts to gain new rights not negotiated away by the company in the contract. Still others are the union's attempt to use the grievance and arbitration procedures to keep management off balance. A fractious union or a union wishing to advertise itself to the employees may file multitudes of specious grievances. The union attempts to cause employee dissatisfaction and lower employee morale, thus unsettling the plant and strengthening its bargaining position.

In each situation, management will find itself attempting to hold on to or at most give a practical application to the terms of the existing agreement. By and large, the union will view even the legitimate grievance as an opportunity for expanding upon the agreement and garnering new concessions not won and often not proposed at the bargaining table.

If the grievance procedure has been properly drafted, each confrontation will arise in the context of a particular problem. Management is attempting to solve the problem within the terms of the collective agreement as written and fairly understood and should only consider a modifying settlement if the agreement itself provides no rational or workable solution to the problem and management acknowledges that the problem needs immediate solution. If, in these rare circumstances, modifications should seem necessary, a written supplement to the collective agreement should be executed by both parties.

To achieve management's overall goals, it is essential that each representative responsible for the handling of a grievance at any step know the agreement thoroughly and the philosophy behind every provision. Particular attention must be paid to the agreed-upon method of handling grievances. The parties should establish regularity at the earliest possible moment and insist upon literal compliance.

In handling grievances, regularity reinforces management's goal which is to have the issues defined by the union and the grievant as clearly and precisely as possible at the earliest possible stage in the grievance procedure. With the issues defined, management can carefully review them and all their ramifications, thereby understanding fully the potential impact of the union's position.

With understanding, management can formulate an effective response and hopefully achieve its aims, which are acceptance of its position with a settlement on its terms. If such a settlement is not achieved in the grievance procedure, the not inconsequential risk is that a supposedly neutral third party, the "arbitrator," will be called in to decide finally and with no effective review a problem which may be of prime importance to the company.

The labor arbitration is a form of civil litigation with the usual inherent risks. Thus, the decision to arbitrate a question must be prefaced with a determination of what may be lost. Of course, in many situations where the potential risk is great, no compromise is possible, in which case arbitration is the only course. However, in other situations, a potential avenue of settlement, if explored, might prove efficacious.

In any event, before a matter is presented to an arbitrator, every effort should be made to assure that the issue is defined and all possible evidence and arguments on the company's behalf are amassed and presented in the best possible form. In this way, the company can minimize the chance of an adverse ruling.

THE RELATIONSHIP WITH THE UNION

In the usual situation, after recognition, the focus of the labor relations function tends to be the union committee and representatives. This group should never be the exclusive focus. Individual and institutional communication with employees is still important. However, the union representatives, having the power to shape or override employee expectations, require consideration.

In negotiations, grievance handling, and strike situations, one factor is all important—leadership. The management must have the respect of the union representatives—just as it must have the respect of the employees. What will create respect will depend on the personalities of the representatives. However, the qualities which are most generally effective in this regard are fairness and firmness. Formulate positions fairly. Explain positions thoroughly. If, in discussing a position, it stands the test of fairness, defend it. Do not retreat merely because of pressure from a position which is fair. When the union recognizes that management will be firm, its respect for management increases.

BIBLIOGRAPHY

CCH Labor Law Reporter, Commerce Clearing House, Inc., Chicago, 1966.

Gregory, Charles O., *Labor and the Law,* 2d ed., W. W. Norton & Company, Inc., New York, 1961.

"Guidebook to Labor Relations," *Labor Law Reports,* published annually by Commerce Clearing House, Inc., Chicago, Ill., 1968.

Industrial Relations Committee, "When Management Negotiates," National Association of Manufacturers, New York, 1967.

Petro, Sylvester, "Union Violence and Administrative Law," *The Kohler Strike,* Henry Regnery Company, Chicago, 1961.

A variety of topical booklets on various aspects of labor relations are available from the National Association of Manufacturers. A complete, up-to-date list of these publications may be obtained by writing to the Association at 277 Park Avenue, New York, N.Y. 10017.

CHAPTER FIVE

Employee Services and Benefits

JAMES L. CENTNER *Vice President—Finance and Administration, The Hess & Eisenhardt Company, Cincinnati, Ohio*

The prime, fundamental concept to be burned into the memory of the manufacturing manager is that a fringe benefit cost, once accepted, becomes a fixed cost rarely ever erased. Irrespective of the accounting language used, these fixed costs add to the overhead burden. Many of the benefits and services granted must be managed as attentively as direct labor costs, or the costs soar.

An estimate of the total cost of the fringe benefit or employee service package in the United States reaches $75 billion a year, and in some specific companies represents 40 to 50 percent of payroll. A good round figure estimate places the average manufacturing organization's benefit cost at 26 to 28 percent of payroll. Although the manufacturing manager is a line executive with staff resources to assist and counsel him on the complexities of the various aspects of the benefit package, he must play a vital role in the supervision and control functions as they affect the ever-mounting costs involved.

BACKGROUND

Why are there fringe benefits in the first place? Do they really accomplish their objective? Obviously, a position can be taken on many sides of these questions; and the current literature of the industrial relations field is full of educated comment on each and every facet, with positions reflecting whether the author hews to the traditional schools of management or has joined the behavioral school.

Practically speaking, fringe benefit programs are in effect because employers granted them, government legislation enabled them, unions demanded them, employees insisted on them, and society smiled on them. The galloping rhythm of the fringe package really began in the United States during the World War II period in the days of wage and price control, excess profits taxes, and a highly competitive labor force situation. Prior to this time, although there were certain minimum fringe benefits (vacations, holidays, group insurance, and pensions) in effect in many organizations, they were unsophisticated by later standards and in many cases were contributory, in that the employee helped pay a portion of the cost through payroll deduction plans.

Many employers granted wide-ranging benefit increases in the World War II period so as to be in a position to recruit new employees, and they did it on the basis that the costs of the additional fringes were deductible expenses against an excess profits tax base. The employer-pay-all philosophy as opposed to the employee-contribute-something one really flamed in this period, with the result that twenty-five years later, few plans remained which included direct employee contributions for insurance, pension, and disability pay plans. Many employers who incepted plans during the excess profits tax era purely because they were deductible, rued that day, when the tax base was lowered in the postwar years and they realized the fixed costs they had accepted and had to live with.

From this beginning, there has been a steadily mounting benefit package. Running the gamut from the more traditional vacation–holiday–pension–group insurance package to paid sabbaticals and bonuses-to-enjoy-vacations-more, there is an unending, myriad diversity in the raising of the ante to satisfy the employee. Constant increases in the benefit package are in the annual bargaining planks of the unions. Rare is the manufacturing manager who, as a member of his company's bargaining team, has not been appalled at the wide range of benefit demands placed on the table in a current contract negotiation series. That some of these are smoke screen and unrealistic is immaterial—significant fringe gains are made in every series of collective bargaining negotiations, and costs increase.

Programs of the Federal government have added to fringe cost, of course, with the most notable being Social Security, destined already to reach an employer-employee rate of 5.9 percent each on the first $7,800 of earnings by 1987. Predictably, both figures in the preceding sentence will have increased by 1987.

Do fringe benefits really accomplish their objective? In the sense that they are now an integral part of personnel management programs and that they do indeed assist in the recruitment and retention of employees: yes. But if adopted in the belief that by and of themselves they motivate employees at all levels to perform better, the answer in most cases has to be a resounding no.

Most workers—union and nonunion alike, salaried or hourly rated, rank and file, administrative, technical, or executive—regard fringe benefits almost as a vested right, an entitlement that goes along with the employment relationship. This is a widespread attitude in the United States and abroad. Industrial relations research has demonstrated time and again that all employees want recognition, security, fair wages, and good working conditions, and they want them precisely in that order. No wonder then that employers have attempted to satisfy these natural wants with a plethora of fringe benefit solutions, some appealing to each of the four categories. From the reserved parking place to the key to the executive washroom, from the special union steward shirt to the removal of time clocks for foremen, from the telephone on the desk of the stenographer to the expense account, the parameters of benefit level are boundless, limited only by the imagination of the beseecher or the bestower. So impressed has the industrial society become with these side aspects of employment that it is not at all unusual for campus recruiters to have framed a virtual litany in response to the frequent first question of the prospect: "What are the fringe benefits?"

On the other side of the coin, there is not a shred of evidence to indicate that the granting of benefit on benefit has increased productivity, individual job performance, promotional aspiration, or general efficiency. Quite the reverse, as the works of Gellerman, Herzberg, McGregor, Mayo, Likert, and others demonstrate. Spiraling wages merely motivate people to seek the next increase, and with fringe benefits at better than 25 percent of spiraling wages, the cry is still for motivation, says Herzberg,[1] as he describes the hygiene factors which do not motivate.

The manufacturing manager is well served who recognizes that efficiency and improvement of both individual and group performance must be based on fundamental management principles, with greater emphasis placed on making work meaningful, rather than looking for golden progress at the end of a fringe benefit rainbow.

RESPONSIBILITY

Ultimate responsibility for the design and administration of the fringe benefit and employee services programs lies squarely on the shoulders of the line organization, with delegation to various staff specialists depending on the size of the company. In a small company, the executive in charge of manufacturing operations may wear two hats in the sense that he is his own personnel administrator. As the size of the company grows, the addition of an individual to assist and counsel the line organization on personnel matters is imperative. In the United States, one person in about ninety is employed full time administering the personnel function. Large companies have staff specialists in dozens of personnel categories such as employment interviewing, insurance administration, and pension planning. The function of the specialist is to relieve the line manager of the details of administration, not of the responsibility for decision making and cost control.

The manufacturing manager must be familiar with the broad concepts involved with each of the employee benefit and services programs and must select his staff advisors with care, whether they be full-time employees or outside consultants contributing an essential staff service. It is common for small- and medium-sized companies to rely heavily on the advice of insurance company personnel in group insurance matters, private actuaries on pension planning, attorneys and bank trust officers in profit sharing trust affairs, and CPA's on cost calculations for these programs. It would make little sense for the manufacturing executive to attempt to become a technical expert in all aspects of fringe benefit programs. First, he could not do it; and even if he tried, by the time he mastered the vagaries of the current program, it would already be obsolete. He should become generally familiar with the program, specifically knowledgeable as to cost, and have the basic humility to know where to look or whom to ask for help and advice.

TYPES OF BENEFITS

There is no commonly accepted definition to separate a benefit from a service. In management literature, the terms are used interchangeably. Where a distinction is made, it would appear that the only discernible distinction is that in some cases, services are optional (for example, financial counseling or group purchasing) while benefits are mandatory entitlements by force of law, contract, or individual company policy.

[1] Frederick Herzberg, "One More Time: How Do You Motivate Employees?" *Harvard Business Review*, January–February, 1968, p. 55.

It is not the purpose of this chapter to cover in depth the virtually unending list of employee benefits, but rather, within time and space limitations, to enunciate the salient features of the more prevalent benefit programs generally in effect, point out others in a cursory manner, and suggest further references in this inexhaustible field. For the sake of some logical order, fringe benefits have been broken down into six general categories:

1. Government-required insurance benefits
2. Employee comfort and protection
3. Employee security
4. Employee pleasure and recreation
5. Employee financial extras
6. Other employee benefits

All these categories require contemporaneous study and consistent communication. Changes in law, details, revenue rulings, interest and premium rates, and national policy are dynamic and constant. The remarks that follow the items by category can at best cover only the essential ingredients of the programs.

GOVERNMENT-REQUIRED INSURANCE BENEFITS

Old Age and Survivor's Insurance. Signed by President Franklin D. Roosevelt on August 14, 1935 and amended many times since, the Social Security Act provides for old age and survivor benefits among other things (such as Medicare). Payroll taxes, shared equally by the employer and employee, finance this ever-expanding program. Tax rates, established by the 1967 amendments for both employer and employee and covering the first $7,800 of income, are as follows:

Year	Rate, %	Maximum tax
1967	4.4	$290.40
1968	4.4	343.20
1969–1970	4.8	374.40
1971–1972	5.2	405.60
1973–1975	5.65	440.70
1976–1979	5.7	444.60
1980–1986	5.8	452.40
1987 and later	5.9	460.20

Note that both employer and employee are subject to these taxes.

Corresponding increases in benefits at all levels were enacted in 1967, owing to the higher tax rate and the higher tax base. As one example, a retired couple began receiving $238 per month maximum benefits in February, 1968, rather than the previous $207. Benefits for survivors were increased as well; children are able to receive benefits based on their mother's earnings; eligibility rules for widows, widowers, and stepchildren were changed; and additional credit was granted members of the armed forces.

Because of their vested interest in and contributions to the Social Security program, employees generally are familiar with the provisions of the law, and there are ample field offices of the Social Security Administration to which specific questions can be referred. The manufacturing manager must keep in mind the constantly increasing cost represented by sizable additional employer tax contribution.

Unemployment Compensation. Under the unemployment title of the Social Security Act, the Federal government is given authority to administer, in cooperation with the states, an unemployment insurance plan. A payroll tax of 3 percent of payroll up to $3,000 per employee is levied by the Federal Unemployment Tax Act. The states administer the plan and have the authority to levy additional taxes against payroll, which most states indeed do, based on the employers' layoff experience. A state-by-state analysis of the distinctive features of individual plans is not practical here. Generally, however, when an employee is laid off for lack of work or through no fault of his own and he has worked a minimum period to qualify (six weeks is a good average), he may then receive weekly benefit payments ranging from a low of $26 to a high of $60, including dependency credits. The employee does not automatically receive these benefits. He must apply for them personally and give evidence that he is actively seeking work, available for work, and physically able to work. He may receive benefits for a period varying between eighteen and thirty-nine weeks. Obviously these plans are subject to almost constant change and the subject of much political oratory in various state legislatures.

It is essential that an individual company's experience under its state unemployment compensation plan be reviewed periodically and that every benefit application be perused to ensure that the laid-off or former employee is actually entitled to receive the benefits allowed. If, in the company's judgment, he is not, an appeal or review procedure is available to challenge the award.

In addition to the Federal and state programs, some companies have adopted a program of supplemental unemployment benefits (SUB) discussed below.

Workmen's Compensation. Whether guaranteed by a state fund or backed by private carrier insurance companies, or in some cases by self-insurance, all states require employers to protect the employee against the direct medical and surgical expense involved in on-the-job injuries, accidents, and occupational disease, and to provide weekly wage indemnity payments. This is a complicated, quasi-legal program of great interest to the manufacturing manager, not only as it relates to his responsibility for compliance with state safety statutes, but also in the control of premium or tax costs through the prompt, accurate reporting of industrial accidents as required by law.

Most state programs provide the following type of benefits:

Medical Benefits Only. When an employee visits his physician as a result of an on-the-job injury and no lost time is involved, the program covers the cost of the visit and any prescription drugs administered.

Temporary Total Disability. Here the employee who loses time from his job as a result of an accident or occupational disease is paid statutory benefits up to a benefit level similar in most states to those prescribed for unemployment compensation.

Temporary Partial Disability. If an employee is injured so as to be not totally disabled but is unable to perform his normal job, benefits may be awarded to compensate him for any loss of earnings from his regular job.

Permanent Partial Disability. This is the same type of program as the preceding one, except that it is expected to be continual for the rest of the employee's life. Rather than partial weekly benefits paid out over a number of years, lump sum settlements are common in these cases.

Permanent Total Disability. The test here is quite specific in the statutes. The impairment must be total and permanent, implying that the employee will never be able to perform any work for the rest of his life.

Occupational Disease. Lead poisoning, anthrax, and silicosis are examples of the occupational disease category, which generally carry certain prescribed, statutory benefit levels in terms of number of weeks of compensation and maximum medical benefits.

Occupational Hernia. The typical award here is recovery of hospital and surgical costs plus six weeks of compensation. A manufacturing manager can help control the costs involved by seeing that employees are properly instructed in lifting techniques, that possible hernia incidents (for example, a sharp pain in the groin while lifting an object of seventy-five pounds) are properly recorded, and that every incident or claim of potential hernia is investigated thoroughly and promptly.

Death Benefits. These are awarded to the survivors, based on maximums prescribed by state statutes.

The above merely point to the multiplicity of benefits available. Costs involved in many states relate directly to the industrial classification of the employer and his own experience within that classification. Payroll taxes to support workmen's compensation programs vary from 0.8 to 5 percent of payroll cost. Periodic actuarial review of individual employer accounts is an essential cost control device.

EMPLOYEE COMFORT AND PROTECTION

Contributing to the protection aspect, insurance programs have long been one of the most common fringe benefits and one in which employee contributions are used to pay a portion of the package. Many of the benefits listed below are combined into one overall group program, administered by a single insurance company and covering all employees with basic benefits. Most major insurers will cover all the risks listed, and premium costs computed on the census list of employees will vary little from insurance company to insurance company. Of essential importance to the manufacturing manager is the service provided by the insurance carrier in the expeditious processing of claims on behalf of employees.

Life Insurance. One of the least expensive benefits to provide is group life insurance which will pay a specific terminal benefit to the employee's named beneficiary in the event of his demise while insured. In a group of as few as twenty-five employees of average age, group life insurance can be purchased without medical examination for $1.039 per $1,000 per month. The amount of life coverage for each employee is determined by negotiations, salary level, or age. Coverage is generally effective automatically when an employee passes a probationary period, say sixty days, and terminates automatically when employment ceases. The employee has the right to name the beneficiary and to convert the policy to an individual contract when he severs employment, although at a much higher cost.

Where the life insurance benefit amount is based on salary increments, the Internal Revenue Service regards up to $50,000 of coverage as tax-free to the employee, and the premium as deductible by the employer.

Group Hospital and Surgical Plans. Closely allied with the group life plan is generally a plan to assist in the payment of hospital and surgical costs incurred by an employee, and in many plans by his dependents. Whether underwritten by Blue Cross–Blue Shield organizations or by commercial insurance carriers, the costs are about the same initially for the same level of benefits for a particular group. Later, premium costs can vary considerably, based on the experience rating of the group. The plans provide the following benefits:

1. A daily hospital room allowance for a specified number of days. The higher the allowance and the longer the period, the higher the premium cost. An allowance equal to the hospital's regular semi-private room rate charge for a period of 120 days is common.
2. A total dollar amount allowed for hospital medical extras such as use of operating room, drugs, laboratory services, and the like. Most insurance companies use a multiplier such as twenty times the room rate allowance.
3. A surgical allowance, usually a dollar amount allocated by schedule in the policy for various types of surgical procedures, with a maximum amount indicated.
4. An allowance for anesthesia, again by schedule as a percentage of the surgical fee.
5. A fixed allowance for maternity benefits both for delivery and hospital expenses.

Group Major Medical Coverage. A frequently adopted addendum to the group hospital and surgical coverage is a form of catastrophe insurance, to indemnify the employee against the tremendous expense of a serious medical-surgical problem or a sustained illness. Generally, these plans provide that 80 percent of the all-inclusive medical expenses, no matter where incurred, will be covered after a basic $100 deductible has been met, with the employee paying the balance. Thus, if total expense incurred were $5,000 beyond basic hospital coverage, the insurance company would pay $3,920 while the employee would pay the initial $100 and the $980 balance, or a total of $1,080. Typical maximum amounts written under these coverages are $10,000 to $15,000 for each period of illness.

Group Accident and Sickness Benefits. Another benefit to indemnify the employee against loss of income due to nonindustrial accident or illness is a sick-pay plan, usually granting weekly benefits. It is common for these to begin on the first day of an accident or the eighth day of an illness and to have a duration of about twenty-six weeks. The benefit amounts vary widely from plan to plan. An average benefit amount is $40 a week. If the benefits are available under a workmen's compensation program, they are of course not available under a nonindustrial program. The one complements the other.

Group Dental and Optical Coverages. Not generally adopted, dental and optical coverages usually appear in the shopping lists of the international unions and have been agreed to in isolated cases. Unless the result of an accident, dental surgery is usually excluded from the plans above, as is the normal dental hygiene program of periodic cleaning, repair, and replacement of teeth. Optical coverage, except for safety glasses, has not been generally popular.

Private Pension Plans. Probably the most widely sought-after benefit, and one of the most widely adopted by employers of fifty or more employees, is the private pension plan designed to augment and reinforce the benefits already granted under the Social Security program. These plans represent one of the most complicated areas of personnel administration and competent outside assistance is essential. Conservatively, it would consume several chapters of a handbook even to scratch the surface of the literature available. The following is a brief look at the six salient points to be considered.

Eligibility. Most plans, because they are designed to supplement a Social Security program to which the employer already contributes substantially, establish rather stringent eligibility requirements such as a minimum of fifteen years of service and attainment of age sixty. In negotiated pension plans, these are established through bargaining. Incidentally, the nature of pension bargaining is so technical that it is a good idea to segregate, if possible, the pension plan negotiations from the labor agreement sessions.

In nonnegotiated plans and particularly where benefits are provided by profit sharing trusts, eligibility is often determined by Internal Revenue Service standards.

Amount of Benefits. The negotiated benefit formulas are fairly precise, for example, $5 per month benefit per year of service with up to a total of thirty years service allowable under the formula. This formula would permit a re-retirement benefit of $150 per month in addition to whatever amount the employee would be entitled to under Social Security formulas.

Where the plan is not negotiated and has no fixed formula, the terminal benefit may be determined by the participating employee's vested interest in the plan and the several options available to him on retirement: lump sum, 120 equal monthly payments, and the like.

Financing. How to pay for the benefits agreed to is a major policy decision for the company. One solution is to pay them out of current general cash at the time due. Another is to fund the plan in trust, with periodic deposits to a trust fund reinvested to assure the terminal benefits. A third solution is to insure the terminal benefit by making deposits through an insurance company, and in effect, to purchase a deposit administration group annuity. Books have been written about each of these solutions and their advantages and disadvantages. Great care and planning are essential.

Contributions. Should there be employee contributions? Generally, unions insist not, and they have been successful in winning major concessions on this point of view at the bargaining table. On the other hand, the most successful plans, in terms of appreciation of capital and size of terminal benefit, do incorporate an employee contribution of up to 5 percent of annual compensation, which the employer may match with up to 15 percent of annual compensation under IRS rulings. These profit sharing trusts are excellent retirement income and estate builders and are particularly attractive to small- and medium-sized companies.

Survivor Benefits. If the employee dies before retirement, what happens? Many plans provide for either a lump sum payment or an annuity for the beneficiary. Other plans provide an additional benefit, particularly where the company has already provided group life coverage.

Administration. Legal requirements, tax considerations, funding requirements, and employee relations activities all dictate scrupulous administration of pension plans. The manufacturing manager must be generally familiar with these aspects and must cooperate with various staff sections in implementing the most sound, error-free administrative procedure possible. Otherwise efficiency is lost, grievances increase, and the major retention facet of the plan is lost.

Salary Continuation Plans. In addition to the sick pay plans described above, many companies have a policy of salary continuation for varying periods when an employee is absent because of illness or accident. Duration of such continuation varies widely and generally is determined by length of service, prior absence record, job level, and direct contribution to the company. These plans are largely discretionary in nature and rarely are formal, written policies, although in larger companies they are indeed formalized.

EMPLOYEE PLEASURE AND RECREATION

In terms of cost, the funds allocated for providing pay for time not worked represent the largest outlay in the fringe benefit programs and exceed the cost of pension and group insurance plans in most cases. With modern-day emphasis on further reduction of the workweek, elongation of holidays, ever-increasing vacation credits based on length of service, longer and more frequent rest periods, and paid sabbatical leaves, the point has been reached in the United States, according to one laconic observer, of the 6½-day weekend. An exaggeration, obviously, but still a caution as to the rapidly mounting fixed costs of these programs. Generally, they take the following forms.

Vacations. Designed as a respite from the routine of week-to-week job commitment, paid vacations have been with us for many years. The old standard of a week's paid vacation after a year of service and two weeks after up to five years of service has been supplanted with an amalgamation of vacation plans almost as diverse as the colors in Joseph's cloak. To attempt to list the multiplicity of vacation solutions here would be futile, for the ink would hardly dry on an already obsolete system. There is no need to argue in favor of the legitimacy of a rest from contributed service, both for the hourly paid worker and the salary paid executive. Current standards call for a week of paid vacation after a year of employment, two weeks after five years, three weeks after ten to fifteen years, and four weeks after twenty years of service. Some rather generous negotiated plans call for as much as thirteen weeks.

The manufacturing manager's chief concern is not restricted to the length of the vacation period, but rather how best to schedule manufacturing operations around it. This is complicated further as the average age of the work force increases, and vacation eligibility with it. Should the plant close? If so, for how long? Is this a negotiated shutdown? How many employees are entitled to one, two, three, or four weeks? Should pay be granted in lieu of time? Is there a contractual right to do so? If the rights of management to direct the running time of the plant are not kept in constant focus as vacation periods are considered, they may well be lost or abrogated in a morass of contract language. No one solution applies. It is a concept that deserves much planning and review, along with constant scrutiny.

Holidays. On the basis of a human relations philosophy which accepted that if a man were denied the opportunity to a day's work solely because a national holiday fell within the normal workweek, employers in general acceded to a demand that employees so affected would not lose a day's pay. From that rather humble beginning, already prevalent before World War II, the situation has progressed from compensating for the six major holidays (Memorial Day, Independence Day, Labor Day, Thanksgiving Day, Christmas Day, and New Year's Day) to compensating for a diverse group of holidays, even though they fall on days not normally within an employee's schedule (Saturday, Sunday, or the sixth and seventh day in shift operations). They are no longer looked upon as vehicles to preclude loss of earnings, but as additional entitlements of employment. As this chapter is written, eight to nine paid holidays are the norm rather than the exception, with the additional days specified by contract or policy as the employee's birthday, Christmas Eve, New Year's Eve, Good Friday, a roving holiday, or many another day specified by the grantor or the negotiator.

Rest Periods. On the basis of cost, a ten-minute rest period per day is the equivalent of a week's paid vacation. Multiply that by two rest periods per day, elongated by the fact that manufacturing managers have long recognized that rarely are rest periods confined to the negotiated or announced time, and a surprisingly high cost results. There are two schools of thought on rest periods, granting that occasional breaks are beneficial. One school believes that rest periods should be established at the same time for all employees, particularly where in-line, high-cycle production methods are employed. The other, quite prevalent in job shop or intermittent production shops, sets no fixed rest periods but permits employees to leave their work stations as their job duties permit.

Whatever the policy, controlling the time spent on breaks, whether by negotiated agreement or informal policy, is a direct responsibility of the manufacturing organization and is often a critical test of good foremanship.

Recreation Programs. The value of company-sponsored recreational programs as an integral part of an employee-relations program is debatable at best and runs the attitudinal gamut from the sublime to the ridiculous. There are company programs well led, financed, and participated in by employees of all levels, highly enjoyed, and certainly contributing to morale. There are others, nominally supported and halfheartedly participated in, that have a negative effect. The most popular have been company-sponsored bowling teams, golf leagues, and softball teams. Financial resources are often provided by commission income generated by vending machines owned by subcontract vending service companies.

Cafeterias. Falling within this general category of employee services is the company cafeteria, generally operated at less than a break-even point with some subsidy provided by the company for the convenience of food service. Few companies now retain their own food service personnel. Most subcontract this function to professional industrial food service or catering organizations. The size of the company, its geographical location, space available, and local conditions determine the efficacy of food service operations. Allocation of space and utilities usually falls to the manufacturing manager, and staff coordination is exercised by the industrial relations function.

EMPLOYEE FINANCIAL BENEFITS

Various programs providing additional financial benefits or incentives are widely used. The more popular are the following.

Bonuses. Cash payments at Christmas, on the basis of profits, for cost saving suggestions, or for discretionary evaluation of performance are often used, sometimes because they are regarded as motivators for better performance, at other times because the company has been doing them for so long that it concludes it cannot quit. Does extra money—that beyond a fair wage or salary—motivate men to greater heights of performance? Yes and no; some men but not all—in fact not even a majority. "The important point is that money derives its compelling power to motivate most people some of the time, and some people all of the time, from the fact that it has no intrinsic meaning of its own. It can therefore absorb whatever meaning people want to find in their lives."[2]

Year-end or profit sharing bonuses are quite prevalent in attracting and retaining executive personnel, of course, and are a vital part of executive recruitment programs.

Merchandise gifts to employees at Christmas are common. Turkeys, fruit baskets, and merchandise certificates usually under $25 in value are widely used.

Severance Pay. Upon termination of employment, many firms grant terminal pay for a varying period to assist the employee in the transition between jobs or between active employment and retirement. This benefit tends to occur chiefly in negotiated agreements and averages four to six weeks of normal compensation.

[2] Saul W. Gellerman, *Motivation and Productivity*, American Management Association, New York, 1963, p. 168.

Supplemental Unemployment Benefits. On the basis, usually emphasized through bargaining, that state-granted unemployment benefit programs are not sufficient to sustain family living, beginning in the 1950s, industry saw the inception of plans designed to add an incremental benefit. The automobile, glass, and steel contracts of this era provided for employer contributions, generally averaging five cents per hour worked, into a fund to be drawn upon when an employee was on layoff status. If he was judged otherwise entitled to state unemployment compensation benefits, he could also draw an additional weekly benefit from the SUB fund. These plans have proved to be a popular bargaining demand, particularly where employment is seasonal or cyclical.

Guaranteed Annual Wage. High on the shopping list of organized labor is a true guaranteed wage. There have been guaranteed annual wage plans in effect in the United States since the 1890s, but because of the calculated cost hazard, there has been no rush for employers to agree to such plans.

Other Financial Benefits. Additional direct financial advantages accrue to employees in such employee services as subsidized or free work uniforms, the laundering of them, low-cost meal plans, shift differentials, free parking, purchase discounts, low interest rate loans through credit unions, and in some cases, company-sponsored low-cost housing. Stock purchase plans and savings programs are also quite common. All these are explained in detail in industrial relations handbooks.

OTHER EMPLOYEE BENEFITS

This is a catchall category. The reader will note that many of these fall in several of the categories above.

Tuition Reimbursement. Continuing education has been accepted as a way of life by most progressive companies, and because it is a way of life, they become directly involved in it by encouraging it and assisting the employee with the cost of it. Most companies no longer insist that evening college or graduate school courses be directly related to job titles. As an incentive to good academic performance, some companies reimburse tuition after course completion based on the grade attained—50% for C, 75% for B, 100% for A. Where pass-fail grading is in effect, this does not apply.

Company support goes far beyond tuition reimbursement. Many provide classroom facilities so that courses can be conducted on plant premises. Others encourage experienced, academically qualified executives to augment evening college teaching faculties. Corporate contributions in support of higher education are widespread.

Leaves of Absence. Excluding illness or accident, other leaves are granted beyond formal vacation periods.

Funeral Leave. Funeral leave with up to three days' pay is standard in many companies. It is designed to permit attendance at the funeral and the making of funeral arrangements in the event of a death in the immediate family. The meaning of "immediate" must be clearly defined. It is also good practice to differentiate funeral leave from bereavement pay, often requested in negotiations to compensate the employee in his sorrow, whether or not he has any intention of attending the funeral.

Military Leave. If an employee is inducted into or volunteers for active military service, he is protected seniority-wise by the Servicemen's Readjustment Act and is entitled to be rehired under certain circumstances. In addition, companies must grant leave for annual active duty training of members of the Reserve or National Guard for up to seventeen days annually. The leave need not be with pay. It is common, however, for the company to make up the difference between normal pay and service pay in the case of an enlisted reservist.

Personal Leave. Leaves of absence for numerous personal reasons are granted by most companies with widely varying policies as to pay, frequency, purpose, and advance notice required.

Employee Counseling. Most modern personnel departments are quite responsive to employee requests for career counseling and related matters. Legal and financial advice should be avoided, because if the employee acts on the advice given and it turns out to have been bad advice, he may have a cause of action against the company.

Physical Examinations. Periodic general physical examination is provided to many employees, particularly executives and managers. Where this is done and the company does not sustain a plant physician, great care must be exercised that the company does not interject itself into the doctor-patient relationship.

In the medical area, manufacturing managers must guard against distribution of patent medicines by unqualified personnel—the frustrated physician in the personnel department can cause much harm and potential legal liability.

Miscellaneous. There are hundreds of other items that could be enumerated here as having a bearing on employee benefits and services. Company parties; open houses; picnics; free inoculation; transportation; use of company cars, tools, or equipment; communications services and publications; and many, many others are in use on a rather widespread basis.

CONCLUSION

Cost and control—the most difficult of all management functions—are the prime considerations of the manufacturing manager. He must be familiar generally with the details of the benefit program in effect in his organization and the staff assistance available to him to implement it.

The nature and diversity of employee services indicate that new, somewhat revolutionary programs will yet be initiated. Keeping abreast of new developments in the total cost structure is a vital aspect of manufacturing management.

BIBLIOGRAPHY

Allen, Donna, *Fringe Benefits: Wages or Social Obligations?* New York State School of Industrial Relations, Cornell University, Ithaca, N.Y., 1964.

Deric, Arthur J., *The Total Approach to Employee Benefits*, American Management Association, New York, 1967.

Gregg, Davis W., *Group Life Insurance*, Richard D. Irwin, Inc., Homewood, Ill., 1962.

Jucius, Michael J., *Personnel Management*, 6th ed., Richard D. Irwin, Inc., Homewood, Ill., 1967.

McGill, D. M., *Fulfilling Pension Expectations*, Richard D. Irwin, Inc., Homewood, Ill., 1962.

Metzger, B. L., *Profit Sharing Plans*, Profit Sharing Research Foundation, Evanston, Ill., 1962.

Pickrell, Jesse F., *Group Health Insurance*, Richard D. Irwin, Inc., Homewood, Ill., 1961.

Strong, Jay V., *Employee Benefit Plans in Operation*, Bureau of National Affairs, Inc., Washington, D.C., 1951.

CHAPTER SIX

Housekeeping

DAVID N. WISE *Manager, Production Planning, Mine Safety Appliances Company, Pittsburgh, Pennsylvania*

In setting corporate objectives, top management tends to emphasize areas such as total sales, percent of market, expected revenue, net profit after taxes, and the like. At the next level, manufacturing management, in setting its own goals, must keep the corporate goals in mind and must develop specific objectives within its own organization to help achieve these goals. Within the definition of manufacturing, the various line and staff functions must set goals of their own to achieve the general manufacturing goals which, in turn, should lead to the achievement of general corporate goals. Within manufacturing, these goals tend to be such things as output per man-hour, reduced level of inventory, higher operator efficiency, lower scrap level, higher yield, cost reduction, and such other appropriate measures of manufacturing performance.

Seldom in the litany of manufacturing objectives does the term "good housekeeping" appear as a specific objective; yet a visitor on a casual trip through a plant can see and feel whether the housekeeping is or is not adequate, and can almost immediately discern the reasons why the housekeeping is what it is. When good housekeeping is apparent, one knows that all the functions of a manufacturing plant are being properly integrated toward the overall manufacturing goal. When the housekeeping is poor, one knows there is a breakdown somewhere.

This chapter will show that housekeeping is a by-product of the proper integration of all the various manufacturing functions. In brief, good housekeeping occurs automatically when material is moved properly and on time.

HOUSEKEEPING

The Federal Register for February 28, 1960, page 13822, section 50, entitled "Housekeeping," touches briefly on the fact that appropriate working areas must be clean and unencumbered, and goes into some detail of minimum general methodology by which this may be accomplished. The Federal Register, however, does not suggest specific detail methodology, thus leaving responsibility to plant management which, of course, is where this responsibility belongs.

Reasons for Housekeeping. Plant management generally wishes the plant to be known as a good place to work. Good housekeeping aids this objective. The morale of factory workers is enhanced if the place in which they work is clean and if they see that their foreman and his assistants care enough to insist that the plant be maintained in a clean condition. Further, insurance costs may be lowered if, as the result of plant housekeeping, goods are speeded up in their flow, making possible lower insurance charges on inventory and work in process. Workmen's compensation may well be lowered if, as the result of good housekeeping, the accident rate is reduced. Good housekeeping aids safety in the plant by the fact that there is less material, if any, to fall over or trip over to cause accidents. This, in turn, contributes to the efficiency of both direct workers and indirect workers.

Similar comments can be made about the office functions that support the factory. In short, all levels and functions of the factory and office contribute to a good housekeeping situation.

Responsibility. A manufacturing plant may be described as a facility which converts raw material and commercial components into finished goods available for sale. The definition includes the functions of receiving, inspection, tooling, laboratory, test facilities, manufacturing processing, warehousing, and the appropriate office functions to support all of the above.

Such functions as industrial engineering, quality control, production control, inventory control, purchasing, and plant maintenance all play a part in the housekeeping program. True enough, the parts that these functions play show up only indirectly in the form of good housekeeping if the functions are being properly performed. If the various functions and the line supervisors do not meld their programs effectively, the result of their failure to do so is quite pronounced—the place is a mess!

Plant general management, being responsible for both the line and staff functions that get out the product, is thus responsible as well for the housekeeping involved.

TYPES OF HOUSEKEEPING

Housekeeping consists of three types: (1) the appropriate movement of material in such a way as to prevent congestion; (2) the appropriate cleanup, during or after manufacturing, of such by-products as scrap, rubbish, process effluents, and other refuse normally generated by people working on goods; (3) appropriate attention to routine and thorough cleaning of nonproducing areas such as passageways, office areas, stairways, and washrooms.

Movement of Material. Briefly stated, congestion equals poor housekeeping. In a smoothly operating factory the amount of goods in process at any time should be relatively small. The proper layout needed to accomplish normal flow of work was decided on at the time that original equipment and workplaces were set up, and it is probable that goods flowed reasonably well in accordance with the original plan. Over a period of time, however, the situation may change. The volume of goods demanded may be higher than was originally planned for the layout. The resulting unbalance may result in a buildup of work ahead of specific machines or ahead of specific operators as work in process and as congestion which deteriorates the housekeeping. The product mix may change. What was once an ideal layout suitable for a given product mix or product line may be inadequate for the new product mix or the new product line. Again, the building up of reservoirs of in-process material here and there along the line impedes the flow and again deteriorates the housekeeping. Rejected material can contribute to congestion in that it is withdrawn from production and placed in a sort of limbo awaiting disposition, rework, or return to the vendor.

Other factors contribute to congestion as well. Suppliers who deliver material in advance of the needed time or deliver quantities more than are desired add to the poor housekeeping and congestion in the receiving department or in the component parts storeroom. Plant managers, although they may originally have been happy with the layout, must adopt the questioning attitude as changes take place and repeatedly ask themselves and their foremen why this congestion is necessary.

It should be observed at this point that all the pressures normally brought by plant managers upon supervision are not sufficient of themselves to clean up the congestion and improve the housekeeping. The basic flaw is the fact that the layout, the operation sequence, and the flow pattern of material are no longer applicable as they once were. It is at this point that various staff departments can make a contribution to eliminating the congestion by improving the layout and concurrently improving the housekeeping.

For example, if there is a chronic situation wherein a vendor repeatedly delivers excess goods or delivers them early, then the purchasing department, as a staff function, should undertake to get this straightened out with the vendor. Similarly, if the feeder departments who make component parts for the main assembly are delivering too early or in quantities higher than needed, the same action must be taken; but in this case it must be taken by the production control department. When some but not all components for an assembly arrive at an assembly location, the fact that the parts are not all available causes some parts to lie about unused until the missing pieces catch up. Here again, the inventory control and scheduling departments must straighten out the matter.

In the case of material rejection while work is in process, the quality control and inspection departments must see to prompt disposition of the material whether by scrap, rework, or return to the original vendor. If the rejected material must go back to an outside vendor, there is a possibility that the purchasing department may have difficulty negotiating the settlement. In this case, congestion and poor housekeeping situations will exist until the problem is resolved.

If, when all these situations are straightened out, it still appears that the layout is basically wrong for the kinds of operations being performed, then the industrial engineering department should reanalyze the flow and reestablish a flow pattern that will reduce or eliminate congestion, improve housekeeping, and add to the general efficiency of the employees in the plant.

Cleanup during or after Process. Depending on the manufacturing process involved, chips, effluents, rubbish, skeleton scrap, trash, trimmings, and the like are generated and must be disposed of. These may have to be removed at frequent intervals during the day to make space for work to be performed. In many cases, the scrap generated is not so great that it cannot be accumulated until after the normal work force has gone home. The janitorial staff is then charged with the task of disposing of the scrap during the off hours.

In many cases, the disposal operation is fairly routine. The material is swept into containers, trash bins, or the like and wheeled or handled by automatic conveyances to scrap bins where the debris can be picked up at intervals by contract collectors or sold or burned.

In some cases, it may be desirable to segregate different types of scrap. For example, after a machining operation, the value of brass chips will be higher if they are not mixed with chips of aluminum. Hence, part of the normal housekeeping routine should be to keep the chips segregated to command the best price at the time that they are sold.

In a foundry operation, it is possible that sprues, gates, and runners trimmed from the original castings can be used along with virgin material to make additional pieces. The housekeeping problem here is to avoid contamination of these salvageable materials.

Disposal of cutting oils, soluble coolants, process acids, and the like can readily be handled if thought is given to these when the layout is first made, and suitable mechanical, chemical, or other means are provided to get rid of them. Laws relating to air and water pollution must be taken into account when such materials are disposed of.

Part of the normal housekeeping services provided by the janitorial staff includes routinely sweeping the plant floors and aisle ways. Automatic sweepers are available which can replace the conventional push broom. To the extent that the plant is large enough to afford these more automatic items, they should be employed. On the other hand, the conventional job shop or small plant probably will do well to train individuals to handle this cleanup task manually at specified time periods.

Nonproducing Areas. Nonproducing areas have been briefly but not totally defined as passageways, office areas, stairways, and washrooms.

These areas produce no product, and yet are occupied, passed through, or used by people during the workday. Here plant management can directly control the state of the housekeeping.

Plant management should establish the standards of housekeeping and cleanliness that are desired, train the janitorial staff to meet these standards, and provide a proper schedule of who will do what and when. This schedule should include a sweeping schedule, a washing and waxing schedule, a schedule for washroom fixture cleaning, and a painting schedule.

JANITORIAL STAFF

In some plants, the janitorial staff may have had no particular training either in the standards of cleanliness and housekeeping desired or in the methods to be followed in attaining these standards. In some plants, too, the janitorial staff may have no particular motivation and may be generally lethargic.

Such situations can be resolved by appropriate training. It is also sometimes desirable to establish a wage payment plan that pays the employee a bonus above base rate when he meets the quality standards desired within the time specified.

CONGESTION BY CHOICE

There may be situations where it will be temporarily desirable to live with congestion rather than to take steps to correct the flow of material. Examples of this are when a company chooses to stockpile in anticipation of a possible strike in the plant of a vendor, or when a purchasing department may get a large price decrease by taking custody of a larger than usual amount of material.

These are managerial decisions to live with a temporary situation under a given set of conditions. Once this choice has been made, the poor housekeeping that occurs is a by-product of the decision.

ENCOURAGING NEATNESS AND ORDER

The personal habits of the people in the plant can contribute to or detract from good housekeeping. If people permit their workplaces to become cluttered and disorderly or are careless in disposing of waste paper, empty bottles, cigarette butts, and the like, the whole plant will appear untidy no matter how well organized the more mechanical aspects, such as work flow and scrap disposal, may be.

Neat and orderly work habits can be encouraged in part if managers and supervisors will set a good example themselves. It will do little good for an office manager to preach neatness to the clerical workers that he supervises if he permits piles of papers and unread books, brochures, and pamphlets to accumulate on his own desk. A foreman cannot expect his workers to pay much attention to the orderliness of their tools, materials, drawings, and time cards if his own office looks like a cluttered closet.

In addition, the plant manager should make it clear that good housekeeping is desired and expected. He should let his people know that he is constantly watching the appearance of the plant. Whenever he finds poor housekeeping practices developing in an area, he should discuss the situation promptly with the area supervisor and encourage him to plan the action that should be taken to bring about improvement. Personal discussions of this sort are usually more effective than written procedures and rules which are all too often ignored.

Housekeeping can sometimes be improved by introducing the element of competition into the plant. For example, one company established a committee whose task it was to survey the housekeeping in the plant each month and to select the best and the poorest departments. The department with the best housekeeping was permitted to display an attractive golden-haired doll during the ensuing month as a symbol of the excellence of its housekeeping. The poorest department was required to suspend a bucket and a mop from the ceiling in a prominent location selected by the committee. No supervisor wanted this "badge of shame" in his department or the inevitable ribbing of his peers which followed its bestowal. Thus a very real incentive to improve housekeeping was provided in a comparatively simple manner. Over the months, the level of housekeeping in the entire plant improved greatly. By rotating membership on the committee among the key supervisors in the plant, a lasting recognition of and interest in good housekeeping was developed throughout the plant.

CONCLUSION

Management will get about what it insists on in the way of good housekeeping. If standards are relaxed, the plant will undoubtedly go on operating for a long period of time. However, as housekeeping deteriorates, inefficiencies will begin to increase, and gradually the profit position of the company will be eroded. Henry Ford was fond of stating a principle which he believed in completely. It was: "No plant ever failed until it had accumulated a large pile of dirt." To him, profitability and good housekeeping went hand in hand. It is a thought well worth pondering.

BIBLIOGRAPHY

Alspach, N. N., "Controlling Factory Housekeeping: Responsibilities of a Supervisor," *Supervision*, January, 1961.
Carson, Gordon B. (ed.), *Production Handbook*, 2d ed., The Ronald Press Company, New York, 1958, pp. 48–53.
"Guides to Good Housekeeping," *Supervisory Management*, June, 1965.
Harrold, W. J., "Good Housekeeping and Accident Prevention," *Personnel Management*, September, 1964.
Kelly, A. S., "Plant Housekeeping: It's More than Pushing a Broom," *Supervisory Management*, June, 1967.
Mayfield, H., "What's So Important about Housekeeping?" *Supervisory Management*, September, 1966.
National Safety Council, "Industrial Housekeeping," in *NSC Supervisors Safety Manual*, 3d ed., National Safety Council, Chicago, Ill., 1967, pp. 181–200.
Person, D. L., "Big-plant Cleaning: Problems and Solutions," *Safety Maintenance*, 1966.
Reid, P. C., "Price of Poor Housekeeping," *Supervisory Management*, August, 1964.
U.S. Bureau of Labor Standards, "Housekeeping for Safety," *Safety in Industry Instructor Outline*, U.S. Government Printing Office, Washington, D.C., 1967.
Williams, C., "Time for a Housekeeping Checkup?" *Supervisory Management*, March, 1968.

CHAPTER SEVEN

Installing and Managing an Accident Prevention Program

M. U. ENINGER *Normax Publications, Incorporated, Pittsburgh, Pennsylvania*

This chapter is written for the manager who is (1) dissatisfied with the accident experience in the plant operation under his direction, (2) without the staff services of a competent safety engineer to advise him, and (3) willing to make a serious effort to reduce his accident problem. It is also written for the man who might be appointed by that manager to see that accidents are reduced in the plant.

What follows is a broad-brush description of the fundamentals of planning, organizing, leading, and controlling a plant accident prevention program. Details are necessarily omitted.

NATURE, CAUSE, AND RESULTS OF ACCIDENTS

It is not possible to implement the tools of accident prevention without having some understanding of (1) the nature, causes, and results of accidents, and (2) the basic concepts and principles of organized accident prevention. The major obstacle to an effective accident prevention program is a management that is so uninformed on the fundamentals that it cannot make a first step in the right direction.

The Nature of Accidents. Prevention must be concerned with two kinds of accidents: employee accidents and equipment accidents.

1. The employee accident is any unplanned, unexpected occurrence—usually a physical contact between an employee and some object, substance, or exposure condition in his surroundings—which interrupts his work activity.
2. The equipment accident is an unplanned, unexpected occurrence to equipment that could, under some circumstances, result in an em-

ployee being contacted by an object, substance, or exposure condition. Usually, although not necessarily, the unexpected occurrence results in an interruption in the use of the equipment.

It should be noted that neither type of accident necessarily involves injuries, yet both have the potential for injuries. The focus of attention must be accident prevention rather than injury prevention.

The physical contact nature of employee accidents is illustrated by how such accidents may be classified: struck by; contacted by; struck against; contact with; caught in, on, or between; fall to below; fall to same level; and exposure to. These expressions describe accident types and emphasize that the prevention of employee accidents is essentially a matter of preventing unexpected contacts.

The Causes of Accidents. An accident cause is anything and everything that has contributed to the occurrence of an accident. This may include the actions of the workman who had the accident; the actions of co-workers; any physical or mental conditions of men that caused or influenced such actions; any defective or otherwise unsafe conditions of tools, equipment, machines, materials, buildings, or atmosphere; the reasons why such hazardous conditions developed or existed; and even the actions of supervisors and higher management.

It is a mistake to think of accidents in terms of single causes. Most accidents involve multiple causes or, to use a better expression, contributing factors. It is practical to think in terms of four major kinds of causes.

1. *Direct Employee Causes.* These are the actions of the man that immediately precede and bring about the accident. They can usually be identified by raising the question: *What did the man do or fail to do that contributed directly to his accident?* Direct employee causes are also called unsafe acts.

2. *Indirect Employee Causes.* These are the conditions or characteristics of the man that caused or influenced him to do what he did or failed to do which, in turn, contributed to his accident. The conditions may be mental, emotional, or physical. The characteristics may be any strongly entrenched feature of his personality. Such indirect causes are very often difficult to determine. The question that must be asked is: *What conditions or personal characteristics of the man caused or influenced him to do what he did?* Indirect employee causes are more conveniently called personal factor causes.

3. *Direct Environment Causes.* These are conditions in the man's physical surroundings that caused or contributed to the accident. They may involve tools, equipment, machines, materials, and buildings, as well as conditions of illumination, noise level, and atmosphere. They are best brought to light by asking the question: *What conditions or absence of conditions in the man's environment contributed to his accident?* Direct environment causes are also called unsafe conditions.

4. *Indirect Environment Causes.* These are the causes that are responsible for the environmental conditions that contributed to the accident. The question that must be raised is: *What brought about the existence of the environmental conditions that contributed to the accident?* Indirect environment causes are also called unsafe condition causes or source causes.

A complete accident investigation will be concerned with establishing the causes or contributing factors in each of the above four categories. For a detailed analysis of the individual types of causes in each of the major cause categories, consult Figure 7-1. Notice that the ultimate causes of accidents have to do with deficiencies in the organization. For example, the employee

ORGANIZATION CAUSES ▶	INDIRECT CAUSES ▶	DIRECT CAUSES
ORGANIZATION CAUSES **Definition:** Any condition or characteristic of a company or plant which causes, permits, or contributes to unsafe conditions or practices.	**PERSONAL FACTOR** **Definition:** Any condition or characteristic of a man that causes or influences him to act unsafely.	**UNSAFE ACT** **Definition:** Any act that deviates from a generally recognized safe way of doing a job and increases the likelihood of an accident.

1. Inadequate hiring or placement standards
2. Lack of standardized safe job procedures
3. Inadequate employee training procedures
4. Failure to establish and enforce safety rules
5. Failure to recognize individual safety effort
6. Inadequate supervisor training in safety
	1. Knowledge and skill deficiencies
	  • Lack of hazard awareness
	  • Lack of job knowledge
	  • Lack of job skill
	
	2. Conflicting motivations
	  • Saving time and effort
	  • Avoiding discomfort
	  • Attracting attention
	  • Asserting independence
	  • Seeking group approval
	  • Expressing resentment
	
	3. Physical and mental incapacities
		BASIC TYPES
		1. Operating without authority
		2. Failure to make secure
		3. Operating at unsafe speed
		4. Failure to warn or signal
		5. Nullifying safety devices
		6. Using defective equipment
		7. Using equipment unsafely
		8. Taking unsafe position
		9. Repairing or servicing moving or energized equipment
		10. Riding hazardous equipment
		11. Horseplay
		12. Failure to use protective equipment

ORGANIZATION CAUSES (Continued) 1. Tolerance of man-made unsafe conditions 2. Failure to design safety into facilities 3. Inadequate safety inspection program 4. Inadequate preventive maintenance program 5. Inadequate safety standards for purchasing 6. Failure to encourage unsafe condition reporting 7. Failure to regulate and supervise contractors	**SOURCE CAUSES** **Definition:** Any circumstance that may cause or contribute to the development of an unsafe condition. **MAJOR SOURCES** 1. Production employees 2. Maintenance employees 3. Design and engineering 4. Purchasing practices 5. Normal wear through use 6. Abnormal wear and tear 7. Lack of preventive maintenance 8. Outside contractors	**UNSAFE CONDITIONS** **Definition:** Any environmental condition that may cause or contribute to an accident. **BASIC TYPES** 1. Inadequate guards and safety devices 2. Inadequate warning systems 3. Fire and explosion hazards 4. Unexpected movement hazards 5. Poor housekeeping 6. Protruding hazards 7. Congestion; close clearance 8. Hazardous atmospheric conditions 9. Hazardous placement or storage 10. Unsafe equipment defects 11. Inadequate illumination; noise 12. Hazardous personal attire

The left margin is labeled, top to bottom: THE EMPLOYEE SIDE / THE ENVIRONMENT SIDE

FIG. 7-1.   The Cause-Effect

failed to shut down the machine before adjusting a part *because* he did not know that to do so was required procedure *because* his initial job instruction failed to cover this point *because* there was no planned and controlled initial job instruction.   Thus, an organization defect must be regarded as a contributing factor to his accident.

The Results of Accidents.   As with causes, there are both direct and indirect consequences of accidents that adversely affect both employees involved and the company.   Consult Figure 7-1 for a summary identification of the results of accidents.

The important thing to know about accident outcomes is that, given the causes and nature of accidents, one cannot with certainty predict what the outcomes will be.   The same set of causes producing the same type of accident in the same work situation may produce a minor injury one time and a disabling injury or even a fatality the next time.   The following two cases illustrate the point: A laborer was cleaning the base of idlers on a conveyor in a sintering plant.   He was using a short-handle brush, and wearing gloves.

► ACCIDENTS	► DIRECT EFFECTS	► INDIRECT EFFECTS
THE ACCIDENT **Definition**: An unexpected occurrence that interrupts work and usually takes the form of an abrupt contact.	**DIRECT RESULTS** **Definition**: The immediate results of an accident.	**INDIRECT RESULTS** **Definition**: The consequences for all concerned that flow from the direct results of accidents.

BASIC TYPES
 	
1. Struck by
 	
2. Contact by
 	
3. Struck against
 	
4. Contact with
 	
5. Trapped in
 	
6. Caught on
 	
7. Caught between
 	
8. Fall to different level
 	
9. Fall on same level
 	
10. Exposure
 	
11. Overexertion/strain
	BASIC TYPES
	
	1. "No results" or near-miss
	
	2. Minor injury
	
	3. Major injury
	
	4. Property damage
	    • Tools
	    • Equipment
	    • Facilities
	    • Materials
	    • Products
		FOR THE INJURED
		
		1. Loss of earnings
		
		2. Disrupted family life
		
		3. Disrupted personal life
		
		4. And other consequences
		
		FOR THE COMPANY
		
		1. Injury costs
		
		2. Production loss costs
		
		3. Property damage costs
		
		4. Lowered employee morale
		
		5. Poor reputation
		
		6. Poor customer relations
		
		7. Lost supervisor time
		
		8. Product damage costs

Accident Sequence.

His right hand brushed against an idler, and his fingers were pinched between the belt and the idler. He suffered minor lacerations and bruises.

A similar case resulted in six months of disability. The injured was using a wooden deck scraper with a 32-inch handle to push coal spillage from the deck underneath a coal conveyor. As he pushed deep, his left gloved hand became caught between the conveyor belt and the idler. His arm was pulled through the pinch-crush point, causing multiple fractures.

The difference in the outcome of these two cases is attributable to how much of the hand and arm were exposed to the pinch-crush point. The first case exposed the fingertips; the second case exposed the arm. In neither case should the decking have been cleaned while the conveyor was in operation.

The key point to remember is: *The causes that produce today's minor result accident may produce tomorrow's crippling injury or fatality if they are ignored and left free to operate again.* All accidents should be assessed from the standpoint of potential for serious injury or property damage. Too often, management shows concern for only those accidents that have had a serious injury or property damage outcome. This is wrong because it neglects to assess the potential of the minor outcome accident.

Some Principles and Procedures. Much that falls under the heading of accident prevention is a circuslike mixture of contests, safety dinners, banners and posters, giveaways and prizes, and other imaginative gimmicks which are at the best only remotely related to accident prevention. Not only are such activities usually ineffective, but they are also often harmful, because they convince management that they have an accident prevention program, when in fact they have none.

The basic principles of accident prevention stem from the recognition that all accidents are covered and that cause analysis and elimination constitute the key to accident prevention. Stated simply, the two foundation principles of accident prevention are:

1. Identify both potential and actual accident causes.
2. Eliminate or nullify both potential and actual accident causes.

The more that accident prevention activities or procedures are directly related to the above principles, the more effective the accident prevention program will be. Thus, for example, a program of planned safety tool, equipment, and facility inspections is a basic tool for detecting potential accident causes (unsafe conditions). By way of contrast, a company safety rally night with prizes, speeches, and hoopla has nothing to do with the above principles.

The first rule for the manager who wants to install an effective accident prevention program is to stick to the fundamental tools of accident prevention and to steer away from the gimmickry. Figure 7-2 identifies in summarized fashion most of the basic tools of accident prevention.

The basic tools identified in Figure 7-2 are not all of equal importance. Indeed, some may not be needed in a given operation, for example, outside contractor controls, medical examinations for mobile equipment operators, industrial hygiene controls, and others that imply a specific operation characteristic. The problem in putting together the elements of a comprehensive accident prevention program is to select the basic tools that are most demanded by the accident causes that characterize the operation. Thus, for example, if a significant percentage of accidents is attributable to unsafe practices caused by inadequate job knowledge, it follows that initial job training should be an integral part of the basic program.

PLANNING AND INSTALLING THE PROGRAM

There is no one best way to plan and install a plant accident prevention program. The experienced consultant knows that before he can develop a master plan, he must take into account the nature of the operation, the management and supervisor organization, the organization deficiencies that contribute to the accident problem, the nature and causes of accidents as they are related to work operations and occupations, and even such difficult-to-assess factors as how far and fast management wants to go to achieve a substantial reduction in the accident problem. What this means is that it is wise to move slowly. A sound, comprehensive accident prevention program can never be achieved as a result of a crash effort. In a large industrial plant, it is not inconceivable to think of a two- or even three-year effort to install a complete program.

What follows are some general guides for developing and installing an accident prevention program. The manager who feels that he has no time for becoming acquainted with the details should consider delegating the

FIG. 7-2. The Basic Tools of the Complete Operation Zero Program.

responsibility to someone in the organization who can take the time. The other alternative is to engage the services of a reputable consultant.

Establish a Planning Committee. The program planning committee is a temporary committee of top plant management personnel whose task it is to plan and develop the various phases of the accident prevention program. A plant manager may designate the department heads who normally report to him, either directly or indirectly through an assistant, as members of the committee. The rule is: include those persons who will play a key role in managing the program or in the planning and development of the program.

The initial session of the committee should be spent with the accident and, if available, cost facts that point out the need to develop a plant accident prevention program. Once the purpose of the committee has been explained, a regular meeting time should be established. Usually, more than two meetings a month is pushing too fast, and less than one a month is going too slow. The first meetings should also set the stage for coming to grips with the planning problem. For example, all members might be requested to study this chapter before the next meeting. This will assure that the committee has a common understanding of what is involved.

Establish Safety Meeting Structure. The development of an accident prevention program requires communication of plans, policies, and procedures from the plant manager to first-line supervisors, and later to hourly employees. Where there are several levels of supervision beneath the management level involved in the planning committee, it is essential that a plan of safety meetings for supervision be implemented. For most plants, two levels of meetings will suffice. The plant manager can meet regularly with his department heads, and the department heads can meet regularly with their supervisors.

During the initial planning and development phase of the program, the department head meetings should be used to communicate the decisions of the planning committee and to discuss and initiate accident prevention steps that do not need to wait for a formal safety program. These meetings can and should be used to discuss recent accidents and suitable corrective actions as well as the causes of accidents generally associated with a department's operation and possible methods for eliminating or reducing these causes. The meetings should be structured as problem solving sessions. The experiences and capabilities of supervisors invariably can be utilized to come up with answers, even though they may have little or no formal training in accident prevention.

A regular monthly meeting schedule is recommended. Where there is urgency, a temporary schedule of two meetings each month may be in order. The meetings indirectly serve notice that management expects a change in accident prevention efforts.

Select the Basic Program Tools. Figure 7-2 identifies all the basic tools that a plant might select from to develop its own accident prevention program. Normally, it is considered good procedure to do a study of the causes of the plant's accidents so that the tools selected will reflect the plant's needs as determined by its accident causes. Unfortunately, most plants with poor safety records also have poor accident reports, and it becomes difficult to do a proper statistical analysis of accident causes. However, the basic organization causes are the same in almost all such plants: inadequate job training, poor control of environmental hazards, no management pressure for safe work performance, inadequate inspection procedures, and so on.

The task of the planning committee is to select those accident prevention tools that will be installed in the first year of the program. Additional tools to complete the program may be added in the second year. The first-year program might be as follows:

1. Supervision training in accident prevention
2. Improved accident investigation procedure
3. Cumulative analysis of accident reports
4. Monthly accident performance reporting
5. Plant general safety rules booklet
6. Written accident prevention responsibilities
7. Planned weekly employee safety contacts
8. Housekeeping and safety inspection program
9. Monthly supervisor safety meetings

Establish Supervisor Responsibilities. An accident prevention program must be a teamwork effort with each level of management doing what it can best do to promote the program. One of the major tasks of the planning committee is to decide who is responsible for doing what with respect to the basic tools of the program. Responsibilities should be specific, put in writing for distribution, and clarified by discussion with all concerned.

Responsibility descriptions should cover all levels of management from and including the plant manager on down the line.

Develop a Training and Installation Schedule.   Once the first-year program has been determined and the related responsibility descriptions have been prepared, the planning committee should develop a schedule which indicates what supervisor training topics will be covered on what dates and when elements of the planned program will be activated.   To develop such a schedule, it is necessary to (1) sequence the tool elements of the program in the order that they will be installed, (2) determine what supervisory training must precede each tool element and how long the training will require to cover all concerned, and (3) assess what else must be done before the installation of the tool.   For example, before installing the improved accident prevention procedure, the accident report forms must be designed and printed, the procedure should be described in a memorandum to all concerned, and supervisors must be trained how to investigate accidents and how to complete the new form.   All this requires time which must be assessed to arrive at a target date on which the new procedure will be activated.

The elements of the schedule should be well spaced.   Those which require the greatest amount of developmental work, such as preparing an employee general safety rule booklet, should be scheduled for late in the first-year implementation period.   Consideration should also be given to the logical sequencing of items.   For example, the accident investigation procedure must be introduced before the monthly accident performance reports.

Train and Install by Plan.   Once the training and installation schedule has been developed, the task of training and installing elements of the program may begin.   The planning committee should establish a procedure for keeping informed of how the program is unfolding.   There will undoubtedly be implementation problems which have to be resolved.   There will also be new problems that come to light as a result of the accident prevention program. Where they are directly concerned with safety, it is desirable to discuss them at the planning committee meetings rather than to resolve them by the usual management decision making practice.

The method of training and the training materials should be closely related to the basic tool to be installed.   For example, a discussion of how to complete the new accident report form may well be followed by a ten-minute practice session in which supervisors write up their latest accident case on the new report form.

MANAGING THE PROGRAM

An organized accident prevention program must be *managed* to be maximally effective.   It will not run itself.   It is not something that can be planned, developed, installed, and then turned over to the lower levels of supervision. It requires the continuing attention of the plant manager and his department heads.

Part of managing the program consists of directing the program activities, leading the program with personal activities, controlling the activities of others, and evaluating the results of the program.   Let us briefly consider each of these functions from the standpoint of the plant manager.   What applies to him also applies to his department heads.

Directing Program Activities.   Many of the basic tools of accident prevention usually are applied by the first-line supervisor who instructs new employees, develops safe job procedures, handles safety contacts with employees, enforces safety rules, and so on. Unless such activities are given direction, the content of what the supervisor concentrates on may not be what he should cover. For example, supervisors making weekly five-minute safety contacts may talk about things that have nothing to do with why people are having accidents.

The manager must create a situation whereby the repetitive accident cases are identified and brought to his attention so that he may direct where and what type of corrective actions need to be taken. The tool for doing this is cumulative accident data analysis. CADA,[1] as it is called, indicates what occupations are contributing to a high percentage of accidents, what specific jobs within occupations involve a relatively high percentage of accidents, what unsafe actions and conditions are major problems, and so on. Such information indicates where corrective action must be directed, because it indicates where the problems are. The major share of such direction may come from the department heads. The manager, however, must broadly direct activities, thereby stimulating his department heads to get closer to the situation and do the same.

Another natural springboard for directing safety activities is the accident investigation. A plant manager should always participate in the investigation of serious injury accident cases, because it provides him with an opportunity to assess causes and direct broad corrective actions. How well he performs in this role may be the most important single determiner of supervisor attitudes toward eliminating accident causes. For example, a clear, ringing statement of dissatisfaction with poor housekeeping that has caused a major injury accident, coupled with an order that all departments put their housekeeping in order within thirty days, can do wonders in setting the climate for accident prevention in a plant.

A third springboard for directing safety activities is what a manager learns about potential accident causes from personal observations of people at work and inspections of their work environment. There are times when a manager must leave his desk and get out into the plant to look for poor housekeeping, hazardous storage, defective equipment, and the many other potential accident causes. This willingness to "see for himself," and to express satisfaction or dissatisfaction to the right people as may be warranted, is an essential ingredient in the process of directing accident prevention efforts.

Leading the Program by Personal Involvement. The work aspects of the safety program cannot be delegated wholly to supervisors. The plant manager and his department heads must lead the program by personal involvement. They must give a reasonable degree of time and effort to the basic safety activities: investigating major accidents, conducting housekeeping and safety inspections, conducting safety meetings with supervisors, and so on.

The purpose of such activities is twofold: (1) to stimulate lower levels of supervision by the personal example of interest and active involvement, and (2) to carry out the function of managing the program. The ways in which a manager can become actively involved in a program are limited only by his imagination and restrictions of time.

The manager can allot only so much of his time to accident prevention. Not all kinds of personal involvement are equally effective. An hour spent lending his presence to a safety meeting by passive participation will certainly not have the same effect as the same hour spent conducting the meeting,

---

[1] M. U. Eninger, *Accident Prevention Fundamentals for Managers and Supervisors*, Normax Publications, Inc., Pittsburgh, Pa., 1965.

raising critical questions, following up on something decided on at the last meeting, or probing for solutions to a problem. Indeed, the manager who is normally very active in meetings related to production or costs conveys a lukewarm interest in safety when he adopts a passive role in such meetings. This silent message is read all too clearly by his subordinates.

The manager should not engage in safety-related activities merely for the sake of demonstrating interest. When that is what prompts his activity, the effect is not the same as when he is carrying out a basic managing function such as planning, organizing, decision making, directing, controlling, and so on. Activity merely to demonstrate interest tends to lean toward gimmicks, speech making, and other surface or superficial activities.

Controlling the Program Activities. An organized accident prevention program consists of a set of action or activity responsibilities assigned to each level of plant management. To control the program means to establish procedures to determine whether assigned responsibilities are being carried out. The procedures may range from a simple question-and-answer check as to whether something was done, to a regular written report indicating that certain activities have taken place according to plan.

Each level of management must control the program activity responsibilities of lower levels of management. The process of control starts at the top. The plant manager must determine what program activities require his control, what methods are appropriate to exercise such controls, and how he will communicate the results of his controlling activities. His controls should be such that they tell him at appropriate intervals to what extent each of his departments is carrying out the activities called for by the program.

The skilled manager will develop an appropriate set of controls that tell him, with the least amount of time expenditure, what is going on. Thus, a manager might conclude that a single question raised at the appropriate time can have the same control effect as a written report. For example, if a major accident resulted in a decision to install a machine guard, the follow-up control may be to inquire about the status of the installation at the next monthly safety meeting.

Obviously, one of the problems in developing a set of controls is to strike the right balance. When the controls become excessively burdensome, one questions their effectiveness in the total accident prevention effort. It is possible to overdo the business of having people report what they have done.

Evaluating the Program. It is the plant manager who must evaluate the effectiveness of the accident prevention program. If he does not do so, those under him will not. If he is satisfied, those who report to him will be satisfied—at least in the sense of not putting out more effort or changing from what they are doing. If he is dissatisfied because of a lack of significant accident rate reduction or accident cost reduction, then the first step has been taken toward greater effectiveness. Therein lies the importance of evaluation.

There are two broad measures by which program effectiveness can be evaluated: (1) reduction in accident frequency rates, and (2) reduction in accident costs. The manager must set up his evaluation yardsticks to assess both dimensions of improvement. Moreover, his evaluative data should be organized to correspond with the plant department organization so that he can evaluate the performance of each department as well as that of the plant as a whole.

The process of evaluation can be helped by adopting reasonable improvement objectives such as a percentage reduction in accident costs or all accident injury rates. There is some merit in asking department heads to establish their own improvement objectives, and then holding them accountable for achieving their objectives. The basic principle of management by objectives applies to accident prevention as well as production.

SUMMARY AND CONCLUSION

Accidents are responsive to the same general management principles and techniques that apply to production and cost control. The basic approaches to organized accident prevention consist of:

PHASE I

Establish a policy and planning committee.
Select the basic program tools.
Establish written responsibilities.
Develop a training and installation schedule.
Train and install according to plan.

PHASE II

Direct basic program activities.
Lead by personal involvement.
Control the program activities.
Evaluate program results.

It is clear that accident prevention must involve all levels of plant management. The key figure is the plant manager, because he is the mainspring that sets into motion the necessary activities to prevent accidents.

BIBLIOGRAPHY

Eninger, M.U., *Accident Prevention Fundamentals for Managers and Supervisors*, Normax Publications, Inc., Pittsburgh, Pa., 1965.
Simons, R. H., and J. V. Grimaldi, *Safety Management*, Richard D. Irwin, Inc., Homewood, Ill., 1956.

MOTIVATING EMPLOYEES

CHAPTER ONE

Motivation Principles

G. H. GUSTAT   *Director, Industrial Engineering Division, Kodak Park Division, Eastman Kodak Company, Rochester, New York*

J. A. RICHARDSON   *Supervisor, Industrial Engineering Division, Kodak Park Division, Eastman Kodak Company, Rochester, New York*

The discussion of motivation principles in this chapter is not intended to be a comprehensive coverage of all human behavior. The primary concern is with those aspects of motivation which relate to human performance in an organizational setting. To be sure, general factors such as the cultural orientation of a work force, the level of economic affluence, and the degree to which basic needs are locally satisfied are relevant. However, this chapter will be concerned with those things within an organization which influence the motivational climate and are susceptible to control by management.

The state of knowledge of motivation principles is such that what is known can scarcely be reduced to simple "do's" and "don'ts." On the other hand, there has been a great deal of research on the subject, and what has been learned can be reduced to general principles which, if followed strategically, over time may increase the probability of higher organizational performance.

This chapter is an attempt to synthesize briefly the best of the research, hopefully in a manner which makes it sound like current common sense. It is based on the work of many of the significant contributors, and the informed reader will recognize patterns of thinking from Douglas McGregor, Frederick Herzberg, Rensis Likert, and others.

DEFINITIONS

The word "motivation" itself is a slippery thing subject to several interpretations. In popular usage, motivation has two major connotations. The noun "motivation" is something which people are thought to have or not to have. The infinitive "to motivate" is thought to be something which person *A* does to person *B* to get the latter to do something *A* wants done.

Both these popular usages are not altogether appropriate. Everyone has motivation all the time, in one way or another. As for the infinitive "to motivate," it is reasonable, if poor usage, to think that if *A* does something to *B* which results in *B*'s (desirable) behavior, *A* has motivated *B*. However, this manipulative form of motivation is generally inappropriate in the modern industrial society, and it will be shown why the infinitive "to motivate" is poor usage.

Finally, "motivation" is a widely used popular word, but behavioral scientists, except when communicating with laymen, tend not to use it—most likely because of this demonstrated lack of precision and potential misunderstanding.

THE MOTIVATION QUESTION

There is an old adage in science to the effect that asking the right questions is the starting place for fruitful inquiry. If the wrong questions are asked, substantial time is spent in searching blind alleys. In this spirit, there are two ways of asking the central question about motivation in an organization: (1) How can I motivate my people to work? or (2) Under what set of conditions are people most likely to achieve our organizational objectives?

Attempts to answer the first question are likely to lead up blind alleys. This question couches the problem in manipulative terms—a "do unto" context. Seeking answers leads one to spend much time examining "carrot and stick" alternatives. To be sure, there are things which can be done unto people which will yield short-term results. In the modern industrial environment, however, legal, moral, and commonsense constraints on the classical hiring, firing, rewarding, punishing, and reprimanding alternatives have significantly limited managements' rights and abilities to use them.

Attempts to answer the second question: Under what set of conditions are people most likely to achieve our organizational objectives?—will yield more positive results. Stating the question this way has a number of advantages:

1. Manipulative overtones are absent.
2. It defines the search as being one of creating conditions in which people will motivate themselves.
3. It focuses on the gist of industrial motivation, the achievement of organizational objectives.
4. The term "work" is absent. Like "motivation," "work" is a word which can lead the search astray. Work is too often associated with activity, with physical busyness. The concern is not with activity or busyness except as related to achievement of objectives. The behavior which more and more makes up modern jobs is that where sheer physical activity has only a loose relationship to achievement.

What has been covered in these introductory paragraphs is more than a play on words. It is fundamental to a healthy understanding of what motivation should mean in a modern industrial environment.

CREATING AN ENVIRONMENT OF ACHIEVEMENT

Having said that the question is: Under what set of conditions are people most likely to achieve our organizational objectives?—it follows that the remainder of this chapter deals with those long-range things that management can do to create such an environment. The approach will be structured as follows:

1. Basic assumptions about people and work
2. Equity—compensation, benefits
3. Communications—goals, measures, information
4. Control and responsibility—job content, work organization
5. Managerial behavior—leadership style
6. Continuing improvement—the ultimate objective

BASIC ASSUMPTIONS ABOUT PEOPLE AND WORK

In 1960, the late Douglas McGregor introduced his now famous Theory X and Theory Y in his book, *The Human Side of Enterprise*. McGregor opined that if one observed most managerial behavior and took account of many management practices, the observer could infer that management held views or assumptions about human behavior which he called, collectively, Theory X. These are basically pessimistic assumptions like "People don't like to work and will avoid it if possible," "People need to be told exactly what to do and how to do it," and several others in the same vein.

McGregor went on to say that these apparent beliefs were rarely, if ever, explicitly stated but tended to be held by managers. They were a form of common sense, because any observant person could find all kinds of evidence to support these beliefs.

Most important, McGregor stated that such beliefs have the property of self-confirming hypotheses. People tend to behave in a manner related to the treatment they receive. Therefore, if treated according to practices based on Theory X assumptions, people will respond in a manner tending to support these assumptions. Observing this behavior, one's theories are confirmed, the theories and practices are reinforced, and the circle is closed.

McGregor suggested that a more valid set of assumptions, which he labeled Theory Y, could be stated. These Theory Y assumptions, if used as a basis of management practice, over time would lead to higher performance, a more satisfied work force, and a generally more efficient organization.

It is the purpose here to suggest, as McGregor did, that a healthy and realistic set of assumptions relating people, work, and organizational performance is the place to start if one is interested in improving motivation.

Work Itself. Work, defined as activity leading to the achievement of meaningful objectives, is a natural human activity. In our society, people basically want to work, to achieve, and under the right conditions will seek the opportunity to do so.

Involvement and Responsibility. People want to be involved in the achievement of the goals of their units. Given the necessary information and opportunity, they will seek voluntarily to advance these goals and gain a sense of responsibility in the doing.

Requisite Control. Given understandable goals and the necessary information, people require the necessary independence and control to achieve the goals for which they are to be held responsible.

Equity. Pay and associated benefits are very important to people. People wish to see a relationship between their contributions and rewards. If inequities exist, these will likely lead to poor performance and conflict. If relative equity is achieved, however, it is no guarantee of high performance. An equitable working climate is the basis and starting point for emphasizing achievement and responsibility.

Supervision and Managment Style. A management style which emphasizes the supportive rather than the directive aspect of management is most likely to lead to high performance. Instead of assuming that it is the boss's responsibility to achieve the objectives and the work force is around to help him, assume that it is the work force's responsibility to achieve the objectives and that the boss is around to help them.

These basic assumptions are not submitted as being literal truth which will hold in individual circumstances. They are submitted as the basis of a management position which, if practiced, will lead to a more effective organization.

The more detailed prescriptions which follow are consistent with these basic assumptions.

EQUITY—COMPENSATION, BENEFITS

The term "equity" is used instead of "pay" or "compensation" because it is the feelings people have about the total equity of their situation, not the factors that cause it, which are most important. Also, "equity" suggests a relative situation. It has been well established that people's relative rather than absolute feelings of equity are of primary importance. Initially, in the discussion of equity, we must confront the issue of "pay" directly. For a very long time, pay was treated by most managements as though it were the be-all and end-all of motivation. People were to consider themselves lucky to have jobs, and nearly the whole employment contract revolved around money. Over time, associated matters, usually called "benefits" and ranging from vacations to insurance plans, came into being. All these, however, because of their economic basis, can be considered part of the compensation package as they relate to equity.

All attempts to place pay or total compensation in a reasonable framework seem to evoke strong reactions such as "Don't tell me money's not important" and the like. The key to understanding the importance of pay is to realize that it is very important, but not all-important. If people have reason to believe that their compensation is not equitable, if it is less than they think it should be, there will be lessened motivation and likely conflict. On the other hand, when people feel equitably treated as to compensation, it is no guarantee of high performance. Where equity exists, management has bought only the opportunity to motivate its people. Having achieved equity, management is in a position to go further in positive efforts to create the climate of achievement.

In its efforts to achieve equity, management's key actions are diligently to maintain compensation relationships. No effort should be spared to keep abreast of all developments in the industry and the community which affect compensation. Within the organization, strong and continual efforts are needed to maintain fair and reasonable job value relationships between jobs through continual review and updating.

A most important consideration in any compensation strategy is the manner in which pay is related to performance. For many years, it was thought that the closer and more incrementally money was related to performance, the better performance would be. The ideal incentive system was considered to be the one which was closest to piecework, or a one-for-one relationship between pay and output. Many economic gains were made by the use of piecework incentives based upon measurement of tasks and objectives.

Reflecting on the history of individual piecework-type incentives, it appears that they are, on balance, not the most effective way of relating pay to performance. In theory, piecework incentives are very attractive. In practice, a variety of problems occur over time to diminish their effectiveness.

A number of factors which enter into the pay/performance relationship have contributed over time to the decrease in popularity of piecework-type incentive plans. Some of these are:

1. Defining and controlling work methods which are nearly always changing is difficult.
2. Selection of units of measure which reflect in a balanced way all the management objectives of quantity, quality, and service has been difficult to incorporate into piecework incentives.
3. Random variables, such as raw material conditions and performance of machines and tools, affect performance results significantly and are difficult to filter out of piecework-type measurement.
4. The precision and accuracy of work measurement techniques for some types of work are questionable.
5. The power of money as a motivator is a key variable which varies by individual and environment and has probably declined over time with rising affluence in our society.

Clearly, the relating of pay to performance is strongly affected by these and other situational factors. The following considerations are submitted as the basis of a healthy pay/performance relationship.

1. Maintain the most technically sound performance measurement, which includes measures of productivity, quality, and service, as these are present in the job and hopefully identified with the objectives that the system is trying to accomplish.
2. Provide for periodic face-to-face review between supervisor and subordinate during which measured performance and ratings and rankings are discussed.
3. Maintain a range of pay rates for each job, and relate total performance to rate step at periodic intervals such as six months or one year. Strictly avoid automatic pay performance relationships which cause pay to fluctuate on a short-term, daily, or weekly basis.

Finally, to repeat, under "equity," the strategy is to strive to create a climate in which people will feel that they are, individually and collectively, compensated fairly in relation to their fellows and to their perceived contribution. Where this has been done, the basis for an environment of achievement has been prepared. It remains, however, to go on from there to achieve positive motivation.

COMMUNICATIONS—GOALS, MEASURES, INFORMATION

So much has been said about the matter of communications that the word itself has lost its utility as a communications medium. It will be used in this chapter in a special sense as it relates to the central purpose of an organization —communication about achievement of objectives.

It seems axiomatic, if the purpose is to create an environment of achievement, that what is to be achieved must be made evident (goals) and that the degree of achievement or scorekeeping must be communicated to the participants (measures of performance).

A widespread awareness of the importance of goals and measures, as fundamental and self-evident as the need for it is, seems to be absent from many management situations. Well-structured goals and meaningful measures are absolutely indispensable to the creation of an environment of achievement. The following criteria are suggested as a basis for designing goals and measures.

Clear, Unambiguous Goals. Clear-cut goals should be established at all levels of an organization—individual, work center, department, division, and so on.

Compatible Goals. Goals should be well related up and down the hierarchy so that at all levels they are mutually supporting and free from conflict.

Multiple Goals. A common mistake is to overstress one kind of goal, like rate or output, at the expense of others, like quality and service. Goal structures always contain multiple goals and should be established so that there is a balance between the goals, relative to their priority and importance.

Quantifiable Goals. It may be said of goals that the more nearly that they can be quantified, the more likely they will actually influence the behavior of participants and thus be achieved.

Measures of performance are, of course, primarily a quantitative medium for communicating the degree of achievement of goals. The suggested criteria are:

Reality-based Measures. To the extent that people can relate measures to apparent phenomena such as physical units, readings on a scale, and the like, the measures are immediately verifiable and are most likely to influence behavior. Abstract measures such as percent of effectiveness or performance indices are less desirable.

Noise-free Measures. Measures of performance are useful to the extent that they are free from noise or extraneous influence. A noisy measure is one which contains much unexplained variability—variability which seems unrelated to the efforts of control of the participants. Frequently, noisy measures indicate the presence of other variables which affect performance and which need to be identified and perhaps expressed as additional measures. Noise in the measures of performance is mainly undesirable because it leads to frustration on the part of the participants and eventual poor performance.

Feedback of Measured Performance. Timely and regular feedback is absolutely essential. Particularly where the measures are not completely understandable, or where "counts" are displaced in time from actual performance, it is important that results be communicated to participants.

Perhaps what has been said above appears painfully obvious. Notwithstanding the truism nature of the criteria, these considerations are all too often overlooked.

CONTROL AND RESPONSIBILITY—WORK ORGANIZATION AND JOB DESIGN

Closely related to goals and measures is the matter of appropriate control and responsibility for the goals and measures.

This is merely repeating the old adage, "authority commensurate with responsibility," but substituting the word control for authority.

It appears obvious that the degree of satisfaction or frustration that an individual gains from his job is related to the extent that he can really control the situation he has been handed.

A most significant piece of research which is related to control and responsibility is the work of Dr. Frederick Herzberg. Dr. Herzberg's initial research, now replicated many times, indicated that the true sources of motivation in a job appeared to be:

1. The sense of achievement
2. The sense of responsibility
3. Recognition for achievement
4. Work itself

Significantly, these revolve around the relationship between goals and measures and the degree of control over or responsibility for them that an individual feels.

The relating of goals and control lies in the specifics of job duties. Hence, the manner in which work is organized or how jobs are designed is the principal place where management can take constructive steps.

What is required is a form of job enrichment. It is important to differentiate between job enrichment and job enlargement. The latter term has been used to refer to attempts to alleviate job boredom and to make work more interesting. Job enlargement includes things such as job rotation and adding elements to jobs. Job rotation is not likely to be enriching, and adding elements to jobs is useful depending only on what the elements are and how they contribute to a sense of control.

Job enrichment should refer to conscious attempts to design jobs where the maximum feasible amount of control is provided to achieve meaningful objectives. This can take many forms in practice, depending on situational factors. It is fundamentally a matter of relating control and objectives where the objectives are substantial enough to provide a challenge.

The following questions have proved helpful in assessing job situations for enrichment:

1. Does the individual or small group have the required control to achieve his objectives?
2. Is there reasonable freedom to adapt to minor changes in conditions and personal preferences?
3. Have "doing" and "thinking" been separated and specialized in different people, or does each job include the necessary thinking related to the doing? (An appropriate example is the matter of inspection. It has been standard practice in many places to have A do a job and B inspects A's work. An enriched job would require A to inspect his own work and bear the responsibility for it.)
4. Does the combination of tasks or elements provide a sense of completion?

Experience has shown that it is very difficult to express universal criteria for job enrichment or job design. Situational factors play a large part in constraining or facilitating job enrichment. What appears most important is the management attitude that this is worthwhile and necessary. Examination of working environments and discussions with workers and line management frequently unearth many opportunities for improvement of this kind.

MANAGERIAL BEHAVIOR—LEADERSHIP STYLE

It has been amply demonstrated through theory and practice that the manner in which a superior manages his immediate subordinates is strongly influential in whether or not an atmosphere of achievement is present.

Paradoxically, the best research indicates that the superior's concern for his people looms as being more important than apparent concern for goals. The style of supervision which has been shown most effective in terms of high producing units is called "supportive" or "employee-centered" as distinct from "directive" or "production-centered."

The differences between these styles is distinct yet subtle. The supportive supervisor is not unconcerned about goals, but manages to convey to his people that achievement is the people's concern and that the supervisor's role is to help them.

Some of the characteristics of employee-centered or supportive supervision are:

1. The supervisor prescribes general goals and allows maximum freedom to subordinates on the means of achieving them.
2. His interest in achievement is evident but is made so without close follow-up or checking.
3. His manner makes him open to suggestion and influence. He is nonthreatening and easy to approach.
4. He is concerned with harmonious relations among his people, is sensitive to grounds for conflict, and is skillful at resolving conflict early without suppression.
5. Basically his style emphasizes the act of supervising people and not preoccupation with getting out production.

CONTINUING IMPROVEMENT, THE ULTIMATE OBJECTIVE

The ultimate objective of a manager's interest in motivation is to create an environment where everyone, as a matter of course, strives for continuing improvement.

The law of survival and growth for organizations requires that they change and adapt to changing conditions. At the same time, effecting changes in methods, procedures, and the like is often a frustrating experience because of resistance to change. So much has been written and said about resistance to change that it is coming to be thought of as an innate human characteristic. It is not so much that, as the manner in which change is brought about that leads to resistance to change.

There are real opportunities in the area of change for a manager to reinforce an environment of achievement. Taken as a whole, the approach to change which is most fruitful is that of participation. This word, too, has been overused and smacks of giving up or losing control. What it really amounts to is realistic sharing of control and information, particularly during conditions of change. The following considerations are suggested to help bring about an innovative environment as well as an environment of achievement.

1. Keep people informed as early as possible about changes in outside demands on the organization.
2. Delegate problems, not solutions
3. Actively solicit ideas for performance improvement through interviews and group discussions. Do not wait; go out and ask!
4. Encourage controlled experimentation on the job—adopt the "let's try it" point of view.

SUMMARY

The attempt in this chapter has been to compress much of what has been written and said about motivation and to express it in commonsense terms. There is far more to the matter of human motivation than is touched upon here. Only that subset of the subject which focuses on how motivation relates to organizational performance has been covered.

The major points selected for emphasis have been:

1. In an organizational setting, motivation should be defined in terms of creating a climate of achievement.
2. The point of departure for creating a climate of achievement is to

adopt a set of assumptions relating people and work, and to use these as a basis for management practices.

3. Equity, the feeling of being treated fairly, particularly in the matter of compensation (pay and benefits), is of crucial importance. However, creating a situation in which equity is positive will not guarantee high performance.

4. Communication, particularly relating to goals and measures of performance, is of prime importance. If the name of the game is achievement of objectives, people must know what the goals are and be kept informed about relative achievement.

5. Given that achievement of objectives is the prime focus, the degree of control and perceived responsibility that people feel for the goals is important. Control and responsibility are largely a function of job duties and tasks, as these are incorporated into jobs in a meaningful way.

6. The manner in which a manager or supervisor relates to his reporting subordinates has a strong influence on the motivational climate. A supportive rather than a directive style is most likely to be effective.

7. The ultimate goal of an organization is continuing improvement, continuing progress. Deliberate efforts to express this point of view and make it part of the organizational norm are desirable.

BIBLIOGRAPHY

Blake, Robert R., and Jane S. Mouton, *The Managerial Grid*, Gulf Publishing Company, Houston, Tex., 1964.

Gellerman, Saul W., *Management by Motivation*, American Management Association, New York, 1968.

Gellerman, Saul W., *Motivation and Productivity*, American Management Association, New York, 1963.

Herzberg, Frederick, B. Mausner, and B. Snyderman, *The Motivation to Work*, John Wiley & Sons, Inc., New York, 1959.

Herzberg, Frederick, *Work and the Nature of Man*, World Publishing Company, Cleveland, Ohio, 1966.

Hughes, C. L., *Goal Setting*, American Management Association, New York, 1965.

Likert, Rensis, *The Human Organization*, McGraw-Hill Book Company, New York, 1967.

Likert, Rensis, *New Patterns of Management*, McGraw-Hill Book Company, New York, 1961.

McGregor, Douglas, *The Human Side of Enterprise*, McGraw-Hill Book Company, New York, 1960.

McGregor, Douglas, *The Professional Manager*, McGraw-Hill Book Company, New York, 1967.

CHAPTER TWO

Wage Payment Plans and Employee Productivity

WALTON M. HANCOCK *Professor, Department of Industrial Engineering, The University of Michigan, Ann Arbor, Michigan*

DUANE C. GEITGEY *Director of Program Development, Maynard Research Council, Inc., Pittsburgh, Pennsylvania*

Managers are increasingly concerned with the problem of establishing an environment for their employees that stimulates high productivity.

Two basic stimuli that have proved effective in improving the working environment and therefore employee output are:

1. Financial—utilization of a monetary stimulus through some form of wage payment plan
2. Social—stimulation of output by assisting people, either singly or in groups, to establish and attain high goals

In this chapter, the major concern will be with various wage payment plans, including the development of a sound and consistent wage structure, to achieve the best working environment for high employee productivity.

If the true capability of an organization is to be realized, an effective and equitable wage payment plan must be present. Wages and salaries represent one of the greatest costs in manufacturing, and consequently, they should receive continuous attention from management. Although other stimuli exist in the industrial environment, wages and salaries represent a combination of financial and social stimuli that directly affect productivity.

ESTABLISHING WHAT EACH JOB IS WORTH

One of the most important tasks the employer must face is that of establishing what each job is worth. In fact, the success of the enterprise may well hinge on this one important task. Job evaluation is a widely used tool for establishing job worth. Properly handled, job evaluation can result in a stable, highly motivated organization. Haphazardly handled, job evaluation can create serious difficulties.

Regardless of the specific approach taken, job evaluation must be done systematically. Criteria must first be established for the equitable determination of the relative importance of each job and then must be applied uniformly and consistently throughout the organization. Job evaluation consists of these steps:

1. Preparation of a description of the job as it is now being performed
2. Development of a final job description and specifications
3. Analysis of each job, using the final description, to determine the relative value of the job

Preparing the Job Description. The first step in the job evaluation procedure is to prepare a description of the content of the job itself. One way that this can be done is by first discussing the job with the worker and his immediate supervisor. Often, workers and management personnel will have differing opinions concerning the job content. The resolution of these differences is an important aspect of job evaluation, and they should be carefully analyzed to make sure that coverage is provided for all necessary job elements. Care should also be taken to avoid including unnecessary elements. Each job must be well defined so that responsibilities do not overlap between jobs. Because these job descriptions will serve as a basis for analysis of the organization itself as well as for providing guidelines for future comparison, each description must be carefully prepared. Also, a job should be clearly defined so that a worker and his immediate supervisor can determine his areas of responsibility exactly. In fact, each worker should be provided with a detailed description of his job responsibilities.

From the job descriptions, job specifications are prepared which clearly describe the job and the qualifications of the person performing the job. Figure 2-1 is a typical job specification. This form is designed to indicate the characteristics of the employee which are of greater than normal expectancy so that, when a person is considered for a position, his abilities can be compared with the requirements of the job. In determining the above average expectancy requirements, it is important to have a list of factors that are important, in relative degrees, to all jobs. The evaluator is then able to consider all the aspects of a job. Skill, responsibility, physical and mental requirements, and working conditions are the factors most frequently considered. In addition, such factors as test scores on various types of dexterity or aptitude tests may also be part of the job specification, and should be included in the form if required.

The "Promote from" row indicates the jobs that would be most likely to produce prospective candidates for promotion. Likewise, "Promote to" serves to indicate the next higher job or jobs. If tools are required by the employee, such as those needed by machinists for example, a list of the tools should be made so that any prospective employee for the job can be questioned on this aspect.

The approvals are necessary because it is important for the evaluator to make sure that everyone is aware of and in agreement with the employee specifications and job description.

With the job description and the associated job specification available, it is possible to determine the relative worth of each job within the organization. Because the relative importance and the status of the job are related, the act of reviewing all the jobs at the same time and establishing the relative worth helps inform everyone of his position and responsibilities in the organization.

MANUAL JOB DESCRIPTION

JOB SPECIFICATION AND EVALUATION

OCCUPATION	FEMALE ☐	CODE NO.
DEPARTMENT	MALE ☐	
COMPANY		DATE

SPECIAL OPERATOR CHARACTERISTICS REQUIRED (CHECK ONLY ESSENTIAL QUALIFICATIONS)

CHECK ONCE IF NORMAL EXPECTANCY IS ADEQUATE BUT REQUIRED—TWICE IF GREATER THAN NORMAL

STRENGTH		EDUCATION		RESPONSIBILITY	
EYESIGHT		EXPERIENCE		MATURITY	
HEARING		COORDINATION		LEADERSHIP	

EMPLOYEE TEST REQUIREMENTS

TYPE OF TEST			
SCORE MINIMUM MAXIMUM			

PROMOTE FROM	PROMOTE TO

TOOLS OPERATOR SHOULD OWN

APPROVED BY		
	FOR	DATE
	FOR	DATE
	FOR	DATE
	FOR	DATE
EVALUATOR		

FIG. 2-1. Manual Job Description.

There are a number of methods of performing this function. In general, they can be classified into three major categories:

1. Point rating
2. Factor comparison
3. Ranking

Point Rating. Under the point rating system of job evaluation, each pertinent factor is weighed to indicate its importance as a job requirement. As mentioned previously, there are four basic factors that are involved in all point rating systems. They are: skill, effort, responsibility, and job conditions. These factors can be further subdivided into more detailed factors.

Figure 2-2 is an example of a typical form used for this purpose. For

MANUAL JOB EVALUATION

FACTORS	REASONS FOR ASSIGNING POINTS		POINTS
SKILL			
EDUCATION AND INTELLIGENCE			
LEARNING TIME			
COORDINATION			
NUMBER OF MAJOR OPERATIONS			
RESPONSIBILITY		POS X PROB	
DAMAGE TO MATERIAL		x =	
TO EQUIP.		x =	
TO TOOLS & JIGS		x =	
SAFETY OF OTHERS		x =	
EFFORT			
PHYSICAL			
NERVOUS			
POSTURE			
EYE STRAIN			
WORKING CONDITIONS		POS X PROB	
ACCIDENT HAZARD TO SELF		x =	
WATER			
LOCATION			
TEMPERATURE			
NOISE			
OIL OR DIRT			
DUST			
FUMES			
CLOTHING EXPENSE			
TOOL EXPENSE			
		TOTAL POINTS	

FIG. 2-2.   Manual Job Evaluation.

each of the subfactors under the major factors, a range of points is allocated. The number of points within the range is then determined for the given job. For example, suppose that a maximum of ten points were allocated for "Education and Intelligence." Then for any given job, the amount of this factor necessary would be related to the point scale, with one-half of the maximum points representing the average condition. In this example, five points would be assigned if average intelligence and education were needed. If a high degree of this factor were necessary, then nine or ten points would be assigned.

It is important to mention that the maximum point allocation represents, in effect, a management decision as to the relative worth of each of the subcategories. For example, if ten points maximum were assigned to "Education and Intelligence" and twenty points maximum to "Physical Effort," then there has, in effect, been a policy decision that physical effort is twice as important as education and intelligence for the range of jobs under consideration.

Under the subareas of "Responsibility" and in the "Accident Hazard to Self" subcategory under "Working Conditions," a separate calculation is sometimes made to avoid assigning points to the extreme conditions which have a small probability of occurring. If the possibility of damage to material exists but the probability of its occurring is low, then points may be assigned under the recognition that damage to material could occur, but this point assignment is multiplied by the estimated likelihood that it will occur. For example, if twenty points are assigned for damage to material but the probability of occurrence is 0.10 (10 percent) then $20 \times 0.10 = 2$ points would be the number entered in the far right column.

The point total is obtained by adding the points in the right-hand column. The total points serve as a basis for comparing this job with other jobs that have been reviewed by the same process. The resulting total can then be related to a specific dollar value for the job. Thereafter, the dollar value can be revised to reflect changes in cost of living, local wage and salary conditions, and agreements with the union.

Although specific job evaluation forms may vary in design, job evaluation factors generally can be categorized into three major areas. The first area is job prerequisites, which are required for the workers to qualify for a specific job. The prerequisites generally fall into four specific areas: strength, mental development, previous experience, and skill. Skill may be further broken down into the three categories of social skill, which includes self-expression and getting along with others; mental skill, which includes judgment, ability to plan, initiative, and resourcefulness; and manual skill, which includes coordination, dexterity, speed, and accuracy.

The second major area covered by job evaluation can be called job deterrents, including working conditions and effort. Working conditions may include such subfactors as surroundings and hazards, while effort may include both physical and mental exertion.

The third major area of job evaluation is job responsibilities, such as responsibility for the work of others and the safety of others, and for materials, tools and equipment, and production.

Factor Comparison. Another method of job evaluation is factor comparison. In the factor comparison method, each factor is ranked individually with other jobs. For example, all jobs may be compared and ranked first by the factor, "mental requirements." Then, the skill factor, physical requirements, responsibility, and working conditions are ranked. Thus, a job may rank near the top in skill, for example, but low in physical requirements. Total point values are then assigned to each factor. The final ranking or total worth of the job is obtained by adding together all the point values for each of the factors considered. The jobs with predominantly low ratings will receive a lower money value, and the jobs with high ratings will receive the higher dollar values.

Ranking Method. The third method of job evaluation is the ranking method. Under the ranking method, each job is ranked in comparison with the other jobs in a given group. The ranking is related to the total worth of the job.

The ranking method is a very limited type of job evaluation. No attempt is made to take an analytical approach to determining the ranking. Jobs are merely arranged in order of rank, usually by a jury. The highest ranking job is at the top of the list.

After the jobs are ranked, they are arranged into groups. All jobs in a group have very little difference in value. Money values are then assigned to each group. The ranking method is sometimes called job classification.

It is sometimes done after the point evaluation method has been used. Here the jobs are arranged into groups where a group is characterized by a small spread in total point rating. Salary ranges are then assigned to each group according to the average point rating within the group.

Although the ranking method is not as accurate as the point system or factor comparison method, it does rank and group jobs by the relative worth of the jobs themselves. This results in a more consistent wage and salary scale than the arbitrary assignment of money values to jobs.

The ranking method is appropriate for small companies that cannot justify the more elaborate point rating or factor comparison methods. It is a practical approach to evaluating supervisory positions and other jobs that require uncommon abilities that are not easily measured in numerical terms.

In effect, job evaluation helps establish the status level of the job. This status level is important to the organization, for it provides a mechanism whereby everyone understands the relative importance of various jobs. The job evaluation system provides the guidelines upon which decisions can be made concerning the placement of personnel. It provides a systematic means of establishing job value, which can be used to identify and adjust inequities in the wage scale. It allows managements to define the extremes of the wage payment scale and to establish the level of each job within these extremes. Properly administered, it ensures that the knowledge, technical competence, and responsibilities expected of each employee are thoroughly spelled out and that each job is defined and evaluated.

One factor that is not included in the job evaluation procedure is the consideration of the competitive situation in certain job specialty areas. The competitive situation in a community may occasionally necessitate the revision of certain portions of the base rate structure derived from job evaluation. Such revision can be a source of difficulty because the wages are not paid on the present worth of a job in relation to other jobs within the organization, but to the present worth of the job in the geographical area. The actual wages that an employee receives, therefore, are sometimes dependent on two factors:

1. The relative worth of the job within the organization
2. The prevailing wages of the area, particularly where a labor shortage exists

For this reason it is usually desirable, as part of a well-maintained job evaluation program, to have periodic wage surveys which will serve as a basis for comparing the relative worth of similar jobs within the community.

WAGE SURVEYS

One of the most important aspects of the wage survey to establish comparable community and industry rates is the problem of determining which jobs are of equal value. Although there are key jobs that are similar in content, particularly in the journeyman trades and unskilled labor areas, the hourly rate of similar jobs can vary considerably between companies. When attempting to establish an equitable wage rate, fringe benefits must be considered. If their dollar value varies widely, it may be necessary to modify base rates to reflect total compensation. Other items that must be considered in a wage survey are the stability of employment and the working environment. Although the fringe benefit package, stability, and working environment may vary considerably between companies, the workers themselves are usually most concerned about their hourly rate or take-home pay. This is because take-home pay is their most immediate reward. Also, they probably have little knowledge of the comparative working conditions and fringe benefits in other companies.

Generally, inconsistencies in wage payment, either within or outside the company, are perceived by employees in two ways:

1. Two jobs appear to be the same, but have different rates.
2. Identical jobs are filled by two persons with different performance levels.

Companies can minimize these apparent inconsistencies by:

1. Appropriate administration of the job evaluation system and the wage payment plans. Because of the amount of information that has to be accumulated, it is highly desirable for the administration to be entrusted to an individual who has a thorough knowledge of the jobs and the competitive situation in the community.
2. Proper employment procedures and periodic review of employee performance, as well as an adequate training program.

THE BASE RATE AS A MOTIVATOR OF PRODUCTIVITY

Method of compensation is one of the factors that cause people to be productive. The base rate (that rate which is guaranteed) is derived from the job evaluation system. The base rate itself does not necessarily relate directly to productivity, except that it represents the security of a constant income to the employee. This income or job security is, for most people, a powerful stimulus to maintain a reasonable level of production. For those who want to perform higher level jobs, the knowledge that base rates increase with jobs of higher evaluation can act as a stimulus for higher than average production in their present jobs. However, the rate of productivity where only a base rate exists is sometimes less than the true capability of the organization. This is true because the wage payment system in itself does not provide a continuing stimulus to improve output.

INCENTIVE SYSTEMS AS MOTIVATORS OF PRODUCTIVITY

Sometimes a wage incentive system provides a social stimulus as well as a monetary stimulus to improve output, but the social stimulus may act in either a positive or negative manner.

Incentive programs must be properly administered and maintained to motivate productivity. Managements that fail to do this may find it necessary to seek other means to stimulate output. Thus, the establishment of a successful financial incentive system demands a high level of competence on the part of management. To achieve the maximum motivational effect from a financial incentive system, managements must provide:

1. A systematic audit of incentive standards
2. Prompt adjustment of inequities

A systematic audit procedure should be so designed that all incentive standards are regularly audited to ensure that the standard accurately reflects the job as it is being performed.

When inaccuracies or inequities develop in incentive standards, it is essential that management take immediate corrective action as soon as the need is determined. Failure to adjust standards promptly will not only minimize the motivational effect of the incentive standard, but may also in some cases act as a negative influence on performance.

THE BEHAVIORAL SCIENCE APPROACH TO MOTIVATION

The social and behavioral scientists have provided knowledge about the actions of management that contribute to high productivity. They have found that employee-centered rather than job-centered managers generally have more productive groups. One of the most meaningful functions of management is to assist the employees in establishing their goals. The best time to do this is at the very beginning of a new production run. For example, it is much easier to establish a high level of productivity with a new group of employees than with a group that has already established its goals. It is therefore important for management to assist the group in establishing goals as soon as a new plant opens or as soon as a new production operation begins. The critical time is the first few weeks or months of the operation. It is much more difficult to establish high productivity goals after social attitudes are established by the group in the absence of any participation by the manager. Management must therefore move quickly to assist the group in establishing a high level of productivity.

MEASURED DAYWORK AND PRODUCTIVITY

Because of the cost and attention required to maintain an incentive system, some organizations have moved in the direction of measured daywork throughout their operations. A measured daywork system provides some degree of motivation, but is not generally as effective as an incentive system. Measured daywork systems do allow management to establish goals by which employees can measure their effectiveness, but the feedback often occurs at much less frequent intervals, such as every month rather than every day or week as in incentive systems.

The measured daywork system is an intermediate form of wage payment that usually arises from an incentive system. Employees are normally given a higher base rate to compensate for the lack of incentive opportunity. The level of production is sometimes, but not always, below an incentive system but above the level of production of nonmeasured work. If properly administered, a measured daywork system can provide a definite incentive to greater productivity. Data on worker performances are usually given to supervisors at the first-line level as well as to the individual employee.

The stimulus for increased output in a measured daywork system must come from management in the form of closer control and better planning, rather than from the incentive stimulus provided by an incentive plan. Successful application of the measured daywork system depends largely on the effectiveness of supervision itself.

MERIT RATING

To maintain a high level of motivation in the work force, management must also maintain a high level of motivation in its own ranks. The merit review procedure is one of the procedures developed by management to assist nonincentive employees in achieving satisfaction from their jobs and to reward these employees for good work or marked improvement. Job evaluation fixes the range of pay which a job is worth. It compares jobs with one another and with jobs outside the company. Merit rating measures the worth of a person in a job evaluation rate range. It tells him and his company how well he is doing and how much he has improved.

The objective of a merit rating procedure is consistent with the behavioral science approach to motivation. Merit rating provides feedback and goal definitions toward which a person can work. These goals are in the area of self-improvement. Characteristics such as level of productivity, quality level, receptiveness toward new ideas, being at work on time, and adherence to safety requirements are evaluated periodically in the case of production workers. In effect, they help provide an environment where an individual can make better use of his assets and increase his strength in his weakest areas.

Figure 2-3 is an example of a typical merit rating form for foremen and supervisory personnel. The traits listed are somewhat different from those of the assembly line worker, but the approach is the same. In this case, the foreman is rated by his immediate supervisor for each of the characteristics listed in bold type along the bottom of the form. The blocks with the cross-hatched lines represent average performance. The blocks above these are for varying degrees of above average performance, and those below for below average performance.

The method of evaluating varies. One method is to assign point values to each of the columns as in the point method of job evaluation. A total score is obtained and compared to the average score which is the sum of the scores of the cross-hatched blocks.

Periodic management review of the performance of an employee is highly desirable. These reviews are normally conducted every six months. However, the interval between reviews can be shorter if the manager or the employee feels a need for a more frequent review. The importance of maintaining a regular schedule of merit reviews cannot be overemphasized. If the frequency of merit reviews is announced publicly, the employees expect to be reviewed at the stated intervals. If management fails to carry out the review as stated, a merit review procedure can actually have a negative motivational effect.

In a typical review procedure, the employee's immediate supervisor discusses the merit rating in detail with the employee in private. One of the problems with the merit review procedure can arise at this point. Most managers find it easy to have a discussion with an individual who has an above average rating, but it is more difficult to talk to an employee who has below average characteristics. This is often so unpleasant that practically all the ratings end up being average or above. This situation can be greatly aggravated if the employee has no reason before the interview to suspect that he or she is not doing as well as other people. Considerable finesse is needed on the part of the manager in these below average cases to accomplish one of the primary purposes of the merit review procedure—helping the employee to become more productive.

Merit review procedures have sometimes become confused with cost of living increases. In these cases, practically everyone who is performing acceptably, not meritoriously, receives an increase. Once this practice starts, it is perceived by the employees as the normal condition and therefore comes to be expected. This practice, in effect, changes the original intent of a merit rating program from rewarding meritorious performance to rewarding average performance.

Perhaps the most important point about merit programs that have regular

Date _____
Dept. _____

Name _____
Job Title _____

FOREMAN AND SUPERVISORY
GRAPHIC PROFILE MERIT RATING PLAN

LEADERSHIP	DEPENDABILITY	ATTITUDE, LOYALTY, AND COOPERATION	RESPONSIBILITY ASSUMED	JUDGMENT APPLIED TO JOB	RESPONSIBILITY FOR SAFETY	METHODS DEVELOPMENT
Marked traits of leadership. Enjoys high regard of employees.	Reliable, dependable, completes assignments as requested, operates without confusion.	High degree of cooperation with other supervisors and management.	Stands on own feet in every decision. Does not blame shortcomings on others.	Good common sense with high degree of initiative and ingenuity.	Insists upon safe working habits. Extremely alert to correct unsafe conditions and practices.	Makes many excellent method changes and improvement of product.
Good leader and well regarded by employees.	Completes assignments with some minor aid. More than average dependability.	Good cooperation with supervisors and management.	Needs occasional help in making decisions. May try to shift responsibility.	Good common sense with fair degree of initiative and/or ingenuity.	Above average regard for safe practices and equipment. Alert to accident hazards.	Makes many excellent method changes and few suggestions for product improvements.
Good leader but neither looked up to nor down upon.	Usually completes assignments or has real reason for not doing so.	Adequate cooperation with most supervisors and management.	Needs some help in making decisions and assumes only assigned responsibilities.	Common sense with occasional evidence of initiative and/or ingenuity.	Adequate regard for safe practices and safety equipment.	Offers some suggestions for methods changes in manufacture.
Some indication of lack of leadership and/or lack of respect.	Realizes assignment will not be completed but does not know what to do about it.	Indications of more than normal conflict with others.	Constantly asks advice in making minor decisions and passes buck to others.	Evidence of lack of common sense with or without initiative or ingenuity.	Little concern about unsafe conditions or practices.	Puts into effect only changes given him. Regards present setup as O.K.
Lacking in leadership and/or respect.	Not reliable. Assignments seldom carried out as assigned. Resorts to alibi.	Definite difficulty with others due to attitude.	Unable to make decisions for self and will not assume even minor responsibility.	Noticeable lack of good judgment.	Inclines to regard injury as the fault of the worker rather than unsafe condition.	Complains about methods, but offers nothing constructive.

Has this person any personality difficulty? _____ What? _____

Would you consider this person for increase? _____ Why? _____

Would training help this person? _____ On what phase of the job? _____

Fig. 2-3. Foreman and Supervisory Graphic Profile Merit Rating Plan.

review periods is that they provide a check on the degree of understanding between the employer and employee. A merit review program should not be a substitute for regular day-to-day contact with the employees. Regular communication with a supervisor is in itself a motivational factor. Problems should be solved on a day-to-day basis. However, because some supervisors find it difficult to criticize employees, a functioning merit review system provides a recurring stimulus to supervisor-employee discussion of problem areas.

CONCLUSION

In conclusion, the area of wage payment and job evaluation is not only of continuing importance to an organization, but also a complex topic with many ramifications. Properly designed and administered, wage payment plans can greatly stimulate productivity. Poorly designed and administered plans can create serious consequences. Thus, management must ensure that wage payment plans are both well designed and carefully administered to achieve maximum motivation and productivity.

BIBLIOGRAPHY

Barret, Richard S., *Performance Rating,* Science Research Associates, Inc., Chicago, 1966.

Cohen, Sanford, *Labor in the United States,* 2d ed., Charles E. Merrill Books, Inc., Columbus, Ohio, 1966.

Davis, Keith, *Human Relations at Work: The Dynamics of Organizational Behavior,* 3d ed., McGraw-Hill Book Company, New York, 1967.

Fogel, Walter A., "Job Rate Ranges: A Theoretical and Empirical Analysis," *Industrial and Labor Relations Review,* July, 1964. Also published by California University Institute of Industrial Relations, Los Angeles, 1964.

Gellerman, Saul W., *The Management of Human Relations,* Holt, Rinehart & Winston, Inc., New York, 1966.

Hughes, Charles L., "Why Goal-oriented Performance Reviews Succeed and Fail," *Personnel Journal,* June, 1966.

Jucius, Michael J., *Personnel Management,* 6th ed., Richard D. Irwin, Inc., Homewood, Ill., 1967.

Kellogg, Marion S., *Closing the Performance Gap,* American Management Association, New York, 1967.

Maynard, H. B. (ed.), *Handbook of Business Administration,* sec. 11, "Management of Human Resources," McGraw-Hill Book Company, New York, 1967.

Megginson, Leon C., *Personnel: A Behavioral Approach to Administration,* Richard D. Irwin, Inc., Homewood, Ill., 1967.

Pigors, Paul, and Charles A. Meyers, *Personnel Administration: A Point of View and a Method,* 6th ed., McGraw-Hill Book Company, New York, 1969.

Raudsepp, Eugene, "Performance Appraisals That Motivate Individual Development," *Management Review,* March, 1967, pp. 62–64.

Scott, Robert C., *Incentives in Manufacturing; Individual and Plant-wide,* vols. 1, 2, and 3, The Eddy-Rucker-Nickels Co., Cambridge, Mass., 1966.

Selected Examples of Performance Reviews, vols. 1 and 2, Bureau of Industrial Relations, University of Michigan, Ann Arbor, 1966.

Sibson, Robert E., *Wages and Salaries: A Handbook for Line Managers,* rev. ed., American Management Association, New York, 1967.

CHAPTER THREE

Incentive Plans for Direct Workers

JAMES W. THOMPSON *Vice President of Manufacturing, Schlegel Manufacturing Company, Rochester, New York*

Incentive plans for direct workers generally have a simple production-pay relationship. The direct worker is aware of the relationship between his performance and production. Pieces completed are evident, and their prompt and accurate counting is encouraged by the complementary requirements of production planning, order follow-up, and inventory evaluation. Quality factors are traceable to the performed operation.

Early incentive plans were applied to direct workers, and their simple concepts have continued to form the bases for direct worker plans. Even simple plans, however, can become unnecessarily complex. Application practices, special application rules, conflicting as well as overriding policies, and special guarantees, generated in the heat of collective bargaining or through management error, tend to change the nature of the plan.

Manufacturing management's role prior to the installation of incentives is usually limited to the selection of the plan to be used. After installation, management has the continuing responsibility for ensuring adequate maintenance of the plan, testing its effectiveness frequently, and planning the strategy for changes that will offset any factors that may be tending to destroy the plan.

DESIRABLE CHARACTERISTICS OF AN INCENTIVE PLAN

There are certain requirements, proved in practice, that an incentive plan must meet if it is to be successful.

1. There must be mutual confidence, between the workers affected by the plan and the management people administering it, that an incentive is advantageous and fair.
2. The plan must be simple, both for ease of understanding and ease of administration.

9–23

3. There must be consistency in task requirements between jobs, achieved by sound standards setting techniques and consistent maintenance of standards.

4. The plan must be sufficiently generous to convince the worker that he is adequately compensated for his effort when compared with other work available to him both within the plant and in the community.

5. The worker's earnings must not be adversely affected by management inadequacies in functions such as planning, scheduling, raw material quality, tool maintenance, and the like. Guaranteed maintenance of earnings cannot offset this requirement.

Types of Plans—Payment Method. Plans are sometimes referred to by method of payment. The manufacturing manager hears plans described as piecework, payment for minutes or hours earned, efficiency bonus, count payment, and the like. These terms do not by themselves completely describe the plan. Indeed, neither does any other system of classification subsequently discussed in this chapter. An understanding of the terminology is necessary, however, for meaningful discussion of and management of an incentive plan.

Piecework. The basic concept of piecework is the payment of a monetary amount for each piece processed through a given operation. Advocates of piecework point to the "instant earning" feature as a strong incentive. Critics of the system point to:

1. Extra administration costs of converting measured time standards to money values

2. Administration costs of recalculating piecework values every time there is a change in the basic wage rates

3. Often conflicting concepts of the value added to the part by the operation when compared with the performance of the direct worker

Piecework earnings may be applied as a bonus on top of a base payment. More commonly, the piecework earnings are the only payment (minimum earnings disregarded). These plans are obviously not alike. This simple example should illustrate why any incentive plan cannot be judged solely by its descriptive title.

Time Earned. The most common form of payment is for time earned. Conceptually, an operation has an allotted "normal" time established for its completion. The incentive operator earns time for each piece produced and is paid at the monetary rate established for the unit of time. Minutes and standard hours are both common units for incentive earnings measurement. Advocates of the time-earned plans list the following advantages.

1. Work measurement techniques give operation time values that are applicable without further adjustment.

2. Adjustments in labor rates can be accomplished without changing the standard time rates.

3. Incentive operators are constantly aware of productivity by noting accomplishment with reference to the clock on the wall.

4. Usually, the time earned and paid for is identical to time units used for establishing the cost and inventory value of a product.

Efficiency Bonus. A variation of the above two classifications is the efficiency bonus plan. Efficiency bonus plans are generally used where there is not a direct relationship between pieces produced and wage payment. A plan such as one offering a flat bonus, say 10 percent, for reaching a quota would fall in the general classification of an efficiency plan. Such plans are relatively rare and are found where a more direct plan is not applicable.

Count Units. Some enterprises measure their output in terms of tons, bags, carloads, or other pertinent units. Such units may not reflect the true performance demand on individual operations. Revolutions of a camshaft or bags of raw material used might be a better type of performance indicator. In either case, plans based on counts offer a form of incentive inducement.

Types of Plans—Performance Structure. Figure 3-1 is typical of charts used to show how operator performance affects pay. Under the plan illustrated, the operator receives a guaranteed rate for any performance up to 100 percent. For performance above 100 percent, he receives a pay increase of 1 percent for each 1 percent increase in performance. This is the most commonly used direct incentive plan. It is usually referred to as a one-for-one, guaranteed rate plan.

Figure 3-2 illustrates a variation of this plan. The incentive worker receives a like guarantee up to 100 percent performance. He receives a 10 percent increase in pay upon reaching 100 percent performance, and thereafter he receives an additional 1.1 percent for each 1 percent increase of performance above 100 percent. This plan has strong financial motivation for holding performance above 100 percent.

Figure 3-3 is representative of the so-called "sharing" plans. For performance above 100 percent, the incentive worker shares the gains, that is, he receives only a portion of the decreased costs resulting from better than 100 percent performance. On examination of the illustrations, it would appear that the sharing plan has less financial motivation for increased performance. This conclusion cannot be accepted, however, without consideration of the other incentive practices contributing to the plan.

Multiple Factor Plans. Financial motivation may be provided where units produced or output is not the major item of accomplishment. Where there

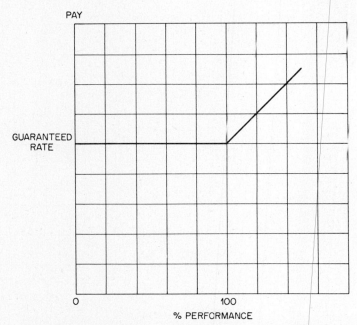

Fɪɢ. 3-1. Pay versus Performance—One-for-One Incentive Plan.

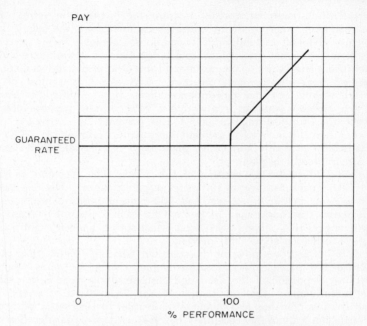

FIG. 3-2. Pay versus Performance—Plan Similar to One-for-One Incentive Plan, with 10% Pay Increase at 100% Performance.

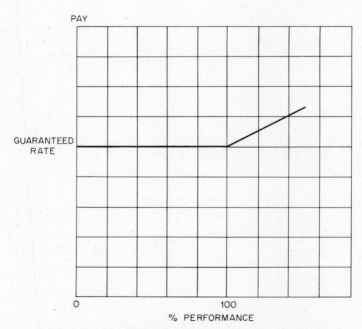

FIG. 3-3. Pay versus Performance—Typical Sharing Incentive Plan.

is a single major item, such as the yield of raw material, a plan can be devised that is not unlike one based on units produced.

Such indirect items, however, are usually interrelated with others. The output of a plastic extruder, for example, is held down by the necessity of minimizing the use of material. An incentive plan can be devised to reward both production and material usage in such a way as to curtail earnings potential for ignoring one item at the expense of the other. Thus, two factors are used to determine earnings. In the interest of simplicity, such plans are usually limited to three or four factors.

MANAGEMENT TESTS OF AN INCENTIVE PLAN

Line and staff groups influence the success of an incentive plan more than is often realized. The equal distribution of work on a process line is often determined more by the fixture designer than by subsequent work measurement. The precedents established by a pattern of grievance settlements sincerely negotiated by the industrial relations director can completely dominate the work standards setting practices. The industrial engineering staff may adjust to these outside influences without management recognition of the trends so initiated. At the extreme, incentives for direct labor have been known to degenerate into no more than ingenious schemes for arriving at mandatory results.

Manufacturing management can request sufficient data and analysis from the staff groups to ascertain the effectiveness of an incentive plan. There are several tests which can be employed.

Observation. Ineffective direct labor incentive plans are relatively simple to detect by direct observation. The work pace is inconsistent between operations, with a general slowdown before coffee breaks and lunch and a more pronounced one before quitting time. There is an attitude of "scorekeeping" rather than effort toward output, with pronounced involvement in pencil and paperwork toward the end of the workday.

The early signs of degeneration are more difficult to detect. Any of the above symptoms is indicative of a loss of financial motivation. Inconsistent work pace indicates lack of incentive maintenance. Both of these symptoms can be further verified.

Task Level. The 100 percent performance level was mentioned above without further definition. This point is a bench mark defined by the procedure used for setting standards. Consistency within a plant is more important than matching the point to that of other plants.

The relative task level is important in the appraisal of an incentive plan. Figure 3-4 superimposes the effect of a low-performance task level (dashed line) and a high-performance task level (dotted line) on the plan portrayed in Figure 3-1.

Industrial engineers are familiar with this concept. With the availability of rating films and predetermined motion-time data, they can readily advise on the relative position of the prevailing performance level in the plant.

Resultant Task Level. Average earnings and average performances are often reported to evaluate the results of the application of an incentive plan. A more meaningful analysis can be made by a plot of the distribution of performance levels for like operations. Figure 3-5 illustrates typical, not too unsatisfactory incentive results. The distribution is skewed to the high-performance side reflecting a high proportion of experienced employees. The performances to the left are those of newer employees. Some curtailment of effort is indicated by the restricted distribution to the right.

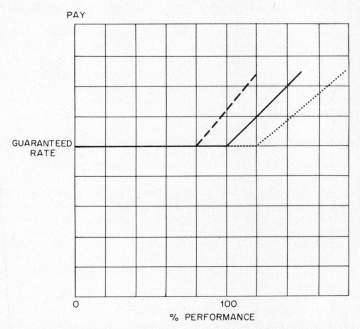

FIG. 3-4.   Effect on Earnings of Performance Level at which Standards Are Set.

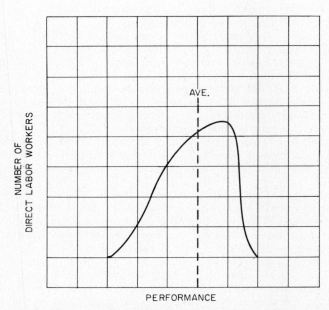

FIG. 3-5.   Typical Distribution of Performances of a Group of Incentive Workers.

The time lapse between methods changes and incentive standard revision is inferred by the degree of skewness to the right. Narrow distribution infers curtailed performance. Wide distribution infers inequities in standards or control of conditions.

Effect of Guarantees. All direct worker incentive plans have some form of guaranteed earnings, even if no more than the legal minimum wage. Excessive guarantees, however, can destroy motivation and lead to an observably inadequate incentive result.

The dashed line in Figure 3-6 illustrates the effect of a "maintenance of earnings" type of guarantee. The incentive worker so affected must produce considerably above the 100 percent level to improve his position. His principal motivation is to maintain his guarantee status, rather than to improve performance.

Effect of Wage Adjustments. The practice of granting "across the board" increases reduces incentive motivation when the increase applies only to the hourly rate and not to the base rate on which incentive earnings are calculated. The production-pay relationship is diminished by the ratio of earnings paid for performance and pay for being present. A better plan is to include the general increase in the base rate of the incentive plan. The relationship of the incentive potential as compared with nonincentive pay is thus maintained.

Over a period of years, the nature of an incentive plan can be radically changed by inappropriate application of wage adjustments. Considerable insight can be obtained by tracing the history of wage adjustments and their effect on a plan's motivation. Future adjustments, properly planned, can be used to enhance motivation.

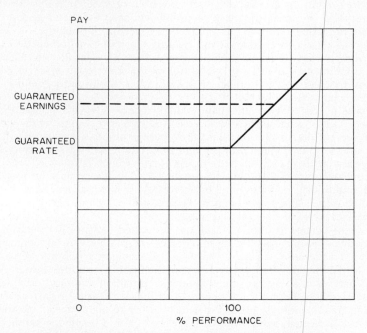

FIG. 3-6. When Earnings Are Guaranteed, Motivation to Improve Performance Is Weakened.

MANAGEMENT OF INCENTIVE MAINTENANCE

The proper maintenance of an incentive plan for direct workers should be a continuing concern of the manufacturing manager. The installation of a new incentive plan is a one-time experience, and the manager should employ competent specialists for the relatively short period involved. The review and analysis of a going plan, both to test its effectiveness and to plan improved motivation, should be a continuing effort. Any plan will degenerate unless it is given continuing maintenance. The manufacturing manager's function is to monitor the effectiveness with which the incentive plan is maintained.

One method of accomplishing this is to schedule a meeting, say once each month, limited to the topic of incentives. Attendees should include, at the minimum, the principal line and staff members involved in the administration of the incentive plan; but the number should be increased, as the topics to be discussed demand, to include others such as personnel from industrial engineering, industrial relations, payroll, budgeting, and inventory control.

Payroll earnings reports can provide clues to the existence of incentive maintenance problems. Disparity of earnings among departments leads the manager to suspect inconsistent standards, the result either of standards setting or of maintenance shortcomings. Operations not on incentive may result from a staff shortage, but may also result from lack of staff coordination. High or low earnings reports should always be followed by an investigation of methods and conditions.

Counts on which incentives are paid are always worthy of surveillance. If production reporting is used for both inventory control and incentive payment purposes, incorrect incentive reporting will sooner or later appear on an inventory adjustment report. If production reporting is separate for the two purposes, a periodic reconciliation will indicate the control action needed.

A review of grievances on incentive problems is of value to the manager as an indicator of worker attitude. Because of the bias involved in grievances, however, they do not give much of an indication of the effectiveness of the incentive maintenance activity.

The size of the staff for adequate maintenance is always a problem for the manager. Tests, such as here discussed, indicate the results being achieved by the present staff. Incentive maintenance is properly the problem of all those who design product process and tools, train and direct workers, and supply them with material. An enlarged involvement is more effective than increasing the size of a single department. Group discussions bring out any lack of uniformity in policy and bring to light incentive problems requiring remedial action. The group tends to become self-policing as understanding of the individual roles of the group members increases.

The sophistication of the organization in methods control is directly related to incentive maintenance. The importance of methods is evident in new incentive installations where savings are considerably greater than those which would be obtained solely from an increase in performance. An important part of the savings stems from the attention required to formulate the best methods and train the operators to follow them as a part of the task of setting time standards. It follows, then, that the maintenance of standards cannot be associated only with work measurement. Ideally, a method card should be provided to each work station, with the operator following the card and the work standard reflecting the method. All changes and improvements should be processed to maintain this condition.

Several indicators are available to the manufacturing manager on how well standards are being kept in line with improved methods. Efforts to improve processes occupy a major portion of the manager's day. If improvements are not reflected in reduced standard direct labor costs or more favorable variance, then it is likely that the time standards have not reflected the improvements. A reverse indicator would be an increase in incentive earnings on an operation where an expected decrease in cost failed to materialize.

MANAGEMENT OF INCENTIVE PLAN CHANGES

A properly functioning incentive for direct workers can enhance the realization of the manufacturing manager's objectives. The manager, through his supporting staff, should direct the administration and maintenance of his incentive plan. He is in the best position to give overall coordination, especially in the direction of corrective changes.

One deterrent to change is the implication that management has been wrong in some phase of operating its incentive plan. One company avoided such a position after an analysis of tests similar to those described above indicated some dangerous trends. A policy paper was written to guide the industrial relations function on the relationship of area wage rates, incentive base rates, and guaranteed daywork rates. Conforming procedures were written for establishing standards, as well as for controls on reporting production and the like. Over a period of time, a very strong incentive was developed without any appearance of change.

When changes must be openly made, such as during negotiations for a labor agreement, preparations should begin early. Direct workers expect leadership from manufacturing management. Desirable changes can be candidly stated, without blame for the causes, with the clear logic that is appropriate for worker understanding.

One company, after the direction it wished to go had been decided upon, followed a policy of open discussion for a year preceding contract negotiations. At every opportunity, such as in grievance meetings, the need for specific change was stated as the basic reason for the disagreement. Inequities in earnings were explained to employees in terms of the need for change. When negotiations began, management's desired change was listed in the union's demands.

When another company met organized resistance to the installation of incentives in a new division, it took the story to the floor through the supervisors. At the next election, a new slate of union officers emerged, pledging cooperation in the incentive installation desired by the members.

The manufacturing manager need not hesitate to assume his leadership role in assuring successful incentives for direct workers.

CONCLUSION

A properly conceived and properly installed wage incentive plan can provide powerful motivation for high performance. Most plans which are installed by competent technicians with the full support of manufacturing management operate satisfactorily during the period immediately following the installation. Change is inevitable in the manufacturing environment, however, and unless the manager constantly evaluates the effects of change on the incentive system and takes whatever steps may be necessary to maintain the soundness of the incentive plan, deterioration in the effectiveness of the plan will be the unhappy result.

It is perhaps quite natural for a manager to feel that once an incentive plan has been installed and is working well, the incentive project has been completed and he can turn his attention to other more pressing matters. The manager who refuses to fall into this trap will in due time find that he has developed an important competitive advantage over the managers who have turned their backs on their incentive plans and left them to others to administer.

BIBLIOGRAPHY

Aiken, William M., "Work Measurement and Incentives," in H. B. Maynard (ed.), *Handbook of Business Administration*, McGraw-Hill Book Company, New York, 1967.

Karger, D. W., and F. H. Bayha, *Engineered Work Measurement*, 2d ed., The Industrial Press, New York, 1965.

Louden, J. Keith, and J. W. Deegan, *Wage Incentives*, 2d ed., John Wiley & Sons, Inc., New York, 1959.

Maynard, H. B. (ed.), *Industrial Engineering Handbook*, 2d ed., sec. 6, McGraw-Hill Book Company, New York, 1963.

Nadler, Gerald, *Work Design*, Richard D. Irwin, Inc., Homewood, Ill., 1963.

Rotroff, Virgil H., *Work Measurement*, Reinhold Publishing Corporation, New York, 1962.

CHAPTER FOUR

Incentive Plans for Indirect Workers

WILLIAM K. HODSON *President, H. B. Maynard and Company, Incorporated, Pittsburgh, Pennsylvania*

The purpose of this chapter is to spell out the advantages and disadvantages of incentives for indirect workers. A number of case examples will be presented; and the relative costs of unmeasured, measured, and incentive applications will be analyzed.

HISTORY OF INCENTIVES

Piecework is one of the oldest forms of incentive. In the early days of an agricultural economy, the farmer traditionally worked under a piecework system. He was compensated for what he produced. The more productive his farm, the higher his income. This is the essential characteristic of any incentive plan. In the early days of the industrial revolution, piecework in the factories was quite common, particularly in the textile mills.

As the industrial system became more and more complex, it became difficult to measure the direct contribution of an individual worker. The worker no longer produced a complete "piece" of work. As a result, piecework gave way to hourly forms of compensation. Early in the 1900s, Frederick W. Taylor introduced his concepts of scientific management. One of these concepts was the use of scientific work measurement techniques. These techniques once more permitted the manager to measure the performance of individuals. This could be done even where the work was complex and interrelated to the work of other workers in the same factory. This ability to measure accurately the productivity of industrial workers gave new life to the old concepts of piecework and incentives. The concept of a piece of work or a complete end product gave way to the concept of the standard hour of work as a measure of performance.

There was a great demand, in the early twenties, for the installation of wage incentive plans based upon the concept of standard hours and accurate work measurement. Unfortunately, this great demand for men skilled in the techniques developed by Taylor, Gilbreth, Gantt, and other pioneers exceeded the supply. In many cases, the shortage was filled by inept practitioners. This resulted in a number of extremely poor incentive installations. As a consequence, a negative reaction toward the use of incentives developed on the part of some unions and managements.

AREAS OF APPLICATION

Because direct labor operations are the easiest to measure, it is only natural that early incentive applications concentrated on this type of work. As work measurement techniques became more sophisticated and as incentive applications began to saturate the direct labor activities, the more progressive managers began to make use of incentives in the indirect labor areas. This usage was accelerated by the rising ratio of indirect to direct workers. In the early factories, it was not at all unusual to have three or four direct workers for only one indirect worker. In many modern plants, the number of indirect workers exceeds the number of direct workers.

There are few, if any, areas of indirect labor that have not been covered by a wage incentive program. Following is a list of typical application areas:

1. Material handling
2. Shipping
3. Receiving
4. Warehousing
5. Tool cribs
6. Toolmaking
7. Maintenance
8. Janitorial
9. Inspect and test
10. Factory service and repair
11. Field installation and servicing
12. Clerical workers
13. Chemical and physical laboratory workers
14. Draftsmen

PROBLEMS OF APPLYING INCENTIVES

There are two fundamental problems in making an incentive application to indirect labor activities. First, it is necessary to establish carefully the methods of doing the work. These methods must then be recorded and documented. Then, a means of measuring the work and recording the output must be developed. This must be done before an installation can be made. The second fundamental problem is to maintain the plan properly after it has been installed.

The importance of maintaining standards to reflect changes in working methods or conditions cannot be overemphasized. If wage incentives are employed, management can expect to be subjected to considerable pressure from time to time to relax the standards in one way or another to permit higher earnings for the same effort or equal earnings for less effort. Despite good intentions when embarking on an incentive program, managers sometimes find it difficult to maintain this position.

A typical example of the pressure that can be exerted on management is illustrated by Figure 4-1. This chart shows the performance of a group of repairmen working under a group incentive plan. The work involved the overhaul and repair of machinery requiring factory rebuilding and servicing. The group had been on incentive for a year before the beginning of the chart, and its performance consistently averaged about 125 percent of standard.

Due to a re-layout of the plant, the rebuild and service operations were moved to a new location. At the same time, new methods, tooling, and equipment were introduced to simplify the work and to reduce costs. The industrial engineers completely reworked all the old standards to reflect the changes in methods, tooling, equipment, and working conditions.

Just before the move, in month 9, the group was allowed credit for a number of miscellaneous jobs which had accumulated over several months but which were cleared out during the move. This accounted for the somewhat higher than normal performance in month 8.

Immediately after the move, the new standards were applied to the work. The employees promptly filed a grievance claiming the standards to be too tight. Production dropped off and performance sank to 60 percent.

Management then had the industrial engineering group review all the new standards to be certain that they truly reflected actual working conditions. This took about one month, and a few changes were made. Management appealed to the employees to give the new standards a fair trial. This trial took place over months 11, 12, and 1. During this period, performance gradually climbed up toward 100 percent. In the meantime, the backlog of work had built up, and customers were complaining about the delays in shipping dates. The employees were also complaining vigorously about their loss in earnings. The industrial engineers held firmly to their position that the standards were correct and that the group could equal their previous performance if they really went to work.

Management was clearly on the spot. What should they do? Should they

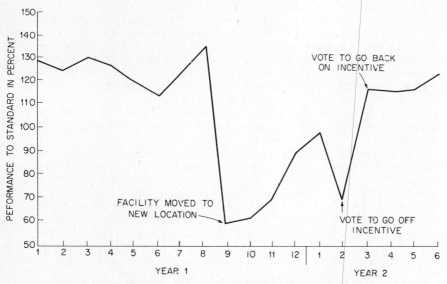

FIG. 4-1.   Effect of Change in Conditions on Incentive Earnings.

instruct the industrial engineers to loosen the standards, or should they "stick to their guns" and put up with the pressure from customers and the union? While management was wrestling with this problem, the employees voted to discontinue the incentive program. In this particular plant, the employees had the option of voting for or against the installation of incentives. They had voted "yes" two years ago and now decided to vote "no."

Performance immediately dropped to 70 percent in month 2. After two weeks of being off incentives, one employee asked to be transferred to another department. The remaining employees then voted to go back on incentives. In the next two weeks, performance went from 70 to 118 percent; and in a few months' time, the group was once again consistently averaging 125 percent.

This example is quite typical of the problems that managers face in the administration of a wage incentive program. It also illustrates the pressures that will be brought to bear to loosen the standards or to relax the maintenance of the standards. If management gives in to these pressures, degeneration of the plan will soon follow and costs will quickly get out of hand. From a manager's viewpoint, an incentive program is something like having a tiger by the tail. It is a powerful tool for controlling indirect labor costs, but it can quickly eat you up if it once gets out of hand.

An incentive plan that is not properly maintained will, in the course of time, become loose and outmoded. As the standards become loose, the workers can maintain the same level of earnings by performing less and less work. The looser the plan becomes, the more difficult it is to correct the conditions causing the looseness. The plan must be strictly maintained from the first day of installation. It cannot be used as a subject for bargaining or negotiation. If it is, it will probably collapse.

ADVANTAGES OF INCENTIVES

The problems of incentives were intentionally discussed first. This was done because the advantages of incentives are so obvious that one might wonder why they are not used universally. Many manufacturing plants do not make use of incentives for indirect workers. Perhaps it is just as well that this is the case, for these companies may not have either the industrial engineering talent or the managerial skills needed to make such a program work effectively over a long period of time. But, for those companies that do have a good industrial engineering staff and a management group interested in obtaining substantial cost reductions and long-term control over indirect labor costs, incentives offer a very powerful and effective tool. It is, however, a sophisticated tool and is not recommended for unsophisticated staffs or managers.

Most indirect labor operations are originally established with very little consideration of work simplification and effective working methods. One reason is that the work is complex. The best way of doing the work is seldom obvious. The one best way of doing a repetitive direct labor job is usually readily determinable. This is not true of indirect work. Because the development of time standards requires a detailed analysis of the work being performed, this analysis will frequently uncover better ways of doing the work. This potential for work improvement is far greater for indirect work than it is for direct work. This is another reason why incentives can produce such excellent returns.

Because indirect work is complex, it is difficult to control. Compare the difference in controlling a group of fifteen maintenance electricians with controlling a group of fifteen people on a production line that is assembling fractional horsepower motors. In the latter case, the work is highly standardized. The same tools and methods are used to turn out the same product day after day. The quantity of product produced is easily measured. In the case of maintenance men, however, no two jobs are alike. Each day's work is quite different from that of the previous day. The men are scattered all over the plant; and it is a job just to find them, let alone gage the effectiveness of their work. Because of these conditions, it is quite natural for indirect workers to be less effective and not as well managed. This means that the potential for improvement is far greater on indirect work than on direct work.

Incentives for indirect workers also offer some advantages to the accountant, in the form of more accurate product costs. Typically, indirect costs such as receiving, warehousing, and shipping are all lumped together in the form of overhead or burden rates. They are then applied to products on the basis of direct labor hours or direct labor dollars. The time standards that are developed as a by-product of the indirect incentive program can frequently permit the allocation of the indirect costs directly to products on the basis of the standard hours required per unit of product. This permits more accurate product costing. It also results in lower overhead or burden rates, and it places the control of the so-called overhead items in the hands of the operating managers. Because of these important advantages, incentives for indirect labor have a strong appeal to managers.

Are there any advantages to the workers? The most obvious advantage, of course, is the opportunity to increase take-home pay in proportion to productivity. The take-home pay of incentive workers is typically 20 to 30 percent above that of nonincentive workers. This difference in earnings is very well illustrated in one company which has a comprehensive system of indirect measurement and control. When the program was first installed, management decided to let each indirect labor group vote on whether or not the standards should be used for incentive pay purposes. Slightly more than half the employees voted for incentives. The other groups voted to operate under a measured daywork plan. The incentive groups have worked consistently at a level of 125 percent of standard. The nonincentive groups have consistently operated at 80 percent of standard.

In addition to the higher earnings opportunity, many of the more conscientious workers prefer to work at the higher work pace that incentives create. They receive some psychological values from the opportunity to work against a goal or standard. In essence, they achieve greater satisfaction from their work.

COST EFFECTIVENESS OF PROGRAM

The principal advantage of indirect incentives to the manager is the opportunity to achieve lower operating costs. How effective has this advantage proved to be in practice? Figure 4-2 shows the effect that one program of indirect labor measurement had on indirect labor costs. The ratio or percentage of indirect labor dollars to direct labor dollars is shown for the six years preceding the installation of indirect labor controls. This ratio was fairly constant around the 80 percent level. The company made extensive use of flexible budgeting during this period and felt that it was fortunate in being able to hold the line against the general tendency for this ratio to inch up

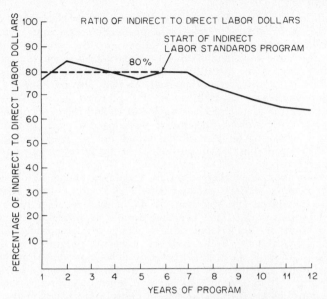

FIG. 4-2.   Effect of Indirect Labor Standards on Indirect Costs.

gradually.   A program of indirect standards was installed on a gradual basis, starting at the beginning of year 7.   Some departments elected to go on incentive and others elected not to do so.   In the latter cases, the standards were used as the basis for a measured daywork program.   The mix of the two methods was about 50–50.   Since the start of the program in year 7, the ratio of indirect to direct gradually declined from 80 to less than 65 percent. This represents a reduction of indirect labor costs of about 20 percent.   Because only 50 percent of the indirect employees were covered by the incentive program, however, the reduction could have been greater if all indirect workers had been on incentive.

LABOR COST PER STANDARD HOUR

Another way of evaluating the savings to be realized by the installation of indirect controls is by calculating the labor cost per standard hour.   A standard hour of work can be defined as the work produced in one hour by a qualified worker performing with average skill and effort.

Without the benefit of a work measurement program, typical indirect labor operations are performed at a level of about 60 percent of standard.   This performance percentage is calculated as follows:

$$\text{Percent performance} = \frac{\text{standard hours allowed}}{\text{actual hours taken}} \times 100$$

If the standard time allowed for a job is six hours, it will usually take an average indirect worker about ten hours to perform the work.   This is a performance of $6/10 \times 100$ or 60 percent.

If the worker is paid a base rate of \$4 per hour worked, then the actual labor cost for the job is \$40.   Because the job represents only six standard hours of work, the actual cost per standard hour produced is \$40/6 hours =

$6.67 per standard hour produced. At 100 percent performance, the cost per standard hour is, by definition, $4. The excess cost per standard hour, therefore, is $6.67 less $4, or $2.67 per standard hour. This excess cost is equal to 40 percent of the actual indirect labor cost:

$$\frac{\$2.67}{\$6.67} \times 100 = 40\%$$

Experience has demonstrated that the performance of workers under the stimulus of an incentive plan will be about 125 percent. For this level of effort, the typical incentive plan will pay a 25 percent bonus. In the example just given, a worker assigned to a job requiring 6 standard hours to produce will, under the stimulus of incentive, do the job in 4.8 hours or 6 standard hours/125% performance. However, he is paid for 6 hours at $4 per standard, or $24, for 4.8 actual hours of work. This represents a rate of pay for him of $24/4.8 hours = $5 per hour, or an incentive bonus of 25 percent over his base rate of $4. The cost per standard hour, however, is $4 per hour.

Experience has also demonstrated that a typical worker operating under a measured daywork plan will increase his normal pace from about 60 percent performance to about 80 percent. In this case, the worker will take 7.5 hours [(6/80%) × 100] to perform a job of 6 standard hours. The cost per standard hour is $4/80%, or $5 per hour. This represents a saving of $1.67 ($6.67 less $5) per standard hour over a daywork performance (60%) but a cost of $1 per hour more than incentive performance.

In summary, the savings that can normally be anticipated by going from a straight day rate of pay to either measured daywork or incentive are:

Rate of pay	Cost per standard hour @ $4	Cost reduction % over day rate
Day rate............................	$6.67	
Measured day rate........................	5.00	25
Incentive rate............................	4.00	40

Of course the percentage cost reduction is the same regardless of the base rate of pay.

The savings calculated above represent gross savings, but to obtain the savings, an investment must be made to develop, apply, and maintain the system. These costs will vary depending upon the type of labor measured, the frequency of changes in product line or plant rearrangement, the proficiency of the technical standards personnel, and a number of other factors. A conservative overall estimate of these costs for typical indirect labor operations is as follows:

Application of standards to new work...................	3%
Maintenance of standard data base....................	2%
Timekeeping and payroll costs........................	1%
Total..	6%

The total cost of operating and maintaining an incentive program on indirect labor operations will be about 6 percent of the indirect labor payroll.

About half the cost is spent on developing standards for new products, new jobs, and new operations. About 33 percent is spent on the routine maintenance of the system to reflect changes in equipment, methods, tooling, new factory locations, and the like. Seventeen percent is spent on keeping track of hours worked and units of work produced and on calculating incentive payrolls.

Generally, these administrative and maintenance costs will start out at a higher rate and gradually reduce. A definite learning effect seems to apply. Figure 4-3 shows the learning effect on standards application and maintenance costs for a typical installation.

A Case Example. Figure 4-4 provides some basic information on the use of indirect labor standards for cost control. This plant employed a total of about 800 indirect workers. An initial survey indicated that about 60 percent of these workers, or about 500, could be measured with conventional work measurement techniques. The survey also indicated a potential labor saving of almost $1.5 million per year. Because the union contract required each group of employees to approve the installation of incentives by a majority vote, the installation of incentives was optional. In those cases where the employees voted against incentives, a conventional measured daywork plan was installed. About half the groups elected to accept incentives.

The installation of indirect labor standards started about the middle of year 1. A management consulting firm was employed to make the survey, train a group of company personnel in the techniques of indirect labor measurement, and supply a bank of standard data for all indirect operations.

Figure 4-4 shows the number of employees covered by incentives or mea-

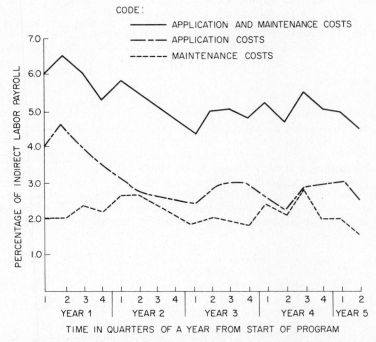

FIG. 4-3. Effect of Learning on Cost of Applying and Maintaining Time Standards.

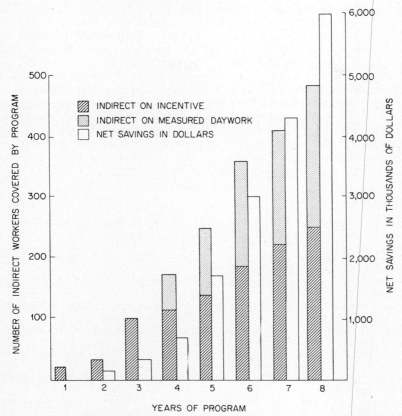

FIG. 4-4 Results Obtained in a Typical Indirect Labor Standards Program.

sured daywork each year. Also shown are the net savings that accrued from this program each year. The cost of consulting services and the cost of the company's personnel were deducted from the gross savings to arrive at the net savings figure.

By the end of the first year, the program was just breaking even; the cost of installation just equaled the gross savings. By the end of the second year, the program showed a net saving of about $100,000. By the end of eight years, the program covered a total of 480 people and was producing savings at an annual rate of $1.7 million per year. The cumulative net saving for the eight-year period amounted to $6 million. These savings would have been almost twice this amount if all employees had elected to accept the incentive program. Employee take-home pay was about 25 percent greater for incentive personnel.

CONCLUSION

One of the major advantages of indirect labor controls based upon sound work measurement standards is that they provide a sound basis for long-term cost reduction and continuous control. Many managers have been tempted to use quick and easy approaches to controlling indirect labor costs. These approaches frequently involve the establishment of approximate or estimated standards and concentrate on the scheduling of work in small batches with close supervision and follow-up. This approach has produced quick results in amazingly short periods of time. The results have generally proved to be short-lived, however, because the standards are not soundly established or clearly based upon given methods, equipment, and working conditions. As is true with so many management problems, the quick and easy approach in the short range turns out to be the least effective and the most expensive in the long range. Although this quick and easy approach is tempting when viewed from a short-range profit viewpoint, a more soundly conceived program, based upon properly developed work standards, is a better long-range solution to the problem of controlling indirect labor costs.

BIBLIOGRAPHY

"Be Practical? or Precise? in Measuring Indirect Work," *Factory*, December, 1964.

Bennett, K. W., "Putting Incentive Back into Wage Incentives," *Iron Age*, Nov. 25, 1965.

Devaney, R. J., and R. G. Lee, "Your Incentive Plan: Does It Need Revising?" *Administrative Management*, July, 1966.

Grove, V. A., and R. Reul, "Wage Incentives for Maintenance: Do They Pay Off?" *Factory*, February, 1964.

Louden, J. Keith, and J. W. Deegan, *Wage Incentives*, 2d ed., John Wiley & Sons, Inc., New York, 1959.

Mangum, G. L., *Wage Incentive Systems*, Institute of Industrial Relations, University of California, Berkeley, 1964.

W. H. Wein, and others, "Sensitivity Analysis for a Wage Incentive System," *Business Topics*, Summer, 1966.

Wilkinson, John J., "How to Manage Maintenance," *Harvard Business Review*, March–April, 1968.

Williams J. A., "Master Plan for Office Incentives," *Administrative Management*, April, 1965.

CHAPTER FIVE

Supervisory Motivation and Compensation

ARTHUR C. BOYDEN *Director, Staff Manufacturing, 3M Company, Saint Paul, Minnesota*

One of the most critical aspects of any manufacturing operation is the effectiveness of the first-line supervisor who generally supervises from five to twenty-five nonsupervisory employees. His effectiveness or ineffectiveness directly influences the results of those supervised, thereby multiplying his own efforts many times. To be effective, the supervisor must be successfully motivated by his manager.

Successful motivation of manufacturing line and staff supervisors results from:

1. The manager's ability to plan, organize, lead, and control the operations
2. The use of specific operation improvement goals
3. Proper selection, placement, and training of supervisors
4. Adequate financial compensation
5. Good interaction between the manager and the supervisor

The term "supervisor" as used in this chapter applies to personnel no more than one or two levels removed from nonsupervisory employees. The supervisor does not generally determine policy but does carry it out. He is concerned with training, work assignment, and control over the work of nonsupervisory employees. He usually has a good technical knowledge of the work to be performed and is very close to daily problems and the solutions to these problems. He may be in a manufacturing line or staff function. The latter may include supervisors of quality control, industrial engineering, production control, plant personnel, plant engineering, process engineering, or other manufacturing support functions.

RESPONSIBILITIES OF THE MANAGER

An understanding of the manager's responsibilities is an important first step to the understanding of how to motivate supervisors. This is because the manager's ability and success in planning, organizing, motivating, and controlling his operations has a major bearing upon the supervisor's effectiveness. A potentially good supervisor under a poor manager may be a poor supervisor. A potentially poor supervisor under a good manager may be a good supervisor.

Planning. The manager must establish the overall objectives of the organization within the framework of division and corporate objectives. He applies developmental and creative thinking to determine the future requirements of the organization. He must be constantly looking ahead.

Organizing. Based upon overall objectives, the manager determines function requirements and proper personnel placement, particularly placement of supervisory personnel.

Motivating. In motivating supervisors, the manager establishes objectives and measurements of performance for individuals. He exerts his leadership through personal enthusiasm and inspiration of personnel and through encouragement of teamwork to meet objectives.

Controlling. The manager must know the status of his operations at all times. To do this, he needs measurements and progress reporting against the major objectives established. He must also counsel with subordinates on objectives and progress.

USE OF SPECIFIC OPERATIONS IMPROVEMENT GOALS

One of the most practical approaches to performing the manager's motivating and controlling functions is the use of specific operations improvement goals with his supervisors. This approach is often referred to as "management by objectives."

The supervisor's stimulation comes from participating in establishing improvement goals, his own development of plans to attain these goals, and his actual accomplishment of the objective which he and the manager can both determine based upon objective measurements. This approach emphasizes goals to be reached rather than activities necessary for reaching them.

The supervisor is held accountable for doing whatever is necessary, within policy and human relations limitations, for reaching the objectives. He uses his own creativeness to develop plans. He is not told how to accomplish the objectives. Relatively few goals are set for any one job, perhaps five to seven. If a supervisor successfully handles each of these, he is successful overall. The supervisor, as well as the manager, is able to judge his performance on a current basis and to derive job satisfaction and further motivation from his accomplishment.

The manager should make every effort to be results oriented, not personality, politically, organizationally, or emotionally oriented. He should establish the climate for management by objectives.

Measurements for all significant factors of the operation should be established and reported on a current basis in index form. From these measurements, the supervisor knows what past performance has been and what present performance is, and can set realistic targets for improved performance based upon specific plans. Accountability for objectives should be personal.

Some requirements of objectives as reviewed by E. C. Schleh in *Management by Results*[1] are:

Should be reasonable (and attainable, set in light of all known existing conditions)

Should be set for a man in any area where he has strong influence on the result, even though he does not have full control

Should require some improvement in operation from each man in each period

Should change from year to year

Are most effective if set in advance of the period they are to cover

Should ordinarily be in writing

CASE HISTORY—MANAGEMENT BY OBJECTIVES

To illustrate the effectiveness of this phase of supervisory motivation, an actual case history of management by objectives will be described.

Objectives for the company used in this case history start at the top of the company, as they do with most companies. These objectives are quite clear and are in terms of sales, profit growth, and return on investment. Profit responsibility is decentralized to product divisions. These divisions forecast sales, expense, profits, return on investment, and new-product growth which are in turn reviewed by a corporate management committee. Objectives are specific at this level of the company organization. Generally, as one moves lower in the organization, objectives become much less quantitative.

This case history was initiated on a pilot basis in the company's finished goods distribution center, an operation of 177 employees servicing the customers of a number of the company's product divisions. Later, the management by objectives approach was extended to several of the firm's manufacturing plants.

Finished Goods Operation. Functions included in finished goods operation were:

1. Ordering finished goods from manufacturing plants
2. Stocking finished goods and controlling inventories
3. Order filling, packing, and shipping for customer order
4. Order filling, packing, and shipping for sixteen regional warehouses
5. Consolidating and shipping goods made to customer order

Supervisory Organization. The supervisory organization included the following: superintendent, general foreman, foremen, order department and data processing supervisors, and industrial engineering supervisor.

Annual Volume Data. At the time of initiation of the pilot management by objectives program, the annual volume data were:

Order filling	43 million pounds
Shipping	79 million pounds
Export packing	5 million pounds
Expense	$2 million
Number of nonsupervisory personnel	155
Number of supervisors	22
Number of items stocked	6,000
Percent of customer orders to total orders	47%

[1] Edward C. Schleh, *Management by Results*, McGraw-Hill Book Company, New York, 1961.

Program Installation. The initial effort in the installation of the program was placed upon obtaining measurements of the major factors affecting the operation. Meaningful measurements were generally lacking. Indices were not available. Service data were inadequate. The cost accounting system had to be revised to provide additional burden centers and to provide for the reporting of unit costs.

Monthly cost and service objectives for the first year were then established upon available crude data. Four or five operations improvement objectives were established with each supervisor. This was done with his participation in operating meetings. Each supervisor then developed plans to attain his objectives. He knew all the organization's objectives as well as his own.

Industrial engineering played a key supportive role by providing measurements of many of the significant factors, by assisting supervisors with project work required to accomplish objectives, and by performing the functions of methods analysis, layout, work measurement, incentive administration, systems and procedure work, work sampling of office operations, space utilization studies, evaluation and selection of equipment, and facilities review. Teamwork was at a very high level.

Primary Measurements. Measurements were first established for the most significant phases of the operation. These were:

Service . . . . % orders shipped same day order received
                                               % orders shipped within 24 hours
Quality of service . . . . % errors, customer orders
                                               % errors, regional warehouse orders
Cost . . . . Unit cost by department
                                               Accounting reported cost reduction projects as a % of
                                               total expense

These measurements were established for individual departments and for the operation as a whole. The targets and actual experience for the first four and one-half years of operation in each primary measurement were as follows:

Service	Year				
	1	2	3	4	5 (6 months)
% orders shipped same day					
Target	. . . . . .	30	50	55	60
Actual	12	26	45	53	59
% orders shipped in 24 hours					
Target	. . . . . .	50	75	85	85
Actual	27	60	82	84	86

Actual service levels are determined daily.

Quality of service	Year				
	1	2	3	4	5 (6 months)
% errors—customer orders					
Target		1.0	0.5	0.3	0.1
Actual	2.0	0.9	0.6	0.2	0.1
% errors—regional warehouse orders*					
Target		2.0	2.0	1.0	1.0
Actual	2.7	2.8	2.6	1.5	1.4

Actual quality levels are determined weekly.
* Errors on regional warehouse orders are internal to the company and orders are not checked before shipment.

Unit cost by department	Year				
	1	2	3	4	5 (6 months)
Storage and order filling, $ cost per 100 pounds:					
Target		1.80	1.40	1.36	1.32
Actual	2.19	1.70	1.41	1.59	1.34
Shipping, $ cost per 100 pounds:					
Target		0.45	0.40	0.36	0.31
Actual	0.51	0.47	0.40	0.32	0.28
Export packing, $ cost per 100 pounds:					
Target		3.45	3.20	2.45	2.25
Actual	4.19	3.36	3.21	2.53	2.31
Order department A, $ cost per order entry item:					
Target		0.65	0.62	0.59	0.44
Actual	0.70	0.66	0.67	0.57	0.41
Order department B, $ cost per order entry item:					
Target		0.55	0.49	0.44	0.40
Actual	0.60	0.49	0.51	0.44	0.38
Computer department $ cost per order entry item:					
Target		0.55	0.51	0.51	0.48
Actual	0.58	0.54	0.48	0.47	0.43
Shipping office, $ cost per order entry item:					
Target		0.45	0.41	0.36	0.30
Actual	0.49	0.44	0.38	0.30	0.20

Unit cost targets for each six months' period are determined by projecting volume, specific cost reduction programs, and cost increases for the period. Actual unit costs are determined monthly.

Cost reduction projects	Year					
					5	
	1	2	3	4	1st quarter	2d quarter
Cost reduction dollars as % of total expense						
Target.................	....	3.0	5.0	6.0	6.0	6.0
Actual...............	1.1	2.4	4.9	6.6	7.2	7.8

Secondary Measurements. During the first two years, a number of necessary changes in supervision were made to strengthen the management by objectives program. Also, a number of secondary measurements were established and progressively emphasized in objectives until improvement and control over each were attained. These secondary measurements were:

1. Percent of back orders
2. Percent of orders shipped in 2, 3, 4, or more days by reason
3. Labor performance percent by department
4. Analysis of orders not shipped on schedule by reason
5. Variable unit cost by department
6. Stock rotation analysis
7. Maintenance cost as percent of total expense
8. Overtime hours as percent of total hours
9. Space utilization as percent of total space
10. Loading quality, percent good to total
11. Drayage cost analysis, per trip and cube utilization
12. Injury experience, severity and frequency
13. Grievance analysis by cause
14. Absenteeism analysis
15. Cycle inventory discrepancies by type
16. Damaged cartons, percent to cartons handled
17. Percent of orders expedited
18. Slow-moving stock report, dollar value to total
19. Inventory usage and balance reports
20. Bin location analysis, activity

Motivation and Personnel Development. Some of the motivation and personnel development results in this case history of management by objectives were:

1. It provided an excellent tool for supervisory development and for objective determination of the capabilities of supervisors based upon results. During the four-year period, seven supervisors were promoted to heavier assignments in other departments of the company.

2. Job satisfaction for supervisors was considerably greater as they had freedom of action to meet their objectives. Their individual objectives were compatible with those of others in the organization.

Supervisors worked independently of one another on specific areas of responsibility with the confidence that they were all going in the same direction (according to overall objectives). This eliminated duplication of effort, contradictory effort, and liaison, communications, and meeting delays.

3. Self-evaluation by most supervisors was easily made. Evaluation by the manager was also easily determined by comparing results with objectives, recognizing happenings beyond the supervisor's control.

4. The organization ran extremely smoothly with very few service complaints compared to the many which existed in the earlier part of the program.

Relationships with other groups in the company improved significantly and these groups, in turn, contributed substantially to the results of the program (divisional planning groups, accounting, traffic, and others).

5. Once the management by objectives program was established and staffed with capable supervisory personnel, the manager's functions relating to motivation and controlling became almost self-administering. This gave him more time for the planning and organizing phases which he found were also of interest to his top-level supervisors. They in turn contributed to these functions.

Case History Summary. Based upon this pilot experience, the program has been successfully extended to a number of the company's manufacturing operations in both domestic and international divisions. In addition, management by objectives is being used by some laboratory, sales, and administrative groups.

Many firms using management by objectives start with the personnel appraisal—defining job responsibilities and identifying objectives for each individual.

The pilot approach for this company and for later applications started with an identification of the specific significant measures of an operation, which if improved, would contribute substantially to the mission of the operation.

Once these measures were identified, individual supervisory improvement goals and plans for attaining them were readily established by each supervisor and manager.

SUPERVISORY SELECTION AND TRAINING

Properly selected, placed, and trained supervisors are more easily motivated because they have the necessary qualifications for their job and can quickly respond to the needs of the organization.

Selection. Too often the procedure used to select supervisors, particularly manufacturing line supervisors, is to select the best producer from the non-supervisory group. This individual often does not have the necessary qualifications for the supervisory position.

Another common problem in supervisory selection results from inadequate planning for filling future supervisory needs. The problem occurs when a supervisor is transferred or leaves the company, or an expanded work volume occurs and a new supervisor is needed. Because of the urgency for filling the job, a supervisor is quickly selected with limited consideration and becomes a supervisor overnight without preparation for the position. Improperly or hastily selected supervisors usually are not able to grow with job requirements.

The recommended selection procedure is as follows:

Establish Qualifications. Qualifications are most important. Intelligence, drive and initiative, personal enthusiasm, human relations ability, job knowledge and experience, and good physical stamina are necessary qualifications. The best way to determine these is by performance in the actual job situation with multiple evaluation by several well-qualified supervisors and or managers.

Establish Candidate Pool. The recommended approach is to develop a supervisory candidate pool of qualified and trained candidates to select from when supervisory vacancies occur. This involves some classroom training, one or more supervisory experiences on the job (such as fill-in supervisor for vacations), and temporary assignment in one or more supporting staff groups such as quality control or industrial engineering.

The following is one company's supervisory candidate program for manufacturing line positions.

SUPERVISORY CANDIDATE PROGRAM—3M COMPANY—DIVISION A

The seven steps followed in this program are:

1. Appointment of a plant supervisory selection and development committee composed of interested and well-qualified line and staff managers of the division manufacturing organization
2. Determination of supervisory qualifications required and tests to supplement on-the-job experience with the candidate
3. Review of plan with all present supervisors and nomination of candidates by supervisors
4. Screening, interviewing, and testing of potential candidates
5. Selection; interview of rejected candidates
6. Training of candidates in pool
7. Selection of future supervisors from this pool

The orientation and training of candidates consist of the following:

1. *Formal instruction.* Survey in approximately sixteen hours of such subjects as:
   a. Supervisor's responsibility
   b. Job training
   c. Human relations
   d. Work measurement and incentive plans
   e. Production control
   f. Quality control
   g. Cost control
   h. Safety
   i. Management responsibilities, expectations, and basic functions
   j. Work simplification

   Instruction is given by person best qualified in following order of desirability:
   a. Immediate supervision
   b. Secondary supervision
   c. Plant staff
   d. Division staff
   e. Training department

2. *On-the-job experience.*
   a. Each supervisory candidate must serve in the capacity of foreman for a temporary period of approximately two to three months.
   b. In addition, while in the candidate pool, he will have limited project assignments in several of the following groups to learn the general responsibilities of these manufacturing staff groups:
      (1) Production control
      (2) Quality control
      (3) Industrial engineering
      (4) Industrial relations
      (5) Plant engineering
      (6) Warehousing

3. *Outside improvement.* Based upon the needs of each individual, guidance is given on ways in which the individual can improve himself through night school, correspondence study, and reading.

Evaluation and selection of new supervisors are then made from the candidate pool.

Training. Once appointed to supervisor, additional training is given by the line manager and his supervisors. It is extremely important that this be the manager's training program, given by him with whatever assistance he requires. The following is an example of a supervisory training program for line manufacturing supervisors.

MANUFACTURING LINE SUPERVISORY TRAINING PROGRAM— 3M COMPANY—DIVISION A

1. *Labor relations and shop discipline—6 hours.* Discussion of labor contract, principles of grievance handling, guides for proper discipline. Case study evaluations and discussion.
2. *Working with individuals—10 hours.* Presentation of the key motivating drives that cause employees to react to shop situations. Evaluation of individual employee's drive pattern. Discussion and suggestions on how each drive can be positively enlisted to improve work habits and attitudes.
3. *Human relations film program and discussion—6 hours.*
   a. The personal problem—recognition of personal problems and how to deal with them.
   b. The hidden grievance—some grievances have deeper roots than appear on the surface. It is important to be able to detect and deal with the real causes.
   c. Delegating work—discussion of effect on foremen and employees of improper work delegation.
   d. Personality conflict—some employee relations problems are caused by personality clashes between supervision and employees.
   e. Enforcing rules and procedures—foremen's consistent and fair application of rules and procedures has a major effect on their enforcement.
4. *Production control and planning—4 hours.* Discussion of shop production control system and ways to improve its application. Critical evaluation and discussion of problems that need solving.
5. *Developing better communications—2 hours.* Film on how to listen effectively. Discussion on practical ways to improve day-to-day shop communications.
6. *Process engineering, job estimating, and work performance control—2 hours.* Discussion of different systems of job estimating and necessity of maintaining accurate estimating for work performance control. What foremen can do to help maintain consistent job estimates. Use of estimates to improve work performance.
7. *Instructing employees on the job—2 hours.* Presentation of four-step method of on-the-job training with practical situation practice.
8. *Cost control and programs for profit—4 hours.* Discussion of "program for profit" approach to cost reduction. Idea sessions with other supervisors on several areas of cost reduction possibilities:
   a. Scrap reduction and control
   b. Downtime and nonproductive time reductions
   c. Small tools, fixtures, and miscellaneous supplies control
   d. Other
9. *Improving manpower and equipment utilization—2 hours.* Discussion of ways in which shop could improve its application of men and equipment for greater efficiency and effectiveness. Evaluation of job structure, skill requirements, and rotation through different skills.
10. *Handling problem employees—2 hours.* A discussion and case study of different problem employee situations:
    a. Poor performer
    b. Chronic absentee
    c. The employee who distracts and affects others

    d. The negative influence

    e. The "needler"

11. *Absenteeism control—1 hour.* Evaluation and discussion of various means of controlling absenteeism.

12. *Selling management ideas and programs—4 hours.* Study of basic elements of persuasion and salesmanship, use of positive tools of selling in presenting common work objectives and programs to employees (role playing and case studies). What part can the union be expected to play in participating in the management program?

13. *Management reporting, record keeping, and paperwork—1 hour.* Discussion of need for good reporting and basic considerations in keeping records and submitting reports.

14. *Handling employee complaints and grievances—2 hours.* Review and discussion of principles in grievance handling. Discussion of basic approach to informal gripes and complaints. Film and discussion on arbitration in action. Mock grievance session.

15. *Maintaining safe, clean, and orderly work conditions—1 hour.* Discussion of ways to improve and maintain housekeeping, safe conditions, and orderly layout in shop.

16. *Encouraging and handling employee suggestions—1 hour.* Discussion of need for employee participation in improving the shop and of ways in which supervision can solicit and promote employee suggestions.

17. *Work simplification and systems improvement—2 hours.* Presentation of basic tools of evaluating present systems. Developing "improvement complex." Discussion of application of work simplification to shop situation.

18. *Basic leadership characteristics—2 hours.* A study of those characteristics that distinguish a leader from a follower and how a man can develop leadership skills.

19. *Evaluating employees and discussing progress with them—1 hour.* Introduction of day-to-day and periodic performance evaluation of employees. Discussion of motivation value of this approach.

20. *A survey of management responsibilities, expectations, and basic functions—10 hours.* A comprehensive presentation of the elements that make up the management function, the manager, and the relationship between superior and subordinate. A review of the many characteristics that make up the management function. Discussion of what employees expect and respect from their boss.

FINANCIAL COMPENSATION

The financial compensation of supervisors is primarily determined by comparisons internal to the company. The pay relationship to the subordinates that he supervises is one factor. Job evaluation, establishing the supervisor's pay relationship with personnel in other functions and those above him in the organization, is the other internal factor. External market pay relationships may indirectly affect the supervisor's pay through salary surveys, by which market conditions are reflected in the company's salary structure and ranges for salary grades.

Pay Differential with Subordinates. The supervisor's pay differential with subordinates is one which must be closely watched. The pay policies for nonsupervisory employees may include base, overtime, shift premium, and incentive pay. The supervisor may not receive all these components of gross pay, and as a result may be outearned by the nonsupervisory employee for equivalent time worked.

An equitable differential pay policy should be established for the supervisor, considering some or all of the components of gross pay of both supervisory and nonsupervisory personnel. Each firm must make its own determination because of its unique interrelationships. Some examples of policies for pay differentials are:

1. Supervisor's base salary at least 15 percent higher than the base, incentive, and shift premium earnings rate of highest employee supervised. In this example, the supervisor does not receive incentive.
2. Supervisor's pay grade at least two grades higher than highest employee supervised. In this example, no incentive is paid to either supervisor or nonsupervisory employee.
3. Supervisor's gross pay at least 10 percent higher than gross pay of highest paid subordinate.
4. Supervisor's gross pay at least 20 percent more than average of all subordinates.

Some companies determine pay groups for line manufacturing foremen based solely upon the pay differential policy established.

Overtime pay and incentive pay are the major contributors to pay differential problems when they do occur. This is because they do not lend themselves to a fixed relationship. For example, in the case of overtime, the supervisor may be paid for overtime work but may not be required to work as many overtime hours as nonsupervisory employees. In the case of incentive payments, there may be a wide variation in nonsupervisory incentive earnings.

Overtime Pay. Most companies treat supervisory overtime in one of four ways:

1. No payment for overtime—compensatory time off
2. Straight time payment
3. Payment of premium rates different from the rates of employees supervised
4. Payment of the same premium rates to both supervisors and nonsupervisors

An excellent review of the overtime subject, including some representative pay plans, is "Overtime Pay for Exempt Employees," National Industrial Conference Board Studies in Personnel Policy Number 208, 1967.

Job Evaluation. Job evaluation establishes the supervisor's pay relationship with other jobs in the company and is a systematic and orderly method for determining the value of his job relative to other company jobs.

The initial step is to draw up a job description outlining the supervisor's responsibilities, organization relationships, and work assignments.

The job is then evaluated against whatever job evaluation plan is in use in the company. There are four commonly used methods of evaluation leading to a variety of plans.

The evaluation places the job in a salary grade which has an assigned dollar range. The dollar range is updated periodically through salary surveys of other companies. The supervisor's actual salary within this range is determined by his manager based upon periodic merit ratings and recommendations for salary increases.

There are many references detailing the establishment of salary administration programs. A concise reference is contained in Section 11 of the *Handbook of Business Administration*.[2]

[2] H. B. Maynard (ed.), *Handbook of Business Administration*, McGraw-Hill Book Company, New York, 1967.

Supervisory Incentives. Incentive plans for the supervisor, where used, are of three general types:
1. Plans based upon the labor performance of subordinates
2. Company or division profit sharing plans
3. Plans based upon measurable factors for which his department is directly responsible

Plans based upon the labor performance of subordinates have a number of disadvantages and are not recommended. They usually cover only one segment of the supervisor's responsibility, labor cost, and have the added disadvantage of encouraging loose standards.

Participation in company or division profit sharing plans has the advantage of helping the supervisor feel that he is a part of management. However, the direct tie-in with the results of his own efforts is somewhat remote, and the incentive is therefore not strong.

The third type of plan is most effective because it emphasizes the several most important controllable cost and effectiveness factors of the supervisor's own job. These plans must be designed for the specific operation to be covered. Generally several factors are a part of the plan, such as labor cost, quality level, absenteeism rate, and schedule performance. Improvement in these factors earns incentive pay usually expressed as a percent of base pay. Incentive pay is most often paid monthly or quarterly in a separate check. Some companies use a comprehensive standard cost system as a measurement upon which the manufacturing line supervisor's incentive is based. The plan should be relatively simple and based upon measurable factors over which the supervisor has direct control.

Several cautions are in order.
1. Initial improvement is often attained the first few years, after which a level of incentive pay is established with little improvement thereafter.
2. Before installing the incentive plan in a department, the supervisor's total pay relationship with subordinates and those above him in the organization as well as supervisors in other departments should be carefully considered.
3. Measurement of results is affected by accounting procedures and reporting.
4. Installation of an incentive plan in one department based upon objectively measured factors may be entirely possible, but may not be practical in other departments.

Another approach is to use this type of incentive plan for a specific period of time, such as one year, to help attain specific improvement goals in a particular department. Experience with this approach has been excellent and is recommended.

Pay as a Motivator. Many studies have been made to determine the effect of pay and other job factors upon motivation. Most of these studies indicate that inequitable or inadequate pay is a "dissatisfier" and contributes to poor job climate. As such, it detracts from the supervisor's motivation.

However, it does not necessarily follow that equitable and adequate pay is a great contributor to the supervisor's motivation. Other factors, such as high-performance goals previously discussed, achievement of these goals, recognition for this achievement, and interest in the work, are major motivators.

SUPERVISOR-MANAGER INTERACTION

A major stimulus to supervisory motivation and accomplishment is the interpersonal action between the supervisor and the manager and the manner in which the manager carries out his responsibilities described earlier. Supervisory performance is very often a direct reflection of the manager's own performance.

Fundamental to good supervisory motivation is a genuine interest on the part of the manager in the supervisor's objectives, progress, and results. This is a very simple and often overlooked means of providing a sense of accomplishment to the supervisor, thereby spurring him on to greater accomplishment.

A great deal has been written by the behavioral scientists on the subject of motivation. Many of these principles have been reviewed in Chapter 1 of this section. Those often referred to are Abraham Maslow's "Need Hierarchy," Douglas McGregor's "Theory X and Y," Frederick Herzberg's "Motivation–Hygiene Concept," and Rensis Likert's studies on leadership. Likert has emphasized supportive management in his *New Patterns of Management*.[3]

Best results are obtained when an organization uses its manpower as members of a well-knit, effectively functioning work group with high-performance goals. The manager makes a conscious effort to use the abilities of each individual in the group as well as the power of the group. Group loyalty is high. Each individual identifies with the organizational goals as well as with his own.

The high-producing manager is viewed by his subordinates as friendly and helpful. He shows confidence in his subordinates and has high expectations of their performance. He sees that subordinates are well trained and helps them get promoted. He coaches and assists supervisors whose performance does not reach goals established. The working relationship among the members of the group is relaxed and objective, with a high degree of trust and confidence displayed. Creativity is stimulated by this supportive atmosphere. Communication among members is good.

CONCLUSION

The successful motivation of supervisors requires much more than adequate financial incentives and compensation. Initial selection of supervisors to meet carefully determined qualifications is an important first step. Proper placement of the supervisor according to job demand and the individual's abilities is a second step. His understanding of what is expected of him is critical to good job performance. On-the-job training and self-improvement programs are important.

A very significant motivator is the supervisor's participation in establishing measurable improvement goals for his operation and the review of progress toward these goals.

Finally, the interaction between the manager and the supervisor; the manager's ability to plan, organize, lead, and control the operations; and his genuine interest in the supervisor's performance against objectives have a major bearing upon the supervisor's effectiveness.

[3] Rensis Likert, *New Patterns of Management*, McGraw-Hill Book Company, New York, 1961.

BIBLIOGRAPHY

Belcher, David W., *Wage and Salary Administration*, 2d ed., Prentice-Hall, Inc., Englewood Cliffs, N.J., 1962.

Blake, Robert R., and Jane S. Mouton, *The Managerial Grid*, Gulf Publishing Company, Houston, Tex., 1964.

Maslow, A. H., *Motivation and Personality*, Harper & Row, Publishers, Incorporated, New York, 1954.

McGregor, Douglas, *The Human Side of Enterprise*, McGraw-Hill Book Company, New York, 1960.

McGregor, Douglas, *Leadership and Motivation*, Massachusetts Institute of Technology, Cambridge, Mass., 1966.

McGregor, Douglas, *The Professional Manager*, McGraw-Hill Book Company, New York, 1967.

Odiorne, George S., *Management by Objectives*, Pitman Publishing Company, New York, 1965.

Pigors, Paul, and Charles A. Myers, *Personnel Administration: A Point of View and a Method*, 6th ed., McGraw-Hill Book Company, New York, 1969.

Schleh, Edward C., *Management by Results*, McGraw-Hill Book Company, New York, 1961.

Scott, Walter D., Robert C. Clothier, and William R. Spriegel, *Personnel Management*, 6th ed., McGraw-Hill Book Company, New York, 1961.

Sibson, Robert E., *Wages and Salaries: A Handbook for Line Supervisors*, rev. ed., American Management Association, New York, 1967.

Strauss, George, and Leonard R. Sayles, *Personnel: The Human Problems of Management*, Prentice-Hall, Inc., Englewood Cliffs, N.J., 1967.

CHAPTER SIX

Salary Determination and Incentives for Managerial Employees

DEAN H. ROSENSTEEL   *Dean H. Rosensteel & Co., Inc., New York, New York*

Management, sometimes defined as the art of getting things done through people, finds compensation administration one of its most important responsibilities. This responsibility cannot be separated from others, but instead must be considered an integral and inseparable part of total management. Experience shows that compensation, equitably and fairly administered, with a genuine purpose of motivation, is a prime factor in accomplishing all the objectives of a business enterprise.

Seldom, if ever, is a compensation program developed only for the manufacturing function. These programs cover all functions and all departments because one of their prime purposes is to maintain equity and consistency among all positions in all functions within a company.

Most well-managed companies have some degree of formalized salary administration and incentive programs, and of course, all such programs are constantly being studied, improved, and refined. The participation of all executives of an organization is universally invited in the development, application, and maintenance of these plans and programs. Therefore an understanding of their underlying principles is vital in any management job.

The elements of a comprehensive salary program are listed below.
1. Philosophy or basic policies
2. Charts or plans of organization
3. Position descriptions
4. Salary ranges and structure
5. Allocation of positions to salary grades
6. Salary administration policies
7. Incentive compensation

8. Relating compensation to accomplishment
9. Deferred compensation
10. Stock acquisition plans
11. Pension and insurance benefits
12. Perquisites and nonfinancial incentives

Although this list serves for all salaried personnel, there are differences in emphasis and interpretation for management personnel, which where applicable will be covered in the discussion of each of the elements.

PHILOSOPHIES OR BASIC POLICIES

Philosophies or basic policies have essentially the same objectives in most companies but there are wide differences in application. For example, over the years some prominent companies have attributed much of their growth and success to liberal incentive systems, particularly for management personnel. They have paid relatively low or modest salaries, but total compensation, including incentive payments, has far exceeded that of corresponding positions in other companies. However, only about 60 percent of the manufacturing companies in the nation have used incentive systems for management employees, and some companies have placed emphasis on security by maintaining attractive pension, insurance, and other benefits. The variations are discernible only from an intimate knowledge of individual company practices.

The following policy statement is for a company which pays relatively high salaries and modest incentive payments, with substantial benefit programs and attractive plans for employee stock ownership.

CORPORATE COMPENSATION PHILOSOPHY

Programs will be maintained which enable the company to employ, retain, and equitably compensate men and women well qualified for the positions to which they are assigned. Its aim is to encourage each individual to produce to the best of his abilities in the best interests of the company.

Salary levels are determined by management judgment with full knowledge of rates paid for comparable positions in other companies, economic trends, ability to employ needed personnel, and any other factors which may have a bearing on the salary structure.

Salary ranges for positions are determined by an evaluation process which recognizes both the value of the jobs in the employment market and the value of the positions within the company. Every job is described in writing for this purpose. Individual employees are paid rates which are within the range established for the position to which each is assigned, and in accordance with approved policies.

In addition to salaries paid according to evaluations and the structure referred to above, annual incentive payments will be made, as has been the practice over a long period of years. Such amounts individually and in total for the corporation may increase or decrease based upon the profitability of the corporation and upon an appraisal of the performance and contribution of individual officers and employees.

These payments may be in the form of cash, company common stock, or certificates of extra compensation, and may be payable currently, or may be deferred over a specified number of years, to retirement, or over a period of years after retirement, all in the sole discretion of the Compensation Committee.

In addition to the foregoing, options to purchase company stock may be granted to selected officers and employees, approved by the Stock Option Committee in accordance with such plans as may, from time to time, be approved by the Board of Directors and the Stockholders.

In addition to its basic compensation policy, the corporation attempts to maintain retirement plans and group life, accident, disability, and health insurance plans which are comparable with the best of such plans maintained by similar and competitive companies.

All management responsibilities with respect to compensation are included in a Corporate Compensation Program. The Corporate Management intends to review these policies and plans periodically for the purpose of making such adjustments and changes as are considered advisable to keep them current and in accord with what is considered good business practice.

Because quite similar companies have been equally successful with widely varying basic policies, it must be concluded that each company must develop the philosophy considered best suited to its own operations.

CHARTS OR PLANS OF ORGANIZATION

Organizational relationships are discussed in detail elsewhere in this Handbook. It is therefore necessary to mention here only their importance to compensation administration. Because one of the prime purposes of compensation programs is to develop consistent and equitable pay relationships, it is necessary to know the position to which each person reports, the number of employees supervised, and the organization through which these employees are directed.

Separate organization plans are not necessary for compensation purposes, but plans in use can be profitably enhanced by the compensation program. For example, while studying organizational relations for compensation purposes, audits can be made to assure that all positions are essential to the accomplishment of the organization's objectives, that they are logically assigned, that optimum skills and abilities are utilized, and that lines of authority and communication are clearly understood and followed.

POSITION DESCRIPTIONS

The need for the use of position descriptions is so widely accepted that again it is necessary to comment here only on their use for compensation purposes. Generally, each description will contain a brief statement of the purpose of the job, the qualifications required, a list of major responsibilities, and references to fundamental relationships inside and outside the organization.

A marked difference between descriptions of management positions and nonsupervisory jobs is that the management position description must contain data on the scope or magnitude of the job. The descriptions of two manufacturing vice presidents could read practically verbatim, but one could be paid $15,000, and the other $50,000, the difference being in the size, scope, or magnitude of the two positions. Plant manager descriptions could also read alike, except for the scope data which are essential to justify differences in pay levels.

These scope data typically include the size of the organization supervised in numbers of employees; the classifications of personnel supervised; the value of the products produced; the investments in supplies, materials, equipment, and property for which the position is held accountable; and any additional financial or statistical data which can be used to compare the position with others within the company and with similar positions elsewhere.

Management employees are normally requested to write their own position descriptions. Uniformity is secured by providing a form or typical description. This creates the needed sense of participation and allows the executive to express what he believes is important in his position.

SALARY RANGES AND STRUCTURES

A few companies use single rates for management jobs, paying individuals in these jobs the amount so established, or somewhat below or above within approved limits. The more common practice, however, is to establish an orderly series of ranges or levels to which all positions can be allocated. These structures have two dimensions: (1) the width or spread of each range or level, and (2) the differential between ranges or levels.

The width of the range is for rewarding employees by increased pay, when earned by increasing ability to perform fully in assigned positions and by improved results. The differential between ranges or levels, often called grades, is for the purpose of reflecting the relative value of jobs from the lowest or least important to the highest or most important positions in the plan. With knowledge of the minimum rates paid in the community or industry for the lowest positions and the highest rates paid for the top jobs, it is possible to construct a salary schedule objectively which will meet the requirements of a salary program.

Width of Ranges. Typically, the range or spread between the minimum and maximum for salaried positions is about 50 percent. This means that if the minimum is $10,000 annually, the maximum would be $15,000. Many schedules have smaller ranges at lower levels than at higher levels, such as 40 percent at the bottom and up to 70 percent at the upper levels.

The ranges for lower level jobs may be smaller because many opportunities exist for promotions, whereas when management employees reach the relatively few jobs at the top, they may expect promotions only after much longer periods of time.

Payments under supplemental incentive plans may also influence the breadth of salary ranges. Companies without these plans often need wider ranges to keep their total compensation competitive; salaries alone, however, seldom make up the difference.

Most salary schedules provide steps between the minimums and maximums within grades to furnish guides for the amounts of increases which may be granted under normal progress.

Increment between Grades. The increment between grades or levels is typically about 10 percent, although schedules can be found with differentials as low as 5 percent and as high as 15 percent. Many schedules provide increasing increments as they progress from lower to higher levels. Differentials of 5 percent assume a rather high degree of accuracy in determining the value of jobs; 15 percent, or higher at the upper levels, may reflect the difference in relative values of actual jobs at these levels.

Rather than adhere strictly to percentage differentials, many companies prefer to use rounded dollar amounts, which eliminate the precision of measurement implied by percentage calculations, even though the progression of the percentages is slightly distorted by the process. This is illustrated by the typical schedule shown by Table 6-1.

Salary schedules are often developed from surveys made in connection with position evaluation installations, which are covered under the next heading.

TABLE 6-1. Typical Salary Schedule

Grade	Minimum	Second step	Midpoint	Percent between grades	Fourth step	Maximum	Percent spread
1	$ 7,500	$ 8,250	$ 9,000	. . . .	$ 9,750	$10,500	40.0
2	8,250	9,125	10,000	11.1	10,875	11,750	42.5
3	9,000	10,000	11,000	10.0	12,000	13,000	44.5
4	10,000	11,250	12,500	11.4	13,750	15,000	50.0
5	11,000	12,375	13,750	10.0	15,125	16,500	50.0
6	12,000	13,500	15,000	9.1	16,500	18,000	50.0
7	13,500	15,375	17,250	15.0	19,125	21,000	55.5
8	15,000	17,250	19,500	11.5	21,750	24,000	60.0
9	16,500	19,000	21,500	10.3	24,000	26,500	60.5
10	18,000	20,750	23,500	9.3	26,250	29,000	66.5
11	20,000	23,250	26,500	12.7	29,750	33,000	65.0
12	22,000	25,750	29,500	11.3	33,250	37,000	68.2
13	25,000	29,250	33,500	13.6	37,750	42,000	68.0
14	28,000	32,750	37,500	11.9	42,250	47,000	68.0
15	31,000	36,500	42,000	10.9	47,500	53,000	69.5
16	35,000	41,250	47,500	14.5	53,750	60,000	71.5

ALLOCATION OF POSITIONS TO SALARY GRADES

Evaluation processes are not intended to change the values placed on jobs by the management or by the market. Instead, they are orderly methods of gathering facts and organizing, analyzing, and presenting them so that management judgment is well informed and consistently directed toward assurance that the salary treatment of all employees is uniform and equitable. This can be done by using survey data, by a ranking method, or by a formalized evaluation system.

Using Survey Data. Relying on survey data alone has limitations because many jobs are unique to particular organizations and similar jobs cannot be found elsewhere. Also, the survey might have to be carried to unjustified and uneconomical extremes to locate management jobs which have similar responsibilities and are of the same magnitude or scope.

In addition, no company would want to admit to allowing other companies to establish its salary standards. It is fundamental in a business enterprise that each manager must be given the opportunity and encouragement to develop fully and to exercise his own initiative and ability, and that contributions and accomplishments of individuals must be rewarded. Skillful judgment must, therefore, be used in applying data from other companies to a company's personnel.

Ranking. The ranking method involves placing all jobs in a plan in order from lowest to highest based on value judgments, usually made by a committee of executives, and fitting the jobs into the salary grades described above. Both completely informed judgment and knowledge of the value of jobs in the market are necessary to make this method successful.

There is a classification system which is quite similar to the ranking method, except that predetermined general definitions are prepared for each salary classification level or grade. This is the early Civil Service method, seldom used in business and practically never for management positions.

Position Evaluation. The foregoing types of plans for grading or classifying jobs involve comparisons on an overall basis. More analytical methods involve establishing and defining the elements or factors which are common to all jobs, and comparing the relative importance and difficulty of each factor.

The number of factors used in these plans ranges from two to thirty, although most plans for management employees use from three to ten. Plans using a smaller number of factors are based on the assumptions that the correlation between factors is sufficiently great to make the measurements just as valid as those using a larger number, and that the managers whose jobs are being evaluated will favor a simpler method.

Plans using a larger number of factors are based on the belief that management jobs are much more involved and complex than nonmanagement jobs and therefore require more factors to measure accurately all the elements involved.

There is no basis or criterion for determining the best type of evaluation plan for management positions, because all types of plans are being successfully used in all sizes and types of companies. Observation of plans in use would indicate, as a generality, that when small numbers of positions are involved and evaluations are done by top management executives, the less formal methods are quite satisfactory. Where evaluations are delegated to job evaluation specialists, the tendency is to use more formal systems.

Evaluations made by key management employees may be accepted because of the confidence placed in the judgment used, whereas analysts should feel compelled and should be required to explain and justify their determinations. This can be done most effectively by breaking each job down into its elements and comparing each element separately.

Evaluation Techniques. Because technical treatments of evaluation systems are available from many sources, it is unnecessary to include them here. It can be said, however, that all systems are intended to measure the qualifications needed to perform a job and the responsibility required of the incumbent. Included in the first broad category are factors such as education, experience, training, and demonstrated ability to exercise the judgment and initiative required. The second category includes responsibilities for supervision, income and assets, policy, methods, and relationships. These in turn can be broken down into components.

Formal evaluation systems usually assign a series of points to each factor, which progress in steps from those for minimum requirements to those for the requirements of the highest positions in the plan. Bench mark jobs representative of all those in the plan are selected, and the points from the scales for each factor are assigned to them by comparing the relative importance of each factor in each job. By this process, definitions of the qualifications needed and the requirements of the jobs are developed for each step of the point scale. These definitions serve as guides for evaluating the remainder of the jobs and for future evaluations.

Typical point relationships are illustrated in Table 6-2.

The total of the assigned points represents the evaluation of the position in comparison with all other jobs in the plan. A scale to convert the point evaluations to the proper salary grade is illustrated in Table 6-3.

TABLE 6-2. Typical Point Relationships

	Professional position		Middle management position		Top management position	
	Points	Percent of total	Points	Percent of total	Points	Percent of total
Knowledge..........	230	34.8	260	27.1	440	22.9
Mental application...	200	30.4	250	26.0	400	20.8
Responsibilities......	230	34.8	450	46.9	1,080	56.3
Total..........	660	100.0	960	100.0	1,920	100.0
Possible salary range.............	$12,000–$18,000		$18,000–$29,000		$35,000–$60,000	

The point ranges shown start with the number of points assigned to the lowest job in the plan. There is a 10 percent spread in each range, to correspond approximately with the differentials in the salary schedule. The top of each range is rounded to the next higher five points. There are five points separating each grade. This will tend to reduce the number of instances where evaluations fall too near the edges of the ranges.

Salary schedules are often constructed as part of the evaluation process. Point values are developed without regard to existing salaries. Survey data are then secured for representative jobs in each of the point ranges, and by plotting the salary data against the point values, structures of salary ranges are constructed.

SALARY ADMINISTRATION POLICIES

Salary administration policies covering payment within established ranges, increases, hiring rates, transfers, and promotions are an integral part of every salary program. Depending upon the needs and the stage of development of the program, they may range from informal understandings between management and employees to detailed written policies covering all the situations which may arise.

Salary policies universally cover all levels of salaried personnel. Nevertheless, it is generally accepted that there will be justification for variations at

TABLE 6-3. Scale to Convert Point Evaluations to Proper Salary Grade

Grade	Point range	Grade	Point range
1	380–420	9	890– 980
2	425–470	10	989–1085
3	475–525	11	1090–1200
4	530–585	12	1205–1330
5	590–650	13	1335–1470
6	655–720	14	1475–1625
7	725–800	15	1630–1795
8	805–885	16	1800–1980

management levels. Written statements of these variations are extremely rare, if any at all can be found. Instead, most companies delegate the responsibility for variations or exceptions to high ranking executives or to a salary committee composed of top management representatives.

Reviews of company manuals and observation of actual practices indicate that annual reviews and adjustments, where justified, are most prevalent for management personnel. Although this is true, it is not uncommon to find that, as management employees reach higher levels and are paid amounts in the upper portion of established ranges, longer periods elapse between increases—two or sometimes even three years.

The size of increases for management employees expressed as percentages of salary may be larger than for other salaried employees. For example, increases to salaried employees in a typical company might range from 5 to 10 percent of salary, with an average of 7 percent. Because of turnover, transfers, or lack of improvement in performance, not all the employees in a group would receive such increases. In the same organization, increases to management employees might range from 10 to 25 percent, justified by their contribution to the growth and prosperity of the company. Because these increases are granted less often, the effect on payroll costs would be about the same.

INCENTIVE COMPENSATION

There are probably more differences in opinions and practice in the use of incentive compensation plans than in any other form of compensation. Only about 60 percent of the manufacturing companies in the United States use such plans continuously, and among these there are an almost unlimited number of policies and philosophies resulting in variations in the provisions of these plans.

For the purpose of discussion, the plans in use can be placed in three categories: (1) current pay profit sharing, (2) bonus plans, and (3) incentive compensation plans.

Profit Sharing. These are plans under which, in addition to regular rates of pay, an employer pays all employees or all salaried employees additional amounts based on the prosperity of the business as a whole. The funds available are usually determined by a formula which allocates a percentage of profits to the plan. These funds are distributed among eligible employees in proportion to the relation that each employee's salary bears to the total salaries of all employees, sometimes weighted by years of service.

Management employees usually participate in these plans on the same basis as other employees, but their participation may be limited by placing a maximum on the amount of salary included. Instances are rare where the relation of payment increases for higher salaries.

Bonus Plans. The difference between bonus plans and incentive compensation plans, as the terms are used here, is that bonus plans are after the fact. They may become traditional and employees may expect the payments usually at the year end, but the company does not make commitments, and requirements are not placed on employees in advance. Both types of plans vary the amounts of payments with profits, but under bonus plans, distribution to individuals is more likely to be based on similar payments in prior years rather than on goals and objectives.

Incentive Compensation. Incentive plans announce to employees their selection for participation in advance of the incentive year. Usually, a form

TABLE 6-4. Number of Employees

Total employment	Key executives	Middle management	Supervisory personnel
Up to 500................................	5–10	10–15	15–20
500–1,000..............................	10–15	15–20	20–30
1,000–3,000...........................	15–20	20–30	30–50
3,000–5,000...........................	20–30	30–50	50–75
5,000–10,000..........................	30–50	50–75	75–100
10,000–25,000.........................	50–75	75–100	100–200
Over 25,000...........................	Over 75	Over 100	Over 200

is provided for recording the results that the individual, in consultation with his superior, can reasonably be expected to accomplish during the period. Payments are determined by value judgments of the degree of attainment of the established objectives. It becomes obvious that strong motivation can be developed under this kind of plan.

The funds for incentive plans are usually based on a formula which states that a specified percentage of profits, usually after a reserve for return on investment to protect stockholder interests and provide for capital growth, will be set aside for incentive compensation. In many plans, the percentage of profits is fixed. In others, the percentage increases with the ratio of profits to sales or to investment. The percentage set aside generally ranges from 5 to 20 percent.

It is practically impossible to generalize on payment practices by types and sizes of companies because of differing philosophies on the size of individual payments required to provide real motivation and the number of positions included in the plans. Some companies apply the percentage before income taxes, and some after. The percentage reserved for return on investment usually varies from 6 to 12 percent. The first considerations when installing a new plan are the employees to be included and the amounts considered adequate for motivation.

Employees Included. Some plans limit eligibility to key executives on the basis that the skill and ability of top management determine the success of the enterprise. Other plans include the middle management group and in some cases the supervisory group. Newer plans are more likely to limit the number of participants at first. Then as experience dictates or as the company grows, the number of participants is increased.

To give some meaning to these generalities, the numbers of participants will generally be within the ranges shown by Table 6-4 for different sizes of companies.

Amount of Payments. The range of concepts of motivating amounts is wide, actually from 5 to 100 percent of salary, or even more in the case of top executives of extremely large corporations. In the majority of cases, however, the percentages of salary are generally between 10 and 50 percent. The percent of salary increases as the amount of salary and the importance of the position increase. Using the same management levels as in the previous table, most actual payments in successful companies fall within the following ranges.

Level	*Percent of salary*
Key executives............................	40–50
Middle management.......................	20–40
Supervisory..............................	10–20

Size of company has little bearing on these figures.

Payments under these plans may be in cash as soon as possible after the incentive period; may be spread over a period of four or five years to level the impact of income taxes; or may be deferred to retirement. In larger companies, payments may also be in the form of company stock, although in most cases only where deferred until retirement.

There are two commonly used methods for incentive compensation in divisions of decentralized companies. One method permits the divisions to establish their own plans independent of corporate plans. The other includes divisional executives in corporate plans, relating payments to both divisional and individual performance.

RELATING COMPENSATION TO ACCOMPLISHMENT

Every management can utilize its compensation program to motivate employees toward the attainment of the company's objectives. To accomplish this, the following are required.

1. A clear statement of company objectives that interprets management's purpose, aims, and standards.

2. The establishment of a sound organization, the delegation of authority, and sharp, clear-cut definitions of both direct line and functional responsibilities.

3. The selection, training, development, and direction of the personnel in the organization.

4. The conversion of company objectives into goals for individual positions, and these into parts or factors which will produce results expected.

5. The participation of each individual in establishing the goals and objectives which become the standards of performance for his job. Each manager agrees upon the specific actions and results that can be reasonably expected from each position reporting to him, and the sum of these will be the goals for his own position. Thus, the company goals will be the sum of those of all of the functions, with top management finally being responsible for decisions on what will be expected for the operation as a whole.

6. Changing goals and objectives where such changes are deemed advisable in the best interests of the employees and the company. Because it is humanly impossible to anticipate all the circumstances and conditions of the future, some objectives may become so easily attainable or so far out of reach as to eliminate their motivational purpose.

7. The regular review and impersonal comparison of results with established objectives. Where facts and figures are available, they should be used, but where such facts and figures do not exist or cannot be efficiently developed, statements should be agreed upon which express the degree of attainment as accurately as possible.

8. The frank acknowledgement of deficiencies. In any business enterprise, it is expected that there will be many instances where aims and objectives will not be fully accomplished. The attainment of perfection would be unrealistic from either the viewpoint of establishing goals or the appraisal of results.

9. The search for and identification of the causes of less than satisfactory performance, and the correction of deficiencies through management assistance and guidance or the removal of the circumstances causing the deficiency.

10. Finally, the use of factual appraisal of accomplishments as the basis for the administration of compensation with fair and equitable reward for the attainment of objectives.

The financial factors for most management jobs can be measured by comparing sales, production costs, and expenses with budgets and standard costs. There can be additional objectives such as the design of new pieces of equipment or the development of new methods to reduce labor costs. Time service is important in most operations and can be factually measured by adherence to schedules. Quality of products or services can usually be measured by inspection reports, number of rejects, or complaints and returns.

In the area of general management performance, objectives can apply to the needs of the organization, such as developing individuals to fill specific positions or delegating responsibility where executives have been reluctant to do so.

No attempt has been made here to list all the factors which should be included as objectives. In fact, any such attempt would be contrary to the principles involved. As previously mentioned, every manager, based on the direction he receives, must discuss with each of his subordinates the results that he hopes to attain, and define in writing specifically what, how, and when the accomplishment is to be expected. It is obvious that under such a concept the objectives will be different for each individual position.

The operation of an incentive program can be utilized to meet new competition and changing economic conditions, and for other good business reasons. The need for new policies or methods may be brought to light. The need for personnel or organization changes or reassignment of responsibilities may become evident. The discussions with individuals should definitely lead to action. Decisions can be reached on the best methods to approach problems and resolve them.

Application to Salaries. The discussion of salary schedules suggested steps within each range for the length of time on a job and for different levels of performance. Length of service alone is not a criterion, but an experienced, seasoned individual can be expected to perform more independently and fulfill the required responsibilities to a greater extent than a new employee.

Typically, the midpoint of a salary range is the amount paid for satisfactory performance by a fully qualified employee. The minimum of the range is intended to be the starting salary, and the maximum is for superior performance. The intermediate steps are typically used as guides to what should be paid as employees gain experience and improve performance.

In most organizations, the salaries of the majority of employees will fall between the second and fourth steps of the schedule, with no more than 10 percent in each of the salaries in the range above and below these steps. If the organization is large enough to contain a representative group of employees, the distribution might be expected to be as follows:

Range steps	Percent of total employment
Minimum salary	5–10
Second step	20–30
Midpoint	30–35
Fourth step	35–20
Maximum salary	10– 5

This table has been constructed to show that one of management's responsibilities is to assist employees at all levels to produce to the utmost of their ability. This will result in an organization performance approaching the percentages on the left-hand side of the percent column. The aggregate performance of all the employees in the group will be much more profitable than if the situation shown on the right-hand side of the column exists.

Caution must be exercised in using a payroll analysis of this kind, because a small group, say of five to ten people, all thoroughly experienced and performing excellently, could all properly be paid at the fourth and maximum steps. The same group in a new installation with excellent performance yet to be developed could all be paid at the midpoint or below. The level of pay must be a matter of management judgment, considering what can be expected under the conditions and opportunities that exist at a given time.

Application to Incentive Payments. The same principles apply to determining the amounts of incentive payments. Having established policies governing the limits of incentive payments, for example from 10 to 50 percent of salary, the attainment of objectives could be appraised in terms of satisfactory, exceptional, excellent, outstanding, and superior. Corresponding percentages of salary would then be established for each overall level of accomplishment.

Most incentive plans state that payments above salaries are for exceptional performance. If employees are told that they are included in these plans but no payments are made over a period of years, they lose their motivating influence. Objectives must be attainable under expected applied effort, and nominal payments should start at levels appraised as satisfactory.

It has not been the purpose here to place emphasis on appraisal techniques or methods used. No two plans in use are alike. Yet they are all based on the concept that desired results will be obtained only if plans are made, objectives are determined, and progress, results, and performance are compared with predetermined goals. It can be accepted that the most effective determination of the action needed to achieve desired results is made through the appraisal of the accomplishments, or lack of them, of the people who have the responsibility for getting the results.

The establishment of objectives or standards of performance is not an exact science. There is no area where more skilled, critical management judgment is involved. Time and effort are necessary, but if these are intelligently applied, the results will be most rewarding.

DEFERRED COMPENSATION

In addition to deferring some part of incentive compensation pay as previously mentioned, employment contracts are sometimes used for this purpose. Deferred pay provisions in incentive plans include certain groups of employees, while employment contracts are designed to fit the needs or wishes of individual executives.

Both types of plans have been used by companies to provide incentives for valuable employees to remain in the employ of the company, to encourage interest in the future progress of the company, and to provide income tax advantages. Companies forego income tax deductions until the amounts involved are actually paid, and executives pay no income taxes until the amounts are actually received.

The income tax benefits of deferred compensation are recognized by the Internal Revenue Service. The rulings are rather involved, but generally require that future payments must be contingent upon the fulfillment of certain requirements by the employee, or that the employee's right to receive the payments when due are based on specific events connected with his employment. Expert tax and legal counsel is needed to be sure that the objectives of these provisions will be accomplished, because determinations are made on the basis of facts in each individual case.

Whether income tax benefits are advantageous to individuals depends upon the level of earnings, income from sources other than employment, allowable deductions, and current financial needs. In most cases, the level of earnings must be between $35,000 and $40,000 annually before there are tax advantages, and cases have been developed to show that there were no tax advantages up to $70,000 annual earnings. Obviously, a great deal of study in addition to technical advice is required before deferred compensation arrangements should be entered into.

STOCK ACQUISITION PLANS

Various plans for acquiring stock in their companies are widely used for motivating and compensating management employees. These plans have as their purpose the promotion of the interests of the company and the other stockholders by encouraging the employees upon whose judgment, initiative, and efforts the company is dependent for its success to invest in the company's stock. As shareholders, these employees have increased interest in the progress of their company, and their desire to continue in the employ of the company is strengthened. Most of the plans provide some advantages to employees over the general public. In addition, these plans:

1. Serve as savings and estate building devices
2. Provide tax advantages, depending on their provisions and the disposition of the stock
3. Can be administered without the discriminating limitations of qualified pension and profit sharing retirement plans
4. Do not require cash outlay, but instead are an inexpensive way of increasing capital funds

The several ways in which stock may be acquired by employees may be classified as: (1) part payments in incentive plans, (2) stock purchase plans, (3) qualified and nonqualified stock option plans, and (4) unit or share plans.

Stock purchase plans are arrangements for the purchase of company common stock on installment payments, usually by payroll deductions and usually at a favorable price. These plans often offer choices among common stock, shares in mutual funds, and government bonds. Companies sometimes contribute to the funds, making them a form of profit sharing. Management employees participate in them on the same basis as other employees.

Stock option plans are mostly designed for management employees. The regulations of the Internal Revenue Code which grant tax advantages to qualified stock options are rather lengthy. The important limiting requirements provide that the option price must not be less than the market value of the stock at the time the option was granted and that no disposition may be made of the shares within a three-year period beginning on the day after the purchase of the shares. If these and other provisions are met, there is no income at the time of granting the option, and none when the stock is acquired. Capital gains provisions apply at the time the shares are sold.

Because of these restrictions, nonqualified stock options have become popular. These do not comply with the Internal Revenue Code regulations and therefore do not receive the favorable tax treatment specified for qualified options. However, because the option price need not be as high as the market price and the holding period need not apply, provisions can be included which offer the opportunity of greater gains for executives than the tax advantages of qualified options.

Unit or share plans have provisions similar to those of other stock acquisition plans except that no shares of stock are actually involved. Instead, participants receive the equivalent of dividends on the units which represent shares of stock and may also receive the equivalent of the appreciation in the value of the stock during the period of participation.

As in the case of deferred compensation, expert tax and legal counsel is needed before entering into stock purchase arrangements.

PENSION AND INSURANCE BENEFITS

Pension and profit sharing retirement and group insurance plans have become nearly universal. Because they provide benefits much more economically for groups than could be purchased individually, their consideration should have priority after sound salaries in any compensation program. Established plans should be reviewed periodically to be sure that they are kept in line with modern business practices.

Because qualified retirement programs are subject to the most favorable tax treatment, there is no more effective way of deferring compensation. To qualify, these plans must not discriminate in favor of highly paid personnel. Employees need not contribute to these plans, but employee contributions can increase the benefits and make the plans more attractive to higher paid employees. Profit sharing retirement plans are particularly attractive, because taxes can be deferred on amounts up to 15 percent of salary.

In the early years of group life insurance, provision was made for amounts just sufficient to avoid hardships. Compensation policies have changed since then, however, and plans have been adopted which provide for benefits up to three times annual salary. In some cases, increasing maximums for different levels of salary are provided. Some states limit these amounts.

Individual life insurance policies are often used to assist executives to build capital. Every life insurance company has experts in this field who will be pleased to provide the advice and counsel necessary on the forms available and the way in which they may be advantageous in individual circumstances.

Health insurance plans include hospitalization, surgical and medical, major medical, disability, and visual and dental care. Prescription drug plans and salary continuation in case of illness may also be included. The lower premium costs through group purchase enable employees to have greater coverage than might otherwise be possible. The security and peace of mind provided are motivating forces toward continuing employment, and indirectly toward greater effort.

PERQUISITES AND NONFINANCIAL INCENTIVES

Nonfinancial incentives comprise those elements of compensation that take the form of advantages, privileges, or services. They deal with size and location of offices, equipment and facilities, private dining facilities, vacations, travel accommodations, subscriptions and club memberships, and the use of automobiles and aircraft. The use of company personnel for medical, legal, tax, and secretarial services is also often offered.

In addition to these perquisites which provide incentive in the form of prestige, there are human or psychological factors present in every organization which may be used and promoted as incentives. Practically everyone wants to work for a company with a good reputation which is making a real contribution to the national or world well-being, security, and standards of living. Evidence of the right to be heard and of participation in decisions that affect products, methods, and policies is a strong incentive. Freedom to think, to venture, and to take calculated risks is a strong stimulant. The announcement of promotions or outstanding accomplishments through a company relations program develops justified pride. Opportunities for writing articles or books or making public appearances are strong motivators to some individuals.

Because anxiety hampers effort, there is need for a sound basis for a sense of security. The elements in a job which lead to pride in accomplishment and personal achievement and to the opportunity for growth and promotion are probably the strongest of motivating forces.

It can be accepted as a truism that financial incentives in a poor atmosphere will be ineffective, whereas the same programs will produce maximum results in an organization striving for character, integrity, a competitive and cooperative spirit of fair play, and outstandingly desirable working conditions.

CONCLUSION

It is well known that the same incentives do not appeal to all people alike. This is because human desires and ambitions do not exist to the same degree in everyone. What may prove a strong incentive to one person may be only mildly motivating to another. The importance of retirement plans increases with age. Deferred pay contracts are not attractive to young executives who need all their earnings for living expenses and nominal savings. Stock option plans are not attractive to people who cannot afford to finance them. Conversely, all types of incentives are attractive to some people.

This is the reason that some companies provide, or at least give serious consideration to, all possible features of a compensation program, and to the extent possible and practical, provide a degree of flexibility or choice within them. Much also depends on basic business factors such as the age and size of the business, its economic stability, its ownership, the cyclical nature of its sales and profits, and outside influences such as general economic conditions and interdependence between companies and industries. As incentive values differ from person to person, so the effectiveness of incentive plans varies from industry to industry and from company to company.

With the recognition that people are induced to greater effort toward whatever they hope to accomplish by incentives of varying kinds, it has been the purpose of this chapter to outline the nature and objectives of all the incentive methods in use for management personnel in manufacturing companies. To develop a program for a specific company requires gathering facts, analyzing them, in many cases securing specialized or professional advice and counsel, and making decisions based on individual company considerations.

The once held opinion that inherent qualities of leadership, loyalty, ambition, and initiative provided sufficient motivation for men in management positions to put forth their best efforts is no longer accepted. With the growth of business organizations, increased complexity of operations, and keen competition for men of high caliber, managements must devote substantial effort to the important responsibility of developing and maintaining rational compensation plans based on sound principles and good management practice.

BIBLIOGRAPHY

Doulton, Joan, and David Hay, *Managerial and Professional Staff Grading*, George Allen and Unwin, Ltd., London, England, 1961.

Evans, Gordon H., *Managerial Job Descriptions in Manufacturing*, Research Study no. 65, American Management Association, New York, 1964.

Executive Compensation Service Reports, American Management Association, New York, continuous.

Fetter, Robert B., and D. C. Johnson, *Compensation and Incentives for Industrial Executives*, Indiana University Press, Bloomington, 1952.

Hall, Harold R., *Executive Retirement*, Graduate School of Business Administration, Harvard University, The Andover Press, Andover, Mass., 1953.

Schleh, Edward C., *Management by Results*, McGraw-Hill Book Company, New York, 1961.

Sellin, Henry, *Taxation of Deferred Employee and Executive Compensation*, Prentice-Hall, Inc., Englewood Cliffs, N.J., 1960.

Sibson, Robert E., "Wages and Salaries," chap. 6 in *Compensation of Exempt Employees*, American Management Association, New York, 1960.

Smyth, Richard C., *Financial Incentives for Management*, McGraw-Hill Book Company, New York, 1960.

"Use and Misuse of Qualified Stock Options," *The Journal of Taxation*, March, 1966.

Washington, George Thomas, and V. Henry Rothschild II, *Compensating the Corporate Executive*, rev. ed., The Ronald Press Company, New York, 1951.

CHAPTER SEVEN

Communications

LEWIS H. McGLASHAN   *Director of Training, Kodak Park Works, East-man Kodak Company, Rochester, New York*

Although enough people dislike certain TV commercials so that the installations of switches to turn off sound is a profitable sideline for some TV repairmen, a lot of viewers are strongly influenced by many of these little screen gems.   If you doubt this, consider the amount of money that American companies spend on television programs to obtain an audience for their commercial messages.

When you, too, have something to say, wouldn't you like to have the same degree of attention?   Although TV commercials represent only one type of communication, their productivity naturally attracts our attention.   There is a lesson to be learned from them.

What makes these communications so effective?

Some say that it is because they are based on a Madison Avenue discovery that you cannot oversell romance or food.   This may account for some TV commercials.   Probably in most communications, however, where the sender wants the receiver to do something (usually buy a product), the point of contact is even more basic.

APPEALING TO AUDIENCE INTEREST

The appeal must be to the listener's (or reader's) self-interest, or group identity.   And this goes beyond food or romance.   It includes fear, aspirations, security, independence, and several other "motivators" (to use a bit of staff Chinese).

The key to getting someone to listen is always the ability of the listener to identify with the subject.   Only when you successfully appeal to that, will the listener continue to listen and, hopefully, to act in the way you would like.

9–73

For example, you would not be reading this chapter unless you expected to profit from it in some way and to make it easier to attain your objectives. You cannot overemphasize the basic rule of self-interest.

Before offering examples of some media through which people are most easily reached, let us identify a couple of other critical trouble spots: how you go about preparing a communication and how you learn to revise it. It is vital to recognize your own limitations and to try to improve your personal skills.

Approach or Method. Having defined your purpose (and, of course, your audience along with it), your choice of approach is not too wide, nor need it be confusing. Suppose that you are trying to reach a large audience all at once, on a matter personally affecting each one. You probably would not personally address yourself to small groups of people. Rather, you would carry a notice in the company news magazine, if you have one. If not, it might be the bulletin boards. That kind of decision is relatively easy. Some others are not.

Evaluation. Evaluation may mean more if it is referred to as "feedback." It is the process of finding out whether you got through to the receiver, and what action followed. Almost no single effort will be as fruitful in improving your ability to communicate well as that expended in evaluating your results.

Identifying the Receiver's Interest. To be more specific about identifying the receiver's interest, let us take an unemployed individual to illustrate a point. He can probably be assumed to have many needs. Obviously, though, the things which will most interest him under those circumstances may be associated with survival or basic standards of living. He will be confused by orders or instructions that do not satisfy him on the score of survival for himself and those with whom he relates. He may even be antagonistic to any kind of communication that does not relate to this survival.

Hopefully, the communication should also give the receiver some expectancy of becoming someone worthwhile, at least by his own standards.

Ordinarily, the kinds of communications just described are created mainly by employment recruiters. If, however, we involve ourselves with some community problems with the "underemployed" or "undereducated," the importance of survival needs is something for us to keep in mind.

Those who are not in advertising are mostly concerned with communications inside the organization. Here the audience may be made up of subordinates, equals, or bosses. All these people generally can be assumed to have satisfied the survival needs and to have moved up the scale to some new needs.

There is another point to be made in connection with the scale of the concerns that people feel: within the scale, the priority will change for any individual from time to time. Fear can be a strong point of appeal, but can easily lose its strength depending on many factors. A promise of financial benefit to come is generally a strong mover; but if other previously unacceptable conditions remain, it may fail to win support.

These points—the scale of needs, and the fluctuations within the scale—are worth emphasis. It is easy to overlook them and to take for granted that common membership in an enterprise provides all the basis necessary for an order or request to get the desired action. To be sure, it limits the size of the group within which you will try to identify your audience. But because there are so many different interests, it seems probable that announcements of concern to everyone will not occur often.

The importance of finding points through which you can appeal to the receiver can backfire if your concern is merely to manipulate him. Most people expect to have to spar with a salesman; similar treatment from a member of their own management could generate a distrust which would be a barrier to later efforts to communicate.

Some Trouble Spots. Emphasis has been on finding the receiver's point of interest. It is taken for granted that you—the communicator—are sure that you represent the company's interest. Even so, you may still stumble into a trap by failing to recognize one of the following taboos:

Are you sure you have the authority to make the communication?

Are you endangering company security by unknowingly divulging proprietary company information? In all companies where this can be a factor, there is always someone with whom you must clear your message.

Are you likely to make a premature disclosure which may embarrass your company, particularly in the marketplace? Both this one and the taboo on proprietary information are real dangers, particularly in preparing talks for technical societies or papers for their publications.

Are you following proper channels? A message which bypasses or undercuts people may be embarrassing.

When you address an outside group, are you allowing yourself to be considered as a company spokesman? If you are, there are all kinds of things to be concerned about. Use this chapter as an illustration. The publishers of this book know, and you should realize, that an author speaks only for himself, and from his *personal* experience.

One more point before we finish the discussion of choosing a subject and directing it toward the listener. Frequently a given situation may appear to you to "write itself." That is, you may feel that a simple, clear exposition of the situation will automatically bring out the desired response in most listeners. Often it will. But have you ever received an instruction like this? The present economic situation makes it necessary for all divisions to cut "travel expenses."

Did you perhaps think:

What economic situation?
How much?
Beginning when?

You must always *try* to put yourself in your listener's place.

ORGANIZING THE COMMUNICATION

Now for the supersized question. What is the best way to organize the communication? Every once in a while someone tries to show how this is to be done in three, five, or ten easy steps. This approach is similar to that of the golf pro who tells you: "The game is simple. . . . Keep your head down, your eye on the ball, and follow through." Then, this same teacher writes one hundred or more syndicated features on how to be a once-a-week golfer and still shoot below ninety.

Organizing the communication is a complex subject, and useful books have been written about just *parts* of it. Even so, if you go no further than employing the principle in the next statement, you will be a lot further ahead than most people.

For anyone preparing a message, the advice given by Lewis Carroll in *Alice in Wonderland* went something like this: "Begin at the beginning. Go on to the end. And then stop."

That is a classic in business, because it reminds you to limit your subject and to organize it.

A professor of dialectics at a well-known eastern seminary used to underline the importance of limiting any one message by repeating over, and over, and over, "There are no souls saved after the first ten minutes."

A time-proved guide in organizing your material has been repeated so often that it has had more influence on English language journalism than any other. It is Kipling's famous jingle—

> I keep six honest serving-men
> (They taught me all I knew);
> Their names are What and Why and When
> And How and Where and Who.

Keep it in mind. It will serve your reader's interest which is, of course, yours as well.

It illustrates that organization is more than: "Tell people what you're going to say. Say it to them. Then, tell them what you've told them." It also illustrates the value of arranging your information so that you do not jump around like an amateur movie maker letting his camera "pan" over too much territory, too fast.

Keep It Simple. A word about "style." This is a word much misused by literary critics, who often write to impress, not to express. In its business connotation, it merely refers to the kind of craftsmanship used in presenting the message. Its most important elements can be illustrated by questions with some examples.

Have you chosen the simple, direct word? What is the matter with referring to the placing of unit products in corrugated cases as "casing," rather than "containerization," or even "finalization"? Have you inserted jargon when there are already good, common English words to use? If so, you may find a practical manager asking you politely but devastatingly if you have invented a solution for which you are now seeking out a problem.

Do not be a contributor to the growing wave of pompous, meaningless phrases or to the proliferation of acronyms.

For example, how about, Enclosed herewith, please find . . ."?

If it is enclosed, where would it be but herewith? If he can find it, where else would it be but enclosed?

And how about the apologetic opener—particularly when you are giving a talk? There you are, and there are all those nice people giving their valuable time to listen to you. You feel rather humble about it—maybe a little frightened. You start with some variant of the old chestnut, "Unaccustomed as I am . . ."

So how does your audience react? Usually by wondering why, if you are so unqualified, you are wasting their time. And then they draw their mental drapes and wander off into some fantasy which is just waiting to be indulged.

Acronyms are badly overdone. They are not only becoming trite, they trip up readers. Just load up a report with them, and you will probably find that it is seldom read through. Why? Because only linguists like to read and translate at the same time.

Sentence Structure. "Sweet Sixteen"—is that a new theme song for Lawrence Welk? No, it is the rule of thumb for the number of words your message should average *per sentence.* That is, providing you do not use many words of more than two syllables. If you want a useful formula for this, known as "Fog Indexing," you will find it in a very helpful little book, *How to Take the*

Fog out of Writing, by Robert Gunning.[1] The editors of at least two nationally known periodicals use something like this.

When you say, "It has been decided that . . ." are you trying to be self-effacing, and placing the organization first? Actually, your reader may think:

1. You are a coward, or
2. Nobody really decided it, but you are trying it on, or
3. You hope to take credit for somebody else's decision.

The cure is simple. Use active, *not passive*, verbs. Try saying, "After study of the available information, I am recommending that . . ."

Use of Visual Aids. The above pointers on writing a letter or report or set of instructions will also apply to a talk. It will certainly apply to the script for a sound-slide presentation or for an instructional movie.

This brings up the matter of visual aids. When do you use them? The answer is easy: Almost always, *IF*. There are really three "ifs."

"If" number one: You may use them when they are of professional viewing quality. The days when you could get away with crudely lettered charts or cartoons are gone. They vanished when people began watching TV. The commercials have set such high standards of lettering, cartooning, charting, and photography that crude stuff produced by well-meaning amateurs will no longer get by.

"If" number two relates to time. As a rule of thumb, sound-slide presentations or movies on anything of an instructional nature should be less than twenty-five minutes in length. Try to avoid showing them in a darkened room after a meal.

"If" number three applies to the appropriateness of the material. The visuals must relate directly to each point as you go along. They must not be left up while you are talking about something else. They must serve to illustrate your topic—not take over for it.

One common error is often made by people giving a talk and using printed charts. *Do* read aloud what is on the chart. *Do not* think you are insulting your audience by repeating what is on the chart. The statement is probably important, or it would not be there. The audience will recognize that you are doing it for emphasis. On the other hand, if you say something else, or elaborate on it while they are trying to read it, you will surely confuse them.

FEEDBACK

Identifying the receiver's interest—pointers which will help you to be better understood—has been discussed briefly. But feedback is the payoff.

For an author, this is usually whether the book sells. For a play or movie, the box office receipts. In television, there are the "ratings."

For your message, it is whether people listen to it or read it, and where called for, produce the desired results.

If it is a talk you have given or program you have conducted and you want to know how it was received, a good way is to ask afterward. Of course, you must ask someone who can be relied on for a candid reply to your basic question, "If you had to sit through that again, how would you like to have it done differently?"

However, candor is rarely shown by your organizational peers or subordinates. Consequently, you should devise a method of asking that keeps the responses anonymous. Questionnaires, where you request the respondent

[1] Robert Gunning, *How to Take the Fog out of Writing*, Dartnell Corporation, Chicago, 1956.

not to sign his name, can partially accomplish this if the questions are carefully drawn not to "lead" the answer. Your Market Research Department or an industrial psychologist can give invaluable assistance in asking good questions.

If you are going to do much speaking, performance as a member of "Toastmasters" or of a Dale Carnegie group will give you both excellent practice and critique.

Assessing the readership of written communications (particularly company newspapers) calls for more sophisticated techniques. Your best help here can be from your advertising agency.

Motion pictures, video tapes, and audio tapes of yourself *and* your audience will give valuable clues. Group restlessness and apathy are things to watch for.

However we may occupy ourselves, it is impossible not to communicate. A little effort, a little sensitivity toward discovering your impact on others will be your most useful tool in making yourself more effective, provided you use the information you get.

SUMMARY

What has been said can be summed up rather simply: talking is for listeners; writing is for readers.

This places the emphasis on the right place in the communication process. It places the emphasis on the receiver of the message. It forces us to define our audience clearly . . . to establish clear-cut objectives . . . to find the means of appealing to the audience. This is how we communicate effectively.

BIBLIOGRAPHY

Classen, H. George, *Better Business English*, Arco Publishing Co., Inc., New York, 1966.

Estrin, Herman, *Technical and Professional Writing*, Harcourt, Brace & World, Inc., 1963.

Flesch, Rudolf, and A. H. Lass, *A New Guide to Better Writing*, Popular Library edition, 1963.

Gunning, Robert, *The Technique of Clear Writing*, McGraw-Hill Book Company, New York, 1952.

Johnson, Thomas P., *Analytical Writing*, Harper & Row, Publishers, Incorporated, New York, 1966.

Lambuth, David, *The Golden Book on Writing*, Viking Press, Inc., New York, 1964.

Menzel, Donald H., Howard M. Jones, and Lyle G. Boyd, *Writing a Technical Paper*, McGraw-Hill Book Company, New York, 1961.

Nirenberg, Jesse S., *Getting Through to People*, Prentice-Hall, Inc., Englewood Cliffs, N.J., 1966.

Rathbone, Robert R., and James B. Stone, *A Writer's Guide for Engineers and Scientists*, Prentice-Hall, Inc., Englewood Cliffs, N.J., 1962.

Shidle, Norman G., *The Art of Successful Communication*, McGraw-Hill Book Company, New York, 1965.

Slattery, James, *Business Letter Writing*, Garden City Books, Garden City, N.Y., 1965.

Smith, Terry C., *How to Write Better and Faster*, Thomas Y. Crowell Co., New York, 1965.

Strunk, William, Jr., and E. B. White, *The Elements of Style*, The Macmillan Company, New York, 1959.

Tichy, H. J., *Effective Writing for Engineers, Managers, Scientists*, John Wiley & Sons, Inc., New York, 1966.

CHAPTER EIGHT

Appraising and Counseling Managerial and Supervisory Employees

HERBERT H. MEYER *Manager, Corporate Personnel Research, General Electric Company, New York, New York*

The performance of any organization will be determined for the most part by the skill with which its activities are managed. A capable managerial staff is obviously very important to the success of the organization. For this reason, manager selection is usually considered to be a very crucial function. But selecting good managers is not as easy as it sounds, for most managers are made, not born. Thus, even more important than selection to the success of the organization is the development of improved skills in managers who now hold key leadership positions in the organization.

In this chapter, we shall attempt to provide some practical and easy-to-apply advice to higher level managers who are interested in helping their subordinate supervisors and managers improve their job performance. This advice will not assume that the manager has had any special training or acquired any unusual capability as a coach or counselor. Rather, it will be directed at the manufacturing manager who has probably been chosen more for his functional knowledge of the product being manufactured and the processes involved than for his proficiency as a teacher or counselor.

THE MANAGER AS A COUNSELOR

Most managers find employee counseling difficult. In fact, experience has shown that managers will avoid this task if they can. Often the personnel department will try to ensure that each employee receives some formal coaching and counseling by establishing a formal performance appraisal feedback program. Under such a program, which has become very popular in American industry, managers are required to sit down with each of their subordinates periodically for a comprehensive review of past performance. The manager is also required to counsel the employee about how he might improve his job performance.

In theory, the performance appraisal program is hard to attack. It certainly makes good sense to expect that if a man is going to improve his present performance, he must have information about his past performance. Moreover, it stands to reason that most people would like to perform as well as they can. We can assume, therefore, that if a person is not performing up to expectation, he could well use some advice and counsel on how he might improve.

Unfortunately, in practice, most performance appraisal programs do not work out as well as it seems they should in theory. Most supervisors find employee counseling very difficult. Performance appraisal discussions are likely to be awkward and strained, especially if the supervisor is attempting to correct some faults that he sees in the performance of the subordinate. Experience has shown that most managers will avoid such discussions if controls are not applied to ensure that they are carried out. And why should the manager not resist? Even the highly trained psychologist or psychiatrist finds that attempting to change another person's behavior through counseling is an extremely delicate and difficult task.

The Subordinate's Needs. Although counseling is difficult, the subordinate manager, on the other hand, at any level in the organization has some needs which counseling or coaching would seem to fulfill. Most subordinates have needs for four kinds of information which the manager might supply:

1. *What Is Expected of Me?* Where a job description or position guide is available, a general framework of expectations is provided for the individual. But this is not enough. The manager at any level needs more detailed information regarding specific task expectations from week to week or month to month. He needs to know, for example, on what specific goals he should focus his energies, what kinds of priorities he should give to various tasks, and which deadlines must be met and which could be moved back if necessary. It is surprising how often employees will say in a survey that they really do not have a clear idea of just what is expected of them.

2. *How Am I Doing?* Almost everyone likes to know whether he is performing up to expectations. He would, of course, like to hear that he is doing well in every case; but if he is not, he wants to know why not. Very often he wants information about his present performance in order to define performance expectations more clearly. In fact, if expectations are defined clearly enough, the individual can get his own feedback. He does not need the manager to tell him whether or not he is meeting his commitments.

3. *What Does Management Think of Me?* Most employees would like to have some general appraisal information over and above the feedback about present job performance. They want to know how they are regarded generally in the organization, not just by their immediate manager, but by higher management, and perhaps the personnel staff as well. They want to know whether they are considered as having future top management potential, or as good, steady, and dependable performers, or as outstanding specialists, or perhaps as over the hill.

4. *Where Can I Go from Here?* Most individuals, especially managers, would like also to know what the future holds. What are the various possibilities for advancement? What are the odds that he may get one of the better jobs? How can he maximize his chances of being advanced?

There are some additional needs for appraisal and counseling which are only indirectly related to the four questions listed above. One of these, for example, is the need to understand the salary program and the reasons for specific salary actions relating to the individual. Certainly the manager should explain to a subordinate the reasons for changes in his salary.

How Serve These Needs? There is no handy-dandy formula or program that managers can use to serve all the information needs of the subordinate regarding his performance and potential. One thing is sure: A single program cannot serve all needs. Many companies have tried to design a single, comprehensive performance appraisal program to serve all four of the needs listed above in addition to communication about salary. Such programs usually fail to serve any of the needs satisfactorily. The approach that serves one of the needs best is often not well suited to another of the needs.

Certainly the "report card" type of rating discussion, where the man is graded on how well he carries out job responsibilities and on traits that are presumably job related, such as dependability, initiative, judgment, personality, and motivation, is not the answer. Careful studies of this approach to counseling have shown that such an appraisal discussion often serves only to break down the working relationship between the manager and subordinate instead of having the intended constructive effect.

A GOAL-ORIENTED APPROACH

The best advice that the manager can get regarding appraisal and counseling with subordinates is that such discussions should be focused on the work to be done and not on the individuals. By work to be done, we do not mean job responsibilities as listed in the position guide, but rather specific job tasks, goals, and problems. Counseling discussions should deal with the actual work itself rather than with generalities. Certainly the manager should avoid talking about relatively intangible personal traits such as dependability, initiative, or judgment.

A second piece of advice which should help any manager with his counseling responsibilities is that he should use a participative approach. Effective counseling is a two-way process. A counselng discussion should be a man-to-man exchange, not a papa-to-boy lecture.

The goal setting and review program, which is becoming increasingly popular, incorporates both principles, that is, focusing on tasks and using the participative approach. In this program, the individual formulates his own goals, reviews them with his manager, and makes changes that they agree upon; then the two working together review and recycle these from time to time in the ensuing months.

Systematic Work Planning. Most managers spend a good deal of their time in planning activities. A work planning approach to subordinate appraisal, therefore, may seem like nothing more than the regular and normal work of the manager. What we are recommending here, however, is a more systematic and highly programmed approach than is normally followed. This approach calls for the definition of and agreement on specific work plans and goals, with results measurements agreed upon in advance, and deadlines set where appropriate. Such a program has been found to be far superior to the performance appraisal approach in serving the first two needs listed above for the subordinate, namely the "What is expected of me?" and "How am I doing?" needs.

A good work planning program for individual managers starts with the objectives of the business. The overall objectives of the business get translated into specific plans for the organization as a whole for a specific time period. Usually these are formulated annually in connection with budgeting.

The overall business plans next get translated into plans for specific components, organizations, or work groups. Component plans then get translated into specific work plans and goals for individuals in the work groups. The job description for each manager should play an important part in determining what aspects of the component plan he will assume responsibility for. Individual capabilities will also play an important part in defining individual responsibilities. Figure 8-1 illustrates the complete planning cycle.

The individual himself should play the leading role in formulating his own plans and goals. Much research has shown that the goals one sets for himself have much stronger motivational effects on his performance than goals or quotas set for him by someone else.

The work plan should be written out, first by the individual in draft form. This document is his own business plan for the subsequent period. The

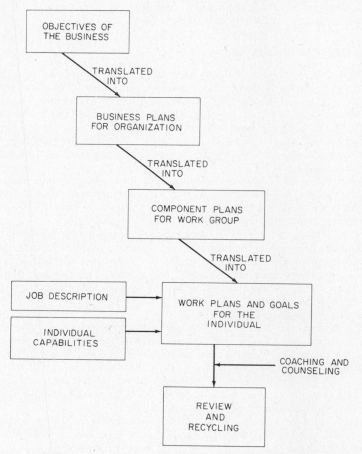

FIG. 8-1. Systematic Work Planning Procedure.

length of time for which such a plan is formulated will depend somewhat on the nature of the job. The first-line supervisor's work plans and goals may be for two- or three-month periods. At higher levels, the work plans and goals may be for longer periods, such as for six months or a full year. Goals should be defined as objectively as possible, with results measurements specified and time deadlines indicated wherever appropriate.

Figure 8-2 presents some sample goals for a manager in a manufacturing operation. Note that the manager has done more than just describe some projects that he will work on. He has set some definite bogeys for himself in terms of percentage improvements which he intends to realize in each area and by what dates.

The sample list of goals presented in Figure 8-2 also illustrates indirectly another advantage of the formal work planning approach. The goals that managers set for themselves usually relate less to the routine day-to-day work of the component than to extra projects that improve the overall performance of the component. Managers who use work planning often testify that they find it possible to accomplish those general projects, designed to improve routine operations, that never seemed to get done before.

Review and Negotiation with the Manager. The next step in the procedure is a review of individual plans with the manager. This review will often take the character of a negotiation. The manager may have some objectives which have not been factored into the man's draft of his work plans. The manager may also feel that some goals the man has set for himself are unrealistically difficult. Others may appear to be too easy—lacking in challenge. Thus, the development of meaningful commitments between manager and man takes place in an atmosphere of give and take. Both are involved, and so the man knows that work planning is not just an academic exercise. The work plan defines for him what he and his manager agree he should devote his efforts to and be held accountable for in the ensuing months.

Some managers who strive to operate their entire work group as a team will

---

SAMPLE WORK PLANS AND GOALS
for
Manager–Inventory Control

Goal: Improve system for identifying parts stock.

Measurement: Complete redesign of system and pilot test of procedures by 6–1. Make it completely operational by 7–1.

Goal: Rearrange parts areas to economize on space and expedite orders.

Measurement: Make available 25% of presently used space. Complete rearrangements by:

J series...................... 6–1
Pts. & vacs.................. 6–15
A's through E's.............. 7–15
All other areas.............. 8–31

Goal: Improve parts inventory control.

Measurement:
Reduce back orders by 40%. (Bring back order list down from 50 to 30.)
Reduce interim orders by 50% (from 4 per month to 2).
Remove overstock. (Inventory should come down by 12%.)

Complete project by 8–31.

Fig. 8-2. Example of Work Plans and Goals.

conduct these reviews as a team. In other words, each subordinate manager reviews his draft of work plans and goals in a group meeting that includes not only his manager, but also his peers. Thus, each subordinate manager has an opportunity to contribute to the total work plans and goals for the entire component. He is truly an important member of the whole team. In every case, the manager will play an important role in the formulation of the final draft of the work plans and goals for each individual. This document will constitute the contract under which the individual works in the ensuing period.

If expected results are defined as specifically and objectively as possible for each goal in the work plan, performance appraisal will become automatic. The individual will not have to be told by his manager whether or not he is performing satisfactorily. He will know as well as the manager whether or not he is meeting his commitments.

Day-to-day Coaching. Needless to say, the manager's responsibilities do not end when the work plan has been completed. He can provide valuable guidance to the subordinate manager on a day-to-day basis. Common sense indicates, and research has proved, that the more immediate the feedback about needed corrective actions is, the more effective it is. It is certainly more appropriate and natural to correct errors when they occur than to wait until the time of a regularly scheduled performance appraisal discussion to call attention to shortcomings. This kind of day-to-day coaching also is a natural management activity. It does not require the kinds of counseling skills demanded in a more intensive and comprehensive formalized appraisal discussion.

Review and Recycling. A formal review session between man and manager should be held at the end of the period agreed upon when goals were set. Usually this is about three months. At this meeting, progress in the achievement of goals is reviewed, new goals are set, and in some cases the old goals are recycled.

As in the original goal setting discussion, the subordinate manager should play a leading role. A few days before this discussion is scheduled, the manager should ask the subordinate to prepare for this review discussion. This is, in a sense, a business review for the subordinate. The manager can help ensure that this review discussion will go well if he uses the following tactics:

1. Keep the discussion on an informal level.
2. Listen as much as possible, rather than talking. Although the manager may feel that he is accomplishing more if he does most of the talking, the odds are that the opposite will be true. The more talking the subordinate does, the more constructive the outcomes are likely to be.
3. Keep the discussion focused on the work, not on the man. Bringing up personal shortcomings of the individual is only likely to put him on the defensive. If he becomes defensive, he is unlikely to take a constructive approach to the solution of problems.
4. Try to encourage the man as much as possible, instead of criticizing.
5. Keep the discussion on an analytical plane rather than on a performance appraisal track. Look for causes and solutions to problems instead of placing blame.

Advantages of Work Planning. The use of a formalized work planning program, as a means of providing coaching and counseling help to subordinate managers, has several advantages. In the first place, this kind of counseling is a normal and natural activity for the manager because it focuses on the work to be done. The manager is not asked to play the role of a psychologist. He is in a sense just performing his assigned duties as a manager.

Second, if the procedure diagrammed in Figure 8-1 is followed, all activities of everyone in the organization will relate directly to the overall plans for the business as a whole. In other words, the activities of all individuals are integrated to accomplish most efficiently the goals of the total organization.

Third, the work planning approach to counseling is by nature a two-way, man-to-man process. Counseling through appraisal, on the other hand, is much more likely to be a one-way process in which the superior manager takes the role of judge and the subordinate manager the role of defendant.

SERVING OTHER COUNSELING NEEDS

The work planning program has been found to serve very well the needs of the subordinate manager for a clear definition of performance expectations and for feedback on how he is performing. The subordinate also has other needs for information or counseling from the manager which the work planning approach may not serve. Discussions of performance on specific work plans and goals may not provide the individual with as clear a picture as he would like of how he is regarded by management in a general sense. Work-oriented discussions also are not likely to provide information about future opportunities and plans for the individual. These are additional counseling needs for which a good manager should provide. The manager will also want to provide some kind of feedback counseling when salary decisions are communicated to the individual.

As we stated earlier, no single program can serve all counseling needs. But two programs can serve most needs. The work planning program serves some needs for appraisal and counseling very well. A second program which should be used in connection with the work planning approach involves periodic discussions with each subordinate manager covering salary status, how he is regarded in the organization in a general sense, and career plans and opportunities. Such a discussion should be held at least annually for the employee who is further along in his career.

This type of career planning discussion should not cover details of performance which are normally discussed in work planning sessions, except as the manager may feel that it is necessary to justify a salary decision. The manager should also avoid passing on judgments regarding a man's personal short-comings. Most judgments of this type are highly subjective. Characteristics that one manager might consider as very handicapping may not be seen as limiting in any way by another manager. It is extremely important that the individual's self-esteem remain intact if he is to be effective in his work.

A counseling interview of this kind is much more difficult to handle than is a work planning and review discussion. The job will be made easier if the manager observes the following precautions:

1. *Don't Try to Play God.* Opinions about performance are legitimate and appropriate. When a manager begins to counsel a man about his future, on the other hand, he is on less firm ground. Remember that the manager's opinion about the man's potential may not be the final word.

2. *Don't Try to Be a Psychologist.* Avoid discussions and advice about personal problems that are not directly related to the job. Also, do not try to look for underlying or devious causes of behavior.

3. *Use a Participative Approach.* In discussing salary action, it may be

difficult to use a participative approach. A manager is obliged to communicate his salary decision and the reasons for it. In talking about career plans and opportunities, on the other hand, most managers will find it easier and more effective to react to the individual's expressed plans and goals than to present ideas to the man. It is only natural to feel that one is not fulfilling his obligations as a counselor if he does not present a plan and give direct advice. It has been demonstrated, however, that a more nondirective approach, where the counselor merely reacts and contributes to the counselee's ideas and plans, almost invariably yields more constructive outcomes.

4. *Avoid Comparisons with Others in the Organization.* Interpersonal comparisons seldom serve a constructive purpose. Certainly, they are not likely to contribute to effective teamwork in the organization. At worst, they can backfire in an embarrassing way.

5. *Tailor the Discussion to the Individual.* A manager may want to give much more direct advice, for example, to a young trainee than to the 55-year-old shop manager who has been around longer than his superior has. Likewise, the very competent and secure individual may be able to use candid information about his development needs more constructively than the person who is less secure and confident.

IN SUMMARY

As stated at the start of this chapter, appraising and counseling subordinate managers is a complex process. It is also a controversial topic. Although most textbooks recommend an annual, comprehensive performance appraisal discussion to serve all counseling needs, we strongly caution against such a program. The most natural and effective counseling for most managers will be that related directly to the work of the subordinate to be counseled. A work planning and goal setting program will serve most of the job-related counseling needs of subordinates.

The manager does not need any special training to handle a work planning and goal setting program successfully. Discussions with subordinates under such a program are aimed directly at the work to be performed. Other needs for counseling may provide a little more difficulty for the manager. Explaining a salary decision, for example, may sometimes be difficult. Advising an individual about what the future holds can be tricky. However, the manager is not likely to get into trouble if he mostly listens rather than talks in such discussions. In other words, he should use a participative approach. The initiative in these discussions should be largely the subordinate's rather than the manager's.

This advice may seem inconsistent with the definition of counseling. It may seem that the manager is not accomplishing anything constructive if he does not give advice. A great deal of experience and research have shown, however, that the outcomes of a counseling discussion where the counselor merely reacts to and clarifies the ideas expressed by the counselee are usually much more constructive and effective than the more directive approach, even when the counselor is a highly trained professional.

Although most managers may prefer to avoid appraisal and counseling sessions, the use of the task-related approach to performance appraisal recommended here, and the indirect approach in counseling discussions for other purposes, should make such sessions relatively easy. The manager who gives these approaches a try will find that the dividends realized in the form of improved performance and motivation on the part of subordinates will pay many times over for the time and energy that he has invested in such appraisal and counseling.

BIBLIOGRAPHY

Hughes, Charles L., "Why Goal Oriented Performance Reviews Succeed and Fail," *Personnel Journal*, June, 1966.

Huse, Edgar F., and Emanuel Kay, "Improving Employee Productivity through Work Planning," in Jerome W. Blood (ed.), *The Personnel Job in a Changing World*, American Management Association, New York, 1964.

Kellogg, Marion S., *Closing the Performance Gap*, American Management Association, New York, 1967.

Maier, Norman R. F., *The Appraisal Interview: Objectives, Methods, and Skills*, John Wiley & Sons, Inc., New York, 1958.

McGregor, Douglas, "An Uneasy Look at Performance Appraisal," *Harvard Business Review*, May–June, 1957.

Meyer, H. H., Emanuel Kay, and J. R. P. French, Jr., "Split Roles in Performance Appraisal," *Harvard Business Review*, January–February, 1965.

SUPPORTING SERVICES AND ACTIVITIES

CHAPTER ONE

How to Utilize Staff Services

THOMAS I. S. BOAK, JR. *Works Manager, Aluminum Company of America, Cressona, Pennsylvania*

Basically, staff organizations are established to perform work for the line which the latter cannot perform as effectively, as inexpensively, or as quickly for itself. The availability of properly established staff groups permits specialization of technique and concentration of effort, beyond that which the line can supply, on solving line problems. At the same time, the line organization can concentrate on the problems of the day, knowing that attention is being devoted to developmental projects vital to continuing progress.

A CONCEPT OF MANUFACTURING STAFF

Before discussing the specific role of the manufacturing staff, it will be well to consider the broad types of duties into which all staff activities may be said to fall:
1. Those that are largely concerned with influencing the "climate" in which work is done
2. Those distinctly corporate duties that must be performed in the manufacturing area
3. Those that are specifically related to getting the work done

In the first activity, one finds public relations, labor relations, salary administration, organizational analysis, and the like. The second category includes such things as the financial programs, pension plan development and administration, and purchasing. The production-related third category includes such things as process engineering, industrial engineering, and product accounting.

Influencing the climate in which work is done is a most significant part of the manufacturing executive's responsibility; therefore the development of practices in these areas requires close contact. Organizationally, those work-

10–3

ing in the areas should report to the executive. The activities in the second area, being of a corporate nature, provide (or require) coordination and uniformity and often a breadth of view independent of local influences. The activities in the third, directly workplace-related area are more common and easily understood.

What staffs perform what types of activity depends on the organization, its history, and the individuals who establish policy. Certain staffs, of course, perform in more than one area of activity. For example, the personnel department might well have responsibility in the climate-influence area through its labor relations or salary administration section. In addition, it might handle development and administration of the pension plan with its requirement of coordination and uniformity. Finally, in the work-related area, personnel might be involved in such activities as employment and training. Another organization might have a different alignment of responsibilities, but in considering those responsibilities, the three-area concept can be helpful.

ROLE OF STAFF

The staff exists to provide the following services to line or other organizational units:
1. Advice
2. Service
3. Coordination
4. Functional direction
   a. Development
   b. Inspection and review of performance
   c. Exercise of control from a technical standpoint
5. Liaison

Advice. Perhaps the most characteristic staff function is advice to the line organization in specialized fields or functional areas. The relations between line and staff in this advisory function should be such that line executives are free to seek such assistance if they require it, and staff executives are free to offer advice if they feel it will be helpful. However, in supplying such advice and counsel, a staff executive does not exercise any direct line authority over operating units.

Service. Various corporate staff departments often offer services to other organizational units, because these services can be performed more effectively and efficiently on a centralized basis, or because the divisions and subsidiaries involved cannot justifiably support the necessary skills. The use of corporate staff services by the divisions may be mandatory in some instances because of the generally more effective performance attainable by a centralized activity. In providing services to the line organization, a staff organizational unit does not attempt to make decisions for the line organization or in any way to assume line authority.

Coordination. Another function performed by various corporate staff departments is coordinating the activities of two or more organizational units to ensure consistency, prevent duplication of effort, avoid omissions in programs, and achieve optimum overall results. Again, however, in performing their coordinating responsibilities, corporate staff executives do not exercise any direct line authority over other segments of the organization. They do not issue directives or orders, and line executives have the right to appeal the recommendations of corporate staff executives when they feel that this is advisable.

Functional Direction. An important area of responsibility of the corporate staff is exercising functional direction over the line organization regarding the performance of certain activities. This important staff role is frequently misunderstood. To state the matter simply, the chief executive officer cannot personally do everything that must be done. He needs specialized assistance in certain key functional areas, not only to provide him with advice but also to represent him in these aspects of his role as the line executive in charge. Key corporate staff executives are then, to all intents and purposes, extensions of the chief executive in the functions which they represent.

Obviously, it is not feasible to permit corporate staff executives to give direct line orders to members of management in other organizational units. Accordingly, corporate staff executives should exercise functional direction over activities only in their specialized areas. This differs significantly from line authority and includes:

1. Development—for approval by the chief executive—of objectives, plans, policies, and related procedures, standards, and programs required to carry out the function for which the corporate staff executive has staff responsibility. Subsequently, a top manager is able to delegate to line executives the responsibility and authority to make decisions within this framework.

2. Inspection and review of the staff function on a company-wide basis and submission of comments and recommendations to divisional personnel and to the chief executive officer. In the inspection and review role, key staff executives are able to bring abnormal conditions to the attention of the chief executive officer. Thereby the chief executive officer can be sure that decisions are being made within the framework of approved policies and procedures.

3. Exercise of control, from a technical standpoint, over the specific practices, procedures, and techniques that govern the function company-wide. It should be reemphasized that, in exercising their responsibilities for functional direction, corporate staff executives do not have line authority. Thus, executives receiving functional direction should have the right to appeal to their line superiors the recommendations of staff executives. However, in a healthy, well-coordinated organization, the occasions on which suggestions of competent staff executives are appealed to higher authority should be few.

Liaison. The way in which communications are handled is also an important aspect of the role of the corporate staff. All major instructions, such as policy changes, emanating from a corporate staff department should be approved by the chief executive officer and transmitted through line executives having key management responsibility and authority. Similarly, approvals of important matters submitted by field line management should be made by corporate line executives, generally after review by corporate staff departments.

Staff instructions involving minor technical matters should not require close adherence to formal line channels, however. Direct interchange of ideas and information, or liaison, regarding the technical or specialized phases of activities should exist at all times between corporate staff executives and their counterparts in the field.

STAFF AT THE PLANT LEVEL

The foregoing discussion has dealt with a concept of the manufacturing staff and the corporate functions and the responsibilities which may be attributed to it. The local plant staff is, of course, an extension of the corporate staff; it is to the plant manager what the corporate staff is to the chief executive officer. In a corporation where all operations are located in one geographic location, the corporate and plant alignments of staff responsibility obviously can be one and the same.

At plant level, the professional skills to be provided in staff services are determined by analysis of such factors as cost-benefit relationship, nature of the manufacturing process, and availability of adequate staff services from the corporate office. The responsibilities of advice, coordination, development, and inspection and review apply to the plant staff as well as the corporate. Questions to be asked when considering the establishment of plant staff might be: What can be afforded—what can be justified by results? Or: What is necessary because of corporate demand? Other questions:

In the skill area: Are the problems faced of sufficient magnitude and frequency to justify local staff? Can the service be provided more economically by corporate staff or by outside consultants?

In company procedural area: Does the control of company-wide procedures and techniques require the establishment of staff?

PROBLEMS IN UTILIZATION OF STAFF SERVICES

One cannot consider how the manufacturing manager can utilize staff services without being aware of certain basic problems that arise in any line-staff relationship. A staff organization exists to provide specific attention to solving problems to which the manufacturing organization cannot give undivided attention because of the press of day-to-day production effort. The staff also has the advantage of familiarity with specialized techniques for solving problems; such techniques are not usually familiar to line organization personnel. The person in charge of the manufacturing operation must know when it is desirable to use staff personnel to recommend solutions to his manufacturing problems and when it is preferable to handle local problems himself. The line group must minimize shifting problem solving assignments to staff. Otherwise the tendency may develop to throw too much routine decision making from line to staff with consequent weakening of the line organization. Problems in which the staff organizations should become involved are those which go beyond routine production problems.

With the introduction of staff personnel to the line operation and the submission of their recommended solutions to line problems, the manufacturing executive may be faced with basic problems in human relations. His solution to these problems may affect the success attained through the use of the staff. The staff problem solver may take a detached, "expert" attitude as he considers the line problem. This at best will cause line organization resentment and at worst will reflect shallow analysis and ineffective solution. The manufacturing manager must recognize these hazards and manage the conflicts which will certainly occur. Control is desirable and a necessary part of progress.

The best staff assistance to the line organization is accomplished when the staff influence is catalytic. In this situation, the staff man will earn the respect of the line organization, and his thoughts and attitudes may be unconsciously adopted by line managers. In such cases, there is an integration of the staff man and of his ideas and plans into the overall manufacturing activity, and the greatest benefit is realized.

MINIMIZING PROBLEMS IN USE OF STAFF

Recognition of line-staff problems is the first step to minimizing those problems. Several basic points should be considered to assure natural promotion of the most effective use of staff functions in the overall operation.

Organizational Placement of Staff. Because there will be differences of opinion between line and staff, there must be a mechanism for resolving such differences. This can be provided by the organizational placement of the staff and line groups. The person in charge of the staff group and the one in charge of the line organization should be at the same organizational level. They should carry equal weight with the person to whom they report as the merits of their cases are argued.

Assignment of Staff Responsibilities. There must be a clear understanding of the responsibilities assigned to individual staffs; that is, a clear statement of the areas that each staff group is responsible for. Thus, while the design and cost estimating for a given capital expenditure may be assigned to one staff organization, its economic justification may be assigned to another. With such responsibilities clearly assigned and understood, duplication of work is avoided and effective specialization may be carried out. It is vital that these specific responsibilities be fully understood and communicated throughout the organization to avoid organizational misunderstandings.

Integration of the Staff Function. The most important aspect of effective utilization of staff is how well the staff responsibility, in the person of the individual performing that responsibility, becomes integrated into the total organization. The person must have the respect of the manufacturing group in which he is working at the time. He must be completely conversant with the operation and must be cognizant of the fact that any solutions which he proposes for operating problems will pay off only after being put into effect by the line organization. His ideas will remain ideas unless the force of his solution and his personal effectiveness influence the line organization to support and implement his plan.

A staff man must not see his work as an end in itself. He will be successful only if he avoids the appearance of being an "expert" and adopts an attitude of serving the manufacturing organization.

Integration of the staff function can often be aided by physical deployment of staff members to the manufacturing areas they serve. This is especially true in the multiproduction-centered operations. Physical proximity helps the staff man to gain an intimate knowledge of the operations being served, a first requirement to effective staff work. Only with such familiarity can the staff man gain the respect of the line organization. Physical location in a department also promotes beneficial personal relationships as staff and line personnel are brought together on a day-to-day basis.

POSITION OF THE MANUFACTURING MANAGER IN THE UTILIZATION OF STAFF SERVICES

The perspective of the manufacturing executive as he views the problems will decide whether the staff can be helpful. He must be entirely objective when the staff initiates a recommendation for study or change. He must avoid becoming partisan. He is in a key position to determine the effectiveness of staff use. He is in the best position to know the scope of problems faced and thus to know the benefits which will accrue from their solution.

He knows the capabilities and responsibilities of the manufacturing personnel and should be able to look objectively at ideas and plans for improving his manufacturing operation.

He, better than any one else, is in a position to assign priority of effort. When he has directed where this effort is to be placed—whether line, staff, or both—he must reap the advantages of this effort by immediate implementation of effective problem solutions. It is in this implementation that the manufacturing executive employs his greatest skill. At this point he is completely dedicated to accomplishing the greatest benefit for the enterprise.

BIBLIOGRAPHY

Dale, Ernest, and Lyndall F. Urwick, *Staff in Organization*, McGraw-Hill Book Company, New York, 1960.

Haire, Mason (ed.), *Modern Organization Theory*, John Wiley & Sons, Inc., New York, 1959.

Hicks, Herbert G., *The Management of Organizations*, McGraw-Hill Book Company, New York, 1967.

Jerome, William Travers III, *Executive Control: The Catalyst*, John Wiley & Sons, Inc., New York, 1961.

Juran, Joseph M., *Managerial Breakthrough*, McGraw-Hill Book Company, New York, 1964.

Maynard, H. B. (ed.), *Handbook of Business Administration*, McGraw-Hill Book Company, New York, 1967.

Moore, Franklin G., *Manufacturing Management*, rev. ed., Richard D. Irwin, Homewood, Ill., 1958.

CHAPTER TWO

Industrial Engineering

ROSS W. HAMMOND *Chief, Industrial Development Division, Georgia Institute of Technology, Atlanta, Georgia*

Industrial engineering can perform a major service role for the manufacturing manager. The generally accepted definition of industrial engineering is that subscribed to and endorsed by the American Institute of Industrial Engineers, Inc.

Industrial engineering is concerned with the design, improvement, and installation of integrated systems of men, materials, and equipment. It draws upon specialized knowledge and skill in the mathematical, physical, and social sciences, together with principles and methods of engineering analysis and design, to specify, predict, and evaluate the results to be obtained from such systems.

This definition, though broad, does not provide the specifics which a manufacturing manager must know to utilize industrial engineering effectively. These specifics will be discussed in this chapter.

GOAL OF INDUSTRIAL ENGINEERING

Industrial engineering practitioners generally agree that the overall goal of the industrial engineering function is profit improvement. This is usually accomplished through programs for controlling production and for reducing costs. Profit improvement is also the goal of top management, middle management, and other elements of the corporate structure. One corporate unit cannot achieve profit improvement by itself—it must be an effort of the entire business enterprise.

Industrial Engineering and the Manufacturing Manager. Industrial engineering, from the manufacturing manager's point of view, should function as a supporting element to the manager. Usually the staff of the industrial engineering department compiles data on the activities for which the department has responsibility. Staff members analyze these data, form conclusions, consider alternatives, and recommend courses of action to the manufacturing manager. Depending on how the industrial engineering department is organized, its place in the organization, and the responsibilities assigned to it, it may provide some or all of the following services to the manufacturing department head:

1. Advise on best work methods and processes—shop and office
2. Establish standards of work performance—production, quality, material
3. Establish standards of measurement
4. Establish cost, budgetary, inventory, and other controls
5. Design materials and quality control specifications
6. Calculate economic lot sizes
7. Assist in increasing productivity
8. Assist in cost reduction
9. Develop and apply production planning and scheduling procedures
10. Apply statistical and other mathematical analyses
11. Simulate systems
12. Develop information systems
13. Provide sound layouts for expansions or production changes
14. Carry out engineering economy comparisons and studies
15. Analyze feasibility of capital expenditure proposals
16. Conduct safety programs
17. Prepare job descriptions and evaluations
18. Develop training programs
19. Prepare wage incentive plans
20. Analyze nonfinancial incentives
21. Perform plant location studies and market analyses

This list is by no means all-inclusive. However, it demonstrates the cross section of activities which may be available to the manufacturing manager through the industrial engineering function.

It would be an unusual company in which all the above-listed activities were assigned to the industrial engineering department. Hence, it is obligatory that the manufacturing manager be aware of the specific responsibilities and capabilities of his company's industrial engineering function. Armed with this knowledge and an awareness of company policies and procedures, the line manufacturing manager can make intelligent use of this support activity.

INDUSTRIAL ENGINEERING FUNCTIONS

As the preceding material indicates, it is possible for a great many varied activities to come under the purview of industrial engineering in a given company. However, all these activities may be grouped into a smaller number of major functional categories. These categories include methods analysis, work measurement, control procedures, plant facilities, material handling, mathematical tools, wage and salary plans, and miscellaneous tools and techniques. Each of these will be discussed in relation to the manufacturing function. These activities are covered in greater detail in the *Industrial Engineering Handbook*.[1]

Methods Analysis. The manufacturing manager is interested in providing the best product at the lowest possible cost. The industrial engineer, through

[1] H. B. Maynard (ed.), *Industrial Engineering Handbook*, 2d ed., McGraw-Hill Book Company, New York, 1963.

methods analysis, can assist the manager in reaching these goals. Methods analysis includes activities which have been variously categorized as motion study, methods engineering, operation analysis, and process planning.

Motion Study. Motion study is the analysis of manual and eye motions occurring in an operation or work cycle for the purpose of eliminating wasted movements and establishing a better sequence and coordination of movements. Its purpose is to permit operators to work with minimum effort and maximum efficiency.

Motion study can be applied to a single operator performing one operation or to the entire flow of material through the plant. The industrial engineer has a number of techniques and types of equipment which he can use in motion study. A full-scale analysis of a complex motion problem might call for use of all techniques and equipment, whereas a simple motion analysis might utilize only one technique or piece of equipment.

Some of the techniques and equipment used by the industrial engineer in motion study are:

1. Process chart
2. Micromotion study—simultaneous-motion-cycle chart (SIMO)
3. Chronocyclegraph
4. Workplace study

The manufacturing manager can call upon the services of the industrial engineer to analyze a particular production operation such as a repetitive drill press operation. The industrial engineer will break the task down, element by element, studying each element in turn and its relationship to other parts of the process. He will analyze the workplace to ensure that parts to be processed are properly located and that the parts which have been processed can be conveniently disposed of by the operator. Everything which can possibly eliminate waste motions will be considered. After having thoroughly studied and analyzed the operation, the industrial engineer will recommend changes in the operation. He will then present his suggested changes to the supervisor for consideration. If the supervisor accepts the recommendations, the operators are trained to use the new and more efficient method of utilizing the drill press.

Methods Engineering. The aim of methods engineering is to improve methods and establish work standards. This technique involves the scrutiny of each operation of a given piece of work to eliminate unnecessary elements or operations and to determine the quickest and best method of performing the work. It includes the improvement and standardization of methods, equipment, and working conditions; operator training; the determination of standard times; and occasionally advice on and administration of various incentive plans.

The manufacturing manager can utilize the industrial engineer to conduct methods engineering studies of operations to great advantage. Such studies are essentially a combination of motion study and other techniques to achieve a standardized approach to the performance of a task in the most efficient manner.

Operation Analysis. Operation analysis is a procedure used in studying the major factors which affect the general method of performing a given operation.

This procedure considers the following environmental factors surrounding the operation to be studied:

1. Repetitiveness of the operation
2. Human attention needed for the operation
3. Life of the operation

From analysis of these factors, the industrial engineer can recommend the type of methods study which can be economically justified. In the course of making this analysis, the industrial engineer may use an analysis chart which will act as a checklist to ensure that he has considered the vital elements involved in a task. Such a chart might include such elements as:

1. Design of part and assembly
2. Material specification
3. Process of manufacture
4. Purpose of operation
5. Tolerances and inspection requirements
6. Tools and speeds
7. Equipment analysis
8. Workplace layout and motion analysis
9. Material flow
10. Plant layout

To carry out this analysis, the industrial engineer may utilize an operation analysis chart, which is an abbreviated outline form covering the above ten elements. A more detailed checklist may also be used. This includes all the questions which should be answered in considering the listed elements. These are only tools, however, to permit the industrial engineer to do a better job of operation analysis.

Process Planning. Process planning consists primarily of planning a method or a series of methods for the economic manufacture of a part or product. A major characteristic of process planning is that it usually is a "before the fact" activity; that is, the planning is done before production is started. Many other methods activities are designed to improve or change existing processes and hence might be considered "after the fact" activities.

This capability of the industrial engineering staff is of great importance to the manufacturing manager. It means that the production of new products can be instituted in a manner which has been studied and designed for optimum operation.

In developing an operation sequence, the process planner, who frequently is an industrial engineer, must have certain basic information:

1. The quantity of products to be produced
2. The nature of the materials to be used in the product
3. Permissible tolerances and precision needed
4. Amounts and kinds of equipment available
5. Current loading of existing machinery
6. Agreement on standard terminology

The process planner uses a variety of tools, including:

1. Analysis sheets
2. Flow process charts
3. Operation process charts
4. Machine load charts
5. Plant layout sheets
6. Standard data charts
7. Cutting speed and feed charts
8. Available equipment listing

Work Measurement. Work measurement is one of the most widely applied industrial engineering techniques. A number of systems for measuring work are in use. They generally fall in two major categories—time study and predetermined elemental time standards. The measurement of work usually leads to the development and use of time standards.

Time standards are applicable to such diverse manufacturing areas as the following:

1. Product design—effect of alternative manufacturing methods, materials, and designs
2. Equipment design—use in considering costs for alternative methods of equipment manufacture and operation and the design of tools, jigs, and fixtures
3. New-equipment selection—standards are helpful in determining new-equipment capital costs as well as setup and operation costs
4. Process planning—determination of time required by the process or operation and evaluation of alternative methods
5. Production scheduling—use in considering work loads of men and machines, time in process, and effect of alternative methods
6. Plant layout and material handling—determination of effective and efficient location of equipment and material handling methods
7. Budgetary control—use for determining direct and indirect costs and man and machine loading
8. Production staffing—application to help determine numbers, types, and training of people for production activities
9. Employee relations—use for job assignment, job evaluation, incentive plans, and collective bargaining

In a manufacturing concern, almost everyone performing a management function can use time standards either directly or indirectly. This accounts for the frequency of occurrence of this function in industrial engineering departments in industry.

There are a number of major techniques and approaches to work measurement. Individual industrial engineers are usually more experienced in one particular technique. However, the good industrial engineer trains himself to have a reasonable familiarity with all the better-known methods of conducting work measurement.

Time Study. Let us suppose that line supervision wishes to establish a standard for an existing plant operation which has not previously been measured. This request is transmitted through the manufacturing manager's office to the industrial engineering department. Here it is assigned to a properly qualified industrial engineer.

The industrial engineer prepares to make the study by first reviewing the history of the operation and the intended purpose of the study. He reviews the way the operation is being performed from the viewpoint of whether the operation is necessary and whether the methods used are optimal.

The line foreman is consulted for information and agreement on suggested method changes. An operator is selected and notified by the supervisor. The reason for the study and the methodology to be used are explained to the operator.

The operation is then broken down into elements by the industrial engineer and described in writing. When the elements have been properly described, the engineer times each element, using any of several procedures and pieces of equipment. Although stopwatches are best known and most used, there are many electronic and optic aids which can be used in time study. The industrial engineer rates the performance of the operator against a defined concept of normal performance. Allowances which are appropriate, such as for maintenance of equipment, interruptions and delays, and personal time, are considered. The data of a number of cycles are reviewed and aberrations eliminated. From the data, a standard time for the performance of the operation is calculated. This in turn can be utilized in establishing a standard rate for the operation, for incentive payment, or for other purposes.

Work Sampling. Work sampling is a procedure, based on statistics, which employs a large number of random observations of an operation. The various activities observed in this procedure tend to fall into categories, such as operation, setup, maintenance, or delay, in the same proportion that they are inherently present in the operation. With this method, it is possible to establish job standards for many operations in industry with the same accuracy found in stopwatch time studies.

From the manufacturing manager's point of view, standards derived from work sampling generally may be achieved at less cost than by traditional time study methods.

Group Timing Technique. Time study and work sampling may be combined in a procedure called group timing technique. It permits the study of a number of operators simultaneously. A great number of observations can be made in a short period. These measurements can be used in the establishment of time standards.

Memomotion Study. Memomotion study utilizes special motion picture cameras for photographing and studying manufacturing and other activities. It provides a permanent record of a job, is accurate, and is relatively easy and economical to use.

Predetermined Elemental Time Standards. Techniques in the predetermined elemental time standard category are based on assigning time values to basic motions. These, in various groupings, can then be combined and totaled for more complicated motions and tasks. From the groupings, time standards can be developed.

Systems which use elemental motions to build predetermined time standards include methods-time measurement (MTM), work factor (WF), motion-time analysis (MTA), and basic motion timestudy (BMT).

The manufacturing manager utilizes these industrial engineering techniques primarily to:

1. Improve existing operations and methods
2. Design new operations
3. Establish time standards
4. Estimate costs of production

There are, of course, other areas of activity to which these techniques can be applied.

Methods-Time Measurement (MTM). The MTM approach to predetermined elemental time standards is widely accepted. It was first described by Maynard, Stegemerten, and Schwab in a book titled *Methods-Time Measurement* (1948).

Methods-time measurement (MTM) is defined as a procedure which analyzes any manual operation or method into the basic motions required to perform it and assigns to each motion a predetermined time standard that is determined by the nature of the motion and the conditions under which it is made.

Much fundamental research on nineteen fundamental motions, and physical and environmental conditions surrounding these motions, has resulted in extensive data tables. In these tables, time is expressed in time measurement units, or TMU's. One TMU is equal to 0.00001 hour.

The industrial engineer, in analyzing the time required for a task by means of MTM, does the same preliminary review of the task and the best method to perform it as does a time study engineer. When the proper way to perform the task has been agreed upon, the task is analyzed in terms of the basic motions involved. For example, motions involved in a task may involve Reach, Move, Turn, Apply Pressure, Grasp, Release, Position, Disengage, and various body motions. The standard MTM data provide different times for different distances and circumstances for each motion.

The combined times for all movements in a task, together with suitable allowances, permit the calculation of standard times.

Work Factor (WF). The bases of the work factor system are a set of fundamental tables of motion and mental process times, and sets of rules, definitions, and procedures for applying the technique. This technique originated with the Work Factor Company, Inc. The words "work factor" relate to an index of motion difficulty in terms of control or weight (or resistance) involved in the performance of a task.

For a given task, the system is based on the body members used, the type of movement or mental process, distance moved, and other considerations. The result is a standard time expressed in work factor units (equal to 0.0001 minute).

Basic Motion Timestudy (BMT). BMT is a system of predetermined motion-time standards. It is based on the definition of a basic motion. This occurs when a body member that has been at rest moves and again comes to rest. The standard times established under BMT are based largely on the major motion(s) with supplementary times for other circumstances such as simultaneous motion, eye time, force factor, and turn.

Motion-Time Analysis (MTA). MTA combines the use of elemental motions (variations of therbligs) and utilization of better methods for performing tasks. The analysis phase revolves largely around the identification and elimination of avoidable loss.

Control Procedures. A major part of the responsibility frequently assigned to the industrial engineering department is the design, installation, and maintenance of control systems and procedures. There are a great many control systems which can be utilized by an industrial enterprise. They include:

1. Production planning and control
2. Inventory control
3. Quality control
4. Reliability
5. Budgetary control
6. Cost control
7. Systems design
8. Network planning techniques

The manufacturing manager must rely on the products of such systems to ascertain whether the manufacturing process is producing the products of the company in sufficient quantity, on time, with proper quality, and at the most economical cost to the enterprise. All the above-mentioned systems are designed in some way to help the manager determine the facts about the manufacturing process.

Production Planning and Control. (This subject is covered in detail in Section 3, Chapter 5.) The primary function of a group responsible for production planning and control is to assist the manufacturing management in the optimization of production. It is defined as the procedure of planning, routing, scheduling, dispatching, and expediting the flow of materials, parts, subassemblies, and assemblies within the plant from the raw state to the finished product in an orderly and efficient manner.

Production planning is generally done in terms of current (one year or less) and long-range planning. Production control is made up of production scheduling and production dispatching and follow-up.

Production planning and control may be a separate department, or it may be a function of the industrial engineering department, depending on the size of the company and the way in which it is organized.

This function is universally needed by all manufacturing companies to assure manufacturing control. Measuring the effectiveness of production planning and control operations is extremely important.

There are four areas in which effectiveness of the function may be measured by the manufacturing manager:

1. Record of delivery, on time, of the finished product
2. Management of inventories
3. Management of production
4. Internal management of the production planning and control function

Relatively simple charts and records can be kept in these four areas to measure effectiveness.

Inventory Control. (This subject is covered in detail in Section 7, Chapter 7.) Inventory control is a complex activity which regulates the amounts of inventory of all kinds on hand to minimize the inventory investment while ensuring that production is maintained on schedule.

For inventory control to be effective, the following conditions must exist:

1. The objective of the inventory control function must be clearly defined.
2. Policies, plans, and standards must be developed.
3. A workable organization must be established.
4. Procedures and methods must be developed.
5. The necessary physical facilities must be provided.
6. Results must be checked to verify the effectiveness of the program.

Inventory control may be done within a structure of the amount of funds available for investment in inventory and on a month-to-month basis, or it may be calculated as a function of the number of times that inventories turn over in a year.

One of the basic activities in inventory control is the determination of when to order an item and how many of the item to order to replenish inventories. This procedure is fundamental to the manufacturing process, because an entire plant can be shut down for want of a single part.

Quality Control. (This subject is covered in detail in Section 7, Chapter 2.) Quality control is a system of inspection, analysis, and action applied to the manufacturing process so that, by inspecting a small portion of the products, an analysis of the quality may be made and action taken on the process to achieve and maintain the desired quality level.

The techniques used are largely statistical in nature and are based largely on probability theory. If quality control responsibility is successfully administered, then the following benefits are possible:

1. Increased production
2. Lower unit costs
3. Improved employee morale
4. Better quality

Reliability. (This subject is also covered in detail in Section 7, Chapter 2.) Reliability is related to quality control. It is defined as the probability that a device will perform satisfactorily in its specified function for a specific period of time under a given set of operating conditions. It can be considered as quality control plus a time element.

Reliability is based largely on mathematical approaches to probability analysis. Use of reliability techniques permits prediction of the ability of a system to perform the intended function. These techniques may be used to analyze the modifications necessary to bring a system up to the desired level of reliability. The ultimate purpose of reliability testing is to provide a statistical estimate of the reliability of the device or system being analyzed.

A successful reliability function produces for management the same benefits previously listed for quality control.

Budgetary Control. (This subject is covered in detail in Section 4, Chapter 4.) Manufacturing managers are always confronted with activities related to budgets. They must prepare budget estimates, live within budgets, explain variances from budgets to top management, and so on.

In essence, budgeting is planning for profits. Budgetary control includes budgeting as one of its elements, but goes beyond it to monitor performance, to analyze causes for deviations from budgets, and to remove the causes for variance or change the budget targets.

The manufacturing goals are obviously related to the sales goals of an enterprise. The properly qualified industrial engineer can be of great practical assistance to the manufacturing manager in helping to design budgetary control systems and in the preparation of the budget itself. By virtue of his background in a company's operation, he can be particularly useful in the following budget considerations:

1. The allowance for staff departments such as engineering and production control
2. The anticipated use of equipment
3. Prices to be paid for new equipment, materials, and supplies
4. Rework and scrap allowances
5. Anticipated labor rates
6. The allowance for maintenance

Cost Control. (This subject is discussed in detail in Section 4, Chapter 5.) Budgetary control is essentially a system to plan for and improve profits. Cost control systems are designed to keep manufacturing management informed about costs after they have been incurred. This knowledge can then permit decisions designed to eliminate or ameliorate cost problems.

The basis of cost control is a system for measuring costs as accurately as possible. Such a system attempts to measure the cost of materials, direct labor, indirect labor, manufacturing overhead, and administrative and sales costs. Basic to its use is the development of standard costs for the various operations to be measured. The differences between actual expenditures and standard costs can then be quickly ascertained, and appropriate action taken. To account for changes in volume of production necessitated by varying conditions, a flexible budget is widely used. This can be established for payroll and materials. A periodic cost-and-variance statement permits analysis of the operation.

Systems Design. (This subject is covered in detail in Section 3, Chapter 1.) The whole operation of an industrial enterprise may be considered to be a complex system. The subsystem, made up of all aspects of the manufacturing function in a company, usually is a complex system in itself. It relates directly or indirectly to all other systems in the company and has complex internal relationships as well.

In recent years, there has been increasing study of the design of systems and subsystems, from the viewpoint of optimizing the operations. These systems vary greatly with the company and the functions being studied.

Network Planning Techniques. (This subject is covered in detail in Section 3, Chapter 6.) The late 1950s saw the first application of network planning techniques. These have subsequently been adapted to many manufacturing control situations.

Program evaluation review technique (PERT) and critical path method (CPM) are the best known of these techniques.

PERT consists essentially of a network model which simulates a complex, simultaneous, and sequential set of events. By analysis of the network, the longest path through the network in terms of time is determined. This is called the critical path. All the activities and events on this path are examined, with the aim of reducing the time on the critical path. By putting additional manpower on the tasks involved in the critical path, it is often possible to shorten that path (and time) considerably.

Critical path scheduling is applicable to many different activities. One of these is the construction business. In this field, a good many activities are dependent on previous events. For example, concrete cannot be poured until the forms have been erected, carpenters cannot erect the studding until the concrete has been poured, and so on. By charting all the jobs to be done and the cost required for each (generally on an optimistic, normal, and pessimistic basis), it is possible to develop the longest or critical path through the network of such activities. Then by analyzing the jobs on the critical path, the scheduled time to completion can be compressed (for example, by adding equipment or personnel to certain jobs or by changing the methods used) so as to complete projects at the least cost.

The use of these techniques by the manufacturing manager (frequently through the industrial engineering department personnel) can affect manufacturing cost and time reduction. However, these are complex techniques, and they should not be applied to simple industrial problems. For involved network systems, the use of the computer becomes necessary.

Plant Facilities. The manufacturing manager should utilize the services of industrial engineers in various activities related to plant facilities. They have competence, generally, in the following areas:

1. Plant location
2. Plant design and layout
3. Equipment selection and replacement
4. Automated processes

The role that industrial engineers can play in these activities is described below:

Plant Location. (This subject is covered in detail in Section 5, Chapter 1.) A decision to locate a plant somewhere is generally a costly one for a company in terms of capital investment, recruiting of employees, and the like. In the long run, the company expects the move to be profitable. However, the profitability may be affected greatly by the ultimate location chosen. The analyses that must be made—first, in the decision to locate a new plant, and second, in the actual choice of the site and community—are extremely important to the overall profit picture of the company.

The industrial engineer, with a background knowledge of the company's policies, products, and markets, is well equipped to conduct the analysis needed. Four major location factors generally must be considered. These are markets, transportation, labor, and in some industries, raw materials. A decision to locate in a given area can usually be made after analysis of these major factors.

When it comes to choosing a specific location within the general area, a number of secondary location factors become important. These include such items as the tax situation, availability of sites properly served by utilities, local financing (where needed), community facilities, business climate, and labor climate in the various communities under consideration.

The manufacturing manager cannot be concerned with the mass of detail involved in the analysis. The industrial engineer, by virtue of background, training, and company knowledge, is well suited to conduct the analysis and make recommendations to management on possible alternative plant locations. Management, of course, must make the final location decision, based on the analysis plus overall considerations.

Plant Design and Layout. (This subject is covered in detail in Section 5, Chapter 2.) Plant design and layout, a traditional industrial engineering activity, embraces the physical arrangement of industrial facilities, both existing and proposed. The manufacturing manager is concerned with having the most efficient and economical layout compatible with employee safety and acceptance.

The industrial engineer brings to plant design and layout the following abilities:

1. To consider all factors affecting the plant layout
2. To minimize material movement distances
3. To optimize flow of work through the plant
4. To utilize all space effectively
5. To provide employee safety and environmental acceptance

When any of the following conditions exist, it should indicate to the manufacturing manager that a review of the present plant design and layout may be desirable:

1. Proposed changes in existing products
2. New products under consideration
3. Need for increased production
4. Failure to meet production and delivery dates
5. Maintenance costs out of control
6. Decline in quality
7. Working environment complaints
8. Higher than usual inventories
9. Increase in worker complaints
10. Congestion and lack of storage space
11. Poor safety record

There may, of course, be other reasons for these conditions arising in a plant, but often they are manifestations of need for improved plant layout.

Equipment Selection and Replacement. (This subject is covered in detail in Section 5, Chapters 4 and 5.) In the case of both initial equipment selection and continuing equipment replacement, the manufacturing manager is usually confronted with making decisions based on two or more possible alternatives.

The replacement study is generally an analysis of these alternatives. It considers the effect of interest and time. Usually, one of the alternatives is not to do anything to replace existing equipment. The cost of doing this is compared with the cost of buying new equipment, taking into account salvage or scrap values of present equipment, and other factors.

The manufacturing manager need not get involved in the details of such an analysis. He should call on the industrial engineering department to make the necessary detailed studies.

For the industrial engineering department to do an effective job, certain policies must be spelled out by management:

1. The stated position of the company on replacement of capital assets
2. Interest rates to be used for various types of equipment
3. Estimates of life of equipment categories
4. Frequency of replacement analyses to be conducted
5. Sources of approval of capital expenditures

Automated Processes. (This subject is covered in detail in Section 5, Chapters 8 and 9.) Automation is the hallmark of American industry. It makes possible mass production, which in turn makes possible low product costs.

The manager of manufacturing must utilize automated processes where they can be economically justified. He also must maintain a state of awareness of new developments in the field of automation.

The industrial engineer, by academic training and experience background, can be helpful to the manager. He has usually had exposure to production lines, automated equipment, numerical control machines, and electronic data processing. Indeed, by virtue of work experience, certain staff industrial engineers may be expert in one or more of these techniques.

Some of the activities in which the industrial engineer is usually adept are the following:

1. Planning and designing a production line
2. Installing and balancing a production line
3. Justifying automated equipment
4. Conducting data processing equipment feasibility studies
5. Designing systems utilizing numerical control machines

It has been predicted that ultimately 85 percent of the dollar sales of machine tools will be for automated machines. In the face of this possibility, the manufacturing manager must utilize the available services of industrial engineers to design, install, and maintain systems of automated computer-controlled machines.

Material Handling. (This subject is covered in detail in Section 5, Chapter 7.) Material handling costs frequently account for 30 to 35 percent of the production costs. The cost-reduction-minded manager can realize substantial production savings through proper and efficient handling of materials. In addition to dollar savings, shortened production time and better utilization of space may also be achieved.

The industrial engineer is expected to have a working knowledge of material handling systems. This may include trucks, forklift trucks, conveyors, pneumatic systems, cranes, containers, and transport vehicles of all kinds. He must be able to design systems which are economically feasible and compatible with the material processing requirements.

The first step in either a new or a replacement material handling situation is to compile information necessary to the analysis. This involves obtaining answers to the following questions:

What material is to be moved?
How much material is to be moved?
How far will it be moved?
What is the frequency of movement?

Then an analysis must be made of the information on hand in the light of the study objectives. This will determine alternative equipment systems for handling the materials. It will also determine the cost to the company of alternative systems.

Finally, the findings and recommendations will be prepared, generally in report form. These will be presented to management for review and decision making.

Mathematical Techniques and Applications. Since World War II, industrial engineering curricula have placed a heavy emphasis on mathematics, especially statistics and matrix algebra, and the formulation of mathematical models. Perhaps the outstanding characteristic of the modern industrial engineer is a strong base of understanding of mathematical theory and applications for solving industrial problems. This body of knowledge forms a powerful set of tools for analysis and decision making on the part of management.

Statistics. Perhaps the most widely used mathematical tool is statistics. This includes such subjects as sampling, testing, variance, regression, correlation, and statistical measures (mean, variability, confidence, and the like). Such tools have been applied to a large number of industrial activities. A few of these are listed below.

1. Determination of economic lot size
2. Inventory analysis and control
3. Warehousing design and layout
4. Capital budgeting
5. Work measurement
6. Man-machine tool scheduling
7. Production scheduling
8. Organization analysis
9. Manpower and facilities needs
10. Forecasting efficiency and output
11. Operation analysis
12. Work sampling

Probability Theory. Much of the mathematical approach used by industrial engineers is based on probability theory. Many business decisions are based on the probability of certain occurrences. Probability can be used to predict sales volume, to forecast market penetration, and in many other company activities. It can be utilized effectively in many manufacturing activities as well. Here are a few areas in which probability is used to assist the manufacturing manager:

1. Process control
2. Downtime control
3. Long-range planning
4. Quality control
5. Maintenance
6. Plant investment decisions
7. Reliability
8. Marketing strategies

Mathematical Programming. Mathematical programming is an advanced mathematical tool which frequently can help in the selection of the most advantageous solution of a problem when a large number of alternatives are present.

One form of mathematical programming is linear programming, which employs matrix algebra. It involves placing the variables in the problem into a set of equations and solving for the unknowns in the equations to obtain an optimum or best solution. Frequently the complexity of the problems requires the use of a computer.

Mathematical programming has been utilized for solving many industrial problems. These include:

1. Process activities such as feed mill or product blending

 2. Inventory control
 3. Production activities
 4. Maintenance inspection intervals
 5. Location of inspection stations
 6. Computer control of multiproduct lines
 7. Manpower requirement estimating
 8. Warehouse location

Waiting Line Theory. Waiting line theory is used to study queuing problems. Wherever waiting lines are formed, people, processes, and production are held up. Queuing theory takes into account waiting times, the ratio of service time to waiting time, arrival rate, and the like. Analysis can indicate how to minimize waiting time and optimize production.

Typical situations to which waiting line mathematics can be applied are:
 1. Conveyor loading
 2. Automatic machines
 3. Idle time utilization
 4. Machine tool cutting time
 5. Production standards
 6. Telephone service

Simulation Concepts. System simulation is a technique for determining through experiment the effect of changing the variables in a system. This may mean varying the flow of materials, location of processes, or the product line or mix. The effect of these changes is determined generally with a mathematical model in which the variables can be changed to simulate changes in the actual system under study.

Many and varied system simulations have been developed in industry. Some representative areas in which they have been utilized are:
 1. Men and equipment allocations
 2. Production and distribution in a plant
 3. Railroad transportation operations
 4. Job shop orders
 5. Manufacturing systems and planning
 6. Competitive management studies
 7. Management control systems

Sampling Concepts. Because examination and analysis of all available data on the operations of a company would be too time consuming and expensive, it is frequently desirable to work with samples of the data. Proper sampling requires a knowledge of statistical techniques. Industrial engineers are usually well versed in these procedures.

Sampling techniques are important in quality control, determination of economic lot size, process control, work sampling, and in various industrial decision making processes.

The wide applicability of these mathematical techniques by the industrial engineer can prove extremely helpful to the manufacturing manager. Because these tools relate to more efficient use of men, machines, and materials, they can provide line management with the data essential to both short- and long-range decision making.

Game Theory. Game theory is a mathematical technique that relates to the strategy to be employed when one is confronted with a number of alternatives. It involves the use of game matrices. Its applications have been relatively few in manufacturing, but it holds promise of providing management guidance under certain circumstances.

Monte Carlo Technique. The Monte Carlo technique is related to probability theory and utilizes random numbers to generate data through unrestricted random sampling. It can be applied to a number of probability-type problems such as maintenance tolerance limits, cycle servicing of semiautomatic machines, time study, and systems simulation.

Wage and Salary Plans. (This subject is covered in detail in Section 9.) There is a close relationship between work measurement and methods engineering on one hand and wage and salary plans on the other. Consequently, industrial engineers are frequently involved in salary administration.

The industrial engineer's work is especially important in the design of standards and of incentive systems which provide the worker with extra pay for extra performance. Incentive plans are numerous in industry and vary greatly from company to company.

To set incentive rates properly, all jobs under the plan must be described and compared with one another. Frequently, the industrial engineer is involved in this job analysis and evaluation process.

Manufacturing managers have found wage incentive plans to be highly effective in obtaining increases in worker productivity. Moreover, they can be applied to most types of work, including maintenance work, office work, supervision, and management itself.

Miscellaneous Tools and Techniques. Industrial engineers increasingly have participated in a number of miscellaneous industrial activities. The location and responsibility for these activities vary from company to company in accordance with organization and policy.

Estimating. Predicting the eventual manufacturing cost of a product by analysis of the components with a reasonable degree of accuracy is usually of sufficient importance to justify a considerable effort.

Office Cost Control. With the expansion of office and clerical work, the control of office-associated costs has become a major segment of total cost control.

Product Design. It is frequently said that half the products that will be in use ten years from now have not even been designed today. If this is true, the design of products will occupy the efforts of a great many individuals in the future.

Safety. The occurrence of accidents and injuries usually indicates that a problem exists in company planning, operation, equipment, construction, or installation. Hence, the industrial engineer is vitally interested in safety because of its effect on company operations.

Tool and Gage Design. The industrial engineer has long been active in tool and gage design. This results from methods engineering and work measurement activities associated with industrial engineering.

Training. The training of operators and supervisors in new methods, processes, and systems is an integral part of the industrial engineering activity.

Work Simplification. Work simplification is an application of methods analysis principles in a systematic way, with the active involvement of supervisors and production workers, and is widely used.

Value Analysis. Developed in World War II, value analysis is a systematic creative approach to ensuring that the essential function of a product, process, or procedure is provided at a minimum overall cost.

Suggestion Systems. The "idea power" of employees is a frequently untapped resource. To utilize this resource more effectively, suggestion systems are frequently designed, implemented, and administered. These benefit the employee as well as the company.

For support and assistance, the manufacturing manager must look to the organization unit that has been assigned the responsibility for the above activities. Where such responsibilities have not been assigned and the need for them exists, consideration should be given to placing them in the industrial engineering department.

UTILIZATION OF THE INDUSTRIAL ENGINEERING FUNCTION

In the first part of this chapter, the impression may have been gained that industrial engineers can be all things to all persons. This is not the case. The industrial engineering manager in a company must not be concerned with building an empire or establishing frontiers. His goal should be the provision of service and technical assistance to the line organization by utilizing the scientific management principles in which he and his staff are grounded.

For an industrial engineering function to operate effectively as staff to a manufacturing operation, a number of decisions must be taken by the company management, including the following:

1. The location of the function in the company organization must be clearly defined and understood throughout the company.
2. The authority and responsibilities of the function must be defined and understood.

Place of the Industrial Engineering Function. The guidelines for locating the industrial engineering department in a company structure are not hard and fast. Generally, it is desirable that the industrial engineering department report to the executive who has line responsibility for the department that it regularly serves. The organization chart (Figure 2-1) is an example of this location in a manufacturing organization. This means that the manager of industrial engineering might report to a manufacturing vice president, a manufacturing manager, a works manager, or whatever the title may be of the individual responsible for production activities.

In small- and medium-size companies, the function is usually vested in a few individuals who report to high-level management. In large companies, industrial engineering is usually a department but occupies a lower place in the organization. Usually the larger and more complex the organization, the larger the industrial engineering department is. Companies with one hundred and more industrial engineers on the payroll are no longer rare.

The responsibilities assigned to industrial engineering vary widely from company to company. There will usually be a number of departments in which the bulk of the industrial engineering work is done. This does not preclude the department providing services to other units of the organization.

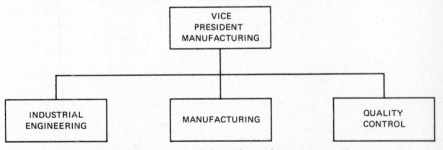

Fig. 2-1. Desirable Location of the Industrial Engineering Department.

Internally, the industrial engineering department may be arranged functionally or organizationally. In the former case, groups of activities are assigned to individuals or groups (time study, methods, wage programs, operations research, facilities, and so on). In the latter, the activities are assigned to individuals or groups by company organization unit (electronics division, appliance division, machine shop).

Some advantages of the functional organization are listed below:

1. When the industrial engineering department is the major service unit in a company, it is generally better to have an industrial engineer operate continuously in a functional field. This will lead to higher technical proficiency in a relatively narrow field.
2. The department can operate with personnel of limited experience.
3. The assignment of tasks and people to tasks is facilitated.

Figure 2-2 shows a functional industrial engineering organization.

Some advantages of the industrial engineering operation which is organized along production activity lines are as follows:

1. In a complex production organization, the industrial engineer with a detailed knowledge of only one phase of the total process can operate more effectively.
2. High priority problems get prompt attention.
3. Closer relationships develop between production supervisors and the industrial engineer working with them.

Figure 2-3 shows a production-organized industrial engineering function.

The multiplant company frequently decentralizes the industrial engineering function, maintaining corporate staff function and industrial engineers in staff or line positions in the plants of the company.

The industrial engineer is frequently called on to perform special projects by company or manufacturing management. This he may do as an individual assignment or as a member of a team. Typical projects might be setting up an assembly line for a new product, an overhaul of the factory incentive system, or the design of a new plant.

Authority, Responsibility, and Accountability. The specific responsibilities assigned to industrial engineering departments vary greatly from company to company. From one or two major responsibilities, such as work measurement and methods, the assigned responsibilities may be a dozen or more. The emphasis given to individual activities will vary, too, in accordance with the importance of the activity to management, the effect that it has on company profits, and the nature of specific problems.

Because of the service nature of its activities, an industrial engineering de-

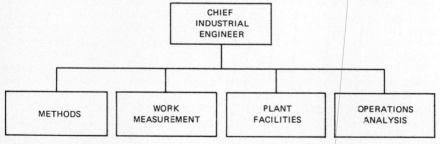

Fig. 2-2. Typical Functional Organization of the Industrial Engineering Department.

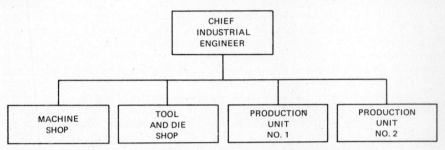

FIG. 2-3. Typical Production Organization of the Industrial Engineering Department.

partment is almost always a staff function. As such, it does not exercise line authority. However, it does exercise functional authority. It cannot tell a line supervisor that something should be done, but it should be able to tell a line supervisor that "if and when you do this, do it this way."

To be truly effective, the industrial engineering function must be given the latitude to initiate programs which will benefit the company operations. The industrial engineer should approach manufacturing management with ideas for studies, analyses, and programs which hold promise of solving problems or improving performance. If line management concurs, then the industrial engineering department should proceed with action.

The authority of the industrial engineering department does not extend to ordering the adoption of a new or changed method, purchasing a specific item of equipment, or installing a specific standard. Its function is to recommend to the appropriate line manager that such actions be taken and to justify its recommendations.

The manufacturing manager should never feel that by involving the industrial engineering function in a line activity, he is yielding part of his authority and decision making function.

Value to the Manufacturing Manager. The principal value to the manufacturing manager of utilizing the industrial engineering department is in the area of potential cost reduction. This obviously can be achieved in many ways, such as better methods, improved equipment, less material handling, and more efficient systems.

The ultimate test of this activity lies in the results which come from changes approved and instituted by manufacturing management.

The line manager must ensure that all recommendations from industrial engineering include the methods by which benefits can be measured—generally, the maintenance of good records and a periodic evaluation of end results. Although line management need not involve itself in all the record keeping, it must follow up on the installation of the change and review progress periodically.

Results may be measured in various ways. Increased production of finished goods, increased productivity per worker, and meeting of production deadlines are examples. Generally, the common denominator applicable to all these should be dollar savings. This is the ultimate test to apply to most change situations. There are, of course, other less tangible benefits which may accrue from changes, such as better employee morale and reduction in turnover or absenteeism.

TABLE 2-1. Management Benefits Available through Industrial Engineering

Industrial engineering activity	Potential benefits to line management
Methods analysis	Simpler methods, increased production, lower costs, better products, estimates of production costs
Work measurement	Standards, incentive rates, increased production, design of new operation
Control procedures	Better control of inventories, better quality, improved employee morale, current status awareness, profit improvement, more efficient management
Plant facilities	Efficient layouts, greater productivity, lower costs, optimum plant locations
Material handling	More effective equipment, lower costs, lower inventories
Mathematical techniques	Problem solving, easier decision making, more effective forecasting
Wage and salary plans	Proper wage scales, less labor friction, improved employee morale
Miscellaneous techniques	Cost reduction, better methods, better procedures

CONCLUSION

This chapter is aimed at describing, for the manufacturing manager, the capabilities of the industrial engineering function in a company. By calling on the services of industrial engineers at appropriate times, the line manager can effect many economies and cost reductions while availing himself of better methods and measures of performance.

Some potential benefits to line management from utilizing the various capabilities of the industrial engineering department in a company are summarized in Table 2-1.

BIBLIOGRAPHY

American Institute of Industrial Engineers, Inc., *Journal of Industrial Engineering,* New York, 1949 to date.

American Institute of Industrial Engineers, Inc., *Proceedings of the Annual Conference and Convention,* New York, 1954 to date.

Hammond, Ross W., *Your Future in Industrial Engineering,* Richards Rosen Press, Inc., New York, 1968.

Ireson, William G., and Eugene L. Grant (eds.), *Handbook of Industrial Engineering and Management,* Prentice-Hall, Inc., Englewood Cliffs, N.J., 1955.

Maynard, H. B. (ed.), *Industrial Engineering Handbook,* 2d ed., McGraw-Hill Book Company, New York, 1963.

Maynard, H. B., G. J. Stegemerten, and John L. Schwab, *Methods-Time Measurement,* McGraw-Hill Book Company, New York, 1948.

Williams, J. B., *The Compleat Strategyst,* McGraw-Hill Book Company, New York, 1954.

CHAPTER THREE

Factory Cost Accounting

DOUGLAS P. GOULD   *Vice President, Trundle Consultants Inc., Cleveland, Ohio*

The basic purpose of the factory cost accounting function is to determine, record, and report the operating costs and conditions which occurred in the course of manufacture and assembly of the products and services comprising the company's output. It is concerned essentially with the recording of the costs of labor, material, and manufacturing expense, according to the most meaningful unit or units of measurement. Cost data developed and reported by the function are required by the manufacturing manager and his subordinates as a foundation for all planning, decision making, measurement, and control of production and plant related activities. It provides the basis of comparison of actual performance against predetermined standards or objectives and enables the manager to evaluate specifically the performance of any component of production or the pertinent costs of any unit of output.

DESCRIPTION OF THE FACTORY COST ACCOUNTING FUNCTION

Factory cost accounting is a staff function, customarily reporting to the controller. It is usually physically located in the plant and under the day-to-day direction of the manufacturing manager. The nature of the subfunctions comprising factory cost accounting in the individual plant, however, as well as the size of the company itself may dictate other reporting relationships. Customarily, factory cost accounting is responsible for timekeeping, payroll accounting, labor distribution and costs, material accounting, factory overhead accounting, and preparation, analysis, and presentation of various cost and expense statements and reports rendered routinely or as a matter of special interest to the manufacturing manager. Whatever the formal reporting relationship may be, maximum flexibility must exist to permit the manufacturing manager access to, and influence on, the function to the degree that cost reports are provided to the manager in the most timely and meaningful form.

The real value of the cost accounting function lies in its ability to provide meaningful cost data with sufficient promptness to permit the manufacturing manager and his subordinates to take corrective action quickly when unfavorable conditions are encountered or when favorable opportunities for change are observed. In this respect, factory cost accounting is a more dynamic function than one associated with the problem of historically reporting costs well after their occurrence, although certain of its activities are concerned with historical reporting. In the furtherance of his own interests, the manufacturing manager must insist on timely reporting in accordance with the realities of his own operation. The factory cost accounting function is responsible not only for identifying the various costs associated with the manufacturing operation, but for identifying their behavior as well. Certain costs increase or decrease with some measure of activity. Other costs remain fairly constant and are a function of time rather than activity. In many organizations, the necessary function of variance explanation falls on the factory cost accountant, and the manufacturing manager must be able to gage the extent to which variances are due to activity and the extent to which they are due to unusual performance. Factory cost accounting must provide insight into this important aspect of cost behavior.

COMMON UNITS OR COMPONENTS ON WHICH COSTS ARE COLLECTED

The elements of the costs of labor, material, and manufacturing expense or overhead are collected and summarized in many different ways. These costs are frequently collected and reported on the following bases:
1. Company-wide
2. By division
3. By plant
4. By function
5. By department
6. By cost center
7. By production line
8. By machine
9. By man
10. By shift
11. By method of manufacture
12. By operation
13. By component
14. By subassembly and assembly
15. By product
16. By product line
17. By job
18. By manufacturing order or batch or by unit of measure as a ton, drum, gallon, pound, or piece
19. By day, week, month, quarter, and year
20. By project or program
21. By customer
22. By vendor

In certain industries, there are undoubtedly other bases on which costs could be collected and summarized for meaningful use by the manufacturing manager. With a suitably designed system, it is possible to determine, for example, the actual cost on a certain date of a particular kind of labor, by man, on the night shift, performing a particular operation, on a specific part, on a given machine, using material from one of several vendors, working under a foreman in a certain department, at a particular plant, using a unique setup or method; and to determine for a unit of output a comparative cost against any chosen alternative or standard. Although the real need for such in-depth reporting on a regular or routine basis is slight in most companies, a well-designed factory cost accounting system, adequate coding on the bills of material and operation sheets, man/machine/department identification, and piece counts on time or production tickets provide the capability for developing costs of material and labor to any level of detail required. With regard to the possibility of providing cost information in depth, it is sufficient to indicate that the manufacturing manager could obtain such data from factory cost accounting on a routine basis if there were sufficient justification for it and if data processing equipment were available to process it. The real question to be answered by factory management is not "What can I get out of factory cost accounting?" but rather "What information do I need in this plant to control the operation adequately and to improve it?" In all probability, that information can be provided on a timely basis.

FUNDAMENTAL REQUIREMENTS FOR SOUND FACTORY COST ACCOUNTING

Because the factory cost accounting function deals with in-plant costs of labor, material, and expense and relates them to units of production or production components, it is evident that there must be:
1. Timely and accurate labor reporting related to accurate production counts
2. Definitive material usage reports
3. Current operation sheets and bills of material or their equivalents
4. A sound numerical coding system providing definitive coding for the several elements on which costs are to be collected and reported
5. Sufficiently detailed account classifications of labor, material, and expense items to permit their individual identification and collection in a consistent manner

The rate and nature of usage of labor, material, and expense must be accurately reported and must be relatable to output. It is of little value to the manufacturing manager to receive cost reports where substantial inaccuracies in time reporting influence the results or where units of output are not sufficiently defined. Similarly, uncontrolled material issuance or sloppy practice in this regard creates cost information which at best is inaccurate, and at worst, completely misleading. It is not possible in every plant to ensure complete accuracy in time reporting and production counts, and in many plants material issuance is only loosely controlled.

When coupled with incomplete or inaccurate piece counts or production count, cost results become overly rough approximations rather than sensitive control tools. The manufacturing manager must evaluate the extent to which poor practices in these two areas materially influence his decision making and control data as reported by factory cost accounting.

Some Frequent Sources of Timekeeping Error. By attention to some of the frequently observed sources of error in labor reporting, the manufacturing manager can substantially improve the quality of the information received from factory cost accounting. Common sources of error in time reporting are:
1. Employee fills in own time card

2. No reconciliation of job tickets with total man time on in-out time cards
3. Inadequate policing of direct labor changeover to indirect or nonproductive operations
4. Failure to segregate setup times from run times
5. Illegible time cards and piece counts
6. Inaccurate reporting of incentive hours and daywork hours when same employee runs both kinds of jobs
7. Automatic approval of time cards by foremen
8. Unidentified similar parts for more than one job run under one job ticket
9. No piece counts on intermediate operations
10. No formal job ticket used or cramped, poorly designed job ticket in use
11. Too few, poorly placed job clocks
12. Part numbers omitted; part name used by employee on time tickets

Modern time clocks and labor reporting equipment and systems have minimized many of these error sources, but where timekeeping procedures are relatively unsophisticated, the alert manufacturing manager will act to minimize the effect of these deterrents to accurate and meaningful labor reporting.

BASIS OF USE OF FACTORY COST ACCOUNTING

As a meaningful analytical, planning and control tool, the factory cost accounting function is a necessary and valued addition to the manager's staff. The manufacturing manager can use the function in one of two broad ways. In its less desirable application, factory cost accounting can be used to justify off-standard or excessive and rising labor, material, and overhead costs in the plant. It can place blame on other functions, vendors, or customers for noted cost increases or failure to perform in the anticipated manner. This defensive application results in different kinds of reports designed to show apparent cost/activity/performance relationships which often conceal the real reasons for out-of-line manufacturing results.

The manufacturing manager interested in continually improving the performance of his function uses factory cost accounting as an investigative and policing activity. He welcomes the imaginative cost manager who can provide him with insights into facets of the manufacturing operation which offer further opportunities for cost reduction and profit improvement. He uses the function to reveal rather than to conceal. He is not as interested in the volume of reports as he is in the quick summary of the significant meaning of the accountant's reports. He is less interested in a "penny-accurate" report in six months than in a reasonably accurate approximation today. His awareness of the fact that his decisions are as good as his timely performance data causes the manufacturing manager to rely heavily on the cost accounting function for assistance in decision making and control in every area of manufacturing. When the manufacturing manager is convinced that the information received from the factory cost reports is accurate, responsive, and timely, he finds new reasons for expanding the capability of the function.

USES OF FACTORY COST ACCOUNTING

The manufacturing manager interested in continually improving his function uses factory cost accounting in many ways to help further his own interests and those of his company. These uses center around planning; control of labor, material, and expense; decision making on significant problems; pricing; evaluating contemplated changes in materials and methods; measuring progress; identifying profit improvement opportunities; training subordinates; reporting results; managing by exception and assigning responsibility; and coordinating the subfunctions of manufacturing in accordance with internal and external objectives.

Labor Effectiveness Reports. Factory cost accounting prepares labor effectiveness reports on a daily basis. These reports provide a percentage measure of actual performance against standard. This is accomplished by comparing standard hours to actual hours required for the planned and scheduled production, or estimated hours required to actual hours spent. The report is available on a man-by-man basis but is customarily summarized daily by department or by foreman for each shift. In certain cases where repetitive production is involved, the comparison of labor effectiveness is made on a part-by-part basis. In standard hour incentive shops, the report may be a summary of the incentive earnings paid the employee. In piecework establishments, an effectiveness percentage can be drawn by comparing actual earnings to a presumed level of normal or expected earnings. In measured daywork shops, actual and standard hours are compared.

This timely report provides the manufacturing manager with the means of identifying production bottlenecks, taking corrective action immediately to improve production situations where excess time is required or spent on given parts or assemblies or product, and directing attention to specific foremen or production employees in a constructive fashion. The progress of new employees can be routinely observed, and the effectiveness of the training effort of supervision in such situations can be measured.

Labor effectiveness reporting need not be restricted to direct labor operations. In those cases where tasks or standards are available on indirect operations, such as maintenance or setup, an equally useful efficiency report can be prepared for those activities.

Effectiveness reports for labor prepared on a broad departmental basis only are useful in measuring the general level of performance in the plant, a fact of general interest in measuring the overall productive capacity of the work force and the quality of the supervision. The more summarized the report becomes, the less effective it becomes as a labor control device, as it is impossible to deal in specific problems concerning men, methods, foremen, or product.

Where direct labor is a substantial part of the cost of production, the factory cost accounting department should provide sufficient timely comparative detail to enable the manufacturing manager to direct specific attention quickly to individual problems and to be in a position to observe the effect of such corrective action in subsequent reports.

Downtime Reports. The proper and complete use of manufacturing facilities and equipment, machine tools, line production facilities, process equipment, and the like is a major concern of the manufacturing manager. When productive facilities are down and not operating for any reason, the plant capacity is in effect curtailed. Certain kinds of downtime are necessary and expected; others can be avoided or minimized. The real effect of downtime is not merely the delay in production which may result, the inconvenience of transferring labor to other operations, or the costs of repair or maintenance involved in correcting the situation. The real loss is represented by the lost dollar contribution of production to payment of fixed expense and profit, the lost marginal income of the time that the equipment is inoperative. When one operation or station is down, the progressive effects of the delay are often substantial, as subsequent operations may depend on a steady flow of production. When operations approach the effective capacity of the plant, the critical nature of downtime becomes readily apparent, although the cost is present to a lesser degree at any operating level. Chronic downtime results in a need for more equipment with higher fixed costs for depreciation to produce a given amount or for unnecessary outside subcontracting in critical cases.

Downtime reports supplied by factory cost accounting identify the nature and extent of the lost time and the reasons for it. Reasons may include routine maintenance, setup or changeover, waiting for material, waiting for instructions, breakdown, no operator, off-specification production, and the like. Depending on the reasons and the critical nature of the downtime involved, the manufacturing manager can take corrective action. The problem may be plant-wide or departmental. Poor maintenance or poor production control may be indicated.

Two aspects of downtime are of particular interest. These involve a determination of the extent and reasons for downtime on equipment scheduled to be in operation, and the relationship of scheduled hours to hours available, scheduled or not.

It is easily possible to have high labor efficiency and yet have poor machine utilization. In certain cases, the latter can be much more costly to operations than low labor effectiveness. The alert manufacturing manager uses factory cost accounting to identify and quantify the extent of downtime and reasons therefor.

Loaned Labor Report. Labor is customarily identified with a particular department. At times, because of temporarily changed needs for labor within that department, interruptions of scheduled production, or critical needs for labor in other departments, productive labor may be loaned or shifted from one department to another.

The manufacturing manager should be aware of the extent, type, and departments involved in such loaned labor transactions. The factory cost accounting department is in possession of the information and should provide it as a matter of regular reporting.

The existence of substantial activity in labor loans to other departments has substantial meaning to the manager, largely in these areas:

1. May indicate changed departmental manning needs.
2. May cause increased production costs through use of higher rated labor on low-rate work.
3. May cause future scheduling problems if labor borrowed actually had scheduled work to perform.
4. Where consistent loans are made by one department, a strong possibility for reduction in the associated indirect expenses of that department may exist, as these are usually related to direct labor.
5. May be indicative of poor scheduling practices and unbalanced work loads.
6. May result in higher production costs which occur when such loaned labor must work at a less familiar skill, as when transferred from fabrication to assembly.

The loaned labor report keeps the manufacturing manager apprised of the extent of the practice and permits corrective action on a timely basis where the need exists.

Use of Productive Labor on Indirect Operations. A report similar in intent to the loaned labor report is a daily or weekly summary of the extent to which productive or direct labor is used on indirect operations. Such assignments are common in many plants where direct labor may be moved temporarily from an operation on the product to that of maintenance, clean up, shipping, packing, counting, or the like. In some instances, such transfers represent "make work" efforts on the part of the foreman. In others, the change is necessary and desirable. Because indirect operations are most frequently unmeasured, a greater part of the hours are relatively uncontrolled where excessive transfers of this nature occur. Similarly, temporary overstaffing of some indirect operations may result during the period. The report provides the manufacturing manager with the opportunity to evaluate the manner in which the labor force is being used, to take corrective action where possible, and to adjust his planning for indirect expenses which must be met if corrective action is not immediately feasible.

Overtime Hours Report. The extent to which overtime is authorized is usually a decision of manufacturing management. The responsibility may be delegated to foremen or superintendents, but in any event, close control of overtime is a practical necessity in any production facility. The factory cost accounting function provides information on overtime hours by department as a matter of routine reporting in most cases. The reasons are obvious. Labor hours under overtime conditions are substantially (50 to 200 percent) more costly than comparable regular shift hours. In certain cases, the desirability of overtime is unquestioned. It is in the best interests of the company and the manufacturing manager to incur the overtime to meet schedules. In some cases, regular overtime is an important part of the plant wage structure and level, compensating for a lower base rate structure. In some cases, regular overtime is an added inducement to attract and hold employees. Notwithstanding these conditions, excessive overtime may reveal opportunities to the manufacturing manager for profit improvement in the following areas:

1. The possibilities of economies to be gained by total or selective second-shift operation
2. The need for more equipment, better equipment, or more automated facilities
3. The need for a definite overtime policy, actively policed
4. The need for adjustment of labor cost estimates in product or job costs
5. Through the comparison of output on overtime versus output on regular time, a complete reappraisal of the value of overtime in this plant
6. The implications of the fact that only certain individuals receive overtime consistently
7. The point at which overtime ceases to be a positive factor in contributing to company profits
8. The extent to which inadequate production control and planning contribute to the need for overtime, and similarly, the relationship of downtime and overtime.

The overtime report can provide insight into departmental operating practice and philosophy, and the alert manufacturing manager does not ignore its implications. Translation of overtime hours into premium labor dollars, related to output during this period, has often resulted in significant changes in manufacturing policy. Factory cost accounting has often been the catalyst.

On-standards Labor Report. The periodic report of the number of labor hours performed on operations on which labor standards exist and the hours incurred on operations not covered by standards provides the manufacturing manager with a factual measurement of the coverage and progress of the standards program in the plant. It often encourages accelerated activity by the standards department when productivity on covered operations is related to productivity on uncovered operations. The report is likewise useful in observing trends of coverage, either favorable or unfavorable, and may influence the costing and estimating factors being applied to future production and bid work.

Scheduling. Actual performance data on time and production of various departments or production centers are required by the manufacturing manager for use in conjunction with the all-important production planning and scheduling function. Where scheduling is accomplished on the basis of standard operating times for the several operations, modification of such standards for scheduling purposes is often necessary to avoid overloading or underloading a department in a given time period, based on existing performance against standards. The factory cost accounting function can provide the information by which scheduling and machine loading can be made realistic.

In other situations where daywork only is paid, it is often necessary to pursue the progress of work performed and operations completed. In the absence of standards, the estimated time may become the effective standard expressed in terms of hours to complete a given operation or group of operations. Factory cost accounting is in a position to record time and cost of completed work, and so determine percent completion and currently the extent to which initial estimates are valid. Such data are used for control and for obtaining a price increase from a customer or perhaps a material price reduction from a vendor. Complete, after-the-fact costing of jobs compared to estimates provides factual information on the performance of the estimating department in respect to labor and related burden used in quoting. Depending on the manufacturing cycle, percent completion estimates on the basis of labor hours may be required for evaluating the work-in-process inventory and obtaining progress payments from customers where this is the trade practice. The manufacturing manager relies upon factory cost accounting for factual information on a timely basis in each of these instances.

Raw Material Utilization Reports. Factory cost accounting can provide the manufacturing manager with a sound basis of material usage control. Information can be provided in terms of operations, departments, jobs, manufacturing orders, plants, machines, cost centers, operators, parts, vendors, or product groups as might be necessary. The practical uses to which the manufacturing manager can put such information include the following:

1. Identification of situations occurring in specific departments where material usage is substantially greater or less than anticipated.
2. Identification of the specific machine, operator, or part responsible for excess usage.
3. Identification of vendor responsible for supplying the material in question.
4. Improvement of yields from raw stock by closer attention to job layout, handling, and preliminary operations such as sawing to length or shearing.
5. Modification of purchase specifications in accordance with present needs.

6. Highlighting increased material purchase costs.
7. Identification of situations where a value analysis approach might be productive in cost reduction.
8. Degree to which material substitutions have been made from that planned on the bill of material and the reasons for those substitutions.
9. Development of labor/material ratios in products manufactured, to determine those items which could be made to best advantage in a tight labor period and those which require high labor/low material in controlling inventory buildup.
10. Determination of the degree to which customer-furnished material affects estimating practices and margin yield from such jobs.
11. Comparative cost effect of mill versus warehouse raw material sourcing.
12. Identification of the material usage factor in conjunction with the development of economic lot quantity calculations, using material cost data in predicting best run size.
13. Determination of opportunities for joint processing of products or components from a material standpoint.
14. Determination of unit material costs in conjunction with make-or-buy decisions.
15. Through the Purchase Variance Report, prices actually paid for materials are compared to the standards used in costing and estimating. The extent of extra, unanticipated cost from this source is specifically identified by type of material. A measure of performance of the purchasing function is likewise possible.

Scrap and Rework Report. From individual scrap tickets and rework orders, factory cost accounting identifies and summarizes the extent of production scrap by type, the physical amount of material requiring rework, and the amount of direct labor invested in the product to that point. Identification of scrap by kind, department, cost center, operation, man, product, or otherwise permits the manufacturing manager to take action depending on the reason that scrap was produced or rework operations were necessary. Explanations might be related to scrap generated in handling the product, scrap due to poor dies or tooling, unusable short ends or the like, careless workmanship, bad material or material unsuited to the purpose at hand, overruns of production which could not be sold, scrap created because of inaccurate prints or instructions, process scrap created in purging systems, or whatever other reasons are appropriate in the particular industry. When costed out, it has often been found that scrap material is a highly significant factor of cost, aggravated by the fact that labor and variable burdens up to the scrapping operation have been incurred.

Rework reports point out the extent to which salvage operations are required, the amount of such activity, and the cost. Painting defects, repackaging, faulty components, regrinding, and other rework operations required indicate to the manufacturing manager the sources of production problems and extra cost. Apart from correcting the indicated difficulties causing a need for rework, the actual performance of the shop in regard to scrap and rework costs must be known in the estimating function, so that allowances can be properly introduced.

Report of Indirect Material and Supplies Usage. Actual usage of various indirect materials is summarized and related to labor or machine hours. This information, periodically supplied by factory cost accounting, enables the manufacturing manager to determine, by departments, trends in usage of such materials. Spot checks have often suggested areas wherein issuance practices can be modified to advantage or possible savings obtained.

OVERHEAD EXPENSE

In factory cost accounting, the unitizing of direct labor and material costs can be accomplished on a basis which is realistic, understandable, and quite directly usable. In most cases, direct labor and material can be associated with an activity or a product as hours or dollars; and with due care within the system, the results will be entirely meaningful.

In the costing process, burdens in the factory are customarily applied in one of two ways.

1. All overhead expense is reduced to a percentage of direct labor dollars, labor hours, machine hours, or other common base and applied to the job, manufacturing order, or product as a function of such labor dollars, hours, or machine hours in the job. Various percentages may be used, reflecting the different overhead-to-labor relationships existing in the several cost centers or departments. In some cases, a single plant overhead rate is used. These rates are likewise used in the presentation of the value of inventories.

2. Overhead or factory burden is recognized as consisting of two distinct and separate parts. The first part is a fixed or set amount, which is not a function of activity but is rather a function of time. It includes such expenses as depreciation, salaries of key personnel, insurance, watchmen, standby power and utilities charges, and the like. The other part of factory burden is regarded as sensitive to changes in activity and is called variable factory burden. Under the direct costing philosophy or marginal income concept only the variable elements of burden are applied as cost factors when unit product costs are under consideration. The degree of variability of like expenses is often a matter of the control philosophy of the individual plant manager, but the existence of both fixed and variable burdens in manufacturing is a fact.

As the factory cost accounting department is engaged in the development and presentation of product and activity costs on both a unit and a total basis, the manufacturing manager must understand the method of overhead application in use. Method 1, or the full absorption method, is primarily useful in inventory evaluation for statement purposes or in a single-product plant operating at a constant level of activity. Its use, when unitized to a machine hour rate or as a percentage factor in product costing or rate setting, becomes of questionable value.

Method 2, wherein only the variable portion of factory burden is applied on a percentage basis, creates a true variable product cost, provides sensitivity to changes in activity for control purposes, and provides manufacturing management with a more useful number in the various decision making areas. In effect, fixed burdens are regarded as common to the entity rather than to a unit of product produced by the plant.

It is desirable in any event to show separately the variable part of burden and any fixed part of burden which is applied. The manager can then take full advantage of the knowledge of incremental costs related to activity and avoid the confusion which results when a fixed or time cost is made apparently variable by reducing it to a percentage across an arbitrarily preselected number of units.

Control of Overheads. Factory cost accounting can furnish to the manufacturing manager the actual cost of expense items for his activity, by type, and in the degree of detail found useful. The control of overhead, either fixed or variable in nature, becomes increasingly important as the degree of automation and mechanization increases. Factory cost accounting can provide both insight into the way that overheads vary and the basis for and extent of change as the activity levels increase or decrease in the plant.

Overheads in the plant consist of people and things. Customarily, factory cost accounting may assist in the development of manning tables for indirect and nonproductive personnel, related to plant activity levels. Variances from plan by department provide the manufacturing manager with the exception control data required to adhere to planned cost levels for varying manufacturing mixes. Control by project or assignment against standards or estimates, with variance reporting in hours or dollars, enables the manufacturing manager to exercise control of authorized maintenance, repair, and construction activities. The imaginative factory cost accountant is constantly striving for improved methods of presenting and identifying areas for potential improvement in the company's factory overhead structure.

PLANNING AND STRATEGY

Inasmuch as the factory cost accounting function is continuously engaged in taking the pulse of the manufacturing operation and transmitting to management frequent readings concerning the plant operation as it behaves and compares to certain norms, the control aspects of factory cost accounting receive heavy emphasis.

The contribution which the function can make in the areas of manufacturing planning, decision making, and strategy, including pricing, can be equally significant. These contributions flow from the basic information sources with which the department routinely deals but on an "as needed" or "requested" basis.

The manufacturing manager uses factory cost accounting to analyze and evaluate:

1. Inventory carrying costs and proper levels to be maintained
2. Economic lot quantities, to ensure that planned economies are secured
3. Manufacturing capital expense proposals
4. Cost effects of proposed and actual labor increases and fringe programs on plant costs
5. Effects of proposed and accomplished component standardization
6. Comparative results of tool and fixture rehabilitation or replacement options
7. Make-or-buy opportunities and alternatives
8. Desirability of subcontracting versus in-house manufacture
9. Effects of proposed revisions in material handling systems and methods
10. Manpower and facilities forecasts
11. Contribution to fixed expense and profit of various products, related to the hours required to produce varying quantities of those products
12. Assignment of production to alternative plants based on the lowest variable cost structure
13. Values added by manufacture

These and similar problems can be clarified by proper, factual cost information developed by factory cost accounting.

Pricing and Estimating. Although there are other conventional bases for pricing than the cost base, it is most important to know the true yield of any price or estimate in terms of what the price produces in profit contribution or marginal income toward the payment of fixed expense and to profit beyond the break-even point. To determine the effect of a price in these terms, it is necessary to know the actual material, labor, and variable aspects of burden and other unit variables such as freight, packaging, and the like. Factory cost accounting provides these data on a unitized basis.

Various comparisons of actual to estimated costs provide a means of modifying standards to reflect the conditions actually experienced in the plant and so permit cost recovery through cost knowledge. Various quantity discounts based on cost differentials are applied through the pricing formula. It is necessary to know the real cost savings which quantity runs produce. Often such savings are in fact nonexistent, and quantity discounts offered in such instances are poorly conceived.

Factory cost accounting is often the lodging point for job cost information on prior similar jobs. Reference to this historic cost information permits better relationship of known unit costs to prices on subsequent bids. This factory cost information may likewise be used in establishing transfer prices between plants or functions.

CAUTIONS FOR BEST USAGE

The obvious trend is toward the use of factual, quantitative data in decision making. The qualitative approach to decision making—reliance on hunch, feel, historical method, or other intangible, unsupported technique—will no longer suffice because of the increasing complexity of the factors involved and rapidly changing conditions. Factory cost accounting can provide the quantitative measurements which the manufacturing manager needs to function as an effective member of management.

In using the factory cost accounting function to advance his own and his company's objectives, there are certain proved principles that the manufacturing manager must remember.

1. The value of average costing is highly questionable. Costs must be determined on the basis of specific runs, pieces, shapes, units, jobs, and departments. When unlike things are averaged, the result is usually misleading. Per ton costs in the foundry, for example, though popular in years past, are being replaced by specific costs per piece.

2. Data must be correct at the source. If not, any subsequent analysis or summary of those data will be inaccurate, no matter how sophisticated the presentation.

3. The cost system itself must be straightforward and understandable. It must report costs and activities in the manner in which they actually occur. Lumping of material, labor, and burden data is unsuitable. Failure to separate the fixed and the variable aspects of burden is a critical fault. Use of outdated standards is a definite weakness no matter how many updates or broad modifiers are applied.

4. Production of extensive cost data, no matter how excellent, is no substitute for action. It is rather a basis for action. Factory cost accounting reports; others must act. Through prompt and proper action, the manufacturing manager makes the cost function meaningful as a decision making activity.

5. "To the penny" accuracy should often be subordinated to timely, reasonably accurate approximations from sound basic data. In most cases, this

approach will be more valuable to the manufacturing manager than late, highly involved, and pseudoprecise costs.

By using the function of factory cost accounting in the above manner for the purposes outlined, and for other related purposes, the manufacturing manager extracts its real value.

BIBLIOGRAPHY

Beyer, Robert, *Profitability Accounting for Planning and Control*, The Ronald Press Company, New York, 1963.

Brummett, R. Lee, *Overhead Costing: The Costing of Manufactured Products*, Bureau of Business Research, School of Business Administration, University of Michigan, Ann Arbor, Mich., 1957.

Bursk, Edward C. (ed.), *New Decision Making Tools for Managers*, Harvard University Press, Cambridge, Mass., 1963.

Davidson, H. Justin, and Robert M. Trueblood, "Accounting for Decision Making," *Accounting Review*, October, 1961, pp. 577–582.

Freidman, I. Paul, *Cost Controls and Profit Improvement through Product Cost Analysis*, Prentice-Hall, Inc., Englewood Cliffs, N.J., 1966.

Gould, Douglas P., *Marketing for Profit*, Reinhold Publishing Corporation, New York, 1961.

Horowitz, Ira, *An Introduction to Quantitative Business Analysis*, McGraw-Hill Book Company, New York, 1965.

Ward, Edwin F., "Making the Proper Make-or-Buy Decision," *NAA Bulletin*, January, 1964, pp. 31–32.

Willson, James D., "Practical Applications of Cost-Volume-Profit Analysis," *NAA Bulletin*, March, 1960, p. 7.

CHAPTER FOUR

Operations Research

HOWARD E. LOVELY *Cresap, McCormick and Paget, Chicago, Illinois*

Although "operations research" as a term is encountered frequently, its meaning and impact are often misunderstood. Fundamentally, operations research enables managers to increase their effectiveness by bringing scientific techniques to bear on recurring day-to-day situations. The result is a quantitative basis for making operational decisions. To the manufacturing manager, operations research is not an essential requirement for successful performance, but it is a significant addition to the traditional tools of management.

Operations research (or OR) techniques are in no sense a substitute for sound management practices, although they can enhance the effectiveness of such practices. The application of operations research methods to the dynamics of the real-world manufacturing environment requires an understanding of OR's limitations as well as its potential benefits. Too often OR's quantitative (mathematical) methods are misconstrued as producing results which can be taken as absolute. This is not so. Solutions to operations research analyses require subjective review on the manager's part before he tries to apply them.

Although general policies have been worked out for selecting appropriate applications, organizing and controlling projects, and measuring performance, OR's potential benefits do not accrue automatically. Each manager must adapt operations research to his own requirements and organization. There have been numerous successful applications of OR in the area of manufacturing; these proved applications should be taken as useful guides and starting points for the introduction and continued development of operations research within the manufacturing function.

DEFINITION OF OPERATIONS RESEARCH

Operations research may be described as a particular method of analysis of the relationships and functions of an organized activity. However, OR projects are so flexible and varied that a precise and generally accepted definition is difficult to formulate. One approach to understanding the concept of operations research is to see how it came into being as an identifiable subject.

Origin of Operations Research. The activity called operations research can be traced to the early days of World War II. Teams of scientists representing different disciplines were assigned the task of analyzing various military management problems. Their objective was to make optimum use of available resources—a management objective within any organization. Included among the problems were such tactical situations as the development of systematic search patterns for naval vessels to be used in combating the submarine menace, and the development of bombing patterns to bring about an increase in the amount of damage.

Although the term "operations research" can be traced to World War II, its fundamental tools, methods, and techniques are as old as the scientific method of problem solving. None of the sciences was created on a specific day, and operations research is no exception. Its origin can be found in the scientific techniques of analysis and synthesis. The way in which these instruments are assembled and applied, as well as the kinds of problems to which they directed, constitute the distinguishing traits and characteristics of operations research.

After World War II, the first attempts to apply operations research to the industrial environment were accompanied by controversy and confusion. Among the reasons that can be cited are the mysticism and jargon that grew up around the quantitative methodology of OR, misunderstanding of what OR is all about, chicanery, and overoptimism regarding what OR could realistically achieve. Since emerging from this formative period, operations research has increasingly developed in scope of application as well as in management acceptance of it as a valuable service.

Characteristics of Operations Research. Operations research has been described as an applied science. Yet the term does not define a clear, concise, generally accepted body of principles, methods, tools, or techniques. It means different things to different people. To many, it means solely the application of sophisticated mathematical techniques. To others, it is synonymous with a systems approach to analysis. To some, the mathematical techniques of statistics and accounting are included within the boundaries of operations research, whereas to others, they are relegated to the category of other management services. And to still another group, operations research means nothing new in principle, but merely an extension of the scientific approach to analysis, applied to executive-type problems and presented with new terminology.

Simply stated, operations research is just what the term implies—research on operations. However, the uniqueness of operations research lies in a particular concept of operations and the specific type of research conducted. This fact may be demonstrated by reviewing the six salient features of OR which establish its uniqueness. These identifying features are discussed individually, but in practice they are inextricably interwoven.

Systems Orientation. The term "system" implies an interaction among individual elements of some process or organization. The individual elements of the system may be viewed as being interdependent in a cause and effect relationship. Fundamental to operations research is the concept that a problem or situation is analyzed in the context of a system. For example, consider an OR project undertaken to reduce the cost of equipment maintenance within a manufacturing plant. The study team would consider the effect of possible solutions not only on the maintenance department, but also on other elements of the plant that would be affected, such as manufacturing, production scheduling and control, and quality control.

The traditional concept of the industrial organization is one of compartmentalized elements, each performing a specialized function. This view of the organization is reflected by the typical organization chart. By contrast, inherent to operations research is the view that an organization is an organic whole and should be approached as such in any analysis of its operations.

Multidiscipline. Operations research has been described as embodying the systems approach to problem solving and analysis. Therefore, where more than a single area of an organization or area of specialization is affected by an OR project, each area must be represented. This concept has resulted in the team or task force approach for conducting OR projects, so that each project will reflect the composition of the team. For this very reason, there is a variety in the detailed method of attack which often makes operations research difficult for managers to understand. Frequently, OR projects take on an exploratory atmosphere which tends to undermine management confidence.

Scientific Method. The approach to analysis, termed the "scientific method," certainly is not peculiar to operations research. For years, the physical sciences have used it as a logical, organized approach to research and analysis. It is based upon the premise that through the analytical array of facts, cause and effect within a system can be identified. As a result, a researcher is able to predict with some accuracy the operations of a system as these interactive relationships become established. Another way to say this is that it now becomes possible for the researcher to simulate the real world by building an analog. Even though such an analog never perfectly duplicates the real-world environment, it can be used to predict causal effects within a system.

Quantitative Basis. The fundamental scientific method used in operations research requires analytical solutions which may be expressed in terms of predictive cause and effect. Such an approach requires a quantitative basis for communicating the results of an analysis. As a result, mathematical reasoning is fundamental to OR. Mathematics thus serves as the common language of operations research.

Model Construction. The use of an analog for simulating the operation of a real-world system requires the development and construction of a model. The model generally takes the form of a series of mathematical equations, so that the relationships among the various elements of the system can be quantitatively expressed. Perhaps one of the most widely known uses of a model in manufacturing is the economic order quantity equation for establishing the optimum number of parts to be ordered. Mathematical models such as this are a significant feature of operations research methodololgy.

Optimized Solution. It is not the aim of operations research to establish a single, definite solution to a problem or analysis. Rather, an operations research solution endeavors to provide management with a quantitative basis for judging among an array of alternatives. Management is thus offered a choice of answers to a problem.   Consider again the OR project which was aimed at reducing equipment maintenance cost within a manufacturing facility. Solutions to this analysis might well be presented in such terms as:

Solution A should reduce maintenance cost by 10 percent but will increase production costs by 15 percent. , Solution B should reduce maintenance cost by 20 percent but will increase production costs by 10 percent and increase the costs of quality control administration by 5 percent.   Solution C should . . . ., and so on.

Solutions of this kind enable managers to judge the total impact of a course of action and to decide which solution is in the best interest of the system or organization as a whole.   Such a solution may be called an optimum one; in contrast, a solution that is best for only one or a limited number of elements of the organization may be called a suboptimum solution.

Operations Research Defined.   On the basis of the foregoing characteristics, a working definition of operations research for this particular discussion may be constructed as follows:

Operations research is the application of scientific methods, tools, and techniques to the analysis of the relationships and functions of a system for the purpose of determining quantitatively the conditions under which optimum results should be achieved.

STEPS IN CONDUCTING OPERATIONS RESEARCH

The team or task force approach constitutes one of the inherent characteristics of operations research.   As suggested previously, one result of this approach is that each project assumes a distinctive tone which reflects the experience and thinking of the team members.   Two projects formulated to deal with similar situations but with two differently composed teams would thus tend to differ somewhat, although they would be conducted in much the same way.   There is general agreement, in fact, that the following are the major steps in conducting an OR project.
1.   Define the objectives of the analysis.
2.   Determine the relationships and constraints that define the system under study.
3.   Construct a mathematical model.
4.   Derive a solution from the model.
5.   Test the model and solution derived from it.
6.   Establish controls over the solution.
7.   Implement the solution.

Defining the Objectives.   As already stated, one of the characteristics of operations research is the systems approach to analysis.   Inherent in this approach is an endeavor to identify all cause and effect relationships of the operations under analysis.   However, there is a practical limitation on the boundaries of most OR projects; such limitations are often established by the organizational span of control of the individual authorizing the OR project. For example, a manufacturing manager may wish to use operations research to increase the effectiveness of his machine loading and scheduling function.   However, the policies of the sales organization, which largely dictate how production orders or work load are generated in the plant, are outside of his authority.   In theory, it would be desirable to include the sales organization in the analysis; in practice, this may not be feasible.

Defining the objectives of an OR project requires more than a statement of purpose describing the end product sought; equally important is establishing the extent to which the OR team may direct its inquiry.   Even though operations research necessarily takes the overall view, successful applications may be undertaken with a limited organizational scope. It is vitally necessary to establish this perspective as part of the project definition.

Determining System Relationships. Once the objectives, including the scope, are clearly defined, the study team may proceed to investigate the relationships that establish cause and effect within the area of analysis. In essence, this is a fact-finding phase. The team becomes familiar with all aspects of the operations under study and sorts the significant from the nonsignificant. During this process, two types of variables are identified—those which are subjective and those which are quantitative. It is important to identify and understand the interaction of both kinds of variables in order to comprehend fully the operations under review. Too often, the impact and qualifying effects of subjective variables are overlooked or minimized.

Constructing a Model. During model construction, the various cause and effect relationships identified in the fact-finding phase are refined and expressed symbolically in the language of mathematics. This expression takes the form of one or a series of mathematical equations. It is essential to identify within the model those variables which may be controlled and those which are not subject to control.

Deriving a Solution from the Model. After the model of the system under study has been defined, the next step is to arrive at an optimum solution. This may be accomplished by either of two techniques. (1) Mathematical techniques such as calculus may be used to optimize the model mathematically. This approach does not involve the substitution of numbers in the equation until after the solution has been obtained. (2) Numbers may be substituted in the equation on an iterative basis until the optimum solution is identified. This approach is often termed the "trial and error" method.

Testing the Model and Solution. There are few systems, if any, in the everyday world where all the cause and effect relationships can be defined in terms of abstract mathematics. Therefore, the model must be tested in its application to the real-world environment which it simulates but which it will never duplicate. The effectiveness of the model can be established by using actual past operating data to measure how well it predicts the various relationships that it expresses. The data must be selected carefully so that the impact of any subjective factors not apparent from the quantitative data can be identified.

Establishing Controls over the Solution. The solution obtained from a model remains valid only as long as (1) the relationships among the elements of the model remain as stated and (2) the fixed and uncontrolled elements maintain their values, or maintain their values within acceptable limits. The solution derived from the model usually becomes invalid when these values or relationships change significantly. For establishing controls over the solutions derived from the model, there must also be established the possible ranges of the variables, the values of fixed constants, and if possible, the qualitative relationships of subjective factors to the model.

Implementing the Solution. To be of value, the final solution must be one that can be incorporated into routine operations. To this end, the changes that are required in existing procedures and policies must be identified and carried through. In addition, working procedures must be prepared which can be understood by the people who will be responsible for their application.

MANUFACTURING APPLICATIONS

Operations research has been successfully employed in every type of industrial environment. It is not limited in its application by the kind of business involved or by the area of application. It can be used to assist decision making across the total spectrum of management responsibilities. The manufacturing function has proved to be one of the most fertile areas for successful operations research projects.

Role and Scope in Manufacturing. Operations research does not represent a cure-all for the varied problems faced by operating managers, nor is it a substitute for management's responsibility for decision making. These truisms are as valid for the area of manufacturing as they are for any other function represented within the modern industrial organization. However, what operations research can give the manager of manufacturing is an opportunity to make his decision making more effective. In this sense, operations research is similar to any other staff capability.

Operations research is not limited in the kinds of situations within manufacturing to which it can be applied. It can be successfully used in all the activities generally found in the manufacturing function. Moreover, operations research need not be limited to problem solving tasks. It may be used to good advantage in the analysis of existing operations where no specific problem, other than achieving better performance, exists.

Criteria for Selecting Applications. In general, there are two situations in which a manufacturing manager may consider operations research. First, specific problems may have defied conventional problem solving techniques. Second, a situation may be selected just to test the use of operations research within the organization. Either way, the following criteria may be used to identify the kinds of applications where operations research may be used with some expectation of success.

1. The operations to be analyzed should be of a recurring rather than a one-time type. Because the typical OR project represents a significant expenditure in staff time and effort, the benefits accruing from continuing application should be sought.
2. The situation should present an opportunity to choose among alternative courses of action.
3. The area to be analyzed should permit the application of quantitative methods and measurement. Furthermore, there should be a large number of controllable variables and a small number of relevant uncontrollable variables. If only a small number of controllable variables need to be coped with, the analysis can often be handled better by more conventional techniques.
4. It should be possible to collect data relevant to the situation.
5. There should be a ready way to evaluate results. The problem or situation should not be so large or so indefinite that a solution cannot be realistically achieved.

Case histories of OR projects have clearly identified the foregoing criteria, which if followed, will significantly increase the chance of success. In fact, one of the most important phases of OR projects is to identify and select areas that lend themselves to OR techniques.

Representative Applications. The following brief description of operations research projects are typical of manufacturing applications.

1. A large midwestern manufacturer of ball-bearing components and assemblies wished to expand component manufacturing capacity by constructing a new factory. Market research studies had already established the anticipated level of demand for finished assemblies. What remained to be established was the required level of component parts inventory to support various levels of assembly production.

Through an OR approach, a production cost model was constructed. The model defined the relationship between the costs generated by shutdown of the assembly areas and the costs involved in various levels of component inventory. As a result, optimum quantities of component inventory were identified for various levels of assembly production.

2. A producer of bulk chemical products encountered highly variable customer demand patterns. Both plant operating costs and product availability were functions of process scheduling. An OR project was formulated with the objectives of minimizing operating costs and maximizing product availability for customer demands.

First, a customer-demand forecasting model employing exponential smoothing was constructed. Second, the output of this model was used as the input to another model that related the costs of the various steps of the production process to the sequence of scheduling. The result was an array of alternatives that allowed management to determine the various levels of operating costs corresponding to variations in product availability which could satisfy varying customer demands.

3. An electronics company wished to improve its operations for the manufacture of television sets. Of specific interest to management were (a) the allocation of plant space to manufacturing tasks and (b) scheduling and loading of designated work centers. Variables included in the analyisis were target levels for in-process and finished goods inventory investment, forecasted orders, equipment and work center capacity, manufacturing flow, and standard manufacturing times. Through the techniques of operations research, these variables were related to identify optimum solutions for plant space allocation and work center scheduling.

4. A job-shop-oriented machine parts manufacturer primarily serving the aerospace industry was faced with increasing equipment downtime and rising maintenance cost for his numerical control equipment. Through the use of linear programming techniques, it was possible to establish (a) an optimum schedule for preventive maintenance and (b) a level of maintenance support to meet acceptable demands for unscheduled service.

Areas of Application. The methodology of operations research must be designed for each specific situation. Real-world situations cannot be forced into preestablished "canned" solutions. Similarly, OR may not be able to solve every problem within identical areas of different organizations. The difference in success and applicability often depends upon varying subjective influences; for this reason, it is dangerous to itemize areas categorically for the application of operations research. However, such areas of successful application can at least serve as general guides.

Included among the areas within manufacturing in which OR has been successfully used are the following:

Production and Inventory Control
    Establishing raw material inventory levels
    Determing traffic procedures and schedules
    Establishing work-in-process inventory levels
    Loading and scheduling machine centers
    Balancing assembly lines
    Establishing inventory reorder rules
    Determining economic production quantities
    Minimizing waiting time between manufacturing operations

Manufacturing Planning
  Matching production resources to sales forecasts
  Determining make-or-buy decisions
  Optimizing equipment utilization
  Establishing process routings and sequencing
  Making cost estimates
  Synthesizing manufacturing operations
  Establishing quality control procedures

Plant Engineering and Maintenance
  Establishing equipment preventive maintenance schedules
  Forecasting maintenance requirements
  Establishing support materials inventory levels

Industrial Engineering
  Allocating manufacturing resources among competing demands
  Establishing labor performance standards
  Determining tool maintenance and replacement schedules
  Establishing plant location and layout
  Determining facilities requirements
  Establishing equipment replacement rules
  Evaluating cost reduction proposals
  Establishing standards for control of indirect costs

Administrative and Cost Control
  Making budget allocations
  Determining direct and indirect personnel levels
  Establishing learning curves
  Assigning personnel in relation to skills versus needs
  Simulating budget performance
  Developing information retrieval systems
  Analyzing scrap losses
  Analyzing contributions to end-product cost

MANAGEMENT IMPLICATIONS

Operations research represents a significant development in the continuing evolvement of modern industrial management, because it extends the quantitative sciences to the area of management. As a result, it can give managers a unique capability for dealing with the growing complexity of daily operations. However, success does not automatically ensue. Success depends largely upon management's intelligent and thoughtful application of this tool.

Understanding when and how to use operations research and the considerations involved in these decisions are perhaps the most important things a manager should know about this subject. He does not need to be a skilled mathematician, a systems analyst, or a computer expert. Rather, he must be able to marshal and organize the resources at his command for applying OR to his special areas of interest.

Organizing for Operations Research. The organizational relationship of operations research to other functional elements within an industrial enterprise may take various forms. This difference, like any other organizational difference, reflects the executive personalities, objectives, and operating policies within each individual firm. However, the manager of manufacturing wishing to apply operations research will in general encounter one of the following two broad organizational situations.

1. There is a centralized corporate or division organizational unit with responsibility for all OR activities. Typically, the personnel who comprise this group are systems and mathematically oriented. They serve as a staff resource capability to line area managers in manufacturing, engineering, material, and so on.

2. There is no separate operations research unit within the overall organization. Each manager organizes and applies OR within his own area of responsibility.

In either situation, the manufacturing manager wishing to organize for operations research must make a series of decisions involving, first, the selection of an area for investigation, and second, selection of personnel to staff the project. Criteria for selecting applications and identification of potential manufacturing areas have already been reviewed. Here, the question is how to select personnel to staff the manufacturing OR project.

The success of an OR project depends in large measure on the staffing of the project task force or team. Generally speaking, two broad categories of skill requirements are necessary: (1) specialized or technical (mathematical, systems) knowledge and (2) operating knowledge and experience in the areas to be studied.

In those organizations where a formal operations research group exists, the technical capability and project leadership may be drawn from this source. Where it does not exist, a manufacturing manager may choose one of three methods to obtain the necessary talents.

1. He may hire an individual skilled in technical aspects of OR techniques into the company.

2. He may train and develop company personnel, using consultant personnel to guide initial projects.

3. He may use consultant personnel on a one-time basis.

Regardless of the approach selected, however, the importance of technical capability to an operations research undertaking is often misunderstood and overemphasized. One of the commonest mistakes made in staffing an OR project is to view the technical skills as the most important ingredient of team resources. On the contrary, in practice, some of the most important contributions to a project team's capability come from those members who are assigned from the line areas being studied. It is through their knowledge that the team is able to analyze the operations in terms of real-world requirements. Unless such people take an active part in the study, there is the strong possibility that the proposed solutions will be neither sufficiently comprehensive nor flexible enough to meet the exigencies of daily operations.

In those companies where responsibility for operations research is centralized, serving on a project tends to be a one-time assignment for personnel within operating areas. For example, personnel from manufacturing would be assigned to a specific OR project that involves some aspect of manufacturing; after completion of that project, they resume their normal responsibilities. During the project, primary responsibility for its direction and leadership generally remains with the OR group.

An advantage offered by this organizational relationship is the capability of cutting across traditional organizational lines. Unfortunately, operating managers often tend to remain aloof from OR endeavors organized in this manner. If success with operations research is to be achieved, it is imperative that all managers affected, including those in manufacturing, select and assign those personnel who are thoroughly familiar with the operations to be studied and who have the respect of other line personnel.

In those organizations not possessing a centralized or identified OR unit, manufacturing managers may choose to establish their own OR function. As noted previously, company personnel selected for this assignment do not need extensive mathematical backgrounds. It is more important that they be familiar with overall operations and possess the basic qualities and traits of inquisitiveness, intelligence, and systems orientation. That is, they should appreciate the necessary interaction among all elements of an organization and not be limited in their viewpoint. They should be capable of adapting to the environment of interdisciplinary views and opinions.

The technical skills and proficiency of the team can be developed through a combination of association with consultants, special on-the-job training programs, and attendance at formal operations research seminars and courses.

Controlling and Measuring Performance. Unfortunately, many OR endeavors are still cloaked in an atmosphere of mystery, not to say mysticism. Too often, managers inexperienced with operations research are led to believe that undertakings involving OR are so esoteric that they cannot be subjected to such operating controls and measures of performance as schedules and budgets. Although it is true that controls may have to be milestoned rather than detailed, there is little substance in the belief that such projects either should not or cannot be scheduled and controlled at all. Actually, the element of risk is reduced when proper controls are applied, because they make potential problems visible in time to permit redirection or recovery.

Establishing adequate controls begins with the inception and definition of the OR project. During this phase, the manufacturing manager sponsoring an OR project should require the preparation of a written study plan before the OR activity is actually begun. This document should include the objectives, scope, and end product of the proposed project, as well as an estimate of the timing, approach to be employed, and required resources. Failure to establish these factors clearly at the beginning of a study is a major reason why OR projects go astray. This approach helps ensure that all significant factors affecting a study have been recognized before the study begins.

Operations research projects do not require unique or special control mechanisms or systems. Existing techniques employed within a company are generally adequate for measuring project progress and performance. Project timing may be depicted in such formats as bar charts or milestone schedules; manpower may be planned and controlled by study activity, by personnel categories, and by the overall project. If the project is large or complicated, it is often helpful to prepare a network of events and activities showing the study interdependencies.

Management Participation. Ensuring a successful OR undertaking does not end with the selection and staffing of a project. In many ways, the most important contribution to the success of operations research comes from management.

It is imperative for a project to have complete management support. Management must exhibit continuing and positive interest in the study. Evidence of a lack of faith or skepticism on the part of management is a sure route to failure. This is particularly true of those situations that affect various activity areas within an organization and that require cooperation and coordination among different managers or supervisors. One way of securing cooperation is to permit all such operating managers or supervisors to participate in the selection of projects for operations research. It is difficult, if not foolhardy, to attempt to force a solution on people who have not participated in establishing the need for a project; the best-designed system and procedures will fail if forced upon unwilling operating personnel.

The last and in many ways the most crucial phase of an operations research endeavor is implementation. It is here that management must be particularly aware of the needs and the psychology of operating personnel. Because most people tend to resist change, management must exhibit the positive attitude that the results to be secured by implementation are worth the trouble to the organization and to those affected by it. Furthermore, operating personnel should have any new systems and procedures explained to them thoroughly. A personnel training or indoctrination program is often a necessary part of the installation process.

Management of the OR project should be ideally vested in someone who not only has technical talent but who also possesses substantial executive capability. A successful operations research endeavor must be properly planned and controlled to produce practical solutions within a reasonable period of time. To further this goal, OR leadership must be capable of providing needed technical guidance and be oriented toward dealing with real-world problems and situations.

Relation to the Computer. Operations research does not require the use of a computer. Many OR solutions can be established in principle—that is, theoretical results identifying optimum solutions for the situation under analysis can be determined by mathematical analysis. However, electronic data processing is useful in operations research because of its ability to process and manipulate large amounts of predominately mathematical data.

It would be difficult and sometimes impractical or impossible to implement many of the solutions to complex business situations represented in the mathematical analogs (models) without this processing capability of the computer. Many study results would remain beautiful theories rather than emerging as practical operating systems and procedures. A typical manufacturing example is the well-known model for computing economic production quantities. The solution to this analysis can be derived through mathematical techniques without the need to process large amounts of data; however, in a manufacturing plant having a large number of active parts, this equation cannot be used easily without electronic data processing capability.

LIMITATIONS AND PROBLEM AREAS

Experience indicates that there are several aspects of operations research which often limit or confuse those managers who do not understand its methodology. The four most frequently recurring situations are discussed below.

Language Barrier. The typical manager is not mathematically oriented. Generally he has difficulty in understanding reasoning expressed in complex mathematical symbols. Unfortunately, the technical OR man often has difficulty in communicating his reasoning without the use of mathematical symbols. A communications gap may develop, as a result of which managers find it difficult to understand and consequently to accept the solution resulting from an operations research analysis.

Furthermore, operations research, like other scientific disciplines, has evolved a body of distinctive terminology. This common language, although facilitating communication among those who practice OR, is generally foreign to operating managers. Thus this situation also contributes to a potential communications gap.

The following list of terms, while not complete, includes those generally considered the most significant in understanding the technical language of OR.

Algorithm. Method for deriving a solution to a problem by using the results from each cycle to refine the following cycle. The process is repeated until a satisfactory answer is obtained.

Allocation Problem. A situation in which there are limited resources to be distributed among competing demands. The problem is to combine resources with demands in a way that will maximize overall effectiveness. There are two primary types of allocation problems: assignment and transportation.

Assignment Problem. A situation in which there is an equal number of resources and demands. The problem is to pair one resource with one, and only one, demand in a way which will produce the maximum effectiveness. A common plant problem would be the assignment of operators to specific machines.

Transportation Problem. A variation of the assignment problem occurs when the number of resources and demands differs. A typical plant example would be assigning one operator to divide his time among several machines.

Game Theory. A method of determining the best strategy in competitive situations where the outcome of various strategies can be precisely predicted. It has proved useful in situations such as the allocation of funds to competing types of advertising media. It generally has limited application to real-world problems, although it has been used extensively as the basis for executive development and training programs involving simulation of competitive business situations.

Inventory Problem. A situation involving one or both of the following decisions: (1) how much to order and (2) when to order. The problem is to optimize the overall impact among such considerations as inventory costs, setup and run costs, cost of delays due to shortage, and the like.

Mathematical Programming. Certain techniques which are useful for solving allocation problems where limited resources must be allocated between competing demands. Mathematical programming can be linear, nonlinear, or dynamic.

Linear programming involves those problem situations in which all relationships are directly proportional (linear). This means that they can be plotted as a straight line. For example, one unit of output costs $2 and fifty units of output cost $100. When all variables behave in this manner, a linear programming problem results.

Nonlinear programming involves those problem situations in which the relationships of the variables are exponential. Graphically, they would plot as a curve. For example, one unit of output costs $2 while fifty units of output cost $75.

Dynamic programming involves sequential multistage problem situations. At each stage, a decision (solution) must be made among alternatives. However, as each decision is made, the parameters of the remaining stages of the problem change. Dynamic programming is thus the most sophisticated of the mathematical programming techniques.

Measure of Effectiveness. The criterion used in evaluating alternative solutions to a problem in order to select the optimum one.

Probability Theory. A method of establishing the predictability of events from the known occurrence of past events.

Queuing Theory. A technique which is applicable to the analysis of waiting line problems—that is, there is an imbalance in the capacity of a service facility and the pattern of demands upon the facility. A typical plant situation would be the number of machines required at a particular production operation in relation to the flow of parts to that operation.

Replacement Theory. Methods of analysis which deal with two types of situations involving the life pattern of the equipment involved. One pertains to equipment that gradually deteriorates in value or efficiency; the other involves equipment that breaks down permanently.

Simulation. A technique which employs mathematical models as analogs of real-world systems. Inputs to the models are varied to establish the effect of decisions on conditions described by the model. Manipulation of the models may take various forms.

Numeric values of variables may be altered to observe their effect. The mathematical relationships expressed by the equations of the model may be subjected to sophisticated analysis to identify when an optimum (maximum, minimum) condition exists. Monte Carlo simulation relies on generating input data to the model by the use of random numbers. Simply stated, Monte Carlo is a simulated sampling technique when actual samples are unavailable. It generates synthetic sample data which are then used as actual data.

Needless Rethinking. An operations research project constitutes an exhaustive search for alternative courses of action which might be taken to solve the problem or improve the situation under review. In many situations, a number of these possible courses of action have already been considered and evaluated and perhaps rejected by line management. This feature of OR methodology often irritates managers, who view this process as a needless rethinking of the problem.

Problem Substitution. A typical operations research solution gives management an array of facts and alternatives from which to choose; the typical manager, by contrast, is conditioned to making yes or no decisions in response to specific problem situations. This type of manager may regard the output of an operations research analysis as indecisive. Many managers view this situation as merely substituting one problem for another—the problem of choice for the problem which was presumably being analyzed.

Model Limitations. The painstaking fact finding and analysis of an OR project culminates in the construction of a model as an analog of the system or situation under review. This model, however precise mathematically, can never hope to duplicate all the real-world considerations that make up the typical industrial environment. Consequently, the solution to many OR projects must be carefully reviewed in relation to the impact of subjective considerations of which a manager is often acutely aware, and many proposed solutions must be discarded or altered. This is why many managers find it difficult to place too much reliance on an operations research endeavor, knowing the limitations that a mathematical model presents.

CONTRIBUTION TO MANUFACTURING MANAGEMENT

In conclusion, in spite of the limitations discussed above, operations research offers the manager of manufacturing a unique addition to the resources upon which he may rely. Although the fundamental premises upon which OR is based may not be new, its application to executive problem solving represents the achievement of a new plateau in management. Operations research intensifies the potential of the manager's decision making role. Through its quantitative analytical methodology, it provides a manager with a factual basis which can guide and support his executive judgment.

BIBLIOGRAPHY

Batchelor, James H., *Operations Research*, Saint Louis University Press, Saint Louis, Mo., 1959.

Bowman, Edward H., and Robert B. Fetter, *Analysis for Production Management*, Richard D. Irwin, Inc., Homewood, Ill., 1957.

Churchman, C. West, Russell L. Ackoff, and E. Leonard Arnoff, *Introduction to Operations Research*, John Wiley & Sons, Inc., New York, 1957.

Herrmann, Cyril C., and John F. Magee, "Operations Research for Management" in Edward C. Bursk and John F. Chapman (eds.), *New Decision Making Tools for Managers*, The New American Library of World Literature, Inc., New York, 1965.

Malcolm, Donald G., "On the Need for Improvement in Implementation of OR," in S. Benjamin (ed.), *Modern Industrial Management*, Chandler Publishing Company, San Francisco, 1967.

Miller, David W., and Martin K. Starr, *Executive Decisions and Operations Research*, Prentice-Hall, Inc., Englewood Cliffs, N.J., 1960.

Morris, William T., *Management Science in Action*, Richard D. Irwin, Inc., Homewood, Ill., 1963.

Solow, Herbert, "Operations Research in Business," *Fortune*, February, 1956.

Trefethen, Florence N., "A History of Operations Research," in Joseph F. McCloskey and Florence N. Trefethen (eds.), *Operations Research for Management*, The Johns Hopkins Press, Baltimore, Md., 1954.

Wagner, Harvey M., "Practical Slants on Operations Research," *Harvard Business Review*, May–June, 1963.

CHAPTER FIVE

Toolmaking

GUY J. BACCI   *General Supervisor—Industrial Engineering, International Harvester Company, Chicago, Illinois*

The toolmaking function is an important part of the supporting services necessary to sustain the manufacturing effort. It represents a sizable investment of company funds in both equipment and labor. Special-purpose toolroom machines such as jig borers, grinders, lathes, and the like are essential if any toolmaking work is to be performed internally. The labor cost of toolmaking has always been well above the average wage costs of production workers. It therefore becomes important to develop and utilize the full potential of the skills inherent in the toolmaking function and make proper use of the highly specialized equipment available.

The toolmaker is one of the key men in modern production manufacturing. In the large body of men engaged in the various phases of machine manufacturing, the toolmaker represents the most skilled, the most inventive, and the most intelligent of the army of mechanics which forms the backbone of our mechanical industries.[1]

Skillful management of the toolmaking function is essential to achieve the objectives of profit-minded manufacturing managers.

PURPOSE AND IMPORTANCE OF THE TOOLMAKING FUNCTION

The function of toolmaking is found in many different business enterprises, probably called by many different names, but utilized as a supporting service to the end result of producing a salable product. The most common use of this function occurs in metalworking industries, which represent approximately one-third of all industries producing consumer and durable goods

[1] Charles Bradford Cole, *Tool Making*, American Technical Society, Chicago, 1941, preface.

in the United States. It is an accessory to the fabrication or manufacturing effort.

With the advent of mass production, including the ultimate sophistication of complete automation, the function has grown in importance. The key to its importance to a manufacturing manager is the large outlay of funds normally associated with the tooling aspects of introducing a new product or the improvement of an existing product. These costs present an excellent potential for cost reduction. Even in industries where toolmaking involves the manufacture of a tool for short-run or limited production, the potential is apparent.

Interchangeability of Parts. An important breakthrough in manufacturing technology resulted from the ability to produce an interchangeable component part. This part, manufactured to specific tolerances, could be produced in high volume at low cost. This concept, referred to as the "Principles of Interchangeable Manufacture," was clearly stated by L. P. Alford in his coverage of the subject in *Principles of Industrial Management*. He states, "The principles of interchangeable manufacture are also called the principles of mass production. There are two, stated in this wise:

1. Large-scale, or mass, production tends to increase operating efficiency and competitive power.
2. In large-scale, or mass, production the unit time of production tends to approach operating time as a limit"[2]

Transfer of Skill. The proper use of the toolmaking function lessens the necessity of using highly skilled employees as production workers. A well-designed and properly constructed tool transfers the skill required to make the part from the worker to the properly functioning tool. This is easily accomplished without sacrificing quality and usually with a large increase of quantity produced per dollar of cost. This was also covered by L. P. Alford and is called the "Principle of Transfer of Skill." He states, "The attention and skill required of a worker to use a tool or operate a machine is inversely as the thought and skill transferred into its mechanism.

Corollary 1: Through the application of the principle of the transfer of skill the worker becomes an adjunct to the tool or machine.

Corollary 2: The transfer of skill from the expert workmen to the machine makes the quality and quantity of work produced dependent upon the machine, not upon the machine operator."[3]

Toolmaking skills also permit building a tool which can help produce production parts from general-purpose machine tools. Without this capability, management would be faced with the expenditure of a larger share of funds to purchase special equipment for the manufacture of these special, unusual parts. A skilled and enterprising toolmaker can return an investment many times his wages in situations such as this.

Classification of Tooling. Tooling provides the necessary and important link in the manufacturing cycle between the machine and the workpiece. It is the device which is used to adapt the standard or special machine to fabricate the workpiece. Its functions consist of changing the form of the workpiece, controlling the workpiece during the operation, and checking the accuracy of the operation. Types of tooling which fall into these three categories are as follows:

2 L. P. Alford, *Principles of Industrial Management,* The Ronald Press Company, New York, 1940, p. 17.
3 *Ibid.,* p. 16.

1. To form or change the shape of the workpiece
   a. Molds, patterns, and coreboxes
   b. Cutting tools and abrasives
   c. Dies for forging and sheet metal work
2. To control the workpiece during the operation
   a. Locators, supports, and clamps
   b. Tool holders
   c. Workpiece holders such as fixtures for assembling, welding, and riveting
3. To check the accuracy of the operation
   a. Gages, templates, and measuring instruments

The first of these categories applies force to the workpiece, utilizing the power of the machine. Through this application, the tool is worn by constant usage, due to friction and heat. The maintenance of the tool is primarily to produce the workpiece to blueprint part tolerances. The machine or tool can normally be adjusted to compensate for wear until the tool must eventually be replaced. This characteristic is the reason why these types of tools are considered as "perishable tools," because they eventually are "expendable." Perishable tools can be classified as follows by the processes they perform.

1. Cutting tools
   a. Drills
   b. Mills
   c. Tool bits
   d. Hobs and the like
2. Forming tools
   a. Punches
   b. Forming rolls
   c. Stamping dies and the like
3. Assembly tools
   a. Welding electrodes
   b. Torch and soldering iron tips
   c. Hand tools and the like

Sources of Tooling. Tooling may be obtained from three principal sources:

1. Commercial tooling—manufactured in large quantities to standardized sizes and specifications and cataloged. This type is normally a stock item and can be purchased on short notice.

2. Regular tooling—not considered commercial enough to permit fabrication in large quantities, but available on short notice because it represents a standard tool specifically used by one company. This type of tool is not produced in large quantities, but because it is standard, it represents a savings over tooling which must be designed and manufactured for each product.

3. Special tooling—when product design is unique and the fabrication of the product demands a process different from the standard operation, special tooling is required. This type of tooling requires a large amount of design time and maximum skill of the toolmaker. The complexity of this type of tooling usually requires the utilization of more intricate and expensive toolroom equipment and fabrication in outside specialty tool shops.

Make or Buy. Both mass production and job shop type industries are faced with the question of whether to manufacture or purchase the necessary tooling. The costs associated with a make-or-buy decision must be carefully scrutinized to arrive at a proper decision. This decision depends heavily on the market life of the product and the production run over which the tool may be amortized. It must be approached on an individual plant basis by weighing all the factors inherent in the decision. These factors are discussed by Franklin Moore in his treatment of tool, jig, and fixture manufacture:

> Tooling is costly, whether you make it or buy it, but if you make your own it usually costs less and usually you have it when you want it. Be sure, though, that if you make your own tooling you give the toolmaking department a steady load of work, because it would be costly to have the highly skilled men and expensive machines in the toolroom idle part of the time.[4]

This conflict of objectives should be carefully scrutinized by analyzing the work load of the toolroom over an extended period of time. The short-range look gives a distorted view of the problem. There are a number of alternatives to consider in making a decision concerning the size of the toolroom. One of these is to maintain a fairly good size toolroom force and in periods of slack tooling work to use the facilities temporarily for close tolerance production work requiring the special skills and facilities of the toolroom. The approach generally prevalent is to maintain a nucleus of skilled toolmakers and machines. This group can be supplemented by outside tool shops. As large tooling projects appear and continue for a reasonable period of time, this core of skilled workers can be increased by permanent employees. Here the manager is faced with the problem of availability of skilled workers if the plant is located in a tight labor market.

ORGANIZATIONAL STATUS AND ROLE OF TOOLMAKING

The successful performance of the manufacturing manager's duties as they pertain to toolmaking can be assisted by many different, well-designed organizational structures. However, there are some basic concepts and elements common to all organizations.

Manufacturing Hierarchy. The manufacturing manager's job can be divided into five principal duties as shown by Figure 5-1. These consist of guiding and directing the work connected with the following functions:

Materials management—procuring, scheduling, and delivering materials, both direct and indirect

[4] Franklin G. Moore, *Production Control*, McGraw-Hill Book Company, New York, 1959, p. 65.

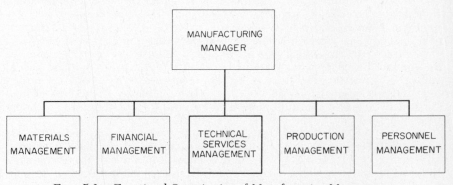

Fig. 5-1. Functional Organization of Manufacturing Management.

Financial management—securing the necessary funds for operation and accounting for their expenditure

Personnel management—establishing employment policies and procedures for operation

Technical services management—the technical staff services necessary to support and sustain the production effort

Production management—the fabrication and shipment of quality products in accordance with specifications and production schedules

Technical Services Organization. The technical services or manufacturing engineering organization, as presented in a typical management hierarchy, may be further subdivided into at least four important functions as shown by Figure 5-2. They comprise the basic elements found in the technical support of fabricating the product.

Machine and Tool Engineering. At the operational level, machine and tool engineering has basic responsibilities for the equipment which helps manufacture the product. An example of this is the design and fabrication of a machine tool to perform a specific operation peculiar to the product. To accomplish this requires excellent knowledge of machine design principles, accurate transmittal of these principles into blueprints and assembly diagrams, and finally, the total efforts of a well-functioning, skilled toolroom. It is important to separate the design of tools from the fabrication because each function has separate and distinct responsibilities. These responsibilities have an interrelationship which contributes equally to the production of manufacturing effort and therefore must be coordinated.

Toolroom Functional Organization. A form of organization, designed for efficient planning and fabrication, starts with establishing a flexible operating budget and comparing operational costs with this budget. Effectiveness is increased through the use of proper job planning, estimating, and scheduling. This, coupled with good supervision of the toolmaking force, leads to an efficient organization.

Traditional Toolmaking versus Specialization. There are two basic forms of toolroom organization. The traditional form, commonly used in smaller shops, utilizes the many skills inherent in the toolmaker craftsman. The assignment to make a complete tool is given to the worker after a superficial

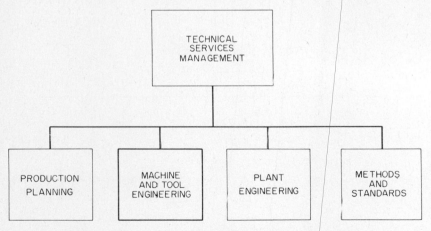

Fig. 5-2. Functional Elements of Technical Services Management.

planning attempt by the supervisor or group leader. The actual planning and fabrication depend on the skill of the worker and his ability to be proficient in all aspects of the craft of toolmaking. Duties under this system entail the detailing, layout, fitting, and assembly work of a complete tooling job.

The other form involves specialization starting with detail planning of the tool to be fabricated, including operational time estimates. The operations as processed or routed consist of logical steps to utilize special skills such as layout, fitting, various specialty machine operations, assembly, and the like. This specialization enables many jobs to be performed concurrently in the toolroom. It also allows supervision the prerogative of assignment to specifically skilled craftsmen at the appropriate rate of pay. All these factors give a decided economic advantage to this method of toolroom operation. A functional organization chart of this form is depicted by Figure 5-3.

MANAGERIAL ASPECTS OF THE TOOLMAKING FUNCTION

The high contribution to profit inherent in the toolmaking function requires the skillful utilization of management techniques. Whether the toolroom is staffed with relatively few skilled tradesmen or contains the degree of specialization just described, proper planning at the shop level is important. The depth of planning varies in proportion to the degree of specialization. At any depth, the essential elements are as follows:

1. Planning—a review of the work order to determine the sequence of work assignments and availability of resources
2. Estimating—a determination of the optimum time required to complete the work assignments
3. Scheduling—a review of the work assignments to determine priority and the actual assignment of the job
4. Follow-up—an assessment by the job planner and supervisor of the procedures utilized and the performance of the toolmaker

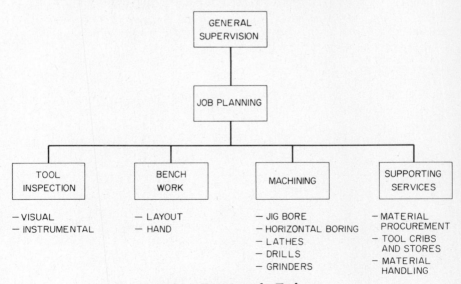

Fig. 5-3. Functions of a Toolroom.

These elements must be properly coordinated by general supervision of the function to assure good liaison between the planning and controlling aspects of the system. The key to improved effectiveness is adequate supervision coverage. The job planning function allows the shop or craft supervisor to spend more time with the craftsmen while the work is being performed. He is also available for consultation with the job planner when necessary.

Work Order Requests. Work orders usually fall into one of three categories, namely, (1) new tools to be fabricated, (2) existing tools to be altered, or (3) existing tools to be repaired. The first two stem from a new or changed product design which results in a new or changed tool design. The last results from damage to the tool or wearing which no longer assures meeting the specified quality limits. These work orders usually are initiated by the tool designer directly or by the production supervisor after receiving consultive service from the tool designer. They normally are formal, written requests as illustrated in Figure 5-4, accompanied by tooling blueprints. There also can be emergency telephone requests which require quick reaction to assure the continuous flow of the production process. These emergency requests must be followed by proper written records to assure cost allocation. It is important to the efficient functioning of the toolroom to keep emergencies to a minimum and have them be the exception rather than the rule of operation.

Planning and Estimating. The initial step of the planning element is the analysis of the work order. With good cooperation from those initiating work orders, sufficient information can be available to permit effective planning. Proper training of the job planner, which results in a questioning attitude, and a checklist of factors to be considered on all work orders assure adequate information even on emergency-type orders.

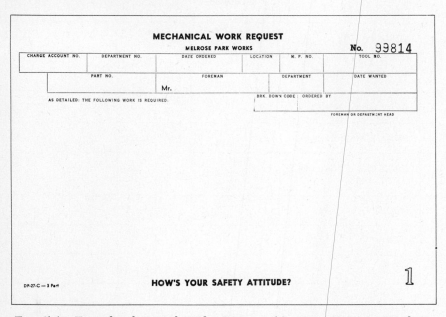

FIG. 5-4. Example of a Work Order Request. (*Courtesy of International Harvester Company, Chicago, Ill.*)

Operational Routing. The next step involves determining the proper sequence of operations, the equipment to be utilized, and the material requirements of each operation. A route sheet (Figure 5-5) is then prepared displaying this information.

Next, the time estimate for each routed operation is determined by reference to catalogs containing time standards for toolmaking tasks. These catalogs are compiled by utilizing industrial engineering work measurement techniques coupled with toolmaking practices information supplied by toolroom supervision. These operational time estimates are important for a number of reasons. They are the basis for accurate cost determination and control, and they also permit the analysis of machine load by types of equipment.

Scheduling. Scheduling requires the maintaining of up-to-date information on toolroom demands, a good knowledge of material availability, and a current feedback of work-in-process status. These are accomplished by effective yet simple inventory records of direct and burden materials. A

ROUTE SHEET

Tool No. __TD-3931 A__   Date __Sept. 10, 19–—__
Drawing No. __A-54932__
Machine No. __D-4295__   Material __Steel & Plastic__

Operation No.	Description of Operation	Time Est. in Hrs.	Machine Name & Number	Due Dates or Time		INSPEC-TION	REMARKS
				Begin	Finish		
1.	MAKE BASE PLATE	.25	SHAPER F4520				
2.	TURN SPACERS	.10	LATHE L1243				
3.	MAKE DRILL PLATE	.20	MILLING M/C M4239				
4.	DRILL GUIDE HOLES	.20	JIG BORE J1892				
5.	DRILL LOCATION HOLES	.15	JIG BORE J1892				
6.	DRILL CLEARANCE HOLE ON JIG BASE	.15	RADIAL DRILL R3140				
7.	MOUNT THE CLAMPS	.25	BENCH WORK				

FIG. 5-5. Typical Route Sheet of a Drill Jig.

job scheduling board,[5] displaying the status of each assigned job and up-dated at regular short intervals, is an effective means of determining the availability of man-machine resources. The sequencing of jobs by priority status is the end result of the scheduling phase.

Follow-up. The effectiveness of job planning procedures requires adequate follow-up. The job planner and supervisor must investigate deviations in performance as compared to the planned procedure. The planner will thus become better acquainted with actual operating conditions and can become more skillful, thereby improving his effectiveness. The supervisor also becomes better acquainted with the planning procedure and its importance in relieving him of administrative work. This permits his full-time concentration on supervision of the craftsmen.

Staffing and Training. The general supervisor of the toolroom must be dedicated to its efficient operation and to fabricating quality tools at optimum cost. He must be technically competent in his field and demonstrate skills of management. Usually, a graduate apprentice toolmaker has an excellent foundation upon which to build the essential management skills required for efficient operation.

The job planner must also be technically competent. In fact, experience has shown the ideal candidate to be a former toolmaker with the education and ambition to progress to supervision. The job requires a questioning attitude and a good knowledge of the usage of industrial engineering techniques. The ability to communicate with supervision and craftsmen is also essential.

It is most essential that the toolroom be staffed with competent, experienced toolmakers. The toolmaking apprentice training course is an excellent beginning, and when supplemented with experience in all major phases of the toolroom, it usually produces skilled tradesmen. However, in many toolmaking shops, there are many skilled and competent workers who are not apprentice graduates.

For overall efficient functioning of the toolroom aimed at fabricating a quality tool, it is also essential to staff and train the tool inspection and supporting services function properly. The tool inspector is usually a former toolmaker who has received specific training in the utilization of inspection methods and equipment. This background and training will help assure the quality and reliability of tools produced.

ASSESSMENT OF TOTAL EFFECTIVENESS

The manufacturing manager must constantly concern himself with the effectiveness of the toolmaking function. The assessment should include:

1. Planned material and labor expenditures compared to actual expenditures
2. Make-or-buy cost analysis
3. Performance evaluation of supervision, job planners, toolmakers, and and other employees
4. Optimum utilization of toolroom equipment

Budget versus Actual. The toolroom should have a variable budget for material and labor based on a fixed and variable cost relationship. General supervision should have the responsibility for preparing the budget and

---

[5] A scheduling board of this type is shown by Fig. 3-5 in Chapter 3 of Section 6.

for coordinating activities and performance to achieve its objectives. All the necessary staff functions such as budgeting, industrial engineering, and so on should be engaged to assist supervision.

Make or Buy. Another aspect requiring attention is the cost relationship of make-or-buy decisions. These must be evaluated not only under present operating conditions, but also with an eye to future requirements of the toolroom. Expansion or contraction of the toolmaking function must be closely scrutinized to prevent past practice or habit from becoming the rule of operation.

Performance Evaluation and Equipment Utilization. The comparison of actual performance to the standard established during job planning is a must. Reasons for deviations should be clearly recorded to plan the corrective action needed to assure better performance on future assignments. Equipment utilization goals and assessment of how well these goals were achieved go hand in hand with manpower performance. Shop supervision must be held responsible for achieving these operating standards.

Techniques of Assessment. Total effectiveness can be evaluated by managerial use of the exception principle. Reports showing present status of the four aspects of (1) operating costs, (2) make or buy, (3) performance, and (4) equipment utilization will permit the manufacturing manager to keep informed of conditions.

An outside evaluation of effectiveness should be conducted periodically by personnel not connected with the function. This will provide the manager with an "audit" of toolmaking and its contribution to the overall manufacturing effort.

CONCLUSION

The toolmaking function plays an important role in assisting the manufacturing manager to achieve low costs and resultant profitability. In a medium- or large-size facility, the manager must delegate many of the procedural decisions to his organization, as described above.

BIBLIOGRAPHY

Allen, Louis A., *Management and Organization*, McGraw-Hill Book Company, New York, 1958.
Bolton, Harold C., "Toolroom Planning," *Proceedings 27th Annual Industrial Management Society Conference*, 1963.
Dale, Ernest, *Planning and Developing the Company Organization Structure*, American Management Association, New York, 1952.
Doyle, Lawrence E., *Tool Engineering*, Prentice-Hall, Inc., Englewood Cliffs, N.J., 1950.
Dwiazdowski, A. P., *Tool Engineering*, C. C. Nelson Publishing Company, Appleton, Wis., 1951.
Eary, Donald F., and Gerald E. Johnson, *Process Engineering for Manufacturing*, Prentice-Hall, Inc., Englewood Cliffs, N.J., 1962.
Moore, Franklin G., *Production Control*, McGraw-Hill Book Company, New York, 1959.
Rusinoff, S. E., *Tool Engineering*, American Technical Society, Chicago, 1959.
"A Toolroom Goes Job Shop," *Steel*, Aug. 20, 1956.

CHAPTER SIX

Tool Crib Management*

RICHARD W. TRUSLER *Manager, Manufacturing Engineering, International Business Machines Corporation, Rochester, Minnesota*

The primary function of a tool crib is to provide the manufacturing areas with the necessary tools at the time that they are needed and in the condition to do the required job.

The function encompasses many internal systems and procedures to get the right tool or supply to the right place at the right time. Simply stated, the basic cycle of the operation consists of:

1. Procurement and stocking of tools
2. Dispensing of tools and supplies
3. Maintenance of tool and gage quality

This basic cycle is not changed by the size of the tool crib operation, but the methods used to accomplish it will vary considerably.

TOOL CRIB ARRANGEMENTS

The tool crib should be located as centrally as possible with respect to its main user areas. It is usually more economical to have one large crib than several smaller ones scattered throughout the plant. Advantages of a single crib are minimum space requirements; maximum use of manpower, facilities, and equipment; and elimination of duplication.

If a single crib is not feasible because of other factors such as plant layout, both satellite cribs and the main crib should be under unified control. This will ensure the use of uniform systems and procedures. The smaller cribs will draw supplies from the main crib which will then be responsible for inventory control.

* Grateful acknowledgement is made to Roger A. Gaio, Manager of Tool Stores, International Business Machines Corporation, Rochester, Minnesota, who provided the principal input data used.

10–65

The crib should be equipped with adjustable shelving units arranged along parallel aisles from the front to the back. Counter units for storage of commonly used items should be under the service window.

Enclosing the crib can be accomplished with the shelving units plus expanded metal screening. A drop area of sufficient size and accessibility should be provided adjacent to the main crib entrance and recessed off the main aisle.

In larger operations, an additional off-site storage area, such as a warehouse, is practical and economical for the storage of large tools, low-usage tools, and miscellaneous bulk items. Storage racks in a warehouse should be of heavier construction and capable of holding skids, tubs, and pallets. Aisle space should be wide enough to accommodate fork trucks. Some precautionary measures to safeguard against rust are usually more necessary than in the main crib.

Staff. Staffing the crib is usually accomplished with clerical-type help. Two skills are generally required: one to perform the window service (Figure 6-1) and tool handling tasks and the other to perform the true clerical functions of typing, records keeping, and filing. The latter should also have the capability of understanding computer printouts and analyzing inventory reports. The overall quality and ability of the staff should be broad enough to deal with a wide range of responsibilities.

Storage. Crib storage requirements fall into two basic categories: storage of jigs and fixtures and storage of supply items.

Jigs and fixtures are usually stored on open shelves as shown in Figure 6-2. Their shelf positions are recorded by tool numbers in a location file. When a tool is needed, the counterman can readily find its location from the file and sign it out to the user. Larger tools may be stored in a warehouse, as mentioned previously.

In special cases, tools may be stored in the user department. These tools are usually single-purpose, high-usage tools such as dies for punch presses, plastic molds, and chases. The size of these tools and their frequency of use make it impractical to transport them back and forth.

Fig. 6-1.   Counterman Delivering Tool to Machine Operator.

Fig. 6-2. Counterman Selects Tool from Its Storage Location.

Crib management should oversee provision of adequate storage facilities in the user departments which then become responsible for the handling and storage of the tools assigned to them. However, the tool crib should still maintain location records of such assigned tools.

Supply items consist mostly of manufacturer's standard catalog items. Upon purchase they are identified with a supply code number before being placed in inventory. Storage may be shelves or drawers.

High-density-type cabinets with variable drawer heights as shown in Figure 6-1 are ideal for small, high-volume items such as drills, taps, reamers, and end mills. Larger items such as grinding wheels, masking tape, and work gloves are more appropriately stored on shelves. Large-bulk items, 55-gallon drums of oil or solvent for example, are best kept on skids in a bulk-type area.

Having the right item at the right time requires the tool crib management to keep track of and order three types of items.

1. Reordering of duplicate and replacement tools. These are special tools of an expendable nature which periodically have to be replaced. All special cutting tools, hydropress tooling, and inexpensive miscellaneous tooling are included. The tool crib processes the orders through a central coordinator, usually in engineering. The crib should not reorder duplicate tools of a permanent nature. It will generally be the engineer's job to determine whether additional tools are needed.

2. Miscellaneous ordering. Quite often, manufacturing managers need items which are not normally stocked. Most manufacturing people are not too familiar with either accounting or purchasing procedures. Therefore, to eliminate confusion, all requests for these items should be made to the tool crib, and it processes the necessary paperwork through the system and assures uniformity in processing. The items are delivered to the tool crib and distributed from there. The paperwork and all records are maintained in the crib, and any inquiries pertaining to the orders are directed to the crib.

3. Inventory ordering. These are the commercially available standard catalog items that are automatically replaced when the inventory reaches a specified minimum level. The supplies are expendable and can represent a sizable percentage of the total yearly expenditure.

There are three quite well-defined areas of supply or expendable inventory items. One area is operating supplies—expendable items necessary to sustain production. These are drills, taps, end mills, grinding wheels, masking tape, cleaning solvents, adhesives, hammers, screwdrivers, pliers, and the like.

The second area is maintenance items—those which are necessary for maintenance of the building and equipment. These include plumbing fittings, electrical supplies, filters, repair parts for fork trucks and equipment, and many more.

The third area is comprised of toolroom supplies which are all the jig and fixture components such as drill bushings, jig feet, clamps, knobs, dowel pins, and screws.

Inventory Control. One of the major responsibilities of the tool crib is the control of inventory. This function represents the largest single outlay of money by the crib. The size of the operation determines whether a computer should be made available or a hand posting system must be used.

Under any system, three questions must be answered for adequate control: When can it be said that the inventory is under control? How can one know whether the inventory is under control? And finally, what can be done to correct the situation?

The first thing to do is to set an objective which will control the size of the inventory. This is set as a turnover ratio rather than a fixed dollar amount. A 4:1 ratio, for example, is considered obtainable with good control in the data processing equipment industry. This means that an inventory dollar value is expended and replaced four times a year.

Based on a 52-week work year, weekly outgo should average 7 to 8 percent of the inventory total. Use of these figures allows frequent checkpoints. If crib outgo is less than 7 percent, it is either overstocked or carrying too many unused items. When outgo rises above 8 percent, the inventory may be in danger in the near future of becoming insufficient to sustain production.

A hand posting system such as that proposed in the *Tool Engineers Handbook*[1] can provide periodic checks on turnover ratio. However, to get the necessary information on a weekly basis from any hand posting system is well nigh impossible and certainly impractical. Thus, whenever possible, a computer should be used to generate the reports for analysis. Figure 6-3 shows a computer-produced report.

The program must give item identity by a code number system. One such system uses nine digits with each group of two representing class, type, or description. The last three digits are an arbitrary size designation sequentially.

For example, the number 76 30 16 381 has the following significance:

76 signifies a machine-type tool.
30 means it is a drill.
16 designates a specific type drill (jobber's length).
381 is the size designation for ¼ inch.

---

[1] American Society of Tool and Manufacturing Engineers, *Tool Engineers Handbook,* 2d ed., McGraw-Hill Book Company, New York, 1959, p. 127.

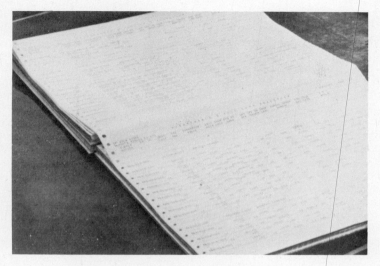

Fig. 6-3. Computer-printed Inventory Listing.

The program then gives the status of three phases of the inventory:
1. Present status (stock on hand)
2. On-order status
3. History, past usage, or year-to-date withdrawal

Minimum and maximum quantities are established for each item, and automatic flagging will be generated when the stock balance reaches the minimum level established. These levels are established based upon the past usage which is reflected in the year-to-date column.

Dollar totals are generated by item and category of items (subtotal) in both stock balance and year-to-date withdrawal.

The grand total gives the dollar value of the inventory, the total dollars of the year-to-date withdrawal, and the dollars committed to on-order status. Analysis of these grand totals will give the inventory picture in one glance.

The difference between one week's year-to-date withdrawal and the next is the second week's usage. Comparison of the total inventory figure and the total year-to-date usage provides the turnover ratio for the calendar time expired. If the totals are not on target, it is time to go through the inventory item by item and category by category and make the necessary adjustments.

ORDERING

To complete the cycle of inventory control, the ordering procedure must be included. The principal objective of an ordering system is to replenish stock in the shortest lead time possible. A short lead time means a lower inventory balance.

To accomplish this short lead time, the tool crib should be authorized to order directly the routine, repetitive inventory items. With tool crib assistance, the purchasing agent negotiates yearly contracts with selected suppliers for certain items.

The crib supplies purchasing with estimated yearly usage of each item. The buyer issues a blanket purchase order for the year. Then the crib can issue releases for part orders at intervals during the year as inventory requires.

This gives purchasing the advantage of minimum cost based on the full yearly quantity, and benefits the supplier in yearly planning and, possibly, reduced salesman activity. Predetermined release quantities are established as well as price. The items are shipped and invoiced only upon a release from the tool crib.

The blanket order-release method considerably shortens lead time, but it can be shortened much more by automating the tool crib portion. This can probably be done best by use of a system such as an IBM 1001 teleprocessing unit in conjunction with a Data-Phone.[2]

Information pertaining to each item is prepunched into a master card. This includes tool crib code number, manufacturing code number, purchase order number, price, and a brief description.

As inventories fall below the specified minimum, master cards are selected for the needed items. A supplier is contacted on the Data-Phone and identification made. All cards for that supler are then processed through the transmitting unit as shown by Figure 6-4.

The unit reads the prepunched information and transmits it via telephone lines to the supplier's location. There cards are reproduced which act as the release orders. The supplier ships the items and invoices the crib. He then proceeds to replenish his stock in anticipation of the next release order.

In summary, the tool crib feeds its transactions to the computer which generates an inventory report. This report reflects the status of the inventory and indicates what to order. The order is then automatically placed with the vendor previously chosen by purchasing.

There are three problems encountered when installing this procedure. The

[2] Telephone company equipment.

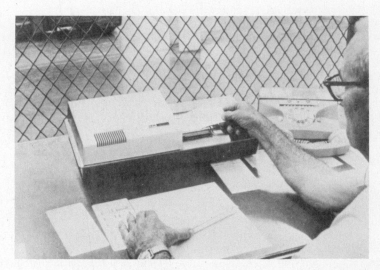

FIG. 6-4.   Order Clerk Inserting Prepunched Order Card into Teleprocessing Unit to Transmit Order Automatically by Data-Phone.

first is difficulty of tying in the accounting aspect. This can readily be overcome once it has been accepted that the tool crib is the logical place for this activity and it is proved that, with the proper staff, the crib can handle the job.

The second problem is convincing the purchasing department that the tool crib is not infringing on purchasing's responsibilities. Actually the buying is performed by purchasing, and the crib merely places the order. The purchasing function has as much to gain as any other function by this system through the reduction of both paperwork and manpower required for performing routine repetitive tasks.

A third problem relates to the availability of the necessary equipment in the suppliers' offices. However, the system still operates well when only part of the crib's suppliers are equipped with Data-Phones. The others are contacted by ordinary phone, and orders are placed verbally.

In addition to inventory control, the computer makes it possible to have catalogs published. Partial computer printouts, such as code number, description, and cost, are printed directly on a multilith master and then printed in sufficient quantity for distribution to manufacturing and process engineering departments for reference. The catalog, shown by Figure 6-5, can be updated and reprinted as often as deemed necessary, depending upon changes.

Yearly physical inventory by counting may be eliminated by spot-checking items at random. An actual count of these items is compared with the latest computer report. If found sufficiently accurate, the computer-run inventory is then accepted as the actual inventory. This eliminates the tedious, time-consuming, and costly operation of inventory counting.

TOOL INSPECTION AND REPAIR

All gages should be on a recall system whereby they are called back to tool inspection after a predetermined time for a complete inspection for accuracy. This includes special gaging as well as standard gages.

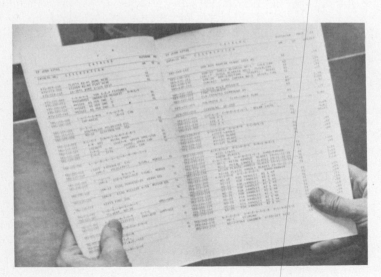

Fig. 6-5.   Computer-prepared Tool Catalog.

It can be presupposed that the gages are used to inspect the parts which are produced with production tooling such as jigs, fixtures, or dies. If the parts are acceptable, the tooling must be good—providing the checking equipment is known to be accurate. A system such as this eliminates the need to inspect the majority of tooling.

If, however, a tool does go bad during use, it should be rejected to tool inspection for repair with a rejection ticket stating the fault. A copy of this rejection ticket is given to the crib so that it will have a record that the tool is being sent to the toolroom for repair. Upon completion of the repair, the tool will be inspected by tool inspection and then sent to the crib. The crib will then reassign the tool to the department if the stub indicates that it is wanted back. If not, it is logged in and replaced in its proper location.

Cutting tools, both special and standard, are handled in a different manner owing to the fact that normal use will cause the need for repair which usually will consist only of resharpening. A cutter grinding department should be located adjacent to the tool crib or even included in the crib. This will minimize the flow of tools between these two areas. All cutting tools are returned directly to the cutter grinding department for resharpening before they are returned to the crib.

PREPACKAGED TOOLING

As previously stated, the primary function of a tool crib is to offer distribution service. Usually it can be assumed that this will be accomplished through what is generally referred to as "window service." This consists of an operator coming to the crib and asking for a tool. The transaction takes place through a window or over a counter.

This system is sufficient for small shops, but for large operations it is obsolete and inefficient. Window service does not allow efficient planning of tool crib work. One man must be available to service the window at all times. Because the crib has no control over the number of people coming to the window, they are often standing in line three and four deep at one time, and a few minutes later there is no one in sight. Also, the time spent by production personnel in walking to and from the crib adds up to a considerable amount of nonproductive time.

The ideal situation is to prepare tools a few days in advance of the time they will be used. This is prepackaging through preplanning. It is accomplished through using both the production scheduling of the production control department and the routings of the manufacturing departments. This, of course, may be done most easily with computer assistance.

The production control department programs its dynamic load report to pick out on a daily basis all the part numbers and operation numbers which are to be run on the third working day in the future. These are then matched against the routing tape, and tooling information is extracted from the routing. A listing is daily sent to the crib. The crib then assembles the tools for each operation as shown by Figure 6-6. It sends the package to the appropriate department a day or two before the tools are needed.

SCRAPPING AND SURPLUS

One of the problems usually encountered in a tool crib operation is that the tools added to the crib for storage exceed the number of tools scrapped

FIG. 6-6. Tools Ready for Production Use Two Days Hence through Prepackaging.

during the same period. It then becomes only a matter of time before the crib runs out of space.

To safeguard against this condition, a procedure for obsoleting and scrapping tools which are no longer useful to the manufacture of the products must be set up. It will usually be under control of manufacturing engineering. On a periodic basis, the tool crib should be notified by manufacturing engineering of the tools to be scrapped. These are then gathered by the crib, identifying numbers are destroyed, and any salvageable components are stripped from each tool. These tools are then scrapped, their records deleted from tool crib files, and the space made available for storage of other tools.

In the case of operating supplies, the tool crib should periodically review the "year-to-date withdrawal" column on the computer report. All items which show no usage for at least a year should be reviewed for possible removal from inventory. If periodic purges are not performed, the crib will become cluttered with useless items and tools.

BIBLIOGRAPHY

Bolz, Harold, and G. Hagemann (eds.), *Materials Handling Handbook*, The Ronald Press Company, New York, 1958, p. 182.

Gaio, R. A., *The Role of the Computer in Expendable Tool Supplies*, ASTME technical paper MS 68-124, 1968.

Marshik, J. A., in *Reliability Handbook*, W. Grant Ireson (ed.), McGraw-Hill Book Company, New York, 1966, p. 13.29.

Martin, J. C., in *Maintenance Engineering Handbook*, 2d ed., L. C. Morrow (ed.), McGraw-Hill Book Company, New York, 1966, p. 11.3.

Moore, Franklin G., *Production Control*, 2d ed., McGraw-Hill Book Company, New York, 1959, pp. 21 and 461.

Raisglid, W., *Better Tool Cribs*, The Industrial Press, New York, 1954.

Reinfield, N. V., *Production Control*, Prentice-Hall, Inc., Englewood Cliffs, N.J., 1959.

Scheele, E., W. Westerman, and R. Nimmert, *Principles and Design of Production Control Systems*, Prentice-Hall, Inc., Englewood Cliffs, N.J., 1960.

CHAPTER SEVEN

Storekeeping

W. F. MASLER, JR. *President, Aero-Corry (Division of Aero-Flow Dynamics, Inc.), Corry, Pennsylvania*

Storekeeping is a cost generating service function which is designed to supply needed materials expeditiously by eliminating procurement lead time from the demand/supply time cycle (see Figure 7-1). The operations performed by a storekeeping department include (1) replenishment and record keeping, (2) receipt verification, (3) storage and protection, (4) selection, and (5) issuance of the needed commodities. The purpose of a storekeeping department is to supply the needed materials to the using function in a timely manner, to the proper location, and at the lowest possible cost.

In manufacturing organizations, raw materials, work in process, finished products, tooling, and maintenance and office supplies are among the many commodities considered in storekeeping operations. Because the stores function adds nothing to the product value except cost, it is important that the operation be carried out in the most efficient fashion to improve the profitability of the business.

In the evaluation or establishment of a storekeeping function, the following elements must be considered:

1. Administration and control
2. Physical requirements
3. Layout
4. Alternatives

ADMINISTRATION AND CONTROL

Good storekeeping management provides the needed commodities to the using function in a timely fashion at the lowest possible cost. It matters little what the products or items to be stored are, whether they be raw materials,

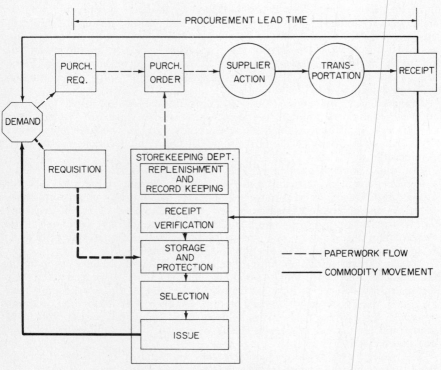

Fig. 7-1. Demand/Supply Cycle.

work in process, maintenance, tooling, office, or other indirect supplies. Once a legitimate need has been established for the item, the lack of availability of it causes production delays and increased factory operating costs. Conversely, excessive supplies of any of the needed materials tie up funds, reduce the company's return on investment, and may be equally costly. Thus, stock must be maintained at the lowest possible level consistent with maintaining production. The storeroom manager's task is that of compromise: He must balance the two extremes, providing sufficient materials to satisfy needs without the luxury of overabundant stocking. He must control his inventory between predetermined maximum and minimum levels, auditing these levels for changes in demand. As demands change, the maximum level may be wasteful of company resources, and the minimum level could cause production delays.

The number of stores personnel must be adequate to minimize production downtime. Storekeeping work loads vary as receipt, storage, and issue cycles vary. Effective utilization of stores manpower is accomplished by balancing the work loads for each operation. Inventory costs and storeroom labor utilization related to production delays caused by shortages are measures of a storekeeper's effectiveness.

The accountability for stores inventory demands that records be maintained and that procedures be consistent with the organization's work system. System analysis is advisable to ensure compatibility and eliminate duplication.

A means for authorization and identification of the materials to be stored must be established.   This is accomplished in the case of manufacturing by having the production control department responsible for establishing the stocking levels of raw, work-in-process, and finished goods.   Maintenance supplies and tooling are usually the responsibility of the manufacturing department, and office supplies the responsibility of the office manager. Figure 7-2 is an organization chart showing typical relationships of storerooms, cribs, and warehouses.

Replenishment and Record Keeping.   Quantitative control of stores inventory is maintained through permanent record cards, usually called stores cards.   For small businesses, these stores cards perform the function not only of recording inventory levels but also of showing the location of the stored commodities.

For some small stores departments, bin tags at the stock location contain the entire inventory status of the commodity.   Posting takes place as new stock is introduced or withdrawals are made.   In large organizations where hand or semiautomated posting is performed, two sets of cards are used. The stores inventory cards are maintained by the clerical function of the storekeeping department.   The issuing function maintains a location card which includes the commodity identification and the location.

The stockroom operation must maintain an adequate balance of materials on hand to meet all normal operating requirements.   A procedure for determining reorder points must be coordinated between the storekeeping manager and the procurement department to establish lead times and maintain adequate stock levels.   An inventory record, by commodity, identifying minimum, maximum, and reorder levels is necessary.   This subject is discussed in detail in Section 7, Chapter 7.

The stores cards which reflect inventory levels must be designed to contain at least the following information if accountability is to be established and maintained.

1. Description of material
2. Material location
3. Maximum stocking level
4. Minimum stocking level
5. Reorder point
6. Accounting columns which reflect the inventory status of the commodity and which may include information such as date, issue quantities, assignment quantities, order quantities, and balance

Depending upon the record keeping system, the size of the company, and its general procedures, it is the storekeeper's responsibility to post receipts, issues, and orders and to maintain a perpetual balance of the materials in storage.

The types of record cards available can range from those designed specifically for the company to standardized forms available from stationery supply houses.   Automatic data processing equipment provides stock status reports which take the place of stores cards.   The purpose of the card or report is to provide the storekeeper and factory management with knowledge of the stocking level of commodities and to provide a check against the inventory of that commodity.

The storekeeping department must provide purchase requisitions to the purchasing organization, identifying the desired receipt date and quantity of the item to be procured.   In some companies, requisitions are compiled and forwarded to the purchasing department on a routine basis once or

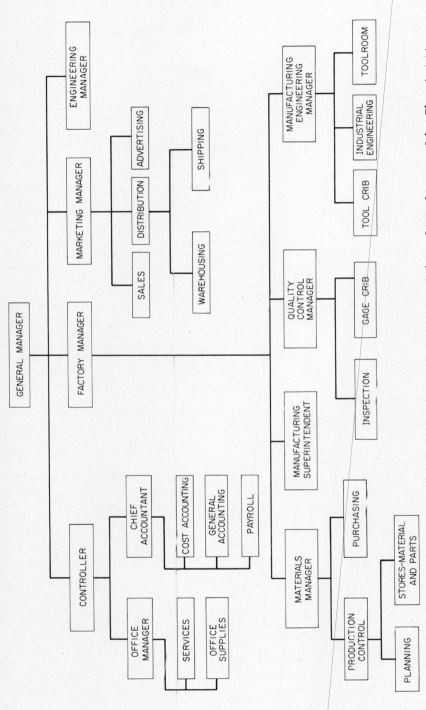

Fig. 7-2. Organization Chart Showing Typical Relationship of Storerooms, Cribs, and Warehouses to Other Plant Activities.

10–77

twice daily. Companies with automatic data processing require only that the user's requisition card, in the form of a punched EDP card, be forwarded to the data center on a scheduled basis for collating and processing. Stock levels are maintained in the computer memory bank. Adjusted by withdrawals and receipts, the computer provides inventory levels and writes purchase orders at the appropriate reorder point.

Requisitions from the user form the basis on which transference of stockroom assets takes place. In small- and medium-sized companies, the posting of these requisitions may take place at the end of the day or during slack periods; in large companies, posting may be a continuous procedure. Where data processing techniques are employed, the requisition cards are delivered to the processing center several times daily and are automatically posted.

Labor is one of the most expensive costs in a business operation. Productive labor is generally more costly than that used for support functions. Thus, the minimum number of people in the stockroom should be the number necessary to maintain productive labor at its peak efficiency.

Accountability for the stores department begins when the needed materials are delivered to the receiving area in the stores department and the stores clerk signs for those materials. Verification of quantity and quality against the appropriate purchase order must be accomplished by stores personnel. Recording the quantity of this material on the appropriate stock card establishes accountability for the increased inventory in the possession of the storekeeping department. Accountability transfer for returned materials (those previously issued but found to be in excess of requirements) is usually accomplished by the use of a "Returned Material" form. For those businesses utilizing hand posting, the format should describe material, quantity, date, and department returning the material. Organizations using data processing cards should have a keypunch machine to accomplish the change in inventory for both returned and new materials.

The storeroom is relieved of accountability for obsolete materials or scrap by the use of a requisition. Usually the next higher level of authority authorizes disposition. These items may be sold by the purchasing department at the highest obtainable selling price, the stores inventories are relieved at cost, and the difference in dollar amount is allocated to a variance account.

As the materials are received and verification is made, they are removed from the temporary storage area inside the stores department and placed in the appropriate permanent storage location. For the materials to be accessible for selection in the future, their location must be identified on a commodity index card or the stores card. Commodity index cards usually are provided for the purpose of locating the commodity within the stockroom area. Stores cards contain additional information including balance on hand.

Storage and Protection. From the administration and control viewpoint, identification, location, and accessibility of the commodities are the responsibilities of the storeroom manager. He must be watchful that materials are stored in the proper, referenced location, or production delays will result when inventories indicate adequate stock levels but materials cannot be located.

Identification of items may be by numeric or mnemonic symbols. Numeric identification is typified by the Dewey Decimal System used in libraries to classify books by subject matter, whereby numbers are assigned in a systematic fashion. For example, 650 identifies a volume under the general classification of factory management and production. The unit identification 658 establishes the general heading of business management, and the decimal figure 658.7 refers to purchasing, warehousing, and shipping. Automatic data processing systems are usually numeric.

Mnemonic identification includes combinations of letters and numbers. For example, SHCS ¼-20-15 identifies a socket head cap screw ¼ inch in diameter, 20 threads per inch, ¹⁵⁄₁₆ths long. This method provides an easily memorized system and is more generally used for hand posting systems.

Commodities may be located by either the symbol or the index method. When symbol identification is used, specific areas (bins, drawers, shelves) are assigned to a particular grouping of commodities. Library book locations are typical of the symbol method. The symbol system can be wasteful of space, because room must always be left available for new items. Unless space is available, entire groups of commodities may have to be shifted to make room for a new item.

Location by index provides flexibility, permitting items to be stored in any location which has space available. The stores or commodity index cards show the location; for example, location A-1-56 might mean bin row A, first bin, fifth shelf, sixth drawer. The index system is the most common.

It is the storekeeping manager's responsibility not only to protect stored materials against damage, pilferage, waste, and deterioration, but also to protect the business from losses which could occur as the result of improper storage. Paints, lacquers, and other volatile materials are usually stored separately from other commodities to minimize fire loss.

Environmental conditions which affect the character of the materials to be stored must be considered. Heat, cold, humidity, and dust are all factors which influence the level of protection necessary. Some adhesives and rubber goods have "shelf life." Deterioration may occur at an accelerated rate unless storage in a controlled environment is provided.

Because the storekeeper is both responsible and accountable for the materials entrusted to his care, many organizations use a check and balance procedure to maintain adequate control. The cost department may be responsible for costing and determining the dollar value of the inventory level. An audit, through inventories taken yearly, compares the physical count and inventory costs against the stock record count and inventory costs. In part, a variance between the two values establishes the efficiency of the stores department.

Selection. Selection (picking) of stored material should be performed only by storekeeping personnel. Unless this is done, responsibility and accountability for stores inventories cannot be assigned to the storekeeping manager. Some organizations prohibit access to stores to all but storekeeping personnel. Thus, the factory manager might be prohibited from entering the storeroom unless accompanied by authorized personnel.

In small companies, one individual may be responsible for all operations in a storeroom. In a large storeroom, however, commodities may be selected by more than one individual and moved to the issue point where the items are rechecked by the issuer.

Issue. Issue of materials to the using function must be accompanied by a receipt for transfer of those assets. Material requisitions and keypunch cards are among the documents used. For jigs, fixtures, and nonconsumable tooling, tool checks are surrendered by the operators. The receipt of these documents or checks relieves the storekeeper of accountability for the materials transferred and acts as a form of "payment" to the stockroom.

PHYSICAL REQUIREMENTS.

The size of a stores department is determined by a number of factors:

1. Maximum quantities and physical configuration of commodities to be stored
2. Use of air space (the volume above the floor area to be utilized) for storage
3. Unusual environmental conditions necessary to protect commodities or the business property
4. The method of storage to be utilized:
   a. Drawers
   b. Racks
   c. Bins
   d. Open and closed shelving
   e. Cabinets
   f. Pallets
   g. Stacking containers
   h. Bulk materials
   i. Gas container storage
   j. Other
5. The material handling equipment to be used:
   a. Forklift trucks
   b. Conveyors (roller and powered, chain or overhead)
   c. Tray trucks
   d. Barrel or hand trucks
6. Areas to be allocated for receipt verification and temporary storage
7. Areas to be assigned for record keeping or administrative functions
8. Aisle space needed for selection of stored items

Centralization or decentralization of storerooms is a policy matter which is dependent upon the size of the factory, character of materials to be stored, needs to be serviced, and cost of providing that service.

Centralized stores operate with the least storekeeping cost. Duplication of items is eliminated and inventories are reduced, less floor space is needed, and stockroom manpower is better utilized.

Decentralized storerooms provide more rapid service to the using function and may reduce transportation costs. Stockroom facilities and personnel are duplicated, however, and inventory may be increased. From the storekeeping viewpoint, decentralization of the stores function should be avoided wherever possible.

Replenishment and Record Keeping. Provision should be made in the storekeeping department for the necessary desks, cabinets, and office equipment required to support the record keeping function.

Receipt Verification. Provision must be made for an area within the storekeeping department proper to provide temporary storage of materials awaiting verification prior to permanent storage. The nature, size, and physical requirements of the commodities, frequency of receipt, and manpower availability determine the amount of stockroom area allocated for this function. Area calculations are also dependent upon the types of racks and shelving utilized.

Storage and Protection. The characteristics of the commodity to be stored —size, shape, weight, value, quantity, and perishability—determine the manner in which the items will be stored. The maximum quantity to be stored of each item determines the cubage required. For planning purposes, consideration should be given to the use of pallets, pallet racks, gravity feed storage, cabinets, shelving, and floor storage. When all the information concerning the stored commodities is available and the storage method chosen, the cubage required solely for storage can be established. Storeroom planning should include provisions for the inevitable changes which occur. Improvement in handling techniques and changes in types of commodities to be stored must be considered to provide flexibility for expansion and contraction of the stores department.

Bagged materials should be skid stored, with plywood separators between layers to spread the unit loading. Boxed materials, if possible, should be procured in quantities most frequently used so that entire containers can be issued. If boxes are skid or floor loaded, provision for spreading the unit loading, similar to that utilized for bagged materials, should be considered.

Through a controlled environment, protection from deterioration must be provided when necessary. Some adhesives require low-temperature storage; refrigerators may be necessary. Certain rubber goods which have a shelf life must be stored away from heat and light to retard deterioration.

Inflammable goods (paints, lacquers, inflammable gases) must be stored in a fashion to protect the company property. Usually the insurance underwriter stipulates, or at least influences, the location of these commodities.

Some commodities must be "cured" or aged before usage; iron castings and green lumber are typical. Usage in the precured state may affect the structural integrity of the final product; thus, storage space for aging must be provided.

Fencing or cribbing is used to enclose the stockroom area to prevent unauthorized selection of materials. It is often possible to use the back of closed shelving or bins as a barrier. This reduces the cost of setting up the stockroom by reducing the need for fencing, and provides flexibility in the event of expansion or contraction of the stockroom.

Bar stock is usually stored on racks designed to support the weight of materials in several places over its length, thus eliminating warping or bending. "A" frame or Christmas tree racks simplify identification, utilize less floor space, and make bar materials more accessible.

Barrels should be stored on end, not stacked on their sides, because the structural integrity of the container is sometimes inadequate to support the weight of the barrels above.

Selection. The material handling equipment, the storage facilities, and the commodities to be selected determine the number and kinds of individuals required for the selection or order picking function. Hand lifting weight limitations for individuals vary from state to state. In most states, female employees are restricted to lifting lesser weights than their male counterparts. The commodity to be selected determines whether female employees can be utilized. Provision for the needed aisle space between storage areas is contingent upon the method of handling material. Identification of the location of the commodities is a prerequisite for efficient stores department operation.

Two general methods of selection may be employed. The first is that which takes place in response to a demand imposed by the using function. A production worker with a requisition or a tool check wishes a commodity immediately. He must wait at the storeroom window while the needed item is selected and issued. Nonproductive or lost time is generated. When more than one individual is waiting for service, significant losses in operating efficiency can occur. The number of stockroom personnel available for selection must be balanced against the lost time incurred.

A second and more efficient procedure is to anticipate commodity demands and have them selected by stockroom personnel prior to production needs. A storage space is required for these preselected items and must be considered when the size of a stockroom is established.

Issue. It is important that the issue window be on a main aisle to facilitate receipt of material by the using function and also to provide a visual indication of the number of people waiting for stockroom service.

If delivery service is provided, either by the stockroom or an internal transportation department, temporary storage for preselected materials to be issued must be provided.

The material handling system and types of commodities determine the floor space required.

LAYOUT

Storerooms should be located adjacent to the using function but out of the normal flow of the production work. The stockroom should occupy the smallest area possible.

The internal arrangement of the storeroom must include provisions for (1) record keeping, (2) receiving, (3) aisles, (4) storage racks, bins, shelving, and the like, and (5) issue point.

When the volumetric calculations for storage of commodities are completed, handling techniques established, and special conditions for protection analyzed, the floor area required can be determined. A floor layout to scale, which identifies obstructions, columns, stairwells, elevator shafts, and permanent partitions, is created. Usually storerooms are designed so that the main internal aisle is parallel to the factory traffic aisle. Storage aisles are at right angles and are usually shorter than the main internal aisle to accelerate the selection process. Pallets or forklift bins are sometimes stored at an angle to the cross aisles to facilitate forklift truck movement. This method requires greater space, but more rapid selection can be achieved. Internal handling techniques establish storeroom aisle size. Where mechanical aids, such as forklift trucks, are used, a six- to ten-foot aisle may be required; for hand selection, a smaller aisle space of three to four feet may be all that is necessary.

When a decision on handling equipment is made, aisle width can be determined and a flow layout developed. Templates to scale for cabinets, racks, shelving, and so on should be employed to evaluate work flow before the establishment of the storeroom. Compromise inevitably is required.

Replenishment and Record Keeping. The size of the stockroom, type of records, and number of employees involved in accountability establish the space required for desks, chairs, record cabinets, and the like.

Receipt Verification. An area for receiving incoming materials should generally be close to the main factory traffic aisle. This area should be used as temporary storage for verification of quality and quantity and should be located in such a fashion that it does not interfere with the selection or the issuing functions.

Storage and Protection. Shelving, pallet racks, bins, and cabinets should be placed in rows, back to back, to minimize internal movement in the stockroom for both storage and selection, as well as to economize on space. The most active materials should be stored close to the point of issue; those items for which there is little demand should be stored on the uppermost portions of the racks and shelving and at the greatest distance from the issue point. If handling equipment, such as forklift trucks, is used, active items should be pallet rack stored in the bottom of the rack to save the time of elevating or lowering the forks of the lift truck. The most active hand-carried items should be stored at waist -or shoulder-height levels.

The degree to which the stores area is protected is a matter of economy and managerial discretion. Most stores areas utilize fencing or the backs of closed bins or shelving to enclose the stockroom.

The weight of the materials to be stored should be checked to be sure that floor loadings are not in excess of building standards.

Issue. Provision should be made at the issue point for necessary record keeping. Stores or index cards should be adjacent to the issue point so that stockroom personnel can rapidly ascertain locations, issue necessary materials, and record changes in stock levels.

ALTERNATIVES

The cost of operating a storeroom is dependent upon inventory and storeroom labor. Production delays from inadequate service by the storekeeping department may have a great impact on the company's profitability. Increasing storekeeping manpower to reduce production delays is many times improper and inefficient and has the effect of increasing permanently the stores operating costs to resolve a temporary problem.

Analyses of the delays and difficulties and consideration of alternatives are the responsibility of the stores manager.

Replenishment and Record Keeping. Automatic delivery by suppliers is common for many commodities such as wiping towels, fuel oils, and industrial gases (oxygen, hydrogen, nitrogen). The stores manager should consider the utilization of this technique for supplies other than those mentioned. Some companies negotiate blanket procurements for mill and office supplies to be furnished on an automatic delivery basis. The supplier guarantees to maintain a certain level of supply, and after notification, to deliver the items within a prescribed period. This technique can reduce the storeroom maximum stocking level. In some instances, the stores department requisitions materials directly from the supplier, sending a copy of the requisition to the purchasing department to support the blanket purchase order.

The company policy on long-term commitments, the integrity of the supplier chosen, and the volatility of the commodity market price are some of the factors which must be evaluated before institution of the procedure.

This procedure can often produce savings not only in purchasing activities but also in the need for storage equipment, floor space, personnel, and inventory.

Storage and Protection. The *ABC* system[1] for inventory control is also successfully employed. Almost all stores inventories consist of a vital few (*A*) high-cost items and the trivial many (*C*) low-cost items, with a small percentage in the (*B*) marginal range. It is possible to eliminate strict control in accountability for low-cost items. Hardware (nuts, bolts, screws, lock washers, cotter pins) can be procured in bulk at relatively low cost. No attempt is made to control the issue of these items, and record keeping is

[1] Joseph M. Juran, *Managerial Breakthrough*, McGraw-Hill Book Company, New York, 1964, chap. 10, p. 168.

simplified; only replenishment and receipt dates and quantities are recorded. As the commodities are received and verified, a quantity equivalent to the reorder point is boxed and tagged with a reorder card. When this container is opened for issue, the reorder card is processed, and the replenishment cycle begins anew.

This procedure reduces the measure of control of materials but without great effect on cost of inventory. Comparison to historic usage will determine whether the procedure is in or out of control.

Issue. A technique successfully used by some manufacturing organizations requires the machine scheduling department to notify the tool crib and storeroom that tooling and material for a particular part number and operation will be required at some designated future date. During slack periods, stockroom personnel select the tools and materials necessary. Similar procedures can be used for maintenance and office supplies. The using function anticipates its needs, thus permitting selection and stockpiling during storekeeping slack periods.

CONCLUSION

It is the storekeeper's responsibility to provide timely service at the lowest cost and to look for methods improvements which will reduce the cost of that service still further.

The purpose of this chapter has been to describe the function of a storekeeping department and briefly explore the actions and procedures necessary for an efficient operation which will increase the profitability of the business.

BIBLIOGRAPHY

Aljian, G. W. (ed.), *Purchasing Handbook*, 2d ed., McGraw-Hill Book Company, New York, 1966.

Bethel, L. L., F. S. Atwater, G. H. E. Smith, and H. A. Stackman, Jr., *Industrial Organization and Management*, 4th ed., McGraw-Hill Book Company, New York, 1966.

Broom, H. N., *Production Management*, Richard D. Irwin, Inc., Homewood, Ill., 1962.

Inventory Control and Material Accounting, rev. ed., general information manual, Data Processing Division, International Business Machines Corporation, Rochester, New York, 1961.

Juran, Joseph M., *Managerial Breakthrough*, McGraw-Hill Book Company, New York, 1964.

Materials Planning and Control, application reference manual 1d, Data Processing Division, Honeywell Electronics Corporation, Framingham, Mass., 1965.

Maynard, H. B. (ed.), *Handbook of Business Administration*, McGraw-Hill Book Company, New York, 1967.

Owens, R. N., *Management of Industrial Enterprises*, Richard D. Irwin, Inc., Homewood, Ill., 1965.

CHAPTER EIGHT

Receiving

WILLIAM J. VALLETTE   *Vice President, Vaule & Company, Inc., Welles-ley, Massachusetts*

The receiving department, its organization, its location, and its paperwork routines are an important segment of the manufacturing cycle, for under receiving's control all material enters the manufacturing facility. Too often, too little importance is placed on the manpower, equipment, layout, and communication media for this activity. In this chapter, the manufacturing manager will find a description of receiving's functions, facilities, and paperwork, plus a brief discussion of incoming inspection.

Increased attention must be focused on the receiving area, if only because of the continually increasing dollar value of the goods handled and the ever-tightening acceptable quality levels demanded of the incoming material. In addition, two other factors have given this area a more dynamic role in the manufacturing activity: (1) the greater use of specialized containers, many returnable for credit and often requiring specialized material handling devices, and (2) the requirement for segregation of material into specific lot sizes or into special lot containers for delivery to production areas.

ORGANIZATION

Like many other service departments, there are a number of places in the organization to which the receiving department may report. If the company is large and uses the materials management concept, the department may report to the materials manager directly. Otherwise receiving may report to the material control department, the purchasing department, the factory superintendent, or the plant manager, depending on the size of the company, the capabilities of the individual department heads, and the company's systems concepts.

Reporting to the purchasing department is a logical arrangement, because it normally initiates the control and the flow of incoming material. Sometimes, because of the need for extensive material handling service, the company may choose to have the material control department handle receiving along with in-plant transportation. Where it is necessary to lend personnel to the receiving department or where receiving has slack periods, it will be important to tie receiving into another department so that manpower may be transferred in and out readily on a temporary basis without disrupting job classifications.

Combination with Shipping. In small companies, it may prove logical to combine the receiving and shipping departments. This combination can aid in reducing supervision and material handling equipment and in providing flexibility of manpower to handle peak load situations. Indeed, the limited area available for truck docks or railroad siding may require that one individual be responsible for that area. Many managements keep the receiving and shipping functions separate, however, not only to avoid possible mix-ups of incoming and outgoing materials, but also because analysis usually reveals that the functions and responsibilities of the two departments are quite different and have only the material handling activity in common.

Combination with a Storeroom. Particularly in a small organization, it may be economical to have the receiving department act as the general supply storeroom and to disburse bulk items such as oil, paint, or adhesives. By planned curtailment of the storeroom open hours, it may be possible to offset the peak load situations which occur in the receiving activity.

Departmental Organization. Probably the most common organizational setup for a receiving department is a salaried supervisor or foreman, a lead man if the size of the department warrants it, one or more clerks, one or more material handlers, and electric truck operators as required. To best handle peak load situations and to provide flexibility in the work force when needed, it is advisable to keep the number of job classifications to a minimum. For example, where possible, the material handlers and clerks should be interchangeable so that either may open cartons and count, record, or handle straightforward records or communications. Broad classifications and work descriptions will increase the capability of the department to respond rapidly to special situations.

FUNCTIONS

The receiving department is concerned primarily with:
1. Quantity—to assure that the count is correct
2. Quality—to assure that quality control has approved the quality of the material
3. Material handling—to deliver the material to the specified area
4. Notification—to advise authorized personnel of status of incoming material

Specific Duties. The personnel in receiving will:
1. Unload and unpack incoming materials
2. Check material for obvious physical damage and make out related claim records
3. Check material against the purchase order
4. Make out receiving reports
5. Provide for temporary storage when necessary
6. Deliver incoming material or selected samples thereof to the incoming inspection department

7. Deliver inspected materials to designated storerooms or storage areas
8. Segregate material into lots when so specified
9. Load material into specialized containers when required
10. Group parts into kits, using bills of material, for delivery to assembly areas or storerooms
11. Report rejected material and hold for disposition

Other Related Duties.   In some manufacturing facilities, the receiving department may perform other duties closely related to the receiving functions, such as advising purchasing of late items, tracing late incoming shipments, and reporting potential delays from impending transportation worker strikes. There are a number of lesser duties which may also be required, such as the making out of identification tags for certain materials or containers, resealing cartons to prevent pilferage, and disposing of waste packaging material.   If the receiving department is also responsible for maintaining and dispensing supplies or commonly used purchase parts, it will also have the clerical and handling duties related to this storeroom effort.

LOCATION

The location of the receiving department is often dictated by the location of railroad tracks or adjacent streets.   Thus, occasionally the receiving and shipping functions are combined or placed in close proximity to each other.   More often, the receiving area will be located at one end of the plant and shipping at the other, sharing the railroad siding but having separate truck docks.   The receiving department should be immediately adjacent to truck docks and to the railroad siding if possible.   The volume and type of incoming product will determine the optimum location, with preference being given to proximity to the truck docks.

Ideally, the receiving department should be located so that materials may be moved readily to the manufacturing areas using them.   Variations in types of materials and their containers may necessitate more than one receiving area for optimum effectiveness and practicability.

Traffic Control.   Care must be taken to provide adequate traffic control in the area of the loading platforms, particularly if on a public way.   Too many times, overtime or overstaffing is necessary only because of traffic congestion which requires time-consuming maneuvering or waiting for the removal of vehicles blocking the way.   Congestion can often be reduced by the introduction and control of one-way streets, traffic lights, no-parking areas, and traffic rerouting during working hours.   Strict in-yard traffic control can be vital to the effective operation of the department.

The incoming inspection department should be as close as possible to the receiving department, for most of the incoming material will move in whole or in part to that area.   Usually, receiving supplies the transportation from both incoming inspection and the receiving department to the storerooms or other factory or office areas, and so the closer receiving and inspection are to each other, the better will be communications and the control of in-transit material.

LAYOUT

When the receiving area is laid out initially or when there is a radical change in product size or volume, a careful review of space requirements should be made.   There should be a calculation of:

1. What volume of items is to be handled and how often
2. How many trucks and freight cars will be handled each day
3. When and how great is the anticipated peak load
4. How much time is required to unload
5. What types of truck and rail facilities are required
6. What types of material handling devices are required
7. What materials can be stored outside
8. How much temporary storage space is necessary
9. What amount of manpower will require how much desk and office space

In spite of the requirement to move material rapidly through the department, there must be adequate room for temporary storage of material which is awaiting:

1. Accurate identification
2. Completion of the quantity or quality check
3. Acceptance notification from the incoming inspection department
4. Disposition authority after rejection
5. Repackaging into special lots or specialized containers where necessary

Arrangement of the Receiving Area.   The receiving area should be arranged with only one entrance and one exit.   It should be enclosed, and only receiving personnel should be permitted within it under normal circumstances. There is a definite need to have a secured area to safeguard the incoming material and to assure the integrity of the count.

Where possible, the receiving office should be adjacent to the receiving docks, with windows permitting ready observation of the dock and the outer yard.   Adequate protection from the weather is necessary in most geographic locations, not only to protect incoming material but also to shield the employees from the adverse effects of wind, rain, and temperature.   Truck docks and railroad cars should be hooded, enclosed, or inside the building when economically feasible, to assure that inclement weather will not adversely affect the receiving activities.

Material Handling Equipment.   Proper material handling devices and equipment can aid in the speed of unloading and the effective use of manpower.   Regularly used truck docks should have built-in leveling devices or hydraulic ramps, and the railroad platform height should be carefully designed for the type of freight car normally handled.   Adequate handling equipment should be available to avoid delays.   Further, to be in a position to take advantage of the increased use of unitized containers and continued improvements in packaging techniques, maximum flexibility must be provided for.   It is well to note, for example, that a trailer truck with pallet-pack containers can be unloaded in approximately one-tenth of the time that single containers can be carried or conveyed out of the same trailer.

Another important consideration is the method of disposition of the waste packaging material.   Temporary storage area (indoors or out) plus transportation equipment must be provided unless there is a baler or an incinerator readily at hand.   Many companies contract for an outside firm to provide a truck body or specialized equipment to be loaded and then hauled away when full.

INCOMING INSPECTION AND COUNT

Immediately on receipt, containers should be checked visually for damage, so that any necessary claim can be registered promptly.   A Polaroid-type camera may be used to document the arrival condition of the merchandise. A further check of the material for damage such as scratches, dents, oxidation, and breakage must be made when the packages are opened.

After unpacking, a quantity check must be made. This may be done by hand count, by weighing, by measuring, or by counting on a proportional scale. It is essential that the receiving area be provided with up-to-date parts specifications and with properly selected equipment to enable the quantity to be checked rapidly. Purchasing the material in standard lot sizes and in standard containers will do much to increase the efficiency of this necessary task.

When shortages or overshipments occur, they must be recorded on the receiving report and flagged to indicate need for action by purchasing and to alert the material control department. In many instances, agreements or contracts made with specific vendors by purchasing will predetermine the method of handling these count variances.

When source inspection (inspection at the vendor's place of business) has been specified, the receiving department should have prior knowledge through appropriate paperwork, so that the material may be moved into manufacturing with a minimum of delay.

Inspection by the Quality Control Department. Normally, the responsibility for other quantitative or qualitative inspections, such as size, color, texture, and electrical characteristics, is the function of the quality control department. These checks are performed primarily in a separate area, under quality control jurisdiction, usually designated as the purchased material inspection department or as the incoming inspection department. The receiving department will send all incoming material or a specified sample of the material to the inspection department and await the results before transporting the material to the manufacturing departments.

If the material is particularly large or bulky, the quality control department's inspection may take place in the receiving department itself or in the area where the material was required to be received, such as bulk storage bins or tank cars. Also, it may be necessary to send certain types of materials to special testing facilities elsewhere in the building, but receiving must maintain control over the material before it is released for use by manufacturing.

The use of statistical quality control procedures, based on Dodge-Romig tables, sequential analysis, and the like, will provide reliable information rapidly, so that except where 100 percent inspection is required, even large lots can be moved rapidly through the receiving area and into manufacturing.

REJECTED MATERIAL

When material is rejected, there must be an accurate record stating the reason for rejection. In the case of goods damaged in transit, the carrier should be notified immediately, and ideally a photograph should be taken to stantiate the claim. Normally, the purchasing department will be tified and will handle the communications relative to the return, advising receiving when and to whom the material should be sent. Rapid action should be taken by purchasing to avoid unnecessary pile-ups of rejected material in the receiving area. The requisitioner and the material/production control department must also be notified of rejections so that they may expedite new material, reschedule, or request material substitution to meet schedule.

Paperwork Procedures. Two methods of reporting and handling rejected material are common.

1. Use of a multicopy Receiving Material Inspection Report, which is made out by the quality department when material is rejected. (See Figure 8-1.) Copies are sent to:
   a. Purchasing—one for file and one to send to the vendor
   b. Manufacturing engineering—so that they may determine whether the material can be designated as substandard and used with restrictions
   c. Production control—one for headquarters control and one for the storeroom

   This type form is intended to get rapid corrective action from the vendor and rapid internal action to evaluate the possibility of using the material in its out-of-specification condition. It may be desirable to attach an identification tag to the actual material until disposition notification is received so that it will not be inadvertently delivered to manufacturing.

2. Use of the purchase order. In this instance, the purchase order form is so designed that when it is originally typed there is a spirit master copy (or a series of multicarbon forms) retaining the essential purchase information, but adding a special format containing space for the posting of material received and inspected. Figure 8-2 shows a typical spirit master format. It is sent to the receiving department which normally fills in the required information; reproduces copies (or separates copies) for purchasing, inspection, material control, the requisitioner, and accounting; and sends these daily to the respective departments. A rejection tag (Figure 8-3) may also be used to identify the material awaiting disposition and to record the disposition instructions when received.

It is essential that the paperwork be kept as simple as possible and the number of copies made be kept to a minimum. This requires a periodic check by the industrial engineers or systems analysts to assure least cost and, most important, rapid notification to the proper people.

RECEIVING REPORT

Upon receipt of material, there must be rapid communication with internal departments, advising them of its arrival. The departments normally concerned are (1) purchasing—to update or close out their records, (2) storerooms—so that they can prepare for storage and distribution, (3) production control or material control—so that they may update their records and schedule or reschedule production as necessary, (4) accounting—so that the vendor will be paid, and (5) issuer of original requisition—to close out his record and notify him of availability.

Required Information. Receiving reports can take many forms. For each shipment received, however, there should be the following information.

1. Date received
2. Vendor's name, identification code, and address
3. Vendor's invoice number
4. Purchase order number
5. Type of material and classification/identification code
6. Quantity
7. Package unit and type of container
8. Carrier identification

UCINITE
Receiving Material Inspection Report

N⁰ 12905

PART NO.	VENDOR		ORDER NO.

DATE REC'D.	QTY. REC'D.	INS. DATE	QUANTITY PASSED

AMOUNT	DESCRIPTION OF DEFECT	USABLE	NON–USABLE
A			
B			
C			
D			
E			
F			
G			
H			
I			
TOTAL	SAMPLES: 1st 2nd		

VENDOR HISTORY AND RATING

Last Five Shipments .... Good .... Defective

Vendor Rating: Approved .... Poor .... Objectionable .... Not Acceptable ....

Signatures ——→   Inspector   Supervisor

To be completed by Vendor and returned to Purchasing

Describe Corrective Action: _____

_____

_____

Date Defect will be corrected: _____   Signed _____

GOODS TO BE RETURNED TO VENDOR	USABLE SUBSTANDARD MATERIAL
Purch. Date	Ch. Eng. Date
Quality Sup. Date	Mfg. Eng. Date
Mfg. Eng. Date	Quality Sup. Date
Shipping # Date	Purch. Date

100%   ☐ At Ucinite Expense
INSPECTION ☐ At Vendor's Expense

Spec. Will ☐ Will Not ☐ Be Changed.

FIG. 8-1.   Receiving Material Inspection Report.

9. Transportation charges
10. Receiver identification
11. Disposition of the material
    a. Delivered to
    b. Charge number
    c. Rejection information

Procedure.   One of the simplest procedures for producing a receiving re-port entails the use of multiple copies of the purchase order.   The pur-chasing department then must provide all necessary delivery information

ANALOG DEVICES

ANALOG DEVICES
241-243 BINNEY ST.
CAMBRIDGE, MASS. 02142
AREA CODE 617 491-7150

TO

No. 15049 — OUR P. O. # PART NO. MUST APPEAR ON ALL BILLS OF LADING, PACKING SLIPS AND INVOICES.

DATE

SHIP TO	SHIP VIA:	F.O.B.	TERMS:	ACCOUNT NO. / DELIVER TO
221 FIFTH ST., CAMBRIDGE, MASS.				

PLEASE SHIP THE FOLLOWING EXACTLY AS SPECIFIED:

ITEM	QUANTITY	DESCRIPTION	UNIT PRICE	
		CONFIRMED TO:		

RECEIVED						INSPECTED					RECEIVED						INSPECTED				
ITEM	QTY.	CUML.	DATE	PACKING SLIP NO.	BY	QTY. ACCEPTED	QTY. REJECTED	REJ. TAG. NO.	DATE	BY	ITEM	QTY.	CUML.	DATE	PACKING SLIP NO.	BY	QTY. ACCEPTED	QTY. REJECTED	REJ. TAG. NO.	DATE	BY

FIG. 8-2. Purchase Order Which Provides Space for Posting Material Received and Inspected.

on the purchase order as well as extra copies—one for the receiving department file, one as a traveler to accompany the material through inspection to its destination, one to the requisitioner, one to be returned to purchasing, and one to be sent to the accounting department. If in-house practices require a receipt, an extra copy or a split portion of the traveler can be returned to receiving to document safe arrival. In many companies, the purchase order will be on a spirit master which is sent to receiving, who will reproduce the necessary copies on receipt of the material (see Figure 8-2). Often the prices will not appear on the copy going to receiving.

When corrections are necessary, they may be handled either by a written memorandum indicating what changes are to be made and signed by the material control personnel or by use of a correction report in simple format. When a spirit master is used by receiving, normally they will make a clear adjustment on the master, reproduce it, and reissue corrected copies.

Daily List. The receiving department may desire to keep a daily list of incoming receipts. This should be arranged in the most convenient manner for each department's use (by part number, by commodity number, and so on) and should include the cost, remainder on order, and other pertinent information. Often the accounting department will use the daily list as a double check against incoming invoices.

File Life. To reduce the space and effort required to maintain files, it is wise

R 20112

ANALOG
DEVICES   **REJECTION TAG**

DATE REJECTED	REJECTED BY			

STATUS OF MATERIAL WHEN REJECTED

RAW ☐	PRE POTTING ☐	FINAL ☐		
VENDOR	P.O. OR RECEIVING RPT. NO.	QTY. ACCEPT	QTY. REJECT	
DESCRIPTION		RUN NO.	REV.	SERIAL NO.

CAUSE FOR REJECTION — TEST SPECS. APPLICABLE

DISPOSITION	REWORK ☐	SCRAP ☐	OTHER ☐

	APP. BY	DATE	APP. BY	DATE	APP. BY	DATE
REWORK COMPLETED BY	DATE		REWORK APPROVED BY		DATE	

Fig. 8-3.   Rejection Tag.

to specify the length of time that each type of record is to be retained: for example, one year by receiving; current use only by purchasing, by expediters, and for the traveler copy; and ten years by accounting.

EVALUATION CHECKLIST

The manufacturing manager will wish to assure himself of the effectiveness of the receiving department either by personal observation and written reports or through one of his assistants. A checklist to aid in such evaluation is provided below.

1. Is the traffic flow satisfactory?
   a. Are there trucks waiting regularly to get into the dock?
   b. Are freight cars unloaded rapidly enough to avoid demurrage payments?
   c. Is purchasing scheduling deliveries to avoid a peak load situation?
2. Are properly selected material handling devices being used?
3. Is the general housekeeping satisfactory?
   a. Are the working and storage areas clearly designated—incoming material awaiting check, material awaiting quality control approval, rejected material, waste material?
   b. Is material clearly identified—with tags where necessary?

    c. Is waste packing material kept under control and off the floor?

    d. Is material left on the dock unprotected overnight?

4. Is manpower handled efficiently?

    a. Are there direct work measurement standards in the kitting area and other areas where the work load is reasonably steady?

    b. Have work sampling techniques or memomotion films been used to aid in man-loading?

    c. Does the department regularly lend out personnel in slack periods?

    d. Does the department regularly borrow personnel for peak loads?

    e. Is part-time help used?

5. Does the department adhere to budget?

    a. Is there excessive overtime?

6. Are the counts accurate?

    a. Are the corrections to the daily receiving report summarized weekly or monthly?

    b. Are errors in kitting summarized and corrective action taken?

7. Is the material moving rapidly into production?

    a. Is there an exception report to show the amount of material not counted within twenty-four hours, not inspected within seventy-two hours, rejected but not disposed of within one hundred and twenty hours?

    b. Is the level of the dollar value held in the area excessive?

    c. Does material arrive on the manufacturing floor uninspected?

SUMMARY

The receiving department has often been the neglected area of the plant—with inadequate or outdated equipment and with incapable personnel often cast off from other departments. If management is to maintain control of material, move it rapidly, and keep inventories at a low level, it is vital that the receiving area receive the same close scrutiny and analysis that would be given to a factory assembly department, and then supplied with the best tools, equipment, and personnel to do the job effectively.

BIBLIOGRAPHY

Bolz, Harold A., and G. Hagemann (eds.), *Materials Handling Handbook,* The Ronald Press Company, New York, 1958.

Carson, Gordon B. (ed.), *Production Handbook,* 2d ed., The Ronald Press Company, New York, 1958.

Ireson, William G., and Eugene L. Grant (eds.), *Handbook of Industrial Engineering and Management,* Prentice-Hall, Inc., Englewood Cliffs, N.J., 1955.

MacNiece, E. H., *Production Forecasting, Planning and Control,* 3d ed., John Wiley & Sons, Inc., New York, 1961.

Maynard H. B. (ed.), *Industrial Engineering Handbook,* 2d ed., McGraw-Hill Book Company, New York, 1963.

CHAPTER NINE

Inspection and Test

HARDY M. COOK, JR.   *Head, Quality Assurance Department, Western Electric Company, Inc., Baltimore, Maryland*

Inspection is the critical examination of product by measurement, test, or visual observation to determine compliance with a specification or standards of good workmanship. A distinction is usually made between inspection and test. When the evaluation of the product requires a test of electrical properties, physical properties, or functional performance, it is called test. The other means of evaluating the product are then classified as inspection. In this chapter the term "inspection" will mean the all-inclusive definition contained in the first sentence.

Inspections are performed (1) to ascertain the product quality, (2) to provide feedback information used to control the quality of product during manufacture, and (3) to assure the quality of the shipped product.

THE INSPECTION FUNCTION

One purpose of inspection is to determine the acceptability of units of product or groups of product. This is called acceptance inspection. The acceptability is related to whether the product meets its design specifications and workmanship standards. Product that fails acceptance inspection may be usable as nonconforming material. This point is discussed later in the chapter.

Another purpose of inspection is to provide feedback information used to control the quality of product during manufacture. A small portion of the output of a manufacturing process is inspected on a periodic time basis. If the evaluation falls within certain prescribed limits, the process is allowed to continue to run. If not, the process machinery is adjusted until the inspection results show it to be within limits. In addition, process control procedures require inspection and calibration of measuring tools, gages, and testing equipment on a regular basis.

Inspection is also performed to assure the quality of the shipped product. A small sample of product is inspected after final acceptance inspection. One procedure is to perform this inspection on a continuous basis with the results for each type of product being compared to an expected level of quality. Through this procedure, known as rating, it can be ascertained whether or not the variability in inspection results from the expected level is normal. Another procedure is to inspect a small portion of product as a part of a periodic survey of the quality control system. The results are used as part of the evidence to judge whether the quality control system is adequate.

Quality, Specifications, and Workmanship Standards. Quality has a twofold meaning. Good quality can mean that an individual unit satisfactorily conforms to its design specifications and workmanship standards. Good quality can also mean that a group or lot of product is satisfactory as determined by an evaluation of a portion of the lot. There is a tacit assumption that product which meets the design specification will perform satisfactorily. Failure to meet a requirement of the specification is designated as a defect. Any individual unit of product that contains one or more defects is called a defective. A product lot can be acceptable even though there are a small number of defectives in the portion of the lot that is examined. The determination of the acceptable number of defectives in a sample or portion of a lot inspected, as well as the appropriate sampling risks, is a quality engineering function.

There are two types of quality: quality of design and quality of conformance. Quality which concerns adherence to specifications is called quality of conformance. Acceptance inspection determines the quality of conformance of a product. A design specification prescribes the requirements for a product that have a certain value to its ultimate user. The design can be modified so that the consumer receives more or less value for the same functional use. The change in value relates to ease of operation, reliability, length of service, appearance, and the like. Grade is the designation given to product having the same value and functional use. The design specification for the different grades of product defines the quality of design. Acceptance inspection does not affect the quality of design of a product.

Workmanship standards may be implied or explicit. In either case, they should be consistent with the objectives of the designer. Workmanship standards usually apply to visual inspection characteristics. It should be realized that workmanship defects are not limited to those caused solely by the operator. Defects caused by tools and machines alone or in conjunction with the operator are considered workmanship defects.

There is a danger when workmanship standards are implied, because it is difficult to obtain consistent judgments among inspectors. There is also a lack of consistency from day to day and from time to time within a shift, even with the same inspector. Because these judgments are subjective, they are also affected by the pressures of shipping schedules with resultant inconsistent evaluation. Training using audiovisual aids is a step in the direction of reducing inspector bias and the difference among inspectors.

Use of explicit workmanship standards results in more consistency among inspectors performing visual inspection. Descriptive standards are inferior to pictorial or illustrative samples. Descriptive standards are subject to the same misunderstandings as any other written communication. The writers are either unable to define clearly and precisely what is desired or the readers misinterpret the written word. Pictorial representations are more easily understood by the inspectors. Better still is the sample board that contains a group of defects ranked in order of severity, with indications of the point of acceptability. Sufficient samples should be used to show the kinds and locations of the defects so that evaluation is not difficult. These types of samples are called limit samples.

Classification of Inspections. Inspection can be classified in a variety of ways. It can be classified by purpose, by point of inspection, by amount of inspection, by measurements classification, and by product flow. Inspection can be for acceptance of product, the control of quality, or the assurance of quality.

Inspection may also be classified by the point in the manufacturing cycle where inspection is performed, such as receiving inspection; process inspection; tool, gage, and testing equipment inspection; and final inspection including test.

Receiving Inspection. Receiving inspection may also be designated by other names such as incoming material inspection, raw material inspection, or purchased material inspection. Purchased material inspection is sometimes performed at the supplier's plant, in which case it is known as source inspection. This is the inspection of all materials that will be manufactured into product, subcontracted piece parts, subcontracted subassemblies, and even completed product that has been subcontracted. The inspection of incoming materials is made in accordance with the purchase order and the specifications and standards for the materials and product. Most of this inspection is by sampling rather than by examination of the complete lot. Some companies have developed extensive instructions for use by both the purchased material inspector and the outside supplier. These instructions include statistical sampling plans for the various characteristics of the incoming parts, assemblies, or raw materials, as well as details on the inspection methods and facilities. These instructions are developed by quality control engineers and are made a part of the purchase order.

Process Inspection. Process inspections take two forms: those that are made to accept product lots before further processing and those that are made to produce information used to control the quality of product during manufacturing. In small-parts fabrication and assembly, an inspection is made of lots of piece parts or subassemblies before they are released to the assembly area. The inspection is usually on a sample of the product with the sampling plans to be used being determined by the quality control engineering group. For some products, there are certain specification requirements that cannot be checked in the complete form of the product. These requirements are inspected in process. This is particularly true of but not limited to those products that are made by continuous-type manufacturing processes. Where the product is very costly, it is economical to make in-process inspections even on those characteristics that could be checked in the completed product. These inspections are usually made on 100 percent of the product. In continuous manufacturing processes, the testing equipment may be built into the process machinery.

In-process inspections made for control purposes may be first-piece inspections, patrol inspections, or inspection of product characteristics for control chart information. The first piece produced on a machine setup is usually inspected by a process inspector before the production run is made. Patrol inspections are made at random during the shift by a process inspector circulating throughout the machining area. Parts manufactured between patrol checks are usually segregated, and good parts separated from bad ones if the check shows that the present parts manufactured by the machine are defective. Control chart methods may be used with first-piece or patrol inspections. These latter procedures may become machine operator duties where statistical quality control methods are used.

Tool, Gage, and Testing Equipment Inspection. Tool, gage, and testing equipment inspection is a very important phase of any program to ensure that parts and product will be manufactured to specification. Dies, jigs, fixtures, and other tools used in production should be periodically checked and, when warranted, repaired or replaced. Measuring equipment, gages, and test equipment should also be checked on a periodic basis and recalibrated when found to be out of adjustment. A master record should be maintained on all tools, gages, and measuring and test equipment showing checking dates, condition, and repairs. Computerized recall systems have been developed to facilitate maintaining calibration schedules. Measuring and testing equipment should have calibration stickers or tags affixed to them showing last or next scheduled calibration date.

Final Inspection and Test. Final inspection and test is an acceptance inspection. It is performed to ascertain whether individual units or groups of units satisfactorily meet their specifications and workmanship standards. Final inspection consists of gaging, measuring, visual inspection, and testing. The testing portion consists of electrical, physical, and functional tests. Usually special test sets are designed to perform the electrical checks on a particular product. Where there is a variety of configurations of a number of similar products, tape-controlled test sets have been designed to accommodate the different configurations.

When final inspection is on a unit basis, defective product is handled as described later in the chapter. When sampling of a lot is used, failure of the acceptance criteria results in the rejection of the lot. The good units may be separated from the defective units in the lot, or the lot may be returned to production for corrective action. Procedures for disposal of nonconforming product described later in the chapter can also apply to rejected lots.

100 Percent and Sampling Inspection. Inspection may be classified according to the amount of inspection performed. If each unit of the product submitted is inspected, it is called 100 percent inspection. If a portion of the units from a lot is inspected, it is called sampling inspection. This latter classification is further amplified by designating the number of times a sample of one or more units is selected from the lot. If the sampling act is performed once, it is known as single sampling. When the inspection scheme requires a second sample if the first sample results are inconclusive, it is known as double sampling. Any sampling scheme that requires more than two selections of samples to determine the acceptability of the lot is designated as multiple or sequential sampling.

It is a well-known fact that 100 percent inspection is not 100 percent effective. Fatigue and boredom affect accuracy when repetitive observations are made over long periods of time. The greater the amount of judgment required for determining conformance, the lower the efficiency. Sampling often can be more accurate than 100 percent inspection because of the reduced fatigue as well as the psychological factor that the acceptability of the lot depends on the results obtained from the small sample. Other reasons for sampling are: (1) testing for some characteristics may be destructive to the product; (2) the cost of the 100 percent inspection may be prohibitive; and (3) the pressure for quality improvement is greater because of the return of rejected lots to production for correction. The determination of which sampling inspection plan to use is a quality engineering function.

Other Classifications. Inspection can also be classified by product flow. When product is submitted as a group of units, it is called lot-by-lot inspection. When the manufacturing process is conveyorized, the inspector selects his sample at random from the flow of product. This is called continuous inspection.

Another method of classifying inspection relates to the way in which the measurements are used to determine conformance of product. When continuous measurements are taken and the amount of deviation from the specification limit is used to determine conformance, the inspection is called variables inspection. When inspection of a quality characteristic does not produce a finite measurement but still permits classification of the unit as conforming or nonconforming, it is called attributes inspection.

A particular inspection scheme may combine several of the different classifications described above. Thus, in final inspection, a double-sampling, lot-by-lot, attributes inspection plan may be used.

Records and Instructions. It is a cardinal principle of inspection that a detailed set of records must be kept. The records should contain product identification, date, number of units in the lot, number of units in the sample, number of defectives in the sample, number of each kind of defect, and disposition of the lot. These records are a source of invaluable information for determining corrective action when multiple cases of trouble occur.

Any reasonable size inspection operation requires a set of inspection instructions to be efficient and orderly. Instructions should be prepared and issued for receiving, process, tool, gage, and test equipment inspections as well as for final inspection and test.

Department of Defense contracts require that the manufacturer have an adequate inspection system. Mil-I-45208A, Inspection System Requirements, describes the procedures and methods of inspection that are considered necessary. Mil-C-45662A, Calibration System Requirements, describes the procedures and methods of an adequate tool, gage, and test equipment calibration system. Mil-Q-9858-A, Quality Program Requirements, also contains provisions that affect the inspection function.

THE NEED FOR INSPECTION

Inspection cannot change the quality of product. The quality is established as the parts are made or when the product is assembled. However, inspection evaluates the quality of product and identifies good parts or good lots from defective ones. The benefits of inspection are not limited to its usefulness for accepting completed product. There is economic advantage to inspecting product during processing or even before processing has begun.

Completed Product Inspection. Inspection of completed product is necessary because manufacturing subordinates quality for quantity and schedules whenever the operator is paid by a wage incentive system based on output. The operator's earnings usually depend on the amount of product produced. He is also faced with producing a certain amount by a certain time. These two pressures may cause him to omit some of his specified measurement checks or may even cause him to include some product that does not meet specifications or workmanship standards.

A number of reasons exist which make these actions justifiable to the operator. He may feel that it is a worthwhile risk to skip some checks in order to deliver the required amount on time. There is considerable judgment associated with determining the acceptability of marginal product, and so he is willing to leave the final acceptance decision up to the inspector. Nonconforming product is sometimes usable, and so he may consider that this substandard product is good enough. Sometimes operator procedures do not provide him with the necessary tools or include adequate time to ascertain the quality of the product that he is producing. Regardless of the reasons for the existence of this situation, inspection of completed product for acceptance purposes is needed.

Another reason for performing completed product inspection is to alleviate the consequences of not doing it. With completed product inspection, customer complaints and warranty costs are minimized, loss of sales from customer dissatisfaction with the quality of the product is reduced, and the company's quality reputation is protected.

If the company has a quality assurance continuing product audit as a part of its quality program, acceptance inspection is necessary to ensure that the specified quality standards are met.

Process Inspection. Although there is a demonstrated need for acceptance inspection, it does not do much to prevent the manufacture of defective product except for the corrective pressures exerted by rejection of product lots. Even in this latter case, the corrective measures will be applied to product manufactured in the future. There will probably be considerable defective product already produced besides that contained in the rejected lot. This substandard product will have to be segregated and disposed of with some financial loss. Therefore, inspection is performed in process to prevent the manufacture of defective parts or assemblies.

The manufacture of defective product is detected by first-piece inspections, patrol inspections, and the inspection of small samples for control chart information. Once the first-piece inspection has established that the process is satisfactory to run, the patrol inspections and control chart inspections are made at periodic intervals during the shift. The product manufactured between checks is kept separate so that it can be sorted should the periodic inspection uncover a defective part. Only a small amount of substandard product is produced before the process is adjusted, and it can be identified. This procedure minimizes scrap, rework, and the use of nonconforming product.

Process inspection is also performed to eliminate additional work on parts that will be scrapped, to eliminate sorting in assembly or future processing operations, and to facilitate repair and rework operations. This is accomplished by having measuring and testing equipment built into continuous manufacturing processes and by the inspection of piece parts, subassemblies, and partially completed product. The integration of measuring and testing into a continuous manufacturing process is also a control procedure that alerts the operator when adjustments are necessary. The other process inspections not only reduce labor losses in future operations, but also give indications when process adjustments should be made without producing a large run of defective product. Rework and repair are easier because additional fabrication has not been performed on the product.

Tool, Gage, and Test Equipment Inspection. Tool, gage, and test equipment inspection also helps to minimize the manufacture of defective product. The inspection of dies, jigs, fixtures, and other tools used in production shows when they should be repaired or replaced before they produce defective parts. The inspection and calibration of measuring and testing equipment ensure that correct measurements are made, thereby preventing incorrect classification of measured product.

Receiving Inspection. Receiving inspection is necessary to detect and thus prevent the use of inferior materials and substandard quality parts as well as to ensure the purchaser that he is getting what he paid for. Identification and rejection of defective subcontracted parts and raw materials which do not meet specification requirements by receiving inspection eliminate labor losses during manufacture and reduce scrap, rework, repair, and the use of nonconforming material. When this inspection is performed at the supplier's plant, costly transportation charges for returned material are also eliminated. In addition, source inspection may eliminate losses from sorting good product from bad when standard lots of subcontracted parts are used to maintain manufacturing operations or shipping schedules.

Receiving inspection ensures that the purchaser is getting not only the proper quality of material, but also the required amount.

Quality Assurance. Even though quality assurance is a separate function from inspection, some quality assurance programs include a continuous product inspection on an audit basis.

These inspections are performed to assure the validity of the inspection acceptance work and prevent the shipment of a run of defective product. The validation of the adequacy of final inspection contributes to the benefits previously described concerning protection of the company's quality reputation, loss of sales, and reduction in customer complaints and warranty costs. Most continuous product audits include a procedure for limiting the shipment of product lots that contain more than a specified percentage of defectives. This identifies and prevents the shipment of a run of bad product.

ORGANIZATIONAL LOCATION OF INSPECTION

The location of the inspection function with relation to other functions in the organizational structure will vary, depending on how a company is organized to accomplish its aims and objectives. To some extent, the location depends on the types of products, processes, and the number of administrative heads required to fulfill corporate responsibilities. However, it is basic that the final responsibility for inspection decisions should be at a managerial level high enough to ensure that company policies on quality are not subordinated to other responsibilities.

One common organizational structure combines the planning and operating functions of inspection and other related functions under one quality manager. The chief inspector, supervisor of quality control engineering, and supervisor of quality assurance report to the quality manager. The quality manager in turn reports to the manufacturing manager or the plant manager. The chief inspector is responsible for carrying out all inspection operations, including receiving inspection; process inspection; tool, gage, and test equipment inspection; and final inspection and test. The quality control engineering organization provides the planning for inspection and the planning for quality control work. The quality assurance group provides the planning for and accomplishing of all quality assurance responsibilities, including performing the continuous product audit. This type of organization has the advantage of bringing together under one head those people who have a common interest in attaining and maintaining the desired quality of the company's products. It also elevates the status of the quality function in the company and reduces the chance that quality will be subordinated to shipping schedules and manufacturing cost pressures.

Another organizational form is to have the separation of functions in line and staff organizations. The chief inspector, with the responsibility for carrying out receiving inspection, process inspection, and final inspection and test, reports to the manufacturing manager. The quality control engineering department, with the same responsibilities as described above, reports to the manufacturing engineering manager. The tool, gage, and test equipment inspection reports to a technical manager, who also has maintenance and construction responsibilities. The quality assurance department reports to the plant manager, or in larger companies, to a separate headquarters organization. The advantage of this organization structure is the ability to coordinate more closely the activities of the production and inspection departments. The inspection and quality control planning are closely allied to the manufacturing planning. The tool, gage, and testing equipment inspection has common interests with the maintenance organization, which results in rapid repairs when needed. The independent quality assurance activity combined with the responsible actions of the manufacturing manager upholds the quality of the completed product.

A few companies have established an organizational structure that integrates the inspection function into the manufacturing department. The operator is furnished with the tools, techniques, and time allowance to assure himself that the product he makes meets its specifications and workmanship standards. Quality control performs a random audit periodically throughout the shift to assure the correctness of the operator's decisions. Quality control also performs the receiving inspection and the acceptance testing of the completed product. There should be an independent quality assurance department which performs a continuous product audit inspection in order to have satisfactory quality protection. The advantage of this type of organization is that it places the full responsibility for quality decisions with the operator who is the person that can do the most about obtaining good quality. The manufacturing costs of this type of inspection system usually are lower than those of other inspection systems.

INSPECTION PLANNING

Inspection planning can generally be divided into two broad categories: those activities that relate to actual performance of the job, and those required to engineer the job. The first classification contains activities such as selection and training of inspectors, assignment of personnel, appraisal and control of work performance, and judgment of conformance. These responsibilities usually belong to the chief inspector and his supervision. The second classification contains activities such as selection of the points of inspection, selection of the amount of inspection, design and layout of the workplace, selection of the method of inspection, design and procurement of measuring and testing equipment, preparation of inspection instructions, and design of paperwork forms and procedures. These activities are usually performed by the quality engineering department.

When the organizational structure is the line and staff type, some of the above duties are performed by the manufacturing engineers. In that case, coordination and cooperation with the quality engineers are necessary, especially with regard to the amount of inspection.

Regardless of who performs the engineering of the inspection operation, it should be coordinated very closely with the inspection supervision, whose practical experience enables them to present suggestions that will be invaluable.

The selection of the points of inspection is related to the need for inspection previously discussed. The completed product should be inspected and tested for acceptance purposes. Purchased items, piece parts, and subassemblies should be inspected so that additional work is not performed on defective items. In addition, to facilitate repair and rework operations, there should be in-process inspection before operations that cover the defects or make permanent assemblies. These inspections are in addition to the first-piece inspection, patrol inspection, and control chart inspection performed to control the quality of product during manufacture.

The amount of inspection is related to the purpose for which the inspection is performed, with the limitations of 100 percent inspection being kept in mind. Functional and electrical tests are usually important enough to be performed on 100 percent of the product, using automatic or semiautomatic testing equipment to ensure efficient inspection. When sampling is used, the selection of the type and level of the plan is based on probabilistic principles.

The determination of the method of inspection and the design and procurement of measuring and testing equipment are complex tasks. Sometimes this responsibility is assigned to manufacturing engineers or to tool, gage, or test set design engineers.

An orderly well-organized inspection operation requires a well-designed workplace and a detailed set of instructions covering the procedures used, measurement equipment, lot and sample sizes, acceptance criteria, results recording, and disposition procedures. The paperwork planning requires the design of various forms for recording the inspection results in an easy and simple manner.

RELATIONSHIP WITH MANUFACTURING

The establishment and maintenance of a good relationship with the manufacturing organization is one of the most difficult tasks that faces inspection management. Manufacturing is endeavoring to make a product of satisfactory quality at the appropriate cost in the amounts required for delivery at a certain time. Inspection judges whether the product quality is satisfactory. An adverse decision can seriously jeopardize the shipping schedule or increase the cost of the product through additional rework, repair, or scrap over that allowed in the standard cost.

Inspection's relationship with manufacturing is affected by the way in which it carries out its responsibilities and by the attitude of its personnel. Good inspection is responsible, knowledgeable performance. The inspector must be skillful in the use of his measuring equipment. Proper care should be taken when making measurements and visual observations. Judgments as to conformance should be in accordance with the specification or workmanship standard. The inspector should not change the specification by his interpretation of it. His application of judgment should be consistent from day to day, and manufacturing should know and understand how the inspector judges subjective characteristics. Decisions should not only be correct, but once made should also be firm. This does not mean that decisions cannot be changed if additional information is uncovered to show that the original rejection was incorrect. However, these reversals should be few in number if adequate investigation of conditions is made before a decision is reached. It should be realized that the product may still be used under procedures to be described later, even though it fails to meet its specification. Finally, the line of authority should be observed, with rejections being processed through the foremen of inspection and manufacturing. This permits review of the decision by inspection supervision before the decision is rendered.

The attitude of the inspector and the inspection supervisor can have a direct effect on their relations with manufacturing. Evaluation of product quality must be made without a trace of vindictiveness. The inspector must not be pious or sanctimonious when more than the usual number of rejections occur. On the other hand, he does not have to be apologetic if his decisions are honest, accurate, and consistent. Relations are not strained when the inspector is open-minded on questions concerning his decisions. The inspector must be mature about reversals of his decisions, whether they are made by higher authority, by his own supervision, or from the procedures for using nonconforming product. He must not relax his standards or become indifferent because of reversals, but must continue his impartial, objective inspections. The reasons for accepting nonconforming product, which had been previously rejected, are complex, economic, or sometimes even arbitrary, but the authority that renders these decisions accepts the risks and consequences.

Another factor that affects the relationship between inspection and manufacturing is the amount of effort that the inspection organization puts forth to help meet the shipping schedules. This cooperation consists of temporary reassignment of personnel to complete inspection without delay, ready identification and assistance in eliminating the cause of a run of defective product, speedily rendering decisions on areas of judgment that have been questioned, and the like.

A good working relationship will exist when manufacturing is convinced that inspection is properly and fairly performing its function.

DISPOSAL OF NONCONFORMING PRODUCT

Not all the product that fails its specification or workmanship standard is thrown away. Some of it may be used as is. Some may be reworked until it conforms to the specification. Some may be repaired so that it is acceptable for use even though it still does not conform to the specification. The unusable remainder is scrapped. When it is a product lot that has been rejected, the disposition may be to use the lot as is, separate the defective product from the conforming, or scrap the lot. The defective product obtained in the second option is reworked, repaired, or scrapped.

Whether nonconforming lots of product should be used as is depends on the margin in the specification or economic considerations. Most characteristics in a design specification contain a margin of safety which is a range of values in which the product will still perform its function. Margin is built into specifications for several reasons. The product may be used for several different applications that have different operating requirements, some of which are more restrictive than others. The design is set to accommodate the most restrictive conditions. Margin, as an addition to the tolerance, is also required to take care of instrument tolerances and instrument drift. In addition, the designer recognizes that not all product will be manufactured to specification. Even a process operating at a satisfactory level produces an occasional bad product lot. Therefore, margin in a specification tolerance permits the acceptance of nonconforming product depending on the extent of the deviation and the specific application of use.

The decision to use nonconforming material as is may depend on economic considerations. A balance is struck between the cost of renovating the defective product in the factory and the extra cost of using it in the field. The extra cost of using substandard quality material in the field arises from the cost of repairing it in the field, the labor losses due to making it perform satisfactorily, and additional product or material required to make the system work satisfactorily.

In most companies, the mechanism for rendering decisions to use nonconforming material is the material review board. The board usually consists of supervisory representatives from inspection, project engineering, and quality assurance. On defense contracts, the board will also include a government representative.

Some industries have an outlet for nonconforming material as downgraded merchandise.

Defective product may be made usable by rework or repair. Rework is the performance of extra operations on defective product to make it meet its specification. Repair consists of the extra operations performed on nonconforming product to make it usable even though the repaired product still does not meet its specification. The cost of the extra operations of the rework and repair should be less than the present value of the product; otherwise, the product should be scrapped. The exception to this economic consideration is when the extra expense of renovating operations is performed to satisfy shipping schedules.

The renovating operations are usually performed in an area separate from the regular production facilities. The repaired product should be properly identified and reinspected to ensure not only that the failings have been corrected, but also that the extra handling and operations have not created additional defects.

When the decision is to scrap, certain procedures should be followed. Where economical, good parts should be segregated or disassembled from the defective product. The product to be junked should be separated, packaged, or baled to bring the highest price for the scrapped material.

For control purposes, records should be kept of all costs associated with reworking, repairing, and scrapping operations. Computerized control systems have been developed by some industries to collect, summarize, and analyze the wasteful costs attributed to rework, repair, and scrap operations.

APPRAISING AND CONTROLLING PERFORMANCE OF INSPECTORS

The successful operation of the inspection function depends on the personnel in the organization and their performance.

It is not uncommon that union contracts and management decisions limit the chief inspector's freedom to fill a job opening with the best qualified person that is available. However, inspector job requirements can be set to require applicants to meet tests for visual acuity at long or short range, depth perception, color vision, and extrinsic muscle balance. Training programs can be instituted to teach the neophyte the reading of drawings, interpretation of specifications, and the skillful use of measuring instruments and testing equipment. College programs have been instituted in inspection or quality control technology to provide the trained personnel needed to perform the ever increasingly complex inspection jobs.

The appraisal and control of the performance of inspectors is related to their methods of wage payment. Inspectors may be on a wage incentive system, on measured daywork, on straight daywork, or salaried. When an incentive system is used, it is common to limit the amount of money earned through output and include a measure of inspector accuracy which adds to or subtracts from the quantity bonus earnings. Appraisal in this case consists of maintaining records of the efficiency of both output and accuracy. On measured daywork, the inspector has time standards that have been set by industrial engineering for completing his tasks. Thus the inspector's output efficiency can be calculated. However, the accuracy of the inspection act must be controlled by direct supervision. Very often, the inspector is required to stamp or tag the product with his number after he has inspected it. Customer complaints or quality assurance inspection reports may include the inspector's number found on the defective product. When the inspector is on salary or straight daywork, the supervisor must establish informal times to complete a task to get a measure of the output efficiency. Rotation of inspectors between jobs gives the supervisor a comparison basis for establishing these informal standards. In this case, however, the appraisal and control of performance are almost totally obtained by direct supervision.

CONCLUSION

Inspection and test constitute the critical examination of product to determine conformance to design specifications and workmanship standards. It is also performed on processes and on incoming material to prevent the manufacture of defective product. The inspection function should be properly organized and staffed to ensure that the company's policies on quality are carried out. An effective inspection operation provides economic benefit from (1) its defect prevention activities, (2) the reduction in customer complaints and warranty costs, and (3) the reduction in loss of sales from the customer's dissatisfaction with the product quality. Inspection protects the company's quality reputation.

BIBLIOGRAPHY

Jacobson, H. J., "Management Methods of Inspection Control," *Industrial Quality Control*, July, 1964.
Juran, Joseph M. (ed.), *Quality Control Handbook*, 2d ed., McGraw-Hill Book Company, New York, 1962.
Kennedy, Clifford W., *Inspection and Gaging*, 3d ed., The Industrial Press, New York, 1962.
Meagley, N. G., "Engineering the Inspection of Industrial Processes," *Transactions Sixth Annual Convention, American Society for Quality Control*, 1952, pp. 397–407.
Michelon, Leno C., *Industrial Inspection Methods*, rev. ed., Harper & Row, Publishers, Incorporated, New York, 1950.
Reynolds, E. A., "Modern Inspection Techniques and Automation," *Industrial Quality Control*, June, 1961.
Schilling, E. G., "The Challenge of Visual Inspection in the Electronic Industry," *Industrial Quality Control*, August, 1961.

CHAPTER TEN

Warehousing and Shipping

CREED H. JENKINS *National Manager, Warehouse Operations, Kaiser Aluminum and Chemical Corporation, Oakland, California*

This chapter considers the problems that manufacturing management deals with in carrying out warehousing and shipping functions. The function of warehousing is to store the finished products from the time they are produced until they are shipped. The shipping function includes the final handling operations and the release of the products to the carrier for transport to destination.

The first problem to consider is whether warehousing should be performed at all. It is sometimes best to ship directly from the production lines to the customer; this eliminates the added problems and costs of warehousing. Assuming that warehousing is required, the problems of location, design requirements, and storage layout must be considered. These physical features of warehousing provide the framework within which the material handling and storing functions are performed.

Considered next are the main operations of warehousing: the receiving, storing, and shipping of finished products. The selection and use of equipment to perform these operations efficiently are important. Equipment is as necessary to modern warehousing as it is to modern manufacturing, and its effective use can reduce costs dramatically.

Warehouse performance controls are discussed next, with particular emphasis on space utilization standards. Last, but very important, are the controls to attain and maintain good housekeeping and safe working conditions.

The purpose of this chapter is to give the manufacturing manager practical guidance in effectively managing his warehousing and shipping operations.

WAREHOUSING VERSUS SHIPPING DIRECT

Whether to warehouse or to ship direct from the production lines is the first question which must usually be asked. The answer is more sophisticated than the simple rule: "Provide warehousing only when it is necessary to meet competition's service level." Warehousing has advantages other than improving the delivery time to the customer. In some cases, the cost saving that warehousing permits is more than the added cost of warehousing; a net saving results. In other cases, however, warehousing causes an overall increase in cost, and its use can only be justified in relation to its value in marketing the product. There are three main reasons for warehousing finished products: (1) to permit longer manufacturing runs, (2) to increase availability of the products, and (3) to reduce transportation costs.

Permit Longer Production Runs. In most manufacturing operations, it is important to have long production runs to make possible low unit costs. Modern manufacturing management has often been able to provide lower production costs via expensive equipment and time-consuming machine setups. Once set up, the equipment can produce units fast and at a low cost. It is necessary, however, to produce enough units to amortize the expensive equipment and long setups; otherwise, less equipment or no equipment at all may be the most economical means of production. Thus, the long production run is often a vital factor in achieving low manufacturing costs.

Manufacturing management should recognize the direct relationship between long production runs and warehousing. To avoid long runs because there are no facilities to store the excess products is shortsighted. The required facilities can be acquired at a price; and this price may be less than the saving that would result from the long production runs. There are other factors to consider, such as the investment tied up in the warehouse inventory, the cost of inventory obsolescence, and the like. However, the point is that warehousing, even with all related costs considered, may make possible the lowest total product cost. Manufacturing management should know the cost of warehousing its products, and should consider producing to inventory as an alternative to producing to order and shipping direct to the customer from production.

Increase Product Availability. Perhaps warehousing is most commonly used to increase the availability of products. What is availability, and how important is it?

A product has value to the customer for two reasons: (1) utility and (2) availability. Utility is the feature of being useful. It is the design and physical properties that enable the product to serve as intended. Availability is the feature of being where it is needed when it is needed. One without the other renders the product useless. Warehousing adds value to the product by making it available when needed.

If the sales department can depend on the product being shipped from warehouse stock instead of waiting for it to be produced, it can often sell more of the product. For some products, delivery time is the key factor in the marketing plan. The increased costs incurred by warehousing may be of minor importance compared to the increased sales income that can be realized. On the other hand, warehousing is not necessary to sell all types of products.

Warehousing should be performed only when the cost of warehousing is more than offset by the profits derived from increased sales, or when it is more than offset by savings from longer production runs or from reduced transportation costs. Sales and marketing departments have a natural tendency to exert pressure on manufacturing to warehouse the products they sell, because this provides a valuable tool in selling the products. Company management, which is responsible for profits, should exercise control to prevent warehousing that increases sales but results in a net loss to the company.

Reduce Transportation Costs. An important factor to be considered in the evaluation of warehousing is its effect on transportation costs. Normally warehousing reduces transportation costs. The highest transportation costs are incurred when LTL (less-than-truckload lot) shipments are made long distances from the manufacturing facility to customers. Warehousing makes possible combining of LTL orders into consolidated TL's (truckload lots), permitting the use of the lowest transporation rates. This process is used when the warehouse is located at the mill or plant site. Warehouses to handle the finished products can also be distant from the manufacturing facility but near the market. In this case, the mill or plant ships in carload or truckload quantity the long distance to field warehouses at the lowest possible freight rates; then the high LTL rates are incurred only for the short distance from the warehouses to local customers. This system of distribution permits a significant reduction in costs compared to shipping LTL all the way from the mill or plant to the customer.

In some distribution systems, the freight savings that result through use of warehouses more than offset the total cost of warehousing. The main purpose of warehouses is to reduce transportation costs.

WAREHOUSE LOCATION

The location of the warehouse is an important consideration in a successful warehouse program. The purpose of the warehouse should largely dictate whether it will be located at the manufacturing facility or at a field location near the customers. If the main purpose of the warehouse is to provide a means to absorb long production runs, it probably should be a part of the manufacturing facility. This will avoid extra transportation and duplicate handling. If the main purpose is to provide better delivery service to customers, the warehouse should be centrally located near the customers that it will serve. If the objective of the warehouse is to reduce transportation costs, it can be either at the plant site or in the field. Generally, the opportunities to effect freight savings are greater when the warehouse is located near the customers, where the high cost of LTL shipments can be minimized.

If reducing delivery time to the customer is the most important consideration, probably a field warehouse or system of field warehouses will be necessary. The location and site selection should be based on sound business principles. Too often the selection of a warehouse location is based on the desire of its management to live in a certain area. This is a consideration, but it should be secondary to business reasons that will directly affect the success of the warehouse operation.

Delivery Time Requirements. The service level objective should be determined in relation to the marketing objective. To be competitive, some products must be delivered within hours after the order is placed on the warehouse. For other types of products, the competitive delivery time is measured in weeks. The specific service level for the products to be warehoused should be realistically established.

The proximity to the customers has a direct relationship to delivery time. A warehouse can serve a definable radius of geography in a specified delivery time. This radius will influence the location of warehouses and the number of warehouses needed to serve a certain market.

Market Area to Be Served. The warehouse should be centrally located to the market that it will serve. The market area, including the specific addresses of major accounts and their service requirements, should be supplied by the sales or marketing departments.

Transportation Service. The warehouse should be convenient to common carrier trucking terminals and service routes. Also, the warehouse should be on the proper railroad line, the same one that services the manufacturing facility or one that has good interconnecting service. Easy access to expressways helps reduce transit time and is particularly important if the warehouse or plant has its own trucks.

Importance of Distribution Center Location. The warehouse should be located in or near the nation's distribution centers unless other factors make this undesirable. Certain cities or regions are recognized as distribution centers. These centers have a high concentration of warehouses, truck terminals, and railroad lines. These centers generally offer the best transportation services, they are centers of population and industry, and they have other factors that are important to successful warehouse operations, such as convenient handling-equipment dealers and repair services.

Importance of Industrial Parks. Most new warehouses are built in modern industrial parks. These parks consist of certain defined areas, generally in the suburbs of the major distribution centers, that are developed and promoted to attract light industry and warehousing. The promoters of these areas establish specific building and zoning ordinances to attract and hold the type of business they are after. Some of the advantages of industrial parks are:

1. Carrier service is better. This is because carriers can economically provide regular and reliable service to an area where they have many customers.
2. Neighbors have common interests. Similar businesses have similar requirements that can be filled best when they are together. Such services include security protection, low tax assessments, labor supply, equipment repair service, restaurants, and the like.
3. Facility investment has better protection. Because of the common interest feature, there is greater likelihood that the community will remain desirable for warehousing.
4. More favorable financing can be obtained. Warehouses located in areas that are suitable to warehousing, and that have a good chance of remaining suitable, attract the most favorable financing. The risk is less for the investor.

WAREHOUSE DESIGN AND LAYOUT

The design of the building and the plans for storing the materials that it houses are very important to the efficiency and effectiveness of the warehouse operation. The building should have adequate space with minimum obstructions and proper dock facilities to receive and ship the materials. The layout of the storage should provide for the optimum combination of efficient space utilization and efficient material handing. The building design and materials layout should be the result of careful analysis and planning. Because almost any dry building *can* be used as a warehouse, and materials *can* always be stacked on the floor, there is a tendency to underrate the importance of scientifically designed buildings and planned layouts. These factors are just as important in warehouse operations as they are in manufacturing operations. If the warehouse is to operate as efficiently as manufacturing, it must receive the same application of scientific management.

Size of Warehouse Building. Possibly the most important characteristic of the warehouse building is its size. The building will have a useful life of between thirty and sixty years. To predict exact warehouse requirements over this period just is not possible. The best that can be done is to project requirements as far into the future as practical and provide for reasonable alternatives to meet the changes that may be required. Avoid designing a warehouse that is specialized to meet only immediate requirements. An example of this would be to build a warehouse with only 12 feet height clearance because the products that are now to be warehoused are best stored in bulk less than 12 feet high. Actually, handling and storing equipment is available to store most products much higher than 12 feet. This warehouse with only 12 feet clearance would be definitely obsolete for most other types of storage. Another example is the size of doors that are used for handling equipment. Often door sizes are determined on the basis of present handling equipment and product loads. If equipment or loads change to a larger size, the doors are too small. The cost of putting in larger doors when the warehouse is built is a lot less than the cost of changing them later.

The size of warehouses should be determined both in (1) usable floor space and (2) usable height. The usable surface and the usable height can then be converted to cubic measurement, which really determines the total usable space that is available. The concept of "usable" is very important when referring to warehouse space. For example, columns to support the roof reduce the usable space. High clearance is good only if it can be used; otherwise the cost of building the greater height, heating it, and paying taxes on it will be wasted.

The building configuration that provides for the most economical construction cost in relation to usable space is a combination of a square, equal sides, and the maximum height in which products can be stored. Generally, it is most economical to provide for an increase in future storage capacity by constructing a building that is higher than needed for present requirements, rather than to provide the equivalent area in floor space. A comparison of two different types of building configurations will illustrate this difference.

Building *A*: 100′ long × 100′ wide × 20′ high = 200,000 cubic feet
Building *B*: 400′ long × 50′ wide × 10′ high = 200,000 cubic feet

Building *A* has 400 linear feet of wall and 10,000 square feet of roof and floor. Building B has 900 linear feet of wall and 20,000 square feet of roof and floor. Both configurations provide the same cubic space. Building *B* would cost considerably more to construct. Though the examples used are extreme, the principle illustrated holds true in less dramatic examples. In summary, the construction cost of warehouse space is greatly influenced by the configuration of the building.

Dock Requirements. A main consideration in warehouse design and layout is the rail and track dock requirements. If the commodities to be handled in the warehouse are to be received or shipped by rail, the warehouse must have a rail spur. The availability of a spur or the possibility of having one put in is then of primary importance. Many warehouses do not use rail service, and so they are not confronted with this problem.

With either rail or truck service, a means of getting from the ground level to the bed of the vehicle must be provided. The most common and efficient means of accomplishing this is to raise the elevation of the warehouse floor to the general elevation of the carriers, about 48 inches. However, if it is necessary to bring in fill to attain this elevation, the cost could be high, and alternatives should be considered. A common alternative is to depress the rail spur or truck approach to bring the beds of the carriers level with the warehouse floor. These are called rail or truck wells. Another alternative is to use fixed or portable ramps. In some types of warehousing, the materials can be efficiently transferred using handling equipment such as a crane, conveyor, or lift truck.

Another important consideration is whether or not docks should be enclosed. Docks that are inside the building have the advantage of being usable in any type of weather, and they provide for greater security. The disadvantage of enclosed docks is that they take up valuable inside space. A common compromise is to cover the outside docks. This reduces the cost of the docks and still provides some protection from the weather. Enclosed docks are naturally more common in areas having cold and stormy weather. Influencing factors are cost, weather conditions, security environment, and type and volume of products handled.

Other Important Design Factors. The building size, configuration, and dock facilities may be considered the most important factors in the design of a warehouse. There are, however, many other factors that are important and should be considered.

1. Construction material (concrete block, metal, tilt wall, brick, wood, combinations of these)
2. Outside storage area
3. Landscaping
4. Parking area
5. Columnar spacing inside
6. Lighting
7. Rest rooms—(men, women)
8. Floor load capacity
9. Offices
10. Sprinkler system
11. Lunchroom
12. Air conditioning, heat, ventilation
13. Security
14. Electric wiring and outlets

Storage Racks. Extensive use is made of storage racks in modern warehousing. Racks are most commonly employed to get better space utilization, but they are also justified to improve handling efficiency. Products should be stored in racks when they are too fragile to stack high in bulk storage or when they have an irregular configuration that prevents bulk storage. Products should be stored in racks when they are not carried in large enough quantities to make efficient bulk storage possible; one product type would have to be stored on another to get good space utilization. Racks may also provide means for efficient order picking. A short-term supply of each common inventory item is stored in convenient order picking racks near the shipping area. The backup inventories for the order picking area are stored high on the same racks or in bulk in a remote part of the warehouse.

A discussion of different types of racks is provided under "Warehousing Equipment" in this chapter.

Aisles. Aisles are necessary to provide access to product storage areas and routes to use in moving materials. The amount of space devoted to aisles should be the minimum necessary to provide convenient product access and to travel through the warehouse efficiently. The nature of the warehousing performed is the main factor in determining the ratio or percentage of aisles to total area. Warehouses that have large quantities but relatively few different items can have efficient layouts with between 10 and 20 percent of the area in aisles. Other warehouses that have many different items stored in small quantities require 40 to 60 percent of the area in aisles. The main reason for this difference is providing for accessibility to different items. Other factors influencing the space devoted to aisles are size and type of handling equipment used, size of items stored, and obstacles in the building such as columns, electrical panels, and the like.

The following are some guides to observe in laying out aisles in a warehouse:

1. Aisles should be laid out in straight lines, avoiding curves and jogs.
2. Main travel aisles should lead as directly as possible from the receiving area to the shipping area.
3. Underpasses (racks over aisles) reduce the loss of storage space to aisles.
4. Width of aisles should be determined by allowing for the maximum width or turning radius of the handling equipment and the load, plus an allowance for maneuverability and safety.
5. Aisles should be clearly marked with yellow lines.

A common error made in laying out aisles is to make them wider than is really necessary. An example of this is aisles left wide enough for the turning radius of equipment and load, when actually the racks that border the aisles are always hand stacked and hand picked. Another example is to make all aisles in the warehouse wide enough for the largest piece of handling equipment, although this is never used in many of the aisles.

Fast-moving Items and Load Ratio. Items should be stored where the travel time to handle them makes the minimum contribution to the total warehouse handling time. Often this means that the fastest moving items should be stored nearest the shipping docks. However this is not always the case. The size relationship between the load carried in receiving and the load carried in shipping also determines where materials should be stored. For example, if the fastest moving item in the warehouse was refrigerators, and refrigerators were handled one at a time in both the receiving and shipping operations, it would not reduce total travel time to store them near the shipping dock. If, however, the fastest moving item was small motors, and if they were received on pallets, one hundred per pallet, and shipped one motor at a time, it would save appreciable travel to store the product near the shipping dock. In this case, there would be only one receiving trip to one hundred order filling trips; therefore, it is the distance of the order filling trips that should be kept to a minimum.

Order Picking Areas. An efficient layout for warehouses that have a large number of orders consisting of many small items commonly includes an area designed specifically for fast order picking. Generally, items in this area are grouped in a sequence that permits minimum motion and travel between items. A small supply of each item is stored in convenient-to-reach racks. The backup supply for each item is stored in bulk in the general warehousing area. This arrangement is similar to the stocking plan for large supermarkets. A small supply of each item is conveniently stocked for fast "order picking" by the customer. The backup for these items is kept in a large stockroom at the back of the store. Often special handling equipment, such as conveyors, monorail systems, and flow-through racks, is used to increase the efficiency of the order picking function.

Staging Areas. In most warehousing operations, it is important to stage shipments as they are received and before they are shipped, in order to inspect and check the accuracy of the shipment. Some warehouses try to get by without the extra staging operation, but this should only be done where inspection and accuracy assurance are not important. Staging is also necessary to consolidate orders for combined shipments. Some warehouses combine many different customer orders into one shipment. This is done to reduce transportation costs and because it would be impractical, or at least inefficient, to load more carriers than are absolutely necessary to make shipment.

Regardless of the reason for staging, if it is necessary, an area must be set aside near the docks to accomplish it. In some warehouses, this area will be the most active part of the warehouse. Storage racks conveniently placed near the docks can be efficiently used to hold staged orders. The racks provide an orderly means of keeping the orders separate and they reduce the space necessary for staging. The practice of using aisles to stage orders should be avoided. Aisles can rarely serve effectively both as aisles and as staging areas.

Layout Drawing. The warehouse layout should be planned on a drawing or with templates as a miniature model. It is much easier to determine an efficient layout with a drawing or model than it is to do it in the warehouse with the actual inventories. The layout drawing provides a convenient means of testing ideas without incurring the high cost of actually moving racks and materials. When the best layout has been determined, prints of the drawing can be run to use in the implementation of the plan. Management should require that the master layout plan is followed. If changes are necessary, the master drawing should be updated so that it currently reflects the actual storage plan.

BASIC WAREHOUSING PROCEDURES

The prime responsibility for warehousing is the accountability for inventories. All operations, procedures, and communications related to warehousing should be geared to fulfill this responsibility. Warehousing's responsibility for providing prompt shipping service or for providing a means of absorbing production runs should be fulfilled only after its responsibility for inventory accountability has been accomplished. Inventory accountability in warehousing means being answerable to the company for all goods received by the warehouse. The concept that establishes accountability is simple and direct. Anything received by a warehouse must still be in the warehouse or have been disposed of by authorized and acceptable means.

To ensure accountability, the warehouse's paperwork systems should provide the company accounting department with documents from two different sources for every inventory transaction. For example, materials received from other company suppliers are documented by the shipper's invoice and by the ware-house's receiving report.   Materials received from a manufacturing facility that is adjacent to the warehouse and in the same company are documented by a report of what production transfers to the warehouse and by another report from the warehouse on what it receives.   The company accounting department should reconcile the two different control documents.   Any discrepancies should be isolated and settled.   For all inventory transactions, the following formulas establish accountability.

$$\text{Inventory on hand} = \text{receipts} - \text{shipments}$$
$$\text{Receipts} = \text{inventory on hand} + \text{shipments}$$
$$\text{Shipments} = \text{receipts} - \text{inventory}$$

These formulas show the interdependence of the three functions, and how one can be isolated from the others for control and investigation.

Inventory Records.   Warehousing must keep inventory records to fulfill its responsibilities for accountability.   The warehouse records are also kept to provide inventory status and to signal stock reordering procedures.   Inventory records are also maintained by the company accounting department. These records are kept as the official record of company assets and for other fiscal and control purposes.   Periodically, the two different sets of records must be reconciled.   Also, physical counts must be taken often enough to assure that record inventories truly reflect the actual inventories.

The following data are commonly found on warehouse inventory records:

Relating to receipts:
    Date order placed
    Supplier name
    Order number
    Quantity ordered
    Date shipped
    Carrier
    Freight bill number
    Date received
    Quantity received
Relating to shipments:
    Date purchase order received
    Purchase order number
    Quantity reserved for shipment
    Date shipped
    Carrier
    Bill of lading number
    Quantity shipped
    Balance on hand (changed with each receipt or shipment)

All this information may not be necessary for every warehouse operation. Some of the data may not be required on the records because they are incorporated into the filing system or because the particular warehouse operation does not require them.   Other types of operations may require additional, specialized information.

Warehousing Documents.   Proper documentation of warehouse transactions is essential to fulfill the responsibility for inventory accountability.   The following are some of the basic documents used in warehouse operations.

1. *Bill of Lading.*   This document contains the general description of the commodities shipped: number of packages, bundles, skids, and so on; the

gross weights; and tariff classification. It includes the terms and conditions governing the shipment. The bill of lading is a contract of carriage and requires the signature of both the carrier and the shipper.

2. *Packing List.* This is a list of all items in the shipment, sufficiently detailed to permit the receiver of the goods to identify each product. It may accompany the shipment or be sent separately to the receiver. The receiver often uses the packing list to determine the description and count of the commodities sent by the shipper. It is not used as a check on the carrier; the bill of lading is used for this purpose.

3. *Freight Bill.* This document is prepared by the carrier. It has the same cargo descriptions as the bill of lading and includes the freight charges. The receiver signs the freight bill to acknowledge receipt of goods. Exceptions are noted on it by the receiver if the quantity is incorrect or if there is damage.

4. *Receiving Report.* This is the formal warehouse report of the commodities and quantities received.

5. *Shipping Report.* This is the formal warehouse report of the commodities released for shipment.

6. *Other Documents.* There are many other documents used in warehousing, such as the sales order, a sales request for shipment, and the waybill—a railroad routing and instruction form. In certain cases, more than one form may be combined into a multiform set to avoid having to record common information several times. The combined form increases accuracy of data as well as providing greater paperwork efficiency. Documents that should be considered for combination are the sales order, shipping report, packing list, bill of lading, customer acknowledgement, customer invoice, and any other forms that are prepared using data that are common to the warehouse shipment. Forms should not be combined when the loss of control or extra effort caused is more important than the accuracy and efficiency achieved.

Taking Physical Inventory. Regardless of how accurate the inventory records are or how effective the warehouse security is, the physical count of the inventories must be verified. All inventory transactions are subject to human error. In addition, the nature of warehouse inventories often makes them attractive to thieves. Therefore, methodical checking of physical inventories is essential to fulfill warehousing's responsibility for accountability, and company and legal requirements for accurate records.

How often should physical inventories be taken? The answer depends on how accurately the inventory records are kept and how effective the warehouse security is. If it is necessary to take physical inventories daily to ensure accuracy and security, they should be taken daily. Normally, with good records and sound security, physical inventories are taken only once a year.

The reason for taking physical inventory is to establish precisely the product items and the quantities of each in the warehouse. To achieve this, it is necessary to have well-designed procedures and a means to ensure that they are followed. Listed here are some of the factors to consider in establishing effective inventory taking procedures.

1. *Effective Date.* The physical inventory should commence with the close of business for a specified date. Normally this date is the end of a fiscal year or the end of a specific accounting period, so that the results will coincide with accounting requirements.

2. *Cutoff Points.* Definitions of what will be counted must be established. Examples of this are: that all fully loaded freight cars on the warehousing

siding shall not be counted, and that no outbound shipments shall be made while the physical inventory is being taken.

3. *Products to Be Inventoried.* Not only should the products to be inventoried be specified, but they should also be classified as salable, unsalable, damaged, obsolete, and the like.

4. *Inventory Taking Method.* Two people should work together as a team to take the inventory. One person should identify and count the objects; the other person should record the information on a two-copy inventory form. Objects that are difficult to count should be counted twice, independently, by both persons. The agreed amount should be recorded. A member of the team should sign and date the form. The second copy of the form should be affixed to the objects to show that they have been inventoried. The first copy should be used to compare with the warehouse inventory records. Any discrepancies between record and physical counts should initiate a recount of the material to verify the physical amount.

5. *Accounting Reconciliation.* Accounting should reconcile the physical counts with their inventory records. Differences should be investigated and true amounts established. Both accounting and warehouse inventory records should be adjusted to the true physical inventory counts. Unless differences between the physical counts and accounting records are within established tolerances, corrective action should be taken.

WAREHOUSE EQUIPMENT

Equipment plays a vital role in modern warehouse operations. Handling and storing equipment for warehouse work has undergone dramatic changes. Where warehousing not too long ago was heavy manual work performed in dingy old buildings, it is now more a matter of skilled technicians operating highly efficient equipment in bright, clean, modern facilities. For centuries, warehousemen stored products as high as they could reach, about 7 feet. Even for years after lift trucks were introduced, they were limited to a reach of about 10 feet high. Now it is common to store about 20 feet high with lift trucks, and over 30 feet with stacker cranes.

Although equipment can be found to assist in performing almost any warehousing function, it should be kept in mind that most functions can be performed without equipment. Some warehouse people have an aversion to manual work and believe that anything done manually is inefficient. This is not the case. Some material handling functions are still, and possibly always will be, best performed manually. Those people who have what can be called a "compulsion" for equipment are as wrong as those who use equipment only for work that cannot be performed manually. Both attitudes are wasteful. Equipment should be used to increase man's productivity when the gain is greater than the cost of the tool. It should also be used to make work safer. It should not be used when it cannot be justified economically or for safety reasons.

Although there is an almost endless list of different types of warehouse equipment available, most of it falls into a few general classifications. Basically, it can be divided into that used for handling and that used for storing. Each of these broad classifications can be subdivided. Handling equipment may be classified as floor based or overhead, fixed route or free driving, electric or gas, and so on. Storing equipment may be classified as pallet racks or cantilever racks. There are many variations of each of these classifications, and there is some equipment that does not fall neatly into either class. Warehouse management must be familiar with the many different kinds of equipment available to make material handling and storing more efficient.

Lift Trucks. Lift trucks comprise the most common type of material handling equipment used in warehousing. This equipment has wide acceptance because of its versatility. It can move materials horizontally and vertically; it can move about freely; and with attachments it can pick up, turn, push, and pull all kinds and shapes of materials. The lift truck, sometimes called forklift or power lift, is the "workhorse" of modern warehousing. Some typical lift trucks are shown in Figure 10-1.

There are two general classifications of lift trucks: the type that uses the counterbalance principle for leverage to pick up loads, and the straddle-arm type that gets its leverage from arms with wheels that extend forward under, or to the side of, the load. The counterbalance type uses the front wheelbase as the fulcrum. The machine is designed so that the weight behind the front wheels is greater than the load and mechanics in front of the wheels. The counterbalance type is the most commonly used lift truck be-

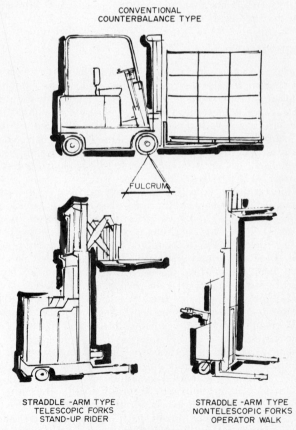

CONVENTIONAL
COUNTERBALANCE TYPE

FULCRUM

STRADDLE -ARM TYPE
TELESCOPIC FORKS
STAND-UP RIDER

STRADDLE -ARM TYPE
NONTELESCOPIC FORKS
OPERATOR WALK

FIG. 10-1. Typical Lift Trucks. (*Reproduced by permission from* Modern Warehouse Management, *by Creed H. Jenkins, McGraw-Hill Book Company, New York, 1968.*)

cause of its versatility. The counterbalance principle also permits lift trucks to be made with almost unlimited lift capacity. Its stability feature enables equipment manufacturers to design units that will reach as high as man's depth perception can practically and safely permit him to use them. Lift trucks with telescopic masts that reach over 20 feet high are not uncommon in modern warehousing.

The main limitation of counterbalance lift trucks is that they require relatively wide aisles to provide clearance for their greater turning radius. It is because of this limitation that the straddle-arm lift trucks, or "narrow-aisle trucks," were developed. For the same capacity, a conventional counterbalance lift truck requires 25 to 50 percent wider aisles than a straddle-arm truck. The disadvantages of the straddle-arm type are that racks and pallets must be designed to allow clearance for the extended arms and that they are not as versatile in loading trucks and in traveling over rough surfaces. Also, problems of stability are encountered in working at heights comparable to those possible with counterbalance design.

There are many variations in the two basic designs which largely overcome their basic disadvantages. Examples of these variations are four-directional lift trucks, side-loader lift trucks, units that the driver walks behind or stands on to ride. Each variation has its advantages and disadvantages. As a general rule, the conventional counterbalance lift trucks are used as multipurpose vehicles where the same trucks must serve many different functions. The straddle-arm, four-directional, and side-loader type lift trucks are more specialized and are used most efficiently when sufficient volume justifies specialization.

Another difference in lift trucks is their source of power: gasoline, compressed gas, or electricity. Normally, the gasoline type costs the least initially, compressed gas slightly more, and electric the most. When operating costs and equipment life are considered, the reverse ranking generally applies. Electric lift trucks are often used when the ignition systems of the gas types can be hazardous. Also, electric lift trucks are used when exhaust fumes are objectionable although compressed gas largely overcomes this objection. Even though the gasoline lift truck costs more to run and produces exhaust fumes, it still is the most commonly used.

Conveyors. Although conveyors are probably more common to manufacturing operations, they find many valuable applications in warehousing. Conveyors are most efficiently used for high-volume material handling, with a fairly constant flow, along a fixed route. Most conveyor systems are designed to specific warehousing requirements.

There are many different kinds of conveyors. The basic differences among them lie in: how they are powered—by gravity or motor; whether they are portable or fixed; and how the materials are carried—on wheels, rollers, belt, slat, screw, and the like. All these variations find application in warehousing. Probably the most common type used in receiving and shipping operations is the gravity-powered, portable, wheel conveyor. Its ready availability in standard lengths from suppliers, its relatively low cost, and the ease of assembly and disassembly are characteristics that contribute to its popularity in warehousing. Far more sophisticated systems are also commonly found, particularly in large-volume warehouses. One of the features of conveyors that makes them such a valuable tool for material handling is that they are relatively easy to equip with automatic control devices. Baggage handling systems at large airline terminals are an example of highly sophisticated conveyor systems that involve many automatic devices and controls. This same type of system finds efficient application in warehouse operations that involve the same type of sorting and cumulation functions.

Cranes. The main advantage of cranes in warehousing is that they provide versatile overhead handling. They can operate independently of the floor. Aisles are not required for maneuvering equipment, and materials can be transported over floor working and storage areas. Cranes also permit handling loads at very high elevations with greater efficiency and safety. Cab or stacker cranes with riders permit the operator to stay above the load or to ride with it.

There are many different kinds of cranes, each designed to accomplish specific functions most efficiently. Possibly the type that offers the greatest advantages to modern warehousing is the stacker crane. The stacker crane is popular because it permits efficient storage at high levels with minimum loss of aisle space and with a relatively high degree of safety. The stacker crane does not have the overall versatility of the conventional lift truck, but for the specific functions cited, it is superior.

There are several basically different stacker crane designs. A common type consists of a vertical column or set of columns that extends from a turntable suspended from a trolley that rides on a bridge. The bridge rides on rails that are supported by structural columns. A load-holding device rides up and down the vertical structure attached to the turntable. An operator can ride with the load to operate the crane, or the system can be designed for control from a remote station, or the system can be further automated to tie into a data processing system. Variations of the stacker design include cranes that ride on rails supported by storage racks, or cranes that ride on rails set in the floor. Another type of stacker system consists of a lift truck that moves up and down the aisles sideways. The four-directional lift truck, which utilizes the straddle-arm leverage principle, and the sideloader, which utilizes the counterbalance principle, are both commonly used with stacker systems. Generally, stacker systems that use lift trucks for the material handling device are less expensive, but they cannot handle and store materials as high as a stacker crane. The lift trucks are more versatile, because they are not confined to a railway, but they generally are not as fast as cranes. Cranes can safely travel under load both horizontally and vertically at the same time. Lift trucks are restricted to one direction at a time.

Other common cranes used in warehousing are the bridge crane, which provides overhead service to a large rectangular area; the jib crane, which provides overhead service to an area defined by the radius of the jib; and mobile and portable cranes, which can be moved as required. Cranes provide the most efficient way, and in some cases the only practical way, of moving certain kinds of materials.

Storage Racks. Apparently because storage racks seem to be such a simple type of equipment, they are too often chosen carelessly. Storage racks are just as important to efficient warehouse operations as handling equipment such as lift trucks, conveyors, and cranes. In addition, storing equipment often requires a greater investment. The acquisition of storage racks should receive the same thorough analysis that is given to handling and manufacturing equipment.

Storage racks are acquired for two basic reasons. The main reason is to increase space utilization. The other is to improve handling efficiency. There are other reasons, such as product protection and good housekeeping, but mainly racks are acquired to take advantage of cubic space and to reduce time in order picking.

Probably the most common type is the *pallet rack* shown in Figure 10-2. It gets its name from its main function, which is to hold pallet loads. The rack consists of upright frames that support sets of load-bearing arms. Although the basic design of pallet racks is relatively simple, there are many specific differences between racks made by different manufacturers. For example, there are pallet racks that cost nearly as much to erect as the purchase price of the racks. Other racks are very easy to put together, and the cost of erection is insignificant. The following factors should be considered in purchasing pallet racks:

Load capacity of both uprights and arms
Spacing between back-to-back rows of racks to allow for overhang of pallets
Length of load-bearing arms—usually two pallet widths plus a minimum of 5 inches clearance per pallet
Height of racks—no greater than the depth perception of lift truck operators
Vertical distance between horizontal arms—about 6 inches clearance above load
Ease of rack erection and ease of arm adjustment
Sets of three horizontal arms instead of the usual set of two arms to accommodate different size pallets
Standardization of pallet racks so that all uprights, bracing, and arms can be used together

Another rack commonly used in warehousing, and one that is becoming more popular, is the *cantilever rack* shown in Figure 10-3. This rack gets its name from the leverage technique used to support the load-bearing arms, which is "cantilever," meaning supported at one end. The rack consists of a row of upright columns, spaced several feet apart, with arms extending from one or both sides of the uprights to form supports for storage. The main advantage of cantilever racks is that they provide a means for long, unobstructed storage. Cantilever racks are particularly efficient for storing long articles such as sofas, rugs, rod, bar, pipe, and sheet.

There are many other types of racks available for warehousing. A few of them are:

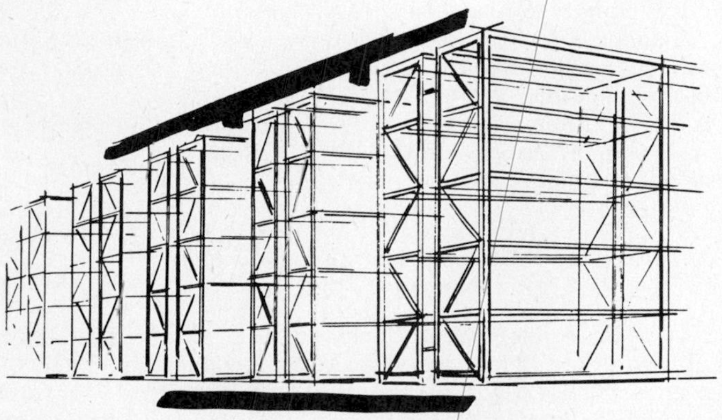

FIG. 10-2. Pallet Racks. (*Reproduced by permission from* Modern Warehouse Management, *by Creed H. Jenkins, McGraw-Hill Book Company, New York, 1968.*)

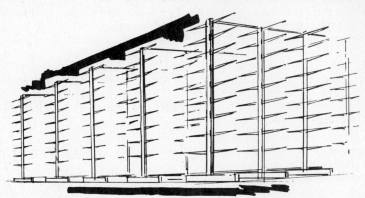

Fig. 10-3. Cantilever Racks. (*Reproduced by permission from* Modern Warehouse Management, *by Creed H. Jenkins, McGraw-Hill Book Company, New York, 1968.*)

Bin Racks. These are like small pallet racks, generally less than 30 inches deep, with solid decking.

Tier Racks. These racks fit on top of pallets to provide a frame that protects the load and provides a means for supporting another pallet.

Flow-through Racks. These racks are similar to bin racks except that they are inclined and use roller conveyors to support and move the stock. Another case moves forward as the front case is removed. The racks are stocked from the back and materials are removed from the front. Their primary purpose is to provide fast order picking.

Drive-through Racks. These are not like flow-through racks. Drive-through, or drive-in, racks are constructed so that a lift truck can place pallets several deep at different elevations. Each tier is supported on cantilever shelves.

A-frame Racks. These are like the cantilever racks described above, except that an A frame is used in place of the single upright column. A-frame racks are generally not as efficient as cantilever racks and are not used for high storage.

Pallets and Skids. The following definitions of pallet and skids are taken from *Modern Warehouse Management* by C. H. Jenkins.

Pallet. A pallet is an elevated platform used for transporting and storing articles; and it is so constructed as to permit tiering for vertical stacking of one pallet load on another.

Skid. A skid is a set of legs or planks used alone or in combination with wheels and platform to elevate and transport articles.

The basic pallet designs are:

Double-faced	Single-wing
Single-faced	Four-way entry
Double-wing	Box

Each of these has special characteristics which make it best for a specific purpose. In addition, there are disposable, or one-way, pallets that are used to transport materials to destination and are discarded after a single use.

Skids are made in even more variations than pallets. They not only exist in standard designs, but are also made to support almost any configuration. They can be made in any shape that enables the load to be elevated and transported.

WAREHOUSING PERFORMANCE CONTROLS

Performance controls for warehousing are essentially the same as those for manufacturing. They consist of budgets, cost standards, handling time standards, space utilization standards, and comparisons of actual performance with these standards. Because budgets, cost standards, and handling time standards are covered elsewhere in the Handbook, only space utilization standards will be considered here.

Space utilization standards are important to warehousing, because in warehousing, the function of storing is as important as the handling function. In manufacturing, secondary importance is generally assigned to the use of space, except when it is needed for another machine. This concept should not carry over into warehousing. To warehousing, space is a commodity. Often the cost of space, in lease or depreciation costs, is more than the salaries of all those employed in the warehouse. The more effectively that space can be used, the more efficient is the warehouse operation.

Space standards are established by determining the proper storage practice and the cubic space required. Allowances are given for all related space such as aisles, building columns, pallets, and staging areas. For example, one case of a product having 1.5 cubic feet measurement might have a space utilization standard of 3.0 cubic feet with the proper allowances added. Also, the standard can be expressed in square feet, instead of cubic feet, by relating the storage practice, including specified height, to floor area. The standard in this example might be 0.15 square foot per case, if the storage practice called for storing the product 20 feet high (3.0 cubic feet ÷ 20 feet high = 0.15 square foot). The use of square feet as the common denominator in space utilization standards has the advantage that it permits easier determination of performance, because it is more convenient to measure in square feet than in cubic feet.

Performance is determined by comparing standard space to actual space. For example, using the standard of 0.15 square foot per case, one thousand cases should require 150 square feet ($1,000 \times 0.15$ ft^2). Now if 200 square feet is used to store the 1,000 cases, the performance would be 75% ($150 \div 200$ ft^2). These figures can be easily converted to costs. For example, if space is worth $0.10 per square foot per month, there would be $5 variance each month ($200 - 150$ ft$^2 \times \$0.10$/ft^2/month).

Some of the uses of standards and performance controls for warehouse operations are:

Measuring and evaluating the handling and storing performance
Determining labor and handling equipment requirements
Determining space and storing equipment requirements
Determining standard costs and charge rates
Planning most efficient operations

HOUSEKEEPING AND SAFETY

Good housekeeping makes a safe and efficient warehouse, and it strongly indicates modern, enlightened management. It is possible to operate efficiently for a short time without due regard for housekeeping and safety, but this condition can only be temporary. High efficiency and poorly kept, unsafe warehouse operations are not compatible. Adequate investment in good housekeeping and safety are prime requisites of modern warehouse management.

The basic requirements of good housekeeping are:

Proper warehouse layout
Orderly stock storage
Clean personnel, equipment, stock, and building
Good waste disposal
Segregated and clearly identified damaged stock
Good lighting
Signs to identify key areas
Aisle and staging area markings
Weather-secure buildings
Liberal use of paint and floor seal

Lack of time to maintain good housekeeping is a poor excuse and should not be accepted. The most efficient warehouse operations have the best housekeeping.

Factors other than good housekeeping that contribute to a safe working environment are proper work assignments, protective devices, safe practices, and effective communications.

Work Assignments. Warehouse supervisors should assign work in such a manner as to assure that it will be carried out safely. Before a job is assigned, the supervisor should appraise what safety factors are involved, such as how many and what kind of personnel are needed, which safe practices apply, and what protective gear should be worn. The supervisor should first decide what he wants done and then clearly convey this to the warehousemen receiving the assignment.

Protective Devices. The purpose of protective and warning devices is to prevent accidents. The old adage, "An ounce of prevention is worth a pound of cure," appropriately applies. Some of the common protective and warning devices used in warehousing are:

Lift truck overhead guard
Handrail guard
Shear, saw, and grinding wheel guards
Removable dock curb
Truck wheel chuck
Trailer jack
Nonslip surfaces
Protective clothing
Warning signs:
   Yellow—caution
   Red—danger
   Green—safe
   Black and white—housekeeping

Safe Practices. Warehouses should have standard, written safe practices for performing all routine handling and storing functions. Being aware of the importance of safety is not enough. There are specific ways to do things that are safer than others. These ways should be established as standard so that they will become habit. A safe practice is determined by analyzing what is to be done, examining the alternative ways of doing it, and then selecting and establishing as standard the safest, best way. Safe practices in warehousing are commonly developed by a safety committee which has representatives from those doing the work as well as those who supervise. The areas in warehousing where standard safe practices should be established include:

Lift truck operation
Hand truck operation
Manual lifting and carrying
Carrier loading and unloading
Use of pallets and skids
Use of small tools
Use of ladders
Crane operation
Conveyor operation

Effective Communications. An effective warehouse safety program must be kept alive with an active interchange of ideas, actions, campaigns, rewards, and penalties. Many excellent programs are written down and put away in an attractive binder but never actually used. To have an effective safety program, every employee must participate, and particularly warehouse management. Everyone in the warehouse must talk and practice safety. Posters and signs should convey certain important messages. A safety committee composed of representatives from all levels of management should actively communicate safety and initiate the correction of safety hazards. A safe practices manual should be made conveniently available to all employees. Formal reports on injury and accidents should be prepared, and the information gained should be used to make the warehouse a safe and healthy place in which to work.

BIBLIOGRAPHY

Bosler, Robert W., "Storeskeeping and Warehouse Management," in H. B. Maynard (ed.), *Handbook of Business Administration*, sec. 6, chap. 9, McGraw-Hill Book Company, New York, 1967.
Jenkins, Creed H., *Modern Warehouse Management*, McGraw-Hill Book Company, New York, 1968.

CHAPTER ELEVEN

Plant Security

RICHARD H. DEHAAN   *Director of Security, Fred Meyer, Inc., Portland, Oregon*

Reliable estimates place theft and fire losses in American industry at over $3 billion annually. Although the professional thief accounts for a sizable amount of this total loss, the overwhelming majority is attributable to the nonprofessional—the average working man or woman—and the staggering loss increases each year.

A considerable number of firms yearly are forced into bankruptcy because of the losses suffered. These statistics deserve the attention and energies of the best men in the company. Most of a company's loss can be prevented if company executives will devote adequate budget, thought, and energy to the security function. This chapter is intended as a guide which, if followed, will greatly reduce losses and increase profits.

PLANT SECURITY

Up to the early part of World War II, plant security to many managements meant someone with a law enforcement background setting up and running a guard service. As a matter of fact, it was difficult if not impossible to find the security function on a company's organizational chart. Security, however, has become a highly trained professional operation. It is a function that no large business can afford to be without, because it more than pays its way. Although in the past security work emphasized the detection of dishonesty, it is now recognized that attention must be centered on the prevention of loss.

A security man must be a man of administrative ability. A police background is not enough. A military background is not enough. The security administrator must be adept in developing and integrating the security program with management's operations and objectives. The security man should report directly to a member of top management, if not to the top man in the firm.

The Security Department. The security department should be set up to protect the properties and personnel of the company, and of others who have permission to be on the premises, from loss and injury. It should operate twenty-four hours a day, every day of the year. The security department's objectives and how they are achieved are shown by Figure 11-1.

To establish a security department, the following alternatives should be considered.

1. Hire an experienced security administrator.
2. Have an executive placement service secure an experienced security administrator.
3. Engage the services of a security consulting firm. A security agency can:
   a. Make a security survey of the plant and systems, if needed, and recommend a profitable security program
   b. Establish contact with a qualified security specialist

Security Consultants. Before the services of a security consultant are engaged, the type required must be determined. There are three choices:

1. The consultant who will conduct a study and recommend a course of action
2. The consultant who will undertake a study, develop recommendations, and put the accepted recommendations into action
3. The consultant who represents a manufacturer or a service

If the last mentioned is the type of consultant desired, it will generally be advantageous to engage the services of not one "services and products" consultant, but several, and to let each know that he is competing with the others.

When selecting a security consulting firm, care must be exercised to choose a firm of the highest ethical and professional standards and technically skilled in all phases of security. References should be obtained and checked closely.

If a problem of theft within the plant is suspected, it is unwise to attempt to solve the problem unaided. The services of a qualified security consulting firm should be obtained to isolate the cause and take whatever remedial action is agreed upon. Industrial theft is an extremely sensitive situation and can backfire into even greater problems unless it is handled with skill and care.

Getting Acceptance for the Security Activity. Not all members of management can be expected to accept a security proposal readily nor to be presold on the need for it. It is therefore important to stress the benefits to be derived from the security program.

The benefit that will sell the security proposal to management is to show how it will contribute to company profits. This is the language that managers understand and the area in which they are most interested.

Employees, quite naturally, often resist a firm's security function and regulations in the same manner that human beings oppose law enforcement. Employees will question a firm's motives and complain about security regulations, but they usually accept them as long as the regulations are uniformly enforced.

To sell security to employees, the security department itself must:

1. Stress the safety and general welfare of the employees and their families
2. Make employees feel at ease with the security department's human

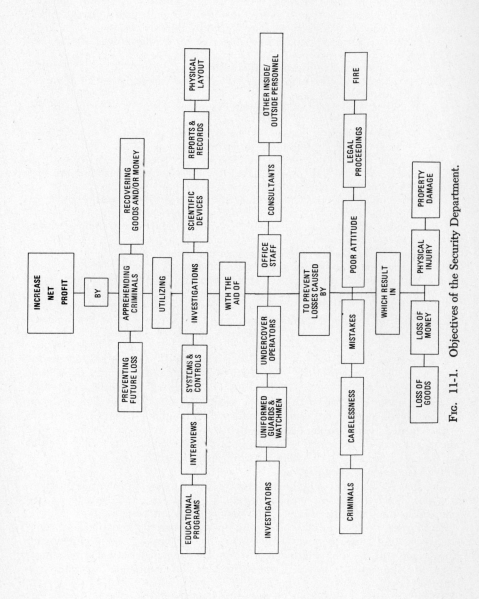

FIG. 11-1.　Objectives of the Security Department.

approach and understanding of the problems involved in attempting to make a profit

3. Impress employees with management's alertness and concern over problems of security
4. Impress on them the advantages of working for a company that recognizes honesty and integrity and practices what it preaches
5. Make employees feel that the company is for them and not against them
6. Tie their job security to the continuation of company profits, and the continuation of company profits in some part to the efforts of the security function and procedures

There are a number of ways of gaining support for the security department, which can be employed as needed. These include:

1. Personal example
2. Induction training for new employees
3. Security manuals
4. Security bulletins
5. Security signs and displays
6. Personal contacts
7. House organ
8. Stuffers in paycheck envelopes
9. Meetings incorporating movies, slides, displays, demonstrations, tape-recorded interviews, speeches, and even lectures by professional thieves

THE SUPERVISOR'S MORAL RESPONSIBILITY

Extremely important to the profitable operation of the business is the leadership role of the supervisor. How he acts will determine the patterns of behavior of those who work for him. His is a serious responsibility. He must set an example of honesty and integrity for his people. He must operate his firm's systems without fear or favor.

It is said that the majority of people seek the motivating guidance for their behavior from others. They look outside themselves for their answers to moral questions. The conscience of these people consists of conforming to the beliefs and actions of those with whom they associate and of those to whom they look for guidance. The actions and beliefs of others become the solutions to their problems. It is on the basis of this emulation of others that they make their decisions.

This conformity increases criminal contamination: that is, one dishonest employee infects another employee. Soon there are several dishonest employees. The disease spreads! Because people must conform, they should be given the opportunity to conform with good principles—principles of honesty and integrity—set up by the company and practiced and enforced by the supervisor. The supervisor must assume the duty of setting moral standards for his people. If he does his job well, all within the firm will profit.

HIRING PRACTICES

It is important to screen well before hiring. A detailed employment application form should be used. It should require the applicant to account for all time for at least the past fifteen years, including beginning and departing dates and specific reasons for leaving all employers. A statement such as: "Were you ever arrested for causes other than violation of traffic regulations? _____" should be included. Immediately above the space for the applicant's signature, a paragraph similar to the following should be inserted.

It is understood that my employment is based upon the truthfulness of the statements contained in this application, and any misrepresentation or omission of facts called for in this application shall constitute cause for immediate discharge. I hereby authorize (the company) to make a complete investigation of all statements contained on this application for determination of fitness for employment.

Signed_____

Preemployment Interview. In the personal interview with the applicant, each item on the application should be reviewed. Particular attention should be paid to:

1. Previous employment. Are there any time lapses between jobs? How long? What was he doing during that time? Can applicant adequately explain? Are his reasons for leaving past positions reasonable and consistent? Discuss this with him. Is he giving the real reason? Was he ever fired?

2. Former employers. Are some of his former employers now out of business? Perhaps he did not work for them as stated, or perhaps he does not want them checked. Has he been in business for himself? If so, why not now? Is applicant new in city? Does he or she have a spotty employment record? If so, it may be an indication of a drifter. Why did he come to this city? If the "ARREST" question is answered in the affirmative, get all the details.

Psychological Tests. Many firms use psychological tests before employing a person, if for no other reason than to isolate those applicants who are: (1) overly concerned with material or monetary gain or wealth, or (2) emotionally unstable or without a great amount of self-control (these persons could succumb to temptation). Firms using such tests are able in most cases to avoid hiring the potentially dishonest employee, and they thereby prevent future problems and loss.

Background Investigation. It is best to employ the services of a reputable agency to do an extensive personal background investigation on each applicant. Job date verifications and reasons for leaving prior positions are important. However, equally important are things such as: How many debts does the applicant have? What are his personal habits? Is he a gambler? Alcoholic? Ladies' man? Does applicant have a criminal record? Most companies do not have the time or resources to conduct such a thorough background investigation on each applicant. A reputable investigative firm specializing in preemployment work can do it for the company and can prevent many future problems.

POST-HIRING PRACTICES

Before beginning work, every employee should be thoroughly instructed in the general rules of the firm, especially as they apply to safety, personal conduct, and causes for discharge. If possible, an acknowledgement, signed by the employee, that the rules and causes for discharge have been reviewed with and are fully understood by him should be made a part of his permanent personnel file.

The new employee should also be informed of the benefits of working for the firm. He should know in advance what is expected of him and what he in turn can expect from the company.

Bonding Employees. At best, the system of internal controls can make embezzling by employees difficult but not impossible. A necessity for the progressive company is fidelity bond protection to guard against financial loss through employee fraud. The purpose of the fidelity bond is to indemnify the company for loss of money or other property occasioned by dishonest acts of its bonded employees. Each employee should be bonded for an amount calculated to offset potential thefts.

There are a number of different forms of fidelity insurance available to meet all requirements. An insurance carrier can suggest the one best suited to the company.

Prosecuting Dishonest Employees. Upon conclusive evidence of dishonesty, dishonest employees should be prosecuted. It is important to let them know that dishonesty will not be tolerated. Merely discharging an employee found committing a dishonest act is not enough and can result in increased dishonesty and losses. Failure to prosecute sets a bad example for others.

PLANT PHYSICAL SECURITY

There are certain physical considerations which are important to plant security. These involve getting into and out of the plant.

Perimeter

1. A fence to surround the entire area that is to be protected is most helpful.
2. The fence should be either high enough to thwart intruders or protected at the top with barbed wire.
3. The fence should be so designed that no one can crawl under it.
4. The fence should be kept in good repair at all times.
5. Materials, trash receptacles, incinerators, and the like that could be used in scaling the fence should be kept a safe distance away.
6. Gates should be solid and in good repair.
7. Gate hinges should be secure.
8. Possibly the dock or wharf area should also be fenced.

Doors

1. All unused doors should be secure.
2. Door frames must be strong and securely in place.
3. Glass in back doors and similar locations should be protected by wire or bars.
4. All doors should be designed so that the lock cannot be reached by breaking the glass or a light sash panel.
5. Hinges should be so designed or located that the pins cannot be broken.
6. Lock bolts should be so designed or placed that they cannot be pried back with a thin instrument.
7. The locks should be designed or the frames placed so that the doors cannot be pried by splitting the frame.
8. Bolts should be protected or constructed so that they cannot be cut.
9. Locks must be securely mounted so that they cannot be pried off.
10. Locks to the doors must be in good working order.

11. Padlock hasps should be constructed so that the screws cannot be removed.
12. The hasps should be heavy.
13. Keys should be in the possession of trusted personnel only, strictly controlled, and of the type that cannot be duplicated except at the factory.

Windows

1. Easily accessible windows should be protected by gratings or bars.
2. Unused windows should be permanently locked.
3. Windows not protected by bars should be kept locked.
4. Window locks should be designed or so located that they cannot be opened by breaking the glass.
5. The use of glass brick in place of windows which are permanently closed is advisable.

Other Openings

1. Unnecessary skylights should be eliminated.
2. Accessible skylights should be protected with gratings, bars, or the like.
3. Roof hatches should be properly secured.
4. Doors to the roof or elevator penthouses should be in good condition and properly locked.
5. All ventilator shafts or vent openings should be protected.
6. Entrances to sewer or service tunnels should be protected.
7. Fire exits and escapes should be so designed that a person can leave easily but would have difficulty in entering.

Lighting. Above all, sufficient high-powered lighting to illuminate the entire area after dark is a necessity.

Plan Plant Physical Security in Advance. It is advisable to plan for the protection of goods, supplies, and equipment with the architects and security advisors before actual building, remodeling, or redesigning the plant. This can result in a substantial saving in the cost of installing security facilities. Installation or addition of some of the newer electronics systems covering exposed walls, ceilings, and floors through vibration detectives, sonic methods, radar, or black light systems will provide improved security.

UNIFORMED SECURITY GUARDS

Uniformed guards are used mainly to safeguard the firm's property against external and internal hazards such as fire, accidents, thefts, vandalism, and sabotage. In deciding whether to have uniformed security guards, the following points should be the basis for the decision.

1. The location of the plant or warehouse
2. Type of products produced
3. The risk of loss
4. The pertinent provisions in any government contract that the firm may have

If the decision is to have uniformed security guards, should the company recruit, hire, train, and carry on the payroll its own guards, or should it obtain guards on contract from an outside guard agency? In making a decision, the following points should be considered.

Company Guards
1. Provide a closer control of personnel.
2. Afford a more flexible system for experimenting with new ideas.
3. Promote better coordination within the entire plant.
4. Costs of recruitment, training, uniforms, guns, badges, insurance, vacations, and other fringe benefits, plus costs of organization and supervision, can be considerable and unpredictable.

Agency Guards
1. Seem to be more acceptable to company personnel.
2. A more thorough security program can be planned by experts of a competent agency.
3. The exact cost of an agency's services can be determined.
4. Some agencies provide receptionists and hostesses who are well trained in security matters.
5. The firm should make sure that it receives from the guard agency a "Hold Harmless" agreement which will relieve it of liability in the event of error by one of the agency's guards.

Uniformed Guard Requirements. Uniformed guards must:
1. Look professional.
2. Be mentally alert and physically fit.
3. Possess integrity above reproach.
4. Be capable of making intelligent decisions.
5. Be well trained in all phases of their duties.
6. Be properly licensed and thoroughly trained in the use and necessity of caution in the use of firearms. Firearms should be used as deterrents rather than as deadly weapons.

Specific Guard Duties. Guard duties and responsibilities such as the following must be well defined and manualized.
1. Be thoroughly familiar with fire and alarm systems, sprinkler systems, and location of fire extinguishers.
2. Be familiar with and alert for accident, fire, and security hazards.
3. Check premises for signs of a break-in or conditions conducive to breaking in.
4. Check employees' adherence to safety and security rules.
5. Administer emergency first aid.
6. Check employees, visitors, cars, and trucks entering and departing the premises.
7. Be alert for suspicious persons or autos nearby.
8. Be familiar with and post locations of equipment, switches, and exits.
9. Train nonguard personnel in security, fire, and safety techniques to be followed in the event of disasters.

General Guard Supervision. It is advisable to alternate guard positions so as to prevent complacency and overfriendliness with company personnel. Routes of guards should also be varied so as to avoid a set pattern that could be discovered by someone with ulterior motives.

If possible, guards should report to a central office or punch a recording clock at stated intervals. These reports indicate that everything is in order and that tours are being made on schedule.

Guards should be required to submit written inspection reports and detailed reports of all irregularities.

It is often worthwhile to hold regular meetings with the guards to discuss possible security problems and to let each relate his experiences. In this way, each benefits from the experiences of others.

Guards, like other employees, need to be checked periodically for integrity, loyalty, and compliance with duties. If company guards are employed, there must be a competent person to supervise the function. If guards are contracted for with an outside agency, a high-level member of the management team must be appointed to whom the supervisor of the guards must report.

TRUCK DRIVERS AND TRUCK SECURITY

As a group, truck drivers, by the very nature of their work, have access to most of the company's physical assets. Freedom of drivers on docks and adjoining sections should be restricted. Drivers should not be allowed to take trucks home at night or to park their own autos near where trucks are parked for the night.

Loading and receiving docks should be kept clear of merchandise to prevent placement of "extra" items on trucks. All truck loadings and receivings should be closely supervised. See that trucks depart promptly after loading or unloading.

If possible, trucks should be sealed or padlocked promptly after loading. A reliable person, other than the driver, should apply the seal or lock the padlock. If trucks are coming in sealed, make sure that they arrive sealed. A reliable person, other than the driver, should remove and record the seal.

Outside areas in which trucks are to be parked during periods of darkness should be brightly and completely lighted.

Truck Control. Recorders are available for installation in trucks which will record the speed at which the truck is driven, how long at that speed, and at what time. The recorder also shows the number and duration of stops made. These recorders are locked. Driver tampering en route should be made a matter for disciplinary action.

As a system check, many companies deliberately route an item or a dummy package to the wrong destination to see if the item is returned to point of origin by the driver.

Truck Audits. It is expensive and difficult to follow and observe delivery trucks, but in the case of company-owned delivery trucks or an exclusive contract carrier, this function should be performed periodically. Such a check gives an opportunity to observe driving habits and courtesy of the drivers. Irregularities such as visits to bars, gathering of drivers, visits to the drivers' homes, unauthorized delivery or pickup, and wasted time can be discovered with these audits.

SECURITY IN WAREHOUSING

No item is too small or too large, too costly or too cheap, that it cannot be or has not been stolen. Much merchandise is stolen from the warehouses which keep business and industry moving.

Many warehouse thefts can be prevented, however, with an effective security program. Such a program must be based first on a sound warehouse operation. Other factors that affect the security program and must be considered when thinking in terms of warehouse security are:
1. Operational layout
2. Control and accountability
3. Inventory and spot checking
4. Shipping and receiving techniques
5. Segregation of attractive items
6. Waste and scrap control

The warehouse layout should afford the maximum number of possible observation aisles. All aisles should permit a clear line of sight from one end to the other.

Control and inventory systems will vary widely from plant to plant. Whatever type of system is in use, it should be made to serve the security program. Inventory and spot checking can alert management to warehouse thefts before they reach serious proportions.

Items particularly susceptible to theft because of their size, usefulness, or value should be placed in storage areas which can be kept under observation easily by supervisory personnel. These special areas should also be kept under lock and key, and special periodic inventory checks should be made of them.

Waste and scrap provide many opportunities to hide items which are stolen from the warehouse and picked up later. Collection of waste and scrap material should aways be carefully supervised to protect against possible collusion between the employees and the persons responsible for disposal. Particular attention should be paid to the drivers and vehicles that are used in the collection of waste and scrap.

Proper warehouse security will more than pay for itself and show a profit by eliminating heavy loss.

SECURITY IN THE SHIPPING AND RECEIVING FUNCTIONS

The shipping and receiving functions need careful regulation and supervision. Where possible, the shipping and receiving functions should be separated.

Shipping and receiving doors are generally out of the department management's sight. Therefore it is often desirable to incorporate a set of lights connected with the doors through a control panel which causes a light to flash in the event that a door is open.

Doors must be kept locked when not actually in authorized use. Keys to the shipping and receiving doors should be kept only by supervisory or management personnel.

Employees should not be allowed to exit through nor park their autos near the shipping or receiving doors. Unauthorized persons should not be allowed in shipping or receiving areas.

Freedom of truck drivers on the shipping and receiving docks and adjoining areas should be restricted, and strict lines should be defined beyond which drivers may not venture. Uniformed guards to oversee the shipping and receiving docks should be considered.

Where possible, all shipping and receiving operations should be performed only in those areas so designated for these functions.

Shipping. The following routines contribute to security at the shipping point.
1. Proper paperwork should always accompany items ordered and prepared for shipment.
2. Order forms and invoices should be numbered in sequence with perforated numbers.
3. An automatic numbering and dating machine should be utilized on bills of lading, shipping orders, shipping labels, and related papers, using the same number as on the invoice. All numbers in sequence should be checked and accounted for.
4. Only one person should be designated to authorize shipments.
   a. All items going into delivery trucks should be physically checked by this person.

    b. This person should not be allowed to take customers' orders or make deliveries.

5. Use of personal autos for deliveries should not be allowed.
6. "Load-out" area should be kept free and clear of all other merchandise.

Receiving. Security requirements indicate that the following receiving practices should be established.

1. All items received should be checked against purchase order, item for item.
2. A receiving record should be made immediately upon receipt of the incoming shipment.
3. Only one person should be entrusted with the responsibility of checking in merchandise.
4. After acceptance of delivery, merchandise should be removed immediately from the receiving area.
5. Receiving department personnel should not perform purchasing duties.

TRADE SECRETS—THEFT AND PREVENTION

A "trade secret" is defined as "any formula, pattern, device, or compilation of information which is used in one's business, and which gives one an opportunity to obtain an advantage over competitors who do not know it or, knowing it, neglect to use it." Generally, it relates to the production of goods such as "a machine or formula for the production of an article."

Industrial espionage is a method used by many businessmen to obtain information about a competitor's new processes, products, materials, and internal operations through many and varied schemes, devices, and techniques.

Sources of Information about the Company's Business

1. Employees and former employees.
2. Counterparts. They exchange information through direct association and at conventions, seminars, and other meetings.
3. Truck drivers who make deliveries to the plant.
4. Salesmen. In some organizations, the gathering of competitive information is a normal part of the salesman's job; in other organizations, information gathering is the salesman's only job.
5. Suppliers. The supplier's desire to better his position with his customer often makes him a furnisher of competitive data.
6. Consultants. Advertising, marketing, and other business specialists sometimes pass on important knowledge about competitors.
7. Waste paper. Drawings, memos, reports, and other documents carelessly discarded as waste can be used by a professional to reconstruct a great deal of the company's activities.

Unfortunately, too many businessmen assume the attitude that their firm's internal workings are either unworthy or in some way immune to theft. All too frequently, they wait until competition has driven them to the brink of bankruptcy before they wake up to the realization that a well-planned and well-executed security program might have meant the difference between success and failure. Firms which are most dependent upon the quality and quantity of their research and development for their competitive position are those most subject to thievery by the trade secret thief.

Some Preventive Measures. There are a number of steps that can and should be taken to discourage the theft of trade secrets.

1. Beginning with the employee's first day and continuing throughout his employment, his supervisor must constantly impress upon him the need for confidentiality with respect to company business, and particularly with respect to trade secrets which the employee may possess.

2. All employees having contact with trade secrets must sign a secrecy agreement, preferably a statement of agreement that, should he leave his present position, he will not work for another firm in a field identical to the one in which he is presently employed, for a stipulated period of time.

3. Speeches and papers should be cleared.

4. All documents containing trade secrets which are to be distributed internally should be clearly labeled with confidential legends and serially numbered.

5. Access to highly important documents should be limited.

6. Control should be kept of visitors.

7. After-hours entrance and departure of personnel should be controlled and recorded, and this record should be reviewed daily.

8. Supervisors must be trained to look for any unusual changes in the attitudes or habits of employees working under them who have access to trade secrets.

High employee morale, integrity, and loyalty are essential to any operation that must protect trade secrets.

SAFEGUARDING VITAL RECORDS

Vital records are those necessary to ensure the survival of the business. They actually constitute only about 2 percent of the firm's records. Therefore it is essential that these vital records be given maximum protection from every disaster, including nuclear.

What records must a company have to continue to function? This varies depending upon the type of business and its complexity, but there are certain fundamental records vital to any corporate organization. For instance, the incorporation certificate, the bylaws, the stock record books, the board of directors' minutes, and certain corporate finance records are vital to any corporation. A manufacturing organization will in addition require engineering records, feasibility and marketing study reports, work processes and procedures, accounts receivable and accounts payable, blueprints, noncurrent payroll records, lists of employee skills required, and similar information.

Selecting the Vital Records. There are three basic questions that should be answered in determining which records are vital:

1. What information is vital?
2. Which records reflect this information?
3. How can these records best be protected?

Most companies assume that in the event of a disaster they would require those records which would enable them to:

1. Resume operations
2. Recreate the company's legal and financial position
3. Fulfill their obligations to their stockholders, employees, and any outside interests

Each company will need to analyze its own operations and its own records to determine which are necessary to the firm's continued existence.

Methods of Safeguarding Vital Records. Vital records may be kept in vaults or safes at the main facility or in a secure location separate from the main facility. These vital records may be in the original form or in duplicate form. Duplication may be by any process—microfilm, magnetic tape, disc pack, punched cards, or photocopy—depending upon the size and volume of the records to be reproduced, how frequently they are to be updated, and like factors.

Regardless of the form, the vital records must be stored in safes or vaults which are specifically designed for the preservation of these records.

Safeguarding Classified Government Information. Companies which have contracts with the Federal government may be required to follow certain procedures and provide suitable facilities for safeguarding classified information. Further details on the necessary course of action for companies with Federal contracts are available in the Department of Defense publication, *Industrial Security Manual for Safeguarding Classified Information.*

Safes. Four out of ten companies in the United States would, in the event of a major fire, be forced out of business owing to loss of irreplaceable records. It is estimated that as many as 70 percent of American firms do not have or do not properly use adequate fire-resistive safes and vaults.

Papers untouched by fire can be destroyed by heat. Water alone can reduce paper to pulp. Magnetic tape and microfilm are even more vulnerable; heat damages tape and film at only 150 degrees—lower than the setting of most sprinkler systems. Humidity, even without heat, damages tape and film; and the combination can be fatal.

There are two basic types of safes: fire-resistive and burglary-resistive. Modern fire-resistive and burglary-resistive safes protect longer, protect better, and offer many more safeguards than the older safes, but there is no single safe on the market that provides protection for everything that requires it. Paper records need one kind of protection, negotiables another, and magnetic tape and microfilm still another.

A "right" choice when selecting a safe for a particular company is extremely important. It must be one designed to fit the company's specific needs, one that can be depended upon to do the job which must be done.

Fire-resistive Safes. The safe that is to contain irreplaceable paper records should have the Underwriters Laboratories (UL) fire protection label. These fire-resistive safes are tested by Underwriters Laboratories for three things: fire endurance, explosion, and impact.

There are three classes of fire-resistive safes. The classes and their fire endurance specifications are as follows:

Class A: 2000 degrees—4 hours
Class B: 1850 degrees—2 hours
Class C: 1700 degrees—1 hour

Burglary-resistive Safes. Ninety-five percent of all safe burglaries involve fire safes. This figure reflects the sad fact that too many safes are used for purposes for which they were not designed.

In purchasing a burglary-resistive safe, consideration must be given to the amount of cash normally held on hand, the length of time that it is held, and the location of the safe. If fire safes are used to hold cash, insurance premiums should be increased by at least 10 percent.

No burglary-resistive safe or money chest is manufactured with a rating less than Class C. Class D rated money chests are no longer manufactured. A Class E rated chest is constructed to resist ripping or cutting with ordinary hand tools. A Class ER rated chest is constructed to resist cutting or ripping and also punching and drilling. A Class F rated chest, in addition to having the desirable qualities of the ER chest, is also designed to resist torch attack. Class G is a rating applied to walk-in vaults such as those used in banks. Class

H and I rated chests are of special construction for high security and offer resistance to extreme and prolonged burglary attack. It is important to know that the above ratings must be in the form of an Underwriters Laboratories (UL) label attached securely to the chest and bearing the Underwriters Registry number for that particular burglary-resistive chest. All present-day burglary-resistive safes are registered for insurance purposes, and specifically govern both the allowable amount of coverage and the cost of such coverage.

A *Third Type of Safe*. The data processing storage equipment safe is classified as a fire-resistive safe. Because of this, and the fact that it is sealed against humidity and moisture, it provides adequate protection and is considered an absolute necessity for the storage of magnetic tapes and microfilm.

FIRE PREVENTION

Loss by fire amounts to over $2 billion annually. It is essential that top management give the fire protection side of security more attention. Top executives must realize that good fire security can, in the long run, save the firm lost man-hours, lost production, and valuable physical assets and help to lower insurance rates. To have an effective fire safety program, top management must desire such a program, encourage it, support it, and participate in it.

Generally speaking, security executives do not pay adequate attention to fire prevention and protection problems. All employees must be conditioned to the need for a fire safety program, the way it affects them, and their part in the program. They must then be made to see how their part may make or break the entire program.

Precautionary Measures. Good management practices can help a firm receive full reimbursement for a fire loss. The following steps will aid the insurer to expedite claims and will substantially reduce losses.

1. Make accurate monthly reports to the insurer of the value of inventories.
2. Have adequate insurance protection on customers' and other firms' property which may be in the custody of the company.
3. Safeguard, in an area separate from the plant's main premises, a duplicate set of those records which will enable substantiation of the loss claim with a minimum of delay.
4. Make sure that the insurance policies protect the firm against all the hazards that could cause serious financial loss.
5. Maintain an up-to-date appraisal of buildings and machinery. This appraisal should be prepared by a reputable appraisal firm.

Fire Alarm Systems. Many different types of fire alarm systems are available:

1. Sprinkler supervisory and water flow alarm service automatically detects water flow and summons the fire department. It also maintains a continuous automatic check on shutoff valves and other elements controlling water supply and distribution.
2. Automatic fire detection and alarm service detects fires and automatically summons the fire department.
3. Manual fire alarm service provides manual fire alarm boxes on premises for the prompt notification of the fire department.
4. Automatic smoke detection and alarm service.
5. Automatic heating and industrial process supervisory service.

Fire Training. A fire training program should have two kinds of objectives: emergency and general.

Emergency Objectives
1. Sound in-plant alarm.
2. Notify fire department.
3. Fight fire.
4. Begin evacuation of building.

Groups of well-trained employee-firemen volunteers many times are of invaluable aid in holding fire loss to a minimum. They are often more effective than the local fire department because not only are they on the spot, but they also are familiar with plant equipment and nearby hazards. However, there should be no delay in calling the fire department.

There should be a master evacuation plan. All employees should be completely familiar with every detail of the plan. Advance assignments should be made to personnel with respect to:
1. Locking all doors, windows, and other openings
2. Shutting off machinery and other equipment
3. Protecting records and documents

Evacuation drills can be used to familiarize employees with what is expected of them during an emergency. This plan should be as simple, quick, and clearly defined as possible.

General Objectives
1. Teach good fire prevention practices.
2. Demonstrate use and care of fire extinguishers and interior hose lines.
3. Instruct all employees as to location and operation of fire doors and cutoffs.

A fire safety manual, designed to be the textbook of the training program, should be prepared.

Fire Department. Professional guidance can usually be secured from local fire departments on the placement of hose lines, fire extinguishers, and fire prevention and detection devices. Guidance should be obtained and policies set up on good housekeeping practices to eliminate safety and fire hazards in the plant.

CONCLUSION

The security function should be integrated into the entire corporate operation. It should be the eyes and ears of management. It should be included in policy making and planning and should be consulted when new physical facilities and systems are being considered. The results will be progressive and profitable.

BIBLIOGRAPHY

Brenton, Myron, *The Privacy Invaders*, Coward-McCann, Inc., New York, 1964.
Gocke, B. W., *Practical Plant Protection and Policing*, Charles C. Thomas Publisher, Springfield, Ill., 1957.
Hartung, Frank E., *Crime, Law, and Society*, Wayne State University Press, Detroit, Mich., 1965.
Rogers, Keith M., *Detection and Prevention of Business Losses*, Arco Publishing Company, New York, 1962.
Security World magazine.
Wade, Worth, *Industrial Espionage and Misuse of Trade Secrets*, Advance House Publishers, Ardmore, Pa., 1964.

CHAPTER TWELVE

The Factory Service Function

HERBERT C. GLOEDE   *Manager of Manufacturing Operations, Asia-Pacific, International Business Machines Corporation, Fujisawa, Japan*

In the high-technology industries, a factory service function has been found necessary to perform certain work that may be beyond the capabilities of the conventional industrial engineering and plant engineering and maintenance functions. Its main goals are to provide maximum equipment availability at the lowest cost and with the optimum utilization of available manpower. This chapter describes the factory service function and how it satisfies these goals.

The activities of a factory service function will be governed by the manufacturing problems and processes existing in a given company. Among those that may be included are manufacturing engineering, tool and test equipment maintenance, instrument services, quality laboratory, measurement standards laboratory, and failure analysis and defect reporting. These will be discussed in this chapter.

MANUFACTURING ENGINEERING

An integral part of most factory service groups is the manufacturing engineering arm that supports the production line or factory floor. As used here, manufacturing engineering is the function which provides the technical link between the development and the manufacturing organizations. Its responsibilities involve the design of tools, test equipment, and the processes necessary to produce a product of high quality at an economic cost.

In a broad sense, manufacturing engineering's responsibilities can be defined as providing the manufacturing systems required to deliver quality products in a timely fashion at an acceptable cost and maintaining these systems once they have been released to manufacturing.

In laying the foundation for a specific manufacturing system, a complete analysis of the product must be made. Manufacturing engineering's entry into this program should be at the start of product design. Manufacturing engineering should analyze each detail part as designed, and recommend any changes which will improve its manufacturability.

Probably the best approach is for the manufacturing engineering organization to build the first unit concurrently with its design by product design personnel. This can be invaluable in eliminating engineering and manufacturing changes after the product is released to the manufacturing floor. Once this foundation has been laid, manufacturing engineering can develop a manufacturing system philosophy with emphasis on the control system to be used, capital equipment, procedures, programs, and expense tools.

At this point, manufacturing engineering is in a position to decide whether the system should be bought or built. If the decision is to build the system, design, including the building and debugging of the special manufacturing and test equipment, should be the first consideration. To complement these efforts, the manufacturing engineering group provides commercially available production equipment as it is required. It also specifies a control system, either manual or computerized, that will meet the demands of the particular operation.

Documentation is another important facet in manufacturing engineering's decision to build a manufacturing system. Control programs, minimum/maximum spare parts lists, and quality control instructions developed with the aid of quality engineering must be prepared. The routing, manufacturing process control procedures, and a test procedure must in many cases be written also.

A routing contains the information necessary to fabricate, assemble, inspect, and test a part or unit to meet all drawings and specifications. Although they are not required for every operation, a manufacturing process control procedure and a test procedure should be generated when more complete manufacturing or test instructions are desired than can be obtained from the routing. When required, the manufacturing engineering group is charged with the preparation of maintenance instructions to accompany the manufacturing process control procedure.

Other manufacturing engineering responsibilities associated with building a manufacturing system include:

1. Assistance in instructing the production operators in accordance with the manufacturing process control procedure, test procedure, and the quality control instructions[1]
2. Arranging with quality engineering and the safety department for a capability or machine acceptance study and eventual approval of this equipment in production[1]
3. Notifying the manufacturing organization and the maintenance department of their jurisdiction over equipment, following written approval from both quality engineering and safety departments
4. Furnishing a minimum-maximum spare parts list in addition to funding and ordering initial spare parts
5. Maintaining tool records
6. Specifying a control system, preparing control programs, writing a routing, and preparing a manufacturing process control procedure and test procedure as needed for all manufacturing operations not requiring special equipment

[1] Also done as required for manufacturing operations not requiring special equipment.

After the release of a manufacturing system to the line or production floor, manufacturing engineering is charged with periodically analyzing engineering changes, manufacturing changes, and manufacturing improvement requests to determine their impact on manufacturing or test processes or equipment. Other follow-up procedures should include a periodic analysis and monitoring of tools, the test equipment or process, the procedures and programs, and the provision of manufacturing support when it is required.

TOOL AND TEST EQUIPMENT MAINTENANCE

Although trouble calls must receive priority, the maintenance work load may be partially smoothed by using preventive maintenance training and new tool checkout as filler activities. Overtime is another tool that may be used to solve knotty scheduling problems. Engineering changes and other rework may be done on overtime to avoid shutting down critical machines or process lines during prime working hours.

It should be the responsibility of any factory service group to summarize all tool and test equipment trouble calls monthly. These data can then be sent to the manufacturing engineering organization for review to determine whether any design changes are needed to improve reliability.

There are two types of maintenance that fall within the responsibility of a factory service group: preventive and corrective. Preventive or scheduled maintenance is maintenance performed to prevent machine breakdown. It may include lubrication, cleaning or replacing filters, replacing parts with a predictable life-span, and assuring that the equipment is operating to its specifications and is properly calibrated. (See Section 6, Chapter 2.) Corrective maintenance is performed to correct any malfunction which prevents a piece of equipment from operating within its functional specifications. Figure 12-1 is a flow chart showing the steps taken to perform corrective maintenance on a typical piece of test equipment.

A factory's product line will determine the types of tooling that its service group may be called upon to maintain. A factory may use any or all of the following types of tooling:

1. General-purpose machine tools such as drills, milling machines, lathes, and jig borers. These may be either manually or numerically controlled.
2. Special product-oriented tooling and test equipment which is frequently designed and built in-house to perform a specific operation on a specific product.
3. Commercially available electronic equipment which may range in complexity from a simple voltmeter to a digital or analog computer.

Maintenance Cost Budgeting. The factory service group may either budget for all parts and labor required to fulfill its mission or charge each user for the service as it is performed. One distinct advantage of having the group budget for all service and parts is that they should have the staff and management most qualified to estimate maintenance costs. This method also allows for easier monitoring of total service costs. The advantage of each user budgeting for his own service and parts lies in making each more aware of the costs associated with tool maintenance. In either case, the cost of maintenance becomes part of the user's overhead.

Stocking spare parts is costly, and it is often a real challenge to provide a maximum amount of spare parts coverage for a minimum dollar expenditure. It is neither practical nor necessary to stock every part number for every tool or piece of test equipment which could conceivably become defec-

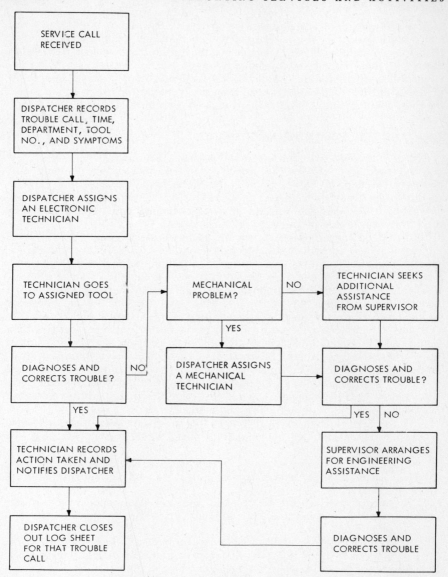

Fig. 12-1.   Flow Chart Showing the Steps Taken to Solve a Problem Relating to a Typical Piece of Test Equipment.

tive.   To minimize the number of incidents of extended downtime due to a lack of replacement parts, it is essential that the maintenance manager give this area of his responsibility a significant amount of attention.

To maintain an efficient spare parts crib, a comprehensive records system is essential.   The records should include the bills of material for each tool or piece of test equipment.   In addition, a record should be kept of each part number stocked, showing where it was used, a history of parts usage, and current stock status.

In determining the quantity of each part number to be stocked, consideration should be given to the following:

1. Manufacturer's recommended spare parts list if purchased; engineer's recommended parts list if designed in-house.
2. Spare parts procurement cycle—parts readily available from local sources or an expected delivery of, say, from three to six months.
3. Projected shifts of equipment utilization. Spare parts utilization will be proportional to the amount of time that the equipment is in service.
4. The actual experience on similar equipment.

The spare parts status information should be kept current. Should any tooling be stored or salvaged, its unique spare parts should also be stored or salvaged. If it shares common parts with other tooling, the stock level of those parts should be reduced proportionately.

Often it is necessary or desirable to obtain vendor support for certain maintenance operations. Examples of such cases are:

1. On rebuild operations requiring special tools, fixtures, or knowledge to perform
2. For technical assistance to identify and repair machine malfunctions when in-house attempts to find the trouble have failed
3. In any case where a manufacturer can perform the service more economically and the turnaround time can be tolerated

Staffing the Group. The type of tooling in a factory will determine the skill level required of its maintenance people. A logical skills-tooling setup might be as follows:

Equipment type	Skill required
1. General purpose machine tools (manual control)	Electromechanical technician
2. General purpose machine tools (numerical control)	Electromechanical technician with some knowledge of electronics and logic; or split the responsibility between electromechanical technician and electronic technician
3. Special product-oriented tooling and test equipment	Electromechanical or electronic technician, depending on tool design
4. Electronic test equipment (commercial)	Electronic technician

The complexity of the equipment being maintained is the determinant of the skill level required of a technician. When in doubt as to the skill level required, it is better to set the standards high.

In addition to possessing the necessary skills, a successful maintenance technician must be able to practice self-supervision. During the greater part of his workday, he will be on his own, answering trouble calls and performing preventive maintenance. Some technicians, although technically qualified, fail in maintenance work because they require close supervision.

The training of maintenance technicians should give them the knowledge necessary to maintain a specific tool or group of tools. Training methods will vary according to the need, but may be of the formal classroom, short seminar, self-study, or on-the-job type. Yet another means of obtaining training is the loan of technicians to an engineering organization allowing them to assist in the design and checkout of advanced tooling. When a complex tool or tester is purchased, it is often possible to arrange for maintenance training at a factory school. Training of this type is often provided by the manufacturer as a service.

Safety and Work Measurement. Teaching safety awareness is a major part of a factory service manager's job responsibility. The maintenance technician must be constantly made aware of the job-related exposure to accidents. He must also be certain that any tool on which maintenance is performed is in safe operating condition before he turns it back to an operator.

Work measurement in the factory service field is discussed in some detail in Chapter 3 of Section 6. Work measurement may be used to help a manager measure the performance of his people and thus obtain a degree of control over maintenance costs.

INSTRUMENT SERVICES

A major responsibility of factory service is the planning, maintenance, and recalibration of measuring instruments and test equipment. In the management of any instrument services organization, historic information relating to the cost and frequency of equipment maintenance is indispensable. It is also imperative that data be available on the spare parts inventory. Information should also be on hand which will allow management to predict the future manpower needs of the department.

The most important factor contributing to the efficient operation of this department involves scheduling the recalibration and maintenance of each instrument at a frequency which will result in minimum cost. A good instrument recall system should consist of identification data such as a description of the equipment to be serviced, its model number, manufacturer, department using the unit, the section which will service the unit, and the date of the next planned maintenance and recalibration service.

From this information, management can receive weekly or monthly reports pertinent to the operation of the department. These reports might include a weekly maintenance schedule, an equipment identification listing, cost information, and the like.

Historic information can tell an instrument services manager how well or how poorly a device has performed on the job over a certain period of time. Such information reveals, for example, how many times a particular piece was returned for unplanned service, a condition which may eventually lead to a readjustment of maintenance scheduling.

Historic information is also valuable in a failure analysis program. Trouble spots can be identified and clues provided on the best and most economical way to make readjustments and modifications to the equipment. The type, quantity, and cost of the spare parts necessary to guard against similar failures can also be predicted.

A good system of instrument recall guides management decisions in the following areas: the purchase of the most reliable type of test equipment, the amount of recalibration and maintenance service that equipment will require, the cost of maintenance and recalibration for any specified period, the degree to which stock levels should be maintained, and the amount of manpower that will be needed to perform test equipment maintenance efficiently.

THE QUALITY LABORATORY

Key elements in any department are the quality and potential of its personnel. Each department or organization has a minimum requirement, a "critical mass," that is needed to function as an effective group. The critical mass required for a quality laboratory will depend primarily on its mission: that is, the type of services provided such as electrical, chemical, metallurgical, plastics, and the like. The total manpower requirements for a laboratory will be the sum of the critical mass plus the personnel required to handle the average work load which cannot be contained by the critical mass.

Projecting the total manpower requirements for a quality laboratory poses a particularly difficult problem. As a service organization, manpower requirements are subject to wide fluctuations because of the impact and priority of manufacturing problems. The normal support efforts required of a quality laboratory for product and process control can usually be well planned and managed with a minimum of effort after the initial planning stage. The support effort required for troubleshooting manufacturing problems, however, and the requests for service from other organizations or departments are factors that are difficult to predict accurately. Several tools are available to the manager to guide him in projecting manpower requirements. These include a labor claiming and retrieval system for studying history, man-hours actually expended, product schedules, quality and manufacturing procedures, engineering proposals on new products, manufacturing engineering plans and schedules, and direct inquiries to areas serviced by the laboratory.

When occasional peaks occur in the total work load, management by priority is a necessity. Each job must be evaluated and assigned a priority rating to ensure that the most important jobs are given precedence.

The basic equipment and facilities required for a quality laboratory will depend on the mission and services expected from the laboratory. The problems facing most laboratory managers are those of justifying the necessity for equipment to satisfy the occasional need, evaluation of its projected utilization, and its availability in other departments. In addition, they must consider the effects of not performing a specific test and the floor space and services required for equipment.

THE MEASUREMENT STANDARDS LABORATORY

Unlike the conventional quality laboratory, a measurement standards laboratory has the responsibility for custody, maintenance, establishment, and dissemination of the highest level of standards for physical measurement commensurate with the needs of the organization which supports the laboratory. The organization must be so established that there is a sufficient balance of both professionally trained and production-oriented personnel. The working environment must be conducive to continuous learning and must place emphasis on the practical application of this learning. The interdisciplinary nature of the work requires an organization which permits infusion of the required disciplines.

Work load control is a necessary provision. The measuring devices and standards needing certification must be scheduled so that they are periodically withdrawn from service for certification before they will deteriorate beyond the established acceptable limits. The scheduling must be arranged to permit a well-regulated work flow. Experience has indicated that not more than 70 percent of the manpower available to perform certification should be scheduled. The unscheduled certification which will be required will account for the remaining 30 percent.

In performing certification, the historical data relative to the numerical values recorded must be plotted and tabulated. This provides the information necessary to justify increasing or decreasing the recall interval. Analysis relating the plotted values and the work-time learning curve will show when the work has become routine. It is at this point that a management decision must be made to determine whether the function should be transferred to a service organization such as a calibration or tool and gage department. In the event that such a transfer is made, measurement personnel will then become available to pursue new investigations.

Another aspect of managing a standards laboratory, one requiring continued surveillance, is the matter of reporting. There is often a tendency for technical and professional personnel to write for their peers. They must, however, also be encouraged to prepare reports for management. A good report format might be first to state specifically what was to be accomplished, then what conclusions were reached, and finally what specific recommendations were made. Any technical discussion should be reserved for the end of the report.

A further need is a follow-up system which will determine whether or not the recommendations were implemented. If they were not, reasons should be assessed to determine whether more work must be done. If, on the other hand, the recommendations were accepted, their worth should be evaluated so that the support of the laboratory can be justified.

FAILURE ANALYSIS AND DEFECT REPORTING

Failure analysis activity has become a key asset in satisfying the industrial world's continued goal and growing concern toward producing a quality product economically. This activity may be defined as a program of systematic collection and analysis of data, the detection and selection of significant deviations or variations from established limits, isolation of the cause, analysis of the defect, and finally the recommendations for corrective action with timely follow-up.

Because failure analysis is by definition a program which deals with history, its effectiveness can be easily measured by the reduction of the resources—mainly time, money, and people—which are required to continue a specific program.

The basic critical skills necessary to meet the objectives of a failure analysis program depend upon the type of industry in which the program is to be instituted. There are, however, some basic skills which have been found to be necessary regardless of the industry. These skills include engineering talents within the discipline of the industry, technically competent personnel, data collection analysts, and data processing knowledge if data analysts use data processing equipment. A statistical background is a must for at least one member of the group.

It would be inconceivable for any failure analysis effort to be able to afford the luxury of having manpower waiting for a crisis to arise. Therefore, a procedure must be available to set and regulate priorities of the individual jobs or crises that occur. As the number of incidences increases, work may have to be delegated to other organizations and facilities to implement a quick response. Studies may be used to fill the gap when serious problems are nonexistent.

Hopefully, the effectiveness of the failure analysis program will eventually reduce the number of serious and catastrophic crises. However, because of the changing technology throughout industry, the probability of this occurring is remote. Early evaluations of development programs, using existing failure analysis history, may ultimately reduce the amount of effort required in the program. One of the greatest assets of a failure analysis group is its ability to respond quickly to emergency situations without disrupting its long-range programs. As industrial technologies change, the disciplines of the critical skills group must be reviewed and altered if necessary, without disrupting the overall objectives of the failure analysis program.

One convenient method for evaluating the effectiveness of the group is to use a standardized reporting system which might include the critical skills discipline, a description of the type of investigation being performed, the number of hours expended on a particular job, the nature of the cause of the problem, the recommended corrective action, a narrative of the follow-up action taken by the group, and a statement relating to the probability of that specific problem recurring. With this information stored in a history file, whether in narrative form or in data processing form, the ability to recall this information is a valuable asset for future planning.

The cost of developing and implementing a failure analysis program is a vital consideration. If 50 percent of the manpower in a failure analysis group is used to attain the objectives of the overall program on a long-range basis, there must be short-range incidences which will result in a current payback of operating costs.

A defect analysis program is quite suitable for providing this payback. Unlike a total failure analysis program, defect analysis is the determination of a significant deviation (circuit, component, or the like) which resulted in an unwanted condition. The cause of the deviation must be determined to effect meaningful corrective measures and to prevent continued deviations of an unwanted condition.

Defect analysis is primarily used to correct the well-known catastrophic, line-stopping situation, where, for example, a final test operation detects a complete failure of some integral part and immediate action is necessary to correct that particular problem.

Failure analysis is primarily used to handle those situations which are not immediately recognized as catastrophic. Defect analysis may or may not be instituted as a result of a situation determined through the early phases of the failure analysis program. In the event that defect analysis is instituted, similarities of the programs become obvious.

The facilities required to accomplish defect analysis depend entirely upon the industry in which the program is implemented. Generally, the basic requirements are those usually found in a well-equipped quality laboratory. The needs specifically could require the following services:

1. Chemical analysis of materials
2. Emission spectrographic analysis
3. Plastic and resin analysis
4. Metallurgical analysis
5. Photographic and radiographic analysis
6. Infrared analysis of organic material
7. Gas analysis
8. Chemical microscopy
9. Environmental testing (temperature and humidity)
10. Electronic evaluation
11. Metallography
12. X-ray diffraction analysis
13. Microsectioning and polishing
14. Eddy current analysis capability
15. Ultrasonic and liquid crystal technology
16. Complete electronic facilities

Personnel must be technically competent in their related disciplines, whether these be physics, electronics, or chemistry, to make a comprehensive defect analysis. Whether performing a total failure analysis program or the defect analysis program, management's responsibility is not lessened. A failure analysis program, to be successful, must be infiltrated with management checkpoints, making the success or failure of the program a reflection of management's involvement.

CONCLUSION

To provide an effective factory service function, it should be recognized that many factors have to be taken into consideration, such as the complexity of the product, the magnitude of production, and the skill level of the available personnel. Organization is obviously an option of management.

A good system of organization, however, might be for the managers of the manufacturing, quality assurance, purchasing, manufacturing engineering, and materials distribution functions to report directly to a works manager. This form of organization will effect close communications among these groups and serve to orient them toward the overall objectives of the factory service function.

Some of the functions described in this chapter, such as calibration and maintenance, can sometimes be effectively subcontracted. With the availability of independent testing laboratories, it is even possible and sometimes desirable to subcontract failure analysis.

BIBLIOGRAPHY

Churchman, C. West, Russell L. Ackoff, and E. Leonard Arnoff, *Introduction to Operations Research*, John Wiley & Sons, Inc., New York, 1957.

DeGarmo, E. P., *Engineering Economy*, The Macmillan Company, New York, 1967.

Feigenbaum, A. V., *Total Quality Control: Engineering and Management*, McGraw-Hill Book Company, New York, 1961.

Grant, E. L., *Statistical Quality Control*, 3d ed., McGraw-Hill Book Company, New York, 1964.

Industrial Quality Control, American Society of Quality Control, circulating journal.

Kepner, C. H., and B. B. Tregoe, *The Rational Manager*, McGraw-Hill Book Company, New York, 1965.

Rutherford, J. G., *Quality Control in Industry*, Pitman Publishing Corporation, New York, 1948.

CHAPTER THIRTEEN

Field Installation and Servicing

JOHN P. SIRLES *Supervisor of Methods, Industrial Engineering Department, Ingersoll-Rand Company, Athens, Pennsylvania*

Large items of major industrial equipment are ordinarily considered fixed assets of a business. Examples are blast furnaces, pumps, turbines, and heavy stamping machines. A leading characteristic of the market for this equipment is the need for satisfactory installation and servicing of the equipment by the equipment manufacturer.

The equipment involved is special—it is generally built to order, and it is built for a given factory setup or to perform a certain operation in making a particular product. Ordinarily, it can be used for no other purpose. Many such installations require great amounts of service from the manufacturer. This service may involve the help of the manufacturer's engineers in planning installations, fitting them into the production routine, installing them, and training the buyer's employees in their use, as well as repair and maintenance service in keeping them in satisfactory working order after installation.

Manufacturers of major industrial equipment often discover that a special engineering department is necessary to install and service equipment, and various personnel involved have to be trained. Production problems with basic equipment are very serious because they always mean costly downtime. Hence the manufacturer must be ready to provide repair service at any time, and a staff of men will have to be maintained to serve as troubleshooters. In many cases, the manufacturer provides periodic inspection service designed to minimize delays in production that are caused by breakdowns of machinery. Thus, manufacturers of major equipment for industrial plants find it necessary to sell service as well as products.

FIELD INSTALLATION

Engineering service is an important factor in the manufacture and distribution of special equipment. This service often involves the preparation of plans and specifications according to which the equipment will be built. It may entail a complete analysis of the buyer's operations and the development of a piece of equipment that will fit into those operations smoothly. It always involves supervision or assistance during the period of equipment installation, performance test operation and demonstration, instruction of the buyer's operators and engineers in operation and maintenance of the equipment, and continuing repair and adjustment service.

Naturally, the nature and extent of such postsales service will differ in each industry. The following categories describe the steps that the manufacturer should take in the installation of major industrial equipment.

Planning. Planning should start from the point of sale. The equipment manufacturer should be aware from the start of the conditions under which the installation will be made and should take the necessary steps to furnish installation drawings and service requirements to the buyer's plant engineer or maintenance staff in advance of the equipment delivery date. This will assure reliable preparation of foundations; necessary relocation of power, water, and air lines; and a generally more favorable atmosphere when the equipment is ready for installation.

Installation Crews. Special installations are frequently built to order. This means that the relation existing between the buyer and the manufacturer must be very close (see Figure 13-1). Successful marketing requires that the manufacturer capture the confidence of the officials of the buying concern and work closely with them in the process of preparing plans and building the machines. Sales engineers may be given the responsibility of installing relatively simple equipment such as parts feeders or standard type machines of the milling machine class. There is a definite advantage to this practice. The sales engineer can utilize his knowledge of both the equipment and the installation. His direct feedback to designers can lead to equipment improvement and provide significant aid in locating additional applications for the equipment—an important fact when the equipment being manufactured is standard, that is, equipment that may be used without material change by several industries or by a number of firms in one industry.

Permanent installation crews are the answer for most manufacturers of basic equipment, as these manufacturers should, if at all practicable, do their own installation. There are several reasons for this.

1. Cost is likely to be less when the manufacturer has his own permanent installation crews. These men, trained at the factory, have the extensive knowledge of the equipment design required to complete the installation and start up without delay.

2. These men are most likely to be the field maintenance crew; their familiarity with the installation will be a definite advantage when the time comes to service the equipment.

3. With a permanent installation crew, there is less need for elaborate paperwork on contracts, prints, specifications, installation drawings, and the like.

4. By having these men do the installation work, the presence of qualified maintenance men is assured in case of emergency.

The use of temporary installation crews is not an economical approach. They require special training and relocation for specific jobs, the cost of which

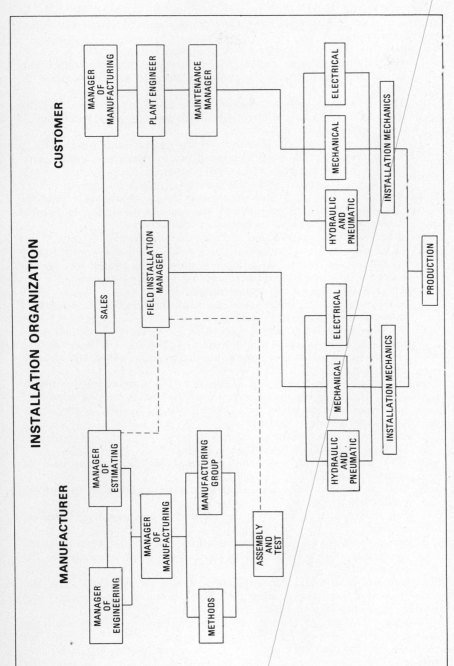

Fig. 13-1. Organization for Optimizing Manufacturer-Customer Installation Liaison.

quickly gets out of hand. Furthermore, because these crews can only be offered short-term employment, the quality of their work does not match that of permanent crews.

The alternative is to call in contractors for the work because:

1. Having done previous similar jobs, these contractors are often highly skilled and familiar with the particular piece of equipment being installed.
2. They have the proper equipment available—eliminating the need for the manufacturer or the buyer to furnish this equipment—and can do a safe, efficient job.
3. Contractors' crews are unionized in the geographical area. This is an important consideration because it means that there are no problems in bringing these crews into customers' plants. As a result, local union resistance to bringing in outside crews is minimized.

Scheduling. The length of time scheduled for the installation must be realistic. It should be based on previous experience with similar equipment or on close estimate if the equipment is new and different.

When scheduling for an installation, the manufacturer should:

1. Make sure that a sales engineer does not oversell delivery and start-up time. This will be no problem if there is the proper interdepartmental teamwork between manufacturing and sales personnel.
2. Allow ample time for debugging equipment.
3. Make sure that the buyer understands all the benefits he will gain if the equipment works right the first time.
4. Put the schedule on paper. Schedule all work in detail; set up a timetable with specific dates and times; and assign a number to each component or subassembly, mark it on an inventory sheet, and check it against a tag.

Installation Site. Foundations and adequate facilities are the responsibility of the buyer. However, the manufacturer must be certain that all aspects of the site have been considered before beginning the installation of the equipment. These aspects include the following:

1. Is the space sufficient for the equipment?
2. Will the foundation support the equipment?
3. What must be done to get the equipment into the buyer's plant; for instance, must walls be knocked out?
4. Will the equipment be located at the proper sequence in the buyer's production arrangement?
5. Has provision been made for air, electricity, and plumbing when required?
6. Has provision been made for extra utilities for use during installation?
7. Are transportation facilities into the buyer's plant adequate for the equipment?

The readiness of the site for installation should be checked. The site should be visited and closely inspected for clearances, interference, and availability of utilities of adequate size.

Installation. Last-minute changes should be anticipated. Things rarely go according to plan. A selected group of spare parts should be carried for emergencies, and the installation manager should report progress regularly.

Start-up. Premature start-up should be avoided. This can be especially applicable if the installation is behind schedule and the desire or tendency arises on the part of the sales engineer, the purchaser, or the manufacturer to accelerate the installation. Installation instructions should be checked to be certain that all have been complied with. Then the start-up procedure, which in all probability is part of the equipment package, should be followed. Figure 13-2 shows a typical start-up procedure.

Cutoff. A deadline for cutoff should be set. However, the equipment should not be turned over to the buyer until it has been operating for a specific period and adjusted, even if the deadline has to be exceeded. If the design is right, and if the equipment has been manufactured in accordance with design specifications, cost of installation will be held to a minimum. However, there is always a possibility of redesign being involved. If changes are made

---

CHECKLIST

STARTING THE FIRST TIME

PRIOR TO STARTING:

1. Make sure all installation instructions have been complied with and foundations and grout are sufficiently hard.

2. Remove one of large crankcase hand hole covers and inspect interior for dirt. If necessary, wipe out thoroughly with clean cloth. DO NOT USE COTTON WASTE.

3. Fill oil sump in bottom of crankcase to high-level mark on oil bayonet gage with a high-grade lubricating oil. (Refer to supplemental instructions for grade and quantity of oil required.)

4. BAR COMPRESSOR OVER A FEW TIMES BY HAND. BE SURE UNIT WORKS FREELY AND THAT EVERYTHING IS CLEAR. THIS IS IMPORTANT.

5. Fill air cylinder force feed lubricator with a high-grade air cylinder lubricating oil. (Refer to supplemental instructions for proper grade of oil, rate of feed and details of lubricating system.)

STARTING

1. Turn on full supply of cooling water. Make sure water is flowing through intercooler and both cylinders.

2. If there is a valve in compressor discharge line to receiver, be sure it is open.

3. Turn three-way valve lever (on semiautomatic unit) on control panel to "START."

4. Start compressor. Make sure crankshaft rotates in direction shown on foundation plan.

5. Be sure oil pressure gage shows pressure of 20 lbs. or more. If not, stop unit immediately.

FIG. 13-2. Start-up Checklist That Can Be Supplied with Equipment.

by the buyer after parts have already been made, the buyer must be charged for the changes. Costs for parts not made in accordance with specification must be assigned to manufacturing expense. Costs for debugging equipment, in excess of anticipated costs, cannot be charged to the buyer. Special consideration must be given to these costs when planning an installation so that estimates are sufficient to cover them and the manufacturer does not have to absorb excessive costs.

For special equipment, when using standard and known components, as much as 30 percent of manufacturing cost may have to be allowed for debugging on the job site; when using new and untried components, debugging costs may amount to as much as 100 percent of manufacturing costs.

When the installation manager is satisfied that all elements of the installation have been fulfilled, the equipment is ready to be turned over to the buyer for maintenance tryout, buyer acceptance, and final cutoff.

SERVICING EQUIPMENT AFTER SALE

Selling policy will partly determine servicing policy. If the equipment is sold under guarantee or with definite performance specifications in the sales contract, the manufacturer will want to follow the equipment into use. If the equipment is sold through distributors or dealers, the manufacturer will want to consider whether or to what extent the servicing of the equipment should be localized in their shops or geographical areas. If the equipment is sold through jobbers or agents, working space, mechanical facilities, and trained workmen to render satisfactory service are probably nonexistent.

Generally, the complicated nature of a piece of major equipment and the delicate adjustments and skilled repairs essential for its proper functioning require the manufacturer to have a supply of properly trained servicemen. He may have to offer a training program for dealers' mechanics. Traveling supervisors or troubleshooter engineers from the main plant should be available to supplement the work of the trainees. Manufacturers of heavy-duty and specialized equipment—such as electric generating and power distribution equipment; electromotive installations; special machine tools; and excavating, conveying, and elevating devices—customarily make sales on the basis of earlier surveys or operating tests and technical recommendations of their sales engineers. The sales specifications and contractual guarantees of performance are definite and usually commit the manufacturer to explicit forms of service after sale.

Repair Service. To meet problems and service needs that arise after acceptance of the equipment by the buyer, it is necessary for the manufacturer to maintain technically competent troubleshooters to cover strategically convenient geographical areas.

Naturally, the nature and extent of such postsale service differ with the industry concerned. In many cases, the most satisfying results for both buyer and manufacturer are obtained where close interdepartmental teamwork exists in the manufacturer's organization. This cooperation combines the technical competency and inventiveness of the engineering and service departments with keen sensitivity to customers' needs and alertness to developmental and promotional opportunities on the part of the sales department.[1]

Schedule Service. Above all, service should be regularly scheduled. Only in this manner can a program of preventive maintenance be implemented. A

[1] Charles F. Phillips, *Marketing by Manufacturers*, Richard D. Irwin, Inc., Homewood, Ill., 1948, p. 213.

good example of this after-sale service is the program devised by each automobile manufacturer to support his guarantee. Various services are scheduled for the guarantee period and are performed by factory-trained personnel. Similarly scheduling postsale service on major equipment will minimize downtime which is costly to the customer from the standpoint of lost production time, and more important here, expensive to the manufacturer from the standpoint of costs over and above those anticipated on service contracts.

Service Organization. From Figure 13-3, it becomes obvious that in a well-functioning organization the service manager deals directly through the customer's plant engineer to the maintenance group. This gives him immediate feedback on equipment performance.

The dotted-line relationship to his engineering group solves the requirement that performance problems and original specification requirements can be transmitted directly to the area of immediate responsibility.

The purchasing department must cooperate closely for the emergencies that arise when standard components are the direct cause of equipment downtime and must be delivered to the job site quickly.

A customer line relationship is shown to clarify proper communication channels with the least duplication of effort. This automatically leads to directness of communications in practice.

Sources of Servicemen. The manufacturing division is the most promising source for competent servicemen. The manufacturer should identify the men who have demonstrated technical competence and then give them specialized training to prepare them to meet the customer, diagnose technical faults, and adjust or repair the faults. Graduates of technical schools are a good source of servicemen. They should be given shop experience and service training under competent supervision. There is also a possibility of obtaining competent men from the staffs of customers. These men are experienced in the industry and in the use of the manufacturer's equipment. With further training, they can become technical servicemen.

What Training to Give Servicemen. The basic requirement for a serviceman is a competent knowledge of the construction and functioning of the equipment that he will be called upon to install. Manufacturing experience is often essential, and field experience in equipment operation or use is equally valuable. Knowledge of the theoretical—the "why" of the functioning—will add confidence and certainty to the serviceman's ability.

Suitable instruction classes, examinations, and controlled shop or laboratory performance experience should be set up together with supervised field service work to summarize, give direction to, and unify these several phases of knowledge.

The customer should have all service people, not just the foreman, participate during machine assembly and debugging. There is no substitute for practical experience with the equipment. If the machine is absorbed smoothly into the customer's operation, this may pave the way for further sales. Competent help in the customer's plant at all times will make a major contribution in this direction—it especially avoids the psychological stress which comes from the switch in responsibilities from the manufacturer to the customer.

Report Preparation. The serviceman should be trained to write an intelligible, correctly phrased report, so that it will provide information required by the service supervisor and by the experts in the engineering department.

Knowledge of Maintenance Standards. Service representatives should be fully informed concerning standards for performance. They should have the capability of locating quickly any inefficiencies in the specified operation.

Personality Factor. The service representative must be able to avoid of-

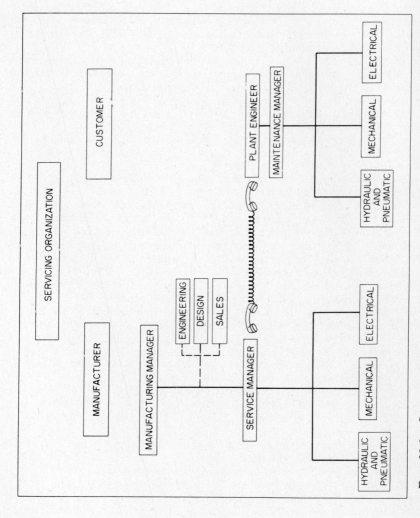

Fɪɢ. 13-3.   Servicing Organization for Optimizing Manufacturer-Customer Servicing Liaison.

fending those whom he is assisting. He must be able to identify the real basis for objections and overcome them tactfully.

Controlling Service Costs. Service costs can be controlled if the reasons for increases in these costs are identified and action is taken to minimize them. To do this, the manufacturer must:

1. Be certain to have sales engineers avoid careless promises which must be redeemed.
2. State clearly exactly what service is to be supplied, on what terms, and for what period of time.
3. Be certain that the buyer is furnished with proper operation and maintenance instructions when the equipment is installed.
4. Train servicemen properly.
5. Institute adequate controls over the dispatching of servicemen between service calls and over the expenditure of their time.
6. Inspect or check up on the results of the servicemen's work.
7. Consider the time required to service modern equipment with more automatic features and often with poorer accessibility to operating parts; provision for this time should be made in any contractual obligations.
8. Consider the possibility of failure of accessories installed with the equipment, and develop a method of recovering service costs in these cases from accessory manufacturers.

Charging for Servicing. Manufacturers of major industrial equipment differ in their service charge policies. During a guarantee period after sale, it may be decided to make no charge for repairs and adjustments of any description; or replacement parts may be furnished without cost to the buyer during that period, his only charge being the actual labor cost of installing the parts.

Service contracts are often offered covering equipment after the guarantee period expires. These cover periodic inspection, cleaning, lubrication, adjustments, and minor repairs. During the course of minor repairs, the serviceman may recommend major repairs, replacement of other parts, or preventive maintenance. Service work may be performed for specified labor costs for the several operations, with replacement parts charged at actual cost or at specified listed prices. The service contract is often best for all concerned. The buyer saves money because he does not have to maintain service crews or replacement parts, and he is assured of competent service when he needs it. The manufacturer benefits through the goodwill built up by competent servicing, and he gains maximum utilization of his installation service crews.

Where there is no service contract, the customer should be billed a minimum service charge. This will discourage requests for servicing trivial needs.

It has been found in various industries that most customers will not complain about paying reasonable charges per hour or per day for necessary service when the problem of the cost of furnishing competent servicing is explained to them intelligently and fairly.[2]

Steps toward Controlling Service Costs. New installations should be routinely inspected within the first day or two of operation, and again within a week or two. This will minimize complaints and service calls which usually follow closely after the installation of new equipment. A competent inspector can detect potential causes of trouble and point out conditions and practices that may contribute to later trouble. He can also make sure that

[2] *Op. cit.*, p. 222.

the buyer's operators know the equipment, thereby eliminating the possibility of complaints which often arise because of lack of knowledge.

Service reports should be carefully analyzed, checking these points: purposes of calls, character of the trouble found, remedial work done, and responsibility for excessive or unusual difficulties or failures.

One of the most important remedial steps will be to identify for production and design personnel the failure-prone characteristics of equipment. These characteristics can then be corrected, significantly reducing heavy demands for service on similar equipment installed in the future.

Controlling Service Performance. Measurements to control service performance are good for supervising purposes, and they are significant factors in controlling service department costs. They help establish efficient work procedures and thus efficient use of manpower, and they may show needs for employee training. The measurements can vary; the manufacturer can:

1. Create work inspection programs to provide indexed ratings on individual servicemen.
2. Compare district and division job performances.
3. Interview individual servicemen periodically.
4. Keep a record of errors per man.
5. Have service supervisors reinspect small percentages of repairs and adjustments made by servicemen. This will help to determine justification for the customer's complaints and whether or not the complaint was rectified in accordance with company policy. Have the inspector complete a checklist which will detail trouble encountered, note any inadequate service work, and state what should have been done.
6. Take remedial steps with the serviceman involved; correct or amplify the training procedure where necessary.
7. Maintain complete service records. Keep a file of cards containing all pertinent information on each installation. Have the service foreman keep duplicates handy in case of off-hour service calls. Be certain that the cards are up to date; they will assure prompt service and provide the serviceman with sufficient background on the installation to perform an efficient job.
8. Demand service reports. Require the serviceman to file a written report on each call. Have him detail all conditions found, remedies applied, and any recommendations for avoiding similar trouble in the future. Have him document temporary repairs and specify permanent work which he thinks should be undertaken.

Controlling Service Obligations under Guarantees. Guarantee policies should be carefully reexamined periodically to make certain that in all cases policies clearly define responsibilities of the manufacturer, the distributor, and anyone else involved in the sale and installation of the equipment. Blanket guarantees covering a specified time period should be reappraised in the light of the costs recorded in actual performance of repair services under such guarantee contracts.

Part Stock and Replacement. For major equipment, repair and replacement parts and subassemblies must be carried by someone. Who carries the stock depends on several factors. For equipment of standard type sold through distributors, such as some electric motors or street and highway pneumatic drills, the distributor carries the immediate obligation of carrying parts and assuring proper servicing. Customers whose production facilities are not convenient to their market, such as certain types of mining operations, often will carry their own extra parts of minor importance. In these cases, the manufacturer must supply parts and repair service promptly and efficiently when major trouble occurs.

When the equipment is highly specialized, the manufacturer should stock spare parts of original grade on a contractual basis. Obviously, the manufacturer will have the direct obligation of assuring prompt and effective servicing.

CUSTOMER EDUCATION

Group Meetings and Clinics. Group meetings and clinics offer a unique opportunity to educate customers or their employees on the proper use and upkeep of equipment. Advantage should be taken of technical associations drawing membership from users of the equipment. They make desired servicing information available to their memberships in a way which would be extremely costly and inefficient to duplicate.

Manuals and Instruction Sheets. Service booklets and manuals should be provided for the customer's use. To reach the less skilled workers who may come into contact with the equipment, instruction sheets should be furnished covering use and operation of the equipment. Clear and detailed explanations and directions for cleaning, lubricating, inspecting, and overhauling the equipment should be provided where this is practicable. The instructions and charts should be placed on or near each piece of equipment.

Technical and Trade Periodicals. Technical and trade periodicals publish special issues or special sections that provide an important medium for exchange of information. The manufacturer should use these publications to explain the proper use and maintenance of his equipment and whenever possible should participate in special issues or sections on such subjects as maintenance, controls, motors, drives, or lubrication. Executives and experts should prepare instructive articles for technical journals and the trade press to assist toward satisfactory service and proper maintenance. After publication, these may be reprinted for use by the sales and technical service personnel.

Consultants. Design engineers and other technical specialists should be made available to customers and prospects for consultation. The manufacturer will benefit not only by uncovering and overcoming possible deficiencies in equipment performance and new problems arising from its actual operation, but also by developing more efficient methods of equipment application and broader utilization.

CONCLUSION

The manufacturer of major industrial equipment must be prepared to supply after-sale engineering service. It is highly important to adhere to a definite policy regarding field installation and servicing. The policy should help in the company's overall marketing operations but should not drain profit from the operations.

Many of the after-sale services that must be furnished are highly technical in nature. They should be supplied by engineers, chemists, service mechanics, or other technically trained representatives. The need for and the cost of such servicing can be reduced by integrated effort on the part of field service supervisors, design engineers, and research technicians to analyze performance data and to correct structural and operating deficiencies of the equipment. The reductions obtained will provide a great impetus toward attaining the twin goals of every successful manufacturer—a satisfied customer and a reasonable profit.

BIBLIOGRAPHY

Drucker, Peter F., *Managing for Results*, Harper & Row Publishers, Incorporated, New York, 1964.

Ewing, David E., *Long-range Planning for Management*, rev. ed., Harper & Row, Publishers, Incorporated, New York, 1964.

Phillips, Charles F., *Marketing by Manufacturers*, Richard D. Irwin, Inc., Homewood, Ill., 1948.

Phillips, Charles F., and Delbert J. Duncan, *Marketing Principles and Methods*, rev. ed., Richard D. Irwin, Inc., Homewood, Ill., 1952.

CHAPTER FOURTEEN

Use of Outside Services

ROBERT E. LEVINSON   *President, The Steelcraft Manufacturing Company, Cincinnati, Ohio*

To expand the work force and the capabilities of the manufacturing organization, consideration should be given to the use of outside services. A company can, if it wishes, take advantage of the organizations or individuals who, on a contract basis, will help perform functions or provide advisory services. These outside services may be divided into two general areas:
1. Those that provide advisory and counseling help
2. Those that actually perform a function within the company
The use of outside services permits expansion of the company's technology without the burden of added overhead on a continuing basis. In both types of services, it is possible to pinpoint the cost and to determine the return on investment. The outside organizations are so constituted that they have highly specialized technicians in specific areas. This specialization can be brought into a company to help accomplish a specific project more effectively. Outside service organizations have a wide experience gained from other organizations with whom they have worked. Therefore, the use of outside services can assist in keeping a company abreast of the industry technology, as well as in solving specific problems.

ADVANTAGES OF USING OUTSIDE SERVICES

Objectivity is an important factor gained by using the services of professional consultants. They are independent, and their outside look at internal problems can usually make an important contribution to the solution of the problems. Even though the solution to a problem may have already been developed by the internal staff, it nevertheless often makes it easier to secure higher management approval if the consultant puts the ideas together and makes the official presentation.

Most companies find that once they enter into a relationship with one or more consulting firms, they began to see their value. Bringing an outside consultant into the organization for a specific job each year has a stimulating effect upon the whole operation. It is important that the consulting firm provide the right type of personnel for the problem to be solved. Should an unsuitable person be placed in the plant, he should be terminated immediately so that a better qualified staff member can be assigned to the job. When employing outside consultants, it is important to match the personalities of the company's own staff and the consultants so that the most effective job can be obtained. Many companies find that the use of outside consultants assists in the training of key staff members. The consultant performs a training function by working with the employee on a project. The discipline of the consultant helps in planning the solution to the problem.

Employing the Outside Service. Whenever a decision is made to obtain the services of an outside consultant, there may be a feeling on the part of the staff that they have failed in their jobs. This may or may not be true, but if properly handled, this somewhat negative attitude can be turned into a positive advantage.

One of the best techniques to use is to have the internal staff itself recommend the outside consultant. They can arrange for and coordinate the preliminary investigation of possible consulting firms. They can be given the authority to select the consulting firm and in addition, if at all possible, the consultant who will be assigned to the work.

If the internal staff can be convinced that it is management's desire to help rather than hinder, then the job is easy. Every effort should be made to show the internal staff that outside services are an extension or an expansion of their own departments and, as such, are temporary aids or assets in performing the job. To a degree, it is like looking up reference material or discussing mutual problems with other companies.

If the internal staff are aware that they have the power to engage and terminate the consultant, it will help to encourage a better understanding and relationship. Once an outside consultant has been successfully used, it will be easier to bring one in the next time. The internal staff should be given full credit for completing the job, and the contribution of the consultant should be played down. This will fortify the idea that the consultant was only "leaning over the shoulders" of the staff.

There are many sources of information about outside services. Local banks and accounting firms can be helpful in providing names of organizations which have been successful and effective in their work. The local management society can also give the names of qualified organizations. Contacting the professional associations to which the consulting firms belong can also provide the names, addresses, and details of the members' expertise.

SERVICES FOR ADVISORY OR COUNSELING HELP

The following are important sources of advisory or counseling help:
1. Management consultants in any field of manufacturing
2. Financial consultants and accounting firms
3. The local public utility companies such as telephone, gas, electric, and waterworks
4. The technical or engineering departments of suppliers
5. Small Business Administration of the United States government

6. City or county health departments
7. State governmental offices such as safety and health departments
8. The industry's own trade associations or other trade associations related to the field

Management Consultants. Many management consulting firms have become very specialized and highly skilled in various areas of the manufacturing field. A representative list of such consultants may be obtained by contacting the Association of Consulting Management Engineers, Inc., 347 Madison Avenue, New York, New York 10017.

In general, the management consultant has the capability of collecting data or ideas and combining them with modern technology to develop plans for definite action or solutions to problems. If a company is installing a data processing facility, for example, many times an outside consultant can help to direct the program rather than relying solely on the data processing company's own technicians. The services of highly trained consultants in setting up systems are important because of the disciplines in which consultants have been trained. The company's own staff easily gets sidetracked from a project because of the pressures of day-to-day business, and therefore, the consultant, who is not influenced by them, can be more effective.

When selecting a management consultant, it is sometimes desirable to discuss his past performance with another company who has used his services. References from a high official in that company will give an overall management viewpoint of the consultant's effectiveness. In some cases, if a consultant has worked for a long period of time with a company, the staff who work with the consultant cannot be as objective in their appraisal of his effectiveness as a higher official in the company would be. Most consultants will present, in advance, an estimate of the cost of the work and a time schedule. An interview in depth with the senior consultant, specifically talking about the people from his firm who will work on the job, is very important. Skill in matching personalities is important to the success of the joint project. The employees of the consulting firm and of the company must establish a rapport and have mutual respect for one another. When the consultant visits the plant and starts working on his assignment, his time should be used wisely. The company staff should be instructed to stay with the assigned project and to work in concert with the consultant.

Financial Consultants. Many accounting firms have developed services for the manufacturing division. Systems for production control, material control, scheduling, and planning are available. Some firms have developed new techniques of timekeeping that work in conjunction with computerized equipment. Having some systems or programs conceived by finance-oriented people can bring stabilized and effective data to the manufacturing division. The organization of data and the proper use of them by the staff are important in the manufacturing division. An accounting-oriented consultant can bring the type of systems organization that will be compatible with the type of services available from the company's own financial function.

Public Utility Companies. Gas, electric, telephone, and water companies can often be of great help to the manufacturing division. Each of these companies employs experts on its staff, who are available to users for consulting purposes. These services can, in many cases, effect production improvement and cost savings. An analysis by the electric company of power requirements and lighting facilities is very important. For example, improper spot welding can many times be caused by an improper power supply and demand situation. A study of this by a qualified consultant from the electric company can usually result in recommendations to correct the problem. The gas company can provide services in heating and ventilating that also can result in reduced costs and improved production.

Because many manufacturing processes use a large quantity of water, consultation with the local waterworks can also result in possible savings in time and money. Surging of boilers is often caused by water conditions, and an analysis of the local water supply can eliminate problems.

The local telephone company maintains communications experts who will analyze phone calls. They will provide schools for teaching the staff how to use the telephone. Technology developed by the telephone company with Data-Phones, internal switchboards, spare phones, and other such equipment can often be used by the manufacturing division for time and cost savings. Consultation with these people is without charge and can prove fruitful.

Technical or Engineering Departments of Suppliers. A seldom tapped source of technical assistance is the technical departments of the company's suppliers. Because supplies are generally handled through the purchasing department, the manufacturing division often does not become involved. However, most suppliers are delighted to give technical assistance when it is needed. The purchasing department can identify the suppliers who have offered services, and the manufacturing division can choose those that it feels are important. Most suppliers have visual aids, such as motion pictures, pertaining to safety and health in relation to their products. For example, fork truck suppliers have produced a great deal of visual material that can be made available to employees. In the area of welding, the welding equipment manufacturers usually are willing to provide trained personnel to teach employees the proper techniques of welding. To keep company staff up to date on technology, the technical services available from suppliers should be used freely. In most cases, this will result in superior knowledge and training for the staff as well as cost savings. A continuing program of this sort can be easily established by inviting a technical representative from a different supplier in each week for a review of his industry's products.

Small Business Administration. The Small Business Administration provides booklets, literature, and conferences on subjects of interest to the manufacturing division. A complete listing of this material is available from any local Small Business Administration Office, or it may be obtained by writing to the Small Business Administration, Washington, D.C. 20416. Many of the pamphlets and booklets are in the form of management aids for small manufacturers, but the data and information are usually applicable to any size organization. Many of the leading businessmen in the United States donate their time for preparing booklets and pamphlets. The Small Business Administration has a minor charge for some of its information.

City and County Health Departments. The local health department can provide vital information on working conditions for the plant. If food services are available at the plant, the health department can also provide the necessary rules for the proper operation of these services. Regulations on employees' working areas are also available. Generally, the local health department receives information from many other outside organizations, and these data sometimes can be applicable to the company's operations. In spray painting, for example, the local health department can supply up-to-date technical data on the proper masks to use. It may be possible that technology has advanced to such a degree that present equipment is outmoded. Using the services of the health department can expand knowledge in the manufacturing area.

State Governmental Offices.   The state sets up various rules pertaining to fire and safety and makes available to manufacturers up-to-date technical data in these fields.   When an inspection of the manufacturing facilities is made by the state fire marshall, advantage should be taken of this to learn of any new technologies available which may aid in making a safer plant and perhaps in saving lives in the event of fire.   Most states conduct industrial safety campaigns, and if the state has its own compensation program, the company rating is based upon safety and health experience.   Close coordination with state agencies will result in a wealth of useful information.

Trade Associations.   Trade associations can often provide technical know-how to the manufacturing division.   Many suppliers belong to trade associations, and if an inquiry is given to the supplier, he in turn can often obtain valuable information on a particular item or point.   For example, the grinding wheel manufacturers have a trade association.   This association has prepared information on safety, proper use of grinding wheels, and other similar data.   By contacting the supplier, data and information can be secured from his trade association.

SERVICES THAT PERFORM ACTUAL FUNCTIONS FOR THE COMPANY

Typical of the services which are available to perform actual functions for the company are:
1. Contract manufacturers who make parts
2. Guards and security police
3. Temporary shop and office help
4. Equipment rental companies
5. Design engineering companies
6. Research and development companies
7. Contract maintenance and janitorial services
8. Outside subcontractors for repairs such as all types of mechanical, roofing, painting, and the like
9. Burglary alarm organizations
10. Miscellaneous organizations for trash removal, landscaping services, yard repair, and so on

Contract Manufacturers Who Make Parts.   Although contract manufacturing organizations are not generally considered as outside services, in effect they are.   Contract manufacturers can perform functions for a company that are too costly to set up on a short-run basis.   A contract manufacturer can often make parts by combining runs with other companies, and the net result is lower costs.   In some cases, a special machine may be needed to produce a particular product or item, and the contract manufacturer who has this machine can do the work much more economically than the company could do it without the machine.

Guards and Security Police.   Many companies have found that hiring independent guards and security police is a most effective way to provide security for their plants.   This eliminates administrative costs because the outside service will handle all employee relations with the guards and see that the plant is adequately protected at all times.   Because the guards are more apt to be specialists and more highly trained, the company usually obtains more technical help in the guard service.   Having outside guard service also prevents collusion with employees, for most outside guard services rotate the guards from time to time.   Generally, the cost per hour is lower with outside guard services when the overhead and administrative costs that are eliminated are taken into consideration. This subject is discussed more fully in Chapter 11 of this section.

Temporary Shop and Office Help. There are many organizations that specialize in providing temporary office and shop help. These companies can provide important assistance to a company by taking care of peak loads of work. For example, when emergencies arise in the factory, the outside service is available to provide additional workmen instantly. In the case of office help, there are many periods within the year when additional typing and clerical work is needed. The use of temporary outside services enables the company to maintain a stable work force.

Equipment Rental Companies. Many outside companies offer equipment rental services. This enables a company to reduce the amount of capital necessary to purchase equipment and, instead, to maintain the year-to-year charges as an ongoing expense. Before entering into a rental arrangement, it is suggested that legal counsel and the financial department be consulted first to discuss the various features of contemplated leasing programs. In one company, fork trucks were rented from a leasing company. When all the costs and expenses were calculated, it was determined that the company would save approximately 25 percent by using leased equipment. Renting often has other advantages in that all maintenance and repair are generally done by the lessor. In addition to this, new equipment is often provided to the company each year. Most of the computer companies primarily lease their equipment, because the technology is such that the equipment becomes easily outmoded. By using leased equipment, companies are able to secure the latest models each year. Many of the machine tool manufacturers will provide a leasing program for their capital equipment. This offers a technique to enlarge company assets with nominal amounts of additional cash. A fuller discussion of the advantages and disadvantages of leasing will be found in Section 5, Chapter 6.

Design Engineering Companies. There are many organizations that will provide detailed design service. This will enable the company's product engineers to devote their time to more creative work. Calling in an outside design engineering company to help with detailed drawings, piece part drawings, bills of material, and other similar items will free engineers' creative time. It is wise to begin working with one outside company and to become familiar with that company's design capability. Then the necessary procedures can be set up to call on this design engineering company as needed for various spot jobs.

Research and Development Companies. There are many independent research and development organizations. Some of these have their own testing facilities. Having one of these services to provide needed information for the company can multiply effectiveness manyfold. Some independent R & D companies can provide a wide access to technology that is not generally known. This technology can usually be made available at reasonable cost by working regularly with an independent outside company. Many production problems can be solved by working with an R & D company that can offer suggestions on the use of materials or equipment. A relationship between staff and outside research in the company's product area can be fostered by establishing a liaison with an R & D company and maintaining it over the years.

Contract Maintenance and Janitorial Services. Contract maintenance companies are able to provide specialized service in various fields. Depending upon the size of the organization, the company may not be able to keep on its payroll a specialist in, say, electrical equipment. On the other hand, it may have a few specialized pieces of machinery that require electrical know-how maintenance. By making a contract with a specialized maintenance firm, it can secure the services of a technician, highly trained in the particular need, at a very nominal cost to the company. In some cases, heating, boiler, plumbing, and electrical contractors will be glad to provide maintenance programs for the company.

Many companies use outside services for janitorial purposes. Usually this is for office areas where the type of cleaning to be performed is somewhat specialized. The janitorial companies have the proper know-how and equipment and also provide the service every day. Using the janitorial service eliminates the administrative costs of cleaning the facilities and reduces the waste of materials and supplies that normally accompany such a job.

Outside Subcontractors for Repairs. The use of subcontractors for repairs and services such as roofing and painting is common among most manufacturers. It is possible to make an arrangement with these companies whereby they provide a yearly service on a continuing basis so that the repairs will not be overlooked or neglected.

Burglary Alarm Organizations. For maximum protection, many companies install an alarm system in their plants or in particular areas of their plants. These alarm systems are generally controlled by an independent company with local offices, who will provide on-the-spot service should the alarm sound. Usually these systems are tied into a sprinkler alarm which will alert the outside service when a sprinkler is turned on. It is possible to secure these alarm services for small areas to protect specialized areas of the facility.

Miscellaneous Organizations. Outside services are commonly available for trash removal, landscaping, and yard repairs. Companies established for this purpose can provide regular, uninterrupted service and can relieve the manufacturing division of the administrative burden which would be involved if these activities were to be handled in-plant.

CONCLUSION

The late Professor Erwin Schell of the Massachusetts Institute of Technology used to point out to his students that "You can have change without improvement, but you cannot have improvement without change." Bringing an outside service into a company almost always produces change in the status quo. It is management's responsibility to see that the change results in ultimate improvement. One of its most important tasks is to see that the internal staff is receptive to change. This is by no means easy, particularly if an organization has become ingrown and has had few outside contacts. One good way to increase receptivity to change is to require staff people to attend seminars, meetings of professional societies, and exhibitions of various sorts where new ideas, methods, and equipment are presented and discussed.

BIBLIOGRAPHY

Advanced Management Journal, special issue on management consulting, January, 1965.
"Consultants: How to Know What You're Getting and Get What You Pay for," *Management Review*, December, 1963, p. 5.

Dunn, Albert H., et al., *Business Consultants: Their Uses and Limitations*, Financial Executives Research Foundation, Inc., New York, 1951.

Dyer, Marshall, "How to Use a Management Consultant," *Foundry*, November, 1959, p. 95.

How to Control the Quality of a Management Consulting Engagement, Association of Consulting Management Engineers, Inc., New York, 1966.

How the Management Consulting Profession Serves Business Enterprise, Association of Consulting Management Engineers, Inc., New York, 1961.

Maynard, H. B., "How to Select a Management Consultant," *Management Methods*, February, 1957.

Rawlings, Gen. Edwin W., "How the Air Force Uses Management Consultants," *Harvard Business Review*, July–August, 1957.

Selected References on Management Consultation, Association of Consulting Management Engineers, Inc., New York, 1967.

Seney, Wilson, *Effective Use of Business Consultants*, Financial Executives Research Foundation, Inc., New York, 1963.

Shay, Philip W., *How to Get the Best Results from Management Consultants*, rev. ed., Association of Consulting Management Engineers, Inc., New York, 1967.

Stanley, C. Maxwell, *The Consulting Engineer*, John Wiley & Sons, Inc., New York, 1961.

INDEX

Prepared by BARBARA HATTEMER, St. Louis, Missouri